THE HUNDRED YEARS WAR
VOLUME V
Triumph and Illusion

by the same author

PILGRIMAGE: An Image of Medieval Religion
THE ALBIGENSIAN CRUSADE
THE HUNDRED YEARS WAR Volume I: Trial by Battle
THE HUNDRED YEARS WAR Volume II: Trial by Fire
THE HUNDRED YEARS WAR Volume III: Divided Houses
THE HUNDRED YEARS WAR Volume IV: Cursed Kings

THE HUNDRED YEARS WAR

JONATHAN SUMPTION

VOLUME V
Triumph and Illusion

faber

First published in 2023
by Faber & Faber Limited
The Bindery, 51 Hatton Garden
London EC1N 8HN

First published in the USA in 2023

Typeset by Donald Sommerville
Printed and bound in England by
CPI Group (UK) Ltd, Croydon CR0 4YY

All rights reserved
© Jonathan Sumption, 2023
Maps © András Bereznay, 2023

The right of Jonathan Sumption to be identified
as author of this work has been asserted in accordance with
Section 77 of the Copyright, Designs and Patents Act 1988

A CIP record for this book
is available from the British Library

ISBN 978–0–571–27457–4

Printed and bound in the UK on FSC® certified paper in line with our continuing commitment to ethical business practices, sustainability and the environment.
For further information see faber.co.uk/environmental-policy

2 4 6 8 10 9 7 5 3 1

To Beatrice, Reuben, Robin, Evie, Sadie and Naomi

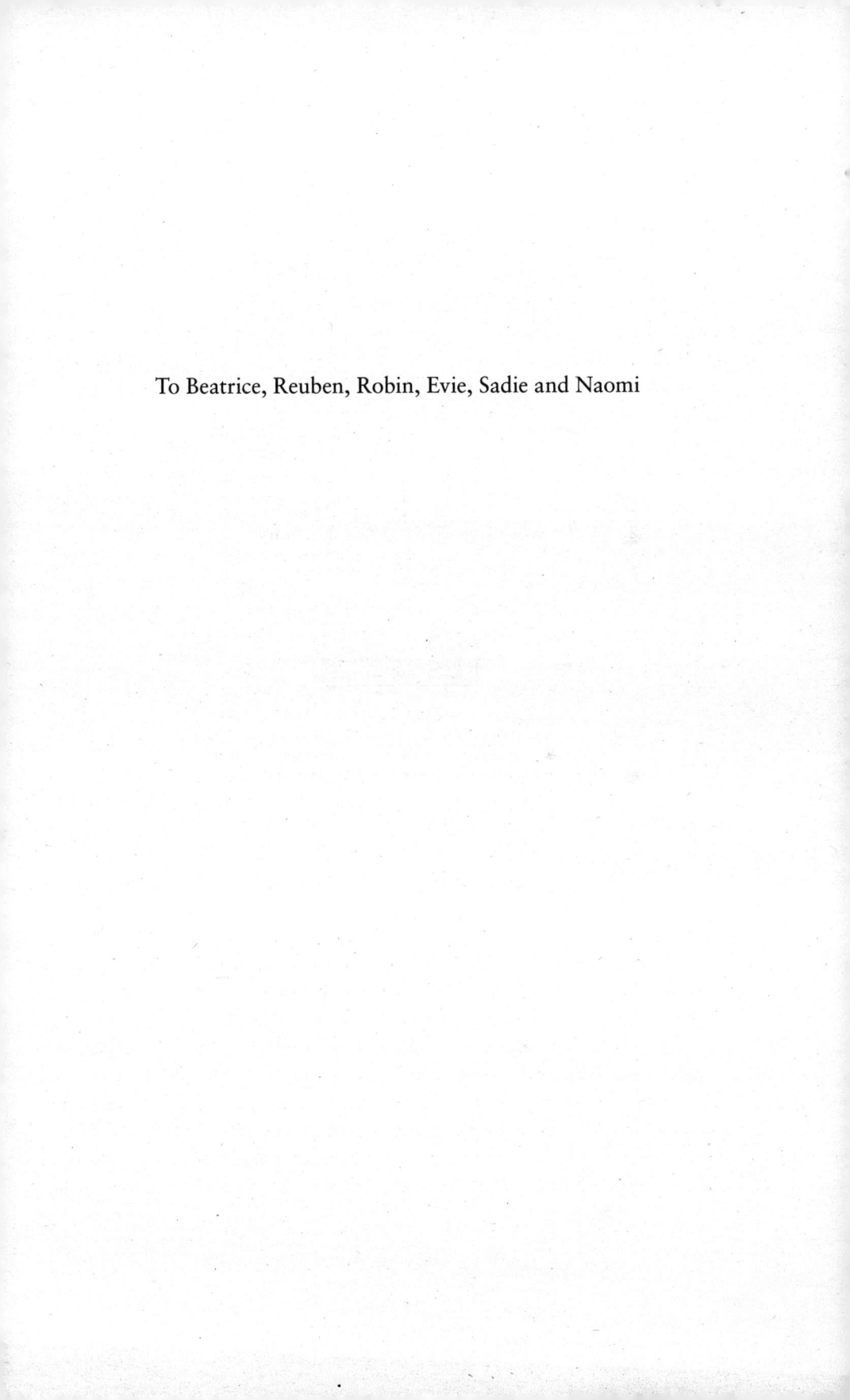

Contents

List of Maps and Tables	ix
Preface	xi
I Crises of Succession, 1422	1
II Allies and Adversaries: The Kingdom of Bourges, 1422–1424	60
III The New Army of Scotland, 1423–1424	108
IV Jacqueline of Bavaria, 1424–1428	150
V The Road to Orléans, 1427–1429	209
VI Joan of Arc: Domrémy to Reims, 1429	252
VII Joan of Arc: Reims to Rouen, 1429–1431	308
VIII The Parting of Friends, 1431–1434	375
IX The Congress of Arras, 1433–1435	431
X The Hinge of Fortune, 1435–1436	479
XI The King's War, 1436–1442	530
XII The King's Peace, 1442–1448	597
XIII The Death of Lancastrian Normandy, 1449–1450	656
XIV Gascony and Beyond, 1450–1453	718
XV The Reckoning	775
General Maps	811
Genealogical Tables: Lancaster, Beaufort and York	818
Note on Money	822
Abbreviations	824
References	825
Bibliography	891
Index	951

Maps and Tables

In the text

1	Dauphinist garrisons of the north, 1422–1428	67
2	The Cravant campaign, July–August 1423	97
3	The Verneuil campaign, July–August 1424; the battle, 17 August 1424	131
4	The siege of Saint-James de Beuvron, 6 March 1426	178
5	The relief of Montargis, September 1427	218
6	The siege of Orléans, October 1428–May 1429	236
7	Garrisons of the Beauvaisis and neighbouring districts, 1432–1433	324
8	The siege of Compiègne, May–October 1430	346
9	Anglo-Burgundian campaign in Burgundy and the Gâtinais, June–September 1433	432
10	The siege of Calais, June–August 1436	511
11	The siege of Pontoise, June–November 1441	582
12	The French invasion of Normandy, July–October 1449	667
13	The battle of Formigny, 15 April 1450	693
14	The siege of Bayonne, August 1451	731
15	The battle of Castillon, 17 July 1453	745
16	The siege of Bordeaux, August–October 1453	749

General Maps

I	France (April 1429)	812
II	Normandy and the *pays de conquête*	813
III	The Île-de-France, Picardy, the Gâtinais and Champagne	814
IV	Maine and its marches	815
V	The Low Countries	816
VI	Gascony	817

Genealogical Tables
The House of Lancaster 819
The Beaufort Family 820
The House of York 821

Preface

The wheel of fortune is one of the most ancient symbols of mankind, an image of capricious fate and the transience of human affairs. In the late middle ages it was everywhere, in illuminated manuscripts, in wall paintings and stained glass, in sermons and homilies, in poetry and prose. 'The wheel of fortune turneth as a ball, sudden climbing axeth a sudden fall,' wrote John Lydgate in *The Fall of Princes*, a work commissioned by one of the dominant figures in this history, Cardinal Henry Beaufort.[1] The present volume traces the remarkable recovery of France in barely two decades from the lowest point of its fortunes to the dominant position in Europe which it had enjoyed before the wars with England. Sudden climbing axeth a sudden fall. These years saw the collapse of the English dream of conquest in France from the opening years of the reign of Henry VI, when the battles of Cravant and Verneuil consolidated their control of most of northern France, until the loss of all their continental dominions except Calais. This sudden reversal of fortune, inexplicable to many contemporary Englishmen, was a seminal event in the history of the two principal nation-states of western Europe. It brought an end to four centuries of the English dynasty's presence in France, separating two countries whose fortunes had once been closely intertwined. It created a new sense of identity in both of them. In large measure, the divergent fortunes of the French and English states over the following centuries flowed from these events.

The passions generated by ancient wars eventually fade, but those provoked by the wars of the English in fifteenth-century France have proved to be surprisingly durable. The foundations of scholarship on the period were laid by patriotic French historians of the nineteenth century, writing under the shadow of Waterloo and Sedan. The passage of the centuries did nothing to soften their indignation about the fate of their country in the time of Henry VI and the Duke of Bedford. The extraordinary life and death of Joan of Arc defied historical objectivity until quite recently. Joan's story became the focus of disparate but powerful political passions: nationalism, Catholicism, royalism and intermittent anglophobia. Much of what has been written falsifies history by attributing to medieval men and women the notions of another age. But myths are powerful agents of national identity. The great French historian Marc Bloch once wrote that no Frenchman could truly understand his country's history unless he thrilled at the story of Charles VII's coronation at Reims. Writing in the summer of 1940 in the aftermath of a terrible defeat, Bloch looked to an earlier recovery from the edge of disaster for reassurance about the survival of France.[2]

If there is a corresponding English myth, it is in the history plays of Shakespeare. The great speeches which he gave to John of Gaunt and Henry V belong to the classic canon of English patriotism. His three plays about Henry VI, a truncated story of discord at home and defeat abroad, never reach the same heights. Yet they serve to remind us that behind the clash of arms and principles were men and women of flesh and blood. I have tried at every page to remember that they were not cardboard cut-outs. They endured hunger, saddle-sores and toothache. They experienced fear and elation, joy and disappointment, shame and pride, ambition and exhaustion. At the level of government, they were trapped by the logic of war, lacking the resources to conquer or even to defend what they had, and yet unable to make peace. It was the tragedy of the English that, after an initial surge of optimism in the 1420s, they realised that the war could not be won, but were forced to fight on by the memory of Henry V's triumphs and the incapacity of his son, until disaster finally engulfed them.

The publication of this volume marks the conclusion of a project on which I embarked in 1979. It is the first full-scale history of the great sequence of wars between England and France, into which all of their neighbours were successively drawn: Scotland, the principalities of the Low Countries and the Rhine, the cantons of the Swiss confederation and the states of Italy and the Iberian peninsula. It is based on a wide range of sources, many of them buried in the archives of England, France, Spain and Belgium. But I could not have written it without the patient work of many earlier scholars who have illuminated specific themes, regions, campaigns or personalities. The bibliography is the

PREFACE

measure of my debt to them. I hesitate to single out individuals, but two modern historians, Philippe Contamine in France and Anne Curry in England, have every historian of the Hundred Years War in their debt.

In the forty-three years in which I have been writing this history, I have incurred many debts of a more personal kind, of which I should mention three. I owe an important part of my education to Sir John Fastolf whose fortune, largely derived from the loot of France, was diverted after his death in 1459 to endow Magdalen College, Oxford. I was a history demy and then a junior history fellow of the college at the outset of my career, before turning to what Fastolf called the 'needless business' of law. I owe my interest in history and my appetite for this fascinating period to the generosity of the college and to two fine scholars, Karl Leyser and Gerald Harriss, who were my mentors there. More recently, I incurred another debt, to the Warden and Fellows of All Souls College, founded by Henry Chichele, councillor to all three Lancastrian Kings, to honour the dead of their wars in France. In the stimulating environment of All Souls, where I was a visiting fellow in 2019–20, I wrote the three chapters on the siege of Orléans and Joan of Arc. Last but certainly not least, I owe more than words can say to Teresa, my infinitely tolerant and encouraging wife. Our marriage has lasted even longer than the writing of these volumes.

J. P. C. S.,
Greenwich,
September 2022

CHAPTER I

Crises of Succession, 1422

On 11 November 1422, Charles VI of France was laid to rest in the Benedictine abbey of Saint-Denis, the great mausoleum of the French monarchy north of Paris. The King never dies. As the coffin was lowered into the ground, the household officers of the dead man broke their staffs of office and threw them into the opening to mark the end of a reign, while the heralds proclaimed the beginning of another: 'God save Henry, by the grace of God King of France and England, our sovereign lord.' Even in the threadbare condition of the French state, the outward decencies had been observed. Mourning robes were distributed to several hundred officers and servants of the royal household. Specially embroidered vestments were issued to the monks. Four thousand pounds of wax were said to have been burned to light up the cavernous gloom of the basilica. The walls and pillars had been draped from top to bottom in blue cloth embroidered with gold fleurs-de-lys that glittered in the candlelight. Alms were distributed to 5,000 beggars pressing round the abbey gates. Even so, it was a dismal occasion in keeping with the wretched final years of the dead King, carefully stage-managed by the enemies who had controlled his every movement since 1418. Not a single French royal prince or great nobleman was present. The only state mourner was the English Regent, John of Lancaster Duke of Bedford, dressed in a black cape and cloak. Around the grave gathered the Bishop of Paris supported by two other bishops, the Chancellor of France, the chamberlains of the royal household, the presidents of the Parlement of Paris and a handful of judges, every one of them a creature of England's ally, Philip the Good Duke of Burgundy. Philip himself, however, had not troubled to attend. As the catafalque was carried from the choir, a sordid fight broke out between the monks and the late King's servants over the cloth of woven gold which covered his effigy, each side claiming it as their spoil. The Duke of Bedford regarded the whole occasion as a distraction from other business. He was not even present at the traditional banquet which followed but dined alone in a nearby chamber before hurrying back to Paris.[1]

The new King was an eleven-month-old baby living beyond the Channel at Windsor castle. Henry VI, by the grace of God King of France and England, was the son of Charles VI's youngest daughter Catherine and the English King Henry V, victor of Agincourt and conqueror of much of northern France. Their marriage at Troyes in June 1420 had been intended to lend legitimacy to the peace treaty which had been sealed in the city a few days earlier. The treaty of Troyes had been negotiated between Henry V and the Duke of Burgundy in the aftermath of the brutal murder of the Duke's father John the Fearless on the bridge of Montereau. The treaty had been authorised by an assembly of French notables of uncertain status shortly before it was sealed, and had received the assent, more or less forced, of the witless Charles VI and his Queen, Isabelle of Bavaria. Six months later, in December 1420, it had been ratified at a meeting of the Estates-General in Paris representing most of northern France. The treaty remained, however, a controversial instrument, repudiated by much of the rest of the country. Under its terms, France and England were to be ruled as separate kingdoms but by the same monarch. The incapable old King disinherited his last surviving son, the Dauphin Charles, who was held responsible for the murder at Montereau, and adopted Henry V as his heir. Pending the French King's death, Henry was to govern in his name as Regent. The treaty envisaged that the dual monarchy would eventually extend its dominion to all of France. The English King undertook to 'labour with all his might' to enforce his authority on the entire national territory.[2] At the time of Henry V's death, however, this labour had only just begun. Almost all of France south of the Loire, together with the provinces of the Massif Central and the French territories of the Rhône basin, acknowledged the authority of the Dauphin.

The men who devised the treaty of Troyes had taken it for granted that Henry V would outlive his sick and ageing father-in-law. Henry's sudden illness and death six weeks earlier at the age of thirty-six provoked a crisis which they had not anticipated. As the English Chancellor told Parliament the following year, Henry had personally embodied the dual monarchy. The conqueror's formidable military and political skills, and the awe with which he was regarded in both countries had alone made it seem realistic. One of the most remarkable rulers of medieval Europe had now given way to a mere symbol of authority. Yet the infant King was wanting, even as a symbol. He was too young for either of the great public ceremonies which traditionally marked the accession of a King of France: the coronation at Reims and the *joyeuse entrée* into the capital. The authority of a medieval king depended on the visible manifestation of power, the public rituals of government and all the theatre of monarchy. For many years, the only visible signs of Henry VI's sovereignty would be the seals on public documents issued in his name and the new coins which shortly appeared on the streets bearing the legend HENRICUS FRANCORUM ET ANGLIE REX over the combined arms of France and England.[3]

As he lay dying in the castle of Vincennes, Henry V had tried to grapple with the problems of his political legacy. He dictated a codicil to his will in which he conferred on his brother Humphrey Duke of Gloucester the '*tutela*' of the infant King and named him as his 'chief guardian and protector'. His uncle Thomas Beaufort Duke of Exeter was appointed the 'director and governor of his person'. In England, the exact meaning of these expressions was to give rise to much debate in the following months. The arrangements for the government of France were even more uncertain. The only wishes that Henry V seems to have expressed were communicated orally to the small group of men gathered round his bed a few hours before his death. He committed the government of Normandy to his other brother John Duke of Bedford for a 'limited period'. Meanwhile, the regency of France was to be offered to Philip Duke of Burgundy, and only if he refused it to Bedford. These were interim measures while Charles VI was still alive. What was to happen after Charles's death remained entirely unclear.[4]

The offer of the regency of France to Philip of Burgundy was a political necessity. As Henry V had reminded the friends gathered round his deathbed, the Burgundian alliance was the foundation of the English position in France. Philip was notoriously prickly about the precedence due to him, and he was the only French prince of the blood actively to support the dual monarchy. But since its future depended on an English child and an English army, a Burgundian regency was not a practical proposition. More durable arrangements were settled by negotiation between Philip and the Duke of Bedford. Immediately after Henry's death, the two men had met at Vincennes. Bedford offered Philip the regency in accordance with his brother's wishes. The matter was discussed over the following days in Paris between their councillors. Philip regarded it as a poisoned chalice. He told Bedford, according to the court historian of Burgundy, that he would 'leave that burden to whoever was willing to bear it'.[5]

That was not the end of the matter. It was also necessary to secure the agreement of the judges and the *grands corps* of the French state, who saw themselves as the guardians of its continuity and integrity. The succession of the infant King was formally acknowledged at the beginning of November 1422, but the lawyers initially refused to countenance a regency. They took the view that the matter was governed by Charles VI's succession ordinance of December 1407. This instrument had been designed to avoid a civil war between the rival branches of the Valois family. It provided that instead of a regency, the government should be vested during a King's minority in the royal council, the officers of state and the princes of the blood. The Duke of Bedford would have none of that. After Charles VI's funeral, he returned to Paris from Saint-Denis with the sword of state carried before him, an ostentatious gesture which provoked much muttering in the streets. The question was only settled after the Duke of Burgundy had been consulted and Bedford himself had agreed to give suitable undertakings about the way in which he would govern. On 19 November 1422 he presided for the first time as Regent at a formal session of the Parlement, the highest court of France, at which he gave the required undertakings. He declared that he would 'apply himself and all that he had to the wellbeing of this realm and ensure that its subjects might live in justice, peace and tranquillity'. Thereupon, he received the oaths of the judges and officers present.[6]

John Duke of Bedford was destined to serve as Regent of France for thirteen years, until his death in 1435. Thirty-three years old at the time of Henry V's death, Bedford was the senior of the dead man's two surviving brothers. But for the birth of the infant Henry VI at the end of 1421, he would himself have succeeded to the thrones of England and France. Yet Bedford never attempted to displace his nephew or to carve out a continental principality for himself. 'Brother', the dying king is reported to have said to him, 'I beseech you by all the love and loyalty that you have always shown to me, that you will be true and loyal to my son Henry, your nephew.' Bedford devoted the rest of his life to this task. He had served his political apprenticeship in England, in the harsh school of the Scottish march. He had acted as his brother's lieutenant in England during the Agincourt campaign of 1415 and again in 1417 when Henry invaded Normandy. He did not arrive in France until May 1420. By then he had already acquired a reputation as a capable administrator and an astute politician with an incisive mind and a sureness of touch that reminded many people of Henry himself.

Opinions differed about Bedford's talents as a soldier. The Earl of Douglas, who had encountered him both on the Scottish march and in France, called him 'John of the leaden sword'. Yet Bedford had commanded the fleet that broke the French blockade of Harfleur in 1416 and the army which fought on the Loire during his brother's last illness. It is true that he was more cautious than Henry V and less dashing than his older brother the Duke of Clarence, which was perhaps the point that Douglas was making. But then Henry had been lucky, and Clarence's bravado had led him to his death at the battle of Baugé, a mistake which Bedford would never have made. Bedford was an able strategist, a careful tactician and a good judge of other captains, as Douglas would discover to his cost. Above all he was a sensitive and skilful politician, who understood the dilemmas of English rule in France better than most of his contemporaries. Although warily received at first, he rapidly established an excellent rapport with his French subjects, whose basic loyalty had always been to Burgundy rather than to England.

A large man with a powerful gaze, high cheekbones and a beak nose, Bedford managed to combine an affable manner with an imposing presence and a habit of authority. He spoke good French. He gave generously to French churches. He patronised French artists and craftsmen. He married two French noblewomen. He mixed easily with the French lords of his obedience and the mandarins of the Parisian legal and administrative world. Bedford acted the part of ruler as the stereotypes of the age conceived it. A year before his death he told the King's council that no one could have been 'to me as loving and as kind' as his French subjects. This was not a mere boast. 'Wise and generous, at once feared and loved', was the verdict of a churchman of Rouen. The querulous anonymous chronicler who recorded the internal life of Paris in these years was no friend of the English. But even he thought Bedford 'quite unlike other Englishmen' with their aggressive ways and love of fighting. Thomas Basin, a man of the next generation, became Bishop of Lisieux and one of Henry VI's Norman councillors in the last years of English rule. Writing in the 1460s, at a time when the English had been expelled and few Frenchmen had a good word to say for them, he made an exception for the Duke of Bedford. He was 'able and energetic ... brave, humane and just', thought Basin, and held in high regard by French and English alike.[7]

When the news of Henry V's death reached Westminster, on about 10 September 1422, most of the principal actors in the drama that followed were still in France. Henry V's youngest brother, the Duke of Gloucester, had been acting as Keeper of the Realm, but his authority automatically terminated upon the King's death. To enable the government to be carried on, a symbolic transfer of power was carried out in the late King's chamber at Windsor castle. On 28 September the Chancellor, Thomas Langley Bishop of Durham, accompanied by the principal councillors who were in England, surrendered the great seal in the presence of the infant King. The Duke of Gloucester delivered it in the King's name to the custody of a chancery official, who sealed acts on the authority of the council until more permanent arrangements could be made. The council immediately authorised the summoning of Parliament, the only body with the authority to approve such arrangements. The meeting was fixed for 9 November. In the meantime, a power struggle developed between the dead King's closest relatives. The main protagonists were Henry V's surviving brothers, the Dukes of Bedford and Gloucester, and his Beaufort uncles.[8]

Humphrey Duke of Gloucester was a year younger than the Duke of Bedford. He was a man of handsome bearing and great culture, charm and eloquence. He also shared the personal courage that was the hallmark of the princes of the house of Lancaster. However, for all his gifts, Gloucester's was a flawed personality. He laid claim to the mantle of Henry V and was clearly taken at his own valuation by many Englishmen, especially in London and in the House of Commons. They called him the 'good duke', but their high estimate of his worth was not shared by those who knew him best. Gloucester inspired some sycophantic verses from his protégé Thomas Hoccleve, portraying him as a new Mars. Years later, he commissioned a long narrative of his brother's conquests from the Italian latinist Tito Livio Frulovisi, in which his own martial deeds featured prominently. Sound judges, however, did not rate him as a commander and he never acquired a significant military following of his own. Gloucester was a disruptive spirit, assertive, opinionated, impulsive and intensely ambitious. He bore grudges readily and nursed them for years. In short, as a contemporary chronicler observed, he was 'noyous with to deal'. Writing in the 1460s, Pope Pius II said of him that he was fitter for pleasure and womanising than for soldiering and could never meet the challenge of living up to his own boasts. It is a harsh judgement, but not unfair.[9]

After the late King's brothers, the dominant figures in English politics at the outset of the new reign were his Beaufort uncles. The Beauforts were the children of Henry V's grandfather John of Gaunt and his mistress Katherine Swynford. Gaunt had married Katherine towards the end of his life and their children had been legitimised by papal bull and royal letters patent. Over the following years, they accumulated grants of land and titles, a tribute not just to their proximity to the royal line but to their conspicuous ability and service to the Crown. John Beaufort Earl of Somerset had died twelve years earlier in 1410. His four sons were destined to play a prominent part in the French wars and the divided politics of fifteenth-century England. The eldest of them, however, had been captured at the battle of Baugé and was currently a prisoner of war in France. His other children were still at the threshold of their careers. The dominant members of the Beaufort clan in 1422 were the two surviving sons of John of Gaunt and Katherine Swynford, Henry and Thomas, both of whom had played important roles in the conquests of Henry V. Thomas, who had been made Duke of Exeter in 1416, had been the closest associate of Henry V's wars. Their relationship dated back to the Welsh wars of the first decade of the century, when Prince Henry had been his father's lieutenant in Wales. When Henry became King and resolved to reopen the war with France, Exeter became the most powerful voice in his counsels and one of his most trusted captains. The fact was noticed by those whose business it was to know who had the King's ear. A Gascon observer reported that Henry 'loved this man and was much guided by his advice'. He was a 'little king', thought another.[10]

Thomas Beaufort's elder brother Henry was a very different kind of man, who was to play an even larger role in the new reign. He was a worldly ecclesiastical politician who had enjoyed the kind of charmed ascent through the ranks of the Church reserved for the scions of great noble families. He had become Bishop of Lincoln in 1398, within a year of taking deacon's orders, and Bishop of Winchester in 1404, when he

7

was not yet thirty. He eventually became a cardinal in 1427. Henry Beaufort was not a holy man. He ate well off silver plate, hunted to hounds, mixed mainly in lay society and fathered at least one bastard. He moved everywhere with a retinue fit for a King. He had sat on the royal council with brief intervals for more than two decades and had served twice as Chancellor. His network of clients and dependents extended through every department of government and across much of provincial England. He had led the English delegation at the Council of Constance and would have become a cardinal in 1418 if the King had allowed it. At one stage he was seriously considered as a candidate for the papacy. As it was, he played a prominent part in the election of Pope Martin V, the first uncontested Pope for nearly forty years.

By 1422, Beaufort was a statesman of European stature. Now in his late forties, he was wise, experienced and completely loyal to the English Crown. However, his most signal service was to act as the government's lender of last resort, intervening with loans at critical moments of the war. In some cases, it is clear that Beaufort was acting as a front for syndicates of lenders, but the major source of his loans was his own immense wealth. In a society where cash was scarce, Beaufort was unusual in keeping much of his wealth in liquid form. A Florentine banker who visited his house in London was shown a chamber with seven large chests bursting with gold, silver plate and jewels. On more than one occasion, he was able to send barrels of cash at short notice to the ports where troops were waiting to be paid before boarding the ships. The exact source of Beaufort's wealth has never been clear. Some of it must have come from the diocese of Winchester, the richest in England. He was widely believed to have speculated successfully in wool, although there is not much evidence of this. The likelihood is that most of his money was obtained by trading on his influence in government, raking in the fees, gifts and perquisites of high office. 'It not ben possible unto the said cardinal to have comen to so great richesse but by such moyens', his nephew and arch-enemy Humphrey Duke of Gloucester alleged in 1440; 'for of his church it might not arise [and] inheritance hath he none.' Whatever its source, his wealth was an important resource of the government. His loans eased its cash-flow problems and gave its financial management a flexibility which few continental governments enjoyed. In the course of Henry V's reign, they had amounted to over £35,000. By the standards of the time, these were prodigious sums. Most of the money was still outstanding at the time of Henry V's death. His loans to the governments of Henry VI were much greater.[11]

The dual monarchy was based on the principle that, although subject to the same King, the two kingdoms would retain their separate identities, with their own laws and institutions and their own resources. However, the Duke of Bedford was well aware that until the finances of the French state recovered from the disasters of the past two decades, the English position in France would depend to a greater or lesser degree on the revenues of England. He was therefore determined to avoid a formal division between the governments of the two realms during the King's minority. In this, he was supported by the English captains in France and by all the closest associates of the dead King. As the elder of Henry V's surviving brothers, Bedford asserted that the government of England belonged to him by the 'ancient usage and custom of the ... realm'. The Duke of Gloucester declined to accept this. He claimed the government for himself under the terms of the codicil to Henry V's will, which had granted him the *tutela* (or tutorship) of the infant King. This expression, which was derived from Roman law, was probably intended to make Gloucester the guardian of the King's property. Gloucester, however, argued that his powers as the King's tutor extended to exercising the government of the realm in his name. He commissioned lawyers to support this claim and scholars to research the precedents from earlier minorities. It was not for want of learning that his claims failed. It was because he was distrusted by many of his peers.[12]

There had always been concerns about Gloucester's ambition and lack of judgement. These concerns were now spectacularly confirmed by a disruptive step on which Humphrey appears to have consulted no one. In September 1422 he declared his intention of marrying Jacqueline of Bavaria. With this act, he blundered into one of most sensitive diplomatic conflicts of the time. Jacqueline stood out even in an age of remarkable women. She was the only legitimate child of William of Bavaria, Count of Hainaut, Holland and Zeeland, the greatest territorial prince of the Low Countries after the Dukes of Burgundy. She was also, on her mother's side, the niece of John the Fearless, the murdered Duke of Burgundy. Now twenty-one years old, Jacqueline would have been the most eligible heiress in Europe, but for the fact that she was already married. At a very young age, she had been married to the ill-fated Dauphin John of Touraine, who had died from an untreated abscess at the age of eighteen in April 1417. When her father followed him to the grave in May of that year, she was recognised as his heir in Hainaut, where female succession was well established. In Holland and Zeeland, however, the position was less clear. Her right to succeed there was challenged by her paternal uncle John of Bavaria, the prince-bishop of Liège. John abandoned his principality and his episcopal title in order to claim the counties for himself as William's closest male relative. He prepared to assert his right by force of arms. In this endeavour, he was supported by the leading commercial cities of Holland and by the German Emperor, Sigismund of Luxembourg.

Faced with opposition on this scale, Jacqueline needed a champion. She turned for help to her mother's family. At the time, John the Fearless was preoccupied by the civil war in France, but his heir, Philip, who was managing the family's affairs in the Low Countries, seized the chance to extend its domains. The acquisition of these three imperial counties would be a spectacular coup. It would extend the possessions of the house of Burgundy from the northern frontier of France to the Wadden Sea. Philip took control of the young heiress and promptly betrothed her to his sickly cousin, the fourteen-year-old John IV Duke of Brabant. The match was legally controversial. The spouses were first cousins, and their union required a papal dispensation. The Emperor, who was firmly opposed to any further expansion of the house of Burgundy in the territory of the Empire, lobbied hard to have it withheld. The Pope, Martin V, under pressure from both sides, first granted the dispensation, then revoked it, and finally reinstated it, but only after the marriage had been solemnised at The Hague in March 1418.

Their union was a personal and political disaster. Jacqueline found her new husband physically inadequate, financially incontinent and politically naive. He for his part found her bossy and demanding and conceived an intense dislike of her. In February 1419, Philip brokered a peace treaty between Jacqueline's husband and her uncle, by which John of Bavaria recognised her rights as Countess of Holland and Zeeland and abandoned his own claims in return for a cash indemnity. But her title was reduced to a shell by a series of improvident transactions which John of Brabant agreed on her behalf, in spite of her objections. He ceded possession of important parts of southern Holland to her rival, and then mortgaged both counties to him. John of Bavaria was allowed into possession of the whole territory, ostensibly as regent for Jacqueline. In April 1420, there was an angry scene between the spouses in Brussels, which ended with him bursting into tears and her walking out and leaving him. Anxious to save his vision of uniting Hainaut, Holland and Zeeland under his family's control, Philip of Burgundy tried to bully the Countess into returning to her husband. But he overreached himself. In March 1421, Jacqueline fled to Calais and from there to England. It soon became apparent that her escape had been managed by Henry V. He had sent an escort of mounted archers to protect her on her way and paid her expenses in England. As soon as she arrived, Jacqueline began proceedings in the papal court for the annulment of her marriage. 'She wanted the liberty to follow her pleasures', wrote the official chronicler of Burgundy with his habitual misogyny, 'and hawked her body around to another man.' Like other high-born young ladies, Jacqueline had been assigned the role of a pawn in the game of marriage, inheritance and power. Unlike most of them, she was a capable and spirited woman who was determined to take control of her own fate.[13]

Why Henry V should have officiously intervened in a quarrel in which he had no obvious interest, is far from clear. Philip the Good's Chancellor Nicolas Rolin came to believe that he deliberately planned a marriage between Humphrey and Jacqueline in order to serve his own territorial ambitions in the Low Countries. But it is unlikely that Henry contemplated a step which would have made an enemy of Philip of Burgundy at a time when his plans in France depended on his cooperation. Jacqueline's own explanation is probably closer to the truth: he acted out of personal sympathy for her plight. It is revealing that Humphrey waited before moving until Henry was dead and then announced his betrothal to Jacqueline within days. The haste was characteristic of the man. He did not even wait for the Pope to annul her existing marriage. It must have been obvious to the other English councillors that if the Duke of Gloucester controlled the government of England, he would use its resources to assert his wife's claims in the Low Countries. The marriage would divert men and money away from the war in France and undermine the Burgundian alliance. This was probably the main reason why Gloucester's pretensions to the regency found so little support. Henry Beaufort made himself the leader of the faction on the council which sought to frustrate them. It was the origin of the venomous feud between the two men that would divide the English government for the rest of their lives.[14]

At the beginning of November 1422, Henry V's funeral procession reached England after its slow progress through Normandy and Picardy. With the catafalque came the widowed Queen, the Duke of Exeter and most of the leading noblemen who had fought with Henry in France. On 5 November, when the full council met for the first time in the Palace of Westminster, Gloucester made his bid for power. He objected to the formal commission which had been drafted empowering him to open Parliament, because it recited that he owed this power to the authority of the council, instead of enjoying it in his own right as the senior peer present in England. His complaint fell on deaf ears. The councillors were asked for their views one by one. Not one of them supported Gloucester's position. The burden of recent history hung heavily over these men. Gloucester was threatening to become another John of Gaunt, whose attempt to found a kingdom for himself in Castile had undermined the war effort in France in the 1370s and 1380s. There were also wider concerns. Resentment of men who monopolised the spoils of office was a long tradition in England. It had overshadowed the dotage of Edward III and brought down the government of Richard II. The councillors were wary of conferring viceregal powers on any one man, especially if that man was the Duke of Gloucester.[15]

Behind the scenes, they had already resolved upon the solution. They would dispense with a regency altogether. When, four days after the council meeting, Parliament opened in the palace of Westminster, Henry Chichele Archbishop of Canterbury proposed in his opening sermon that the powers of the Crown should be exercised by a representative council. The Lords, whose role it was to resolve the issue, commissioned researches into past precedents and consulted the lawyers. They concluded that Gloucester's demands were 'naught caused nor grounded in precedent, nor in the law of the land'. They recognised that the late King may well have intended to make him regent. But, they observed, Henry V had had no power to dispose of the government otherwise than according to law and English law knew nothing of *tutela* or other such Roman law concepts. The Lords adopted the consensus of their leaders that the King's powers should be vested in the council, acting collectively. In all but name, it was a council of regency. There would be standing orders to prevent power falling into the hands of a cabal. There would be rules requiring a quorum to be present at every meeting and a majority in favour of any important decision. The Duke of Bedford was to become 'Protector and Defender of the Realm' and head of the council when he was in England. As a sop to Gloucester's self-esteem, he would perform these offices when Bedford was in France, but the Lords were careful to explain that they conferred no viceregal powers. Gloucester did not accept defeat. He presented an irritable memorandum in which the Lords' views were rejected as legally and historically unsound. He invoked the authority of the Commons who, he suggested, must have expected him to enjoy substantially greater power than this. His objections were overruled. On 5 December 1422, after three weeks of wrangling, the Lords announced their decision. Gloucester was obliged to submit. He no doubt hoped that Bedford's absences in France would be frequent and long enough to leave the substance of power in his hands. In this too, he was to be disappointed. When, shortly afterwards, the Lords announced the composition of the new council, it turned out to be dominated by the two Beaufort brothers and their associates, and by men prominently associated with the conduct of the war in France whose priorities were much the same as the Duke of Bedford's.[16]

Fifteenth-century England was a middling power with a population of about two and a half million. In addition, it could draw on the manpower of Wales and, occasionally, Ireland, both of which were separate principalities under the Crown. England was less industrialised than the Low Countries and less populous than France or even than that part of France which recognised the authority of the Dauphin. The country had suffered, like the rest of Europe, from severe depopulation during the epidemics of the previous century. Its population was still declining, albeit at a gentler pace. In 1422 England was in the grip of a prolonged agricultural recession that had lasted with brief intermissions since the 1370s. The previous years had been difficult, and the following ones would be worse: abandoned fields, declining agricultural prices, shrinking rent-rolls, falling land values, scarce and expensive labour. These changes were gradual but disruptive. They brought about a significant transfer of wealth from landowners to wage-earners. 'For the plough, none gaineth thereby but he that layeth his eye or hand daily upon it,' wrote the seventeenth-century historian of the Berkeleys of Berkeley castle after reviewing their estate accounts for this period.[17] The nobility and the richer gentry were particularly hard hit. Some of them were able to maintain their fortunes by successful military careers, skilful estate management, mergers with other landed families or the ruthless deployment of political power. Overall, the power of land, the traditional bedrock of English political and military society, was declining.

Long wars between established states are ultimately contests in the deployment of economic power. In the series of French wars which had begun at the end of the thirteenth century, England's main asset had been an elaborate governmental machine which had enabled its kings to deploy the country's limited resources more efficiently than its enemies. The ability of its kings to raise taxes, recruit troops and requisition ships had been impressive. The fourteenth-century Count of Saint-Pol, who had spent several years as a prisoner of war in England, was certainly not the only one to be 'amazed at how the English ever mustered the strength to achieve the conquests that they had'. But the system depended on the authority and personality of the King, and above all on his relations with the nobility. They were the captains of his armies, the recruiters of his troops and his chief creditors, frequently serving for years before they were paid. They were also, in effect, an intermediate level of government in England itself. In a world where influence and status were the chief instruments of political power, it was the elaborate networks of clientage and mutual dependence maintained by the nobility and the greater landowners which assured basic levels of public order in the English counties.

Ultimately, however, this precarious balance depended on their common need for the goodwill of the monarch. That shrewd northerner John Hardyng said of Henry V that his shadow fell across all England, even when he was campaigning in France. Looking back at his reign in old age, he thought that the King's ability to maintain order at home had been the 'rote and head' of all his foreign conquests. Hardyng's view is borne out by the sudden revival of a number of ancient aristocratic vendettas as soon as the news of Henry's death reached England. For some years into the new reign, the council was able to contain the worst symptoms of this renewed lawlessness. But in the nature of things, they could never entirely replace the firm hand of the dead King. In the longer term, the institutions of the English state would be engulfed by a rising tide of brigandage, piracy and aristocratic gang-warfare, classic symptoms of political breakdown and social fragmentation.[18]

Financial failure was the first symptom of England's ills. The current system of public finance had served the country well, but it was not equal to the cost of keeping a permanent army of occupation in France. At the time of Henry V's death, the English government's permanent revenue was about £67,000 a year. Of this, about a third came from the King's 'ordinary' revenues, in other words from the demesne lands of the Crown, the profits of justice and the proceeds of feudal rights of one kind or another. The rest came from the customs. The customs had for many years been the Crown's single largest source of revenue. They comprised a variety of historic duties, levied mainly on exports, which had been granted to the kings as a permanent addition to their revenues; and the wool subsidy, or *maltolt* ('bad tax'), a supplementary export duty on wool which depended on regular Parliamentary grants but had come to be regarded as a permanent tax. The financial statements presented to Parliament in May 1421 suggested that the King's permanent revenues were entirely consumed by the cost of the royal household, the ordinary administration of England and Ireland, and the garrisons of Calais and the Scottish march, leaving nothing at all for military operations in France.[19]

The problems of Henry V's successors were considerably worse. In the first place, they inherited the dead King's leaden legacy of debt. Henry had left an insolvent personal estate which took more than twenty years to wind up. The deficiency was met in part from the ordinary receipts of the royal demesne over the next decade, and in part out of the revenues of the duchy of Lancaster, which had been placed in the hands of trustees charged with the payment of his debts and the support of his widow. The result was a substantial burden on the new King's hereditary revenues, from which he was not freed until the 1440s. In addition, there were the much larger public debts amassed during seven years of intensive military operations. Their total amount cannot be determined, but some examples will give an idea of their scale. Arrears from the Agincourt campaign of 1415 were still being settled in the 1430s, and some remained outstanding a decade later. John Holland Earl of Huntingdon, who had been captured at the battle of Baugé in 1421, claimed to have accumulated arrears of more than £8,000 in war wages for himself and his company in addition to £1,000 in prize money for the capture of some Genoese carracks in 1416. At the beginning of the new reign, the arrears of wages owing to the garrisons of Calais and its outlying forts alone exceeded £30,000.

Henry V had managed to sustain his cash-flow in his final years only by borrowing against future revenues and by allowing unpaid debts to accumulate.[20]

More serious, because its effects would be felt for longer, was the decline of the customs revenues. This had been a problem since the last years of Edward III, but it reached crisis proportions under Henry VI. The main reason was the rise of the domestic cloth industry, which provided a steadily growing market for wool that would otherwise have been exported. Already in the 1370s, Chaucer's Wife of Bath made cloth which 'passed hem of Ypres and of Gaunt'. By 1422, finished cloth had overtaken raw wool in England's export markets. East Anglia and the Cotswolds, which were the main centres of cloth-making, became the richest regions of the country, their fine halls and churches standing to this day as visible monuments to the prosperity of the trade. For the Crown, however, it was an unmitigated misfortune. The English Kings had been able to tax wool exports as heavily as they did because the country was the only significant source of high-quality raw wool in northern Europe. But English cloth faced stiff competition from the domestic cloth industries of Flanders and Brabant and could not be taxed at comparable rates without killing the trade. The result can be seen in the figures. In the golden age of English public finance, in the 1350s, the customs had yielded more than £100,000 in a good year, but the receipts in 1422 were just £45,800. At their nadir a decade later, they would fall below £30,000. This not only reduced the King's revenues, but drastically reduced his borrowing capacity, for assignments from the regular stream of customs revenue had traditionally provided the most attractive security for loans. The mercantile interest was well represented in the Commons and was in no mood to help. The wool subsidy had been granted to Henry V for life, but his son's first Parliament would not renew it for more than two years and then at a reduced rate.[21]

The English government had no access to long-term loans. The wars of Edward I and Edward II and the early campaigns of Edward III had been funded in large part by the great Italian banking houses. Their fingers had been burned when the Kings defaulted, and their successors withdrew from the market. Thereafter, the government's credit was never good enough to support an ambitious programme of foreign borrowing. Henry V and Henry VI borrowed almost entirely from their own subjects. Their borrowing was short-term, intended to meet pressure on their cash-flow at critical moments, and did not therefore constitute an addition to the government's resources. Money was advanced for terms of weeks or months and secured against future revenues or pledges of jewellery or plate. Much of the debt had to be repaid from further borrowing, sometimes from the same lenders. The largest single creditor by far was the supremely wealthy Henry Beaufort. Over the next twenty-four years he lent over £180,000 to the Crown. Further large sums were borrowed from the merchants of the Calais Staple (nearly £87,000 in the course of the reign), the corporation of London (over £56,000), individual Londoners (nearly £50,000), the trustees of the Duchy of Lancaster (nearly £42,000), the Italian merchant community in England (about £16,000), the Archbishop of Canterbury (over £14,000) and innumerable municipal and religious corporations and private individuals in the shires (about £40,000).

During the reign of Henry V Parliament had begun the practice of authorising the King to borrow against future tax revenues up to a given limit. Initially, the government was only authorised to anticipate taxes already granted. But in 1421 Parliament began to authorise borrowing up to specified amounts against the proceeds of taxes not yet granted. This practice continued throughout the reign of Henry VI and became a significant feature of English public finance.

Government borrowing was expensive, even with first class security. Interest was a sensitive subject because of the Church's prohibition of usury, but it was an almost universal commercial practice. That well-informed councillor and judge Sir John Fortescue, writing in the 1460s, recorded that Henry VI had generally paid between 25 and 33 per cent on his borrowings, 'and thus be thereby always poorer and poorer as usury and chevisance increaseth the poverty of him that borroweth'.[22]

The only durable solution was regular Parliamentary taxation. Parliamentary subsidies were unpopular and politically problematic. The objections were partly principled and partly practical. The principled objection was the ancient idea that the ordinary cost of government should be met from the King's personal resources, which retained its grip on men's minds long after it had ceased to be realistic. Parliamentary subsidies were regarded as one-off emergency taxes. They were reserved for cases of 'evident necessity', generally wars in defence of the realm, when the Commons were conventionally bound to support the King with their purses. The practical problem was that Parliamentary subsidies were direct taxes levied as a standard proportion of the value of movable property, a tenth in the towns and a fifteenth in the country, according to an assessment dating back to 1334. A standard subsidy was reckoned to produce about £37,000, or £52,000 if matched by a grant of the clergy, as it usually was. In 1334 the population had been larger and the geographical distribution of wealth very different. A century later, parts of the country had real difficulty in raising the amount of their assessment. Taxes had to be paid in cash, which was hard to find in an economy still partly based on barter, where silver coin was in short supply. England had been a precociously developed tax state in the early years of the war, but its failure to develop a sales tax like the French *aides* had ossified the system and meant that by the fifteenth century the tax base bore little relation to the real resources of the country. In the afterglow of his victories, Henry V had been able to impose heavier burdens on his subjects than any king had done before, or indeed for many years afterwards. But by the end of his reign, the Parliamentary Commons had had enough. In October 1419, amid growing signs of tax exhaustion, they had bluntly told the King's representatives that while they were willing to pay for the defence of England, they would vote no more taxes to support the war in France. Apart from a solitary subsidy granted to Henry V at the end of 1421, they stuck to this line for nine years, until 1428. Coming on top of the decline of the customs, the result was to cut the English government's annual revenues from all sources to barely half those which Henry V had enjoyed.[23]

The Commons' indifference to the government's financial embarrassment was symptomatic of a more general disengagement of English society from the French war. After the treaty of Troyes, England and France were nominally at peace. The Commons took the view that English taxes should not be used to support the civil administration of France or to pay for military operations there. They regarded the continuing struggle with the Dauphin as an internal crisis of the French state, rather than an English national enterprise. The signs are that most Englishmen agreed with this. They were not entirely deluded. With Normandy occupied, the Duke of Burgundy an ally and Brittany neutral, England no longer had an enemy on the opposite side of the Channel. The frontier of Valois France was more than 200 miles away on the Loire. The Dauphin had few ships and no Atlantic ports apart from La Rochelle in Poitou. A Dauphinist garrison still clung on to the fortress of Le Crotoy at the mouth of the Somme, surrounded by hostile territory, but the French were never able to base a fleet there, and in any event its days in their hands were numbered. As a result, French seaborne attacks on the English coast and English shipping had almost ceased. As for France's allies, Scotland and Castile, they both had important contingents serving in the Dauphin's armies in France, but neither was willing to attack England directly. The northern marches of England had been quiescent for five years; and Castile, although still willing to furnish transports for Scottish companies crossing to France, had abandoned the cruiser wars and resumed active trading links with England.[24]

The patriotic fervour which had sustained Henry V's enterprise was already fading when he died. In some regions, such as Lancashire, an older tradition of military service in France was still vigorous. London and East Anglia were also important recruiting grounds for English armies. But in most of England, the government had difficulty in recruiting troops to serve overseas. These difficulties mounted in the new reign, especially among the nobility and the larger landowners who had been the backbone of past continental expeditions. Their contribution was important not just in itself, but because their networks of clients and dependents in the English counties were a major source of recruits. Most of them fought for status, not money. The honour of serving under the King's eye had always been the biggest draw, and military service was a route to royal favour even when the King was not present in person. Nearly four-fifths of the Parliamentary peerage served in the army that accompanied Henry V to France in 1415, but an infant king whose patronage was controlled by his council could never have matched the draw of Henry V. Only half of the peerage accompanied the eight-year-old Henry VI to France in 1430, and the number serving in less glamorous campaigns was much smaller.[25]

These problems reflected profound changes in English society, which was becoming progressively demilitarised. Men-at-arms were traditionally drawn from the nobility and gentry, who had trained from their early teens to fight on horseback with lance and sword. Noblemen of every rank continued to pay lip-service to martial ideals, which were still a mark of status, but the high rates of participation attained in the reigns of Edward III and Henry V were never matched under their successors. Every company which had fought at Agincourt had been commanded by a belted knight. However, the number of men willing to become knights had been in decline for many years. After a short-lived improvement in the reign of Henry V, the decline was noticeably steeper in his son's time. Captains commonly mustered their contingents with numbers of knights well below those specified in their indentures of service. By the 1430s there were probably only 250 to 300 English knights in all of England. Fewer than half of these ever served in France and only a handful served at any one time. In 1434, when a survey was carried out, there were only twenty-nine English knights in France out of a military establishment of about 6,000. Reflecting on the ultimate failure of English arms, Sir John Fastolf, who lived through the last years of Lancastrian France, put it down to the abandonment by noble families of the traditions of chivalrous education. Men 'descended of noble blood and born to arms as knights' sons, esquires and of other gentle blood', now devoted themselves to law and other 'needless business'. 'There beeth few captains as of knights or squires that wollen go,' as the council complained in the mid-1430s. Their numbers had to be made up by recruiting rougher men. They were the 'poor fellows' whom the herald Nicholas Upton observed, men who had 'become noble through their service in the wars of France by their own wisdom, strength or valour or by the divers other virtues which ennoble a man'. However, even with a broader social base for recruitment, the proportion of men-at-arms in English armies persistently declined during his reign. The balance was usually made up with archers, who were more plentiful and cheaper. The standard ratio of men-at-arms to archers was one to three. But as the war continued, the proportion progressively declined, reaching one to five or six or worse in the final years of the English occupation.[26]

The tactical requirements of war eased these changes. Most fourteenth-century campaigns had been cavalcades ('*chevauchées*'), involving rapid and destructive movement through enemy country, lasting no more than a few months. The fifteenth-century war was different. It was a war of sieges, calling for a permanent army of occupation. Service was mainly in garrisons and required long-term commitment. Most of the leading captains, all the principal garrison commanders and many of their humbler followers were career soldiers who spent years, even decades in France. The more successful of them received grants of land or office in Normandy. But this kind of service held little attraction for men with interests to safeguard and estates to manage at home.

With English armies increasingly recruited in a lower social stratum and the men passing many years abroad, the military community in France and the political community at home drifted apart. Gone were the veterans who had played such a prominent part in the county politics of fourteenth-century England and filled the benches of the House of Commons. In the first Parliaments of Henry VI's reign, nearly half the knights of the shires had served in France at least once in his father's time. Some had had military careers dating back to the 1380s. Over the following years, the number of men with military experience serving as justices of the peace or returned to Parliament progressively dwindled. The Speaker of the House of Commons was invariably a substantial landowner representing a county seat, and usually a belted knight, but of the ten men to hold the office in the first two decades of the new reign, only one had any military experience at all. The indifference of the Commons to the government's dreams of conquest probably mirrored that of the population at large. English chronicles from these years have remarkably little to say about it. France seemed a world away.[27]

Few people in England understood how complex the English position in France was. At the accession of Henry VI, slightly over half of the French kingdom acknowledged his authority. It comprised the duchy of Guyenne in the south-west and all the provinces north of the Loire valley with the exception of Anjou and Maine. But Lancastrian France was a political patchwork, not a monolithic block (*Map I*). Calais was a military and commercial colony, an outpost of the city of London populated by Englishmen and dominated by the powerful corporation of English Merchants of the Staple. It was generally regarded as an extra-territorial enclave of England: 'beyond the boundaries of this realm', as one of Henry VI's French tax officials once put it.[28] The ancestral lands of the English royal house in the duchy of Guyenne, now reduced to a modest part of the province of Gascony, were geographically remote, economically vulnerable and under constant threat from the Dauphinist provinces on its borders. The possessions of the house of Burgundy and the duchies of Brittany and Lorraine were autonomous principalities whose rulers were allies rather than subjects, and not always dependable ones. Paris and the Île-de-France,

Picardy, Champagne, the Gâtinais and the Beauce were governed by the English Regent through the existing administrative structures of the French kingdom. These were staffed by French officials, most of whom owed their careers and their allegiance to the Dukes of Burgundy. Only Normandy was firmly under direct English control, with an administration dominated by English officials and an English army of occupation.

Philip the Good, Duke of Burgundy, occupied a pivotal position in English calculations. Burgundy had been the richest and most powerful of the princely houses of France for more than half a century. The Dukes possessed two large blocks of territory in France. A western block with its administrative capital at Lille comprised Flanders, Artois, the county of Boulogne and the three castleries of Montdidier, Péronne and Roye in Picardy. A south-eastern block administered from Dijon comprised the duchy of Burgundy, the county of Burgundy beyond the Saône (technically part of the German Empire), the Charolais and the Nivernais. In addition, the Dukes effectively controlled the adjoining regions of the Auxerrois and the Mâconnais, although neither had been formally granted to them. Between these two blocks lay a broad crescent of territory which was not strictly speaking part of the Duke's domains but which he dominated politically. This was a region of populous industrial cities which had been won for the Burgundian cause in 1417 by John the Fearless's cynical promise of honest government and tax cuts.

The Valois Dukes of Burgundy were not just great princes of France. They also controlled important territories to the east and north of the French kingdom which belonged politically to the enfeebled German Empire. By a shrewd mixture of dynastic marriage, purchase and political pressure, Philip's grandfather had planted branches of his family in the imperial counties of Brabant, Hainaut, Holland and Zeeland. His father had married one of his daughters into the ducal family of Cleves and established a Burgundian protectorate in Luxembourg. Philip himself had purchased the succession to the imperial county of Namur from its childless ruler in 1421. In the late middle ages these regions were, together with northern Italy, the richest, most densely populated and most heavily industrialised in Europe. Philip's revenues in the first decade of his reign averaged about 200,000 *livres* (about £33,300 sterling). In the next decade, when the Burgundian empire expanded to absorb most of the Low Countries, they nearly doubled. This made them comparable to the ordinary revenues of England.[29]

The Dukes of Burgundy had been able to endow their disparate territories with all the trappings of a state, apart from a crown. They held a magnificent court. They rode from city to city with large armed escorts and clattering crowds of mounted courtiers, clients and officials. They issued documents 'by the grace of God'. They minted coins. They nominated bishops. They sponsored crusades. They conducted diplomatic relations with the papacy and the kingdoms of Europe. They deployed armies and fleets commanded by their own marshals and admirals. Flanders was rarely willing to furnish armies to fight in France and produced only a small number of troops, generally noblemen and their retainers attached to the Duke's household. From his other French territories, however, Philip the Good could raise up to 6,000 men. The armies of the duchy and county of Burgundy, which accounted for slightly under half of this number, were recruited in the traditional way from the kinsmen, retainers and clients of the nobility and consisted mainly of cavalrymen. Artois and Picardy produced the rest, disciplined, well-equipped companies, mounted for movement but fighting on foot in the English manner. In both regions, but particularly in the more heavily urbanised north, the proportion of bowmen rose rapidly in this period, reflecting the growing power of modern crossbows, the demands of siege warfare and the influence of English tactical doctrine. Bowmen had accounted for little more than a tenth of Burgundian armies of the previous century. But by the 1430s they comprised about a third of the forces recruited in the two Burgundies and three-quarters of those raised in Picardy and Artois. The Dukes were also quick to exploit the technological advances of the age. Their artillery arm was among the most advanced in Europe.[30]

The obligation to extend Lancastrian rule to the whole of France was one of the critical provisions of the treaty of Troyes. The prospect of preserving the country's territorial integrity was one of the main reasons why the dual monarchy was accepted by so many sincere French patriots. The completion of the English conquest would mean the end of the murderous civil war between Armagnac and Burgundy which had divided the country for twelve years and laid waste to much of its territory. It would settle the secular conflict with England, which had been almost as destructive. It would resolve the question of the succession, at any rate for those who believed that the Dauphin was barred by his complicity in the murder of John the Fearless. For much of the administrative and ecclesiastical elite, it offered a way out of the impossible dilemmas of a venomous past. Writing from Troyes as the treaty's terms were being settled, the King's proctor in the Parlement told the Parisians that he was certain that it would bring about 'a definitive peace between the two realms which, God willing, will endure forever.'[31] At the time, many people had shared this man's confidence.

Whether this ambition could ever have been achieved is an unanswerable question. In the event it was frustrated even before the death of Henry V by the success of the Dauphin's ministers in creating a parallel government based at Bourges and Poitiers, with duplicates of the principal political and judicial institutions of Paris. The Dauphin's enemies derisorily referred to it as the 'kingdom of Bourges'. But the kingdom of Bourges was a reality. The Dauphin's officers had effective administrative control and the strong support of the population in the regions which recognised him as King. The frontier between the two kingdoms of France was never impermeable. But it gradually hardened as each side sequestered the property of the other's subjects and treated contacts across the line as treason. The final campaigns of Henry V and the early campaigns of the Duke of Bedford concentrated on eliminating Dauphinist pockets in the north instead of pursuing the Dauphin into the heartlands of his power, thus reinforcing the partition. Once the kingdom of Bourges was securely established, its conquest would have required money and manpower on a scale well beyond the combined resources of the insolvent English kingdom and the war-torn provinces of northern France. The result was a frustrating stalemate with no obvious way out.

At the end of his life, Henry V himself seems to have recognised this. The war, he had declared, would be 'a long, dangerous, risky and very difficult business, between well-matched parties'. This had been his declared reason for accepting the mediation of Amadeus VIII Duke of Savoy. He had also welcomed the mission of the Carthusian Niccolò Albergati, the legate sent by the Pope to the courts of all three protagonists to support the process. We do not know what kind of deal Henry had in mind, but some reports of his final words to the friends gathered round his deathbed suggest that if his title to Normandy and, presumably, Guyenne had been recognised, he might have surrendered his claim to the rest of France along with the throne. This would have left England with a manageable block of territory in northern France which would have been easier to defend.

Henry V would have had the natural authority to agree to this without discrediting himself in the eyes of his countrymen. His successors were in a more delicate position. The Regent and the councillors lived under the shadow of the dead King. They were trustees for his infant son. As such, they could make any number of provisional arrangements but, as they saw it, they could not surrender his rights without his consent, which he was incapable of giving until he reached his majority. As a result, the English had nothing of real value to offer the Dauphin and abandoned the talks after Henry V's death. They were condemned to fight on indefinitely in a cause which they gradually realised was hopeless. The implicit promise of peace which had justified the treaty of Troyes in the eyes of so many Frenchmen, proved to be an illusion. The Chancellor of Burgundy Nicolas Rolin had been among the treaty's first champions but was quickly disillusioned. 'They called it a treaty of peace,' he wrote years later, 'but it might as well have been called a treaty of war and destruction.'[32]

What above all lent plausibility to the claim of the English to be the true government of France was the possession of Paris. In 1422 the city was a shadow of its former self. It had suffered from years of intermittent blockade, punitive taxation, political proscription and mob violence. After the death of Charles VI, there was no longer a royal residence in the city, for the first time in centuries. The Louvre had become a state prison and arsenal, its gatehouse let out for a workshop. The courtiers who had once filled the courts and gardens of the Hôtel Saint-Pol had vanished, leaving Charles VI's widow Isabelle as its only notable resident, a lonely, forgotten figure living behind closed doors in an apartment overlooking the Rue Saint-Antoine. The palaces of the great territorial noblemen and the mansions of the ministers and financiers of the Valois kings had been confiscated or abandoned. England's few allies among the French princes shunned a city which had been the centre of the civilised world only two decades earlier. The Duke of Burgundy rarely visited Paris and allowed the Hôtel d'Artois, his father's old headquarters, to fall into ruin. The Duke of Brittany's mansion by the Louvre was described in 1429 as 'empty, ruinous and uninhabited'. He had not set foot in it since the summer of 1417 and finally gave it away for nothing. The great Italian banking and merchant houses had left for Bruges and Antwerp, never to return.

Not one notable new church, mansion or public building was built in the half-century following the Cabochian revolution of 1413, the only comparable period of emptiness in the city's architectural history. The characteristic monument of these years was a celebration of death: the frescoed Dance of Death in the cemetery of the Holy Innocents by the market of Les Halles, which was completed in 1425. The skeletal figure of Death coming for men and women clinging vainly to life remained the most familiar image of fifteenth-century France for generations of Parisians until the cemetery was finally swept away in 1785.[33]

The flight of the rich and powerful was the visible symptom of a profound demographic and economic crisis in the life of Paris. Its population had halved since the turn of the century. Every contemporary description of the city in these years remarked on the spectacle of dilapidated and deserted buildings and empty workshops, 24,000 of them according to a plausible estimate in 1424. Their sombre accounts are borne out by the records. In its golden years, the bridges over the Seine had been lined with shops and houses, but a third of the buildings on the Pont Notre-Dame were now shut up and abandoned. Rents fell to historically low levels. The luxury trades were particularly badly affected. A handful of outstanding craftsmen found work from the Duke of Bedford and his circle, but most of the workshops closed down. One manuscript illuminator claimed that the fall-off of work had forced him to take a job as a sergeant at the Châtelet. In 1433 a jeweller declared that his craft was the poorest in the city. At least there were customers for those who sold bread, shoes and other basics, he said. Yet even that was not always true. Much of the market of Les Halles, once the centre of the city's food distribution, was deserted and its buildings in a state of collapse. The butchers' guild, formerly the richest in the city, complained in 1427 that some of their number were unemployed and starving. In the first decade of the English regime in Paris, the number of licensed wholesalers of wine fell from sixty to thirty-four, and even that was thought to be more than the market could sustain.[34]

For all its shabby indigence, Paris still had a powerful symbolic status. As a Burgundian councillor observed, it was 'the heart of the mystic body of the realm'. In a country of strong provincial loyalties, the monarchy was the only truly national institution, and Paris had been its seat since the twelfth century. The organs of government were all based there: the royal council, the judicial offices of the royal household, the Parlement which served as the ultimate court of appeal, the Treasury and the Chambre des Comptes, the departments which administered the mints and the royal demesne. On the Île de la Cité the old palace, abandoned to the bureaucrats since the 1350s, still hummed with busy officials, judges and clerks who proclaimed their jurisdiction over every French province, even if their writ in practice ran no further than the Loire.

With the Duke of Bedford's installation as Regent, a new nobility installed itself amid the debris of the old. The Earl of Salisbury moved into the Hôtel d'Arras in the Rue Saint-André des Arts on the left bank. The Earl of Suffolk installed his household nearby in the Hôtel d'Aligré, in what is now the Rue de l'Université. Robert Lord Willoughby, one of Bedford's most dependable captains who served almost continuously in France throughout his regency, lived in Hôtel de Bohême, the great mansion of Louis Duke of Orléans near the Halles quarter, with its vast gardens extending on both sides of the old city wall. Lesser men snapped up empty lots at knock-down prices. Bedford himself took over the Hôtel des Tournelles on the Rue Saint-Antoine. This rambling mansion, with its turreted façade opposite the Hôtel Saint-Pol and its gardens and tilting yard extending over what is now the Place des Vosges, was to be the headquarters of the English in Paris for fourteen years until they were finally expelled in 1436.[35]

The English were in power in the French capital, but it was borrowed power. When Henry V entered Paris for the first time as Regent in December 1420, he was ostensibly stepping into the shoes of King Charles VI. In reality, he was stepping into the shoes of Philip of Burgundy's father, John the Fearless, the ruthless faction leader whose partisans had taken over the city in the bloody coup d'état of May 1418. The figure of the murdered Duke cast a long shadow over the Lancastrian regime in France. The *grands corps* of the royal government, the municipality and the University were all filled with men who owed their places to the Burgundian coup and the brutal proscriptions which had followed it. Their first loyalty was to the house of Burgundy. Their sentiments were echoed by most Parisians. They loved the Duke of Burgundy, one of them wrote, as much as it was possible to love any prince. At crises of the war, it was the Burgundian crimson sash that men wore to proclaim their allegiance in the streets, and the St Andrew's cross of Burgundy that they unfurled on the ramparts. Bedford himself was under no illusions about this.

Nowhere was his dependence on the Burgundian alliance more obvious. 'Without his support,' he said of Philip the Good some years later, 'Paris and everything else would have been lost at a stroke.'[36]

Bedford was astute enough to treat the Parisians as allies and subjects, and not as a conquered race. He tried to persuade them that Henry VI was as much French as English. The painted genealogy which he ordered to be hung in Notre-Dame cathedral traced the English King's descent through successive Kings of France back to St Louis. The lion's share, about 95 per cent, of property confiscated from Dauphinists in Paris went to French partisans of the dual monarchy, not to Englishmen. He surrounded himself with French councillors. But there still were plenty of reminders of the foreign character of English rule. Ordinary English soldiers and officials tended to speak poor French and pronounce it badly, while hardly any Frenchmen spoke English. 'We don't understand what they say, and they don't understand us,' complained the curmudgeonly contemporary chronicler of the city. There were the inevitable curses and insults, brawls in taverns and fights at street corners. A priest taking part in a religious procession described in his journal how as he approached the Porte Saint-Martin the Duke of Bedford's cavalcade rode furiously through the opening, forcing the crowd out of the way and spattering them with freezing mud. Thomas Lord Roos caused much irritation by having himself preceded by buglers and trumpeters blowing their instruments as he came through the city gates, 'as if he were some kind of King, Duke or Earl'. This kind of insensitivity was no different from that of the French princes who had been cocks of the roost at the court of Charles VI before the civil wars but coming from foreigners it left a sourer taste. From time to time, there were more serious incidents. At Christmas 1422, the Duke of Bedford had to hurry back from Rouen when a plot was uncovered to deliver up the city to the Dauphin. The plot was foiled and the ringleaders executed. But the discovery provoked weeks of panic. A large number of suspected Dauphinists were rounded up and thrown into the Châtelet. Oaths of loyalty were exacted from all the more substantial citizens. Some of them were said to have sworn 'with very ill grace'.[37]

On the whole, however, there was very little overt opposition to the Lancastrian regime in Paris in Bedford's time. The main concern of the inhabitants was the security of their city. Much the most important factor in the English administration's relations with them was its ability to keep open the main road and river routes of the Seine basin, on which Paris depended for its trade and its supplies of food and burning wood. The English occupation of Normandy and the Vexin on its eastern march more or less guaranteed the free flow of supplies through the lower valleys of the Seine and the Oise. The eastern and southern approaches were more vulnerable. Their security depended on the shifting fortunes of war. Food prices in the city's markets were a sensitive index of the English military position and a powerful generator of popular discontent. Fortunately for Bedford, a succession of good harvests and the favourable military situation in the Île-de-France meant that the early years of his regency were years of relative plenty and low prices.[38]

The anonymous Parisian chronicler thought that 'the English did everything' in government. This was probably most people's impression, for the English, with their loud ways and armed escorts, were a visible presence. But it was in fact untrue. The personnel of the Lancastrian government in the capital was almost entirely French. The principal officers and departments of state inherited from the Valois Kings continued to operate exactly as they had in the last years of Charles VI, with the same personnel and the same procedures. The main organ of the Lancastrian state in France was the Grand Conseil, an executive committee responsible for the day-to-day business of government, comprising the officers of state such as the Chancellor and the Treasurer, some senior administrators and judges, and permanent councillors with no official 'portfolio' who were there because Bedford had learned to value their advice. In addition, there were the occasional members, generally powerful political or military figures, who received no formal retainer and rarely attended but whose voice was indispensable at critical moments. Almost all of these men were French. Bedford brought in a small contingent of Englishmen but none of them were regular attenders.[39]

The bedrock of the Lancastrian regime was a group of Frenchmen who had begun their political careers as Burgundian protégés in the time of John the Fearless. At the outset of the new reign, most of them were veterans of the Cabochian revolution of 1413 and the Burgundian coup of 1418, or else they were John's partisans nominated to offices in the King's government during the purges which followed. Some of these men regarded themselves primarily as servants of the

Duke of Burgundy. Others became committed supporters of the dual monarchy and remained so even after Philip of Burgundy had broken with it. The most significant of them were John of Luxembourg and his brother Louis, Pierre Cauchon and Jean Rinel. The Luxembourg brothers belonged to a cadet branch of the imperial house which had settled in Picardy, a region which had long looked for patronage to the house of Burgundy. John of Luxembourg had been the most talented Burgundian commander of the civil wars. Louis, the younger brother, had entered the church and become Bishop of Thérouanne in Artois. He had been responsible for burying the French dead after the battle of Agincourt, an experience which can have given him little reason to love the English. In fact, both brothers had initially opposed the treaty of Troyes and refused to swear the oath to abide by it until Philip of Burgundy made them. Yet both were ultimately seduced by Henry V and later became his son's most loyal supporters in France. Louis of Luxembourg was the nearest thing that Lancastrian France had to a prime minister. Bedford made him Treasurer and ultimately, in February 1425, Chancellor. He was a princely figure, haughty and authoritarian, a lover of luxury who held court with a grand household in his many residences in Paris and Normandy. He was also a man of martial tastes who, in spite of his clerical status, was entirely comfortable in the saddle taking command in moments of crisis. His brother John followed a similar trajectory. He became a permanent councillor and took command in a succession of campaigns in Picardy and Champagne for both the Regent and the Duke of Burgundy.

Most of those who worked for the Lancastrian administration had been propelled into the English camp by the fears and hatreds generated by the civil wars. Pierre Cauchon, Bishop of Beauvais, later notorious as the judge of Joan of Arc, had more modest origins than the Luxembourg brothers and belonged to an older generation. He was born in Champagne and had made his career in the golden years of Charles VI as a canon lawyer at the University of Paris. Cauchon had been drawn to John the Fearless by his campaign against government corruption, a cause dear to the University's heart. He had sat on the reform commission that produced the Cabochian Ordinance of 1413 and was appointed by John to the judicial service of the royal household after the coup of 1418. To a man like him, the austere rectitude of Henry V and Bedford was attractive. In 1423 Cauchon became the first permanent member of the Grand Conseil to be appointed by the

Duke of Bedford and he remained one of its most active members until his death in 1442.

Jean Rinel, who came from Lorraine, had first risen to prominence as a young man on the staff of the Dauphin Louis of Guyenne, who died in 1415. Like Cauchon, to whom he was related by marriage, he became a partisan of John the Fearless during the Cabochian revolution, which briefly overthrew the old bureaucratic establishment in 1413. When John recovered control of Charles VI's government in 1418 Rinel emerged as an influential member of the secretariat serving the Burgundian council in Paris. He played an active part in the negotiation of the treaty of Troyes and may have been one of its draftsmen. He was never a councillor, but he became Henry V's principal French secretary and performed the same service for the Duke of Bedford after Henry's death, achieving as much influence behind the scenes as most councillors enjoyed in front of it. Judging by his later writings, Rinel was genuinely convinced that the dual monarchy was the only guarantee of domestic peace in France. Yet he remained in the service of the house of Lancaster long after the dream had faded, right up to his death in 1449 on the eve of its final collapse. All the evidence suggests that the same was true of several hundred other Frenchmen who made their careers in less visible positions in the service of the house of Lancaster during the thirty years that their government in France survived.[40]

In addition to the council and the administrative and judicial departments in Paris, the English maintained a separate capital in Rouen, where a burgeoning bureaucracy was housed in the castle at the northern end of the city. This untidy arrangement was due to one of the abiding dilemmas of the Lancastrian regime. According to the treaty of Troyes, once the King of England had mounted the throne of France, the separate administration which Henry V had set up in Normandy should have been wound up and merged with the royal government. For French supporters of the dual monarchy, this was a point of principle. The unity and integrity of the French kingdom depended on it. The English saw things differently. They distinguished between the territories which they held by right of conquest and those which they held by treaty. The first comprised the duchy of Normandy and the so-called *pays de conquête* on its fringes, which Henry V and Bedford had forcibly incorporated into it: Perche, Alençon and later Maine on the south-west; the verdant plateau of the French Vexin which extended to the river Oise on the east and had historically been part of the Île-de-France; and a handful of fortresses like Dreux, Mantes, Poissy and Saint-Germain-en-Laye west of Paris. The treaty territories comprised the rest of Lancastrian France. The promise to merge their administrations had originally been made in the expectation that the Dauphin's cause would have collapsed by the time that Charles VI died. When the time came and the war was still being fought with unabated fury, this promise was honoured only in name. The Regent spent as much time in Rouen as in Paris. The King's council in Normandy continued to function, albeit ostensibly as a branch of the Grand Conseil in Paris and with some of the same members. The Norman Chambre des Comptes at Caen was abolished and its audit function transferred to Paris, but the finances of the duchy continued to be separately administered by the Treasurer and the Receiver-General of Normandy, both of whom were based at Rouen. Normandy retained its own hierarchy of courts and the Parlement of Paris had some difficulty in asserting its right to hear Norman appeals.[41]

The truth was that Normandy was too important to the English to be merged with the rest of Lancastrian France. It was their main military base and chief source of revenue. It had valuable ports, readily accessible from England. Together with the neighbouring provinces of Picardy and Artois, the possession of Normandy gave the English control of the Channel from both sides. In addition, large numbers of English soldiers and officials had been endowed with Norman lands confiscated from loyalists of the house of Valois who had fled before the invaders. Henry V had set out to create a new nobility of settlers committed to the Norman duchy's defence, very much as his ancestors had done in Ireland and Wales. It has been estimated that the nominal value of the English nobility's land holdings in Normandy was about a sixth of the entire value of its English holdings. The more important of these men took Norman territorial titles, becoming counts of Harcourt, Aumale, Mortain, Perche, Tancarville or Eu. Substantial English communities settled in the principal towns, notably Rouen and Caen, the 'English town' par excellence. Bedford broadened the Lancastrian land settlement, extending it to large numbers of humbler men, ordinary men-at-arms and even archers, who might form the kernel of a resident military class. By comparison, apart from some adoptive Parisians, Henry VI's English subjects rarely settled in other parts of France. His ministers never really felt secure in the provinces which they owed to the treaty, a political arrangement which they knew was no more solid than the alliances which had brought it about. To these men, as to the dying Henry V, Normandy was the redoubt to which they might one day have to retreat.[42]

The main constraints on English military operations were finance and manpower. At the time when he assumed the regency, the Duke of Bedford had a permanent force of about 5,500 English troops at his disposal. Thereafter, the permanent establishment fluctuated between 3,000 and 6,000 men. In addition, ad hoc armies up to about 2,000 strong could be recruited from the indigenous population for particular operations. Most of these men came from Normandy or from regions dominated by the Duke of Burgundy, mainly Artois and Picardy. They generally served under the command of John of Luxembourg or Bedford's French Marshal Villiers de L'Isle-Adam. In theory, responsibility for financing the war was shared between the French and the Norman treasuries. The war on the marches of Normandy was fought mainly by the English army in Normandy and funded from Norman revenues. The revenues of the rest of Lancastrian France were supposed to pay for the war in Picardy, Champagne, the Gâtinais and the Île-de-France, which was fought partly by English captains with English companies, but mainly by indigenous troops in English service.[43]

In practice, this neat scheme broke down, because of the collapse of tax revenues everywhere except Normandy and Paris. During the civil wars, John the Fearless had curried favour with the northern towns by abolishing the *aides* and the *taille*, the two main war taxes of the French state. He funded his government by resorting to coinage manipulation. The resulting economic disruption, combined with a Europe-wide scarcity of silver, had ultimately made this policy unsustainable. Henry V reversed it, reinstating the war taxes abolished by John the Fearless but promising his French subjects sound money. The Duke of Bedford stuck to Henry's policy, but the results were disappointing. The machinery of tax collection was successfully re-established in Normandy and the *pays de conquête* but not in the treaty provinces. In the early years of the regency, total receipts from the treaty provinces averaged only about 169,000 *livres* (about £28,000) a year, a small fraction of what they had yielded before the civil wars. In spite of the efforts of Bedford and Louis of Luxembourg, receipts actually declined over the first decade of the new reign. The corresponding figure for the year ending 30 September 1428, according to an estimate prepared by the English administration, was 129,240 *livres* (£14,360), about half of the projected expenses. Picardy and the Île-de-France, which had once been among the richest regions of France, yielded no revenues at all in the only complete account to survive, which covers a period of nineteen months in 1427 and 1428. The position was only marginally better in other regions.[44]

War damage was the main reason for these dismal figures. These regions had been fought over for a decade before the treaty of Troyes. Much of the land had been abandoned by the inhabitants to anarchy and scrub. The chronicler Thomas Basin, who was a student in Paris in the 1420s, remembered travelling across the plains of northern France and finding desolation around him as far as the eye could see. From the Loire to the Somme, he reported, the land was a sea of brambles, except in islands of security around the walled towns and castles. The only signs of life were beasts of burden, abandoned to fend for themselves.

In addition to the poverty of the land, there was a problem of authority. The Valois monarchy at its apogee had been able to impose taxes without consent by mere royal fiat. The English lacked the political capital and the administrative infrastructure to do that in regions where their hold was always precarious. Across Europe national or regional assemblies were the main means of legitimising taxation. The English made effective use of them in Normandy but there was no functioning system of representative assemblies in the treaty provinces. In the whole of Henry VI's reign, there was only one certain meeting of the Estates-General of Lancastrian France, at Paris in October 1424, and one possible meeting, at Amiens earlier in the same year. The practice was to levy local taxes for specific military operations in the regions directly affected. Thus, the siege of the Dauphinist stronghold of Le Crotoy in 1424 was funded partly by *tailles* levied in the towns of the Somme valley. The costs of the campaigns in Champagne in 1426 and 1427 were met mainly from contributions exacted from the cities of Champagne. The city of Paris was regularly mulcted for campaigns against the Dauphinist bands operating in the surrounding river valleys. Some process of negotiation and consent was generally involved in these cases. At least one local tax for defence was authorised by a meeting of the provincial Estates of Champagne.

Others were painstakingly negotiated with individual towns and cities. These ad hoc procedures hardly amounted to a system, and the yield rarely covered the cost of the relevant operation. The taxes levied for the campaigns in Champagne in 1426 and 1427 covered only about 60 per cent of the cost. The rest was met by diverting revenues from Normandy. As the Earl of Suffolk complained in 1425, there was never enough money to meet the wage bill of John of Luxembourg's army. He was inclined to put the problem down to waste and incompetence on the part of the Treasurer, John's brother Louis. But the truth was that the necessary revenues were not there. There was not even enough to pay the ordinary expenses of government. Bedford's government repeatedly defaulted on the salaries of judges and officials, a source of ill-feeling which more than once threatened to bring the business of government to a halt.[45]

As a result of the financial travails of the government in Paris, the burden of funding the war fell mainly on the taxpayers of Normandy. Normandy was one of the richest and most fertile regions of France, a 'fine duchy, powerful and wealthy', Charles VII's principal herald enthused, 'a land of wheat, of white and brown cattle, of lush forests watered by countless streams, and abundant plantations of apples and pears'. Before the civil wars, it had accounted for between 10 and 40 per cent of the revenues of the French Crown, more than any other region. It had suffered less from physical destruction than other provinces, but the wars had taken their toll nonetheless. The parish tax records reveal a picture of severe depopulation as people fled before the armies, taking with them all that they could carry. By 1422, however, a semblance of order had been restored and the refugees had begun to return. The duchy, which was better defended than the rest of Lancastrian France, became an island of relative peace and prosperity amid the surrounding desolation, enjoying a brief economic renaissance which lasted into the 1430s. The population rose by about a quarter. Boosted by a run of good harvests, agricultural production recovered. In the towns these were fat years, probably the best of the century. Cash flooded into the region in the pockets of English soldiers and officials. The trade of the ports enjoyed a resurgence from the depths of the civil war depression, as old commercial links with England and the Low Countries were restored. At Dieppe, the best-recorded case, the number of ships using the port rose from a low of 67 in the year of Agincourt to 269 a decade later. The textile quarters of Rouen expanded rapidly. In sharp contrast to Paris, with its depressed property and labour markets, the city saw a steep rise in craft earnings, rents and property values during the 1420s.[46]

Normandy was destined to be the milch cow of Lancastrian France. The English Kings took over the Norman demesne of the Valois Kings and their various public rights, such as confiscations, profits of justice and coinage profits. In addition to the heavy permanent taxes, the *quatrième* on sales and the *gabelle* on salt, local garrisons collected a tax known as the *guet*, which was in theory an alternative to watch duty in places with a professional garrison. The provincial Estates of Normandy were summoned year after year and sometimes several times a year to grant extraordinary taxes (*aides*) for war. In the 1420s, extraordinary taxation contributed at least half of the English Kings' Norman revenues. In addition, assemblies representing particular districts were summoned to fund local military operations. All of these imposts, except for the *guet*, were managed by a network of local receivers, *vicomtes* and salt *greniers* which Henry V had inherited from the Valois kings. Collection was always in arrears, and the yield of each tax was usually less than its nominal value, problems which were endemic in medieval financial administration. Overall, however, the English succeeded in mulcting the duchy for considerable amounts. At the accession of Henry VI, the government's net revenues from Normandy stood at about 292,000 *livres* a year. These revenues were drained by the cost of the permanent military establishment. In 1424, the English army in the duchy and the *pays de conquête* consumed between 22,000 and 25,000 *livres* a month, leaving very little to meet the ordinary costs of government. As the council at Rouen pointed out in the autumn of 1425, it was 'generally acknowledged that revenue will have to be increased if the government of this kingdom is to be carried on and the needs of the war satisfied'. As the military pressures intensified and the revenues of other provinces declined, Bedford squeezed more and more out of his Norman subjects, until by the end of the decade the duchy was contributing some 424,000 *livres* net to his coffers. This was more than three times the revenues of the rest of Lancastrian France.[47]

The English military organisation in France was based on a highly flexible system of mutually supporting garrisons. The scheme can be seen from Map II. The spinal cord of the English defensive system was the river Seine between Paris and the sea. Paris itself was defended by its citizens, who were organised in watches, district by district, for that purpose. The only English troops permanently based there were the garrison of the Bastille, which was probably about eighty strong. Small detachments occupied the gatehouses and the fort of Saint-Victor commanding the river entrance to the city. There were also English garrisons in the suburbs, at Vincennes and in the towers of the fortified bridge over the Seine at Pont-de-Charenton. West of the capital a cluster of garrisoned towns marked the eastern extremity of the *pays de conquête*: Saint-Germain-en-Laye, Poissy, Pontoise and Mantes. At the beginning of the reign and again during the two years that Henry VI passed in his French realm during 1430 and 1432, there was a major concentration of troops in Rouen. In the west the Seine opened out into a broad estuary guarded from either side by the twin ports of Harfleur and Honfleur, both of which were refortified in the early 1420s. On the northern march of Normandy, the main line of defence followed the road from Paris to Dieppe, which passed beneath the walls of the major fortresses of Gisors, Gournay, Neufchâtel, Torcy and Arques. In addition, there was an important garrison at Eu, at the mouth of the river Bresle, which marked the northern limit of the duchy. The main strength of the English, however, was concentrated on the exposed southern flank of Normandy. A line of powerfully garrisoned towns and castles extended along the Paris–Cherbourg road and another, further south, followed the chain of hills running from Dreux to Avranches. The most significant of these places were Verneuil, Falaise, Vire, Alençon, Fresnay and Domfront, which had originally been built by the Anglo-Norman kings of the eleventh and twelfth centuries to defend an earlier frontier.[48]

There were forty-four royal garrisons in Normandy and the *pays de conquête* in 1422. Most of them occupied the citadels of the larger walled towns, which were integrated into the towns' defensive systems. Their captains were nominated by the Regent for a year at a time, counting from Michaelmas (29 September), although the higher-ranking captains were usually allowed to perform their duties through deputies. The captains and their deputies were almost invariably English, or sometimes Welsh or Gascon. They were the pivotal figures in the English war effort. They enjoyed a wide discretion, high status and in some regions outstanding opportunities for enrichment. Some of them were reappointed year after year and acquired considerable knowledge of their districts. Every autumn, garrison strengths were reviewed. Each captain was assigned a specified number of men-at-arms and archers for the year ahead, some of whom were required to be mounted and some unmounted. The numbers varied from two or three hundred in the fortresses of the notoriously insecure marches of Alençon and Maine, down to a dozen or fewer in places further from the front. Altogether, about 3,300 men were serving in Norman garrisons when Bedford became Regent, rising to 4,000 during the first year of his tenure. Like their captains, almost all of these men were English, although as recruitment at home became more difficult there was a tendency to fill gaps with native Normans, Brabanters, or 'Picards', the generic term for French-speakers from the north whether or not they came from Picardy proper. Outside Normandy and the *pays de conquête*, the evidence is thinner. But we know that in 1425 the Grand Conseil was maintaining another twelve garrisons supported from the revenues of the treasury in Paris in addition to garrisons living on the local population. Royal castles were the visible arm of the dual monarchy. Proclamations were made beneath their walls, to the sound of trumpets. The cross of St George flew from their towers. The King's arms, carved and brightly painted, were displayed above their gates. Their garrisons assisted the *baillis* to keep order in their districts, suppressing brigandage and patrolling the road and river routes. They provided escorts for royal officials. They gathered intelligence and distributed it to other garrisons and to the councillors at Paris and Rouen. They were centres of local government, agents and symbols of the King's authority. But their prime functions were to serve as the first line of defence against the enemy, and as reservoirs of manpower from which to recruit field armies.[49]

In addition to the royal castles, several hundred other walled places were defended by local men or private garrisons. Some of them were performing customary watch duty. Some were freelance companies in English or Burgundian service. In Normandy, some were occupied by English proprietors who had been granted them on condition of military service. These arrangements did not work well. A handful of private castles occupied strategically important positions. Tancarville, standing on a high spur of rock at the mouth of the Seine, was probably the most significant of these. After the English conquest, Tancarville was confiscated from the heirs of the viscounts of Melun and granted to the Grey of Heton family from Northumberland. They held it on terms that they were to maintain a garrison of forty-five men. But it is unlikely that the Greys met their manpower obligation, and on the only occasion when the castle is known to have been attacked, by peasant rebels in 1435, it was captured without difficulty. Many other private fortresses proved to be equally vulnerable. Minor walled towns and privately owned castles served to safeguard the inhabitants and provide refuges for the surrounding district, but they were incapable of resisting a sustained attack. Their walls were usually ancient, thinly manned and poorly maintained.[50]

In the early 1420s, between a quarter and a third of the troops on the payroll of the Lancastrian government were not attached to any garrison. These men were the kernel of every English field army. Most of them belonged to the military retinues of the leading English noblemen in France. The Duke of Bedford alone maintained a military retinue of 400 men, which accompanied him wherever he went. The Earls of Salisbury and Suffolk both had large personal retinues in addition to the garrisons under their command. The same was true, later, of the Earl of Warwick and the Duke of York. The principal officers of the Norman administration and the district *baillis* also had small mobile forces at their disposal to serve as personal escorts and as a tactical reserve. For larger operations, however, it was necessary to draw on the mounted contingents of the garrisons. Generally, up to half of the total garrison strength was available for this purpose, but there were occasions when bigger risks were taken and garrisons were pared to the bone to supply men for field service. However, even with detachments from the garrisons, the Lancastrian administration in France could rarely raise more than 3,000 men for service in the field. To deal with a serious crisis, it had to tap other local sources of manpower. Englishmen holding grants of land in Normandy in return for military service could in theory be called on to furnish another 1,400 men at their own expense, although in practice there were many absentees and defaulters who never responded to the summons. An unruly underworld of unemployed English soldiery had settled in Normandy but were not attached to any garrison or retinue. These men, mostly deserters or men who had completed their indentures and decided to stay, were known as 'people living off the land'. They provided another important pool of military manpower which could be pressed into service when needed. Urban levies, generally crossbowmen and infantry, were conscripted in Paris and the principal towns. Noblemen, French or English, holding land in the duchy could be summoned to the colours at any time, and many came. The proclamation of the *arrière-ban* widened the obligation to all able-bodied men, noble or otherwise, but experience showed that it produced disappointing numbers of generally unenthusiastic troops.[51]

It did not take long for the Duke of Bedford to realise that even with these additions to its strength, the English army in France was not strong enough to mount major offensive operations. The burden was bound to fall mainly on England. Within days of assuming power as Regent, Bedford sent Louis of Luxembourg to England, accompanied by several of his most senior colleagues on the Grand Conseil and a delegation of the city of Paris. Their task was to explain to the councillors at Westminster that without reinforcements from across the Channel the war could not be carried on. Louis arrived at Westminster towards the end of January 1423. He persuaded the English council to send Thomas Beaufort Duke of Exeter and Thomas Mowbray Earl Marshal of England at the head of an expeditionary force of more than 1,400 men. A precedent had been set. Thereafter, expeditionary armies between 800 and 2,500 strong sailed year after year in spring from the harbours of Kent, Sussex and Hampshire to reinforce the English army in France. They served on short indentures, generally of six months. During that period their wages were paid from English revenues, together with the cost of shipping. Some of them volunteered to stay on at the expense of the war treasurers of Rouen or Paris, to replace the high levels of wastage and attrition that were a constant feature of military life in France. The annual expeditionary armies from England were a significant exception to the principle that the King's French dominions should be financially self-sustaining. In the first five years of the new reign, an average of about £8,300 a year was spent from English revenues on expeditionary armies. This was more than 12 per cent of the government's English revenues at a time when Parliament was refusing to grant taxes for the war in France. In the 1420s, the Exchequer was always able to pay the expeditionary armies promptly and in cash. But it achieved this only by building up trouble for the future: borrowing on onerous terms, defaulting on older debts and deferring other important expenditure.[52]

The critical issue for England's military administration in Normandy was discipline, which depended on regular pay. In principle, soldiers on the King's payroll were well rewarded. At a shilling a day, a man-at-arms could earn more in a year than the revenues of a small manor in England. An archer in garrison service got sixpence a day, half as much again as the skilled mason working on the walls. There were also benefits in kind. Garrison troops were accommodated free in royal castles. There was also the prospect of legitimate (and illegitimate) plunder. In Rouen, an elaborate military administration grew up, whose job it was to see that troops were promptly paid their due. But the administration always operated on a financial knife-edge, and there were times when the payment of army wages failed.

At the outset of the regency, the Duke of Bedford was faced with a serious disciplinary crisis. The sudden withdrawal of Henry V's heavy hand and the exhaustion of his war treasury was followed by several months of political uncertainty. Unpaid soldiers deserted or turned to looting. Captains unsure of the chain of command abandoned their posts. There were widespread reports of rape, burglary, cattle rustling and extortion by garrison troops. The Duke of Bedford appointed a judicial commission to enquire into the facts and punish those responsible. The Estates of Normandy were persuaded to vote a special grant to cover the arrears that had gone unpaid in the last months of Henry V and in the opening months of the regency. Such crises were rare in the 1420s. There were no mutinies, and desertion was not yet a serious problem. But discipline began to break down as the military situation deteriorated in the following decade and financial problems accumulated.[53]

Problems like these were endemic among medieval soldiery, but they represented a particular challenge for the English in Normandy. The breakdown of discipline not only undermined the military effectiveness of the army as an instrument of war but threatened to poison the relations between the English government and its Norman subjects. As Henry V's councillors had succinctly observed, the regular payment of wages was essential, 'the which must needs be done or else ... Normandy should be lost from him.' The Duke of Bedford understood this very well. In December 1423, he supplemented his brother's ordinances of war, which had been mainly concerned with field operations, by issuing a disciplinary code for garrisons. It regulated the appointment and powers of garrison commanders and captains of retinues and placed them under the authority of the King's *baillis* and judges. It required garrison troops to reside in their castles and not in lodgings in the town or in the surrounding country. Their servants, pages and armed varlets were subject to military discipline even though they were not on the King's payroll. Soldiers were required to pay for everything they took and were strictly forbidden to live off the land. Pillage, protection money ('*pâtis*'), ransoms and unauthorised tolls, the traditional methods by which soldiers supplied their needs when their pay was in arrears, were all banned in territory under English administration. Bedford's ordinance was ordered to be proclaimed to the sound of trumpets in every *bailliage* of Normandy.

It was true, and perhaps inevitable, that the reality never quite lived up to the promise. But the ordinance was more than window dressing. Undertakings were inserted into officers' indentures. Oaths were administered to them. Courts martial sat to try offenders. Captains were required to certify, before they could be credited with the legitimate gains of war, that they had levied no *pâtis* and taken no provisions without payment. 'Controllers' were appointed to the larger garrisons, who checked the captains' accounts and reported infractions. There were frequent inspections at which local men were invited to put their grievances before a royal commissioner. Their complaints were investigated with every sign of impartiality even when the alleged miscreant was one of the great captains of the day. Bedford's measures did not completely put an end to abuses and outrages, but it is significant that we know about these mainly from records of the action taken against those responsible. The worst breaches of discipline were visited with restitution orders, fines, confiscation of horses and equipment, imprisonment and even occasional executions. In the nature of things, compliance passed unrecorded. What is clear is that in Bedford's time contemporaries spoke well of English military discipline. Even the Dauphin's ministers acknowledged that it was better kept in English armies than in their own.[54]

The English military machine in Normandy depended on an exceptional generation of commanders. Most of them were career soldiers serving for long periods in Normandy, who had learned their trade under Henry V. At the outset of Henry VI's reign two earls, Salisbury and Suffolk, were more or less permanently based in France. Thomas Montagu Earl of Salisbury was the principal English commander of the 1420s. Salisbury was thirty-four years old at Henry VI's accession and had been a soldier all his adult life. He had fought with the Duke of Clarence in France in 1412, with Henry V at Harfleur and Agincourt in 1415 and with the Duke of Bedford in the sea battle off Harfleur in the following year. He had crossed to Normandy with the invading army of 1417 and had been given important commands at the siege of Rouen and in Lower Normandy. As the King's lieutenant-general in Normandy during Henry V's brief absence in England in 1421, he had been mainly responsible for retrieving the military situation after the Duke of Clarence's disastrous defeat at Baugé. Salisbury was a hot-tempered and undiplomatic man. He quarrelled openly with the Duke of Burgundy, and his relations with the Duke of Bedford were often difficult, but he was a hero to those who served under him. One of them, the chronicler Jean de Waurin, thought him 'the most skilful, cunning and fortunate captain to bear arms for two centuries past'.

Like many of those who served in France, Salisbury was driven by financial pressures at home. When he was twelve years old, his father had been lynched by a mob while leading a rebellion against Henry IV, and the family's titles and assets had been forfeited. Although the sentence was reversed in 1421 in recognition of Thomas's own war service, his earldom was one of the poorest in England. He rarely let slip a chance to make money out of the war. He took a hard-nosed line on ransoms, had a sharp eye for booty and carefully husbanded his profits. Like many successful war captains, he was a persistent litigant. The Earl of Suffolk once joked that Salisbury 'worried more about his money than his life'. He had good reason to. The war made him a great figure, rich and respected. Henry V made him Count of Perche, with a Norman endowment theoretically worth almost as much as his English estates. Bedford added grants of land and revenue, including a grand mansion in Paris. Salisbury's *état*, a kind of discretionary merit award paid to captains on top of their ordinary war wages, was higher than anyone else's.[55]

William de la Pole Earl of Suffolk was ten years younger than Salisbury and never acquired the same military reputation. His initiation as a soldier came in 1415, when he served in the Agincourt campaign. Like Salisbury, he probably embarked on a military career for financial reasons. He had unexpectedly inherited his earldom at the age of nineteen after his father had died at the siege of Harfleur and his elder brother a month later at Agincourt. But he was still a minor and his patrimony was burdened with the dower rights of two widows. So it was logical for him to return to France with Henry V in 1417. As it happened, the dowagers were both dead by 1419 and Suffolk was able to take complete control of the earldom lands by the time he was twenty-three. But by then he had acquired extensive domains in Normandy and a taste for diplomacy and war. He served continuously in France for twelve years. He was entrusted with major regional commands and was appointed Admiral of Normandy. Under Henry V, he became one of the richest landowners in the Cotentin peninsula. Bedford made him Count of Dreux with another large endowment in the valley of the Eure. He evidently thought better of Suffolk's judgement than he did of Salisbury's and relied heavily on him as a political and diplomatic adviser as well as a field commander.[56]

After the two earls, the man closest to the Duke of Bedford was probably Sir John Fastolf. Fastolf is famous as the supposed model for Shakespeare's Falstaff, but he had nothing in common with the rowdy drunkard of *Henry IV* and *The Merry Wives of Windsor*. His story was typical of the combination of patronage and talent on which successful military careers were so often built. His family were minor gentry in Norfolk. He came to the attention of his first important patron, the Duke of Clarence, while serving in his retinue in Ireland in 1408. Fastolf followed Clarence to France in 1412 and was entrusted with important commands in Gascony. He fought at Harfleur in 1415 and was invalided home but returned later to serve in its garrison. He joined in the conquest of Normandy in 1417. There, he caught the eye of the senior member of the Beaufort clan, Thomas Duke of Exeter, who appointed him as his lieutenant at Harfleur and later as the first English captain of the Bastille in Paris. But Fastolf's big break came in 1422, when he joined the household of the Duke of Bedford after Exeter had returned to England. He rose rapidly in Bedford's service, becoming his chief steward within a few months and then a permanent member of the Grand Conseil, only the second English soldier to be admitted to it.

Fastolf had by now escaped his threadbare origins. But wealth never dulled his acquisitive instincts. Even before the death of Henry V he had embarked on the steady process of self-enrichment that would lead him to accumulate property holdings in East Anglia, Southwark and Normandy and make a fortune matching that of many peers of the realm. His prime motive, however, may not have been money, for all the time and effort that he spent in getting and managing it. Fastolf relished the sheer excitement and challenges of war. He was already in his early forties when he entered Bedford's service and continued to take an active part in military operations until 1438, when he was nearly sixty. His surviving papers, preserved by his long-serving amanuensis William Worcester, show him to have been more than a brutal man of war with a lust for gain. He was a shrewd and reflective adviser with a sound grasp of strategy until the very end, when age and bitterness warped his judgement and people stopped listening to him.[57]

Beyond the tight circle of trusted military men around the Regent a group of competent and resourceful captains reappeared year after year in the major engagements of the war. They waxed rich in the prosperous 1420s before defeat and decline set in. Robert Lord Willoughby fought at Agincourt and served in France with only brief interruptions from 1417 to 1438. Willoughby was not a great commander in the mould of the Earl of Salisbury, but he was a reliable one, whose growing reputation can be measured by the expansion of his company. It trebled in size in the first seven years of his service. Family connections probably accounted for his choice of career, but there were handsome material rewards as well. Willoughby received generous grants of cash and land from the Duke of Bedford, and in a decade and a half of adept dealings built up a considerable property empire in Paris. The Norfolk knight Sir William Oldhall, another veteran of Agincourt, had begun his career as a household knight of the Duke of Exeter. He had fought in the Duke's retinue at Agincourt and Rouen, and held a succession of offices and commands in Normandy until 1449. The Nottinghamshire knight Sir Thomas Rempston fought at Agincourt, then returned to France in 1417 and stayed there for almost the entire duration of the war. He almost certainly came to France to escape financial pressures at home. His family estates in England were extensive and those of his wife even more so, but both were burdened by the dower rights of very long-lived widows. For some years after his arrival, he must have felt that the bet had paid off. He earned a formidable reputation in the dangerous south-western march of Normandy and received a handsome landed endowment there. More than a decade younger than these men, Thomas Lord Scales arrived in France in 1417 at the age of eighteen, and by the time he was twenty-three was already in command of 400 men in two critical garrisons of the southern march. He too would remain in Normandy almost to the end.[58]

The English army in Normandy was for practical purposes a standing army, something which England would not have again until the time of Oliver Cromwell. The long terms served by captains and ordinary soldiers made possible intensive training, accumulated experience and a habit of fighting together which greatly increased their effectiveness. For many years, the shared memory of past victory made these men confident that they could do it again. The military implications of this would be hard to overstate. There was a world of difference between a scratch force recruited for a particular operation, and a permanent army. Power, as William Worcester wrote, echoing his master Sir John Fastolf, lay not in numbers but in men 'well learned and exercised in arms'. Soldiers risk their lives for each other. Jean de Bueil, the French author of the *Jouvencel* who wrote what was perhaps the most evocative account of military life to survive from either side, captured something of the spirit of professional fellowship among soldiers. 'Men grow to love each other in war,' he wrote, 'your heart fills with pity and fellow feeling when a friend puts his life on the line before your eyes . . . You want to go and live or die with him, to love him, never to abandon him. No man who has not experienced these feelings can understand the elation that they bring.'[59]

Many of these men were united by much more than the war. They still belonged to the small, interconnected world of the English landowning class, even if they had left that world behind to make a career in France. The captains who contracted to lead their companies to France commonly recruited them in the English regions from which they themselves came. Men fighting together in Normandy were often neighbours at home. They had sat on each others' councils, acted as each others' trustees and witnessed each others' wills. They had served in the households of the same great men or risen by the same patrons. The retinues of the Dukes of Clarence and Exeter were great schools of future captains, in which Fastolf, Oldhall and Rempston among others had refined their skills. Some men fought with their sons, brothers or cousins. Others were related by marriage. Willoughby was the Earl of Salisbury's brother-in-law. His sister married Sir William Oldhall. The Earl of Suffolk married Salisbury's widow after his death in action.

A notebook jotting of William Worcester allows us to peer into an even smaller world: the billet of the Suffolk knight Sir William Bowet during the siege of Rouen in 1419. Eight 'lodging fellows' shared this cramped accommodation. These men's friendship was founded on much more than the common effort to conquer Rouen. All but one of them came from East Anglia, one of the most heavily militarised regions of England. Most had had dealings with each other in

Norfolk and Suffolk, like their fathers before them. Four had served in the household of the Duke of Exeter. Three were related by blood or marriage. Two were cousins. Two were brothers-in-arms, sharing the gains and losses of war. And at least five were destined to serve in France through the following decade. Behind the mutual loyalty of friends engaged in the common endeavour to make or mend their fortunes, lay deeper layers of sociability whose roots lay in the provincial communities of England.[60]

The English army was the most effective fighting force in France and possibly in Europe until it was overshadowed in the 1440s by the reformed army of Charles VII. Its fighting quality was probably at its peak in the decade after the battle of Agincourt. But its advantages were gradually eroded over the following years. Its discipline and training would eventually be matched by French armies, and technical advances in weaponry undermined its traditional strengths. English field armies were heavily dependent on longbowmen, who constituted at least three-quarters of their numbers. 'The power of England', wrote Sir John Fortescue a generation later, 'standeth most upon our poor archers.' The longbow was the English weapon par excellence. Its use called for long training and considerable physical strength, as a result of which it was deployed by no one else apart from the Scots. It had been the decisive weapon at Agincourt and in most of the great pitched battles of the previous century. For speed of fire and force of penetration, it was still unequalled. However, although the English retained their faith in it to the end, its domination of French battlefields was coming to an end. The longbow could achieve a range of as much as 300 yards but was at its most effective at much shorter ranges. It was outranged by modern steel-armed crossbows, which were rapidly replacing older models made of laminated wood. Firearms would eventually reduce its relative advantage even further. At the same time advances in the manufacture of plate armour were making men-at-arms less vulnerable to arrow fire. Lighter, harder steels had been developed in Italy. Angled, ribbed and fluted surfaces were designed to present glancing surfaces to deflect arrows and bolts. Horses were now routinely armoured ('barded').[61]

These developments undermined some of the old verities of English military practice. English armies were organised for field service in integrated units of mutually supporting men-at-arms and archers. Men-at-arms, although trained as cavalrymen, generally fought on foot in battle, using their lances as pikes. Trenches were dug in front of their lines to hinder cavalry attack. Sharpened stakes, planted in the ground and pointed diagonally outward, protected packed bodies of archers, generally stationed at the wings a little forward of the main body. They poured devastating volleys of enfilading fire on an enemy advancing against the centre. In the course of the fourteenth century, the French themselves had cautiously adopted elements of the English system. In the following century, however, the increased range of crossbows and firearms made these tactics less effective, while improvements in the armour and equipment of both men and horses led to a revival of the traditional cavalry action. This development was assisted by the invention of the *arrêt de cuirasse*, a hinged steel projection riveted to the right side of the breastplate which served as a rest and fulcrum for a couched lance. It made it possible for mounted cavalrymen to use longer and heavier lances. When properly handled, the heavier French lances greatly increased the impact of the cavalry charge and made it possible to disperse concentrated bodies of archers. Jean de Bueil thought that in his day horse and lance were 'the most effective weapons in the world', something which no one would have said a century before. English men-at-arms were not blind to these changes. They wore modern armour, as their wills and funerary monuments show. There were excellent armourers in London, and dealers who imported plate armour from Milan and other continental centres. But the French were quicker to perceive the tactical significance of the revival of cavalry warfare, and the higher proportions of cavalry in their armies made it easier to exploit.[62]

The design and construction of artillery underwent considerable changes in the first three decades of the fifteenth century. The English deployed two main types of artillery. 'Bombards', the largest type of cannon, were used as siege artillery. Examples are known weighing up to sixteen tons, although English bombards generally weighed less than that, between two and five tons. They were muzzle-loading pieces with long barrels, made from wrought-iron staves, butt-joined, then welded and bound together with iron hoops. They were bedded down in shallow pits dug in the ground to contain the recoil and elevated by placing timber wedges under the mouth. Improvements in the formulation of gunpowder increased its speed of ignition and force of propulsion. With a bore of between 14 and 20 inches, a bombard could propel a heavy stone ball in a high parabola over 1,200 yards in the

1420s. However, to inflict serious damage on stone walls it needed to achieve a nearly horizontal impact, and that required a firing position within 200 yards. Two guns of this kind, the 'Michelettes', still stand by the water gate of Mont-Saint-Michel, which are plausibly believed to have been captured from the English in 1425.

The other type of cannon were known as *veuglaires* in French, or 'fowlers' in English. They were lighter pieces, also made of welded wrought-iron staves. *Veuglaires* were cheaper to manufacture, easier to transport and quicker to cool down and refire. They were anti-personnel weapons, firing stone pellets or lead shot. They were often used between the salvoes of the bombards to prevent the defenders from repairing the damage or, occasionally, against the massed ranks of the enemy in the preliminary stages of a battle. In addition, English soldiers were beginning to use 'culverins'. The original culverins were hand-held field pieces made of cast iron, weighing about fifteen pounds, with a long barrel mounted on a wooden stock and firing lead shot. But in the course of the fifteenth century, the word came to be applied to larger field pieces. The accuracy and range of all these machines improved rapidly over the years.[63]

There were two main constraints on the deployment of artillery. One was financial. Artillery was expensive. The ironmasters who made the cannon and the gunmasters who operated them commanded high wages. The manufacture of gunpowder required costly materials. Bombards required long intervals between firings while the metal cooled down, which meant that for maximum effect they had to be deployed in large numbers. They had a short life, because repeated use wore away the inside of their barrels, reducing their range and accuracy. Early weapons were apt to shatter, wrecking them beyond repair and killing the men around. The other constraint was logistical. It was some time before adequate wheeled gun-carriages were devised for the heavier pieces. Unless the target could be reached by water, they had to be transported in strengthened wooden carts or on large timber panels hauled forward on rollers. Teams of oxen were employed to drag them overland at a speed which rarely exceeded five miles a day. These difficulties explain why armies so often abandoned their artillery when they retreated after a reverse.

Henry V had been fascinated by artillery and made effective use of it in his conquest of Normandy. However, English artillery really came into its own when the conquest of Normandy was complete and a

Lancastrian administration was created for much of northern France. Operating on internal lines of communication and controlling the Channel coast and the basin of the Seine, the English were now able to store equipment at strategic centres such as Paris, Rouen, Harfleur and Caen, and to move it relatively quickly by barge over considerable distances. They were also able to provide the administrative and logistical support on which artillery warfare depended. An ordnance office for Normandy was created at Rouen under the supervision of a series of English or German artillery-masters. Another was set up in Paris by the Duke of Bedford, headed by a 'Master of the King's Artillery in France'. In both Rouen and Paris there was a permanent staff of gunners, smiths, carpenters, masons, carters and clerks as well as an escort of archers to protect the machines while they were being transported. These men were charged with making and repairing the guns, building the wooden carriages on which they were carried and the large swivelling shields of timber ('mantlets') that protected the gunners as they worked. They carved stone cannonballs to exact dimensions. They bought in materials, distributed them to garrisons and organised transport. They also acted as general procurement offices for basic equipment such as arrows, scaling ladders and trenching tools. Most artillery-masters were just administrators, but some were true specialists. William Forsted, who was Master of the King's Artillery at the end of the 1430s, declared that he had been an artillery-master in Ireland, Scotland, Wales, Gascony, Normandy and the Île-de-France.[64]

Fifteenth-century warfare was first and foremost siege warfare, the perennial struggle to capture walled places from which the surrounding country could be controlled. Most French towns were still defended by walls dating from the first age of urbanisation in the eleventh and twelfth centuries. Some still had their old Gallo-Roman walls. In the face of the English invasions of the fourteenth century, the richer towns had rebuilt their walls and some castles had been modernised. But the development of artillery made their defences out of date very quickly. High walls had been built to resist assault and undermining but presented ideal targets for the more powerful cannon that came into use at the beginning of the fifteenth century. However, like other technical advantages which the English and their Burgundian allies enjoyed at the start of the period, their superiority in artillery waned over time.

The French learned how to counter siege artillery and became extremely skilled at defending walled places. They developed tactics for keeping the besiegers out of artillery range. Guns were mounted on top of the walls and gates to kill or maim the exposed gunners of the besiegers. Sorties were launched against the gun sites. Defensive bulwarks ('*boulevards*'), generally of earth and stones, were built in front of the gates, armed with their own artillery and manned by their own garrisons, which subjected assault parties to a murderous enfilading fire. The effect was to increase the distance from which the besiegers had to operate and greatly reduce their effectiveness. The improvised forts ('*bastides*') which besieging armies customarily built in front of the gates had to be sited further back, sometimes as much as a mile away.

The growing distance from which the besiegers had to work had a significant impact on the course of the war. It progressively increased the length of their siege lines. Building and manning them required ever larger numbers of troops and pioneers, a particular problem for the English, who were constantly coming up against the limits of available manpower. As a result, major cities and towns, although vulnerable to treachery and surprise, were rarely captured in the face of determined resistance, even with the aid of powerful artillery pieces. Rouen, which was captured after a siege of six months in 1419–20, was the last major city to fall to the English in the fifteenth-century wars. Lesser places commonly held out for many months before surrendering. Much depended on the morale of the defenders, which was intimately connected with the political situation. If there was a good prospect of relief or they were confident that the war was going their way, garrisons and townsmen could achieve astonishing feats of endurance, defying great armies led by talented captains and equipped with powerful artillery trains. When their political world was collapsing, they would often put up no more than a token resistance. Henry V swept through Normandy taking one place after another as the French civil wars raged between 1417 and 1419. The same thing happened in reverse when Normandy was reconquered by Charles VII in 1449 and 1450 at the lowest point in England's political fortunes.

Unless the walls could be swiftly carried by assault, a risky and bloody business, a successful siege usually ended with a negotiated surrender. The surrender of walled places was governed by an elaborate body of law and practice. The defenders were encouraged to surrender by the brutality of their fate if they did not. The customs of late medieval warfare allowed almost unlimited licence to soldiers who captured a walled place by storm. Once over the walls, the assault parties would force open the gates, and the besieging army would pour in. In towns, the attackers would spread through the dense network of streets with cries of '*Ville prise!*', indiscriminately killing, looting and burning. As the war continued, it became increasingly common to refuse any quarter to the defenders, even if they were worth a ransom. The more ruthless captains had entire garrisons hanged from trees or improvised gibbets outside the gates. Professional garrisons were often forced to abandon the fight by terrified inhabitants unwilling to run the risk of an assault.

Terms of surrender varied according to the defenders' power of resistance. At one extreme, the besiegers might insist on unconditional surrender, leaving the defenders at their mercy. At the other, the defenders were allowed to leave '*baston au poing*' (staff in hand), carrying the white stick which traditionally served as their safe-conduct through the enemy lines. Negotiations usually revolved around the question of how much the garrison would be allowed to take away with them. They almost always had to leave their artillery and heavy equipment behind, and usually their prisoners as well. They might be made to leave everything else, including their horses, armour and weapons. Money sometimes changed hands, especially if the captain was a freelance operating for his own account. The decision to negotiate a surrender was one of the most difficult that faced a fifteenth-century garrison commander. If he surrendered too soon, while his walls were intact and his supplies plentiful, he was likely to be accused of treachery and disgraced by his own side. If he waited until the place had become indefensible, he would have little to bargain with in negotiations with the besiegers.

The immediate surrender of a garrison was rare. The almost invariable practice was to enter into a conditional surrender agreement. The usual form was a promise to surrender at an agreed future date conditionally on the place not being relieved. In the interval, a truce was usually agreed, during which the garrison could forage for food but could not take in extra men or equipment. This arrangement saved the honour of the captain and cast on his masters the onus of raising an army of relief. The time allowed for relief depended on the strength of the defence and the state of the defenders' supplies. It could be as long as six months or as short as a day. Hostages were taken from the garrison as security, who were liable to be executed or held for ransom if the place was not duly surrendered on the appointed day.

The result of a conditional surrender agreement was what, in contemporary military jargon, was called a *journée*. It was in effect a challenge to an arranged battle. The besieging army would be reinforced to match whatever relief force might appear. On the appointed day, they would be found drawn up in battle order across the approaches to the beleaguered place from sunrise to sunset. Sometimes a specific site was agreed, sometimes a precise time. The enemy might accept the risks of battle and appear on the appointed day. More commonly, he would decline the challenge and fail to appear, allowing the place to be lost. This practice had a considerable influence on the strategy of all belligerents. It meant that successful siege warfare required a field army in reserve. Both sides needed to be able to bring in large additional forces so as to appear with credit at a *journée*. English commanders in Normandy were adept at this. The flexibility of the defensive system enabled troops to be withdrawn from garrisons and rapidly concentrated against intruders.

How the Normans looked upon their Lancastrian rulers is a difficult and contentious question. The evidence is plentiful, but it is anecdotal and inconsistent. All Normans were required to swear an oath of allegiance to Henry VI and were given a certificate (or *bullette*) to prove it. This gave them a measure of protection against being harassed or arrested by English soldiers or officials. The same system was applied, less consistently, in Paris and some other northern towns. Those who failed to swear were expelled and their property was confiscated. Those who swore and were then found fighting against the English were treated as traitors and executed. Agreements for the surrender of enemy garrisons invariably contained clauses requiring such people to be delivered up to the King's justice.[65]

These policies were characteristic of a government that never felt entirely secure. The Lancastrian regime in Normandy was not seen as a mere continuation of the French monarchy under a new dynasty. It was very obviously an alien administration. Soldiers generally lived apart in the fortresses to which they were assigned. The garrison commanders who exercised police powers in their districts and the regional *baillis* of Normandy were almost all Englishmen, unlike most of their opposite numbers in the treaty provinces. They had unfamiliar ways. They swore heartily and often (Joan of Arc referred to them as '*Godons*' – 'God Damns'). Many of them were ignorant of French laws and customs. The execrable French spoken by their subordinates was a standard trope of contemporary satire. Many of them spoke no French at all. 'Speak English – I know you can,' said an English soldier, provoking a fight at a local smithy in which he met his death. French townsmen doing watch duty on the walls were sometimes issued with passwords in English which they did not understand and could not pronounce. The common reaction showed itself in unthinking but revealing turns of phrase. In spite of heavy fines and the threat of imprisonment and forfeiture, Normans and English alike tended to refer to the enemy as 'French' and Charles VII as King, instead of saying 'Armagnac' and 'Dauphin' in accordance with the approved usage. The dual monarchy aspired to be as French in France as it was English in England, but its continuing dependence on English money and men made a mockery of the aspiration.[66]

Nonetheless, in the 1420s the Lancastrian regime clearly did enjoy a large measure of tacit support from the indigenous population of Normandy, especially in the towns. It could not otherwise have survived as long as it did, for the English were never strong enough to impose their will by mere force. This state of affairs, which seemed so unnatural to the Dauphin's advisers at the time and to patriotic French historians of a later age, should not have surprised anyone else. For a man like Charles VII's secretary Alain Chartier, loyalty to the indigenous dynasty was part of the law of nature. It was based on the simple facts of geography. 'Show that you were born Frenchmen,' he urged his fellow countrymen. Charles VII adopted the same formula in his public documents. He intended, he said, that 'Our subjects, natives of this realm, should recognise in us their sovereign and natural lord and obey us as they ought.' Every Norman who supported the English government was a traitor, according to a ballad of the time. Yet when Frenchmen were divided, what was treason? For the English, it was a question of law. Those who opposed them were traitors, regardless of where they were born, if they had sworn allegiance to Henry V or lived under the protection of his officers. For the Dauphinists, it was a question of natural identity, of geographical origin and above all of language. Some French captains routinely hanged native French speakers who were captured serving in English armies. The practice became increasingly common as the war lost the trappings of a French civil war and evolved into something that was more obviously a war of nations.[67]

National sentiment was slow to develop in France. It had traditionally been the preserve of an official and ecclesiastical elite. Beyond the small circle of the Dauphin's ministers, captains and propagandists, an authentically French patriotism only gradually emerged under the pressures of war. In the 1420s patriotism remained essentially local. The *patria* was not France but the province, the town, even the village. The civil wars had dissolved wider patterns of loyalty. Normandy in particular had a strong tradition of provincial separatism dating back to the Anglo-Norman dynasties of the eleventh and twelfth centuries and the Norman Charter extracted from Louis X in 1315. It had its own customary law, its own dialect and accent, its own solidarities. Henry V went to some length to flatter these instincts, reviving old offices and institutions dating back in some cases to the Angevin empire. The Duke of Bedford followed the same policy, endowing Rouen with new courts and government offices and Caen with a university. The most important and enduring institution was the provincial Estates, which had been virtually defunct for more than three decades at the time of the English conquest. Henry V summoned the Estates only once, at the beginning of 1421. But Bedford transformed them into an instrument of government, serving as a forum dealing not just with grants of taxation but with strategy, law and order, coinage policy and other matters. They fostered a sense of provincial solidarity and became an important source of political and financial support for the Lancastrian government throughout the period of English occupation.[68]

One of the most difficult and controversial questions about these years is the significance of rural banditry. Was it mere criminality? Or was it political resistance? Rural banditry was not a new phenomenon. It had been endemic in Normandy for many years before the English conquest, as it had in other parts of France. The scale of the problem varied with the economic fortunes of the countryside. Recession and war drove men from the land and into crime. The mass flight of the peasantry which followed the arrival of the English armies in 1417 led to a powerful upsurge of rural violence. Men lurked in the dense forest that then covered much of Normandy or, in the words of one of Henry V's ordinances, 'took to the caves, marshes and fastnesses to become looters and brigands, contrary to their oaths and their allegiance'. The surviving documentation, which is plentiful, suggests that the great majority of them were young men, generally peasants, agricultural labourers or rural tradesmen, and that their operations were mainly concentrated in Lower Normandy in the *bailliages* of Caen and Bayeux. Rural unemployment was high in these regions and the life of the countryside was regularly disrupted by raiders from Mont-Saint-Michel or Maine.[69]

Some brigandage was undoubtedly political. Very occasionally, those who were caught were accorded the status of prisoners of war and allowed to ransom themselves as enemy soldiers. They must have been regarded as fighting in the Dauphin's name. The gangs referred to in English records as 'brigands and others of the French party' or 'Armagnac brigands' were probably political resistants. The gang which roamed the *bocage* south of Pont-Audemer in the mid-1420s and administered an oath to recruits to 'do all that they could to harm the English' certainly were. Some brigands were found cooperating with nearby French garrisons. But it is difficult to generalise from cases like these. A price of six *livres* was put on the head of every brigand taken alive, and large numbers of them were caught and put to death. They were commonly charged as traitors and beheaded, or buried alive in the case of women, instead of being hanged as common criminals. This has led to their being claimed by historians as political resistants. But treason was too loosely defined to make the label 'traitor' a reliable guide. As the law developed in the course of the fourteenth and fifteenth centuries, French lawyers increasingly resorted to Roman law definitions of treason which could embrace any violent subversion of public order. The Norman chronicler Thomas Basin observed that whether they had abandoned the land out of hostility to the English or out of moral depravity or because they were on the run, these men 'did not fight in the ranks of the French but like the wild beasts and wolves in the remotest parts of the forest'. This is probably a fair summary. The great majority of their victims were fellow Normans, not English soldiers or officials.[70]

For years after the English conquest, the attitudes of prominent Normans were shaped by the memory of the civil wars. Rouen and other Norman towns had been strong partisans of the house of Burgundy. For them, the Dauphin was not the natural ruler of France but a party leader. That he was French was less important than the fact that he had allowed himself to be the puppet of the hated Count of Armagnac, had occupied their city by force in July 1417 and been privy to the murder of John the Fearless two years later. The bonfires, peals of bells and street parties at Rouen which greeted the news of Henry VI's landing at Calais in April 1430, and the crowds which came out to cheer his entry into the city three months later were probably sincere.

There were certainly Normans who took a different view. Most of the oldest and richest noble families of Normandy, the Harcourts, the Meluns, the Maunys, the Estoutevilles and their like, saw themselves as actors on a national stage. They had long traditions of service to the French Crown, and many of them also had domains in regions under Dauphinist control. They withdrew from the duchy after the English conquest and joined the Dauphin. But lesser men whose interests were concentrated in Normandy generally accepted the Lancastrian regime. Many of them actively supported it. Most bishops and abbots remained at their posts. Substantially the whole provincial administration did the same. Norman noblemen served in English armies and accepted office in the English administration. One of them declared in 1425 that he had been captured three times and had lost two of his uncles, four cousins and thirty of his friends, all in the service of the English King. How typical this man was is hard to say. But such actions are probably a better guide to the sentiments of the great majority of Normans in the high times of the English regime than the melancholy toll of executions in market squares across the province.[71]

What is clear is that the traditional distinction made by Dauphinists between 'good' and 'bad' Frenchmen, 'loyalists' and 'traitors', is an inadequate taxonomy. Prominent Normans faced impossible dilemmas in the aftermath of the civil wars and the English conquest. Guy Le Bouteillier, a minor nobleman from the Caux, had been the leader of the Burgundian party in Normandy during the civil wars and had commanded the defence of Rouen during the siege by Henry V. His change of allegiance was due to his disgust at the inability of the Valois monarchy to resist the English invasion or relieve the Norman capital during the six-month siege. When the city fell, Guy did homage to Henry V and threw himself into the English cause. He fought in their armies, serving briefly as captain of Paris in the opening weeks of Bedford's regency and later as master of his household. He was well rewarded for his pains. But personal advancement was not the only factor in his decision and probably not even the main one.

If Guy Le Bouteillier came to the English allegiance through the Burgundian party, Robert Jolivet Abbot of Mont-Saint-Michel had been a declared Armagnac. Nominated as Abbot at a young age in 1411, he refortified the island monastery and took command of its defence against the English during the invasion of 1417. The Dauphin was still referring to him as his 'councillor' at the end of 1419. But Jolivet was above all a loyal Norman, who found that the world of his kinsmen and friends had become part of an English polity. No doubt he also realised that with his abbey in enemy hands, he would be able to appropriate its Norman revenues, which were in English-held territory. In the spring of 1420, he fell out with the monks, left the abbey and submitted to Henry V. Within six months of the English King's death he had joined the Duke of Bedford's council in both Paris and Rouen, and embarked on a new career in English service which ended only with his death in 1444. Jolivet's books, some of which survive and one of which he may have written himself, suggest a committed Frenchman who found himself on what proved to be the wrong side of history, like so many others. The same was probably true of his friend Raoul le Sage, lord of Saint-Pierre. Le Sage, a native of the Cotentin like Jolivet, had had a distinguished administrative career under Charles VI, but entered English service shortly after Henry V's invasion of the duchy in 1417. He was a stalwart of the Rouen administration for many years and was eventually naturalised in England.[72]

For most of the population, these were not ideological choices. Their priorities were the mundane imperatives of security and survival. The English government was financially demanding, but it promised to restore, and to some extent did restore, basic standards of administration, justice and public order after the disasters of Charles VI's final years. This was a powerful generator of loyalty. If a ruler was able and willing to keep the peace and do justice, wrote the French sage Jean Juvénal, people driven crazy by the war would give him their allegiance 'even if he was a Muslim'. As Sir John Fastolf used to remark, '"*Vive le plus fort*," that is to say, "Let the greatest mastery have the field."' Something like that judgement must have been made by very many Normans. The success of the Duke of Bedford in defending Normandy in the 1420s and the rising economic fortunes of Rouen and other Norman towns did much to justify their choice. What these men had in common was a belief that the Lancastrian government would endure, a belief which persisted in Normandy long after it had given way to doubt and fear in Paris and the rest of Lancastrian France. But that belief was based on the myth of English invincibility and was sensitive to the changing fortunes of war. When the military tide turned and confidence began to fade in Normandy as well, men would once more be forced to remake their plans for a different future.[73]

CHAPTER II

Allies and Adversaries:
The Kingdom of Bourges, 1422–1424

The news of his father's death was brought to the nineteen-year-old Dauphin at Mehun, the imposing castle on the banks of the Yèvre west of Bourges, whose ruins are today among the most romantic in France. On 30 October 1422, he was proclaimed King Charles VII by the small group of courtiers and ministers around him. It was a subdued occasion. The heralds' cries of *'Vive le Roi!'* rang out unheard by the world in the confined space of the castle chapel. The Pope, Martin V, recognised the new King's title, and so did his allies in Scotland and Castile. But there was something provisional about Charles's accession. The old coinage of Charles VI continued to be minted until 1429. The English continued to refer to him as 'the Dauphin'. For many of his supporters too, among them Joan of Arc, he would remain 'the Dauphin' until he was crowned, a claimant to a kingdom that he might never possess. Charles's ministers were very conscious of this. For years after his accession, their plans were dominated by the hope of capturing Reims, the coronation city of Kings of France, and crowning him there as King.[1]

Charles VII is celebrated as one of France's greatest medieval kings, the ruler who brought a decisive end to more than a century and a half of Anglo-French wars. *Le Très Victorieux Roy de France Charles, Septième de ce Nom*, runs the inscription on Jean Fouquet's famous portrait in the Louvre. Yet the personality of the man is an enigma, and for more than a decade after his accession he scarcely emerges from behind the overbearing figures of successive ministers. The new king was physically unimpressive: pallid, thin and sickly, with spindly legs that gave him a rather awkward gait. In the 1420s he was not the authoritative figure of his later years. He was withdrawn and taciturn, moody and depressive and uncomfortable in company, all symptoms of a basic lack of self-confidence which lasted into middle age and shines out of the melancholy figure in the portrait. It meant that he

ALLIES AND ADVERSARIES: THE KINGDOM OF BOURGES, 1422–1424

was easily led by strong-willed men. In spite of his youth, Charles had already experienced politics in all its raw brutality. At the age of fifteen, he had been plucked half-naked from the palace enclosure in Paris and hustled away as the Burgundian mobs took over the streets. He had been present a year later on the bridge of Montereau when his cousin John the Fearless Duke of Burgundy was hacked to death beneath his eyes by his ministers, an event which gave him a lifelong fear of plotters and assassins. Medieval princes learned their trade young, but Charles had acquired little experience of statecraft or war. He owed his accession to the premature deaths of his elder brothers. He had been brought up in the protective environment of the Angevin court in Provence far away from the turmoil of the royal court. Even after coming to the throne, he was sheltered from the daily dilemmas of diplomacy by determined ministers and distanced from the strategic decisions by overbearing mercenary captains. He was kept away from the fighting, for he was the last male of the Valois line apart from his son Louis, a fragile child born in July 1423, and his cousin Charles of Orléans, a prisoner in England. It is sometimes said that even in his early years, Charles's passivity was just a façade, and that behind it he manipulated his servants, not the other way round. It is a possible view, but difficult to reconcile with the evidence.[2]

There was very little in the Dauphin's situation to foretell the triumphs of his later years. The Duke of Burgundy's official chronicler Georges Chastellain, a young man in 1422, would one day paint a vivid picture of the condition of Charles's realm at his accession: a country 'devastated, exhausted and torn apart, like a half-demolished edifice, ruinous on every side, its foundations undermined, a mere wreck of its former beauty and grandeur'. Images like these were often deployed in later years to heighten the dramatic impact of Charles's ultimate victory. But the contrast was a real one. A ditty which mothers sang to their children plaintively asked what was left of the great kingdom which the Dauphin had inherited.

> Aujourd'hui que reste t'il
> A ce Dauphin si gentil
> De tout son beau royaume?

It comprised less than half of the territory which his father had inherited in 1380.[3]

The 'kingdom of Bourges' controlled the whole of the territory south of the Loire, apart from the diminished English duchy of Guyenne in the south-west. In addition, it included Anjou and Maine in the west, the great city of Lyon and its region on the eastern march of the kingdom, and the large and rich province of Dauphiné, east of the Rhône, which was technically a part of the German Empire but had become the traditional endowment of the heir to the French throne. The political and economic heart of the Dauphin's territory was a cluster of princely appanages in the basin of the Loire belonging to the various branches of the royal house. These comprised Touraine, which had been part of Charles's own appanage as Dauphin; the extensive territories formerly owned by his great-uncle Jean de Berry in Poitou and Berry, which had passed to him by inheritance; the lands of the Duke of Bourbon in the Bourbonnais and Forez, which were governed by the Duchess Marie de Berry while her husband languished in an English prison; the duchy of Orléans, another appanage belonging to a prisoner of war in England, which was administered by the Duke's officials from the castle of Blois; and finally the domains of the dukes of Anjou in Anjou and Maine. These provinces constituted a broad belt of rich agricultural land and important commercial cities extending in an arc from the Atlantic seaboard in the west to the foothills of the Massif Central in the east. They provided the Dauphin with the greater part of his revenues, his manpower and his political standing.

In due course, Charles would acquire the soubriquet *'le Bien-Servi'*, the 'well-served'. The government of the kingdom of Bourges was staffed by a talented generation of administrators, lawyers and financiers, most of whom had risen through the patronage of the leading Armagnac princes and had fled from Paris after the Burgundian coup. It was these men who had created the institutions of Bourges and Poitiers from nothing after Charles broke with his father's government in 1418. But the new king was not well-served. The problem lay at the highest levels of his government. The royal council was dominated by a clique of impetuous and violent men of the old Armagnac party, who had risen to prominence during the dictatorship of the Count of Armagnac in Paris. The most influential of them were compromised by their involvement in the two most disastrous acts of the Dauphin's early years: the murder of John the Fearless in 1419 and the abduction of John V Duke of Brittany a year later. The unscrupulous and conspiratorial Jean Louvet, who had been the prime mover behind both decisions, was effectively the Dauphin's first minister. We have it on Charles's own authority that before his eventual removal in 1425 he had enjoyed 'excessive and unreasonable powers' over the whole machinery of government, including unlimited authority to deal with foreign governments and to dispose of the government's revenues. He was said to have a pile of blank warrants bearing the Dauphin's seal, with which to authorise whatever he chose. Like Louvet, and almost as influential, the Maine nobleman Guillaume d'Avaugour was a protégé of the dukes of Anjou. He had been present on the bridge of Montereau and was among the small caucus of councillors behind the attack on the Duke of Brittany. Tanneguy du Châtel, the headstrong and impulsive Breton soldier of fortune who served as Master of Charles's household, had struck the first blow against John the Fearless on the bridge. William Viscount of Narbonne, a southerner and a son-in-law of the Count of Armagnac, had been in on the plot and joined in the affray around the dying Duke. Pierre Frotier, the ill-tempered bully who served as the captain of Charles's personal bodyguard, had finished off the Duke by plunging a sword into his belly. The Picard Jean Cadart, the Dauphin's physician since childhood and perhaps the nearest that Charles had to an adult friend, was admitted to the Dauphin's council at about the time of his accession and became increasingly influential. He had not been present at Montereau but was believed to have helped persuade his master to authorise the deed. These were 'scandalous and dishonest men', in the words of a well-placed official of the Duke of Orléans. They controlled access to the Dauphin and directed his every move in the disastrous opening years of his reign, all the while busily lining their pockets. As a result, they had many enemies and were forever looking over their shoulders.[4]

Other men about the new King had a more creditable past and a more balanced judgement of the future, but perforce lived under the shadow of Louvet and his friends. Robert le Maçon, the Dauphin's former Chancellor, was a 'wise and cautious' adviser according to a sound judge. He had been deliberately kept in the dark when the murder of John the Fearless was being planned. He had resigned his office early in 1422 but remained an influential member of Charles's council until his retirement in 1436. Robert was one of an important contingent of dedicated churchmen largely unsullied by the crimes of the civil wars. They included his successor as Chancellor, Martin Gouge

Bishop of Clermont, who had also been kept at arm's length from the planning of the murder. A lawyer and career administrator born in Bourges who had risen in the service of Jean de Berry, Gouge had sat on the council since 1413 and was one of the most experienced men there. Regnault de Chartres, Archbishop of Reims, was the Dauphin's principal diplomatic adviser and himself a future Chancellor. Scion of a prominent Orléanist family, he was the only figure of international stature on the council. These men had as much reason as anyone to feel bitter about the English and their Burgundian allies. Regnault de Chartres had lost all three of his brothers at Agincourt. His father had been murdered in Paris by a Burgundian lynch mob. Martin Gouge had fled from Paris in disguise during the coup of 1418, losing almost everything he had. But in spite of all that they had suffered, theirs were moderating voices in the Dauphin's counsels. Men like Louvet and Tanneguy were committed by their past to opposing a reconciliation with the Duke of Burgundy, which would certainly have entailed their dismissal and quite possibly their execution. Wiser advisers knew that the Dauphin could not recover the lost provinces of the north without coming to terms with Philip the Good. It was probably Gouge who initiated the policy which would remain the constant theme of the Dauphin's diplomacy for the next thirteen years. The great object was to detach the Duke of Burgundy from the English alliance. There would be no direct negotiations with the English, except perhaps when their participation was an unavoidable incident of negotiation with Burgundy, and even then, the plan would be to drive a wedge between them.[5]

Conventional opinion expected a king to be surrounded by the princes of his blood and the foremost noblemen of the land, not by carpetbaggers on the make. Charles's chief ministers and councillors were generally drawn from the minor nobility. They were *'de povre, bas et petit lieu'* ('poor fellows of low birth and station'), sneered the Duke of Brittany. At the outset of the new reign, the only royal prince in the Dauphin's inner counsels was the Duke of Orléans's nineteen-year-old half-brother John Bastard of Orléans, the future Count of Dunois. He was one of the ablest men there, but he was only there because he had married Jean Louvet's daughter. The council was a large body of fluctuating membership, but real power depended on the favour of Louvet and his allies. The rest were outsiders or makeweights. Looking back in later years, the lawyer-bishop Jean Juvénal des Ursins remembered councillors who were ribald, arrogant, loud-mouthed or drunk in council, 'ignorant young men . . . without wisdom, caution, moral judgement or sound reason, who gave their opinion without a moment's thought'.[6]

While Charles VI was alive, the English had ruled northern France in his name. Once he was dead, their claim to govern depended entirely on the legitimacy of Henry VI's succession. Many of the Dauphin's courtiers and officials were convinced that the alliance of England and Burgundy would collapse once the true heir mounted the throne. People would surely see that the treaty of Troyes was no longer the way to peace and national unity that it had once seemed to be. The Dauphin's ministers told the Estates-General at Selles in August 1423 that three years would be more than enough to see the English expelled from France.[7] They reckoned without the tenacity of the English and the resilience of their military organisation in Normandy, as well as the tacit support which they could command in the regions under their control.

The strategic options of both sides were shaped by geography. The Loire provided the kingdom of Bourges with an almost impermeable barrier to invasion from the north. The river was a fuller, faster torrent in the late middle ages than it is now. Before the construction of the embankments, it was vulnerable to sudden floods which rapidly inundated large areas on both banks, producing an inhospitable landscape of alternating forest, scrub and marsh. There were few fords. All the bridges were defended by walled towns and cities, except for the Ponts-de-Cé south of Angers, where a line of fortified and garrisoned bridges carried the road over the channels and islets of the river at one of its broadest points. Apart from Nantes, whose passage depended on the fickle sympathies of the Duke of Brittany, all of these crossings were held for the Dauphin. His followers were able to pass freely over the river, while the English were rarely able to force their way in the opposite direction. Henry V had once ventured to cross the Loire at a ford near Saint-Dyé in September 1421 but suffered heavy losses and was almost cut off. Apart from a brief and unsuccessful raid on Bourges in 1423, the English did not try again until the ill-fated siege of Orléans in 1428-9. In other circumstances, Guyenne might have served them as a base from which to attack the kingdom of Bourges in the rear. But the English did not have the manpower to mount a major offensive from the south-west and defend Normandy and Paris at the same time.[8]

Seen from Bourges, there were three main fighting fronts.

The northern front extended in a broad belt from the Channel to Champagne. In 1422, all the major towns and cities of this region acknowledged the authority of the Lancastrian government in Paris except for Tournai, an isolated enclave of the kingdom of Bourges on the march of Flanders. The Dauphin's battles on the northern front were fought by irregular forces which had captured smaller places and turned them into bases for raids against the main centres of English and Burgundian administration. The raiders struck without warning, often far away from their bases, carrying off cattle and people and visiting wanton destruction on unwalled settlements. In spite of the irregular and incoherent character of their operations, they represented a serious threat to the Lancastrian regime. They undermined its authority, damaged its ability to levy taxes and threatened to choke off the flow of supplies to the capital. In the last fifteen months of his life, Henry V had come close to eliminating them. English and Burgundian troops had established control of all the passages of the Seine and the whole course of the Marne from Paris to Châlons, thus cutting off the northern regions from all assistance from the Dauphinist heartlands further south.

At the end of 1422, *routier* bands loyal to the Dauphin were still clinging to three major bases north of the Seine and the Marne: Le Crotoy at the mouth of the Somme, Guise in the upper valley of the Oise and Vitry-en-Perthois overlooking the Marne in eastern Champagne. Each of them served as the headquarters of a group of satellite garrisons which swelled their numbers and extended their reach. In spite of the fact that they were spread over a distance of about 200 miles, these clusters of garrisons were able to coordinate their operations, wreaking havoc and destruction across the whole of the sensitive northern march of Henry VI's French kingdom.

Le Crotoy was held by the resourceful Jacques d'Harcourt, a former Burgundian captain who had fallen out with the English and declared for the Dauphin in 1421. Charles had appointed him as his lieutenant in the valley of the Somme and the northern march of Normandy. Recently, Harcourt's operations had been curtailed by the installation of a large English garrison at Saint-Valéry on the opposite side of the Somme estuary, which pinned his companies to their base and made

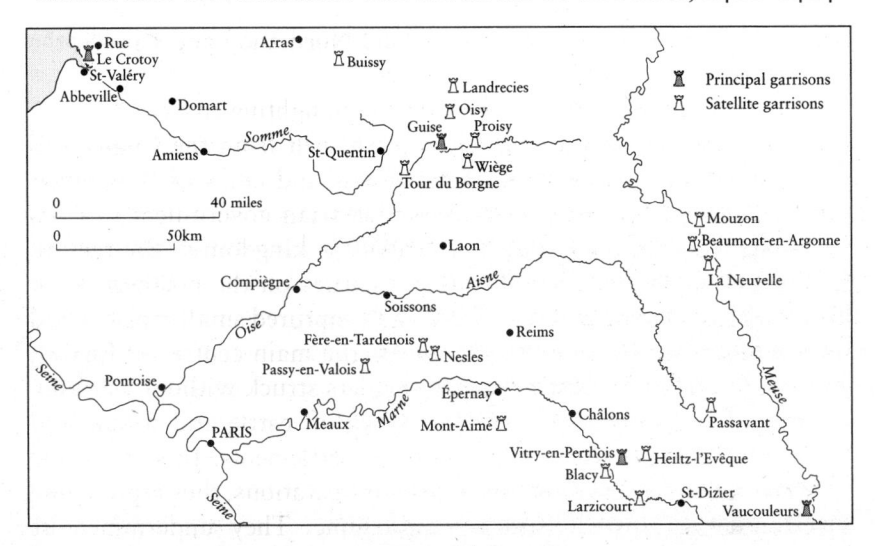

ALLIES AND ADVERSARIES: THE KINGDOM OF BOURGES, 1422–1424

1 Dauphinist garrisons of the north, 1422–1428

it difficult for them to get supplies. But Harcourt was still capable of spectacular strikes, like the plundering of the rich town of Domart, east of Abbeville, in March 1423, which spread terror across much of western Picardy.

Guise was the headquarters of the Gascon captain Jean ('Poton') de Saintrailles, a former retainer of the Count of Armagnac who had come north with him in 1416 and had made the town his base in 1418 after the fall of the Armagnac regime in Paris. Poton was one of the most effective guerrilla leaders of the age. At Guise, he controlled the largest Dauphinist garrison in northern France, comprising a number of independent companies in addition to his own band of some 300 men.

Further east, a cluster of castles in northern Champagne was occupied by another notable Gascon captain, Étienne de Vignolles, better known as La Hire, who had once been Poton de Saintrailles's brother-in-arms. La Hire first came to the notice of his contemporaries when he was serving in the Orléanist garrison of Coucy. He had been an active and highly effective partisan of the Dauphin in Picardy and the valley of the Oise before moving into Lorraine and then into Champagne. La Hire was an improbable hero. He was a man of modest origins. He was lame, the result of an accident when the chimney of an inn collapsed on top of him. But he was a brilliant strategist and a charismatic leader who drew to his standard not just the rough military underworld from which *routier* bands were usually recruited but many minor noblemen serving their apprenticeships in the profession of arms. He was a master of rapid movement and surprise. 'Strike first,' he used to say, 'so as not to be afraid.' In 1422 La Hire and his lieutenants occupied five castles in eastern Champagne and later that year he increased their range by occupying Vitry-en-Perthois. The old castle of the counts of Champagne at Vitry dominated the valley of the Marne upstream of Châlons and gave the Dauphinists a secure crossing of the river. La Hire's lieutenant, the Breton soldier of fortune Jean Raoulet, made it the headquarters of an important group of garrisoned castles extending west to Vertus and the great keep of Mont-Aimé on the road from Reims to Troyes; and north to Mouzon and Beaumont-en-Argonne in the valley of the Meuse.[9]

Eastern France, between the Loire and the Rhône, was a distinct theatre of war which followed its own logic. The great bend of the Loire marked the boundary between the kingdom of Bourges and the southern domains of the house of Burgundy (*Map I*). In 1422 the Burgundian territories were under severe pressure. The county of Nevers, on the east bank of the Loire, was Burgundy's first line of defence. The previous Count of Nevers, a cadet of the house of Burgundy, had been killed at Agincourt. The county was ruled by his widow, Bonne d'Artois, as regent for their young son. In June 1422, an army commanded by Tanneguy du Châtel had invaded the Nivernais and seized a large number of walled places, including La Charité with its great stone bridge over the Loire and the important administrative centre of Saint-Pierre-le-Moutier further south. These events left the Dauphin's captains with a bridgehead into Burgundian territory. East of the Nivernais, beyond the Morvan hills, the disputed region of the Mâconnais and the Burgundian county of Charolais had for four years been the targets of large and well organised Dauphinist companies operating from the Lyonnais and the Dauphiné. In the summer of 1422 the Dauphin's ministers sent Bernard of Armagnac Count of Pardiac, a son of the late Constable, and Amaury de Sévérac, one of the Marshals, to take command in the region. Their arrival marked a notable escalation in the scale of operations and threatened to carry the war up the valley of the Saône into the heart of Burgundy. In September 1422, a few days after the death of Henry V, Amaury de Sévérac came up the valley and surprised the monastic town of Tournus, only thirty miles from Beaune. The town was captured by escalade and sacked. Hardly anything was left standing apart from the abbey and the town church. This event spread alarm through much of Burgundy. At least eighty men, women and children were drowned trying to flee across the Saône in a boat as the Dauphinists burst into the town. From Mâcon came reports that a mob of Dauphinist partisans in the town had seized the Duke of Burgundy's representatives and imprisoned them in the citadel.[10]

The most active theatre of war was the long southern front extending from the Atlantic coast at Avranches to the Auxerrois and southern Champagne. The Lancastrian territories were wide open to attack there through the coastal plain around Avranches and the open plains of the Beauce and the Gâtinais. Three major river valleys, the Sarthe, the Eure and the Loing, served as highways into this broad band of contested territory. Dauphinist forces were concentrated in the west, in the heavily wooded hills of Perche and the Norman *massif* and in the island monastery of Mont-Saint-Michel. The epicentre of the war in the west was the duchy of Alençon and the adjoining domains of the dukes of Alençon in Perche and northern Maine (*Map II*). The ducal family had been evicted by Henry V in 1417 when the current Duke, John II, was only eight years old. But he remained an important focus of loyalty and his partisans were to be a threat to the security of the English throughout the period of their occupation. They found an effective leader in a local nobleman, Ambroise de Loré, a committed Armagnac who had fought at Agincourt and served in the garrison of Paris during the Count of Armagnac's regime before 1418. The Duke of Alençon eventually named him as his marshal. A dense cluster of garrisons commanded by Ambroise and his lieutenants conducted a persistent guerrilla war against the English garrisons of the region. Their operations received powerful support in 1420, when Mont-Saint-Michel was placed under the command of the Dauphin's lieutenant on the western march, Jean d'Harcourt Count of Aumale. He filled it with troops and integrated it into the defence of the sector. Its location was ideal for his purposes. It stood close to the old Roman roads to Carhaix, Rennes and Le Mans and at the centre of a great network of pilgrims' tracks extending across much of western France. At low tide, mounted men could ride over the sands to the Cotentin peninsula north of the bay. As a result, nearly half of the entire English garrison strength in Normandy had to be concentrated on the south-western marches of the duchy. For the Dauphinists, Mont-Saint-Michel became a potent symbol of resistance. Charles VII adopted St Michael as the patron saint of Dauphinist France in place of the 'English' St Denis. The Archangel slaying the dragon became the emblem on his banners.[11]

The Dauphin's war was largely shaped by his financial resources, or lack of them. Very little survives of the financial records of the kingdom of Bourges, but the main lines of the Dauphin's finances can be reconstructed from fragments. The ordinary costs of government were high, even before taking account of the heavy burden of military expenditure. In the late middle ages display was an instrument of government. A showy court was a political necessity, especially for a ruler who could not take his royal status for granted. This implied a high level of expenditure on the royal households. At the beginning of his reign, the separate households of Charles VII and his Queen consumed well over 400,000 *livres* (£67,000) a year and constituted the largest single call on his revenues. Diplomacy was another heavy cost. Ambassadors had to travel with an entourage consistent with their dignity and an armed escort for their safety. With three administrative centres at Bourges, Poitiers and Toulouse, the civil and judicial services of the Dauphin's realm drained his treasury year after year. A pamphlet written in 1425 by an anonymous official lamented the poor standards of audit and cost control in the kingdom of Bourges. He thought that they ordered things better in England. He reckoned that the Dauphin's government cost as much in salaries alone as the bloated administration of Charles VI, which had been responsible for the whole of France. The burden was significantly increased by the survival of many of the corrupt practices which had characterised that administration: lavish discretionary rewards paid to ministers, councillors and senior officials and open-handed grants to favoured figures. The Dauphin's private secretary Alain Chartier described his expenditure as a 'bottomless abyss'.[12]

The kingdom of Bourges had three main sources of revenue: the royal demesne, the mints and taxation. Of these, only the last was of any real significance. The most productive parts of the royal demesne were located in provinces occupied by the English and what remained was poorly managed and disrupted by war. Devaluation of the silver coinage was a traditional resort of French governments. But it was extremely unpopular, especially with the Church and the nobility, much of whose income was derived from fixed nominal rents. In

September 1422, in a bid to rally support for his government, the Dauphin had resolved to restore the old coinage values, a policy which he stuck to for the next four years, but which left a large hole in his budget. The tacit understanding was that the goodwill generated by this measure would enable the hole to be filled by taxation. Yet taxation was a precarious resource. The traditional war tax of the French state was the *aides*, a sales tax usually levied at a rate of 5 per cent on goods exposed for sale and 25 per cent on wine. This had been supplemented since the 1380s by periodic *tailles*, which were direct taxes, assessed on the value of the taxpayer's movable goods. John the Fearless's abolition of these taxes had crippled the governments of Charles VI in his final years, but the Dauphin had had no choice but to follow suit in the regions which he controlled. His ministers were in no position to impose taxes by royal command, as French governments had done before the civil wars. This left them with no permanent taxes apart from the *gabelle*, an excise duty on salt. The Dauphin's ability to raise armies for operations against the English and Burgundians depended on special taxes granted at irregular intervals by provincial and national assemblies. The willingness of these bodies to support the war could not be counted on. It depended on a variety of unpredictable factors, including the fortunes of war, the political mood and current economic conditions.[13]

For fiscal purposes, France had been divided since the middle of the fourteenth century into two regions of unequal weight, each with its own representative assembly. The Estates-General of the Dauphin's entire territory rarely met. The Estates of Languedoc represented Languedoc proper, that is to say the three seneschalsies of Toulouse, Carcassonne and Nîmes, and usually also the neighbouring provinces of Quercy, Rouergue, Agenais and Périgord, and those parts of Guyenne which had been reconquered from the English. It met frequently and was politically very active. The taxes which it voted were generally modest and the Dauphin's ministers did not have unfettered disposal of them. They were often voted on terms which required them to be spent on local defence against *routier* bands and incursions from the English duchy of Guyenne. As a result, the burden of supporting the war against the English and Burgundians fell mainly on the Estates of Languedoil, which represented the rest of the country. Much of Languedoil was now under English control, but it had a substantial taxable capacity even in its truncated form.

In May 1421, the Dauphin had taken advantage of the euphoria following his victory over the English at Baugé to obtain an *aide* of 800,000 *livres* from the Estates-General meeting at Clermont in Auvergne. Charles's accession to the throne produced a fresh surge of goodwill. In January 1423, an assembly meeting at Bourges granted an *aide* of 1,000,000 *livres* 'for the recovery of the King's dominions and the expulsion of his enemies'. The results, however, were disappointing. As a result, a fresh meeting of the Estates of Languedoil was summoned to the small town of Selles in Berry in August 1423. They adopted a more radical approach. They agreed to grant a further 200,000 *livres* to make good at least part of the shortfall on the earlier grant. More remarkably, they were persuaded that the abolition of the *aides* had been a mistake and agreed to restore them for a limited period of three years starting on 1 October 1423. The revived *aides*, levied at the old rates, were expected to bring in 1,000,000 *livres* in each year, to be spent exclusively on the war. This appears to have been subject to annual reconfirmation at further meetings of the Estates. An additional *aide* of 1,000,000 *livres* was voted by the Estates at Poitiers and Riom in the autumn of 1424, bringing the nominal value of taxes imposed in the first three years of the new reign to 4,550,000 *livres*. These are impressive figures, comparable to the *aides* imposed by the monarchy in its heyday in the 1380s, which were paid by the whole of France. If all of the sums voted had been collected, the Dauphin would have enjoyed vastly greater resources than the Duke of Bedford.[14]

In fact, the position was much less satisfactory. Taxes on sales were sensitive to economic conditions. They shrank in a recession and in regions suffering from depopulation or war damage. Peculation and corruption gnawed at funds in the collectors' hands. The clergy and the nobility 'living nobly' and participating in the King's wars, were exempt by law. Many other exemptions were conceded in practice. Local assessments had to be negotiated with provincial assemblies and local officials who did their best to lighten the burden on their own regions. The corps of collectors and accountants who had administered the *aides* before 1418 had dispersed and the job was now done mainly by local functionaries who were less expert and more indulgent. A number of provinces were able to negotiate special arrangements by which the new *aides* were replaced by 'equivalents' levied on a different and less transparent basis. Some towns obtained reductions or were allowed to divert part of the proceeds to local purposes, such as the repair of their walls. The whole process was painfully slow. In the end, the amounts collected fell a long way short of the original expectations. In the rich city of Lyon, for example, where the records are unusually complete, the city authorities managed to negotiate its contribution to the *aides* down to just over half of the original assessment.

To make up the shortfall of revenue, the Dauphin's ministers pursued a disastrous policy of large-scale alienations from his demesne. His ministers lent him money and his captains served on credit, until they were eventually satisfied by grants of land which were often worth considerably more than the debt. Regnault de Chartres acquired the town of Vierzon in satisfaction of loans worth 16,000 *livres*. The Duke of Alençon acquired Niort, the second city of Poitou, in the same way. Marshal Sévérac's credits reached the enormous sum of 92,000 *livres*, which was eventually discharged by mortgaging to him the entire tax revenues of Languedoc and Auvergne.[15]

The kingdom of Bourges had one important financial advantage which was not available to the English. Politically, the English could not support their Norman garrisons by plundering their subjects. But the Dauphin's partisans operating in enemy territory had no such inhibitions. Companies like those of Le Crotoy, Guise or Mont-Saint-Michel, drew little or nothing from the Dauphin's war treasurers. They funded their operations from loot, the sale of safe-conducts and above all from *pâtis*, the traditional process of exacting protection money from the local populations. The Count of Aumale's garrison at Mont-Saint-Michel, for example, received modest financial support from the Dauphin up to 1425. It sustained itself mainly by looting 77,000 *livres* worth of precious objects from the abbey treasury and exacting another 3,000 *livres* in 'loans' from the monks. Louis d'Estouteville, who succeeded Aumale in 1425, received not a penny for himself or his garrison for the next twenty years. His operations were funded by *pâtis*. At Mont-Saint-Michel the exaction of *pâtis* achieved a high degree of sophistication. A network of local assessors and collectors was established, generally recruited from local officials or parish priests, the two main literate groups. Villages and towns within raiding distance were assessed for what they could afford, not so much that the population would be driven away or too little to sustain the soldiers of the garrison. On the mount itself, a staff of clerks drew up the demands and kept the accounts. In 1425, the Duke of Bedford remitted a sentence of death passed on a parish priest whose story spoke volumes. He had been captured on the road three years earlier by soldiers from Mont-Saint-Michel and released without ransom in return for agreeing to act as their assessor and collector in his native village and five other parishes near Caen. His demands on his fellow villagers were enforced by the threat that 'if they did not like it they would be attacked and sacked instead'. From this and other documents of the kind, it is clear that the garrison of Mont-Saint-Michel was collecting *pâtis* under the noses of the Duke of Bedford's officers from the whole of the Cotentin outside the main walled towns.[16]

The garrison of Mont-Saint-Michel operated in enemy territory, but that was not true of all the Dauphin's troops. Many of them were based in garrisons on the marches of his own territory or were cantoned in regions like Touraine or Berry at the heart of his domains. They supported themselves in the same way, by levying *pâtis* on the inhabitants and pillaging travellers on the roads. The laws of war were in the process of adapting themselves to this state of affairs. In November 1424 there was a minor but revealing incident in the Dauphinist city of Tournai. A soldier called Colard de Verly from the Dauphinist garrison of Guise was captured in the city's territory while trying to carry off some local people for ransom. Colard was imprisoned in the felons' jail pending his appearance in the city's criminal court. The Dauphin's representative demanded his release, asserting that this was 'not a crime but a simple act of war'. 'In conducting his wars', this officer explained, 'the King does not have the means to pay his troops, who therefore have no choice but to burn down buildings and kill or kidnap people.' The judges accepted this argument, and Colard was released. There were many such incidents, even if they were not always justified so bluntly. 'If it should please our lord the King to provide us with supplies and pay us wages, then we will serve him in all his affairs and obey his orders without levying anything on the inhabitants of this place,' declared the semi-fictional hero of Jean de Bueil's novel, *Le Jouvencel*, 'but if there are too many other calls on his resources, or he is for some other reason advised not to pay for our supplies or wages, then we shall have to collect them from his subjects and enemies alike.'[17]

This practice became a serious issue at successive meetings of the Estates of Languedoil. The assembly at Selles in August 1423 complained bitterly about the intolerable damage inflicted by the Dauphin's troops on his own subjects. Charles did not deny it.

Indeed, it became an organised system, a form of taxation implicitly and sometimes explicitly authorised by his ministers. During the long intervals between active operations, the Dauphin's mercenaries were distributed through the frontier provinces of the kingdom of Bourges and directed to live off the land. Touraine suffered grievously throughout the 1420s at their hands. The Duke of Anjou complained that his duchy had paid more than 100,000 *livres* a year in *pâtis* to support a dozen garrisons which were ostensibly there to defend it. Allowing troops to live off the land depressed tax revenues, leaving still less to pay the troops and provoking yet more looting. It was a vicious spiral from which there was no escape. The temporary reimposition of the *aides*, which was authorised at Selles, was intended to break the spiral by enabling the Dauphin's government to pay its troops regularly. But the plan failed. Only a pause in the war long enough to allow people to return to their homes, trade to revive and agricultural yields to recover could have done it.[18]

The human cost was high. The great limestone plain of the Beauce had once been a rich agricultural region crossed by important trade routes and dotted with prosperous market towns. A persistent guerrilla war between the English garrisons of Chartres and the Norman march and Dauphinist companies from the Loire all but destroyed its economic and social fabric. Kidnapping, highway robbery and economic sanctions extinguished ancient patterns of trade. People living in English-controlled areas could no longer trade with their traditional markets in Dauphinist Touraine and Orléanais, while those living in Dauphinist areas had to buy expensive safe-conducts from English captains in order to get their goods to Paris or Rouen. Cash was scarce and people hid what they had in cavities in the walls of their homes or under the roots of trees, to be discovered centuries later by builders, archaeologists and museum curators.

The town of Bonneval, which changed hands several times in this period, told the Dauphin in 1424, when it was temporarily controlled by his officers, that the region had been ruined 'not just by our enemies but by captains claiming to be our own'. The suburbs of the town had been destroyed. It was overrun by refugees from the surrounding country. The destruction of crops and theft of working animals had led to the progressive abandonment of the land by the sharecroppers who had tilled it for centuries. The nearby town of Gallardon was besieged five times in the decade after the battle of Agincourt. When, years later, it was finally recovered from the English, the Duke of Alençon, who was the lord of the region, commissioned a survey of what had once been among his richest domains. The report made dismal reading. At one village there were no inhabitants to be seen and the land was given over to bushes and brambles. At another the tenants had died many years before and no one had come in to replace them. At another, the village's nominal tax assessment had been halved after Agincourt, but there was no longer anything to tax for the place had been deserted for years. Barns, mills, baking ovens and wine presses had been wrecked and never rebuilt. The local courts had ceased to function. Seigneurial rights had fallen into desuetude. As farms reverted to weed and scrub, families left for the comparative safety of Normandy or the Loire. Those who stayed behind sank into abject poverty. We cannot know what private tragedy lay behind the deed of amicable separation executed by Robin and Jeanne Porcher of Châteaudun in 1422, which declared that they could no longer live together as husband and wife or support a common table 'on account of the wars and the dearth of food'. The Beauce was by no means an exceptional case.[19]

The problem of the Dauphin's ministers was that if they were to make any significant inroads into Lancastrian territory they needed a field army, which would have to be paid. French field armies, unlike English ones, consisted mainly of cavalry. Men-at-arms were recruited in the traditional way from the landed classes, by personal or general summons. An army on the march could not be sustained from loot and *pâtis*. Even garrison troops used to living on the land at their bases, demanded pay when they were withdrawn for field service. In theory they were entitled to a daily wage dependent on rank: two *livres* for a banneret, one for a knight and half for a squire. In practice, from 1422 onward, the Dauphin's war treasurers gradually ceased to pay the standard rates and started paying arbitrary lump sums to captains for distribution to their companies. The amounts depended on what funds were available and were always less than the men's due. Many were unwilling to serve on these terms. The higher ranks, the bannerets and knights and the nobles and country gentlemen, who had once stood at the summit of the military hierarchy, almost disappeared from the Dauphin's armies.

The Dauphin's ministers reckoned that the provinces under their control could produce about 4,000 men-at-arms to serve in the field, barely a third of the number recruited for the great armies of the previous century. Many of these men were unreliable, undisciplined and poorly trained and equipped. Alain Chartier complained that they answered the King's summons out of duty, arrived late, served without enthusiasm and left as soon as they could. Bowmen, generally armed with crossbows, were recruited in modest numbers in the towns, but their skills were poor and they were not obliged to serve for long periods or far from their homes. Ordinary foot-soldiers were hardly used at all. The traditional explanation was that the government was afraid to arm the populace for fear of revolution. The Berry Herald voiced the common opinion when he observed that the 'lords did not send them to war if they could help it'. This became a cliché of military writers from Froissart to Macchiavelli, but the main reason for the lack of any organised French infantry was a different one. Peasants and townsmen lacked the training required to acquit themselves with credit in battle. The Norman bishop Thomas Basin remembered the disorderly bands of French troops roaming over the country, with little knowledge or experience of war. Like all monochrome pictures, these generalisations concealed a more complex situation and probably contained a measure of exaggeration. But there is little doubt that the early 1420s marked a low point in the history of French arms.[20]

These pressures forced the kingdom of Bourges to rely mainly on professional mercenaries. They were hired for long periods and were available when required. They were politically more dependable and militarily more skilful. And they were relatively cheap. According to Henry V's informants in 1421, their rates of pay were less than a third of the traditional rates for French troops. Some of these men were French, often men of low birth who had gained their experience of arms in *routier* companies. Their leaders were commonly minor noblemen, dispossessed victims of war, landless younger sons or bastards excluded by tradition or law from their fathers' succession. These days, complained Chartier, anyone could call himself a man-at-arms who knew how to wear a sword and a coat of mail, even if he had not a house to live in or a plot of land to his name. The great majority of the Dauphin's professional troops, however, were not drawn from the military underworld of France itself. In the early years of his reign, well over half of them had been recruited in Castile, Italy or Scotland.

Castilian soldiers of fortune had operated in France ever since Charles V had forged his alliance with the Trastámaran dynasty in the 1360s. Several hundred of them were serving under the Dauphin's banner in 1422. The Dauphin continued the French monarchy's long tradition of hiring companies of crossbowmen in Genoa, by reputation the most skilful in Europe. Recently, his ministers had also begun to hire cavalry in Lombardy and Piedmont. The dukes of Orléans were the hereditary lords of the Piedmontese principality of Asti, an important centre of military recruitment. Others were hired through the good offices of France's long-standing allies the Visconti dukes of Milan. The heavily armoured Italian horsemen were regarded as the supreme practitioners of cavalry warfare. It was hoped that they would be able to disperse the massed archers which were such a formidable component of English armies of the period.[21]

The Scots had first appeared in France in significant numbers in 1419. Since the winter of 1420–1, they had been organised as a self-governing corps, calling themselves the 'Army of Scotland' and operating under their own commanders: John Stewart Earl of Buchan, Archibald Douglas Earl of Wigtown and John Stewart of Darnley. The first two were respectively the son and son-in-law of the Duke of Albany, Governor of Scotland, and the third, who served as constable of the army, was a cousin of the Scottish royal line. Numbering about 6,500 men at its highest point, the army of Scotland was by far the largest mercenary corps in the Dauphin's service. It was comparable in size to the English army under Bedford, although drawn from a country with perhaps a tenth of England's population. Casualties and desertion had reduced the Scottish numbers since then, but they were still a formidable force, inspiring fear and contempt among the English and French alike. They supported themselves from loot, *pâtis* and contributions exacted from the towns by overt threats of violence. There were occasional atrocities, which were no doubt magnified in the telling. But the Scots had proved their military value at the battle of Baugé in March 1421, when a largely Scottish army had routed the English under the Duke of Clarence, the only significant English defeat to date. The Scots fought with reckless courage in battle. Their bowmen were the only match for the English archers. Buchan, who had been appointed Constable of France after the battle of Baugé, proved to be a skilful tactician, bringing a new boldness to the conduct of the war after years in which French captains had been cowed by the memory of Agincourt.[22]

All of the Dauphin's problems of military organisation and finance were on show in the first major military incident of the new reign.

Meulan was a walled town on the north bank of the Seine, thirty miles west of Paris. It was joined to the opposite bank by a fortified bridge, defended at the southern end by a massive keep. The bridge was of great strategic importance. It carried the main road from the Loire into the Vexin and the Oise valley and controlled the river traffic between the capital and Normandy. The defence of Meulan was the responsibility of the English captain of the nearby town of Poissy, Sir John Fastolf's nephew Robert Harling. He had more than a hundred men under his command, but most of them were probably stationed at Poissy. At the beginning of January 1423, the bridge was surprised and captured by a company of Dauphinist partisans led by Jean de Garencières, a Norman nobleman who had lost most of his lands in the English conquest. Garencières's men seem to have lured the guards from the gate with the aid of a traitor within, and then ambushed them, before taking over the tower and massacring most of the garrison. It so happened that the council in Paris had recently resolved to besiege Le Crotoy and forces were being built up in Picardy for this operation. On 3 January Bedford postponed these plans and withdrew 500 men from Picardy. Within days he had laid siege to the bridge of Meulan from both ends and brought up an artillery train.[23]

The Dauphin's ministers did their best to exploit the opportunity presented by Jean de Garencières's coup. They had high hopes of crossing the Seine in force over the bridge and rolling up the English positions in the Vexin and eastern Normandy. They promised the defenders in the bridge-tower that an army would arrive to relieve them by 20 February. Tanneguy du Châtel and the Earl of Buchan were put in charge of the operation. They summoned troops from Brittany and from every frontier region between Maine and Berry. All of these contingents were ordered to assemble outside the small town of Janville in the southern Beauce by mid-February to advance on Meulan. The Duke of Bedford responded by summoning the entire feudal service of Normandy, together with every man who could safely be withdrawn from the Norman garrisons. In Rouen and Paris, there was a scramble for money. Bedford ordered the sale of all the remaining jewels of Charles VI. Paris was in a state of high excitement. Daily street processions were organised by the Bishop. The sittings of the courts were suspended to allow the judges to take part in them.

The threatened battle never happened. The Dauphinists raised a substantial force. A contemporary estimate of 6,000 men is probably roughly accurate. The Earl of Buchan gathered his Scottish troops and the contingents of the west at Janville on time and advanced to Gallardon, about fifty miles south of Meulan. There he halted and waited for Tanneguy to appear with the contingents of Berry and the Orléanais. But Tanneguy set out late and then, when he eventually reached Janville, he abruptly cancelled the campaign and disbanded his army. He had run out of money to pay his men. The first instalment of the *aides* voted by the Estates in December had not yet come in. Writing to Marshal Sévérac from Bourges, the Dauphin reported that all his financial officials had left the city to scavenge for funds in receivers' offices across France. Tanneguy had received part of the funds owed to his contingents and found more from his own resources. But all this was exhausted by the time he reached Janville and his men evidently refused to go into battle on empty purses. Left in the lurch, Buchan had no choice but to retreat. Some of the garrison in the bridge of Meulan mounted the battlements to hurl abuse of the Dauphin into the empty air. Conditions inside the bridge-tower deteriorated fast. February was bitterly cold, with heavy snowfalls and the worst frosts for many years. The defenders had found the stores almost empty and were nearly out of food. Garencières himself had withdrawn, leaving a deputy in command, who was shortly struck dead by a cannonball. The remaining captains concluded that the situation was hopeless. On 1 March, they capitulated.

For the Dauphin, it was an expensive defeat. The defenders of the bridge were given just one day to open their gates. Those of them who controlled garrisons elsewhere in France had to agree to procure their surrender as well. They included the major fortresses of Montlhéry, Marcoussis and Étampes on the Orléans road south of Paris. In return, the Duke of Bedford agreed 'out of pure grace and in view of the Lenten season' to spare their lives. But there was a limit to Bedford's clemency even in Lent. The amnesty excluded the ringleaders of the ambush party which had first forced its way into the tower as well as every artilleryman in the place. Their fate is not recorded, but they were probably hanged. In Paris, Bedford's report of the surrender was posted in the windows of the palace on the Cité. The capital erupted with joy.[24]

The first task of the Duke of Bedford, once he had taken control of the machinery of government, was to rebuild the alliances which his brother had made, none of which could be taken for granted after Henry's death. In the long run the Lancastrian regime in France could not survive without regional allies and could not extend its reach beyond the Loire without significant defections by the Dauphin's principal supporters there. The critical power brokers were the great territorial princes, pre-eminently the Dukes of Burgundy and Brittany, but also the other local potentates who occasionally flirted with the idea of throwing their lot in with the English: the Dukes of Orléans and Bourbon with their great appanages in the Loire valley, and the Counts of Armagnac and Foix in Languedoc.

Philip the Good was an indispensable ally, but an awkward one. He was twenty-six years old in 1422. He had been associated with his father's government since he was seventeen and already had a good deal of political experience when he had succeeded him three years before. Philip was a conventional, pleasure-loving man, bored by the bureaucratic details of government. But he had inherited a well-oiled government machine from his father and grandfather and was an excellent judge of councillors and ministers to operate it. Shrewd and cautious, he was nevertheless completely ruthless in his pursuit of the dynastic ambitions of his house. Philip had entered into the English alliance as a result of his father's murder. Avenging it was a point of personal and family honour. He conserved a lifelong repugnance for Charles VII personally. According to Olivier de la Marche, the court chronicler of the next generation, who had been Philip's page, he never really warmed to the English either. But he got on well enough with the Duke of Bedford until the latter's final years. The two men had 'an unusually relaxed and good-humoured friendship', said Olivier. When events threw them together after the death of Henry V, they found that they were able talk candidly in private in a way that had never been true in the time of Bedford's chilly and statuesque older brother. But Philip hedged his bets. He was never willing to break off all contact with the Dauphin's court. Within a month of Henry V's death, there were reports of exploratory talks between the councillors of the two Valois princes. The intermediary was the Duke of Savoy, Amadeus VIII, who had played such a prominent part in the peace negotiations of Henry V's final months. Amadeus, the perennial peacemaker, was a man of genuine piety. He was appalled by the bitterness of a war between French princes, all of whom were his kinsmen. In about October 1422, Philip the Good accepted a proposal for a peace conference under his auspices in December. The English were not invited.[25]

Amadeus's initiative was a real threat to the English position in France, and much of the Duke of Bedford's energy over the following months was directed to frustrating it. Bedford planned to tie the house of Burgundy into the English alliance with a pair of political marriages. Philip faced a grave dynastic problem throughout the 1420s. He had no brothers, and no male heir. His first wife, Charles VI's daughter Michelle, had recently died childless at the age of twenty-nine. His presumptive heiresses were his two surviving sisters, Anne and Margaret. The whole elaborate edifice of the Burgundian empire threatened to disintegrate if he were to die. Within a few weeks of Henry V's death, negotiations were under way for a marriage between Bedford and Anne, who was the presumptive heiress to Artois and the Burgundian interests in Picardy. At the same time, Philip and Bedford revived an old project to marry Margaret to Arthur Count of Richemont and make her the heiress to the duchy of Burgundy.

Richemont was destined to be one of the major figures in French politics during the next three decades. He was the ambitious but impoverished younger brother of John V Duke of Brittany. Now thirty years old, he had acquired a reputation during the civil wars as one of the great French captains of his day. He was not, it is true, an impressive strategist or battlefield tactician. But, like that earlier Breton paladin Bertrand du Guesclin, he was a charismatic personality with the power to draw men to his banner. Richemont had been captured at the battle of Agincourt and then released by Henry V without a ransom in return for his homage, his military service and his influence in Brittany. Henry had had high hopes of him. He had invested him with the castle and county of Ivry in Normandy and put him in command of the sensitive south-eastern sector of the Norman march. Philip the Good's sister Margaret was the widow of the late Dauphin Louis of Guyenne, who had died in 1415. She was currently living in retirement at the castle of Montbard in Burgundy. She was not keen on the idea of marrying a notoriously ugly, almost landless soldier of fortune. Philip sent some of his principal councillors to Montbard to persuade her. The marriage, they told her, was of the utmost importance. The destinies of the family might depend on it. As for Richemont, he might not be her equal in birth, but he was 'a valiant knight, renowned for his loyalty, wisdom and prowess, well-loved, with a distinguished retinue, and likely to enjoy a great position in the kingdom'.[26]

The next piece of Bedford's diplomatic jigsaw was Brittany, the strongest of the princely states of France after Burgundy itself. Brittany was a region apart. Since the 1380s it had been untouched by the fighting which engulfed the rest of the country. As a result, in spite of the poverty of the soil and the dense forests which then covered much of the peninsula, it had emerged from the crises of the early fifteenth century with its towns intact and prosperous and its population growing. The duchy had been administratively independent of the French Crown for many years, with its own regional institutions, each of them miniatures of the corresponding offices of the French monarchy. 'The Duke of Brittany,' wrote Pope Pius II, 'lives under his own laws and acknowledges no earthly superior.' This was not quite true, for the dukes had always done homage to the kings of France. But it was only 'simple' homage, and not the liege homage that the French Kings claimed, which would have prevailed over every other political obligation. The exact form of legal dependence, however, hardly mattered. The civil wars of France and the war with England had in practice freed the dukes of Brittany from interference from any quarter. Like the dukes of Burgundy, they enjoyed most of the outward marks of sovereignty. They celebrated their accession with an elaborate coronation service and *joyeuses entrées* into the principal cities of their duchy. They issued their own coinage, founded chivalric orders, prosecuted rebels for *lèse-majesté* and maintained their own diplomatic relations with other rulers. An increasingly efficient financial administration furnished them with substantial revenues derived from the ducal lands, regular hearth taxes, and duties on wine and seaborne trade. The dispersal of most of the financial records of Brittany during the Revolution makes it impossible to make even an approximate estimate of their amount, but fragmentary survivals suggest that they may well have been comparable to the revenues of Lancastrian Normandy.[27]

The main objective of John V, who had inherited the duchy from his father in 1399, was to stay out of the Anglo-French war. His enemies put this down to idleness and cowardice. Writing at the court of the Duke's son and successor, Robert Blondel regarded John as a snake. He would 'call the night the day, dining at daybreak and breakfasting after noon' rather than take a stand on principle. But the Duke's motives were simpler than this and his methods subtler. He did not wish to see his domains turned into a battlefield or to exhaust his treasure by recruiting armies year after year to fight in a war in which no interest of his own was at stake. Brittany had close connections with both sides. It was the principal maritime province of France, lying across both land and sea routes between England and Gascony. Its commercial interests were aligned with England, which was an important market for Breton merchants and controlled the sea passage through the Channel to the markets of Flanders and the Low Countries. Politically, the interests of the dukes were closely aligned with Burgundy, which had been an ally since the 1380s.

All of this pointed to an alliance with England. Some of John's ministers, notably his Chancellor Jean de Malestroit, consistently favoured this course. But although John was anxious to keep the peace with England, he was viscerally averse to a formal alliance because of the divisions that it was likely to provoke among his subjects. Most of the Breton nobility had supported the Armagnacs against the house of Burgundy during the civil wars. The duchy's Estates, which were dominated by the nobility, persistently opposed entanglements with the Lancastrian government. Like many harsh agricultural regions, Brittany produced a large diaspora of professional soldiers of fortune, drawn for the most part from impoverished landowners and the younger sons of minor noble houses. Most of them were currently serving in the armies and garrisons of the Dauphin. The divisions of Brittany were reflected within John V's own family. Of his two surviving brothers, one was a prominent French captain while the other, Arthur himself, was currently fighting with the English. In the next generation, John's heir would be a firm ally of Charles VII, while his younger son became an ardent English partisan who ultimately paid for it with his life.

In the longer term, John V hoped to resolve his dilemma by brokering a general peace between all three parties, England, the Dauphin and the Duke of Burgundy. Meanwhile, he pursued a sinuous course between England and France, buying off whichever side appeared to be stronger with an alliance which always promised more than it delivered.

The marriage of Arthur de Richemont to Margaret of Guyenne was designed to draw John V into the Anglo-Burgundian alliance. Philip offered Richemont the prospect of succeeding to the duchy of Burgundy if he should die childless, a move which would have made the house of Montfort the greatest territorial princes of France. The

ALLIES AND ADVERSARIES: THE KINGDOM OF BOURGES, 1422–1424

Montfort brothers took the bait. By the end of December 1422, all of the pieces had fallen into place. The marriage of Bedford and Anne of Burgundy was settled. Her sister Margaret had submitted to her brother's wishes and agreed to her union with Richemont. And John V had finally resolved to throw in his lot with the representatives of the new English King. He appointed ambassadors to go to Paris and declare his intention to adhere to the treaty of Troyes. The deal opened the prospect of a triple alliance controlling all of the Atlantic provinces of France apart from La Rochelle and its hinterland.[28]

The immediate result was to kill off current moves to reconcile the Dauphin and the house of Burgundy, as Bedford had always intended. The peace conference sponsored by the Duke of Savoy opened nearly a month late in early January 1423, in the town of Bourg-en-Bresse, beneath the mountains of the Jura. The Dauphin took the occasion seriously. He told his Chancellor Martin Gouge that he was genuinely intent on making peace with Burgundy and would commit himself to accepting whatever terms Amadeus might recommend. But by this time the tripartite alliance was almost a done deal. So Philip's Chancellor Nicolas Rolin, who led the Burgundian delegation, arrived determined to agree nothing. Indeed, he would not even deal directly with the Dauphin's ambassadors, insisting that he would discuss the business with no one but Amadeus himself. He and his colleagues had come, he said, only 'to hear what it might please him to tell them'. The Burgundians produced from their satchels copies of the 'treaties, undertaking and oaths' that bound their master to the English. As a man of honour, they said, Philip was bound to observe them. On that basis, there was nothing more to be said.

Amadeus pressed Rolin and his colleagues to tell him privately their own opinion. What terms should the Dauphin offer that they would recommend Philip to accept? After some hesitation and protesting their lack of instructions they agreed to tell him. A memorandum was drafted. Philip, they thought, ought to be prepared to accept a sufficient offer of amends for the murder of his father. The men responsible should be expelled from Charles's counsels and delivered up to Philip the Good's justice. Perpetual chantries should be founded for the repose of the dead man's soul. His companions who had been with him on the bridge of Montereau should be compensated for their losses and injuries. The counties of Gien and Étampes, which had belonged to Philip the Good, should be restored to him, together with an indemnity for all his war expenditure to date. There should be a general amnesty for all misdeeds committed by the Burgundians during the civil wars and a mutual restoration of confiscated property. Philip's French domains would naturally be treated as fiefs of the French Crown, but he must be excused from having to do personal homage to his father's murderer, at any rate for an initial period.

Amadeus put these proposals to the French as coming from himself and got the impression that the Dauphin would have accepted all of them except the last. He had draft articles drawn up, recording the terms of a possible agreement. The problem was that it did not mention the English. The Duke of Savoy had hoped to keep them out of it after his bruising experience of their obdurate negotiating methods under Henry V. But since Philip was determined to honour the treaty of Troyes, it was clearly pointless to discuss peace without them. Accordingly, Amadeus proposed to both delegations that a peace conference should be convened at Chalon-sur-Saône in April 1423, at which the English Regent would be invited to appear. The Burgundian delegation declined to commit itself. On that note the conference broke up.[29]

Although the delegates went away empty-handed, the conference at Bourg was not a complete waste of effort, for it resulted in an important limitation on the geographic scope of the war. A local and temporary truce was agreed covering the south-eastern block of the Burgundian domains: the duchy of Burgundy itself, the Charolais and the Mâconnais. Another truce, agreed at the same time, covered the territory of the Countess of Nevers. The ostensible purpose of these agreements was to hold the position pending the peace conference at Chalon-sur-Saône. But it was convenient to both sides for broader reasons. For the Dauphin, the war against Burgundy was a distraction from the more important task of dislodging the English. Indeed, it was worse than a distraction, for ultimately the Dauphin needed an accommodation with the Duke of Burgundy. As for Philip, the guerrilla war in his southern territories was destructive, expensive and ultimately unwinnable. In the event, the peace conference never opened. But the councillors of the Dauphin and the Duke of Burgundy met discreetly at Chalon in June 1423 and renewed the truces anyway.[30]

The triple alliance of England, Burgundy and Brittany was finally proclaimed with much pomp at a summit meeting at Amiens in the middle of April 1423. Philip the Bold arrived with the usual crowd of courtiers, councillors and officials. The Duke of Bedford came with most of his Paris council and installed himself in the bishop's palace, where he entertained royally. John V arrived in the Picard capital accompanied by an enormous suite, including his brother Arthur, many of the leading barons of Brittany and a large military escort, all paid for from the Duke of Bedford's treasury. There was 'much bowing and outward show of affection', according to the chronicler Monstrelet, who may have been present. Lavish gifts were exchanged. The costumes and jewellery had to be seen to be believed. The two marriages were publicly proclaimed. On 17 April, the triple alliance was sealed by all three parties. They declared their mutual 'love, brotherhood and union ... with no secret reservations or dissimulation'. They promised to concert their plans, to defend each other's territory, to furnish each other on demand with up to 500 men-at-arms for a month at their own expense, and more upon payment. They committed themselves to work together to pacify the entire kingdom of France 'for the relief of its wretched inhabitants who have suffered so much'. They supported these undertakings with solemn oaths, sworn on consecrated hosts at the high altar of the great gothic cathedral.[31]

Once the powers at Amiens had dealt with their own obligations, they turned to the urgent need to enlarge their alliance to embrace powerful figures south of the Loire. They had high hopes of Jean de Grailly, Count of Foix, who was the most powerful of the Pyrenean princes. A year earlier, in March 1422, Jean de Grailly had done a deal with Henry V. His ambassadors had sworn on his behalf to adhere to the treaty of Troyes and he had accepted the lieutenancy of Languedoc from the English King. A large cash advance had been paid to him to fund a campaign in the Dauphin's rear that summer. But the Count had held off in the hope of a better offer from the Dauphin. The death of Henry V had finally put these plans into abeyance and the promised campaign had never materialised. On the day after the sealing of the triple alliance Bedford held a council attended by Philip the Good and the two Montfort brothers. They resolved to confirm the Count of Foix's lieutenancy and the terms of the earlier treaty. Bedford issued letters retaining him as his captain with a force of 1,000 to 1,500 men-at-arms and 1,000 mounted archers, or 'whatever greater number may be needed to reduce our provinces of Languedoc and Bigorre to obedience and to defeat the man who calls himself Dauphin or King of France, along with other rebels, recalcitrants and enemies'.[32]

The conference at Amiens represented the high point of the Lancastrian system of alliances. Everything thereafter marked its decline. The attempt to find allies south of the Loire failed completely. The Count of Foix was already looking for a way out of his commitments of the previous year and was gratified to be told by his lawyers that the treaty of Troyes was void. The Dauphin, who was well informed about the discussions at Amiens, let it be known that he might be willing to make him a better offer. So, while the Count pursued his negotiations with the Dauphin's councillors, the emissary sent by Bedford from Paris was made to cool his heels in Bordeaux for more than six months trying to get an audience. He never completed his mission. Eventually, after two more years of cautious evasion, the Count of Foix threw in his lot with the Dauphin.[33]

For a few months, the English government hoped to gain another foothold south of the Loire by suborning the royal princes captured at Agincourt, who were languishing in various provincial castles of England. The Duke of Bourbon had already succumbed before the death of Henry V and had undertaken to do homage to him as King of France. But Bourbon was a broken reed. In the end he was unable to raise his ransom or to induce his officers to deliver up the eight major fortresses of the Bourbonnais which he had promised the English as an earnest of performance. His appanage was governed by his wife and son, who were not prepared to line up with the Duke of Bedford. Charles of Orléans would have been a bigger catch. But he persistently refused to follow Bourbon's example. Three weeks after the gathering at Amiens, he was moved to London for another round of negotiations with the English council. His Chancellor and several of his principal officers came over from France to participate. But these exchanges proved to be no more fruitful than earlier rounds.[34]

Even the Dukes of Brittany and Burgundy never fully lived up to their undertakings at Amiens. They needed an insurance against the collapse of the English cause. So they entered into a secret protocol with each other in which they contemplated the possibility of an accommodation with the kingdom of Bourges.[35] In the event, John V stood aside from the war after the conference at Amiens, just as he had done before. Given his long record of double-dealing, Bedford can hardly have been surprised. Philip of Burgundy was a bigger disappointment. Philip cared about his public reputation, which was very much bound up with the oaths that he had sworn at Troyes in 1420 and at Amiens in 1423. Bedford's marriage to his sister created a more personal but durable bond between the two men. Some of Philip's closest advisers, however, had always taken a more calculating view of his alliance with the English. The shrewd Chancellor of Burgundy Nicolas Rolin had supported the alliance in 1419 for want of a better option but was never a committed anglophile. He was associated with the policy of progressively withdrawing from the actual conduct of military operations.

Beneath the surface, there were other problems. In the fourteenth century, the economies of England and the Low Countries had been largely complementary. England was the source of raw materials and the Low Countries were the great industrial centre. But the rise of the domestic English cloth industry had turned them into increasingly bitter competitors. This was an uncomfortable background for a close political and military alliance. The alliance was welcomed by most of the English political community, but it was never popular among the wider population. For English townsmen of the late middle ages the archetypal subjects of the Duke of Burgundy were not the knightly paladins of Philip's court or the polished diplomats with whom Bedford was used to dealing, but Flemish merchants whom the English associated with espionage, social deviance and commercial sharp practice. Humphrey Duke of Gloucester, whose main power base was in London and the mercantile towns, was always ready to harness these rivalries to his own cause.

For much of the 1420s Gloucester's antics were the biggest single obstacle to the smooth running of the Anglo-Burgundian alliance. Humphrey married Jacqueline of Bavaria at the end of January 1423, four months after the announcement of their betrothal. Shortly afterwards, he took the title of Count of Hainaut, Holland and Zeeland. 'By the celebration of this marriage,' he declared, 'I have acquired the government not just of the lady but of all her lands.' That was the legal orthodoxy. But it depended on the validity of the marriage, which was within the exclusive jurisdiction of the Church. The matter was currently before the papal Curia, a cumbersome tribunal whose deliberate and unhurried procedures were profoundly frustrating for all parties. In the meantime, Jacqueline's rivals had the advantage of possession. Her uncle John of Bavaria effectively controlled Holland and Zeeland, while her estranged husband John of Brabant controlled most of Hainaut. Humphrey made it clear that he was not prepared to wait for the Pope's judgment. Urged on by Jacqueline, he wanted possession of Hainaut at once.[36]

These claims put the Duke of Bedford in an impossible position. He could not openly defy his brother. The Lancastrian monarchy was a family partnership and likely to remain so while Henry VI was a minor. However inconvenient, Gloucester's ambitions could not be ignored. Instead, Bedford played for time in the hope that the validity of the marriage would be determined by the Pope before Humphrey proceeded to extremes. The issue must have been discussed with Philip the Good at Amiens, for shortly after the summit Philip convened a series of conferences at Bruges in an attempt to negotiate an interim agreement about the government of Hainaut pending the Pope's decision. When that failed, an attempt was made to resolve the issue by arbitration. Philip persuaded John of Brabant to submit the question to the joint arbitration of himself and Bedford. He gave John an assurance that nothing would be decided against his interest. Gloucester was naturally more difficult to persuade, especially when Philip's assurances to John of Brabant became public. He refused to cooperate. For Philip, this situation was intolerable. Humphrey's claims struck at the heart of his dynastic ambitions in the Low Countries.[37]

The claims of the Duke of Gloucester and Jacqueline of Bavaria were an unexpected complication, but even without them, the course of Anglo-Burgundian relations would never have run smooth. There were other sources of tension. The war was expensive for Philip, who bore the main burden of the fighting in Picardy and on the southern marches of Burgundy. War damage significantly diminished his revenues. Most of the damage was done by the Dauphin's armies, but some of it was due to garrisons serving under English command. In 1425, Philip the Good's officials prepared two reports running to more than fifty pages on the depredations of the Earl of Salisbury's garrisons in the sensitive regions of southern Champagne bordering on the duchy of Burgundy. One company, when challenged by the Duke's officials, is said to have responded that 'when they had run out of things to eat in France they were free to enter the duchy, for the Regent was a greater prince than my lord of Burgundy'. Other irritants were nothing to do with the war but arose from the kind of issues which had always pitted the French Crown against its most powerful vassals: issues about royal jurisdiction, military obligation and territory among others. Royal judges and officials in Paris were just as tenacious in defending the rights of the French Crown under Bedford's regency as they had been under the Valois Kings. The Parlement of Paris was particularly reluctant to concede the rights which the Duke of Burgundy asserted in territories which he effectively governed but which had never been formally or unconditionally granted to him.[38]

The Burgundian alliance was always likely to falter as the shock of John the Fearless's murder receded into the past. Like his father and grandfather, Philip the Good was an ambitious international politician. Like them, he felt himself to be French. He 'lived and died ... completely French, by blood, by instinct and by desire,' wrote his official historiographer. But his position in France was different from his predecessors'. They had been first and foremost French politicians. Philip the Bold, the first Valois duke, had founded his state by exploiting his position at the heart of the French monarchy to plunder its public revenues and deploy its military and diplomatic strength in his own interest. John the Fearless had devoted the whole of his fifteen-year reign to the struggle to control the government of France and maintain the position which his father had established. Both men had owed their chances to the prolonged illness and incapacity of Charles VI. But once Charles was dead, France could never be as central to Philip's interests. With its government in more capable and determined hands, he would not be able to deploy the revenues and the power of the Crown in his own interest as his forebears had done. As the Burgundian state expanded to absorb Hainaut, Holland and Zeeland (1428), Namur (1429) and Brabant (1430), its centre of gravity moved away from its cradle in war-torn France to the richer domains of Flanders and the Low Countries, then at the height of their medieval prosperity. In 1445, when Philip the Good's empire reached its greatest extent, these territories contributed about 60 per cent of his gross revenues. In the course of his long reign, Philip the Good would tighten his personal control over his northern territories, creating a centralised transnational empire. His court and administration were French but most of his subjects spoke Dutch ('Thiois') and were indifferent to the fortunes of France. French-speaking Lille and Dijon competed with Dutch-speaking Bruges and Ghent. In due course all of them would be overshadowed by a new Burgundian capital at Brussels, beyond the frontiers of France in Dutch-speaking Brabant.[39]

*

The Duke of Bedford's main strategic priority after the Amiens summit was to eliminate the Dauphinist enclaves in northern France, before trying to extend the war into the heartlands of the kingdom of Bourges. The plan, which must have been discussed at Amiens, was for the English to open the campaign with an attack on Jacques d'Harcourt's garrisons of the Somme. When they had been dealt with, there would be a joint operation with the Burgundians against the other major centre of resistance in the north, the town of Guise and its satellite fortresses in the upper valley of the Oise. Operations on the Somme were confided to Ralph Butler, who was the *bailli* of Caux, captain of Arques and Eu, and for practical purposes the English sector commander on the northern march of Normandy. With the English in control of all the major river valleys of the north, the Dauphin's partisans were in no position to interfere directly. But they were able to stop the English concentrating their forces by launching widely dispersed spoiling operations against selected targets elsewhere. In the following months the Duke of Bedford would discover how difficult it was to mount an offensive while protecting a vast front against an enemy who could choose the time and place to strike. The English, complained the chronicler of the city of Paris, with pardonable exaggeration, took a castle in the morning and lost two by the evening.[40]

Butler arrived without warning outside Le Crotoy in the middle of April 1423 with about 600 men. He achieved complete surprise. Within a few days, Noyelles-sur-Mer at the head of the estuary surrendered. The other outlying Dauphinist garrison at Rue was withdrawn to reinforce the main fortress. Harcourt did not give much for his chances. Two messengers from the beleaguered fortress succeeded in getting through the English lines with an appeal to the Dauphin for help. They told him that Le Crotoy could hold out for a time but would have to surrender sooner or later unless it was relieved. The Dauphin's ministers replied that they would send what help they could. But that was very little. Le Crotoy was beyond their reach. In spite of the bleak prospects, the garrison resisted with a ferocity that evidently took the English by surprise. Butler brought in reinforcements from the surrounding towns. Three great cannon which had been specially built at Rouen arrived by sea. A fleet of twelve ships was fitted out in the Channel ports of Normandy to blockade the mouth of the Somme. But the marshy ground around the town made it difficult to invest the place closely. Artillery sank into the mud, while Harcourt's guns, securely mounted on the walls of the town, covered all the main approaches. High winds made life miserable for the besiegers and continual rain waterlogged their trenches. Sorties from the gates created havoc in their encampments. At the end of May 1423, when very little progress had been made, Butler travelled to Paris to discuss the situation with the Regent and the Grand Conseil.[41]

Butler arrived in Paris to find the Duke of Bedford overwhelmed by other pressures. He had married Anne of Burgundy at Troyes on 13 May. As soon as the festivities were over, he had left to deal with a dangerous incursion into the valley of the Seine south-east of Paris by a group of Breton companies commanded by Tanneguy du Châtel's twenty-four-year-old nephew Prégent de Coëtivy. Their objective was the important bridge-town of Nogent-sur-Seine. They had already captured several walled places around Nogent and the town itself was in danger of falling. Its loss would have been a grave setback for the English. It would have given the Dauphin a powerful fortress on the Seine, blocking an important river route to Paris. It would also have enabled his partisans to penetrate into Brie and southern Champagne and perhaps even to open a route to Reims. The Regent marched against the intruders, accompanied by the Earl of Salisbury and the lord of L'Isle-Adam. All of the lost strongholds were recovered by assault, except for the castle of Montaiguillon in Brie, just north of Nogent, where Prégent had his headquarters. Ostensibly, this brief campaign was a success. But the resistance of Montaiguillon cost the English much grief. Little remains today of this powerful fortress, but what there is, hemmed in by forest and brambles, is enough to show how formidable it must once have been, with its great square footprint, its nine high towers and its single entrance defended by a massive gateway. Prégent's garrison was destined to be a thorn in the side of the English for months to come.[42]

When Bedford returned to Paris at the end of May, he was greeted by clamorous calls from the Provost of the Merchants and the citizens for action against predatory Dauphinist garrisons which had established themselves on the main routes to the city. Prégent de Coëtivy's garrison at Montaiguillon was under siege by the Earls of Salisbury and Suffolk. At Passy-en-Valois, fifty miles north-east of Paris, another enemy garrison was blocking the important road to the capital from Soissons and Laon. The garrison of Orsay on the Orléans road south of the capital was raiding right up to the southern suburbs. One of the most effective of the Dauphin's guerrilla captains, the Gascon nobleman Géraud de la Paillière, had captured the town and castle of Ivry (modern Ivry-la-Bataille), the strongest fortress of the Eure valley, in a surprise night-time attack. Since then, he had planted satellite garrisons in ancient and dilapidated castles along the roads from Paris, blocking the traffic between Paris and its main source of grain in the Beauce.

Bedford was obliged to submit to the clamour. Sir John Fastolf was sent to deal with Passy. He swiftly captured it, taking a rich harvest of ransoms. Bedford himself retook Orsay. Its garrison was paraded through the streets of Paris with nooses round their necks, their captains holding drawn swords pressed against their chests. They would have been taken to the Châtelet and executed if Anne of Burgundy had not interceded for them. All of this activity put the Lancastrian administration under severe strain. The garrisons had been stripped to the bone to provide troops for offensive operations in four directions at once. At the beginning of June, Bedford's financial officials reported that they had run out of money to pay the Norman garrisons their next quarter's wages. It had all been spent on showmanship at Amiens, the siege of Le Crotoy and operations in Champagne and Brie. Nothing could be done for Ralph Butler.[43]

The Dauphin's next move took both the Regent and the Duke of Burgundy by surprise. Early in June 1423, his ministers decided on another attempt to open the way to Reims. They resolved to send the Earl of Buchan, Constable of France, into Champagne with the army of Scotland. This entailed a difficult negotiation with the Scots. They would not take part in any field operation without an assurance of payment. With some difficulty the Dauphin's officers managed to find 10,000 *livres* for an advance payment and promised another 20,000 *livres* later for what was expected to be a two-month campaign. Buchan's orders were to relieve Prégent de Coëtivy at Montaiguillon and then to penetrate into the plain of Champagne. He set out from Bourges on about 22 June 1423. His army crossed the Loire at Gien and reached the Yonne near Auxerre a few days later. There, he fatally allowed himself to be diverted from his task.[44]

Cravant was a walled town on the Yonne at the point where the river valley begins to open out into the plain of the Auxerrois. It was one of the river ports at which the wines of Burgundy were loaded onto barges for carriage to Paris. The surrounding region had been a target of Dauphinist partisans for some time, for one of the principal routes from the Loire valley to Champagne passed through it. There was already a Dauphinist garrison at Mailly-le-Château, in the hills a short distance to the south-west. At the end of May, Cravant had been occupied by Imbert, Bastard of La Baume, a Savoyard *routier* whose band had been operating in the area in the Dauphin's name. His tenure was brief. On about 26 June, his company was expelled from the town by the combined efforts of the townsmen and Claude de Beauvoir lord of Chastellux, the Duke of Burgundy's lieutenant in the region. At this point, the Earl of Buchan was approaching from the west. The Bastard of La Baume went to meet him on the road to recruit his help. The Scottish commander was told, presumably by La Baume, that some of his men were still holding out in the keep of Cravant and others had been put in irons in dungeons in the town. This was not true. But by the time Buchan realised his mistake, he had already committed himself to a siege. The Scottish army arrived outside Cravant towards the end of June. They had no artillery and were ill-equipped for a siege. But the place seemed weak. The walls were low and ancient. The defenders had not had time to lay in supplies. Buchan evidently felt that the operation would present no great difficulty.[45]

The Earl of Buchan's decision to besiege Cravant was a serious mistake. The truce covering the southern domains of the Duke of Burgundy, which had been agreed under the auspices of the Duke of Savoy in January, had been renewed only a few days earlier. The siege was a repudiation of the truce and a direct challenge to the Duke of Burgundy at a time when some of the Dauphin's councillors were trying to detach him from the English alliance. It also meant that, provided that Chastellux and his companions could hold out in Cravant for long enough, the Scots would be immobilised on the Yonne while the English and Burgundians concentrated their forces against them. They saw their opportunity at once. Philip the Good was in Flanders, but the crisis was efficiently handled by his officers at Dijon. The Marshal of Burgundy, Jean de Toulongeon, succeeded in collecting an army within a month of Buchan's arrival on the Yonne.

The Duke of Bedford was in Paris. He was in a difficult position, for all the available field forces were tied down in sieges, and the garrisons of Normandy were already reduced to dangerously low levels. It was therefore decided to detach part of the Earl of Salisbury's army outside Montaiguillon and divert it to the Auxerrois to support the Burgundians. By a stroke of good fortune, the expeditionary army from England, which had been promised in very different circumstances in February, began to arrive in the Channel ports at the beginning of June. It was more than 1,500 strong. Most of the men were directed straight to Montaiguillon. There they were shortly joined by Thomas Lord Scales with more companies withdrawn from Norman garrisons. Messengers passed between Montaiguillon and Dijon, coordinating the plans of the two armies. Salisbury and Jean de Toulongeon finally agreed to join forces at Auxerre on 27 July.[46]

In Bourges there was much irritation with the Earl of Buchan, who was supposed to be relieving Montaiguillon and invading Champagne, not wasting time and effort in the Auxerrois. But since he was now in serious danger, they had no choice but to support him. They recalled troops from across the whole of the extended southern front. A contingent of Italian mercenaries was diverted to Cravant. Marshal Sévérac, who was based in Lyon, was ordered to leave at once for the town, bringing with him, in addition to his own company, some 400 Castilian mercenaries and several hired bands of *routiers*. By the end of July, Buchan's numbers had swollen to between 6,000 and 7,000 men. Inside Cravant, the defenders were by now in desperate straits. They were exhausted by successive alarms and assaults on the walls. Their limited stocks of victuals had run out. Before long, they were reduced to butchering their horses for food and scavenging in the streets and cellars for other animals.[47]

On 17 July 1423, the Earls of Salisbury and Suffolk marched south from Montaiguillon, leaving a screen of troops to contain Prégent de Coëtivy's garrison. Auxerre was some sixty miles away, and they did not reach it until 30 July. There, Jean de Toulongeon's Burgundian army was waiting for them. The captains met that evening in the cathedral to plan their campaign. Between them, they had about 1,500 men-at-arms, roughly equally divided between English and Burgundians. On the assumption that the English supplied the great majority of the archers, this suggests a total strength of about 3,000 English and between 1,000 and 2,000 Burgundians. There were also three small cannon (*veuglaires*) mounted on wheeled wooden chassis, which had been brought from the arsenal at Dijon. A set of ordinances of war, bearing the mark of English drafting, was drawn up to ensure that two armies with very different traditions remained 'united in friendship and

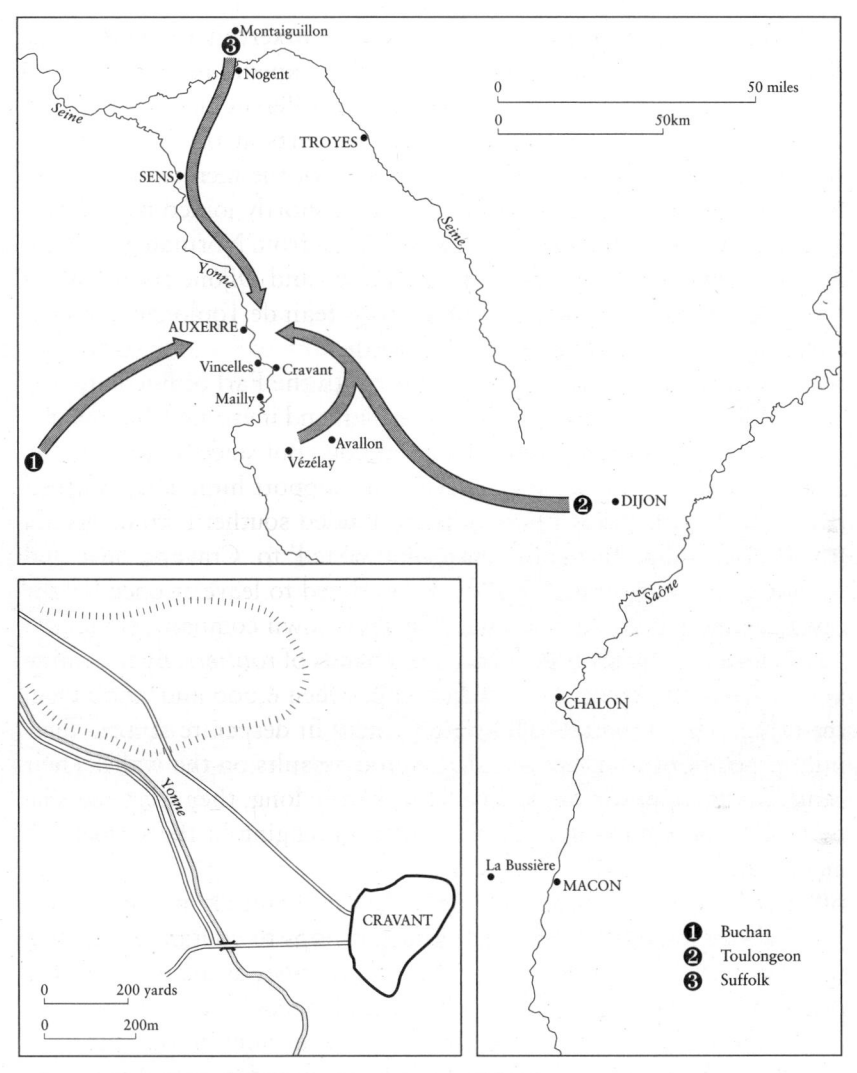

ALLIES AND ADVERSARIES: THE KINGDOM OF BOURGES, 1422–1424

2 The Cravant campaign, July–August 1423

alliance'. At dawn on the following morning, a Mass was said in the cathedral for the whole army. The ordinances of war were read out to the men at street corners to the sound of trumpets. Then the combined host marched south, up the right bank of the Yonne followed by a fleet of barges with the artillery and foot-soldiers.[48]

Cravant stands on the right bank of the Yonne, twelve miles south of Auxerre. A short distance west of the town, the ground rises steeply from the riverbank to form a high plateau overlooking the river and the old road from Auxerre. The Earl of Buchan had divided his forces into three divisions. One of them had advanced to occupy these heights to block the approach of the relief army. They were drawn up in battle order on the hillside when the English and Burgundians approached. Another division had occupied a strong position on rising ground overlooking the river on the other side of the town. The largest division was drawn up in battle order between the river and the town walls. At about ten o'clock on the night of 31 July, Salisbury and Toulongeon called a halt opposite the village of Vincelles and reconnoitred the road ahead. It became clear that it would be suicidal to go further. So they crossed the river on barges and approached the town from the opposite bank, arriving at about eight o'clock on the morning of 1 August.

The Yonne at Cravant was diverted in the eighteenth century when the present bridge was built so as to flow beneath the ramparts, as it still does today. In the fifteenth century the river was broader and shallower, and separated from the town by some 400 yards of flat open ground where Buchan's main division had taken up position the day before. The approach to this space was by a stone bridge of nine arches over the Yonne. When the Anglo-Burgundian army reached the bridge, they found that Buchan had withdrawn his men from their hilltop positions on either side to reinforce the men standing in their ranks on the opposite bank. The Scots were stationed in the front line and the French, Italians and Castilians behind. The two armies glared at each other across the water in the intense summer heat. The stand-off lasted for three hours.

At about midday, the English attacked. They brought cannon up to the western end of the bridge and began to fire stone shot into the dense ranks of the Scots on the other side. Then, without warning, the English longbowmen began to shoot volleys of arrows over the river causing carnage in the front ranks. While the Scots reeled from the onslaught, the cry of 'St George!' went up. Salisbury charged the bridge on foot at the head of his company and fought his way to the other side. Once his men had established a foothold on the east bank, the rest poured over the bridge after them, attacking the enemy lines with swords, axes and lances and driving them back from the river towards the town. A short distance upstream, Robert Willoughby and his men waded across the river with water up to their waists, while the archers covered them from the riverbank. Scrambling up the opposite bank, they attacked the Scots from the flank. Panic set in in the Dauphinists' ranks. As the Scottish lines broke, the Italians standing behind found themselves taking the brunt of the arrow fire. The dense flights of arrows entered the joints between their armour plates, causing severe injuries in the thighs and groin. The Italians had been placed under the command of the Bastard of La Baume. But seeing which way the battle was turning, he decided to flee. He ran for the horses, taking the whole Italian corps with him, pursued by oaths and curses in bad French shouted in thick Scottish accents. Marshal Sévérac followed the example of the Italians, leading his company and his Castilian mercenaries to safety while they could still get away. At the critical moment, Claude de Chastellux ordered a sortie from the town. Several hundred men poured out of the main gate and attacked the Scots and the remaining French in the rear. Resistance swiftly collapsed as the survivors of Buchan's army fled in all directions. It was all over, bar the pursuit. Years later, Jean de Bueil would cite the fight as an object lesson in the importance of not fighting a battle against an army of relief beneath the walls of the besieged town.[49]

The English casualties were small, about thirty men-at-arms according to the Earl of Suffolk's report to the council in Paris. As usual in medieval battles, it was the defeated side which suffered almost all the losses. Most of the slaughter occurred in the final moments of the fighting and in the pursuit, after the victory had been won. The pursuit from Cravant was particularly vicious. Most of those who escaped the carnage of the battlefield tried to reach the Dauphinist outpost at Mailly-le-Château. But men running away had little chance against mounted pursuers. It was the job of the heralds, those workhorses of late medieval armies who served as messengers, diplomats and experts on the law of arms, to count the dead and identify the more notable casualties by their coats of arms. They reported 1,000 dead on the field of battle and another 1,500 killed in the pursuit, whose corpses were scattered across the countryside for miles around. Some 400 prisoners were taken. They included the Earl of Buchan, who was cornered by the sortie from the town and lost an eye in the fight before surrendering to one of Chastellux's squires. John Stewart of Darnley, the constable of the Scottish army, was captured with him, together with most of the French captains who had brought their companies from the Loire provinces and the west during the panic of July.

The army of Scotland was a broken force. They had fought in the front line and stayed on the field to the bitter end, losing at least a third of their numbers. Decimated and leaderless, the survivors were scattered across the Auxerrois and the Nivernais and took no part in operations for the rest of the year. When Suffolk's report reached Paris, the citizens lit bonfires and danced in the streets. They should have been weeping at so much loss of life, wrote the anonymous Parisian chronicler, once a belligerent Burgundian, whose gradual turn against the war in these years is one of the most revealing signs of things to come.[50]

At the Dauphin's court at Bourges, the news of the battle was received with surprising indifference. Writing to the inhabitants of Lyon, the Dauphin declared that there was no cause for alarm. After all, he wrote, the casualties were not French noblemen or people of any consequence, but 'only Scots, Castilians and other foreigners who have been living on the land and are not much loss'. He was confident of recovering his strength quickly enough. For a time, events seemed to bear him out. The victory of the English and their Burgundian allies made very little difference to their strategic position, for they had great difficulty in following it up.

With his customary energy, Tanneguy du Châtel reinforced the garrisons of the Loire frontier within days of the defeat. His agents were busy recruiting fresh companies in Brittany. A mixed force of English and Burgundians tried to test the defences of Berry and Orléanais. They crossed the Loire in late August, probably at the bridge of Cosne in the Nivernais. They raided up to the gates of Bourges, where the Dauphin was in residence, and penetrated as far as Issoudun. But they made no conquests and were soon forced to withdraw.[51]

At the end of August 1423, the leading spirits of the alliance gathered in Paris to review the future conduct of the war. The Duke of Bedford presided. Most of the leading English captains were present. Philip the Good arrived, accompanied by Arthur de Richemont and a crowd of soldiers, advisers, courtiers and servants, behaving 'like pigs' according to the disgruntled chronicler of the city and driving up prices in the city's food markets. On the face of it, the strategic situation seemed favourable. The mauling of the army of Scotland ruled out a full-scale French offensive for the rest of the year. It was possible to take the risk of stripping even more men from the Norman garrisons to boost the field armies. The Grand Conseil was determined to exploit the opportunity while it lasted. Their first priority was the elimination of Le Crotoy, Guise and Montaiguillon and the garrisons of La Hire in northern Champagne. The English also needed to deal with the dangerous situation developing south-west of Paris as a result of the operations of Géraud de la Paillière at Ivry. Philip the Good had his own, different priorities. The Cravant campaign had reignited the war on the southern march of the duchy of Burgundy after six months of delicate truce. A crisis was developing in the Mâconnais and the Charolais. Philip demanded English support in a region where they had never previously operated.

The outcome was the dispersal of England's military manpower in France among half a dozen task forces, none of which was strong enough to achieve its objective. Three large military governorships were created. The Earl of Salisbury was given command of operations in the whole eastern half of Lancastrian France, including Champagne and the Burgundian counties of Mâcon and Nevers. Sir John Fastolf was appointed as Bedford's lieutenant throughout Lower Normandy and charged with the conquest of Maine. Bedford himself and his Marshal Villiers de L'Isle-Adam, proposed to besiege Ivry. Suffolk was given responsibility for the Beauce and the western and south-western approaches to Paris but was also expected to go to the aid of the Duke of Burgundy in the Mâconnais.[52]

The Dauphinist commander in the Charolais and Mâconnais was the Admiral of France Louis de Culant. In addition to his own retinue, he had some 1,600 mercenaries under his command who had recently arrived from Italy under the command of Borno dei Cacherani (known in France as Caqueran 'Le Borgne') a veteran from the Italian domains of the Duke of Orléans at Asti in Piedmont. The Italians were experienced professional cavalrymen who quickly transformed the Admiral's campaign. In a short time, they occupied several Burgundian strongholds. While the Duke's officials at Dijon were preoccupied by the threat from the Earl of Buchan, Louis de Culant had laid siege to La Bussière, the principal garrisoned fortress of the Mâconnais. He captured the outer bailey, leaving the defenders holding out in the keep. A few days later, Jean de Toulongeon arrived with the Earl of Suffolk. They brought with them part of the Burgundian contingent from Cravant and a force of English archers. The Earl rapidly recovered many of the walled places that the Italians had captured. Most of the garrisons were 'sent away in their shirtsleeves'. But disaster befell Jean de Toulongeon at La Bussière. He arrived there too late to save the keep, which had already surrendered. The new Dauphinist captain of the place did not rate his chances against Toulongeon's army and was persuaded to enter into a conditional surrender agreement. The *journée* was appointed for 7 September. When the day came, the Marshal duly appeared outside the gates at the head of several hundred men to accept what he expected to be an uncontentious surrender. He walked straight into a trap. Entering the outer bailey alone, he was at once taken prisoner. Outside the gates, a large Italian force concealed nearby fell on his men and massacred them. Jean de Toulongeon himself was carried off to Lyon, where he was imprisoned in harsh conditions for two years before being released, broken in health, in exchange for a large ransom.[53]

News of the disaster at La Bussière caused a panic among the Burgundians comparable to the one which had followed the fall of Tournus the year before. The Duke of Burgundy, who was still in Paris, left the city at once and made for Troyes, where a group of his councillors and captains gathered to discuss the situation. Jean de Toulongeon's brother Antoine was hastily appointed as acting Marshal of Burgundy in his place and sent to Mâcon to take command. Troops were recruited across Burgundy and rushed south to hold the line. The Earl of Suffolk left the Mâconnais at the end of September, but he was persuaded to leave most of his force behind him. They were placed under the command of one of the more remarkable English captains of the day. William Glasdale was a Yorkshireman of modest origins who had joined the English invasion of Normandy in 1417 as an archer in Salisbury's retinue and had risen rapidly to become the steward of his household. Glasdale was given more than 200 men and nominated as Salisbury's lieutenant in the region. His company was progressively reinforced over the following months, eventually comprising 400 men.[54]

Glasdale and Antoine de Toulongeon were able to stabilise the southern march of Burgundy over the following months, but the most significant Anglo-Burgundian success in the sector was a private enterprise which owed little to either of them. A day or two before Christmas 1423, the town of La Charité on the Loire north of Nevers was surprised by a company of *routiers* and occupied in the name of Henry VI. The author of this coup was Perrinet Gressart, the archetype of those low-born, self-taught soldiers, 'ennobled by the profession of arms though not by birth' as Jean de Bueil put it. He was probably the son of a local tax farmer in Poitou. Contemporaries believed that he had begun his career as a builder. He had learned the soldier's trade in the free companies in the later stages of the civil war, first in Picardy and then in the Nivernais and the southern march of Burgundy. It was in the Nivernais that Gressart formed his lifelong alliance with the adventurer François de Surienne, a minor nobleman from Aragon who had settled in France in his teens and eventually married Gressart's niece. Gressart and Surienne were freelance captains, but throughout their careers they coordinated their operations with Philip the Good and his officers at Dijon and with the officers of the Regent in Paris and Rouen. Gressart had put his plan for capturing La Charité to Philip the Good at Chalon-sur-Saône earlier in December 1423 and received his endorsement and a company of Burgundian troops.

The taking of La Charité was a considerable boost to the Anglo-Burgundian cause. The town controlled the traffic of the upper Loire valley and stood across the main road from Bourges to Mâcon and Lyon. It served as a back door into the heart of the Dauphin's territory in Berry. Gressart set about repairing the walls and gates of the town, restoring the famous stone bridge and rebuilding the citadel in the north-east corner of the town. He built up a large company of Picards, Italians, Spaniards and Germans as well as local men, expanding his reach along the river valley and into the hinterland to the east. These men were fed and paid from the plunder of the Nivernais, ostensibly a Burgundian territory. But their main target was Berry and the Dauphin's capital at Bourges, just thirty miles away. For the Dauphin it was a costly defeat. He was obliged to create a screen of garrisoned castles on the left bank of the Loire and to divert substantial resources, military and financial, to defending the new front which Gressart had opened up.[55]

At the opposite extremity of the extended front, the English plan to conquer the western county of Maine was stillborn when their forces in the region suffered a serious reverse. The English commander in the sector was the Earl of Suffolk's younger brother, John de la Pole. Back in July, he had been instructed to take advantage of the depletion of the French garrisons to lay siege to Mont-Saint-Michel. To do this, he had raised an army of about 2,000 men, partly by stripping the English garrisons of the march of as many men as he dared and partly by calling on the feudal service of the nobility. But Pole did not lay siege to Mont-Saint-Michel. Instead, he used the troops that he had raised to lead a heavy raid deep into Anjou. His reasons are unclear. The probability is that he expected the raid to be more glorious, and perhaps more profitable than a difficult siege.

Pole's decision drew him into a fight with superior forces commanded by the Count of Aumale, the Dauphin's lieutenant in the region. When Aumale learned of the army that Pole was forming on the march of Normandy, he withdrew to the Loire where he gathered a large force of his own. By September 1423, Aumale had some 2,500 men under arms at Tours, including the Scottish company of Stewart of Darnley. On 20 September he left Tours and marched north to Laval, where he joined forces with Ambroise de Loré and the Dauphinist garrisons of Maine. By this time Pole's army had turned for home encumbered with prisoners, booty and an immense herd of rustled cattle. The French scouts located him near the castle of La Gravelle on the Breton march.

At dawn on 26 September 1423, Aumale and de Loré cut the English off by the hamlet of La Brécinière, some six miles north of La Gravelle. As the English approached, they saw the enemy arrayed in battle order on gently rising ground ahead of them. Careful choice of site and meticulous tactical preparation had been hallmarks of the English military method, but that morning there was no time for either. The English dismounted, planted stakes in front of their line and began to dig a trench to hold off the assault. They were still building their field defences when the French attacked. Aumale's direction of the battle which followed was one of the earliest successful deployments of heavy cavalry against massed archers. His horsemen worked their way round the rows of stakes and charged the English line in the flank, pinning them against their own trenches and breaking up their order. The main body of his army, advancing on foot, then fell on them by the front. The battle lasted some seven hours. By 2 p.m., almost all of the English force had been wiped out. The Alençon Herald counted more than 1,400 men dead on the field, in addition to those who died in the pursuit and whose bodies lay scattered across the countryside. About eighty prisoners were taken, including several captains of garrisons in Lower Normandy, among them Pole himself.[56]

The crisis provoked by Pole's defeat tested the resilience of the English system of defence, which responded well. The Count of Aumale tried to follow up his victory by laying siege to Avranches, the English headquarters on the south-western march. But the English were able to reinforce Avranches with troops transferred from other fortresses. The Duke of Bedford was at Ivry with his Marshal Villiers de L'Isle-Adam, the companies of Willoughby and Scales, and part of the expeditionary force from England. He had just begun the siege of the town. He abruptly abandoned the operation and made for Avranches. The Count of Aumale was not willing to risk another engagement, and swiftly withdrew to the Loire. He had plenty to be satisfied about. In a short campaign, he had inflicted heavy casualties on the English, disrupted all of Bedford's plans for operations south of the Seine and relieved Ivry. In the following year, a small chapel was erected at La Brécinière at the expense of the Dauphin and the Count of Aumale to mark the most significant Dauphinist victory since the death of the Duke of Clarence at Baugé.[57]

North of the Seine, the English made strenuous efforts to exploit their victory at Cravant, but with equally poor results. Three major sieges, at Montaiguillon, Le Crotoy and Guise, tied down large numbers of men without making any significant progress. Prégent de Coëtivy's garrison hung on with grim determination at Montaiguillon. Their walls were undermined. Their keep was partially destroyed by artillery. They had exhausted their stores and were reduced to eating their horses. Many of them had already deserted, escaping through the English siege lines at night. The garrison was reduced to a quarter of its original strength. Yet, although several assaults were attempted, the English seem to have lacked the manpower to carry the walls even in the debilitated state of the defences.[58]

At Le Crotoy, after five months of siege the garrison was by no means at the end of its resistance. When, at the end of September 1423, Jacques d'Harcourt finally agreed to enter into a conditional surrender agreement, it was not because he needed to, but in order to pressure the Dauphin's ministers into sending an army of relief. The instrument of surrender allowed an unprecedented five months for relief to arrive. The terms provided that on each of the first three days of March 1424, the Duke of Bedford or his lieutenant was to be standing in battle order at dawn in the fields north of the town. Unless an opponent appeared to fight him and won the day, Le Crotoy would surrender at 3 p.m. on the third day. The garrison would then be allowed to leave with their lives and property and even part of their artillery, and would be entitled to safe-conducts wherever they chose to go. The fact that the besiegers were prepared to agree such generous terms was some indication of the gloom which had descended upon them. Harcourt left at once to persuade the Dauphin to raise an army of relief.[59]

Guise proved to be an even tougher nut to crack. Poton de Saintrailles's stronghold on the Oise was heavily fortified and defended by several hundred men. It was surrounded by satellite forts, whose garrisons were able to harass a besieging army, attacking them in the rear and cutting their supply lines. The task of taking these places had been assigned to John of Luxembourg. John had already tried and failed in the previous year. In the late summer of 1423, he embarked upon a second attempt, supported by some of the men who had come over from England with the expeditionary army. John methodically took out the outlying forts of Guise one by one, with the brutality that was his hallmark. His army left behind it a trail of burned-out villages, looted houses and corpses hanging from trees outside the gates of captured castles. But terror had little impact, and progress was slow.

John's army did not have the numbers to invest Guise and was only ever able to blockade two of the three main gates. It rained incessantly. The soft ground made it difficult to deploy artillery. In November, both sides were reinforced. The Duke of Bedford sent Villiers de L'Isle-Adam to the region with several hundred fresh troops raised in Paris and the Île-de-France and a company of 120 English. Poton's forces were reinforced by La Hire, who arrived with some 300 men drawn from his garrisons in the Laonnais and Champagne. They were joined by some companies from beyond the Loire, who had succeeded in making their way to the Oise valley, probably via La Hire's fortress at Vitry-en-Perthois.

With these additions to his strength, Poton launched a highly successful diversion. On 13 December, a large sortie party from Guise captured the town of Ham on the Somme by escalade. The town, which commanded an important bridge on the road from Arras to Paris, belonged to John of Luxembourg. He was forced to interrupt his campaign to retake the place. His men entered the town early in the morning, coming over the walls and landing on the strands of the river from boats. The defenders were all put to death. One of the abiding images of this brutal campaign was the soldier appearing above the gate of Ham with the severed head of the Dauphinist captain Waleran de Saint-Germain and impaling it on a spike, as the man's mother waited in the crowd below with a bag full of money for his ransom.

'This is the fourth son that this war has cost me,' she screamed. As for Poton de Saintrailles, he managed to escape back to Guise with a handful of followers in the confusion which followed the fall of the town. Like the Count of Aumale, he had every reason to be satisfied. Early in the new year, John of Luxembourg was forced to abandon his campaign and pay off his men until the spring. In spite of the Anglo-Burgundian victory at Cravant, the two sides had reached a stalemate which would not be broken until the following year.[60]

CHAPTER III

The New Army of Scotland, 1423–1424

In the winter after the battle of Cravant, the Dauphin's ministers reviewed their policy on the employment of foreign mercenaries. They decided to retain only the Scots and the Italians, who were the largest and the most effective of their mercenary corps. The perennial problems of indiscipline and looting would be addressed by raising taxes and paying the men regularly. The rest of the foreign troops, mostly German or Spanish, were to be dismissed and ordered out of the realm. In practice the policy was not consistently applied. The Spanish companies in particular largely escaped the cull. But there is no doubt that the Scottish and the Italian contingents were specially favoured. Both had suffered heavy casualties at Cravant, and the gaps in their ranks needed to be filled. Six weeks after the battle the Dauphin's council, meeting at Mehun, decided to apply for recruits to Filippo Maria Visconti Duke of Milan. A discreet embassy was sent to his court, which obtained fresh promises of Milanese cavalry for the summer of 1424.[1] However, the Dauphin's hopes of breaking the stalemate rested mainly on the prospect of a new army from Scotland.

Scotland was in the middle of a prolonged and complex power struggle, whose origins went back to 1420. James King of Scots had been a prisoner in England since he had been captured at sea in 1406 at the age of eleven while on his way to complete his education at the court of France. James succeeded to the throne when his father, Robert III, died less than a month later. In his absence, Scotland had been ruled by his formidable uncle Robert Stewart Duke of Albany, who took the title of Governor. Albany had two surviving sons: Murdoch Stewart, his designated successor, and Murdoch's younger brother the Earl of Buchan, Constable of France and commander of the Scottish army on the continent. There was no love lost between the Scottish King and the Albany Stewarts. The Governor had shown little interest in negotiating James's release, which would have put an end to his dominant position in Scotland. Nor did he take any trouble to conceal his ultimate ambition to take the Scottish throne for his own branch of the family. They were next in line to the throne if James died childless. James was well aware of this, and greatly resented it.

Desperate to regain his liberty after a decade and a half of gilded captivity, James had thrown in his lot with his English captors. Early in 1420, he entered into a personal alliance with Henry V. James's object was to earn his release on clement terms. Henry's was to use him to put an end to the operations of the Scottish army in France, which had significantly altered the military balance. The Scottish King allowed himself to be taken to France and carried about in the English King's baggage train. The English supplied him with money, armour, horses and banners. James attended the ceremonies which marked the sealing of the treaty of Troyes and the marriage of Henry V and Catherine of France. He was present at the surrender of Melun to Henry V, when twenty Scots found in the Dauphinist garrison were hanged for treason to their sovereign. He opened negotiations with some of the Scottish captains with a view to detaching them from the Dauphin's cause. The tactic appears to have had some initial success. But the manipulative hand of England was too obvious. The scheme ultimately failed, due mainly to the energy and personal prestige of the Earl of Buchan. There was never any doubt about his loyalties. In France, he had found fame, wealth and status beyond the dreams of a younger son, whereas there was no future for him in a Scotland ruled by King James. In the summer of 1420, the Earl of Buchan returned to Scotland with the Dauphin's Chancellor Regnault de Chartres. There, the Duke of Albany promised to raise a second army of Scotland to fight in France.[2]

The Duke of Albany died at a great age in Stirling castle in September 1420, before this promise could be honoured. The hopes of the Dauphin and the Albany Stewarts now devolved upon Murdoch. He succeeded to all his father's titles and powers, but not to his natural authority or his political skills. He was 'remiss', said the principal chronicler of his reign. He was a poor administrator and a clumsy politician, who allowed the elaborate network of alliances which his father had made with the leading Scottish lords to fall apart. He quarrelled with his sons, who had political ambitions of their own. Most serious of all, he fell out with the most powerful of the Scottish lords, the flamboyant head of the Black Douglases, Archibald Earl of Douglas. The Black

Douglases, the dynasty founded by the current Earl's father Archibald 'the Grim', were the dominant noble family of southern Scotland, on whose support, or at least acceptance, every Scottish government had depended since the closing years of the fourteenth century. Douglas was the warden of all three marches facing England as well as the captain of Edinburgh castle. His domains extended across the whole of southern Scotland from Galloway to Berwickshire. As a well-informed insider at the Scottish court put it some years later, the implicit understanding between the Douglases and the Albany Stewarts had involved a division of their interests at the Firth of Forth. 'The Duke of Albany governed & took upon him the rule of Scotland beyond the Scottish sea, and in the same wise did th'earl Douglas both govern and rule all on this side the Scottish sea.' Douglas had got on well enough with the old Governor. But he had no time for Murdoch and resented his increasingly obvious designs on the throne. The way to thwart him was to procure the release of King James so that he could return to Scotland and take over its government.[3]

Henry V had every reason to favour this plan. If James's alliance with England could be cemented before his release, he might even be induced to withdraw his kingdom from its 'auld alliance' with France and recall his subjects serving in the Dauphin's armies, or at least to ensure that there was no addition to their numbers. The problem, as Edward III had learned when he tried to do a deal with another captive Scottish King, was that agreement with James himself would not have been enough. Scotland's King had few means of imposing his will on an unruly and recalcitrant nobility with strong regional power bases. Moreover, the English were badly in need of money and determined to extract a ransom for their prisoner. The Scots would have to consent to the necessary taxation, and to provide hostages to secure its payment. All of this meant that a deal would have to be negotiated not only with James but with one or other of the main factions in Scotland.

The Earl of Douglas took the initiative. Within months of the old Governor's death, he was plotting with the English. Douglas was in an exceptionally delicate position. He was personally committed to the 'auld alliance' and to the deployment of Scottish troops in France. When, during the second decade of the fifteenth century, the border war died down, it was Douglas who had promoted the idea of taking a Scottish army to France. His power rested on an extensive network of kinsmen, tenants, followers and friends in the Lowlands who looked to him for the opportunities which only war could offer. His son, although quickly overshadowed by the Earl of Buchan, had been the joint leader of the first army of Scotland in 1419. Many of his tenants, kinsmen and clients had fought in its ranks. These things resonated in Scotland, where the operations of the Scottish army in France were avidly followed and very popular. In April 1421, Douglas travelled to London to negotiate directly with Henry V and James.[4] It must have been an awkward encounter. All three men wanted to be rid of the Albany Stewarts, but there the common ground ended. The English saw it as a way of installing a friendly government in Scotland which would stop military assistance to the Dauphin, while Douglas was committed to the continuance of the French alliance. This union of opposites required a large measure of duplicity on all sides.

The outcome was an agreement that James would be provisionally released on parole to return to Scotland, provided that he could persuade twenty named Scottish magnates to surrender themselves as hostages for his return. The English hoped that once Murdoch Stewart had been pushed aside, James would be able to cajole his subjects into an acceptable peace. In return, James agreed to 'order' the Earl of Douglas to join the English army in France, and Douglas for his part entered into an indenture promising to appear there at Easter 1422 with a company of 400 men ready to fight for Henry V.[5] This was all window dressing. Douglas can never have intended to fight in France against a Scottish army in which his son and many of his tenants were serving. Nor did he. Easter 1422 came and went without any sign that he would appear in France. How far James himself had been party to this subterfuge is far from clear.

After Henry V's death, the project to return the King of Scots to his realm took on fresh urgency as a result of the Dauphin's attempts to raise another army in Scotland. The new army promised by the former Governor before his death was finally recruited in the summer of 1422. It was expected to sail from the Clyde that autumn. The Dauphin's ministers assembled a fleet at La Rochelle to transport them. A large sum in coin and jewels was collected in bags to hire more tonnage in Scotland and to pay the advances of the men. The Dauphin's council had high expectations. They planned to use the new army to force a way to Reims and fulfil their long-standing ambition to have the Dauphin crowned there. They looked forward to the rapid collapse of the English positions in the north. But their hopes were rudely dashed. The English government found out about these plans. The fleet of La Rochelle was intercepted in the Bay of Biscay shortly after setting out for Scotland. Some of the French ships were captured and the rest dispersed. Most of the money and jewels were lost. The Scottish expedition was abandoned.[6]

Support for a new army, however, remained strong in Scotland. Over the winter of 1422–3, the Dauphin wrote to a number of prominent lords in Scotland to canvass support for another attempt. The response was encouraging. In May 1423, the Dauphin's ministers decided to send the Earl of Buchan back to Scotland, for the second time, to press Murdoch Stewart to push the enterprise forward. Buchan was to be accompanied by a number of Charles's councillors, including John Cranach, a Scottish clergyman naturalised in France who had been instrumental in arranging the original army of Scotland back in 1419. Their task was to raise the largest possible army on the most favourable possible financial terms. The Dauphin fantasised about the possibility of 8,000 recruits, a figure which was probably well beyond Scotland's military capacity.[7]

At Westminster the English council closely followed these developments. Its response to the new threat was to resurrect the old project of returning James Stewart to Scotland and unseating Murdoch Stewart. The case was urgent. They needed to act before the new army could be recruited. They moved James to Westminster, where he passed the winter of 1422–3 in discussions with the English council and his Scottish allies. The Earl of Douglas played his old double game. He sent his discreet private secretary William Fowles to London to support the Scottish King's negotiations with the English council. In February 1423, the English council decided to convene a conference between all parties. The venue was to be the immense and secure Lancastrian fortress at Pontefract in Yorkshire, where the matter could be more conveniently and less noisily discussed than in the open palaces of southern England.

At the beginning of July, the English council formulated its proposals in preparation for its opening of the conference. They had probably already been agreed at least in outline with James himself. They had three main demands to make of the Scots. First, the Scottish King was to be released in return for an enormous ransom of £40,000, euphemistically described as 'costs and expenses' of his captivity. This sum, which was to be secured by the delivery of hostages from the richest of the Scottish lords, was several times the gross annual revenues of the Scottish Crown. Secondly, there was to be a long-term truce, during which the Scots must agree not to support the Dauphin's cause by land or sea. Ideally, they should immediately recall all Scottish troops fighting in France. Thirdly, there should be a marriage alliance between the King of Scots and an English noblewoman, although the English diplomats charged with the negotiations were told to be coy on this subject. They were to encourage the Scots to raise it, since 'English women, and especially noble English women, are not in the habit of offering themselves in marriage unasked.' At Westminster, the chief proponents of this deal were the Beaufort brothers, Thomas and Henry. They had a personal interest in the project, for the noble bride whom they had in mind for James was their niece, Joan Beaufort. The Beauforts, ever sensitive to the stain of illegitimacy on the descendants of John of Gaunt and Katherine Swynford, saw in the marriage a way of boosting their status in England and beyond. But the idea was just as welcome to James himself. If we are to believe the autobiographical poem which he wrote in the following year, he had spied Joan from a window, walking in the garden beneath the walls of Windsor castle, and thought her 'beauty enough to make a world to dote'. In mid-July 1423, James's jailers moved him to Pontefract. He was followed there by a large English embassy led by Thomas Langley Bishop of Durham, an experienced border politician, and Henry V's old diplomatic secretary Philip Morgan, now Bishop of Worcester.[8]

The Pontefract conference brought the divisions of the Scottish politicians into the open. Murdoch Stewart had not been party to the discussions with the English. He had everything to lose by the release of the King, especially if it came with a marriage and the prospect of children whose birth would put an end forever to his family's hopes of succeeding to the throne. Many of Murdoch's allies among the Scottish nobility shared his fears. They had waxed rich and expanded their Scottish domains during the long rule of the house of Albany. They worried about how they would fare under a restored monarchy. They were opposed by the Douglas interest and by the King's Scottish friends, as well as by many churchmen and others who had tired of the Albany dynasty and its hapless current chief. Among them were important elements within Murdoch's own administration, including his Chancellor, William Lauder Bishop of Glasgow. It was these men who finally forced Murdoch's hand.

In August 1423, the Governor was forced to call a meeting of the General Council of the realm at Perth. There was a long discussion at Perth about the best way of securing Scotland's interests. The outcome was a decision to send a Scottish delegation to Pontefract, led by Bishop Lauder. The delegates' powers were carefully limited. They were authorised to negotiate a ransom agreement for the King but had no power to deal with future relations with England and France. In particular, they had no power to negotiate the truce for which the English were pressing. The Scots knew that the despatch of a new army to France would no longer be possible once the truce was agreed. They were determined to delay it until after it had sailed. The negotiations at Pontefract concluded with an agreement in principle, which was sealed on 10 September 1423 in the chapter house of York Minster. The English demand for a ransom of £40,000 was accepted and seven years were allowed for its payment. James was to be freed in exchange for hostages, but not until the following March. Nothing was said in the agreement about the marriage except that it could be expected to promote mutual affection and goodwill between the two realms and was therefore 'expedient'. There was nothing at all about the truce. It was agreed that these matters would all be discussed in London in October.[9]

While this was happening, the Dauphin's ministers were struggling to get their own ambassadors to the Scottish court before the auld alliance was irrevocably compromised. The French ambassadors had been delayed, first by Buchan's deployment to Champagne and then by his capture at Cravant. There might have been no embassy at all but for the fact that his captor, a squire serving in the company of the lord of Chastellux, sold him to the Duke of Burgundy. Philip the Good was more interested in the financial than the political value of his prisoner. He assessed Buchan's ransom at the enormous sum of 100,000 *écus* and quickly released him on parole. At the beginning of October 1423, Buchan and his fellow emissaries finally reached Scotland and arrived at the Governor's court at Stirling castle. The conference at Pontefract had just closed, and negotiations for James's marriage and the Anglo-Scottish truce were reaching their critical stage.[10]

The arrival of the Dauphin's ambassadors provoked a fresh crisis in the affairs of the northern kingdom. It strengthened the hand of those in Scotland who opposed the return of the King. The leader of the malcontents was Murdoch Stewart's eldest son Sir Walter Stewart.

He was an ambitious young man then in his early twenties, who had already succeeded in building up a strong power base in Lennox in western Scotland. He was also the keeper of the castle at Dumbarton on the Clyde, which was the most convenient port at which to embark a Scottish army for La Rochelle. A contemporary called Walter an 'insolent' spirit, indifferent to the law and intent on getting his own way. As the heir of the house of Albany, he had as much interest as his father in keeping James out of Scotland and a great deal more energy and determination in pursuing it. Walter saw the truce with England as the issue that might galvanise opposition to the ransoming of the King. On 6 October 1423, he entered into a personal alliance with the Dauphin's envoys. He issued a declaration from Stirling in their presence, which can only be described as a manifesto. He promised to 'honour the ancient bonds of alliance between the kingdoms of France and Scotland'. He declared that if he became King or Governor of Scotland, he would make no truce with the common enemy but would carry on the war. In the meantime, he would ensure that the French had access to the port of Dumbarton and would assist any agents of the Dauphin who might come to recruit troops in Scotland.

Shortly after this declaration, on about 22 October, a large French fleet from La Rochelle with twelve great carracks hired by the Dauphin's agents in Castile appeared in the Clyde and anchored beneath the walls of Dumbarton castle. More were to arrive in the following days. The awkward balancing act in which the Earl of Douglas was engaged was rudely upset. To draw support away from Sir Walter Stewart, Douglas was obliged to outbid him. He made his own private agreement with the French ambassadors. He not only promised them that he would observe the alliance with France but declared that he would join the new army himself along with other lords of his affinity and a large body of men-at-arms and archers drawn from his own followers. He undertook that the army would be ready to sail by 6 December 1423.[11]

It was the worst possible season for the long passage through the Irish sea and across the Bay of Biscay. The fleet sailed in about the middle of December, only a week after the promised date, but was forced to turn back by winter storms. There was a further delay while the ships were resupplied, the men on board were disembarked and the masters waited for the wind. In London, the Scottish delegation, led once again by Bishop Lauder, continued to put off agreement on the truce by one stratagem after another while the shipmasters on the

Clyde struggled with the wind and weather. The ransom agreement, which was finalised on 4 December, said nothing about it. In the event, James and Joan Beaufort were married in February 1424 without anything being agreed about future relations between England and Scotland. It was a Beaufort occasion. The ceremony was performed by Henry Beaufort himself in the abbey church of St Mary Overy in Southwark. The wedding feast was held in his palace nearby. In lieu of a dowry, 10,000 marks (£6,666) was remitted from the agreed ransom, thus effectively ensuring that the bride's dowry was provided at the expense of the English treasury. After the ceremony, James and his bride were taken to Brancepeth, the great castle of the Neville Earls of Westmorland north of Durham.

In the second week of February the new army of Scotland finally sailed from the Clyde. It had reached France by 7 March. James I finally sealed a truce with England in Durham cathedral three weeks later on 28 March, by which time the news must have reached him. It was to last for seven years, starting on 1 May 1424. There was a special clause dealing with Scottish troops in the Dauphin's service. The King of Scots, it declared, would prevent those who were within his realm from committing acts of war against the English. But those who were already in France were beyond his control and he would not be held responsible for them. This was politically realistic and was no doubt necessary in order to placate powerful interests in Scotland which would otherwise have resisted the King's return. James was formally released in Durham cathedral later that day. Two months later he was crowned as King of Scotland at Scone.[12]

Years later, the Duke of Gloucester would number the release of James of Scotland among the misdeeds of Henry Beaufort. It was, he said, an abuse of power, unauthorised by Parliament and a 'defraudacion' of the infant Henry VI. There was a large element of malice and hindsight about this accusation. At the time, Humphrey had been happy to accept the congratulations of the House of Commons on a deal which was thought to be 'good and profitable for our lord the King and for all his realm'. The deal did not achieve all that the English had hoped for. The ransom was well beyond Scotland's financial capacity and less than a quarter of it was ever paid. Restored to his kingdom, James ended up by maintaining the French alliance just as his forebears had done. The auld allies remained closely aligned politically and Scottish volunteers continued to go in small groups to fight in France for the rest of the war. But the treaty with James nevertheless brought considerable benefits to England. The new army of 1424 was the last fully formed army to leave Scotland's shores for France. The northern border became more secure than it had been for a century past. The truce was repeatedly extended until 1436 and then, after a two-year hiatus, from 1438 onwards. The march courts for settling cross-border disputes, which Henry IV and Henry V had allowed to fall into disuse, began to function again. There were brief periods when large Scottish raiding parties came over the border, but they were minor affairs by comparison with the great invasions which the Black Douglases had organised at the height of their power. All of this meant that the English government was no longer obliged to maintain large garrisons continuously in the north or to reserve the military manpower of the region for the defence of the border.[13]

In France, Montaiguillon finally surrendered to the Earl of Salisbury in February 1424 in the ninth month of the siege. The survivors paid dearly for their long resistance. Salisbury exacted a promise of 22,000 gold *saluts* (about £5,500 sterling), an enormous sum, to spare their lives. Four prominent hostages were taken as security for its payment. Prégent de Coëtivy and another Breton captain were released but had to swear never again to make war against Henry VI or his Regent north of the Loire. As soon as the garrison had departed, the fortress was partially demolished. This, however, was the only gleam of light in a lacklustre winter campaign.

In Picardy the Anglo-Burgundian position had sharply deteriorated. The disbanding of John of Luxembourg's campaign in December had left a void which Poton de Saintrailles and La Hire rapidly moved to exploit. Shortly before dawn on 7 January 1424 La Hire and about 300 men came over the walls of Compiègne from ladders under cover of a dense fog. Compiègne was a major fortress on the south bank of the Oise, standing at the hub of the road and river routes between Paris, Picardy and Flanders. For four years before its capture by Henry V in 1422 it had been the base of the largest concentration of Dauphinist troops in northern France. The memory of that period was graven in English minds. Villiers de L'Isle-Adam rushed to the town, hoping to recapture it before La Hire's garrison were securely established. In Paris, the Provost of the Merchants hastily assembled a citizen army to support him. They were beaten off without difficulty, and while they were distracted La Hire's companies captured the island fortress of Creil, further down the Oise, another formidable *routier* base of earlier years.[14]

The capture of Compiègne and Creil had an electrifying effect on both sides. The *journée* of Le Crotoy had been fixed for 3 March 1424. Jacques d'Harcourt had been unable to persuade the Dauphin to relieve the place. But the concentration of Dauphinist companies on the Oise and the capture of two major fortresses on the river in addition to Guise, had altered the picture. In the second half of January the Dauphin's ministers changed their minds about an army of relief and began to make frantic efforts to send troops to the Oise. They recognised that Le Crotoy was out of reach from the Loire. Instead, they devised an ingenious scheme to recruit troops in the Low Countries. The prince-bishopric of Liège was a large ecclesiastical state in the lower valley of the Meuse, with a long history of hostility to the Dukes of Burgundy. French agents had been discreetly fanning the flames for several years. In early February 1424, two commissioners of the Dauphin arrived in the city to hire 1,400 men-at-arms and 500 bowmen. They planned to pay for them out of the proceeds of a tax of 14,000 *écus* granted by the French city of Tournai.[15]

The Duke of Bedford was suddenly faced with the task of finding an army to recover Compiègne and Creil, while at the same time appearing in strength at the *journée* of Le Crotoy and defending the Seine valley and the southern march of Normandy against incursions from the Loire. He lacked the men to do all these things at once. He had with him his own retinue of 400 men, together with the retinue of the Earl of Suffolk and some garrison troops withdrawn from the castles of the northern march of Normandy, probably no more than about 800 men in all. It was not enough. Bedford appealed to the council in England and to the Duke of Burgundy. At Westminster, the council agreed to raise an army in England and send it by sea to Le Crotoy under the command of the Duke of Gloucester. The Burgundians supplied additional contingents from Artois and Picardy, including the companies of John of Luxembourg and the Count of Saint-Pol. In the event, few of these forces were needed. By the middle of February, it became clear to everyone that the Dauphin's attempts to raise an army of relief had failed. He had not left himself enough time.[16]

This sealed the fate of both Le Crotoy and Compiègne. Most of the Anglo-Burgundian army was diverted to Compiègne, which was besieged on about 21 February. Bedford marched with a reduced force to Le Crotoy, which opened its gates in accordance with the surrender agreement on 3 March. Compiègne held out for only a few days longer. Bedford resorted to a tactic which Henry V had employed at the last siege of Compiègne in 1422. Guillaume Remon was a prominent Dauphinist partisan who had been one of the captains at Guise. He had been taken prisoner when the satellite garrison at Passy-en-Valois surrendered to Sir John Fastolf in June 1423 and was currently lying in the cells of Rouen castle. Bedford threatened to hang him unless the town was given up. The wretched Remon was brought to Compiègne and paraded before the walls in a tumbril with a noose around his neck. Many of the defenders of Compiègne had served under him. Their stores were well-stocked, but with no prospect of relief the defence seemed hopeless anyway. So, on 15 March 1424, they saved the life of their friend by entering into a conditional surrender agreement. To salve their honour, they were given a month to open their gates. Bedford moved on to Creil. Both places were in his hands by mid-April.[17]

In March 1424, Philip the Good and the Duke of Bedford held a three-day conference at Amiens with their chief political and military advisers. The main business was the awkward problem of Humphrey Duke of Gloucester's claim to Hainaut and Holland, to which we shall return. But the military situation was high on the agenda and plans had to be made for the summer. Most of the leading Anglo-Burgundian captains, among them Arthur de Richemont, John of Luxembourg and the Earl of Salisbury, were there. Apart from Mont-Saint-Michel, the Dauphin's surviving enclaves in the regions under Lancastrian rule were now Guise in the upper valley of the Oise, Ivry and its satellites south-west of Paris, and the strongholds of La Hire in northern Champagne. The plan was to capture all of these places before the arrival of the Scots shifted the military balance in the Dauphin's favour.

At the beginning of April 1424, the Earl of Salisbury invaded Champagne with a large company and an artillery train, while John of Luxembourg embarked on his third attempt in as many years to conquer Guise. Poton's empire on the Oise was weaker now. Many of his men had been lost at Compiègne and La Hire had withdrawn to Champagne. With the dry weather, artillery could once more be used to good effect. This time, the surviving satellite garrisons quickly succumbed. In about the middle of April 1424, a large Anglo-

Burgundian army, supported by an artillery train, appeared outside Guise and began to dig itself in.[18]

The new army of Scotland arrived in France after a difficult sea passage in which the fleet was scattered by storms and four of the largest ships foundered. Part of the army was landed at Saint-Matthieu in western Brittany at the end of February 1424. The rest, including the Earl of Douglas and his men, disembarked at La Rochelle a few days later. The Dauphin had been told by his ambassadors to expect 2,000 men-at-arms, 6,000 archers and 2,000 'wild Scottish axemen', a total of 10,000 men. In fact, the numbers were smaller than that, partly because the ambassadors had been too optimistic and partly because of losses at sea. Between them, Buchan, Douglas and Stewart of Darnley indented with the Dauphin in April for 2,650 men-at-arms and 4,000 archers, a total payroll strength of 6,650 men. Of these, the well-informed Berry Herald reported that 4,000 had just arrived from Scotland. The rest were survivors of the battle of Cravant. They were rapturously received, a stark contrast to the surly reception of the first army of Scotland five years earlier. The Earl of Douglas was welcomed as a hero. He was received with wine and spices at the gates of towns on his march from La Rochelle. The Dauphin showered honours on him and appointed him his lieutenant for the conduct of the war throughout France. He made him Duke of Touraine, a title traditionally reserved to members of the royal family, and granted him the whole province apart from the royal residences of Chinon and Loches. On 7 May 1424, Douglas was received in his new capital at Tours with an awkward mixture of joy and foreboding. There was every reason for the foreboding. The Scots were cantoned in the countryside around and told by the Dauphin's ministers to live off the land.[19]

The Dauphin's council now set about creating the largest possible field army for what they expected to be the decisive campaign of the war. The kernel of the new army was to be the various mercenary corps: 6,500 Scots, some 2,000 Italians and a few hundred Castilians and Aragonese. In addition, they recalled their French troops from the Mâconnais and the march of Maine and issued a general summons to all nobles and others proficient in arms. All of these forces were ordered to assemble on the Loire by 15 May. Later, they were joined by contingents from the northern front. Poton de Saintrailles's company from Guise came south, together with La Hire's companies from northern Champagne, adding several hundred men to the Dauphin's strength. In all, the Dauphin could count on between 12,000 and 13,000 men, about a quarter of them French. It was the greatest military effort undertaken by the kingdom of Bourges since 1421. Nothing on the same scale would be attempted again until the 1440s. The decisions about the deployment of this great host were taken at a council at Bourges in the third week of April 1424, at which both Buchan and Douglas were present. They decided against an invasion of Champagne and a thrust on Reims. The bulk of the English forces were concentrated in Normandy. There was unlikely to be another chance to confront them on such favourable terms. The captains at Bourges resolved to invade Normandy across the plain of the Beauce and bring their enemies to battle. Reports of the decision were passed within days to the Regent in Paris by an English spy in Bourges.[20]

It was a dangerous moment for the Lancastrian regime. The loyalties of England's princely allies were more fluid in the spring of 1424 than they had been at any time since the treaty of Troyes. Philip the Good and John V of Brittany were watching the Dauphin's military build-up with anxiety, uncertain whether it was a disaster or an opportunity. For some months the thoughts of both men had been turning to the possibility of an accommodation with the Dauphin.

The main broker involved was Yolande of Anjou, another of the remarkable women who played such a prominent part in the politics of these years. Yolande was the daughter of John I King of Aragon and the widow of Louis II Duke of Anjou, who had died in 1417. She was also the mother-in-law of Charles VII, who had been betrothed as a child to her daughter Marie and brought up in her household. Yolande had left France after the murder of John the Fearless and taken refuge in the domains of the house of Anjou in Provence. Her son Louis III of Anjou had left shortly afterwards to pursue his family's dreams of a kingdom in southern Italy, leaving the affairs of his house in her hands. In August 1423, at a low point in the Dauphin's fortunes (the battle of Cravant had been fought a few days before), Yolande returned to Anjou and began to take an active part in the affairs of the kingdom of Bourges.[21] For this role, she had many advantages. She was a shrewd politician and a patient diplomat. Intensely pious, she had a moral stature that lent force to her political positions and won allies among those at court and in government who normally stood aloof from the factions and cabals about the Dauphin. She was the only person whose influence over the young King was comparable to that of the all-powerful caucus of ministers gathered around Jean Louvet. Yolande had a clear view of the Dauphin's situation. She strongly disapproved of those who had plotted the murder of John the Fearless. She thought that her son-in-law's only hope of victory lay in a reconciliation with the two major autonomous princes of France, the Dukes of Burgundy and Brittany. In this, she had the support of a number of Charles's ablest advisers.

It was Yolande who identified John V's brother Arthur Count of Richemont as the man who might be able to reconcile both John V and Philip the Good with the Dauphin. Richemont was still nominally in the English camp. But his relations with the English were strained. He did not get on well with the Duke of Bedford, who had never taken him as seriously as Henry V had. He had taken almost no part in the English war effort since Bedford became Regent.[22] In November 1423 Yolande travelled to Nantes for a preliminary meeting with the Duke of Brittany. Towards the end of February 1424, she was followed by an embassy from the Dauphin. In May the representatives of all parties met again in the Breton capital of Nantes. Yolande travelled to join them from Angers. The Dauphin was represented by his Chancellor Martin Gouge and Jean d'Harcourt Count of Aumale, who were among his more accommodating councillors. The Duke of Burgundy sent an embassy, led by Arthur de Richemont himself. A protocol was drawn up recording the discussions. It was framed as an agreement. But it was really no more than an agenda for further negotiations, based on the proposals which Amadeus of Savoy had originally made two years earlier at Bourg-en-Bresse. The protocol envisaged that the Duke of Burgundy would repudiate the treaty of Troyes and return to the allegiance of the Valois. It provided for the endowment by the Dauphin of a chantry to pray for the soul of John the Fearless, for the mutual forgiveness of past offences and the mutual restitution of confiscated property. The parties agreed in principle that the Dauphin's household and council were to be strengthened by the addition of 'persons of rank' who could be relied upon to honour these terms. But all of the thornier questions were left to be resolved by John V and Yolande of Anjou, who were nominated as joint mediators. They included the identity of the 'persons of rank' and the sensitive question whether Philip would be required to do homage and court service in person to his father's murderer. The instrument was also distinctly coy about the fate of the Dauphin's chief councillors, who had been responsible for planning the murder at Montereau and the subsequent abduction of John V. As for the English, the Dauphin's ambassadors refused to be drawn. They had no instructions about that, they declared. So the document merely recorded the Duke of Brittany's 'request' that the Dauphin should make 'such proposals as, by God and reason, should satisfy them'.[23]

The Duke of Bedford's situation was now exceptionally difficult. His principal allies were threatening to desert him. The Dauphin was planning to invade Normandy with more than 12,000 men. His own troops were dispersed across northern France in a large number of small-scale operations. John of Luxembourg's army of Picardy and Artois was tied down at the siege of Guise, along with some 400 English troops sent to support him under the command of Sir Thomas Rempston. Another 400 men were with William Glasdale in the Mâconnais. Several hundred more were engaged in operations in the Ardennes and the Rethelois on the north-east march of Champagne. At Sézanne, a walled town of the Dukes of Orléans standing at a major cross-roads in the plain of Champagne, two associates of La Hire were holding out against the Earl of Salisbury. Faced with loud complaints from the city of Reims about Dauphinist garrisons in Champagne, Bedford had sent yet another task force into Champagne under the command of Villiers de L'Isle-Adam, which was currently engaged in the siege of Nesles-en-Tardenois. Yet another siege, of which very little is known, was in progress at Nangis in Brie. Much of the rest of the Regent's manpower was needed to maintain minimum garrison strengths in Normandy.[24]

To add to Bedford's woes, a serious situation was developing in the valley of the Eure. The valley was the main route into Normandy from Touraine and the Orléanais. A chain of castles, extending along both sides of the river and dating for the most part from the eleventh and twelfth centuries, served as a reminder that historically this had been the Paris region's main line of defence against aggressive powers based in France's Atlantic provinces. Géraud de la Paillière was still holding out behind the massive walls of Ivry, the most powerful of these castles, with a garrison believed to be about 400 strong. He had recently been reinforced by soldiers from the Dauphinist garrison of Compiègne, who had been given safe-conducts to pass through Normandy and placed themselves under Géraud's command as soon as they crossed the Seine. On 16 April 1424, Palm Sunday, they surprised the castle of Gaillon while the garrison was at Mass. Gaillon stood on a steep escarpment overlooking the Seine twenty-five miles north of Ivry. Its capture threatened to open a corridor into the heart of Normandy. A few days later, La Paillière's men advanced on Louviers, close to where the Eure flows into the Seine. They raided up to the gates of the town and captured its captain when he attempted a sortie. A wave of panic broke over the region. The Seine towns from Rouen to Paris were ordered to close their gates and guard their walls. Landowners were told to take all of their movable property north of the Seine. The English commander in the sector was Thomas Lord Scales. The Duke of Bedford ordered him to find 800 men from the garrisons and retake Gaillon. But in the current crisis garrison commanders were reluctant to part with troops. Scales arrived outside the walls of Gaillon in the middle of May, but with less than half the force that Bedford had envisaged and no artillery train.[25]

With so many of his men tied down in sieges and garrisons, Bedford was badly in need of extra numbers in the field. After several weeks of hard bargaining at Westminster, a delegation of the Grand Conseil led by Pierre Cauchon succeeded in extracting a promise of 1,600 men for six months' service over the summer and autumn. These men were due to embark at Dover by 1 May. On 8 May 1424, the Regent summoned the whole nobility of Normandy, Norman and English, to gather in arms to defend the duchy against invasion.[26]

Early in June 1424, the Duke of Burgundy entered Paris for talks with the Regent, accompanied by Arthur de Richemont. The principals met in an atmosphere of intense mutual suspicion. The Regent, who had plenty of friends at the Breton court, must have known about the provisional agreement made at Nantes less than a month before, which envisaged that Philip would repudiate the English alliance. Richemont had been party to the Nantes protocol. Philip himself was nominally committed but keeping his options open.

The main item on the agenda in Paris was the continuing demand of Humphrey Duke of Gloucester for possession of Hainaut. Humphrey had been persuaded to yield a little. He had declared that he would, after all, submit his demand to the joint arbitration of Bedford and Philip of Burgundy. But the arbitration proved to be a dead end. The arbitrators issued an advisory award from Paris which proposed that

John of Brabant should remain in possession of Hainaut. Jacqueline was told to content herself with her dower lands from her first marriage to the Dauphin John of Touraine, which Bedford had annexed to the royal domain, plus a pension of 4,000 *francs* secured on the receipts of Philip's county of Ostrevant. It was in effect an award in the Duke of Brabant's favour, coupled with an offer of compensation for Jacqueline, at the expense of the two arbitrators. Neither of them can have been surprised when the Duke of Gloucester rejected it. Having failed to get Hainaut by negotiation or arbitration, he now resolved to get it by force. He had already begun noisily recruiting an army in England. For the Regent, his brother's timing could not have been worse. For his part, the Duke of Brabant responded by summoning the feudal service of his duchy. They were ordered to muster at Nivelles, on the eastern march of Hainaut.[27]

Against this difficult background, the parties in Paris fell out. The Regent's preferred strategy was to concentrate his forces against the Dauphin's army on the Loire. Philip, no doubt under pressure from his Parisian allies, demanded that priority should be given to clearing the remaining Dauphinist garrisons of the Île-de-France. Bedford was obliged to accept this. With Anglo-Burgundian forces committed to no less than five sieges already, it was decided to risk a sixth. Bedford ordered the Earl of Suffolk to besiege Ivry. This provoked an immediate protest from Richemont, who claimed the command of operations around Paris for himself. Bedford was dismissive. He told him that he had done too little fighting since Agincourt and needed more experience before he was given a command. He probably doubted Richemont's loyalty in the aftermath of the meeting at Nantes. Both of them were hot-tempered men. The gossip was that in the ensuing row the Regent struck Richemont, whereupon he walked out. For their part, the English military leaders were becoming increasingly resentful of the Duke of Burgundy. They believed that he was not making a sufficient contribution to the war. What is clear is that both visitors left Paris in a highly discontented frame of mind. Richemont resolved to break openly with the English masters whom he had nominally served ever since his release from prison in 1420. The Duke of Burgundy renewed his contacts with the Dauphin's court. It seems likely that he was asked to contribute troops to the Regent's current campaign. If so, it is clear that he refused. The Earl of Suffolk confided to one of his squires that Philip the Good was a source of 'much grief' to his English allies. Sometimes, he said, it seemed that there was 'more to fear from him than from the Armagnacs'.[28]

In the end, the Duke of Bedford got his confrontation with the Dauphin's army. The Earl of Suffolk arrived outside Ivry on 22 June 1424 with a force of nearly 350 men, the advance guard of a larger force which gathered over the following fortnight as men were stripped from nearby garrisons to join him. The move provoked a change of strategy by both sides. The Dauphin's captains saw in the sieges of Ivry and Gaillon the chance to force the enemy to battle while they had the advantage of numbers and their enemy's forces were dispersed. They resolved to relieve Ivry. Within days, reports of their decision had reached the Duke of Bedford. He decided to accept the challenge to battle. On 24 June, midsummer day, Bedford directed the nobility of Normandy, who were gathering at Caen and Rouen, to join him at Vernon on the Seine on 3 July. Over the following weeks, his manpower situation slowly improved as other operations came to an end. On about 24 June Salisbury succeeded in undermining the walls of Sézanne and stormed the fortress through the breach, massacring the entire garrison and much of the population. The walls were razed to the ground. At Gaillon, the belated arrival of an artillery train from Paris turned the fortunes of the besiegers at the end of June. The guns quickly made the fortress untenable, and the garrison surrendered in return for their lives. These events released between 800 and 1,000 men to swell the ranks of Bedford's field army. Finally, on 1 August 1424, the garrison of Ivry itself entered into a conditional surrender agreement. They promised to open their gates unless they had been relieved by midday on 15 August. The Duke of Bedford established his headquarters at Rouen and began to collect an army for the *journée*.[29]

Bedford had with him his own retinue and that of the Earl of Salisbury, the garrison of Rouen and most of the expeditionary army from England, which had landed at Calais early in June. The troops of Lord Scales and the Earl of Suffolk were encamped outside Ivry. Together, these contingents amounted to about 3,000 men. In addition, there were the noblemen of Normandy, of uncertain number and quality, who were encamped around Vernon. An urgent call went out for reinforcements. Garrisons across the whole of Normandy were ordered to send every available man. Altogether, forty of the forty-four garrisons of Normandy and the *pays de conquête* were called on for contingents amounting to more than 1,800 men, nearly half the total garrison strength of the province. In Lower Normandy, some major fortresses were left with barely a quarter of their normal establishments. Urban militias were summoned from Paris, Chartres, Senlis and the principal towns of Normandy and Picardy. Only the subjects of Philip the Good stayed away. Villiers de L'Isle-Adam, who came to join the Regent from Champagne with a contingent of indigenous troops, was sent away after a few days. Bedford may have been unsure of his loyalty. But L'Isle-Adam was Philip's protégé and it is more likely that he withdrew at Philip's insistence.

On 11 August 1424, the Duke of Bedford marched out of Rouen at the head of his army. Three days later he arrived before Ivry. The best estimate that can be made is that the army was about 8,000 strong, of whom about 5,000 were English. Bedford chose a site for the battle on high ground south of Ivry, lying across the road by which the enemy was expected to approach. Here, he drew up his army in battle order, riding up and down in front of the lines wearing a tunic with the upright white cross of France superimposed on the red cross of England. Close by, in full view of the lines, the priests were consecrating a burial ground with a tall cross in the middle, for those who would die in the coming battle.[30]

The Dauphin was at Tours when the news of Ivry's conditional capitulation was brought to him. It took his councillors by surprise. They had assumed that there was plenty of time to relieve the town and were waiting for all their dispersed forces to be concentrated. The designated assembly point of their army was at Châteaudun at the southern edge of the Beauce. The Count of Aumale and the fifteen-year-old Duke of Alençon were already there with the troops of the western provinces. Buchan, Douglas and the army of Scotland were with the Dauphin at Tours. The reason for the lack of action more than two months after the date originally appointed seems to have been the absence of the contingents of the eastern provinces commanded by Marshal Lafayette and the Viscount of Narbonne. They included the Italian heavy cavalry with their barded horses and plate armour, on whom the commanders of the army were counting to disperse the English archers at the beginning of a battle. They had only reached France in July. They had then been incorporated in the existing Italian corps under Borno dei Cacherani and the Piedmontese captain Teodoro di Valperga. But instead of making for Châteaudun the Italians had been diverted to the eastern march of Berry, where a serious crisis seemed to be developing in a region only a day or two's march from the Dauphin's capital at Bourges. Perrinet Gressart's seizure of the bridge-town of La Charité the previous winter had been followed in the spring by the occupation of a number of enclaves of the county of Nevers on the left bank of the Loire by companies operating in the name of Henry VI. They included several contingents of English troops. As a result, the Dauphin's ministers had resolved to eliminate the threat in their rear before advancing against the English in Normandy. The most important of these enclaves, lying west of the confluence of the Loire and the Allier, was guarded by two powerful castles at Cuffy and La Guerche-sur-l'Aubois. Their garrisons were still holding out when the captain of Ivry made his agreement with the Earl of Suffolk.[31]

At the beginning of August, the troops were urgently recalled from Berry. Marshal Lafayette and the Viscount of Narbonne left at once for Châteaudun. Terms were offered to the garrison of Cuffy, which brought the siege to an end and released the Italians a few days later. On 4 August 1424, the Dauphin marched out of Tours together with Buchan, Douglas and the army of Scotland and headed north to join forces with Aumale and Alençon. They must have reached Châteaudun on the following day. By about 8 August, the whole army was gathered there, except for the Italians, who were still making their way across Berry and Touraine. The captains held a council of war. With only ten days to go before the *journée* of Ivry, they resolved to advance on the beleaguered fortress without waiting for the Italians. A letter, sealed by the eighteen prominent noblemen present, was sent forward to Géraud de la Paillière at Ivry, promising him that relief was on its way. The Dauphin must have been present at the council, but his ministers were not prepared to risk allowing him to participate in the campaign. After the meeting, he was led off to safety in the castle of Amboise on the Loire to wait upon events. On about 12 August, the French army marched out of Châteaudun along the high road through the Beauce towards Rouen. They had left it too late. On 15 August, the day appointed for the surrender of Ivry, they had got no further than the walled town of Nonancourt on the river Avre, some twenty miles away. At midday, when Buchan's army failed to appear, the Duke of Bedford came up to the gates and summoned the garrison to surrender according to their promise. He was met by Géraud de la Paillière bearing the keys of the fortress.[32]

The attempt to relieve Ivry had failed. But the Dauphinists would still have their battle. Early on the morning of the 15th, they sent a mounted scouting party forward to reconnoitre the Duke of Bedford's positions. The scouts found the English army arrayed and waiting with banners flying, well dug in in a strong position on rising ground. The English had posted mounted units along the approaches, who captured several of the scouts. The rest brought a gloomy report back to the Dauphin's commanders. They thought that there was no prospect of dislodging Bedford's army. Buchan and Douglas advised against trying. Instead, they suggested that the army should take advantage of the fact that the English garrisons of the region had been stripped to the bone. They resolved to march on Verneuil, the principal English garrison of the region, which was thirteen miles away to the west. If the Duke of Bedford came after them in pursuit, they would have the advantage of a full day's lead, a battlefield of their own choice, and the support of the Italian cavalry. The Italians, some 2,000 strong, had passed through Tours on 9 August, and were fast approaching.

On the evening of 15 August, the French army arrived before Verneuil. The garrison's strength had been sharply reduced since the previous year and most of it was probably with its captain Lord Scales outside Ivry. Stores were low and no provision had been made for a siege. The Dauphinists sent parlementaires ahead to talk to the townsmen. They told them that a great battle had been fought outside Ivry that morning, in which the English had been routed with heavy losses. According to a story repeated by the chronicler of Paris, several hundred Scottish troops pretended to be English prisoners of war, parading before the walls with their hands tied behind their backs and their faces and arms smeared with blood, wailing loudly in English. One of the 'prisoners', Jean d'Estouteville lord of Torcy, a Norman who had deserted from Bedford's army and was known to some of the townsmen, endorsed their story. Believing that the English cause was lost, they opened their gates and were promptly massacred and their town sacked. The English garrison fled to the keep. Later that evening they were able to trade the keep for their lives.[33]

The Duke of Bedford held a council of his principal captains at Ivry on the afternoon of 15 August. By this time, it was known that the French had withdrawn west from Nonancourt and were heading for Verneuil. The captured French scouts had been interrogated and had given a clear picture of the strength and composition of the enemy army. This was presumably the source of Bedford's intelligence that the opposing army was 14,000 strong, a figure which was probably too high. But the prisoners had no knowledge of the French commanders' plans. So it was agreed that the Earl of Salisbury would take a mounted scouting force to follow them at a safe distance, while the Earl of Suffolk shadowed them by the north. Bedford himself would withdraw to Evreux with the greater part of the army to cover the approaches to Rouen. He had every intention of bringing the Dauphinists to battle if he could.[34]

The Regent spent that night at Evreux. When he rose in the morning of 16 August, he was met by a courier from the Earl of Suffolk reporting that the Dauphinists had tricked their way into Verneuil and were now encamped in the fields around the town. Bedford called his captains together and 'swore by St George that he would not rest until he had found and fought these base fly-by-nights'. He heard Mass, while in the streets and fields around the trumpeters sounded the signal to march. At about mid-morning, the Duke led his army out towards Verneuil. According to Jean de Waurin, who was serving in the company of the Earl of Salisbury and whose chronicle has the most vivid account of these events, Bedford rode along the units as they marched, telling them that they had left behind their country, their lands, their parents, wives and children to serve their sovereign in a just and worthy cause. France, he said, was 'their true heritage'. As evening drew in, the English army halted for the night south of the village of Damville to allow Salisbury and Suffolk to join them and the men to rest, examine their consciences and pray for the salvation of their souls. The English, remarked Waurin observing the scene, were 'by nature extremely devout until they have had a drink'.[35]

The news of Bedford's approach was brought to the Dauphin's commanders at Verneuil in the late afternoon of 16 August as they were in council. Initial reports suggested that the English army was 18,000 strong, but the heralds returning from Bedford's camp dismissed that idea. They thought that he had no more than 10,000. In fact, he had substantially fewer than that, certainly no more than 8,000. The Dauphinists had half as many again, but their army was even more disparate than their enemy's, for about half of them were Scots and many of the rest Italian or Spanish. There cannot have been more than 3,000 to 4,000 French, some of whom were of low quality. As so often in large French armies, in the absence of firm political leadership, there

THE NEW ARMY OF SCOTLAND, 1423–1424

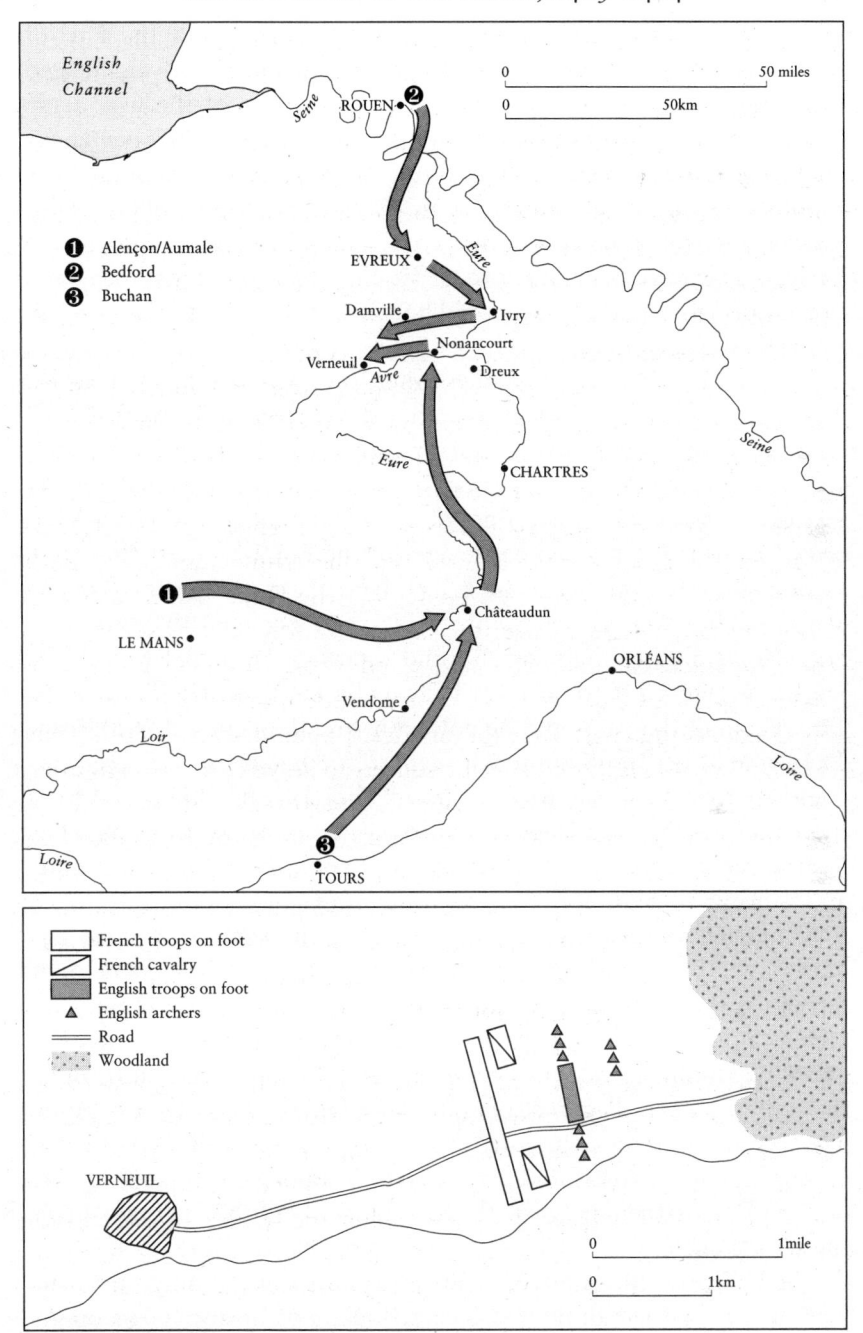

❶ Alençon/Aumale
❷ Bedford
❸ Buchan

French troops on foot
French cavalry
English troops on foot
▲ English archers
═ Road
Woodland

3 The Verneuil campaign, July–August 1424; the battle, 17 August 1424

was no clear line of command. As Constable of France the Earl of
Buchan outranked everyone there, but found his authority challenged
by others. Douglas, who was the effective captain of the new army
of Scotland, claimed precedence over him as Charles VII's lieutenant
for the conduct of the war. The young Duke of Alençon claimed the
command as the senior peer present, although he was wholly without
experience. The French captains were riven by past slights and present
jealousies. Jean de la Haye lord of Coulonces, who commanded the
cavalry of Anjou and Maine, could hardly bear to be in the same army
as the Count of Aumale.

The main question before these men was whether to fight at all.
Aumale, Narbonne and other experienced French captains were against
a battle. They thought that the right course was to garrison Verneuil
and withdraw, with a view to attacking other thinly garrisoned English
fortresses of the region. No one, they said, should ever advise a King
of France to risk a pitched battle against the English unless there was
a compelling reason. With the fall of Ivry, there no longer was. The
Scots, Buchan and Douglas, put aside their personal differences to
argue for standing their ground and fighting. They had beaten the
English in pitched battle before. They had archers to match Bedford's.
They thought that it would be cowardly and damaging to withdraw.
The Duke of Bedford's approach silenced further argument. Everyone
could see that there was now no choice. Shortly, a herald arrived from
the Regent with a challenge to battle on the following morning. The
French captains charged him to tell his master that they were ready
and waiting for him.[36]

Militarily, there was much to be said for the view of Aumale and
Narbonne, but politically the Scots were undoubtedly right. The
retreat of the army on the approach of the enemy would have been
seen as a defeat. The fiasco at the bridge of Meulan must have been in
everyone's mind. There was a great deal at stake, for in the background
the contest for the allegiance of Frenchmen had reached a critical point.
The formation of the Dauphin's great army aroused high expectations
among his supporters, and consternation among prominent figures
who had made their peace with the English. Had they perhaps made
the wrong choice?

The Dukes of Burgundy and Brittany were not the only ones who
were revisiting their options. Charles II Duke of Lorraine was one of
many prominent French noblemen who had tried to stay in with both

sides until the direction of events became clear. He had done homage to Henry V and was a long-standing ally of the Duke of Burgundy, but his son-in-law and heir was the Dauphinist prince Réné of Anjou. He was counting on an English defeat and was collecting troops to break the siege of Guise in the interest of his son-in-law, who was lord of the town. In Picardy, where John of Luxembourg's crude ambition and destructive way of war had made him many enemies, a group of noblemen holding important towns and castles met at Roye and resolved to abandon them to the enemy in the event of a Dauphinist victory.

In Normandy, many people had accepted English rule without being committed to it. As the Grand Conseil observed, they were 'waiting to see which side would turn out to have the advantage'. Robert de Carrouges, a substantial landowner in the Cotentin and the Bernay area, gathered his servants and left to join the French army forming on the Loire. Jean d'Estouteville, the man who had helped persuade the men of Verneuil to open their gates, was the nineteen-year-old heir to one of the great landed fortunes of Normandy. He had defected from Bedford's army before the surrender of Ivry, taking his whole retinue with him. Others were tempted to follow his example. The Picard nobleman Charles de Longueval, the ringleader of the plotters of Roye, slipped away from the English encampment outside Damville on the eve of the battle and went over to the other side. Several Norman companies followed him believing, says Jean de Waurin, that the superior numbers of the French would win the day. There was a palpable tension in the towns of Normandy, where reports were circulating that the Duke of Burgundy was about to abandon the English cause. Like the hapless inhabitants of Verneuil, they wanted nothing more than to be on the winning side. The rich Rouen merchant Richard Mites had been among the commissioners who negotiated the city's terms of surrender in 1419. He was an important tax farmer and purveyor for the English administration. He collected a group of citizens around him to plan for the event of an English defeat. They intended to raise the inhabitants of the city, seize the English stores of artillery and lay siege to the citadel, before inviting in the Dauphin's officers.[37]

On the morning of 17 August, the English rose early. They had about twelve miles to cover, and it was early afternoon before they approached Verneuil. Nearly three miles from the town, the forest which then covered much of the region opened up into a broad open plain. As the English army emerged from the forest, the ground rose gently ahead. About half a mile away, the whole Dauphinist army could be seen in battle order before them, drawn up along a broad front about a mile wide. Jean de Waurin, an experienced soldier who had fought at Agincourt and Cravant, thought he had never seen a finer or more confident array. The French commanders had placed their cavalry in the front line. It comprised some 2,000 Italians on the right and a smaller body of French horsemen on the left, including the companies of La Hire and Poton de Saintrailles and some mounted troops of Anjou and Maine under the lord of Coulonces. The whole of the rest of the army was arrayed on foot behind them in a single battalion, a forest of banners and raised lances. The plan was for them to exploit the advantages of the defensive and wait in their starting positions until the English attacked. As the English came forward, the cavalry were to outflank them, disperse the archers and then wheel round to attack them from behind.[38]

Bedford halted his columns and ordered them to dismount. Like the French, he arrayed his men-at-arms in a single battalion. The archers constituted more than half of his army. Most of them were massed at the wings, with sharpened stakes planted in the ground before them, pointing outward for protection against the enemy's cavalry, 'according to the English practice' says Jean de Waurin. Bedford had anticipated the French battle plan. He expected the enemy cavalry to attempt a flanking movement. His left flank was protected by the river Avre, but there was open country on his right. There was no time to dig trenches. So he ordered the creation of an artificial barrier by having the horses and baggage carts tied together and stationed on the right flank behind the archers. About 2,000 archers were stationed at the rear to protect the baggage park and deal with any enemy troops who succeeded in getting behind the English lines. The Duke placed himself in the centre, flanked by his standard-bearer Henry Tilleman, now aged well over seventy, whose military service dated back to the Black Prince's campaign in Castile in 1367. The commanders on both sides observed the long-standing tradition of dubbing new knights before a great battle. On the English side they included prominent military settlers in Normandy: Ralph Butler, the lieutenant on the north-western march and William Oldhall, the future seneschal of Normandy. Sir John Fastolf, already a knight, flew the square banner of a banneret for the first time.[39]

The English made the first move. At about four o'clock in the afternoon, a great shout went up from more than 7,000 throats as the whole English line began to move slowly and methodically forward. Every few feet, they paused to keep formation, let out another shout and advanced again. As the English began to close on the enemy, the French cavalry on their left charged the English wing opposite according to the plan. Avoiding the barriers of horses and baggage carts and the stakes in front of them, they directed their lances at the junction of the archers and the men-at-arms. Couching their lances in the charge, they struck the massed archers with immense force, breaking up their formations and driving them back in disorder. On the opposite wing the heavy Italian cavalry inflicted even greater damage. The English reeled under the impact of the charge. The archers were scattered. The men-at-arms who tried to fight back were flung to the ground and trampled underfoot. Shortly, the English line failed and a gap opened up. The horsemen poured through it and suddenly appeared in the English rear. Panic spread through the English army. There was a brief collapse of discipline, as parts of the line began to break up. The Duke of Bedford's standard was seen to fall. Many men-at-arms on the English right wing, including an entire company some hundreds strong, fled the field. They ran through the surrounding villages shouting that all was lost. Panic spread across the region as men decided that English rule was over. There were spontaneous outbreaks of violence and looting. At Pont-Audemer a mob sacked the house of the English captain.

The day was not lost. The cavalry charges lost their impetus. The Italian horsemen, their vision restricted by their visors and their ears deafened by the noise, found it hard to follow the course of the battle. Some of them, seeing English soldiers taking flight, assumed that their job was done and made their way to the baggage park at the rear, where they killed the pages standing by and started looting. Meanwhile, a Norman gentleman, Jean de Saane, managed to reach Bedford's standard and lift it. The English men-at-arms let out a great shout, rallied and recovered their formation. The archers, who had been held at the rear for just such a crisis, loosed volleys of arrows against the Italians who remained in the fight. The dense shower of arrows penetrated the eye-slits of their visors or found the gaps protected only by chain mail or leather. The cavalrymen, French and Italian alike, retreated pell-mell back through openings in the English ranks towards their own lines.

At this point, the Viscount of Narbonne decided to abandon the defensive strategy agreed before the battle. He ordered his dismounted French and Spanish troops forward on foot, lances lowered, to meet the advancing English men-at-arms. The Earl of Douglas, furious at this breach of discipline, had no choice but to order the Scots to follow suit. But the damage was done. As they moved forward, the Scots encountered the retreating Italian cavalry which barged into their lines, completing the chaos. The Dauphinist line broke up into separate units, attacking piecemeal and unable to support each other. The men-at-arms on both sides fought desperately with swords and lances, and finally with their bare hands. The English and Scottish archers joined in with daggers and axes as soon as they had emptied their quivers. Jean de Waurin, who was with the Earl of Salisbury in the midst of the melée, recalled the ebb and flow of men, the terrible din, the cries of 'St Denis!' and 'St George!', the tangled mass of weapons, the sight and sound of men dying, mutilated or crushed underfoot, the ground thick with blood, and everywhere the prospect of instant death for any man who could not fight his way through. The Earl of Salisbury could barely stay upright, as he urged on his company. Bedford himself fought surrounded by his company, fighting off assailants with a battleaxe. In the French ranks, the Earl of Douglas and his company threw themselves into the fray in a desperate bid to maintain the momentum of their attack.

The melée had lasted less than an hour when the French began to fall back everywhere. As they retreated, wide gaps appeared in their lines. The English broke through, surrounding those who were still fighting and hacking them to death. Seeing the chance of victory slipping away, Jean de la Haye fled the field followed by the French cavalry. Others, without horses and encumbered by their armour, turned and fled towards the walls of Verneuil, pursued by their assailants. The townsmen, who had been watching the battle from the walls, did not dare to open the gates. They were afraid that the pursuing English cavalry would force their way in after their prey. Unable to find sanctuary in the town, several hundred Dauphinists were trapped against the town ditch, where they were pitilessly cut down or drowned in the moat.[40]

The battle of Verneuil was the bloodiest fight of the Hundred Years War. The English and French heralds spent the next day counting and identifying the dead. They found 7,262 of the Dauphin's army dead on the field, about 60 per cent of its strength. The cavalry had been able to escape the carnage on their horses. But among those who fought on foot, the casualty rate must have approached 80 per cent. The Scots were all but wiped out. Most of the principal commanders on the Dauphinist side perished. The Earl of Buchan, the Earl of Douglas and his son James, the Count of Aumale and the Viscount of Narbonne were all killed. About 200 prisoners were taken at the end of the day. Their ransoms were believed by Sir John Fastolf, a considerable authority in these matters, to have been worth 160,000 gold *saluts* (about £40,000 sterling) to Bedford alone. They included the Duke of Alençon and Marshal Lafayette. Alençon had been lucky to survive. He was pulled out alive from a pile of corpses. His bastard half-brother, a prominent captain on the western march, was captured with him, but was so badly wounded that he died shortly afterwards. Unusually, most of the casualties were suffered in the heat of battle, not in the pursuit. The victor's losses, although much lower than those of the vanquished, were higher than those suffered in any other English victory of the period. Writing after the battle to John of Luxembourg and Sir Thomas Rempston outside Guise, the Duke of Bedford reported that he had lost only two gentlemen, both Norman, and a few archers. Bedford's boast was misleading, for he was only counting the more notable casualties. Jean de Waurin records that his own side lost 1,600 men, English or Norman.

There were several reasons for the exceptionally high casualty rate. The two sides were roughly evenly matched once the force of the cavalry charges was spent. The Scots, even with defeat staring them in the face, fought with ferocious courage while they still had breath in their bodies. Ill-feeling against the Scots, whose participation in the French war was bitterly resented by the English, banished whatever chivalrous instincts they might otherwise have felt towards their ancient enemies. 'A Clarence! A Clarence' they cried as they remembered the Scottish massacre of the Earl of Clarence and his companions at Baugé three years before. The main reason for the slaughter was the ban on taking prisoners during the battle, which applied in both English and Scottish armies. The Earl of Douglas was believed to have ordered that the English were to be killed on the field and not taken, a rumour which is confirmed by Scottish sources. This was not rancour, but a practical disciplinary measure. Many fights over the past century had been lost as a result of men withdrawing prematurely from their lines to take lucrative prisoners before their fellows could get them. English soldiers had been strictly forbidden to do this since at least the 1380s. 'Attend not to covetise . . .', Bedford had reminded them in his harangue before Verneuil, 'but only to worship [sc. honour] and to do that that you came for.'[41]

Bedford passed the night near the battlefield. On the following day there was unfinished business to attend to. The corpses of the Viscount of Narbonne and François de Grignaux, both of whom had been involved in the murder of John the Fearless, were identified by the heralds. They were hanged from gibbets by order of the Regent, together with two others who were probably Norman defectors. A hunt was ordered for other defectors. They were executed if they were caught and their property forfeited. The man who was believed to have led the flight from the field after the initial cavalry charge was found and drawn, hanged and quartered, 'as he was well worthy', said an English chronicler. Several hundred French troops who had been assigned to guard the town of Verneuil were summoned to surrender and after a brief negotiation were allowed to depart with their lives and personal possessions. The Scots who survived were given safe-conducts to return to Scotland. As for the Duke of Alençon, he was taken to the keep of Le Crotoy on the Somme, where he came under heavy pressure to acknowledge Henry VI as King of France and defect to the English. He was eventually released in 1427 in return for a ruinous ransom. For the English who had distinguished themselves in the fight, there would be a lavish distribution of land grants in France, many of them small holdings granted to mere archers.[42]

On the evening of 18 August, the Regent left for Pont-de-l'Arche where his army was disbanded. The field of battle was left as it was, strewn with corpses rotting in the summer heat. Scavengers descended on the site to strip them bare and hunt for rings and jewels. The bodies of the Scottish captains, Buchan, Douglas and his son, were eventually retrieved and taken to Tours cathedral to be buried 'without ceremony'. The Viscount of Narbonne's kinsmen came to take his mutilated body down from the gibbet and carry it for burial to the beautiful Cistercian abbey which his ancestors had founded at Fontfroide near Narbonne. Across the Dauphinist provinces, whole communities mourned their dead, even if their bodies were never recovered. The Estates of the Dauphiné raised money to endow perpetual Masses in the Dominican church of Grenoble and the

Benedictine abbey of Saint-Antoine-de-Viennois. They commissioned paintings of the dead of Verneuil, their salvation assured, sheltering beneath the Virgin's cloak. The image was copied in other churches of the region. In the parish church of Laval, a fresco discovered beneath the whitewash in 1885 commemorates no fewer than 120 gentlemen of the region who never returned from the battle. Most of the other casualties had no monument to recall their violent deaths. Sometime after the battle, a hermit consecrated the field on which they had died, collected up the bleached bones still scattered over the ground and built an ossuary and a chapel to house them. It became the site of a pilgrimage and an annual market, before it finally disappeared without trace many years later.[43]

A few days after the battle the Duke of Bedford made his entry into Rouen, to be cheered by delighted crowds as he walked to the cathedral through streets hung with bunting and decorated with commemorative tableaux. The scenes were repeated in September when the Duke and his wife, accompanied by the Earl of Salisbury, entered Paris to be greeted by bonfires, cries of *'Noel!'* ('Hurrah!') and massed choirs singing the *Te Deum*, accompanied by organs, trumpets and pealing church bells. The chronicler of the city likened it to a Roman triumph. They had good reason to celebrate. The battle of Verneuil was the decisive victory which the English had failed to achieve the year before at Cravant. One day, in unhappier times, Parliament would remind the English King that Verneuil was 'the greatest feat of arms performed by Englishmen in our time, apart from the battle of Agincourt'.[44]

Its first and most direct impact was on the military capacity of the kingdom of Bourges. The army of Scotland, on which the Dauphin had depended for his ability to challenge the English in the field, was destroyed as a fighting formation. Stewart of Darnley had not been present at the battle, probably because his ransom from Cravant was still unpaid. He did his best to gather the remnants of the Scots and reconstitute them as an organised unit. A number of Scots resolved to return home. Those that remained amounted to just 150 men-at-arms and about 400 archers. The Dauphin nursed hopes of a third army of Scotland, and even opened negotiations with the Earl of Mar, whom he hoped might be persuaded to lead it. But these plans were never realistic. James I, newly restored to his kingdom, had promised the English that he would stop the recruitment of a fresh army for the

Dauphin's service. The Earl of Mar, sixty years old and preoccupied with the affairs of the Highlands, was perhaps the least likely candidate to take over Buchan's role in France. But Scotland could not have raised another army for France even if James and Mar had been willing. The northern kingdom had lost the best part of a generation of its military manpower at Cravant and Verneuil.

Politically, the country was in turmoil. Within months of his return, King James moved against the Albany Stewarts, the Dauphin's chief allies in Scotland. Murdoch Stewart was executed. His sons followed him to the block. Their closest associates were imprisoned. The Black Douglases, who had been the main recruiting agents for the first two armies of Scotland, fared better. They reached an understanding with the King. But the death of the Earl of Douglas and many of his tenants and clients at Verneuil had dealt a blow to their influence from which they never recovered. The new Earl succeeded to none of his father's offices and was gradually shouldered from power over the following years. No substantial reinforcements reached the Dauphin from Scotland until 1428, when a few hundred men arrived in the retinue of a Scottish embassy.[45]

The Italians had escaped the slaughter and remained in France, but they never again played the important role that they had played in 1423 and 1424. Borno dei Cacherani appears to have withdrawn to the domains which the Dauphin had granted him in the Dauphiné and took no further part in the war. Teodoro di Valperga remained in the Dauphin's service for thirty years, but his company dwindled to two or three hundred as men deserted, died or went home. For a time, the Dauphin's ministers considered recruiting more Italians to replace them. They approached Niccolo d'Este, the despot of Ferrara and the most notable Italian *condottier* of the day. He was friendly, but unhelpful.

Within France, the main of sources of mercenary manpower had traditionally been Brittany and the great Gascon lords of the Pyrenees. Efforts to draw John V of Brittany into a military alliance were redoubled and appeals were made to the Gascons. In the aftermath of the disaster, neither initiative got anywhere. This left Charles with a small corps of Italians, about 600 Scots, a few Castilian companies and up to 4,000 French, of whom perhaps a third were professionals in full-time service. There was no prospect of raising a field army from these sources capable of matching the highly professional army of the English and their Norman auxiliaries. For the next five years, the Dauphin's captains were forced to abandon the offensive strategy conceived in the wave of optimism that followed his accession, and to conduct a largely defensive war, distributing their exiguous resources across a large number of garrisons on the southern marches of Lancastrian France.[46]

The Duke of Bedford was determined not to repeat the mistakes made after the battle of Cravant, when his advantage had been frittered away in a series of limited and unproductive operations. Within a few days of the victory, detailed plans to follow it up were prepared in the citadel of Rouen. The destruction of the Dauphin's field army at Verneuil made it possible to redeploy much of the English army in France. With effect from the end of September 1424, the total garrison strength of Normandy and the *pays de conquête* was reduced to less than 2,000 men, about half of the figure for the previous year. It remained at roughly that level for the next four years. At the same time garrison troops were withdrawn from the northern march and William Glasdale's small army was recalled from the Mâconnais. They were concentrated on the marches of Maine and the Avranchin. It was decided to launch a great offensive in the west to conquer Maine and Anjou. This was a project dear to the Duke of Bedford's heart. He had recently appropriated both counties to his own appanage in anticipation of their conquest. He had high, perhaps excessive, expectations of what their annexation might achieve. It would relieve pressure on the southern march of Normandy and open a route to the Loire. It would bring a new source of revenue to the Norman treasury, and new lands to be granted out to loyal supporters. Above all, it would bring the war to the enemy and show the waverers who were waiting on events that the English were still committed to the conquest of the whole of France. Two simultaneous operations were planned. One army would invade Maine while another would lay siege to Mont-Saint-Michel. 'By this means,' the Grand Conseil observed, 'the war will be brought swiftly to an end.'

On 1 October 1424, the Duke of Bedford explained his intentions to a joint meeting in Paris of the Estates-General of Lancastrian France and the provincial Estates of Normandy. Taking account of casualties and the return of some of the latest expeditionary force to England, the army's permanent strength currently stood at 4,800 men. Of these, Bedford intended to assign 1,600 men to the defence of Normandy, 1,600 to garrisons and field operations in the rest of Lancastrian France, and 1,600 to the conquest of Mont-Saint-Michel and the invasion of Maine and Anjou. In addition, he proposed to call for a fresh expeditionary army from England in the next season. These arrangements marked a notable shift of military resources away from Normandy and towards the Île-de-France and Champagne and operations against the Dauphinist provinces of the west. In future, there would be a stronger emphasis on the formation of field armies for offensive operations. In keeping with this approach, the personal retinues of the greater captains, which were intended mainly for service in the field, were progressively increased. The Earl of Warwick went out to France in 1426 with 400 men, which was shortly increased to 800 and then to 1,200 when he took over from the Earl of Salisbury in the following year.[47]

The first task was to complete the operations which had been begun in the spring to clear the Dauphinist garrisons at Guise and in northern Champagne. It was also urgent to remove the smaller Dauphinist garrisons which had established themselves on the route between Paris and Lower Normandy while attention had been focused on Ivry. The Earls of Salisbury and Suffolk were charged with these tasks. They were accomplished relatively swiftly as isolated and demoralised Dauphinist garrisons lost the will to resist. The Dauphin was condemned to watch impotently as they surrendered one after the other. Writing to the council of Tournai, the only major city of the north to acknowledge his authority, Charles declared that he had exhausted the funds voted to him by the Estates and could no longer undertake large-scale field operations. Nesles-en-Tardenois in the Laonnais opened its gates to Villiers de L'Isle-Adam at the end of August 1424. The nearby fortress of Fère-en-Tardenois, whose gaunt ruins are still one of the most striking sights of the region, surrendered shortly afterwards. Most of the garrisoned forts south-west of Paris were mopped up by the Earls of Salisbury and Suffolk over the following month. On 18 September 1424, the defenders of Guise entered into a conditional surrender agreement. The place was still strong, a fact which was reflected in the unusually long time allowed for relief. The *journée* was fixed for 1 March 1425, more than five months ahead. But no one seriously expected such an army of relief to appear. In the event Guise surrendered early without waiting for the *journée*. La Hire's headquarters at Vitry-en-Perthois agreed to surrender together with its satellite forts with a delay until 2 April 1425 and a large cash payment on the side to La Hire himself.[48]

The Duke of Burgundy mounted a similar campaign against isolated Dauphinist garrisons in his own domains. The first news of the battle of Verneuil was brought to him at Chalon-sur-Saône, four days after it was fought, by two members of the Earl of Salisbury's household who had ridden post-haste from Normandy. Philip had contributed nothing to the victory, but he was highly satisfied with their report and made them a generous gift. He returned at once to Dijon, to exploit the Dauphin's disarray. An army was hastily recruited to expel Charles's partisans from the Nivernais. Another, which Philip intended to lead in person, was summoned to invade the Mâconnais. The Dauphinists still held two powerful fortresses there, at La Bussière, the scene of the embarrassing ambush of Jean de Toulongeon a year earlier, and the impressive natural fortress of La Roche Solutré, perched on its limestone escarpment a thousand feet above the plain west of Mâcon. William Glasdale took the field with a mixed force of English and Burgundian troops and a powerful artillery train from the ducal arsenals. By the time Philip reached Mâcon with his army, at the beginning of October, Glasdale had already captured La Bussière and obtained the conditional surrender of La Roche Solutré. The Count of Clermont, the Dauphin's current lieutenant in the region, was completely wrong-footed by the speed of events. He reacted too late to save La Bussière. He tried to gather an army to relieve La Roche Solutré at the *journée* appointed for its surrender. But when the day came, he was nowhere to be seen.[49]

While the parties waited for the *journée* of La Roche Solutré, their masters' ambassadors were deep in conclave in the castle of Amadeus of Savoy at Chambéry, south of Geneva. On 28 September 1424, they agreed upon a new truce covering the whole of the southern block of Burgundian territory including the duchy of Burgundy itself, the Mâconnais, the Charolais and the Lyonnais on its southern marches, as well as the domains of the house of Bourbon in the Bourbonnais, Beaujolais and Forez. It also extended to the Nivernais, the strategic cross-roads between the kingdom of Bourges and the domains of the house of Burgundy. The truce came into effect at dawn on 5 October 1424, the day after the *journée*. It was a seminal moment in the history of the region. Like the earlier truce, it was intended as a temporary measure to allow for the negotiation of a more general reconciliation between the two branches of the house of Valois. A fresh peace conference was to be convened at Mâcon at the end of the year under Amadeus's auspices. But the regional truce was too convenient to both sides to be allowed to expire. It was in fact continually renewed at successive conferences under the auspices of the Duke of Savoy until 1435.[50]

These operations left the territory of the Lancastrian regime and its Burgundian ally more or less free of Dauphinist garrisons for the first time since the treaty of Troyes. The only significant hostile bands still operating were now the garrison of Vaucouleurs in Lorraine and the group of castles far away in the Meuse valley held by La Hire's associate Jean Raoulet. However, no region could ever be entirely pacified in a war which was fought mainly by irregular forces dependent on fighting for their living. Countless abandoned castles, the monuments of past wars, survived to be occupied and refortified without warning by free-lance companies. Even garrisoned castles were vulnerable, as routine blunted the attention of sentries, stores were allowed to become run down and vital repairs were deferred. The government in Paris responded rapidly to the more dangerous intruders, sending troops to expel them before they could establish themselves securely. But it did not have the resources to garrison every place that it recaptured, and demolition was not always enough.

The story of Mont-Aimé in Champagne illustrated the scale of the problem. The ancient fortress stood on a rock pinnacle some 250 feet above the main road from Paris to Châlons-sur-Marne (modern Châlons-en-Champagne). It was easily surprised but difficult to besiege. Too steep for artillery, the mountain required very large numbers to invest it completely. Mont-Aimé had been occupied in about 1422 by associates of La Hire and by 1425 had passed into the control of a Champagne nobleman, Eustache de Conflans. Eustache was expelled in June 1425 by the Earl of Salisbury, but the place was almost immediately reoccupied by another company and at the end of September 1425 Salisbury had to besiege it again. The fortress held out for at least three months before surrendering. This time, it was partially dismantled apart from a single tower, which was retained in order to accommodate a small garrison. But by the following summer, the ruins left by Salisbury were once more in enemy hands after two members of the garrison had been bribed to let them in. Within a short time, the defences had been repaired and occupied by 300 men, who used it as a base for raiding across much of central Champagne. In September 1426, the newcomers captured the important town of Vertus nearby. The garrison of Vertus, a mixed force of English and French, took refuge in two fortified gatehouses and waited to be relieved. The Grand Conseil in Paris finally resolved to be done with the companies of Mont-Aimé. They ordered the Earl of Salisbury and John of Luxembourg to take 1,200 men into Champagne to recover it. Vertus was besieged first and surrendered by Christmas. But at Mont-Aimé itself even Salisbury's large force proved to be insufficient. Some 400 reinforcements had to be sent to join them from Normandy. The garrison ultimately surrendered at the end of April 1427 after withstanding a siege of four months. The men who had betrayed it were identified and executed. The fortress was then comprehensively destroyed and was not reoccupied again.[51]

Perhaps more important even than the military impact of these operations was their profound effect on the political psychology of the regions recognising the dual monarchy. They pushed the fighting fronts further from the centres of English power, ushering in a period of relative tranquillity and prosperity which lasted until the end of the decade. The victory restored for a time the aura of English invincibility and persuaded the populations of the north that the English were there to stay. Men thought, as Bedford told the Parlement of Paris that October, that the English owed their victory 'more to the grace of God than to mere numbers or force of arms'. The importance of these intangible factors had been dramatically demonstrated by the plots formed in Rouen in the expectation of an English defeat and the riots which broke out on the afternoon of the battle when reports circulated that they had been beaten. After the battle, the rioters dispersed. The plotters of Roye and Rouen forgot their plans and were eventually denounced and forced to flee or sue for pardons. A few days after the battle the Duke of Lorraine received an angry rebuke from Bedford for his attempt to march to the relief of Guise, and promptly abandoned it. Less than a year after their last substantial grant, the Normans authorised a large increase in the *gabelle* and voted an *aide* of 200,000 *livres* to pay off the arrears accumulated during the military operations of the summer and to fund the siege of Mont-Saint-Michel.[52]

The great western offensive planned in Rouen castle in the aftermath of the battle began within days of the decision to launch it. The officer charged with the siege of Mont-Saint-Michel was the *bailli* of Cotentin, Nicholas Burdet, a man with a violent past in his native Warwickshire, who had fought at Agincourt and been knighted at Verneuil. Burdet arrived at the mouth of the river Couesnon opposite Mont-Saint-Michel on 12 September 1424 at the head of some 500 soldiers. The great island monastery, dominating the shoreline at the eastern end of the Gulf of Saint-Malo, was a natural fortress comprising the abbey church, its conventual buildings and a small town, crammed onto a rock of some seventeen acres. It looked less dramatic than it does today, for the old romanesque church had partially collapsed in 1421 and the great gothic choir with its spire and flying buttresses did not begin to rise from the ruins until the 1440s.

The fortress presented unique problems for a besieging army. The tides in the bay are the highest in continental Europe, with a difference of up to fifty feet between high and low water. Today, five centuries of alluvial and tidal deposits have raised the level of the coastal land, bringing it closer to the rock. In 1424, the abbey was more remote. On the coast opposite the mount, the river Couesnon spread over a broad delta, creating an impassable landscape of rivulets and marsh. At high tide, the sea lapped the walls of Pontorson, which is now five miles inland, and sometimes penetrated up the valley as far as Antrain, seven miles further south. At low tide, it retreated some ten miles beyond the mount, leaving it accessible by land twice a day for just a few hours. The saturated ground was too soft and the intervals of accessibility too brief to allow the deployment of siege artillery at effective range. These natural defences had been reinforced since the 1390s by the construction of towers and barbicans around the abbey buildings. After Henry V's invasion of Normandy in 1417, the town clustered around the base of the rock was enclosed by a second line of fortified gates, towers and ramparts at the water's edge, armed with artillery. Mont-Saint-Michel was virtually impregnable, unless its defenders could be starved out, and that presented its own difficulties. Fresh water was the critical factor. There was only one small spring on the mount. A large lead-lined cistern had recently been excavated in the rock behind the ruins of the apse, which collected rainwater from the roofs of the church and abbey buildings. But the cistern often ran dry and had to be regularly refilled by hauling water in barrels from the mainland. Fresh food and other supplies had to be supplied by sea from Saint-Malo. In 1424 the defence of the mount was directed by

Nicolas Paynel, lord of Bricqueville, a resourceful Norman nobleman who had defended Cherbourg against the army of Henry V in 1418 and had withdrawn to the mount after it had fallen. Paynel had at least 120 noblemen under his command, whose arms, still visible in the eighteenth century, were once painted on the walls of the church together with contemporary verses celebrating their valour. Including common men-at-arms, bowmen and townsmen, the defenders of Mont-Saint-Michel must have been several hundred strong.[53]

Nicholas Burdet had hoped to capture the mount by a coup de main with the aid of a traitor serving in the garrison. Henri Murdrac, a minor nobleman of the Cotentin, had been paid the enormous sum of 1,000 *écus* back in July to let them in. The plot came to nothing. Either Murdrac double-crossed his paymasters or he was discovered. It was already clear by the time Burdet arrived on 8 September 1424 that the defenders would have to be starved out. He had brought with him a large crew of craftsmen and labourers. He set them to work to build a timber bastide by the hamlet of Ardevon on the shore south-east of the mount. Funded by levies on the surrounding villages and ready for occupation within two months, the fort was an impressive structure, defended by a walled moat with a fortified gate and drawbridge, and large enough to hold 240 men with their horses. Burdet established his headquarters there in mid-November 1424.

Burdet's main challenge was to blockade the mount from the sea. Some four years earlier the English had occupied Tombelaine, a bleak granite rock rising out of the tidal waters a little over a mile north of Mont-Saint-Michel, on which there was an abandoned castle dating from the beginning of the thirteenth century. Burdet took over Tombelaine and turned it into the base for a small squadron of ships hired in Rouen and Harfleur in the hope of controlling the sea around the mount. But the English never succeeded in closing the ring. The Dauphin sent one of his private secretaries to organise supplies for the beleaguered garrison. A victualling base was set up at Saint-Malo. The Malouins responded energetically. They loaded food, water and equipment onto armed ships which provided a regular ferry service to the mount. There were frequent fights with the English ships from Tombelaine, but the flow of supplies was never interrupted for long.[54]

The English invasion of Maine began in the second week of September 1424, shortly after Burdet laid siege to Mont-Saint-Michel. Maine had been a frontier region for centuries and bore the marks of it in its landscape. A rash of ancient castles dating from the tenth, eleventh and twelfth centuries extended across the granite hills and heavily wooded valleys of the northern highlands (*Map IV*). Further south, beyond the line of hills, the ground fell away, descending into the fertile plain of Le Mans and the broad valley of the Sarthe. When, at the end of 1417, Henry V had conquered the neighbouring duchy of Alençon, the English had occupied much of the northern highlands and a number of important castles in the plain. But over the following years they had gradually withdrawn or been expelled from these outposts and by 1424 only the powerful border fortress of Fresnay-le-Vicomte in the upper valley of the Sarthe was still in their hands. Three major strongholds in the northern highlands, Mayenne, Sillé-le-Guillaume and Beaumont-le-Vicomte, served as the bases of large Dauphinist companies.

After the battle of Verneuil Maine was seriously exposed. The battle had taken a heavy toll of the nobility of Maine and had depleted its garrisons. The county was without coherent military leadership. The Duke of Anjou, Louis III, was an impecunious absentee. The barony of Laval, the greatest lordship of the county, was in the hands of a widow whose young heir lived at the court of John V of Brittany. The Duke of Alençon, who had important lordships in Maine, was currently languishing in the English fortress of Le Crotoy. The Dauphin's able lieutenant in the west, Jean d'Harcourt Count of Aumale, had been killed and was not replaced. His role was informally assumed by his old enemy Jean de la Haye, baron of Coulonces, who had led the French cavalry at Verneuil and escaped on horseback when the day was lost. He had recently occupied the fortress of Mayenne in the north-west of the county. But La Haye never enjoyed the authority or reputation of his predecessor.[55]

Although the command was nominally shared between several English captains, the real leader of the army of invasion was Sir John Fastolf. Fastolf had no artillery train. He was counting on surprise and speed of movement to achieve his objectives. He entered the county by the valley of the Sarthe with more than 800 men at his back towards the end of September 1424. Within a day or two, the army had arrived outside Beaumont-le-Vicomte (modern Beaumont-sur-Sarthe), a walled town belonging to the Duke of Alençon which commanded the valley of the Sarthe as it opened out into the plain of Le Mans. The defences of the town were three centuries old and the castle standing on the rock above it was even older. But it took Fastolf more than two weeks to overcome the resistance of the garrison. He made them pay for their determination by taking half of them for ransom. The fall of Beaumont provoked a chain reaction, as one castle after another surrendered with only nominal resistance. The roads to Le Mans, the provincial capital, lay open. Fastolf's army began to close in on the city. Shortly, they occupied and repaired the abandoned castle of Montfort-le-Rotrou (modern Montfort-le-Gesnois), standing above the Roman bridge over the river Huisne, just ten miles from the city. They now controlled both of the rivers passing beneath the walls of Le Mans and were in a position to blockade the city on every side.[56]

CHAPTER IV

Jacqueline of Bavaria, 1424–1428

On 16 October 1424 Humphrey, Duke of Gloucester, accompanied by Jacqueline of Bavaria, landed at Calais with the advance guard of an army in the first stage of a planned invasion of Hainaut. The couple established their headquarters in the walled town of Guines at the southern edge of the pale of Calais. In England, the bulk of Gloucester's army was still being assembled by his friend and chief lieutenant John Mowbray, the Earl Marshal. Mowbray's companies crossed the Channel in stages over the following month, bringing the army's total strength to more than 4,000 men. It is far from clear how Humphrey had been able to recruit and pay such a large force. He was not a rich man and he received no support from English public revenues. He must have enjoyed some financial support from friends and clients among the nobility. But he appears to have funded the venture mainly through a public appeal. He had always made a pitch for the support of the mercantile interest and his appeal was addressed mainly to the towns. 'The will of us and of this our viage,' he told them, 'is like to turn to right great ease of the people, and specially of this merchants of this realm.' They responded with substantial grants and loans. The Common Council of London gave him 500 marks.[1]

The news of Gloucester's landing at Calais was received with predictable fury in Paris. The mood there was summed up in a letter addressed to Humphrey by that pillar of the Lancastrian regime, the University of Paris. What, they asked, could have possessed him to commit such a gross breach of the alliance with Burgundy, which he had himself sworn to respect? 'For the love of God ... think what scandal your perjury has brought down on your head, what damage you have done to your king, what injury you are causing to us, what joy to your enemies and confusion among your friends.' Among the English, opinion was divided. Gloucester was a flamboyant figure whose aggressive methods had their admirers. The Earl of Suffolk was one of them. Sir Thomas Rempston, who had once served in Gloucester's retinue, was another. They doubted the military value of the Burgundian alliance and lacked Bedford's larger view of England's interests. Why not join forces with the English, Suffolk had once suggested to the Duke of Brittany. Together they could have done with the Duke of Burgundy. Rather later, the Earl of Salisbury joined their number. He had very publicly fallen out with Philip, a lecherous man who was said to have made clumsy advances to his wife. Gossip had it that at one point, Salisbury had to be talked out of returning to England and throwing in his lot with the Duke of Gloucester.[2]

The Regent was already under pressure when Humphrey arrived in France. The Duke of Savoy's peace conference was due to open at Mâcon in just over a month. The English had not been invited, and the implicit threat of a reconciliation between Burgundy and Valois must have been in everyone's minds. Up to now, Bedford had refused to break with his erratic younger brother. He had tried to keep the peace by acting as broker, mediator and then arbitrator. Gloucester's resort to force changed all that. It compelled Bedford to abandon his neutrality and turned him into a discreet but active opponent of his brother's adventure, both in France and at Westminster. There were some in Bedford's circle who thought that this was just for show, and that he would continue to ride both horses at once or even offer covert support to his brother. Perhaps Gloucester himself thought so. If so, events were to prove him wrong.

As soon as Humphrey had disembarked, the Duke of Burgundy set out for Paris with his principal councillors. They found the ambassadors of the Duke of Brabant already there. They were all closeted with the Regent for several days. At the end of October, the Dukes of Bedford and Burgundy issued a joint declaration as arbitrators. They ordered the rival claimants to take part in yet another mediation and announced their intention of convening a conference between all interested parties. Failing agreement, they threatened to impose a reasonable settlement of their own making. In the meantime, neither claimant was to resort to arms. Ambassadors were sent to both claimants bearing copies of the joint declaration and instructions to press for compliance. John of Brabant did comply. He was unwilling to defy Philip the Good, on whose support he depended. So he put garrisons into the main towns and castles of western Hainaut, and dismissed the army which he had gathered at Nivelles near the eastern border of Hainaut. He then withdrew to Louvain, where he proposed that the conference with Humphrey's representatives should be held. This was a serious misjudgement, for the Duke of Gloucester was temperamentally averse to negotiation and declined to reciprocate. Once he learned that the army at Nivelles had been stood down, he sent a fresh message to Paris announcing that he intended to march at once on Hainaut. When this uncompromising statement reached Paris, Philip told Bedford that in that case he would support his cousin by force. On 18 November 1424, Gloucester and Mowbray marched out of Guines at the head of their army and headed east.[3]

Hainaut was a francophone territory of the Empire occupying the southern part of the broad fertile plateau between the Scheldt and the Meuse (*Map V*). It was one of the least urbanised regions of the Low Countries, sparsely populated, with few fortresses, little industry and just one large town, Valenciennes. The region had barely been touched by the war since the early campaigns of Edward III and it was ill-prepared to resist an invasion. Its only significant line of defence from the west was the natural barrier of the river Scheldt. The Duke of Brabant had expected Gloucester to approach by the direct route from Calais through Flanders and the Tournaisis, entering Hainaut by the north. Most of his garrisons were concentrated there. But the Duke, who had been accurately informed of the dispositions of John's troops, avoided them by taking a southerly course through Artois. He crossed the Scheldt near Bouchain in the south-west of the county, which was held by Jacqueline's mother, the dowager countess, and was not defended.[4]

In Hainaut there was much sympathy for Jacqueline, who was the heiress of the Bavarian dynasty that had ruled the county for eighty years. But the sympathy did not extend to the Duke of Gloucester. In the towns there was serious concern about the prospect of a military occupation by an English army. A delegation of the Estates of Hainaut had visited the couple at Canterbury before their departure to protest. Jacqueline's mother Margaret of Burgundy, a vigorous lady in her fifties whose dower lands included much of the south-east of the county, was Jacqueline's main advocate in the territory. She wrote to all the towns and leading noblemen of Hainaut urging them to accept Gloucester and Jacqueline as their rulers.

Once Humphrey had entered the county, sentiment changed. The absence of the Duke of Brabant and the dispersal of his army proved to be decisive. Resistance collapsed almost overnight. The lord of Havré, whom John of Brabant had appointed to command the defence, was among the first to submit. His example was followed by all of the towns and the nobility except for the Flemish-speaking town of Halle on the northern march and a handful of powerful lords who were closely associated with the courts of Burgundy and Brabant. On 27 November 1424, the Duke of Gloucester entered Mons, the political capital of Hainaut, accompanied by Jacqueline and Margaret of Burgundy. Over the following days, the Estates of Hainaut gathered in the town and renounced their allegiance to the Duke of Brabant, acknowledging Jacqueline and her husband as their lords and voting them a subsidy of 80,000 *livres* towards the cost of their army.[5]

Faced with the sudden loss of Hainaut, Philip the Good did what he had threatened to do at the conferences in Paris. On 21 November 1424, he summoned troops from every part of his domains to support his cousin. Over the next six weeks, Burgundian troops began to mass on the northern and eastern marches of Hainaut. Raiding parties poured over the border, burning villages, killing and robbing, and provoking a tidal flow of refugees across what had recently been one of the most peaceful regions of northern Europe. John Mowbray responded in kind. He gathered his men from the garrisons to which they had been posted and led a large raiding force across the border into Brabant. They marched to within a few miles of Brussels, leaving a trail of burned-out villages in their wake and seizing large numbers of cattle and horses. John of Brabant, who had never been a robust man, could not cope. He suffered a physical and mental breakdown. His own council worried that he 'did not behave as such a great lord should', and doubted whether he was capable of handling the crisis. In January 1425, the Estates of Brabant met in Brussels and forced him to cede command of the army to his more capable younger brother, the twenty-year-old Philip Count of Saint-Pol. Overall direction of the campaign was placed in the experienced hands of John of Luxembourg's brother Peter, who as lord of Enghien was the principal territorial magnate of northern Hainaut.

Peter was a shrewd choice. He was well liked at the Burgundian court and at the same time a notable anglophile who had fought with Henry V at the siege of Melun and consistently supported the dual monarchy. His intervention in Hainaut was discreetly supported by the Duke of Bedford. His lieutenants included a number of Bedford's

French officers, among them John of Luxembourg and Villiers de L'Isle-Adam, who are unlikely to have served without his blessing. There is some evidence that Bedford even agreed to contribute to their war wages. It was a strange alliance. They found themselves fighting alongside some unlikely companions in arms, including Dauphinist captains such as Poton de Saintrailles who had sold their services to their former enemies.[6]

At the beginning of March 1425, the Count of Saint-Pol's army entered Hainaut from Nivelles and laid siege to the walled town of Braine-le-Comte, the principal fortress of the eastern march. The Duke of Gloucester had installed a garrison of 200 men in the town. But its defences were old and in poor repair. The first artillery salvoes brought down a number of towers and made several breaches in the walls. Humphrey, who was twenty miles away at Mons, marched on the town on 5 March with the bulk of his army, accompanied by the redoubtable Jacqueline. He made a poor show at Braine. Saint-Pol's army was larger than his own, but much of its strength comprised undisciplined infantry levies from the towns of Brabant while Gloucester's own force consisted mainly of experienced soldiers. Yet Humphrey made no attempt to attack. The besiegers launched a series of assaults on the walls from ladders, while the English army stood by a short distance away without intervening.

Inside the town, the English garrison finally lost hope. On 11 March, they agreed to surrender both town and castle in return for their lives and personal possessions. The townsmen, who had fought valiantly beside them, were abandoned to their fate. They proffered a large cash indemnity to avoid a sack, but in vain. Saint-Pol's captains took the money but were unable to control their men. The troops ran riot in the streets, slaughtering much of the population and leaving the place a heap of charred ruins. Prominent figures who had submitted to the Duke of Gloucester were rounded up and summarily executed. The fate of the English garrison was not much better. Many of them were lynched as they left the fortress in spite of the terms of surrender.

The fall of Braine was followed by an uncomfortable stalemate. Humphrey withdrew to the town of Soignies on the road to Mons. From there, he sent his heralds into Saint-Pol's lines with a challenge to battle. The two armies faced each other for four days, drawn up in battle order between Soignies and Braine. As each side waited for the other to move, the weather deteriorated. A heavy fall of snow dampened morale on both sides. Saint-Pol's infantry finally decided that they had had enough and mutinied, leaving the field in defiance of their captains' orders. Without them, Saint-Pol decided that he was not strong enough to confront the English. In the middle of March, he withdrew with the rest of his men to Brussels.[7]

The Duke of Gloucester was left in possession, but his adventure ended in farce within days. He had been engaged in an acrimonious public correspondence with Philip the Good since the beginning of the year. He had taken exception to a manifesto issued by Philip which had accused him of needlessly shedding Christian blood by rejecting the proposal for arbitration. Humphrey was stung by the accusation and accused Philip of making up the facts. In any event, he added, the whole dispute was a private matter between Jacqueline and John of Brabant, which was no business of Philip's. Indeed, given his close kinship with Jacqueline and his adherence to the treaty of Troyes, if Philip was going to intervene on anyone's side it should have been hers. The Duke of Burgundy responded from Bruges on 13 March with a challenge to a duel. Writing from Soignies on 26 March, Gloucester accepted Philip's challenge. It was agreed that the duel should be fought before the Duke of Bedford on St George's Day, 23 April 1425. It is a measure of Philip's fury at the conduct of the Duke of Gloucester that he had embarked upon this impetuous course. His councillors were aghast. They urged him to put off the day in the hope that some other solution would be found. But Philip would not hear of it. He was serious about fighting Humphrey in single combat. He left at once for his country house at Hesdin in Artois for a period of intensive training. He summoned noblemen to accompany him in suitably magnificent style. He spent some 14,000 *livres* on embroidered hangings, armorial horse-coverings, banners, pennons and stately tented pavilions.[8]

Whether the Duke of Gloucester was serious is a more difficult question. In the last few days of March, he abruptly left Hainaut and marched back to Calais with his whole army, leaving Jacqueline behind. His explanation was that he was going home to get suitable weapons and to prepare himself for the duel. He said that he expected to return shortly with another army. The real reason was probably that he could no longer support the army that he already had. Desertions had taken their toll on its strength. Six months after the soldiers had mustered by the Kent coast, the indentures of the rest were probably about to expire. More personal factors weighed on Humphrey. He was in bad health.

He was already tiring of his forceful wife. He took back with him on the march one of her ladies-in-waiting, Eleanor Cobham, who was later to become his wife and may already have been his mistress. On 12 April, just eleven days before the date on which he was supposed to meet the Duke of Burgundy in single combat, Humphrey sailed for England. He was frostily received. He reported his exchanges with Philip the Good to the King's council. He told them that his main object was now to stop the Duke of Brabant usurping his wife's inheritance. For this, he said, he urgently needed money and men. The council's answer was delivered by his enemy Henry Beaufort, who had recently become Chancellor of England. According to reports reaching the continent, it was brief and uncompromising. Gloucester's invasion of Hainaut and his intemperate exchanges with the most powerful territorial prince in France, said Beaufort, were utterly reprehensible. They threatened to destroy England's alliance with the Duke of Burgundy and to undo the English conquests in France. He would have neither money nor men to support another such enterprise.[9]

In Paris, the Duke of Bedford moved to put a stop to the duel. As the judge in a court of honour, it was his role to resolve the issue without bloodshed if he could. After consulting bishops, noblemen and doctors of civil and canon law, Bedford theatrically entered the Great Hall of St Louis in the palace on the Île de la Cité on 22 September 1425. Sitting beneath the gilded and painted statues of the kings of France, he delivered his ruling. He declared that neither side's letters went beyond the limits of courtesy and neither had lost face or honour. The fight was forbidden and the parties ordered to maintain 'perpetual silence' on the subject. The ambassadors of the Duke of Burgundy, who were present, protested in his name. Privately, they breathed a sigh of relief.[10]

By this time Jacqueline's brief reign in Hainaut had come to an end. Humphrey had left her in Mons with only a handful of attendants and a small personal bodyguard. Her supporters had wanted her to stay. She was a focus of loyalty and a more valuable asset in Hainaut than she could ever be in England. But without her husband and his army her cause collapsed. Almost all of those who had acknowledged her and Humphrey the previous autumn now deserted her. They included most of the nobility and all of the towns except for Mons. The citizens of Mons had sworn before Humphrey's departure to defend Jacqueline against her enemies and for a time they stuck to their resolve. They laid in stores for a siege. They demolished their suburbs and broke the bridges over the moat. They hired professional garrison troops. They placed artillery on the walls. In the third week of May 1425, John of Brabant arrived before the walls of Mons with an army and an artillery train. He cut the watercourses that supplied the city and began to batter the walls. The citizens had already opened discreet negotiations with the Duke of Burgundy. He made them an offer designed to avoid the destruction of their town. Jacqueline should surrender to him and live under his 'protection' until the Pope had decided whether she was married to Humphrey of Gloucester or John of Brabant. In the meantime, Hainaut should be restored to the Duke of Brabant, who was in a position to occupy it by force anyway.[11]

Philip summoned all parties to a conference in the Flemish town of Douai to hear his proposals. Jacqueline declined to participate, but her mother the dowager countess attended. The Duke of Brabant was there. So too was a delegation from the town of Mons. But the discussion was entirely one-sided. The Duke told them that he had come to tell them his terms, not to negotiate. All of them submitted, even the dowager countess. She never forgot that Philip the Good was 'the head of the family from which she had sprung and the one whom she relied on most in the whole world'. The chronicler Jean de Waurin, who lived through these events, was probably right to say that the ruthlessness of Philip the Good's response was a shock for many people in Hainaut. But to anyone familiar with the way in which the various branches of the house of Burgundy had always operated as a family enterprise, Philip the Good's intervention should not have come as a surprise. Only Jacqueline remained defiant. Early in June 1425 the men of Mons forced her hand. They arrested all her supporters in the town and put some of them to death. At a tense meeting in the town hall, they told her that unless she accepted Philip's terms, they would kill her attendants and deliver her up to the Duke of Brabant. When she reminded them of their oath, they replied that they were not strong enough to save her. Declaring herself 'a lost woman, the most basely betrayed alive', Jacqueline addressed an emotional appeal to Humphrey in England. But Humphrey could not have done anything for her even if the message had reached him, instead of being intercepted by Philip's agents on the road. On 13 June 1425, Mons opened its gates to John of Brabant. Jacqueline, weeping copiously, begged to be allowed to settle in Brabant rather than being handed over to Philip the Good. Her pleas were ignored. She was delivered up to Philip's representative the Prince of Orange, who took her under guard to Ghent. There, she was installed in luxury with an ample household but under strict surveillance in the Posteerne, the town mansion of the counts of Flanders, while preparations were made to move her to more secure facilities at Lille.[12]

Events in Hainaut cast a long shadow over the Anglo-Burgundian alliance. With the north cleared of Dauphinist garrisons and the duchy of Burgundy and its satellite regions protected by the truce of Chambéry, Philip the Good had for practical purposes withdrawn from the Anglo-French war. He flirted with the idea of a reconciliation with the Dauphin and from time to time engaged in active negotiations with his agents but was never willing to commit himself. Philip was content to leave both allies and enemies guessing about his plans. It cost him nothing and reinforced his bargaining power. John V of Brittany was less cynical. He openly declared himself in favour of a reconciliation between the Dauphin and the house of Burgundy. He believed that, deprived of the support of the Duke of Burgundy, the English would be forced to agree to a general peace which would put an end to his own dangerously exposed position between the two main belligerents.

The leading spirit in the long-drawn-out and ultimately fruitless discussions which followed was Arthur de Richemont. He returned to Brittany after his ill-tempered exchanges with the Duke of Bedford in Paris in June 1424. From there, he signalled to the Dauphin's ministers that he wanted to change sides. He was not rich, he explained, and had always depended on the favour of more powerful men than himself. He had submitted to Henry V only to please his brother John V and Philip the Good, and to escape from his English prison. But his allegiance had been purely personal, he declared. He owed nothing to the English now that Henry V was dead.[13] Richemont was genuinely interested in restoring peace between the princes of France. He was less interested than either John V or Philip the Good in brokering a peace with the English, whom he viewed with the resentment of a convert. Knowing them as he did, he may have regarded any accommodation with them as unattainable. But his dominant motive was personal ambition. He could never have been more than a marginal player in Brittany or Lancastrian France but was determined to become a major figure in the kingdom of Bourges.

JACQUELINE OF BAVARIA, 1424–1428

In August 1424 Yolande of Anjou had arranged a meeting between Richemont and the Dauphin, to take place in her capital at Angers in October. Extraordinary steps were taken to assure the pathologically distrustful Richemont that he would not be walking into a trap. Hostages were delivered up to secure his safety, including the Dauphin's cousin the Bastard of Orléans. He was granted temporary custody of four of the Dauphin's finest castles, at Chinon and Loches in Touraine, Mehun-sur-Yèvre in Berry and Lusignan in Poitou, for the duration of the conference. Ostensibly, Richemont was acting for himself. But standing behind him was his brother the Duke of Brittany, who met the cost of his impressive entourage and placed a number of his own councillors among them. The Dauphin had high hopes of the meeting. He told his supporters that he expected Brittany to supply him with a new army after the destruction of the Scots at Verneuil, which would escort him to Reims to be crowned.[14]

On 20 October 1424 Richemont entered Angers. He was greeted as a state visitor. He was met outside the gates by a crowd of ministers and courtiers, who received him with extravagant honours. They brought him before the Dauphin in the cloister of the Benedictine abbey of St Aubin. The meeting was carefully choreographed, as such occasions almost always were. Richemont told Charles that his true sympathies had not changed since he had fought in the French lines at Agincourt. The English allegiance that he had borne for the past four years had been no more than a charade. He was now willing to serve the Dauphin with his heart as well as his right arm. The Dauphin offered Richemont the office of Constable of France, the highest rank at his court, which had been vacant since the death of the Earl of Buchan at Verneuil. But Richemont and John V were determined to drive a hard bargain. Richemont declined to accept the Dauphin's offer at once. He would need, he said, to consult Philip the Good and Amadeus of Savoy. Before the Montfort brothers committed themselves, they intended to stake out their claim to a dominant role in the Dauphin's government.[15]

On 30 November 1424, Philip the Good celebrated his marriage to Bonne d'Artois, dowager Countess of Nevers, in the castle of the counts at Moulins-Engilbert. It was a family gathering of cousins and in-laws, bringing together the courts of Burgundy, Brittany and the kingdom of Bourges for the first time since the civil wars. As soon as the festivities were over, the whole cavalcade travelled to Mâcon for the opening of the Duke of Savoy's peace conference. The importance which all parties attached to the conference was reflected in the status of the participants. Philip the Good attended in person. John V of Brittany was represented by Richemont and a delegation from his council. The Dauphin sent the Count of Clermont accompanied by his Chancellor Martin Gouge and his senior diplomat Regnault de Chartres. The English were not represented. Amadeus had written off the chances of a general peace. The hubris in Rouen and Paris after the battle of Verneuil had put that out of reach. His objective was to douse the embers of the civil war and reunite the French princes against the English.

The discussions took as their starting point the Duke of Savoy's proposals at Bourg-en-Bresse in 1423 and the protocol drawn up at Nantes in May. It quickly became apparent that the main obstacle to agreement was the prominent position at the Dauphin's court of the men who had been behind the murder at Montereau and the subsequent attempt to overthrow John V in Brittany. This intractable issue had been evaded in all their discussions to date. When the Dauphin's ambassadors tried to excuse the Dauphin's role in the murder, saying that he been young and easily led astray by bad advice, Philip replied that in that case, he should dismiss the men who gave him the advice. Amadeus observed that the vendetta was unlikely to end while the Dauphin was surrounded by men like Louvet and his friends. On that note, the conference was adjourned after only two or three days. Philip had made his position very clear. John V was just as blunt when Tanneguy du Châtel came before him in the new year. Tanneguy's mission was to get military support against England. The Duke curtly told him that there was no prospect of Breton assistance until he and his associates had left the Dauphin's circle. The Dukes of Burgundy and Savoy sent messages saying the same thing in equally uncompromising terms. When the peacemakers reassembled in the new year, it was at the magnificent castle of the Duke of Savoy at Montluel, standing over the valley of the Rhône upstream of Lyon. But Martin Gouge had no more to offer at Montluel than he had had at Mâcon. The hated councillors of the Dauphin remained in place, and the talks broke down.[16]

The conference was not completely devoid of effect, for the Dauphin's representatives agreed to a considerable enlargement of the area covered by his truce with Burgundy. Hitherto, it had covered only the territory east of the Loire and the Allier, essentially the southern domains of the Dukes of Burgundy and the appanages of the Dukes of Bourbon and the Counts of Nevers. At Montluel, it was extended to cover the adjacent regions which were either held by the Dauphin or contested between him and Philip. This meant the Dauphiné and a large belt of territory on the eastern march of the kingdom of Bourges, including the whole of Berry, the Auxerrois and the Gâtinais. The revised truce, which was proclaimed by the Duke of Savoy from the small town of Bâgé in Bresse, marked a further stage in the Burgundian withdrawal from active prosecution of the war. It left the English to fight alone in the critical region south of Paris. It also more or less ruled out an English invasion of the upper Loire, which would have had to be launched from Burgundian territory comprised in the truce.[17]

Richemont and the Duke of Savoy regarded the conference as a failure, for there had been no tangible progress towards detaching the Duke of Burgundy from his English allies. They blamed the Dauphin's ministers, whose continued presence at the Dauphin's court had become the main obstacle to agreement. Left to themselves at Montluel after the diplomats had dispersed, the two men agreed upon a plan, which they recorded in a short memorandum of four articles. The articles were nothing less than a proposal for taking over the Dauphin's government. The Dukes of Brittany and Savoy would insist on nominating enough members of his council to be able to conduct its business, together with well-disposed existing members. The Dauphin would be required to act in accordance with their advice. The new councillors would have to report regularly to the two dukes on the work of the council and the conduct of the war. They would also be charged with drawing up suitable terms of agreement with the Dukes of Burgundy and Brittany. Few documents are more revealing of their contempt for the 21-year-old Dauphin's political capacities.[18]

In February 1425, the Dauphin's court moved to the immense twelfth-century fortress of Henry II of England on the banks of the Vienne at Chinon. Towards the end of that month, Richemont arrived, accompanied by the ambassadors of the Dukes of Brittany and Savoy. They brought with them the articles of Montluel and laid them before the Dauphin and his council. The future of the peace negotiations and Richemont's own acceptance of the office of Constable, they said, depended on their being agreed. Their demands were supported by Yolande of Anjou. The Dauphin's ministers were divided. Tanneguy du Châtel, as a Breton, was reluctant to break with John V. He declared himself willing to resign for the sake of peace and pressed the same course on his colleagues with his customary intemperance. But Jean Louvet loved power too much. He refused to surrender the dominant position in government that he had enjoyed for the past six years, even if it wrecked the talks with the Dukes of Burgundy and Brittany. There were angry recriminations between the councillors about where the blame lay for the murder of John the Fearless at Montereau. At one point, Tanneguy was said to have come to blows with one of Louvet's supporters in the Dauphin's presence. The Dauphin was incapable of resolving a schism between the men on whom he had been dependent for so long. He summoned what was nominally a meeting of the Estates-General, although the speed with which it assembled meant that only those within a short distance of Chinon can have attended. The Estates endorsed the articles of Montluel.

The result was an untidy compromise. The Dauphin accepted the articles and Richemont agreed to become Constable. But Louvet and his friends were to remain in post. Indeed, Richemont was required, as a condition of taking office, to swear 'on the Holy Gospels and by his baptism and his place in Paradise' that he would do nothing to undermine their position. He readily swore the oath, but without the least intention of honouring it. On that equivocal basis, he was solemnly invested with the sword of office in the meadows beneath the walls of the fortress, in the presence of the Estates-General and a crowd of ministers and courtiers. The letters patent which formalised his appointment, praised his valour at Agincourt and his 'intelligence, industry, wisdom and courage, both in the profession of arms and in other ways'. It then laid out his plan. He would provide leadership in the conduct of the war, which gone badly for want of a unified command; and he would bring organisation and discipline to the Dauphin's armies, so that they would no longer have to live by looting his subjects.

There were other elements in this plan, which were not recorded in the document but were laid out in a circular sent by Yolande of Anjou to the principal towns of the realm. This was overtly hostile to the ministers. It declared that Richemont and Yolande, together with like-minded men on the Dauphin's council, intended to reconcile the Dauphin with Brittany and Burgundy and clean up his administration, which they believed was being pillaged by his councillors to line their own pockets and those of their clients. For many of those present at the new Constable's investiture, his appointment seemed to draw a line under the failures of the past. Reporting to their constituents on the day after the Estates-General dispersed, the delegates of Tours detected a significant change of mood. There was palpable optimism that the worst was over and that peace would shortly be made between the French princes. But their optimism was not shared by those who knew the situation best. The new Constable himself told the men of Lyon that he believed that the kingdom of the Valois was 'tottering towards its utter destruction'.[19]

It is easy to understand why Richemont was so gloomy. Louvet and his associates had been conspicuously absent from the council which approved his appointment. Behind the scenes they were actively resisting the implementation of his plan to reform the government. The conflict between the Constable and the ministers provoked a crisis which lasted for the next four months and brought the kingdom of Bourges to the edge of civil war. For most of that period, Louvet continued to control the person of the Dauphin and the machinery of government. He had himself appointed 'supreme director' of the finances of the kingdom, with authority over all the receivers of revenue. He removed from the Dauphin's council all of those who had supported the project for a deal with Burgundy and Brittany. He replaced a large number of officials and household officers by men loyal to himself. Martin Gouge was dismissed as the Dauphin's Chancellor and Tanneguy du Châtel was expelled from court. Richemont's appointment could not be undone, but he was not allowed access to the Dauphin and there were rumours of plots to murder him. The new Constable had been retained with a personal retinue of 3,000 men to fight the English in Maine. Louvet believed that these men would be turned against himself. He cancelled the musters of Richemont's troops in the regions under his control and cut off the funds destined for the payment of their wages.

In April 1425, Louvet's leading opponents, Richemont, Yolande of Anjou and the two dismissed ministers Martin Gouge and Tanneguy du Châtel, met in the castle of the Dukes of Anjou at Angers to plan their next move. They declared their intention of liberating the Dauphin from the clutches of 'evil traitors'. They recruited troops in Brittany. They appealed for more from the nobility and the major towns. It shortly became clear how widely hated Louvet was. From Poitou, Berry and Auvergne prominent noblemen brought their retainers to Richemont's banner. From Brittany, John V announced that his youngest brother Richard would join them with an army of Bretons. All the more substantial towns declared their support except for Vierzon and Selles in Berry. Early in May, Richemont and his allies occupied Bourges, one of the Dauphin's two capitals, where they were received with acclamation by the townspeople. They took control of the financial departments. The machinery of tax collection ground to a halt. Meanwhile, Louvet hunkered down with the Dauphin in his other capital, at Poitiers, protected by Italian and Scottish mercenaries and by the retinue of Pierre Frotier, that other much-hated man of 1419.[20]

At the beginning of June 1425 Louvet and the Dauphin left Poitiers with a small army to march on Bourges and confront the Constable. Their advance was stopped at Vierzon, twenty miles west of the city, by Yolande of Anjou. The Dauphin's formidable mother-in-law was the only person with the influence and status to penetrate the barriers which Louvet had placed around his master. No account of the encounter at Vierzon survives, but it is clear that Yolande's intervention was decisive. She persuaded the Dauphin to withdraw to Selles on the marches of Berry and Touraine, and then to dismiss his troops and remove Louvet from his service. A spurious mission to Languedoc was invented for the minister, and he left within a few days. Yolande returned from Selles to Bourges, bringing the Dauphin with her. In the city, Richemont convened an assembly of his supporters. It comprised the captains of his army, the noblemen who had responded to his summons, and what representatives of the towns could be found at short notice. The Dauphin addressed them in a speech scripted for him by Richemont and his allies. He acknowledged the vices of his government. He had been led astray, he said, by bad advice. But from now on he would do 'all that his brother-in-law of Brittany and his Constable might advise him to do'. Charles and what remained of his court were escorted back to Poitiers, where the new arrangements for the government of his realm were to be finalised. On 5 July 1425, he issued an ordinance formally dismissing Louvet from his service and annulling all the powers which he had previously granted to him.[21]

Charles's weakness had rarely been more obvious. He looked as much a puppet in Richemont's hands as he had previously been in Louvet's. He never forgave Richemont for the public humiliations of these weeks. Even after submitting to his demands at Bourges, he refused to receive him in audience until 9 July and then only after a delicate negotiation conducted by Yolande of Anjou. But, however brutally, Richemont had achieved the change of regime which he had planned ever since he agreed to become Constable. Louvet was taken under escort to Provence where, beyond the frontiers of France, he lived in retirement for the fifteen years of life that remained to him. Guillaume d'Avaugour and the physician Jean Cadart followed him into exile in the south. Tanneguy du Châtel was banished to Languedoc, where he was honourably employed as Seneschal of Beaucaire. Louvet's son-in-law the Bastard of Orléans was temporarily disgraced. Pierre Frotier was summarily dismissed, and the Dauphin's bodyguard, which he had commanded, was replaced by another under more reliable captains. It was the end of the old Armagnac party which had held sway in Paris before the Burgundian coup of 1418 and had dominated the kingdom of Bourges ever since. The Dauphin had grown up under their tutelage. He parted with them under constraint and with obvious regret and continued to protect them from the vengeance of Philip the Good. They received handsome gratuities and pensions. Many years later, when he was once more in control of his own affairs, they would be welcomed back to his court, although they never recovered their former influence.[22]

After the initial invasion of Maine, in the autumn of 1424, the English offensive in the west had stalled. Sir Nicholas Burdet failed to make any impression on Mont-Saint-Michel. The Dauphinist captains in Anjou and Maine had mounted a successful counterattack, recovering most of the castles which the English had conquered in the Sarthe valley, including Beaumont-le-Vicomte. In the opening months of 1425, the Duke of Bedford took steps to breathe new life into the western offensive. His trusted councillor Robert Jolivet was sent into Lower Normandy to raise fresh troops for Burdet's army at Mont-Saint-Michel. Twenty ships were chartered, most of them in the ports of England, to strengthen the blockade of the mount from the sea. In Maine, Fastolf was reinforced and moved back onto the offensive. He launched a raid into the valley of the Loir and occupied the important bridge-town of La Chartre-sur-le-Loir. Substantial forces were sent there under Thomas Lord Scales and William Glasdale, who planned to turn it into an advance base for the conquest of Anjou. Within a month, they were creating ransom districts extending as far south as Tours. From Rouen, the Regent commissioned the Earl of Salisbury to complete the conquest of Maine in the spring with an army of 1,600 men and a powerful artillery train.[23]

The renewed attempt to capture Mont-Saint-Michel was a failure. At about the end of April 1425, Burdet launched an assault on the fortress from the tidal sands between Ardevon and the mount. The defenders had got wind of the plan. They called for reinforcements from Jean de la Haye's companies at Mayenne. The captain of Mayenne left the town for Mont-Saint-Michel before dawn with an all-mounted force and managed to cover the whole distance by early afternoon. It was a remarkable feat. They arrived to find the tide out and a battle in progress on the sands beneath the water gate. The defenders of the fortress had sortied from the gate to drive the English from the walls. The English were steadily pushing them back when La Haye's companies appeared in their rear. They now found themselves attacked from both sides. More than 200 of them were killed or captured according to the defenders' reckoning. Burdet himself was among the prisoners. This was an unexpected setback. The Earl of Suffolk had to be sent urgently from Normandy with reinforcements to shore up the English position. Worse was to follow. The chartered ships, stuffed with men-at-arms and archers, arrived off the mount in the course of April and early May and for a time succeeded in stopping the regular supply run from Saint-Malo. But at about the end of June a fleet of armed merchantmen from the Breton port broke through the blockade, dispersing the besiegers' ships and killing many of the men on board. Shortly afterwards, the English abandoned the siege.[24]

The conquest of Maine by contrast proved to be one of the Earl of Salisbury's most successful campaigns. Its opening was delayed by several months, mainly because of the late arrival of the annual expeditionary army from England. They did not reach Calais until about the middle of June. It also took a long time for teams of oxen to haul the heavy artillery pieces through the hills of Perche to the Earl's forward base at Alençon. As a result, the offensive was not launched until the last days of June, but it then proceeded with impressive speed. The two main Dauphinist garrisons of the Sarthe valley, at Beaumont-le-Vicomte and La Guierche, were battered into submission within a few days and the way to Le Mans opened up.[25]

It was Salisbury's good fortune that the Dauphin's government was paralysed by Richemont's feud against Jean Louvet and his friends. When he entered Maine, the Dauphin's ministers were at Poitiers, preoccupied with their internal struggles, which were then approaching their climax. They tried to react to each item of bad news as it arrived but were repeatedly overtaken by the speed of the English advance. At about the beginning of July, Richemont summoned every available man to muster at Saumur. He hoped to have an army of 3,000 men on the Loire by the beginning of August, ready to reverse the dismal course of events in Maine. The Count of Foix was believed to be on his way north from Toulouse with at least 1,600 Gascon soldiers. Richemont was counting on Le Mans to hold out until these forces could arrive. But until then there was only a small Dauphinist force in the province, commanded by Jean Girard. On 17 July, when it became clear that Salisbury was heading for Le Mans, Girard was ordered to take sixty men-at-arms and make for the city at once to reinforce its garrison. It was already too late. The first English contingents had reached Le Mans a week earlier. On 20 July 1425, the Earl of Salisbury arrived outside the walls with the main body of his army.[26]

Le Mans was situated on steeply rising ground on the east bank of the river Sarthe. It had a professional captain but few professional troops. The city's stores were low. Its walls, which were manned by the citizens, were unfit to resist artillery. Most of them dated from Roman times. Salisbury established his headquarters in the Dominican convent on the east side of the city beneath the great gothic apse of the cathedral. Here, he called on the inhabitants to surrender. Unusually, the text has been preserved in a herald's commonplace book. The Earl declared that he had come to bring the city back to its rightful obedience. If the inhabitants submitted, they would be treated with 'courtesy' and enjoy all their traditional privileges. But if they did not, they could expect the fate that had befallen so many other towns that had been taken by assault after vainly hoping to be relieved. With the aid of God, he said, he would 'visit such punishment upon them as men would speak of forever'. When Salisbury's demands were rejected, his artillery began to pound the walls. After two weeks, large sections of them had been reduced to rubble, along with much of the cathedral quarter. The English gunners consumed a prodigious 3,000 pounds of powder. On 2 August, the citizens sent their bishop into the Earl's camp to sue for terms. Agreement was reached on the same day.

Salisbury imposed what was by now the standard capitulation agreement. The garrison and those who declined to live under English rule were allowed to leave with their personal possessions. The rest were required to swear oaths of loyalty and to submit to a contribution of 1,000 *livres* towards the cost of the siege. The usual exceptions were made for English renegades, Frenchmen who had sworn allegiance to Henry VI, anyone involved in the murder of John the Fearless in 1419 or the kidnapping of John V of Brittany in 1420 and all professional gunners. The inhabitants were allowed just eight days to await a relief force. On the day of the capitulation, Richemont's army had only just begun to assemble. Stewart of Darnley was at Ponts-de-Cé, south of Angers, with 450 Scots. Richemont himself had more than 300 men with him at Poitiers. But only a handful had so far appeared at the designated muster-point at Saumur. The Constable announced that he would leave for Saumur on the following day and march against the English, but the slow progress of the muster made such haste pointless. In fact, he did not set out for another week. At midday on 10 August 1425, the day that he marched out of Poitiers, Le Mans opened its gates to the Earl of Salisbury. The Berry Herald, who was at the Dauphin's court, blamed the quarrels of his ministers, which had made it impossible to organise an effective counterattack earlier. 'By these disputes and divisions,' he wrote, 'Le Mans was lost.'[27]

Salisbury remained in Le Mans for some three weeks, while detachments of his army spread out across the plain, taking possession of defensible castles and demolishing others. At the end of August 1425, he was joined by the Earl of Suffolk from Mont-Saint-Michel with reinforcements from Burdet's broken siege army. Together, they marched on the headquarters of Ambroise de Loré at Sainte-Suzanne. Sainte-Suzanne was an outpost of the barony of Beaumont belonging to the dukes of Alençon. Sited on a spur of rock overlooking the river Erve, it remains one of the best-preserved walled towns of the region. Salisbury's artillery train took some days to come from Le Mans, but once it had arrived it made short work of the ancient walls. At the end of September, after two weeks of bombardment round the clock, de Loré surrendered on terms. They were harsh. The captain of Sainte-Suzanne had held out for too long, and the ferocity of his defence had infuriated the Earl of Salisbury. De Loré and his men were allowed to leave. But they had to abandon their horses and possessions and to swear not to fight against the English for at least a year. Those who remained in the town had to pay an indemnity of 2,000 *écus*, more than twice the sum demanded of the much larger and richer city of Le Mans. The professional gunners in the garrison were all hanged from gibbets outside the gates, with cannonballs chained to their feet.[28]

Of the field army of 3,000 men planned for Richemont's counter-attack, fewer than 1,300 had appeared by the beginning of September 1425. It is a measure of the chaos and division in the kingdom of Bourges that hardly any of these men came from the Dauphin's territory. They were almost all Bretons or Scots. Richemont marched to Angers in the third week of August and then up the valley of the Sarthe towards Le Mans early in September. But his numbers were reduced by desertion and the need to leave garrisons in the more important castles. The men had been paid nothing since leaving Saumur and they were threatening mutiny. In about the middle of October, Richemont's army penetrated into Maine in what appears to have been an attempt to surprise Le Mans. They were met by a detachment of Salisbury's army at the small hamlet of Saint-Julien, ten miles east of Le Mans, and put to flight. This was the last to be heard of Richemont's much heralded counterattack.[29]

At the beginning of October 1425, the first detachments of the English army reached the valley of the river Mayenne in western Maine. The town of Mayenne stood on the west bank of the river in the foothills of the northern highlands. It housed a large garrison, the last substantial Dauphinist force remaining in the county. For the past two and a half years, it had been the headquarters of Jean de la Haye, but he had withdrawn from the place after Salisbury's invasion, leaving its defence to two local noblemen. The old fortress had been built in the tenth century and strengthened by the addition of towers in the thirteenth. Like other fortifications of Maine, it was in poor condition and not designed for modern siege warfare. Even so, it held out against the Earl of Salisbury for more than six weeks, longer than any other fortress. The Earl's gunners consumed as much gunpowder there as they had at Le Mans and Sainte-Suzanne combined, without making any real impression on the walls. The English tried to undermine them without success. They mounted an assault on the main keep from ladders but were thrown back with heavy casualties. It was growing late in the season, and Salisbury was obliged to offer the garrison generous terms to induce them to surrender in early November 1425.[30]

Salisbury left the region after the surrender of Mayenne, but the campaign was not quite over. Shortly after his departure a group of Dauphinist partisans seized La Ferté-Bernard, a garrisoned fortress on the river Huisne which marked the eastern limit of Maine. It was an unwelcome reminder that the Dauphinist garrisons of Maine had consisted mainly of local noblemen, who did not leave the province when their strongholds were taken but lay low waiting for their opportunities. The author of this coup was Louis d'Avaugour, the younger brother of the Dauphin's disgraced minister. He was a local officer of Yolande of Anjou, who had commanded at La Ferté-Bernard before the English invasion and returned when the English moved into winter quarters.

In Paris, the Earl of Salisbury decided to go back to Maine as soon as material could be collected for a siege. He established an advance base at Bellême in Perche and arrived there at about the end of January 1426. On about 2 February, he came before La Ferté-Bernard. The castle, which adjoined the walled town at its southern end, was defended by two concentric lines of walls and surrounded by water and marsh. Salisbury tried to take it by the traditional method of an artillery barrage followed by an assault, but in the end, he was obliged to starve it out. In the Earl's rear, other groups of local noblemen made a bold attempt to draw the English away by attacking the major fortress of Alençon while its captain Sir John Fastolf and much of his garrison were away at the siege. They hoped to be let in by a Gascon traitor in the garrison. But the Gascon took their money and disclosed the plot to the Earl of Salisbury. As a result, they walked into an ambush as they approached the town and lost most of their men. At La Ferté-Bernard, the garrison's supplies were almost exhausted. Early in April 1426, Louis d'Avaugour surrendered.[31]

In the space of nine months, the Earl of Salisbury had conquered almost all of Maine except for the barony of Laval in the south-west of the county. The result was to push the frontier of English power south from the march of Normandy to the valley of the Loir, where a belt of disputed territory marked the boundary with Anjou. Here, however, the English advance stopped. The officers of Yolande of Anjou established a powerful line of garrisoned castles extending from Craon to Château-du-Loir which the English were not able to penetrate except for short hit-and-run raids. The occupation of Maine gave some protection for the Cotentin and the south-western march of Normandy from enemy raids and helped to isolate the garrison of Mont-Saint-Michel. But these advantages came at a high cost. Salisbury left behind him an army of occupation spread among no fewer than fourteen garrisoned castles, most of them on the southern march of the county. Over the following year, the English established at least five more. Even so, they were never secure in Maine. Their rule was not accepted by the population as readily as it was in Normandy. They encountered persistent tacit, and sometimes active opposition from the local nobility. Craon in northern Anjou became the base of a large raiding force commanded by one of the Dauphin's household squires, Gauthier de Brusac, which repeatedly raided up the valleys of the Oudon and the Mayenne. Laval received a Dauphinist garrison of 270 men, one of the largest in the region. On the east march, Maine was wide open to raids up the valley of the Loir by the companies of La Hire, who had established themselves around Vendôme.[32]

As a source of revenue and patronage, Maine proved to be a disappointment to its conquerors. The fighting had been immensely destructive. The passage and repassage of troops of both sides made sowing and harvesting impossible and reduced grain yields by three-quarters or more. The destruction of barns and mills completed the disaster. The English occupation was followed by years of guerrilla warfare which retarded recovery. Peasants and farmers abandoned the land to brambles and nettles and migrated to neighbouring Brittany. Maine became part of the personal appanage of the Duke of Bedford. The germ of a civil administration was set up in 1425 under a military governor, Sir John Fastolf, and a Chancellor, the experienced soldier and administrator Sir John Popham. Maine had its own council, sitting at Le Mans, and an independent financial administration. English settlers arrived in large numbers. Some of the principal captains, including Fastolf, were endowed with ample estates. Land worth up to 60,000 *livres* a year was reserved for humbler soldiers who had fought at Verneuil. The English made no attempt to reconcile the population of Maine to the new regime, as they had done with some success in Normandy. They treated it as enemy territory under military occupation. The cost of the occupation, which was considerable, was met by the inhabitants as, in one way or another, military occupations almost always were. Garrisons regularly requisitioned victuals and other supplies from local villages without payment. The county was taxed on the same basis as Normandy, but unlike Normandy it was also required to pay *pâtis*. A highly centralised system was set up at three local centres, Le Mans, Sainte-Suzanne and Mayenne, for collecting *pâtis* and selling the safe-conducts and certificates of allegiance without which movement was almost impossible. Writing many years later, Sir John Fastolf reckoned that Maine generated war profits of

4,000 marks (£2,666) a year for Bedford's personal exchequer. But all of this and more must have been expended on the costs of occupation and defence.[33]

Measured against the high ambitions of Richemont and Yolande of Anjou, the palace revolution of 1425 was a failure. The Dauphin's council was reorganised so as to include a much larger aristocratic element, thus meeting one of the most persistent criticisms of the Louvet regime. The only list that we have contains nineteen names, including twelve great noblemen and four bishops. The council's business was dominated by a triumvirate of Yolande of Anjou, the Constable and Pierre de Giac. Yolande, the only woman to serve as a permanent member of the council in this period, resided almost continuously at court for the next two years and was usually present at its meetings. Richemont's was a powerful voice but he was preoccupied with the armies and bored by the details of administration.

Pierre de Giac was the odd man out in this group. He was a nobleman from Auvergne whose family had long-standing connections with the royal house (his grandfather had been Chancellor for five years in the 1380s). Pierre himself had risen in the service of John the Fearless and had been among the companions who were with him when he was murdered. He had changed sides immediately afterwards, prompting suspicions that he had been privy to the deed. This was probably untrue, but it would not have been out of character. Pierre de Giac was a man with an instinctive preference for violent solutions. His record included at least one forcible abduction and he was widely believed to have poisoned his first wife. Admitted to the Dauphin's court, he worked his way into Jean Louvet's inner circle, and stood by him to the end. He now became First Chamberlain and took over Louvet's role as the Dauphin's gatekeeper. The choice was probably the Dauphin's. Charles, perennially insecure, had always needed the reassurance of friends. Giac was a man of very limited ability, but he was an archetypal court favourite, by turns haughty and ingratiating. In a short time, he acquired the same possessive influence over his master that Louvet had enjoyed. 'Men said that the King loved him dearly and would do whatever he wanted,' wrote a contemporary observer of the court, 'for which reason things went very badly.' The workhorses of the new council were the bishops: the well-respected Martin Gouge, who was reinstated as Chancellor, the diplomat Regnault de Chartres, and Guillaume de Champeaux Bishop of Laon, an old associate of Louvet's who was responsible for the financial administration and was widely thought to lack both judgement and integrity.[34]

The fundamental problem of the new regime was the same as the one which had frustrated the efforts of its predecessor: the absence of any dependable source of tax revenue from which to pay the troops. The Estates of Languedoil met at Poitiers in October 1425, and the Estates of Languedoc a month later at Mehun-sur-Yèvre. These assemblies set the seal on the changes of government of July. They also endorsed the Constable's proposed reorganisation of the army as a regularly paid force which would not need to live off the land. Between them, the two assemblies granted taxes amounting to 1,050,000 *livres*, marking the last part of the three-year programme of taxation inaugurated by the Estates-General in 1423. The grants, however, did not resolve the Dauphin's financial problems. In the first place, the yield was depressed by the usual problems of administrative disorganisation and petty corruption. Secondly, the taxes had been granted without regard to the capacity of people to pay them. Recession, depopulation and war damage had all taken their toll on the population of the kingdom of Bourges. Thirdly, old habits died hard and promiscuous grants of annuities, stipends and cash to favoured courtiers continued unabated. The new councillors were the largest beneficiaries, just as the old ones had been. Richemont once told an agent of the city of Lyon that he 'did not bother with matters of finance'. He never really understood the deep-rooted financial problems which defeated his hopes of creating a paid army on the model of the English army in Normandy. Most of his fellow councillors were no better. When the Bishop of Poitiers, Hughes de Combarel, spoke out against the depredations of the Dauphin's unpaid troops and called for reform in the Estates, there was no answer. Returning to the Dauphin's quarters after the session, Pierre de Giac uttered a mighty oath and declared that the Bishop should be thrown in the river, along with anyone else of the same mind.[35]

On 18 September 1425, the Count of Foix finally arrived in the Loire valley from Languedoc with a brilliant company of southern lords and at least 2,000 Gascon troops, only to discover that there was no money to pay them. The Gascon leaders followed the court, collecting grants and favours, but showed no inclination to fight without pay. Lesser captains were deputed to lead the men west across the Beauce to join Richemont on the marches of Maine, but they were no more willing to serve for nothing. They got no further than Bonneval and Saumur before turning back for want of pay. Over the winter months, they rewarded themselves by pillaging the population of the Orléanais. The Dauphin's ministers tried to limit the damage by dispersing them in garrisons spread across the Loire provinces. But their persistent looting and violence came close to provoking an uprising. When, in November, the city of Tours was ordered by the Dauphin and Yolande of Anjou to accept a Gascon garrison, the town council, supported by their Archbishop and a general assembly of the inhabitants, were defiant. They had only recently got rid of the Scots and regarded this new tribe of marauding aliens as no better than the enemy. They pointed to the desolation to which the Gascons had reduced other towns of the region and threatened to resist them by force. At one point, when the Gascons were thought to be approaching, they closed their gates, manned their walls, and posted watches day and night in the towers of the cathedral and the abbey of St Martin to ring their great bells if the Gascons should appear across the fields.[36]

The Scots and most of the Bretons who had served with Richemont were eventually laid off and cantoned in the towns and castles of northern Anjou, where they too were allowed to live on the land. The region's transformation into a frontier zone was a disaster for its population. In the worst-affected areas, the courts ceased to function; rents and crop yields collapsed; sharecroppers and tenants deserted the land, leaving abandoned buildings, burned-out barns and scrub behind them. The damage was aggravated by the exactions of the English garrisons of Maine. But the greater part of it was the work of soldiers in the service of the Dauphin. His officials travelling through the region needed a military escort to protect them from his own Scottish garrisons. By June 1426, the Dauphin's ministers had concluded that the depredations of unpaid soldiery made it impossible to collect the taxes which had been voted to pay them. They resorted instead to one-off expedients. In December 1426, they reverted to the unpopular and destructive policy of coinage devaluation. A new silver coinage was introduced with a reduced bullion content. Within three years, the new coins had themselves lost much of their value in the course of successive reissues.[37]

After the coup which had disposed of the Dauphin's old ministers, the Dauphin's council sent an embassy to the Duke of Savoy asking him to resume his role as mediator. Another was despatched to the court of John V at Nantes inviting him to meet the Dauphin now that the councillors behind the Penthièvre plot of 1420 had been banished. The meeting finally took place over several days at Saumur at the beginning of October 1425. The entry of the two principals was carefully staged in accordance with the demands of precedence and status, the Duke arriving first, followed at a day's interval by the Dauphin, each with an imposing cavalcade of noblemen and advisers around him. The two men met in the fields outside the town, ostentatiously embraced twice, and proceeded together to Yolande of Anjou's castle overlooking the Loire, where the discussions were to take place.

The Dauphin was prepared to pay a high price for John V's support, politically and financially. He declared that he would be guided by John V in all matters both public and private. John responded by laying out his proposals, which he declared to be 'necessary and profitable' if any progress was to be made. These were essentially a restatement of the four articles agreed by Richemont and Amadeus of Savoy at Montluel. First and foremost, Charles must make peace with the Duke of Burgundy. The Dauphin would have to make him a generous offer based on the abortive proposals made at the earlier conferences at Bourg-en-Bresse, Nantes, Mâcon and Montluel. Secondly, to discharge his duty to God and his own conscience, the Dauphin must make a reasonable offer to the English, with a view to achieving at least a pause in the fighting. Thirdly, while the war continued, it should have the first call on the Dauphin's resources. The problem, as John V saw it, was not shortage of revenue but the wasting of what revenue there was. He therefore proposed that the Dauphin should be deprived of control of his finances. The revenues of Languedoil should be confided to two commissioners, one appointed by the Dauphin and the other by himself. The commissioners would have to agree on any item of expenditure or, in the absence of agreement, refer the matter to John V or his brother the Constable for decision. The councillors of the two sides met for two full sessions each day to discuss these proposals. The talks were interspersed with banquets, balls and jousts. 'Fine and notable speeches' were made on both sides according to an agent of the city of Lyon who hung about the antechambers of the castle. Finally, the Dauphin accepted the Duke's terms in their entirety and swore a solemn oath to observe them. Only his desperate position could have warranted what amounted to an abdication of his government into the hands of the Duke of Brittany. In return, John V promised to give him military assistance against the English to the full extent of his resources. The Counts of Foix, Clermont and Vendôme and the lord of Albret, all of whom were present, promised to do the same. The Duke then did homage to the Dauphin for his duchy amid cries of 'Noel!' from the dense throng of ministers and courtiers standing around. Yolande of Anjou was highly satisfied. Writing to the citizens of Tours, she declared that the negotiations had gone well. 'Shortly,' she told them, 'all the princes of France will be united.' Her hopes may never have been realistic. They were certainly destined to be disappointed.[38]

The conference at Saumur had been a very public and noisy affair, which did not escape the attention of the English. They reacted with predictable fury. When John V returned to Brittany, he received an embassy from the Duke of Bedford. The ambassadors had come to find out what was going on and to call on him to honour the alliance to which he had sworn at Amiens two years before. The Duke of Bedford, they said, was particularly concerned about the large number of Breton soldiers in the service of the Dauphin. John replied rather disingenuously that the agreements sealed with Bedford at Amiens and the arrangements made at Saumur were both steps towards a general peace which would include England. He assumed that the English would welcome this prospect as much as he did. As for the soldiers, he was in no position to tell his subjects which side they should fight for. Bedford's response was uncompromising. He had no interest in a general peace, he told John, except on terms that Henry VI was acknowledged as King of all France. Anyway, a diplomatic project on the lines proposed would have to be discussed first with the Duke of Gloucester as Protector of England and Philip the Good, whose consent would be necessary. But since John V had now become an ally of the Dauphin, the Regent proposed to treat him as an enemy and take up the cause of his mortal rivals the counts of Penthièvre. John professed to be shocked by this reaction. But it was consistent with the line that the English had taken ever since the treaty of Troyes. Bedford's threats were meant, and taken, seriously. John V panicked. He sent a herald to the Duke of Burgundy, begging him to intercede for him not just with Bedford himself but with Henry Beaufort, the Duke of Exeter, Parliament and anyone else in England who might be able to soften Bedford's anger.[39]

By the time this message reached Philip, it was too late for compromise. At Westminster, the council declared 'open war' on Brittany and authorised English ships to attack Breton merchantmen at sea. For the first time in years an English war fleet was mobilised to patrol the Channel. Trade between Brittany and England collapsed. The Count of Penthièvre and his brother, who were still plotting the downfall of the house of Montfort from their exile in the Low Countries, were invited to Paris or Westminster to discuss matters of common interest. More ominously for John V, the Earl of Suffolk, the English sector commander in Lower Normandy, began to concentrate troops on the border of Brittany. He occupied Pontorson, south of Mont-Saint-Michel, whose powerful moated citadel and fortified bridge marked the border of the Breton duchy. Further south the dilapidated fortress of Saint-James de Beuvron, abandoned by the English after 1418, was repaired to serve as the base of another force commanded by the energetic Sir Thomas Rempston. Early in 1426, Suffolk and Rempston invaded Brittany with about 500 mounted men and penetrated almost as far as Rennes, where John V was then residing. The region had been fattened by half a century of peace and yielded a rich haul of loot and prisoners.[40]

Suffolk's raid provoked a brief but destructive war on the marches of Brittany. John V summoned the whole baronage of his duchy to defend the border. His brothers Arthur de Richemont and Richard Count of Étampes were recalled to take command. Their first task was to eliminate the Earl of Suffolk's new bases on the border of the duchy. In about the middle of February 1426, the Bretons carried the walls of Pontorson in a bloody assault, which left most of the defenders dead or prisoners. The castle was slighted and breaches blown in the walls of the town to make it indefensible. In the closing days of February, Richemont marched south against Saint-James de Beuvron. There, his army came to grief for the same reason as the army of Maine the year before. He ran out of money to pay them. The Bretons had so far served on promises, but their patience was running out. Some of them could no longer buy food in the itinerant markets which followed in the wake of every army. They began to desert.

On 6 March, about a week into the siege, Richemont called a council of war. The assembled captains realised that they did not have time to starve the place out. They would have to storm it before their unpaid army disintegrated. Saint-James was built on a spur of rock towering over a tight bend in the river Beuvron. The river protected it on three sides, while the fourth was defended by a powerful moated

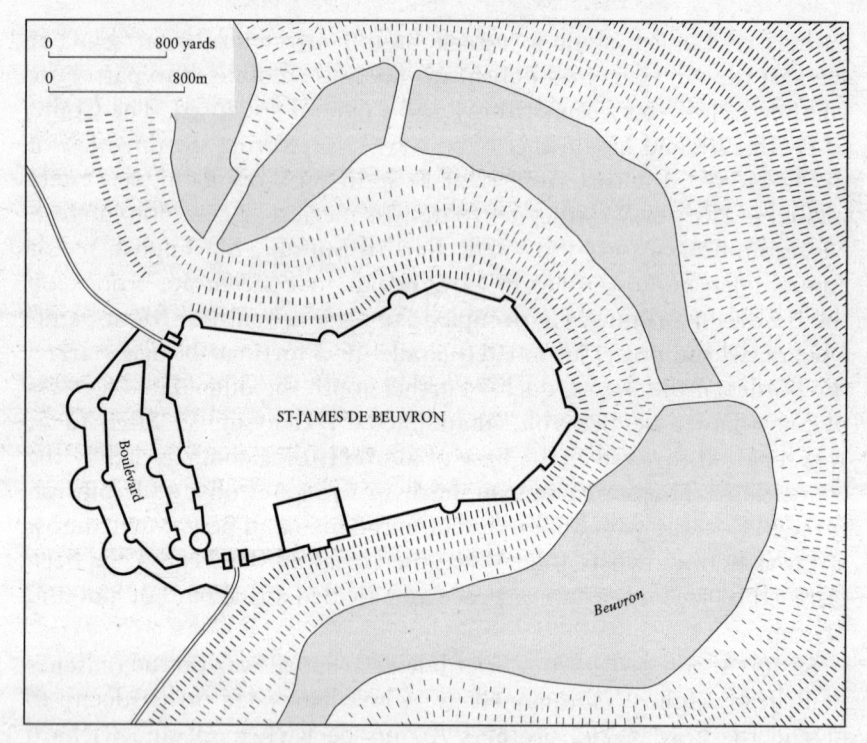

4 The siege of Saint-James de Beuvron, 6 March 1426

boulevard with its own garrison. A double assault was ordered. The Breton-speakers were detailed to go over the walls on the north side of the town, while Richemont and the French-speakers attacked the boulevard from the west. The attack opened later that day with an artillery barrage before the assault parties ran forward with their ladders. Inside the town, Sir Thomas Rempston had several hundred men under his command. They fought back 'like lions'.

After three or four hours of bitter hand-to-hand fighting on the ramparts, a mounted force was seen approaching from the north. It was the Breton troops whom Richemont had stationed around Avranches to contain the English garrison. They had come to reinforce their fellows. But both sides believed that it was an English army of relief. The English cried 'Salisbury!' and 'Suffolk!' from the top of the walls. The Breton-speakers panicked and abandoned the assault, retreating in disorder towards their encampments. At this point the river Beuvron broadened out into a chain of deep ponds crossed by narrow causeways which were quickly clogged up with fleeing men. The defenders opened the gates and sortied out, falling on them from behind. There was a massacre. Those who could not get across the causeways threw themselves into the water, where many of them drowned. As night fell the survivors, many nursing serious wounds, fled into the forest. Their captains mounted their horses and tried in vain to stop them. The panic spread to the rest of the army which joined the exodus. At about 2 a.m., a fire was seen spreading through the Breton encampment. Richemont, although wounded in the thigh and deserted by most of his army, remained at his post until his brother Richard Count of Étampes persuaded him to leave, one of the bitterest moments of his life according to his squire and biographer, who was with him. The brothers left by the light of the flames, together with the few men who remained with them. A great quantity of stores and equipment was abandoned to the enemy, including 14 artillery pieces and 141 standards. Reports reaching England, which were probably based on the heralds' count, put the Breton casualties at 1,500 men dead on the field, including 800 noblemen in coat armour.

Two days later, the Earl of Suffolk arrived from Avranches with a large company of fresh men and took command. He gathered up the men at Saint-James who were still fit to fight and invaded Brittany by the northern road, making for Dol-de-Bretagne. John V was at Rennes. With no army, he was defenceless. There was no alternative to a humiliating surrender. John sent a herald into Suffolk's camp to ask for a truce. Suffolk demanded a cash indemnity before he would even consider it. After some haggling, he was paid 4,500 *francs* in return for a short truce until the end of June 1426.[41]

The disaster at Saint-James de Beuvron and the truce of Rennes put an end of the Dauphin's hopes of a great offensive against the English in 1426. The Bretons, who were to have served as its spearhead, were forced to withdraw from the fighting. The Gascons, in whom such high hopes had been reposed, were still cantoned in Berry and Touraine but were stood down in March. They returned to the south in the spring without having struck a single blow against the enemy in the whole six months that they had been in the north. The Dauphin's ministers resorted to counsels of desperation to find a new army. They tried to recall Louis Duke of Anjou and his followers from Naples. Ten thousand *livres* were laid out to pay his expenses. But Louis did not come. Attempts to recruit 2,000 or 3,000 men on credit in Castile were equally unsuccessful. The rosy picture which the Dauphin's ambassadors were instructed to paint of the Dauphin's political and military situation can have cut little ice with the well-informed advisers of the Castilian king. They replied with unctuous insincerity that they would have offered the Dauphin all the support that he wanted and more, if they had not already taxed their subjects to the limit.[42]

Richemont never understood that money could not be conjured up at will to pay his armies. He blamed the debacle on John V's Chancellor Jean de Malestroit. He had always regarded Malestroit as an English agent and accused him of having taken a bribe to withhold his soldiers' wages in order to force the raising of the siege. In April 1426, he appeared at the Chancellor's manor house near Nantes and arrested him, carrying him off to captivity at Chinon. He was not released until he promised to do 'marvels' to detach Philip the Good from the English. This, as Richemont saw it, was now the only way of keeping Brittany in the Dauphin's camp and reversing the increasingly unfavourable military balance.[43]

Everything now depended on the attitude of the Duke of Burgundy. John V had only been willing to make peace with the Dauphin at Saumur because he thought that Philip the Good would do the same. Richemont believed that he had Philip's assurance that he would abandon the English once the authors of his father's murder had been banished. After the conference at Saumur, John sent a formal embassy to the Duke of Burgundy, pointing out that with their departure the only impediment to his reconciliation with the Dauphin had gone. If there was going to be a reconciliation between the two branches of the house of Valois, they were instructed to say, it had to be now, before irreversible damage was done to the French Crown ('of which the Duke is the chief ornament'). The drafting of these instructions bore the marks of Richemont's influence, and one of the two ambassadors, Philibert de Vaudrey, was certainly Richemont's agent. Another plea followed after Christmas, when John had received the Duke of Bedford's threats of retaliation and was beginning to feel seriously exposed. The Dauphin added his own urgings, using his private secretary Alain Chartier and the Poitevin nobleman Georges de la Trémoille as intermediaries with the court of Burgundy. None of these approaches elicited a clear response. To some extent, this was due to the cumbrous methods of communication available. Philip was campaigning in Holland throughout the autumn of 1425 and the following winter and was difficult to reach. But there is every reason to think that he welcomed the slow pace of diplomacy. It suited him to remain inscrutable for as long as possible.[44]

Philip the Good's position was particularly delicate as a result of a political crisis in England and another in the Low Countries, both of them provoked by the ambitions of Humphrey Duke of Gloucester. In the course of 1425, Humphrey tacitly recognised defeat in Hainaut. But his covetous eye moved to the Dutch-speaking counties of Holland and Zeeland (*Map V*). Hainaut, with its serene landscapes and fine castles, had been the residence of choice of the princes of the house of Bavaria, and before them of the counts of the house of Avesnes. But Holland and Zeeland, which had been ruled as a single principality since the eleventh century, were much the wealthiest parts of Jacqueline's inheritance from her father. Holland was the most populous territory of the Low Countries after Flanders. Its expanding towns had become major centres of the north European cloth industry. Middelburg was an important entrepot for international trade at a time when the port of Sluys was slowly silting up and Antwerp was just beginning its ascent. Standing at the crossroads of the rich trade routes that joined the Atlantic, the Baltic and the Rhineland, these towns would soon challenge the great industrial and commercial centres of Flanders.[45]

The politics of Holland and Zeeland had been dominated for many years by two loose political federations, the Hooks (*Hoeken* in Dutch) and the Cods (*Kabeljauwen*). Both factions were led by noblemen, but by this time, the Cods had come to be associated with the industrial and mercantile elites of the larger towns. The Hooks drew their support mainly from the landed nobility, but they controlled a few towns, notably Gouda, and had partisans in many more. The differences between the parties corresponded to no consistent ideological or social divisions. They depended on tradition, on local rivalries, on the networks of patronage run by urban party bosses, but above all on the need to find allies against enemies of the opposite party. The counts of Holland had found it necessary to associate themselves with one group or the other in order to build a power base in a region from which they were usually absent. Jacqueline's father had been a consistent patron and supporter of the Hooks and had made many enemies by appointing only Hooks to important offices. During the war of succession which followed his death, Jacqueline had succeeded naturally to his alliances, while her uncle and rival John of Bavaria had equally naturally found his support among the leading Cod cities. John of Bavaria's regime in Holland and Zeeland was detested by the leaders of the Hooks, whom he systematically pushed out of office and influence during the six years that he was in power.[46]

On 6 January 1425, John of Bavaria died at The Hague, murdered, it was believed, by his marshal Jan van Vliet with a slow poison applied to the leaves of his prayer book. Allegations of poisoning were too common in the late middle ages to be taken entirely at face value. But in his confession, which was extracted by torture, van Vliet claimed with a wealth of circumstantial detail to have been paid to do the deed by an English merchant and a group of Hook noblemen. This, and the fact that van Vliet was married to Jacqueline of Bavaria's half-sister, meant that she never entirely shook off the suspicion of complicity. John died childless. His succession was a complex business. He had taken the title of Count of Holland and Zeeland and was generally treated as such. In strict law, however, he was only a mortgagee and regent for Jacqueline. A year before his death, he had nominated Philip the Good as the heir to his private estate. This included his rights as mortgagee of Holland and Zeeland as well as his extensive personal domains in south Holland, among them Dordrecht, then Holland's chief city. It did not include the government of the two counties. Even John of Bavaria had recognised that his regency would end with his death and that the government of Holland and Zeeland would then revert to Jacqueline and her husband (whoever that was). His sudden disappearance from the scene was therefore a seismic event in the history of the region.[47]

When John of Bavaria died, Humphrey of Gloucester and Jacqueline were still in Hainaut. They immediately asserted their claim to the government of the two counties and sent messengers into the territories calling on its people to recognise them. But they were not content with propaganda. Jacqueline made contact with a prominent Hook nobleman, Floris van Kijfhoek. He assembled a group of supporters and tried unsuccessfully to raise Gouda for her. Then, at the end of January 1425, he and his companions occupied the river port of Schoonhoven on the river Lek in Jacqueline's name, expelling the garrison and seizing the castle. For some months, the town became an isolated beacon of her cause in Holland.

Philip was in Burgundy when John of Bavaria died. In his absence, his affairs in the Low Countries were dealt with by the Council of

Flanders, which sat in Ghent. They acted fast. The initiative was taken by Roland van Uitkerke, a Dutch-speaking nobleman from Flanders who served as Philip's principal adviser and agent in Holland. Within days of John of Bavaria's death, he left for the north with other councillors to take possession of the towns and regions which had belonged to the dead man personally. The Cod nobility declared almost immediately for John of Brabant, as Jacqueline's true husband, and took control of the government of both counties. The Duke of Brabant arrived at The Hague at the beginning of February 1425 and received the homage of the Dutch towns. When he returned to Brabant, he left behind two stadtholders to govern in his name, whose authority was accepted in most of the territories. In March 1425, Jacqueline's partisans were besieged in Schoonhoven by a large army drawn from all the main Cod towns of Holland. The last embers of the revolt of the Hooks were suppressed by the end of June 1425 with the aid of troops brought over from Burgundy. Jacqueline's cause appeared to have collapsed. Gloucester had returned to England with his army and Jacqueline herself was immured in the Posteerne at Ghent.[48]

The Cods had taken over Holland and Zeeland in the name of the Duke of Brabant, but the real beneficiary of their coup was Philip the Good. He had no intention of leaving Holland and Zeeland in the hands of John of Brabant. He had long ago concluded that his cousin had neither the wit nor the energy to hold the prize that had fallen into his lap, and was determined to take Holland and Zeeland for himself. He employed the methods that he always preferred: diplomacy and bullying. The cousins met at Mechelen in the middle of July, and John submitted to his fate. On 19 July 1425, 'considering the many domains and territories that have come to him by inheritance or marriage, which he cannot conveniently govern himself', he appointed Philip as his lieutenant in Holland and Zeeland for a period of twelve years with a free hand to do with them as he wished.[49]

At the beginning of July 1425, a fortnight after Jacqueline's confinement at Ghent, the Duke of Bedford, accompanied by his wife and his principal councillors, arrived at Philip the Good's country retreat at Hesdin in Artois for discussions extending over nearly a week. It was an occasion for mutual flattery, hunting, dancing and feasting, and for talks about matters of common interest. Two of the Burgundian noblemen present, who had fought in Hainaut, were seen to be wearing embroidered roundels on their shoulder declaring their readiness to accept challenges from the English and their allies. Bedford took offence and demanded their removal until it was explained to him that they referred only to the English supporters of the Duke of Gloucester. Humphrey of Gloucester's humiliation in Hainaut was evidently a source of satisfaction to everyone.[50]

Within two months the comfortable harmony of the allies was disturbed by an unexpected and unwelcome event. On 2 September 1425, in the early hours of the morning, Jacqueline escaped from her gilded cage at Ghent. Her servants smuggled her out of the Posteerne dressed as a man and took her through the streets of the sleeping city to a gate. There, a group of Hook noblemen from Holland was waiting with horses. She rode to Antwerp and from there across northern Brabant into Holland. In the second week of September, she arrived at Gouda, the principal Hook town of Holland, to an ecstatic welcome from her supporters. There, she installed herself in the castle which was to be her base for most of the next three years. As the news of her return spread through Holland, noblemen of the Hook party made their way to Gouda to do homage to her. They included the heads of many of the leading noble families, who arrived with their retainers. We do not know how many troops she was able to raise, but they cannot have come close to matching the numbers available to the Duke of Burgundy. Nor does she appear to have had any artillery. One of her first acts was to write to Humphrey of Gloucester in England, calling on him to bring the largest possible army to help her to capture the urban strongholds of her enemies.[51]

Philip the Good was at Bruges when he learned of Jacqueline's escape. At first, he assumed that she was heading for England, and ordered a watch to be kept on the ports. When it became clear that she was making for Holland, he reacted with remarkable speed. On 6 September, four days after Jacqueline's disappearance, Philip called on the chivalry of his domains to accompany him to Holland. On the 15th he embarked at Sluys on a fleet of 200 requisitioned ships with an army of 3,000 men. On the 18th they disembarked at Rotterdam. He was received on the quayside by representatives of the leading Cod towns, Leiden, Haarlem and Amsterdam. From Rotterdam, Philip went to The Hague and then began a tour of the towns of Holland, receiving the homage of the inhabitants. The triumphal progress, however, was suddenly interrupted by a serious military defeat. On 22 October 1425, when Philip was back at Rotterdam, a large force of militia from the leading Cod towns was advancing on Jacqueline's headquarters at Gouda when they were ambushed by her partisans in the village of Alphen, ten miles north of the town. They were slaughtered and lost all their standards, which were carried back in triumph to decorate the hall of the castle at Gouda. As yet Jacqueline controlled only a modest territory north of the river Lek, around the towns of Gouda, Schoonhoven and Oudewater. She also occupied, at about this time, the port of Zevenbergen, further south on the Merwede, which gave her access to shipping and allowed her to communicate with England. The victory boosted her standing with the Dutch, encouraging trimmers to declare for her. It marked the start of a destructive guerrilla war between Hook and Cod partisans, which eventually extended over much of Holland and Zeeland. Dordrecht was particularly badly hit. At about the same time rumours began to circulate that the Duke of Gloucester was trying to respond to his wife's appeal from Gouda. Troops were reported to be assembling in England to invade Holland. For Philip the Good, what had begun as a showy military promenade began to look like a real war. To reassure the leading Cod towns, he had to promise them that he would not leave Holland and Zeeland until Jacqueline had been defeated. In the meantime, frantic messages were sent back to the Council of Flanders calling on them to send another 4,000 troops urgently to Holland.[52]

Holland and Zeeland were of much greater interest to England than Hainaut. The two counties were an important market for English wool. They were the main destination for English cloth exports, most of which reached their northern European markets through middle-men based there. There were communities of English merchants at Middelburg and Dordrecht, which were for practical purposes outposts of the London mercers' guild. For England's merchants, the prospect of a Burgundian takeover of Holland and Zeeland was extremely unwelcome. It threatened to introduce into one of their most important markets the kind of protectionism and retaliatory seizures which they associated with Burgundian Flanders. Feelings ran particularly high in London, where most of the trade with Holland and Zeeland was concentrated and hostility to the Duke of Burgundy and his Flemish subjects was strong.[53]

The Duke of Gloucester's close relationship with London was one of his chief political assets, and he worked hard to cultivate it.

As Chancellor, Henry Beaufort had become the effective governor of England. He was thought to bear a 'heavy heart' against the Londoners, a fact which Gloucester skilfully exploited to wrong-foot his rival. In February 1425, while Gloucester was still in Hainaut, there was an upsurge of anger in the city against foreign merchants, which was mainly directed against the Flemings, the largest and most prosperous of the city's alien communities. Beaufort had made himself the protector of these subjects of the Duke of Burgundy. After some inflammatory handbills against them had been distributed across the city, he overreacted. He had several prominent Londoners arrested and charged with treason on the basis of doubtful information from a paid informer. To overawe the city, he put a large garrison into the Tower under the command of Bedford's chamberlain Sir Richard Woodville, who had been sent back to England to reinforce his authority. When, six weeks later, Humphrey returned to England from Hainaut, he took the Londoners' part. He appeared outside the Tower and demanded admittance. Woodville, who had been ordered to admit no one without the authority of the council, refused, and Beaufort backed him up. Later, Gloucester returned when Woodville was away and bullied his deputy into releasing one of the prisoners held there. Overriding the council's authority, he told the lieutenant that his own order should be a sufficient warrant. Addressing the city authorities not long afterwards, he told them that he could well understand why they had found Beaufort's behaviour overbearing. They could expect better treatment from him, he said.[54]

On 30 April 1425, Parliament opened at Westminster, with the three-year-old King symbolically presiding from the throne. The session was dominated by the dispute between Gloucester and Henry Beaufort. Humphrey had never forgiven Beaufort for leading the group which had cut him down to size in 1422, when he had tried to obtain the regency of England for himself. The Chancellor was firmly opposed to Gloucester's adventures in the Low Country. His stinging rebuke for Gloucester's operations in Hainaut must have rung in his ears for weeks. The Duke's emergence as the champion of the Londoners against the Chancellor brought their relations to their nadir. 'The lord of Gloucester', as the council would later observe, 'hath long borne and had heaviness and displeasure against the person of my lord the Chancellor, his uncle.' The atmosphere at Westminster was poisonous. Beaufort claimed to have received credible reports that Humphrey planned to assault him. Violent handbills against him circulated in London. A mob gathered in the warren of lanes in Vintry, at the western end of the city, shouting that if they could get their hands on Beaufort, they would throw him into the Thames 'to have taught him to swim with wings'. Beaufort was in a strong position, for the settlement of 1422 had vested the powers of the Crown in the council, which he and his allies dominated. Gloucester was determined to outflank them in Parliament in order to get support for his wife's claim to her inheritance. Parliament sat for two and a half months, until the middle of July. The official record is, as always, discreet. What is clear is that Gloucester outmanoeuvred his rival. The Commons had a good deal of sympathy for Jacqueline of Bavaria. They invited the council to press Philip the Good to release her into 'indifferent' (that is neutral) hands. On 14 July 1425, the last sitting day, they authorised a loan of 20,000 marks to be made to Humphrey in four annual instalments to pay for his 'diverse necessities'. By this, they presumably meant the payment of the arrears of war wages due to the troops who had served him in Hainaut. Thus, said a London chronicler, one of the most ill-tempered Parliamentary sessions for many years came to 'an evil faring end, too shamefully for to be named of any well-advised man'.[55]

The Duke of Gloucester must have received Jacqueline's appeal for help in about the middle of September 1425. With his usual impetuousness, he immediately resolved to send an army to Holland. At the end of that month, he was actively recruiting troops. The poet John Lydgate, taking his cue from his patron, looked forward to the imminent union of England and Holland, 'a new sun to shine of gladness in both lands'. This time, however, Humphrey did not intend to lead the army himself. He had learned on the last occasion how much his influence in council waned when he was out of England. Instead, his choice of general fell on the Essex magnate Walter Lord Fitzwalter, who was then serving in the Earl of Salisbury's army in Maine. Although only twenty-five years old, Fitzwalter was already an experienced soldier. He had fought in France for years, acquiring a reputation for lawlessness and violence which had once earned him a spell in a Paris prison. But apart from a brief appointment as captain of Vire, he had no experience of command. Money was probably his reason for joining Gloucester's adventure. He had been captured at the battle of Baugé and was having difficulty in paying his ransom. He no doubt hoped for a measure of glory and a chance to repair his battered fortunes.[56]

Reports of Gloucester's military preparations reached the Council of Flanders at Ghent early in October 1425. In Paris, the Duke of Bedford sent Sir Ralph Butler urgently to England with a group of his councillors to talk to Gloucester and find out what was going on. At Westminster, the Chancellor and the council took fright. The gathering of a private army in England, they declared, was a serious breach of the King's peace. They were uncertain what the Duke planned to do with it. They feared that he planned to mount a coup. His behaviour certainly encouraged their fear. In the last days of October 1425, the Duke was at Baynard's Castle, his walled mansion by the Thames next to Blackfriars. On the evening of 29 October 1425, he had summonses distributed through the city calling on the citizens to assemble, fully armed and arrayed in their sections. On the following morning, he ordered the mayor and aldermen to provide him with 300 mounted men, apparently in order to take possession of the child-King, who was then at Eltham Palace in Kent. Henry VI was a mere symbol of royal authority, but the prospect of his passing under Gloucester's control was intolerable to Beaufort. He was also concerned for his own safety, for Gloucester's route to Eltham would have taken his supporters over London Bridge and through the densely populated streets of Southwark. Southwark was home to the chief targets of the London mob. It housed the largest concentration of immigrants in England as well as the manor of the bishops of Winchester where Beaufort himself lodged. He resolved to stop Gloucester's horde by closing London Bridge. The chains were drawn across the road at the southern end and soldiers were brought in to defend the gatehouse. As the news spread, the city exploded. Shops were closed everywhere as men converged on the bridge to confront the Chancellor's men. The stand-off continued for the rest of the day and through the following night. A battle was only avoided by the intervention of Archbishop Chichele and Pedro, the son of the King of Portugal, who was visiting England. They negotiated a truce which enabled each side to withdraw its forces without bloodshed. But Gloucester eventually got his way. He was allowed to bring the child-King to London, accompanied by the rest of the council, the mayor and aldermen of London and a great mob of Londoners. He presided over the next meeting of the council in his own mansion at Baynard's Castle. A few days later, the council authorised payment of the first instalment of Gloucester's Parliamentary loan.[57]

JACQUELINE OF BAVARIA, 1424–1428

Outmanoeuvred in London and at Westminster, on 31 October 1425 Henry Beaufort wrote to the Duke of Bedford in Paris, pressing him to return at once to England. Under the political settlement of 1422, Gloucester's authority as Protector of the Realm would automatically be suspended when his elder brother was in the country. 'As ye desire the welfare of the King our sovereign lord and of his realms of England and of France and your own well and our[s] also, haste ye hither,' Beaufort wrote, 'such a brother ye have here, God make him a good man.' For Beaufort, and no doubt for Bedford too, nothing less than the future of the dual monarchy was at stake. 'Your wisdom knoweth well,' wrote Beaufort, 'that the prosperity of France stands in the welfare of England.' Beaufort's letter was carried post-haste to France and delivered to the Duke of Bedford on 3 November, just three days after it was written. Bedford agreed to return, but he could not return as quickly as Beaufort would have liked. There were current problems to be resolved in Brittany, in Maine and in Champagne. In the event, the Regent was unable to leave Paris until the beginning of December. He arrived in England shortly before Christmas. On 7 January 1426, Parliament was summoned. Making his formal entry into London three days later, on 10 January, Bedford lost no time in showing where his sympathies lay. He rode into Westminster with Chancellor Beaufort at his side and Gloucester pointedly absent. The mayor and aldermen welcomed him with trepidation. They presented him with two silver basins, for which they 'had but little thanks'.[58]

By the time Bedford reached England, Fitzwalter's army must already have been embarking. On about Christmas Day 1425, it sailed from the Thames with 1,500 men in twenty-four large ships. Gloucester Herald, who travelled with them, claimed that it comprised 'the flower of England's archers, the elect of the elect'. Philip the Good got plenty of warning of their coming. Bedford had received the latest reports of Fitzwalter's progress while he was waiting at Calais for a passage and had passed them on to Philip's officials in Flanders. Further information came from the captain of the castle at the entrance to the harbour of Sluys, who counted them as they sailed past. Fitzwalter was accompanied by a group of Hook leaders who served as his advisers and guides. They had agreed a rendezvous with one of Jacqueline's chief supporters, Jan lord of Heemstede, on Schouwen, one of the larger islands of Zeeland. Van Heemstede was waiting for them there with about 2,000 Zeelanders. Fitzwalter had an accident-prone passage. His ships got separated in bad weather and did not all make the rendezvous. Some of the stragglers were attacked at sea. Most of them were too big for the shallow inlets of Zeeland, making it necessary to find a deep-water port. The fleet arrived late on 5 January 1426 off Zierikzee, which had the best deep-water harbour on Schouwen. The population of Zierikzee was hostile. The invaders were forced to withdraw to Brouwershaven, a small fortified bastide town with a sheltered but shallow harbour on the other side of the island. Fitzwalter's men had a difficult landfall. They had lost about a third of their numbers to casualties and navigational errors. The survivors had to disembark into lighters to reach the shore.

The Duke of Burgundy passed Christmas and New Year at Leiden. He was informed of the English landing on the evening it happened. On the following day, 6 January 1426, he marched with his army to Rotterdam. By his own estimate he had about 6,000 men with him. Of these, rather less than half were French or Flemish and the rest were local contingents furnished by the Cod towns of Holland. In a remarkably short time, the shipmen of Rotterdam collected a fleet of shallow draft vessels to carry these men down the coast. For several days, high winds prevented Philip's fleet from approaching Brouwershaven. But on 13 January, a fine clear day, they were able to anchor about a mile and a half west of the town. The English and their Zeeland allies had followed them along the shore and were waiting for them.

An army disembarking over the side onto beaches and tidal flats is extremely vulnerable. The process was particularly difficult for Philip's army because the tide was going out and they had to wade a considerable distance ashore with their heavy equipment. Inexplicably, Fitzwalter failed to exploit their difficulties. He drew up his men behind the dykes, leaving the Burgundians free to land most of their army without interference and to occupy the dykes themselves. By the time Fitzwalter decided to attack, the Burgundians had got about two-thirds of their force ashore, some 4,000 men, and had formed them up in battle order on the dykes. The English and their Zeeland allies were drawn up in the classic English battle formation, with the archers at the wings. They advanced towards Philip's lines in perfect step, letting out a fearsome yell and sounding trumpets and bugles. The Burgundians were the larger of the two armies and had the advantages of the defensive and the higher ground. They had placed about a thousand crossbowmen of the allied towns in front of their lines. But although these men held their fire until the enemy was well within range, the bolts made no impression on the steel helmets and cuirasses of the English men-at-arms. They might as well have shot rotten apples at them, an eyewitness remarked. The English longbows rapidly scattered the Dutch townsmen and forced them to withdraw to the rear. However, the heavily armoured French and Flemish men-at-arms, who were standing in line behind them, counter-attacked with devastating effect. They drove Fitzwalter's men back until their lines broke and they turned and fled. It was all over very quickly. The pursuit was left to the lightly armed Dutch townsmen. They killed indiscriminately.

Some of the defeated army managed to escape across the sands and were picked up by the English ships anchored in the strait. They included Fitzwalter himself. He threw off his armour and cast his banner on the ground, where they were later found by the victors. Others were less fortunate. They drowned in the sea or the drainage canals or were chased along the dykes and cut down in their hundreds. When the killing was over, Gloucester Herald came before the Duke of Burgundy wearing his gorgeous brocade tunic embroidered with Humphrey of Gloucester's arms and accompanied by the herald of Lord Fitzwalter. He reported the fate of the men-at-arms. All dead, he announced. And the archers? All but 300. The prisoners included Jan van Heemstede and some 200 Englishmen. The battle of Brouwershaven, fought in a distant corner of northern Europe by a private army, was rarely remembered in later years, but it had lessons to teach. It was a striking demonstration of the power of the longbow even at this late stage in its development, and of the excellence of modern plate armour. The only notable casualty on the Burgundian side was killed by an arrow in the eye, because he was not wearing his helmet.[59]

The Duke of Bedford arrived at Westminster in January 1426 with an ambitious agenda. He wanted to put an end to the vendetta between Henry Beaufort and the Duke of Gloucester. He wanted to repair relations with the Duke of Burgundy after two abortive attempts by English armies to prise the inheritance of Jacqueline of Bavaria from his grasp. And he had to persuade the political community to recognise the war in France as an English commitment, not just a foreign adventure of the house of Lancaster. Some councillors were already wondering whether it was worth carrying on the fight for the treaty provinces of France. Once it became clear that unending war was the price of keeping them, would Henry V himself not have contented himself with Normandy?[60]

On 18 February 1426, Parliament opened in the unfamiliar surroundings of the great hall of Leicester castle. The midlands town had been chosen because it was an important centre of Lancastrian power, far away from the London mob and the influence of the Duke of Gloucester. But the threat of violence was never far beneath the surface, even in Leicester. The peers came with their crowds of unruly and partisan retainers, expecting trouble. Members of the two houses had to be reminded to leave their swords and knives in their lodgings but responded by bringing in clubs hidden 'in their necks' and stones 'in their bosoms and their sleeves'. The Duke of Gloucester sulked in his quarters. Vexed by being supplanted in what he saw as his own government, he had declined to attend either of the preparatory meetings of the council to discuss his dispute with Beaufort unless the Chancellor was first dismissed, a demand which was rejected out of hand. News from the continent darkened his mood. The cardinal commissary charged with examining Jacqueline's case in Rome had recently pronounced her marriage to Humphrey to be adulterous and void. This was a serious setback although not a conclusive one, since the final verdict was reserved to the Pope himself. The news was quickly followed by the first reports of the destruction of Fitzwalter's army at Brouwershaven.[61]

The issue between Gloucester and Beaufort called for all of Bedford's reserves of tact. Gloucester had prepared a long list of charges against the Chancellor, including some extravagant allegations of treason dating back to the previous reign. Beaufort submitted a detailed written response. Both rivals were pressured into submitting the dispute to the judgment of a committee of councillors. On 12 March 1425 the child-King was brought into the hall to hear the committee's judgment pronounced by the Archbishop of Canterbury. Beaufort was exonerated from all of Gloucester's charges and Gloucester had to make a public statement acknowledging the fact. The two men were ordered to 'clasp each other by the hand as a sign and proof of the complete and steadfast love and affection to be maintained between them'. But in reality Gloucester had won. Beaufort was made to resign the chancellorship and was permitted to withdraw from the council to go abroad on pilgrimage. By way of compensation, he was allowed to accept the offer of a cardinal's hat which Henry V had required him to refuse a decade earlier.[62]

The vendetta of Gloucester and Beaufort diverted attention from the vital question of the level of English support for the war in France. The immediate problem was the persistent refusal of the House of Commons to recognise the scale of the financial challenge involved. In 1422 and again in 1425, Parliament had authorised further government borrowing against future tax revenues but had voted no new taxes from which the borrowing could be repaid. At the same time the government's permanent revenues were under pressure. The customs revenues had been badly affected by the dispute between Gloucester and Philip the Good, which sharply depressed the volume of trade. English merchants had been arrested in the towns which Philip controlled in Holland and Zeeland, while Flemish ships and cargoes had been seized in England. The expeditionary armies sent to France in 1424 and 1425 had been funded by borrowing, but borrowing on this scale without fresh sources of revenue was unsustainable for more than a short period. In the autumn of 1425, the flow of loans stopped. For the first time since the King's accession, no expeditionary army from England was planned for 1426.

The Duke of Bedford was furious. Unless a fresh Parliamentary subsidy was granted, he declared, he would refuse to return to France or accept responsibility for the defence of the young King's interests there. The Lords called for a report on the state of the government's finances. The records of the Exchequer were brought up from Westminster to enable the Treasurer, John Stafford Bishop of Bath and Wells, to present it. The Commons were presumably dissatisfied, for Stafford, who had struggled to contain the deficit for the past three years, refused to bear the burden any longer and resigned his office. A fresh report was presented to Parliament by his successor Sir Walter Hungerford in May. The Commons were still unmoved. They declined to grant a subsidy. All that they would do was authorise the government to borrow another £40,000 for up to a year.[63]

On the strength of this decision the Earl of Warwick was commissioned in July 1426 to raise 800 men in England, the smallest expeditionary army to date. But the borrowing campaign which was supposed to fund it was a failure. The council could no longer rely on Henry Beaufort for loans after his withdrawal from the government.

The other large lender, the Corporation of London, made a small cash gift, but that was all. The Italian mercantile community took their cue from the Corporation. In desperation, the council resorted to a device last used by Henry V in the crisis of 1421. They appealed to the public, hoping to close the deficit with a large number of small loans. Commissioners were appointed for each county with instructions to summon 'the better sort of persons' before them and call on them to lend money to the King in his hour of need. In the event, less than £4,400 was borrowed, and of this, the county commissioners accounted for barely a quarter. The variety of excuses related in their returns spoke volumes about the declining enthusiasm for the war since 1421. Most pleaded poverty. In Norfolk and Northamptonshire men pointed out that they had not yet been repaid their loans to Henry V. In East Anglia, they protested that their goods had been seized in Holland and Zeeland. In Berkshire and Oxfordshire, twenty-two men turned up in answer to the commissioners' summonses, but not a single one of them would lend. Many of the 'better sort' failed to turn up at all.[64]

To get money for the army that he planned to bring with him when he returned to France, Bedford was obliged to stop the payment of other expenses of government. The main victim of these forced economies was the garrison of Calais. In May 1426, all payments from English revenues to the Treasurer of Calais were suspended. They were not resumed until nearly a year later. There was a similar squeeze on payments for the defence of Gascony. As a result, some £18,000 in cash built up at the Exchequer. It was used to pay the advances of Warwick's army, which sailed for France at the end of August 1426 and the 1,200 men that Bedford eventually took to France with him in the following March. The protests of the garrison of Calais were fobbed off with an assignment of the first instalment of the ransom of King James of Scotland, a highly uncertain debt which was less than their due and already in arrears.[65]

Parliament was dissolved on 1 June 1426, and the council returned to Westminster. The Duke of Bedford had hoped to go back to France at this point. In fact, he was detained in England for another ten months by unfinished business, financial and political. Foremost among these was the need to contain the activities of his brother. Jacqueline of Bavaria, the 'battle-hardened lady' as an admiring Jean de Waurin called her, had succeeded in holding her own in Holland throughout the months of crisis in England. The town of Alkmaar and the whole of the surrounding maritime province of Kennemerland in northern Holland came over to her. With the assistance of the Kennemers, her forces laid siege to Haarlem, one of the leading Cod towns of Holland, where Philip's lieutenant Roland van Uitkerke held out in increasingly straitened circumstances. The army of relief that Roland's son brought from Flanders was wiped out at a second battle of Alphen. Philip the Good was obliged to return to Holland with a fresh army in July to restore the situation. Meanwhile in England Bedford obstructed any attempt to send help to Jacqueline. The Duke of Gloucester bided his time. 'Let my brother govern as him lust while he is in this land,' he said, 'for after his going over into France I will govern as me seemeth good.'[66]

While Bedford did his best to repair England's strained alliance with Burgundy, the Duke of Brittany and his brother the Constable made their most determined attempt yet to disrupt it. At about the end of July John V appointed an embassy, to be led by Jean de Malestroit, to do a grand tour of the principal courts, starting with the Dauphin's, then visiting the Duke of Savoy in Geneva and finally appearing before the Duke of Burgundy in the Low Countries. Jean de Malestroit's mission opened a winter of intensive diplomacy, whose object was to persuade Philip the Good to abandon the English alliance and join forces with the Dauphin and the Duke of Brittany against the English.[67]

Richemont and his advisers had a large part in the drafting of Malestroit's instructions. They recited all the old arguments which had failed to move Philip before. But they added a startling new one. John V claimed to have discovered that the English had been plotting to assassinate Philip in the interest of the Duke of Gloucester. This allegation was supported by a dossier containing what were said to be original documents of the Regent, the Duke of Gloucester and the Earl of Suffolk. The story which these documents told was an elaborate fantasy. It was alleged that in the autumn of 1424, when Gloucester was embarking on his conquest of Hainaut, the English were concerned about the imminent marriage of Philip the Good to Bonne d'Artois. She was thought to be hostile to England and a firm ally of the Dauphin, who would push Philip to turn his arms against his erstwhile allies. Philip, so the story went, had to be stopped before this happened. The original idea, which was said to have been suggested by the Duke of Gloucester, was that he should be arrested when he next came to Paris, and carried off as a prisoner to England. According to this document, the Duke of Bedford accepted the idea in principle, but thought that it was impractical to arrest Philip in the middle of Paris. The attempt would provoke an immediate rising in the capital. Better to kill him and make it look like an accident. Bedford proposed that Philip should be invited to a joust at which he could be felled by a 'subtle blow' that would not look deliberate. This idea was endorsed by Bedford's council in Rouen as well as the council at Westminster.

There were many implausible things about these documents, not least the fact that such things had been committed to writing at all. But they were circumstantially plausible. They referred to real events and gave accurate dates when the supposed authors were indeed in the places where they were said to be. Moreover, Suffolk's letters were apparently signed by him and sealed with his seal. In fact, the documents had been skilfully forged by a Norman squire, formerly in Suffolk's service, called Guillaume Benoît. Suffolk had shared many confidences with Benoît, which he used to give verisimilitude to the documents. He had also allowed him custody of his seal, which Benoît used to forge one of the documents and to authenticate blanks that were later used to forge others. Benoît's motive was money. He had hawked the documents around to various Burgundian officials in search of a buyer. Eventually, he obtained an introduction to Arthur de Richemont, who promised him a handsome reward for his pains. Richemont knew that the documents were forgeries. He and his closest advisers even suggested 'improvements' to one of them and used one of the blanks to create another. John V and his Chancellor, however, appear to have been genuinely taken in. They agreed that Benoît should accompany Jean de Malestroit to the Duke of Burgundy to vouch for their contents.[68]

Jean de Malestroit arrived at the Dauphin's court at Mehun-sur-Yèvre in August 1426 to unfold his mission. The Dauphin was enthusiastic. So was the Duke of Savoy, whose representatives joined Malestroit at Mehun some weeks later. Charles summoned a meeting of the Estates of Languedoil, whose main business was to consider the plan. According to the report of the representatives of the city of Tours, those present enthusiastically supported it. They believed that a reconciliation with Philip the Good was the only way out of the unending cycle of tax exhaustion and looting by unpaid soldiers.

Charles nominated Jean de Malestroit as his own ambassador, and appointed four men, including a councillor and the Berry Herald, to accompany him on his mission.[69]

While Jean de Malestroit was on his way to the court of Savoy at Geneva, the Constable and the Count of Clermont were meeting the Marshal of Burgundy Jean de Toulongeon and his fellow commissioners at Bourbon-Lancy and then at Moulins, the capital of the Dukes of Bourbon. It was the latest of the regular series of conferences called to review and extend the regional truces between the Dauphin and the Duke of Burgundy. But at its conclusion, Clermont and Richemont delivered a 'remonstrance' to their Burgundian opposite numbers, to be passed on to Philip personally. Richemont, they declared, had accepted the office of Constable of France with Philip's consent on the understanding that if he succeeded in banishing the men responsible for the murder of his father, the Duke would make his peace with the Dauphin. He, Richemont, had been as good as his word. The current position was that all of Charles's councillors and subjects wanted a reconciliation between the two branches of the Valois dynasty. Only Philip's agreement was wanting. When Jean de Malestroit reached Geneva, these arguments were seconded by the Duke of Savoy, who added his own representatives to the growing diplomatic train following the Chancellor of Brittany.[70]

One of the hazards of medieval diplomacy was that events tended to move faster than ambassadors, especially if they were bishops or other great lords whose status called for a large entourage and a stately pace of travel. Jean de Malestroit did not reach the march of Flanders until the end of January 1427. By this time, the military pressure on John V had intensified. The Earl of Salisbury had been replaced as the sector commander in the west by the Earl of Warwick. Warwick was a masterful politician who had been Henry V's right-hand man for five years. He was probably the only adjutant that Bedford ever had who matched his own intelligence or his political skills. The truce on the march of Brittany which John V had agreed in March 1426 expired in June. English raids into Brittany, mounted from Saint-James de Beuvron and their fortresses in Maine, resumed with devastating effects. As winter drew in, a human catastrophe was in the making on the Breton march. Walled towns like Vitré were overwhelmed by refugees. The main hospital of the town no longer had revenues to support its mission or food to hand out to the crowds of beggars and wounded men outside its doors. Much of the border area east of Rennes had to be exempted from castle guard because the fit males were all dead or prisoners of the English or else had fled to more secure areas. The Duke's officers in the region reported that no one had ever experienced such a situation in the memory of man. It was the beginning of a new and sombre period in the history of the Breton marches, when they shared the destruction and desolation which had become the common fate of other march regions of France. Over the following years the northern sector of the march lost between half and three-quarters of its population.[71]

In desperation, the Duke of Brittany decided to try for another truce with the English. He made common cause with Yolande of Anjou, who was as worried as he was. If Brittany collapsed into the arms of the English, the domains of the house of Anjou would no doubt be next. John V and Yolande worked on a joint approach to the English. They had in mind something very similar to the arrangement which they had jointly made with Henry V at the end of 1417, after an earlier string of defeats. They planned to ask for a regional truce. Under this proposal, a vast expanse of western France comprising the duchies of Brittany and Anjou, what was left of the county of Maine and the whole of Touraine, would become effectively neutral. The idea was supported by the Duke of Savoy and by the provincial Estates of both Anjou and Touraine. That such a thing should have been contemplated by the chief princely supporter on the Dauphin's council and the mother of his Queen was some indication of the parlous state of the kingdom of Bourges. In the end, they were wasting their time, because the Earl of Warwick made it clear that a truce would not be good enough. He wanted the complete submission of Brittany. In December 1426, he called on John V to return to the English alliance and renew his homage to Henry VI. The Duke's response was to play for time. He would make his own proposals in due course, he said. He would send an embassy to Paris, and another to Westminster. Meanwhile, John V piled the pressure onto the Duke of Burgundy to come to his aid. The war damage on the eastern marches of Brittany was more than he could bear, he said. Unless Philip committed himself soon to joining his alliance with the Dauphin and taking active steps to support him, he would have to make the best deal he could with the English.[72]

It was not until the beginning of March 1427 that Jean de Malestroit's swollen diplomatic cortege was finally received by the

Duke of Burgundy. They found him at Dordrecht in Holland. Philip was unimpressed by both the number of ambassadors and the intensity of the clamour. Apart from the alleged English plot, he had heard all their arguments before. His advisers saw through Benoît's forgeries in no time. Their author was arrested and thrown into prison. Philip's substantive response to the ambassadors' message is not recorded, but it was evidently unhelpful. He declined to follow the Duke of Brittany into the Dauphin's camp or to commit himself to any particular course of action. As for the unhappy Benoît, he was later taken to Flanders in Philip's baggage train and shut in the cells of the ducal castle at Lille. There he confessed everything, revealing the full extent of Richemont's duplicity. The failure of Jean de Malestroit's mission was a decisive moment. It left the Duke of Brittany with no alternative but to make his peace with the English on the best terms that he could get. The Dauphin's ministers for their part were disheartened by Philip's response and lost interest in negotiating with him. The next peace conference organised by the Duke of Savoy was due to open at Geneva in March. Charles's ministers did not even bother to send a delegation.[73]

In the new year, the Earl of Warwick assembled the largest field army that the English had yet deployed on the Breton march: 600 men-at-arms and 1,800 archers. The focus of both sides' attention was the great border fortress of Pontorson, south of Mont-Saint-Michel. Richemont had partially dismantled its defences a year before, but then thought better of it and installed a mixed force of Bretons, French and Scots among the ruins, commanded by one of his Breton lieutenants, Jean de Rostrenen. He carried out some repairs and turned the place into a base for raids into Lower Normandy and Maine. The whole venture was dogged by misfortune. Jean de Rostrenen was captured along with a large part of his force in the course of a raid against the English garrison of Avranches. The garrison seriously considered abandoning the fortress to the English. But Richemont urged them to stay and promised to bring fresh troops from the Loire to reinforce them. Bertrand de Dinan, lord of Châteaubriand, who succeeded Rostrenen as captain, called for volunteers to hold the town until Richemont arrived. Almost all the garrison volunteered apart from the Scots, who thought the place indefensible and left. Their misgivings proved to be entirely justified.

At the end of February 1427, the Earl of Warwick arrived before the walls of Pontorson. The defenders fought a valiant but hopeless defence against overwhelming odds. On 17 April 1427, when the siege had been in progress for some seven weeks, a large force under the command of Jean de la Haye tried to ambush an English food convoy on the coast road east of Mont-Saint-Michel. Although La Haye's men outnumbered the English, they were routed with considerable losses. When the news of this disaster reached Pontorson the garrison sued for terms. They were allowed three weeks for relief. A relief operation would probably have been feasible, for there were two substantial armies within marching distance of Pontorson. Richemont was on the Sarthe with his army, about five days' march away. The Duke of Brittany had proclaimed the *arrière-ban* in his duchy, and was thirty miles away at Dinan, where his officers were mustering his own army. Richemont rode to Dinan to confer with his brother. He brought his principal captains with him, including John Stewart of Darnley and the Dauphin's newly promoted Marshal Jean de Brosse lord of Boussac. They were all keen to relieve the town. But John V would not hear of it. He had never wanted a major confrontation with the English on his border and he was averse to the risks of battle. He had also, by now, probably received Jean de Malestroit's report on the failure of his mission to the Duke of Burgundy. He decided to submit to the English.[74]

The Duke of Bedford left England towards the end of March 1427. He paused at Calais to witness a papal legate presenting a cardinal's hat to Henry Beaufort in the town church, and at Amiens to confer with John of Luxembourg and other French captains of his allegiance. On 5 April, he entered Paris. His first task when he got there was to complete the subjugation of the Duke of Brittany. On 28 April 1427, the Regent tightened the screw on John V. He granted all of the Duke's valuable possessions outside Brittany, most of which were in English-occupied areas, to the Earl of Salisbury. When Pontorson opened its gates to the Earl of Warwick a few days later, on 8 May, John V gave up the unequal struggle. His ambassadors came before the Duke of Bedford to enquire on what terms the English were prepared to cease hostilities. Bedford told them that John would have to reinstate the agreements which John had made at Amiens in 1423. An oath to abide by the treaty of Troyes would have to be sworn not just by the Duke himself but by his brother Richard Count of Étampes, both of his sons and all the leading magnates and towns of Brittany represented in the duchy's Estates. John was to do homage to Henry VI in person within three months of the King's first appearance in his French kingdom. On 3 July 1427, these terms were accepted by John's ambassadors. The treaty was sealed by the Regent in Paris on the same day. Bedford's commissioners carried it back to Brittany to present it to the Duke and the Estates of the duchy for ratification.[75]

The abject submission of the Duke of Brittany did not take long to reach the ears of the Dauphin's ministers. Towards the end of July 1427, a delegation from Chinon came before John V at Redon. Its leader was the Archbishop of Tours, Jacques Gélu. Gélu was a man to whom the Dauphin sometimes turned for advice, although he did not sit on his council. He was an eminent canon lawyer and an international ecclesiastical politician, a man of strong moral convictions who had once told a Pope to his face that the time had come for him to abdicate. He did not mince his words on this occasion. There had been reports, he said, that the Duke had abandoned his rightful King in his moment of need and had agreed to transfer his homage to his rival. John did not deny it. He had made his peace with the English, he explained, for two reasons. First, the promises that the Dauphin had made to him had not been honoured. This was presumably a reference to the arrangements agreed at Saumur to give him the decisive voice in the Dauphin's affairs. Secondly, he was 'not strong enough to carry the burden of so much war, now that the English were sitting at the very gates of his domains'. Gélu thought that these were trivial reasons by comparison with the demands of justice and reason. As far as John was concerned, he assumed that the die was cast. But there might still be a chance of persuading the Estates of Brittany. Gélu offered to go to Rennes, where they were about to meet, and to reason with them. In the event, he did not go to Rennes, perhaps because John would not allow him to. But he wrote an angry protest to be read out before them. It was one of the most eloquent and emotional statements ever made in support of the Valois cause. Their Duke, he told them, was set on a course which was 'ill-advised, underhand, unjust and neither honest nor honourable'. Had he ignored Brittany's history? Had he forgotten the ties of kinship that joined him to the French Crown? Had he overlooked the favour which earlier French monarchs had shown to his house? Was a Breton heart as hard as marble, that it could lightly pass over these things? Did it not trouble them to be passing on to future generations the indelible stain of treachery? 'To build your fortunes on the ruin of the coming generation may bring you some short-lived advantages,' he wrote, 'but it is as clear as the brightness of the midday sun and the darkness of a moonless night that it is not an honourable thing that you are doing but a badge of shame.' His words fell on deaf ears. The Duke, he reported to the Dauphin, was 'stiff and inflexible in the face of all my protests'.[76]

After Gélu had left Brittany the Estates ratified John V's acts under the eyes of the Duke of Bedford's commissioners. The Duke's brother and two sons swore the oath that Bedford had demanded of them, together with five bishops, seven cathedral chapters, three towns and thirty-four lay magnates. It is clear that despite the show of assent, Breton society was fractured, especially in the French-speaking regions of the east which had traditionally supported the Valois monarchy. Some significant figures, like the lord of Retz, stayed away. Others, like the lord of Beaumanoir, swore the oath but were soon found fighting in the Dauphin's cause. The heir to the great viscounty of Rohan, whose family had been pillars of the royalist cause during the Breton civil wars of the previous century, formally recorded before a notary that he had sworn under duress. He would not regard himself as bound once the present crisis had passed, he said. His father, the old viscount, would not swear even on these terms. He registered a formal protest against his son's failure to stand up to the Duke's 'terrible persuasiveness'. A year later, the Dauphin reckoned that there were still a few noble houses of Brittany that he could count on, including Retz and Rohan. But looking back on the 'desertion' of the Duke of Brittany, he regarded it as nothing less than a disaster. Without that, he declared, he would have reconquered most of the territory held by the English in France. This was a fantasy. It assumed that if John V had remained in the Dauphin's allegiance, he would have supplied thousands of experienced Breton soldiers that he did not have and whom the Dauphin could not have paid anyway.[77]

On 17 April 1427 occurred one of those transformative events which had so often disturbed the expectations of all the parties to the dispute over Jacqueline of Bavaria's inheritance. John IV Duke of Brabant died in Brussels at the age of twenty-three of a mysterious illness which had struck him a week before as he rode out of the city. His death greatly strengthened Jacqueline's legal position and weakened Philip's. The duchy of Brabant automatically passed to the dead man's brother Philip Count of Saint-Pol. But John's title to Hainaut, Holland and

Zeeland had been entirely derived from Jacqueline, and Philip the Good's powers in Holland and Zeeland were derived from John's. Once John was dead the government of all three counties reverted to her. Philip's lawyers devoted all their ingenuity to justifying Philip's continued control over her inheritance. They pointed out that Jacqueline's marriage to Humphrey was still void, even if her marriage to John of Brabant had ended with his death. They argued that unless she publicly acknowledged the fact, she was debarred from the government of her domains, which must be regarded as vacant. In that event, Philip considered that he himself, as Jacqueline's closest relative, was entitled to succeed. In the meantime, he would assume the government of all three territories as 'stakeholder' for whoever should prove entitled to them. Most of this was highly questionable in point of law. But that hardly mattered in the face of Philip's dominant political position in the region. A combined meeting of the Estates of Flanders, Picardy and Hainaut was summoned to Valenciennes in June. They were there, as everyone knew, to formalise what was expected by then to be a fait accompli. With Jacqueline herself tied down in Holland, the only resistance came from her mother, Margaret of Burgundy, and from the town of Mons. Margaret summoned a rival assembly in the hope of pre-empting the Duke. Mons despatched agents to Holland to discover what Jacqueline's own views were. Both initiatives were quickly snuffed out. Philip arrived at Valenciennes at the beginning of June accompanied by a large body of Burgundian magnates to watch over the proceedings of the Estates. They passed off very satisfactorily. All the representatives of Hainaut acknowledged Philip as their ruler including, in the end, those of Mons.[78]

From Gouda, Jacqueline protested against Philip's high-handed procedures. But her position was weak. Over the past eighteen months, Philip the Good had conducted three extended campaigns in Holland and Zeeland. He had deployed troops from all his other dominions in addition to the nobility and the urban levies of the Cod party. He had deployed fleets chartered in Artois and Flanders and commandeered the ships of the northern territories. Between 1425 and 1428, he poured money into the conquest, by his own reckoning more than a million gold *saluts* (about £250,000 sterling). The siege of Haarlem, the only siege of a major Cod town that Jacqueline had attempted, had been broken the previous July. Kennemerland and Alkmaar had submitted to the Duke of Burgundy, paying a heavy indemnity. After withstanding two sieges, the island port of Zevenbergen had finally surrendered in April 1427. As a result Jacqueline had lost control of southern Holland and the whole of Zeeland and was reduced to fighting a rearguard action in the fastnesses of Utrecht and the Zuiderzee. Writing to the council at Westminster a few days before the Duke of Brabant's last illness, she declared that she 'could not hold out much longer without your help and my husband's'.[79]

Jacqueline's latest appeal to the English government was brought to them by one her closest advisers, Louis van Montfoort, one of the men who had engineered her first entry into Gouda two years before. Montfoort and his companions arrived at Westminster in about the middle of May 1427. The council was evidently embarrassed, by both the timing and the substance of Jacqueline's appeal. With Bedford and Beaufort out of the country, it would be necessary to face down the Duke of Gloucester's inevitable demands for support. They decided to put off a decision while they consulted Bedford and Philip the Good in France. Their chosen emissaries were William Alnwick Bishop of Norwich and the soldier-administrator John Lord Tiptoft. In Paris, the Duke of Bedford was dismayed by the sudden return of an issue which he thought had gone away. He left Paris in a great hurry to confer with the Duke of Burgundy. The two men met at Lille on 6 June and after a week of discussion they rode together to Arras to meet Alnwick and Tiptoft. The upshot was a compromise. They agreed that Jacqueline could be rescued from Holland and brought back to safety in England. But she was to have no help to recover her inheritance. On 23 June, the council at Westminster agreed to lend Gloucester 9,000 marks (£6,000) on strict conditions. It was to be spent exclusively on raising troops to rescue Jacqueline and on paying her existing garrisons. On no account was any of it to be spent on new conquests or other offensive operations in Holland. To ensure that these conditions were observed, the money was to be paid to two special treasurers, who were directed to disburse it for authorised purposes only.[80]

The council had done their duty by the Duke of Bedford. But they clearly felt that their decision did not measure up to the personal tragedy of Jacqueline of Bavaria. They wrote a remarkable letter to Bedford. They pointed out that the English people had taken Jacqueline's cause to their hearts. She had undoubtedly suffered a grave injustice. She was also a dedicated ally of England who had remained loyal to the Duke of Gloucester through thick and thin. She had been through extraordinary hardships and had now thrown herself on their mercy. It was time, they said, for Bedford to recognise these things and prevail on the Duke of Burgundy to stop the course of 'oppression, usurpation and insult' on which he seemed to be set. It was hard to disagree with any of this, but Bedford was unmoved. Writing to them from Corbeil at the end of July 1427, he took exception to their criticisms of Philip's behaviour. He accused them of taking Gloucester's side without having heard Philip's case. He reminded them that their first duty was to the child-King. Philip was a great and powerful prince. His support was the foundation of the dual monarchy and offered the only prospect of peace. By comparison the interests of Jacqueline of Bavaria were of no importance to England. Bedford sent a copy of this correspondence to Philip. Doubtless, he was satisfied.

The Duke of Gloucester was not. He declined to accept the restrictions that the council had imposed on him and attracted a number of powerful allies to his cause. They included the Earl of Salisbury, who arrived in London from France in the middle of July, ostensibly to support the Duke of Bedford's demands for a more generous level of support for the war in France. Gloucester began to look about for other sources of support which might trump the hostility of the Westminster council and the Duke of Bedford. One was the city of London. Another was Parliament, which was due to meet in October. In the meantime, he began once more to recruit troops in England. His efforts enjoyed the active support of the Earl of Salisbury, who may even have contemplated commanding Gloucester's army himself. What Bedford thought of the behaviour of his emissary is not recorded but can be imagined. Two agents were promptly sent to England to reason with Humphrey. They brought with them a personal letter, calling on him to show some loyalty to the young King whose heritage he was duty-bound to protect. 'Listen now to the advice of those who wish you well,' Bedford wrote to his brother. His own advice could not have been more blunt: 'If you care for the greatness of our family and the reputation of your name,' he wrote, 'you must stop trying to achieve your objectives by force and try the way of consensus and peace.'[81]

In the event it was Jacqueline and not Humphrey who looked to the way of consensus and peace. In September 1427, after receiving the report of Louis van Montfoort, she sent word to Philip the Good in Flanders that she was ready to negotiate. A short truce was agreed so that their councillors could meet. Philip sent Hughes de Lannoy, who knew his mind well and had recently discussed the same issues with both Bedford and Gloucester. He was accompanied by another experienced diplomat, John lord of Roubaix. It became clear at their first meetings how little Jacqueline had to bargain with. Philip's councillors did not waste time with the legal arguments which decorated their master's public statements. He did not dispute her legal title to the three counties, they told her. But he regarded the Duke of Gloucester as his mortal enemy, her marriage to him as disreputable and the prospect of England becoming a power in his back yard as intolerable. If she wanted to recover possession of her domains, she would have to repudiate her marriage and her alliance with England and agree never to allow her domains to pass under anyone else's control. Jacqueline rejected these terms. She had not yet given up hope of English support. Knowing that the council at Westminster was unwilling to intervene and that Bedford was hoping for some kind of compromise settlement, she sent her private secretary Jean Grenier to England with a final appeal. Perhaps, she suggested in her instructions, her earlier emissaries had not been men of sufficient status. Perhaps they had failed to convey the true awfulness of her situation. There was no compromise peace to be had, she said, for she was not willing to repudiate Humphrey or to do a deal with Philip the Good on his terms. But unless she received armed support urgently, she was unlikely to be offered anything better. What she needed now, she said, was 'not conferences or ambassadors but an army worthy of the name and strong enough to defeat her enemies'.[82]

Philip the Good responded to Jacqueline's defiance by reopening the war. He returned to Holland at the end of September 1427 to begin his fourth campaign there in the space of two years. The campaign, which was intended to complete the conquest once and for all, was laborious and the results disappointing. Much of the autumn was taken up with the long siege of Amersfoort in the territory of Utrecht. An assault on the town, directed by Philip in person, failed with heavy casualties. The floating blockhouse with which he tried to blockade the town's river outlet to the Zuiderzee was battered by Jacqueline's artillery and then carried away by ice floes.[83]

At Westminster, Parliament opened on 13 October 1427. The Duke of Gloucester was determined to get Parliamentary support for the despatch of an army to Holland, outflanking the council in a forum where his views and his eloquence would count for more. The Duke of Bedford sent two emissaries to put his own views to the peers. A negotiated solution to the crisis in Holland, they argued, was now the only possible course. In spite of the eloquence of Jacqueline's secretary and a 'lamentable' letter addressed by her to both houses, that view seems to have been accepted by the English political community. All Gloucester's pent-up resentments against the conciliar system of government which had been imposed on him by the Lords in 1422 now came to the surface. He referred to his earlier demand to be recognised as Regent and the learning that his advisers had deployed in support of it. He called on the Lords to revisit the issue and redefine his powers on a broader basis. The Lords were unenthusiastic. They deferred the question and turned to other matters. Eventually, on 3 March 1428, they rejected his demands in their entirety. They told him that he would have to be satisfied with what authority he already had. In Parliament, they added, he had no status except as a peer like any other. Gloucester's plans for an invasion of Holland were dropped. For a time, he clung to the more limited plan proposed by the council to rescue Jacqueline and bring her back to England, but eventually abandoned even that idea.[84]

The final act of Jacqueline's five-year adventure was written in Rome by Pope Martin V. On 9 January 1428, he declared that her marriage to John of Brabant had been valid and her marriage to Humphrey void. Philip the Good, whose agents had conducted the litigation in Rome on behalf of the Duke of Brabant, was the real party interested. His satisfaction was recorded by the accounts clerks who totted up the cost. 'By the Pope's definitive judgment, my lord has now achieved his objective,' they wrote against the relevant entry. The Duke of Gloucester thought so too. His interest in Jacqueline vanished. Within weeks of the Pope's decision, he married his mistress, Eleanor Cobham.[85]

Jacqueline could probably have continued the fight for a time. Her long personal struggle against the Duke of Burgundy was in reality a Dutch civil war which had been intermittently fought for decades before she assumed the leadership of the Hook party. But although she still had substantial support among the nobility and a powerful ally in the prince-bishop of Utrecht, she controlled none of the great commercial towns of Holland and Zeeland except for Gouda. She had lost her fleet. She had never enjoyed administrative control of the two counties, which was securely in the hands of Philip the Good and his

Flemish governors and captains. A militant Burgundian author gave it as his opinion that an English army supported by a fleet of shallow-draft ships could have overrun the whole land. Philip himself may have taken the same view. But the political and logistical problems were too great. In England, Jacqueline was now no more than a stirring symbol, 'beloved so entirely through all the land', as John Lydgate sang in his *Complainte for my Lady of Gloucester*. This was hyperbole, but it had a real resonance in public opinion. The mayor and aldermen of London petitioned that she be given some financial support, and themselves raised at least 1,000 marks for Jacqueline's cause. A delegation of women from the main food market put on their best clothes and appeared before Parliament to criticise her treatment at the hands of the Duke of Burgundy. They took a swipe at the Duke of Gloucester for failing to rescue her and then marrying another woman. The Commons themselves made it a condition of the subsidy that proper provision should be made for an ally 'that liveth in so great dolour and heaviness, and hath so lamentably written to our said sovereign lord and to all the estates of this noble royaume'.[86]

On 3 July 1428, Jacqueline was forced to sign the treaty of Delft with Philip the Good. The treaty formally recognised her title to the three counties which she had inherited from her father but emptied it of any content. Their government was to be vested in Philip himself, together with all of Jacqueline's castles. The revenues of the territories were assigned to him apart from an allowance for her maintenance. If she married again without Philip's consent, the sovereignty of her domains was to be forfeited and transferred to him unconditionally. In fact, Philip had no intention of allowing her to marry again, for any child of hers would have succeeded to her domains in priority to himself. When, some years later, she secretly married the Dutch nobleman Frank van Borselen, her husband was arrested and she was forced to abdicate. Once destined to be Queen of France and Countess of Hainaut, Holland and Zeeland, Jacqueline died almost landless in October 1436 in the austere thirteenth-century castle of Teylingen, whose ruins still tower over the flat landscape north of Leiden. She was thirty-five, a young woman even in a world where old age came early.[87]

CHAPTER V

The Road to Orléans, 1427–1429

In February 1427 the Dauphin's favourite Pierre de Giac, who had served as his chief counsellor for the past eighteen months, was murdered. The authors of the deed were a group of noblemen led by the Constable Arthur de Richemont, the Poitevin nobleman Georges de la Trémoille and the Gascon Charles of Albret. All three were prominent members of the Dauphin's council, and their act is said to have been approved by most of the others, including Yolande of Anjou. On 8 February, while the court was residing at Issoudun in Berry, La Trémoille entered Giac's bedroom at dawn with a company of soldiers. The Dauphin, who was sleeping in a room nearby, was woken by the noise. His guard arrived at the scene to find out what was happening. 'Go away,' the Constable told them, 'what we are doing is for the King's benefit.' Giac was taken down to the street below still in his nightgown. He was mounted on a horse and escorted to Richemont's castle at Dun-sur-Auroy, south of Bourges. There he confessed, probably under torture, to a catalogue of crimes including the murder of his first wife and the embezzlement of the proceeds of the taxes recently granted by the Estates. Once the interrogators had done their work, Giac was summarily sentenced to death. They fetched an executioner from Bourges, who tied him up in a sack and drowned him in the river Auron.[1]

The Dauphin's court was riven by feuds, jealousies and political faction-fighting which frequently erupted into violence and gang warfare. An observer writing in 1425 was struck by the presence in every doorway and corner of gossips, backbiters and cabals, promoters of 'noise and conflict'. Pierre de Giac had certainly been profligate with the Dauphin's revenues. But his real offence was to have monopolised the Dauphin's favour, marginalised other councillors and then added insult to injury by slapping them down in council and treating them with overt disdain. For their part, the councillors found it convenient to blame him for disappointing the high hopes that they had entertained at the time of Louvet's disgrace. Writing to his supporters in Lyon, Richemont said that Giac had simply continued the vices of Louvet and his gang. The Dauphin's opinion was not consulted. He looked on with furious impotence as the plotters ignored him. He was apparently unaware, said Richemont, of Giac's 'disloyalty and treasons', and for some weeks refused to receive his murderers. Giac was not the only victim. Within six weeks of his death the Count of Clermont, one of the Dauphin's principal councillors and captains, seized the Chancellor Martin Gouge, whom he had identified as an enemy, and held him for ransom for several months. Few incidents said as much about the poisonous atmosphere around the Dauphin. It provoked outrage in the Parlement of Poitiers and angry debate in the country, but the Dauphin barely reacted. 'Have I not witnessed in my own lifetime,' remarked Jean Juvénal des Ursins years later, 'a bishop of Clermont . . . kidnapped by a prince of the blood royal and held for ransom without the King or his council or courts lifting a finger to stop them?'[2]

Once the dust had settled, the Dauphin looked around for someone else on whom he could depend. Giac was replaced as his First Chamberlain by Louis lord of Chalençon, one of the junior chamberlains, who was presumably nominated by Richemont and his allies. But before long he had been supplanted by a new royal favourite, the equerry Jean du Vernet, also known as Le Camus de Beaulieu. Like Giac, Vernet was a minor nobleman of Auvergne. He had begun his career at court as a protégé of the discredited Pierre Frotier, a fact which probably did him no harm in the Dauphin's eyes. Shortly, he began to sit in council. He was appointed as captain of Poitiers, Frotier's old job, which gave him oversight of the Dauphin's security when he was in the city. Vernet rigorously controlled access to the Dauphin, and once he felt secure in Charles's favour began to display all the generosity to friends and arrogance to rivals which had characterised his predecessors. The Berry Herald was not the only one to notice that Vernet had acquired 'more power over the King than it was his business to have'. Yolande of Anjou noticed it too. So did Richemont. He was 'worse than Giac', he complained. At the end of June 1427, after an unsatisfactory audience with the Dauphin, Richemont told Marshal Boussac to get rid of him. Vernet did not even have the travesty of a trial accorded to Giac. He was killed by a hit-squad of five armed men as he rode with a single companion through the meadows of the river Clain beneath the walls of Poitiers. One of them split open his skull with his sword. The Dauphin, seeing the companion returning alone with Vernet's riderless mule, knew at once what had happened. He ordered his guards to pursue the killers, but they had vanished. An investigation was ordered, which had little difficulty in identifying them. But they were never brought to justice.[3]

All of these appointments, which Richemont could have prevented, of men whom he ended up by hating, testified to his poor judgement of character. The same was true of the next man to serve as the Dauphin's chief minister. Georges de la Trémoille was destined to be Richemont's nemesis and the dominant figure in government for the next six years. He was forty-five years old when he became Charles VII's first minister. Like Pierre de Giac, indeed like Richemont himself, he had an ambiguous past with a foot in both of the princely camps that divided France. As a young man, he had served in the household of John the Fearless, who had made him First Chamberlain to Charles VI during the short-lived Burgundian régime of 1413. La Trémoille came over to the Dauphin's side in 1418, but doubts about his true loyalties persisted throughout his career. Everyone knew that he retained strong connections with the court of Burgundy. His younger brother, Jean de la Trémoille lord of Jonvelle, was one of Philip the Good's most influential councillors. The Constable had found Georges to be a useful confederate in the plot against Pierre de Giac and encouraged the Dauphin to employ him. With that strange and distant passivity with which Charles viewed all ministerial changes in these years, he hardly resisted. He merely warned the Constable that he would live to regret it. 'I know him better than you do,' he said. In spite of Charles's initial suspicion, he was intimidated by his new minister, who swiftly took control over every aspect of the administration, the first person to do so since Louvet's dismissal.[4]

La Trémoille's dominant instincts were a ready resort to violence and a passion for riches which was highly developed even by the venal standards of the Dauphin's court. He had made his fortune by marrying the immensely rich widow of John Duke of Berry, Jeanne de Boulogne, who had died in 1422 after years of maltreatment at her husband's hands. In 1427 La Trémoille astonished the court by marrying Catherine de l'Île-Bouchard, the widow of Pierre de Giac, whom he had murdered only five months before. This brought him the dead minister's ample movable assets and provoked strong suspicions that she had been his mistress and was privy to the plot. La Trémoille knew how to manage his money. In an age when cash was scarce and most noble fortunes were illiquid, he was cash rich. He was an active moneylender, lending large sums to the Dauphin and to many towns and individuals who had been ruined by the war, on good security and at rates of interest reported to be up to 100 per cent per annum. Moneylenders are rarely popular, and La Trémoille was no exception.[5]

Georges de la Trémoille has a poor historical reputation. French historians have never forgiven him for his coolness towards Joan of Arc in the later stages of her career. Philippe de Commynes, perhaps the shrewdest observer of the next generation, compared him to his English contemporary Warwick the Kingmaker. Both of them, he thought, illustrated the golden rule that if a favourite wanted to survive, he should be loved by his master, not feared. Some favourites served their master too well to be popular. In one sense La Trémoille served Charles VII well. He was clever, politically astute and hard-working. He was an effective administrator, the first since Jean Louvet. He understood better than most of Charles's councillors the limits of the kingdom's resources. His consistent advocacy of a reconciliation with the Duke of Burgundy was vindicated by subsequent events. But he had many faults. He was an unimaginative strategist. He was greedy and corrupt. He was a divisive figure, who made enemies easily and relentlessly pursued his vendettas, often with men who might have done good service to the King.[6]

The summer of 1427 can be seen in hindsight as the high point of the house of Lancaster's fortunes in France. Years later, in more troubled times, Bedford himself remembered it as a time when 'all things there prospered'. The threat to the English flank from Brittany had been neutralised. There were no notable enemy garrisons in Normandy, Picardy, Champagne or the Île-de-France. The road and river routes around the capital were clear. In the summer of 1426, the Lendit fairs had been held in their traditional site in the plain of Saint-Denis for the first time since 1418. Cherries sold at Les Halles for a ha'penny a pound and oats on the strands of the Seine for less than 10 sous a bushel, the lowest prices for over a decade.

The Duke of Bedford's return to France was marked by a spectacular coup which substantially completed this tale of good fortune. He appointed Sir John Talbot, who had accompanied him back to France, to replace Fastolf as military governor of Maine. Early in May, Talbot fell on the town of Laval on the west bank of the Mayenne. The barony of Laval belonged to the formidable dowager Anne, Dame de Laval, who was in the town at the time. When the English came over the walls, her nineteen-year-old son André lord of Lohéac fought a losing battle in the streets before withdrawing into the citadel with many of the inhabitants. The citadel had not been stocked for a siege and its defenders did not have much to bargain with. They surrendered after four days. They were allowed to leave in return for a collective ransom of 20,000 gold *écus* (£3,333). Shortly afterwards the Dame de Laval bought peace for the rest of the barony by agreeing to pay *pâtis*. The conquest of Maine was almost complete.[7]

The Regent met his principal commanders in Paris in the middle of May 1427 to decide upon the next steps. After five years passed in consolidating his hold on northern France, Bedford believed that the time had come to penetrate the Loire barrier and take the war to the heart of the kingdom of Bourges. The strategic challenge was to capture and hold a secure crossing of the river. That meant either the line of heavily fortified bridges at Ponts-de-Cé, in open country south of Angers, or else at least one of the four walled bridge-towns on the north bank of the river, at Orléans, Blois, Beaugency or Meung. The Regent had always favoured a western strategy, advancing to the Loire through Anjou. The advantages of this course were that it opened up the prospect of conquering the rich plain of Poitou, closing off the Dauphin's access to the Atlantic and linking Normandy and Gascony. The alternative was to attack the kingdom of Bourges further east. This was the preferred strategy of the Earls of Salisbury and Warwick and several of Bedford's French councillors. Their eyes were fixed on Orléans, a rich, populous and politically important city close to the administrative centres of the Dauphin's territory. There were logistical as well as political arguments for an attack on Orléans. The Paris–Orléans road was under English control to within twenty miles of the city. Heavy artillery pieces could be carried south by the river Loing, a tributary of the Seine which was navigable in the fifteenth century to within ten miles of the Loire and was controlled for most of its course by English garrisons. Sharp differences between the partisans of these two strategies were destined to complicate the conduct of the war for the next eighteen months.[8]

The main difficulty about the eastern strategy was the delicate position of Charles Duke of Orléans. Charles was the son of Louis of Orléans, the previous King's brother, whose murder by John the Fearless in 1407 had sparked off the civil wars of France. He had been captured at Agincourt at the age of twenty-one and had been held in various fortresses in England ever since, pouring out his heart in melancholy poems in French and English, many of them on the themes of captivity, loneliness and sexual frustration. Charles of Orléans was the highest-ranking prince of the French royal house after Charles VII and had been the heir presumptive to the throne until the birth of the Dauphin Louis in 1423. He remained an important political figure in France in spite of his long absence, a 'great and fell-witted man', as the council in England once described him. He maintained an active correspondence with French politicians from his prison and was kept in touch with events by a stream of visitors, officials and messengers. The English had always regarded their princely captives as political pawns and not just financial assets. They sedulously worked to turn them into subjects or allies as the price of their release. Charles of Orléans was the most valuable potential turncoat in their hands, given his proximity to the royal line, his network of political alliances in France and his strategically located domains. His appanage, one of the richest in France, comprised the whole of the duchy of Orléans together with the adjacent counties of Blois and Dunois. It included all four bridge-towns on the north bank of the middle Loire by which the English hoped one day to penetrate into the heartlands of the kingdom of Bourges.

It was commonly held that the laws of war protected the domains of a prisoner of war from attack by his captor. That well-travelled observer of the European scene Pope Pius II held that 'every man of honour thought it a base deed to attack the strongholds of a man whose person you have in your power'. In fact, the authority for this rule was uncertain, and the English had never accepted it. But in 1427 they had pragmatic reasons for wanting to spare the Duke's appanage. In his last will, Henry V had directed that Charles was not to be ransomed unless he adhered to the treaty of Troyes and acknowledged the right of the house of Lancaster to the Crown of France. In Henry's time, he had always refused to do this. But his position had begun to soften since the battle of Verneuil and the successive palace revolutions at the Dauphin's court.

The Duke of Orléans was now in his twelfth year of captivity and had begun to despair of ever recovering his liberty. He had become increasingly bitter about what he saw as his betrayal by the Dauphin and his ministers, who seemed to have abandoned him to his fate in England. While Bedford was in England, he arrived at an understanding with the Duke of Orléans. The terms are not recorded, but their general tenor can be inferred from subsequent events. The essence of it was that Charles's lands in the Loire valley would be protected from attack and he himself released from captivity. In return, he would do homage to Henry VI and use his political influence in France to organise support for a general peace on England's terms. Bedford was already engaged in discussions along these lines with another notable prisoner of war, the Duke of Bourbon. In March 1427, the English council had met over several days at Canterbury as Bedford waited to embark with his army for France. The Duke of Bourbon came into the council's presence and renewed the undertakings that he had given six years earlier to Henry V. Charles of Orléans was at Canterbury at about the same time, probably on the same business. Indeed, this may have been the occasion, recorded in a document executed by him some years later, when he formally recognised Henry VI as King of France. The agreements with these two prisoners, if they had been carried out, would have brought under Anglo-Burgundian control a solid block of territory comprising the whole of the middle and upper valley of the Loire from Blois to the mountains of Auvergne. The difficulty, as always, was to get the promises of prisoners living under constraint in England honoured by their representatives in France. Successive deals with the Duke of Bourbon had failed for this reason. But there was good reason to think that more could be expected of Charles of Orléans. He had no wife, children or siblings. His half-brother the Bastard of Orléans and his Chancellor Guillaume Cousinot, who managed his affairs in France, were no friends of England but were both wholly devoted to his interests.[9]

The military outlook was promising. The Duke of Bedford had brought with him from England an expeditionary army of 1,200 men, thus taking the payroll strength of the English army in France to at least 6,000. In addition, there were about 1,800 indigenous troops serving under John of Luxembourg. The Dauphin could muster only half of those numbers at best. But the outcome of the Regent's conference with his captains was a decision that stronger forces would be needed to force a crossing of the Loire. Bedford decided to send his best commander, the Earl of Salisbury, back to England to negotiate with Parliament. The hope was that the Earl's military reputation would persuade the Commons to vote a generous subsidy, the first in six years, to fund a larger than usual expeditionary army in 1428.

In the meantime, Bedford planned to secure advanced bases in preparation for a major campaign on the Loire. The Earl of Suffolk was put in command of 2,000 men, including the whole of the expeditionary army which Bedford had brought with him from England. His area of operations was carefully delimited. He was ordered to capture all towns and castles occupied by the enemy in a broad belt of territory north of the Loire, comprising the Vendômois, the Beauce, the Chartrain and the Gâtinais. However, he was expressly forbidden to operate in the domains of the Duke of Orléans. There were only three major enemy fortresses in the area assigned to Suffolk. One was Châteaudun, which was out of bounds because it was the capital of Charles's county of Dunois. The other two were Vendôme in the west, which was held by the companies of La Hire, and Montargis in the east, which belonged to the Constable and his wife. The original plan for 1427 was to open the campaign by besieging Vendôme, presumably in preparation for an attack on Anjou and the Ponts-de-Cé. Extensive preparations were made. An advance base was set up at Mondoubleau north of the town. Large quantities of artillery and stores were transported there. Special taxes for the conquest of Vendôme were negotiated with the main cities of Lancastrian France.[10]

Not everyone was content with these decisions, and about a month after they were made, they were abruptly changed. The preparations for the siege of Vendôme were abandoned. Instead, the principal target was to be Montargis, which had little strategic value except as a staging post on the way to Orléans. It is unclear who was responsible for the change of plan, but it was probably the Earl of Warwick, who was appointed to command the operation in place of the Earl of Suffolk. On 2 July 1427, Warwick's marshals mustered his men at Verneuil and they began their march east across the Beauce and the Gâtinais. On about 15 July, they arrived before Montargis. Meanwhile, however, the Earl of Suffolk was occupied in taking forward the arrangements which Bedford had made with the Duke of Orléans in England. Suffolk met the Bastard of Orléans at Orléans and on 16 July the two men agreed on a truce. The terms did not prevent the Duke's officers and subjects from fighting the English, but they protected Orléans and all the Duke's other domains in the Loire valley from attack. The instrument was sealed by the captains of all the principal towns of the appanage and proclaimed a few days later with much ceremony at Chartres by the heralds of the Dukes of Bedford and Orléans. It is hard to say what lay behind these contradictory moves. The answer probably lies in the complex and secretive dealings between the English government and the Duke of Orléans, which are only intermittently recorded in the surviving documents. The most plausible hypothesis is that the Regent hoped that Charles of Orléans would declare publicly for Henry VI, as the Duke of Bourbon had done, and allow his domains to be used as a highway into the kingdom of Bourges without the need to capture a bridge by force of arms.[11]

Montargis was not an easy place to surround, even for a relatively large army. The town stood in a marshy plain crossed by a lacework of intersecting watercourses formed by the branches of the Loing and its tributaries. A formidable circular keep stood on a high rock at its western end, dominating the surrounding country. To lay siege to the place, it was necessary to divide the English army into three parts, separated by water, thus exposing each part to the danger of being defeated in detail. This problem was only partly mitigated by the construction of temporary timber bridges over the main waterways. The Earl of Warwick established his headquarters in the walled enclosure of a Dominican convent east of the town. Suffolk rejoined the army and took the southern sector by the road to Gien. A third sector lay north and west of the castle, which was divided between Sir Henry Bisset and Suffolk's younger brother Sir John de la Pole. The English built bastides opposite the gates, dug trenches and made improvised field works around their positions. The height of the rock on which the castle was built made it a difficult target for artillery. But the English bombards did serious damage to the low-lying town, while their sappers began to undermine its walls. Neither town nor castle had been provisioned for a siege, and stocks of food soon fell to dangerously low levels. At some point in the first half of August, the defenders managed to get a message out warning the Dauphin that unless they were relieved soon, they would be forced to surrender.[12]

The English attack on Montargis caught the Dauphin's ministers unawares. La Trémoille was in the process of taking over the administration. The government was in disarray. The garrison, which was commanded by the Gascon captain Bouzon de Fages, was understrength. The Constable, who was the lord of the town, was far

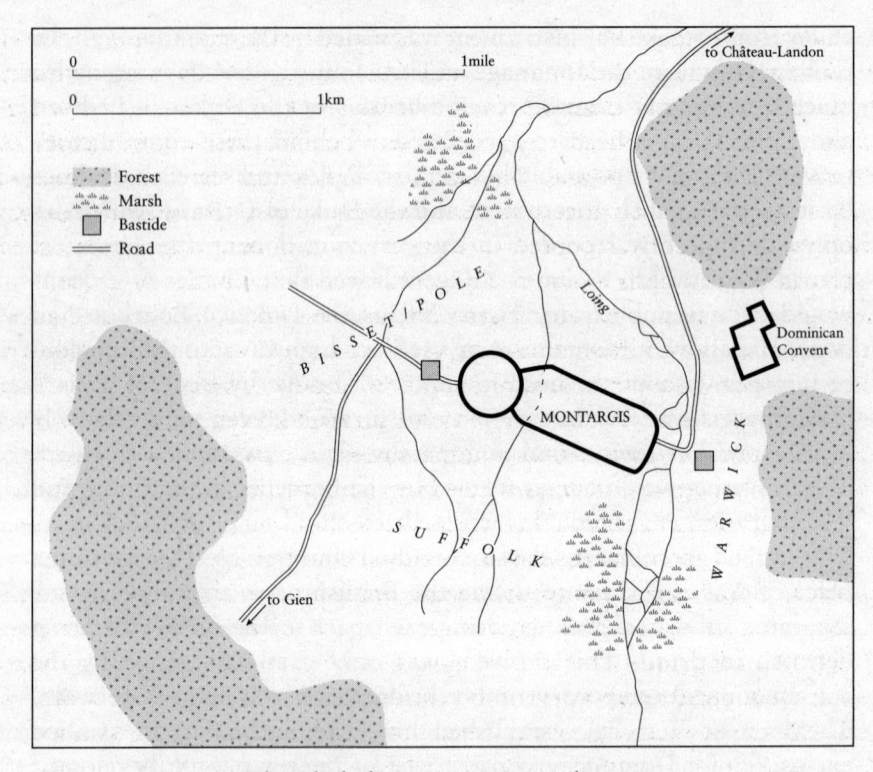

5 The relief of Montargis, September 1427

away at Chinon. He initially proposed a limited intervention to get reinforcements and supplies into the castle before the English arrived. This operation was entrusted to Jean Girard, the man who had been sent too late to reinforce Le Mans in 1425. He was also too late to help Montargis. His troops had to come from Niort in Poitou and by the time they reached Montargis the English were already building their siege lines. Lacking the numbers to attack them, Girard was forced to withdraw. Richemont now faced the difficult task of recruiting an army of relief on a much larger scale. The Bastard of Orléans had a number of troops in garrison in the Orléanais. They were commanded by Raoul de Gaucourt, an old officer of the house of Orléans who had recently returned from ten years' captivity in England. The only other troops immediately available were the personal retinues of the military officers, La Hire's companies at Vendôme, the Scots of Stewart of Darnley and the garrisons serving on the marches of Anjou and Maine. Richemont summoned them all to Gien on the Loire and then to Jargeau. A large quantity of victuals and other supplies was collected and loaded onto wagons. About 1,600 men mustered to escort the wagon train to Montargis. The Dauphin mortgaged one of his crowns to pay their wages. Richemont pawned his jewels to the moneylenders of Bourges. Then at the last moment the Constable got cold feet. The enterprise was too risky, he decided. Almost all of the Dauphin's permanent forces had been assigned to the operation. He could not afford to lose them in another Verneuil.

The Dauphin's exasperated councillors responded by taking the operation out of Richemont's hands and appointing the Bastard of Orléans to take command in his place. He was given the Master of the Royal Archers Jean Malet de Graville and the Gascon captain Guillaume d'Albret as his principal lieutenants. All the captains of Richemont's army, including La Hire, agreed to join them, except for Stewart of Darnley and Richemont himself. Command of what was left of the Scottish corps passed to the Ayrshire knight Hugh Kennedy of Ardstynchar, a veteran who had come over with the first army of Scotland in 1419. On 4 September 1427, the whole army crossed the bridge of Jargeau and made for Montargis, followed at a short distance by the supply train.[13]

Montargis is thirty-two miles east of Jargeau. Apart from clearings around the rare settlements, the whole route was covered by the dense forest of Orléans, which in the late middle ages was vastly more extensive than it is today. The Dauphinist army was able to approach Montargis unseen through the forest. Their task was made easier by the carelessness of the English. Pole and Bisset had posted scouts along the approaches to their lines, but for reasons which are unclear had recalled them. As a result, the French arrived unnoticed within a few miles of Montargis early on the morning of 5 September. La Hire and Hugh Kennedy rode ahead of the main body to reconnoitre the English positions. They were accompanied by members of the castle garrison who had stolen out at night to guide them. They found an unguarded gap in the field works behind Henry Bisset's corps. The army paused some two miles away as its leaders made their plans. They decided to attack through the gap. Between seven and eight o'clock in the morning the French burst out of the forest and charged the gap on horseback. The English were taken completely by surprise. There was a fierce fight around the opening, but the defenders were swept aside. Bisset was at the bastide in front of the west gate of the castle. The Bastard of

Orléans attacked the bastide, while La Hire made for Pole's command post. Pole fled the scene heading for Warwick's sector, taking much of his force with him. The rest of his men rallied but were quickly forced back towards the improvised bridge over the river Loing north of the castle. Pushed forward by those behind them, they struggled onto the bridge, which collapsed under their weight. The defenders of Montargis completed the disaster by opening the lock gates in the town, flooding the valley and causing the Loing to break its banks. Many of Pole's corps were drowned or trapped and killed on the banks of the river as they tried to escape. Around the bastide, Bisset and about 200 Englishmen were still fighting, but it was an unequal struggle. Bisset himself was captured and most of those around him were killed. Warwick rallied the troops stationed beyond the Loing, but by then the French had taken possession of the whole of the western sector of the English siege lines. Warwick challenged the Dauphinist commanders to a pitched battle. But they knew better than to risk battle against the hardened English veterans. The French held the field until nightfall, when the supply train emerged from the forest and was escorted through the western gate of the castle. Warwick took the realistic view that there was no longer any prospect of reorganising the siege and capturing the place. He and Suffolk gathered the survivors and marched away in good order that night, heading north up the valley of the Loing towards the nearest English garrison, which was twelve miles away at Château-Landon. Most of their artillery had been in Pole's sector of the siege and had to be abandoned to the enemy, along with the baggage and large stocks of food.[14]

The Dauphin and his councillors were elated by the first reports of the battle. These suggested that the English had lost 1,400 men killed or captured, three-quarters of their army, and that both earls might be among the casualties. The true figure is unknown but was certainly much lower. Only the sectors commanded by Pole and Bisset had been attacked, and many of Pole's men had been able to get away before the bridge collapsed. However, there was no doubt that the battle was a serious reverse. With Montargis in enemy hands, the English would not be able use the valley of the Loing to supply an army on the Loire in 1428. To complete their embarrassment, a few days before the relief of Montargis, the companies which La Hire had left behind in the Beauce had put an end to the other English project of 1427 by capturing the castle of Mondoubleau and all of the artillery stored there for a siege of Vendôme. That autumn, the Duke of Bedford found himself seriously short of artillery as a result of losses at Montargis and Mondoubleau, and wear and tear in other operations. He tried to collect enough bombards from the garrisons to attempt another siege of Montargis but eventually had to recognise that it could not be done. Four years later, the Dauphin would look back on it as the 'first and chief victory that we won over our enemies, and the beginning of the reconquest of the provinces which they had occupied'.[15]

The relief of Montargis made the reputation of the Bastard of Orléans, who had pressed the plan against Richemont's advice and then led the decisive cavalry charge that scattered the besiegers. John of Orléans had been a soldier from the age of fifteen and a councillor at seventeen. He had fought with distinction at Baugé. But he had been closely associated with his father-in-law Jean Louvet and had fallen into disgrace after Louvet's fall. The autumn of 1427 saw him reinstated on the council and granted 2,000 *livres* for his valour at Montargis. In the following years, he would become, along with La Hire, the leading figure in the Dauphinists' military revival. Just as the operation made the military reputation of the Bastard of Orléans, it destroyed that of Arthur de Richemont. The Constable's career had been marked by a string of failures. He never recovered from his refusal to support the one successful operation since his appointment. The aloofness of the Duke of Burgundy and the desertion of John V to the English destroyed what political value he ever had.[16]

'Power tolerates no colleagues', remarked Alain Chartier, that shrewd observer of the Dauphin's court. La Trémoille seized the opportunity offered by Richemont's indecision over Montargis to discredit him. He found a willing supporter in the Dauphin. After the bullying that Charles had endured at Richemont's hands and the murder of two of his favourites in succession, he had come to loathe his Constable. Richemont could not be dismissed from the Constableship, which was conventionally held for life. But he was removed from the important governorship of Berry in favour of La Trémoille and shouldered out of influence and power at court. He no longer had access to the Dauphin and he ceased to attend council meetings. With the loss of his power to reward clients and supporters much of his influence drained away.

Richemont was a determined man who refused to accept his relegation to the margins. He began to collect allies for a showdown with La Trémoille, hoping to remove him as he had removed Louvet,

Giac and Vernet. He entered into an alliance with three other disaffected noblemen, Charles Count of Clermont, the heir to the duchy of Bourbon, his cousin Jacques de Bourbon Count of La Marche, and Bernard Count of Pardiac, the younger brother of the Count of Armagnac. These were angry and violent men. Clermont had withdrawn from court and was still holding the Dauphin's Chancellor prisoner. The Armagnac brothers had been seriously discountenanced by the award of the lieutenancy of Languedoc, which their family had held for most of the past half-century, to their great regional rival the Count of Foix. They were widely believed to have been responsible for the murder of the Dauphin's Marshal Amaury de Sévérac, who had recently been found hanged from a window of the Armagnac castle of Gages in the valley of the Aveyron. The conspirators gathered around them some important allies, including Richemont's close colleague Marshal Boussac. From a distance, they received encouragement and support from the Duke of Brittany, and perhaps also from Yolande of Anjou.[17]

In October 1427, their resentment erupted into open rebellion. Richemont was on the march of Maine. He was gathering his forces for the *journée* of La Gravelle, the last important castle to hold out for the Dauphin in the barony of Laval, which had recently entered into a conditional surrender agreement. Sir John Fastolf was directing the siege and the Duke of Bedford was on his way with an army for the *journée*. Suddenly, the Constable abandoned the whole operation. He put a new garrison into La Gravelle and repudiated the surrender agreement. Then he led his army into Poitou to join his confederates, leaving Bedford to have one of the old garrison's hostages beheaded beneath the walls of the castle. Richemont made first for Châtellerault, where the rebels had agreed to meet. When Richemont arrived at Châtellerault, he found the gates shut in his face by La Trémoille's order. The allies eventually joined forces at Chauvigny on the river Vienne, and from there withdrew to Chinon, where they succeeded in occupying the royal castle. For some weeks it remained unclear what they wanted, or what they would do next. Then, in the new year, they showed their hand. They issued a manifesto declaring they would reform the state and remove the Dauphin from the evil influence of Georges de la Tremoille and the ex-Chancellor Robert Le Mâcon. Richemont tried to repeat the tactics that he had successfully employed in 1425. He summoned an assembly in the castle of the Dukes of

Bourbon at Montluçon on the western march of the Bourbonnais. There, the rebels planned to announce their programme of reform, rally their supporters and call for a meeting of the Estates-General. But they did not intend to limit themselves to political pressure. They were preparing for a show of force. They had substantial forces at Chinon. From Brittany, John V promised to send more. The allies were recruiting troops in Auvergne. Richemont left for his great fortress of Parthenay in southern Poitou, to create a second centre of resistance there. Meanwhile, a group of his supporters seized La Trémoille's castle at Gençay, south of Poitiers. The minister, who was staying there, was lucky to escape with his life.[18]

Considering that the kingdom of Bourges was on the edge of civil war, it is remarkable that the Dauphinists made significant advances across the whole of the southern front from Maine to the Gâtinais during the winter of 1427–8. The Dauphin's ministers contributed little or nothing to these operations. They were the work of enterprising Dauphinist captains, apparently acting on their own initiative. The Gascon captain Géraud de la Paillière, former captain of Ivry, and Florent d'Illiers, captain of the Duke of Orléans's garrison at Châteaudun, launched an invasion of the region south-west of Paris, which brought the fighting uncomfortably close to the capital and threatened to obstruct the English offensive to the Loire planned for the summer. It is poorly recorded, but there can be no doubt about its scale or importance. Over the winter months, Dauphinist companies invaded Perche, the Beauce and the valley of the Eure, capturing at least nine walled towns and castles. None of these places had a professional garrison. There is no evidence that any of them resisted for long. The English were caught unprepared. They found themselves having to divert troops to hold the crossings of the Seine and reinforce Dreux and Chartres, the principal towns of the region. The Earls of Warwick and Suffolk were both withdrawn from other sectors to concentrate their forces against the new offensive.[19]

The result was to weaken English forces in the west, where the Dauphin's forces were able to make some striking gains. The French commanders in this sector were two Breton noblemen, Gilles de Retz, the Dauphin's lieutenant in Anjou, and Jacques de Dinan lord of Beaumanoir, captain of Sablé. Both men came from families with long traditions of service to the Valois monarchy and had refused to swear the oath demanded by the Duke of Brittany to abide by his agreement with the English. In about November 1427 they attacked Le Lude, a fortress on the river Loir which had been occupied by the Earl of Warwick in the previous year and served as the eastern anchor of the English defences of Maine. Le Lude was battered with artillery and its broken walls were carried by assault. The English lieutenant captain was among the prisoners. Shortly after the fall of Le Lude, the companies of La Hire came up from Vendôme, joined forces with the Maine nobleman Louis d'Avaugour and attacked the fortress-town of La Ferté-Bernard. These incidents illustrated the difficulties which the English would always have in Maine, too thinly spread across a broad front, constantly under threat from a hostile population and from enemy garrisons nearby. Robert Stafford, the English captain of La Ferté-Bernard, was away at Le Mans when La Hire struck. He rushed back and occupied the castle. But his garrison was only twenty-four strong. They were unable to prevent the townsmen from opening their gates to the enemy on about 20 January 1428. Stafford's men told him that with the town in enemy hands, the castle was untenable. They refused to fight. When La Hire's troops assaulted the walls of the citadel, they laid down their arms and surrendered. It was the third time in two years that La Ferté-Bernard had changed hands. Its capture enabled La Hire to establish a new base there and to link up with the Dauphinist garrisons of Anjou.[20]

The first fruit of their collaboration was an attack on the provincial capital of Le Mans. On 25 May 1428, a force of several hundred men commanded by La Hire and Beaumanoir appeared before the city. One of the city gates was opened for them with the connivance of the bishop and some prominent citizens. However, La Hire's men, many of whom were old-style *routiers* living on plunder, alienated their natural allies among the citizenry by spreading through the town shouting '*Ville prise!*', the traditional call to indiscriminate looting and violence. There was a large English garrison in the citadel, 120 men under the command of two prominent Welsh captains, Matthew Gough and Thomas Gower. They did not react fast enough to stop the French from occupying the city below. But Gower was able to send a messenger to Alençon, where Gough was conferring with the sector commander Sir John Talbot. In less than two days, Talbot and Gough had collected a formidable force, including the companies of Scales, Oldhall, Rempston and Glasdale. They rode through the night, arriving outside Le Mans shortly before dawn on the 28th. They were let into the citadel by a postern gate and from there burst out into the streets. The Dauphinists were unprepared. Beaumanoir had left with most of his army. Most of La Hire's men were asleep in their billets. As the English spread through the city crying 'Notre Dame!', 'St George!' and 'Talbot!', householders took their revenge for the sack of their homes by hurling heavy objects from upper windows on the heads of La Hire's men as they tried to rally. Heavily outnumbered, they turned and fled through the gates, many of them still in their night-shirts. Beaumanoir had hastily retraced his steps and appeared outside the town later that day. He had hoped that his appearance would provoke a rising of the inhabitants. But they refused to move and he marched away empty-handed. Over the following days, the ringleaders of the group which had helped the Dauphinists to enter the city were denounced and executed.[21]

At Westminster, the Earl of Salisbury was struggling to raise support for the great offensive planned for the following summer. According to Jean de Waurin, Bedford was expecting an expeditionary army of 6,000 men. With the kingdom of Bourges divided and bankrupt, Salisbury hoped to persuade the sceptical political community of England that a supreme effort would finally break the Dauphinists' resistance and bring an end to the war. When Parliament opened on 13 October, the opening address of the Chancellor, Archbishop Kemp of York, left them in no doubt about what was expected of them. They had been summoned, he said, 'to offer their willing support to the King and the state, and to aid them with their bodies and their wealth'. For the first few weeks, however, the war in France was pushed into the background by the Duke of Gloucester's bid for a regency and his plans to intervene in Holland. It was not until the new year, when Humphrey's hopes had finally been extinguished, that there is any evidence of active preparation for an expeditionary army to France. The Duke of Bedford's plans were eventually considered by the Lords in March 1428. They resolved, unanimously according to the only surviving account, that the Earl of Salisbury should return to France in the summer at the head of the largest expeditionary army to leave England's shores since the death of Henry V. It would not be 6,000 strong, as the Regent had hoped. That was well beyond the government's means and England's military capacity. By 24 March

1428, when Salisbury sealed his indenture with the King, the size of his force had been fixed at 2,400 men, including 600 men-at-arms. They were to be ready to embark on 30 June. In addition, the Seneschal of Aquitaine Sir John Radcliffe, who was in England, was to accompany Salisbury with another 800 men. The intention was probably that once the English had established themselves south of the Loire, Radcliffe would march overland with his company to Bordeaux.[22]

The Commons were finally persuaded to abandon their policy of refusing to vote direct taxes for the war in France. They voted two new taxes to support the Earl of Salisbury's expedition. One was a so-called parish tax, imposed on householders and graduated according to the wealth of their parish church, which was taken to be a rough indication of the prosperity of the parish. The second was a tax on holdings of land, according to the number of knight's fees that they represented, which meant that the amount paid was approximately proportionate to area. Both of the new taxes were ingenious attempts to devise a progressive tax, related to ability to pay, which did not depend on a long and complex process of individual assessment. The drawback of the new taxes was that, being experimental, their yield was unpredictable. In the event they raised only just over £12,000, about a third of the value of a standard subsidy. Salisbury launched his own appeal for loans on his personal credit. He is said to have raised 3,000 marks from the public, with contributions coming in as small as ten shillings. These early signs of changing attitudes to the French war among the English at home, must have been welcome. But the main financial burden continued to rest on the government's ordinary revenues. Lord Hungerford, who had taken over as Treasurer in 1426, had brought a new efficiency to the management of the Crown's demesne revenues. He was also helped by a temporary spike in the customs receipts. But Salisbury's army was financed mainly by allowing yet more old debts to pile up unpaid and deferring other expenditure. This stored up financial problems for future years. But it enabled Hungerford to put off the evil moment when a fundamental review of war finance would be unavoidable.[23]

The bigger problem proved to be manpower. A decade of annual expeditionary armies to France had come close to exhausting the supply of trained men willing to serve abroad. The shortage of men-at-arms was particularly acute. Of the six bannerets and thirty-four knights that Salisbury had contracted to provide, only one banneret and eight knights could be found. He was unable to find more than three-quarters of the ordinary men-at-arms required, and had to scrape the barrel to get that many. Hardly any of the recorded participants are known to have fought in France or indeed anywhere else. The numbers had to be made up by recruiting more archers. As for Radcliffe's force, his participation was cancelled, probably because of recruitment problems. Instead, he was ordered to Gascony by sea with just 200 archers and no men-at-arms. Even this reduced force was shortly cancelled.[24]

Previous expeditionary armies had comprised a number of independent companies, each under its own captain, with no common link except that they were all at the service of the Duke of Bedford. But the army of 1428 was different. It was to be Salisbury's army. He indented for the entire force, taking personal responsibility for its recruitment and to some extent for its financing. He also organised his own ancillary services. He created his own artillery train to make good the serious losses suffered at Montargis and Mondoubleau, and recruited his own corps of master gunners, miners, carpenters, masons, bowyers and fletchers. John Parker, the Cheshunt ironmaster hired by the Earl as his artillery-master, assembled a formidable artillery train comprising seven iron bombards weighing on average more than two tons each, sixty-four smaller bronze pieces, more than 1,200 dressed stone cannonballs and a train of massive carts with reinforced axles to carry them. These arrangements gave Salisbury an unprecedented measure of autonomy, and a dominant voice in the army's deployment. They probably reflected the views of Humphrey Duke of Gloucester, a close ally of Salisbury, ever jealous of his brother Bedford and happy to prise strategic control from his grip. In due course, Salisbury would be appointed lieutenant-general of both King and Regent for the conduct of the war in France.[25]

In view of the pole position accorded to the Earl of Salisbury, it was unfortunate that he was still in England when the Grand Conseil met in Paris at the end of May 1428 to decide upon the strategy for the coming campaign. The Regent presided. The principal members of the Norman council came from Rouen. The Duke of Burgundy arrived from Flanders with his own advisers. The conference resolved to adopt the western strategy which Bedford had always favoured. The first objective would be Angers. Possession of the city was expected to lead to the occupation of the duchy of Anjou and the capture of the bridges at Ponts-de-Cé. Salisbury's numbers were by now known. It was proposed to reinforce them with 400 men-at-arms and 1,200 archers already serving in France. Half of these men would be drawn from English companies serving in Normandy. They were to muster on 15 July at Vernon on the Seine. The rest would be raised from English and French troops serving in the treaty provinces. They were to muster on the same day at Poissy, west of Paris. With this accession of strength, Salisbury would have some 4,300 men under his command. To meet the heavy cost of these arrangements an *aide* was imposed on the whole of Lancastrian France.[26]

The Dauphin's ministers learned of the scale of the English preparations early in 1428 and discovered their objective not long afterwards. Their first thought was to appeal to the King of Scotland for another Scottish army. In April 1428, three ambassadors were appointed to proceed urgently to Scotland. John Stewart of Darnley, constable of the small Scottish corps already in France, led the embassy. He was supported by Regnault de Chartres and the King's private secretary, the poet and pamphleteer Alain Chartier. Their instructions were to ask for the immediate dispatch of 6,000 Scottish troops to La Rochelle. With such an army, they were to say, the Dauphin would be able to create an 'impenetrable wall' against English incursions. In return, the Dauphin proposed a marriage between his only son Louis, who was then nearly five years old, and the three-year-old Margaret Stewart, daughter of James I and Joan Beaufort. The ambassadors' departure was delayed by difficulties in finding ships for their passage and money for their expenses. They did not reach James's court at Linlithgow castle until about the end of June 1428. In the great hall of the castle, Alain Chartier delivered a flowery encomium in Latin on the auld alliance and the valour of Scottish men-at-arms. 'Truly,' he said, 'this alliance is not recorded in a charter on vellum but on the very flesh and skin of men, nor written in ink but in the mingled blood of friends.' James was seduced by the flattery and the proffered marriage. Agreement was reached at a gathering of the General Council of Scotland at Perth on 17 July 1428. James undertook to send Margaret to France accompanied by the 6,000 troops demanded. However, they were not expected to be ready until the spring of 1429. When Stewart of Darnley left for France immediately after the assembly, he brought with him a Scottish embassy led by James's most experienced diplomat, Henry Leighton

Bishop of Aberdeen. Leighton was charged with finalising the marriage alliance and the terms of service of the new Scottish army. In reality, this was an empty gesture. It is unlikely that so many men could have been found after the heavy losses suffered by two previous Scottish armies. James must have known this. In the event, the departure of the child-bride was delayed for several years and the new army of Scotland never materialised. The only reinforcement received from Scotland in 1428 was a company of several hundred soldiers raised by the Angus magnate Patrick Ogilvy of Auchterhouse, which served as Bishop Leighton's escort and stayed behind when his mission was completed.[27]

At the end of June 1428, when it became clear that any Scottish army would arrive too late for the coming campaign, the Dauphin appealed for troops to Castile, which had so often disappointed him before. Guillaume de Quiefdeville, a veteran of similar missions in the past, was despatched to the court of King John II with an enthusiastic account of the battle of Montargis, a highly optimistic view of the Dauphin's military situation and an ambitious shopping list. He was instructed to ask for two Castilian armies. The first was to consist of 2,000 to 3,000 men-at-arms and 5,000 to 6,000 crossbowmen with their pavisers, making a total of at least 10,000 men, all to be ready within weeks. The second army, which was to be carried to Brittany in a fleet of forty to fifty Castilian ships, was to invade Brittany from the sea and force its duke to return to his proper allegiance. In return, there was a vague promise of reimbursement when the Dauphin's financial situation improved. There is no record of the Castilian response to these unrealistic demands, but it is clear that Quiefdeville got nowhere.[28]

In the result, the Dauphin was left with only his garrison troops and the small companies of Scots and Italians already in his service. They were tied down dealing with the rebellion of the Constable and his allies. At the beginning of March 1428, the Dauphin had recovered possession of Chinon. The rebels withdrew to the domains of the Count of Clermont in Auvergne and the Bourbonnais. In about the middle of May 1428 Clermont, accompanied by the Castilian *routier* Rodrigo de Villandrando, invaded Berry and occupied Bourges. Bourges had backed the revolt against the Louvet ministry two years earlier, and it backed the revolt against La Trémoille now. The citizens opened their gates without a fight. Once in possession of Bourges, the princes summoned the inhabitants to a public meeting, at which they announced a vague programme of reform, the main element of which was a promise to deliver the region from soldiers living off the land. Meanwhile, the rebels took control of the mint and the warehouses of the collectors of the *gabelle* and began to impose their own taxes. The royal officers in Bourges were divided. The captain of the town threw in his lot with the rebels. The others refused and withdrew to the great circular keep standing over the southern gate of the city. There, they were besieged by the rebel princes.[29]

The Dauphin was at Loches, the fortress-town on the Indre some seventy miles west of Bourges. His government was only enabled to go on functioning by regular cash loans from La Trémoille. The minister dug deep into his chests to pay for the embassies to Scotland and Castile, and deeper still to pay for an army to confront the rebels at Bourges. The Bastard of Orléans and Raoul de Gaucourt came with their companies from the Orléanais. The principal captains arrived from the marches of Maine and the Beauce: La Hire, Poton de Saintrailles, Géraud de la Paillière, Florent d'Illiers, Guillaume d'Albret and Hugh Kennedy. In early July 1428, as the Earl of Salisbury's army was mustering on Barham Down in Kent, all the troops that the kingdom of Bourges could raise were deployed against each other. The Dauphin and La Trémoille marched on Bourges. Richemont tried to reach the city in time to save it with his personal military retinue and another 600 men supplied by the Duke of Brittany. He headed east into the Limousin, hoping to get to Auvergne and approach Bourges by the south. But he found his way blocked by that mortal enemy of the house of Montfort, Jean de Penthièvre, Viscount of Limoges. The Dauphin's army reached Bourges first.[30]

Faced with superior forces commanded by the Dauphin in person, the princes in Bourges lost their nerve. They declared that they had never intended to cross their King and backed away from their more extreme demands. They even dropped their call for the dismissal of La Trémoille and Robert Le Maçon. Instead, they called for the Estates-General to be summoned to Poitiers, at which all should be free to speak their minds about the future government of the kingdom. They also demanded the dismissal of the Dauphin's foreign mercenaries, for fear that La Trémoille might use them to destroy his rivals. The Dauphin refused to disband his mercenaries. But otherwise, he accepted their terms. On 17 July 1428, he issued letters of remission pardoning all of the rebel leaders. Five days later, on 22 July, the Estates-General of the whole kingdom of Bourges were summoned to meet at Tours on 10 September. All the princes except for Arthur de Richemont laid down their arms and dispersed to their own lands.[31]

Richemont had been included in the general pardon, but he had no interest in an accommodation with La Trémoille. He returned to Parthenay, and doggedly continued to defy the minister from there. The main theatre of their rivalry was Poitou, a rich province at the political heart of Charles VII's realm which had historically been an important source of soldiers and tax revenues. Richemont and La Trémoille were both powers in Poitou. La Trémoille already had large, landed domains there when he became Charles's chief minister. The opportunities of office enabled him to build a territorial power base in the province designed to put him on a par with the scions of the great noble houses at Charles VII's court. He took great castles and extensive lordships, such as Lusignan and Melle, as security for his loans to the Dauphin. He nominated his creatures to command royal castles like Luçon. He used his powers of patronage to draw others into his alliance. Later, in 1431, he would take possession of the vast domains around Thouars confiscated by the Crown from Louis of Amboise. For his part, Richemont had major lordships in Poitou at Parthenay and Fontenay. He was allied to some of the leading princely houses: Anjou, Bourbon-Clermont, La Marche and Armagnac. He could call on the political and military support of his brother, John V of Brittany. He had a large personal following among the Breton companies. For the next five years, the two men pursued their vendetta through surrogates: on Richemont's side, his principal Breton lieutenant Prégent de Coëtivy and his allies among the nobility of Poitou; on La Trémoille's, Olivier de Penthièvre, the exiled head of the family which had for years been the main opposition to the Montfort dynasty in Brittany, and the Périgord nobleman Jean de Rochechouart (alias Jean de la Roche), whom the minister had appointed as Seneschal of Poitou.[32]

The Earl of Salisbury disembarked with his army at Calais in the third week of July 1428 just as the Dauphin's stand-off with the rebels was approaching its climax. Salisbury left his army in the charge of his lieutenants while he rode to Paris to confer with the Duke of Bedford. In the French capital, the Regent presided at a council of war. In addition to Salisbury himself, many of the leading English captains in France were present. After several days of argument, the campaign strategy was radically changed. It was decided that instead of making for Angers, Salisbury's army would clear the Dauphinist garrisons which had established themselves between Paris and the Beauce during the previous winter and would then turn south to besiege Orléans. A fresh indenture was drawn up which entrenched Salisbury's authority over the army. He was given plenary power over both the expeditionary army and the men recruited in France and was authorised to conduct the campaign in whatever way he judged to be in the interests of the King. These were fateful decisions. Years later, Bedford denied any responsibility for them. The siege of Orléans, he said, had been undertaken, 'God knoweth by what advice'. Yet Bedford knew very well who was responsible. The Earl of Salisbury was the one captain with the stature and the power to insist on his own plan. The change marked the end of the western strategy which Bedford had espoused for years. It also involved the repudiation of the truce with Charles of Orléans. In a broader sense, it meant the triumph of a more aggressive approach to the conduct of the war, which eschewed the patient construction of political alliances that Bedford had always favoured. Like Humphrey of Gloucester, with whom he often saw eye to eye, the Earl of Salisbury disliked and distrusted the French princes, especially Burgundy and Orléans, and looked for a purely military solution to the current strategic impasse.[33]

Salisbury opened his campaign with characteristic brutality and speed. In the second week of August 1428, he rejoined his army and marched on Nogent-le-Roi, just south of Dreux. The Dauphinist defenders of Nogent were unwilling to risk an assault and surrendered on terms. A large number of them were found to have sworn allegiance to the English King and were summarily hanged, while the rest were made to pay heavy ransoms. From here, Salisbury divided his army into several divisions which advanced on parallel routes across the plain of the Beauce mopping up one walled place after another. All of them surrendered on terms and opened their gates. The first serious resistance which they encountered was at Le Puiset, Toury and Janville, a line of walled places commanded by Géraud de la Paillière which defended the approach to Orléans. Géraud fled on Salisbury's approach, leaving his garrison to make terms with the conqueror. Le Puiset was swiftly taken by assault and the entire garrison hanged. Janville held out for ten days. The town fell after a ferocious battle on the walls, in which most of the defenders were wounded, 'the most notable assault that we ever saw' as Salisbury reported to the citizens of London. The rest retreated to the castle and bargained in vain for their lives. A number of the defenders were hanged and the rest ransomed. In the space of three weeks Salisbury captured thirty-nine walled towns and castles, sweeping away all the enemy garrisons of the Beauce except for Châteaudun. The Earl paused to rest his men and allow the contingents from Normandy to join him. He was still hoping to conceal his real objective. In early September the Regent assured the Estates of Normandy that Angers was the target. But the pretence was wearing thin. The Dauphin's ministers had already realised that the direction of the English offensive pointed to an attack on Orléans and had begun to reinforce its garrison. The Earl tried to surprise it but found that he was too late. The English approached Orléans to find the walls bristling with armed men. On 8 September the English stood in battle order outside the city from midday to dusk before returning to Janville. No one answered their challenge. It would be necessary to undertake a major siege.[34]

Salisbury had already secured his rear and his communications with Paris and Rouen. His next task was to obtain control of the Loire on either side of Orléans so as to impede the carriage of supplies and reinforcements to the city. The fate of Le Puiset and Janville shocked the inhabitants of the Loire towns, many of whom opened their gates to the English without a fight. Meung, thirteen miles downstream of the city, was one of the first. A delegation from the town came into the Earl's quarters at Janville with their submission. Salisbury sent one of his lieutenants to occupy it, fortify the bridge and take possession of the valuable supplies in its stores. With Meung's bridge over the Loire in his hands, Salisbury was able to lay siege to Beaugency, five miles further downstream on about 10 September.[35]

On the day that the English appeared outside Beaugency, the Estates-General opened to face the worst military crisis in the history of the kingdom of Bourges. They had been summoned to Tours, but in the event met at Chinon, which was thought to be more secure. It was the first time since Charles's accession that the representatives of all his domains had met in a single assembly. Raoul de Gaucourt, the captain of Orléans, appeared with La Hire to report on the military situation. It was essential, they said, to hold Beaugency. Money must be found to pay the troops. The Treasury was empty. La Trémoille opened his chests once more and contributed 10,000 *écus* on top of the large sums that he had already lent. Other councillors chipped in. The delegates put their hands in their pockets. A total of 15,000 *écus* (£2,500) was borrowed, enough for one month's wages. The whole sum was paid over to Gaucourt and La Hire. The delegates then voted a general *aide* of 500,000 *francs* (about £55,000). Their political demands were predictable but unattainable. They urged the princes of the blood to unite behind the Dauphin. They called for a fresh attempt to win over the Duke of Burgundy, in spite of the Dauphin's protest that he had already done his best. They wanted Richemont recalled to court, something which neither Charles nor La Trémoille was willing to contemplate. Richemont was absent throughout the sessions, sulking at his brother's court in Brittany. Shortly, he returned to Parthenay and remained there throughout the winter, as his allies deserted him one after the other to swell the Dauphin's forces.[36]

The English offensive continued on its inexorable course. Beaugency was a heavily fortified town dominated by an imposing eleventh-century keep. It withstood continuous bombardment for a fortnight before finally surrendering on 25 September. The terms were harsh. The captains of the garrison surrendered as prisoners of war. The inhabitants were spared a sack but had to pay a large fine for their contumacy and to swear allegiance to Henry VI or leave. Upstream of Orléans, the principal French fortress was the bridge-town of Jargeau. Many of the garrison troops whose bases had been overrun during the English offensive had taken refuge there. Sir John de la Pole, the Earl of Suffolk's brother, captured the fortified bridge at Jargeau at the beginning of October and, after battering the walls of the town with artillery for three days, accepted its surrender. Morale among the defenders was low. They were allowed to leave, but some of them are said to have sworn allegiance to the English King and joined the Earl of Salisbury's army. Châteauneuf, a short distance up the river, surrendered without striking a blow as soon as the English appeared before the walls. From the Nivernais, the Burgundian captain Guillaume de Rochefort, one of Philip the Good's chamberlains, advanced down the Loire to occupy Georges de la Trémoille's castle at Sully. By the end of the first week of October, Salisbury controlled the whole course of the middle Loire. Between Blois and Gien, a distance of some eighty miles, not a single bridge remained in the Dauphin's hands except at Orléans itself. The English crossed the Loire at Meung, Beaugency and Jargeau and approached Orléans along the south bank from both directions. On 12 October 1428, the whole army stood once more before the city.[37]

Orléans, the largest city of the Loire, was built on rising ground on the north bank of the river. Approaching from the south, the English captains would have seen a densely built walled city, its skyline pierced by the high watchtower of the Tour Neuve at the eastern end of the strand, the belltowers of some fifteen parish churches, the spires and crosses of a dozen chapels, and the romanesque west towers of its incomplete gothic cathedral. The kernel of the city was the rectangular Roman *castrum*. On the west side of the *castrum*, stood the populous suburb of Avenum, containing the city's principal markets, which had been enclosed by a new rampart in the early fourteenth century. Even with this extension, however, the area within the walls was small. About half of Orléans's 12,000 or so inhabitants still lived in extensive unwalled suburbs on the north and east sides and on the south bank of the Loire.

A great deal of work had been done on the defences since the last time that they had faced a serious threat from the English, in the 1370s. The dilapidated Gallo-Roman walls, towers and gates had been largely replaced by modern ramparts some thirty feet high, defended by deep dry moats and thirty towers. The approaches to the five principal gates had been protected by boulevards of stone and timber breastworks and palisades. On the opposite bank of the Loire stood the unwalled suburb of Porteriau and the walled enclosure of an Augustinian convent. The suburb was joined to the city by a long stone bridge of twenty arches, originally built in the twelfth century. The bridge, which stood a short distance upstream of the position of the modern Pont George V, was destined to play an important part in the siege. It was defended at its northern end by the castle of the Dukes of Orléans, built on the foundations of the old Roman fort. At the southern end it was defended by an imposing fourteenth-century fortress known as Les Tourelles, which rose out of the crowded buildings of Porteriau, protected on either side by a drawbridge. In the middle of the bridge stood a hospital, a chapel and the Bastille Saint-Antoine, a small fort constructed a decade earlier. Beneath the bridge, floating water mills provided the city's bakers with milled grain.

When the English arrived, there were already more than 600 professional troops in Orléans. The Dauphin had appointed the Bastard of Orléans as his lieutenant for its defence. He was supported by a

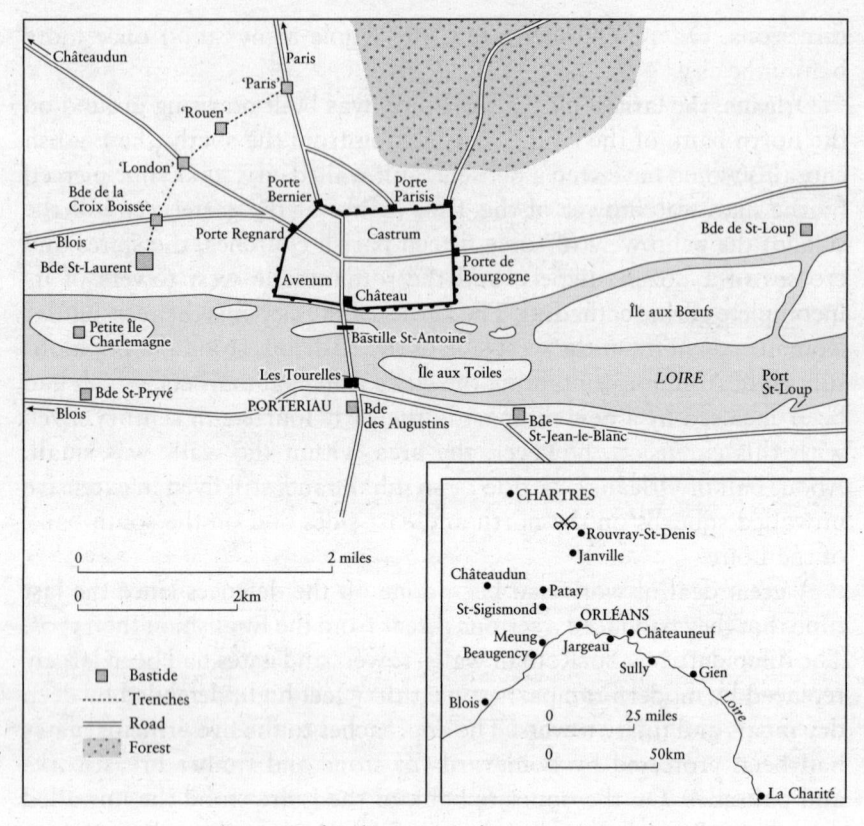

6 The siege of Orléans, October 1428–May 1429

formidable group of captains, including Raoul de Gaucourt, La Hire and Poton de Saintrailles. The Dauphin's treasurers emptied out their chests to fund the garrison's wages, but most of the burden fell on the citizens themselves. A heavy *taille* was imposed on them, in addition to the large quantities of silver coin and plate which they had voluntarily contributed. The municipality laid in great stocks of food from which to supply the garrison.[38]

At the outset of the siege, Salisbury's army had a payroll strength of at least 4,500 men. Of these, about 2,700 had come with the Earl from England, and about 1,600 from English and indigenous troops already in France. A few hundred more had been recruited from the urban militias of Paris, Chartres, Rouen and other cities under English control. Some of Salisbury's men had been detached for garrison service in the recently captured bridge-towns along the Loire. That would have left about 4,000 men for the siege. The Earl of Salisbury does not seem to have had a very clear idea of the topography of Orléans. To surround it at a sufficient distance to avoid artillery fire from the walls, it would be necessary to build and man siege lines about six miles long extending to both sides of the Loire. Communications between different sectors of the siege would be difficult, for it was not practical to build pontoon bridges over the fast-flowing river, with its tendency to sudden floods. So there would have to be enough men on each side to hold their own against an army of relief. To make matters worse, the troops from England had indented to serve for only six months, more than half of which had already elapsed when the siege began.

The Earl therefore needed to take the city quickly by assault. He might have been expected to concentrate his attack on the long northern wall, but he was evidently deterred by its strength and by the four fortified gateways from which sorties could emerge to attack the assault parties in the rear. He therefore planned an assault from the south side of the river. This was a formidable undertaking. It involved capturing the fortress of Les Tourelles and using it as a base from which to batter his way across the bridge and into the town. The defenders had had time to demolish the suburb of Porteriau and the adjoining village of Saint-Marceau in order to give the defenders of Les Tourelles a clear field of fire. They had used the debris from the demolitions to build an improvised boulevard of timber and rubble in front of the fortress. As the defenders retreated over the bridge into the town, they set fire to the remaining buildings of Porteriau, including the Augustinian convent. When the English arrived, the ruins were still burning and the heat was so intense that they had to wait until the following day before entering. Once inside, they took possession of the ruins of the convent and began to fortify them, digging deep trenches around the buildings and installing their artillery in the enclosure. Here, the Earl of Salisbury established his headquarters.[39]

From the Augustinian convent, the English opened a relentless bombardment of the city. In a single day, the citizens counted 120 stone projectiles, some as large as a hundredweight, crashing into houses at random. Twelve of the floating water mills beneath the bridge were destroyed in the first few days, forcing the defenders to build horse-powered mills within the walls. Les Tourelles took several direct hits and began to suffer serious damage. Meanwhile, the English started to dig a mine from the Augustinian enclosure to the fortress. On 21 October, they launched their assault. They first had to take the boulevard, which was stormed by massed men from scaling ladders. There was a fierce battle on the walls, lasting four hours. The defenders broke the ladders and poured red hot cinders and boiling water and grease over the assailants as they came up the sides of the moat. The women of the city formed a human chain the length of the bridge to bring rocks and pails of burning matter to the men on the walls. Both sides had suffered heavy casualties by the time that the English called off the assault and withdrew. Over the next two days, the English completed their mine, penetrating beneath the boulevard, and prepared to fire the timber props and assault the breach. The defenders decided that the boulevard could no longer be defended. On 23 October they set fire to the walls and retreated into Les Tourelles, pulling the drawbridge up behind them. A rapid survey persuaded them that the fortress had been too badly damaged by artillery fire to be held. So they resolved to hold off the English from the walls while they built a new boulevard in the middle of the bridge. On 24 October, the English planted their ladders against the walls of Les Tourelles from the bridgehead and the bed of the river. In two hours of hard fighting, they captured it. Salisbury appointed William Glasdale, one of his favourite lieutenants, as captain of the fortress. From the upper windows Glasdale hurled abuse at the defenders of Orléans, threatening to kill every one of them, men and women alike, when he finally got into the city.[40]

Disaster struck the English in their moment of triumph. On the evening that they occupied Les Tourelles, the Earl of Salisbury climbed to the top of the building to survey the city, accompanied by Glasdale and other captains. As he peered through a barred opening, it was struck by a cannonball fired from a tower on the waterfront opposite. The Earl flung himself against a wall, but the iron grating shattered and he was hit by a fragment which took away an eye and a quarter of his face. The surgeons could do nothing for him. His attendants took him in a litter to Meung, where he lingered on for ten days. He died on 3 November 1428, the last of the Montagu Earls of Salisbury. His body was taken back to England and buried in St Paul's cathedral in London. In his will, in addition to bequests to various charitable purposes in both England and France, he left money to be distributed among the poor of France, 'men and women, friends and enemies alike'. 'And sith forth that he was slain,' a London chronicler wrote,

'English men never gat ne prevailed in France, but ever after began to leave by little and little till all was lost.'[41]

The death of the Earl of Salisbury altered the whole direction of the campaign. The Duke of Bedford, who was in Paris, took charge as soon as the news was brought to him. He appointed the Earl of Suffolk as director of the siege. Bedford and Suffolk were more cautious, perhaps more realistic strategists than Salisbury. They quickly concluded that Salisbury's plan to force his way into Orléans across the bridge was impractical. The assaults had cost the English many men, including some prominent captains. The situation on the bridge had resolved itself into a bloody stalemate. The French defenders of Les Tourelles had broken one of the arches of the bridge as they retreated into the city. The English for their part broke two more arches in front of Les Tourelles and built their own boulevard at the break to ward off any attempt to counterattack. Glasdale transformed Les Tourelles into a great artillery platform, from which he exchanged continual artillery fire with the defenders of the French boulevard on the bridge. Both constructions suffered serious damage. But neither side was able to dislodge the other from their positions.

Meanwhile, the city's garrison was being reinforced. On 25 October, the day after Salisbury's fatal injury, the Bastard of Orléans and La Hire brought some 800 fresh men into the city by the north bank. They included the companies of Marshal Boussac, the famous paladins Jean de Bueil and Jacques de Chabannes, Valperga's Italian corps and a company of Aragonese mercenaries. They were followed in November by some 500 Scots of the Dauphin's personal guard. By the end of that month, the garrison of Orléans stood at about 1,700 professional soldiers. The Dauphin was still at Chinon, more than a hundred miles away in Touraine, where he remained for most of the siege. His captains established a forward base on the Loire at Blois, forty-five miles downstream from Orléans. The Count of Clermont, until recently the leader of the rebellion against the Dauphin's authority, took command there. In October and November, he recruited a substantial field army, most of it drawn from his family's domains in the Bourbonnais and Auvergne.[42]

Once they had abandoned the plan to assault Orléans across the bridge, Bedford and Suffolk had to resign themselves to starving it into submission. They now had to confront the problems that the Earl of Salisbury's strategy had aimed to avoid. They did not have enough men. The low quality of the 2,700 men brought from England in the summer was beginning to show. There had already been a fair number of desertions, and the trickle became a flood after the Earl of Salisbury's death. Most of those who stayed refused to go on serving after their indentures expired at the end of December. Only six companies, comprising about a quarter of the expeditionary army, could be persuaded to sign new indentures with the Regent. This meant that the army outside Orléans would lose about half of its nominal strength in the new year. At least 2,000 men had to be found to replace them, in addition to the substantial extra forces required to man the long siege lines. Writing to the council in England in November, the Duke of Bedford told them that at least 1,400 more men would have to be sent out urgently from England, or he did not see how the siege could be sustained. Since Salisbury had already exhausted the available reserves of manpower, Bedford's appeal fell on deaf ears at Westminster. He had to find the extra men from the English and French companies already in his service and from the nobility of Normandy. The *arrière-ban* was proclaimed throughout Normandy at the end of October. The English garrisons were stripped of every man that could be spared. Troops were recalled from all other fronts. Even on the most optimistic view, however, these measures would not produce the numbers required to invest Orléans on all sides.[43]

In this extremity, the Regent appealed to the Duke of Burgundy. Philip the Good's record as a military ally was poor. Since the death of Henry V the only significant military operations in which Burgundian forces had fought side by side with the English had been the Cravant campaign in July 1423, the siege of Guise in the winter of 1424–5 and some of the campaigns in the Mâconnais. In November 1428, the position looked more hopeful. The long-drawn-out dispute between Philip and the Duke of Gloucester was at an end. The treaty of Delft had settled the war with Jacqueline of Bavaria, and Philip had returned from Holland. He not only promised to raise another army in his own domains but declared that he would lead it himself. He proposed to march south from Flanders with the contingents of Artois and Picardy. Another sixty companies from the duchy and county of Burgundy were summoned to assemble at Montbard to cross the Auxerrois and join him outside Orléans. The projected size of Philip's army is not known, but the scale of his preparations suggests a substantial force.[44]

The new plan made it necessary for the English forces outside Orléans to regroup. On 8 November, the siege was suspended. Glasdale was left with about 500 men to hold Les Tourelles. The rest of the army was temporarily withdrawn to the bridge-towns of Meung and Jargeau. On 9 November 1428, the Regent left Paris to confer with his principal advisers at Mantes. Towards the end of November, he and his Chancellor Louis of Luxembourg arrived at Chartres, where they established an advance base and prepared to resume the siege. It took nearly two months for the additional forces to be raised. An extra 1,200 men were found from the English companies in France. This was in itself a remarkable achievement, which was possible only because of the collapse of the Dauphinist cause almost everywhere north of the Loire. In addition, there were important contingents drawn from the Norman nobility and from indigenous troops recruited in the treaty provinces.

The major disappointment was the Duke of Burgundy. He abandoned his plan to lead an army to France from Artois and Picardy within a fortnight of announcing it. At the end of November 1428, when the army of Burgundy was gathering at Montbard, he abruptly cancelled it. Philip's sudden change of heart is hard to explain. The most likely reason is that he had a sudden access of guilt about attacking a city belonging to Charles of Orléans at a time when Charles was a prisoner of war. Philip valued his reputation as a chivalrous prince and had probably already arrived at the view which he firmly expressed four months later, that a prisoner was entitled to be treated as a non-combatant and his property was immune from attack. Some companies from Burgundy, presumably volunteers, did join the English army over the winter in spite of Philip's decision. But the Burgundian forces at the siege fell a long way short of the numbers that Bedford had been counting on.[45]

The Regent appointed Talbot and Scales to take joint command of the siege under the overall direction of the Earl of Suffolk. Talbot, who quickly eclipsed his fellow commanders, had been in France for eighteen months, most of it spent on the marches of Maine. He stood out as a man of exceptionally violent instincts, even by the standards of his age. Now about forty years old, his earlier career had left a trail of lawlessness and disorder in his native Shropshire, in Wales where he had served during the rebellion of Owen Glendower and in Ireland where he had passed five years as Henry V's lieutenant. Talbot was idolised in England but inspired mixed feelings in France among English and French alike. He was a man of reckless courage, a master of bold planning, rapid movement and surprise, who was willing to take big risks. But in spite of a reputation for chivalry, he was crudely aggressive and foul-mouthed to both friend and foe. 'A hot-head with an uncertain temper, always angry when things were done badly ... terribly brutal and cruel,' was the verdict of a Burgundian contemporary.[46]

The main lines of the campaign were agreed at a series of conferences of the English captains in late November 1428. The English expected to have about 5,000 men available for the siege by the end of December. Glasdale's troops on the south bank of the Loire were reinforced with another 400 men, bringing his total strength to about 900. About 2,000 men were held back for garrison duties in the occupied towns of the Loire valley and for service in a mobile reserve to escort supply convoys and fight off any attempt at relief from Blois. This left only about 2,500 men to blockade the city by the north. These dispositions were probably the best available, but they meant that the men stationed in the siege lines around the city would be thinly spread and vulnerable to sorties from the gates. By way of comparison, in 1412 John the Fearless had had more than 8,000 men in the siege lines at Bourges, a city of comparable size, and Henry V had needed about the same number at Rouen in 1419.[47]

Glasdale's reinforcements reached him at the beginning of December, accompanied by some additional artillery and a large store of projectiles. The relentless bombardment from either end of the bridge was resumed. There was a brief truce for six hours on Christmas Day, when the guns fell silent, and musicians serenaded the English from the ramparts of the city. Then the fighting resumed in earnest, huge projectiles landing several times a day to crush buildings in the crowded streets of the city. The main body of the new English army mustered at Janville, Beaugency, Meung and Jargeau during the last two weeks of December. Bedford himself arrived at Meung shortly before Christmas to supervise the final arrangements, but he stayed away from the siege itself, following events from his headquarters at Chartres. The three commanders, Suffolk, Talbot and Scales, arrived before the city walls on 30 December. They were greeted by a scene of utter desolation. The garrison of Orléans had taken advantage of the pause in November and December to demolish all of the northern and eastern suburbs as well as the villages that had grown up outside the Porte Bernier and the Porte Regnard on the west. Those suburbs included some of the richest residential and commercial districts of the city, the great monastic church of St Aignan with its beautiful cloister, the monastery of St Loup, the convents of the mendicant orders, no less than sixteen chapels and parish churches, and whole streets of mansions and hovels. All went up in flames. By the time the destruction was completed, there was no cover for the besiegers close to the walls, while the garrison had a clear field of fire for their artillery.[48]

Over the following weeks, the English prepared their siege lines. Downstream from the city walls, they built three forts to block access to the city by water. There was one by the hamlet of Saint-Pryvé on the south bank and another on the Petite-Île-Charlemagne, an island of sand and scrub which has long since disappeared. Opposite these works, the ruined parish church of Saint-Laurent on the north bank was transformed into a powerful bastide which served as the principal store house for the western sector of the siege. From here, the English dug a line of trenches extending in an arc west and north-west of the city from the Loire to the Paris road. This scheme had a number of weaknesses. In the first place, the city was not completely invested. The English lines served only to guard against a relief force approaching from the west. On the north, attempts to build siege works were obstructed by dense forest. The eastern approaches to Orléans remained wide open. There was nothing to stop the enemy bringing in reinforcements and supplies by river from upstream. Secondly, the strength of the French garrison and the risk of powerful mounted sorties from the gates made it necessary to site the English siege lines a long way from the walls. The closest artillery batteries were about 1,000 yards away. At that range they could and did inflict serious damage on buildings inside the city by firing high, but they were ineffective against the walls and gates.[49]

The Dauphin's council believed that the fall of the city would be the beginning of the end. At Chinon they met several times to discuss contingency plans in case the English broke through. The open plain of Berry would be defenceless. With the English penetrating south from Orléans, the kingdom of Bourges would be split in two. The Dauphin's advisers seriously contemplated abandoning the western provinces and retreating east beyond the upper Loire, leaving them with only Languedoc, the uplands of the Bourbonnais and Auvergne, and the Rhône provinces of the Dauphiné and the Lyonnais. This shrunken kingdom could not have survived for long. It would have lacked the economic resources to carry on the war and would have been beyond the reach of Scottish armies or Castilian fleets. Brittany would have been lost beyond recall. Others made the same gloomy assessment. 'If the English take Orléans,' the Giustiniani factor in Bruges reported to his father in Venice, 'they will have no difficulty in making themselves lords of all France and sending the Dauphin packing to beg his bread at almshouses.' The Dauphin's officials embarked on a desperate scramble for money. Local collectors of revenue were cleaned out. Commissioners were sent to the principal towns to borrow money. By a supreme effort, the Dauphin's ministers succeeded in raising an average of about 13,500 *livres* a month for the defence of Orléans over the eight months of the siege, which was about two-thirds of what the English were spending. But it was enough to allow the defenders to be progressively reinforced in the course of January and February 1429.

All the great captains of the kingdom of Bourges, except for Richemont, fought at one time or another at Orléans. The Admiral of France Louis de Culant entered the city on 5 January 1429 with 200 men under the noses of the besieging army. On 8 February, no fewer than 1,620 fresh men arrived under the command of Marshal Lafayette, Stewart of Darnley's brother William, and the Gascon captains Guillaume d'Albret and La Hire. Allowing for casualties, these reinforcements must have brought the strength of the professional garrison to between 2,500 and 3,000 men. The result was a dramatic increase in the scale of their sorties against the English lines.[50]

By mid-January 1429, the siege of Orléans had settled down to a routine of continual exchanges of artillery fire and murderous raids across the charred ruins of the suburbs. The critical factor on both sides now was the flow of supplies. The destruction of Orléans's suburbs had provoked a tidal wave of refugees into the city. This, and the reinforcement of the garrison, roughly doubled the population within the walls, intensifying pressure on the city's stocks. At first, the defenders were able to bring in supplies without difficulty from the south-east, which was not covered by the English siege works. Carts and herds of animals were brought overland to Saint-Denis-en-Val, some four miles upstream of Orléans, where they were loaded onto barges and taken down to the river port of Saint-Loup on the south bank a short distance from the city. Here they were trans-shipped onto flat-bottomed ferries and carried to the opposite bank, then brought through the massive Porte de Bourgogne. But although heavily armed companies of mounted men were able to move freely in and out throughout the siege, the slow-moving food convoys were more vulnerable. On 18 January 1429 a large convoy was intercepted by Glasdale's garrison from Les Tourelles as it approached Saint-Denis-en-Val. Most of it, including some 500 head of cattle, was captured. The next major convoy to get through was not until April. After January, the defenders stopped bringing in live animals and resorted to bringing in sacks or barrels loaded onto packhorses, which were more agile but had very limited carrying capacity.[51]

Besieging armies in the middle ages were almost as vulnerable to starvation as the population within the walls. Tied to their siege lines, they quickly exhausted the supplies available nearby, and were obliged to forage at ever greater distances, often over hostile territory. The combined numbers of English around Orléans and in the occupied towns of the middle Loire were equivalent to the population of a substantial town. Food had to be found for them by purveyors and wholesalers in the Paris markets, in quantities so large that prices in the capital rose to twice their previous level. Long wagon trains snaked their way across the Beauce in heavily escorted convoys. Carts and horses were requisitioned in Paris and across the whole of the Île-de-France. Because food was not issued to the troops as rations but sold to them by middlemen at markets set up behind the siege lines, it was necessary for the convoys to be accompanied by treasury clerks with chests full of coin to pay them their wages, at a total cost of up to 20,000 *livres* a month. The man responsible for organising the operation was Sir John Fastolf, the head of Bedford's military household. The army was already feeling the pangs of hunger when his first convoy reached them in the middle of January. Protecting it had required an escort of as many as 1,200 men accompanied by two artillery trains, one from the arsenal in Paris and the other from Rouen. Yet it took only three weeks for stocks to fall once more to perilously low levels.[52]

On 9 February 1429 Fastolf's second convoy left Paris. It comprised at least 300 wagons loaded with grain and flour, pickled fish and other supplies, as well as nearly 17,000 *livres* in cash and yet more artillery. It was escorted by a force of about 1,500 men under the command of Fastolf himself and Sir Thomas Rempston. Some 600 of them were English and the rest Normans, Picards and Parisian militia under their Provost Simon Morhier. The Dauphinist captains in Orléans learned about it as it was being made ready. It seems to have been La Hire who resolved to intercept the convoy. The plans were laid in great secrecy. On 10 February, the Bastard of Orléans and Stewart of Darnley left Orléans with an escort of some 200 men to confer with the Count of Clermont and Marshal Lafayette at Blois. Clermont and Lafayette had at least 2,000 men with them. But since this was thought not to be enough, they decided to recall as many as possible of the garrison of Orléans to join them on the road. Clermont left Blois with Lafayette early on 11 February and marched rapidly north. On the same day, La Hire left Orléans with some 1,500 men of the garrison, more than half of its total strength. The combined force, at 3,500 men, would outnumber the convoy's escort by more than two to one.

Clermont believed that his march from Blois had passed unobserved. He was mistaken. His cavalcade had been seen from the walls of Beaugency and Meung and the news passed on to Fastolf on the road. On the morning of 12 February Fastolf's scouts, riding ahead of the convoy, located both Dauphinist forces. It was early afternoon when the scouts reported to Fastolf at the village of Rouvray-Saint-Denis, on the Orléans road eight miles north of Janville. Shortly after this La Hire's force from Orléans appeared from the south across the plain. There was an altercation among the Dauphinist captains. Stewart of Darnley wanted to attack the convoy at once. La Hire restrained him, for Clermont, who was still some distance away, had given them strict orders to wait until he could join them. It was probably the right decision. But the delay allowed the English time to organise their defence. Rouvray stood in a flat, featureless landscape. It was bitterly cold. The ground was hard with frost. These were difficult conditions in which to fight a battle against a superior force. Fastolf ordered the wagons to form a large circle with a single narrow opening. The wagons and dray horses were tied together to make a firm barrier. Inside this improvised wall, the escort force was drawn up in battle order facing the opening. The archers were arrayed on foot with sharpened stakes planted in the ground in front of their positions. But contrary to the standard English battle tactics the men-at-arms were ordered to remain in the saddle.

La Hire's force approached the opening and stopped. They arrayed their bowmen, sited their culverins in front of their lines and then waited for Clermont's force to reach them. After some two hours of waiting in line, the light was beginning to fade. The Dauphinists saw their opportunity slipping away. They could no longer contain their impatience. There was a brief skirmish between the French and some English archers who had ventured outside the ring of wagons. The archers, who had the worst of it, hastily retreated into the circle. Stewart of Darnley, seeing this, decided that this was his chance. Ignoring his orders, he dismounted his Scottish troops, broke ranks, and rushed the opening on foot. A disorderly mass of Gascons and French followed him on horseback. It was the same indiscipline which had cost them the day at Verneuil and it had the same consequence now. The attackers were received with persistent volleys from the English archers. The Scots tried to rush the English line on foot through the rain of arrows and a soldiers' battle developed. The mounted French and Gascon troops came up from behind and charged the Normans, Picards and Parisians with axes and couched lances. Many of their horses were impaled on the stakes or turned and fled. The attackers were gradually driven back and put to flight. The Bastard of Orléans was pulled out alive from a pile of dead with an arrow in his foot but was able to follow them. The Count of Clermont's army came upon the scene too late. When they saw the English in possession and the dead strewn across the field, they too fled. La Hire rallied a group of sixty to eighty men-at-arms who conducted an effective fighting retreat and saved many lives. Most of the survivors of the Dauphinist army crept past the English forts under cover of darkness that night and found their way into Orléans. Fastolf's slow-moving convoy safely reached the English siege lines five days later.

English casualties were light. Some of the merchants and carters had been killed while trying to take their wagons out of the line and escape. At least one of the clerks guarding the cash was felled. But the escort force was intact. La Hire's army had fared much worse. He lost 300 to 400 men, a quarter of his strength. The Scottish corps took the brunt of the casualties. 'They were every mother's son slain,' crowed the London chronicler. The most famous casualty was Stewart of Darnley. His body was later recovered from the field and buried in the cathedral of Orléans, where Masses were said for the repose of his soul until the Revolution. His descendants were naturalised in France as lords of Aubigny in Berry and would fight in French armies until the seventeenth century. The battle at Rouvray became known as the 'battle of the Herrings', after the commodity loaded onto most of the wagons. It was Lent, and herrings were in demand.[53]

The battle of the Herrings was a minor affair by the standard of the great battles of the war, but it came at a difficult moment for the Dauphin and his councillors. They were cast into the deepest gloom. A week after the battle, on 18 February, the principal Dauphinist captains in Orléans, including Clermont, Louis de Culant, La Hire and Poton de Saintrailles, left the city to confer with the Dauphin and his council at Chinon. It was a sombre meeting. The blame for the debacle at Rouvray seems to have been laid mainly on the shoulders of Clermont and Lafayette, who had first ordered La Hire's corps to wait for them and then tarried on their approach until it was too late. Clermont retired soon afterwards to the Bourbonnais, taking his men with him. Lafayette was later dismissed from the marshalsy. The general view was that Orléans was likely to fall. It was not easy to see how the position could be retrieved. It was known that Margaret of Scotland would not be coming to France in the current year, and neither would the 6,000 trained men which King James had promised to send with her. Patrick Ogilvy, who took over command of the Scots in France after Stewart of Darnley's death, was said by the Scottish chronicler Walter Bower to be a man of 'acute mind, lofty speech, and manly spirit, small in stature but honourable and trustworthy in every way'. But he had only sixty men-at-arms and 300 archers, less than half the strength of the Scottish corps six months before. As for the troops in Orléans, about a tenth of their strength had been lost in the battle, and their numbers continued to dwindle over the next six weeks as men were killed in skirmishes or withdrawn for field service. There were only 1,000 troops in the city by the end of March 1429. Revenue was still dribbling in and the garrison was being paid at least part of its due. But there was no money to pay for another field army. The Dauphin's borrowing capacity was exhausted. There were no reserves. At one point, his receiver-general confided to his wife that he had only four *écus* in hand. The last chance of relieving Orléans, he told her, had passed.[54]

In the Loire valley, panic set in. Well-placed individuals were reported to be deserting the Dauphin's cause to make peace with the English. At Chinon, contingency plans to withdraw to the Lyonnais and Dauphiné were revisited. In Charles of Orleans's castle of Blois and his mansion at Saumur, his servants were packing up his books and tapestries and the records of his administration to be evacuated to La Rochelle for safety. There were rumours that the Dauphin was contemplating leaving France for exile in Castile. They were almost certainly false, but the fact that they circulated at all spoke volumes about the mood of the moment.[55]

Before leaving Orléans for the conference at Chinon, the Count of Clermont had assured the citizens that he would be back with reinforcements and supplies to boost the city's dwindling stocks. It was an unrealistic promise, and when it became clear that it could not be honoured, the morale of the Orléanais plumbed new depths. Towards the end of February 1429, they gave up hope and resolved to open negotiations with the enemy. According to the usually well-informed Pope Pius II it was Charles of Orléans who suggested, in a letter to the city authorities, that they should place themselves under the protection of the Duke of Burgundy. It seems likely that before making this suggestion, Charles had sounded out Philip himself. At any rate, the men of Orléans acted on his advice. At the beginning of March, a delegation consisting of Poton de Saintrailles and two prominent citizens left the city to lobby Philip in Flanders. Their instructions were to persuade him of the injustice of attacking the domains of a prisoner of war, and to propose a truce covering the whole of Charles's appanage. Philip had probably already come to this view, but if not, he was easily persuaded. He was in any event due to go to Paris to confer with the Regent and the other English leaders. He agreed to raise the matter with them. Poton returned to Orléans for discussions with the Dauphin's officers while his two colleagues accompanied Philip to Paris.[56]

Philip the Good entered Paris on 4 April 1429. A few days later Poton de Saintrailles arrived, accompanied by representatives of the Dauphin. He brought with him a proposal, which was shrewdly calculated to appeal to Philip's chivalrous instincts as well as his self-esteem and to drive a wedge between him and the Duke of Bedford. He suggested that Orléans should be surrendered to Philip himself, to hold as stakeholder pending a political settlement between the Dauphin and the English. Meanwhile a truce would be proclaimed covering Charles of Orléans's appanage. Its revenues would be equally divided between the Duke and the English. In addition, the city offered to pay the English 10,000 *écus* as a contribution to the costs of the siege. Philip adopted these proposals as his own and pressed them on the Duke of Bedford. The war, he said, was nothing to do with Charles of Orléans. As a prisoner of war, he was unable to defend his domains and was entitled to protection.

Faced with this unwelcome pressure, Bedford's usual tact deserted him. The duchy of Orléans was an appanage of its Duke, he replied, but it was also a fief of the French Crown. He was astonished to hear the Duke of Burgundy, who was duty bound to uphold the rights of Henry VI, suggest that anyone else should hold conquered territory in France. Whose side did Philip think he was on? Before reaching a final decision, Bedford withdrew to consult his council. They were as indignant as he was. The government had spent large sums on the siege and had lost some of its finest troops, they said. The city was on the verge of collapse, and the Regent would soon be in a position to impose his own terms. Why back down now? The Duke of Bedford agreed. He declined to accept that he should 'beat the bushes only for someone else to get the birds'. Raoul le Sage put it more crudely. 'We have chewed the dish; why let the Duke of Burgundy swallow it?' Throughout these exchanges, Poton and his fellow delegates were waiting to be admitted to the Regent's presence. They never were. Bedford would not receive them except to negotiate the surrender of their city to the English commanders. When this was put to them, they replied that they had no instructions to discuss such a thing. On that note, the negotiations came to an end. Poton de Saintrailles returned to Orléans with the citizen delegates.

Philip the Good was furious about the lost opportunity and the slight to himself. He sent a herald to Orléans in Poton's company to order all those in his obedience to withdraw from the siege. It is not clear how many of the men encamped around Orléans left as a result of this order. Given that Philip had cancelled the substantial army that he had once intended to bring to the Loire, the effect of the new order was probably largely symbolic. The Burgundian garrison of Sully withdrew to the Nivernais. Some companies of volunteers withdrew from the siege, but they are unlikely to have been numerous enough to make much difference.[57]

In the course of March and April 1429, the English redoubled their efforts to overcome the city's resistance. The Duke of Bedford moved his headquarters from Chartres to Corbeil on the Seine, within easy reach of both Paris and Orléans. There was another summons of the Norman feudal host. They began to arrive in substantial numbers. The cost of Bedford's army rose to 40,000 *livres* a month, a figure which was bound to rise further as reinforcements arrived from Normandy. In the past six months, the Regent had already extracted two grants of taxation from the Norman Estates and one from the Norman Church, representing a total nominal yield of 270,000 *livres* (£30,000). He persuaded the Pope, instead of just confirming the clerical tenth in the ordinary way, to double it, something that Martin V was happy to do in return for the right to levy a third tenth for his own account. There were howls of protest from the clergy and some resistance to the collectors. More howls greeted Bedford's order that all officials of the dual monarchy in France must lend a quarter's wages to the government, on pain of forfeiting half a year's pay.[58]

Outside Orléans, five new English forts were rising from the ground. The line of trenches across the north-western approach, was reinforced by the construction of three garrisoned bastides, which the English nicknamed 'London', 'Rouen' and 'Paris'. Powerful batteries of artillery were sited on top of them. Another bastide was built in the ruins of the church of Saint-Loup on the north bank upstream of the city to command the course of the river. This finally stopped the flow of supplies to the city through the river port of Saint-Loup on the opposite bank. Later, after a small convoy of animals had been successfully driven overland and ferried over the Loire by the hamlet of Saint-Jean-le-Blanc, a bastide was built there to block this route too. At Corbeil, the Duke of Bedford was planning for the day that the city fell. He hoped to bring Henry VI, now seven years old, to France to be crowned and receive the homage of his French subjects. He would be accompanied by a great army to follow up the victory. A seaborne expedition from England would finally put an end to the operations of the Dauphinist garrison of Mont-Saint-Michel.[59]

'No one on earth, no king or duke or princess of Scotland can save France,' Joan of Arc had declared a few weeks earlier; 'I alone can save her.'[60]

CHAPTER VI

Joan of Arc:
Domrémy to Reims, 1429

Joan of Arc's brief public career lasted barely two years, from her first appearance at the Dauphin's court at Chinon at the age of seventeen in February 1429 to her execution for blasphemy and heresy at Rouen in May 1431. Her military campaigns lasted less than half of that, from the campaign to relieve Orléans, which began in April 1429, to her capture at the siege of Compiègne in May 1430. Joan's life was the subject of two elaborate judicial investigations: in the trial at Rouen which led to her execution, and a quarter of a century later in the inquiry conducted after the final defeat of the English, which resulted in her posthumous exoneration in 1456. Joan was the only witness at her trial, but more than 120 witnesses who had known her at different points of her life gave evidence at the posthumous inquiry. Thanks to the detailed records of these proceedings, we know more about Joan of Arc than any other person of her class and time. Yet much of this material is treacherous. Both proceedings were intensely political. Joan's evidence at her trial was given in response to questions carefully framed by trained theologians and inquisitors in order to fit her into conventional legal or religious categories. For their part, the politicians had their own stereotypes. It suited both sides to portray Joan as possessed of supernatural powers. For the Dauphinists she was the instrument of God's redemption of his chosen people. The English and their French allies, on the other hand, needed to blunt the moral force of her victories by showing that they were the work of the Devil. Whether she was an instrument of God or Satan, or perhaps no more than a charismatic leader, became a contentious political issue. Pope Pius II, writing three decades after her death, confessed to being unable to decide. But Pius was an Italian, an intellectual and a pragmatic politician. Few contemporaries viewed Joan's career with the same detachment. The crust of myth had already begun to form around her story within days of her first appearance at Chinon. 'Many marvellous things are told of her birth and life as if they were true', wrote the churchmen appointed to consider her case less than six weeks later. As a Parisian cleric remarked with disgust, Masses were said in her honour and portraits and statues made of her within weeks of the relief of Orléans, 'as if she were already beatified'.[1]

Joan did not know the date of her birth but told her judges that she thought that she was nineteen years old. She was born at Domrémy in Lorraine, probably early in 1412, at the height of the French civil wars and three years before Henry V's first invasion of France. Her father's name was Jacques Darc, but she never called herself Joan 'of Arc'. In Lorraine, girls took the surname of their mother. She was known simply as Jeannette at home and as Jeanne after she had left for the Dauphin's court. Throughout her public career she referred to herself as 'La Pucelle', the 'Maid', which meant a young girl between the ages of puberty and marriage. Legend made her a shepherdess, because it suited the image which people had of her. In St Luke's Gospel the birth of Christ was first revealed to the shepherds, and Christian tradition held them to be mild, innocent, loving and open to the revelations of God. 'Be shepherds of the Church of God,' St Paul had enjoined his followers. But Joan was not a shepherdess. Her father was an agricultural labourer. Like other villagers, he was a serf, owing labour services to the lords of Bourlémont, the feudal lords of Domrémy. He had a smallholding of his own, with some cattle and draught animals. But by her own account Joan rarely looked after animals. She had been taught to sew and spin and at her trial gave her trade as seamstress.[2]

Domrémy stood on the west bank of the Meuse, which in the early fifteenth century marked the north-eastern limit of France. The region was a complex and unstable mosaic of fragmented territories and overlapping jurisdictions, which had recently assumed growing political significance. The northern part of Domrémy belonged to the castlery of Vaucouleurs, an important frontier fortress twelve miles downriver, which in the past had been the traditional meeting place of the kings of France and the German emperors. Vaucouleurs belonged to the county of Champagne and was part of the French royal demesne. The rest of the village, where Joan's family lived, belonged to the duchy of Bar. The duchy comprised scattered lands on both sides of the frontier, but Domrémy belonged to France. Beyond the Meuse, the duchy of Lorraine was the dominant local power. Lorraine was a francophone principality of the German Empire, but its dukes had moved in the political orbit of France for more than a century. Other regional powers, the Bishops of Metz, Toul and Verdun, and the Counts of Vaudémont, Sarrebrück and Salm, occupied an ambiguous position between the Empire and France, and between Lancaster and Valois.

The Dukes of Burgundy were a more distant but also a more powerful presence. They had a vital interest in the region, because it lay across one of the main corridors between Burgundy and the Low Countries. The Dukes had manoeuvred for influence there for many years. They were closely allied to the Dukes of Lorraine and to a number of lesser lords of the region, both French and German. Their main regional rival was the house of Anjou. Yolande of Anjou was descended on her mother's side from the Dukes of Bar. In 1419, she had achieved a spectacular dynastic coup. Her kinsman Louis, Cardinal of Bar and Bishop of Châlons-sur-Marne, had unexpectedly inherited the duchy of Bar in 1415 after the death of two brothers and a nephew at the battle of Agincourt. She persuaded him to adopt her second son, the ten-year-old Réné of Anjou, and to designate him as his heir. At about the same time, Charles II Duke of Lorraine, who had no legitimate sons, agreed that Réné would marry his elder daughter and succeed to the duchy of Lorraine as well. The Dukes of Anjou were the chief princely supporters of the Dauphin. These transactions were therefore a serious threat to the Dukes of Burgundy and indirectly to their English allies. The Dukes of Burgundy had gone to great lengths to draw Lorraine and Bar into the orbit of England. In 1422 Charles of Lorraine did homage to Henry V and adhered to the treaty of Troyes. In April 1429, during the closing stages of the siege of Orléans, Réné, now twenty years old and already in control of the duchy of Bar, was persuaded by his father-in-law to follow suit and seal a document promising to do homage to Henry VI. The act was performed by proxy at the beginning of May and confirmed by Réné himself in June.[3]

The English had occupied most of the royal *bailliage* of Chaumont, in which Domrémy was situated, since 1421. They had three major garrisons there, in the castle of Coiffy and the towns of Montigny-le-Roi (modern Val-de-Meuse) and Nogent-le-Roi (modern Nogent-en-Bassigny). In the late 1420s, all three places were commanded by the Yorkshire knight Sir Thomas Gargrave, a veteran of Agincourt and Verneuil. For some years, the English position in the region had been challenged by the companies of La Hire and his protégés. But by 1425, most of the Dauphin's partisans had been cleared from Champagne. The valley of the Meuse was the only area north of the Seine where there were still important Dauphinist garrisons. In August 1428, an Anglo-Burgundian army commanded by John of Luxembourg had invaded the valley and overrun every one of them except for Vaucouleurs, which became the sole beacon of the Dauphinist cause in the region. In the fortress, a large garrison held out against the incoming Anglo-Burgundian tide under the command of the Lorraine nobleman Robert de Baudricourt, a friend and counsellor of Réné of Anjou and a loyal follower of the Dauphin with good connections at his court. Vaucouleurs and Robert de Baudricourt became the targets of a sustained guerrilla war fought by Antoine de Vergy, Henry VI's governor of Champagne and captain of Langres.[4]

Domrémy was far away from Paris and Bourges, but it was not a backwater. Its inhabitants lived constantly under the threat of war. Companies of *routiers* loosely affiliated to one or other local potentate infested the Barrois. Mounted raiding parties from the French garrison of Vaucouleurs and the English garrisons of Montigny and Nogent passed within a few miles of their homes. The companies of Antoine de Vergy invaded the district in pursuit of Robert of Baudricourt. Domrémy itself was burned at least once and its church left in ruins. Joan was eleven years old when a cousin living a few miles away was killed by a cannonball fired at the church where he had fled for safety. In the same year, the villagers were obliged to pay *pâtis* to Robert of Sarrebrück lord of Commercy, at that stage a Dauphinist partisan. Joan's father was one of those who put his name to the agreement. Two years later a company of Savoyard *routiers* in the service of the Duke of Burgundy carried off all their cattle. When Domrémy was threatened the villagers fled with their animals to a nearby island in the Meuse or took refuge in the walled town of Neufchâteau six miles away. The threats came indiscriminately from Dauphinists and Burgundians alike. But like much of northern France, Domrémy took sides. It was an Armagnac village. There was only one Burgundian there, and Joan told her judges that she would have been happy for him to be beheaded 'if such was God's will'. Her venom against Burgundians was shared by her neighbours. Young men would go out to fight the villagers of Maxey across the river, who were Burgundians, and would return covered in blood. This was war in miniature. News of the wider conflict percolated through to Domrémy by many routes. It was carried by merchants, preachers and other travellers on the old Roman road from Langres to Verdun, which passed within three miles of the village; or picked up at Neufchâteau, an important market town whose trading links extended into France, Germany and the Low Countries. Local noblemen had their own informants. The captain of Vaucouleurs maintained a regular correspondence with the court of Réné of Anjou. At Domrémy, they knew about the military vicissitudes of the kingdom of Bourges; about the wickedness of Isabelle of Bavaria, who was commonly blamed for the treaty of Troyes; about the captivity of Charles of Orléans in England; about the King of Scotland's promise to send a fresh army to France; and about the siege of Orléans.[5]

Joan of Arc was an intelligent, self-confident and articulate young woman with a formidable presence but no formal education. A shrewd witness, who thought well of her and had a good opportunity to observe her at close quarters, described her as a 'very simple and ignorant woman'. She spoke French with the pronounced accent of Lorraine. She may have learned the rudiments of reading in the final months of her life, but at the outset of her public career she was certainly illiterate. She signed her name with a cross or sometimes with another's hand to guide her fingers across the page. 'I know neither A nor B,' she told the churchmen who interrogated her after her first appearance at Chinon. She had learned her faith from her mother, but as she grew older, she developed an intense religious and emotional sensibility which was very much her own. She attended every service in the church of Domrémy, and not only Mass on Sunday. She prayed often. In church, she prostrated herself before the crucifix and the image of the Virgin. She confessed and took communion several times a week at a time when most lay people took the sacrament only once a year at Easter. Those who observed her at Chinon reported that she was highly emotional, alternating readily between grief and joy. She wept copious tears while praying or receiving the eucharist. Like many other holy women of the time, Joan was anorexic, a condition sometimes regarded as an overt sign of sanctity and often associated with ecstatic and mystical experiences.[6]

In the summer of 1425, when Joan was thirteen years old, she had an intense spiritual experience in the garden of her father's house at Domrémy. She believed that she had seen a bright light from the direction of the parish church and heard a 'voice coming from God to guide her'. The experience recurred frequently over the following months, perhaps two or three times a week, in the garden, in the fields, or in the woods nearby. The source of the voice gradually became clearer in her mind. She came to believe that an angel was speaking to her, whom she eventually identified as the Archangel Michael, the chief of the celestial host and the patron saint of the Dauphin's cause. She visualised him as she had seen him painted in local churches: beautiful, young, winged, robed in white and carrying a sword and buckler. Later came other voices: the Archangel Gabriel; then St Catherine and St Margaret, both of whom were the objects of local cults around Domrémy. Episodes of this kind are well documented in the history of Christianity and other religions. Modern psychology has shown how strongly sensory perceptions are influenced by prior expectations and beliefs. The expectations and beliefs of people were very different in the self-contained communities of late medieval Europe, in which almost everything was experienced within a framework of intense religious faith and the omnipresence of God. It is unnecessary to be a believer oneself in order to accept that Joan of Arc genuinely believed in the reality of her voices and in the visions that gave them bodily form. 'I saw them with my eyes, as clearly as I see you now,' she told the judges at her trial.

At first, the voices gave her only spiritual guidance. But later they acquired a more overtly political tone, which may have been associated with the growing insecurity and violence of life in wartime Lorraine and the deterioration of the Dauphin's political fortunes. Joan believed that her voices were messengers of God, commanding her to go before the Dauphin and expel the English from France. As time went on, the commands became more specific. Initially, her mission was to be to lead the Dauphin to Reims to be crowned. After the English laid siege to Orléans, Joan's voices told her that she was God's instrument for breaking the English siege. They promised to guide and support her in her mission. They foretold that the English would be defeated and that Charles VII would live to rule over his entire kingdom. Some of this may have been associated with a rejection of her parents' authority. Joan resolved to leave home without telling them. She rejected the fiancé whom they found for her. She made a private vow of virginity, an assertion of female autonomy in a world dominated by men, and a dedication of her life to God in the eyes of a Christian tradition which rejected sexuality as impure. Shortly, Joan acquired a local reputation as a holy woman. Her fame spread. It even reached the ears of the Duke of Lorraine.[7]

That a seventeen-year-old girl claiming direct communication with God and his saints should have been taken seriously, both in Lorraine and later at Chinon, seemed less surprising to her contemporaries than it does now. The attitude of medieval people to the miraculous reflected an approach to the natural world which has vanished from the canon of European thought since the seventeenth century. God and nature did not exist on separate planes. The world was not ordered by impersonal forces or by laws of nature reflecting empirical experience. It was governed at every point by the direct action of divine providence. The will of God lay behind every event, great or small. Seen in this light, the miraculous became normal, a mere manifestation of God's changing intentions. It was a commonplace of contemporary belief that the civil wars of France and the victories of the English pointed to a profound rupture between God and the French kingdom, provoked by the sins of France. Joan herself believed this, as she told the judges at her trial. Prophets and seers were symptoms of crisis. People looked to spiritual heroes, to a saviour of spotless purity and virtue who would appease the divine wrath, saving them from the consequences of their sins, as Christ himself had done. An age of anxiety, pessimism and violence, of political instability and defeat, was receptive to myths of redemption.[8]

Joan's was a well-beaten path. In the previous century St Bridget of Sweden and St Catherine of Siena had commanded attention across Europe for their imprecations against the papal schism and their prophecies of disaster if the sins which had brought about this catastrophe were not amended. The same message came from a variety of more heterodox figures. Many of them were women, usually young, poor and without education, characteristics which were an important part of their appeal. They were models of purity in a corrupted world. Marie of Avignon (alias Marie Robine), who pushed her way into the presence of a Pope and a Queen of France at the end of the fourteenth century with prophecies of calamity, was an uneducated peasant girl from Gascony. Like Joan, she claimed to have been guided by divine voices. 'Go and seek out the King of France', they had told her. Writing in the closing years of the fourteenth century, the Paris-trained theologian Henry of Langenstein believed that eschatological revelations of this kind had multiplied in his own day and all the contemporary evidence tends to bear this out. It was, he thought, the product of political and social disintegration, a sign of the imminent advent of Antichrist which would precede the second coming.[9]

The royal line of France had a special place in the apocalyptic literature of the time. More than any other European monarchs, the kings of France had developed a public mythology of kingship. It endowed them with a sacral status and priestly powers. Their special relationship with God was symbolised by their coronation, their anointment with holy oil, their gift of touching for scrofula (the 'King's evil'), the memory of St Louis and the ritual theatre of the court. A popular myth held that they would be the kings of the Fourth Empire, a line of rulers blessed of God who in the last days of the world would expel the wicked, recover the Holy Land and receive the empire of the world. The calamities of fourteenth- and fifteenth-century France provoked the appearance of a succession of seers and prophets declaring that they were charged to bring the word of God to its kings. Some of them had powerful political patrons, like the tertiary Franciscan Colette of Corbie, who was supported by Jacques de Bourbon Count of La Marche; or the aristocratic visionary Jeanne-Marie de Maillé, also closely associated with the Franciscans, who until her death in 1414 was a protégé of the house of Anjou and widely regarded as the 'Armagnac' saint. At least twenty such figures can be traced in the chronicles of the time, some of whom had messages uncannily like Joan's. There were no doubt others whose brief appearances on the political scene passed unrecorded.[10]

It was as a seer in this tradition that Joan of Arc first emerged into public light. She 'declared herself to be a prophetess, saying "Truly this or that thing will happen",' wrote the choleric contemporary chronicler of Paris. Her youth, simplicity and humble origins placed Joan in a classic line of redemptive holy women. She was 'an angel of the God of armies', wrote an early admirer, 'sent to achieve the redemption of His people and the restoration of the kingdom'. Like Jeanne-Marie de Maillé, her message was overtly political. She was opposed to the Regent of France, the English and their French supporters. Joan was not the only one, even in her own time. She had at least three rivals, all of them associated with opposition to the English. They included the visionary Pierrone 'the Breton', sometime companion of Joan's campaigns, who preached her word in English-held territory until she was arrested and burned at the stake in Paris; the stigmatic William 'the Shepherd', a young seer from the Gevaudan who rode like Joan with the armies; and Catherine of La Rochelle, who went from town to town calling on people to surrender their gold and silver for the Dauphin's cause, and whom Joan denounced as a fraud and told to 'go home to her housework'. There is some evidence that all three had been groomed for their role by the same itinerant Franciscan friar, who called himself Brother Richard, a man of uncertain orthodoxy and strong Dauphinist loyalties who eventually exhausted the patience of even his own side.[11]

In the spring of 1429, tensions were high and prophecies proliferated on both sides of the political divide. An Italian newsletter written from Bruges reported that France was awash with reports of prophecies said to have been 'found in Paris', announcing an imminent turn in the Dauphin's fortunes. It was in this electric atmosphere that Brother Richard, who had spent more than a month preaching in Orléans during the siege, turned up in Paris and began to draw large crowds with highly charged sermons based on his own brand of eschatological mysticism. He declared that Antichrist had already been born and that the day of judgement was at hand. He foretold 'the greatest wonders ever seen' for the coming year, claims which were generally regarded as hinting at a Dauphinist victory. Brother Richard was preaching in Paris shortly after Joan of Arc had publicly announced her mission. The authorities in the capital believed that he was in league with her and expelled him from the city. But well before Brother Richard's advent, prophecies had been circulating which foretold that the kingdom of France would be saved by a virgin warrior. Some of them were adapted from the celebrated prophecies of Merlin in the works of the twelfth-century Welsh writer Geoffrey of Monmouth. Some were derived from the opaque words of an author known to contemporaries as 'Bede' (actually the fourteenth-century Englishman John of Bridlington). Others were prophecies of uncertain origin, more or less altered to fit current circumstances. 'Merlin, the Sybils and Bede, had seen her coming for 500 years,' declared the poet and novelist Christine de Pisan.

These utterances were widely known and extremely influential, especially among those around the Dauphin. Charles himself was a superstitious man, who had long been fascinated by astrology, chronograms and other forms of political prognostication. He had patronised John of Ghent, the hermit of the Jura, who foretold the death of Henry V. He had received prophecies of victory by a virgin's intervention from the Italian astrologer Giovanni da Montalcino. Prophecies of this kind were familiar to several of his closest friends and councillors. His confessor Gérard Machet is unlikely to have approved of astrology, but he had heard the legend of the virgin redeemer of France and believed it. He was destined to play an important part in launching Joan of Arc's military career. If the witnesses to the inquiry of the 1450s are to be believed, Joan herself had heard similar prophecies at Domrémy. In June 1428, she was telling villagers that within a year a young girl would lead the Dauphin to Reims to be crowned. This girl, she said, would come from their own region. She may already have come to believe that she herself was the redeemer. 'Has it not been said that France will be devasted by the act of a woman,' she asked her cousin, referring to Isabelle of Bavaria, '... and then rescued by a virgin?' Joan's own apparent belief in prophecies of the warlike mission of an armed virgin explains much. One reason for her credibility in the eyes of contemporaries was that she deliberately modelled herself on the heroine imagined in stories like these which already had a wide circulation.[12]

It was probably in about the middle of December 1428 that Joan decided that her time had come. She resolved to leave home and find her way to the Dauphin. She needed money, a horse, an escort for the long and dangerous journey to the Loire, and patronage to enable her to obtain an audience when she got there. She resolved to apply to Robert de Baudricourt, the captain of Vaucouleurs. She told her judges that it was her voices who told her to do this. But it was the natural course to take in any event. Joan did not know Baudricourt, but he was the only Dauphinist notable in the district and an obvious point of contact with the wider political world. She confided her plan to an older cousin who lived in a village near Vaucouleurs, and he agreed to take her into his home and then bring her to Baudricourt.

Robert de Baudricourt was a tough soldier with little time for fantasists. Joan had three difficult meetings with him over a period of about six weeks. On the first occasion, she told him that she was charged by God with an important message for the Dauphin. The message was that he should on no account risk a pitched battle against the English. Instead, God, who was the true lord and protector of the French kingdom, would send him help by mid-Lent which would enable him to triumph over his enemies. She, Joan, would then lead him to Reims to be crowned King. Baudricourt refused to take all this seriously and sent her away. She tried again and received an even more brutal rebuff. Turning to her cousin, who was with her, Baudricourt told him to give her a good hiding and take her back to her parents. Joan, however, persisted. At about the end of January 1429, Baudricourt visited her at the house in which she was staying at Vaucouleurs, accompanied by the parish priest, who attempted to perform an exorcism upon her. The scene was described by her landlady in her evidence to the rehabilitation inquiry in 1455. At the end of the ceremony, Joan called on Baudricourt for the third time to help her reach the Dauphin. She told him that she would go before the Dauphin whatever he said, even if she had to get there on her hands and knees. 'Have you not heard the prophecy that France will be destroyed by a woman and saved by a young girl from the marches of Lorraine?', she asked. Her passion made a powerful impression, and some time afterwards Baudricourt relented.[13]

The most plausible hypothesis is that he changed his mind as a result of exchanges with Charles Duke of Lorraine and Réné of Anjou. Both men had their own reasons to be interested in Joan. Charles was in failing health and hoped that the holy woman might heal him. Réné may have heard, or been told, about the prophecies, and thought that there could be something in her claims. Shortly after Joan's third encounter with Robert de Baudricourt, a safe-conduct arrived for her to come before Charles of Lorraine. Réné, who was then at Saint-Mihiel, left at once to join Charles. Joan met the Duke, probably at Toul, an independent episcopal city on the marches of the duchy of Lorraine. Réné may have been present. Very little is known about what happened there. What is clear is that Joan told the Duke about her plan to go before the Dauphin and made a bid for Réné's patronage. She wanted him to accompany her to Chinon. This request was turned down, either by Charles of Lorraine or by Réné himself. But Charles supported her adventure. He gave her a horse and some money for the journey. The patronage of these powerful men seems to have made the difference. When Joan returned to Vaucouleurs, Robert de Baudricourt paid for another horse and provided her with a sword and an escort of four men-at-arms and two servants. He gave her a letter of recommendation to the Dauphin. Her companions and the inhabitants of Vaucouleurs found her some male clothing, a necessary precaution for a young woman travelling through country infested by soldiers and brigands. Her landlady cropped her hair to make her look like a page. Thus clothed and equipped, Joan and her escort set out for Chinon, probably on 13 February 1429. Although she did not know it, it was the day after the battle of the Herrings. 'Go, go, whatever fate may hold in store,' Baudricourt told her as she left.[14]

Their route took them through Champagne, northern Burgundy and the Auxerrois, territory controlled by the English and their Burgundian allies. At about the beginning of March they reached Gien, the only bridge-town of the middle Loire still held by the Dauphin's partisans and a vital communications hub for his armies. Here, she publicly announced her mission. She had come, she said, at the command of God to raise the siege of Orléans and lead the Dauphin to Reims to be crowned. The news was rapidly carried to Orléans, where it generated much curiosity and excitement. The Bastard of Orléans sent two of his officers to Chinon to warn the Dauphin and his councillors. While they digested these reports, Joan made her way to Sainte-Catherine-de-Fierbois, a small town some twenty miles east of Chinon where there was a sanctuary dedicated to Ste Catherine, one of her guiding spirits. From here she wrote to the Dauphin telling him that she had travelled 150 leagues to bring him important news and aid in his war and asking for an audience.[15]

The reports from Vaucouleurs, Gien and Orléans had already provoked much discussion and a fair amount of scepticism at the Dauphin's court. There was a vigorous debate in the Dauphin's council. Some councillors thought that she was a charlatan and that Charles should have nothing to do with her. Others said that there was no harm in listening to what she had to say. They were impressed by Robert of Baudricourt's letter of recommendation and by the fact that she had crossed several hundred miles of enemy-occupied territory to reach them. There may have been some truth in the suggestion made years later to Pope Pius II by a well-placed French diplomat that an unnamed 'cunning individual' saw in Joan a way of uniting the quarrelling factions at the Dauphin's court against the English. Towards the end of February 1429, at midday, Joan entered Chinon with her small group of companions. Emissaries were sent to her lodgings in the town to ask what her business was. She told them that she had been commanded by God to raise the siege of Orléans and lead the Dauphin to Reims. They interrogated her travelling companions, who were unable to add anything. A committee of councillors examined her. They were unable to reach any firm conclusion. They advised the Dauphin to have her claims properly investigated before deciding whether to receive her. This was expected to take two or three days. But Charles overruled them. He decided to see Joan straight away.[16]

Shortly after her arrival at Chinon, Joan was received by the Dauphin. Their meeting is one of the most celebrated moments in the history of France and, like other such occasions, quickly acquired a veneer of spurious miraculous detail. Apart from Joan's own brief summary at her trial, the most reliable accounts are those given to the posthumous enquiry of 1456 by Raoul de Gaucourt, who had been present, and by her confessor, who had not been present but said that he had the details from Joan herself. Joan and her four companions were admitted to the castle and received by the Count of Vendôme. In the late afternoon they were introduced into an audience hall overlooking the river Vienne. The hall was packed with more than 300 gentlemen of the court, their faces lit in the fading daylight by fifty torches. Her appearance was striking. She wore male clothes: a black tunic over a short grey robe and a black hat covering her close-cropped dark hair. The Dauphin asked her name. Addressing him as '*gentil Dauphin*', she replied, 'I am called Joan La Pucelle, and the King of Heaven has commanded that through me you are to be consecrated and crowned in the city of Reims.' Then she told him, 'On behalf of my God, I tell you that you are the true heir of France and that He has sent me to take you to Reims.'[17]

Charles was an impressionable man, who was fascinated by Joan. According to his former secretary Alain Chartier, who was probably present, it was obvious that their brief exchange had thrilled him. He ordered the lieutenant governor of the fortress to take charge of her. He had her lodged in rooms in the Tour du Coudray, the great circular keep of Philip Augustus on the west side of the castle. He assigned a young nobleman to serve as her page. On the day after her first appearance before him, they had a private interview, and on the day after that another in the presence of Georges de la Trémoille and the Duke of Alençon. Joan expanded on her message. She called on the Dauphin to surrender the kingdom of France to God, who would then re-grant it to him 'as he had done with all of his predecessors'. His title to the Crown would then be beyond question. Over the following days, there were more meetings, sometimes with the Dauphin alone, sometimes with one or two selected advisers in attendance.

Charles was keen to take Joan at her own valuation. Some influential figures at court encouraged him. His confessor Gérard Machet, who had recently been admitted to the council, was one of the first to connect Joan with older prophecies of a virgin saviour. Another early supporter, John II Duke of Alençon, who shared the Dauphin's obsession with astrology and the supernatural, befriended Joan, taking his meals with her and attending her meetings with Charles. He seems to have been among the first to realise that Joan's utter conviction in her divinely ordained mission might make her an inspirational leader of armies. Even Georges de la Trémoille, who was later to turn against Joan, was prepared to swallow whatever scepticism he may have felt.[18]

Not all of Charles's councillors were convinced. Some of them regarded Joan's project as rash and the impression that she had obviously made on the Dauphin as dangerous. They had lost confidence in the prospects of military action and thought that in the long run the only way out of the Dauphin's predicament was a reconciliation with the Duke of Burgundy. Their attitude to Joan was probably faithfully represented by Jacques Gélu, the outspoken former Archbishop of Tours and a man firmly grounded in the traditions of the royal administration. Gélu had retired to Provence but still maintained an active correspondence with influential figures at court. Asked for his advice shortly after Joan's arrival at Chinon, he replied that although the English invasion was an offence against all morality and law the Dauphin should not be too ready to listen to an impressionable young peasant girl. She might well be deluded or turn out to belong to some questionable sect. Gélu thought that Charles was in danger of making a fool of himself. France's international standing was low enough as it was, without allowing its King to be taken for a dupe. He accepted that Joan should not be dismissed out of hand, in case she truly was the agent of the Almighty for chastising the English. But he knew Charles's weakness. He warned him, too late, against any attempt to assess the girl himself. On no account should he allow her access to him or receive her in private audience. She should be properly examined by experts.[19]

The medieval Church had an ambivalent attitude to visionaries and prophets. They could not simply be ignored, for there was scriptural and patristic authority that God did occasionally communicate with mankind through prophets and other holy men and women. No one doubted that some visions and revelations were authentic.

But orthodox opinion instinctively distrusted people who claimed a direct relationship with God. Thomas Aquinas had set the tone two centuries before by observing that while true prophets could be instructive, they should be regarded as altogether exceptional. 'Beware of false prophets', warned the French theologian Pierre d'Ailly, whose treatise, written at the end of the previous century, was regarded as the authoritative work on the subject. They were often fantasists or charlatans or possessed by the Devil. They escaped the mediation of the clergy and the authority of the Church. They were liable to favour a variety of heterodox beliefs and practices, especially if they were lowly, uneducated or female.

The investigations that the council would have preferred to carry out before Joan's first audience in the end took place afterwards. Joan was physically examined by various noble ladies, who confirmed that she was a woman and a virgin. She was interviewed by a group of clerics at court, including Gérard Machet. They reported that she appeared to be orthodox, devout, sober, temperate and chaste, and that her answers were so articulate and pertinent that, given her lack of education, the hand of God was the only plausible explanation. But they recommended that before a final decision was made, she should be sent to Poitiers for a more thorough interrogation. At the same time, the Dauphin's officials were directed to write seeking the opinion of eminent scholars, including the celebrated theologian Jean Gerson, the titular Chancellor of the University of Paris then living in exile at Lyon, who was the author of a well-known treatise on visions and other paranormal phenomena.[20]

About a week after Joan's appearance at Chinon, the Dauphin left for Poitiers, bringing Joan and his principal councillors with him. Poitiers was the judicial capital of the kingdom of Bourges and the refuge of many of the theologians of the University of Paris who had fled from the Burgundians after their entry into the capital in 1418. The Dauphin's Chancellor Regnault de Chartres assembled a commission of theologians, lawyers and councillors to interview Joan and report their findings. In the early fifteenth century, there were recognised criteria for assessing the authenticity of visions and prophecies. There were two stages. The first was an examination of the supposed prophet's character, to ensure that she led a blameless life, held orthodox opinions and behaved with suitable decorum. One should be particularly careful about people whose motives or methods seemed to be manipulative. Any sign of arrogance or pride, pretentiousness or spiritual exhibitionism was to be distrusted. The commissioners' main difficulty in Joan's case was the warlike role that she envisaged for herself and her male dress, which she had continued to wear after her journey from Lorraine. The outside experts who were consulted also had difficulty with this. The concept of killing other Christians in battle had always posed difficulties to the Church even when it was done by men. In the end, they turned to biblical precedents. Had not Judith saved her city by beheading the Assyrian general Holofernes? Was it not natural for God to use the weaker sex for his purposes, in order to demonstrate his power and the worthlessness of mere human skills? As for her clothes, transvestism was a long-standing religious taboo dating back to the Book of Deuteronomy ('The woman shall not wear that which pertaineth unto a man, neither shall a man put on a woman's garment, for all that do so are abomination unto the Lord thy God.'). For reasons which were never clear, Joan regarded the wearing of male clothing as an issue of principle. She claimed that she had been ordered by her voices to wear it. She wore it not only on campaign or on horseback, contexts in which there were practical considerations in its favour, but at all times. What was more, she wore short tunics and robes of a kind that moralists regarded as indecent. Gerson, who is unlikely to have known the exact cut of her clothes, boldly declared that the Deuteronomic code was no part of the law of Christ and in any event could not apply to a woman appointed by God to be a warrior.[21]

The second stage of the inquiry was even more problematic. It consisted of a search for evidence that God had performed wonders through the supposed prophet (*signa*) and for older prophecies, preferably biblical, which could be said to relate to her (*scripta*). The commissioners questioned her about her voices, her long journey to Chinon and her mission. But this was not enough. God, they told her, could not possibly wish them to advise the Dauphin to entrust soldiers to her command and put their lives at risk without positive evidence of the divine character of her mission. What could she tell them that went beyond mere assertion? She replied that she had not come to Poitiers to work wonders. Let her have enough troops and she would lead them to Orléans, defeat the English and raise the siege. That would be their *signum*. As for the *scripta*, the commissioners consulted a wide range of prophetic writings. They appear to have examined an anthology of prophecies including those of Merlin and 'Bede', some of which appeared to foretell the raising of a great siege by a warrior 'clothed like a man, with the body of a woman'. One of the commissioners recalled a prophecy of Marie Robine of the calamities soon to befall France, from which the land would be rescued by a pure young girl.[22]

The Poitiers commission reported in early April 1429. Only a summary of their report survives, together with some fragmentary evidence of its contents given to the posthumous inquiry in the 1450s. The commissioners' advice was a masterpiece of equivocation. It was couched in the kind of reticent language which suggested that they were unwilling to go against the Dauphin's obvious desire to believe in Joan, but reluctant to be blamed if the result was a disaster. Joan's answers, they said, amply demonstrated her personal holiness and this was confirmed by the reports of those who had had to do with her since her arrival at Chinon. She appeared to have simple but orthodox opinions. The commissioners were satisfied for the time being with Joan's declaration that the relief of Orléans would be the 'sign' of her divine mission. But they recommended that the Dauphin should be cautious about this until she had proved it by her actions. They seem also to have accepted that older prophecies could at least arguably be said to relate to her. For the rest, they had nothing to say, at any rate so far as the summary shows. They were probably divided. So they passed over in silence the problems of Joan's transvestism and the warlike nature of her mission. They said nothing about her voices and visions, remarking only that she 'claimed' to have been sent by God. All in all, they reported that they had found nothing against her and concluded that, given the desperate military situation and the sufferings of the French people, it would be wrong to advise the Dauphin to turn her away.[23]

One of Joan's last acts before the hearings at Poitiers concluded was to dictate to one of the commissioners a letter addressed to Henry VI and the Duke of Bedford ('so-called Regent of France') and to the leaders of the English army outside Orléans. It was dated 22 March, and headed 'JHESU MARIA', which was to become the motto with which she opened every document which she dictated. In it, she announced her mission to the enemy. 'Surrender the keys of every town that you have taken in France to the Maid, who is the emissary of God the King of Heaven,' she commanded. If they complied and paid reparations for the damage that they had done, she would be merciful. But if not

'I will make them leave whether they like it or not and, if they decline to obey, I will have every one of them killed.' There is a good deal of evidence from the Lancastrian side that this missive, together with others of the same kind which followed, had an unsettling effect on the English. It was something new in their experience of war. But in a world which acknowledged the interventions of the God of battles it could not be ignored. The English were infuriated, but at the same time frightened. They declined to treat her interventions as legitimate acts of war, or even to recognise the customary immunity of her heralds. The herald who delivered her first challenge was treated as an emissary of Satan and thrown in prison. When, weeks later, Sir John Talbot came to respond, his answer consisted of foul-mouthed abuse. Joan, he said, was a whore who should go back to her cows unless she wanted to be burned as a witch.[24]

The report of the Poitiers commission cleared the way for Joan's employment in the relief of Orléans. She was brought back to Chinon at about the end of March 1429. In the castle the Dauphin's councillors were considering the report and arguing about what to make of it. Most of the clergymen were profoundly sceptical of her claims and were pressing the Dauphin to ignore her. Her evidence at her trial was that she went before him to confute the doubters in person. She embellished this evidence with fantastic detail, as she later admitted. But she did not resile from the essence of her story. She said that she was received by the Dauphin in the presence of the Chancellor Regnault de Chartres, La Trémoille, Clermont, Alençon and a number of other advisers, both clerical and lay. At some point, Charles asked her how he might be sure that she was sent by God. According to her own account at her trial, she responded with a 'sign', a spectacular affirmation of the divine character of her mission, the nature of which she refused to disclose to her judges. She had sworn, she declared, to reveal it to no one else and would not perjure herself. None of those said to have been present survived to give evidence to the inquiry of 1456 except for the Duke of Alençon, who said nothing about it. We shall never know what finally persuaded the Dauphin to believe in her mission. What is clear is that the doubters among his councillors were silenced. It was decided to try her out in an operation currently being planned to resupply Orléans.[25]

While the supplies and the escort force were being prepared, Joan was equipped for the task ahead. She was given her own military household, as much to control and protect her as to fight with her. It was headed by Jean d'Aulon, an experienced soldier and a 'wise and honourable man' according to the Bastard of Orléans, who had been present at the critical council meeting. The rest comprised a small group of men-at-arms including two of those who had accompanied her from Vaucouleurs and eventually two of her brothers who came to join her from Domrémy. There were also the friar Jean Pesquerel, who served as her confessor and amanuensis, two pages and an accounts clerk. They took her from Poitiers to Tours. Joan called for a sword from the collection of ex-voto offerings at the sanctuary of Sainte-Catherine-de-Fierbois, which she had visited on her journey to Chinon in February. The sanctuary was the site of an important pilgrimage closely associated with the war. Soldiers would offer up armour plates, chains or weapons as mementos of the saint's miraculous intervention to release them from captivity or cure them of their wounds. A sword with a distinctive hilt marked with five crosses was fetched by an armourer, who cleaned and repaired it. A set of scabbards was made for her, and a suit of armour. Joan was allowed her own standard. The famous silk banner, which she claimed to value forty times higher than her sword, was painted to her own design: a central figure of Christ with two angels, against a ground of fleurs-de-lys on a white background, with the motto 'JHESU MARIA'. By the time she left Tours in mid-April 1429, she must already have looked as Guy de Laval would describe her a few weeks later in a letter to his mother: a young girl mounted on a large black charger, wearing heavy plate armour from neck to toe and carrying a lance and an axe. Meanwhile, a dossier was prepared for distribution to the principal towns of France. It included a summary of the conclusions of the Poitiers commission, a copy of Joan's letter to the English and a selection of pertinent prophecies. The publicity given to these documents was a mark of the hopes that the Dauphin reposed in Joan.[26]

By her own account Joan of Arc had no martial skills when she left Domrémy. She could not even ride a horse. Yet at Chinon a number of people remarked that although she was simple and ignorant, she seemed to know a great deal about the arts of war. Some of this was exaggeration by witnesses to the enquiry of 1456 who had every incentive to play up the miraculous side of Joan's achievement. Some of it was probably bluff on Joan's part. But for all that, she clearly did have skills beyond her years or experience. How did she acquire them, or seem to have done? She appears to have learned to ride on the long journey from Vaucouleurs to Chinon. She probably learned how to handle a lance at the same time, presumably from her companions. Shortly after her arrival at Chinon, she was seen practising running with a lance in a meadow below the walls. But Joan cannot have had the physical strength and endurance to match the rough professionals who filled the ranks of fifteenth-century armies, most of whom had trained for war from the age of fourteen and had years of combat experience behind them. Nor did she need to. For although she was present in the midst of many fights, there is no evidence that she ever herself engaged in actual combat. She acquired a number of swords and wore one most of the time, but never had to strike an enemy with it. She had twelve horses including five chargers and learned to handle them expertly, but she never participated in a mass cavalry charge in serried ranks with couched lances. What she brought to the battles around Orléans was not military skill or experience but the ability to inspire others. Her real weapons were her charisma and her faith in herself and her voices, qualities which made her immune from fear, oblivious of pain and indifferent to danger. She had no objection to killing in battle but told her judges that she herself had never killed a man and preferred to carry her own standard so that she would never be in a position to.[27]

'I am a captain of war', Joan told the English captains in her famous first letter. At her trial, the prosecutors took her at her word. Contrary to the law of God and His saints, they alleged, she had constituted herself 'commander and captain of the army', outranking princes, barons and other noblemen. In fact, Joan's status was never clearly defined and she was not entrusted with the command of armies. This was a continual source of tension between her and the professional captains who were responsible for operations, as well as the ministers who had overall conduct of the war. They regarded Joan as a useful morale-booster. But she had an altogether larger view of her role. She had strong and rather crude views about strategy and an imperious way of conveying them. She believed in confronting the enemy at his strongest point, the reverse of every experienced commander's instinct. Victory would come from God, she said, and not from numbers or tactics. Joan's interference with strategic and tactical judgements and her habit of placing herself in the front line in every skirmish surprised and irritated the professionals. At a personal level, she got on well with the Bastard of Orléans and the Duke of Alençon, both of whom admired her courage and strength of purpose. But the Bastard deliberately kept her in the dark about his plans and held his councils of war when she was not about, while Alençon assigned her to the rearguard whenever he expected a pitched battle. Later, Joan's insistence on military outcomes would cut across the Dauphin's attempts at diplomacy or compromise. When crossed, she frequently resorted to her voices to support her demands, too frequently perhaps to be credible, even to some of those who believed in her.[28]

By April 1429, the situation in Orléans had become exceptionally serious. The garrison's strength was at a low ebb. No major food convoy had reached the city since January. A large food convoy was being formed at Blois to fight its way through. Yolande of Anjou had been charged with making bulk purchases of grain, salted meat and other victuals. A plausible contemporary estimate reckoned the whole convoy at nearly 500 wagons in addition to driven cattle. In preparation for the attempt, the Dauphin's garrisons from Berry to Maine had been stripped of troops to create a powerful escort and to build up the forces in the city. By the last few days of April, the professional garrison had been increased to about 1,500 men in addition to able-bodied citizens. The escort force comprised between 2,200 and 2,400 men in addition to an unknown number of infantry contingents from the cities of Berry and the Loire. The Dauphin's treasury was emptied out to pay their advances. Crossbow bolts, gunpowder and other stores were being sent forward in small quantities on packhorses and entering the city inconspicuously to refill its depleted magazines. By the time that Joan arrived at Blois on 25 April, everything was ready. Two days later, on the 27th, the convoy set out.[29]

The command of the escort force had been given to the Marshal Jean de Boussac and the twenty-four-year-old Gilles de Retz, an experienced soldier from the march of Brittany. They coordinated their plans with the Bastard of Orléans, who as the Dauphin's lieutenant in the sector was responsible for the whole operation and commanded the troops in Orléans itself. Joan's reputation had preceded her, and she quickly acquired a strong moral power over the army. The march was organised like an armed pilgrimage. The column was preceded by a corps of priests singing hymns. The troops were urged to confess their sins daily, for God could not be expected to achieve victory through sinners. The prostitutes who customarily hung about every army on the march were sent packing. La Hire was told to swear by his baton, not by the Lord or his saints. How the men responded to this unusual regime is unclear. Many of them found it inspiring. Others must have found it an irritating distraction.

Differences about the direction of the campaign arose almost immediately. The ambitions of the Dauphinist commanders were limited to resupplying the city. They did not think it feasible to raise the siege. They did not have enough men and after Verneuil and the Herrings were unwilling to risk a pitched battle against a concentrated English force. They therefore resolved to approach Orléans by the south side of the Loire and load the supplies on barges upstream of the walls. Joan had other ideas. She wanted to attack the English by the north, where they were strongest and where victory would be decisive. But the convoy's chosen route ruled this out, as there was no bridge in friendly hands between Blois and Gien. The professional captains responded to her attempts to take over their plans in the same way as they would do throughout her public career. They held their councils in her absence whenever they could and declined to explain what was going on. She was apparently unaware of the problem of the bridges and the captains were careful not to tell her.

On the night of 28 April, the convoy arrived at Olivet, four miles south of Orléans. The captains rode forward to the river port opposite the bastide of Saint-Loup to meet the Bastard of Orléans and his principal officers. Joan went with them. It was a stormy meeting, the first time that she had met the Bastard of Orléans. She soon realised that she had been duped. 'Are you the Bastard of Orléans?' she asked him. 'And was it on your advice that I have been brought here, on this side of the river, instead of going directly against Talbot and the English?' The Bastard replied that he had had to make a judgement, and that wiser heads than his had agreed with it. 'The advice of the Lord my God is wiser and better than yours,' she answered. 'You have tried to take advantage of me, but you are the dupes for I have brought you the best reinforcement that any soldier or city ever had, the support of the King of Heaven.'[30]

On the following morning the captains of the army met again. Once more Joan attended. Since she could not attack the English on the north bank, she told them that she was determined to attack the new bastide of Saint-Jean-le-Blanc. This course was rejected by the captains. Their priority was to get the convoy into the city. The old river port of Saint-Loup was no longer usable because of the English artillery on the opposite bank. So they decided to take the convoy six miles upriver and load the carts onto barges there. When they got there, however, they found that the barges had been prevented from reaching them by the current and a strong east wind. Three decades later the Bastard of Orléans remembered Joan praying for divine assistance, whereupon the wind fell and the barges came up from the city. He said that this was the moment when he learned to trust Joan's miraculous powers. That was the conventional line in 1456. But there were a number of different versions of this story, and at the time it is clear that the Bastard and his captains continued to treat Joan's tactical and strategic interventions with reserve. Over the next few hours, the convoy was safely ferried over the river. Some 200 men-at-arms were detached from the escort force to bring it into Orléans, while the rest of the men began the march back to Blois. The defenders of the city mounted a sortie from the gates of the city against the bastide of Saint-Loup to tie down its English garrison, while the convoy with its small escort made its way from the riverbank to the Porte de Bourgogne, the immense fortified gateway guarding the eastern entrance to the city. That night, the seventeen-year-old Joan of Arc entered Orléans in full armour on a white charger, flanked by La Hire and the Bastard of Orléans, with a page carrying her banner aloft before her. She was greeted by extraordinary scenes. The citizens crammed the streets, lighting up the darkness with burning torches, surging forward to touch the hem of her robes and hailing her 'like God, come down among them from Heaven'.[31]

The joy of the people of Orléans was due to their belief that Joan had come to raise the siege, and not just to resupply the city for the next stage. They had suffered seven months of privations. Their houses had been smashed by English artillery. Casualties had been high. The city's treasury was depleted and its trade ruined. When it became clear that the escort force had come only to guard the convoy and that most of it had already left for Blois, morale collapsed. It became clear to the Bastard of Orléans that unless the siege was raised soon, the city was likely to surrender. On 1 May, he left Joan at Orléans and rode post-haste to Blois to confer with the captains there. The Chancellor Regnault de Chartres, who was in the town, presided at a council of war. The troops of the western garrisons declared that they needed to return to their bases. The rest seem to have assumed that the army would disperse once the revictualling operation was completed. The Bastard told them that in that case Orléans would probably surrender. The only way that the city could be saved was for them to raise the siege. The assembled captains were persuaded. The new strategy would involve returning to Orléans by the north, as Joan had always demanded. The army would either have to fight its way through the English lines or enter the city and attack them from the gates.[32]

On 3 May 1429, the Bastard of Orléans marched out of Blois at the head of the army and advanced along the north bank of the Loire. They brought with them another wagon train loaded with victuals and large quantities of powder and ammunition. On the following day, 4 May, in the late morning, they approached Orléans by the north-west. Inside the city, the defenders had been reinforced by the garrisons of Montargis, Gien and Châteaurenard, bringing their total strength to at least 2,000. A sortie party of some 500 mounted men was formed under La Hire. Accompanied by Joan of Arc, they advanced from the gates to meet the army of Blois. The English did not react. They had recently reinforced their own lines from the feudal service of Normandy. But even with these additions to their strength they were dangerously dispersed. Between 3,000 and 4,000 English and Norman troops were distributed among eleven forts and several encampments around the city. At least a third of these were out of reach on the south side of the Loire. Another 1,500 men were being held back as a strategic reserve under the command of Sir John Fastolf at Janville, twenty-five miles away, for exactly this eventuality. But Fastolf's field intelligence had failed him and he did not learn of the approach of the French army until it was too late. Towards the end of the morning the Bastard of Orléans entered the city unopposed. There were now about 4,500 professional troops in Orléans in addition to citizen soldiers. The two sides were roughly evenly matched for the first time since the beginning of the siege. But unlike the English forces the Dauphinist forces were concentrated and under unified command.[33]

At about midday on 4 May, the troops in Orléans launched a powerful sortie against the English bastide of Saint-Loup with about 1,500 men. Saint-Loup was the most exposed of the English forts. It lay east of the city, some distance from the rest of the siege lines and was garrisoned by fewer than 200 men. Joan of Arc had told the

Bastard of Orléans that she would 'have his head off' if he kept her in the dark about operations. But she was not told about this one, almost certainly by his decision. As she rested in her quarters, the noise in the streets outside alerted her to what was happening. She rose hurriedly and sent her page to fetch her horse while the lady of the house and her daughter struggled to help her on with her armour. Her banner was passed to her through an upper window as she left. Jean d'Aulon, who was quartered in the same house, followed her a few minutes later. By now the battle around the bastide had been in progress for some time. As Joan and Jean d'Aulon made their way towards the fighting they encountered a stream of wounded men coming in the opposite direction. The Dauphinists had initially taken the garrison of Saint-Loup by surprise. But by the time that Joan arrived on the scene a successful counterattack had driven them back. It was Joan's first experience of combat. She rallied the retreating French and led them back to the walls of the bastide. Sir John Talbot, who was based in the fort known as 'Paris', north-west of the city, realised what was happening and tried to collect a mounted force to intervene. But he was stopped by Marshal Boussac, who led a sortie against 'Paris' from one of the northern gates and forced him to turn back. After some hours of close combat Saint-Loup was stormed from scaling ladders. The English defenders retreated to the bell tower of the abbey church, where they were eventually forced to surrender. A handful of prisoners were taken, but otherwise the defenders of the bastide were killed to a man and its ramparts destroyed. The fall of Saint-Loup, and Joan's part in it, had an electrifying effect on the French army in Orléans. It showed them how vulnerable the English defensive works, apparently so imposing, really were.[34]

5 May was the feast of the Ascension, a major festival which was marked by a temporary truce. Inside Orléans, the principal French captains met to plan the next move. It was decided to attack Les Tourelles, the great keep at the south end of the bridge. It would be a difficult operation. Les Tourelles was heavily garrisoned and defended by boulevards on both sides. It would be necessary to cross the Loire. Once across the river, the French would first have to capture the outworks which guarded the approaches: the small fort which the English had recently built at Saint-Jean-le-Blanc and the much larger one which they had created in the ruins of the Augustinian convent directly south of the bridge. A large part of the army inside Orléans was

assigned to the operation. Joan was not present and was not consulted about any of these decisions. It was agreed that she would not be told. It was only when she detected that something was afoot and insisted, that she discovered the plan and was allowed to take part. On the evening of 5 May she dispatched her next letter of defiance. The letter, signed 'JHESU MARIA – Jeanne la Pucelle' commanded the English to leave France. It was tied to an arrow and shot from the walls into a group of English soldiers, followed by a yell of 'News for you!' from Joan herself.[35]

On the following morning, 6 May, before dawn, the troops gathered on the riverbank under the Tour Neuve, the high tower at the south-east corner of the city walls. From here they were ferried in barges in two groups to the Île-aux-Toiles, a long island of sand and scrub. A bridge of boats was formed to join the island to the south bank. The first group to land on the south side was commanded by Raoul de Gaucourt. They had little difficulty in occupying Saint-Jean-le-Blanc. The English garrison retreated as soon as the French appeared. Pursuing them, Gaucourt's force came up against the formidable defences of the Augustinian convent. Their initial assessment was that it was too strong to be taken by assault. So they withdrew towards the barges. There they found the second force, which was commanded by La Hire, in the process of disembarking. Joan of Arc was with them. A hurried conference was interrupted by the sudden appearance of an English sortie party from the Augustinian convent. The combined French force turned to meet the threat, and drove them back, pursuing them to the walls of the convent. An immediate assault was ordered. The English fought back fiercely, but the Dauphinists were able to get over the walls, and once inside the fort their numbers prevailed. The defenders withdrew in good order to the keep of Les Tourelles, abandoning the convent to the Dauphinists. Characteristically, Joan pressed for an immediate assault on the keep. But the men were tired and Joan herself, who had been wounded in the foot by a spiked caltrop, was persuaded to return to the city to rest.[36]

Once Joan was safely out of the way Gaucourt and La Hire called the captains of the assault force to a council of war in the Augustinian convent. They decided that they did not have the numbers to assault the besiegers' largest and most heavily defended fort. Orléans had now been resupplied and the pressure was off. It would be wiser to wait until reinforcements could be sent from Blois. Joan did not learn of this decision until late that night. She was furious. They had conferred among themselves, she said, but she had conferred with God Himself. They would see whose was the better counsel. Early the next morning, 7 May, the Dauphinists in the Augustinian convent were reinforced from the city. Joan came with them and spoke at a new council of war. She persuaded the captains to reverse the decision of the previous evening and attack Les Tourelles at once.

The assault was launched later that morning with a barrage of bombard and culverin fire. The assault parties surged forward with scaling ladders to the heavily defended boulevard protecting the south side of the keep. Joan was at the head of them. The defenders of the boulevard fought back with every weapon to hand: artillery, crossbows, swords, axes, mallets and cascades of rocks. It was some time before the assault parties were able to cross the ditch to reach the foot of the rampart. As Joan climbed her ladder, she was struck in the neck by a crossbow bolt which penetrated several inches into her flesh and flung her back into the ditch. She was forced to withdraw to have the wound treated with olive oil (a commonly used disinfectant) and staunched with animal fat. The assault flagged as the men saw her standard leaving the fight. Eventually, the captains decided to call it off until artillery could be brought over from the city the next morning. The trumpets sounded the retreat. But in the midst of the confusion Joan's bodyguard Jean d'Aulon and a Basque soldier who was with him seized her standard and relaunched the assault. Standing at the edge of the ditch, Joan shouted encouragement: 'The place is yours, get in there!'

As the French came over the walls of the boulevard, on the opposite side of Les Tourelles another assault force emerged onto the bridge from the city. They threw an improvised timber pontoon across the broken arches. From here, they launched a second assault on Les Tourelles from the north. Attacked on both sides at once, the English defenders panicked. They abandoned the southern boulevard and retreated across the drawbridge into the main structure. Unfortunately for them, the drawbridge had been damaged in the artillery bombardment, and the timber planks gave way under their weight. The men were cast into the torrent below. Four prominent English captains were drowned, including the commander of the garrison William Glasdale and his deputy William Molyns. From the bridge side, the assault force poured into Les Tourelles and massacred the garrison. Some 400 to 500 English were killed. The fighting lasted all day, from dawn to dusk. Glasdale had been a hate-figure among the defenders of Orléans because of his habit of shouting blood-curdling threats at them from the windows of his fortress. His name, distorted as 'Glassidas', became a symbol of the arrogance of the invaders. Yet this former archer of modest birth deserved to be remembered for more than his foul language. He had had a remarkable career, culminating in the courageous defence of the crumbling keep of Les Tourelles. His body was eventually recovered from the river and taken back to Paris, where vigils fit for a prince were observed in the church of St Merri before his remains were taken back for burial in England.[37]

Joan and her companions made their way back into Orléans across the bridge with the bells of every church in the city ringing in their ears. The English met, probably in their headquarters in the bastide of Saint-Laurent, to review the situation. They still had a substantial army. But they had lost between 700 and 800 men, a great deal of artillery and all their south bank forts except one. The city had been revictualled. The bridge was open, allowing the Dauphinists to bring men and supplies freely across the Loire as soon as repairs were carried out. It was obvious that the attempt to take Orléans had failed. The English commanders, Suffolk, Scales and Talbot, resolved to abandon the siege.

There was a final, face-saving gesture on the following morning, 8 May. The entire English army emerged from its forts and camps and drew up in battle order in the plain north of the walls. For a time, it seemed that the challenge would be accepted. The whole of the French army in the city came out of the gates, followed by most of the citizens capable of bearing arms, and formed up in their own battle order. The two armies faced each other across the plain. The French declined to attack, according to one source because Joan would not let them fight an offensive battle on a Sunday, more probably because the Bastard of Orléans thought that there was no point in risking everything that they had gained on a single encounter. After waiting for an hour in their ranks, the English turned away and marched back along the road to Meung. They abandoned their heavy artillery and great stores of victuals and left their encampments in flames. La Hire and Ambroise de Loré pursued them for part of the way and succeeded in seizing some of the lighter artillery pieces which they had been able to carry away. The citizens took possession of the abandoned siege lines and joyfully demolished what remained of the forts and field works.[38]

The relief of Orléans provoked a prolonged crisis in the affairs of Lancastrian France. Five years later, the Duke of Bedford summarised its impact in a memorandum addressed to Henry VI and his English council. After 1422, he wrote, he had re-established the English position in France as it had been before Henry V's death. 'Divers great and fair days and victorious were had there for you and in your quarrel upon your enemies.' He had expanded the territory under English control in the Île-de-France, in Champagne and Brie, the Auxerrois, the Nivernais, the Mâconnais, Maine and Anjou. Everything had gone well until the siege of Orléans. But after the Earl of Salisbury's death,

there fell by the hand of God as it seemeth a great stroke upon your courage that was assembled there in great number, caused in great part as I trow of lack of sad belief and of unlieful doubt that they had of a disciple... of the fiend called the Pucelle that used false enchantment and sorcery, the which stroke and discomfiture not only lessened in great part the number of your people there but as well withdrew the courage of the remnant in marvellous wise and couraged your adverse party the enemies to assemble them forthwith in great number.

Bedford identified as the main factors at work a general collapse of English morale, leading to large-scale desertions from the army and a corresponding rise in the self-confidence of their enemies. He was defending his own conduct of the war, and his account of the situation before the death of Salisbury was perhaps too glowing. But all the contemporary evidence bears out his assessment of the results of Joan's intervention. The same view was expressed by the Bastard of Orléans who, like Bedford, attributed the change mainly to her. Before her appearance, he told the posthumous inquiry, 200 English soldiers could put a Dauphinist army four or five times their size to flight; but afterwards 400 or 500 Dauphinist troops were able to take on the whole of the besieging army, none of whom dared to emerge from their siege works. The English were stunned by what had happened. They did not know how to cope with something that seemed inexplicable except by reference to supernatural forces beyond their control. A number of observers on the Anglo-Burgundian side remarked on the fear that gripped the English army after the siege of Orléans. English prisoners of war told the same story to their captors. They had never known the French to fight so powerfully, while their own courage seemed to drain away.[39]

'In war,' wrote Napoleon in one of his many hectoring lectures to his brother Joseph, 'morale is three-quarters of the business; numbers count for no more than a quarter.' Recruitment, courage, endurance and discipline are all in one way or another dependent on morale. If this was true of the great European wars of the modern age, it was truer still of the middle ages, when the state's means of coercion were more limited, the material rewards of service more uncertain and the structures of command more fluid. Joan of Arc's main contribution to victory was to transform the morale of the Dauphin's troops. She persuaded them that victory was within their grasp. As a citizen of Orléans observed in his evidence to the rehabilitation inquiry, Joan did it by telling them that God was with them and proving it by her own example. She put herself in the way of danger and survived. They had only to trust in God as she did. Joan had been asked by the commissioners at Poitiers why soldiers were needed if God had determined to lift France out of its wretched condition. It was a classic theological conundrum. She had replied that the soldiers were God's instrument for performing His task. 'The men-at-arms must fight, and God will grant victory.' This was always her message. It not only inspired the troops in service but proved to be a powerful agent of recruitment among many who had previously stayed away.[40]

Joan's intervention had an equally powerful impact on those living in regions under English control whose main object was to be on the winning side. Writing in 1435, the Duke of Bedford's loyal French secretary Jean Rinel endorsed his master's view of the 1420s as a golden age. He believed that the people of northern France had been happy to accept the government of Henry VI and his Regent until that 'wild woman, sorcerer, idolater and heretic' suborned them. Sceptical churchmen, hard-nosed politicians, and some of England's allies of convenience may have doubted whether the 1420s were really as golden as Rinel suggested, but they were agreed on the seminal role of Joan of Arc in transforming Charles's political prospects. Jean Gerson, whose treatise on the detection of false visionaries had recommended an attitude of cautious scepticism, completed his response to the Dauphin's request for advice a week after the relief of Orléans. He threw caution to the winds. 'This is the work of the Lord,' he declared.

Jacques Gélu, the author of the deeply pessimistic advice to the Dauphin and his council in March, did a volte-face. That Joan was inspired by God was now plain. It was the Dauphin's duty, he argued, to follow her advice rather than put his trust in mere human judgement. Even the Duke of Brittany, cynical, calculating, a weathervane of the changing fortunes of war, sent his confessor, accompanied by a herald, to present Joan with horses and a jewelled dagger, and to report back on her claim to have been sent by God. If the Duke was satisfied of that, the confessor told her, he would send a contingent of troops to fight for the Dauphin. John V was not yet ready to break with the Duke of Bedford. But he gingerly resumed diplomatic contact with the Dauphin's court and allowed him to recruit troops in Brittany. The Dauphin worked hard to foster the aura of the miraculous which surrounded these events. Circulars were dispatched to the four corners of his territory recounting what had happened 'by means of the grace of Our Lord'. As for Joan, she had accomplished the 'sign' which she had promised would prove the divine character of her mission. For the next three months, the strategic judgements of the Dauphin would be largely determined by her single-minded focus on the central part of her mission, the coronation at Reims.[41]

Joan met the Dauphin on 11 May on the road to Tours. Charles was an undemonstrative man, but to the surprise of his entourage he was so elated that he took her in his arms and looked as if he might even kiss her. In the ancient citadel of Tours, an enlarged meeting of his council gathered to consider the next move. Everyone agreed that the first task must be to recapture the bridge-towns of the Loire. They had to protect Orléans against a renewed English attack and secure the army's rear before moving north against the centres of English power. But which centres? Joan was adamant that as soon as the English garrisons had been cleared from the valley of the Loire, the Dauphin must march on Reims. In the eyes of the lawyers, Reims was an irrelevance. It had been established since the thirteenth century that the kings of France derived their status and powers from inheritance alone, not from the coronation ceremony or the forms of election which accompanied it. These were no more than the blessing of the Church upon an accomplished fact. But the coronation had a more fundamental significance for Joan. Kingship was a grant of God and not a mere legal construct. Once Charles had been crowned, Joan argued, the prestige of the English would start to wane and would never recover. In an age when public display was an essential element of legitimacy and ceremony was a basic tool of government, hers was not an unreasonable view. Beyond the official world most ordinary people probably shared it. 'The French believe... that he who has not been anointed with oil is no true king,' wrote Pope Pius II.[42]

Most of the Dauphin's councillors viewed the question in narrower and purely military terms. They favoured an invasion of Normandy, not Champagne. The duchy, with its dense network of English garrisons, was a difficult target, but in the hubristic mood which followed the relief of Orléans, the Dauphin's advisers believed that the Duke of Bedford's government might collapse. Normandy was the main pillar of the Lancastrian regime, the one theatre where a military collapse might be decisive. There was another reason for avoiding an offensive in Champagne. This was the delicate question of relations with the Duke of Burgundy, which now emerged as a strategic issue for the first time since Joan's appearance on the scene. For years, the Dauphin's ministers had been trying to drive a wedge between Burgundy and England. These efforts had recently hung fire, but Philip's objections to the English siege of Orléans seemed to open the prospect of restarting the dialogue. Joan's plan to lead an army to Reims would have cut across any initiative of this kind. The only feasible route to Reims lay through the Auxerrois and southern Champagne, which was a region of vital interest to Philip the Good. For Joan, none of this mattered. Philip was 'false Burgundy', not a potential ally to be wooed but a traitor to be bludgeoned into submission.[43]

The issue was still unresolved when the Dauphin left Tours on about 20 May for the fortress-town of Loches. Shortly after his arrival there, Joan burst into his private apartments as he was conferring with a small group of advisers. According to the Bastard of Orléans, recalling the scene a quarter of a century later, she fell to her knees in front of him, throwing her arms around his legs. 'Noble Dauphin,' she said, 'enough of these windy deliberations; come as soon as you can to Reims to receive a worthy crown.' One of those present asked her whether it was her voices who had told her to say this. She replied that it was. When she was frustrated by other people's scepticism, she said, she would withdraw to pray. A voice had come to her urging her to persevere: 'Onward, onward, I shall be at your side,' it had said. At the mere repetition of the words, Joan went into a trance. It was one of a number of occasions when one suspects her of acting a part at convenient moments. But it achieved her object. Joan could do little wrong in Charles's eyes. He was persuaded and, with whatever misgivings, his advisers followed his lead.[44]

The army of Orléans had been disbanded two days after the city had been relieved. There was no money to pay their wages in full or victuals to feed them. The troops withdrawn from garrisons were needed back at their posts. The rapid formation of a new army was perhaps the most remarkable evidence of the impact of the relief of Orléans. The Dauphin resorted to a feudal summons of a kind which had not been used for many years. Fief-holders were called on to serve with their tenants and retainers with no assurance that they would be paid anything. The Dauphin planned to lead the army himself, for the first time since 1421. 'Everyone, knights, squires and others was content to serve in his presence,' wrote the squire of the Duke of Alençon, 'even for virtually no pay.' Joan's presence was almost as important. She had become the most famous figure in France. The soldiers viewed her as a saint, the reason why they were bound to win.

By early June, just three weeks after the summonses had been issued, nearly 5,000 men had arrived at the appointed meeting place at Selles in Berry. This was less than half the size of the great hosts which the Dauphin's ministers had deployed in 1421 and 1424. But they had been composed mainly of foreign mercenaries. The new army was an indigenous French army, representing substantially the whole military capacity of the kingdom of Bourges. The Scottish companies of Patrick Ogilvy and Hugh Kennedy and the Italians of Teodoro di Valperga fought in it too but accounted for fewer than 1,000 men between them. For many great noblemen, service in the King's army involved considerable financial sacrifice. Guy de Laval sold land to meet the cost. The Duke of Alençon was required by the laws of war to pay off his ransom before he could be allowed to fight and was obliged to mortgage valuable fiefs to the Duke of Brittany. His reward was to be nominated by the Dauphin as commander of the army. Alençon was just twenty years old. His only substantial experience of war had been gained at Verneuil, the battle in which he had been captured. But by birth he outranked everyone else and that was enough. As always, Joan's own status was ambiguous. She had no formal command. But Alençon's instructions from the Dauphin were to 'act in all matters by her advice'. She was seen everywhere in Alençon's company. She mixed easily with the soldiers, joking and swapping stories. Her ambitions grew with her confidence. She told Guy de Laval over a pot of mediocre wine that she would stand him a better one in Paris.[45]

The Duke of Bedford and his captains watched these preparations with dismay. Having failed before Orléans, their main priority now was to hold on to the three bridge-towns of Meung, Beaugency and Jargeau, which had been captured by the Earl of Salisbury the previous August. These places offered the only prospect of a successful counterattack on the Loire. The English army had been diminished by casualties and desertion and by the departure of garrison troops who had been recalled to their bases. There remained between 3,500 and 4,000 men in the field. The Earl of Suffolk adopted a largely defensive strategy. He assigned between 500 and 600 men to each of the three bridge-towns. The rest, about 1,500 to 2,000 men, were retained as a strategic reserve at Janville. Suffolk was deeply pessimistic about the prospects. Writing to the Duke of Bedford, he warned that unless reinforcements could be found quickly all the English strongholds of the region were likely to fall.[46]

Suffolk's messenger arrived in Paris to find the government in a state of panic. The Duke of Bedford, fearing a revolution in the capital, had temporarily withdrawn to Vincennes for safety. Some days later he gingerly returned to the city and presided at a council of war attended by his principal captains. They decided to raise a new army to confront the Dauphin's army in the field. It was a formidable task. Men were once more pulled out of garrisons and directed to muster at Mantes and Pontoise. The feudal service of Normandy and Picardy was summoned to join them. Orders were sent to the captains of every Norman port to round up deserters before they could escape to England. The *baillis* were told to root out English settlers in their districts and send them to muster with the rest. The military organisation in Normandy, which had been placed under severe strain by the siege of Orléans, suffered a partial breakdown under the weight of these demands. Garrison troops had only just returned to their bases. Their captains were alarmed by the signs of disintegration all around them and by the threat of attack from the south. They did not dare to release men. The indigenous nobility waited to see what would happen before moving.

It soon became clear that if the Regent wanted to raise a fresh army most of it would have to recruited in England.[47] The Duke of Bedford had been pressing the English council for men for several months before the disaster at Orléans. Jean Rinel was in England in April with a deputation from the Grand Conseil, negotiating with the council at Westminster. They were calling for the adoption of Bedford's plan to send the young Henry VI to France with a powerful new army. The English councillors were sceptical. The need for a major expedition to France was not as obvious as it became a few weeks later. They assumed, like Bedford himself, that Orléans would shortly fall. A big push beyond the Loire would no doubt follow, but that could wait. The Treasurer, Lord Hungerford, reported that with revenues falling short of expenditure by 20,000 marks (£13,332) a year, Bedford's demands were unaffordable. The whole issue was referred to a great council, an assembly of the whole Parliamentary peerage reinforced by selected officials and captains, which was summoned at irregular intervals to consider great issues of state. The larger body met on 15 April 1429 and took the same view as the permanent councillors. The most that they were willing to do was divert Sir John Radcliffe, who was once again preparing to sail for Gascony, to bring his company of 800 men to the Duke of Bedford instead.[48]

Manpower was an even bigger problem than money, for while the council was warding off the Duke of Bedford's emissaries, they were also having to deal with insistent claims on their resources from a new direction: a quixotic project of Henry Beaufort to lead an English army against the Hussites of Bohemia. The Hussites were a heterodox Christian community drawing their inspiration from the teachings of the Czech theologian Jan Hus, who had been condemned and executed for heresy by the Council of Constance in 1415. Their creed had acquired a dominant position among the Czech population of Bohemia. They had taken control of Prague and evicted the Catholic Church from most of the kingdom. They had defeated three successive German crusades sent against them. In June 1427, shortly after Beaufort had left England to receive his cardinal's hat, he had accepted appointment as papal legate in Germany, Hungary and Bohemia, and had been charged with organising a fourth crusade against them. It fared no better than its predecessors. The predominantly German army of the Church was routed in Beaufort's presence near the Bohemian town of Tachov in August 1427. Beaufort is said to have exclaimed that if he had only had 10,000 English archers, the heretics would now be in full retreat. The story is probably apocryphal, but the sentiment was real enough. Early in 1428, Martin V and Beaufort had resolved to broaden the anti-Hussite coalition beyond Germany to other countries, in particular Burgundy and England. The plan was for Philip the Good to lead a crusading army drawn from his own territories with a small contingent of English men-at-arms and between 4,000 and 6,000 English archers. On 1 September 1428, after long discussions with Philip in Flanders, Beaufort returned to England. There, he exhibited his new status with a grandiose entry into London on horseback, wearing a robe and cap of red velvet, with his legate's cross and cardinal's hat carried before him. In his luggage he brought a papal bull charging him with preaching the crusade in England.[49]

The presence of a papal legate on English soil provoked instinctive hostility even among the cardinal's traditional allies, especially as he proposed to retain his English bishopric and his place on the royal council at the same time. Beaufort's call for troops added to the controversy. He pitched his demands high: 500 men-at-arms and 5,000 archers. As Chancellor Kemp pointed out in a letter to the English agents at the Curia, this involved raising troops 'in such numbers as have not been seen to leave England for a long time, except in the presence of the King'. It was a direct threat to the Duke of Bedford, who needed the dwindling reservoir of English military manpower to make good his losses in France. The council told Beaufort that losses from war and disease had already significantly reduced the number of available soldiers. His demands were 'perilous and dangerous', they said. They cut down his numbers to 250 men-at-arms and 2,500 archers and imposed tight conditions. The men were to be found exclusively in England, not in France, and they were to be paid by the papal chamber, not from English revenues. The council also reserved the right to approve each of Beaufort's captains individually. Yet Beaufort's project proved to be unrealistic even on the reduced scale demanded by the council.[50]

While the councillors at Westminster grappled with these problems, yet more disasters befell the English in France. On the afternoon of 11 June 1429, the army of the Duke of Alençon arrived outside the town of Jargeau, accompanied by Joan of Arc. Jargeau was a compact walled town upstream of Orléans with an important fortified bridge. The defence was directed by the Earl of Suffolk. He had 300 to 400 English under his command. All of them had fought at Orléans and they had little enthusiasm for the fight. The French occupied the suburbs on the evening of their arrival after a fierce battle in the streets. Inside the town, Suffolk retired to bed, it was said with his mistress, a renegade nun from a French convent. During the night, the French brought up their artillery.

When day broke, the guns began to take a heavy toll on the defences of the town. One of the bombards, rechristened 'La Bergère' in honour of Joan of Arc's supposed occupation, brought down the keep at the south end of the town after three hits. At this point, Suffolk offered a conditional surrender. He approached La Hire, who had a healthy respect for the fighting qualities of English troops and was inclined to negotiate. Suffolk asked for fifteen days. But with substantial English forces still in the region neither Alençon nor Joan was willing to accept anything less than the immediate surrender of the town. Suffolk would not agree to that. So, at about nine o'clock, the trumpeters in the French lines sounded the assault. The French rushed the dry moat with their scaling ladders. Joan, holding her standard in the front line, urged them on. 'Fight hard, and God will fight hard with you,' she cried, 'God has doomed the English.' The French suffered heavy casualties in the assault. Joan herself was hit by a stone thrown from above, which struck her helmet and briefly stunned her. After four hours of bitter fighting, the French obtained a foothold on the ramparts and then poured over the walls. Suffolk recognised that the town could no longer be held. He rallied his troops and retreated onto the fortified bridge, pursued by the victorious French. He tried to make contact with Alençon to agree a general surrender but was unable to make himself heard above the noise of battle.

In the end, the English were fought to a standstill and the bridge was captured. About sixty English were taken prisoner. Suffolk surrendered to a French squire, a gentleman but not a knight. Unwilling to be disparaged, he knighted his enemy on the spot before giving him his word as a prisoner. His brother John was captured with him. They were quickly taken to the barges in the river with other notable prisoners and carried for safety to Orléans. They were the fortunate ones. Most of their men were killed in the final moments of the fighting, as the French rampaged through the town and across the bridge, killing and looting indiscriminately. The dead included another of the Pole brothers, Alexander, who like many of his fellows was drowned in the river while trying to get away.[51]

The rapid collapse of resistance at Jargeau forced the English to change their strategy. Events were moving faster than they had anticipated. Rather than conduct a static defence from behind the walls of their remaining strongholds on the Loire and wait for them be picked off one by one, they decided to concentrate as many men as possible at Janville under the command of Sir John Fastolf, in the hope of forming an army capable of meeting the Duke of Alençon in the field. Fastolf already had about 2,000 men at Janville. Lord Scales was withdrawn from Meung, bringing part of his garrison with him. Sir John Talbot was recalled from Beaugency with 240 men, nearly half his garrison. Troops were withdrawn from the garrisons of Normandy and the Île-de-France and mustered outside Paris. The chronicler Waurin left his garrison at Nemours on the Loing with 120 men, which must have been close to its entire strength. But even with these additions to his strength, Fastolf's army would have only about 3,500 men. Radcliffe's company from England was not expected to arrive until the end of June at the earliest.[52]

The Duke of Alençon rested his men for two days before resuming the campaign with simultaneous attacks on Meung and Beaugency (*Map 6*). His army was gaining strength by the day as fresh men, inspired by the victories of the past two months, arrived to join them from every part of the Dauphin's territory. The whole army marched downstream on both banks of the Loire and arrived outside Meung on 15 June. They almost immediately captured the fortified bridge joining the town to the south bank of the river. They then divided their forces, leaving part of the army to contain the English garrison of Meung while the rest marched on Beaugency, five miles downstream.[53]

There, they received significant reinforcements from an unexpected quarter. Arthur de Richemont was still nominally the Constable of France, but he had not fought with a French army for more than two years. The turn of the tide in the Loire valley gave him a chance, as he thought, to return to favour and perhaps even to power. On his own initiative, he had recruited a large force, about 1,200 men, mostly from Brittany and the marches of Maine. To the Dauphin and his councillors this was most unwelcome. Richemont was disruptive, treacherous and conspiratorial, and venomously opposed to the Dauphin's principal minister. The French council had sent a nobleman to meet him on the road at Loudun with a written order to turn back. Richemont ignored it and continued on his way, arriving at Beaugency on 16 June, shortly after Alençon himself. Alençon's orders were not to accept his help. But Richemont had many friends in the army who had fought with him on the western march and welcomed his support. The stand-off was resolved by Joan of Arc. She had a frosty meeting with Richemont. The hard-bitten warrior had no time for women or seers. But Joan knew that 1,200 experienced Breton troops would be a valuable addition to the army's strength. She welcomed him and undertook to reconcile him to the Dauphin. Alençon had no choice but to go along with this. His total strength must now have been between 6,000 and 7,000 men, nearly twice the number at Fastolf's disposal.[54]

The ramparts of Beaugency were old and indefensible. Once the French had sited their artillery, large sections of wall were brought down within a few hours. The real strength of the town lay in its fortified bridge over the Loire and its citadel, set back from the river and dominated by the tall square keep now known as the Tour de César. In Talbot's absence, the defence was directed by his two Welsh deputies, Sir Richard Gethin of Builth and Matthew Gough. Their orders were to hold out in the citadel and the bridge until help could arrive. They did not rate their chances highly. According to Jean de Waurin, they knew that Joan of Arc was with the enemy host and were frightened by her reputation. They managed to get a messenger out with an appeal to the captains gathered at Janville to come at once or they would be forced to surrender. On the evening of 16 June, Fastolf held a council of war at Janville. He was reluctant to go to the aid of Beaugency and Meung. The English, he said, had suffered a succession of serious defeats. The courage of the French was up, while the English were badly demoralised. They were also heavily outnumbered. It would be a mistake, Fastolf thought, to court further disaster now. They should wait for further reinforcements to arrive from the army assembling outside Paris. Gethin and Gough would have to hold on or make the best deal that they could with the French. This view was badly received by the other captains present. It was particularly unwelcome to Talbot, who had just arrived from Beaugency and joined the meeting after it had begun. There was no love lost between Fastolf and Talbot, who had partly eclipsed him in Bedford's favour since his arrival in France. Fastolf was the more cautious soldier and in this instance he was right. But Talbot's overpowering personality carried the day. He thought that they should fight. The other captains followed his line. The men were ordered to be ready to march the next morning.[55]

Early on 17 June 1429, the English army marched out of Janville, pennons flying, with Fastolf continuing to protest from the saddle. They arrived outside Meung towards the end of the afternoon, only to find the French siege lines abandoned. The besiegers had withdrawn their men to Beaugency, leaving only a small force behind to hold the bridge. The English prepared to assault the bridge the next morning. Outside Beaugency, Alençon and his captains resolved to march on Meung and confront the English army the next day. But they were unwilling to leave the English garrison of Beaugency in their rear. So they sent a message to the defenders of the town telling them that Fastolf's force had abandoned the campaign and was on its way back to Paris. They invited them to negotiate the surrender of their town. The defenders were taken in. Negotiations continued into the night until agreement was finally reached at about midnight. Gethin and Gough agreed to deliver up Beaugency at dawn the next morning. They would be allowed to leave with their horses and weapons and personal property worth up to one mark but had to promise not to fight against the Dauphin's forces for the next ten days. Gethin and Gough were held as hostages for the due performance of these undertakings. At dawn the English garrison of Beaugency marched away.

At Meung, the troops of Fastolf and Talbot had already begun the assault on the bridge, when a herald arrived with the news that Beaugency had surrendered and Alençon's army was approaching in battle order. The English captains hastily conferred. With Beaugency taken, the point of the campaign was lost and the risk of engaging the superior forces of the French was no longer worth taking. They decided to retreat before Alençon's army arrived. The assault parties were recalled from the bridge. The army formed up outside the gates. They marched north, making for their base at Janville, pursued at a distance by the whole of Alençon's army.[56]

The way to Janville passed through the forest of Bucy to reach the old road from Paris to Blois at the hamlet of Saint-Sigismond. The English army was encumbered by baggage carts, artillery and a mob of victuallers. Their progress was slow. The French sent a large detachment of cavalry forward under La Hire's command to stop them. When the French horsemen caught up with them, the English were spread out along the road between Saint-Sigismond and the village of Patay, a distance of some five miles. Sir John Talbot was the first to see the enemy approaching. He stationed his archers on a ridge behind a hedge. They were ordered to hold back the approaching French, in order to allow time for the rest of the army to close up and form a line. But the French cavalry force reached the archers while they were still taking up their positions, and slaughtered them. Talbot himself was captured by one of Poton de Saintrailles's men. The rest of the French army pressed forward along the road and caught the English rearguard in a state of disarray. The fighting lasted only a few minutes. The English were scattered by the first charge and fled in all directions. Joan of Arc had been placed in the rearguard of the French army, much to her dismay. She shouted encouragement from the rear but otherwise took almost no part in the fighting.

The English vanguard, which was still intact, had by now reached a point just south of the village of Patay. Sir John Fastolf rode as fast as he could towards the village to rally them. But they assumed that he was running away and joined in the general flight. According to the chronicler Jean de Waurin, who was near him, Fastolf originally resolved to stand and fight with the small number of men that remained. But his companions, who included experienced captains, persuaded him to save himself and his company rather than indulge in pointless heroics. As always in medieval battles, most of the casualties were suffered in the pursuit. The French pursued the fleeing English over a distance of some fifteen miles. The most reliable body count was made by the heralds after the fighting was over. They counted 2,200 English dead. Estimates of the final tally of prisoners ranged from 400 to 1,500. In addition to Talbot, they included Lord Scales, Walter Hungerford, son of the Treasurer of England, William Neville Lord Fauconberg and Sir Thomas Rempston. Talbot was brought to the Duke of Alençon after the battle. 'Such are the chances of war,' he said.

The battle of Patay was a disaster for the English. It was the first time that they had been defeated in the field since the battle of Baugé in 1421. They suffered heavy losses at a particularly difficult moment. A large part of the army of Normandy had been killed or captured. Most of the principal English commanders in France were prisoners. Scales was free within a year on terms which are not recorded. Talbot was eventually released after four years in captivity when his captor, Poton de Saintrailles, was himself captured and the two men were exchanged. Rempston was held in harsh conditions for seven years and eventually released in exchange for a crippling ransom. As for Fastolf, he rode off 'with the greatest grief that I ever saw in a man', wrote Waurin. He succeeded in reaching Janville with about two dozen men-at-arms, but found the gates shut in his face. He eventually made his way to Paris followed by angry recriminations from those who accused him of fleeing the field at the crisis of the battle. The Duke of Bedford was shocked by the defeat and suspended Fastolf's membership of the Order of the Garter. Once the anger had subsided a review of the facts established that Fastolf had not left the field until after the battle was lost. He was officially exonerated and his Garter restored. But the smell of cowardice never dissipated. Six years later, in litigation in the Parlement of Paris, Fastolf was still being described by an opponent as the 'fugitive', which is 'the worst thing that a man can say about a knight'. Talbot never forgave him. After years of simmering resentment, he finally had the case brought before a tribunal presided over by the King, which exonerated the old knight once more. But Fastolf's flight from Patay still discredited his memory more than a century and a half later. 'I vowed, base knight, when I did meet thee next, to tear the garter from thy craven's leg,' says Talbot in Shakespeare's *Henry VI Part I*.[57]

The total number of English troops remaining to the Regent after the battle cannot have been more than about 3,500 including men in garrisons, a historic low. The citizens of Janville, who had refused to admit Fastolf, expelled their English garrison soon after. Their example was followed by all the English-occupied towns of the Orléanais and the southern Beauce. The damage to English prestige was irreparable. Wild, eschatological rumours circulated: that the Archangel Michael had been seen in the sky over Brittany mounted on a white horse; that conjoined twins and double-headed cattle had been born in the suburbs of Paris; that Rouen and Paris had risen in rebellion and had opened their gates to Joan of Arc; that the Duke of Bedford had fled to save his life; that Charles of Orléans had escaped and fled to Scotland, where King James was on the point of invading England; that the Dauphin was marching on Rome to be crowned by the Pope. Writing from Avignon, a Venetian shipmaster reported the universal opinion that all of this had happened because at the point where the French were about to be overwhelmed a pure young girl had 'redeemed them of their sins and pride'.[58]

Paris was in a state of high alarm. The Duke of Bedford, who learned of the battle on the day after it was fought, presided at a meeting of the Grand Conseil to assess the situation. Several councillors were in tears.

A major Dauphinist offensive must now be expected. But Bedford no longer had the English manpower to meet it and it was uncertain how much reliance could be placed on his indigenous troops. The council decided that the first priority should be to defend Normandy. All the garrisons of the duchy were put on alert. The main fortresses were revictualled. Men who had been withdrawn from garrisons to serve in the field were sent back to their bases. Places such as Pontorson which were judged to be indefensible except at excessive cost in men and money were demolished. All this meant that for the next few weeks the English had no field army. The rest of Lancastrian France, especially the Île-de-France and Champagne, was left exposed. The Grand Conseil turned in despair to the Duke of Burgundy. A high-powered delegation left for Hesdin to flatter and cajole him into coming at once to Paris. Letters were despatched to England, calling on the council there to increase the expeditionary army of Sir John Radcliffe and speed up its departure.[59]

At Westminster the council immediately grasped the gravity of the situation. The King's French dominions, they said, 'standen in like to be lost and subverted unless than hasty and undelayed provision of socours and relief out of his realm of England be disposed and sent thither'. All English holders of Norman land were ordered to cross the Channel at once to the duchy to perform their military obligations. England's available military manpower was already committed to Radcliffe's small expeditionary army and the army of the Hussite crusade. Both forces were currently mustering at Barham Down in Kent. A fleet was waiting in the Downs to carry them to Calais. In this extremity the council made a drastic decision. They resolved to take over Beaufort's crusading army and use it to shore up the position of the Duke of Bedford. Beaufort's numbers were disappointing. Instead of the 2,750 men which he had been authorised to recruit, he had managed to find only 1,000 men, of whom only fifty were men-at-arms. But together with Radcliffe's force, they constituted a corps of some 1,800 men, which was enough to replace most of the losses at Patay.

The diversion of the crusading army was a gross breach of faith. The men had been recruited by the promise of indulgences and had received their first quarter's wages from the papal chamber, in effect out of revenues raised in Italy. The English treasury did not have the money in hand to reimburse the papal chamber. Undeterred, a group of councillors met Cardinal Beaufort in Rochester castle on 1 July. He was readily persuaded to cooperate 'for the most singular love, zeal and tenderness that he beareth to the surety, welfare and prosperity of the King'. He also received a douceur of 1,000 marks which went into his own pocket. It was agreed that once the army had landed at Calais, the Duke of Bedford would issue an order forbidding subjects of Henry VI to leave France for a period of six months. The men would then be conscripted to serve under his orders. The Pope would be reimbursed what he had paid out as soon as the money could be found. He would be told that Beaufort had complied only with the utmost reluctance and under duress. In a sense, this was true, for as the cardinal's emissary later explained to Martin V, his men would not have followed him to Bohemia anyway if their fellow countrymen needed them in France. Martin was outraged and protested loudly. But there was nothing that he could do.[60]

The French army was already mustering outside the bridge-town of Gien for the march on Reims. The kernel of the army was the 5,000 or 6,000 men who had fought under the Duke of Alençon at Jargeau and Patay. But the excitement provoked by their victories and the threats of forfeiture had drawn men to Gien from far and wide. Some gentlemen, lacking armour, weapons or war-horses, came on ponies or mustered as mere archers or dagger-men (*coutilliers*). There was only enough money in the Treasury to pay them three *francs* apiece, but in the encampments around the town, there was a carnival atmosphere. The crowds of soldiers expected to participate in a miracle. No one, said one of Alençon's squires, had seen anything like it.[61]

The Dauphin was staying in the castle of Georges de la Trémoille at Sully. There, a major row broke out in the Dauphin's inner circle, which continued after the court arrived at Gien on 24 June. A group of councillors led by La Trémoille had become uncomfortable about the enthusiasm all around them. They were pushing back against the idolisation of Joan of Arc and her influence over the Dauphin. Joan had planned to make a triumphal entry into Orléans with Charles at her side, and to begin the march of Reims from there. It was probably La Trémoille who put a stop to that. He was certainly responsible for Charles's rejection of Joan's pleas in favour of the Constable Arthur de Richemont. He refused to let Richemont return to court or participate in the coming campaign. Richemont, who was waiting for the call at

Beaugency, was obliged to return to Parthenay. A number of other captains whom La Trémoille regarded as his enemies were sent away from the muster. Much of the opposition to Joan on the council can be ascribed to La Trémoille's pathological suspicion of anyone who might supplant him or undermine his authority. But resentment of Joan's influence was not just a matter of political jealousy, nor was it confined to La Trémoille. Other councillors feared that Joan might push the Dauphin into unwise decisions on a tide of emotion. Judging by their later actions, they included the Chancellor Regnault de Chartres and the ex-Chancellor Robert le Maçon, both of them experienced and influential councillors.[62]

These issues came to a head at Gien in the final days of June 1429, as it became ever clearer that the coming campaign would be directed at least as much against the Duke of Burgundy as against the English. La Trémoille and his allies believed that by going ahead with the campaign the Dauphin would simply drive the Duke of Burgundy into the arms of the English at a time when their alliance was beginning to look fragile. This was a real risk. Philip the Good's officers in Burgundy were already becoming alarmed at the concentration of Dauphinist troops on their frontiers. Reports were coming in of incursions into the Nivernais, Charolais and southern Burgundy, as the old Dauphinist companies began to resume their operations in anticipation of the collapse of the Dauphin's truce with Burgundy. Philip himself was beginning to regret falling out with the English over Orléans. He had not expected their positions on the Loire to collapse so dramatically, and when they did, he did not take long to realise the implications for his own domains. At the beginning of July, when he received the news of the fall of the Loire towns and the battle of Patay, he ordered troops to be raised throughout his French domains. Talk of a march on Reims by the triumphant Dauphinist captains added to the general alarm at his court. His Chamberlain Jean de la Trémoille lord of Jonvelle sent one of his squires to find out from his brother how the Dauphin proposed to lead an army to Reims without breaking the truce. For Philip, this was a critical question. He was counting on the truce to protect his eastern territories. If it was repudiated, he would need the English as much as they needed him.[63]

For the French captains gathered at Gien, there were logistical as well as political problems to be faced. There had been no time to organise a proper supply train. The army's route would lie across the main river valleys, so that any heavy artillery would have to be left behind or dragged laboriously overland. As a result, there would be neither equipment for an assault nor supplies for a siege. Even those councillors who were content to repudiate the truces with Burgundy thought that an invasion of Champagne was too risky. One group favoured a preliminary campaign to invade the Burgundian county of Nevers and capture the crossings of the upper Loire. They were afraid that otherwise the Burgundians might respond by invading Berry while the Dauphin's back was turned and all his best captains were away. At one point this strategy appeared to have been adopted. Two Burgundian fortresses at the edge of the Nivernais were actually attacked and captured by detachments from the army at Gien in the last days of June. Joan, however, was adamantly opposed to any diversion of effort from her main objective. Her response to the dissenters was to put emotional pressure on the Dauphin, sulking and weeping and complaining bitterly about the frustration of her mission. She brushed aside the logistical difficulties. The enemy in Champagne would not fight against the agents of God's will, she declared. After a series of acrimonious council meetings, the Dauphin finally accepted her advice. On 29 June 1429 the army, now about 6,000 or 7,000 strong, marched out of Gien on the road to Auxerre.[64]

The French host crossed into the Auxerrois on 1 July. Philip the Good's officers had no army with which to confront them. There was no prospect of help from the English, whose own army was below strength and tied down in the garrisons of Normandy. The council of Burgundy, which was sitting at Dole in the Jura, was urgently recalled to Dijon to deal with what was rapidly becoming a serious crisis. They sent Philip's *bailli* of the Mountains Guillaume de la Tournelle, his principal officer in northern Burgundy, to meet the Dauphin and La Trémoille on the road. He had an interview with them beneath the walls of Auxerre. Their response seems to have been to try to negotiate some arrangement which would allow the army to cross Champagne without an open breach with Philip the Good. The *bailli* sent to the Duke for instructions. But this took time. Philip was far away at Hesdin in Artois. In the meantime, the Dauphin pressed on with his campaign. He sent his heralds forward to summon Auxerre to submit. When they were met with a refusal, Joan proposed to assault the city at once. She was supported by the captains of the army. They believed that the walls would easily be carried and looked forward to the pillage that would follow. But they were thwarted by La Trémoille, who was horrified by the prospect of a sack of one of the Duke's principal cities. He brokered a deal under which the city was granted a local truce in return for a large supply of victuals for the army and a bribe of 2,000 *écus* for himself.[65]

The Dukes of Burgundy had been the dominant political power in Champagne since the civil wars. The region looked mainly to Philip's officers to defend them. Some of the towns and castles had Burgundian garrisons. It fell to the council of Burgundy to decide what to do. They gathered at Dijon on 5 July. They resolved to summon the whole nobility of the two Burgundies to assemble in arms at Châtillon-sur-Seine to stop the advance of the Dauphin's army. It was already too late. The Dauphin had entered Champagne the day before by the bridge over the river Armance at Saint-Florentin. The town had opened its gates without striking a blow. That very morning, the French had arrived before Troyes. The earliest that the Burgundian army could be ready was the end of July.[66]

Troyes should have been able to hold out for a long time. It was the richest and most populous city of Champagne, well-stocked with food and defended by broad ditches and a double circuit of modern walls. Like most northern cities, Troyes was governed by a council drawn from patrician families and the mercantile oligarchy, whose main loyalty was to Philip the Good. The city was responsible for its own defence. There was normally no professional garrison. On this occasion, however, its defence had been taken over by the principal officers of the Lancastrian government in the region: Jean de Dinteville, a Burgundian partisan who was *bailli* of Troyes and captain of the Burgundian garrison at Bar-sur-Aube; and Philibert de Moulant, who was Bedford's Master of Artillery and captain of the royal fortress of Nogent-sur-Seine. On the approach of the Dauphin's army, they had been able to bring some 500 to 600 professional troops into Troyes drawn from their own companies and the retinues of local noblemen. The councillors of Troyes were thought to be reliable. They had recently renewed their oaths of allegiance to Henry VI and had declared their intention of resisting the Dauphin 'to the death'.

The sentiments of the citizens were more equivocal. They were frightened. They had heard about Joan of Arc's achievements at Orléans and the miracles attributed to her. They did not care to fight against the cause of God. Someone declared that he had seen her standard carried aloft in the host outside, surrounded by an angelic halo of white butterflies. Many of them were followers of the Franciscan preacher Brother Richard, an overt partisan of the Dauphin who had recently arrived in the city. On 4 July 1429, as the Dauphin's army approached, the townsmen sent him out to meet Joan on the road and report back on whether she was truly an agent of God or an instrument of Satan. He came into her presence as if about to perform an exorcism, crossing himself and sprinkling holy water before him. He was presumably impressed, for he returned to Troyes with a characteristic letter from Joan headed 'JHESU MARIA'. It commanded the inhabitants 'in the name of the King of Heaven, in whose royal service she is', to open their gates to the Dauphin.

The summons was brought to the city authorities. They rejected it out of hand and briefly threw Brother Richard in prison. When the Dauphin's army appeared outside the walls early on the morning of the 5th, they were bristling with armed men. The heralds came forward to summon them to submit. The town's spokesman shouted his answer from the walls. They had received a letter, he said, which made no sense, from a madwoman possessed by the devil who called herself Jeanne la Pucelle. Troyes had sworn to admit no armed force without express orders from the Duke of Burgundy and they intended to honour their oath. In the meantime, they had thrown Joan's letter in the fire.

The decision of Troyes to fight shocked the Dauphin's captains. They had been expecting an easy victory. The stores which they had acquired at Auxerre were nearly finished and the army had already exhausted the food supplies within foraging distance. It had to keep moving in order to eat. On 8 July, the Dauphin called his captains and councillors to a council of war. Joan was not invited. It was a critical moment. When the meeting opened, the lead was taken by the Chancellor Regnault de Chartres. This august and cautious churchman had had misgivings about Joan of Arc, probably from the outset. Troyes, he said, was a much more powerful city than Auxerre. They had no artillery capable of supporting an assault. The city could not be encircled because the army was not large enough and had no food. The men present were asked for their opinions one by one. Some of them thought that the army should return to the Loire. Others proposed that they should leave Troyes behind them and press on to Reims, living on the land as they went. When it came to Robert le Maçon's turn, he observed that the Dauphin had launched his campaign without enough men to take cities or money to keep the army in being, and with few prospects of success. He had done this because Joan of Arc had persuaded him that it was the will of God and that there would be little resistance. He suggested that they should ask her what she would have them do next. Unless she had some new idea that had not occurred to anyone else, the army should return to the Loire.

At this point Joan herself arrived outside the council chamber and beat at the door. When she was admitted, Regnault de Chartres told her how the debate had gone. She knew from experience that her best tactic was to appeal to the Dauphin personally. Addressing him directly, she asked whether if she prophesied what lay ahead, she would be believed. In principle yes, Charles replied, depending on what she said. Then, she declared, Troyes would be his within two or three days, either by force or treaty. The Chancellor was unconvinced. If it was certain that the city would fall within six days, he said, he would be inclined to stay, but he did not believe it. Joan replied that she had no doubt. Her confidence and force of personality carried the meeting. Many of those present must have remained doubtful. But Joan retained the confidence of the Dauphin and of the army outside, and that was what counted.

As the council dispersed, Joan prepared an elaborate feint. A direct assault was not feasible, but she proposed to make the defenders believe that one was being prepared. She rode through the French camp, ordering everyone to collect lumber to build shelters and to approach the walls with bundles of branches and twigs to fill the moat. She told them to bring forward the few light pieces of artillery that were all that they had. The men worked at these tasks through the night. When the sun rose the next morning, the sight of the preparations provoked alarm and division among the defenders. Many of the townsfolk fled to the churches. The professional garrison was not impressed, and they were supported by the city authorities. But ranged against them was much of the clergy, led by the Bishop, Jean Lesguisé.

Lesguisé belonged to the long royalist tradition of the French Church and had many contacts with influential figures at the Dauphin's court. He had been elected to the see in 1426 in spite of the opposition of the Duke of Bedford, who regarded him as politically unreliable. He was supported by Brother Richard and by the heads of a number of monastic houses. They made contact with the Dauphin's confessor

Gérard Machet. Machet entered the city for preliminary discussions in the bishops' palace. The leaders of the guilds called for a preliminary conference with the Dauphin's officers. They wanted, they said, to discover what terms might be available to them. But the Bishop, who was appointed to represent the town, quickly went beyond that. He entered the Dauphin's camp and negotiated draft terms of surrender. They provided that the garrison was to withdraw with their possessions and their prisoners. The city was to be granted a general amnesty for past acts of disloyalty. It would receive extensive fiscal privileges and exemptions and a promise that no royal garrison would be imposed on them. Its commerce would not be subject to the prohibitions against trading with the enemy which were in force elsewhere in the kingdom of Bourges. These terms were brought back into the city and ratified at a general meeting of the inhabitants. The streets exploded with joy. Not everyone shared the joy. Many prominent citizens felt that they had been overborne. The captains of the garrison had only agreed to exploratory talks, not to a negotiated surrender, and they rejected the terms. But without the support of the inhabitants there was nothing that they could do. In the end an intimidating mob of townsmen appeared and told them that they would admit the Dauphin with or without their agreement. On the following morning, 10 July, at nine o'clock in the morning, the citizens opened their gates. Joan was first into the city, accompanied by a large body of bowmen whom she posted in the streets to maintain order. The city's storehouses were opened up and their contents distributed among the Dauphin's famished troops. Joan personally supervised the withdrawal of the garrison. Ignoring the terms of surrender, she relieved them of their prisoners 'in the name of God' as they passed through the gates, as a result of which the Dauphin later had to pay compensation to their captors.[67]

On the afternoon of 10 July 1429, Philip the Good arrived in Paris for urgent talks with the Regent and his advisers. Philip found the capital in a state of panic. Troyes had surrendered that morning. On the following day the Bishop of Châlons, whose city commanded the passage of the Marne south of Reims, met the Dauphin on the road bearing the keys of his city. Over the next few days, while the conferences were in progress in Paris, support for the Anglo-Burgundian cause collapsed across most of Champagne. The Dauphin and Joan of Arc were received into Châlons by enthusiastic crowds of citizens on 14 July. The Duke of Bedford warned the council at Westminster that Reims would probably fall and Paris would be next. Many thousands of Parisians, led by the councillors of the Parlement and the canons of the major churches, joined the religious processions which wound their way through the streets, habitual symptoms of a burgeoning crisis.[68]

The Duke of Bedford needed two things from Philip the Good: military support on a generous scale, and political support to shore up his position in Paris. The outcome confirmed all La Trémoille's fears that the march on Reims would drive the Burgundians into the arms of the English. Philip and Bedford solemnly renewed their alliance. They agreed that each would draw on all their resources to deal with the current crisis. Writing to the council in England, Bedford reported that in this extremity Philip had shown himself to be a 'true kinsman, friend and vassal' of the King. Philip had brought 400 or 500 men with him to Paris to help secure the city against attack. His officers were already recruiting a new army across his territories. The Regent promised a subsidy of 40,000 *livres* for their wages, half of it cash down in advance and the rest secured by a pledge of jewellery belonging to himself and his wife. Beaufort and Radcliffe were expected to arrive from England in a few days with another 1,800 men. In fact, the first transports sailed from Sandwich on 13 July. The English council promised to send more men as soon as they could be found and paid. Meanwhile Bedford planned to do a tour of Normandy to pull as many troops as possible out of garrisons. Another 1,750 men were found from this source by the end of the month. The cost of all this fell on the English Exchequer and on the Treasury of Normandy. By now Bedford had given up any hope of defending the treaty provinces from their own resources.[69]

Philip the Good had neglected Paris for years, but the head of the house of Burgundy was still an important focus of party loyalty among the guilds and *grands corps* of the capital. Bedford joined him in the palace on the Île de la Cité for a dramatic re-enactment of the murder of John the Fearless, at the end of which the spectators, all prominent citizens, were asked to swear a collective oath of loyalty, raising their arms in assent as in a twentieth-century political rally. The Provost of the Merchants and all four of the city's *échevins* (councillors) were replaced by reliable Burgundian loyalists, and Villiers de L'Isle-Adam, another stalwart Burgundian, was named as captain of the city.

Much of this was whistling in the dark, for the truth was that neither Bedford nor Philip was confident of the future. When Philip left the city, he took his sister the Duchess of Bedford with him, 'on account of the great perils that seem likely to be threatening the Île-de-France'. Concluding his report to his colleagues in England, Bedford chided them for resisting his previous calls for the young Henry VI to come to France and asked them to think again. The sudden renaissance of the Dauphin had shown the value of a visible focus of loyalty in a world where the theatre of monarchy counted for so much. If the King had been in France, Bedford observed, the situation would not have got out of hand in the way it had.[70]

On about 11 July 1429, Villiers de L'Isle-Adam arrived at Reims with the Picard nobleman Philippe de Saveuse and a company of soldiers. Their task was to suppress any movement among the citizens to defect to the Dauphin and persuade them to hold out until more substantial forces could arrive. They cannot have been reassured by what they found. As at Troyes, there was a schism between the city government and the townsmen. The councillors had proclaimed their intention of defending their city and had taken energetic steps to prepare it. The watches had been reinforced; repairs had been carried out on the walls, towers and gates; chains had been stretched across the streets; and action had been taken against strangers and known partisans of the Dauphin. After the surrender of Troyes, these measures had been intensified, and the inhabitants of the surrounding countryside had been ordered into the city bringing all the food that they could carry.

The townspeople demurred. They were terrified of Joan and inclined to follow the line of least resistance. Upon entering Champagne, the Dauphin had sent his heralds to the city with a summons calling on the inhabitants to submit to him. He reminded them of his victories on the Loire. He gave them an exaggerated picture of the English losses. He hinted at the dire consequences of refusal. When this was ignored, another, more insistent message was sent. The Dauphin's claims were backed up by the councillors of Troyes. Charles, they wrote, was a prince of 'great discretion, wisdom and courage' who had been exceedingly gracious and generous to them. The citizens of Reims should submit to him as they had done. Writing from his castle at Châtillon-sur-Marne, the Burgundian partisan Jean de Châtillon wrote to the city with a different version of the facts. Troyes, he said, had in fact been tricked into surrendering by its treacherous bishop against the wishes of the inhabitants. The Dauphin's army could never have taken the place by force. As for Joan, he had spoken to a squire of the garrison who had seen her and reported that she was 'the simplest thing he had ever seen', with no more sense in her than any dumb fool.[71]

The captain of Reims, Guillaume de Châtillon, was forty miles away at Château-Thierry, an important fortress for which he was also responsible. From there, he engaged in an acrimonious stand-off with the townsfolk. He refused to be responsible for the defence of the city unless he was allowed to bring in 300 or 400 professional troops, the minimum that was necessary in his view. The townsmen, who had a long tradition of hostility to professional garrisons, would not let him bring more than fifty. They also declined to let him occupy the Porte-Mars, a Roman monumental gateway converted into a fortress, which Guillaume believed to be necessary for his personal security. He was afraid of being trapped in the city in the event of an uprising in Charles's favour.

On the morning of 16 July, as the French army approached from Châlons, Philippe de Saveuse and Guillaume de Châtillon appeared together at an assembly of the citizens. The two men asked the townsmen whether they were prepared to resist the Dauphin's army. They responded with another question. If they resisted, was the Lancastrian government in a position to relieve them? Saveuse answered that at the moment it was not, but if the city could hold out for six weeks it would be relieved by a large Anglo-Burgundian army which was in the process of being formed in Paris. There were plenty of people at Reims who wanted to stand by the city's Burgundian allegiance. But the majority thought that Saveuse's answer was not good enough. The English were paying a heavy price for their inability to put an army into the field after Patay. Saveuse and Châtillon decided that there was nothing more to be done. As they left, Reims sent a delegation to meet the Dauphin on the road with an offer of submission. They reported back that they had found him 'kind, gracious, compassionate, merciful and handsome, with a fine bearing and a quick understanding'. They were granted substantially the same terms as Troyes. The Chancellor Regnault de Chartres entered the city as its Archbishop, the first time for more than a decade that he had set foot in it. That evening, Charles and Joan made their own ceremonial entry, watched by a cheering crowd of citizens.[72]

The whole of the night was occupied in feverish preparations for a coronation ceremony that was usually organised over several weeks. The last one had happened forty-nine years before, and there was much that had to be improvised. The current order of service dated back to the coronation of Charles V in 1364, but it was under English control in the treasury of the abbey of Saint-Denis, along with the crown and other regalia. It was necessary to rediscover the old *ordo* of the thirteenth century, a copy of which was found in the cathedral library. They had to manufacture a simple crown overnight and find replacements for the other regalia. The holy oil with which the kings of France were anointed was fetched from the abbey of St Rémy beyond the walls, in accordance with ancient and half-forgotten rituals. The Constable of France as the custodian of the sword of state was absent. The Duke of Burgundy as the senior of the twelve peers and a number of bishops with important ceremonial roles were in the Anglo-Burgundian camp. Others had to stand in for them.

The next day, 17 July 1429, was a Sunday. At nine o'clock in the morning, the ceremony opened in the vast space of Reims cathedral. It lasted for five hours. Charles was knighted by the Duke of Alençon at the high altar, and then anointed by Regnault de Chartres on his head, chest, shoulders and arms. He swore the traditional oath to protect his people, support the Church and administer justice and equity. The crown was placed on his head to the sound of trumpets and cries of '*Noel!*' so loud that some of the congregation feared that the vault would collapse. At the conclusion of the ceremony the King promoted Guy de Laval and Georges de la Trémoille to be counts and Gilles de Retz to be a Marshal. Several hundred others were knighted. Joan of Arc stood beside the King at the altar throughout, holding her famous banner aloft. It was a 'fine thing to see their noble bearing', three servants of the house of Anjou wrote to the Queen and Yolande of Anjou at Bourges. Among the congregation were Joan's father, one of her brothers and several inhabitants of Domrémy, for whom the experience must have been overwhelming. At the end of the proceedings, Joan threw herself at Charles's feet declaring through her tears: 'Noble King, thus is accomplished the will of the Lord.'[73]

Joan had earned her place of honour. The relief of Orléans had owed much to the boost which she gave to the morale of the defenders, but it would probably have happened anyway. The English never had enough men for the siege, and all the tactical decisions had been made and carried out by professional captains, notably the Bastard of Orléans and La Hire. The same was true of the operations to expel the English from the Loire fortresses. Joan's role at Patay had been marginal. The march on Reims was different. It would not have happened without her. Her indifference to risk might have led to disaster and had been opposed for that reason by the most experienced heads on the Dauphin's council. In a sense they were right. The capture of Troyes, Châlons and Reims were achieved by bluff, which might have been called. But in war strategists have to take chances. Joan's arguments were emotional and spiritual, not strategic. But as it happened there were better strategic reasons for marching on Reims than she knew. The Dauphinists were able to exploit the psychological momentum created by the victories of May and June and the fame of Joan to whom those victories were attributed. The timing was fortunate. A month later and the Duke of Bedford would have had an army in the field. As it was, there was a void of authority in Champagne, and no effective resistance.

The coronation of Charles VII was an event of incalculable moment. For many Frenchmen living in regions under English rule, its effect was to remove the doubts created by the treaty of Troyes about his right to succeed his father. For Christine de Pisan, writing from retirement in the convent of Poissy after a decade of silence, it transformed Charles from a mere contestant, the rejected child of the last unquestionably legitimate monarch, into a true king. In the sacral theology of French kingship, it made him the elect of God, the successor of earlier kings who had been through the same rituals and enjoyed the same powers uncontested. In Paris, the clerk of the Parlement, a servant of the dual monarchy, recorded in his register that Charles had been 'crowned in Reims cathedral, like his father and every King of France before him'. The coronation accelerated the spread of national sentiment beyond the limited circles traditionally reached by Valois propaganda. Charles VII was unequivocally identified with France in a way that Henry VI never could be. 'Loyal Frenchmen, come before King Charles,' Joan had said in her summons to the inhabitants of Troyes. France was for Frenchmen, England for Englishmen. 'Go back to your own country,' she had told the English in her famous first letter. Joan's words were widely distributed, fostering the idea that this was a conflict of nations, and no longer a French civil war. Even among the English and Burgundians, people understood that a new chapter had opened. Those who had habitually referred to Charles as 'Dauphin' now began to call him King. The belligerently Burgundian chronicler of Paris, who was probably a canon of Notre-Dame, affected neutrality and began from this point to refer to both Charles and Henry as 'self-styled' kings. The Lancastrian government naturally continued to follow the prescribed usage, but the poor parody of the coronation which it organised for Henry VI at Notre-Dame in Paris in 1431 showed that its ministers were uncomfortably aware of the impact of the authentic ceremony at Reims.[74]

Just as the coronation seemed to undo the legal effect of the treaty of Troyes, so the expulsion of the English from the Loire valley undid the moral effect of Agincourt and Verneuil. The English tacitly abandoned the ambition to extend their government to the whole of France, even if it was politically impossible to admit it. They never again tried to break through the Loire barrier. North of the Loire they were fatally weakened. Bedford's most potent advantage had always been the myth of English invincibility. The inhabitants of Champagne no longer believed it. Over the three weeks following the coronation, the trickle of submissions became a flood. Laon, the fourth cathedral city of Champagne, admitted Charles VII's officers. Château-Thierry expelled Guillaume de Châtillon's garrison and opened its gates to the King's captains. Soissons and Provins sent delegations with their submissions and their homage. By the beginning of August 1429, the English and their Burgundian allies had lost most of Brie and western Champagne. Charles's captains were collecting artillery from the urban arsenals of the region to move against Lagny and Meaux with their important crossings of the Marne east of Paris. The King began to rebuild the provincial administration, appointing his own *baillis* and castellans after twelve years in which the region had been in the hands of officials of the Dukes of Burgundy and the English Regent. These events resonated across all of northern France. On the Moselle, where Charles of Lorraine and Réné of Anjou were engaged in the siege of the German city of Metz, Réné broke away from the operation and marched west to join Charles VII at Provins, bringing with him a band of noblemen and a large body of troops from the duchies of Bar and Lorraine. A few days later Réné renounced the homage that he had done to Henry VI just three days before the relief of Orléans.[75]

CHAPTER VII

Joan of Arc:
Reims to Rouen, 1429–1431

Philip the Good was the first to appreciate the significance of the coronation. He learned of the surrender of Reims shortly after leaving Paris, as his cavalcade approached Laon. In spite of the arrangements that he had just made with the Duke of Bedford, he decided at once to re-establish diplomatic relations with Charles VII. On the afternoon of the coronation, a Burgundian embassy led by David de Brimeu, one of Philip's closest confidants, appeared at Reims with a message of congratulation and an invitation to negotiate. Another message was sent to the Duke of Savoy, inviting him to resume his old role as mediator. In Charles's camp, Regnault de Chartres and La Trémoille grasped the opportunity with both hands. A short truce of two weeks was agreed on about 24 July, which appears to have covered the Île-de-France and Champagne. An exploratory conference was arranged for the beginning of August at the castle of the lords of Coucy at La Fère on the Oise. The English were not invited.[1]

Strategically, the loss of Champagne was a disaster for both England and Burgundy. It was a rich agricultural region with important commercial and industrial cities, one of the few provinces outside Normandy from which the dual monarchy derived any substantial tax revenues. Its reconquest opened up the regions north of Paris to Charles's partisans for the first time since the expulsion of their northern garrisons five years before. Charles VII advanced west from Reims a few days after the coronation. On 23 July 1429 he reached Soissons, which opened its gates to him. Soissons was an important bridge-town on the Aisne and a major hub of the road system north-east of Paris. From here, the French army was poised to march on the capital. The captains of the army were keen to exploit the momentum of the past month and attack the city before the Regent could concentrate his scattered forces and bring in reinforcements from England. They were outraged by the truce with Burgundy, which gave Bedford a vital fortnight's breathing space. Joan of Arc, who had been determined to attack Paris from the outset, was furious and threatened to ignore it. Her attitude to the Duke of Burgundy was uncompromising. On the day of the coronation, she had dictated a letter to him calling for a complete Burgundian surrender. Let Philip make peace with Charles VII, recall all his garrisons from France and withdraw from the war. There was no point, she told him, in waging war against the King of Heaven. Her view was that there was no peace to be had from him, 'except at the point of a lance'.[2]

The last contingents of the army of Cardinal Beaufort and Sir John Radcliffe disembarked at Calais a few days after the coronation. They marched to Amiens, where they joined forces with some 700 Picards under the command of Villiers de L'Isle-Adam. The Regent went to Rouen to meet them there. On 25 July, Beaufort, Bedford and L'Isle-Adam entered Paris together, accompanied by some 2,500 men. The city was volatile and fearful, the streets filled with refugees from the surrounding region. The troops were retained for the defence of the city. As further contingents arrived, they were deployed to guard the approaches to Paris. About 1,750 men from the English garrisons of Normandy and the indigenous nobility of the province arrived at Pontoise during the last week of July. They were sent to defend Lagny, the vital bridge-town over the Marne twenty-five miles east of Paris. John of Luxembourg was sent to defend the valley of the Oise between Saint-Quentin and Noyon. Another force under his cousin the Bastard of Saint-Pol was ordered to hold Meaux. The Duke of Bedford now had between 5,000 and 6,000 men at his disposal in the Paris area. Philip the Good's army from Artois and Picardy, which was mustering at Corbie on the Somme, was expected to arrive in a few days.[3]

At Soissons, Charles VII's advisers briefly lost their nerve. They thought that an attack of Paris was no longer possible. They were unwilling to risk another Verneuil and persuaded him to abandon the idea and withdraw to the Loire. This was very ill-advised. It would have exposed the cities of Champagne to the vengeance of the Duke of Bedford's new army. The cities protested energetically when they heard about it. Nonetheless, the French King showed every sign of acting on it. On about 28 July, he left Soissons, heading south towards Bray-sur-Seine, the only crossing of the Seine in friendly hands. On 2 August, his army reached Provins, the capital of Brie, some fifteen miles north of the crossing. There followed a game of cat and mouse between the two armies as they manoeuvred for advantage (*see Map III*). The Duke of Bedford sent a contingent of troops to occupy Bray, blocking the French line of retreat. He recalled as many men as he could spare from the garrisons of the Marne, and on 4 August led his whole host up the Seine to the island-fortress of Melun, which lay directly west of the French encampments around Provins.

In Provins, French strategy was undergoing another volte-face. The talks with the Duke of Burgundy had failed. Regnault de Chartres and Georges de la Trémoille, accompanied by La Hire and Poton de Saintrailles, had met Philip's Chancellor Nicolas Rolin at La Fère at the beginning of August. The conference had been brief and unproductive. It proved impossible to agree on anything, even an extension of the truce, which was accordingly allowed to expire. The outcome greatly weakened the hand of those who were looking for a diplomatic solution and strengthened the more aggressive ideas of Joan of Arc and the captains of the army. The plan to withdraw to the Loire was abandoned as lightly as it had been adopted. Instead, they decided to challenge the Anglo-Burgundian army to battle in the plain of Brie and then, if the challenge was declined, to resume the offensive in the north.[4]

Early on 5 August 1429, the French army advanced west from Provins to Nangis, a small town twenty miles from Melun, dominated by the immense thirteenth-century fortress whose ruins still stand above the plain. They stood in battle order beyond the town for the whole day waiting for the English to attack. Bedford decided not to take the risk. With at least 6,000 men, the French commanders had a slight advantage of numbers. The flat, featureless plain around Nangis was a difficult place for a battle against superior forces. The Anglo-Burgundian army stayed behind the walls of Melun throughout the day. Then, thinking that Charles was still planning to escape to the Loire, Bedford led his army south along the left bank of the Seine to Montereau to head them off. He realised his mistake when he reached the fortress on 7 August and discovered that the French had marched north out of Provins, not south. From Montereau, the Regent issued a challenge to submit their dispute to the God of battles. The purpose of such challenges was usually propagandist, and this one was no exception. It consisted mainly of crude abuse of 'Charles de Valois who calls himself Dauphin' and his acolytes, the one a 'loose, infamous and immoral woman dressed as a man', and the other a 'seditious and heretical friar' (this was a reference to Brother Richard). With the French army now heading back to the Marne, Bedford and his army raced back to defend Paris. The French army crossed the Marne at Château-Thierry, and on 11 August reached Crépy-en-Valois on the main road from Soissons to Paris. For the next few days, the old castle of the Counts of Valois at the edge of the town would be the headquarters from which French operations were directed. It was here that the Duke of Bedford's heralds caught up with Charles VII and delivered his challenge. On the following morning the French army began its advance along the Paris road towards the capital.[5]

The Duke of Bedford, who was receiving regular reports of the enemy's movements, left Paris early on 14 August at the head of his army. That afternoon, he established his headquarters in the ruins of the abbey of Notre-Dame de la Victoire, south-east of Senlis. With the French army still the stronger force, the cautious Bedford decided to stand on the defensive. He dismounted his men and drew them up in a single line extending for about a mile across the countryside. The English were stationed on the left of the line and the Burgundians on the right, with their rear and flanks protected by dense hawthorn hedges. The archers were posted in front with sharpened stakes pointing outward. Two tall banners, one with cross of St George and the other with the lilies of France, floated side-by-side above their lines. The French halted some three miles away, beneath the imposing fortress of Montépilloy. Much thought was given to their order of battle. They dismounted and formed up in three battalions. The Duke of Alençon and the Count of Vendôme were stationed in the vanguard. Behind them a second battalion was commanded by Réné of Anjou. The King took nominal command of the rearguard, but real direction was exercised by the Count of Clermont. Separate units were posted at each wing, commanded by the marshals, together with a mounted reserve under the Bastard of Orléans, the lord of Albret and La Hire. As at Patay, Joan of Arc was posted well away from the front line, in the reserve.

On the following morning, 15 August, La Hire led a mounted scouting party forward to reconnoitre the Anglo-Burgundian lines. The English had laboured through the night to complete their field works. A line of trenches had been dug in front of their positions. La Hire surveyed the scene and quickly decided against an attack. The enemy's position was too strong, he said, and the French superiority of numbers not big enough. The French tactic should be to draw the Anglo-Burgundians out from behind their field works and tempt them to take the offensive. Joan of Arc was for once uncertain what to do, alternating between the defensive tactics proposed by the professional captains and a full-scale assault on the enemy lines. The French formations advanced from Montépilloy to within two bowshots of the Anglo-Burgundian line. There they halted and challenged them to come out from behind their defences. The Duke of Bedford was not to be tempted. His men stood all day in the baking heat amid the clouds of dust stirred up by the horses. There were vicious skirmishes between the lines and some exchanges of archery, which caused several hundred casualties. Some Picard companies briefly broke out of their stockade and captured a number of French culverins. Charles himself rode up and down in front of the English lines with La Trémoille and the Count of Clermont, taunting the enemy. La Trémoille was mounted on a fine and richly caparisoned horse, which bucked and threw him into the enemy lines, where his heavy armour made it impossible for him to get up. He had to be rescued or he would have been captured.[6]

Neither side was willing to risk a full-scale battle. The French King withdrew at nightfall to Crépy-en-Valois. The next morning, he and his advisers at Crépy learned that the English and their Burgundian allies had abandoned their position and retreated towards Paris. There was no attempt at pursuit. Tactically, the encounter was a stalemate. But strategically, the English had suffered a serious reverse. Bedford had successfully blocked the French King's advance on Paris, but his retreat left the northern Île-de-France, the Oise valley and the Beauvaisis exposed and defenceless. None of the towns had professional garrisons except for Clermont-en-Beauvaisis, the island fortress of Creil and the great fortified bridge of Pont-Sainte-Maxence (*Map III*). The French captains moved quickly to exploit their advantage. The King had already sent heralds to the major walled towns of these regions, summoning them to submit. Resistance collapsed everywhere. In the cathedral city of Beauvais, a major crossroads lying across the route from Paris to Amiens, the townsmen submitted as soon as they saw the fleur-de-lys on the herald's tabard. At Compiègne, the principal walled town of the Oise valley, the inhabitants hesitated for a time, but gave up once the Regent had withdrawn to Paris. They sent a delegation to the King at Crépy with the keys of the town. Supporters of the Lancastrian government abandoned their homes and left. Even Senlis, traditionally the most pro-Burgundian town of the region, surrendered to the Count of Vendôme and Marshal Boussac on the day after Bedford's retreat. The townsmen reasoned that Charles VII had conquered a vast territory very quickly and the Regent had not dared to fight him.[7]

Charles VII made his formal entry into Compiègne on 18 August and established his headquarters there for the next ten days. During that period his officers took possession of most of the surrounding region including the Oise fortresses of Creil and Pont-Sainte-Maxence. Their inhabitants and garrisons 'yolde hem without resistance or [waiting for] succour', as Bedford later complained. Contemporaries were shocked by the speed of the Anglo-Burgundian collapse. According to a Picard chronicler who lived through these events, Joan of Arc had only to summon a town to surrender for it to open its gates. Her 'miracles persuaded them that it was God's purpose'. If Charles had chosen to invade the Somme valley, the chronicler thought that he could have had Saint-Quentin, Corbie, Abbeville and Amiens for the asking. Some people thought that he could have recovered the whole of Lancastrian France.[8]

The loss of the fortresses of the Oise, which lay across the main road and river communications between Paris and Picardy, was a grievous blow to the Lancastrian government. It was followed at the end of August by the loss of Lagny, whose garrison had been withdrawn to shore up the position on other fronts. As soon as the soldiers had left, the inhabitants of Lagny sent a delegation to Charles VII bearing their submission. This was an even more serious blow, for Lagny was a strong walled town controlling an important fortified bridge over the Marne. Its fall closed the approach to Paris by the valley of the Marne, and left Meaux as the only major garrisoned fortress in the valley still under English control. In the hands of Charles VII's partisans, the newly conquered cities became bases for the seizure of a large number of isolated and undefended castles, from which they preyed on the traffic of the roads and rivers. They choked off supplies to the capital, threatening a return to the loose siege which had made life so wretched for its inhabitants before 1422. Panic gripped the city's palaces, streets and warrens. The Parlement suspended its sittings. Some of the city gates were walled up. The suburbs were cut off and their inhabitants brought within the walls. The religious life of the city acquired the intensity which always came with danger. Special Masses were ordered. The fragments of the True Cross were brought out of the Sainte-Chapelle to be displayed to the people. Great processions wound their way through the streets to appease the God of battles.[9]

As the crisis deepened, there were alarming signs that it would spread to Normandy, where the withdrawal of men for the defence of Paris had left garrison strengths at dangerously low levels. In Maine and the duchy of Alençon, local partisans took advantage of the situation to occupy a number of powerful fortresses, including the old castles of the Dukes of Alençon at Bonsmoulins on the river Iton and Saint-Céneri on the Sarthe, both of which would cause much grief to the English over the following years (*Map IV*). In south-eastern Normandy Arthur de Richemont, frustrated by his exclusion from the King's army, unexpectedly burst into the Eure valley at the beginning of August at the head of his Breton company. Conches-en-Ouche, a twelfth-century fortress whose ruins still stand over the road from Rouen to Verneuil, was captured. Evreux, the principal town of the region and the anchor of the defence of the south-eastern march, entered into a conditional surrender agreement.

On the northern march, the English garrisons, after five years of relative peace, had been reduced in number and depleted in strength even before the siege of Orléans. This region was rich in ancient and vulnerable seigneurial castles. With the French reoccupation of the Beauvaisis and the Oise valley, partisan loyalties were awakened that had been dormant for years. Old allies of La Hire and Jacques d'Harcourt reappeared with fresh companies in the valleys of the Bresle and the Varenne (*Map II*). The leading figure was André de Rambures, head of one of the great noble families of Picardy. In August 1429, Rambures's company, guided by the local priest, surprised the old castle of the Harcourts at Aumale on the river Bresle, which now belonged to the Earl of Warwick. Warwick's garrison, just six strong, was swiftly overpowered. Rambures's men were shortly joined not just by other Picards but by men from English-occupied regions of western Normandy. A month after his capture of Aumale, André de Rambures moved into the Norman Vexin and captured the old twelfth-century fortress of Étrépagny, which belonged to the Greys of Heton. Like other places, it seems to have been betrayed by its locally recruited garrison. An Italian company in French service occupied and fortified the buildings of a priory at Blangy, a short distance downstream of Aumale. Together the invaders mounted destructive raids across the whole region north of the Seine, penetrating to the gates of Rouen and driving flocks of refugees to the towns.[10]

These incursions into what had recently been the most secure province of Lancastrian France happened at a time when the Duke of Bedford was struggling to defend his capital against a superior French army. On about 21 August, just five days after his return from Montépilloy, he was forced to leave the city to relieve Evreux on the day appointed for its *journée*. He took with him all the men who had been withdrawn from the garrisons of Normandy in July, leaving the capital to be held by a reduced force of English and Burgundian companies. In Rouen, Bedford hurriedly reordered the defences of the Norman marches, creating a number of new military commands. The northern march was placed in the hands of Robert Willoughby and the 23-year-old Edmund Beaufort, a nephew of the Cardinal at the outset of a long career in Normandy. Beaufort was made captain of Neufchâtel, Gournay and Gisors, while Willoughby took command at Pontoise. South of the Seine, two field forces were created, one under Richard Wallier *bailli* of Evreux covering the south-east march and the other under Ralph Butler covering the south-west. All of these forces, however, were thinly spread across large areas. Bedford did not have enough men to fight off Charles VII's army north of Paris and at the same time to defend the vast area of Normandy against potential attacks from both north and south.[11]

Philip the Good followed these events from Arras. The once invincible English army was overstretched and seemed to be on the verge of collapse, leaving him to face the vengeance of Charles VII alone. The invasion of Picardy and the Oise valley had transformed Philip's domains in northern France into a war zone. His policy, sedulously pursued over the past six years, of sheltering his domains in France behind a wall of truces and leaving the active prosecution of the war to the English, had finally proved to be a dead end. His council, whose leading members were with him at Arras, was divided. Most of them were for pursuing the negotiations with Charles VII even if it meant undermining the English alliance. Some of the councillors openly argued that the treaty of Troyes had been a mistake. A minority, led by Hughes de Lannoy and the aged Jean de Thoisy, Philip's former tutor and Rolin's predecessor as Chancellor of Burgundy, took a different view. They had just returned from a conference with the Duke of Bedford in Paris. They believed that the English would pull through and that Philip should stand by them.[12] Without the English alliance, Philip would have very little to bargain with in any negotiations with Charles VII. In the end, Philip decided upon a middle course. He would stand by the English alliance and shore up the defence of Paris, which was in a sense his city more than it was ever Bedford's. At the same time, he would open negotiations with Charles VII for another regional truce covering his own domains. The emissaries of the Duke of Savoy, who had arrived at Arras a few days earlier, were ready to act as intermediaries.

The French negotiators, led by Regnault de Chartres, entered Arras in the middle of August 1429. They were received by Philip the Good in the presence of his council and a large body of captains and courtiers. Regnault delivered a flowery oration of the sort which usually marked the beginning of a difficult negotiation. He declared that Charles had a 'real desire' for reconciliation with the house of Burgundy. The ambassadors of Savoy produced a ready-made plan for a comprehensive peace. This marked a significant advance on previous proposals. Charles VII, they suggested, should agree various public acts of expiation for the 'evil and execrable' murder of John the Fearless, perpetrated by his advisers at a time when he was young and immature. The advisers in question would be named and punished. He should confirm Philip in the possession of all the territory which he currently occupied, including lands which had been granted to him by the English. There would be a mutual pardon for all offences arising out of the civil war and a general restitution of confiscated property on both sides. Philip would acknowledge Charles as his sovereign, but while the King lived, he would be exempted from doing homage to him in person, and his domains would be exempt from the jurisdiction of Charles's judges and officials. The Savoyards had discussed these proposals with the French delegation in advance. They were broadly satisfied with them. The more difficult question was what to do about the English. The French acknowledged that Philip could not make peace without them. They proposed that Henry VI should be allowed to retain his territory in the south-west beyond the river Dordogne, but the English would have to forfeit all of their conquests in northern France and release the remaining prisoners of Agincourt. The ambassadors of Savoy were sceptical. They thought that the French would have to offer more than that. The French proposed a general truce until midsummer 1430, to allow for a peace conference in which all three parties would be represented. But they doubted whether the English were willing to negotiate and insisted on an earnest of good faith. They must, said Regnault de Chartres, at least bring the prisoners of Agincourt with them to the conference. On this note, the discussions stalled.[13]

The main problem about the proposed truce was the status of Paris. Charles VII's diplomats, supported by the ambassadors of Savoy and the more experienced voices on his council, wanted to pause the military offensive for the greater prize of an accommodation with Burgundy. Joan of Arc on the other hand, who was with Charles at Compiègne, wanted to press on with the attack on the capital, which she believed would fall like a ripe plum into their hands, just as the towns of Champagne and Picardy had done. Her view was shared by the Duke of Alençon and by most of the captains of the army. On 21 August, negotiations with the Burgundians were transferred from Arras to Charles VII's temporary headquarters at Compiègne. Two days later, on the 22nd, as discussions about the truce were resuming, Joan resolved to force the King's hand. She left Compiègne with Alençon to rejoin the army at Senlis. Two days later the two of them led the troops into the plain north of Paris and occupied Saint-Denis, which they found undefended and abandoned. Here, in the burial place of the kings of France, one of the centres of French royal mythology, they set up their headquarters. The main body of the army encamped outside the capital, around the suburban villages of Montmartre, La Chapelle and Aubervilliers.[14]

The Regent received the news of the occupation of Saint-Denis at Vernon on the Seine, where he was trying to cover both the Norman and the Paris fronts. He called Cardinal Beaufort and the principal members of his council to an urgent conference. It was by now obvious that his withdrawal from Montépilloy had been a mistake. This time, he decided, the French would have to be confronted at whatever cost. He had with him at Vernon the army which had been employed in the relief of Evreux. A fresh call was made for troops from the garrisons, leaving them once again stripped to the bone and dangerously exposed. On 27 August the whole *arrière-ban* of Normandy was summoned to muster at Rouen by 10 September. Bedford declared that he would lead the combined force to fight Charles VII's army outside Paris. Although service in response to this summons was traditionally unpaid, he promised that this time they would have 'due and reasonable money' in advance. To fund this commitment, he resorted to extreme measures. A forced loan was imposed on the Parisians. The churches of the capital were raided for cash. Deposits, many of which had been placed there for safe-keeping by citizens, were seized. Henry Beaufort dug into his chests and advanced 10,000 *livres*, his first loan to the English Crown for more than four years.[15]

On 28 August 1429, the councillors of Charles VII and the Duke of Burgundy reached a provisional agreement at Compiègne. It was a messy compromise, which had been agreed in haste before the clash of arms drowned out the voices of the diplomats. A partial cease-fire was declared with immediate effect until Christmas. It covered all regions north of the Seine from Nogent-sur-Seine in Champagne to the sea. The main beneficiary of this arrangement was the Duke of Burgundy, who achieved his objective of protecting his territorial interests in Artois and Picardy. There was also an informal side-agreement whose terms were disputed and were destined to cause much trouble later. Philip believed that he had been promised possession of Beauvais, Senlis, Compiègne and Creil for the duration of the cease-fire. These places were important to him. They were part of the network of influence and clientage by which he extended his political influence beyond his own domains into northern France. The weakness of the new agreement was that the English were not party to it. For that reason, it was necessary to include some significant provisos. To accommodate the demands of his army, Charles VII reserved the right to attack towns controlling bridges over the Seine, including Paris. To this, the Burgundians responded by reserving the right to fight in defence of Paris. Both exceptions were embodied in the final text.[16]

The French King and his councillors had left open the possibility of attempting the conquest of Paris, but their hearts were not in it. They hoped to be able to restrain the enthusiasm of the soldiers and avoid an open war with Philip the Good. So when Charles VII left Compiègne immediately after the proclamation of the cease-fire, he did not join the army as Alençon and Joan had urged him to do. Instead, he installed himself in the old royal palace of Senlis. The captains outside Paris wanted to launch their assault before the Duke of Bedford arrived with reinforcements. They needed the King to be there. Charles repeatedly promised to come but put it off from day to day. It was not until 7 September that, under heavy pressure from

Alençon, he finally appeared at Saint-Denis. The assault on the capital was launched on the next day, 8 September 1429.

There had been no proper reconnaissance of the defences, which would have revealed the formidable character of the undertaking. Paris was one the best defended cities in Europe. The northern walls of the city had been rebuilt by the King's grandfather Charles V in the 1360s and 1370s to enclose the new quarters of the right bank. They were some sixty feet high, ten feet thick at the base, and reinforced by towers and internal buttresses. The approaches were defended by a double line of ditches: a deep, water-filled moat about 100 feet wide preceded by a dry ditch. A steep earthwork separated the two, which made it difficult to deploy artillery against the base of the wall and exposed assault parties to murderous fire from the ramparts as they tried to scramble over it. The six gates which penetrated the new wall were protected by drawbridges, fortified boulevards in front, and artillery above. A dense line of men armed with crossbows, culverins and other weapons could be seen drawn up along the top of the wall, with a forest of standards and banners floating over their heads.[17]

Joan of Arc had hoped that the mere appearance of the assault parties would provoke a loyalist rising in the capital and that the gates would open before her. But this was never likely to happen in 1429. Paris was the heart of the Burgundian party in France. During August, prominent citizens had been summoned to swear an oath to 'live in union with the city under the obedience of the King of France and England according to the treaty'. For the great majority of these men, Charles VII remained what he had always been, the figurehead of the hated Armagnac party. There had been yet another round of proscriptions, in which anyone suspected of Armagnac sympathies was arrested and their property seized. There was a garrison, mostly Burgundian, of some 2,000 men. But the main burden of the defence fell on armed citizens, organised in companies of ten under the command of the *dizainiers* or recruited to the city's corps of bowmen. They manned the walls while the professionals stood behind in reserve to deal with any assault parties that succeeded in coming over the top. When the Duke of Alençon's herald came before the Provost of the Merchants with his call to rally to the Valois cause, he was laughed out. They told him not to waste good paper.[18]

In keeping with her usual method, Joan of Arc had resolved upon a direct frontal assault from ladders. The sector chosen for the attack was the 1,500-yard length of wall on the north-west side, between the Porte Saint-Honoré in the Louvre quarter and the massively fortified Porte Saint-Denis. Towards the end of the morning the French advanced on foot in battle order towards the wall. At their head marched Marshal de Retz, Joan of Arc and her standard-bearer carrying her banner aloft. They were accompanied by artillery pieces and a convoy of wagons filled with bales of straw, bundles of twigs and the wreckage of demolished houses with which to fill in the moat. At about two o'clock in the afternoon, the assault was sounded. An artillery bombardment made no impression on the defences. Joan and the Marshal rushed the dry ditch and climbed into it and then onto the earthwork on the other side. They were followed by a large number of men with armfuls of material to fill the moat. Joan tested the water level with a lance. She had underestimated its depth. There was no chance of filling it. Undeterred, she shouted up to the defenders on the walls, calling on them to surrender. Otherwise, she said, the city would be carried by force and they would all be killed. 'Shall we now, you brassy trollop?' a crossbowman shouted back. Then he took aim and shot her in the thigh. She fell back into the dry ditch, while her standard-bearer was felled by a bolt which struck him in the eye.

Prone on the ground and racked with pain, Joan urged on the soldiers around her. But because of the breadth and depth of the moat, the only place where they were able to attack was the Marché aux Porceaux, a large open space outside the Porte Saint-Honoré, which was the site of a weekly cattle market and the traditional place of execution by burning or boiling of forgers, heretics and women. The ditches were narrower here and the ground rose steeply, making it possible to reach the top of the walls from ladders. Inside the city hysterics screamed that all was lost. The enemy was within. People boarded up their homes and fled to the churches. But the attackers were not within. For nearly two hours, they tried to fight their way over the rampart. But their assault had had to be channelled into a relatively narrow section of wall, where the defenders were able to concentrate their strength. By four o'clock in the afternoon it was clear that the attack had failed. Joan, who was still lying wounded at the bottom of the dry ditch, refused to recognise defeat. She urged the troops to launch a second assault. But they were exhausted and disillusioned by the first notable failure of their prophetess. In the early evening they withdrew. About 500 men had been killed or mortally wounded according to a preliminary count by the heralds. Forty carts were required to carry the wounded back to Saint-Denis. Joan, dazed and baffled, surrounded by her small personal guard, refused to leave. After nightfall, Raoul de Gaucourt came to find her and lead her back to the camp at La Chapelle, still complaining about the failure of the troops to attempt another assault. 'By my staff,' she kept saying, 'the place would have fallen.'[19]

On the morning after the fight, Joan sought out the Duke of Alençon and persuaded him to lead another attack on the city. Alençon thought that the best chance of success lay in an assault mounted from the south bank, against the older and weaker rampart of Philip Augustus. This involved building a temporary bridge over the Seine west of Saint-Denis, and embarking on a long march, laden with equipment, around the broad bend of the river. In spite of the high risks, a number of companies volunteered to join them. The bridge, probably a line of barges with a timber carriageway, was built, but before Joan and Alençon had got very far, the Count of Clermont and Réné of Anjou rode up with the King's order recalling them. Joan was distressed. But she reluctantly returned to Saint-Denis. In the abbey buildings where Charles was lodging, there was a long council of war. Opinion was divided, even among the professional captains. They were full of praise for Joan's courage, but most of them thought that the city's defences were too strong. Charles's councillors agreed. The only chance of taking the city lay in a loyalist rising among its inhabitants, and after all the purges of 'Armagnacs' in the capital this was not going to happen. The King accepted their advice. Initially, the response of Joan and Alençon was defiant. After the council had dispersed, they plotted to pursue their plan of attack. But the King got wind of their intentions. When they reached the site of the improvised bridge they found that it had been dismantled on his orders.[20]

Over the next two days, the King and his ministers resolved to call a halt to the campaign. The army had been in the field since June and could not be kept together any longer. There was neither money to pay them nor supplies to feed them. The French King's hopes now rested on the prospect of a deal with the Duke of Burgundy. Philip the Good sedulously encouraged these hopes. His representative, the Burgundian nobleman Pierre de Bauffremont, passed to and fro between Arras and the French King's headquarters with reassuring messages. According to one well-informed source, Bauffremont told Charles that his master was confident of being able to arrange the peaceable submission of Paris. On 12 September, Charles's council decided to withdraw to the Loire. A commission of senior councillors headed by Regnault de Chartres was appointed to administer the newly conquered territories. The Count of Clermont was nominated as the military commander everywhere north of the Seine. Powerful forces were assigned to him, including the Italian corps of Teodoro di Valperga and the company of Poton de Saintrailles, which were based at Compiègne. In addition, there were five large garrisons. The Count of Vendôme was at Saint-Denis to cover the roads north out of Paris. A garrison of several hundred men was installed at Lagny under the command of the energetic Maine partisan Ambroise de Loré to guard the passage of the Marne. Other garrisons were based at Senlis, Beauvais and Creil (*Map III*). On the following day, 13 September 1429, Charles VII withdrew with the rest of his army to Senlis. There, on 18 September, he effectively declared the campaign to be at an end by extending the cease-fire to cover the capital together with the suburban fortresses of Vincennes and Saint-Denis and the fortified bridges of Saint-Cloud and Pont-de-Charenton. The army began its retreat to the Loire on the same day.[21]

The great Anglo-Burgundian counterattack never materialised. The Duke of Bedford arrived in Paris with his army just as the French King was withdrawing. Together with his Burgundian ally, he had between 4,000 and 5,000 men. There were about 2,000 men of the army of Normandy under his own command, and between 2,000 and 2,500 English and Burgundian troops in Paris under Villiers de L'Isle-Adam. Another 1,700 men recruited by Philip the Good were mustering at Beauquesne in the Somme valley. Saint-Denis was reoccupied without difficulty. The Count of Vendôme withdrew to Senlis rather than risk being blockaded behind the weak defences of the town. Villiers de L'Isle-Adam made a half-hearted move against Lagny with the troops of the Paris garrison, but quickly abandoned it in the face of stiff resistance. The Duke of Bedford was reluctant to embark on a war of sieges in the muddy plains of the north at the onset of winter and was worried about the security of Normandy. In the last week of October, his field army was dispersed to its garrisons. The English took down the armour which Joan of Arc had left as a devotional offering on the high altar of the abbey church of Saint-Denis and sent it to England to be presented to Henry VI as a trophy. It was a poor return for so much effort.[22]

The regions which the French had occupied in July and August were spared a major campaign of reconquest, but the fate which they actually suffered was worse. They became eternal battlegrounds. In Champagne, Charles VII's invasion had won him nearly all the major cities of the province but left many small towns and rural castles in the hands of English and Burgundian partisans. Charles VII's companies embarked on the unending task of eliminating them, but for every one that they took another sprang up. In the north of the province, the English and Burgundians raided around Laon and Reims. In the south, the Burgundian garrison of Chappes planted a ring of satellites around Troyes. In the east, the Burgundians still held Chaumont and the cathedral city of Langres, while Sir Thomas Gargrave commanded a force of several hundred Englishmen in the Bassigny region. All of these garrisons lived from hand to mouth on the land. The unpaid French and Scottish garrisons of Charles VII completed the destruction with their own raids and impositions. The French garrison stationed at Laon, for example, paid themselves by taking 100 of the richest citizens for ransom, while the soldiers invaded the houses of the townspeople, breaking open their chests and helping themselves to their wine.[23]

If the situation in Champagne was bad, the situation in the Beauvaisis and the Oise valley was catastrophic. The Count of Clermont's troops had to fight continual battles with mounted raiding parties from the large Burgundian garrison at Clermont-en-Beauvaisis and the English at Gournay and Gisors on the Norman march. Charles VII tried to limit the number and size of his own garrisons, ordering the abandonment and demolition of a large number of subsidiary castles, and regulating the requisitioning of food and equipment and the levying of *pâtis*. But there was a limit to the control that Charles's officers could exercise over troops whom they could not pay. The result, as Jean Juvénal des Ursins pointed out, was the utter destruction of the region. Villages were wasted or burdened with heavy *pâtis*. The peasantry abandoned the land, leaving the crops unharvested in the fields. 'And there was no God or Church and none that feared Justice,' wrote one observer of these terrible scenes.

The experience of Beauvais, the provincial capital, is recorded almost daily in the minutes of the town clerk. The city had already suffered grievously from the misfortunes of the past century. Once a rich clothmaking centre, it had lost 85 per cent of its population since the 1350s and had barely 1,500 inhabitants left in 1429. Most of the

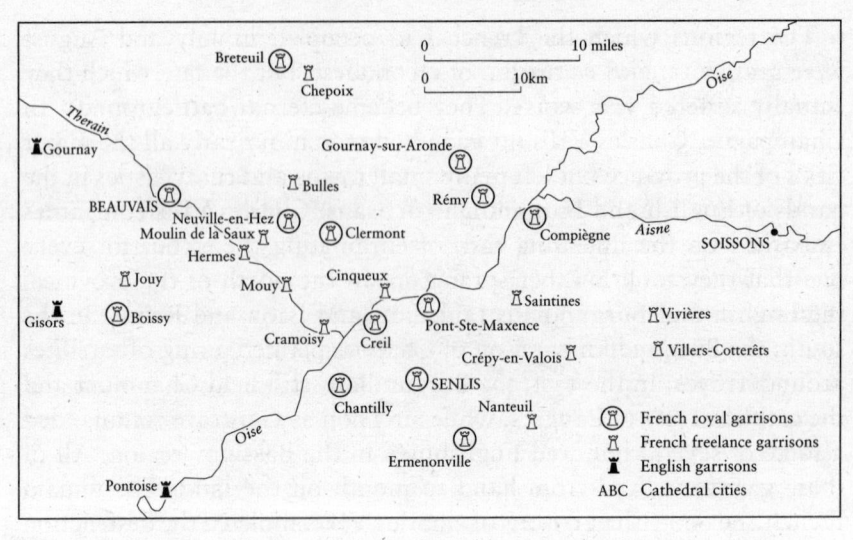

7 Garrisons of the Beauvaisis and neighbouring districts, 1432–1433

skilled textile workers had vanished. The spectacular gothic cathedral, the highest in France, stood incomplete, a monument to past greatness and current decay. Beauvais received a royal garrison of 200 men, the largest in the region after Compiègne, and became an important centre of military activity. This made it a frequent target for the English. Their Norman garrisons were only twenty miles away. At some stage, the terms of service of these garrisons were changed, so that instead of being paid a daily wage like other English garrisons in Normandy, they paid themselves from *pâtis* imposed on French-occupied areas of the Beauvaisis and Picardy. Within six weeks of its submission to Charles VII, Beauvais was attacked by Edmund Beaufort and Robert Willoughby. They carried off cattle, killed a number of townsmen and took many more for ransom. Four months later Sir Thomas Kyriel led a devastating raid into the same region. The Count of Clermont assembled several hundred troops and a large crowd of peasants and townsmen but arrived too late and was beaten off in a battle outside the walls. Serious as the incursions of the English were, much more damage was done by the partisans of Charles VII, who sustained themselves by fortifying manors, millhouses and church towers, occupying abandoned and dilapidated castles and looting and ransoming the surrounding districts. In 1432–3 there were at least a dozen of these improvised fortresses around Beauvais and as many more further east towards Senlis and Soissons, all of them ostensibly in Charles VII's allegiance. A region barely forty miles across was supporting nearly thirty predatory garrisons of both sides. For Beauvais, this was a tragedy. The river Thérain, which passed beneath its walls, was not navigable, leaving the city dependent on a vulnerable road network. Its trade withered. Food supplies dried up. Heavy municipal taxes were imposed to pay the wages of the garrison and the cost of repairing the walls and gates. Onerous guard duties had to be performed. Men lived in constant fear of surprise attack and betrayal. Prominent partisans of the English government were rounded up and expelled together with their families. The men of Beauvais, said Jean Juvénal who later became their bishop, were profoundly loyal to the Valois cause but they would have been better off under English rule.[24]

In six months, Charles VII had moved from the despair which had characterised his counsels during the siege of Orléans to elation and confidence in his ultimate victory. In the mood of hubris which prevailed around him, the King issued a fateful ordinance from Compiègne on 22 August, dealing with rights over property confiscated in the course of the wars. Many of Charles's loyal followers, in his household and council, in the armies, in the administration at Bourges and Poitiers, had owned property which they had had to abandon in May 1418 when John the Fearless had occupied Paris and taken over the government of Charles VI. Under the Burgundian and English regimes which followed, their lands had been granted to others, who had often sold, mortgaged or charged them or allowed them to be taken in execution of their debts. Some of these properties had passed through many hands and were currently occupied by people who had purchased them in good faith. The edict of Compiègne authorised the original owners to recover what had previously been theirs from whoever was found in possession, regardless of their nationality or allegiance or the circumstances by which it had come into their hands and without compensation or any form of legal process. Charles VII was under pressure from the large class of exiles to whom he owed his political survival. But his intransigent decree must have stiffened resistance to his cause in the territory which was still under English or Burgundian occupation and it was to bring serious practical problems later. It was perhaps the last notable act of the French civil wars and the first of the renascent monarchy.[25]

*

On 21 September 1429 the French army reached the Loire at Gien, where it was disbanded. There remained an unanswered question about Joan of Arc's future role. She had initially refused to leave Saint-Denis and announced that she would stay there with the Count of Vendôme and his garrison. She had had to be peremptorily ordered to leave with the King and the army. Was her mission now over? Joan's own definition of her mission had varied. At her trial she was sensitive to suggestions that the failure of her subsequent campaigns showed that she could not be the instrument of God's will. Her answer was that the coronation campaign had been the last enterprise which had been demanded of her by her voices. Her later military ventures had been undertaken on her own initiative and at the insistence of the troops. But this was not what she had said at the time. She spoke of a continuing role: of capturing Paris, of expelling the English from France and even of invading England to rescue Charles of Orléans from his prison.

Joan's public fame was undimmed by recent reverses. In November, the Giustiniani factor in Bruges reported that 'everyone hangs on the Maid's words'. Stories of her deeds were recounted across France and Europe, belittled or exaggerated according to the speaker's point of view, but everyone agreed that she was the 'wonder of the world'. Charles VII himself took the remarkable step of ennobling her and her entire family and their descendants in perpetuity. Among the King's councillors, however, she was viewed with an increasingly jaundiced eye. The failure of the assault on Paris had armed her enemies at court and broken her spell in the eyes of many of the professional captains. Some of them were heartily fed up with her histrionics, her crude military methods and her insensitivity to political realities. Joan's critics were probably behind an attempt to interest the King in a rival prophet, Catherine of La Rochelle, who began to hang about the court that autumn. She preached a more convenient political message, emphasising the necessity of making peace with the Duke of Burgundy. Rather later, Charles was persuaded to receive another seer, William the Gevaudan shepherd, who uttered prophecies very similar to Joan's and, like Joan, declared that he had a divine mission to lead the King's armies against the English. Regnault de Chartres accused Joan of the sin of pride. He objected to her swagger and her showy clothes. He thought that she was headstrong, unwilling to listen to professional advice, and far too ready to confuse her own instincts with the will of God.[26]

These issues came to a head in mid-October 1429, when the court was at Mehun-sur-Yèvre in Berry. The Duke of Alençon came before the council with a plan to mount a winter campaign in Maine and the Breton march, and then invade south-western Normandy. Alençon, whose domains in this region had been occupied by the English since 1417, was desperate to recover them and repair his battered finances. He had already recruited a number of companies and if Joan joined him he would be able to raise more. La Trémoille vetoed her participation, with the support of other councillors. The councillors' misgivings were as much about the Duke of Alençon as they were about Joan. He was a peer of high status but he was inexperienced and impulsive, and at twenty he was only three years older than Joan herself. He had become her uncritical ally and was unlikely to restrain her wilder impulses. According to the Duke's squire, the council did not trust them together.[27]

For the time being, Charles's ministers were still willing to employ her in less sensitive theatres of the war. A limited campaign was in preparation against Perrinet Gressart's strongholds in the Nivernais. The operation was to be led by those reliable captains Charles of Albret and Marshal Boussac. The council proposed that Joan should accompany them. But the campaign was a sideshow, as Joan must have known. It was also a failure, which did much to undermine what remained of her reputation for military miracles. Saint-Pierre was taken by storm at about the beginning of November. But La Charité, which was the more significant target, withstood a siege of a month before the army ran out supplies and the war treasurers of money. Albret finally called off the siege, abandoned most of his artillery and returned empty-handed with the army to Bourges just before Christmas.[28]

On 30 September 1429, Philip the Good made his entry into Paris. It was an impressive show. He was preceded by a crowd of heralds, trumpeters and courtiers and escorted by more than 2,000 troops. The Parisians gathered in the streets and cheered him to the echo as his cavalcade passed by. The Duke established his headquarters in the dilapidated buildings of the Hôtel d'Artois, his father's old headquarters in the north of the city. This quarter, once one of the most opulent of the capital, was a sorry sight now. Philip's entire army was accommodated in empty and abandoned mansions around, while their horses were stabled in the many humbler residences that had been turned into cowsheds and pigsties. The Duke had arrived deeply pessimistic about the English government's prospects of survival and determined to press for a peace with Charles VII. He had met Regnault de Chartres and a group of Charles VII's councillors on his way south at Montdidier in Picardy and had agreed to attend a peace conference at Auxerre on 1 April 1430. He had assured the French King's officers that he would see Paris delivered to them. He saw it as the main purpose of his visit to discuss a change of allegiance with his partisans in the city. The English alliance seemed to be approaching its end.[29]

When Philip left Paris two and a half weeks later, it was stronger than ever. How had this sudden change come about? One reason was a serious dispute with Charles VII's ministers which came to a head while he was in the capital. An important part of the cease-fire agreement as far as Philip was concerned was the informal understanding that the French would surrender some of their garrisoned towns in the Beauvaisis and the Île-de-France to his officers. Charles VII's officers were backtracking on these promises. They denied having promised to surrender Beauvais and Senlis, and although they acknowledged an obligation to surrender Compiègne and Creil, they had never done so. At Compiègne they had reckoned without the citizens, who were afraid that Philip would punish them for delivering the place up to Charles VII. They refused to accept Philip's officers. Charles's captain in the town was ordered to deliver it up in spite of their objections, but he refused. The French offered Philip Pont-Sainte-Maxence instead. But their commanders on the spot thought that these places were too important to be relinquished. They delayed the surrender of Pont-Sainte-Maxence and never gave up Creil.[30]

There was, however, another reason for the mercurial Duke of Burgundy's change of mind. Over the past few weeks, the Duke of Bedford had returned to his project of bringing Henry VI to France to be crowned. In the aftermath of the disasters of the summer, the English council had finally accepted the idea in principle. Parliament was in session at Westminster during Philip's visit to Paris. The main business of the assembly was to approve the crowning of the young King and vote fresh subsidies to support the war in France. The Regent persuaded Philip the Good and his advisers that there was every prospect of a dramatic military recovery in the following year. The

English would expect their King to be nobly accompanied by an army large enough to reverse the disasters of 1429, an army comparable perhaps to the great hosts which Henry V had led to France in 1415 and 1417. Even at the age of eight, the King's presence would be a powerful recruiting agent.

Meanwhile the Lancastrian government would have to be sustained through the winter. The Regent had enough manpower and revenue to defend Normandy and the *pays de conquête*, but not Paris and the Île-de-France as well. It was therefore agreed to divide responsibility for the defence of Lancastrian France between Bedford and the Duke of Burgundy. Bedford would concentrate on Normandy, Maine and the *pays de conquête*, while Philip would assume the government of Paris and the rest of Lancastrian France as Henry VI's lieutenant. In particular, he would be responsible for the defence of Chartres, Melun and Sens, the three major provincial cities outside Normandy which remained under English control. The revenues of these places, such as they were, would be at his disposal. The decision marked a step change in the Duke of Burgundy's engagement with the dual monarchy. He appointed Villiers de L'Isle-Adam as Captain of Paris. A Burgundian garrison of 640 men, more than the English had ever had, was stationed in the city under the command of two of Philip's closest lieutenants, Philippe de Saveuse and Jean de Brimeu. These arrangements were initially expected to last for six months until Easter 1430 when, all being well, Henry VI was expected to arrive. Philip refused to commit himself to operations after that. In practice, however, the division of responsibility agreed in October 1429 continued to apply to the dwindling area under Anglo-Burgundian control until the final breach between the allies in 1435.[31]

This left the awkward question of what to do about the cease-fire and the proposed peace conference at Auxerre. Philip had committed himself to the conference while at Montdidier and was not prepared to abandon it. But the English had not signed up to the cease-fire and were uncomfortable about the conference. They had nothing to offer the French, at any rate while Henry VI was still a minor, and were unwilling to allow diplomacy to frustrate their plans for a major campaign in 1430. The ambassadors of the Duke of Savoy made a determined effort to draw them in. On 10 October 1429, Amadeus's councillors arrived at Saint-Denis, accompanied by Regnault de Chartres, to settle the preliminaries of the conference. The Duke of

Burgundy was represented at these discussions by the two leading anglophiles on his council, Hughes de Lannoy and John of Luxembourg. They confirmed the Duke's agreement to the peace conference. They also agreed on the appointment of mediators. The French had already been in contact with Pope Martin V, who had agreed to nominate a cardinal. His co-mediator was to be John of Luxembourg. The English stood aside from all this. Their representatives at Saint-Denis would not commit themselves to anything, and the discussions ended within the day. As for the truce between France and Burgundy, the English declared that they would observe it, but without formally acceding to it. An untidy arrangement was made with the Count of Clermont that eight days' notice would be given before hostilities were resumed. On 17 October 1429, the Dukes of Burgundy and Bedford left Paris together, Bedford for Normandy and Philip for Flanders. In a symbolic move, Bedford's valuable library, the fruit of nearly a decade of connoisseurship, followed him to Rouen, and his Paris librarian was discharged. Rouen was to be his main base for the rest of his life and, as the English progressively withdrew from Paris, it became the real capital of Lancastrian France.[32]

Henry VI was crowned as King of England in Westminster abbey on 6 November 1429. Considering the short time available for its preparation, it was a magnificent occasion. Cardinal Beaufort arrived from France with two members of the Grand Conseil, Pierre Cauchon and Robert Jolivet, to take part in the ceremony and press the case in Parliament for a second coronation in France. London was full of bishops and abbots, lay peers and members of the Commons. The abbey was packed. The child-King, wearing scarlet robes trimmed with fur, was brought from the Tower to the abbey by his tutor the Earl of Warwick and seated upon a high scaffold in the choir next to the Cardinal. 'Sirs,' intoned Archbishop Chichele, 'here cometh Harry, King Harry the Fifth's son.' The boy cannot have understood much of the event's political significance. An onlooker described him looking around 'sadly and wisely' from his seat as they presented him with the sceptre and sword of state and placed the crown of Edward the Confessor on his head. It was so heavy that it had to be held over him by two bishops. At the banquet in Westminster Hall which followed, there were plenty of reminders of the high expectations of a son of Henry V. He sat at the head of the hall, with Beaufort on his right and Cauchon on his left. Richard Neville, the new Earl of Salisbury, stood behind him as the representative of the Regent of France. Even the 'subtleties' (pastries) were decorated with figures of St George and St Denis presenting the young King to Our Lady, over the words 'born by descent and title of right, justly to reign in England and in France'.[33]

It took longer to get the Commons to commit themselves to the coronation expedition. Beaufort and the two French councillors were joined at Westminster by an embassy from Philip the Good, led by Hughes de Lannoy. This 'sharp-witted, ingenious and clear-sighted man', as the court chronicler of Burgundy called him, had been a committed supporter of the dual monarchy ever since he had served in the Burgundian team responsible for negotiating the treaty of Troyes. After several previous missions to England, he had become almost as much an adviser to the English as he was to Philip. He took his cue from a memorandum on the current situation, which provides an insight into the thoughts of Philip and his councillors at a critical stage of the war. Lannoy reminded his audience that the English could not succeed without Burgundian support. The Dukes of Burgundy were not only militarily powerful but enjoyed status and popular support in France which was politically indispensable. The Duke was willing to help, he said, but the English would have to meet his terms. The first of them was that they must take the forthcoming peace conference at Auxerre seriously and send a delegation with full power to reach agreement. Otherwise, they would lose support among the many people in France who were desperate for an end to the fighting. Lannoy suggested that Henry Beaufort, who was highly regarded at the Burgundian court, should return to the continent as soon as possible as England's ambassador. Secondly, there would have to be a commitment to increase the scale of English military intervention in France. Reinforcements were urgently needed. They must be sent out by Christmas, together with a powerful artillery train, before the current truce with Charles VII expired on 31 December. Philip himself expected to take the field at the beginning of January 1430 with 1,000 men-at-arms and 1,000 bowmen. Some of the English reinforcements would have to be deployed to the garrisons of Normandy. The rest should join Philip's army and help to clear the French garrisons of the Île-de-France by March. The Burgundians were counting on Henry VI landing in France with the main English army before 1 April, when the conference was due to open. This was essential if the diplomats were to have anything to bargain with at Auxerre. At the same time another army should be sent to Guyenne to fight the Counts of Armagnac and Foix and the lord of Albret and to threaten the French rear. Thirdly, the English would have to meet the cost of Philip's army. He would have to be granted territory, either in lieu of payment or by way of security. Lannoy hoped that by April the Anglo-Burgundian army would already have opened a route to Reims so that Henry could be crowned there. Finally, the English must repair their other alliances. Brittany was particularly important. An embassy should be sent to John V to persuade him to contribute to the campaign and to recall his brothers from Charles VII's service.[34]

Apart from the proposed expedition to Guyenne, which was hardly realistic on top of the other burdens that the government was expected to bear, all of these terms were agreed in principle by the English council. They accepted Lannoy's advice that Cardinal Beaufort should be sent as ambassador to the court of Burgundy. They also decided to send an emissary to the Pope declaring that they would participate in the conference at Auxerre. The advance guard of the expeditionary army was already being recruited. By the end of November, indentures for six months' service had been sealed with various English captains for 2,200 men. They were due to muster at Winchelsea between 19 and 21 December 1429 and to arrive in France by Christmas, as Lannoy had proposed. The designated commander was the King's cousin Sir John Clarence, a bastard son of the Duke of Clarence who had been killed at Baugé. He was not an obvious candidate for this command, for he had limited experience of the war in France. But he was living in penury and like so many others had petitioned for a command in France to repair his fortunes.[35]

The next question was how all this would be paid for. Customs revenues were at their lowest level ever. The expected receipts from the ransoms of James I of Scotland and the Duke of Bourbon had not materialised. The arrears of the Calais garrison had risen to £20,000 as a result of the diversion of funds to the expeditionary armies of 1427 and 1428. The need for direct taxation had never been greater. There had been various experiments with new forms of taxation, all unsuccessful, but no standard lay subsidy had been voted since the King's accession. Beaufort, supported by Cauchon and Jolivet, worked on the Commons during November. They explained the predicament of the Lancastrian government in France in the aftermath of the relief of Orléans and the coronation of Charles VII. They implored them to support the King's expedition. On 12 December, the Commons yielded. They announced a grant of a full subsidy, to be collected and paid in just one month, by 14 January 1430. It was not enough, and sustained pressure was brought to bear on them to increase it. A few days later the Commons agreed by Beaufort's 'special advice' to grant a second lay subsidy payable by Christmas 1430. The council was authorised to borrow up to £50,000 on the security of future revenues. The Canterbury Convocation of the Church agreed to add one and a half clerical subsidies, bringing the total value of the new taxes to about £90,000, the largest tax package since 1416. On 20 December, the day that Parliament was prorogued for Christmas, letters were sent out in Henry VI's name to the principal towns of Lancastrian France announcing his decision to visit his French realm in the following year. He would bring with him, he said, a great army to push the war front far away from their homes. They would once more be able to live, labour and trade in peace.[36]

While these negotiations were making slow progress at Westminster, the military situation in Normandy and Maine rapidly deteriorated. On 25 September 1429, the English lost Laval, the key to the lower valley of the Mayenne. Raoul du Bouchet, the captain of the nearby castle of Jeanne de Laval at Meslay-du-Maine, hid a company of men overnight in a millhouse on the bridge leading to the town. When the gate was opened at sunrise, they jumped the gatekeepers and poured into the streets. The captain of Laval, Matthew Gough, was with Bedford's army with much of his garrison. The English never tried to recapture Laval. They were at their wits' end to defend Normandy itself. The Estates of the duchy met at Rouen in November and granted an *aide* of 140,000 *livres* to reinforce the garrisons of the march and recover the castles captured by raiders during the summer. But the perennial shortage of troops crippled English attempts at recovery. They were condemned to rush from place to place putting out fires. Beaufort and Willoughby laid siege to Étrépagny and battered its old walls until the garrison surrendered in return for their lives. But the castle's defenders merely withdrew to continue their depredations from Aumale. Then, on 26 October, builders working on the walls let another French raiding force into the old castle of the Estoutevilles at Torcy south of Dieppe, the 'finest and best-built castle of the region' according to

Jean de Waurin. Within two days a task force drawn from nearby English garrisons was mobilised to retake it before the occupiers could establish themselves. But they were almost immediately recalled by the Regent to deal with a fresh crisis beyond the Seine in Perche, where the French had just captured Verneuil. They held it for more than a month before they were evicted. The captain of Verneuil was Sir John Fastolf. Like Matthew Gough at Laval, he was serving in the Regent's field army with most of his garrison when the blow struck.[37]

By the end of 1429, the French were threatening the valley of the Seine, the spinal cord of the English defensive system in France. When, on 8 December, La Hire and Géraud de la Paillière came up the valley of the Eure with several hundred men, a small group of French partisans in Louviers let them into the town. The alarm went up, but too late. The garrison and the citizen guard were overwhelmed. Louviers was one of the largest towns of Normandy, with a population of about 4,000 souls. Situated on the west bank of the Eure close to its confluence with the Seine, it was defended by a circuit of modern walls three-quarters of a mile long with a triple line of ditches. La Hire established himself as governor of Louviers. The inhabitants were made to swear an oath of loyalty to him or forfeit their property and leave. They had to pay a heavy indemnity to be spared a sack. From Louviers, La Hire was able to cut the road and river communications between Lower Normandy and Paris and to raid up to the gates of Rouen. Companies operating from Louviers occupied Bernay and Beaumont-le-Roger on the road to Cherbourg. On 24 February 1430, they capped these achievements by making their way up the Seine in barges and capturing the fortress of Château-Gaillard at Les Andelys by escalade. They got in with the connivance of a Frenchman in the garrison and an English soldier whom he had suborned. This was a serious embarrassment. Standing over the great bend of the Seine east of Louviers, Château-Gaillard was one of the strongest places in France and was guarded by a garrison of eighty men. Its capture completed the rupture of the river traffic between Rouen and Paris and provided La Hire with a secure base on the north bank of the Seine. It also resulted in the release of a number of valuable prisoners of war who were being held there, including Charles VII's redoubtable former Marshal Arnaud-Guilhem de Barbazan.[38]

These incidents were symptoms of a general collapse of morale among both the English and French subjects of Henry VI. Desertions spiked during the winter. A chance survival records the situation at Evreux in January and February 1430. Eighteen men left the garrison of Evreux in just two months, more than a tenth of the establishment. Most of them were English deserters who disappeared into the military underworld of the towns or tried to get back home. But a Norman deserted to the enemy and three more changed sides in the course of a skirmish outside the walls. Evreux was in the eye of the storm, but the experience of other garrisons is likely to have been similar. The situation in Normandy was not stabilised until January, when the Bastard of Clarence arrived from England with much-needed reinforcements. All of these men were deployed to the marches of Normandy. At the end of January Clarence laid siege to Torcy. By the end of March Edmund Beaufort was besieging Château-Gaillard.[39]

For the Regent, one of the most troubling features of recent reverses was that French commanders had generally been able to find collaborators among native Normans and even among the English. Almost all the towns and garrisoned castles captured by French partisans had been betrayed from within. The triumphant progress of Charles VII's armies in Champagne and Picardy persuaded many people that the days of the English in France were numbered and provoked a rash of plots and conspiracies such as had not been seen since the eve of the battle of Verneuil. At Mantes, a sympathiser let the French into the town, but they were swiftly expelled by the garrison. Conspiracies were discovered at Dreux and Meulan before they came to anything. Towards the end of 1429 some citizens of Rouen plotted to let the Count of Clermont's troops into the city by night. Poor planning and execution defeated this enterprise. The plot was only discovered because the troops lost their way in the dark and stumbled into an English patrol. Rumours of further plots proliferated, magnified by gossip. 'We will ... that ye take good heed ... both day and night,' wrote Bedford to his lieutenant at Falaise, 'and that ye be well wary of treasons.'

Some of those who plotted with the enemy were lone operators. The men who let La Hire into Château-Gaillard had probably been bribed. A single well-placed citizen of Gournay was behind a plot to let the French in there. The ladders were already placed against the walls when he was betrayed by a double agent in English pay. But sometimes, as with the plots at Louviers and Pont-de-l'Arche, significant numbers were involved. The same double agent sold to the English a substantial list of people living in Rouen who were in touch with the French, and identified a large group of plotters at Gisors. They were rounded up and executed. In March 1430 another informer disclosed plans to seize the Porte Saint-Antoine in Paris and let in a company of Scots. This enterprise might well have succeeded. Rumour had it that more than 4,000 Parisians were involved, including members of forty of the *dizaines* which constituted the basic units of the watch. The rumours were probably exaggerated, but the Regent was sufficiently alarmed to divert the Bastard of Clarence from the siege of Torcy and send him urgently to support Villiers de L'Isle-Adam in the capital. More than 150 people were arrested. Six of them were executed in the market of Les Halles. They included a clerk of the Chambre des Comptes and two senior officials of the Châtelet.[40]

Treason made the English edgy. A revealing symptom was the progressive exclusion of indigenous Norman and French troops from service in their garrisons. Some garrisons, especially in south-west Normandy and Rouen, had traditionally recruited heavily from the local population. But in March 1430 orders were given that only native Englishmen were to serve in the critically important garrison at the fortified bridge of Meulan, which had already been betrayed once from within. With effect from Michaelmas 1430, a similar restriction was generalised across Normandy. Garrison troops were no longer to be recruited in the neighbourhood, where they were apt to form attachments among the indigenous population. Archers were to be English, or else Welsh, Irish or Gascon. Of the men-at-arms, no more than half were to be French. In 1430 that shrewd judge of the direction of events Sir John Fastolf began to move part of his fortune out of France, realising large sums and investing them in land in Norfolk.[41]

Philip the Good was preoccupied with his own affairs. Twice widowed, on 7 January the Duke took a third wife, Isabella of Portugal. In the same month, Philip founded the Order of the Golden Fleece 'for the great love that we have for the estate and order of chivalry, which we desire to honour and increase'. The Order was conceived mainly as a means of creating a shared identity for the nobility of the disparate principalities of the Burgundian empire. But it was also, in a sense, a declaration of Philip's independence of the dual monarchy, for he had more than once refused the Order of the Garter, and knights of the Golden Fleece were forbidden to belong to other orders, including

English ones. In the wider conflict of England and France Philip hedged his bets for most of the winter. He did not react when the cathedral city of Sens, one of the places which he had undertaken to defend, submitted to Charles VII in the new year. He sent ambassadors to the court of Charles VII to finalise the arrangements for the peace conference at Auxerre. He did not take the field on 1 January 1430, as Lannoy had promised when he was at Westminster, but instead agreed to extend the cease-fire agreement with the Dauphin to 25 January and then to 15 March.[42]

Early in February 1430, Cardinal Beaufort left England to meet Philip the Good at Ghent. Diplomatically, it was Beaufort's finest hour. He persuaded Philip finally to throw his weight behind the English war effort. On 12 February, the Duke sealed a new treaty with the English. He promised to serve Henry VI with an army of 1,500 men-at-arms and 1,500 bowmen for three months. The English agreed to pay a lump sum of 50,000 gold *saluts* (£8,333) in advance for each of the first two months, with Philip serving the third month at his own expense. Thereafter he would serve with reduced forces, 600 men-at-arms and 600 bowmen, for up to nine months at the standard rates for service in France. The Burgundian army was to operate independently of the English, but Beaufort agreed that 500 English troops would serve under Burgundian command as soon as they could be released from current siege operations in Normandy. In return for the Duke's commitment, Beaufort agreed that he would be granted the whole of Champagne and Brie as an addition to his French appanage. It was a shrewd concession, and cheap for the English to make since most of these provinces had already been overrun by the French. But the recovery of Champagne would be a great prize for the Duke of Burgundy, since it would create a bridge between his western and south-eastern domains. As for the peace conference at Auxerre, Beaufort persuaded Philip that it would have to be postponed to 1 June. Privately, neither of them now expected it to happen.[43]

Beaufort raced back to England to get the terms of the agreement confirmed by the council. He funded Philip's advance from his own chests. The money was carried over the Channel in cash and counted out at Lille in the middle of March. Active preparations were already in train in England. The practised routines for recruiting troops, requisitioning shipping and procuring equipment were put into operation. A campaign of borrowing generated large cash funds including a loan of no less than 10,000 marks (£6,666) from the City of London. The King, accompanied by his court, attended a service at St Paul's cathedral in London on 24 February and took formal leave of the mayor and aldermen of the city, before departing on the first stage of his progress to the Kent coast. The Duke of Burgundy summoned his own army to muster at Péronne.

It fell to his Chancellor Nicolas Rolin to explain to the Duke of Savoy why his peace proposals had fallen by the wayside. Rolin appeared before Amadeus in the Château de Ripaille on the shores of Lake Geneva on 26 March, five days before the peace conference was due to open at Auxerre. His explanation was extremely disingenuous. He produced a written schedule of French breaches of the truce, starting with their failure to deliver up Compiègne and Creil. He blamed the administrative disorganisation of the English. Nevertheless, he said, he would have been happy for the conference to proceed, but Cardinal Beaufort had complained that the distance was too great and the notice too short. The Savoyard delegation to the conference was already on the road. The Duke of Savoy sent riders out to recall them.[44]

The fighting had already reopened with an explosion of violence on all fronts: in Champagne, on the march of Burgundy, in the Oise valley and around Paris. Within days of the expiry of the truce, a large French raiding force defeated the garrison of Paris beneath the walls and captured its commander, Philippe de Saveuse. They followed this up by entering Saint-Denis by night, slaughtering much of the garrison and looting the town before withdrawing in the morning. Operations like these were plundering raids, destructive but strategically marginal. One of them, however, inflicted serious damage on the Anglo-Burgundian cause. In the third week of April 1430, the citizens of Melun rose up against the Paris government, threw out their Burgundian garrison and declared for Charles VII. Melun was a powerful island fortress in the Seine about forty miles upstream of Paris with two fortified bridges connecting it to either bank of the river. Ten men held out in the citadel while Burgundian troops from Paris and Corbeil rushed to relieve them. But the citizens summoned help from nearby French garrisons, and they got there first. By the time that the Burgundians arrived, the town gates were closed and the citadel was about to surrender. The loss of Melun was a major strategic setback for the English. The island was almost impregnable (in 1420 it had taken Henry V four and a half months and more than

8,000 men to starve it out). Its capture gave the French control of the main crossing of the Seine upstream of the capital and opened the way from the Gâtinais into Brie and Champagne, avoiding the need for them to fight their way through the Auxerrois.[45]

Henry VI landed at Calais on the morning of 23 April 1430, St George's Day. He was accompanied by Cardinal Beaufort, the Earl of Warwick and a large number of prominent peers, councillors and captains, as well as by the troops of the royal household. The rest of the English army followed over the next three weeks. The whole force numbered 4,800 men, in addition to the usual crowd of officials, clerks, chaplains, servants, pages and varlets, heralds, surgeons, trumpeters, cannoneers, craftsmen and labourers. Most of these men had indented to serve for a year, twice the usual duration of an expeditionary army in France. The King's presence had drawn a wider range of recruits than any earlier expeditionary force of his reign, with twenty-one peers, including two dukes and six earls. An impressive artillery train was shipped over with the army, including three large bombards, sixteen other cannon and eighty gun-crew and artificers. Together with the advance guard of Sir John Clarence and the other men already in Normandy, the arrival of the army brought the total number of English troops in France to over 10,000 men, the largest force which the English had deployed there since Henry V landed in Normandy in 1417. Five days before, the Duke of Burgundy's army, nearly 3,400 strong, had mustered at Péronne. It represented substantially the whole military capacity of Artois and Picardy, in addition to a significant contribution from the duchy of Burgundy. With a total strength of over 14,000 men, the allies now had a unique opportunity to transform the strategic situation. In prayers, handbills and verses circulating at home, anxiety for the King's safety mingled with high hopes for a reversal of England's fortunes:

> And though fortune hath cast us late behind
> Yet fail us not when that we cry thy name,
> For with thine help we hope recure good fame.[46]

The arrival of the English King entailed some radical changes to the government of Lancastrian France. These were mainly the work of Cardinal Beaufort, whose political standing was now at its height. At his insistence, an ordinance regulating the government of both kingdoms was drawn up and approved by the English council at Canterbury shortly before the King sailed. It is clear that Henry's English councillors had lost confidence in the Duke of Bedford and the group of military leaders around him. The main purpose of the new ordinance was to take the conduct of the war out of their hands. Bedford's title and powers as Regent of France were to be suspended as soon as Henry VI set foot on French soil. Major decisions were to be made in the King's name by a small group of English councillors who had come over with him.

The most striking thing about these men was that most of them had been confidants of Henry V. Some of them had not been in France since his death. They had experienced the war in its most dramatically successful period. Richard Beauchamp Earl of Warwick was 'a man of impressive bearing, exceptional judgement and great military experience, with a practised and accomplished eloquence on any subject' according to an admiring contemporary. He had been present at the late King's deathbed and was one of the few advisers whom he would have counted as a friend. Philip Morgan, now Bishop of Ely, had been Henry V's Chancellor of Normandy and principal diplomatic adviser in his final years. William Alnwick Bishop of Norwich was a civil lawyer who had learned his diplomatic skills as Henry V's private secretary during his last campaigns. The veteran soldier and administrator John Lord Tiptoft had been one of the late King's most trusted administrators in Normandy. John Stafford Bishop of Bath and Wells had been keeper of his privy seal. The existing members of Bedford's council had to apply to be reconfirmed by the new regime. In due course the young King's council in France was reinforced by the principal members of the Grand Conseil, including Louis of Luxembourg, Pierre Cauchon, Robert Jolivet, Raoul le Sage and Sir John Fastolf. But they had less influence than the men who had come from England.

There were significant changes in the military leadership. Some important garrisoned towns in Normandy were transferred to men who had come from England with the King. All major military operations outside the duchy were entrusted to the newcomers. The dominant figure throughout was the Cardinal himself. Bedford seems to have had only a limited role in the formation of strategy and did not even attend council meetings except during a brief period in December 1431 when the King was in Paris. He was stripped of his most valuable lordships in France, including the duchy of Alençon, whose revenues had supported the cost of his household for years. For Bedford, who had exercised absolute power in Lancastrian France for eight years, these changes came as a shock. There is some evidence that he resented it and fell out with the Cardinal as a result.[47]

There had been much discussion of strategy before Henry VI left England, both in his English council and among the advisers of the Duke of Burgundy. The original idea had been for Sir John Clarence's advance guard to join forces with a Burgundian army and recover the Île-de-France before Henry VI arrived with the main army. With the way clear into Champagne, they would advance on Reims to crown the child-King in the cathedral. By the time that Henry VI arrived in France, this plan had been abandoned. The timetable had been disrupted by the extension of the truce, which ruled out joint operations in advance of his arrival. The situation in Paris had deteriorated. The marches of Normandy were insecure. The Dauphinist hold on the routes into Champagne was as tight as ever. At Calais, Henry VI's councillors found an elaborate memorandum waiting for them in which Lannoy explained the current thinking of Philip's council. They were opposed to any strategy which involved besieging major walled towns and cities. The siege of Orléans had shown that these operations required a great deal of time and manpower and posed formidable difficulties of supply. They were also unnecessary, the Burgundians thought, for if the smaller garrisons were cleared and the open country secured, the great strongholds like Reims, Beauvais, Compiègne, Melun and Sens would surely wither on the vine.

Philip's advisers seem to have persuaded their English allies that their first priority should be to secure the Île-de-France and clear the approaches to Paris, which was being slowly strangled by Dauphinist garrisons in the surrounding river valleys. Reims would have to wait. It would be too time-consuming to besiege, and Paris might not be able to hold out that long. The allies differed, however, about the best way of achieving this. The English wanted to open up the valley of the Oise and clear the approach to Paris from the north. They believed that the first task should be the recapture of the Count of Clermont's base at Compiègne. The Burgundians objected to a major siege of a powerfully defended town like Compiègne. Their preferred plan involved two powerful offensives. The greater part of the Burgundian army, supported by 1,000 English archers, would advance on Soissons and Laon, opening the way for a future invasion of Champagne.

The main body of Henry VI's army would reconquer the Beauvaisis, seize the crossing of the Oise at Creil and from there invade the Île-de-France. In addition to these major operations, Philip's advisers proposed a number of smaller ones. Some 700 to 800 men should be detached from the English army and deployed to Normandy, to secure the English base there. Torcy and Château-Gaillard, which were already under siege, were expected to fall soon. Aumale should follow and then Louviers. A joint Anglo-Burgundian task force should hold the line of the Seine and the Yonne south-east of Paris. Another joint force should be sent to reinforce Perrinet Gressart in the Nivernais and from there invade Berry and the Orléanais to tie down as much as possible of Charles VII's strength. Lannoy also suggested that a separate expeditionary army should be sent out from England to Bordeaux to prevent the southern lords from coming to the French King's aid.[48]

Not all of this complex plan was practicable, but there was much sense in the advice to avoid major sieges, as the sequel would show. Nevertheless, the English commanders rejected it and insisted on their own strategy. Philip the Good yielded to the demands of his paymasters and agreed to open the campaign with an attack on Compiègne. The Duke raised his standard at Péronne on 18 April 1430, a few days before Henry VI's arrival at Calais. Two days later, on the 20th, John of Luxembourg arrived within sight of Compiègne. A forward base was established in the cathedral city of Noyon by the Oise twenty miles upstream of the town. The Burgundians had a garrison at Pont-Sainte-Maxence twenty miles downstream and another in the great fortress of the Duke of Orléans at Pierrefonds. From these places, they took control of all the bridges of the Oise in the region and planted garrisons in an arc around Compiègne. On 7 May Philip and John of Luxembourg laid siege to Choisy (modern Choisy-au-Bac), an important castle and fortified bridge on the Aisne close to its confluence with the Oise, which was the key to the northern approach to Compiègne. The English offered to support the siege with a detachment of their army. In the second week of May, the 500 troops which Henry Beaufort had promised to contribute in February arrived at Noyon under the command of the Welsh knight Sir John Montgomery.[49]

Charles VII and his court passed most of February and March 1430 with Georges de la Trémoille at Sully. The developing diplomatic and military situation gave rise to intense discussion among his councillors. They had once hoped to return to Champagne and resume the conquest of the provinces north of the Seine and the Marne with another great army on the model of 1429. But if the events of 1429 had transformed his military situation, they had not changed the implacable financial realities. Over the winter, a number of regional assemblies had been planned in order to fund a continuation of Charles's winning streak. There had been no grant of taxation in Languedoil since the Estates of Chinon in October 1428, which had funded the relief of Orléans. Only Languedoc seems to have voted funds, and most of those were spent on the defence of Languedoc itself. The representatives of the newly conquered provinces of the north gathered before the King at Chinon at Christmas but they had been ruined by war damage and do not seem to have granted any taxes. By the end of March 1430 reality had dawned on Charles's councillors. They met in the King's presence and decided that the plan to resume the conquest of the north would have to be postponed.[50]

Joan of Arc's was an insistent voice in the background throughout these debates. She behaved as if she was in command of affairs. She wrote to Reims and no doubt to other northern towns telling them to expect a large French army. She breezily declared that all Brittany had come over to the King's side and that 3,000 Bretons were on the way to fight for Charles VII. She addressed a threatening letter to the Hussites of Bohemia warning them that as soon as she had finished with the English, she would come to put them to the sword unless they abandoned their 'worthless heresy'. Increasingly, Joan inhabited a fantasy world of her own.

Never one to appreciate the realities of state finance or the subtleties of diplomacy, Joan was disgusted by the decision to defer the campaign in the north. She left Sully as soon as it had been made, without even taking leave of the King. No one knew what her plans were. She may have feared that she would be stopped if she disclosed them. From Sully, Joan marched north in search of action, accompanied by her brother Pierre, her small military household, a few companies of volunteers and a band of Italian soldiers of fortune under a mercenary captain called Bartolomeo Barretta. She appears to have participated in the siege of the citadel of Melun after the rising which delivered the town into French hands. Towards the end of April, she made for Lagny, the French outpost on the Marne, where a large garrison was engaged in a series of running battles with the Burgundian garrison of Paris. Joan was at Lagny for at least two weeks and took part in a brutal battle outside the walls. She was still there when news began to arrive of the Duke of Burgundy's advance to Compiègne. Joan was determined to be there. She could still inspire men and rally them to her banner. She gathered about her several hundred recruits from the garrisons of Lagny and other French garrisons nearby, bringing her total force to about 1,000 men. With these troops at her back, she left Lagny in the second week of May 1430 and entered Compiègne on the 13th or 14th.[51]

The town was in a state of panic, expecting a close siege at any moment. The streets were full of soldiers, frightened citizens and refugees. Food supplies were low. The defence of Choisy-au-Bac was going badly. The castle had been severely damaged by Burgundian artillery. A sortie against the besiegers' lines had failed, and the captain of the place had abandoned his men and fled for safety by boat in the middle of the night. The Count of Vendôme and the Chancellor Regnault de Chartres were in Compiègne to organise its defence, but it was known that they planned to leave while it was still possible to get out. Joan immediately began to behave as if she were in command. A day or two after her arrival, she led her own company and a large part of the garrison up the west bank of the Oise by night. Just before dawn, they fell on Sir John Montgomery's English contingent, which was encamped outside Noyon. There was a bloody fight. The English were outnumbered, but the battle turned against the attackers when the garrison of Noyon came out and joined the fight. Joan and her companions were driven back to Compiègne. This probably happened on 15 May. The garrison of Choisy surrendered on the following day.[52]

Two days later, on 18 May, Joan attempted another sortie. She left Compiègne accompanied by Regnault de Chartres, the Count of Vendôme and a number of other captains, in the hope of taking the Burgundians at Choisy in the rear. This venture was as ill-starred as the earlier one. To carry out her plan she needed to find a crossing of the Aisne. With Choisy in Burgundian hands, the nearest one was twenty-five miles away at Soissons. The captain of Soissons, a lieutenant of the Count of Clermont called Guichard Bournel, held it for Charles VII. But like others in the region his loyalties were divided. As a native of Artois, he was a subject of the Duke of Burgundy, and he was in the process of negotiating a change of allegiance with Philip's officers. Joan's arrival at this point was embarrassing, and possibly dangerous. Bournel let her in with a handful of companions. But he would not admit her army. As a result, they were blocked south of the Aisne, where they could find no food. On the following day most of them abandoned the enterprise and withdrew to Senlis. Joan of Arc was left with fewer than 400 men. She resolved to lead them back to Compiègne. Meanwhile, on 20 May 1429, while she was still away, Philip the Good's heralds summoned the defenders of the town to surrender, and the siege began.[53]

Compiègne was an ancient royal city standing on the east bank of the Oise at the hub of the road and river routes from Champagne to Normandy and from Paris to Flanders. It had once been rich, living well off the trade in wine and grain and the annual mid-Lent fair. But the wars had put an end to that. It had been a frontier town throughout the civil wars and the English occupation, changing hands no fewer than eight times between 1414 and 1429. Its trade had been ruined and many of its buildings destroyed. Its defences, however, had been constantly improved during successive periods of occupation by free companies. In 1429 Compiègne was defended by a circuit of walls a mile and a half long, reinforced by more than seventy towers and protected by a broad, water-filled moat. To the east the dense forest of Compiègne, the playground of royal huntsmen from the twelfth century to the nineteenth, extended into the Valois and the Soissonnais as far as Pierrefonds and Morienval. On the west, the town was joined to the opposite bank of the Oise by a wooden bridge resting on stone piers. The town end of the bridge was defended by a massive, fortified gatehouse and a drawbridge. At the other end there was a powerful moated barbican with its own garrison.

In 1430 the defence of Compiègne was directed by the captain of the town, the Picard squire Guillaume de Flavy. He was a man of strong will and boundless energy with a hot temper who had participated in some of the boldest military ventures of the wars. He refused the rich marriage and large bribe that the Duke of Burgundy offered him to surrender the town. But he was hard put to defend it. Earlier in the year, a large number of troops had been based in Compiègne, but they had all withdrawn before the opening of the siege. The town was left to be defended by its citizens and a corps of 600 professional troops hired by the municipality at their own expense. The Count of Clermont, the ranking French commander in the region, was with

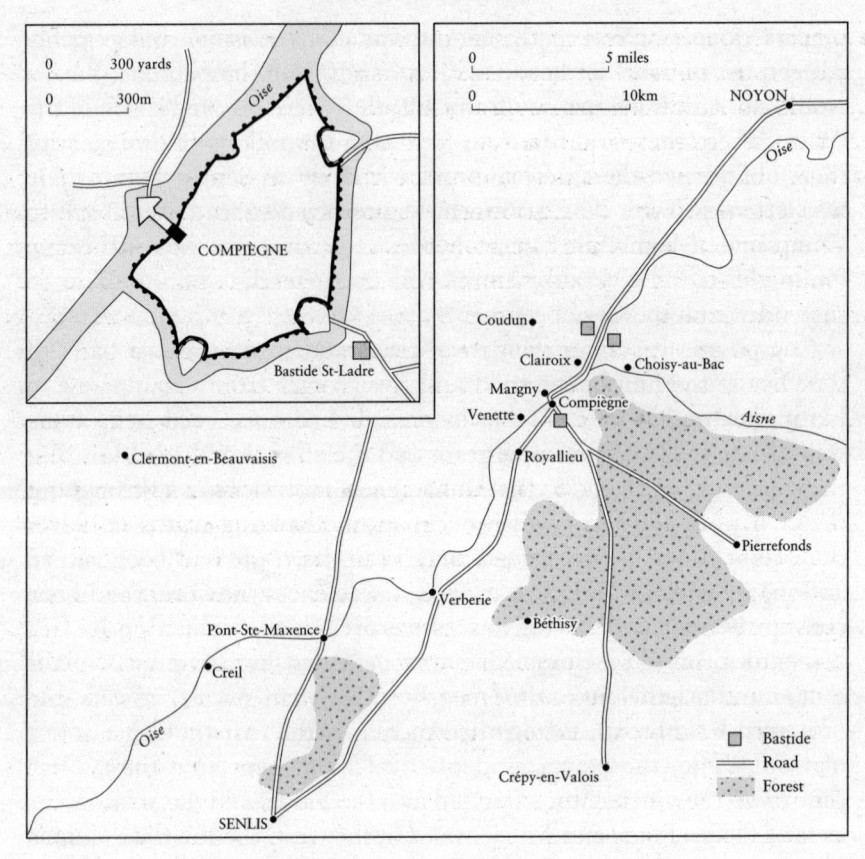

8 The siege of Compiègne, May–October 1430

the King in the Loire valley. In his absence the Count of Vendôme assumed the command of the sector. He established his headquarters at Senlis, twenty-two miles away. Some of the companies who had left the beleaguered town joined him there. In addition, he controlled the important French garrisons at Creil and Crépy-en-Valois.[54]

The Burgundians and their English allies deployed their forces in the meadows of the Oise, opposite the town. The marshal of the army, Baudot de Noyelles, established himself in the tower of Margny, with his troops encamped between the hamlet below and the river. John of Luxembourg, who commanded much the largest division, occupied the old castle of Clairoix further upstream at the foot of the steep wooded hill now known at Mont Ganelon. The English contingent encamped downstream of Margny around the grange of the abbey of St Corneille at Venette. There, they built a pontoon bridge giving the besieging army access to both banks. Philip the Good was based well to the rear in the comfort of the castle of Coudun. Hughes de Lannoy's fears about the army's supplies proved to be unfounded. Supplies flowed into the siege lines through Noyon from Picardy and, less securely, from Normandy through the Burgundian-held town of Clermont-en-Beauvaisis. In the opening weeks of the siege no attempt was made to invest Compiègne on the town side. The Burgundians did not want to lose time by trying to starve it out. They hoped to take it by storm and move on. The plan was to capture the barbican at the open end of the bridge and to batter the river walls and the gatehouse with artillery. They would then assault the town over the bridge. It was the strategy which had failed at Orléans.[55]

Joan of Arc and her company returned to Compiègne from Soissons shortly before dawn on 23 May 1430, having ridden through the night. Once in the town, she immediately took charge as was her way. She passed the morning devising plans and sharing visions, prophecies and 'all sorts of mad fantasies' with her companions. Then she had the gates of the city closed and the garrison and townspeople assembled. She told them that St Catherine had been sent by God to tell her that she must conduct a sortie against the Burgundian positions outside the town. Her voices had told her that victory was certain. The Duke of Burgundy would be captured, and all his followers killed, captured or put to flight. That evening, at about six o'clock, there was a mounted sortie over the Oise bridge by about 400 or 500 men. Joan did not lead it. She was at the rear, surrounded by her usual companions. But she was a conspicuous figure, dressed in a scarlet and gold robe worn over her dazzling white armour, mounted on a richly dressed horse and holding her famous banner aloft. The sortie force emerged from the bridge barbican and charged Baudot de Noyelles's division in front of Margny. Baudot was unprepared. Many of his men were unarmed. They rushed for their weapons and put up a stiff resistance, winning precious time for the commanders of neighbouring sectors to come to their aid. John of Luxembourg brought his men through the meadows from Clairoix and led the counterattack. The battle ebbed and flowed. The French charged John of Luxembourg's line three times, with diminishing force. But as more men joined the fight from other parts of the siege lines, it became an unequal struggle. The French trumpeters sounded the retreat.

In the age of walled and gated towns, a sortie into the siege lines of the enemy was one of the most dangerous operations of war. It was necessary to hold open the sortie force's line of retreat into the town. That carried the risk that the besiegers would follow them, forcing their way in through the open gates. To cover the sortie force's line of retreat, Guillaume de Flavy had mounted culverins on the barbican at the head of the bridge and stationed a large force of bowmen at the barriers in front of it. More bowmen had been posted on barges moored in the river. When the retreat was sounded, Joan of Arc was urged to make for the bridge before she was cut off. She refused and precious seconds were lost. Her companions eventually seized the bridle of her horse and forced her after them. Most of the sortie force managed to reach the barriers and escape over the bridge into the town. Some were cut down by their pursuers. Others fell over the sides in the crush and drowned. But in spite of Guillaume de Flavy's bowmen and artillery the English, who had come up from Venette, were able to fight their way through the press of retreating French troops to reach the barriers before the rearguard in which Joan was fighting. Guillaume de Flavy, who was following the fight from the gatehouse, feared that the pursuing English troops would reach the city gate. He took the difficult decision to close the gate and raise the drawbridge. The rearguard was cut off. Joan found herself surrounded. At least half a dozen men tried to seize her. Some grabbed her armour, others the bridle of her horse. 'Surrender and pledge your faith to me,' they all shouted, the classic formula prescribed by the conventions of chivalric warfare. Joan shouted back, 'I have pledged my faith to another, and will honour my oath.' It was bravado. An archer grabbed her long robe and dragged her from her horse. She rose from the ground among the press of enemies and pledged her faith to two members of John of Luxembourg's household. Her brother Pierre and her faithful protector Jean d'Aulon were captured alongside her. Joan was taken to Baudot de Noyelles's headquarters in the tower of Margny.

As the fighting subsided, Philip the Good arrived on the scene, accompanied by the usual swarm of courtiers and attendants, among them the chronicler Enguerrand de Monstrelet. Philip had a brief conversation with Joan, but Monstrelet confessed that he had forgotten their exchange by the time he came to write his chronicle. Later that evening Joan was handed over to John of Luxembourg's officers. She was held in John's quarters at Clairoix for a few days and then taken to his castle at Beaulieu in Picardy. Philip the Good announced the news in a circular to his allies and the towns of his domains. 'Her capture', he wrote, 'will show what a foolish mistake it was for all those people to be impressed by her deeds.'[56]

In the days following Joan of Arc's capture, the Duke of Burgundy and John of Luxembourg mounted their assault on the town. To storm it from the west bank of the river, they first had to capture the barbican at the open end of the bridge. Its defenders fought back with ferocity. They had a clear field of fire around them. Their bowmen and culverins repelled all the initial attacks, inflicting heavy casualties on the assault parties. John of Luxembourg was forced to sound the retreat and turn to more deliberate methods. He had a powerful artillery train, including five large bombards firing stone balls up to a foot in diameter. These were set up along the banks of the river, where they destroyed part of the timber carriageway, along with several of the water mills beneath the arches. To supply and reinforce the barbican the defenders of the town were obliged to improvise a rope-bridge across the gap, but it was a dangerous business which cost them many lives including one of Guillaume de Flavy's brothers. Meanwhile the besiegers built a boulevard of earth opposite the barbican at a distance of a bowshot. From here, they began digging long trenches to enable troops to approach it unseen and in safety. They dug mines under the barbican walls. The defenders dug countermines. There was hand-to-hand fighting in the tunnels. Progress was slow. By the end of May, it was already clear that the Burgundians were getting bogged down in the long siege that they had hoped to avoid.[57]

Both sides called for reinforcements. At about the beginning of June Sir John Montgomery withdrew with his troops to Normandy. He was replaced by a larger English force, more than 1,000 strong, commanded by the Earls of Huntingdon and Arundel. The town council sent a succession of emissaries to Charles VII, appealing in ever more urgent terms for help. Guillaume de Flavy made no fewer than four visits to the royal court during the siege to press the King for relief. Charles gave him written authority to surrender the town if he concluded that it could not be held, but he promised him an army of relief as soon as the troops could be found. This was easier said than done. The only field forces immediately available to the King were the company of the Bastard of Orléans and the Scottish corps, a few hundred men at the most. The Bastard of Orléans left at once on the long march round Paris by Melun and Lagny. He joined the Count of Vendôme at Senlis early in June. The Scottish corps left Touraine soon after. A small contingent of troops entered Compiègne in mid-July. But the main army of relief was still being assembled by Marshal Boussac on the Loire. He did not arrive at Senlis until September.[58]

The barbican, battered by the Duke of Burgundy's army and undermined by his sappers, was finally captured in the third week of July 1430. After two months of resistance, the defenders were overwhelmed by a surprise night-time assault. The damage to the bridge made it impossible for them to retreat into the town. Most of them were cut down or captured or drowned in the river as they tried to flee. After the battle was over, Philip the Good bought the commander of the barbican from his captor for the sole purpose of having him hanged from a gibbet at the top of the ruins in full view of the gatehouse. However, instead of being the beginning of the end, as the Burgundian captains had hoped, the capture of the barbican opened a frustrating period of stalemate which lasted nearly three months. The Burgundians repaired and garrisoned the barbican and installed their bombards there. They began the systematic destruction of the riverside defences and the western quarters of the town at point-blank range. A later survey enumerated nearly 350 buildings destroyed by artillery during the siege. In some quarters whole streets were reduced to rubble. But the besiegers were unable to fight their way across the bridge or mount an assault across the river.[59]

Philip the Good was under growing pressure from other parts of his far-flung empire. The first challenge came on the marches of Burgundy. Early in June 1430, Philip's captain in the region, Louis de Chalon Prince of Orange, had invaded the Dauphiné on Philip's instructions. His army was drawn from his native Franche-Comté, stiffened with several companies of Savoyard and English mercenaries. On 11 June, less than a week into the campaign, he was ambushed near Anthon east of Lyon by a French army led by Raoul de Gaucourt, supported by the formidable Seneschal of Lyon Imbert de Grolée and the Castilian *routier* Rodrigo de Villandrando. Louis's army was almost completely destroyed. He himself was lucky to escape on horseback, wounded in several places and covered in blood. He and another knight of the Golden Fleece were later expelled from the order for this disgrace. The event marked the start of a broad offensive by Gaucourt's two lieutenants against Philip the Good's domains in the Charolais and the Mâconnais. News of the battle of Anthon reached Philip at Compiègne about a week after it was fought, followed almost immediately by reports of a crisis at the opposite end of his empire, on the border between the county of Namur and the prince-bishopric of Liège. This was a region where local rivalries had simmered beneath the surface for many years. The men of Liège, counting on the fact that Philip was tied down on the Oise, were preparing to invade Namur and besiege the town of Bouvignes. Shortly afterwards the prince-bishop of Liège sent a formal declaration of war into Philip's camp. The Duke was forced to detach Antoine de Croÿ, one of the principal captains of his army, with 600 men and send them urgently to Namur.[60]

Early in July 1430, the Chancellor of Burgundy Nicolas Rolin arrived at the castle of Coudun to review the situation with his master. Philip was overstretched. He had more men under arms on different fronts in the summer of 1430 than at any time since 1422. The army at Compiègne alone was currently costing him about 33,000 *livres* a month in war wages. He was being forced to make drastic economies, including putting all his officials and annuitants on half-pay. The three-month period for which he had agreed to serve with his army expired on 10 July. The third month, which he had agreed to serve at his own cost, left his treasury seriously depleted. Under the terms of Philip's agreement with Cardinal Beaufort in February, his military contribution to the campaign in France was supposed to be cut to 600 men-at-arms and 600 bowmen at the end of the third month. This would have reduced the size of the Burgundian army outside Compiègne by two-thirds and would probably lead to the abandonment of the siege. In the event, Philip struck a new agreement with his English allies. The Duke agreed to serve for another six months in France with 800 men-at-arms and 1,000 bowmen in return for a subsidy of 19,500 *francs* a month. The English also agreed to reimburse all his expenditure on artillery. Henry VI's war treasurer John Hotoft arrived on 12 July to count out the first month's payment in coin. Like the original payments to Philip in March, this sum was advanced by Cardinal Beaufort from his own chests.[61]

In the second week of August 1430 a fresh crisis arose. News arrived that Philip's cousin Philip of Saint-Pol, Duke of Brabant, had died at Louvain. He had been ill for some time and his death was not unexpected. He had no children. The Dukes of Burgundy had long regarded the duchy as their own. There were others who arguably had a better claim, but Philip was the most powerful and had the support of most of Brabant's nobility. He also acted fast. On 15 August, he abruptly left the siege of Compiègne and marched to Ghent and from there to Mechelen. He never returned to Compiègne.[62]

Before leaving, the Duke appointed John of Luxembourg and Philippe de Saveuse to command the army in his absence, leaving them with instructions to do everything in consultation with the two English earls. The siege operation was left in disarray. John of Luxembourg was absent on a long military promenade in the Laonnais and the Valois. He did not return until the end of August. Many of the men participating in the siege had deserted and had either gone home or left on plundering expeditions into the surrounding region. It took a month to recall them and reconstitute the siege army. From the middle of September 1430 new energy was injected into the siege. The Burgundian and English captains abandoned the idea of an assault over the bridge. Instead, they resolved upon a close investment of the town from both sides of the river with a view to starving it into submission, a course that should probably have been adopted from the outset. It was a more difficult strategy in September because of the reduced forces available. A review of the army's strength was carried out on 19 September. The Burgundian division had about 700 men-at-arms and 1,600 bowmen, about two-thirds of its original strength. There is some evidence of an even steeper decline in the strength of the English division. The Earl of Arundel appears to have left the siege, and other companies may have been withdrawn for operations elsewhere. The chronicler Monstrelet, who was probably present, believed that English numbers had fallen to about 600 men, making a total of fewer than 3,000 for the combined allied force outside the town.

The west bank was assigned to the English, and the east bank to the Burgundians. On the east side, the main entrance to the town was the Pierrefonds gate in the centre of the circuit of walls, which opened via a barbican onto the road through the forest to the fortress of Pierrefonds nine miles away. The gate had been open throughout the siege. The Burgundians now began to build a large bastide in front of it. They called it the bastide Saint-Ladre. A garrison of 300 men was put into this place under the command of Jean de Créqui, a prominent captain and counsellor of the Duke, along with Jacques de Brimeu and his nephew Florimond, all three of them founding knights of the Golden Fleece. At the same time, the barbican at the end of the Oise bridge was refortified and received another large Burgundian garrison. Two smaller bastides of timber were constructed across the roads leading north to Noyon, one on either side of the river. John of Luxembourg and the leading Burgundian captains established their headquarters in the buildings of the Augustinian priory of Royallieu, a short distance south of the town. The new measures had an immediate impact. The situation of the defenders began to deteriorate. Their shops and storerooms emptied out. Hunger set in. The garrison sent desperate appeals to the French King's officers to hasten the arrival of the promised army of relief.[63]

Towards the end of September 1430, Marshal Boussac finally arrived in the region with the first companies of his army. He made for Senlis where he joined forces with the companies of the Count of Vendôme, Poton de Saintrailles and Teodoro di Valperga. Several more companies recruited by Guillaume de Flavy among the garrisons of Champagne arrived in the third week of October and established a base some ten miles south of Compiègne in the village of Béthisy. But even with the new arrivals, the French had only 1,200 men. This was disappointing. It was about a third of the number available to the Anglo-Burgundians. The Count of Vendôme had expected to have more, but many of the troops that he had been promised failed to appear. Vendôme could not afford to wait for them. The deteriorating situation inside Compiègne left him with no option but to do his best with the forces available. He did not expect to be able to raise the siege, but he hoped at least to resupply the town. On 24 October the Count and Marshal Boussac led their troops out of Senlis, followed by a large food convoy. They marched up the valley of the Oise to the bridge at Verberie, where they joined forces with the men from Champagne and encamped for the night in the meadows.

Eight miles away in the priory of Royallieu, the English and Burgundian captains were debating their own strategy. They faced the classic dilemma of any besieging army in this situation: how to confront an army of relief in front of them, while containing the garrison in their rear. There were now at least 500 professional troops in Compiègne in addition to armed townsmen. They were capable of mounting a powerful sortie. Some of the captains at Royallieu were in favour of abandoning their siege lines and advancing to attack the French. However, the majority were for fighting a defensive battle in prepared positions in the broad open plain south of the town. It was agreed that the English division would cross the river by the pontoon bridge at dawn on the following morning and join forces with the rest of the Burgundian army at Royallieu. The Burgundian garrisons holding the bridge barbican and the three bastides would remain in place. The calculation was that together with the rearguard of the main army they would be able to deal with any sortie from the gates.

At Verberie, the French commanders resolved upon a stratagem. A column of 200 to 300 men was placed under the command of Poton de Saintrailles and sent ahead by night through the forest of Compiègne. They planned to make their way unseen round the Anglo-Burgundian positions under cover of the forest. They would then surprise the bastide of Saint-Ladre and enter the town by the Pierrefonds gate before the English and Burgundians realised that they were there. A convoy of food wagons would follow them through the forest, escorted by another 100 men. The French scouts reported that the Burgundians appeared to have anticipated some such manoeuvre. They had blocked the paths through the forest with felled trees. But the French recruited the local peasantry to help clear the trees and hack a way through the thick vegetation. Meanwhile, early the next morning, the rest of the French army planned to advance in battle order on Compiègne, giving every impression that they intended to fight a battle. They hoped to pin down the enemy forces and draw them away from the Pierrefonds gate while Poton de Saintrailles and the food convoy went round their backs.

Early on 25 October, the English crossed the river and joined the Burgundians at Royallieu. The combined army took up a position on open ground south of the priory, with their right wing protected by the river and their left by the forest. They dug a deep line of trenches in front of their line to serve as a cavalry obstacle. The Count of Vendôme approached during the morning with the main body of the French army through the broad band of meadowland by the river. They advanced into the plain and formed up in front of the Anglo-Burgundian line, a bowshot away. The two forces faced each other across the gap for several hours, while the bolder spirits in both armies showed off their prowess by skirmishing between the lines. But the allies were unwilling to abandon the defensive and the French had no intention of attacking.

Early in the afternoon, Poton de Saintrailles emerged from the forest into the clearing opposite the bastide Saint-Ladre. The garrison of the town had been forewarned. Poton's appearance was the signal for a powerful sortie against the bastide. The Burgundian works were still unfinished. The ditches were only half-dug. The fixed defences were incomplete. The sortie party from the town had no difficulty in reaching the walls with their scaling ladders and grappling irons. The Burgundian garrison beat back the first two assaults. But a third assault, by the combined forces of Poton and Guillaume de Flavy, overwhelmed them. A crowd of angry townsfolk, both men and women, joined in the fight with whatever weapons they could find. More than half the garrison of the bastide was killed and most of the rest, including two of the three commanders, were captured. The townsmen set about demolishing the structure as the food convoy came out of the forest and was escorted in triumph through the gate.

Outside Royallieu, John of Luxembourg conferred with his captains. He thought that they should abandon their positions and march at once to the aid of their companions in the bastide. But he was persuaded instead to hold the army's existing positions, in the hope that a decisive engagement with the troops of Vendôme and Boussac would restore the situation. A herald was sent across no-man's-land with a challenge to battle. But the French commanders were not going to gamble everything on the outcome of a pitched battle against superior forces. In the failing light of evening, they made use of their superior mobility (they were all mounted) to escape around the wings of the Anglo-Burgundian army and make for the town. As they rode through the gates of Compiègne, the garrison was already following up their victory. They had improvised a bridge of boats over the Oise and fell on one of the two smaller Burgundian bastides north of the town, killing its defenders and burning the timber structure. On the opposite bank the defenders of the other bastide set fire to it and fled before they suffered the same fate.

John of Luxembourg and the Earl of Huntingdon had a hasty conference in the field. They decided to return to their encampments on either side of the river to regroup. They would reassemble in battle array the next morning and challenge the French to fight them in front of the town. But it must have been obvious to them that the siege was over. The French were unlikely to accept the challenge. The town had been reprovisioned and its garrison reinforced. Three of the four bastides had been destroyed. Morale was so poor in the allied ranks that both commanders were obliged to post guards to prevent their men from deserting. These precautions proved to be useless. The desertions began in the English division. Men formed themselves into improvised bands, swept aside the guards and made off towards Normandy. The Burgundians began to follow suit. In the morning the two commanders surveyed what was left of their army. There could be no question of challenging the French in Compiègne now. They agreed to retreat to Noyon and wait there until Philip the Good and the English King's council could agree upon the next step. As they left, the townsmen gleefully began to break up the pontoon bridge at Venette. In the barbican at the end of the town bridge, Baudot de Noyelles burned his buildings and withdrew with the rest of the army. The French took a great haul of spoil. The allies' wagons and stores were recovered from the encampments at Royallieu and Venette. The Duke of Burgundy's great bombards were found abandoned in the fields. It was a 'shameful and most dishonourable thing', the Count of Vendôme remarked. On 26 October 1430 the retreating allied army reached Noyon and encamped by the Oise around the suburban village of Pont-l'Evêque.[64]

Philip the Good was at Brussels when the news of the disaster was brought to him. He hurriedly completed his business and left at once for France. On 2 November, his cavalcade entered Arras. By this time the commanders at Noyon were no longer in control of events. The French had received more reinforcements from the Loire and had launched a powerful counterattack against the Burgundian forces in Picardy and the Beauvaisis. In a matter of days, they had retaken all the towns and castles which the allies had occupied since April, except for Soissons. They captured the fortified bridge over the Oise at Pont-Sainte-Maxence. Marshal Boussac occupied the town of Clermont-en-Beauvaisis and laid siege to the citadel. Poton de Saintrailles was advancing north towards the Somme. From Arras, the Duke summoned all available troops to Corbie and urgently set about putting garrisons into the principal towns of Picardy. As his officers struggled to organise a new army, what remained of the old one fell apart. The English troops at Noyon mutinied. The period of service covered by their advances had ended in September, and they had received no wages since then. They declared that they would leave at once for Normandy. The Burgundian captains begged the Earl of Huntingdon to wait a few more days until further orders could reach them from Arras and Rouen. But Huntingdon, who was no longer obeyed by his men, was immovable. John of Luxembourg is said to have 'cursed the lot of them and the whole nation from which they had sprung'. But the situation of his own troops was no better. Their wages were also in arrears, and their mood was just as ugly. On 4 November, the campaign was abandoned.[65]

The debacle at Compiègne did lasting damage to relations between the Duke of Burgundy and the English. Philip the Good believed that the English had betrayed him. He sent several testy messages to Rouen in the final days of the siege. Then, on 4 November 1430, he wrote a stinging rebuke to Henry VI's council and sent two of his councillors before them at Rouen to reinforce the message. Philip's immediate cause for complaint was that the English had not paid him. The monthly payments for his army were two months in arrears and the 40,000 *saluts* which he claimed to have spent on artillery had not been reimbursed. In fact, by the time that the emissaries reached Rouen, the war wages of Philip's army had been paid up to date, together with half of his claim for artillery. The Duke was on stronger ground when he complained that the English had failed to pay their own troops, thus causing them to desert and leave him dangerously exposed to a French counterattack in Picardy. Philip's real grievance, however, was more fundamental. He protested about the whole course which the war had taken and the burden which it was imposing on him. His warnings about the risks of a major siege had been ignored. He had lost valued friends, including four prominent members of his household who had been captured in the bastide of Saint-Ladre. His domains in Burgundy had been wasted by the French. His county of Namur had been invaded by the men of Liège. Behind this litany of complaints lay Philip's unspoken fear that he might have been backing a losing cause ever since 1420.[66]

The English council was alarmed by the tone of Philip the Good's messages. They scrambled for troops to shore up the Burgundian positions in Picardy and the Beauvaisis. The Earl of Huntingdon, who had withdrawn to Gournay with the remnants of his army, was sent straight back to relieve Clermont-en-Beauvaisis. Sir Thomas Kyriel, who was based on the northern march of Normandy, was sent with several hundred men to join Philip on the Somme. Men were pulled from the garrison of Calais. The Earls of Stafford and Arundel were recalled from the Gâtinais and the Île-de-France. The Cardinal's nephew Thomas Beaufort Count of Perche, who had been ordered to reinforce the defences of the Nivernais, was abruptly transferred to Picardy. The promised counterattack began well. Marshal Boussac's troops around the citadel of Clermont fled on the approach of Huntingdon's army, leaving behind them much of the artillery that had been captured at Compiègne. But disaster struck further north. On 20 November about 600 English and Burgundian troops under Kyriel's command were ambushed by Poton de Saintrailles as they passed through the village of Bouchoir. Kyriel had allowed his men to disperse across the countryside to hunt hares. They were easy targets for their mounted assailants. Most of them were cut down in the fields as they fled. A few were able to rally and make a stand beneath Kyriel's banner, but they were overwhelmed. About eighty men were captured, including Kyriel himself.

Philip advanced south with his army as far as the river Avre at Roye and halted there. For some days, the French and Burgundian armies were only five miles apart. Boussac sent a herald forward with a challenge to battle. Philip, who wanted to regain his lost prestige, would have liked to accept it. He drew up his army in battle order south of Roye. But his council persuaded him to back down. He had more than twice the numbers of the French, but his men were demoralised by recent defeats and in no condition to fight. Besides, the councillors added, it was beneath him to accept a challenge from an army with not a single royal prince in its ranks. So the message went back that John of Luxembourg would fight them instead. The French were relieved to be offered a get-out. They said that they would only fight Philip, and overnight withdrew to Compiègne.

As for the promised English reinforcements, none of them arrived in time except for Kyriel's ill-fated company. The Earl of Stafford did not appear until Philip had begun to retreat. The companies from Calais seem to have left too late. Lewis Robesart and Thomas Beaufort got as far as Conty, south of Amiens, with 500 to 600 men but were attacked and defeated by a much larger force under Poton de Saintrailles as they tried to cross the river Evoissons. Robesart, who had refused to flee because he was a knight of the Garter, was killed. In the final days of December 1430, Philip's councillors met the principal English commanders at Amiens. They were joined there by Bishop Cauchon. It must have been a tense meeting. The allies agreed that the campaign must be abandoned. Philip presented his bill. His accountants reckoned that he was still owed 113,000 *livres* which the English had failed to pay him. In the second week of December, he returned in an angry frame of mind to Brabant, where he spent most of the winter.[67]

The drama of Joan of Arc was being played out in the background throughout the siege of Compiègne. She did not remain long at Beaulieu. While she was there, she tried to escape. She locked her guards in her room and slipped through a gap in a timber partition. But she was stopped by a gatekeeper. As a result, she was transferred early in June 1430 to another fortress of John of Luxembourg at Beaurevoir, further north on the borders of the prince-bishopric of Cambrai. Beaurevoir has disappeared, apart from the stumps of a single tower, but a seventeenth-century traveller described it as a 'massive fortress, powerfully built and heavily turreted'. It was remote and extremely secure.[68]

Joan's exact legal status was unclear. She had surrendered to a retainer of John of Luxembourg. If she was a prisoner of war, she was John's property, and he was entitled to ransom or sell her as he pleased. According to English practice, that right was subject to some important exceptions. The King could claim any prisoner of high rank who had been captured by men employed on his service. In Normandy, a distinct principle had grown up that the King's officers of justice could claim a prisoner who was required to answer criminal charges. Brigands, freebooters and other irregulars were often claimed by Henry VI's Norman officials in this way, even if they had been captured in the course of ordinary operations of war. But Joan had been captured in the Beauvaisis by an officer of the Duke of Burgundy, and neither English nor Norman practice applied. There was some authority that as King of France Henry VI was entitled to buy any prisoner worth 10,000 *livres* or more, but the English council initially declined to recognise that Joan was worth that much, for fear that they might have to pay it.

The claims of the Church added another layer of complexity. The Church had exclusive jurisdiction over heresy and other offences against the faith such as sorcery and blasphemy. Responsibility for dealing with these crimes was shared between the diocesan bishop and the Holy Office of the Inquisition, a loosely organised institution staffed mainly by Dominican friars and deriving its authority directly from the Pope. In 1430 the office of Inquisitor of France was held by the prior of the Dominican house in Paris. His powers were delegated to vicars-general appointed for each diocese. Three days after Joan's capture, Martin Billorel, vicar-general for the diocese of Paris, wrote to the Duke of Burgundy declaring that Joan was suspected of a variety of crimes 'smelling of heresy'. It was, he said, the duty of every Christian of whatever rank to cooperate in the suppression of such crimes. He called for Joan to be sent under guard to Paris to be tried there by the Inquisition.

Behind this initiative stood the University of Paris, of which Billorel was a prominent member. The University was a mere shadow its former self in 1430, 'Alas, much reduced from its former glory' as it admitted in a candid petition to the Pope. The Burgundian proscriptions after 1418 had eliminated every prominent Armagnac from its ranks and transformed it into an aggressive partisan of the house of Burgundy and, by extension, of the Lancastrian Kings. Its interest in Joan of Arc was intensified by the political implications of her case. But there was more to this than politics. The University remained the guardian of religious orthodoxy and the ultimate authority on matters of doctrine. It had been extremely active in the persecution of sorcery, taking a close interest in Brother Richard and Pierrone the Breton. Even to an austerely apolitical churchman, the religious implications of Joan's claim to speak with the authority of God were disturbing. Writing in 1431 to the Pope, the scholars of the University deplored the 'surge of new prophets announcing revelations from God and his saints', agents of chaos and harbingers of the social disintegration which would precede the end of the world.[69]

Henry VI's council had not instigated Billorel's intervention and did not welcome it. They had reservations about trying Joan of Arc in the politically volatile atmosphere of Paris. But they were determined to try Joan one way or another. They believed that they had good grounds for prosecuting her in an ordinary criminal court as a traitor and a brigand. However, there were obvious propaganda advantages in a show trial before an ecclesiastical court for heresy and sorcery. Her conviction by the Church would make an impression beyond anything that an ordinary criminal court could achieve. If her triumphs were seen to be the work of Satan, their moral impact on both sides would be dissipated. So the English resolved to extract Joan from the hands of John of Luxembourg and were not inclined to bandy law with him.

The man whom they employed to try her was Pierre Cauchon. So far as is known, Cauchon had no personal experience of inquisitorial proceedings. But he was a careful lawyer and close to the University, of which he had once been an active member. He was also politically reliable, the most prominent and influential French member of the Grand Conseil after Louis of Luxembourg. Cauchon's chief advantage, however, was a more narrowly legal one. He was the Bishop of Beauvais. Joan had been captured in his diocese. Technically, therefore, he could claim jurisdiction over her case. Cauchon understood the political sensitivity of Joan's case and the importance of a trial which would look good in the eyes of the outside world. It must be procedurally unimpeachable. He told his colleagues at an early procedural meeting that he intended at one and the same time to 'serve the King and conduct a fine trial'.[70]

On 14 July 1430, while Philip the Good was still at Compiègne, Cauchon appeared at his headquarters. Philip was surrounded by his councillors and captains, including John of Luxembourg. The Bishop delivered a formal command on behalf of Henry VI and the Church for the surrender of Joan of Arc. She was accused of sorcery, idolatry and conjuring demons, he said, and was not entitled to the status of a prisoner of war. Nonetheless, the King in his largesse would agree to pay John of Luxembourg 6,000 *francs* for his prisoner as well as a life pension to the squire to whom she had surrendered. John of Luxembourg received this missive without comment. In the course of the next two weeks, he drove a hard bargain. The English were ultimately forced to pay the 10,000 *livres* at which the Crown could claim her as of right. In August the Estates of Normandy met at Rouen and agreed to a tax of 120,000 *livres*, part of which was earmarked for the purchase of 'Jeanne la Pucelle, accused of sorcery, a prisoner of war commanding the armies of the Dauphin'. Pending the laborious process of assessment and collection, Joan's purchase price was advanced by Cardinal Beaufort.[71]

When Joan was told that she was to be handed over to the English, she threw herself from the top of a tower into the dry moat of Beaurevoir, a fall of some sixty feet. It was never clear whether this was an attempt at suicide or at escape. Her own evidence on the point was ambiguous. She was concussed, and badly injured her back and her kidneys. It was some time before she could be moved. But by September 1430 she had sufficiently recovered to be taken to Arras, where she was delivered to the English in exchange for the money. Early in November, they took her to the coastal fortress of Le Crotoy at the mouth of the Somme, which was often used to hold important prisoners of state, while a military escort was collected to bring her to Rouen.

On 23 December 1430, Joan entered the city where she was to pass the brief remainder of her life. The arrangements for her custody were in the hands of the Earl of Warwick. Normally, she would have been held in an ecclesiastical prison, but they were notoriously insecure and Warwick was determined that the prisoner should not escape or kill herself. She was taken to the castle at the north end of Rouen, the symbol of English power in the city and the seat of the Norman administration. An iron cage had been specially made to hold her. But its use was shortly abandoned and she was transferred to a cell in what is now known as the Tour de la Pucelle. It was a large, cold and sparsely furnished chamber in an upper storey, lit only by two arrow-slits looking out over the fields. Here, she was attached by chains and leg-irons to a heavy wooden beam and watched around the clock by a team of four English jailers under the direction of a squire of the King's household. No one was allowed to visit or speak to her without leave. According to the evidence given at the posthumous inquiry, Warwick dealt brutally with anyone who tried to help or advise her, or even uttered a word in her defence. Joan had to face her ordeal alone. Her physical and mental health suffered. She experienced long periods of depression and several bouts of fever and gastroenteritis. Warwick ensured that she received the best medical attention that the uncertain skills of the age could provide. One of the doctors who attended her was told that she must on no account be allowed to die of natural causes; the King had paid a high price for her so that she might be publicly convicted and burned. On 3 January 1431, Joan was formally transferred to Bishop Cauchon for examination and trial, although she remained throughout in the physical custody of her English jailers. She was under no illusions about her likely fate. She told John of Luxembourg, who visited her in her cell, that she 'knew well that these English will put me to death, because they think that once I am dead, they will be able to conquer the kingdom of France'.[72]

An inquisitorial trial was a cumbersome process governed by the elaborate procedural rules of canon law and two centuries of accumulated practice. Cauchon's desire for a 'fine trial' made it even more cumbersome in Joan's case. Canon law required alleged heretics to be brought before a tribunal comprising the diocesan bishop and the relevant inquisitor acting jointly. The tribunal which was to try Joan consisted of Bishop Cauchon and Jean le Maistre, the prior of the Dominican house at Rouen and vicar-general of the Inquisitor of France for the diocese. Of the two men, Cauchon took by far the more active part. He was involved throughout. He held procedural sessions in his own lodgings near the cathedral. He intervened frequently in the hearings. Le Maistre's presence was essential to the validity of the proceedings, but he was generally a passive participant. Very little is known about his background or sympathies, but it is clear that he was a reluctant judge. He told one of the notaries charged with recording the proceedings that he 'disapproved of the whole business and did as little as he could'. A third participant had an important role to play. This was the prosecutor Jean d'Estivet, a Paris-trained canon lawyer and the official prosecutor of the diocese of Beauvais. Unlike Cauchon, whose manner was at least outwardly judicial, Estivet made no attempt to conceal his hatred of Joan. An ardent Burgundian partisan, he was an aggressive advocate. He called Joan a 'tart' and a 'shit' to her face in the course of encounters in her cell. Even the Earl of Warwick had to warn him to mind his language.

Unusually, there was a large and fluctuating body of assessors in addition to the two judges and the prosecutor. Forty-two assessors attended the first public session and more than a hundred participated in the trial at one time or another. Most of them were canons of the cathedral or Norman clergymen, many with degrees in theology or law. There was also a delegation of six doctors of the University of Paris, who were among the most active participants. Some of the assessors were closely associated with the Lancastrian administration. Gilles de Duremort Abbot of Fécamp, for example, a particularly active assessor, was a veteran of many diplomatic missions for the Duke of Bedford and one of the most assiduous members of the Grand Conseil. Only three assessors were native Englishmen. William Hatton was a civil lawyer who had served in Henry V's secretariat in France and now in Henry VI's. The two others were Oxford theologians belonging to the chapel royal.

The palpable hostility to Joan during the trial owed little if anything to the occasional presence of the English. The leading actors at the trial were all native Frenchmen. Politically, they were Burgundians before they were ever English. Most of them were men filled with the venom of the French civil wars, who had staked their careers on the change of dynasty effected by Philip the Good and Henry V in 1420. Above all, they were churchmen with their own interest in the suppression of unauthorised and heterodox revelations. They shared the rising hysteria about sorcery and witchcraft that was becoming endemic in Europe at the time of Joan's trial. Like most men of their cloth, they had a real horror of heresy, which they saw as an insidious poison liable to infect the whole population and destroy the religious and political order, as Hussitism had done in Bohemia and Lollardy threatened to do in England.[73]

Inquisitorial proceedings were usually initiated by the tribunal itself, which was entitled to take notice of notorious facts. Bishop Cauchon opened the proceedings by declaring that her words and deeds were matters of 'common report'. The trial which followed proceeded in two stages. The first was a preliminary examination of the facts, known as the *processus preparatorius*, during which provisional charges were formulated. Only then could they proceed to summon the accused before them and interrogate her. On the basis of the material collected and the accused's answers, formal charges were then drawn up and put to the accused, who was called upon to admit or reject them one by one. The tribunal then proceeded to the second stage, the trial proper, known as the *processus ordinarius*. The prosecutor was called on to prove, by evidence, all the charges which the accused had denied.[74]

The legal basis of the proceedings against Joan of Arc was that the accused's reputation was notorious. Technically, therefore, no evidence was required at the preliminary stage. But Cauchon decided to gather evidence anyway in order in order to reinforce the prosecution case. The search for incriminating material had already been initiated by the King's council. They instructed local officials to collect evidence in Lorraine and possibly elsewhere. The first six weeks of the process were taken up with the assessment of this material and the examination of witnesses. In the event, none of the information was used and none of it has survived. As several witnesses told the posthumous inquiry of 1455–6, this was because none of it incriminated the prisoner. Indeed, one of the witnesses was accused of being a covert Armagnac and another was refused his expenses when he failed to produce anything of use to the prosecution. So, in the end Cauchon decided to proceed on the basis of the notorious facts and Joan's evidence alone. On 20 February 1431, she was formally summoned to appear before the tribunal on the following morning.[75]

At eight o'clock on the morning of 21 February 1431, Joan was taken from her cell in the tower and brought across the courtyard to appear at the first public hearing of the tribunal in the castle chapel. The intimidating atmosphere was described, a quarter of a century later, in the evidence given to the posthumous inquiry by one of the official notaries. Joan was brought in by the bailiff and seated in front of the prosecutor and judges and the serried ranks of assessors, notaries and clerks. Around them stood a large and noisy crowd of spectators who kept up a constant background hubbub and frequently interrupted her answers. As a result, the subsequent hearings, although still ostensibly public, were moved to the small antechamber of the great hall, with two English soldiers posted at the door to restrict access. Later they were moved again to her room in the tower, where there was only room for the judges and a select group of assessors to participate. Even in these more intimate spaces, however, the mood must have been oppressive. Although the tribunal was almost entirely French, the English presence was felt everywhere. Rouen was a Lancastrian city. The proceedings were conducted in a fortress occupied by the English King and his court. Its courtyards and towers were full of English soldiers. The prisoner was escorted everywhere by English guards. The English were paying for the whole cost of the trial, including the wages and expenses of the judges, the prosecutor and the delegates of the University of Paris. They also undertook to indemnify all those involved against any untoward consequences for them personally. Several of Henry's French secretaries attended the hearings, recording points of interest for the council. The Earl of Warwick was constantly in the wings.[76]

Over twelve sessions Joan of Arc was interrogated about her beliefs, her childhood and upbringing, her voices, her arrival at Chinon, her male dress, and her participation in the military campaigns of 1429 and 1430. The procedure was undoubtedly unfair, although no more so than inquisitorial trials generally. It compared favourably with ordinary criminal trials, which in this period could be extremely summary. In Joan's case, the sessions lasted between three and four hours in the morning and were often continued after a short break in the afternoon. The questioning was relentless, physically and mentally taxing and sometimes tendentious. Occasionally, assessors would intervene with a word of advice for the prisoner or a suggestion that she should not be required to answer some question, but they were brusquely told by Cauchon to hold their tongues. As Cauchon himself observed, the judges and assessors were men learned in theology and law, whereas Joan had no knowledge of such things. Yet canon law restricted the use of counsel by a defendant. It was not until well after the end of the interrogations, when the tribunal was embarking on the trial proper, that she was offered any professional assistance, and then only from among the assessors. She replied that she would be content with the counsel of God.

In spite of all these difficulties, it is impossible to read the detailed record of Joan's interrogations without being struck by her intelligence, spirit and presence of mind. She refused to swear to tell the truth, except on the footing that she reserved the right not to answer some questions at all. In the early hearings, she would not discuss her visions. She was never willing to reveal her private exchanges with Charles VII. She skilfully avoided most of the rhetorical traps that were set for her. She offered some tart answers and had her own views about what were proper questions. She would say 'This is nothing to do with your case,' or 'Look back at your notes and you will see that I have already answered that,' or 'One question at a time, good Sirs', or just 'Next question?' (*'passez outre'*). Her answers rarely gave any ammunition to the prosecution. The impression given was of a woman impelled by a genuine belief in her voices and her mission. Forced to be her own lawyer, she proved to be a good one. The tribunal was clearly disconcerted by her candour and directness.[77]

On 26 March 1431, the tribunal proceeded to the trial proper, the *processus ordinarius*. It began with a private meeting of the judges and some of the assessors, at which Jean d'Estivet presented a list of no fewer than seventy articles which he undertook to prove. Estivet's articles accused Joan of sorcery, divining, false prophecy, conjuring demons, superstition and magic, heresy, schism, sacrilege, idolatry, apostasy, blasphemy, sedition, fomenting war, shedding blood, wearing male dress, subverting ecclesiastical discipline, seducing people of every class from princes to simple souls into the ways of wickedness, and usurping the place of God by inviting people to adore and venerate herself. It was an indiscriminate indictment, embellished with points of detail which had no basis either in Joan's evidence or in any other material in the record. Perhaps its most striking feature was that it did not suggest that Joan had invented her voices or the accompanying visions. On the contrary, the suggestion was that they were genuine but diabolical. On the following day, 27 March, the proceedings moved back to the antechamber of the great hall, and the articles were put to her one by one for her to answer Yes or No. Over three days, she responded to each of them by denying either the whole article or the tendentious terms in which it was formulated.[78]

It soon became clear that the judges were uncomfortable with Estivet's approach. In the first few days of April, they produced a new set of just twelve articles, couched in less extravagant terms, which were substantially based on Joan's answers in cross-examination. These focused almost entirely on her voices and visions. She was said to have put her trust in them without consulting her parents or respectable churchmen who might have warned her of the dangers. And, trusting them as she did, she had been led to adopt male dress and to fight the English, blasphemously invoking the name of God ('JHESU MARIA') in support of her acts. Joan's notorious first letter, addressed to the Duke of Bedford and the English captains outside Orléans, was the prime item in the new indictment as it had been in the old.

The new articles were certainly easier to prove. But they raised problems of their own which went to the heart of the judges' dilemma. Cauchon was wary of making the proceedings too obviously political. But politics could never have been kept out of it. The message of Joan's voices was that the English must be expelled from France. The question whether the voices were true or false, divine or diabolical, was therefore inevitably a political question. Ultimately, the issue was the legitimacy of the dual monarchy. Joan's judges could not regard her voices as true without accepting the divine character of her mission. Even, however, on the footing that the voices were false, as the judges and assessors were bound to believe, many difficulties remained. It was far from clear that it was heretical for Joan to have been taken in by them. Cauchon was uncharacteristically hesitant in the face of these problems. He decided to submit the articles to twenty-two notable academic theologians. Their opinion was unequivocal. They advised unanimously that Joan's voices and visions were false and that she had no good reason for believing in them. Either she had invented them, or they were the work of the Devil. In either case, they declared, her belief in them was a crime against the faith. The judges were inclined to agree but were not confident enough to go ahead on that basis. They resolved to collect further opinions and to submit the whole question to the University of Paris for a ruling. These authorities expressed the same view, but with varying degrees of conviction. The University was unequivocal in its condemnation of the accused. Some of the theologians consulted were equally forthright. But others regarded the question as difficult and uncertain, and answered with much hesitation. One of them thought it so difficult that no decision should be made until it had been submitted to the Pope, a suggestion which would have derailed the whole procedure.[79]

Meanwhile, Cauchon made a sustained attempt to avoid the issue by trying to persuade Joan to confess her errors and recant. Politically, a public act of recantation on Joan's part would have been as valuable to the English and their French supporters as her execution. Over the following days, Cauchon sent several emissaries to talk her round in her cell. In the end, he even came himself. On another occasion he tried a trick which was entirely in accordance with inquisitorial procedure and recommended in standard textbooks on the subject. He employed a stool pigeon. One of the assessors was placed in the cell next to Joan's pretending to be a cobbler from Lorraine, who gained her confidence and tried to trap her into incriminating herself while Cauchon and Warwick listened in.

When all these efforts failed, other approaches were tried. On 2 May, Joan was brought into the great hall of the castle, the largest space available, there to be publicly admonished by Jean de Châtillon, a Parisian professor of theology. His message was subtle. He transformed the issue from a question of truth or falsehood to one of authority. It was the duty of every good Christian, he said, to submit to the authority of God's Church. Refusal to do so would itself be a heretical and schismatic. Was she willing to submit to the guidance of the tribunal? She was immovable. 'You will get nothing more out of me', she said. They asked her whether she would submit to the authority of the Pope. 'Take me to him,' she answered, 'and I will tell him directly.' A week later, they threatened her with violence. They took her to the Grosse Tour, which served as a courthouse and prison, and told her that she would be tortured unless she acknowledged her errors. The executioner was brought in to show her the instruments which would be used. She replied that she would say nothing different if they tore her limb from limb, or if she did, it would be worthless for she would resile as soon as the torture ended. The judges backed off. Torture was authorised by canon law in inquisitorial proceedings, but there were plenty of contemporaries who objected to the practice, including several of the assessors. They thought that it would discredit the trial in the eyes of public opinion. The general view was that they already had enough to convict her, and nothing would be gained by torturing her.[80]

Joan's adversaries were by now becoming impatient of the delay. The University of Paris wrote to Cauchon and to Henry VI, urging them that the time had come to bring matters to a conclusion. This seems to have been decisive. A final attempt was made to persuade her to recant on 23 May. A group of assessors entered her cell. They were accompanied by Louis of Luxembourg, Henry VI's Chancellor of France. The twelve articles were read to her. She was told that the judges were satisfied that she was guilty. Unless she recanted, she would be burned. One of the Paris theologians tried to convince her of the folly of holding out any longer. She replied that she 'stood by all that she had said and done'. She would not renounce her voices even if the fire was ready and the executioner waiting.[81]

In canon law, the fate of a convicted heretic depended on whether she abjured her heresy. If she did, a 'penance' was ordinarily imposed. In the more serious cases, the penance was indefinite imprisonment on bread and water, generally in an ecclesiastical prison. If she did not abjure, or if having previously abjured she apostasised and returned to her heresy, the penalty was death. In theory, ecclesiastical tribunals did not pass death sentences. It was inconsistent with the clerical status of their judges. Instead, the formal sentencing followed a well-settled ritual. The condemned person was brought to a public place, where a sermon was preached describing her sins and explaining for the edification of the audience why she had been convicted. The preacher then called on her three times to recant her heresy. When he had finished, the inquisitor read out the formal sentence, which was that she should be 'released to the secular arm' with a hypocritical prayer for mercy. The sequel was automatic. She was summarily sentenced to death by a secular judge and burned at the stake, while the churchmen hurriedly left the scene so as not to be involved.

On 24 May 1431 Joan of Arc was brought in a tumbril through the streets of Rouen to the cemetery of the Benedictine Abbey of St Ouen, the largest open space in the city, where a crowd of several thousand people had gathered. Two large stages had been built. On one of them the two judges sat, surrounded by some forty ecclesiastical dignitaries, including the principal assessors at the trial, together with their chaplains, notaries and clerks. Prominent among them were Henry VI's chief English and French councillors: Cardinal Beaufort, Louis of Luxembourg, Bishop Alnwick of Norwich, Jean de Mailly Bishop of Noyon and President of the Chambre des Comptes of Paris, and Robert Jolivet Abbot of Mont-Saint-Michel. On the other stage stood the *bailli* of Rouen with the lay officials. Joan was taken to a third platform occupied by the solitary figure of Guillaume Erard, the Parisian theologian who was to preach the sermon. The executioner waited by the tumbril. The stake and bonfire had been prepared but they were out of sight, for executions could not be carried out on consecrated ground. Erard delivered the kind of sermon that was standard on these occasions. He dwelt on the duty of every Christian to adhere to the teaching of the Church and retailed all of the ways in which Joan had separated herself from the Church by her acts and beliefs. He made no attempt to disguise the essentially political character of Joan's crimes. He damned the cause of the Valois King. In a phrase which several members of the audience remembered a quarter of a century later, he declared that the 'noble house of France had always been without stain or reproach'. No true King of France could possibly depend for support on a sorcerer and a heretic, as Charles VII had done. When Erard had finished, there was a brief altercation between the preacher and Joan, in which she defended the honour of Charles VII and then tried, too late, to appeal to the Pope. The appeal was brushed aside as Erard called on her the prescribed three times to repent. He was received each time by silence.

Cauchon then began to read the sentence of the tribunal. It was a long document and he read it slowly, while Erard continued to urge Joan to recant. Joan, said Cauchon, was an 'inventor of revelations and visions, a seducer of the faithful, a presumptuous, credulous, obstinate, superstitious pseudo-prophetess, and a seditious and cruel apostate and schismatic'. Before he had finished reading there was unexpected *coup de théâtre*. Joan interrupted him to declare that she would recant after all. She said that she would observe all the commands of the Church and do everything that the tribunal required of her. She added that since the churchmen had said that her voices were not to be believed, she no longer desired to believe in them.

'Thus,' recorded the notary, 'before a great crowd of clergy and people she declared her revocation and abjuration.' There was consternation among the ecclesiastical dignitaries. Cauchon was taken by surprise. He turned to Henry Beaufort and asked him what to do. Beaufort replied that in the light of her abjuration, she had to be treated as a penitent. A penitent could not be released to the secular arm. Some of the assessors came up to the bishop and remonstrated with him. Harsh words were exchanged. But Cauchon and Erard insisted. A written form of abjuration was produced, and Joan marked it with a cross by way of signature. Cauchon then took up a fresh document from which he read out a sentence of life imprisonment on the 'bread of anguish and the water of sorrow'. At that, she was delivered into the custody of the *bailli* and taken back under guard to her prison cell. There, she was given woman's clothing to wear, and her head was shaved so that it would grow back as a woman's.[82]

Four days later, Joan was found by her jailers to be wearing a tunic, a cap and other items of male clothing. The captain of her guards went to fetch Cauchon and Le Maistre, who arrived with some of the assessors to see for themselves. They were joined by the Earl of Warwick with some notaries to record the scene. The wearing of male clothing had been a prominent part of the case against her. Her resumption of the practice was taken to be clear evidence of apostasy. How did it come about? There is no doubt that many of the English at Rouen had wanted Joan burned and were furious at what they saw as the technicality that had enabled her to escape her fate. According to the evidence given to the posthumous inquiry by the tribunal's bailiff, when Cauchon asked Joan for an explanation, she claimed to have been framed by her English jailers, who had taken away her female clothes at night leaving her nothing but male clothes to wear. But the bailiff had not been present and neither of the notaries present endorsed this version, either in their record or in their own evidence to the inquiry. It is impossible to be sure what happened, but the most probable explanation is the one which Joan herself gave according to the official record. Surrounded by male guards, she felt sexually vulnerable in woman's clothing. She told Cauchon and his colleagues that if she was transferred to an ecclesiastical prison, she would wear women's clothes.

In itself, the issue of Joan's clothing might not have been enough to damn her. But it was clear from her answers that she had changed her mind about her abjuration. She had abjured, she said, to save her life. She may not have appreciated in the cemetery of St Ouen that the alternative to a death sentence would be life imprisonment on bread and water. But whether or not she appreciated it at the time, her return to the cell in the castle of Rouen must have brought home to her what that meant. She was still watched all the time by English guards, still locked in leg-irons and chains every night, still unable to attend Mass or take the Eucharist. She told Cauchon that she would rather die than live in such conditions. There was also a belated onset of depression and remorse. She seems to have felt that by renouncing her belief that God spoke to her through her voices, she had renounced God himself. Her voices had returned since the ceremony at St Ouen to rebuke her for betraying them, and she told Cauchon that she had never really intended to do so. In the margin of the record, the notary wrote against these words: 'fatal answer' (*responsio mortifera*). On 29 May 1431, Cauchon, Le Maistre and twenty-nine of the assessors met in the chapel of the Archbishop's palace and resolved to release her to the *bailli* of Rouen to be put to death.[83]

At nine o'clock on 30 May 1431, an hour after the advertised time, Joan was brought weeping from the castle with a large escort of English soldiers and taken to the market square. She was wearing her male clothes and a mitre-shaped cap with the words 'Heretic, Relapsed, Apostate, Idolater'. The great triangular square was packed with onlookers. A bonfire had been built beneath a high platform with a notice in front announcing Joan's sins to the crowd. The ritual of six days earlier was repeated in every detail except for the outcome. This time the sermon was preached by the Paris theologian Nicolas Midi, who had been the most assiduous of the assessors and the chief author of the twelve articles. As soon as it was over, Cauchon and Le Maistre read out the sentence. Then, in accordance with the ordinary ritual, they and the assessors hurriedly left the scene to avoid any overt involvement in the sentence of blood which they had instigated. Joan was delivered to the *bailli* of Rouen, the English soldier Sir Ralph Butler. He was in such a hurry to get the business over that he forgot to pass sentence of death on her as form required, but simply delivered her up to the executioner crying 'Take her away!' ('*Emmenez! Emmenez!*'). Joan was dragged to the stake, praying and clutching a makeshift crucifix as they bound her to the post and lit the fire. Her screams, invoking the names of Jesus, St Michael and St Catherine, carried over the crackling of the flames. Even Cardinal Beaufort, who watched her destruction with the other officials and dignitaries, was moved to tears. When it was all over, he ordered her ashes to be gathered up and cast in the Seine so that they would not become an object of veneration.[84]

The servants of the dual monarchy had always viewed the trial of Joan of Arc as a tool of propaganda. Her 'relapse' into the heresies of which she had been convicted had deprived them of the advantages of a public confession. The judges did their best to make good the loss. On 7 June 1431, a week after Joan's death, they took evidence about her last hours from those who had attended her, including some who had heard her last confession. According to these witnesses she had told them that she had believed that her voices would save her from the executioner. Now she realised that they were really devils sent to deceive her. She was even said to have asked the English to forgive the harm that she had caused them. The circumstances in which this material was collected make it of very slight evidential value. But that did not stop the English from deploying it in letters sent out over the following days in Henry VI's name to the princes of Europe and the bishops and towns of France. After reciting the history of Joan's life and death, the circular declared that Joan was one of a number of false prophets and teachers of heresy who had infected the people of France. By her visions and revelations, she had inflicted 'very grave damage to our nation'. But now, it was said, she had unequivocally confessed that they were false and deceptive. The same message was delivered to the populace from pulpits in Paris and no doubt other towns of the Lancastrian obedience.[85]

The ashes were hardly cold on Joan's funeral pyre when the first reports of her miraculous survival began to circulate. It was only a matter of time before impostors appeared. The most successful of them, a woman from Lorraine of roughly the right age and appearance called Claude des Armoises, was even endorsed by the real Joan's brothers. She acquired a considerable following. She drew enthusiastic crowds wherever she went, was feted at Orléans, and was briefly taken into the service of the Marshal Gilles de Retz for a projected attack of Le Mans, before being publicly exposed as a fraud in 1440 by the University of Paris and the Parlement.[86] The episode testified to Joan's continuing hold on the popular imagination. But among the more influential figures on both sides of the political divide, the English propaganda offensive succeeded in burying Joan's memory for a generation. She had had plenty of enemies among the French

King's captains, ministers and courtiers. Many of them had always felt uncomfortable about her visions and her male dress. She had now been condemned in accordance with an apparently regular procedure by the Church, the one institution which transcended the political divisions of France. The University of Paris, still the most prestigious authority on theological orthodoxy in Europe, had pronounced against her. Most people were probably inclined to accept these judgements.

Writing from his cathedral in Provence after Joan's capture at Compiègne, Jacques Gélu had urged Charles VII to spare no effort or money to obtain her release. The English certainly anticipated a campaign of litigation at the papal Curia against those involved, or an appeal to the Council of the Church which was about to open at Basel. In the event Charles did nothing. There were no attempts to recapture or ransom her, no moves in Rome or Basel, and no campaign of counter-propaganda. From the court of Charles VII and the bishops of royalist France there was only an embarrassed silence. Brother Richard, the seer who had acted as Joan's John the Baptist and groomed some of her imitators, was arrested by order of Charles VII's Parlement, and forbidden to preach by the Bishop and the Inquisitor of Poitiers. It no longer suited Charles VII's ministers to associate his victories with a convicted sorcerer and heretic.

Only in the 1450s, when Joan's prophecy that the English would be expelled from France had finally come true, was it safe to revisit her extraordinary life in an elaborate posthumous inquiry at least as political as the original trial. By then the principal protagonists, Cauchon and Beaufort, La Trémoille and Regnault de Chartres, were all dead and their ambivalent attitudes to Joan irrelevant. Very few of those involved in her trial had objected to the procedure at the time, but by the 1450s most of them were keen to distance themselves from her fate and cast the whole responsibility for it on the English. It was a version that suited the politics of the time and the patriotism of another age.[87]

CHAPTER VIII

The Parting of Friends, 1431–1434

The arrival of Henry VI in his French realm had been expected to rekindle loyalty to the dual monarchy among the increasingly uncertain populations of northern France. In fact, much of the benefit was lost because the insecurity of the northern provinces prevented the King from showing himself. In April 1430, when Henry arrived at Calais, all the main routes from Calais to Paris were threatened by French garrisons in the Oise valley and the Île-de-France. Rouen was more secure than Paris, but the French companies at Aumale and Torcy had blocked the direct route from Calais and reduced the pays de Caux to chaos. The young King's guardians and councillors were unwilling to risk taking him through a war zone. They had bonfires lit and church bells rung in Paris to mark his arrival, but with a *setier* of wheat rising to forty *sous* and a pint of oil fetching six, Parisians found little to celebrate. Some of them even wondered whether the reports of his arrival in France were true. Pierre Cochon, the chronicler of Rouen, cannot have been the only one to remark on the oddity of celebrating the arrival of a King who came no closer than Calais.[1]

Any residual hopes of a coronation at Reims were eliminated by the inability of the allies to break through to Champagne. The key Dauphinist positions were the cathedral city of Laon and the bridge-town of Lagny on the Marne, which lay across the two main routes to the coronation city. During the siege of Compiègne, John of Luxembourg had detached part of the Burgundian forces around the town and tried to occupy the Laonnais. He succeeded in establishing a base at Crépy-en-Valois, but his army was not strong enough to overcome the large force which the French had established in the fortified abbey of St Vincent beneath the walls of Laon. He was shortly recalled to Compiègne to participate in the last disastrous days of the siege. The English succeeded no better against Lagny. Charles VII's garrison there had been reinforced, and had spread into two subsidiary strongholds, the old but still powerful fortress at Montjay on the hillside opposite, where Louis of Orléans was said to have dabbled in magic and satanic rites, and the walled town and castle of Gournay on the right bank of the Marne eight miles downstream. In March 1431, the Duke of Bedford tried to take Lagny with a force drawn mainly from the garrison of Paris. But, like John of Luxembourg, he did not have the numbers or the time to do it. Gournay and Montjay, which had surrendered to him as he advanced, were swiftly reoccupied by the enemy as soon as he withdrew.[2]

The only plausible alternative venue for the coronation was Paris. The capital, however, was scarcely more accessible than Reims, owing to the disturbed military situation in the Île-de-France. Freelance garrisons fighting in the Dauphin's name sprang up everywhere like mushrooms after rain. A large French company occupied the castle of La Chasse in the forest of Montmorency north of the city, and another occupied and fortified the buildings of the Benedictine abbey of Saint-Maur-les-Fossés by the forest of Vincennes. Substantial forces were sent to the Île-de-France, which quickly recaptured both of these places. Others were cleared in September and October 1430, when the Duke of Norfolk led a sweep across the north of the Île-de-France, and the Earl of Stafford conducted a parallel operation in the Gâtinais and the marches of Brie. But with the transfer of large forces to support Philip the Good in Picardy after the disaster at Compiègne, the situation sharply deteriorated again. The French companies returned to take over abandoned castles, church towers and fortified houses. They choked off the traffic of the roads and rivers, leaving the markets of the towns and cities bare and their populations starving. In the open country, peasants were driven to banditry, fortifying isolated farmhouses or roaming through the region in large and intimidating gangs.[3]

While the King waited in Calais, most of the English army which had accompanied him from England was deployed to Normandy. The Bastard of Clarence was reinforced outside Torcy. The Earl of Stafford opened a new siege at Aumale. Edmund Beaufort took the surrender of La Hire's garrison at Château-Gaillard in early June 1430. Torcy and Aumale followed in July. André de Rambures, who was captured at Aumale, was sent as a prisoner to England where he remained in captivity for more than six years. In July 1430, the northern march of Normandy was finally judged to be secure enough to allow Henry VI to leave Calais for Rouen with a large military escort. He passed through successive towns of Picardy, to be received at the gates in carefully choreographed demonstrations of loyalty. Henry finally made his ceremonial entry into Rouen on 29 July. Everything was done to mark the occasion. The leading citizens received him in their uniform robes of scarlet and purple. The gates were decked with armorial banners and gilded models of heraldic beasts. The street corners were decorated with tableaux ('mysteries'). Every church bell in the city rang out as the King processed through the streets to the cathedral, a 'beautiful child' as one observer remarked. The King did not live up to the occasion. His only audible utterance was a protest against the enthusiastic cries of '*Noel*' from the crowds. He asked them to be less noisy. Then he disappeared into the citadel and was rarely seen in public for the next eighteen months.[4]

The winter of 1430–1 was the worst on record. Anarchy in the north indiscriminately affected communities of both allegiances. But by far the most serious effects were felt in Paris. The traffic of the Oise and the Marne was blocked. Food had had to be brought into the capital over the insecure roads of the Beauce or in escorted convoys of barges from Normandy. They were frequently attacked and suffered heavy losses at the hands of La Hire's men at Louviers and the French companies of the Oise valley. Prices in the city's markets rose to unheard-of levels. The poor, who had nothing to eat but nuts and bread, died in the streets and garrets or fled out of the gates to take their chances in the desolate countryside beyond.[5]

In the course of these terrible months, it became clear that Henry VI's presence in France would have to be extended well beyond the year originally envisaged. This posed serious problems of finance and recruitment. The army's strength was by now well below its peak. In addition to the usual wastage from casualties, disease and desertion, Sir John Clarence's force appears to have gone home after the fall of Torcy in July 1430, when their indentures expired. A number of other companies left in December for the same reason. The men who had come over with the King had indented for twelve months' service until March 1431, but most of them had not been paid since September 1430. The King's council at Rouen had not forgotten the mutiny of the English army at Compiègne. Their correspondence took on an air of desperation. Writing in the King's name to the Corporation of London, they declared that a loan of 10,000 marks now 'would do more ease and service in our present necessity than peradventure should the double and much more at other time'. Yet, like other lenders, the Corporation was unable to help until there was some prospect of tax revenues against which a loan could be secured. At Westminster, the council had already decided that Parliament would have to be summoned in the new year. Cardinal Beaufort returned to England to put the government's case for a further round of taxation.[6]

Parliament opened in the Painted Chamber in the palace of Westminster on 12 January 1431. The opening sermon was delivered by the learned Dr Lyndwood, Keeper of the Privy Seal. He said very little about the war in France, but his text said everything: 'The throne of his Kingdom will be established' (1 Chronicles 22:10). The Commons rose to the occasion. New taxes, although not publicly announced until the last day of the session on 20 March 1431, were probably agreed within a few days of the opening. In addition to the customary trade duties, the Commons granted a standard subsidy payable in November 1431 and another third of a subsidy payable in April 1432. There was also to be a tax of a pound on every knight's fee, in effect a land tax. With matching grants from the clergy, these taxes were expected to bring in about £75,000. The King's ministers in England diverted every penny that they could find to the French war, putting off other calls on their resources, such as the defence of Ireland, the garrison of Calais and the payment of outstanding arrears from previous campaigns. But until the subsidies came in their main resource was borrowing. The council embarked on the most successful campaign of borrowing in the whole of the fifteenth century. Nearly £65,000 was raised in the first half of 1431. Even Henry V at his most masterful had not managed such a feat. The Cardinal had become the dominant figure on both sides of the Channel. He contributed no less than £20,000. The recruitment of the new expeditionary army was mainly the work of his nephews, Edmund Count of Mortain and Thomas Count of Perche. In the space of three months, some 3,500 men were raised, the largest expedition of the reign to date after the one that had come over with the King the year before.[7]

The new army sailed for France in stages between April and July 1431. It brought the total number serving in northern France back to something like the peak figure of 10,000 to 11,000 men achieved in the summer of 1430. The surge enabled the council at Rouen to harden the defences of Normandy and to open a way to Paris for the King's coronation. The main obstacle which they still had to clear was La Hire's garrison at Louviers. It was probably the largest French garrison north of the Loire and certainly the most dangerous, owing to its position at the heart of Normandy. Willoughby and Scales had laid siege to the place in the previous September but had underestimated the forces required and abandoned the operation after a month. With the prospect of fresh troops crossing the Channel, the council decided to try again in April 1431. By then the place presented an even more formidable challenge, for the defenders had refortified it over the winter and the Bastard of Orléans had brought in additional troops. Willoughby arrived outside the town in April with an advance guard of 1,200 men. When the Beaufort brothers landed at Calais in May with the first division of the expeditionary army, they were directed to join him. At an early stage, they enjoyed a stroke of luck. La Hire left the town to organise an army of relief, but as he crossed the Beauce he ran into a company from the Burgundian garrison of Dourdan. He was recognised and captured and remained a prisoner until the following year. La Hire's capture nearly led to the fall of Louviers. His Gascon companions lost heart and secretly negotiated a deal with the besiegers. La Hire's brother Amadoc, who had taken over the command of the defence, eventually recovered control and repudiated the deal, and the Gascons fought on. The English redoubled their efforts. They bridged the Eure with pontoons. They brought in several hundred more men from Rouen and Lower Normandy. At its highest point, the besieging army was well over 4,000 strong, comparable to the army which had besieged Orléans.[8]

Charles VII's captains did what they could to relieve Louviers. On the northern march of Normandy, Marshal Boussac had established his headquarters at Beauvais. Boussac and Poton de Saintrailles mounted a series of diversions in the hope of drawing off at least part of the besieging army. In August 1431, when the position of the defenders of Louviers was becoming desperate, they assembled a large force to march on Rouen. Hoping to recover some of the spirit of 1429, they brought with them William the Gevaudan shepherd, the seer who preached a message very similar to Joan of Arc's. According to an unfriendly English source, they thought that 'if he had laid his hand on a castle wall ... it should have fallen down by the power of his holiness'. But Boussac's plans were discovered by English spies. As the Marshal's army gathered in the village of Milly outside Beauvais, it was surprised by an English force from Gournay commanded by the Earls of Warwick and Stafford. The French only just had time to collect on high ground and form up in battle order. As the English advanced up the hill on foot, the French Marshal ordered a cavalry charge. It was a disorderly affair. The leading horsemen were enveloped by the enemy. The rest of the cavalry, including the whole of one wing, turned and fled, the Marshal among them. Sixty prominent prisoners were taken, including Poton de Saintrailles and the hapless shepherd. The battle of Milly sealed the fate of Louviers. The garrison capitulated a few days later on 22 October in the seventh month of the siege. Three days later the defenders marched out of the gates with what property they could carry. The defences of the town were methodically razed to the ground. The siege had consumed the entire summer and occupied a large part of the English army in France.[9]

At Rouen, the final decision to go ahead with the coronation in Paris was made as soon as the capitulation of Louviers was sealed. Invitations were sent out on the day that the English entered the town. The letters, drafted in Henry VI's name by Jean Rinel, made a virtue of necessity. The coronation ceremony, he argued, had not always been performed at Reims. A list of kings who had been crowned elsewhere was given, starting with Pepin the Short. Was not Paris the capital and chief city of France? Custodian of the relics of the passion of Christ conserved in the Sainte-Chapelle, was it not also among the holiest?[10]

Since the raising of the siege of Compiègne, Charles VII's ministers had reoriented their strategy so as to make Philip the Good their main target. They hoped, by reminding the Duke of the heavy cost of the alliance, to drive a bigger wedge between him and the English. The main focus of the French offensive was the duchy of Burgundy itself. In the summer of 1430 Arnaud-Guilhem de Barbazan, recently released from his prison at Château-Gaillard, was appointed as Charles VII's Captain-General in Champagne. Barbazan was an extremely capable soldier. '*Expert, subtil et renommé en fait de guerre*', was what a contemporary said about him. His long captivity had not blunted his skills. He concentrated his forces in southern Champagne, where a chain of Burgundian garrisons controlled most of the crossings of the Seine and the Aube. During the calamitous winter of 1430–1, Barbazan captured all of these Burgundian bridge-towns except for Bar-sur-Seine. Chappes, the strongest of them and the last to be attacked, briefly became the flashpoint of an intense regional struggle. The Marshal of Burgundy, Antoine de Toulongeon, made a determined attempt to relieve it with 1,800 men from the duchy and 600 Englishmen sent by Sir Thomas Gargrave from the Bassigny. For his part, Barbazan summoned help from Réné of Anjou, who arrived with 500 Lorrainers in the later stages of the siege. On 13 December 1430, the Burgundians and their English auxiliaries were defeated in a pitched battle south of the fortress and retreated into Burgundy, abandoning their baggage and artillery and leaving Barbazan to take the surrender of the garrison. The result of this campaign was to expose the whole of the northern march of Burgundy to incursions from Champagne.[11]

Parallel offensives against the duchy of Burgundy were launched from the west and south. In November 1430, Georges de la Trémoille was appointed as Charles's lieutenant in the Auxerrois and Burgundy. In the opening months of 1431, a fresh wave of freelance captains moved into the region from the Loire under his patronage. Auxerre was shortly surrounded by hostile garrisons, and by June was threatening to submit to Charles VII. At the same time, the Count of Clermont was nominated as lieutenant on the southern march of the duchy and opened an aggressive campaign in the Charolais and the Mâconnais in conjunction with the Castilian *routier* captain Rodrigo de Villandrando. Faced with simultaneous attacks from three directions at once, Philip's councillors at Lille and Dijon were unable to cope. They were maintaining nearly 4,000 men permanently under arms, distributed between the Somme front, the county of Rethel in north-eastern Champagne, and the marches of Burgundy. It was more than the army which they had deployed at Compiègne. The cost was punitive. Philip's search for an exit from the Anglo-French war took on a new urgency.[12]

In the spring of 1431, a fresh crisis added to Philip's burdens. Charles Duke of Lorraine died at Nancy on 25 January 1431 after a long illness, leaving his domains to be contested in a bitter war of succession. With his last breath the old Duke had urged his son-in-law and designated successor Réné of Anjou never to cross the Dukes of Burgundy if he wished to live happy and powerful. But Réné was never likely to heed this advice. He was Charles VII's brother-in-law and he needed the French King's support to survive a powerful challenge from Antoine Count of Vaudémont. The Count was one of the leading barons of Champagne and Lorraine and the principal regional ally of the Dukes of Burgundy. He was also the last Duke's nephew and closest male relative. He had never accepted the diversion of the succession to the house of Anjou. In April 1431, Réné declared war on him. Vaudémont did not have the manpower to hold his own against the combined strength of the nobility of Lorraine and Bar, almost all of whom supported Réné. So, leaving his wife in charge of his lands, he fled to the court of Burgundy to appeal for help. He found Philip the Good closeted with his principal councillors at Hesdin. The Marshal of Burgundy Antoine de Toulongeon and a number of Burgundian councillors had arrived from Dijon with gloomy reports of the military situation in the aftermath of Barbazan's campaigns. Philip's advisers were divided. The men of Artois and Picardy were alarmed by recent French incursions in the Somme valley. Three weeks before, an attempt on the important town of Corbie had very nearly succeeded. They wanted Philip to husband his strength in the north. The Marshal of Burgundy on the other hand saw the worst of the crisis emerging in his own region, where the forces at his disposal were too thinly spread. He wanted troops transferred there from the north. For Philip, the acquisition of Lorraine by the leading princely house of Armagnac France would be a geopolitical disaster. He sided with Toulongeon. On 4 May he ordered the transfer to the north-east of all the men that could be spared from the Somme front.[13]

In about the middle of May 1431, Réné of Anjou invaded the county of Vaudémont with an army of Lorrainers and Germans. They were joined there by all of Charles VII's partisans who were within reach. Robert of Baudricourt came from Vaucouleurs, and Arnaud-Guilhem de Barbazan from Champagne. Contemporaries estimated their total strength at about 6,000 mounted men-at-arms and some 1,500 foot-soldiers. It was a large army, but of very uneven quality. The cavalry contingents of Baudricourt and Barbazan were experienced veterans. But the Lorraine cavalry was a formless mass. The foot-soldiers were poorly armed urban levies. There were hardly any archers. With this motley force Réné laid siege to the castle of Vaudémont on its spur of rock towering 500 feet above the valley of the Moselle. Some 200 miles away Antoine de Toulongeon mustered about 1,500 men from Picardy and Artois made available by Philip's council. In about the middle of June, they joined forces in northern Burgundy with some 1,800 mounted men raised by Philip's officers at Dijon. Sir Thomas Gargrave arrived from the Bassigny with a contingent of English troops, mostly archers. Altogether, Antoine de Toulongeon must have had between 3,500 and 4,000 men at his disposal when he finally advanced against Réné's host. They were heavily outnumbered, but their army was composed of veterans with better discipline, better equipment and better leaders.

The two armies met on 2 July near Bulgnéville, a castle by the old road from Neufchâtel to Nancy about twenty-five miles south of Vaudémont. Sir Thomas Gargrave took charge of the array, ordering it according to classic English tactical doctrine. The men dug themselves into a prepared position across the path of Réné's army, on rising ground with the sun behind them. They stood on the defensive, dismounted, with their archers and artillery on the wings. The cavalrymen of the two Burgundies, who had wanted to fight a chivalrous battle on horseback, were firmly told that this would not be allowed. The men of Bar and Lorraine launched a frontal attack on them on foot. The battle lasted barely a quarter of an hour. Réné's army was scattered in the opening moments. The Burgundian cavalry remounted and pursued them for three hours across the plain. More than 2,000 of them were killed and several hundred captured. Barbazan, who had advised against a frontal attack, was among the dead. Réné himself was taken prisoner by a Hainaut squire and sold to his arch-enemy, Philip of Burgundy.[14]

The battle of Bulgnéville relieved some of the pressure on the Duke but it did nothing to mitigate his grievances against the English. Early in May 1431, Quentin Ménard, one of Philip the Good's household officers, arrived at Westminster to discuss the military situation with Cardinal Beaufort and the English council. Ménard brought with him an ultimatum. Unless by the end of June the English agreed to support the defence of the Duke's territory with their own troops and at their own expense, Philip would resort to 'other measures' to safeguard his interests. The reference to 'other measures' was not lost on Henry VI's ministers. It was a scarcely veiled threat to open direct negotiations with Charles VII and withdraw from the war. Neither Beaufort nor the English council at Westminster was willing to take that risk. They referred Philip's ultimatum to the King's councillors at Rouen, who took the same view. In spite of the financial and military constraints, they agreed to send John of Luxembourg with 1,800 men to support the defence of Philip's northern territories. But they confessed themselves unable to help in Burgundy.[15]

In fact, the Duke had already opened negotiations with Charles VII without waiting for the expiry of his ultimatum. While Ménard was at Westminster, his Chamberlain Jean de la Trémoille lord of Jonvelle was discussing an extended truce, initially limited to eastern France, with his brother Georges at Chinon. In September, they agreed upon a truce of two years limited to Burgundy and Champagne. Three months later, in December 1431, Regnault de Chartres led an embassy to Philip's headquarters at Lille and agreed a six-year truce covering all fronts. The terms included a proviso which allowed Philip to perform his treaty obligations to the English. But that meant very little, since the only firm military obligation that Philip had ever assumed was the promise given at Amiens in 1423 to provide 500 troops when required. There was a secret side-agreement which effectively prevented Philip from assuming any greater obligation to the English. If these terms had been observed, they would in practice have put an end to military cooperation between Burgundy and England. Philip understood this perfectly well. On the day before the instrument was sealed, he notified his ally of its terms and offered an explanation. The English had not sent him the troops he needed. They had not paid for his armies. He could no longer support the cost of defending his domains. He had given them plenty of warning of the likely consequences. The war had to come to an end as far as he was concerned. It was the letter of a man who had always acknowledged his political obligations to the English government but had never regarded the war as a joint enterprise. The Duke of Bedford replied in equally abrasive terms. It was the beginning of a long period of coolness between the brothers-in-law.[16]

What saved the Anglo-Burgundian alliance in 1431 was the inability of either party to the new truces to enforce them on their partisans. According to a hostile report, Charles VII's representatives candidly admitted this. Their master, they said, 'employed only outsiders in his wars, to whom he abandoned the countryside, and on this point they would not obey him'. The French King's ministers made the same point about the soldiers of the Duke of Burgundy. In a list of their complaints about Burgundian breaches of the truce in Picardy, they put their finger on the problem. Philip's officers could not enforce discipline on soldiers who were not employed full time in paid service. The fact that the truce did not bind the English made matters worse. A number of Burgundian captains simply declared themselves to be in English service and carried on the fight. The duchy of Burgundy was particularly badly affected. On the southern march of the duchy, companies operating under the nominal command of the Count of Clermont continued their operations in the Charolais and the Mâconnais as if nothing had changed. On the eastern and northern marches of Burgundy, the *routier* offensive inaugurated by La Trémoille the year before continued with unabated fury. One of La Trémoille's captains, the notorious Jacques d'Espailly ('Forte-Épice') had come over the walls of Avallon on New Year's Eve 1431 with 200 men. They sacked the town and remained in occupation for nearly two years, planting subsidiary garrisons across northern Burgundy and threatening Auxerre, Tonnerre and Vézélay. Large bands of irregulars fortified themselves in Cravant, in the nearby castle and town of Mailly and in the walled town of Chablis. Ducal revenues collapsed across much of the region.[17]

On 2 December 1430 Henry VI, then four days short of his tenth birthday, approached the walls of his capital across the plain of Saint-Denis. It was a bitterly cold day with the frost lying thick on the ground. The King was mounted on a white horse, dressed in robes of gold and blue and wearing a black cloth hat. Four squires bearing his sword and crown rode ahead of him, escorted by a cloud of liveried heralds and trumpeters. The young King was accompanied by his French Chancellor Louis of Luxembourg, Cardinal Beaufort and the Duke of Bedford, Bishop Alnwick, the young Duke of York, the Earls of Warwick, Arundel, Salisbury and Stafford, and a dense throng of native French captains, bishops and officials. The Parisians had given much thought to the King's reception. In spite of the surrounding poverty, the citizens had spared no expense to make it as spectacular as possible. The municipality laid out nearly a year's revenue. The Provost of the Merchants met the royal cavalcade in the open plain between Paris and Saint-Denis. He was followed by all the leading citizens of official Paris: the magistrates, the officers of the watch, the councillors of the Parlement and the Chambre des Comptes, the staff of the government offices and the state secretariat and the faculties of the University, all in the uniform robes and caps of their offices.

The Rue Saint-Denis, the paved street which led from the Porte Saint-Denis to the Châtelet, was the royal road of medieval Paris, the scene of the arrivals and departures of armies and embassies, of emperors, princes and royal brides, the traditional route of the *joyeuses entrées* by which every King of France marked his accession, and of the state funerals which awaited them at the end. The street was packed. As Henry's procession made its way into the city the guilds took it in turns to walk beside him holding over his head a blue silk canopy embroidered with gold fleurs-de-lys. Outside the churches the clergy stood wearing their robes and holding their relics. At intervals, there were displays, mimes, 'mysteries' and *tableaux vivants*. The captured seer William the Shepherd was brought from his cell at Rouen trussed up with rope to be exhibited from a stand by the roadside, his last appearance in public before they quietly drowned him in the Seine. On a platform in front of the Châtelet, just before the procession reached the Pont aux Change, an image of the child-King was shown, surmounted by the two crowns of England and France, and flanked by actors representing the Duke of Burgundy and his brothers and principal captains offering him the arms of France from one side, while figures representing the Duke of Bedford, Cardinal Beaufort, and the leading English noblemen presented the arms of England on the other. Henry was taken to the palace on the Cité to inspect more holy relics and to the Hôtel Saint-Pol to meet his grandmother, Isabelle of Bavaria, an almost forgotten figure from France's contentious past, before retiring to the Hôtel des Tournelles opposite. The men around him were too suspicious of the turbulent environment of Paris to let him stay for long in his subjects' sight. On the next morning he was carried off to the safety of Vincennes, where he remained for the next fortnight.[18]

Henry VI was crowned in Notre-Dame cathedral on 16 December 1431. A high platform had been built beneath the crossing of the church, preceded by a great staircase, all covered in royal blue cloth embroidered with gold fleurs-de-lys. The King processed up the nave with two crowns, for England and France, carried before him. He ascended the stairs and was seated on a broad stool in the middle of the platform. He swore to protect the liberties of the French Church and govern his French subjects with wisdom and mercy. He was anointed with holy oil. The regalia were retrieved from the treasury of the abbey of Saint-Denis. The spurs and the sword of state were presented to him, followed by ring, sceptre and orb. At the end of the ceremony the King was seated on the throne, holding the crown of England in his hands, as the crown of France was placed on his head and the Cardinal led the packed congregation in the acclamation: '*Vivat rex in aeternum*'.

The chroniclers reported that the service was conducted according to the rite of England, not France. This was untrue, but it was probably what most people believed. The order of service used was the coronation order of Charles V, carefully modified to omit references to Reims and its Archbishop. But the chroniclers' mistake was a revealing one, for very little was done to manage French sensitivities or live up to the ideology of the dual monarchy. The claims of the Bishop of Paris to conduct the ceremony were brushed aside by Cardinal Beaufort, who insisted on performing it himself. The canons of Notre-Dame were outraged when an official carried off the gold goblet from which the King drank the communion wine, instead of lodging it in the cathedral treasury as tradition demanded (it was later recovered after an unseemly wrangle). The Mass which followed the coronation ceremony was sung by English choristers of the Chapel Royal, perhaps in the beautiful polyphonic setting (*Missa da gaudiorum premia*) which John Dunstaple is thought to have composed to mark the marriage of the King's parents and the conclusion of the treaty of Troyes. The traditional order of ceremony had a large place for the twelve peers of France and the officers of state, but the only peers present were the Bishops of Beauvais and Noyon. The Duke of Burgundy, the senior peer of France, was at Lille, negotiating the six-year truce with Charles VII's chancellor. He later claimed to have disapproved of the whole ceremony, because it damaged the prospects of a general peace, on which his hopes now rested. The Duke of Brittany, nominally an English ally, was not there either. His presence would have compromised his attempts to stay in with both sides. The roles of the six lay peers of France appear to have been taken by English noblemen. The Constable of France, whose part it was to place the sword of state in the King's hands, was an Englishman, Humphrey Earl of Stafford. Other Englishmen occupied most of the places of honour, both in the cathedral and at the state banquet which followed in the palace. The banquet was a public relations disaster. No seating had been reserved for the municipality, the councillors of the Parlement or the representatives of the University. They found themselves obliged to sit with common tradesmen in the body of the hall, to be served indifferent meat cooked four days in advance which was pronounced to be inedible. Even the sick from the Hôtel-Dieu, who traditionally attended the ceremony to receive alms, declared themselves to be ill-served.[19]

'The English were in charge of all of this and cared nothing for the honour of the occasion', the city's chronicler grumbled. They had done less for the depressed luxury trades than the average bourgeois marrying his daughter. 'Truly no one had a good word to say about it.' Except for the English. They at least were satisfied. It was 'worthily done, with all the solemnity that might be done and ordained', they told themselves. Yet the occasion manifestly failed in its main object, which was to promote the legitimacy of the dual monarchy to the French. None of the traditional gestures were observed. No prisoners were amnestied. No taxes were remitted. The King presided at a formal session of the Parlement, at which he was surrounded by English noblemen and, although brought up to speak excellent French, addressed the councillors briefly and in English. On the day after Christmas, a flowery letter was issued in the young King's name lauding the city of Paris and declaring that he felt as much at home there as the Roman Emperors in Rome. The whole court then left for Rouen, and from there rode to Calais. With him went most of the great lords who had crossed with him to France in 1430. On 16 February 1432, they sailed for England.[20]

Henry VI received an extravagant welcome in London. Blackheath was packed as the Mayor and aldermen went out by the Old Kent Road to meet him. From London Bridge to Ludgate the streets were filled with cheering crowds. The tableaux of London were more stridently political than anything that had been seen in Paris. At London Bridge, model giants flanked by heraldic beasts bearing the arms of England and France proclaimed that they would lay low the King's enemies. At Cheapside a mock castle was flanked by figures of Edward the Confessor and St Louis and a divided genealogical tree showed Henry's descent from the royal houses of both realms.

> And all the people glad of look and cheer
> Thanked God with all their hearts entire
> To see their King with two crowns shine
> From two trees truly set the line.[21]

The King returned to a political crisis at Westminster, of which he must have been conscious even at his age. Its origin was the unremitting hostility of Humphrey Duke of Gloucester to Cardinal Beaufort, and his desire to stamp his personal authority on the government of England after nearly two years in which Beaufort had directed policy in both realms. Humphrey's plans had been maturing for months. But they acquired a fresh urgency with the prospect of the return of the King and the councillors who had been with him in France. His weapon was the fourteenth-century statute of praemunire, which had been passed to counter the claims of the papacy to international jurisdiction in ecclesiastical matters. It forbade the introduction of papal bulls into England without licence, on pain of forfeiture. Beaufort was believed to have obtained a papal bull exempting him as a cardinal and papal legate from the jurisdiction of the Archbishop of Canterbury. At the same time, Gloucester prepared charges of treason against his rival, which although never used were widely publicised. His object was to ruin Beaufort financially and to deprive him of his political influence, which was mainly based on his wealth. He hoped to garner support by arguing that Beaufort's forfeited assets would fund the war without recourse to Parliamentary taxation.[22]

At the end of November 1431, the Duke of Gloucester had persuaded the council to authorise the opening of criminal proceedings against Beaufort. News of this development must have reached the Cardinal in Paris as he was about to officiate at the coronation ceremony in Notre-Dame cathedral. His first instinct was to stay out of England until the storm had blown over. He accompanied Henry VI as far as Calais on his return to England, and then excused himself on the ground that the Pope had called him to the Curia at Rome. But while the royal party was at Calais, news arrived that changed his mind. On the night of 6 February, the Duke of Gloucester discovered four great chests containing all Beaufort's liquid riches, gold and silver plate, bullion and coin, being loaded by night into a ship at Sandwich to be carried to their owner on the continent. The export of these commodities required a royal licence, which Beaufort had not had the foresight to obtain. Gloucester impounded the chests in the King's name. Without his wealth, Beaufort could neither maintain himself on the continent nor retain his political influence in England. He now had no choice but to return to fight his corner.

In the first instance, Beaufort withdrew to the court of Philip the Good in Flanders, where he would be well placed to follow developments in England as they unfolded. From Ghent, he wrote to rally potential allies in England. He told them that the charges against him were baseless and that he would go before Parliament 'to know the causes why I am thus strangely demeaned and declare myself as a man that have not deserved so to be treated'. Meanwhile, Gloucester set about destroying Beaufort's network of friends and clients. On

25 February, he used the King's authority to dismiss all Beaufort's allies from their offices and replace them with his friends. When one of the old councillors, Ralph Lord Cromwell, complained that this had happened without notice and contrary to the standing orders, he was told that it was a sufficient justification that 'it pleased the lord of Gloucester and the others on the council present that it should be done'.[23]

On the day of Gloucester's purge, the reconstituted council summoned Parliament. This was intended to be the scene of Gloucester's showdown with the Cardinal. The Duke anticipated an easy ride. But when the session opened on 12 May, he found that he had overplayed his hand. The purged officers and councillors were sitting on the benches with their friends and allies. Many of the Lords had served in France and knew the value of Beaufort's services. Others were personal guarantors of his loans and were becoming worried about the consequences of his destruction for their own fortunes. When Beaufort himself arrived from Flanders in June, his friends rallied to his defence. The Cardinal appeared in Parliament, and from his seat among the Lords called on anyone who accused him of treason to come forward with the charge and justify it. Gloucester's bluff had been called. He hastily conferred with the Lords. They agreed that the King would declare from the throne that Beaufort was not accused of any treason, and that he, Henry, regarded him as his loyal subject. The Commons petitioned the King to cancel the writ of praemunire. The council took fright. On 3 July, they negotiated a deal with the Cardinal. The writ was cancelled and all proceedings against him were dropped. Beaufort's treasure was restored to him in return for a loan of another £6,000 for the war in France and a deposit of £6,000 to abide a decision about its illegal export. His existing loans, amounting to 13,000 marks (£8,667) would be satisfied from the proceeds of the next Parliamentary subsidy in priority to all other debts. But in spite of this setback to his campaign, Gloucester won one notable victory. The council continued for the time being to be packed with his nominees. Beaufort was excluded. This enabled his rival to dominate the government in England for the next year.[24]

In France, the Duke of Bedford resumed his powers as Regent as soon as Henry VI boarded his ship at Calais. The pageants of Paris and London had pushed uncomfortable truths into the background which now had to be faced. In spite of the King's two years in France with the largest English army to serve there since Henry V's time, England's strategic situation had not fundamentally changed. The lesson of the coronation expedition was that in the face of the revived Valois monarchy, a temporary surge was not enough. The occupation of northern France would require a continuous effort by larger forces for longer periods than England could sustain. The English were never likely to recover control of the vital river valleys while cities and towns like Orléans, Compiègne and Louviers were able to hold out against them for months. In a series of letters addressed to the King in England, the municipality of Paris expressed themselves in strong terms. The King's presence, they reported, had generated high expectations which had been disappointed. England's political credit was spent. People felt abandoned when Henry returned to England with most of his army. Their loyalty to his cause, the Parisians declared, had been rewarded only by poverty and misery. Their message was the same as the Duke of Burgundy's. The house of Lancaster would have to maintain a much larger permanent establishment in France if it was to be taken seriously.[25]

With the departure of the King, the number of English troops at the Regent's disposal declined to somewhere between 5,000 and 5,600 men, about the level which had been normal before their arrival. The English had given much thought to the best way of deploying these forces. The existing system for withdrawing troops from garrisons for service in the field had worked well enough when the English were on the offensive, as they generally had been before 1429. But it had proved to be incapable of defending its territory against multiple threats from several directions at once. The English had been forced to adopt a defensive strategy, tying down almost all their available forces in more than forty royal garrisons. This had made it exceptionally difficult to put an army into the field. Only the diversion of Beaufort's crusading army had enabled them to confront Charles VII's armies after the disaster at Patay. The Regent's government took the lesson to heart. Over the following years, the defence of Normandy was reorganised to create larger field armies. In 1429 Bedford had introduced a system of *creus* (increases) to enable the strength of particular garrisons to be varied as the local situation required. The larger garrisons were boosted by additional forces stationed there for 'lodging and accommodation', which could be withdrawn at any time to serve in field armies. They served under the command of regional captains for long periods, generally from spring to October. In the early 1430s, the regional captains usually employed were the Earl of Arundel and Robert Lord Willoughby. They commanded what amounted to large mobile reserves capable of intervening rapidly at critical points. The new system was formalised in the terms of service for garrisons introduced in the autumn of 1434, but it had been in force for some time before that. In the spring of 1432, after Henry VI's return to England, a third of English troops serving in Normandy were assigned to field service. A year later more than half of them were serving in the field in different parts of the duchy.[26]

The limiting factor for everything that the English did in France was money. The financial administration in Normandy was operating in conditions of mounting difficulty. The cost of the duchy's defence was met mainly from the periodical *aides* granted by the Estates of Normandy. In principle the Estates aimed to cover the full cost of the duchy's defence. At times of peak military activity, their grants could be very large. In 1431, when military activity was at its height, the Estates had met no less than three times and voted a total of 410,000 *livres*, the largest amount that they ever granted in a single year. But the Estates were sensitive to economic conditions and to the complaints of the population. After the King's departure, they reverted to the earlier pattern of making lower grants, generally with a nominal value between 160,000 and 200,000 *livres* a year. A budget prepared for the Duke of Bedford by his Norman accounting staff at the end of 1433 gives a good idea of the state of the finances of Normandy (excluding Maine). Since the crisis of 1429 the administration had sweated its assets in the duchy and increased the government's permanent revenues by nearly 30 per cent to some 180,000 *livres* a year. In the current year, the Estates had voted an *aide* of 160,000 *livres*, making a total revenue of 340,000 *livres*. But budgeted expenditure came to 377,622 *livres*, of which about two-thirds represented the cost of the army in Normandy. The accountants were therefore assuming a deficit of nearly 40,000 *livres*.[27]

In the first half of the 1430s, Normandy could probably still just about fund its own government and defence. It could not fund the government and defence of the rest of Lancastrian France. The French conquests had reduced tax receipts outside Normandy to zero, except for the exiguous revenues of the city of Paris and of a handful of towns in Picardy such as Amiens and Abbeville. This posed serious problems for the Regent's government, which was still meeting the wage bill of the English garrisons but was unable to pay either the civil service or the indigenous troops on its payroll. The English councillors with the King at Rouen struggled to find money for the indigenous troops but were distinctly unsympathetic to the claims of the civil servants. When, in October 1430, the councillors of the Parlement complained that their pay was now two years in arrears, they were told that there were more urgent priorities. In February 1431 they were still waiting and went on strike. Bedford, when he resumed his powers, took a softer line with a body of men whose status and influence had never been properly appreciated by the more abrasive English councillors. He agreed to make the pay of the council and the Parlement the first charge on the revenues of France. Even this was only possible because of a drastic reduction in the number of judges and officers on the payroll. The other *grands corps* suffered the same mixture of defaults and redundancies. When, in November 1431, the Grand Conseil reviewed the government's finances, they ordered a sale of all confiscated land in the government's hands to clear some of the mounting arrears. But they recognised that this was no more than a temporary patch. In the longer term, they advised, not even the heaviest taxes levied in Normandy for years and the '*très grosses finances*' currently coming from England would enable Lancastrian France to be defended.[28]

The '*très grosses finances*' from England were becoming a significant issue on both sides of the Channel. Henry VI's return to England was followed by a prolonged financial crisis. The coronation expedition had been the most expensive campaign of the reign. The cost, including the advance guard of Sir John Clarence and the subsidies paid to the Duke of Burgundy, came to more than £170,000. Normally, the cost to English revenues would have been limited to the advances paid to the men in England and their shipping costs. Expenditure in France would have been met by the Treasurers at Rouen and Paris. This time, the English Exchequer had to pay most of the charges incurred in France as well. Normandy contributed only about £40,000 and the rest of Lancastrian France nothing at all. In the final year of the coronation expedition, chests of English coin had been regularly laden into ships in Kent and Sussex and carried across the Channel for delivery to the King's officers at Rouen or Dieppe. These chests marked the beginning of a significant shift of the burden of the war from French to English revenues.[29]

Early in 1431 the council at Westminster decided that there was no alternative but to treat the wages of the French *grands corps* and the 1,800 indigenous soldiers currently in English service as a charge on the revenues of England. The new policy was never systematically followed because the revenues of England were not equal to the task. But large transfers were made to meet the most pressing commitments. John of Luxembourg received his retainer from English funds. His army received its wages from the same source when they mustered in July 1431. His cousin, the Bastard of Saint-Pol, who commanded the important garrison on the Marne at Meaux, was also paid from England. Over the following months, English revenues were used on an ad hoc basis to patch holes in the funding of operations beyond the marches of Normandy whenever disaster threatened to overwhelm them. But the high levels of direct taxation achieved between 1428 and 1431 produced protest and tax exhaustion in England, while the failure to achieve a military breakthrough prompted a more general cynicism about the real value of these sacrifices. As the new Chancellor, John Stafford Bishop of Bath, acknowledged in his opening address to the Parliament of May 1432, the English had lately 'lived under a lengthy and continuing hardship'. All that the Commons would grant that year was a half-subsidy to replace the land tax of the previous year which had proved to be uncollectable. There was no new money. Since government borrowing was usually secured on future tax revenues, that too dried up. In the three years after the King's return from France, revenue declined steeply and borrowing fell to less than half the previous average.[30]

The financial situation was aggravated by a clumsy piece of mercantilist legislation. The so-called Partition Act was passed by Parliament in 1429 and came into force in the following year. The Act was an attempt to deal with the growing problem of the export of bullion and coin. The war had important implications for England's balance of payments. It was necessary to export considerable quantities of silver in the purses of English soldiers or in chests destined for the war treasurers in France. This was only possible because England was a large exporter of primary commodities, in particular wool, with a trade surplus that traditionally made it a net receiver of bullion. The bullion cost of the war in France was derived from that surplus.

However, the continental purchasers of English wool were increasingly paying for the commodity in continental coin of the same nominal value but lower quality. Much of this inferior coin originated in Philip the Bold's mints in the Low Countries, which had successfully competed with English mints by debasing their silver coinage. Bad money drives out good. The Partition Act sought to address this by requiring foreign merchants buying wool or fleeces at the Calais Staple (the sole authorised outlet) to pay for it in bullion, Sellers were required to take at least a third of the proceeds to the Calais mint to be melted down and struck into English coin. To aid enforcement, goods had to be sold at a fixed price laid down by the Staple and sellers were forbidden to sell on credit. These changes played havoc with the trade, which had traditionally operated on the basis that only part of the price was paid in cash down and the rest in bills of exchange at varying terms. This implicit credit was essential to the financing of the textile manufacturing industries of Flanders and the Low Countries. The new rules also enabled the Calais Staplers to operate as a cartel, pushing up wool prices to unheard-of levels. The Act provoked an outcry in the Low Countries and precipitated a prolonged slump in the continental textile industries. Between 1429 and 1433, the volume of English wool exports declined sharply. Customs receipts, which had been the mainstay of English government finance for decades, halved over the same period.[31]

It was fortunate for the English that these years coincided with a fresh series of political crises in the kingdom of Bourges. When, in 1430, the Parlement of Poitiers complained that anarchy was diverting resources from the struggle with England and Burgundy, the main culprit in its sights was the King's minister Georges de la Trémoille. His vendetta with Arthur de Richemont in Poitou was much the most destructive of France's many private wars and politically the most damaging. His protégé Jean de la Roche was identified by the Parlement as one of the worst domestic plunderers. Nothing had changed two years later. The divisions of Valois France were observed from a distance by both the Duke of Bedford and Philip the Good. In a memorandum prepared for the English council, Hughes de Lannoy urged the English to take advantage of the situation. John V of Brittany and his brother Richemont were the key figures, he thought, who might turn the course of the war if they could be drawn to England's side. Both were at loggerheads with Charles VII's overbearing minister. Lannoy thought that they would be tempted if Henry VI were to promise Poitou to the Duke of Brittany and the office of Constable to Richemont. Over the winter of 1431–2, a serious incident on the march of Brittany exposed all of these tensions and showed how dangerous the continuing stand-off between La Trémoille and his enemies had become.[32]

At the end of September 1431, the Duke of Alençon kidnapped the Chancellor of Brittany Jean de Malestroit as he returned from an embassy to the French court. Alençon was an embittered and hot-headed man. Few men had paid a higher price for their loyalty to the Valois cause. He had lost his duchy to Henry V in 1417. Most of his domains in Maine had been overrun by the English in 1424 and 1425. After his capture at Verneuil, he had rejected an offer from the Duke of Bedford to reinstate him in all his domains and release him without ransom in return for doing homage to Henry VI, saying that he would never renounce his allegiance to his rightful lord. Instead, he had had to pay a steep ransom which he had funded by mortgaging Fougères, his most valuable remaining property, to his uncle, John V Duke of Brittany. He had hoped to repair his fortunes by his prominent role in the epic of Joan of Arc, but in the event the victor of Patay gained nothing for his efforts. Alençon regarded the mortgage of Fougères to his uncle as exploitative and wanted to amend it. He resurrected some old claims of his family against the house of Montfort. He declared that he would hold John's Chancellor until those claims were satisfied. At the beginning of January 1432 John V and Richemont laid siege to the Duke in his castle at Pouancé, whose impressive ruins can still be seen standing over the river Verzée on the old border between Brittany and Maine.[33]

John V believed that Alençon's rash act had been encouraged by the French court, and in particular by Georges de la Trémoille. He appealed for help, first to the English garrison commanders of Lower Normandy and Maine and then to the Duke of Bedford in Paris. Bedford seized the opportunity to fish in the troubled waters of French politics. As it happened, he was well placed to intervene, because an English army of some 1,200 men was operating on the south-west march, where it was engaged in the siege of Alençon's partisans in the castle of Bonsmoulins. Bedford sent Thomas Lord Scales to negotiate with the Duke of Brittany at Rennes. Scales offered John V a deal along the lines previously suggested by Hughes de Lannoy. The English would put an army at his disposal to complete the siege of Pouancé and defend him against a French counterattack. Once Pouancé had fallen, the English and Breton armies would cross the Loire together at Nantes and jointly embark on the conquest of Poitou. Scales brought with him a formal grant in Henry VI's name of the whole county of Poitou to the Duke of Brittany, with an option for the English to buy it back at any time in the next twenty years for 200,000 *francs*. John V took the bait. He agreed to Scales's terms. In a separate agreement, he promised to cede Pouancé to Bedford personally once he had conquered it.

Within days, nearly 2,000 English troops drawn from the siege lines at Bonsmoulins and the garrisons of the south-west were on their way to Pouancé under the command of Robert Lord Willoughby and Sir John Fastolf. Their appearance outside the fortress brought the total strength of the besieging army to about 4,500 men. Alençon, whose castle was poorly garrisoned and supplied, had no hope of fighting off this great host. He fled through a postern gate with half a dozen companions and made for Château-Gontier, leaving his pregnant wife to hold out in the castle. From there he appealed to Charles VII for support. What Alençon proposed was nothing less than an all-out war between France and Brittany. This would have suited the Duke of Bedford very well. It suited La Trémoille too. He made Alençon's fight his own. His garrison at Craon, one of the largest on the march of Maine, was sent to reinforce the defence of Pouancé. Jean de la Roche came north from Poitou with his companies. Raoul de Gaucourt, still at this point an ally of the minister, was sent to the region from the Loire with more men.[34]

Unfortunately for Bedford, he had made too good a bargain with the Breton Duke. Frightened by the implications of what they had agreed, the Montfort brothers lost their nerve. They made contact with Raoul de Gaucourt and Yolande of Anjou and asked them to broker a settlement. On 19 February 1432, just as the besiegers had undermined the curtain wall of Pouancé and were poised to storm the fortress, the Duke of Alençon reached an agreement with John V. John agreed to lift the siege. Alençon for his part promised to release Jean de Malestroit and to surrender another of his castles on the march of Brittany. John no longer needed the dangerous support of an English army and called off the invasion of Poitou. The English were furious. They refused to go away unless they were paid off. The embarrassing grant of Pouancé to Bedford was bought out for another 4,000 *saluts*.

As soon as he had got rid of his awkward English allies, the Duke of Brittany withdrew to Rennes with Richemont and Raoul de Gaucourt. Within two weeks they had reached a provisional agreement settling all of the outstanding bones of contention between Charles VII and the two Montfort brothers, including those arising from the war between Richemont and La Trémoille in Poitou.[35]

The principal loser, apart from the English, was La Trémoille. The treaty of Rennes marked the beginning of Charles VII's emancipation from his influence. The minister's nemesis was Yolande of Anjou, an old ally of Richemont whose intervention with the King had already brought down one favourite. She had been the inspiration behind the treaty of Rennes and she accompanied the negotiators to Chinon to persuade the King to ratify it. After a two-year interval in which she is not recorded as sitting in the royal council, she had begun to sit again. Shortly, a rival to Le Trémoille emerged in the shape of her third son, Charles of Anjou. Charles was only eighteen years old in 1432 but he had many advantages in the contest for influence and power at court. He had a close personal relationship with the King, who was his brother-in-law and had been brought up with him in the ducal household of Anjou. He had sat on the royal council since March 1430 when he was just sixteen. Later that year he was appointed as royal lieutenant in Anjou and Maine. Even as a very young man, said the Burgundian chronicler Georges Chastellain, he enjoyed a reputation for judgement, eloquence and largesse. Over the following year he and his mother became increasingly powerful figures at the fractured court of Charles VII.[36]

In spite of the domestic preoccupations of Charles VII's ministers, 1432 was a terrible year for English arms. It started badly at Pouancé. Then, on 3 February, French partisans captured Rouen castle and held it against the English for some six weeks. Marshal Boussac had decided to make another attempt against the Norman capital after the fiasco of the previous year, this time with the aid of a member of the castle garrison, a Béarnais *échelleur* (a professional scaler of walls) called Pierrot de Biou, who agreed to admit them to the citadel. About 600 men took part in this operation. They left Beauvais and made their way west through the dense forests that then covered most of the route. When they were within two or three miles of Rouen, they sent one of their number, Guillaume de Ricarville, forward by night with

120 men to make contact with Pierrot. With his assistance, Ricarville's men descended into the dry ditch and scaled the walls of the Grosse Tour, the huge circular tower of Philip Augustus at the northern corner of the castle. They took over the tower and overran the whole castle, killing every man of the garrison that they encountered, as the rest fled over the walls into the town. The Earl of Arundel, who had taken over from Warwick as captain of Rouen, escaped by abseiling down the wall into the ditch.

At this point, the adventure began to go wrong. Ricarville left to get help from the men waiting with Boussac in the forest. But the alarm had by then gone up in Rouen, and Boussac lost his nerve. He left in haste, accompanied by his army and Ricarville himself. The men in the castle were abandoned to their fate. They retreated into the Grosse Tour with what little food they could find in the castle stores and barricaded themselves in. The tower was quickly surrounded by English troops, supported by a mob of angry citizens. The Earl of Arundel summoned reinforcements from nearby garrisons. He brought up artillery and ordered the gunners to batter the upper stories of the tower and bury the defenders in masonry. On 14 February the 105 men who were still alive surrendered unconditionally. They were all put to death. Pierrot de Biou was drawn, hanged and quartered in the market square of Rouen. The plot had failed, but it shook English nerves and illustrated the vulnerability of even the strongest and best garrisoned castles to treachery and surprise.[37]

On the marches of Alençon and Maine, the English suffered a succession of reverses. Robert Willoughby laid siege to Ambroise de Loré's headquarters at Saint-Céneri after the debacle at Pouancé. De Loré and Jean de Bueil collected a relief force and came up the valley of the Sarthe with some 1,400 men at their backs. At Beaumont-le-Vicomte, some fifteen miles from Saint-Céneri, they were attacked in the early hours of 1 May 1432 by a detachment from the besieging army under the command of Sir John Montagu, bastard son of the late Earl of Salisbury. They had made the mistake of separating themselves into two groups encamped on opposite sides of the Sarthe. Montagu surprised one of the French encampments. The French were captured or fled before they had time to arm or array themselves. But the English threw their victory away by breaking ranks to secure their prisoners and loot the French camp. While they were at this, Jean de Bueil's force on the opposite side of the Sarthe came over the bridge of Beaumont and fell on them from behind. The French prisoners seized their weapons, turned on their captors and joined in the rout. Montagu fled the field, and much of his force was lost. Willoughby was obliged to abandon the siege of Saint-Céneri.

Shortly afterwards Willoughby was recalled to deal with crises elsewhere, leaving the field clear for de Loré's partisans. Over the following months they expanded their reach across Maine and occupied much of the duchy of Alençon. They entered the vast walled enclosure of the abbey of Saint-Evroul by the banks of the river Charentonne and turned it into a fortress. The Duke of Alençon captured L'Aigle, a major road-hub on the marches of the Beauce. The ungarrisoned cathedral city of Séez fell into their hands. They put garrisons into Sillé-le-Guillaume and Beaumont-le-Vicomte, two of the most hotly contested prizes of the campaigns of 1424 and 1425. The English administration in Maine seemed to be on the verge of collapse. They were reduced to just the three principal garrisons, at Le Mans, Mayenne and Sainte-Suzanne. From their bases in Alençon and Maine, the French were now able to launch raids deep into regions hitherto securely under English control. At the end of September 1432, de Loré attacked the Michaelmas fair in front of the gates of Caen, taking so many prisoners for ransom that his men could not cope with the numbers and had to release most of them.[38]

Worse was to follow. On 23 March 1432, the French captured Chartres, the capital of the Beauce and the hub of the road network of the region. Chartres had an ageing circuit of walls dating from the twelfth century, and an even older citadel defended by a Burgundian garrison of about 100 men. As with Rouen castle, its capture was made possible by traitors within. The French suborned two merchants of the city. Early in the morning, they went forward at the head of forty or fifty men dressed as carters and a number of wagons with weapons concealed beneath the merchandise. The porters recognised the merchants and let them in. A Dominican friar, who was in on the plot, had called the citizens to an open-air sermon at the other end of the town. The intruders seized the gateway, killed the gatekeepers and spread through the city. The Bastard of Orléans, who was lying in wait with a large force in a nearby wood, followed them in. The professional garrison mounted their horses and rode hard for Evreux without striking a blow. The citizens panicked. Some of them fled to guard their homes. Others took up weapons and put themselves under the command of the governor of the city and the Bishop, Jean de Frétigny, a stalwart Burgundian sympathiser who had been nominated in 1419 at the instance of John the Fearless. They tried to make a stand in the marketplace, but they were swiftly overwhelmed. More than sixty townsmen were killed and more than 500 were reported to have been taken prisoner. The Bishop and the governor were among the casualties. The city was a *'ville prise'* to which the laws of war gave no protection. It was brutally sacked, and the leading Burgundian partisans rounded up and executed.

In the hands of the Bastard of Orléans Chartres became a major military base, from which he conducted the war on the southern march of Normandy for the next twelve years. His companies spread out to occupy a line of castles spread along the old Roman roads from Paris to Ivry and Dreux. They included Houdan, which belonged to the Provost of Paris Simon Morhier, the great fortress of the Dukes of Brittany at Montfort l'Amaury, and the castles of Rambouillet and Beynes. Like most privately owned castles, these places were old, inadequately garrisoned and badly maintained. The important town of Mantes on the south bank of the Seine, which had a royal garrison, suffered repeated raids and at least one internal plot to open the gates to the enemy.[39]

For Paris, the consequences were exceptionally serious. French operations from Chartres brought most of the Beauce under French control and blocked the routes to the capital, cutting off much of the city's grain supply. With the Oise held by the French companies at Creil and Compiègne and the upper valley of the Seine barred by the garrison of Melun, the feeding of Paris now depended more than ever on reopening the road and river routes through the valley of the Marne. The Parisians told Henry VI in March that Lagny had to be recovered and its ramparts thrown down, 'otherwise you will not be master of your own kingdom, as you should be'. Henry VI's councillors in England followed these events from a distance, but the full fury of the Parisians fell upon the Regent. In March 1432 the Grand Conseil resolved to launch another attack on Lagny. The experience of Orléans and Compiègne, and of the attempt on Lagny in the previous year, had taught them that very large forces would be needed. This was to be the main military operation of the year. The kernel of the army was provided by the companies in Bedford's service, English and French. In addition, they withdrew some 1,500 men from the garrisons of Normandy, nearly half of their total strength at the time, and called for reinforcements from England. At the beginning of May, an advance guard of 1,200 men was sent forward from Paris under the command of the Earl of Arundel and the newly appointed Marshal of France, Villiers de L'Isle-Adam.[40]

To begin with they enjoyed some success. They overran the outlying satellite garrisons without difficulty. Towards the end of the first week of May, they arrived opposite the town. Lagny stood on the south bank of the river. A stone bridge joined it to a barbican on the north bank, where the English were encamped. The defenders were well prepared. They had more than 800 men in the town under the command of the Limousin knight Jean Foucault and the Scottish captain Sir Hugh Kennedy. Arundel's first target was the bridge. One arch was broken by a bombard at its first shot. The barbican, which had thus been severed from the town, was assaulted shortly afterwards and captured after a fierce fight. Within a few days, much of the bridge had been destroyed by artillery. Pontoon bridges were constructed over the Marne a short distance downstream. At this point Arundel's good fortune ran out. He crossed the river and ordered an assault on Lagny from several points at once. It was a costly failure. The assault parties suffered heavy casualties and lost five of their standards before the retreat was sounded.[41]

Lagny was critically important to both sides. Its fall would have been a severe setback to the French campaign to blockade Paris. It would also have undermined their positions in the north, for the bridge at Lagny was the main route by which their troops were able to pass between Picardy and the centres of royal power in the Loire valley. The siege became a public trial of strength which neither side could afford to lose. Its progress was watched intently, not just in Paris but across Picardy and the Beauvaisis, where the French occupation was beginning to provoke a backlash among the population. The experience of Beauvais was probably typical. The municipality's support for the Valois cause was questioned by a vocal party of citizens who objected to the presence of Marshal Boussac's large and unruly garrison in their town. They openly declared that they would not allow him to return and that if Lagny fell they would open their gates to the English.[42]

Once Arundel's assault on the walls of Lagny had failed, the siege went from bad to worse. The setback hit morale badly and was followed by mass desertions among the English. The war treasurers in Paris had no money to pay the indigenous troops, who threatened to desert in their turn. As a result, although the English succeeded in surrounding the town, their troops were too thinly spread. In Paris, the Duke of Bedford scrambled for reinforcements. He called up the feudal service of Normandy. The response was tepid and the summonses had to be repeated several times. Officers were sent through the duchy rooting out defaulters. Robert Willoughby, who was struggling to contain the French offensive in Maine, was urgently recalled. In England, the council agreed to send 1,200 reinforcements to France under the command of Sir Walter Hungerford. But their plans remained on hold while the vendetta between the Duke of Gloucester and Cardinal Beaufort was played out at Westminster. Gloucester had hoped to fund Hungerford's force from the spoils of Beaufort's destruction. It was not until the middle of July, when the council forced a settlement on the two rivals, that the Commons voted a half-subsidy, and Beaufort was able to resume his lending. On 19 July Hungerford's captains sealed their indentures, and the cumbersome process of requisitioning shipping for his passage began.[43]

In the meantime, the army outside Lagny suffered a succession of defeats. On 24 May Marshal Boussac appeared without warning with a task force drawn from the French garrisons of Beauvaisis and the Oise. They attacked Arundel's artillery parks, killing many of the skilled cannoneers, and then successfully fought their way through the siege lines with a convoy of supplies. On 2 June, a pitched battle outside the walls appears to have gone badly for the English, although the details are obscure. Shortly after this event, the Duke of Bedford arrived with the main army to breathe life into the siege. The English settled down to starve the defenders out.[44]

At the beginning of August 1432, Charles VII's ministers succeeded in assembling another relief force. It was not large, just 800 men. They had been raised with much difficulty from the companies of Marshal Boussac in the north, the Bastard of Orléans's men in the Beauce, the bands of the Castilian *routier* Rodrigo de Villandrando and a corps of Scottish archers. The enterprise was funded by another large advance from La Trémoille's capacious chests. On 10 August, just as the garrison of Lagny had opened negotiations for their surrender, English scouts detected Boussac's force coming up the Melun road. The negotiations were put on hold. The Duke of Bedford drew up his men across the road in front of a stream south of the town. The

French approached across the open fields in the intense August heat and drew up their own array. They were greatly outnumbered and had no intention of fighting. But they drew Bedford away from the town while Rodrigo de Villandrando broke away and went round the English flank with a small force of some eighty men, a herd of cattle and a train of wagons with flour and other supplies. They fought their way through the depleted siege lines. There was a fierce battle around one of the gates. Finally, Rodrigo forced his way into the town with the supplies. The Duke of Bedford was now in an impossible position. The garrison of Lagny had been resupplied. Marshal Boussac's army had withdrawn intact and appeared to be heading for the Île-de-France. There were no English forces between Boussac's army and Paris. Walter Hungerford and his men were still waiting to cross the Channel from Winchelsea. With them were two officers of the Exchequer with chests containing £2,500 in cash to pay the army's wages for September and October. With his own army on the point of breaking up, Bedford decided to stake everything on a final assault. It very nearly succeeded. At one point the Regent's standard could be seen floating above the walls. But fresh waves of defenders drove them back until the retreat was sounded. A week later, Marshal Boussac was reported to have reached Mitry, just twenty miles from Paris. Bedford called off the siege. Abandoning his artillery in the fields, he hurried back to defend his capital. The expeditionary army and the cash arrived, too late, in September.[45]

Bedford's failure before Lagny was a heavy blow to his reputation. It was the last time that he commanded an army in person. At forty-three, he was already worn out. His health had begun to fail. In November his wife Anne of Burgundy, to whom he was devoted, died in the Hôtel de Bourbon in Paris, a victim of the latest epidemic to hit the distressed city. Morale in the capital sank to a new low. That autumn, there were fresh reports of plots by royalist groups to let the enemy into the city. The citizens dared not go out of the gates, even to bring in the vintage from their suburban vineyards. The price of wheat in the city's markets rose by 70 per cent from levels that were already historically high. In England, grain was being bought up in bulk and shipped to the Seine to relieve the distress of the French capital.[46]

By this time, all of England's dilemmas, military, financial and diplomatic, had been sharpened by a fresh diplomatic initiative of the papacy, the first for eight years. At the end of November 1430, Pope Martin V had appointed a papal legate to broker a permanent peace between all three belligerents. His choice fell on the Italian Carthusian Cardinal Niccolò Albergati. Albergati already had a European reputation. At a time when most cardinals led a worldly existence, he observed all the austerities of his order, fasting, avoiding meat and wearing a hair-shirt next to his skin. Over the years in which he was employed as a papal diplomat, he drove himself forward in spite of the weakness caused by his way of life and the effects of bladder stones and gout. Albergati was perhaps the most experienced peacemaker in Europe. He had conducted an earlier peacemaking mission in France in 1422 in the time of Henry V. He had served as a mediator in the quarrels of the German princes, and had recently presided over the conference at Ferrara which put an end to the war between Venice, Florence and Milan. His portrait by Jan van Eyck in the Kunsthistorisches Museum in Vienna (if it is indeed him) accords with what we know about him from other sources. It shows a serene, avuncular and slightly world-weary figure in his late fifties, at once shrewd and good-humoured. Martin V did not live to see the start of Albergati's mission. He died in February 1431. But the legate's appointment was renewed by his successor Eugenius IV.[47]

This happened at a difficult moment in England's relations with the papacy. They had been strained for many years, mainly because of Martin V's long and fruitless struggle to secure the repeal of the fourteenth-century statutes which restricted the exercise of papal jurisdiction in England. Martin had eventually accepted defeat on this issue. But he had been profoundly shocked by the diversion of Cardinal Beaufort's crusading army to fight in France in 1429. He became overtly hostile to England's war aims. Writing to Philip the Good, he doubted whether the English had any interest in peace and urged him to make a separate peace with Charles VII regardless of the treaty of Troyes. Eugenius IV thought no better of England's claims. Jean Juvénal des Ursins, who met him as a member of a French embassy to Rome at the beginning of his reign, reported that the new Pope regarded England's pretensions as 'irrational and wicked'. Albergati was more discreet, but his view was no different. In the course of his earlier mission, he had acquired a profound knowledge of the political background. Above all, he had grasped the lesson of France's wretched recent history. The English invasion had been made possible by a

French civil war. The only way of bringing an end to the conflict of England and France was to reconcile the Valois King with the house of Burgundy.[48]

There had been several attempts to broker peace since the collapse of Albergati's first mission, most of them under the auspices of the Duke of Savoy. They had all come to nothing while the English seemed to be prevailing. The reverses which the English had suffered more recently offered fresh hope of an accommodation. Philip the Good, whose main objective was now to bring an end to the war, hoped that papal mediation would push the English into making concessions. Philip's attitude made it difficult for the English to ignore Albergati as they had ignored Amadeus of Savoy. In February 1431, the situation was examined at Westminster in the course of a remarkably candid discussion in the council. The occasion was the imminent departure of some of their number, including Cardinal Beaufort, Bishop Alnwick and Lords Tiptoft and Cromwell, to join the councillors about the King at Rouen. Developments in France were profoundly discouraging. The siege of Compiègne had failed. The Duke of Burgundy had disbanded his army. The optimism that had surrounded the King's departure for France the year before had evaporated. Financial problems were crowding in. England, said the councillors destined for France, 'may not bear the charges of a continual war'. The rest of them agreed. The war could not be fought at England's expense nor at the expense of Henry's French subjects. The only way that they could see of recovering the territories lost since 1429 was to grant them to anyone who could recover them, in effect farming out the prosecution of the war to free companies operating at their own financial risk. It was what Edward III had done in the late 1350s and Richard II's ministers in the 1380s, with disastrous consequences in both cases. As for Albergati's peace mission, it was agreed on all sides that it must be welcomed, at least outwardly. It was important to the government's public reputation, both in England and France, to be seen to be open to reasonable proposals. But the council had the same misgivings that they had always had about peace initiatives. They had nothing to offer at a peace conference. The coronation of Henry VI in Notre-Dame cathedral was a public proclamation of his pretensions, which made concessions difficult. These men were prisoners of their own claims, condemned by the logic of the past to carry on a war that they knew they could no longer win. In March 1431, about a month after this discussion, the council obtained Parliamentary authority to negotiate with the Valois King. But they never had a coherent negotiating position. Their objective as it emerged was to get a long-term truce which would decide nothing but would at least protect their current positions until their fortunes improved or their King came of age. This strategy was to be the undoing of the alliance with the Duke of Burgundy. He had learned to distrust truces and genuinely wanted peace.[49]

Cardinal Albergati arrived at the French court at Amboise in late September 1431. He soon established a common understanding with Charles VII and his ministers. Like the legate, they believed that the first essential was a reconciliation with the Duke of Burgundy. They regarded Albergati's mission as a way of separating Burgundy from England. But, unlike the legate, they had no expectation that this would lead to a general peace. They had already concluded years before that the English were not serious about peace. How much of this was understood by Albergati himself is difficult to say, but it must soon have become obvious. Early in October, the Cardinal entered Rouen. Henry VI's councillors in the Norman capital were expecting him. They had already discussed the options among themselves. They had consulted the Grand Conseil in Paris and the leading English noblemen in Normandy, including the Duke of Bedford. They had also sounded out Philip the Good. They had their answer ready. They said that they were willing in principle to discuss peace on honourable terms and meanwhile to consider a truce on all fronts. But they were not prepared to suspend military operations in mid-campaign. They believed that the same was true of Philip the Good.

Philip, however, was in a difficult position, as Albergati no doubt discovered when he went on to meet him at Lille. Although he was desperate for an end to the war, he was bound by his seal on the treaty of Troyes and his oath to observe it. His negotiating position was subsequently set out in his instructions to his diplomats and remained substantially unchanged until 1435. His priorities were an end to the war, honourable amends for the murder of his father and confirmation of the territorial gains that he had made during the civil wars and the period of English rule. But he was not yet prepared to break formally with the English or to make a separate peace with Charles VII. These positions meant that the prospects of peace depended on the willingness of the English to make concessions, in particular on their claim to the Crown of France. Philip must have hoped that they would be persuaded to agree in return for a sufficiently generous territorial settlement, as they had done at Brétigny in 1360.[50]

The calculations of all three belligerents were complicated by a major constitutional crisis in the Latin Church. The 1430s were a dark period in the history of the Church, faced with the internecine wars of Christendom, the challenge of heresy in Bohemia and the threat from renascent Islam. A General Council of the Church had been sitting in the Swiss city of Basel since July 1431. It had been summoned by Martin V in accordance with the decrees of the earlier Council at Constance, which had required a General Council to meet at regular intervals. The fathers at Basel were almost immediately diverted into a long and tortuous dispute with Eugenius IV over its claim to ultimate authority in the Church, which was to overshadow the rest of the Pope's long reign. Eugenius, a mercurial and impulsive man, weakened by a stroke shortly after his accession, was ill-equipped to meet this challenge. In November 1431 he dissolved the Council of Basel and tried to reconstitute it in the more congenial atmosphere of Italy. The fathers were defiant. They refused to disperse. Supported by the Emperor Sigismund and by most of the cardinals, they proclaimed that a General Council was the supreme authority in the Church and could not be dissolved or suspended by the Pope without its own consent. They followed these pronouncements with a diplomatic offensive in the courts of Europe and a barrage of propaganda in favour of their claims.[51]

Among the sovereigns of Europe, there was much sympathy for the Council's position. A conciliar regime in the Church would weaken the central authority of the papacy and strengthen their own control over their national Churches. The French Church on both sides of the political divide had a strong Gallican and conciliar tradition, and ancient concerns about the long reach of papal jurisdiction. In Lancastrian France, conciliar sentiment was strongly entrenched in the Parlement and the University of Paris, and in a number of cathedral chapters, including Rouen and Paris. In Valois France, a Church Council which Charles VII summoned to Bourges in February 1432 pronounced unanimously in favour of the Council. Most European rulers accepted the Council's legitimacy, while trying to avoid another schism or an open breach with the papacy. They allowed their clergy to send delegations to Basel, and in due course sent their own official embassies. Charles VII was represented at Basel from November 1432. Philip the Good, John V of Brittany and James I of Scotland had all followed suit by the beginning of 1434.[52]

England's position was more equivocal and took longer to resolve. In the summer of 1432, rival embassies from the Pope and the Council appeared at Westminster to argue their respective cases. After much internal debate and a decisive intervention by the Duke of Gloucester, Henry VI's ministers decided to participate in the Council. A contingent from the English Church appeared at Basel in February 1433. The government announced that it would send its own ambassadors on behalf of both of Henry VI's realms later in the year. Their main reason for wishing to participate in the Council was unconnected with the French war. They were concerned about the Hussites and their links with the English Lollards, who were regarded as political revolutionaries. They believed that the Council might be a valuable instrument for dealing with the menace of heresy. But another important factor was the desire for an alternative mediator if Albergati should fail or turn against them. Philip the Good took the same view.

England's relations with the Council, however, got off to a bad start. When the government resolved to participate, they were unaware of a number of important procedural decisions which the fathers at Basel had made at the outset of their proceedings. The Council had abandoned the system of voting by nations which had been used at Constance and which had given the English the same weight as France. They had also insisted that delegates swear a so-called 'oath of incorporation', which in effect required them to work for the collective purposes of the Council and not in the interests of the countries from which they had come. When the councillors at Westminster discovered this, they were outraged. They protested against both decrees and forbade the English who were already at Basel to take the oath of incorporation or to enter the Council unless the system of voting by nations was restored. As a result, the English contingent found itself excluded from almost all of the Council's business. In May 1433, shortly after the official English embassy had set out for Basel, it was recalled. A letter of protest was addressed to the Council in Henry VI's name. His subjects, he said, had been prevented from labouring in the Lord's vineyard, but instead had been 'left standing there in the marketplace like idle and rejected hands'. This missive provoked an angry debate when it was read out before the Council, but not because of its content. The Archbishop of Tours objected to Henry's use of the title 'King of England and France' and embarked of a long defence of Charles VII's claims. This generated an aggressive response from the Burgundian delegation about the murder of John the Fearless. The Burgundian spokesman ended with a rousing declaration that Henry VI was the true and only King of France, while his words were drowned out by loud cries of 'Burgundian traitors' from the French benches.[53]

The Council of Basel had its own claim to perform the Church's classic function of mediating international disputes. From the outset, it had declared the peace of Europe to be an essential part of its role. These pretensions became more plausible as the number of national delegations increased. The Pope was left a lonely figure in Rome, while Basel became the capital of the Church and the scene of a major international gathering of representatives of the princes of Europe. The fathers initially contemplated setting up a rival peace process under their own auspices. In an encyclical addressed to the whole people of France in March 1432, they called on all the belligerents to send delegations to Basel to participate in a peace conference there. None of them took up this idea, which was shortly abandoned. Albergati was the Pope's legate, not the Council's. But, conscious perhaps of the risk that the belligerents might play off Basel against Rome, he took care to involve the fathers of Basel at every stage in his work. He invited them to send delegates to successive conferences in France and reported to the Council as well as the Pope on his progress. As relations between Rome and Basel grew more acrimonious, only Albergati's tact and high reputation in both cities enabled this even-handed approach to be sustained.[54]

Cardinal Albergati struggled to organise his peace conference against the noise of the clash of arms. For six months after his initial meetings with the three powers, the 58-year-old Cardinal trekked along the frozen roads of northern France with his small staff from one capital to the next in the coldest and longest winter for years. The first challenge was to get agreement on the venue. The English council wanted the conference to be held in the Low Countries, away from a war zone and easily accessible from England. They had initially proposed Cambrai, the seat of an independent ecclesiastical principality on France's northern frontier. Charles VII refused to agree to any place north of the Seine. He suggested Auxerre or Nevers, both of which were rejected by the Duke of Bedford on the ground that they were too far away and too dangerous. Bedford suggested Brie-Comte-Robert, a small walled town south-east of Paris on the road to Melun, which was currently in English hands. Before this difference could be resolved, the Duke of Burgundy lost patience. He met Charles VII's representatives at Dijon. At the beginning of May 1432, they agreed that the conference would open at Auxerre on 8 July. Philip sent one of his private secretaries to Paris to notify the Grand Conseil of the fait accompli, and to ask them what they proposed to do. They replied that they would have to consult the council in England, but they told the emissary confidentially that they expected the English to be represented. But they reckoned without the councillors at Westminster. The council in England was infuriated by the French King's obduracy on the question of venue and were not as keen as Bedford was to remain in step with the Duke of Burgundy. By mid-June, when there was still no response from England, the conference was postponed to the end of September.[55]

Albergati summoned the delegations of each side to a preliminary meeting in the Burgundian town of Semur-en-Auxois to discuss how the main conference should proceed. The delegations of Charles VII and Philip the Good appeared before him there in the first week of August 1432, each led by their respective Chancellors. The Council of Basel also sent representatives. The English did not appear. According to Albergati, they applied at the last moment for safe-conducts and then complained that they had arrived too late and were defective. The French and Burgundians agreed to another postponement of the main conference, to the end of October, to allow the English more time. But what if they still stayed away? Albergati had by now identified the English government as the main obstacle to peace. He suspected that they would not appear at Auxerre. In that event he declared, Charles VII and Philip the Good should make a separate peace without them. This was naturally acceptable to the French. But Nicolas Rolin would have none of it. In the absence of the English, he said, they would be unable to agree anything, or to do more than report back what had been said. In the margins of the sessions, the parties tested each others' positions on the substantive issues. The answers were not reassuring. It became clear that the French had no desire to negotiate with the English, any more than the English wished to negotiate with them. They only tolerated English participation at Auxerre because Philip the Good insisted on it. But when asked what territorial concessions they were prepared to make for the sake of peace, Regnault de Chartres answered none. The Burgundian Chancellor reported back to the Duke in gloomy terms. Philip told his minister that he would not contemplate abandoning the peace process, even if the conference of Auxerre failed. If necessary, they would have to refer the issues to a further conference or find some other mediator such as the Council of Basel.[56]

To many people's surprise, when the peace conference eventually opened at Auxerre a month late on 27 November 1432, the English were there. Their representation was neither as distinguished nor as experienced as that of the other parties, whose delegations were once again led by their Chancellors. The English spokesman was John Langdon Bishop of Rochester, who had only recently begun to take an active part in the business of the English council. He was supported by the Yorkshire knight Sir Henry Bromflete, who had served in France some years earlier as one of Henry V's household knights. In some ways the most interesting member of the English team was the third member, the civil lawyer Thomas Beckington, a protégé and former Chancellor of the Duke of Gloucester, now embarking on his first major diplomatic mission. He was destined to become Henry VI's private secretary and one of his principal diplomatic advisers. These men were joined from Paris by members of the Grand Conseil including Gilles de Clamécy and Sir John Fastolf.

In spite, or perhaps because of the full attendance, the atmosphere was every bit as poisonous as Rolin had anticipated. Albergati thought that the English bore most of the blame. They opened with a demand for the recognition of the dual monarchy, as they always did. This provoked the usual French refusal to discuss the point. The fall-back position of the English was a long truce, ideally of three years, but at the very least of a year. For their part, the French were no more cooperative. They made no proposals for a permanent peace and rejected outright the alternative suggestion of a truce. A truce would be unenforceable anyway, they pointed out, given the scale on which irregulars were employed to do the fighting. They then raised a new demand. Before any serious negotiation could occur, the French prisoners in England, the Duke of Orléans, his brother the Count of Angoulême and the Duke of Bourbon, must be brought to France so that Charles's councillors could consult them. The French were concerned about the dealings of the princely prisoners with their captors. Both Bourbon and Orléans had come close to abandoning the Valois cause. The French King's ministers hoped to counter the pressures to which these lonely and desperate men were subject in England.

In reality, the positions taken at Auxerre by both the English and the French were a charade. For different reasons, neither of them really wanted a deal. Albergati thought, or so he later told the Duke, that only the Burgundian delegation was really interested in peace. This was probably true, but even the Burgundians had their hands tied by the Duke's treaty obligations to the English. Their instructions were to support the English dynasty's claim to the Crown of France so far as it was based on the treaty of Troyes, but not so far as it was based on its 'old quarrels', in other words on hereditary right. The breakdown of the conference at Auxerre can have come as no surprise to the participants. But unrealistically high hopes had been entertained elsewhere. In Paris, where the loose siege of the city continued to cause real hardship, criticism of the government became so vehement that the authorities, fearing riots, arrested a number of the principal malcontents.[57]

During the spring and summer of 1433, Albergati's mission collapsed. The Cardinal, mindful of English sensitivities about the venue, proposed that another conference should be convened between the English-held town of Corbeil on the Seine and the French-held town of Melun twelve miles upstream. The delegations reassembled in their respective strongholds on 21 March 1433. Albergati installed himself and his staff at Seine-Port half-way between the two, probably in the empty buildings of the Cistercian abbey which had been abandoned by the monks during the civil wars. It was here that the plenary sessions were held. The whole conference was taken up with the question of the princely prisoners in England. The English announced that they were being held at Dover and would if necessary be brought across the Channel to Calais. The French would have to confer with them there. Alternatively, the conference could be moved to somewhere in Picardy and the prisoners brought as close to the chosen site as possible. The French replied that they had no power to proceed unless the prisoners were brought at least as far as Rouen. The argument continued for more than two weeks until the legate suspended the conference while he travelled to the French court to resolve the issue with Charles VII in person. Albergati returned to Seine-Port in June having persuaded the French King to agree to the English proposals about the prisoners, and to accept a short truce of four months until the conference could resume. The Burgundians were happy to agree. A formal agreement was drawn up ready to be sealed. But by this time the English had developed plans for a major offensive in the west. Louis of Luxembourg came out from Paris and appeared in person at Corbeil to announce that the proposed truce was unacceptable.

Albergati gave his mission up as hopeless. France was divided into two armed camps waiting for the signal to attack, he wrote in his report to the Council of Basel. It was time, he suggested, for the Council to send its own ambassadors to all three belligerents to see if they could succeed better than he had. On 10 September 1433, the legate was received at the gates of Basel by all the cardinals in the city and conducted to the Council where, six days later, he delivered the same gloomy message in person.[58]

At the beginning of 1433, as England's military position deteriorated on both sides of the Channel, the Duke of Bedford arranged a joint conference of the Westminster and Paris councils. It was to be held at Calais in April. The business of the meeting was to be the current state of negotiations with France and the future direction and financing of the war on the assumption (which seemed likely) that Albergati's peace mission would fail. Behind the formal agenda lay the Regent's broader concerns about the competence of the Duke of Gloucester's government in England and the management of its finances, on which the fortunes of the war in France were now increasingly dependent. The long dispute between Gloucester and Beaufort the previous summer had arguably cost him Lagny. In the new year, several serious incidents advertised the extent of the financial disorganisation at Westminster.[59]

In February 1433 there was a mutiny in the garrison of Calais, the second in ten years. Calais was perhaps the worst example of the English council's habit of funding current operations by deferring necessary expenditure elsewhere. The town with its castle and dependencies had a large garrison in addition to a staff of builders, officials and clerks, whose wages were the largest recurring item in the government's accounts. For years, the men had received only part of their due. The slump in the wool trade following the Partition Ordinance of 1429 aggravated the problem, since the Treasurer of Calais derived his funds mainly from assignments of the wool customs. At some point in 1432, the payments seem to have stopped altogether. Assignments from the Exchequer fell to a fraction of their usual levels, and much of what was paid to the Treasurer of Calais was diverted to settle arrears due to the Earl of Warwick from the time that he had been captain. As a result, about half of the garrison rose up, expelled Bedford's lieutenant Sir William Oldhall, and seized the Staplers' stocks of wool as security for their back pay. Bedford had already experienced one mutiny by an English army, outside Compiègne in October 1430, and was not prepared to countenance another. At the end of March 1433, he left Rouen and marched on the town. On 7 April he arrived at the outlying fort of Balinghem, where he opened negotiations with the mutineers. Bedford tricked them into submission. He gave them written assignments on the customs, which had no prospect of being honoured, and in return they agreed to admit him to the town. In the last week of April, he entered the town with his retinue to a tumultuous welcome from citizens and garrison alike. As soon he was inside, the gates were closed and the mutineers were arrested and taken to various prisons in the town. Their assignments were confiscated and cancelled. Eventually, 200 of them, nearly half the garrison, were banished and their wage claims forfeited. Four ringleaders were summarily condemned to death and beheaded in the market square.[60]

The mutiny of the Calais garrison was quickly followed by the chaotic business of the expeditionary army for 1433. The English council had decided early in the year to send an army to Normandy under the command of the Earl of Huntingdon. As originally conceived, it was going to be comparable to the great expedition of the Earl of Salisbury, who had led 2,700 men to France in 1428. But when Huntingdon eventually sailed in May it was with only half that number. Even that proved to be more than the Exchequer could afford. Their pay for the first quarter's service was borrowed from money that the trustees of the duchy of Lancaster had earmarked for the unpaid debts of Henry V. The second quarter's pay was due on embarkation, but in April, as ships and men were assembling at Winchelsea, the new Treasurer Lord Scrope of Masham reported that the government's coffers were empty. He could not even pay the expenses of diplomatic missions or the costs of shipping councillors to Calais for Bedford's conference. The money was eventually borrowed from Cardinal Beaufort, although there were now no unencumbered revenues to offer him as security. He was reduced to taking personal guarantees from each member of the council.[61]

The conference of the two councils finally took place at about the beginning of May 1433. It was a large affair. A flotilla of ships carried the Duke of Gloucester, Chancellor Stafford, his predecessor Archbishop Kemp, Bishop Alnwick, the Earl of Suffolk, Lords Hungerford and Cromwell and other councillors across the Channel to Calais, together with a crowd of retainers and officials. No fewer than fifteen ships were loaded with food and other supplies. From Paris and Rouen came Bedford and Louis of Luxembourg, together with other members of the Grand Conseil including Raoul le Sage, Sir John Fastolf and the President of the Parlement of Paris. Cardinal Beaufort, who had been in France since March, was also there. John of Luxembourg and the Count of Saint-Pol attended in their dual capacities as councillors of the Duke of Burgundy and the principal French commanders in Lancastrian service. The Duke of Brittany was represented by his English private secretary James Godart.[62]

Shortly after the conference opened, the participants had another uncomfortable reminder of the vulnerable state of Lancastrian France. Saint-Valéry was a walled town on the south side of the estuary of the Somme with a Burgundian garrison. In theory it was protected by the six-year truce between Charles VII and the Duke of Burgundy. But Louis de Wancourt, a French captain based at Beauvais, crossed Picardy unseen and captured the place by escalade one morning at dawn. He sacked the town, killed much of the garrison, and then installed his own men. They began to raid far and wide across the Somme valley. Experience showed that unless these seizures were quickly reversed, the intruders dug themselves in and became extremely difficult to expel. The councillors at Calais had to take urgent action. The English garrison at Le Crotoy on the opposite side of the estuary was reinforced by loyal contingents from the Calais garrison. The Count of Saint-Pol left at once to blockade Saint-Valéry while John of Luxembourg set about raising the forces required for a full-scale siege. These measures called for immediate payments of cash. The council's way of getting it perfectly illustrated the patches and improvisation which characterised English public finance at this point. Archbishop Kemp, who was due to proceed to Basel once the conference was over, emptied out his satchels so that the £1,000 that he had received for his expenses could be used as an initial payment for Saint-Pol's army. For more substantial funds, the councillors turned in desperation to Cardinal Beaufort, who had at least part of his treasure with him at Calais. Beaufort laid down his terms. He was restored, in the teeth of Gloucester's hostility, to the royal council. In return, he agreed to lend 10,000 marks (£6,667), which was paid over at once to Louis of Luxembourg. Once again, there were no unencumbered revenues to offer him as security, and he was obliged to take further guarantees from councillors personally. It was a sign of the English council's divisions that only Beaufort's allies among them would subscribe the guarantee. Gloucester's friends kept their purses resolutely closed.[63]

Plainly, the war could not be funded any longer on this hand-to-mouth basis. The Duke of Bedford pressed the English councillors to say what plans they had for the future. Were they in a position, he asked, to send to France 'a more chargeable and abiding succour than ever they did before'? Their answer was not reassuring. They had no plans. In spite of the critical state of affairs in France, Bedford decided that he must return to England to take the government there in hand. He told the assembly of his intention. He needed, he said, to explain to the King's English subjects how close France was to being lost, and to his French subjects what help they could realistically hope to receive from England. It was agreed that Parliament would be summoned urgently to Westminster and that Bedford himself would be present.[64]

Parliament opened on 8 July 1433 in the Painted Chamber of the palace of Westminster in an atmosphere of menace. The Duke of Bedford dominated the proceedings. He was entitled to take precedence over the Duke of Gloucester as soon as he set foot on English soil, a fact which Humphrey acknowledged but deeply resented. He muttered about his brother's mishandling of the war in France and began preparing accusations against him which, like the allegation of treason against the Cardinal the year before, were spread about but never formally made. Bedford responded as Beaufort had done. Shortly after the opening he made a statement to both Houses challenging those who were circulating such rumours and calling on them to make them openly and justify them. Once again, Gloucester was willing to wound but afraid to strike. He disingenuously declared that no such rumours had come to his ears. The King was made to back Bedford from the throne, declaring that special thanks were due to him for his 'good, laudable and fruitful services' in France. There is little doubt that this reflected the feelings of both Houses. Bedford's stewardship of the Lancastrian cause in France was widely admired, while Gloucester's year-long experiment in personal government had sown divisions which alienated much of the political community.[65]

Bedford applied himself first to the personnel of government and the restoration of financial discipline. The council was refashioned again. Several of its less competent members were discarded. Gloucester's allies were dismissed or marginalised. Treasurer Scrope's power to authorise expenditure was severely curtailed, and on 11 August he was replaced by Ralph Lord Cromwell. Cromwell was an old Normandy hand, whose experience of the war went back to Harfleur and Agincourt. He was also a reliable ally of Bedford and no friend of Gloucester. He was destined to hold office for a decade and proved to be one of the few ministers who really understood the problems of royal finance. Within days of his appointment, he temporarily stopped all payments out of the Exchequer until proper provision could be made for the expenses of the King's household. He then established some priorities for other payments, restricting the payment of annuities to those recipients whose political or military support was indispensable. The crown jewels were inventoried. A variety of corrupt practices at the Exchequer were suppressed.[66]

The autumn, declared Chancellor Stafford as Parliament was prorogued in August, was the season when it was 'fitting for the lords to occupy themselves in recreation and hunting and the commons to attend to the harvest'. Before agreeing to accept the office, Cromwell had made it a condition that he should be allowed to present a comprehensive financial statement to Parliament. He wanted them to understand how bad a situation he had inherited. 'It is behoveful', Sir John Fortescue later wrote, 'that we first esteem what his early charges and expenses beeth likely to draw unto, for after that needeth his revenues to be proportioned.' Yet this was rarely done. The accounts of the English state for this period are impressive in their bulk, but they were designed to detect fraud, not to present the current state of the King's finances. Over the summer, the staff of the Exchequer laboured at the records to produce something like a budget. The result was the remarkable document which was laid before Parliament on 18 October 1433, after they had returned from their recess. Based on the figures for the financial years 1429–32, it showed that the Crown's permanent revenues came to less than £60,000 a year, which just about covered the cost of the domestic government of England. When the defence of Ireland, Gascony, Calais and the Scottish march was taken into account, there was a structural deficit of nearly £16,000 a year, leaving nothing at all for the war in France. The government's total outstanding debt had risen uncontrollably as vital expenditure had been deferred and arrears due to soldiers and contractors accumulated unpaid. At the time of Cromwell's statement to Parliament the debt stood at more than £168,000, an astronomical sum equivalent to nearly three years' ordinary revenue or five Parliamentary subsidies. Some £45,000 of this was attributable to Calais alone. These figures lent precision and authority to Cromwell's words, but the broad picture cannot have come as a surprise. The lesson was that if the English were to fight on in France there had to be a step change in the level of Parliamentary taxation.[67]

The Parliamentary session was an occasion to review, once again, the prospects of war and peace. Both of England's princely allies, the Dukes of Burgundy and Brittany, had sent their ambassadors to Westminster for the occasion. John V was represented once again by James Godart. He was joined by the Irish knight Sir Thomas Cusack, an Agincourt veteran then serving as the captain of John V's corps of English archers. The Duke of Burgundy's embassy was headed by Hughes de Lannoy, by now a familiar figure at Westminster.

Relations between Bedford and Philip the Good were glacial. The death of Anne of Burgundy the previous November had severed the strongest personal link between the two men. Bedford's subsequent re-marriage to Jacquetta of Luxembourg completed the breach as far as Philip was concerned. Jacquetta was the seventeen-year-old daughter of John of Luxembourg's elder brother Peter Count of Saint-Pol, a 'vivacious, beautiful and gracious' woman according to the chronicler Monstrelet, who had probably met her. The marriage was celebrated in Louis of Luxembourg's cathedral at Thérouanne in April 1433, a few days before the conference at Calais. It cemented Bedford's personal alliance with the house of Luxembourg, whose leading members had been pillars of the dual monarchy for years. But it infuriated the Duke of Burgundy. The Luxembourgs were the leading noble house of Picardy, at once his most powerful vassals and his principal regional rivals. The marriage threatened to detach them from Philip's political network in France and make them directly dependent on the English dynasty. Cardinal Beaufort had tried to arrange a meeting between Philip and Bedford at Saint-Omer at the beginning of June, in the hope of effecting a reconciliation. But although they both came to Saint-Omer, feelings were so high that neither would consent to call first on the other, and the meeting never took place.[68]

Because of the delicate nature of his mission, Hughes de Lannoy had received his instructions by word of mouth from Philip himself in the garden of the ducal mansion at Arras. Philip gave free rein to all his accumulated resentments against the English. He complained that they would neither make peace with the Valois King nor put resources into the war on a scale which might bring them victory. He believed that a negotiated peace was now the only way out of a war which neither side could win. If the English wanted to fight on with his support, they would have to make a much larger commitment of money and manpower and to take a more active part in the defence of his domains as well as their own. The English were in no position to do that, as Philip must have known. In July 1433 they were already maintaining about 6,000 troops in northern France. About 4,800 of these were Englishmen stationed in the marches and garrisons of Normandy. The rest were French troops in English service under the command of the Luxembourg brothers. About a third of these forces were currently engaged in the siege of Saint-Valéry, which had begun in early July and lasted until Louis de Wancourt's garrison was bought out in late August. In addition, Philip the Good claimed to have paid 4,500 troops in the course of the past year to serve in garrisons and field forces in Burgundy alone, not to speak of the forces which he was having to maintain on the Somme. Lannoy was told to make sure that the English understood how strongly he felt about this.[69]

Philip charged his envoy to discover the state of opinion in England at a time when the whole political community would be gathered at Westminster for the Parliament. Lannoy prolonged his stay until the day after the opening and kept his ear to the ground. His impressions were shrewd and revealing. Fortunately, Philip ignored his request that his report should be destroyed as soon as he had read it. Lannoy attended two council meetings and had an audience with the King ('a very beautiful child with a good presence'). He also spoke privately to a number of councillors including Cardinal Beaufort, the Duke of Bedford and the Earls of Warwick and Suffolk. He had met all these men before, on previous missions to England or in Flanders, and found their mood darker than usual. They had given up hope of victory. Beaufort was affable but 'somewhat strange' and more guarded than before. Warwick was gracious but sombre. People were depressed by the turn that the war had taken and hostile to Philip, who was evidently thought to demand too much and contribute too little. Lannoy heard harsh words and ugly threats spoken against his master every day that he was in London. Only the lower orders spoke like that, Warwick assured him, although the Earl himself admitted that those about the King were angry that he had not once visited Henry in the two years that Henry had spent in France. The Duke of Bedford was conscious that Philip no longer regarded him as a friend, but he remained Philip's firmest supporter at Westminster. He reminded the council that Philip was indispensable. They were evidently sceptical, but Lannoy found no evidence that they were secretly negotiating with Charles VII, as Philip had feared.

What was clear was that most of those in positions of power realised, as Lannoy put it, that 'the French business cannot go on like this'. They must now decide whether to make peace with the Valois King on the best terms that they could get or send a 'very large and powerful' army to France. There was no other option. Lannoy had two interviews with Cardinal Beaufort. The Cardinal told him that the decision was in the hands of the current Parliament. Until they decided whether to fund a new offensive it was impossible to know whether England would negotiate its way out of the war or prosecute it on a larger scale. The Earl of Suffolk told Lannoy that the general view of the council was that a negotiated peace was essential. But the Dukes of Bedford and Gloucester took their own line. Hughes de Lannoy had only a brief and uninformative exchange with Bedford and none with Gloucester. But although the brothers were divided by personal animosity and competing strategies for France, they were at one in their reverence for the legacy of Henry V.

Bedford himself shared the general desire to extricate England from the war but could not bring himself to abandon an ambition which his elder brother had come so close to achieving. His view was stated with characteristic eloquence in the declaration that he would make to Henry VI the following summer before returning to France:

How great a pity it were that that noble royaume [should be lost], for getting and keeping of the which my lord that was your father ... and other many noble princes, lords, knights and squires and other persons in full great number have paid their lives, many that ... yet ... live shed their blood more precious to them than any temporal good and spended their days and their noble and true labours, and as well they as in general the co[mmons] of this land have also spended an infinite good . . . So that the loss of your said country and subjects . . . should cause me a perpetual heart's heaviness and sorrow.

Bedford's sincerity was palpable, but his position was impossible. If Parliament would not support his plans financially, then some way would have to be found of placating his allies and keeping the peace process alive. But he was not willing to make the concessions on which alone peace with France could be made.[70]

In this extraordinary situation, the council clutched at straws in their effort to find a way out of the war on acceptable terms. Their chosen instrument, once again, was the Duke of Orléans. After eighteen years as a prisoner in England, the Duke was willing to do almost anything to return to his homeland. His herald told Hughes de Lannoy that his master had 'no intention of allowing himself to be ruined or putting up with his current situation a moment longer'. It had always been clear that Charles's only hope of release was through a political deal with his captors. He had already secretly acknowledged Henry VI as King of France some years earlier and had made several offers to mediate. He had made his own peace proposals in 1427 and had begun to canvas support for them in France, but that plan had fallen away as a result of the siege of Orléans. He felt, he said, 'like a sword shut in its scabbard, useless until it is drawn'.

In 1433, the council decided that the time had come to make better use of the Duke of Orléans. There is every reason to believe that the man behind this was the Earl of Suffolk. Suffolk had been one of England's longest-serving commanders in France until his military career was cut short by the disasters of 1429. He had been captured at the storming of Jargeau and had become the prisoner of the Bastard of Orléans, Charles's half-brother. Suffolk was released on parole early in 1430 and returned to England. There, he married Alice Chaucer, the wealthy widow of the last Montagu Earl of Salisbury, and began to build up an important regional power base in East Anglia and another in Oxfordshire. Suffolk had traditionally been an ally of the Duke of Gloucester, and his appointment to the council in November 1431 seems to have been Gloucester's doing. But he had quickly established himself as one of the King's most diligent and independent-minded councillors, as well as a forceful advocate of a negotiated peace. Suffolk befriended Charles of Orléans. The two men had many common interests, political and literary. In 1432, he successfully applied to have custody of the prisoner transferred to him, and from August of that year, Charles's usual residence was the Earl's castle at Wingfield. Suffolk encouraged Charles to revive his earlier schemes of mediation. Within three weeks of the transfer, safe-conducts were issued for the Bastard of Orléans to visit Charles in England, together with members of his staff from Blois. Charles made contact with other prominent figures in France, including Yolande and Charles of Anjou, the Montfort brothers John V and Richemont, the Duke of Alençon, the Count of Clermont, the southern lords, Foix, Armagnac and Pardiac, and some of Charles VII's officers including his Chancellor Regnault de Chartres. He was confident, he told Hughes de Lannoy, that these people, 'the greatest lords of the French King's court and party', would take their lead from him when it came to the terms of peace. In July 1433, he was brought back from Dover to the Earl of Suffolk's mansion in London, where he put his detailed proposals before the council.[71]

On 14 August 1433, after six weeks of negotiation, the Duke of Orléans sealed letters patent in which he announced his intention of convening a peace conference of his own sometime after 15 October, either at Calais or somewhere in Normandy. Referring to Henry VI as 'my lord the King of France and England' and to Charles VII as 'the Dauphin', he declared himself confident that the great lords of France with whom he had discussed the matter would support a permanent peace on terms that Henry VI would be recognised as King of France, provided that proper territorial and financial provision was made for his Valois rival. Charles of Orléans cannot have imagined that the Valois King would submit voluntarily to such a treaty. What he must have had in mind was an aristocratic coup against his cousin. If peace could not be made on these terms within a year, he promised to do homage to Henry VI as King of France and England and to serve him against Charles VII. He would then be released without ransom. Once at large, the Duke undertook to arrange for his subjects and allies in France to perform their own homage to the English King. A large number of strongholds distributed across the French kingdom were to be delivered up to the English. They included Mont-Saint-Michel and La Rochelle, the only walled places in Charles VII's allegiance on the Atlantic seaboard, the towns of Orléans, Blois and Châteaudun, which were part of the appanage of Orléans, the walled places of Bourges, Poitiers, Tours, Loches and Chinon, which were the principal centres of Charles VII's government, the provincial capitals of Limoges and Saintes, and the city of Béziers in Languedoc.[72]

It is difficult to know how seriously this extraordinary prospectus was taken by the English King's ministers or indeed by Charles of Orléans himself. The council made arrangements for a high-ranking delegation of their own to attend Orléans's conference. They invited Philip the Good to be there in person, or at least to send a suitably impressive embassy. We do not know what Charles of Orléans's correspondents in France had told him, but it is clear that in his dealings with the English council the Duke greatly exaggerated the vulnerability of Charles VII and his own influence in a country that he had not seen for nearly two decades. He seems to have hoped to exploit discontent with the dominant role of Georges de la Trémoille at Charles VII's court, for almost all of those whom he had named as his supporters were known enemies of the minister. But if that was the plan, it was undone before even the letters patent were sealed. When, in mid-July, Hughes de Lannoy passed through Calais on his way home, he encountered another Burgundian diplomat who had just returned from the French court. He told him that La Trémoille had fallen.[73]

The minister's fall from grace had begun with the treaty of Rennes, which forced him to settle his dispute with Richemont and marked the return of Yolande of Anjou to influence at court. La Trémoille viewed the treaty as an act of war. In August 1432, immediately after the relief of Lagny, he took another notable *routier* into his service, the Castilian soldier of fortune Rodrigo de Villandrando, and unleashed him upon Anjou. Rodrigo invaded Yolande's duchy from Touraine, uttering dire threats. Charles of Anjou, the effective governor of the duchy in his brother's absence, refused to be intimidated. His lieutenant Jean de Bueil summoned the nobility of the duchy and confronted Rodrigo south of Ponts-de-Cé in September. There was a pitched battle, in which Rodrigo's companies were put to flight. The Castilians retreated into Touraine, where they passed several weeks in looting and destruction before withdrawing to Languedoc.

As La Trémoille's behaviour became more erratic and extreme, a powerful coalition built up at court waiting for the occasion to unseat him. Even the minister's former friends, like Raoul de Gaucourt and La Hire, were now ready to desert him. The occasion arose at the end of June 1433. The peace talks at Seine-Port had just collapsed. The English were concentrating for a fresh offensive. Charles VII and La

Trémoille arrived with the court at Chinon. The captain of Chinon was Raoul de Gaucourt. That night, his deputy admitted a band of forty or fifty armed men to the fortress through a postern gate. They were led by four men: Charles of Anjou's lieutenant Jean de Bueil, Bueil's fellow captain on the march of Anjou Pierre de Brézé, Richemont's adjutant Prégent de Coëtivy and a kinsman of the minister's most prominent victim Louis of Amboise. La Trémoille was surprised in his bed and arrested. There was a struggle, in the course of which he was stabbed in the belly. The King realised what was happening as soon as he heard the noise. He sent his attendants to investigate. The Queen, who may have been in on the plot, calmed him and Charles submitted passively to events which he made no attempt to control. La Trémoille, wounded but alive, was taken under escort to Jean de Bueil's castle at Montrésor near Loches and was eventually allowed to retire to his castle at Sully, still a rich man but no longer a powerful one.[74]

There was naturally much speculation in England and Burgundy about who would replace the man who had dominated the French government for six years. Charles VII, perennially lacking in confidence and bored by the details of administration, needed ministers who were friends as well as servants. He tended to leave more to them than contemporary convention thought proper for a King. But he never again surrendered his government so completely to one man as he had done to La Trémoille. Observing the scene from his exile in Provence, Jean Louvet had lost none of his shrewdness or understanding of the workings of government. In a memorandum written for the Duke of Savoy, he reported that the King now had 'no one servant with power over all the others'. But Charles of Anjou, his mother Yolande and his sister the Queen nonetheless enjoyed an unrivalled influence. They were supported by the authors of the coup, Jean de Bueil, Prégent de Coëtivy and Pierre de Brézé, and by the solid corps of professional administrators who had been trained in the Angevin administration at Angers or Tarascon. Between them, these people would dominate the French government for years to come. Nothing was decided without their consent. Richemont had resumed his functions as Constable, but not his former political power. It was, initially at least, a government of Charles VII's kinsmen, the kind of government that contemporaries thought in keeping with the fitness of things. The consequences for the course of the war, however, were modest. There was a greater emphasis on the western front in Maine and Alençon and on relations with

Brittany, always the dominant concerns of the house of Anjou. But the constraints of money and manpower remained the limiting factors that they had always been. La Trémoille's view, shared by Regnault de Chartres, had been that the essential condition of victory was to detach Burgundy from England. That remained the orthodoxy of the political class. No one was inclined to make significant concession to the English, least of all on the intractable questions of sovereignty and title to the Crown.[75]

The palace revolution at the French court put an end to any hopes that Charles of Orléans might have entertained for his conference. The English government appointed Calais as the venue and issued safe-conducts to a large number of French councillors and noblemen whom they hoped would attend. Not one of them did. At the end of October 1433 Sir William Oldhall reported from Calais that there was no sign of any delegates. He thought that they might appear by Christmas. There was some talk of extending the date, and the project was still theoretically on foot in the new year. The French were probably unaware of the terms of Charles of Orléans's deal with the English, but they were wary of the initiatives of desperate prisoners in England and had decided to boycott the conference.[76]

The English were no more successful in their attempt to extricate themselves from the war with Scotland. One of Bedford's first tasks in England had been to take a fresh look at relations with the northern kingdom. So far, James had stuck to the letter of his agreement with the English council. But he was unable to stop Scottish soldiers of fortune from volunteering to fight for Charles VII. In 1430, the council at Westminster reported that Scots were passing 'daily' through Dieppe and other ports under the noses of English officials, on their way to fight for Charles VII.[77] While things were going well in France, the English had been content to ignore the latent threat from Scotland. But with the reversal of their fortunes Scotland loomed larger in their thoughts. Berwick and Roxburgh, England's last surviving garrisons in the Scottish Lowlands, were in poor condition and hardly worth the cost of their defence. Guarding the border was expensive and made it difficult to recruit troops in the northern counties for service in France. Margaret Stewart was still in Scotland, but the threat that James might one day send her to France with another Scottish army hung over the English like the sword of Damocles.

THE PARTING OF FRIENDS, 1431–1434

In August 1433, an embassy was sent to Scotland under the leadership of King James's brother-in-law, Edmund Beaufort Count of Mortain, to try to negotiate a permanent peace. Beaufort was authorised to make attractive offers: the restitution of Berwick and Roxburgh and the abandonment of the English claim to the homage of the Scottish Kings. A treaty on these terms would have restored the territorial integrity of Scotland as it had been before Edward III's fateful intervention in the country a century before. James took the bait. He summoned a General Council (in effect a Parliament) to meet in the Dominican convent in Perth in October 1433. But although the King was keen to accept the English offer, the council rejected it after two days of acrimonious debate. The chronicler Walter Bower attended in his capacity as Abbot of Inchcolm. He was one of the commissioners charged with canvassing opinion in the assembly. His account shows that the decisive factor was the treaty with France, which ruled out a separate peace with the English. James's confessor, Abbot Fogo of Melrose, tried to persuade the assembly that a promise not to make peace with an enemy was contrary to God's law and not binding. But he was ignored and later accused of heresy by the Inquisitor of Scotland. Bower himself thought that the English offers were not made in good faith. They were a crafty trick to detach the Scots from the French. Many of those present must have shared his view. Others pointed to England's 'inveterate resentment' of the Scots. The legacy of Edward I and Edward III was not so easily forgotten. The Scots did not trust the English enough to want to abandon their only continental ally. The practical effect was that no peace could be made with Scotland except as part of a general settlement with France. In the following year, the English improved their offers, adding a proposal for a marriage alliance between the young Henry VI and a daughter of the Scottish King. The Scots were immovable.[78]

Shortly before Christmas 1433, the Commons finally came to grips with the problems of war and finance. They had digested Cromwell's gloomy report on the state of the King's finances but were unwilling to grant more than a single standard subsidy. It was not a generous grant, and it was payable in four instalments over two years, an unusually long period. The Commons also began the practice of directing that discounts should be given to towns and counties which found it difficult to raise the sums due under the antiquated scheme of assessment, now nearly a century old. The discounts were declared to be necessary for the relief of communities 'desolate, laid wasted or destroyed, overgreatly impoverished, or to the said tax over greatly charged'. The effect was to reduce the value of the standard subsidy by about a tenth. It was a watershed moment. The Commons had made it plain that they were not willing to increase the scale of England's commitment to the war in France. The Church was even more resistant than the Commons. A vocal minority of the Canterbury Convocation, meeting at St Paul's in London, would have refused to grant any subsidy at all, citing poverty, plague and past fiscal burdens. Two successive delegations of the House of Lords tried to impress on them the growing numbers and strength of the French, but to no avail. The assembly declined to match the Parliamentary grant with a full tenth, as they had done in the past, but voted only a proportion. Well over half the combined value of these grants was already committed to the repayment of Beaufort's recent loans. Over the next two years, the government's cash receipts fell to historically low levels. The Duke of Bedford did not hide his disappointment. He had pressed the English political community with the perilous position of Lancastrian France and called on them to fund the powerful army that might finally reverse the tide of fortune. 'Nevertheless ... the means thereof have not as yet be found, to my full great heaviness God knoweth.'[79]

Bedford remained in England for the first six months of 1434, during which argument raged about the future government of both England and France. The Commons, who had learned to distrust the Duke of Gloucester's abrasive style of government, wanted Bedford to remain in England. Bedford himself was determined to return to France, in spite of Parliament's inability to supply him with the tools of victory. He undertook to return regularly to England as and when he was needed there. He insisted, however, that even when he was in France, he must retain the decisive voice in the selection of the councillors at Westminster. In the final days of the Parliament, Bedford obtained its consent to new rules about the conduct of business, all of which were designed to limit the ability of the Duke of Gloucester to reshape the government in his own image. Until the King came of age the council's membership must be publicly disclosed and all new appointments submitted for his approval, wherever he was. He, Bedford, must be consulted about all appointments to offices of state, bishoprics and even lesser appointments in government service. These changes in effect made him regent in both countries.[80]

The Duke of Gloucester was intensely irritated by the new ordinances. He responded by challenging the whole conduct of the war by his brother. He produced an alternative plan of his own, which has not survived, but appears to have been a more ambitious variant of the one which Bedford had proposed to Parliament and which they had refused to fund. It envisaged another military surge with a view to winning a victory that would reverse the whole course of recent events. Gloucester rallied his supporters. He put it about that his plan would avoid the need for further war taxes in England for many years to come. Presumably this was to be achieved by recovering the conquered provinces of northern France and taxing or looting them.

A great council was summoned to consider the Duke's plan. It met at Westminster in the last week of April 1434 amid high public expectations. The lords temporal and spiritual and the crowd of experienced soldiers and officials who attended were under strong pressure to endorse Gloucester's proposals. The fractious sessions of the assembly continued well into May. Gloucester set out his plan in abrasive terms that were highly critical of Bedford. Bedford responded with his own document which Gloucester in turn found offensive. The assembly reconvened on 12 May in the undercroft of the Bishop of Durham's London mansion to present their advice in writing. Their view was that Gloucester's plan was admirable in principle but unaffordable. It would require a large army to be recruited immediately at a cost of between £48,000 and £50,000. Treasurer Cromwell reported that he could not find even half this sum. The commissioners who had been sent into the counties to raise loans reported that no one would lend. People were wary of default given the scale of the government's existing debt and the lack of unencumbered revenues to offer as security. The King's jewels, which had often been pawned, were now sadly depleted. The Duke of Gloucester's project was stillborn.[81]

In June 1434, in his final days in England, the Duke of Bedford attempted to put the flow of money from England to France on a more regular and sustainable footing, in place of the constant improvisations which had characterised the past three years. The Rouen administration had prepared analyses of military expenditure in Normandy, summaries of the finances of Bedford's personal domains, budgets, garrison lists and no doubt other documents which have not survived. The result of all this effort was a new financial plan. In future, the Chancellor of France, Louis of Luxembourg, was to receive 5,000 marks (£3,333) each half year from English revenues towards the cost of garrisons and field operations outside Normandy. To fund these payments, the trustees of the duchy of Lancaster agreed that once their existing loans to the government had been repaid, they would surrender their assets back to the Crown. This arrangement was expected to pay for a permanent force of 200 men-at-arms and 600 archers. Bedford for his part agreed that the revenues of his personal appanage in Normandy and Maine should be applied to military expenditure instead of being used to support his status and household in France. This was expected to pay for another 200 men-at-arms and 600 archers. In addition, the soldiers of the Calais garrison (who had always been paid from English revenues) were to be placed at his disposal to deploy elsewhere in France when they were needed.

Theoretically, these arrangements gave Bedford the wherewithal to support up to 2,000 men without additional calls on the King's ordinary revenues. It was an ingenious scheme, but less satisfactory than Bedford thought. Even if these revenues had been paid over promptly and in full, they could not have supported much more than half the number of troops envisaged. In fact, they rarely were. Bedford's appanage lands were already charged with the payment of salaries and pensions, a fact which he appears to have overlooked. As for the revenues of the duchy of Lancaster, they would not be available until trustees' existing loans had been repaid and that was unlikely to happen soon. The assets were not in the event returned to the Crown until 1443. The money had to be found from the King's ordinary revenues after all. Ultimately the payments promised to Louis of Luxembourg were made at irregular intervals and were funded by defaulting on obligations to the King's officers in Calais, Guyenne and Ireland. The Regent's immediate financial requirements had to be met by borrowing. This required a new settlement with Cardinal Beaufort. The council agreed to release him from the charge of trying to export his treasure illegally in 1432 and repaid the money that he had deposited to secure payment of any judgment against him. In the course of May and June, Beaufort's loans paid for the advances of the army which was to accompany Bedford back to France. In July 1434, the Duke left London for the coast and sailed for France. He never saw England again.[82]

CHAPTER IX

The Congress of Arras, 1433–1435

During Bedford's absence, the English commanders in France had devoted most of their energy and resources to the defence of the Duke of Burgundy's domains, for fear that he would make a separate peace with Charles VII. The main decisions were made by Bedford himself at the joint conference of the English and French councils at Calais, before he left for England. The siege of Saint-Valéry, which was conducted mainly by troops in English pay, represented the first fruit of this policy. The most vulnerable of Philip the Good's domains, however, was the duchy of Burgundy. The French offensives of the past three years had left the marches of the duchy dotted with predatory enemy garrisons. In the spring of 1433, Philip the Good decided to raise a large army in Artois and Picardy and lead it across Champagne to reinforce the local forces already operating there. The Duke of Bedford agreed to deploy the largest possible force in support of this operation. The command was given to the Earl of Arundel, whose effective use of speed, surprise and artillery had already begun to mark him out as the natural successor of the late Earl of Salisbury.[1]

Arundel was operating on the marches of Alençon and Maine in the spring of 1433. Bedford created a vast new military governorship for him, extending from the Atlantic to Champagne, and directed him to concentrate his forces on the marches of Burgundy. The Earl of Huntingdon's expeditionary army, which was due to arrive in Normandy at the end of May, was ordered to join him there. Arundel's movements were closely coordinated with Philip's. On 24 June 1433, the Duke marched out of Rethel with the men of Picardy and Artois and advanced across Champagne. Once he had joined forces with the troops of the duchy, south of Troyes, he had more than 3,000 men under his command. In addition, he had brought an artillery train from Flanders. Meanwhile, English forces converged on the Gâtinais.

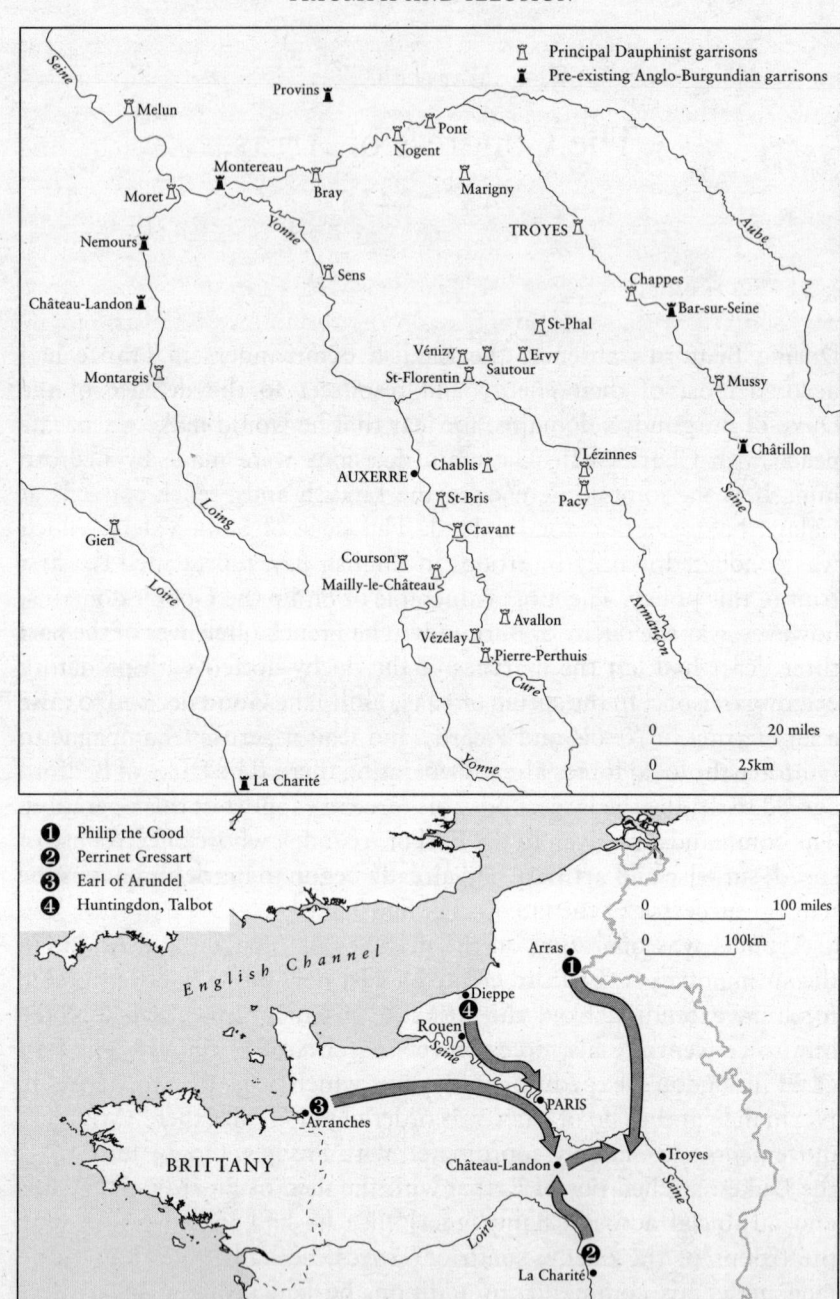

9 Anglo-Burgundian campaign in Burgundy and the Gâtinais,
June–September 1433

The English had four major garrisons in this region: Montereau at the confluence of the Seine and the Yonne, Nemours and Château-Landon in the Loing valley, and Provins in Brie which they had recently recaptured from the French. Towards the end of June, Arundel and Huntingdon arrived at Château-Landon with some 2,200 men. They were joined there by Villiers de L'Isle-Adam with several hundred Picards from Paris and by two freelance captains who transferred from Burgundian service: Perrinet Gressart, captain of the *routier* garrison at La Charité, and a Gascon captain known as the Bourc de Jardre. The combined strength of the army at Château-Landon came to over 3,000 men, making it comparable to Philip's own. More were on their way. At Westminster, the Duke of Bedford arranged for Sir John Talbot, who had recently returned to England from his French prison, to join Arundel with his company. He sailed for France in July. The commanders agreed upon a plan. They intended to clear the French garrisons from the valley of the Seine between Paris and Troyes and from the valley of the Yonne as far as Auxerre, while Philip the Good concentrated his efforts on the territory east and south of Troyes. Perrinet Gressart and the Bourc de Jardre were given the task of recovering Montargis, which the English had lost in humiliating circumstances six years before. The Duke of Bedford promised Gressart a reward of 10,000 *saluts* if he could take it.[2]

The English campaign opened spectacularly with the fall of Montargis. The captain of the town was a protégé of La Trémoille called Raymond de Villars. The Bourc de Jardre had suborned the girl-friend of his barber. Before dawn on 27 June 1433, she let him and a professional *échelleur* into the citadel from ladders through a high opening in the wall. They were followed by several hundred armed men. They took over the castle and then fought a bitter battle with the garrison in the streets of the town until the French finally fled out of the gates. The response of Charles VII's ministers was rapid but ineffectual. About a fortnight later, Jean Malet de Graville, Charles VII's Master of the Archers, appeared outside Montargis with 500 to 600 men. He succeeded in reoccupying the town and laid siege to the castle. But when the Earl of Huntingdon approached with a relief force Malet hastily demolished as much as he could of the town walls and left. Perrinet Gressart's companion in arms, the Aragonese adventurer François de Surienne, took possession of the citadel in the name of Henry VI. He was to remain there for the next five years.[3]

The Earls of Arundel and Huntingdon opened their campaign at the end of June 1433. They fought their way up the Seine valley into Champagne, clearing the valley of French garrisons, including those in the important walled town of Nogent and the fortified bridges at Bray and Pont. Within two weeks they had recovered the whole valley as far as Troyes. By the middle of July they were advancing up the Yonne taking every enemy garrison in their path until they were finally stopped by the walls of Sens. Philip the Good's campaign in Champagne and northern Burgundy was a triumphant promenade. He completed the reconquest of the upper Seine valley which the Earl of Arundel had begun. Mussy, the largest enemy garrison of the region, surrendered after a brief bombardment. Chappes, south of Troyes, an important Burgundian base which had been lost to Barbazan two years before, was captured after a siege of a week. Most places succumbed with the first salvo of artillery or entered into conditional surrender agreements after only a nominal resistance.

Serious opposition was encountered only at Pacy and Avallon, where the largest freelance companies were concentrated. Pacy on the river Armançon entered into a conditional surrender agreement in the middle of August. The Burgundians fully expected a royalist army to try to relieve it. They summoned help from all the English and Burgundian troops within marching distance to boost their forces at the *journée*. L'Isle-Adam came from the Gâtinais and Talbot from Paris. But the castle surrendered without incident. At Avallon, Forte-Épice put up a tougher fight. He held out for more than two months as the town around him was reduced to rubble by the Duke's bombards. Finally, he fled by night through a postern gate, leaving his wife, small son and most of his company to their fate.

These conquests provoked a string of submissions from other French garrisons. The companies occupying Chablis, Mailly and Saint-Bris were persuaded to surrender by a liberal distribution of bribes and the threat to execute all 200 of their fellows at Avallon. The fortress of Pierre-Perthuis below the hilltop abbey of Vézelay surrendered after the curtain wall had been carried by assault and the keep undermined. The French garrison of Cravant, which was under the same command, was the last place to open its gates. Between them, the Earl of Arundel and the Duke of Burgundy had achieved remarkable results in a short time. Some fifty walled places had fallen. All the enemy garrisons planted since 1430 in the Auxerrois and the marches of Burgundy and

Champagne were swept away except for Saint-Florentin, the frontier fortress on the Armançon. With François de Surienne's garrison holding Montargis, the English had closed the main route by which the French had been able to penetrate into the region from the Loire. The Earl of Arundel left in August with most of the contingents that had been withdrawn from Norman garrisons. The rest of the army dispersed after the *journée* of Pacy. Huntingdon and Talbot returned with their men to England in the autumn.[4]

In August 1433, the Earl of Arundel launched a fresh offensive in the duchy of Alençon and the frontier areas of Maine. The main targets of this campaign were the bases of Ambroise de Loré's partisans at Bonsmoulins and Saint-Céneri, both of them long-standing centres of armed resistance to English rule. The Earl had about 2,200 English troops under his command, about half of the English strength in Normandy, plus a large contingent of indigenous troops drawn from the feudal service of the duchy. They were supported by an artillery train laboriously assembled from the depots at Rouen and Louviers and dragged overland from Caen.

In the course of an eight-month campaign, Arundel recaptured almost all the French strongholds of the region which had been lost since the spring of 1429. Ambroise de Loré's headquarters at Bonsmoulins was besieged in September and quickly succumbed. The place was razed to the ground and never resurrected. Only a few stumps of masonry survive today to testify to its brief celebrity as a centre of partisan operations. Arundel met tougher resistance at de Loré's other base at Saint-Céneri (modern Saint-Céneri-le-Gérei). An attempt to surprise it failed, and in November Arundel sat down to batter it into submission with artillery. Charles of Anjou set about forming an army of relief. It was a powerful force, which included Charles himself, the Duke of Alençon, the Constable and both Marshals of France, as well as Jean de Bueil and Ambroise de Loré. They were too late to save Saint-Céneri. The place succumbed in January 1434 and was demolished like Bonsmoulins. But when, a few days later, Sillé-le-Guillaume entered into a conditional surrender agreement, Charles of Anjou determined to be present at the *journée*. Not everyone agreed with his decision. There was much to be said for Richemont's view that it was not worth saving. But Charles was concerned about the impact on his following in the region if the place was allowed to fall with no attempt at relief. His army duly appeared at Sillé on the appointed day. According to Richemont's contemporary biographer, it was the first time in living memory that a French army had actually turned up at a *journée*. But it was an empty victory, for they were forced to withdraw by concerns about their supplies and their line of retreat. As soon as they had gone, the English returned to Sillé and launched an assault. Three days later, on 12 March 1434, the place surrendered. From the marches of Alençon and Maine, the Earl of Arundel then marched across Lower Normandy to confront the French garrisons which had established themselves along the roads to Paris. In the course of April 1434, they were all cleared and most of their castles demolished. There was little if any resistance.[5]

In a purely military sense, these were successful campaigns. They also significantly disrupted French communications with Burgundy and Champagne. But the position of Paris remained as precarious as ever. Arundel had not had the numbers, the time or the equipment to besiege large towns. He had cleared the Yonne and the upper valley of the Seine, but with a powerful French garrison still installed at Melun, neither of these important navigable rivers could be used to supply the capital. He had cleared the roads south-west of Paris, but with the Bastard of Orléans still occupying Chartres the granary of the Beauce was still out of reach. This had been the abiding strategic problem of the English ever since the siege of Orléans. It took only one major river fortress to cut the capital off from a whole region.

The winter of 1433–4 was as difficult for Paris as the previous one. Supporters of the Valois cause in the city became bolder and more numerous. At the end of September 1433, some Parisians were found to have taken bribes to bring enemy troops over the walls from rafts floated in the moat. In the same week an even more alarming plot came to light, to admit 200 Scots disguised in English uniforms by the Porte Saint-Denis. When those involved were questioned under torture it became obvious that the scheme had extensive support among the city's patrician groups, men who had traditionally been among the Lancastrian regime's most reliable supporters. Their grievances included the collapse of trade, the failure of the legal system and the dwindling prestige of the once-great city. 'Things can't go on like this,' one of the plotters had said in the course of an indiscreet exchange in a city tavern. The ringleaders fled to the French garrison at Lagny after the first arrests, but a number were caught and six of them were beheaded in the market of Les Halles.

THE CONGRESS OF ARRAS, 1433-1435

With the appointment of La Hire in December 1433 to succeed Marshal Boussac as military governor north of the Seine and the Marne, the war around the walls of the capital took on a new savagery. La Hire's companies routinely attacked the heavily guarded food convoys on which supplies to the capital now depended. They cut the throats of every man in the escort who wore English insignia or spoke English. Among the records of the Corporation of London is a Parisian verse pamphlet from the spring of 1434, which probably reached England with a newsletter or a petition. The author lamented the disappearance of kings and nobles from the palaces and streets of Paris, the destruction of its crafts and its trade, the raiders who kidnapped or murdered those who ventured from the gates, the youth and naivety of the English King at a time which called for strength of purpose and experience. 'Come, fight and save me,' ran the refrain, 'or you will lose Paris and with it all of France.'[6]

At the beginning of May 1434, the Earl of Arundel was in Paris conferring with Sir John Talbot and the Grand Conseil. Talbot had recently returned to France with more than 900 men, the advance guard of what was intended to be a 2,000-strong expeditionary army. The question was what use to make of them. The Grand Conseil's priority, as always, was the security of the supply routes around Paris. But there was also growing concern about the Somme, where there had been an alarming upsurge in partisan activity. The leading figure was a captain called Charles Desmarais, who had assumed the mantle of Jacques d'Harcourt. Desmarais was an unusual figure who was said to have begun his career as a builder's labourer. He had risen to prominence in 1432, when he had captured the castle of Rambures in the valley of the Bresle. At the beginning on 1434, he led a raiding force north from the Beauvaisis and reoccupied Saint-Valéry less than six months after Robert Willoughby and the Count of Saint-Pol had recovered it. Much of their work in Picardy the year before was undone. From their base at Saint-Valéry, Desmarais's companies were able to occupy a number of castles around Amiens, establishing a loose blockade of the region's principal industrial city.[7]

The Grand Conseil resolved to employ the new forces from England in yet another attempt to clear the enemy garrisons which had blocked the valley of the Oise since 1429. At the same time the officers of the Duke of Burgundy planned to expel the garrisons which the French had planted in the valley of the Somme. The command of the campaign on the Oise was entrusted to Talbot, who was appointed lieutenant in the Île-de-France. He was given authority over an area extending from the Seine to the Somme and control of the Norman border fortresses of Gisors and Neufchâtel. He joined forces with the Earl of Arundel and Villiers de L'Isle-Adam to create a field army of some 1,600 men. Their operations marked a new pitch of savagery, matching that of La Hire. Talbot hanged entire garrisons that failed to surrender, with no quarter being given or ransoms taken. Arundel, a less aggressive temperament than Talbot, is said to have promised to 'join every man to a gibbet' who tried to hold a town against him. Beaumont-sur-Oise, an important fortified bridge twelve miles upstream of the English fortress-town of Pontoise, which had been occupied by the French in February, was recaptured in May. La Hire's brother Amadoc de Vignolles, who had been in command of the place, had fled north to Creil with most of his garrison on the English army's approach. The men left to defend the castle were hanged at the gates to the last man. The island fortress of Creil, a much stronger place than Beaumont, withstood a six-week siege before surrendering on terms on 20 June 1434. In July some 800 more men of the expeditionary army from England crossed the Channel and joined Talbot's army. The combined force cleared the French from Pont-Sainte-Maxence, Crépy-en-Valois and Clermont-en-Beauvaisis in about three weeks. Meanwhile, the Burgundians with about 1,000 men under the command of Philip the Good's nineteen-year-old cousin John of Nevers, expelled all the main French garrisons of the valley of the Somme, culminating on about 24 July in the conditional surrender of Saint-Valéry. The *journée* of Saint-Valéry was fixed for 1 August.[8]

At this point the progress of both allies was checked by the unexpected arrival of a French field army. The army, about 2,000 strong, was commanded by the Constable Arthur de Richemont and Pierre de Rieux, a figure from the past who had served as a Marshal under Charles VI. The new army had originally been intended for Champagne but it was diverted to Picardy when the English seemed to be sweeping all before them. At about the end of July 1434, Richemont entered Compiègne. He came too late to save Saint-Valéry. On the appointed day, John of Nevers was reinforced for the *journée* by the Count of Saint-Pol and Robert Willoughby with 500 English troops from Normandy. No one appeared to challenge them, and the place surrendered in accordance with its agreement. But Richemont's appearance put an end to any plans that Talbot might have had to advance further up the Oise or to join up with the Burgundians on the Somme. It also meant that for all his triumphs, Talbot's campaign was devoid of significant results. He had expelled the French garrisons from all their fortresses on the Oise downstream of Compiègne, but with Compiègne in French hands the capital's main supply route through the valley was still closed. The English army conducted a brief demonstration in front of Beauvais in the middle of August and then withdrew to Paris. This decision proved to be a disaster. It left Richemont free to turn his entire strength against the Burgundians. As Talbot retreated, Richemont reached the Somme and arrived before the town of Ham with its powerful castle and fortified bridge over the river. Most of its garrison had been withdrawn for operations elsewhere. The depleted company which remained was overwhelmed in the first assault. John of Nevers was left to fight off the French on his own.[9]

Like the English, Philip the Good was facing the classic problems of defensive warfare. The initiative was always with the enemy, who could pounce and withdraw at will, feeding and paying themselves from loot and *pâtis*. The war was disintegrating into an unending succession of firefights, which required the Duke to maintain a standing army and many garrisons at prodigious cost. Philip had hoped for a new expeditionary army from England comparable to the coronation expedition of 1430. He wanted up to 4,000 English troops to be placed under his own command. He demanded a large subsidy to pay his own troops. None of this was possible after the English Parliament's refusal to increase the scale of funding for the war. As the Westminster council pointed out to Philip's ambassador Quentin Ménard, who was back in England in June 1434, they were already paying more than forty garrisons and three field forces. For the past year, they had been spending English revenues on trying to make good the gap left by the financial collapse of the Paris government. All of this was true, and familiar. There had been countless earlier diplomatic exchanges of the same kind. But the council's assurances that they had done their best to reach agreement with Charles VII at Auxerre and Pont-de-Seine cut no ice with Philip. He knew that English intransigence over the claim to the French throne made agreement impossible. The English reply served only to confirm Philip's conviction that the time had come for them both to recognise reality and negotiate the best deal that they could with Charles VII. As he later told them, he had received letters from 'several kings and Christian princes' urging him to make his own peace and expressing their astonishment that he was still fighting. In Brittany, England's only other ally, John V, with his acute sense of the direction of the wind, had reached the same conclusion. He sent his Chancellor Jean de Malestroit to urge the English council to make peace. Malestroit was at Westminster at the same time as Ménard and received a very similar answer.[10]

While Ménard was in England, the already tense relationship between Philip the Good and his English ally took another turn for the worse. Philip chose this moment to retaliate for the English Partition Act. He issued an ordinance from Ghent banning the importation of English cloth into any part of the Burgundian Low Countries. Any consignments found there were ordered to be impounded and burned. A boycott of English cloth had been in force in Flanders for a number of years but had simply served to divert the trade to the ports of Holland, Zeeland and Brabant. The extension of the boycott to these territories resulted in a drop of more than 40 per cent in the volume of English cloth exports over the next two years. Philip's measures were a symptom of the decline of the alliance with England. He was no longer willing to resist the fury provoked by the English legislation among his subjects. The trade embargo marked a significant and permanent change in Flanders' relations with England.[11]

The Duke of Bedford landed at Dieppe in the middle of August 1434 after a fourteen-month absence in England. Within days of his return, a major rural rebellion shook the foundations of English rule in Normandy. Peasant uprisings in France had a long history. The peasant armies of the Jacquerie had risen in the 1350s against the indiscriminate violence of the *routier* companies. The rebellion of the Tuchins, who formed themselves into large roving bands of brigands in central France in the 1370s and 1380s, was a protest against the gratuitous violence of soldiers and the crushing burden of war taxes and *pâtis*. These things had happened, as Charles V had once put it, 'in the shadow of the war'. War intensified common grievances, until distinct incidents of low-level banditry coalesced into explosive insurrection. The 1430s were difficult years across the whole of northern Europe. Exceptionally severe winters followed by wet summers brought harvest failure, famine, disease and social unrest in their wake. In northern France the rivers froze and stopped the movement of foodstuffs. 1433 had been a particularly bad year. An epidemic of plague had persisted through the winter and well into the summer. The fruit harvest was killed by late frosts. October gales uprooted trees, while torrential rain in November rotted the newly sown grain in the fields.[12]

Saint-Pierre-sur-Dives was an unwalled village south of Caen, living under the shadow of a famous Benedictine abbey. There had been some ugly incidents in the region, in which English garrison troops had attacked and plundered open villages. The peasants of Saint-Pierre, like those of other villages, had gathered in their units to defend themselves. Some English had been killed. In August 1434, an English squire called Richard Venables led a company of men to Saint-Pierre-sur-Dives and killed about a dozen peasants in retaliation. In some ways, Venables was a characteristic figure of the last years of Lancastrian Normandy. He had been in Normandy for at least five years. For much of that time he served in the garrison of the Duke of Bedford's castle at Harcourt, before abandoning garrison service to set up as a freelance captain living on booty. In 1434, he commanded a large company which had installed itself in the abandoned Cistercian abbey of Savigny and had taken to looting on the marches of Brittany and Maine. The alarm went up immediately after the incident at Saint-Pierre. The peasantry of the whole surrounding region was summoned to arms by church bells and assembled in the hamlet of Vicques near Saint-Pierre. There, they were suddenly attacked by a force of mounted English troops commanded by Venables and two associates called Thomas Waterhouse and Roger Yker. They cut down everyone in their path and pursued the survivors across the country as they fled. About 1,200 peasants were killed. English opinion was divided. Some were loud in their approval. They thought that the peasants had it coming to them. The official reaction was horror. The *bailli* of Caen ordered an inquiry. The Grand Conseil sent Jean Rinel to confront Venables at Savigny. A number of ringleaders, including Waterhouse and Yker, were arrested and taken to Falaise where they confessed and were summarily beheaded on the orders of Sir John Fastolf. Venables fled, but he was quickly found when a price of 1,000 *saluts* was put on his head. At the end of November 1434, the Duke of Bedford personally ordered him to be drawn, hanged and quartered in the marketplace at Rouen.[13]

By this time reports of the massacre had provoked a spontaneous uprising across much of the Cotentin. By October 1434, tens of thousands of men were in arms. Most of them were peasants with only rudimentary weapons. But they were joined by some well-armed gentry and found a leader in a local squire called Pierre Chantepie. The rebels sent messages to the Duke of Alençon, asking him to serve as their captain. Alençon sent Ambroise de Loré with 300 professional troops to support them, while he set about recruiting more. At Poitiers, Charles VII's ministers began to organise another army. Men were summoned to muster at Angers in January. Meanwhile, the rebels advanced on Caen and occupied the fortified enclosure of the suburban abbey of St Stephen (the 'Abbaye aux Hommes'). Sir John Fastolf, who was at Le Mans, left the city at once with 120 men, more than a third of his garrison, to support the defence of Caen. He stumbled on the peasant army at night a short distance from the town and killed a large number of them. Shortly afterwards, he entered the town and organised a sortie from the gates which claimed another 400 casualties, including Pierre Chantepie. The peasant army had no proper organisation. No arrangements had been made for feeding such a large host. It was bitterly cold. Most of them abandoned the struggle over the following days. Some, fearing the vengeance of the English, hid in the forests. Others left, disheartened, for their homes.

There was only a rump of about 5,000 or 6,000 men still in arms when Ambroise de Loré finally reached them on the road a few miles from Caen by the Cistercian abbey of Aunay-sur-Odon. De Loré could see that the attempt to take Caen was hopeless. He decided to lead the peasant army against the important English garrison of Avranches, which was thought to be weaker. Towards the end of January 1435, the rebel army met the Duke of Alençon east of Avranches and a few days later laid siege to the town. But their advance had been too slow. Powerful English forces were building up north of Avranches under the command of the Earl of Arundel. The peasants became anxious. Desertions depleted their numbers every day. There was no sign yet of the French army which was supposed to be assembling at Angers. After a week they abandoned the siege and headed aimlessly south along the march of Brittany, until they reached Fougères, where their army broke up.[14]

The revolt in the Cotentin, and the far more damaging one in the Caux the following year, were the first movements of resistance to English rule to organise themselves on a large scale. The English were shocked. They made a serious attempt to address the underlying problem of undisciplined garrison troops and freelance soldiers 'living on the land'. The Earl of Arundel was ordered to round them up and put those who were of any use into royal service or send them back to England. Several hundred of these men were drafted into field forces during the summer. Commissioners were appointed to investigate acts of violence against the local population and punish those responsible. But the damage was done and it proved to be irreparable. There was a general loss of nerve among the Regent's councillors and captains. When the peasants of the Cotentin rose, Thomas Lord Scales had been methodically preparing to starve out the garrison of Mont-Saint-Michel. He had rebuilt the bastide at Ardevon and started to build another on the ruins of an old seigneurial castle at Saint-Jean-le-Thomas on the north shore of the bay. But in January 1435, while the peasant army was outside Avranches, the 320 men in garrison at Ardevon, believing that Alençon's peasant army was about to attack them, sloped away by night to join the Earl of Arundel, leaving all their stores and artillery to be seized by the garrison of the mount. Five months later, in June 1435, the English abandoned Saint-Jean-le-Thomas in order to free up men for the defence of Paris. It was a symbolic moment, the abandonment of the last attempt to capture a fortress whose garrison had mocked every English attempt to subdue it for the past eighteen years.[15]

This loss of nerve marked a profound change in the political mentality of the English in Normandy. Soldiers and administrators became more suspicious of their Norman subjects. Sir John Fastolf had been concerned about the deteriorating security situation ever since the debacle of Orléans. By 1435 he had concluded that Henry VI would never enjoy the affection of the French 'which of their nature love his adversary more than him'. They understood nothing but the language of force. The English, he declared, should not be 'demeaned so much by the French counsel as it hath be done heretofore'. He called for the Rouen council to be filled with experienced English soldiers, and not with French administrators as it had been in the past. Fastolf's views came to be shared by a generation of English captains and administrators in Normandy and perhaps even by the Duke of Bedford, on whose behalf those words were written. Summonses of the indigenous nobility for field service became rarer and the response weaker. In the new forms of indenture issued to garrison commanders six weeks after the outbreak, the rules about recruiting local men to royal garrisons were tightened up. No more than an eighth of any garrison could henceforth be French, regardless of rank. At private castles, French garrison commanders were required to find family members to give bonds for their loyalty. At royal castles Frenchmen had rarely been appointed as captains or deputies, but the few exceptions were squeezed out, or else arrangements were made to ensure that they had only Englishmen serving under them. A few years later, Englishmen were being paid to keep watch on the walls of Rouen, and no doubt other places, instead of townsmen who owed guard duty for free but could no longer be trusted. A government dedicated to the defence of the population against external enemies, gradually became an army of occupation whose priorities were internal control and counterinsurgency.[16]

The change of mood was visible in the built landscape. In the northern Beauce, the imposing twelfth-century castle of Houdan stood over the Roman road from Paris to Dreux, 150 miles from the epicentre of the peasant rising. Its private owner, Simon Morhier, was the Provost of Paris and an influential member of the Grand Conseil. Houdan had already been betrayed once to the French by local men. When, in January 1435, Morhier entered into an indenture with a French squire for its defence, the new captain was required to build a new timber fortification 'in case the townsmen rise up and try to force the castle'. In the valley of the Risle, Edmund Beaufort's steward undertook substantial building work to strengthen his castle of Harcourt against another local rising. Beaufort's new country residence at Elbeuf, on the Seine south of Rouen, had been conceived as a place for pleasure, but it was built like a fortress, with a drawbridge, gunports, arrow-slits and raised walkways. Few buildings were as evocative as the new royal palace of Rouen, which had been planned by Henry V as an impressive royal residence destined to display the power and prestige of the Lancastrian Kings. The site by the Seine in the south-west corner of the city had been marked out by Henry himself before his death. But when the building finally began to rise from the ground in 1435, it was as a brutal fortress designed to shelter the English from the townsmen.[17]

In his report on the failure of his efforts in France, Cardinal Albergati had urged the fathers at Basel to appoint their own peacemaking mission. In May 1434 the Council took him at his word. They appointed an embassy headed by Cardinal Hughes de Lusignan, a member of the French dynasty which ruled the crusader kingdom of Cyprus. They gave him the portentous but empty title of legate '*a latere*', which normally signified a legate with all the powers of the body which sent him. In the end, Hughes and his colleagues did very little. They briefly met Charles VII and his councillors at Vienne on the Rhône and then returned to Basel. Philip the Good, however, seized upon this opening to keep the peace process alive. In May 1434, he persuaded a reluctant English council to send another English delegation to Basel after the debacle of the previous year.[18]

The new delegation had an eye-opening exposure to the politics of the Council. It entered the Swiss city with great show on 5 August 1434. Greeted by the cardinals at the gates, their cavalcade passed through the streets led by Edmund Beaufort Count of Mortain and escorted by 150 mounted archers in livery. But when, twelve days after their arrival, they came to the cathedral to present their credentials, the French objected once more to the form of Henry VI's letters, which described him as King of England and France. Their anger mounted as the Bishop of London, in his opening homily, repeatedly referred to Henry by that title. The chief French spokesman was Amadée Talaru Archbishop of Lyon. Henry VI's ambassadors, he protested, could speak for England but not for any part of France. The Englishmen were eventually incorporated in the Council in October, but the issue came back in December, when the Bishops of Lisieux and Bayeux arrived to join the English delegates as representatives of Lancastrian France. These people, said the Archbishop of Lyon, could not be accepted as emissaries of the French kingdom by virtue of Henry VI's objectionable claim to be its king. This provoked a loud outburst of 'insults and noise' from the English benches which drowned out the rest of the Archbishop's words. But the French were supported by the delegations of the Valois kingdom's political allies: Castile, the Angevin kingdom of Naples, Cyprus and Scotland. The two Norman bishops were excluded while the issue was referred to a commission. There it festered, and when the English finally withdrew from the Council in the following summer it was still unresolved.[19]

The truth was that the subjects of Charles VII had come to dominate the assembly. The French provinces of the Church accounted for more than a third of the 3,500 fathers of the Council, and almost all of them came from Valois France. They had been present almost from the start. They were highly organised, ably led and wholly dedicated to the interests of their King. They also had the support of France's traditional allies and the francophone territories of the Empire which were politically dominated by France, as the affair of the Norman bishops had shown. But it was not just numbers and tactical skill which accounted for French influence at Basel. For centuries before the English wars, France had been the dominant continental power and French the dominant European culture. The Council's view of France was coloured by long historical experience, reflected in the instructions which it would later give to its delegation at the Congress of Arras. The fathers declared that France's power, the skills and intelligence of its nobility, the stature of its churchmen, its great wealth and large population, had made it over the centuries the mainstay of the Church until the current crisis had laid it low. Remember the great Kings of France from Charles Martel to Charlemagne and Louis the Pious, who had been the pre-eminent European figures of their day. Remember the pivotal role of France in the crusades. The Christian Church was facing grave internal and external challenges in the 1430s. History, they said, showed that when France was incapable of playing its traditional role among nations, all Christendom was weakened.[20]

All of this reflected the growing international prestige of the Valois monarchy in the aftermath of its reconquest of much of the north, just as, two decades earlier, the English had been able to dominate the Council of Constance after the battle of Agincourt. Charles VII's ministers pressed home their advantage. They embarked on a prolonged diplomatic offensive across Europe. They courted those in Germany who resented the aggressive incursions of the house of Burgundy in the western territories of the Empire. Charles VII renewed his alliance with the Austrian Habsburgs, who had fallen out with Philip the Good over the succession to Brabant and the Burgundian expansion in the Rhineland. The Emperor Sigismund, a persistent enemy of the house of Burgundy still smarting from his diplomatic reverses in Holland, Zeeland and Brabant, was no longer the reliable ally of England that he had been at Constance. He too ultimately entered into an alliance with France in June 1434 which was specifically directed against Philip the Good ('disobedient rebel and so-called Duke of Burgundy'). After a long hiatus, in which his relations with Castile had been indifferent, Charles sent an embassy to Castile, the first for six years, which renewed the old treaties at the beginning of 1435. Another neglected ally, Scotland, received two French embassies. The marriage alliance of 1428, which had been a dead letter from the moment it had been sealed, was reinstated in February 1435. None of these alliances produced military support, although the French had high hopes of the Austrians and the Scots. But they did much to reinforce the international influence of Valois France. By 1435, Charles VII was well on the way to re-establishing the great network of alliances which had made France such a formidable diplomatic power in the time of his grandfather, while the English had allowed their own international connections to wither. The loss of confidence of the English in France was matched by a decline in their international stature. No European power apart from Burgundy regarded the Lancastrian claim to France as anything but a reminder of the brief and anomalous period from 1415 to 1425 when English armies had swept all before them in the midst of a French civil war. By 1434, even the Burgundians at Basel had been instructed to avoid antagonising the French, now that Philip the Good was bent on finding an accommodation with them. They had vociferously supported the English claims to the French throne the year before but sat in stony silence through the angry exchanges of August and December 1434.[21]

At the end of July 1434, Philip the Good finally lost patience with his allies and determined to go ahead with the peace process with or without them. The last straw was the retreat of Sir John Talbot's army when Richemont entered Compiègne. The Duke was on the road to Burgundy when he learned of this reverse. The news of the Constable's advance to the Somme and the fall of Ham followed soon after. The forces of John of Nevers, Philip's cousin and lieutenant in the region, were outnumbered and his northern domains were at Richemont's mercy. Philip sent one of his chamberlains, Pierre de Vaudrey, with a herald to speak to the French Constable at Ham. Negotiations between the French leaders and John of Nevers opened early in September. The Chancellor Regnault de Chartres hurried north to join them, bringing large powers of negotiation with him in his satchels. On 17 September they entered into a six-month truce which was intended to pave the way to a permanent peace. It covered the whole of the sector north of Normandy and the river Aisne, in other words Picardy, Artois, the Beauvaisis and the Laonnais. Ham was to be restored to John of Luxembourg. La Hire's headquarters at the castle of Breteuil, half-way between Beauvais and Amiens, which had for years had been a thorn in the side of the Burgundians, was to be surrendered and demolished. Richemont demanded a large sum of money to pay his army before he would agree to put his seal to the instrument. Philip's captains were too desperate to make an issue of this. John of Nevers held a series of meetings with delegates of the surrounding towns, calling for loans and grants. They had little choice but to agree if they wanted to be rid of Richemont's army and La Hire's companies. The Burgundians eventually paid them an indemnity of 50,000 gold *saluts*.[22]

The truce of Ham did not cover the southern domains of the house of Burgundy. The situation there was complicated by the fact that the war was being fought by the Count of Clermont (now Duke of Bourbon since the death of his father in England). He was acting not only as Charles VII's lieutenant but also in his own right as the ruler of the princely appanage of Bourbonnais and Auvergne and Burgundy's principal regional rival. Philip the Good passed most of the last four months of 1434 in a debilitating campaign in the southern march of Burgundy, while his representatives negotiated with Charles VII's ambassadors in the castle of Amadeus of Savoy at Pont-de-Veyle beyond the Saône. This subsidiary war ground on until the last of Bourbon's strongholds, at La Roche Solutré, surrendered on 13 December. The parties then proclaimed a three-month truce covering the rest of the Duke of Burgundy's territories. At the same time, they informally agreed to hold a preliminary conference in the new year to prepare a framework for peace. The truces agreed at Ham and Pont-de-Veyle marked the final withdrawal of the Duke of Burgundy from the English war effort.[23]

The preliminary conference opened on 20 January 1435 at Nevers. Charles VII was represented by Regnault de Chartres, Christophe d'Harcourt and Marshal Lafayette. They were joined a few days after the opening by Arthur de Richemont. The Duke of Bourbon arrived to support his own claims against Burgundy. Philip the Good marked the significance of the gathering by attending in person, travelling across the snowbound Morvan in the depth of winter to be there. He installed himself in the bishop's palace, while the other delegates and attendants filled the mansions of the city. It was a family gathering. Bourbon and Richemont were both married to Philip's sisters. The sessions were held in an atmosphere of conviviality which astonished those present. 'No one would have guessed that they had ever been at war,' wrote a Burgundian herald. Others were more cynical. 'We must be fools to risk our lives and souls at the whim of lords and princes,' one of them declared in his cups, 'they make peace when it pleases them and leave us with the poverty and destruction.' In spite of the cynicism, the discussions at Nevers marked the turning point of the peace process. There was a settlement of the long-running disputes between the Dukes of Burgundy and Bourbon, and an agreement in principle on the amends which Charles VII would make for the murder of John the Fearless. The diplomats then turned to the larger issues of peace and war. The English were not present at Nevers, but they were in everyone's mind. The French delegates made it plain, as they had at Semur-en-Auxois and Auxerre, that they did not wish to negotiate with them. They wanted a separate peace with the Duke of Burgundy, which would put them in a better position to deal with the English later. As Richemont recalled many years later, the French feared that the mere presence of the English would deter the Burgundians from doing a deal with Charles VII. But Philip was adamant, and they were obliged to submit. The issues were referred to a diplomatic congress involving all three parties and, it was hoped, Brittany as well. They agreed that it would open on 1 July 1435. There were the usual arguments about the venue. The French wanted Auxerre, Mâcon or Nevers itself, knowing that the English would be reluctant to come to these places. Philip insisted on Arras, which was more accessible from both Westminster and Paris. Arras was finally agreed. The Pope would be invited to appoint Cardinal Albergati to serve as mediator alongside a representative of the Council of Basel.

The rest of the agreed document addressed the role of the parties at the proposed Congress. Philip the Good agreed to attend it himself and to invite the English to send ambassadors. The French agreed that they would make offers at Arras with which the English ought in all reason to be content. If the English did not appear, then Philip would do all that he could ('saving his honour') to negotiate something that ought in all justice to satisfy them. If they were represented, he would work on their delegation to agree terms of peace and would make his displeasure clear if they refused. In that case, the agreement envisaged that ('saving his honour' again) Philip would make a separate peace with Charles VII. To make this outcome more attractive, Charles VII's representatives promised that if peace was made between them, he would cede territory to Philip on both banks of the Somme, subject to an option for the King to reacquire it at a price of 400,000 gold *écus*.[24]

The agreement reached at Nevers largely determined the outcome at Arras. It was in effect a provisional resolution of the main issues between the French King and the Duke of Burgundy, coupled with a joint ultimatum to the English to make peace on any terms that appeared reasonable to both of them. Philip had clearly signalled his intention of abandoning his ally and making a separate peace with Charles VII if the English stuck to their current position. In the agreed text, he referred to Charles VII for the first time as 'King of France'. But the reservation for his honour was meant seriously. He had sworn an oath in 1420 to abide by the treaty of Troyes. The oath was therefore beginning to assume great importance. The English knew that the Pope could dispense the faithful from honouring their oaths, and they suspected that Eugenius might already have done so in this case. The civil lawyer Adam Moleyns, a rising star in the royal administration, was about to leave for the papal court on other diplomatic business. He was instructed to find out. In response, the Pope wrote assuring the English government that he had not dispensed anyone from any oaths that they might have sworn to Henry V or the current King. This was the truth, but it was not the whole truth. Eugenius IV had reappointed Albergati as his mediator, as the signatories at Nevers had asked. He had given him two procurations. The first empowered the legate to make peace between England and France. The other empowered him to make a separate peace between Charles VII and the Dukes of Burgundy and Brittany, and to annul any oath or other obligation that might stand in the way. Eugenius intended these powers to be used. His instructions to Albergati were that if negotiations between England and France broke down, he was to press the Duke of Burgundy to make a separate peace with France in spite of the treaty of Troyes.[25]

The loud negotiations at Nevers cannot have passed unnoticed by the Lancastrian government in Paris, and some idea of what was afoot must soon have reached Westminster. But the English council received no official notification of the outcome until 8 May 1435, when Toison d'Or, the herald of the Order of the Golden Fleece, arrived at Westminster with a formal invitation to attend the Congress, now only seven weeks away. The herald had set out for England in February, a few days after the date had been fixed, but had been delayed by illness. The English reaction was described by Chancellor Stafford to Parliament later in the year. They were outraged by the lack of consultation, the short notice, and the apparent breach of the restrictions in the treaty of Troyes on unilateral negotiations with the enemy. They would have been even more outraged if they had known the terms agreed at Nevers.[26]

Toison d'Or was followed to Westminster by an embassy led by Hughes de Lannoy, which arrived in late May 1435. Lannoy had come to justify his master's conduct and to persuade the English to participate in the Congress. His instructions were a remarkable document, a heartfelt plea for an end to the war which loses none of its emotional force, even in the ancient French of a diplomatic draftsman (probably Lannoy himself). The ambassador pointed out that the treaty of Troyes had not turned out as its authors had expected. It had not healed the scars of the civil wars or settled the dynastic issue between England and France. The peace which it promised had not come about. He reminded the English councillors that Henry V himself had warned of the risks and costs of a long war. He claimed that at the end of his life Henry had been looking for a negotiated way out, as those of his councillors who were still alive would confirm. Lannoy himself had been party to some of these exchanges.

Lannoy was brutally frank about the current military position. The war could not be won. Neither party was strong enough to overcome the other. Most Frenchmen backed Charles VII. The northern towns who had acknowledged the house of Lancaster had only done so under Burgundian influence. These towns were now facing ruin and their loyalty to the dual monarchy could no longer be counted on. Many of them had already surrendered without striking a blow and were beyond recovery, save at a cost in money, blood and effort which the allies could not afford to pay. Travelling between Flanders and Burgundy, Philip the Good had seen the charred villages and abandoned fields for himself and had heard at first hand the demands of the people for an end to the war. The Duke knew that the English favoured a long truce as a way of avoiding the issue of the claim to the throne. But this too was unrealistic. No truce would hold. There were too many French garrisons in English and Burgundian regions made up of irregulars living on loot. Lannoy ended ominously. If the English council ignored the Duke's plea, the Duke would have done his duty. He would 'hold himself discharged of it, and for witnesses will call on all of my lords here present and listening'.[27]

The English did not need to be persuaded to come to the Congress. They realised that they would be wrong-footed if they failed to appear. They originally hoped to bind Philip the Good to their cause by making him their principal ambassador, but no one can have been surprised when he declined the honour. To make him Henry VI's ambassador, his spokesman explained, would inhibit his direct dealings with the French if the English fell out with them. 'In this matter, there are three parties: the King, his adversary and my lord of Burgundy for his own particular interest.' In the event, the English appointed a particularly grand embassy. It consisted of twenty-six ambassadors led by the Archbishop of York, John Kemp. Its membership roll was an overt statement of the ideal of the dual monarchy. Apart from Kemp there were ten English and fifteen French delegates, with a quorum of eight, half English and half French, and a secretariat of lawyers and clerks drawn from both realms. The English members included two other bishops, the Earls of Suffolk and Huntingdon, Walter Lord Hungerford, the Seneschal of Aquitaine Sir John Radcliffe and the keeper of Henry VI's privy seal William Lyndwood. The French members of the Lancastrian delegation were nominated by the Duke of Bedford. They included Louis of Luxembourg, Bishop Cauchon, and the three principal French soldiers in English service, John of Luxembourg, his nephew Louis Count of Saint-Pol and Villiers de L'Isle-Adam, together with the senior state secretary Jean Rinel. Not all of these men were present throughout. Louis of Luxembourg and Villiers de L'Isle-Adam were detained by a burgeoning crisis in Paris and did not appear at all. What was never clear was the role of Cardinal Beaufort. Beaufort was England's most famous and experienced international statesman, a dominant figure in the English government and well regarded by the Duke of Burgundy. He was told to cross the Channel but to remain at Calais. The main reason for this arrangement appears to have been to hold him in reserve to break a deadlock between the parties at Arras, either by intervening on his own authority or perhaps by authorising concessions beyond the powers of the ambassadors.[28]

The instructions of the English delegation were drawn up in late June 1435. They left little room for manoeuvre. The ambassadors were told to make no concessions about Henry VI's status or rights as King of France. The whole subject was said to be 'difficult and very dangerous' in view of the King's minority. Cardinal Beaufort may have had a secret authority to enlarge the ambassadors' powers, but there is no reason to think that it extended to this point. The English council recognised that this would rule out a permanent peace. So, in spite of Lannoy's warning, the ambassadors were enjoined to seek a long truce of twenty, thirty, forty or even fifty years. When the King was of full age, he would be able to revisit the question himself. With goodwill on each side, the council suggested, a long truce would confer many of the advantages of a permanent peace. The goodwill could be secured by a marriage between Henry and one of Charles VII's four infant daughters, 'the eldest or the one who, after inspection, is found likely to be most pleasing to the King'. The Earl of Suffolk and Sir John Radcliffe were nominated as the appropriate experts to carry out this examination. These powers were supplemented by at least three further sets of instructions dealing with the territorial partition of France during the truce and the release of the Duke of Orléans. To enable the Duke of Orléans to participate in the negotiations, he was brought to Calais in the company of Cardinal Beaufort, but for reasons of security was not allowed to proceed further. Any French diplomats who wished to confer with him would have to apply for safe-conducts to visit him in the fortress.[29]

Both sides set out to improve their strategic position in advance of the Congress by seizing as much territory as they could in the short time left. But Charles VII was better prepared and better armed than his enemies. In May 1435, he presided over an assembly of notables in the city of Tours. It was one of those grand consultative gatherings which the Valois kings had traditionally summoned in order to rally support for their plans at critical moments. The assembly approved the King's participation in the Congress. Its main business, however, was to formulate plans for immediate military action against the English. The Constable Arthur de Richemont was formally restored to royal favour, the King expressing his regret that 'certain malevolent persons then in power' had deprived him of his services. But it was the Bastard of Orléans, much the best captain in Charles's service, who took the lead. He proposed to step up operations on both flanks of the duchy of Normandy and to mount a major offensive in the Île-de-France with a view to putting the King in a position to capture Paris. He obtained the council's approval for a bold plan to seize the abbey town of Saint-Denis and establish a permanent base within five miles of the capital.[30]

The fighting had already begun to intensify as the assembly at Tours was sitting. Towards the end of April 1435, some 300 French troops from the Beauvaisis made their way by night over the ford of the Somme at Blanchetaque and took Rue by escalade. The leading spirit in this enterprise was once again Charles Desmarais. Rue was a river port on the north side of the bay of the Somme. It was defended by a detachment from the nearby English garrison at Le Crotoy. The loss of the town imperilled the security of Le Crotoy and threatened the sea traffic of the Somme ports. Bedford ordered the Earl of Arundel to march at once on the town. Arundel received these orders at Mantes, where he was commanding a field force of some 800 men guarding the valley of the Eure and the western approaches to Paris. He led his men north to Gournay, the principal English fortress of the northern march, where about 200 more men and a crowd of armed peasants and townsmen joined him. At Gournay, he decided on a diversion to capture Gerberoy, a walled town dominated by an ancient castle which the French were refortifying.

On the evening of 8 May the Earl marched north out of Gournay with his army in two divisions. One of them was encumbered with the artillery, which slowed down its progress. Arundel marched through the night hoping to achieve surprise. Unknown to him, La Hire, Poton de Saintrailles and other French captains had occupied Gerberoy during the night with some 400 men. They were waiting for him in the morning. Arundel's force was stronger, but his divisions were too widely separated. La Hire's company, which included some of the most experienced cavalrymen in France, was able to charge and scatter each of them in turn. The Earl rallied all the men he could gather and made a stand in an enclosed field on a hill with a hedge at his back. The French attacked on foot and took the hill. Their cavalry charged straight through the line of stakes in front of the archers and completed the rout. Arundel himself was captured. He had suffered a bad wound in his leg from a culverin. It became infected and the leg had to be amputated. Gangrene was a common killer of medieval soldiers. Arundel survived for about a month but died in captivity at Beauvais on 12 June. The English had failed to retake Rue and had lost one of their best commanders along with some 400 or 500 men killed or captured, about a tenth of their entire strength in Normandy. Over the following weeks the French garrison at Rue was heavily reinforced by French freelance companies. They ranged at will across the region from the Somme to the march of Flanders. The 'Armagnacs of Rue', complained the men of Calais, 'press us close'.[31]

The withdrawal of Arundel's field army from Mantes, followed by transfers to the northern march after the defeat at Gerberoy, weakened the defences of the southern march, a fact which was quickly noticed and exploited by the Bastard of Orléans. Moving north from Chartres towards the end of May 1435, his companies occupied Verneuil for the third time in a decade and Houdan for the second time in two years. In the following days, they moved into the valley of the Eure, threatening Evreux. Meanwhile, Saint-Denis fell to a French raiding force drawn from Charles VII's northern garrisons. The watch were asleep or absent when 300 or 400 men came over the walls from ladders in the early hours of 1 June. By the time that the alarm was raised it was too late. The captain of the town fought a hopeless rearguard action through the streets, while the inhabitants welcomed in the conquerors. Within two weeks the companies of La Hire, Poton de Saintrailles and Guillaume de Flavy were all concentrated in the plain of Saint-Denis north of Paris. Eventually there were about 1,600 men lodged in or around the town. From here, they extended their reach into the Oise valley, where they recaptured the bridge-town of Pont-Sainte-Maxence. They raided every day up to the gates of the capital, killing every man they found beyond the walls.[32]

The English were caught on the wrong foot. No reinforcements had been sent to Normandy, and no expeditionary army had been planned for that year. It was not for want of advice. Hughes de Lannoy had warned them that the French were likely to mount a powerful offensive in the weeks before the Congress opened. As he pointed out, events on the ground would have a significant impact on the parties' bargaining power at Arras. Unless the English quickly sent an army to France, they would find themselves negotiating at the point of a lance with an adversary who would have no reason to make concessions. Lannoy's warning was justified sooner than he could have imagined, for the news of the battle of Gerberoy and the loss of Saint-Denis arrived while he was still in England. It was followed by a panic-stricken review of the military situation at Westminster. There were some 4,300 English troops in Normandy, about 40 per cent of them assigned to mobile field forces and the rest in garrisons. More than half of the troops at the Regent's disposal were based along the vulnerable southern front facing the Orléanais and the Beauce, where the Bastard of Orléans had substantial forces. The northern march was dangerously denuded of troops and just as vulnerable to the companies of La Hire and Poton de Saintrailles.[33]

Given the current nervousness about the possible defection of the Duke of Burgundy, the defence of Paris was a serious problem. Philip the Good visited the city unexpectedly on 14 April 1435 in the absence of the Regent. It was only too obvious that his purpose was to reinforce his personal authority there. The Parisians were impressed by his great cortege of courtiers, his imposing military escort, his wagons full of meat, fish, wine and cheese, and his train of bastard children. They received him with acclamation and flocked to his open audiences. The only English troops in the capital were a company of eighty men retained by Sir John Talbot, who were probably based in the Bastille. The main burden of defending the city fell on the Chancellor Louis of Luxembourg and the Grand Conseil. But their hands were tied. They depended on regular cash subsidies from England, which had not been paid since the previous October. As a result, they had been forced to lay off most of their men. After the French capture of Saint-Denis, urgent steps were taken to rebuild the defenders' strength in Paris. Louis of Luxembourg raised more than 1,300 men, including 500 Picards commanded by his cousin the Bastard of Saint-Pol. The English government assumed responsibility for their wages and paid off the arrears of the subsidy owing to the Grand Conseil. Another 60 men-at-arms and 600 archers were hastily recruited by the councillors at Rouen from the freelance and unemployed soldiery of Normandy and sent to the city under the command of the *bailli* of Evreux, Sir George Rigmaiden. By the end of June 1435, there must have been about 2,000 troops in Paris.[34]

At Westminster, the council belatedly changed its mind about sending a new expeditionary army to France. In May 1435, Talbot and Willoughby were urgently recalled to England to recruit it. In spite of the short notice, indentures were sealed on 8 and 9 June for companies totalling about 2,000 men. Coming on top of the subsidies sent to Louis of Luxembourg and the cost of a large and expensive delegation to the Congress of Arras, this represented a heavy financial commitment. Cardinal Beaufort lent more than £7,000, with no security other than the personal bonds of the Westminster councillors. He put relentless pressure on other lenders. The trustees of the duchy of Lancaster (of whom Beaufort was one) lent more than £3,000, again without effective security. £2,000 more was taken from the accumulated revenues of Beaufort's nephew John Earl of Somerset, a prisoner in France. There was no time to send commissioners into the counties, but selected individuals were mulcted for loans. It is measure of the gravity of the situation as it was perceived in England that in six weeks the government succeeded in borrowing £22,000 from lenders who had very little prospect of prompt repayment. The army of Talbot and Willoughby eventually mustered at Barham Down in Kent on 19 and 20 July and sailed for France at about the same time as the English delegation's arrival at the Congress.[35]

Charles VII's delegation met his own council on 6 July 1435 in the castle at Amboise on the Loire in order to complete the preparations for the Congress. Twelve ambassadors were nominated to represent him. The nominal head of the embassy and personal representative of the King was the Duke of Bourbon, formerly Count of Clermont. He was appointed on account of his status as the senior prince of the royal line, and perhaps because he was the Duke of Burgundy's brother-in-law. But his acerbic temperament made him a poor diplomat. The real head of the embassy and its spokesman at formal sessions of the Congress was Regnault de Chartres, a more gracious negotiator. He had been at Nevers and had attended all the earlier conferences under Albergati's auspices. His experience of negotiation with the English went back nearly twenty years, longer than anyone else's. He was supported by the Constable Arthur de Richemont, the Count of Vendôme, Christophe d'Harcourt and seven prominent councillors and officials. They were given two procurations defining their formal powers, one to negotiate a general peace and the other to make a separate peace with Philip the Good along the lines provisionally agreed at Nevers. Their detailed instructions have not survived, but the broad lines can be inferred from the subsequent course of events. The ambassadors were empowered to make large territorial concessions to the English, extending to nearly everything that Henry VI's subjects currently occupied in France. But the instructions were uncompromising on two points. The first was that there could be no concession to the Lancastrian claim to the French Crown. Secondly, it followed from this that any lands which the English occupied in France must be held under French sovereignty, and homage must be done for them. These stipulations were in line with consistent French policy for the past sixty years and no amount of debate would ever have shifted them.

None of the French councillors present at Amboise can have been under any illusions about the prospects of peace. They expected their terms to be rejected. The real object of the Congress as far as the French ministers were concerned was to achieve a reconciliation with Burgundy. The only reason for making any concessions at all to the English was to persuade Philip the Good that they had made a reasonable offer which would justify him in repudiating the treaty of Troyes. In many conversations in the passages and anterooms of Nevers, the French councillors had been able to form an accurate idea of the balance of opinion on the Duke's council and to identify those who were inclined to support a separate peace. To encourage them to persevere, the French ambassadors were authorised to offer 60,000 *saluts* (£10,000 sterling) in bribes, 'considering that peace and reconciliation can more easily be achieved through our cousin's principal ministers and closest advisers whom he trusts with the conduct of his affairs'. The largest payments, 10,000 *saluts* each, were to go to Nicolas Rolin, probably the most influential councillor of all, and Antoine de Croÿ, Philip's favourite throughout his long reign and the leading francophile on his council. Seven other men were favoured with cash gifts, including Antoine's brother Jean de Croÿ, Pierre de Bauffremont, the former captain-general in the duchy of Burgundy, and Guy Guilbaut, Philip's Treasurer and a man second only to Rolin in the Burgundian administration.[36]

Arras was the capital of the Burgundian county of Artois. It was a walled city on the banks of the river Scarpe which had once, at the height of its thirteenth-century prosperity, been among the richest textile manufacturing centres in Europe. Like many French cities it was divided between the old *cité* and the newer *bourg*, each with its own walls, gates and ditches and its own municipal organisation. The *cité* to the west was the old town, with its broad, straight streets and open spaces, dominated by the cathedral and inhabited mainly by churchmen, judges and officials. The *bourg*, originally a suburb, had grown up organically around the Benedictine abbey of St Vaast. It was larger, more densely built and packed with narrow, crooked lanes, which accommodated the commercial and industrial districts and most of the population. Artois had suffered less from war damage than Picardy and the Île-de-France. But the landscape still bore the scars of the civil wars, especially in Arras itself. The suburbs beyond the walls, with the churches of the mendicant orders and the mansions of the new rich, had been demolished at the time of the siege of 1414. Artillery damage to the walls and gates was still unrepaired. The long recession and the decline in revenues from land had left its mark on ecclesiastical and patrician proprietors, while the disruption of trade had depopulated *bourg* and *cité* alike.[37]

It was rare for a major diplomatic conference to open on the appointed day. An advance party from England arrived at Arras at the end of June and found nobody there except for a few Burgundian officials. The first significant arrival was the legate of the Council of Basel, Hughes de Lusignan Cardinal of Cyprus, who entered Arras at the head of an imposing delegation on 8 July 1435. His cavalcade, 150 strong, was ceremonially received at the gate by the Bishop and the whole clergy of the town. In addition to the Cardinal, the Council had sent four other ambassadors and a small army of lawyers, chaplains, secretaries, clerks and gentlemen. Albergati, who disliked pomp, made his own, more modest entry four days later. He brought with him a small but distinguished personal staff, including two Italian secretaries, Tomasso Parentucelli and Aeneas Silvius Piccolomini, both of them future popes. Albergati's company was a third of the size of Hughes de Lusignan's. He gave so little notice of his coming that there was no time to organise a ceremonial entry. The smaller reception committee which was hastily gathered to receive them reached the gate only to find that they had already passed through it.[38]

Relations between Albergati and the delegates of Basel were outwardly courteous, but the tensions were never far from the surface. Albergati firmly resisted the Council's attempt to take over the Congress. The fathers of Basel had initially nominated him to act as a joint mediator with the Cardinal of Cyprus for their own account, but the Carthusian declined to go along with that. He insisted that he was the Pope's legate and Hughes de Lusignan was the Council's. Hughes was a bombastic man, forever standing on his dignity as the son of a king and the emissary of a body claiming ultimate authority in the Church. When Albergati was given a retiring room in the abbey buildings of St Vaast because of his infirmity, Hughes de Lusignan demanded the same privilege. He claimed precedence over Albergati in the conference chamber, an issue which the Carthusian settled by arriving early and sitting in the principal's seat. Temperamentally, Albergati hated squabbles like these, but he was pressed to make a stand by his secretary Parentucelli, a firm opponent of the Council's pretensions. His other secretary, Piccolomini, recorded in his memoirs that by the end the two mediators were no longer on speaking terms.

In practice, Albergati's high reputation, transparent integrity and long experience of the issues ensured that his was the dominant role. By comparison, although Hughes de Lusignan had met Charles VII and his principal councillors the year before, neither he nor his fellow ambassadors had any real experience of the issues or the parties. The commission at Basel which had been charged with drawing up their instructions was no wiser. Their proposal was that if a permanent peace proved impossible to achieve, the Council's delegation should press for a long truce, a solution that Albergati knew would not work and which the French and Burgundians had already rejected for good reasons. So far as the records show, the Basel delegation's role was largely ceremonial. Its members preached on notable occasions, led processions, said Masses, and occupied the benches assigned to them in the conference chamber. If they made a difference to the course of events, it passed unnoticed. It did not take long for observers to realise where real power lay. To the visible consternation of Hughes de Lusignan, the crowds gathered every morning outside Albergati's lodgings while the street outside his own quarters was empty.[39]

The entry of each national delegation was a carefully choreographed moment of political theatre, involving the cardinal mediators and their entourages, the Bishop of Arras with the canons of the cathedral and the clergy of the town, the abbot and monks of St Vaast, the ducal governor and the delegations already at Arras, all arrayed in their robes, vestments and habits in front of the gates. It had been the same at earlier international conferences, at Avignon in 1344 and Bruges in 1377. The English delegation crossed the Channel with an entourage of some 800 men in mid-July. Cardinal Beaufort remained at Calais with about half of this great horde, while the ambassadors, led by Archbishop Kemp and the Earl of Suffolk, rode into Arras on 25 July, escorted by a large company of mounted archers and attendants. The Duke of Burgundy arrived four days later on 27 July, as the bells were ringing for vespers. His ambassadors, led by his Chancellor Nicolas Rolin, were already in the city, but in reality, Philip was his own ambassador. He had brought with him most of his council. All of the great names of Burgundian chivalry and the principal administrative and diplomatic officers of his household were there. The herald Toison d'Or listed eighty-eight prominent individuals drawn from all of Philip's scattered territories, not to speak of the lawyers, clerks and household staff. The French delegation made the last and grandest entry of all. They arrived on the evening of 31 July, having waited for several days at Saint-Quentin so as to time their arrival for maximum impact. The four principal ambassadors, the Duke of Bourbon, Regnault de Chartres, the Count of Vendôme and Christophe d'Harcourt, arrived at the head of a cavalcade of 900 to 1,000 horsemen, including a large body of gorgeously dressed noblemen, a crowd of heralds, trumpeters, musicians, chaplains, clerks, officials and captains, and a corps of liveried crossbowmen. The Duke of Burgundy decided to attend their reception after a long debate in his council in which it is clear that there were some dissenting voices. Indeed, he did more than attend. He rode three miles out of town to greet them on the road and accompanied them back. The three Dukes of Burgundy, Bourbon and Guelders approached the city gates side by side, preceded by the Constable of France, seven trumpeters, and a host of heralds and pursuivants led by Montjoie the herald of France. They processed through streets filled with crowds cheering and crying 'Noel!' The English sulked in their lodgings.[40]

Over the following six weeks more delegations arrived from the many parties whose interests would be affected by the remaking of the political map of western Europe. The Duke of Guelders had arrived with Philip the Good. Delegations followed from the other princes of the Low Countries. The prince-bishop of Liège came wearing plate armour and a straw hat, escorted by 200 outriders. Embassies came from Angevin Naples, Milan, Castile, Navarre and Portugal. A number of interested parties from both sides of the political divide in France sent their own delegates. Three ambassadors and a pursuivant represented the Duke of Brittany. Yolande of Anjou, the Duke of Alençon and the Count of Foix all sent their own representatives. As the peace process faltered and then failed, more delegations appeared, from the municipality, Parlement and University of Paris and the chapter of Notre-Dame, as well as from the principal cities of Burgundy, northern France and Flanders. All of these people came with own their armed escorts and crowds of servants and attendants.[41]

The arrangements for accommodating all these people had been made by officials of the Duke of Burgundy, who had been at Arras since May. Jean Chartier, the French official historiographer, had it from them that between 9,000 and 10,000 strangers were accommodated in Arras for the Congress, more than its normal population. About half of them were lodged in the *bourg*, and the rest in the *cité* and the outlying villages. Most of the grander houses of Arras had been requisitioned for the use of delegates. Their allocation was a delicate matter. With national ill-feeling strong and large numbers of armed men in the suites of the delegations, public order was a serious challenge. Fine political judgements were required, and careful attention to the rank of every participant. The only recorded complaint came from the Duke of Bourbon. He thought his lodgings unfit for the premier ambassador of France and demanded to be given those occupied by Cardinal Albergati, threatening that otherwise he would leave the Congress. Albergati refused to move, and Bourbon was eventually pacified. The Duke of Burgundy and his personal household were lodged in the Cour-le-Comte, the old castle of the Counts of Artois in the centre of the *bourg* opposite the abbey of St Vaast. The mediators, the French ambassadors and the principal councillors of the Duke of Burgundy were all accommodated in houses in the *bourg*, where they were able to confer freely outside the formal sessions of the Congress. The French delegation were regular visitors to the Cour-le-Comte. They partied with the Burgundians until well past midnight. Philip the Good played paume with the Duke of Bourbon. However, in what was surely a deliberate decision, the English were lodged in the *cité*, separated from the centre of activity by a water-filled ditch and a fortified gate which was closed at night. They had a number of meetings with the Duke of Burgundy and his councillors in the Cour-le-Comte but their dealings with him were not as cordial as those of the French. Kemp and his colleagues consulted Philip about their negotiating position and conference tactics and did their best to involve him in their decisions, His response was generally chilly and perfunctory.[42]

It was presumably the cardinal mediators, with their uncomfortable recollections of noisy scenes at Basel and direct confrontations between English and French delegations at earlier conferences, who devised the procedures used at Arras. They were designed to keep the delegations apart. The seat of the Congress was the abbey of St Vaast, an imposing but incomplete gothic church in the middle of the *bourg*, surrounded by an untidy jumble of monastic buildings and estate offices. The two cardinal mediators and the ambassadors of the Council of Basel occupied one of the abbot's parlours which had been converted into an audience chamber. The room had been hung with tapestries and the floor covered with carpets. Separate chambers in the abbot's lodgings, hung with costly silks and cloth of gold, were assigned to each national delegation. They were required to appear in their rooms twice a day, between seven and eight o'clock in the morning and between three and four o'clock in the afternoon. There were no plenary sessions. The delegations were called into the audience chamber separately, one after the other, to hear and comment on the other side's proposals. Except on one occasion towards the end, they never confronted each other directly, but only indirectly, through the mediators. The English hardly encountered the French, even outside the curtilage of St Vaast. In order to avoid disputes about precedence, they would not even worship in the same churches, insisting that they would hear Mass in the cathedral while the French and Burgundians could go to the abbey church of St Vaast, with one of the cardinal mediators attending in each place.[43]

The mutual incomprehension was aggravated by the very different negotiating methods of the English and French delegations. The French were politicians trading for advantage and exploiting a strong military and political position. They had no interest in discussing unrealistic proposals or debating abstract ideas. The English behaved like forensic advocates appealing to precedent and authority, as they had always done. An exasperated French diplomat of the previous century had once complained of their habit of arriving armed with 'beautiful and important-looking books' in which they had recorded all their claims together with the juridical and historical evidence to support them. A generation later nothing had changed. In 1435 the English invoked their past victories, which had been partly undone, the treaty of Brétigny, which Charles V had repudiated in 1369, the treaty of Paris of 1396, which Henry V had repudiated in 1415, the treaty of Troyes, which the French had never recognised, and the concessions made by the Dauphin at the abortive conference at Alençon in 1418, when Henry V had been at the height of his military fortune and France crippled by civil war. The Bishop of Nevers was one of those who openly expressed his irritation. 'Coffers are raided, documents extracted from archives, chests broken open, deeds produced out of cupboards, charters emerge from corners of their treasury, registers are examined and ancient parchments conjured up from their graves,' he complained.[44]

The first week of August was filled with the ritual preliminaries which had become routine features of diplomatic conferences. There were formal Latin orations from the Basel delegation and responses lauding the virtues of peace from Regnault de Chartres and Archbishop Kemp. There was a long wrangle about the form of the ambassadors' procurations. Discussion of the real issues did not begin until 10 August. The opening positions of each side revealed the gulf between them. The English had already informed the cardinal mediators that they did not intend to debate Henry VI's right to the French Crown. It was a grace derived from God and unsuitable for discussion among mere mortals. Accordingly, they proposed that Charles VII should recognise Henry's title and abandon the provinces that he had usurped, in exchange for a reasonable appanage and assets and titles befitting his station. The French for their part demanded possession of the entire kingdom and compensation for the war damage caused by the English in France. These were simply rhetorical declarations, designed to avoid suggestions that their claims had been dropped. On 12 August the English made their first serious proposal. They suggested that all the contentious issues should be deferred until their King's majority and that in the meantime there should be a truce of between twenty and fifty years supported by a marriage alliance. The French responded that they were not interested in a truce. They had come to discuss a permanent peace. Until the English put forward proposals for one, they would not make any of their own. They were pressed by the mediators to soften this line, and eventually came back with an opening offer. Henry VI must renounce his claim to the French throne and all the territories that he occupied in France. In return, he would be confirmed in possession of the duchy of Guyenne in the south-west, including Périgord and Quercy, most of which the English had lost to French armies in the 1370s. This would have to be held under French sovereignty, in return for homage, as it had been before the wars began in the 1330s. As for the proposed marriage alliance, they did not reject the idea out of hand but thought that further progress would have to be made on other issues before it could be considered. They added later that they doubted the value of marriage alliances as a way of securing a truce. This had been the basis of the marriage of Richard II and Isabelle of France, which had secured the peace for barely three years.[45]

The following days were mainly taken up with haggling for territory. The French gradually increased their territorial offer, but always on the footing that Henry VI must renounce the claim to the French Crown and hold any territory in France under French sovereignty. They added the Agenais, Limousin and Saintonge south of the river Charente to the territories that they were prepared to cede in the south-west and threw in a cash indemnity of 600,000 *écus*. This would have reconstituted almost all the enlarged duchy of Guyenne which had been ceded to England by John II in 1360, although without the rich province of Poitou. The problem about these offers, apart from the perennial issue of sovereignty, was that they would have required the English to give up everything that they held north of the Loire. This would have been regarded as a betrayal of the legacy of Henry V and would have been deeply unpopular in England, where Normandy was much more highly prized by public opinion than Guyenne. The English pressed for concessions in the north. The cardinal mediators pressed the French into making them. The French initially offered to cede the Cotentin, and then the whole of Lower Normandy apart from the duchy of Alençon, the counties of Harcourt and Tancarville and the still unconquered Mont-Saint-Michel. When the English countered that they had been offered more than this in earlier negotiations, the French replied that that was then. The boot was on the other foot now.[46]

The English declined to talk in terms of French cessions of territory to Henry VI. That was putting things the wrong way round. The question, as they saw it, was what they would allow Charles VII to retain. On the morning of 16 August, they offered him Berry, Touraine, the Vivarais and Languedoc, provinces which they reckoned to be worth 120,000 gold *saluts* a year. The English for their part would have the 'ancient heritage' of the English royal line, by which they meant the duchy of Guyenne including the Agenais and the Bazadais, Périgord, Quercy, Limousin and Poitou. In the north, they demanded all of France north of the Loire and the portion of the duchy of Anjou which lay south of it. But Henry VI was to have the Crown. It is difficult to know how seriously the English themselves took these extraordinary proposals, which bore no relation to the current balance of power. They would have deprived Charles VII of the heartlands of his kingdom and dispossessed some of the principal royal princes including the Dukes of Anjou, Alençon and Orléans. When the English ambassadors returned to the conference chamber in the afternoon, the cardinal mediators reported that they had passed their proposals on to the French, who had simply laughed and left the room.[47]

In the town, plans were already being made on the assumption that the peace negotiations would collapse. The French and Burgundian delegations had attended Mass together on the feast of the Assumption and after the service repaired to the Cour-le-Comte where an agreeable banquet was put on in the hall. From their quarters in the *cité*, the English looked on with suspicion, fearing that the other delegations were already plotting a separate peace.[48] There was good reason for their concern. An inner group of the French embassy had been meeting regularly at night in the utmost secrecy in Arthur de Richemont's lodgings to plan how they would work on Philip and his advisers. Richemont himself was a regular visitor at the Cour-le-Comte, discussing the progress of the Congress into the night with Philip the Good. He held several meetings in the lodgings of Chancellor Rolin, Antoine de Croÿ and other 'partisans of peace' who had come to believe that the treaty of Troyes must be repudiated. But Richemont's most powerful ally at Philip's court was probably the Duchess, Isabella of Portugal. This intelligent and forceful woman had quickly learned to manoeuvre her way to influence and power among the complex cabals of the Burgundian court and was proving to be an astute negotiator. The French ambassadors reported that she was wholly converted to the cause of reconciliation between the estranged branches of the Valois house and had worked tirelessly with them to promote it.[49]

On 17 August there was a full meeting of the Duke's council in the Cour-le-Comte to consider the implications of the looming breach with England. It was a difficult occasion, lasting five hours and attended by some 200 councillors drawn from all of Philip's territories. Everyone there was sworn to secrecy at the beginning of the meeting and again at the end. It was probably for this occasion that a number of memoranda were produced rehearsing the arguments for and against the repudiation of the treaty of Troyes. One of them was probably by Nicolas Rolin. He urged the Duke not to regard himself as bound by the treaty. It was technically defective. The diversion of the succession away from the Valois line was probably beyond the powers of Charles VI even if he had been sane. He thought that the provision in the treaty which prevented Philip from making peace was impossible to justify. It was contrary to natural and divine law to contract not to make peace. Politically, the treaty of Troyes had completely failed in its main object, which had been to bring peace to France after a decade of civil war. Adherence to it now would serve only to prolong the fighting. Rolin thought that the English demands for a truce were unrealistic and their position on other points unduly rigid. He advised Philip to try to moderate the more extreme English positions, while secretly preparing to make a separate peace with Charles VII. The main problem that Rolin foresaw was not so much the treaty itself as the oath which Philip had sworn to observe it. He would need to enlist the help of the cardinal mediators to get round that.

The arguments of the anglophiles were recorded in a memorandum which was probably due to Hughes de Lannoy. They believed that Philip the Good would suffer serious reputational damage if he dishonoured his treaty and his oath. The ingenious legal arguments about their validity would cut no ice with foreign powers. But their main arguments, like Rolin's, were political. They pointed out that the Duke was unlikely ever to be fully reconciled to Charles VII, whatever agreement might be made with him now. Charles had been privy to the murder of his father. Philip had been the main actor behind the treaty of Troyes and had been at war with France for sixteen years. These things would leave a lasting legacy of bitterness, not just in Charles's mind but in the hearts of his courtiers and councillors and the leading noblemen of his realm. Sooner or later, a war between the houses of Burgundy and Valois must be expected. If Philip broke with the English, they would no longer be there as allies and might even side with France. A treaty with Charles VII, they argued, could not even be relied upon to deliver peace. The French King had only limited control over captains like La Hire and Poton de Saintrailles. The English would become a formidable enemy. They would reinforce their garrisons in the marches of Flanders and Artois, exposing Philip's northern territories to serious war damage and commercial disruption.

The proponents of a separate peace acknowledged the force of this last point. They accepted that it would probably involve war with England and that such a war would be destructive. But the threat from England on the march of Flanders could be mitigated if Calais and its subsidiary forts were captured. What seemed clear, they argued, was that a hostile France was in a position to do much more damage to Burgundian interests than a hostile England. In a powerful riposte to the anglophiles, Rolin rehearsed all of these points but added emotional arguments of a kind that had rarely been deployed in the Burgundian chancery. Philip, he wrote, should make peace with Charles VII for moral reasons and not just for political ones. France was a great kingdom. Philip himself was a Frenchman, born in France. He was a peer of the French realm. He was a close kinsman of its King. Charles had made reasonable offers of settlement, whereas the English were obdurately clinging to immoral and unachievable hopes of conquest. As a Christian prince who valued his honour and reputation, Philip could not ignore the catastrophic damage and loss of life that the conflict had caused and would continue to cause until the English were finally expelled from France. Rolin's counterblast was a remarkable assertion of French national identity and a measure of the transformation of France's fortunes since 1429. It is hard to imagine these arguments being pressed on a Duke of Burgundy by a councillor a decade earlier.[50]

All of the political arguments rehearsed in these documents turned in one way or another on the long-term future of the Burgundian state, and on dilemmas which had divided Philip's advisers ever since the resurgence of French military power. Some of them harked back to the original debates surrounding the treaty of Troyes in 1419 and 1420. The problem then had been that the Dauphin was incapable of standing up to the combined strength of England and Burgundy. The problem now was that the renascent power of France was a threat to Burgundy as well as to England. Was the physical destruction and ruinous expenditure associated with the war a burden worth bearing in order to preserve Burgundy's alliance with the one European power capable of acting as a counterweight to Valois France? Would the reopening of the trade routes between the Low Countries and France compensate for severance of commercial relations with England, on which its textile industries had traditionally depended? Would a trade war with England destabilise Flanders, as it had done during the fourteenth century? Much depended on whether the English occupation of Normandy and parts of the Île-de-France was sustainable in the long term. That in turn depended on the resources and military capacities of England and France. It is clear that a substantial body of opinion on the Duke's council did not believe that the English had the will or the resources to keep up the fight.

On 18 August 1435, the diplomats had reached the impasse to which their instructions had always pointed. When they appeared before the cardinal mediators, the French declared that they would make no further proposal unless the English agreed to renounce their claim to the French Crown. It was clear, they said, that with each party claiming to be King of France, there could be no peace. The cardinals duly reported this position to the English, who withdrew to consider their response. Archbishop Kemp was ill, and when the English returned it was the belligerent Bishop Cauchon who served as their spokesman. Henry VI's representatives, he said, had always been willing to make territorial concessions to Charles VII. They had made what seemed to them to be generous offers. But Henry VI had been crowned and anointed as King of France, and they had not come to Arras to dethrone him. If France was now delivered up to fire and sword, it would be because the French had not really wanted to make peace.[51]

So far, Cardinal Beaufort had remained at Calais with the Earl of Huntingdon and the Duke of Orléans. At the outset of the Congress, Albergati had expressed his surprise at this. He told the Duke of Burgundy that Beaufort's 'authority, prudence and strong desire for peace' would be missed at Arras. At Albergati's suggestion, Philip now wrote to Beaufort urging him to come. But Beaufort did not come until 23 August, when the peace negotiations were on the verge of collapse. He had to take the long route through Flanders to avoid the unsettled roads of western Artois and entered Arras in characteristically grand style with a company of some 300 mounted men. He was received in front of the gate by the Cardinal of Cyprus and the Duke of Burgundy with his whole court, together with the English delegation and the representatives of Lancastrian France. Beaufort was lodged close to the rest of the English embassy in the bishop's palace in the *cité*. Here he embarked upon an intensive round of talks with the English delegation, the cardinal mediators and the Duke of Burgundy.[52]

Once Beaufort had arrived at Arras, the English delegation took their instructions from him. Archbishop Kemp told the cardinal mediators that they 'neither could nor would proceed' without his approval. The mediators naturally assumed that Beaufort must have brought wider powers to reach an accommodation with France. Why else would he have come at this late stage? In fact, he had none. His hands were tied by the views of the two great absentees, the King's uncles Gloucester and Bedford. Gloucester was viscerally hostile to any arrangement with Charles VII and deeply suspicious of Philip the Good. Judging by his later criticisms he believed that the Congress of Arras should never have been allowed to happen at all. He would have objected to any concessions to the French on the question of sovereignty. That was also the position of the Duke of Bedford, who was lying sick at Rouen, but still in control of affairs. The Regent and the Grand Conseil were adamantly opposed to the surrender of Henry VI's claim to the French Crown. At about the end of August, they instructed Sir John Fastolf to write an uncompromising memorandum for the ambassadors at Arras, explaining why they 'in no wise would grant or condescend' such a thing.[53]

At St Vaast, the English and French delegations briefly resumed their haggling against a background of fraying tempers. Both sides enlarged their territorial offers. The English said that they were content for Charles VII to occupy all the territory which he currently occupied on either side of the Loire. The French eventually agreed that the English might have the whole of Normandy in addition to those parts of Guyenne which they currently occupied, but not Paris, the Île-de-France or Maine. All of these exchanges, however, were conducted on an artificial basis, because neither side was willing to move on sovereignty. When the cardinal mediators called on the English to say what instructions Beaufort had on that point, Kemp's reply was uncompromising. They had no intention of abandoning Henry VI's title to the French Crown, and the mediators should not imagine that Beaufort had come to Arras to uncrown his King or make him the subject of another man.

By the end of August, Archbishop Kemp acknowledged that the peace process had reached its term. For the first time since the start of his mission four years earlier, Albergati lost patience and gave the English his own opinion. In the end, he said, the only point of real substance that separated the parties was the English claim to the Crown of France. The Crown of England was a noble thing, and the English should be content with that. The claim of Henry VI to be King of France was a good deal weaker than that of his rival, whose ancestors had worn the crown from time immemorial. Since a permanent peace had proved to be impossible, he and his colleague would now use the power conferred upon them by the Pope and the Council to bring about a separate peace between France and Burgundy. According to his private secretary Piccolomini, Albergati

thought it better to save one kingdom by making peace between the French parties than to allow both kingdoms to be ruined by the continuance of old hatreds, for he was convinced that if the Duke of Burgundy and the King of France made friends the English would soon be driven out of France. They would then have to be satisfied with their own kingdom and stay quietly on their island without troubling France any more.

Kemp responded in equally forthright terms. He embarked on a long and angry defence of the English claim to France founded on inheritance, on treaty and on victory in the field. It is clear that the cardinals' threat to use their powers to promote a separate treaty between France and Burgundy had riled him. He could not believe, he said, that either the Pope or the Council could have authorised something so unreasonable.[54]
Beaufort made no attempt to resurrect the peace negotiations. He concentrated on trying to save the Burgundian alliance. The tide was flowing strongly against him. A venomous debate opened up over the validity of the treaty of Troyes, which was emerging as the sole obstacle to a reconciliation between Burgundy and France. Albergati's legal adviser, a civil lawyer trained in the famous law school of Bologna, prepared a long opinion arguing that the treaty was of no effect, mainly because Charles VI had not had the constitutional right or the mental capacity to alienate his kingdom. Jean Rinel answered him at equal length, arguing that the treaty was valid but pointing out that, valid or not, Philip the Good had personally negotiated it and sworn to observe it. This was the argument that had always concerned Nicolas Rolin. On the afternoon of 3 September Philip the Good met his council for another long and fractious meeting in the Cour-le-Comte, which ran five hours over its expected time. The spokesmen for the anglophile party were John of Luxembourg and Hughes de Lannoy. They were supported by a number of senior councillors. But they knew that they were losing the argument. They pleaded with Philip to listen to the 'older knights and squires' of his council and pull back from a course which could only dishonour his name. As these words suggest, it was in large measure a generational divide. The spokesmen and the 'older knights and squires' behind them were all veterans of the civil wars who had begun their careers under John the Fearless. In contrast, the leading francophiles like Nicolas Rolin and Jean de Croÿ tended to be younger men who had come to the fore after the murder at Montereau. Antoine de la Taverne, the observant Provost of St Vaast whose daily journal is one of our main sources for the Congress, believed that the

francophiles had strong support in the corridors and antechambers of the Cour-le-Comte and in the streets outside.[55]

Philip himself was inscrutable. The only way out of his dilemma was to pressure the French for some concession which would put off the intractable question of sovereignty to another day. With both parties bidding for his support, he was in a strong position to do this. 4 September was a decisive day. Philip spent much of the morning closeted with Rolin and Croÿ, while Cardinal Beaufort and the English ambassadors met their French opposite numbers face to face for the first and only time in the lady chapel of St Vaast. That afternoon, Philip had an audience with the cardinal mediators, and then with the French ambassadors.

The outcome of all this activity was a fresh French offer, their last. The cardinals summoned the English delegation before them to explain it. The territorial provisions were much the same as in earlier French proposals. The English King was to remain in possession of his ancestral domains in France, namely the regions currently occupied by his officers in Guyenne and the county of Ponthieu at the mouth of the Somme. He was also to retain Normandy and hold it on the same terms as John II and Charles V when they were Dauphins of France, in other words as an appanage with a high degree of political autonomy. But there were a number of conditions. First, the English must renounce their claim to the Crown of France. Secondly, they must hold all their French domains as fiefs of the Valois monarchy. Third, they must surrender all other places occupied by them in France, including Paris and Maine. Fourth, landowners who had been exiled from the regions which the English retained and whose land had been confiscated must be allowed to return and reclaim their own. Finally, the Duke of Orléans must be released for a reasonable ransom. The new feature of these proposals was that Henry VI's renunciation of his claim to the French Crown and his act of homage were to be deferred for seven years, when he would be of age. In the meantime, the settlement would take effect only provisionally.

The mediators believed this to be a generous offer and strongly recommended it. It gave the English, they suggested, a third of the area of the French kingdom, including some of its richest regions, and resolved the problem of ceding sovereignty during the English King's minority. The English had probably received some advance notice of what was proposed, for they were ready with their answer.

Archbishop Kemp said that their authority did not extend to accepting such arrangements. In the ordinary course, the English would have been expected to ask for the Congress to be prorogued while they sought further instructions. But they did not. They merely undertook to report the French proposals to the King's council in England, which might or might not choose to respond. They knew that the English council would reject them. On the following morning they went before Philip the Good to tell him that they would leave Arras the next day. Philip, angered by the failure of his attempt at mediation, told them that in that case he would make a separate peace with Charles VII. He then recited all the accumulated grievances of the past decade: the destruction of his domains, the want of military support, the Duke of Gloucester's attempt to take possession of Hainaut and Holland and his challenge to Philip, all indignities which still rankled. According to a story which is probably apocryphal, Beaufort's last words were that he had two million nobles to spare to support the continued prosecution of the war. Early on 6 September, the whole English cavalcade rode out of Arras behind Cardinal Beaufort, wearing uniform purple liveries with the motto 'Honour' embroidered on their sleeves.[56]

Writing after the English had been expelled from both Normandy and Gascony, that astute observer Philippe de Commynes observed that the English won most of their battles, but always lost out at the conference table. Prominent English politicians had ruefully admitted it in his presence. The English could have made peace at Arras on terms which would have secured them Normandy and Guyenne. If that was not quite a third of France, as the cardinal mediators had suggested, the final French offer nevertheless represented a significant concession. The cardinal mediators had expected it to be accepted and were shocked when it was not. They put it down to the obtuseness of the English and their love of war. Yet the politicians on Henry's English council did not love war. Although few of them thought that England could win it, their rejection of the French terms was not irrational. The French offer had dealt effectively with the problem of Henry VI's minority. But it did not address the legacy of the past. Conceding the claim to the throne would have undermined the basis on which England had fought in France for a century. 'It might be said, noised and deemed in all Christian lands where it should be spoken of,' Fastolf had written in his memorandum, 'that not Henry the King nor his noble progenitors had, nor have, no right in the crown of France and that all their wars and conquest hath been but usurpation and tyranny.' Medieval statesmen cared about what was 'said, noised and deemed in all Christian lands'. The English could not bring themselves to admit that they had fought an unjust war. For Bedford himself it would have dishonoured the memory of his brother and marked the abandonment of the cause to which he had devoted the last thirteen years of his life.

There was more than emotional commitment involved. The mediators had underestimated the practical difficulty of restoring Paris and Normandy to Valois sovereignty. Too many people had acquired a vested interest in English rule. The *grands corps* of the Parisian government were full of prominent officials who would have no future under a Valois monarchy. Many of them occupied houses which had been confiscated from 'Armagnacs' and other enemies of the dual monarchy. The Edict of Compiègne, Charles VII's ill-advised declaration of August 1429, would in effect abolish all titles derived directly or indirectly from the vast turnover of property since 1418. The records of confiscations ordered by the English authorities filled thirty-two volumes in the archives of the Chambre des Comptes before their destruction by fire in 1737. No one can have been surprised that the Grand Conseil was the strongest opponent of concessions at Arras. The problems of restitution were even greater in Normandy than they were in Paris. Henry V and the Duke of Bedford had presided over a landowning revolution in Normandy. The largest domains belonging to the higher nobility, and very many smaller ones, had been resettled on English noblemen, soldiers and officials and on loyal Normans. French demands for the restitution of confiscated land would have meant the expropriation of nearly every English landowner in Normandy and the destruction of the whole infrastructure on which the occupation and defence of the duchy were based. If the English had remained in possession of Normandy on the terms proposed, they would sooner or later have found it impossible to hold it.

There was another, broader problem which had taxed English diplomats for many years. Fastolf's memorandum asserted that the French had broken every treaty that they had ever made with the English. This was a tendentious interpretation of a complex history. But it was undoubtedly true that the eighty years between the treaty of Paris of 1259 and Edward III's assumption of the Crown of France in 1340 had demonstrated the practical impossibility of the King of England being at the same time a sovereign in his own country and a vassal in France. It had led to continual disputes about homage, jurisdiction and feudal obligation, which had poisoned relations between the two countries, undermined the English dynasty's authority over its French vassals and resulted in a succession of forfeitures in the French King's courts, followed by disastrous wars. English medieval diplomats were dedicated students of history. The lesson was not lost on them.[57]

10 September 1435 was the anniversary of the murder of John the Fearless at Montereau. Philip the Good had Mass said in the cathedral for the repose of his father's soul, and then presided at a long meeting of his council at which it was finally agreed to make a separate peace with the man who had presided at his murder. There was a strong dissenting minority, but the outcome was never in doubt. The terms of the peace had already in large measure been agreed at the conference at Nevers and in many discreet conversations between French and Burgundian diplomats over the past month. On 20 September there was a prolix ceremony in the abbey church of St Vaast. Cardinal Albergati, with Hughes de Lusignan standing beside him, recited the desolate state of France, the history of the peace process, the final offers made by both sides, the breakdown of the talks and the abrupt departure of the English delegation. The two cardinals then formally pronounced the annulment of the treaty of Troyes and of the oath that Philip the Good had sworn to observe it. They declared it to be 'notoriously null and void as being contrary to the public interest, to good relations between men and to all morality'. Not only would it be lawful for the Duke of Burgundy to make a separate peace with Charles VII, but it would be a grave sin not to do so. The treaty between Charles VII and the Duke of Burgundy was sealed the next morning and read out to a packed congregation in the abbey church.[58]

Charles VII paid a high price for his reconciliation with Philip the Good. The terms were so favourable to Philip that the Duke of Bourbon, who had been mainly responsible for negotiating them, was suspected of selling out his master in order to boost his own standing with Philip. The treaty provided at length and with much elaboration the symbolic gestures of atonement required of Charles VII for the murder of Philip's father: the Masses to be funded, the monuments to be built, the religious houses to be endowed. Compensation of 150,000 *écus* was to be paid for the jewellery and other property seized in the aftermath of the murder. The culprits were to be named and punished.

Generous territorial concessions were made to the Duke, so generous in fact that they aroused concern among some of the French King's more cautious advisers. On the marches of Burgundy Charles VII ceded the Mâconnais and the Auxerrois, which Philip and his father had held for many years without any clear title. In the north, he ceded the three castleries of Péronne, Montdidier and Roye in Picardy, which had been granted to Philip by the English. Charles VII was given the right to reacquire them on terms which were never properly recorded and inevitably gave rise to dispute later. In addition, the French King was to cede all the towns of the Somme valley and the Boulonnais. A number of lordships were regranted to the Duke which had belonged to his father and grandfather but were either disputed or situated in territory controlled by the Valois King. The effect of these provisions was that Philip obtained from Charles VII everything that he had ever had from the English except for the county of Champagne, which he had never been able to occupy. For Philip's lifetime his domains were to be exempt from the jurisdiction of the French Crown, and he himself was to be spared the ordeal of doing homage to his father's murderer. There was to be a general amnesty for all acts done in the course of the wars. Very little was said about the English. But Charles VII undertook to support Philip against them in the event that he was attacked and to make no peace with them without including him. It was a long treaty, and the reading must have taken more than an hour to complete. When it was finished, cries of 'Noel!' went up from the congregation. A *Te Deum* was sung. Many sermons were delivered. People wept. The Dukes of Burgundy and Bourbon emerged from the church arm-in-arm. As the feasting and dancing began in the Cour-le-Comte, tables were set up in the streets outside, and free bread and wine served to all comers. An unhappy chapter of France's history seemed to have ended.[59]

When, towards the end of the ceremony in St Vaast, the oaths were about to be administered, Hughes de Lannoy and Roland of Dunkirk slipped quietly out of the church. They subsequently relented and took the oath. John of Luxembourg stayed but publicly refused to swear, and unlike the others persisted in his refusal until his death in 1441. For the last six years of his life, he never renounced his English allegiance and defended his castles in Picardy against all comers, while many of his retainers and vassals continued in English service.

Men like Lannoy and John of Luxembourg had backed a cause that was doomed to fail in the end. But their warnings in the fraught council meetings at Arras proved to be prescient. The passing of the years never did appease the anger provoked in the breast of Charles VII and his ministers by the treaty of Troyes and Philip's fifteen-year alliance with England. Charles never shook off the idea that the treaty of Arras conceded too much to Philip. The Angevins who dominated his council had their own reasons to resent the house of Burgundy. The two princely houses had fallen out during the civil wars, and an extra layer of bitterness was later added by the brutal terms of the ransom treaty imposed on Réné of Anjou after his capture at Bulgnéville. Twelve years after the treaty of Arras had been sealed, the Elector of Saxony's ambassador at the French court reported that Philip the Good was as much detested there as he had ever been. The monuments to John the Fearless which were to be constructed at Montereau were never built, the Masses for the repose of his soul never endowed and the men responsible for his death never brought to justice although their identity was by now known to everyone. Philip's domains, especially in the two Burgundies, continued to be the prey of French *routier* companies, whom Charles VII was unable to control. A persistent juridical offensive undermined Philip's authority within his own domains. Burgundian officials were shortly drawing up long lists of breaches of the treaty of Arras and intrusions on his jurisdiction.

Once England was disarmed, between 1449 and 1453, a triumphant France, freed from the continual threat of war from across the Channel, would one day challenge Burgundian influence in Lorraine, in Luxembourg and in the Rhineland, all vital Burgundian spheres of interest. 'When a man wants to bring down a great and ancient tree anchored to the ground by long and deep roots, he first digs a great trench around it ... so as to sever those roots,' wrote Thomas Basin. 'Just so, in order to bring down the house of Burgundy, then the richest and most successful principality in either France or Germany, Charles, King of France, set about undermining it and severing its roots.' Philip was shortly to learn what the English had never forgotten, that in the long run his political autonomy could not survive once he accepted the status of a vassal of Valois France. It is not only in hindsight that the treaty of Arras can be seen to have prepared the way for the eventual destruction of the Burgundian state. The more far-seeing members of Philip's council warned him at the time that if Charles VII ever succeeded in ridding France of the English, the house of Burgundy would be next.[60]

On 14 September 1435, a week before the treaty of Arras was sealed, the Duke of Bedford died in his mansion at Rouen. He was forty-six years old. For the English too, a chapter had ended. Within a few days, they had lost their only significant continental ally and their only statesman who understood the challenges of the dual monarchy or, by the end, truly believed in it. In his will, which was drawn up four days before his death, Bedford asked to be buried in Rouen cathedral, of which he was an honorary canon and to which he had given many precious objects. A fine tomb of black marble standing on columns was erected in accordance with his instructions on the left side of the high altar, with a copper plaque engraved with his arms and the insignia of the Order of the Garter. According to the Tudor chronicler Edward Hall, a faithful plagiarist of older sources, Charles VII's successor Louis XI was walking one day in the cathedral when one of his attendants pointed out the tomb, suggesting that it was too grandiose for an enemy of France and should be broken open and the bones scattered. The King is supposed to have answered:

What honour shall it be to us or you to break this monument and to pull out of the ground and take up the bones of him who in his life neither my father nor your progenitors with all their power, puissance and friends were once able to make fly one foot backward, but by his strength, wit and policy kept them all out of the principal dominions of the realm of France and out of this noble and famous duchy of Normandy; wherefore I say first God have his soul and let his body now lie in rest, which when he was alive would have disquieted the proudest of us all.

Bedford's tomb survived the expulsion of the English from France. It was eventually mutilated in the name of puritanism, not nationalism, by the Huguenots who sacked the churches of Rouen in 1562. As with so many monuments in French cathedrals, it was cleared away in the eighteenth century in the name of modernisation. Today, there is only a plain, incised slab of stone.[61]

CHAPTER X

The Hinge of Fortune, 1435–1436

The collapse of the peace negotiations with France came as no surprise in England, where the familiar trope of French treachery and obduracy was widely accepted. But few Englishmen had expected the Duke of Burgundy to desert them, or the cardinals to ease his way out of a treaty and an oath. Returning from a mission to Scotland that autumn, Cardinal Albergati's secretary Aeneas Silvius Piccolomini fell in with an English judge on the road to London. The judge, who had no idea who he was, told him all about the Congress of Arras. He thought that the outcome of the Congress was Albergati's doing and roundly cursed him as a 'wolf in sheep's clothing'. Most people blamed Philip the Good. Even the cautious and equable Archbishop of Canterbury Henry Chichele thought that the Duke's breach of faith was 'wicked and criminal', papal dispensation notwithstanding. The West Country seamen declared open war on the merchants of Flanders and began to seize their cargoes at sea, citing the authority of the Duke of Gloucester. In London, the mood was venomous. Philip was denounced in street songs as the 'founder of new falsehood. disturber of peace, captain of cowardice, sower of discord, reproof of all knighthood'. Anger was intensified by fear. There was a 'great noise' that an attack on Calais was imminent and perhaps even an invasion of England.[1]

When, early in October, two Burgundian heralds, Toison d'Or and Franche-Comté, landed at Dover, they were received as enemies. They had come bearing the written record of the French government's final offer. Philip the Good and the cardinal mediators hoped that calmer reflection might still lead the English council to accept it. They persuaded the French ambassadors to keep the offer open until the end of the year. The heralds also brought two other documents. One was an emollient letter from the Duke himself declaring that he had no desire to make war on England and would continue to work for peace between Henry VI and Charles VII. The other was a proposal from the French that, to spare the Kings of England the humiliation of an act of personal homage, Normandy should be treated as an appanage of their eldest sons, like Wales or the Dauphiné. The heralds were met on the Dover road and escorted to London, but instead of being granted the usual honours they were lodged with a cobbler, locked in their rooms and forbidden to go out even to attend Mass. As the news of their mission spread, mobs gathered in the streets. Flemish, Dutch and Brabant merchants were attacked. The heralds' letters were taken from them and read out at an enlarged meeting of the council in the presence of the King, Cardinal Beaufort and the Duke of Gloucester. It was an emotional meeting. There was much fury when they heard Henry addressed as King of England but not France. The young King is said to have wept tears of rage. The Duke of Gloucester and Cardinal Beaufort walked out. Several others followed them. Further discussion was suspended and the issue was referred to Parliament.[2]

Parliament opened on 10 October 1435. In his opening address, Chancellor Stafford presented them with the stark choice that the council had left unresolved. Either the final French offer, which he described as 'trifling and derisory', must be accepted and the King suffer the humiliation of renouncing his title of King of France; or they must fight on. The mood darkened as reports trickled in of the contents of the treaty of Arras. Opinion was divided. Some people, according to the chronicler Monstrelet's informants, wondered whether it was worth trying to defend Henry VI's claim in the face of the combined strength of France and Burgundy. Some would have accepted the final French offer, although Hughes de Lannoy was probably wrong to think that public opinion was behind them. The failure of the Congress briefly changed the dynamic of English politics. With the Duke of Bedford dead, Humphrey Duke of Gloucester was now the heir apparent to the Crown. With Henry Beaufort discredited by the failure of his pro-Burgundian policy, the main political constraints on Humphrey were gone. For some months his was the dominant voice in England's strategic and political judgements. The consensus was that Philip the Good's letters should be left unanswered. After a month in England, the heralds were finally received by Chancellor Stafford. He curtly informed them that the King had received their letters with 'understandable displeasure', and that they were at liberty to go. That was all. They left for the Channel, running a gauntlet of abuse as they made their way back down the Dover Road.[3]

The Duke of Gloucester believed in the strategy of the knock-out blow, as opposed to the policy of sieges and static defence adopted hitherto. His views were close to those which Sir John Fastolf had expressed in the memorandum which he had prepared for the ambassadors at Arras shortly before Bedford's death. Fastolf had learned the lesson of Orléans and Compiègne. He thought that siege warfare should be avoided at all costs. The French had become too good at holding walled places. Instead, he proposed a return to the *chevauchées* which had been such a terrifying but ineffective strategy under Edward III. Regions under French or Burgundian control 'must needs have another manner of war, and more sharp and more cruel war than a natural and ancient enemy'. Two expeditionary armies of 3,000 men each, supported by light artillery, should descend each year on France at the beginning of June, with a period of service of five months. They should pass through northern France destroying everything in their path. Buildings should be burned, grain wasted, vines and fruit trees uprooted. All cattle that could not be rounded up and driven back to Paris or Normandy should be killed and left. No time should be wasted in taking prisoners or imposing *pâtis*. Traitors should be hanged. Even tonsured clergymen should not be spared. It was a scorched earth strategy. The object was to seize the strategic initiative and divert French energies away from offensive operations and into static defence. Fastolf believed that the resulting destruction and famine would terrorise the French into submission within three years. 'Better is a country to be wasted for a time than lost,' he wrote. At the same time, he called for economic warfare against the Duke of Burgundy's Flemish subjects. Exports of wool to Flanders should be embargoed and alternative export markets found in Italy. What Parliament thought of these ideas is not recorded. But at the end of October, they approved the appointment of the Duke of Gloucester as the captain of Calais and its subsidiary forts, and presumably also his appointment as royal lieutenant in Picardy, Artois and Flanders, which followed a few days later.[4]

While these matters were being considered at Westminster, the military situation was rapidly deteriorating in France. In the final days of the Congress of Arras, a great struggle developed for control of the plain north of Paris and ultimately for Paris itself. The large French garrison at Saint-Denis had begun to expand into the walled places around.

Écouen, to the north, had been taken by storm, and Orville on the Senlis road had entered into a conditional surrender agreement. In Paris the defence was directed by Villiers de L'Isle-Adam and the Bastard of Saint-Pol with about 2,000 men. Talbot and Willoughby arrived in Normandy towards the end of July 1435 with the expeditionary army from England. They were joined by several hundred men withdrawn from the Norman garrisons. The whole army made for Paris, bringing the total number of professional troops there to between 4,000 and 5,000 men. Heavily outnumbered, the French abandoned their outlying strongholds and concentrated their forces in Saint-Denis. The English planted garrisons in the forts and castles around the town and built a large timber bastide armed with artillery on an island in the Seine. On about 24 August they laid siege to Saint-Denis.[5]

The defences of Saint-Denis were weak. The walls were in poor repair. The stores were too low to sustain such a large garrison for long. The town was some way from the Seine and the garrison depended on wells for fresh water. There could be no question of the defenders confronting an army three times their size in the open plain. The French captains held a council of war in the town. They decided that the Bastard of Orléans should return to the Loire valley to raise an army of relief, while Pierre de Rieux held out in Saint-Denis. On 9 September, after John of Orléans had left and two weeks of bombardment had fractured the walls and gates, the English launched a major assault. They waded neck-high across the moat and climbed the walls from ladders at several points at once. The assault lasted for two hours before the attackers withdrew. Both sides suffered heavy losses, most of them from gunshot. The garrison's courage bought them a little more time.

Two armies of relief were formed. On 22 September, the day after the conclusion of the treaty of Arras, Arthur de Richemont and the Count of Vendôme marched out of Arras at the head of a modest army recruited from the retinues of the French lords at the Congress. They got as far as Senlis, eleven miles from the beleaguered town, before giving up. Reports of the strength of the English siege lines persuaded Richemont that the task was beyond his strength. Meanwhile, the Bastard of Orléans had assembled some 4,000 men at Chartres. Rather than make his way round east of Paris via Melun and Lagny, which would have taken too long, he decided to try to force a crossing of the Seine west of Paris. Before dawn on 25 September his men tried to surprise Mantes. But there was a strong and vigilant English garrison there and the attempt failed. At this point an unexpected event looked as if it might save the venture. That very night, ten miles upstream, two French partisans with a small company of fishermen, acting on their own initiative, had captured the bridge of Meulan. They had entered the fortress at the southern end with ladders from boats moored in the river, bribed the lone watchman, killed about twenty of the garrison, and forced the captain and the rest of his men to surrender. The Bastard of Orléans made straight for the bridge, only to discover when he got there that the defenders of Saint-Denis had entered into a conditional surrender agreement the day before. The *journée* was fixed for 4 October, only a week ahead. He considered trying to fight his way into Meulan from the bridge but concluded that it could not be done in time. On the appointed day, the gates of Saint-Denis were opened and the French garrison marched out under safe-conduct with what personal possessions they could carry.[6]

In any other circumstances the English recapture of Saint-Denis would have been hailed as a great victory. But it was overshadowed by the news of the treaty of Arras. A significant proportion of the Anglo-Burgundian army in Paris and most of the remaining Lancastrian garrisons of Picardy and Champagne were subjects of the Duke of Burgundy. Many of them had fought alongside the English for years and now found their loyalties divided. The large Picard contingent in Talbot's army at Saint-Denis left for their homes immediately after the surrender of the town. The Burgundian troops who had assured the defence of Paris for the past six years left with them. Their captains, who had had personal obligations to the Lancastrian government, were in a more difficult position. Villiers de L'Isle-Adam was a councillor of Philip the Good, but he also held the offices of Marshal of France and Captain of Paris from Henry VI and had sworn allegiance to him. His lands were in disputed territory in the Oise valley. He decided that he could not honourably abandon the English until after the final surrender of Saint-Denis, and then sought the advice of his fellow knights at the next chapter of the Order of the Golden Fleece in December. 'Considering the treaty which it has recently pleased you to make in your town of Arras,' he asked, addressing Philip the Good, 'may it please you to advise me what I should do concerning my office, my oath and my honour.' The Bastard of Saint-Pol, also a knight of the Golden Fleece, followed his example. His lands were in Picardy and Walloon Flanders, but he had received the lordship of Montmorency in the Île-de-France from the Duke of Bedford and had done homage for it. 'Affairs now stand otherwise and are very much changed,' he told his brother knights. Both men eventually threw in their lot with the Duke of Burgundy. A few Burgundians went the other way, like the Picard knight Guy de Roye, who commanded the important garrison at Soissons. He was heard to say that he would not honour the treaty of Arras even if it meant that he had to go and live in England. His men exchanged their St Andrew's crosses for the upright red crosses of England. In Paris, the departing Burgundians had to be replaced by English troops withdrawn from Normandy, thus adding to the burdens of the already overstretched English army. They were put under the command of Robert Willoughby, who was appointed as captain of Pontoise, and shortly afterwards assumed responsibility for the defence of the capital as well.[7]

At Rouen, the death of the Duke of Bedford had left the English administration leaderless. The news reached the English ambassadors at Calais as they were waiting to cross the Channel. Cardinal Beaufort sent the Earl of Suffolk with a small escort to Rouen to 'put the country in rule'. He arrived in the city towards the end of September to find it in ferment. The streets were filled with refugees. There were constant reports of plots, and regular executions in the market square. Beyond the city walls, the Norman garrisons had been severely depleted to reinforce Talbot's army at Saint-Denis. Of the estimated 7,000 English troops in France at the beginning of October 1435, at least 4,000 were concentrated in and around Paris. About half of these had been withdrawn from the Norman garrisons, mostly on the vulnerable north march and in the region between the Seine and the Eure. Meanwhile, a menacing concentration of French troops was building up on the north march. The companies of La Hire and Poton de Saintrailles, which had been operating in Artois and the Somme valley, returned to their bases in the Beauvaisis after the treaty of Arras. Charles Desmarais abandoned Rue to the officers of the Duke of Burgundy and returned to Rambures with his companies. They were joined in mid-October by Pierre de Rieux with many of the men who had fought in the defence of Saint-Denis.[8]

On 16 November 1435, some 300 men of the companies of Desmarais and Rieux captured Dieppe. This was a grave setback for the English. With the loss of Burgundian Picardy, control of the

Norman coast was critical to the province's communications with England. Dieppe was an important commercial port and the usual landing point for soldiers and officials from England. It also housed a subtreasury which was used to receive bullion destined for the English treasuries at Rouen and Paris. Yet it had one of the smallest garrisons of Normandy, with just sixteen men. Relations between the town and the garrison were poor. When Desmarais's company waded across the river Varenne at low tide before dawn, a gate in the harbour wall was opened for them by accomplices. They passed silently through the streets and opened the Rouen gate to admit Marshal Rieux, who was waiting outside with his men. With banners unfurled and cries of '*Ville gagnée!*' they sacked the town and seized most of the ships in the harbour, the cash in the subtreasury and the artillery. The French established a permanent base at Dieppe. They expelled everyone who refused to swear an oath of allegiance to Charles VII, and then set about reinforcing the walls and building a citadel on the cliff at the western end of the ramparts. A large raiding force was installed in the town under the command of Desmarais himself, which supported itself from the plunder of western Normandy. The harbour became a base for French privateers, who raided the Thames estuary and the coasts of south-eastern England, seizing ships and going ashore to rob isolated settlements and carry men off for ransom.[9]

The capture of Dieppe was the signal for a peasant rising in the Caux which provoked the worst crisis of Lancastrian Normandy since its conquest by Henry V. The Caux was a broad limestone plateau lying west and north of Rouen between the Seine and the sea. It was the richest agricultural region of Normandy and its main grain-growing area. The 1420s had been a prosperous decade for the region, but its fortunes had dramatically turned with the occupation by French companies of Torcy and the castles of the Bresle valley in 1429. They had been expelled in the following year but were followed by others operating from the garrisoned castles of the French in Picardy and the Beauvaisis. The raiders destroyed crops and buildings, driving the peasants off the land and into the woods, where they added to the swelling tide of rural brigandage. By 1435, the Caux had lost a large part of its population, and those who remained subsisted in increasingly difficult conditions. The previous year's harvest had been lost to autumn rains and frosts which rotted the grain in the fields and left peasants without seed-corn. Outbreaks of plague found many victims in a population weakened by famine.

The Caux was more densely settled by English landowners than any other part of Normandy, but it was not well defended. There were large royal garrisons at Arques and Eu, which were reinforced when Dieppe fell. However, in the interior of the region the only garrisons were the custodians of privately owned castles, whose owners were often absentees and even when present were notoriously lax in performing their military obligations. In June 1435, the *bailli* of Caux, Sir John Montgomery, had poured oil on the flames with an ill-advised decision to conscript and arm the local peasantry. When the Earl of Suffolk took charge in Rouen, he tried to retrieve the position by having the peasants mustered into organised units under the control of companies of English archers with English captains. But it was too late for that. Within days of the fall of Dieppe, the peasantry had risen across the whole region. It was a better planned affair than the revolt of the Cotentin the year before. The peasants were well equipped, many of them carrying arms provided by the English authorities. They found an effective leader by the name of Caruyer who quickly created an army of some 4,000 men. The rebel leaders approached the French at Dieppe for support. Desmarais and Rieux responded much faster than the Duke of Alençon had managed to do in the Cotentin. They brought in La Hire with a large number of French companies from the Beauvaisis to exploit the unexpected opportunity which had opened up. By the end of the year, there were reported to be more than 3,000 French troops in the Caux.[10]

The Earl of Suffolk left Normandy at the end of November to attend Parliament at Westminster, leaving the duchy once again without political leadership. If he thought that the worst was over, he was mistaken. Shortly before Christmas, the peasant army joined forces with the French. The combined army numbered about 6,000 men. In December they launched a powerful offensive against the English positions in the region. Moving west along the coast from Dieppe, Marshal de Rieux occupied the abbey town of Fécamp. There was no garrison at Fécamp. A local nobleman persuaded the inhabitants to open their gates. Two days later, the garrisoned fortress of Montivilliers, which guarded the approach to Harfleur, was surrendered by its Gascon captain after the townsmen made common cause with the attackers. On 27 December 1435 the French came before Harfleur itself, where they encountered the first serious resistance. The town's defences had been expensively rebuilt by the English since the famous siege of 1415. Its garrison had recently been reinforced with additional companies brought across the estuary from Caen. Rieux ordered an immediate assault, which was thrown back from the walls with heavy casualties. But a rising by the French inhabitants of the town cut the ground from under the defenders' feet and forced the captain, William Minors, to negotiate a surrender. The entire English population was expelled along with the garrison. The loss of Harfleur was a disaster for the English. The town's arsenal, where important reserves of artillery were stored, fell into French hands. French ships from the harbour were able to play havoc with the trade of Rouen and other Seine towns, as well as imperilling the transport of troops between England and Normandy. In the new year, English troops were being rushed to Rouen, which was expected to be attacked next.[11]

Across the Caux, spontaneous local risings coalesced into a great conflagration. Within days, the rebels had occupied every notable town and fortress of the region except for the garrisoned towns of Arques and Eu in the north and Caudebec in the south. At the turn of the year, the rebellion showed signs of spreading across the estuary of the Seine into Lower Normandy, where the embers of revolt were still red from the rebellion of the previous year. A rising in the district of Vire quickly spread across the Cotentin. Its leader, a man called Boschier, was reported early in January to have raised a peasant army several thousand strong and to be concerting his plans with the French garrisons of the neighbouring regions. In the short time since the Congress of Arras, the English had lost control of the entire Channel coast of France from Flanders to the Seine and were facing the prospect of losing the ports of the Cotentin as well. There was serious concern about the security of Cherbourg, which was now the only major port in English hands apart from Honfleur. At Westminster, the council was gripped by panic. With the troops in Normandy heavily committed in Rouen and the Caux, they even toyed with the idea of raising yet another army in the west of England to sail directly to the Cotentin.[12]

The disaster lay not only in the losses themselves, serious as these were, but in what they revealed about the state of opinion in Normandy. The Normans, like the Parisians and the citizens of countless towns of Picardy and Champagne, had submitted to Henry V and supported the English regime in the 1420s because it looked like the only authority strong enough to give them security. That calculation no longer held good. Few people in Normandy or Paris would have followed the diplomatic haggling at Arras or understood the complex issues involved. But they did understand that the failure of the Congress meant the continuance of the war, and this fundamentally affected their attitude to the English occupation. The Earl of Suffolk knew this. One of his first acts on reaching Rouen was to distribute to the Norman *baillis* a paper prepared by the English delegation at Arras justifying their conduct at the Congress. The clergy were ordered to preach the message from their pulpits.

Sentiment in the duchy was divided. The English retained the support of most of the greater landowners, the higher clergy and the patrician oligarchies of the larger towns. These groups had a strong vested interest in the survival of the Lancastrian regime, to which many of them owed their places, their lands and their fortunes. The Norman Estates, which represented them, met at Rouen in November. They expressed their desire to remain under Lancastrian rule. But they thought that the final French offer, which would have restored peace to the duchy and left the English dynasty in place, should be accepted. As they pointed out, the only alternative was a more vigorous defence of Normandy than the 'feeble resistance' seen so far. The Estates called for a large English army, led by a prince of royal blood, 'virtuous, valiant and diligent, loved, renowned and feared by all'. They granted fresh taxes nominally worth 190,000 *livres*, but recognised that it would be nothing like enough to fund the effort now required. The main burden would have to be carried by the revenues of England. A delegation left to press these views on the government and Parliament at Westminster. But their loyalty to their English rulers was not widely shared in the Norman countryside or the smaller towns, where the new taxes served only to remind men of the burdens of the war. Conditions were particularly difficult in the north of the duchy where there was frequent contact between the inhabitants of the towns and the French garrisons of Picardy and the Beauvaisis. In the following year, Poton de Saintrailles briefly occupied Gisors after the townsmen went over to the French in a body. The English sensed the change. 'There was so much treason walking that men wist not what to do,' a London chronicler wrote.[13]

At Westminster, where Parliament was still sitting, the capture of Dieppe and the peasant rising overshadowed the proceedings. The

Earl of Suffolk arrived at the end of November to take his seat in the Lords with a first-hand account of events in Normandy. He was accompanied by Jean Rinel, by the ambassadors of the Norman Estates and by delegations from the municipalities of Paris and Rouen, 'loyal subjects of your wrecked and broken kingdom of France' as they called themselves. They told their hosts that another invasion in force by French companies would probably enjoy popular support. People were 'angry and oppressed by this long war and the inadequate steps taken to defend them'. They no longer believed that the English were there to stay, or that loyalty to Henry VI was the surest route to peace. The air of crisis at Westminster was intensified by reports of the activities of French agents in Scotland. A French embassy had been in the country for several months. The presence in its ranks of Sir Hugh Kennedy, one of the principal Scottish captains in France, revived fears of the new 'army of Scotland' that the Scottish King had promised to the French King as long ago as 1428.[14]

At the end of November 1435, the council won the support of the Lords for a dramatic increase in the scale of English operations in Normandy. A fresh expeditionary army would cross the Channel that winter, 'the biggest that has passed the sea in the memory of man' according to the council's grandiloquent announcement to the Normans. The plan was to raise 2,000 men-at-arms and 9,000 archers, which would bring the total strength of the English in France to at least 16,000 men. Some of these men would be expected to serve for long terms, two or even three years instead of the traditional six months. The command seems to have been offered first to the Earl of Suffolk. But Suffolk was reluctant to leave his influential place as steward of Henry VI's household and had no desire to assume responsibility for the 'misfortunes' that he clearly regarded as likely. Instead, the choice fell on the King's cousin, the twenty-four-year-old Richard Duke of York. Richard was the grandson of Edmund Langley Duke of York, Edward III's fourth son, whose title he had inherited on Edmund's death at the battle of Agincourt. Through his mother, he was also descended from Edward's second son Lionel of Antwerp Duke of Clarence. When in 1425 his uncle Edmund Earl of March died childless, Richard acquired the vast inheritance of the Mortimers in Wales and Ireland. In 1435 he was a Knight of the Garter and the richest peer in England. No one could have answered better the call of the Norman Estates for a prince of royal blood. But Richard had few other qualifications for the job. He had no military or administrative experience. His knowledge of France was limited to what he would have picked up at Henry VI's court during the coronation expedition, in which he had played an inconspicuous part. His appointment, which was limited to a year, seems to have been intended as a stopgap while more durable arrangements were made. To make up for these deficiencies he was given an impressive array of experienced captains to support him, including Suffolk, Salisbury, Fauconberg and Edmund Beaufort as well as the formidable Talbot and Fastolf who were already in France.[15]

The council had an ambitious timetable. An advance guard of nearly 1,800 men was expected to sail for France at the end of December 1435, followed by the rest a month later. The overall strategy was the one which had been tried and failed in 1428 and again in 1430: to bring an end to the war by a single blow in overwhelming strength. The task of the new armies would be to close the gaping wounds that had already opened in western Normandy and the Paris area, and then mount a major offensive against the territory recently occupied by Charles VII. Two independent forces were envisaged. The main body, 7,000 strong, was to operate in conjunction with the forces of Talbot and Willoughby in the Île-de-France and the marches of Normandy. A separate command was created for Edmund Beaufort, who was to take 2,000 men to recover territory lost in Maine and invade Anjou. On the success of these offensives the council pinned its hopes of extracting better terms from the Valois King than it had been possible to achieve at Arras. In due course the Duke of York was appointed as the King's lieutenant in France and given power to prosecute the war and to negotiate the permanent peace or the long truce which had eluded the English so far.[16]

An army of the size planned represented a severe test for the uncertain finances of the English state. It would cost about £60,000 in cash advances before it sailed, in addition to more than £9,000 due to Louis of Luxembourg for troops directly retained by the Grand Conseil. On top of that there would be the constant drain of cash while the army remained in France drawing pay every quarter. The Commons eventually voted a single subsidy to be paid in four instalments over the next two years and an increase in the taxes on trade. The Church matched this with a clerical tenth. The hope was that substantial further sums would be raised from another fiscal experiment, a graduated tax on incomes from land and from offices and annuities over five pounds, levied at progressive rates varying from sixpence to two shillings in the pound. The Commons appear to have hoped that the whole package would yield at least £100,000, for they authorised the government to borrow up to that amount against it. About half of this was expected to come from the income tax, which was to be paid in one lump sum in April and was to be the main source of funding for the new army. In fact, the income tax was slow to come in and its yield was disappointing. The inquisitorial powers of the fifteenth-century state were limited. Incomes were self-assessed. In the event, the tax produced less than £9,000. Worse, the failure of the new tax coincided with the collapse of customs revenues as a result of the Burgundian trade boycott and piracy in the Channel and the North Sea.

The Treasurer, Ralph Cromwell, had been trying ever since his appointment to break out of the vicious cycle of borrowing and assignment required by the continual demands of the French war. Much of the record-breaking borrowing of the past few years was still outstanding. But the insistent demand for cash to pay the new army left Cromwell with no choice but to go deeper into debt. Between November 1435 and August 1436, the government borrowed more than £48,000. Of this sum, nearly two-thirds was advanced by Cardinal Beaufort or by lenders such as the trustees of the duchy of Lancaster and the attorneys of his captive nephew the Earl of Somerset, who took their cue from him. Another £16,000 was found by commercial interests such as the corporation of London and the merchants of London and Calais, who were profoundly affected by the loss of the French Channel ports. The rest came from a large number of individual lenders, more than 450 of whom received direct commands to lend against the proceeds of the Parliamentary subsidy. These sums were fed straight to the troops as they arrived at the ports, in the hand to mouth way to which the Exchequer clerks had grown accustomed.[17]

In the new year, the war in the Caux took a new turn. Marshal Rieux's companies and Caruyer's peasant army captured the mighty fortress of the Greys of Heton at Tancarville on its clifftop site at the head of the Seine estuary. The fortress served as a secure base from which they were able to advance up the Seine valley, occupying the walled town of Lillebonne on the main road to Rouen. The Norman capital was in a state of panic. Some of the citizens were believed to be in touch with the French. The council was not at all confident that it could be held. Talbot, who took command on New Year's Day 1436, conducted the defence with his habitual decisiveness. He had troops brought into Rouen from other garrisons. Sir Henry Norbury, who arrived in early January from England with the first thousand men of the great expeditionary army, was directed straight to the city.[18]

Fortunately for the English, their enemies fell out. The leaders of the peasant army wanted to push further up the valley to take Caudebec. The French captains wanted to pause and regroup. So the peasants went forward on their own, hurling insults at the professional troops as they left. The soldiers withdrew to their coastal fortresses, leaving the peasants to their fate. Talbot sent 400 men forward under the command of the Shropshire knight Sir Fulk Eyton to hold Caudebec. He arrived in the town on 4 January 1436. Caudebec stood on the north bank of the Seine nineteen miles west of Rouen. It was defended by modern walls dating from the previous century with two massive towers and five heavily fortified gateways. The peasants seem to have approached along the strand, intending to occupy the strip of ground between the walls and the river. They found their path barred by the river Ambion. The river was crossed by a narrow bridge defended by a large force of English archers. The peasants attacked the bridge in a disorderly mob. As they did so, Eyton and his company emerged from the Harfleur gate on horseback and fell on them from behind. They were dispersed by the horsemen and cut down as they fled across the fields. The few who were taken alive were brought into the town, where they were butchered in the streets or drowned in the Seine.[19]

From Rouen, Talbot, Scales, Kyriel and other English captains followed up the rout with two devastating punitive raids into the Caux. The fighting took on the character of a class war as the peasants, abandoned by Rieux and Desmarais, turned to face the professional soldiers of the English alone. The repression was actively supported by the gentry and minor nobility of Normandy. The Norman chronicler Thomas Basin believed that these men were privately as hostile to the English occupation as the peasants but that class solidarity kept them loyal to the government in Rouen. They saw 'great danger for themselves and all France if the common people liberated their land from the English by their own efforts'. The peasants were not even accorded the small measure of humanity which the laws of war accorded to gentlemen. The English and their Norman auxiliaries burned down whole villages. They rode through the streets of market towns, killing indiscriminately. They seized men for ransom in the fields and cut their throats or drowned them in the rivers if they could not pay. They rounded up thousands of head of cattle and drove them back to Rouen. They looted everything worth taking. At Lillebonne, they joined forces with Eyton's garrison from Caudebec. The town's citadel was held by a company of Marshal Rieux's men. The town was packed with refugees. The English tricked their way into the gatehouse with the assistance of a French prisoner of war who had been promised his release without ransom. They killed or captured the whole garrison and sacked the town. Some 800 people are said to have lost their lives in this incident alone. When the English finally withdrew, they set up a blockade of the Caux, stopping all food supplies destined for the region. The result was a famine and the rapid spread of plague which together killed even more people than Talbot's soldiers. The campaign swiftly extinguished the peasant rebellion in the Caux. Boschier's rising in Lower Normandy was suppressed with equal violence by Lord Scales at the end of March. The rebels were cornered south of Saint-Lô, before help could reach them from the French strongholds further south. They were slaughtered in their thousands like Caruyer's followers at Caudebec and Lillebonne.[20]

The rebellion of the Caux left a terrible legacy. Whole communities fled before the soldiers, abandoning the land, leaving their fields untilled and the charred ruins of their homes behind them. Some took to the forests and became outlaws. Some emigrated to neighbouring provinces. The richer migrants found passages on ships bound for Brittany, the one island of relative security in western France. The poorer ones left for Picardy, which was beginning to rise from the wreckage of the past six years. Others made their way to Rouen and other Norman towns, where they were reduced to begging in the streets. The hospitals and houses of charity were overwhelmed. The destruction was completed by the garrisons of Marshal Rieux and La Hire, which preyed on the survivors, sustaining themselves from *pâtis* and loot. The tax records told their own melancholy story. Ten years after the rebellion, the region was still being described as a scene of 'total destruction and desolation'. One district was 'utterly destroyed and depopulated', another 'uninhabited, abandoned and close to destruction'. When the English judge Sir John Fortescue was living in exile in France in the 1460s, he cited the pays de Caux as the worst example of rural poverty that he had seen. It was 'almost desert for lack of tillers, as it now well appeareth by the new husbandry that is done there, namely in grubbing and stocking [rooting] of trees, bushes and groves grown while we were their lords of the country'. Half a century after the rebellion, much of the region was still a wasteland. 'The land knew not the plough, nor the footsteps of friends,' declared the representatives of the Caux at the Estates-General at Tours in 1484.[21]

At the end of January 1436, La Hire and Poton de Saintrailles tried to surprise Rouen with a force of about 1,500 men. They had allies among the citizens, who had promised to rise against the English. But Talbot had got wind of the plan, and when they arrived, they found the city's defenders ready for them. The French withdrew to regroup in the village of Ry, in the forest east of Rouen. There, at dawn on 2 February, they were attacked by an English force led by Lord Scales. They had no time to arm or array themselves. Many of them were killed and there was a rich haul of prisoners. Scales was reported to have made 20,000 *saluts* from just one of them. La Hire and Poton escaped, but lost their horses, their baggage and much of their weaponry. The battle at Ry saved Rouen. But shortly afterwards Talbot was forced to withdraw his troops by an incipient calamity in the Paris area. As soon as they had left, the French garrisons resumed their expansion. In March, Desmarais's force at Dieppe captured the town and the castle of Eu, overcoming one of the largest English garrisons in the region and leaving Arques and Caudebec as the only remaining English garrisons in the Caux.[22]

The final ordeal of Paris began with the French capture of the fortified bridge over the Seine at Meulan in September 1435. Control of the bridge enabled the French to stop most of the supplies reaching the city from Normandy, which had hitherto been its only reliable source of grain and its main source of meat and dairy products. The price of wheat in the city's markets doubled overnight and doubled again during the winter. The English laid siege to Meulan on 24 October, but with other pressures on their manpower they were unable to invest the place from both sides of the river. The operation dragged on until February 1436, when it was abandoned after the rapid disintegration of the English military positions around Paris had made the fight pointless. In the capital, the central institutions of the dual monarchy began to fall apart. The Chancellor, Louis of Luxembourg, had been at Rouen for weeks, along with most of the Grand Conseil. In his absence, the senior members of the council in the city were the ineffective Jacques du Châtellier Bishop of Paris, and the firmly anglophile Gilles de Clamécy. In government offices men worked under the shadow of imminent disaster. Those members of the *grands corps* who were not too obviously compromised by their association with the English had already begun to slope away. The principal clerk of the Parlement abandoned his post and left the city. These men lived in fear of their jobs, isolated in the face of a citizen body which was heart and soul with the Duke of Burgundy and increasingly hostile to the agents of a discredited Lancastrian government. Those who stayed at their posts had very little business. The Parlement seriously considered indefinitely suspending its sittings.[23]

The captain of Paris, Robert Willoughby, had a permanent garrison of about 400 English troops under his command. In addition, some troops had been withdrawn from English garrisons in eastern Normandy, and there were a few indigenous troops under the command of Burgundian captains of uncertain loyalty. The men were based partly in the Bastille and partly in the ring of suburban garrisons which guarded the main road and river approaches. These forces were pitifully inadequate for the task. None of them had been paid for months. The administration was now entirely dependent on cash sent from England and although money was still reaching Rouen, none of it got as far as Paris. The dearth of cash to pay the troops had the predictable consequences. The captain of Corbeil, the main river port for supplies reaching the city from the Gâtinais, was Guillaume de Ferrière, a Burgundian nobleman who had remained in English service after the treaty of Arras. He was owed more than 1,000 *livres* for the back wages of his garrison. Early in January he was bought by the Duke of Bourbon and entered French service, delivering up Corbeil together with Brie-Comte-Robert, the only remaining English strongholds between Paris and Montereau. A few days later, the fortified bridge of Charenton, a vital element of Paris's outer defences, which was also garrisoned by indigenous troops, went over to Charles VII.

A crisis meeting was summoned to the Parlement chamber on the Île de la Cité. It was attended by Willoughby, the handful of members of the Grand Conseil in the city, the Provost, the officers of the municipality, and all the councillors of the Parlement who could be found. They set up a committee to meet daily at the Hôtel de Ville to organise the defence and rally support in the streets. But they saw no way of defending the city against an all-out attack. They sent yet another delegation to Rouen to appeal for help. They even tentatively opened negotiations with the Duke of Burgundy. The city authorities reported a 'great murmur' and much seditious talk in the streets. Not long afterwards mobs gathered demanding the right to replace Willoughby with a captain of their own choice. They wanted to elect the French captain Jean de la Haye lord of Coulonces, the old cavalry commander in Anjou and Maine. He had been captured when the Earl of Stafford took Brie-Comte-Robert in 1430 and was currently languishing in the Conciergerie. The Parisians threatened to invade the prison and release him by force if their demands were not met.[24]

On 19 February 1436, the fortress of Vincennes east of the city walls was captured by the French. Twenty partisans came over the walls from ladders, with the connivance of a Scottish member of the watch. On the following day, the citizens of Pontoise, which commanded the main road to Rouen, rose up against the English, arrested the garrison in their billets and took over the town. Willoughby, who remained captain of Pontoise, had depleted the garrison to reinforce his troops in Paris. His lieutenant in the town, Sir John Ripley, took refuge in one of the gatehouses with a handful of men and fought off the citizens by hurling down stones and tiles from the roof until he was finally forced to surrender. The citizens invited in Villiers de L'Isle-Adam, who chose this moment to declare for Charles VII. He arrived in the town and was shortly joined there by about 150 troops sent by the Duke of Burgundy. At about the same time, the French occupied the bridge-town of Poissy, on the Seine south of Pontoise. Of the ring of forts around Paris, only Saint-Germain-en-Laye, guarding the southwest approach from the Beauce, was still in English hands. The capital was almost completely cut off. At Poitiers, Charles VII and his advisers believed that their time had come. They nominated Richemont as the King's lieutenant in the Île-de-France and ordered him to reoccupy the city. A general pardon was drawn up for all the years of opposition to Charles as Dauphin and King since 1418, and Richemont was authorised to issue it when the time was ripe. They expected the city to fall into their hands without a fight.[25]

Early in March 1436, Louis of Luxembourg arrived from Rouen to take a grip on a rapidly deteriorating situation. Many people in the capital who had sworn allegiance to Henry VI, he declared, were now actively preparing to submit to his rival. All the most prominent officials and citizens were summoned to the chamber of the Parlement to swear a fresh oath of allegiance. Any who refused were expelled, together with their families. Paris was put in a state of siege. Police powers were tightened. Passes were required to go through the gates. There were rumours that suspected opponents of the government were being arrested and obscurely drowned in the Seine. An ordinance was published to organise guard duty on the walls and gates and require citizen soldiers to wear the uniform red cross of England, not the traditional St Andrew's cross of Burgundy. The canons of Notre-Dame with houses giving onto the river were required to block their doors and windows. Beyond the city walls, a scorched earth campaign was ordered around Pontoise to prevent its Burgundian garrison from resupplying itself. The English passed through the country burning down the grain stores and invading houses to destroy stocks of winter vegetables, enough, thought the contemporary chronicler of Paris, to feed 6,000 people for half a year at a time when the city was facing starvation. The council at Rouen made a serious attempt to break through the ring of French garrisons surrounding the capital. They began to build up their forces at Mantes, the closest bridge-town downstream of the capital still under their control. A great wagon train of food and herds of cattle were assembled to be convoyed to the city. But they never succeeded in getting through, and the attempt was eventually abandoned.[26]

If the plans made at Westminster in December 1435 had worked out, there should by now have been an extra 10,000 English troops in France, many of whom would have been available to repel a French assault on Paris. But the Westminster council's ambitious timetable quickly went awry. Sir Henry Norbury had sailed from Portsmouth with 1,000 men at the end of December. But the rest were still held up in England. The loss of the Somme towns and the ports of the Caux had challenged the traditional logistics of English expeditionary armies. It was no longer possible to ship them to Normandy through Calais or Dieppe on packed barges. They had to take the longer passage to the Seine estuary, which required more and larger ships. These were expensive and took two or three months to requisition. Sir Thomas Beaumont, who should have sailed with Norbury in December, did not reach Paris until late March.

The main body of the expeditionary army should have sailed with Edmund Beaufort and the Duke of York by the end of January, but it was delayed by a combination of logistical problems and distractions at home. A full-scale invasion scare was in progress in England. Men were being arrayed in their counties for defence against invasion for the first time since the early years of the century. Along the south and east coasts, towns were laying in stocks of weapons, setting up warning systems and building improvised fortifications. There was continuing concern about the security of the north. The two northern bishops of Durham and Carlisle had been instructed to negotiate a renewal of the truce with Scotland, which was due to expire on 1 May 1436. They got nowhere, and may not even have been received. The need to retain troops for the defence of England inevitably added to the risks associated with the shipment of great armies to France and slowed down their recruitment. The Duke of York's army was reduced from 7,000 to 5,000 men and its embarkation postponed from January to April.[27]

It shortly dawned on the council that the biggest threat was to the English outpost at Calais, now surrounded by hostile territory. They toned down the fiercely anti-Burgundian rhetoric which had been heard in the aftermath of the treaty of Arras. They took steps to suppress attacks on Flemish cargoes in the Channel and the North Sea. In January 1436 they even approached the Duke through the Luxembourg brothers, with a proposal for a mutual non-aggression pact. But the time for that had passed. Philip had already decided that with the English facing a crisis in Paris and Normandy, there would never be a better time to eliminate the threat to his dominions from Calais and Le Crotoy. As his advisers had pointed out at Arras, if the object of his deal with Charles VII was to bring peace to his territories, it would not be achieved while these powerful fortresses with their secure harbours and large permanent garrisons remained in English hands. Those who at Arras had supported a separate peace with France had insisted that capturing these places would be a straightforward operation. Hughes de Lannoy, who knew England better than anyone at the Burgundian court, thought that this was unrealistic. He had pointed out at the time that the English were in a position to put up to 3,000 men into the two fortresses by sea relatively quickly. Philip's domains, he said, would be a prime target. Flanders was rich and vulnerable, and the English could put 14,000 or 15,000 men into the county through Calais to attack it.

This was in fact the strategy favoured by the Duke of Gloucester, as Lannoy probably knew. Much of what he had to say was prescient, but it was essentially a rehearsal of the arguments against a breach with England which had already been rejected. At the end of January 1436, Philip summoned his council to obtain their advice. But he knew what advice he wanted to receive and did not invite councillors who were known to disagree. Most of the voices were with Nicolas Rolin and the Croÿ brothers who favoured a trial of strength at Calais. The council's advice was to attack the town in overwhelming force. On 19 February 1436, Philip answered the English olive branch with what amounted to a declaration of war. By the end of March the first reports reached England of active preparations for a siege of Calais.[28]

The council at Westminster was paralysed by disagreements about the priority of the different fronts. Calais or Normandy? One of Louis of Luxembourg's secretaries arrived in London to find out what was going on, but could get no answer. Another servant of the French Chancellor arrived a month later with the same mission and was equally unsuccessful. The issue was ultimately decided in favour of Calais, but not until the beginning of April. Edmund Beaufort's army of 2,000 men was gathering at Winchelsea to embark for the Seine when they were redirected to Calais. A large artillery train which was due to be shipped with Beaufort's army to Normandy and was badly needed there, was eventually sent to Calais instead. Substantial sums in cash destined for the payment of the Duke of York's army were diverted to the Treasurer of Calais. These delays and diversions repeatedly put back the embarkation of the army of Normandy. The result was to extinguish the last hope of saving Paris.[29]

Arthur de Richemont opened his offensive against Paris from Lagny on 1 April 1436. Two days later, on the 3rd, he entered Pontoise. He was joined there by the Bastard of Orléans. Their combined force was small, no more than 500 or 600 men. Their hopes rested on the prospects of a general insurrection in the city. Richemont made contact with sympathisers within the walls. In better days, these men had been pillars of the Anglo-Burgundian establishment. Guillaume Sanguin was a rich jeweller of the quarter of St-Germain-l'Auxerrois who had lent money to both John the Fearless and the Duke of Bedford. He had been the Provost of the Merchants in charge of the defence during the siege of 1429. Michel de Lallier, one of the most senior financial officers of the Lancastrian government, was a councillor of the Chambre des Comptes who had sworn allegiance to Henry VI as recently as 15 March, one of many who had done so with their fingers crossed behind their backs. Pierre de Landes was a former master of the Paris mint. Jean de Belloy was a former *échevin* of Paris whose loyalty in the early years of the regency had been well rewarded by the Duke of Bedford, but who like so many others regarded himself as primarily a partisan of the Duke of Burgundy. Philip the Good discreetly encouraged them. But they were cautious men. They told Richemont's emissaries that they were willing to let him in but could not do it until there was a large enough French army at the gates to guarantee success. Reinforcements were already on their way to join Richemont from the French garrisons of Champagne. The Bastard of Orléans left to recruit more in the Beauce and the Loire valley.[30]

At the beginning of April 1436 Jean Chartier, who was following these events from the abbey of Saint-Denis, reckoned Robert Willoughby's total strength in Paris after Sir Thomas Beaumont's arrival at about 1,500 men. But a series of disasters shortly reduced their numbers. On 4 April, the 400 men of Willoughby's English garrison troops mutinied for want of pay and marched out of the southern gates of the city. They occupied the suburb of Notre-Dame-des-Champs, looted the churches, invaded houses in search of food and then marched away leaving the whole district in flames. Beaumont's companies did not join the mutiny. They had been paid for half a year before leaving England, and had money in hand. But on 10 April, they had a disastrous encounter with a detachment of the French army from Pontoise. Richemont had ordered Villiers de L'Isle-Adam to occupy Saint-Denis in the name of Charles VII. The walls of the town had been demolished by Talbot the previous autumn. There was only a small English garrison in a tower of the abbey enclosure. The defence committee in Paris ordered Beaumont to stop L'Isle-Adam's force as it approached. He marched out of the Porte Saint-Denis at midnight with about 500 men and took possession of the abbey town in the early hours.

As the sun rose, Beaumont advanced to meet the approaching French force. His men took up a position in front of the narrow stone bridge over the river Rouillon near the point at which it flowed into the Seine. The place has long ago disappeared beneath the industrial ugliness of modern Saint-Denis. Beaumont had the advantage of numbers and charged L'Isle-Adam's lines, driving his men back for more than a mile. But Richemont came up with the rest of the French army from Pontoise and reversed the course of the battle. The English were defeated in fierce fighting in the meadows of the Seine. The pursuit was murderous. Most of the surviving English troops made for Paris. But the gatekeepers closed the gates and raised the drawbridge against them for fear of letting in their pursuers. As a result, most of the fugitives were killed beside the ditches and barriers of the city. The English lost about 200 dead. The whole of the rest of Beaumont's force was captured, including Beaumont himself. The thirty or forty English troops in Saint-Denis were soon winkled out of their tower and the town occupied by the French. Willoughby was left with barely 600 English troops to defend the capital.[31]

The centres of Burgundian sentiment in Paris were the University quarter on the left bank with its large and unruly student population, and the densely populated district around Les Halles dominated by the butchers' guilds. Assemblies were held in both quarters on the day after Beaumont's defeat. They decided that their moment had come. A message was sent to Pontoise that night inviting Richemont to take possession of the city. The Porte Saint-Jacques, they said, would be opened for him by the *dizainier* on watch duty. On 12 April 1436, the Constable marched south from Pontoise and crossed the Seine at Poissy. Here, he joined forces with the Bastard of Orléans. The whole army, now about 2,000 strong, rode at night through the vast forests of Laye and Saint-Cloud which then extended from Poissy to the southern suburbs of Paris. Shortly after dawn on the 13th, Richemont was met on the road a few miles outside the city by one of the conspirators. The plot, he reported, had been discovered. The men who had planned to open the gate had been replaced. The Constable decided to press on regardless and try the citizens' will to resist.

The Porte Saint-Jacques was the principal southern entrance to Paris, a massive, fortified gateway defended by a dry ditch and a drawbridge, where today the Rue Saint-Jacques crosses the Rue Soufflot. At about seven o'clock in the morning, Richemont's army approached the gate. Villiers de L'Isle-Adam was sent forward to parley with the men on the walls. He told them that the Duke of Burgundy had called on them to submit to Charles VII. He produced the royal pardon, with the King's wax seal hanging from the vellum. The alternative to submission, he said, would be famine and death, for no supplies would be allowed to reach the city while it remained in the hands of the King's enemies.

By now, the streets were filling with armed citizens. The defenders of the gateway looked down at the crowd gathering below and took fright. They did not have the keys, but a ladder was found and passed down. L'Isle-Adam climbed onto the wall, followed by the Bastard of Orléans and a standard-bearer who planted the Valois King's banner on the ramparts. The gates below were broken open and the Constable and his troops poured in. It was almost exactly eighteen years since Burgundian partisans had let L'Isle-Adam into the city to proclaim the violent revolution which brought John the Fearless to power. This time, the coup was almost bloodless. As the news spread, people came out of their houses wearing the upright white cross of the Valois or the St Andrew's cross of Burgundy, and crying, 'Peace! Long live the King and the Duke of Burgundy!'[32]

The English were alerted by the noise. Louis of Luxembourg, Robert Willoughby and the Provost Simon Morhier met to organise the defence. They pulled as many Englishmen and die-hard French loyalists as they could find out of their lodgings and formed them into three armed battalions. The Chancellor took command of one, and Willoughby and Morhier of another. The third was commanded by Jean l'Archer, the long-serving officer of the Châtelet responsible for the city's police and criminal court. The three Frenchmen passed through the northern quarters of the city with their men, trying to rally support. 'St George! St George!' l'Archer shouted as he made his way up the Rue Saint-Martin, 'French traitors, we will kill the lot of you!' Not a single person joined him. Simon Morhier led his battalion into the Les Halles quarter. There, he approached a friend, a rich wholesale miller whom he was sure he could depend on. 'Have pity, my friend,' this man said, 'we have to make peace now or we are done for.' 'What, you too?' replied Morhier, striking him across the face with the flat of his sword and leaving him to be lynched by his followers.

Resistance to Willoughby's battalions quickly built up. Michel de Lallier and his allies distributed arms to 3,000 or 4,000 supporters. The heavy chains traditionally piled up at corners were stretched across the streets and lanes, the first time that they had been used since 1418. Improvised barricades were constructed from logs, stones and lumber. People threw rocks down on the heads of Willoughby's men as they struggled through the streets. The English and their allies were finally dispersed by artillery fire as they approached the northern ramparts. Simon Morhier, who was afraid that he would be lynched, fled to Charenton and surrendered to the French captain at the fortified bridge. Willoughby, Louis of Luxembourg and Jean l'Archer made their way through the streets of eastern Paris pursued by a vengeful mob and shut themselves in the Bastille. They found Pierre Cauchon already there with a crowd of refugees, flotsam from the wreckage of the Lancastrian government. Across the city, mobs broke into the houses that the English and their French associates had abandoned, trashing the buildings and carrying off their contents.

The Bastille was not stocked for a siege, and Willoughby soon realised that there was no prospect of holding it. Louis of Luxembourg was deputed to open negotiations with the Constable. The French captains were divided. Some of them called for the unconditional surrender of the men in the fortress and proposed to starve them out if they had to. But the wiser course seemed to be to let them leave. They were eventually allowed to abandon the fortress in return for a large sum of money. On 17 April, they left with safe-conducts for Rouen, pursued by howls of mockery and abuse from the crowd gathered round the gates. The loudest abuse was reserved for the leading French partisans of the house of Lancaster: Louis of Luxembourg, whose haughty manner had always been resented; Jean l'Archer, an obese and undignified figure whose function as chief of police had made him few friends; the master of the butchers' guild Jean de Saint-Yon, the great mob leader of the civil wars who, like other prominent Parisians on the Grand Conseil, had done too well in the last fifteen years to have any future under the new regime.[33]

The loss of Paris marked the end of the dual monarchy. Without the capital or the central institutions of the French state, it was no longer a credible idea. Henry VI clung to the titles conferred on him by the treaty of Troyes, but they had become empty formulae. The English became a provincial power in France whose first priority was the conservation of their territorial base in Normandy. The Grand Conseil transferred its operations to Rouen, where in practice the major decisions had been made anyway since the Duke of Bedford's move from Paris in 1429. The judicial arm of the council at Rouen (sometimes called the Cour du Conseil), had already begun to claim the authority of an independent sovereign court even before the fall of Paris, a development which was completed afterwards. A new Chambre des Comptes was created for Normandy in place of the 'rebellious and disobedient' officers of the Paris institution. Many of the official refugees who had gathered around Robert Willoughby in the Bastille in the last days of the occupation found new roles in the English administration in Rouen.[34]

The Norman administration was now very obviously an outpost of the government of England. Even its French officers increasingly saw themselves as the agents of an English monarchy. Jean Rinel retained his post as the French secretary to the King, serving successive lieutenants at Rouen. He had already taken the precaution of acquiring letters of denization in England, and ultimately moved to England to serve in Henry's diplomatic secretariat. In 1437, Henry VI granted him two manors in Hampshire to compensate him for the loss of his property in Paris. Laurent Calot, another member of the Paris state secretariat, was said by his family to have lost 'country, kinsmen, friends, and all his property, houses, possessions and inheritances' on account of his loyalty to the King of England. He was employed in both Normandy and England, receiving an annuity of 100 marks a year from the English Exchequer and eventually buying a house in London where he settled with his family. Gervase le Vulre had worked for the Lancastrian administration in Paris from 1421 but moved to England in 1437 to serve as the King's French secretary. Like Calot he settled there permanently with his wife and family. Many other current or former officials who fled from Paris received pensions and grants from English revenues. The most remarkable case was Louis of Luxembourg. He moved to Normandy but made frequent visits to England and was naturalised there in June 1437. From 1439 he was summoned to sit among the Lords in Parliament. The Pope was prevailed upon to translate him from the diocese of Thérouanne, which was in Burgundian territory, to the archbishopric of Rouen. But the revenues of the archbishopric were badly depleted by war damage. His income was derived mainly from the English Exchequer, which paid him an annuity of £1,666 marks a year (equivalent to the income of an earl). The diocese of Ely, one of the richest in England, was kept vacant for eight years so that he could draw the revenues. He probably never visited Ely, but when he died (in England) he was buried there, as he had directed in his will. His tomb and effigy can still be seen at the east end of the cathedral, a curious monument to a stranded life.[35]

Charles VII and his ministers lost no time in dismantling the structures of English rule in Paris. There was an almost complete turnover of civic officers. The royal Provost and all but one of the officers of the Châtelet were replaced. So were the officers of the municipality: the Provost of the Merchants and the four *échevins*. In every case the incoming officers who replaced them were Parisian partisans of the Duke of Burgundy. Paris had been a Burgundian city for a generation, and for the moment it was destined to remain one. The civil service and the judiciary were viewed with undisguised hostility by the servants of the Valois King. In their eyes, they were the creatures of John the Fearless, who had expelled a generation of Armagnac officials in 1418 and replaced them with Burgundian intruders. The fifty-nine notaries who conducted the routine business of the Chancery in Paris were all dismissed, and only those who had been appointed before the Burgundian coup were reinstated. On 15 May 1436, the King ordered the closure of all the *grands corps* in Paris: the Parlement, the judicial offices of the royal household, the Chambre des Comptes, the Treasury and the administration of the mints and archives. Their premises were sealed up and their personnel dispersed. In December, after a seven-month hiatus, the corresponding institutions in Bourges and Poitiers, the only ones that Charles VII regarded as legitimate, were transferred to Paris with trumpet fanfares at street corners.[36]

In spite of these dramatic assertions of official doctrine, there was a limited measure of continuity between the old regime and the new. When the Parlement was reconstituted, half of its membership either had sat in the Anglo-Burgundian Parlement or were newcomers nominated by the Duke of Burgundy. At the Chambre des Comptes, there was more of a clean sweep, but two of the ten former councillors were reinstated alongside the men brought in from Bourges. The biggest change was at the top. Charles VII had never liked Paris. He had bad memories of the riots and massacres of the civil war, in which many of his friends had been killed. He did not visit his capital until November 1437, more than a year and a half after its capture, and stayed for only three weeks. 'It seemed that he had only come to look at the place', wrote the bilious chronicler of Paris, who found the new regime little better than the old. Thereafter, Charles's visits were rare, brief and formal. He appeared there 'like a tourist' but continued to live mainly in the Loire provinces like most of his successors until the end of the sixteenth century. This meant that the Chancellor, the royal council and the political organs of the monarchy which followed the King did not return to Paris. Nor did the princes and noblemen whose crowded courts had been hubs of Parisian life before the civil wars and whose patronage had kept generations of craftsmen and bankers in business. Their mansions in the capital were left empty, leaving a void at the heart of the city's life.[37]

Inevitably, the sixteen-year English occupation of Paris left traces which could not be obliterated overnight. A handful of the Lancastrian government's indigenous French servants stayed behind and conducted a clandestine resistance to the city's new masters. In March 1437, three officials were beheaded, and a herald was consigned to an oubliette for passing information to the English about plans to seize walled places in the Île-de-France. Another man, a former advocate in the Parlement, left the city to conduct his own guerrilla war against French-held towns of the Île-de-France until he too was captured and executed. There cannot have been many fifth columnists like them.

A more important legacy of the years of English rule was the Lancastrian property settlement. A very large number of Parisians had property the title to which depended directly or indirectly on grants, forfeitures or court decrees during the English occupation. An ordinance was issued repeating the substance of the Edict of Compiègne. It annulled every forfeiture or confiscation since 1418 and invited the former owners or their heirs to resume possession. All property abandoned by the English or belonging to their supporters was ordered to be forfeited. Informers were rewarded with a quarter of the spoil.

Others found their social and business relations severed by the erection of a legal wall between Paris and the territories still under English occupation. Jacques Bernardini, a Lucchese merchant in Paris, had done good business with the English and followed them to Rouen. His Parisian wife eventually succeeded in joining him there, an offence for which all her property in the capital was confiscated. Her duty as the King's subject, declared the newly reconstituted Parlement, prevailed over her duty as a wife. The fact that she had four children was an aggravating factor for, they said, it was treasonable to boost the population of the enemy. The fate of another Parisian, Jeanette Roland, was harsher still. She was engaged to Sir John Talbot's Irish herald. As long as she lived, she declared, she would have no other husband than him. The Parlement prevented her from joining him in Rouen by ordering her indefinite detention in her parents' house.[38]

Those Parisians, probably the majority, who expected the return of the Valois to restore a measure of security were destined to be disappointed. By the time that Richemont entered Paris, the French had recovered all the fortresses in the immediate vicinity of the city, except for Saint-Germain-en-Laye which was sold to them a month later. But the English still retained a ring of garrisoned fortresses on the river routes leading to Paris. From these places, they were able to maintain a distant siege of the capital, just as the French had done for years before 1436. They blocked the valley of the Marne at Meaux where the French had blocked it at Lagny. They stopped the traffic of the Oise at Creil where the French had stopped it at Compiègne or Pont-Sainte-Maxence. The Seine was blocked by English garrisons upstream of the capital at Montereau and downstream at Mantes; the Loing at Montargis and Nemours. The roads from Amiens were blocked at Orville, the roads from the Beauce at Chevreuse. It took more than five years to winkle the English garrisons out of these places. In the meantime, they raided regularly up to the walls of Paris, killing, raping, kidnapping and looting within sight of the guards manning the gates. 'Hey you, what's up with your King,' they would shout up at them, 'is he in hiding?' The French garrisons of the region, which were paid irregularly or not at all, behaved no better. The Constable Arthur de Richemont made Paris his headquarters and imposed heavy taxes on its citizens. Poverty and administrative collapse depressed the yield of these taxes, and for most of the time Richemont was unable to pay his troops or maintain discipline. The garrisons of Vincennes, Pont-de-Charenton and Saint-Cloud lived on loot. They took eight or ten hogsheads of wine as *pâtis* from every suburban village and mounted destructive night-time plundering raids around the capital. The French captain of Corbeil was said to be taking *pâtis* from the whole of the Île-de-France.

The years which followed the reoccupation of Paris proved to be the worst in the memory of men. The population continued to decline, rents and wages to fall. The devastation of the countryside combined with a succession of bad harvests to push food prices up sharply. Grain reached the highest levels of the century in 1438. Wine and meat disappeared from the markets. Famine and cold, followed by a serious epidemic of smallpox, killed thousands in the streets and tenements.

Between June and December of that year 5,000 people were reported to have died in the Hôtel-Dieu, the main hospital of Paris, and 45,000 in the city at large.[39]

When Paris fell, the Duke of Burgundy's preparations to take Calais were already at an advanced stage. The Duke planned to recruit most of the men-at-arms from Picardy. But the lesson of Orléans and Compiègne was that very large numbers of infantry were required for a major siege. They would have to come from the populous industrial cities of Flanders, with their large armed militias. Much of February and March 1436 was passed in delicate negotiations with urban communities who were initially fearful of the economic fallout from a war with England. As the authorities of Ghent had declared in the aftermath of the treaty of Arras, 'the Flemings do not believe in war with England'. When the delegates of the Four Members, representing the cities and regions of Flanders, appeared before Philip at Brussels at the end of November 1435, they urged him to let Flanders remain neutral. It was a 'commercial region', they said. Over the following weeks, he won them over. On 8 March there was a great assembly of the municipality and guildsmen of Ghent. The delegates of the Four Members also attended. Philip presided while the *bailli* of Flanders recounted the proceedings at Arras and the history of his recent dealings with England. He explained why the commercial interests of Flanders, which had traditionally required peace with England, now pointed to war. The English occupation of Calais not only threatened the security of the whole region but enabled the Staple merchants to control the market in wool and impose monopoly terms of trade. The Duke intended to attack Calais, he said, in order to defend the interests of Flemish industry 'as the good shepherd expels the wolf from the sheepfold'. When the *bailli* had finished, opinion in the hall was divided. But the guild leaders and the city magistrates had been softened up in advance and loudly declared their support. Dissent was silenced. The final decision lay with the Grote Raad, the 'Great Council' of Ghent comprising three men, representing the inhabitants of the city, the weavers and the minor guilds. They delivered their consent to the Duke the next morning. The delegates of the rest of Flanders imposed a number of terms, including an equitable sharing out of the wool stocks of Calais, but they too gave their support. Ghent, which was much the largest of the industrial cities of Flanders, proposed to send a contingent of 15,000 men. It was expected that Bruges, Ypres and the Franc would provide another 15,000 men between them.[40]

Although the main burden of the siege would fall on Flanders, the operation represented a collective effort by the whole of the Burgundian domains. Philip the Good's other territories were expected to make their contribution in cash. Their promises had to be laboriously negotiated territory by territory, in some cases by Philip in person. But the results were remarkable. The nominal total of tax grants came to nearly 250,000 *livres* of Flanders (about £20,000 sterling). Only the duchy and county of Burgundy, impoverished by war damage and threatened by freelance companies, stood aside. The Duke raised more or less forced loans from towns, religious houses and officials, some of which were not repaid for many years. Over the whole of the calendar year his net receipts from all sources came to 718,000 *livres* (about £80,000 sterling), by far the highest figure of his reign.[41]

The English council received a detailed report of the proceedings at Ghent from 'special friends' in Flanders. From the same source, they also received an exaggerated report of the current state of Philip's preparations. He was said to have assembled a fleet of 400 large ships at Sluys, Biervliet and Rotterdam, loaded with artillery and siege equipment and poised to descend on Calais. The loss of Calais was a terrifying prospect for Henry VI's councillors. It was widely regarded as the wall of England, its fall the precursor to an invasion. In fact, Philip's naval and military preparations had hardly begun, and the fleet of 400 was a fiction. But the spies' reports provoked panic at Westminster, which shortly spread to the four corners of the land as the council distributed copies to towns, cathedrals and abbeys, accompanied by insistent demands for money. 'There hath not been seen so great an ordinance disposed for any siege in our days,' the council wrote. 'How great a jewel the said town with his marches is to us and to our land . . . [as] to caste this land out of all reputation and into perpetual reproach, villany and shame through the world if [it] so fell . . . that it were gotten by our enemies for lack of convenable defence in time.'

There was an extraordinary outburst of fear, anger and emotion across England. Ugly mobs gathered to threaten Flemings and Brabanters. A great council was hurriedly convened, comprising all the peers and prelates who were at hand. The Duke of Gloucester was in his element. He declared that he would lead an army to Calais to confront Philip the Good's horde and then carry the war into his domains. The young King came personally to the meeting to persuade the lay peers to find men to serve for six weeks under Gloucester's command. Some of them even agreed to dispense with advances and serve on credit. Many towns offered to recruit and pay their own contingents. Bishops and abbots dug into their chests to find money on top of the taxes granted by the last Convocation and the forced loans earlier in the year. Some £15,000 was raised in this way. As usual, the largest contributions came from Cardinal Beaufort (£6,000) and the trustees of the duchy of Lancaster (£5,000). The recruitment drive was equally successful. Although more than 7,000 men had already been raised for service in France in addition to the men already there, by July another 7,600 men were found to go to the defence of Calais. Not since the original siege of Calais in 1346–7 had so many English troops served at one time beyond the sea.[42]

Calais was as close to being impregnable as any fortress in Europe. The town was a rectangle some 5,000 feet long by 1,700 feet wide, enclosed by limestone walls. At its north-west corner, a powerful castle overlooked the estuary of the river Hammes, separated from the town and the surrounding country by its own moat. On the seaward side the town and castle were defended by a water-filled moat and a long spit of sand enclosing the harbour, at the end of which, dominating the entrance, stood a fort known as the Rysbank Tower. On the landward sides, the walls were protected by a double line of broad ditches, which were filled from the sea and could not be diverted or drained. There was a permanent garrison varying between 500 and 2,000 men, and a civilian population of about 3,000, almost entirely English. The approaches to the town were guarded by a ring of six subsidiary forts, pushing the border of the English 'pale' out for ten miles into the hinterland and enclosing an area of about 120 square miles. Guines, the most important of these places and the only significant population centre apart from Calais itself, was a walled town at the southern extremity of the pale, dominated by a large moated castle standing over the road from Saint-Omer. There were five smaller forts at Oye, Marck, Balinghem, Hammes and Sangatte. Calais had formidable natural defences as well as man-made ones. A vast marsh extended from the cliffs of Escalles on the west to the river Aa on the east. The soft ground meant that there were very few places where a besieger could set up artillery. Along the shore, a line of dykes held back the

THE HINGE OF FORTUNE, 1435–1436

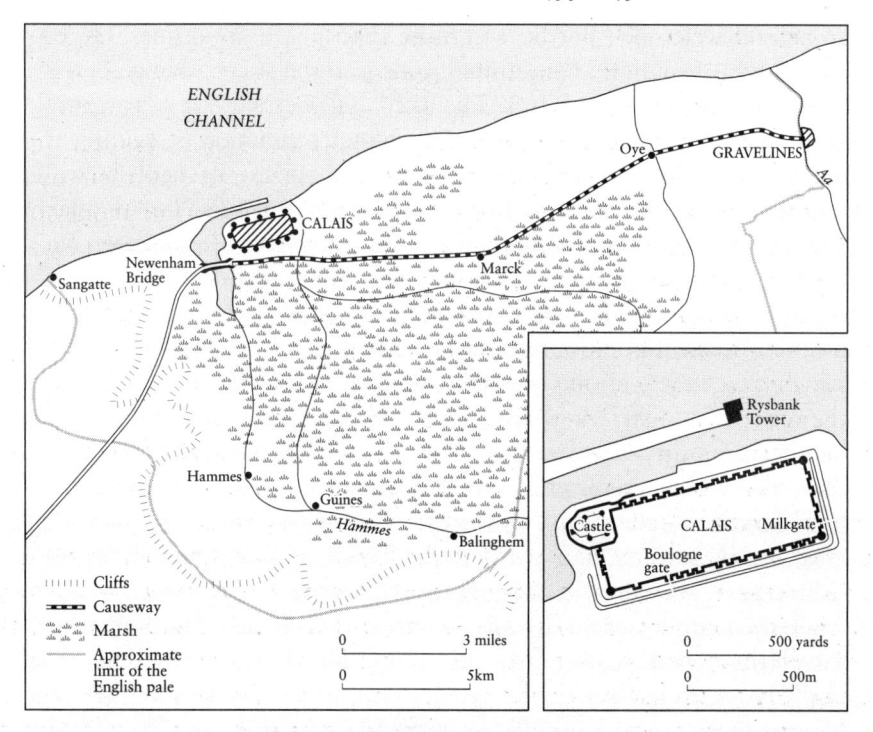

10 The siege of Calais, June–August 1436

sea. Sluice gates at Oye and Newenham Bridge allowed the whole plain to be flooded with sea water in a matter of hours. Separated by just twenty miles of sea from the Kent coast and linked to the outlying forts by a dense network of waterways, Calais was relatively easy to reinforce and supply, and impossible to starve into submission without a large fleet to blockade it from the sea. That was no mean undertaking, even for a major maritime power. The English Channel is stormy, making it difficult for ships to keep station off the coast. Philip the Good must have had a fair idea of what he was taking on by besieging Calais. He commissioned painters to produce plans of the defences and presumably studied them. It is one of the earliest recorded examples of the use of military cartography in Europe.[43]

The Duke of Gloucester was the nominal captain of Calais, but effective command was in the hands of his deputy Sir John Radcliffe. Radcliffe had passed much of his career on the march of Aquitaine. He was a popular commander. According to the London chronicler, he 'kept and held a good and open household to who that would come and welcome'. But he was more than just a good host. He was a resourceful soldier. He mounted raids into the surrounding country. He organised practice alarms. The fixed defences were in a lamentable state of disrepair as a result of the council's practice of raiding the budget of the Treasurer of Calais for other purposes. Parts of the walls and towers were perilously close to collapse and breaches regularly appeared in the sea walls. Radcliffe embarked on a series of emergency repairs, building new dykes west of the town and earth boulevards outside the gates. He installed additional artillery and repaired the outlying forts. The nominal establishment in 1436 was 720 men, of which 520 were stationed in the town and castle of Calais itself, and the other 200 distributed among the outlying forts. But the garrison had been reinforced at intervals since the threat from Philip the Good first arose. The arrival of Edmund Beaufort in late April brought the total English strength in Calais to something like the 3,000 men that Hughes de Lannoy had warned the Duke of Burgundy to expect. In addition, there was a large staff of masons, carpenters and other tradesmen employed on the maintenance of the defences, all of whom were armed and expected to fight alongside the garrison. The able-bodied townsmen were organised in support teams, and even the women 'both young and old ... spared no sweat ne swynk'. Writing to a friend who was worried about the fate of Calais, an anonymous English official declared that there was nothing to worry about. 'I will have you know that at Calais there are more gigantic men, more ferocious lions and more terrible dragons mounted on the highest horses.'[44]

It took the Duke of Burgundy more than two months to negotiate grants of taxation with the assemblies of the various provinces of his far-flung empire. The money came in with painful slowness, causing severe cash-flow problems and losing him much time. As a result, the English were ready for the attack several weeks before it materialised. In April 1436, when Edmund Beaufort arrived at Calais, the only Burgundian troops based in the region were the garrisons of Ardres and Boulogne. A month later, another 600 mounted men appeared under the command of Jean de Croÿ, who established himself at Gravelines, the walled port on the river Aa which marked the western boundary of Flanders. Edmund Beaufort immediately took command and embarked on a series of heavy mounted raids into the surrounding region. The suburbs of all three Burgundian garrison towns were destroyed. His men penetrated into western Flanders on large-scale rustling operations which produced several thousand head of cattle to fill the stores of the town. They destroyed the open villages, burning the entire population of one place in the church where they had taken refuge, and massacring the ill-prepared local militias mobilised to confront them. In June they inflicted a bloody defeat on Jean de Croÿ east of Boulogne: 'iii hundred lay stretched on the sands' according to the verses in which the English celebrated this encounter. There was a rich haul of prisoners. The council at Westminster was highly satisfied with these operations. They made Beaufort a knight of the Garter and sent a herald to bring the insignia to him at Calais.[45]

In the second and third weeks of June 1436, the contingents of the Duke of Burgundy's army mustered in market squares and suburban meadows across Flanders and began to converge on Gravelines. On 25 June, Philip the Good reviewed the whole army outside the walls. The promise of 30,000 men which had been made at Ghent in March had never been realistic. The Ypres alderman Oliver van Dixmude, who may well have been there, reckoned the whole Flemish army at about 10,000 fighting men, not counting auxiliaries. These were impressive numbers, but the men were of poor quality. The Duke himself thought them untrained and undisciplined, while the English dismissed them as 'nothing else worth but great words'. They were good enough to contain the garrison of Calais but performed poorly in major assaults on the walls and were notoriously unreliable in pitched battles against disciplined men-at-arms. The Duke of Gloucester's army was known to be gathering in England. To meet them on equal terms Philip needed experienced mounted troops. His northern domains could produce about 3,000 men. Nearly 900 more were expected to arrive from Burgundy. In the great enclosed harbour of Sluys, the Admiral of Flanders had assembled the eight ships belonging to the Duke, a galley contributed by the King of Portugal and thirty-one requisitioned merchantmen including two large Italian carracks. Another thirteen chartered ships were waiting in the harbour of Dunkirk. At Saint-Omer, the abbey buildings of St Bertin had been converted into a storage depot and workshop for an immense artillery train drawn from the four corners of Philip's domains. From there, they were carried down the Aa on barges to Gravelines. There were ten bombards firing stones of up to 250 pounds, sixty *veuglaires* of different sizes, fifty-five of the light shot-firing pieces known as *crappaudaux* and 450 hand-held culverins. Three huge bombards were on their way from the arsenals of Burgundy. The largest of these monsters had a bore of twenty inches and required eighty-four horses to haul it in pieces across France at seven miles a day.

The chronicler Monstrelet thought that Philip had deployed only half the strength available to him. But he must have been satisfied that he had enough, for he turned away a number of companies from Picardy who appeared at the muster and rejected an offer from Arthur de Richemont to bring 3,000 experienced men up from the Beauvaisis and the Caux. He also released Holland and Zeeland, whose seamen and shipowners were reluctant to become involved in a naval war with their chief trading partner, from their promise to provide 100 ships. In hindsight, these proved to be unwise decisions.[46]

On 28 June 1436 the Burgundian army crossed the Aa into the pale of Calais. At about the same time, Philip's Seneschal of Ponthieu, Florimond de Brimeu, attacked Le Crotoy. In England, recruitment of the Duke of Gloucester's army had been delayed by the usual combination of administrative confusion and shortage of cash. There were also debilitating arguments about the command. Not everyone was happy with Gloucester's appointment of himself as commander, least of all Cardinal Beaufort, whose money would be needed to bridge the gap between receipts at the Exchequer and payments to the troops. At one point, the fourteen-year-old King was proposed as the nominal commander, which would have allowed effective control of the operation to be shared between several captains. Then the choice fell on the Admiral of England, the Earl of Huntingdon. Gloucester was not confirmed as commander until the end of June, and the army was not expected to be ready until the last week of July. Until then, the defence of Calais was left to Edmund Beaufort and Sir John Radcliffe. Their problem was that although they had enough men to man the walls of the town and mount rapid sorties, they did not have enough to relieve the outlying forts. That would have risked an engagement in open country with the whole of the Burgundian army and imperilled the town. As a result, the Burgundians were able to overwhelm the forts one after the other with only limited opposition.[47]

Between the Aa and Newenham Bridge lay fifteen miles of scrub and dunes crossed by a raised causeway. Two garrisoned forts barred the causeway east of the town, at Oye and Marck. The Duke of Burgundy came before Oye on the first day of his invasion. Its captain, with a garrison of just fifty men, did not think that it could be defended and immediately opened negotiations with the Duke. But while he was parleying in the Duke's tent, the Flemings entered the fort through a grating that had carelessly been left open. They took the entire garrison prisoner and hanged all but three of them in front of the gate. The next day, they lit fires inside and threw down the walls into the ditch. On 2 July, the Burgundians came before Marck, where they encountered stronger resistance. The assault on Marck was led by the Picards. The defenders, who had just been reinforced, were more than a hundred strong. They fought off successive assaults over six days, repairing the breaches made by the Duke's artillery with lumber and rubble. On 8 July the Picards captured the boulevard in front of the gate. The defenders decided that the place could no longer be held and surrendered in return for their lives. Seven subjects of the Duke of Burgundy, a Dutchman and six Flemings, were found among the garrison. They had been excluded from the terms of surrender and were beheaded. Marck was thoroughly looted and then, like Oye, demolished.[48]

The Picards and other experienced troops were given the task of capturing the remaining garrisoned forts at Guines, Balinghem and Sangatte. They made short work of Balinghem and Sangatte, both of which surrendered without striking a blow. The garrison of Balinghem traded the fort with its ample stores for their lives and a safe-conduct out. They withdrew to Guines in their shirtsleeves, where their captain was arrested and charged with cowardice. The entire garrison of Sangatte surrendered as prisoners of war after the chaplain persuaded the captain that resistance was hopeless. Both places were demolished, apart from a single tower at Sangatte which resisted all attempts to destroy it. Of the six forts around Calais the only ones to survive were now Hammes and Guines. Hammes is not mentioned in any of the narratives of the siege. It was in a bad state of repair and seems to have been left unmanned. At Guines, the Picards under the command of Jean de Croÿ captured the town and the lower ward. But the captain of the place held out with his garrison in a tower. The Picards brought up three large guns, which battered the tower day in day out, but Guines held out to the end.[49]

On 9 July, the Burgundians laid siege to Calais itself. Philip the Good initially pitched his camp near Newenham Bridge, a fortified bridge over the river Hammes about a mile west of the town walls on the site now occupied by Vauban's Fort Nieulay. It was strongly defended. The

Duke's encampment was soon made untenable by artillery fire from behind the river. After a cannonball had stuck his tent, he moved his command post to the east side of the town. He was followed there by the whole contingent of Ghent. The men of Bruges, Ypres and the Franc encamped around the church of St Pierre, which stood on the causeway directly south of the town walls.[50]

The besiegers made no impression on the town. Only one attempt was made to assault the walls, on the opening day of the siege. This was probably directed against the castle at the western end of the town during the brief period when the Duke was encamped nearby. La Hire, who was in the Duke's camp for discussions, took part in the fight and was wounded in the leg by a crossbow bolt. Once the outlying forts had been lost, the English opened the sluice gates at Newenham Bridge and flooded the pale, leaving only the causeway and a few islands of dry ground above water and breaking up communications between different sections of the besieging army. The defenders were able to keep the town gates open and pasture their cattle by the moat in full view of the besiegers with impunity. Attempts to capture the animals were repeatedly fought off by sorties from the gates. The siege turned into a series of artillery duels. The English generally had the better of these exchanges. The Burgundian gunners could not get close enough to the walls for their weapons to have much impact. They tried to build bastides closer in but were constantly frustrated by the floodwaters, by sorties from the town, and by the greater height and range of the English cannon mounted at the top of the walls and towers. Philip the Good, who had already been forced to move his camp once by artillery fire, had underestimated its effectiveness in the hands of the defenders. On one occasion a cannonball felled a trumpeter next to him as they rode over the dunes. His own gunners, forced to shoot high to achieve range, found their projectiles sailing over the walls into the town, where they did some damage to buildings but caused no casualties. These problems might have been resolved if the great bombards from Burgundy, with their long, broad-bore barrels, had been available, but they were still being hauled laboriously across Picardy and in the event arrived too late.[51]

On 25 July 1436, Jan van Hoorn, the Admiral of Burgundy, arrived off Calais with his fleet. He had been delayed, initially by the difficulty of finding the money to pay the seamen and troops on board, and then by south-westerly gales in the Channel. He had about seventy ships under his command. Great hopes had been invested in them by the besiegers. They were expected to stop the continual flow of supplies and reinforcements reaching the town under the noses of the besiegers, and to prevent the landing of the Duke of Gloucester's army. Philip the Good rode out to the dykes with a great crowd of followers to watch them coming in. The Admiral had brought six large blockships filled with bricks and stone which were kept afloat by continuous pumping by teams of men working in shifts. Over the next twenty-four hours he tried to scuttle them in the entrance to the harbour. One of them was sunk by artillery fire from the walls before it reached the harbour mouth. The other five reached the entrance, but the seamen on board were working under fire and in a hurry to escape. They sank their blockships at a point which was exposed at low tide. When the sea receded, the townsmen swarmed out of the gates onto the strand and broke them up in full view of the Burgundian fleet and the crowds of Flemings watching from the dykes. That evening, the wind got up and the fleet could no longer keep station off the town. Reports were arriving that the Duke of Gloucester's fleet was about to sail from Sandwich. Hoorn decided that his fleet was not large enough to confront it. The fireships which had been assembled at Sluys to be released into the English fleet had been held up by adverse winds and had not arrived. On 26 July the Admiral withdrew to Flanders and did not return. It was a severe blow to the besiegers' morale.[52]

In England, newsletters from Calais had raised public emotions to fever pitch. Reports of the fall of Oye and the execution of its garrison, which were distributed across the land by the government, aroused much indignation. Sermons were delivered in parish churches denouncing the Duke of Burgundy as a perjurer and a warmonger. In Kent, the Duke of Gloucester was straining at the leash. His army was encamped by the coast near Sandwich, but the men could not be mustered because there was no money to pay their advances. The ships to carry them were waiting offshore in the Downs but the seamen had not yet been paid. The treasury was empty. Everything now depended on Cardinal Beaufort's willingness to advance money at the critical moment as he had so often done before. So far, Beaufort had shown little inclination to fund an expedition led by his rival in accordance with a strategy for which he had no sympathy. On 22 July, there was a crisis meeting of the council at Canterbury. The fourteen-year-old King presided, one of the earliest occasions when he can be seen to have taken an active part in affairs. All the lords who were to participate in the army were there. The fate of the expedition hung in the balance. Beaufort was finally prevailed upon to open his chests and fund the initial costs, and the decision was made to go ahead. Orders were issued as soon as the meeting was over. Gloucester's herald Pembroke was sent over the Channel to deliver a challenge to battle to the Duke of Burgundy. A small advance guard sailed for Calais on 29 July and landed that evening. The rest of the army was expected to reach the town in stages over the following days.[53]

Pembroke Herald arrived in the Duke of Burgundy's tents on the evening of 27 July and delivered his master's challenge. Having failed to blockade the harbour against Gloucester's army, Philip was now faced with the choice between a battle and a humiliating retreat. He called an urgent meeting of his council. Philip famously hated the chances of the battlefield. His councillors were of the same mind but agreed that he could not honourably withdraw now. They had misgivings about his current position by the causeway close to the southern wall of the town. It was decided to fight Gloucester's army further east by the river Aa, where the ground was firmer and the risk of a sortie from Calais more easily managed. In the meantime, an appeal was sent out to the whole nobility of his domains to come urgently to swell the ranks of experienced soldiers in the army. Florimond de Brimeu, who had succeeded in capturing the town of Le Crotoy and was besieging the citadel, appears to have been ordered to abandon the operation and recalled to join the main army.

On the following morning, Philip went to the tents of the captains of Ghent and obtained their consent to the decision to fight. However, when the captains went to tell their men, they encountered unexpected resistance. The morale of the urban contingents was low. The men of Bruges had recently tried to mount an assault against the Boulogne Gate at the western end of the town and had met with a humiliating defeat. The men of Ghent had jeered as the Brugeois fled, but their own turn came soon after. They had been building a large timber bastide on an island of high ground between their lines and the town wall. The bastide was designed as a solid platform for artillery, closer to the walls than the Flemings had hitherto been able to get. It had a high tower from which it was possible to see into the town and direct the gunners' fire. The incomplete works were defended by 300 to 400 men, who had so far beaten back every attempt to destroy them. In the early hours of 28 July, there was a carefully planned night-time attack. Edmund Beaufort and his principal lieutenant Sir Roger Camoys sortied from the Boulogne Gate while another sortie party emerged from the gate at the east end known as Milkgate. They converged on the bastide. The mounted men occupied the ground behind the bastide to stop the Flemings intervening, while the rest attacked the works on foot. The men on watch were found in a drunken sleep. Their throats were cut. The men inside were taken by surprise. About 160 of them were killed, and most of the rest captured. The works were left in flames. Townsmen were rarely worth a ransom, and half of those who were taken were found to be too much trouble to hold. They were put to death outside the gates by Edmund Beaufort's order.[54]

Later that day there was an angry meeting in the Ghent encampment as the captains tried to prepare their men for the coming battle. The soldiers complained that they had borne the brunt of the fighting and were losing men every day, while the Picard noblemen had done nothing of note since the capture of the outlying forts. The blockade of Calais had failed. A large English army was about to descend on them. There was no longer any prospect of victory. They thought the whole venture ill-conceived. They blamed the Duke's councillors, especially Jean de Croÿ, Jean de Brimeu and Baudot de Noyelles who were with him in his camp. Some of them threatened to go there at once and kill them. Their captains tried to calm them, but the majority were determined to abandon the siege. Late that night, the captains of Ghent came before the Duke to report that their men would leave that night and withdraw beyond the river Aa to await events. Philip was aghast. He protested that he would be dishonoured. He begged them to stay. They were not to be moved. On the morning of 29 July, the men of Bruges, Ypres and the Franc woke up to a reveille sounded from the top of Milkgate by an English trumpeter, only to find that the men of Ghent had gone. They decided to follow them. That evening they abandoned their equipment and stores and left in a disorderly mob up the Gravelines road. The Duke was left with only about 3,000 Picards. The reinforcements expected from Burgundy had not yet left. The Duke would be hopelessly outnumbered once Gloucester's army arrived. Philip had no choice but to withdraw to Gravelines. By his own account, he left 'with more bitterness in his heart than he had thought possible'. The chronicler Jean de Waurin, who had fought in the Picard contingent at Calais and Guines, deplored the behaviour of the mutineers of Ghent but agreed that the venture had been ill-conceived from the start. It could never have succeeded without an effective blockade from the sea, and a more disciplined army than the Flemish towns could provide.[55]

Henry VI and the leaders of the army were still at Canterbury when the news reached them that the Burgundian siege had been abandoned. The expedition no longer had any purpose, but the musters were already being taken and the Duke of Gloucester was determined not to waste the opportunity of showing his mettle as a commander. He proposed to follow up Edmund Beaufort's victory at Calais by leading a punitive raid into Flanders. On 30 July, a document drawn up in Henry's name as King of France, declared that Philip 'commonly called the Duke of Burgundy' had forfeited his French territories by his rebellion, and purported to confer the county of Flanders on the Duke of Gloucester. On 2 August, Humphrey landed at Calais, followed over the next few days by the rest of his army.[56]

By the middle of August, there were between 9,000 and 10,000 English troops in Calais in addition to the garrison. The Burgundians were in no position to resist such a force. Philip the Good presided at a sombre council meeting at Gravelines. The Flemish units refused to stand on the Aa to defend their county, and Philip disbanded them. It was decided to put the Picards into garrison at Gravelines, Ardres and other walled places along the march of Flanders. The troops from Burgundy, who had just reached Arras, were sent to hold the region of Boulogne. Meanwhile the Duke returned to Lille to raise a new field army. In the first two weeks of August, his secretariat despatched no fewer than 718 letters to the nobility and professional soldiery of his northern domains, summoning them to his banner. He wrote personally to the Duke of Bourbon begging him to send the French troops that he had cavalierly rejected when Richemont had offered them in June. In Burgundy, the ducal council at Dijon struggled to find more men to add to the companies that they had already sent. Philip planned to concentrate these forces outside the cathedral city of Thérouanne in Artois. But they were unlikely to be there in less than a month and the men of Burgundy would take at least six weeks to arrive. He did not have that long.[57]

On 13 August, while Philip's messengers were still riding across his domains with his summonses, the Duke of Gloucester marched out of the gates of Calais at the head of his army and advanced along the coast road into West Flanders. The Earl of Huntingdon was standing off the coast with the English fleet, which Philip's officers reckoned at 200 ships. It was a short, brutal campaign by land and sea, with no strategic objective other than revenge and destruction. Gloucester's army had no siege equipment or supply train, and its companies had indented for only a month. The fleet had no troops on board, but only armed seamen. The army gave a wide berth to Gravelines, Dunkirk, Berghes and other well walled and garrisoned towns, before turning inland. They began to burn and loot their way across the territory of Ypres. Only two substantial towns were captured, Poperinghe and Bailleul, both of them by assault. Their fate was as terrible as that of any place entered by force. Poperinghe lost its church and 2,500 houses.

From Lille castle, Philip the Good watched the ring of fire spreading across the northern horizon. The English met with only sporadic resistance from local militias, and occasional sorties from garrisoned towns. Philip made a final attempt to rally the Flemish towns. On the day after the sack of Poperinghe his representative urged the general assembly of Ghent to send troops to Ypres to defend 'their land, their property, their privileges, liberties and franchises, their whole lives and those of their wives and children, their honour and reputation in the eyes of posterity'. But the most that they could be persuaded to do was send a handful of archers up to the north coast to help guard against English landings from the sea. An attempt to rouse the people of Bruges was equally unsuccessful.

By now, however, the English were beginning to suffer from hunger and sickness. Shortly, they turned back towards Calais. On about 24 August the army returned to the town driving great herds of stolen cattle before them and hauling a long wagon train full of looted valuables. The Earl of Huntingdon's fleet left a similar trail of destruction along the coast of the Franc of Bruges. They entered the lagoon of Sluys and burned many of the ships at anchor in the port. They sacked villages along the coast and the exposed offshore islands (as they then were) of Wulpen and Cadzand.[58]

The news of Philip's humiliation was greeted in England with explosions of joy, and a great outpouring of boasts, mockery and venom in doggerel verse. 'Such and many other rhymes were made amongst

Englishmen,' wrote the scribe who wrote out one of these pieces. The Duke of Gloucester was received as a hero. He commissioned a bombastic celebration of his deeds in mediocre Latin hexameters from the Italian versifier Tito Livio Frulovisi, modelled on the *Aeneid* (it was called the *Humphroidos*).

Perhaps the most reflective monument of this brief moment of English hubris was the *Libel of English Policy*. The *Libel* was not a handbill written for the streets. It was a verse pamphlet intended for Walter Lord Hungerford and a select group of councillors and members of the royal household. The author was an unnamed but well-placed official, possibly Richard Caudray, a former clerk of the council who was currently serving as private secretary to the Admiral, the Earl of Huntingdon. The poem is a forthright defence of a strategy based on the exercise of economic power and control of Calais and the Channel. 'The true process of English policy ... is this: cherish merchandise, keep th'admiralty, that we been masters of the narrow sea.' The poet conceived the sea as the 'wall of England'. But it was also an offensive weapon. Flanders and the Low Countries could not do without English wool to feed their looms. The seaway between Dover and Calais, those 'two eyes' of England, was the artery through which northern Europe received the commodities of Brittany, Spain and Italy. A naval blockade, he thought, was at least as good a way of bringing the enemy to terms as sending an army of 10,000 men into France. By building up English sea power and controlling the traffic of the Channel, the Burgundian state could be brought to its knees. The author's omissions are as revealing as his argument. He assumes throughout that the enemy is the Duke of Burgundy. He has nothing to say about the war against Charles VII or the defence of English-occupied territory in France. The value of England's French conquests seemed to him to consist only in its Channel ports, which were now in enemy hands with the solitary exception of Calais. 'Cherish ye Calais better than it is,' he wrote. Nothing else counted.[59]

The *Libel*'s advocacy of an aggressive naval strategy and a mercantilist trade policy won it many admirers in the following centuries. Queen Elizabeth's minister William Cecil owned a copy. His chaplain Richard Hakluyt, the great Tudor historian of English maritime enterprise, owned two, and printed the text in his *Principal Navigations of the English Nation*. The Stuart lawyer and politician John Selden cited it in *Mare Clausum*, his celebrated defence of English rights over the adjacent seas. Samuel Pepys, clerk of Charles II's Navy Board, had a copy in his library. The blockade proposed by the author became an orthodoxy of the Royal Navy from the eighteenth to the twentieth centuries. In his own day it proved less influential. The poet spoke for some important interests: the Staple merchants of Calais, the financiers and wholesalers of London and the shipowners of the south and east coast ports. Theirs, however, was a minority view. The dominant opinion in England's political community remained unchanged. The enemy who mattered was not the Duke of Burgundy but the King of France. His territories did not depend on international trade and were only marginally vulnerable to sea power. Without a powerful military presence in France, there was no prospect of a durable political solution to the wider war. Once the crisis of the siege had passed, Calais reverted to its secondary place in England's strategic calculations as attention was once more focused on Normandy. In the next Parliament, which met in January 1437, the Duke of Gloucester personally petitioned the Commons for funding and went on his knees before the King, begging him to make proper provision for the cost of the Calais garrison. He was wasting his breath. Calais continued to be seriously underfunded, and Gloucester never recovered the brief dominance of English strategy that he had enjoyed in the twelve months following the Congress of Arras.[60]

'Where ben our ships, where ben our swords become?' asked the author of the *Libel of English Policy*. It was a good question. The loss of the French Channel ports from the Scheldt to the Seine had transformed the balance of power in the Channel and the North Sea. For the first time in twenty years, these seas became a battleground in which the Flemings and the Dutch were the dominant powers and the Castilians a latent threat. As the council had explained in its appeal for funds, the result was to expose the south and east coasts of England to the coastal raids which been such a terrifying feature of life in the 1370s and again in the opening decade of the fifteenth century. Yet maintaining a powerful English presence at sea was unaffordable on top of the heavy cost of military operations in France. England never had the kind of naval arsenals which enabled Castile, Portugal and the Italian republics to build and maintain permanent war fleets. Merchant ships continued to be requisitioned as transports, but there was no return to the great requisitioned war fleets of Edward III. Of

Henry V's fine fleet of thirty warships, only one refitted balinger (or whaling barge), scarcely larger than a ship's boat, was still in service. This, and two more small balingers purchased to keep the garrison of Le Crotoy supplied, constituted the entire Royal Navy of the 1430s. The rest of Henry V's fleet had been sold off to pay his debts, apart from four 'great ships' whose hulls, stripped of their fittings, were rotting away on the river Hamble. Henry V's great ship *Grace Dieu*, at 1,400 tons the largest vessel built for the Royal Navy before the seventeenth century, was struck by lightning and burned to the waterline in 1439.[61]

Instead, the council turned to privateers, as Richard II and Henry IV had done in their time, with equally unsatisfactory results. In the course of the year 1436 a total of twenty privateering licences were issued to merchants or commercial syndicates on terms that, after satisfying the customary shares of the Admiral and the Warden of the Cinque Ports, they could keep the spoil for themselves. Their efforts were seconded by unlicensed pirates, whose activities were encouraged by Parliament's suspension of the statute that visited the penalties of treason on them. The government had no control over either category. Licensed privateers elected their own admiral, who received a royal commission but was not subject to the orders of the King's officers. Pirates were a law unto themselves. The only notable naval operation in 1436 and 1437 was the capture of a Flemish fleet carrying wine from La Rochelle in April as it was passing Finistère. The triumph was brief, for on the following day a Castilian fleet appeared, attacked the English ships, and after capturing a number of them released the Flemings. The experiment was not repeated. After 1437, the government gave up the task of 'keeping of the seas' until the 1460s.[62]

For Philip the Good, the immediate effect of his defeat before Calais was to provoke a crisis in his relations with the industrial towns of Flanders and the maritime communities of Holland and Zeeland. The Flemish towns had supported the attack on Calais because they were persuaded that its capture would destroy the English wool Staplers' monopoly and allow the wool in their warehouses to be released. The failure of the siege put an end to these hopes. The English council tightened the screw by banning all trade with Flanders. The Flemings were now confronted with the old reality that they could not do without English wool. This was one thing that the author of the *Libel* of *English Policy* got right. 'If England would his wool restrain,' he argued, 'Flanders of need must with us have peace, or else he is destroyed.'

The return of the urban contingents, armed and organised, after a major military campaign was always a dangerous moment in the life of Flemish towns, and especially so in the autumn of 1436. The men had been recruited mainly from the craft guilds whose members were being ruined by the trade wars and from journeymen and rural artisans who had no work to come back to. When Philip the Good entered Ghent on 3 September, there was a spontaneous rising in the streets in which the returning soldiers played a leading part. The mob occupied the Friday Market, disarmed the Duke's bodyguard and demanded a response to a long written list of grievances. Several of these arose from the chaos of the last days of the siege of Calais and the *chevauchée* of the Duke of Gloucester. Why had Calais not been blockaded from the sea? Why had fire-ships not been used against the English fleet? Why had non-Flemings (they meant Picards and Burgundians) been put into garrisons on the march of Flanders? At Bruges the discontent merged with wider grievances and events took a more serious turn. The returning troops occupied the marketplace, declared a general strike and installed a new town government dominated by the deans of the guilds. They murdered the city sheriff (a ducal official) and summoned all those who had held the principal offices of the town in the past three decades to answer for their administration. The tensions eased over the winter as the firebrands who had led the revolt were edged aside by more moderate spirits. But they flared up again the following April. The burgomaster of Bruges was lynched by members of the coopers' guild who alleged that he was a stooge of the Duke. A month later, on 22 May 1437, Philip forced his way into the town with an army of 3,000 Picards, provoking a fresh uprising from which he was lucky to escape with his life. These events led to a prolonged economic blockade of the rebellious city which lasted until February 1438 and brought it close to ruin.[63]

The war with England not only divided Flanders but opened a schism between Flanders and the rest of Philip's empire in the Low Countries. The Flemings were both the strongest supporters of the Duke's ban on imports of English cloth and the main victims of the English embargo on wool exports. Holland, Zeeland and Brabant, on the other hand, although they had indigenous textile industries of their own, were heavily dependent on the carrying and entrepot trades, and profited mightily from the trade in English cloth. They had always objected to the Duke's attempts to extend the cloth embargo to them and had resisted its enforcement when it was imposed on them. In early 1436 the council at Westminster had conducted an energetic diplomatic offensive in Holland and Zeeland through John Middleton, the leading English factor in Middelburg. Middleton's campaign had enjoyed some success. The Dutch refused to enforce the ban on trade with England in spite of the complaints of Philip's ministers. In Brabant, industrial cities like Brussels and Mechelen shared the instincts of Flanders, while the rising ports of Antwerp and Bergen op Zoom, with their important international trade fairs, continued to receive English cloth in defiance of Philip's legislation. At Middelburg, when the Duke's *bailli* seized an English ship bound for Antwerp, a mob broke open the prison, released the crew and forced him to restore the cargo. Philip, weakened by the disaster at Calais and the revolt of the Flemish towns, was unable to insist. In the years following the siege, English wool exports via Calais, which traditionally went almost entirely to Flanders, fell to close to zero, while cloth exports to the rest of the Burgundian Low Countries rebounded to well above their previous level. In the spring of 1437, Bruges and Ypres began to press the Duke hard for an accommodation with England.[64]

Six weeks after the abandonment of the siege of Calais Hughes de Lannoy addressed another long memorandum to the Duke of Burgundy. Recent events had largely vindicated his earlier advice, as he was tactful enough not to point out. Like all of Lannoy's memoranda, it was perceptive. The war with England had only just begun, he argued, but it was already proving to be a disaster. Having failed to take Calais, the Duke would now have to maintain a large permanent force around the English pale in order to contain its garrison. This would be expensive. Philip was crippled by debt and threatened by the divisions among his subjects. With Holland and Zeeland continuing to ignore it, his embargo on trade with England was achieving nothing, whereas the stoppage of wool deliveries risked driving the Flemish towns into the arms of the English. All of Philip's territories were experiencing severe economic disruption, aggravated by high levels of taxation. 'Strange and angry things have been said about you, your government and your leading councillors,' he told his master. Military assistance could no doubt be had from the King of France, but it would come at a price. French companies would expect to be paid. Without that, they would 'destroy your domains as efficiently as they defend it'.

Lannoy thought that it was imperative to make peace with England. Under the terms of the treaty of Arras, Philip was prevented from making a separate peace with England. He would therefore have to offer himself as a mediator to bring about a general peace between all three parties. Lannoy was optimistic, too optimistic, about the outcome. France and England, he thought, were both exhausted by the war and ready to make peace. There was a workable basis for agreement if Normandy was ceded to England. Lannoy thought that there were several things that Philip could do to ease the way. He could surrender the Somme towns to the French King without charging the 400,000 *livres* agreed at Arras, which would sweeten the pill of ceding Normandy. He could release his prisoner Réné of Anjou without ransom, which would win him the favour of the dominant Angevin faction at the French court. He could encourage the English to release Charles of Orléans, which would win him the support of the Bastard of Orléans, a man of growing influence with Charles VII. Above all, Philip should learn the lessons of his failure before Calais. He should not imagine that his honour was committed to continuing the war or that the Flemish rebellions could simply be ignored or put down by force.[65]

Philip's initial response to Lannoy's advice was to ignore it. He did nothing to cultivate his relations with the French court. His acquisitive instincts would not allow him to abandon the Somme towns or release Réné of Anjou. Réné was eventually made to pay a punishing ransom. The result was to make enemies of the Angevins at the court of France and to alienate his allies in Lorraine and Bar who had hoped to see Réné forced to abandon his rights there. At the same time, Philip pursued his vendetta with England with vigour but little success. A full-scale siege of Le Crotoy by land and sea was attempted in the autumn of 1437, but was broken by a fleet from England and an army from Normandy. In the following year another attempt was made on Calais. Philip had been persuaded that the town could be destroyed if the sea dykes were broken. An army of pioneers, escorted by 1,600 troops, entered the pale, but they were unable to break the dykes and no serious damage was done. In the longer term Philip came to appreciate the wisdom of Lannoy's words. These were the last significant military operations that he undertook against the English.[66]

*

The fiasco of Calais claimed another victim before the year was out. The attack on the town encouraged James of Scotland to burnish his military reputation in the eyes of his domestic enemies and to demonstrate his value to his French allies. On about 1 August 1436, as the Duke of Gloucester's army was embarking for France, a large Scottish army commanded by the King in person laid siege to Berwick and shortly afterwards to Roxburgh. With England denuded of troops and the garrison of Berwick on the edge of mutiny for want of pay, the opportunity seemed too good to miss. James had made elaborate preparations. He had summoned all men of military age and assembled a large artillery train. But the result was a military and personal disaster. The noisy build-up of forces had given the English wardens of the march plenty of notice of what was afoot. Within two weeks, they were approaching the Scottish siege lines around Roxburgh with the levies of the northern counties. The Scots melted away, leaving their siege equipment behind them. The sieges of Berwick and Roxburgh were the last notable Scottish military operations on the border for more than a decade.[67] King James had done much to restore the power and finances of the Scottish Crown after the long regency of the Albany Stewarts and might in time have become a formidable antagonist of England. But his humiliation at Roxburgh badly dented his authority in Scotland. In February 1437, he was murdered in the course of a failed coup by a group of conspirators led by his uncle, Walter Stewart Earl of Atholl. His son James II came to the throne at the age of six. In the following year, the truce with England was formally re-established after a hiatus of nearly two years. Scotland would endure a troubled minority and a brutal civil war before it could again become a significant factor in English strategic calculations.

Margaret Stewart had made her long-delayed voyage to France to marry the Dauphin in the spring of 1436, shortly before her father's ill-conceived adventure at Roxburgh. The marriage was celebrated with much splendour in Tours cathedral on 25 June 1436, but it never lived up to the hopes which either country had reposed in it. The bride had been escorted to France by some 2,000 Scottish soldiers, but to the surprise of their hosts they announced as soon as they arrived that they had come only to defend their fleet against English attacks and not to strengthen Charles VII's land forces. When the ceremony was over, they returned to Scotland leaving only a handful of adventurers behind. Charles VII continued to maintain a personal guard of

Scottish archers and a shrinking corps of survivors from the army of Stewart of Darnley, but there would be no new army of Scotland to fight in France. As for Margaret herself, her marriage opened the most wretched period of her life, ignored by her husband and shunned by the court until her premature death at the age of twenty-one.[68]

CHAPTER XI

The King's War, 1436–1442

On 6 December 1435, Henry VI was fourteen years old, the time when Kings traditionally came of age. Royal minorities were difficult periods in the history of any European state, but the years which followed them were often worse. The King took up the reins of power without the apprenticeship in statecraft which an adult heir in waiting would have had. Henry V had fought a pitched battle at the age of sixteen and had ten years of political and military activity behind him when he succeeded his father at the age of twenty-six. By comparison Henry VI, like Richard II of England and Charles VI of France before him, came of age with little more to draw on than the enclosed world of childhood.

Henry VI is one of the most enigmatic English rulers of the middle ages. We have a sharply drawn portrait of the young King from Piero da Monte, the papal nuncio in England, who arrived in the country in August 1435 and met him several times. He found himself in the presence of a tall, handsome and friendly young man of dignified bearing with a rather solemn manner. Da Monte remarked on Henry's prim religiosity: his regular fasts, his daily devotions, his abhorrence of low games, obscene swearing or the pleasures of the flesh. He thought that Henry seemed unworldly, more like a monk than a prince. Much that we think we know about Henry is derived from the propagandists of the first two Tudors. They lauded him to damn the Yorkists who had deposed and murdered him. But even they were equivocal about his statecraft. Writing at the beginning of the sixteenth century at the request of Henry VII, the Italian publicist Polydore Vergil described him as a 'man of mild and plain-dealing disposition, who preferred peace to war, quietness to trouble, honesty to utility and leisure to business and, to be short, there was not in this world a more pure, more honest and more holy creature'. Accounts like these have moulded Henry's historical reputation as a holy simpleton. There is plenty of contemporary evidence to bear out parts of the picture. Henry was kind, generous and compassionate. He was also gauche and unworldly, and oblivious of the poor impression that he sometimes made on public occasions. But although unquestionably holy, he was not a simpleton, at any rate before his mental breakdown in 1453. Nor was he a mindless cipher in the hands of his councillors. But he was a man of limited intelligence, with little interest in business and no aptitude for it. He had a small stock of experience and learned little from it.[1]

Henry VI's public personality was shaped by his unusual upbringing. He had been King of England since he was nine months old and had grown up surrounded by the veneration due to monarchy. Inevitably, this gave him a precocious sense of his own dignity and importance, which was reinforced by the flattering ceremonial of his two coronations. His tutor from the age of seven was the cultivated and experienced Earl of Warwick. But the King was barely eleven years old when he began to kick back against Warwick's authority. Henry, as the Earl reported to the council in November 1432, was 'grown in years in stature of his person and also in conceit and knowledge of his high and royal authority and estate, the which naturally causen him more and more to grouch with chastising and to loathe it'. Others noticed this too, and some of them took advantage of it for their own purposes. Two years after Warwick's report the Duke of Gloucester, frustrated by the council's hold on power, seems to have encouraged the young King to rule in person, presumably under his own guidance. The council rode in a body to Cirencester, where Henry was then staying, to protest against the 'motions and stirrings' to which they feared that he had been subjected. He did not yet have the knowledge, wisdom or experience to make his own decisions or dispense with the advice of the councillors who had been appointed for him, they said. After the death of the Duke of Bedford the council gradually introduced him to affairs of state. He began to attend council meetings in October 1435. He was present at the difficult meeting at Canterbury in July 1436 which finally authorised the Duke of Gloucester's expedition to Calais and Flanders. He took control of his own privy seal and began to make grants to servants and favourites with a profligacy which alarmed his councillors.[2]

Henry's French subjects were told in December 1435 that having come of age he was now attending to affairs of state 'continually'. In fact, the process was more gradual. For a time, very little changed. Military and diplomatic business continued to be conducted by the council. However, two years after Henry had formally come of age, his role was reviewed at a great council which met in his presence in the house of the London Hospitallers at Clerkenwell. After two days of discussion a declaration was issued defining his relations with his councillors. They were to continue to carry on the day-to-day business of government as before. But grants and appointments were reserved to the King in person, and all 'matters of great weight and charge' were to be referred to him, together with any lesser matters on which the council was unable to agree. The change was marked by the formal reappointment and re-swearing of the existing councillors, with a few additions. The council remained an important organ of government, but its influence as a body tended to decline. This was unfortunate. During the minority, the council had generally maintained a delicate balance between competing interests. Henry was subject to no such constraint. Lacking experience and self-confidence, he relied heavily on his household companions and officers, men whom he had learned to trust and who were unconditionally loyal to him. They were well rewarded, with a very public show of royal favour and a shower of offices, wardships and riches. This inevitably exacerbated the jealousies and tensions which were never far below the surface of English public life.[3]

After the successful relief of Calais and the destructive invasion of Flanders, Humphrey Duke of Gloucester might have expected to succeed to his elder brother's place as the dominant figure in the English government. But as the awful reality of the English position in France dawned on the political world, he became an increasingly marginal figure. The real successors of the Duke of Bedford were Cardinal Beaufort and the Earl of Suffolk. Beaufort's influence was founded on his status as Henry's closest kinsman after Gloucester himself, as well as on his diplomatic experience and his importance as the Crown's principal source of emergency finance. His power base was the council, in which his was the dominant voice. Over the following years he took a growing interest in the conduct of the war, pushing his nephews forward to positions of power in Normandy and taking control of attempts to negotiate peace. His efforts were seconded by the Earl of Suffolk, whose rise to power from 1436 onward was charted in a spectacular succession of royal grants and favours. His position as

Steward of the royal household since 1431 gave him both unrestricted access to the impressionable King and a large measure of control over who else had access to him.[4]

The evolution of Henry VI's attitude to the war in France is difficult to follow, partly because as business moved away from formal sessions of the council, discussions were not as well recorded. It is clear that Henry was strongly attached to his title as King of France. There is no evidence that he was ever willing to surrender it. He held it against Philip the Good for the rest of his life that he had 'abandoned him in his youth, in spite of his oaths'. But the consensus of the men around him was that the war could not be sustained for much longer. Beaufort had probably been persuaded of the need for a settlement since the disappointing outcome of the coronation expedition of 1430-2, Suffolk for even longer. Other influential figures about the King shared their judgement. One of them was Archbishop Kemp of York, whom Humphrey of Gloucester accused of having the King under his thumb. Others included the clerk of the council Adam Moleyns and probably also Henry's diplomatic secretary Thomas Beckington. All this chimed in with the King's own ideas. Henry had received the traditional martial education of a nobleman. He had been knighted by the Duke of Bedford at the age of four. The Earl of Warwick saw to it that he was given a miniature suit of armour and a long sword 'for to learn ... to play in his tender age'. But for all that, Henry grew to manhood without any martial instincts whatever. He never commanded an army. He was genuinely distressed by the divisions of Europe, and over the decade which followed his majority he developed a kind of Christian pacifism which was a good deal more than the familiar rhetorical trope.[5]

The problem of Henry's ministers was that they had to make war to make peace. Without a strong military position in France, England had little to bargain with. The collapse of the English positions in the Île-de-France, Picardy and Champagne had persuaded many of Charles VII's councillors that they did not need to concede much. 'What kind of peace would you want, when you can have the lot by force of arms?' Jean Juvénal imagined them saying. Henry VI and his leading councillors would have been content to retain Normandy in full sovereignty, in effect as an annex of England like Calais, if the French had been willing to contemplate a partition of their country. Beaufort and Kemp, who knew that they were not, might have gone further and dropped the claim to the Crown of France if that was the price of peace. According to the Duke of Gloucester, they urged this course on Henry in 1439. But they were never able to persuade the King or the political community in England to accept such a policy. Caught between an uncomprehending public, unbending financial realities, and an impossible diplomatic situation, Henry's ministers were forced to go on rolling the stone of Sisyphus. In the decade after the fall of Paris, they successfully held on to Normandy and most of the *pays de conquête* but were winkled out of all their remaining fortresses in the Oise valley, the Gâtinais and the Île-de-France one after the other.[6]

The Duke of York landed with his army on the south shore of the Seine estuary on 7 June 1436, five months after the date originally planned and two months after the fall of Paris. At the time of his arrival, a large French army was besieging Creil on the Oise under the command of the Constable and the Bastard of Orléans. They viewed York's arrival with trepidation. They expected him to try to recover the capital. They abandoned the siege as soon as they received the news and withdrew to Paris to defend it against the expected attack. In fact, their fears were groundless. Paris was irrecoverable and untenable anyway without the support of the Duke of Burgundy. The English knew that and had given it up for lost. York's main priority was Normandy. He needed to restore English authority there after the death of the Duke of Bedford and the peasant rebellions, and to strengthen the marches of the duchy against the increasingly aggressive incursions of the French King's captains. He marched straight to Rouen and remained there, buried under the burden of administration, for most of his term of office. The fighting was left to Sir John Talbot. He was appointed Marshal of France and assumed command of the great army that York had brought with him from England.[7]

The military fortunes of the English in Normandy were at a low ebb when the Duke of York arrived. In the Caux, French garrisons at Dieppe, Fécamp, Harfleur and Tancarville still controlled a continuous band of territory along the Channel coast. From these bases, they had begun to penetrate inland. A similar process was occurring at the opposite end of the duchy, where the French garrison at Pontoise had gradually extended its tentacles through much of the Vexin and eastern Normandy. In these districts, a dense network of castles and small walled towns and villages enabled the French to control large tracts of open country, to levy *pâtis* to pay their garrisons, and to roam freely across Upper Normandy. Their operations not only presented a serious military threat. They undermined the Lancastrian land settlement and with it the economic foundation of the English occupation. In areas under threat from rebels or enemies, land values and revenues collapsed. Tenants either fled or were unable to pay their dues. Untenanted land could not be let. The same refrains recur time and again in the valuations, estate accounts and charters of these years: 'gone away to live in Rouen because of the war' – 'no one will take the lease on account of the war' – 'buildings collapsed due to the wars and the timber pillaged by neighbours'. The accounts which William Worcester prepared for his master Sir John Fastolf showed that his holdings in the Caux were worth only £8 a year as against £200 before the rebellion. The barony of Le Neubourg south of Rouen saw its revenues more than halved in the decade after 1435. Those whose land was charged with military obligations or rentcharges often found that their revenues were entirely swallowed up by expenses. Some of them even renounced their holdings to the Crown.[8]

Talbot's strategy was to recover control of the open country to stop the French garrisons taxing the population or resupplying themselves. This involved capturing the secondary castles occupied by the French, which were generally weakly defended, before concentrating his forces against the main French garrisons. In the weeks following the Duke of York's arrival, Talbot cleared most of the minor castles occupied by the French north and west of Rouen, while Lord Fauconberg carried out a similar sweep in the Vexin to the east. These operations continued sporadically into the following year. In June 1437, Talbot invaded the pays de Caux again, clearing all the lesser walled places still in enemy hands.

Talbot's clearances revived old issues about minor fortifications whose private proprietors lacked the will or the means to defend them properly. Those which had been captured from enemy garrisons were commonly demolished, but for some years the council at Westminster had been calling for a more systematic and pre-emptive approach. They wanted a survey of all walled places, followed by the demolition of those which were indefensible, without waiting for them to be occupied by the enemy. 'For as much as there is a great multitude of walled towns and castle[s] in Normandy and in France, as well of the King's as of other men's,' they observed in 1431, 'and the keeping of so many is a great charge to the land and oppression to the people, it seemeth necessary to be advised which should be kept and which should be disempared as well of the King's as of other men's.' The call was taken up by the Grand Conseil at Rouen. A programme of demolitions was ordered on the marches of Alençon, a sensitive region frequently disturbed by partisan activity. But otherwise very little was done until the arrival of the Duke of York. During his time at Rouen, teams of masons and labourers dismantled at least fifteen castles, nine of them in the Caux alone. But the project was expensive and unpopular, and never comprehensive enough to make a real difference. Landowners were understandably reluctant to lose their castles, which were a source of status and revenue. Local communities, although they resented the burdens of maintenance and watch duty, objected to the loss of their places of refuge. In parts of the Caux the demolitions had a catastrophic effect as people had nowhere to go for safety. When Talbot expelled the French garrison from the small town of Neufmarché and threw down its walls, the inhabitants and the monks of its Benedictine priory found themselves at the mercy of every passing troop of soldiers. Within a few years its commerce had come to a halt. Shortly afterwards, the town was abandoned.[9]

Talbot's finest achievement was to recapture Pontoise, which had been the most grievous loss of the previous winter apart from Paris itself. It was the kind of operation in which he excelled. On 12 February 1437, the moat around the town had frozen over. The English crossed it at night, camouflaged in white sheets and clutching their ladders. They came over the walls before the alarm could be raised. Villiers de L'Isle-Adam, the captain of the town, fled with most of his garrison, leaving the men in the citadel to surrender on the best terms they could get. This feat did much to secure the Vexin and the eastern marches of Normandy. The record was more chequered in the Caux. Talbot began to attack the major garrisons there in 1437. He laid siege to Tancarville in August and the Earl of Salisbury to Fécamp in September. Both places were low on victuals and Tancarville was also in a poor state of repair. But their defenders proved to be unexpectedly resilient. Fécamp surrendered on terms in late October 1437 but was recaptured by the French within days. At Tancarville, the siege involved an army of 800, several ships moored in the river below, and a great crowd of labourers to construct siege works. The besiegers lost large numbers of men from desertion and had to be reinforced several times before the fortress finally surrendered at the end of November after an epic resistance of four months.[10]

Richard of York brought about some improvement in the discipline of the English army in Normandy. He halted the decline that had followed the disappearance of the Duke of Bedford. He provided some redress to those who had suffered from the 'outrages' of English soldiers. But measured against the high expectations entertained in England, his lieutenancy was a failure. He had been expected to achieve a decisive change in the strategic balance, paving the way for a more favourable settlement than the French had been willing to offer at Arras. In the end he presided over the consolidation of the English position on the eastern march of Normandy towards Paris, but little more. His term of office ended with a whimper. His great army wasted away. Casualties, desertion and men going home at the end of their indentures ate into its strength. The Norman treasury was empty, and by the end he was having to pay his men out of his own pocket. In March 1437, a month after Talbot's triumph at Pontoise, York declined to extend his term of office and announced his intention of returning to England as soon as a successor could be found to relieve him. He left in November 1437.[11]

As the English and Norman treasuries slid into bankruptcy, the French King's financial position underwent a dramatic improvement. The early 1430s had marked the nadir of the French tax system. The Estates are not known to have met in either Languedoil or Languedoc for two years after the siege of Orléans. The King's ministers had tried to exploit the prestige of his coronation at Reims by sending commissioners into the provinces to negotiate directly with local communities, but this policy appears to have enjoyed only limited success. Assemblies of the Estates were resumed in Languedoil in 1431 and over the following years were held roughly annually. Most of these meetings were dominated by complaints about the violence and looting of the King's troops. *Aides* were voted in the hope that regular pay would improve the situation, but the machinery of collection functioned badly, and the yield appears to have been poor. As a result, the King's armies and garrisons continued to draw their pay directly from his subjects. The French garrisons in Champagne, Picardy, the Beauvaisis and the Île-de-France lived off the land. The same was largely true of the troops standing on the marches of Anjou and Maine. Even at the heart of Charles VII's territory, soldiers, whether on active service or laid off, lived on plunder and *pâtis*. The result of their activities was the destruction of the tax base. In the absence of adequate tax revenues, the King's ministers reverted to the policy of alienations of demesne land which they had pursued in the opening years of his reign. In La Trémoille's time, large sums were borrowed from ministers and courtiers in transactions which were often disguised sales of land at a gross undervalue. The loans were secured on major assets of the royal demesne in circumstances where default was inevitable. La Trémoille and his allies had been the main beneficiaries of this system. He took over the rich lordships of Lusignan and Melle in Poitou, and Amboise, Montrichard and Bléré in Touraine, as a result of his loans to the King during the crisis occasioned by the English siege of Orléans.[12]

The recovery began in 1435. In January of that year Charles VII presided over a meeting of the Estate of Languedoil at Poitiers. They voted a modest *taille* of 120,000 *francs*. More significantly, they authorised the revival for the next four years of the *aides* at the rates in force under Charles VI before the destruction of the French tax system by John the Fearless. In practice, this decision was a dead letter. The provincial estates called for the substitution of different and almost certainly less productive taxes. In the lead-up to the Congress, Charles was in a hurry and in no position to resist these demands. But an important psychological barrier had been crossed. In the following year the King, fortified by the successful outcome of the Congress, tried again. The Estates met in February, also at Poitiers. The King laid out in detail the problems of financing the war. The assembly agreed to the permanent re-establishment of the *aides* and granted a further 200,000 *livres* to compensate for the failure of the previous grant. This time, the reform proved to be more durable. Charles VII was enabled to dispense with consent to one of the two main war taxes. In practice, he dispensed with consent to the *taille* as well. In February 1437, he imposed a supplementary *taille* of 200,000 *livres* on his own authority. The experiment was repeated year after year, and the amounts tended to increase. As taxation gradually became a royal prerogative, the Estates of Languedoil became redundant. It met for the last time in Charles's reign at Orléans in 1439 to consider proposals for peace, but no financial business was put before it. These assemblies, the King would later say, were an unnecessary expense for the towns and provinces of the realm. In conducting a great war for their defence, his royal authority would have to suffice. At the same time, the administration which had been responsible for the collection of these taxes before the civil wars was revived and reorganised with extended powers.

Events followed a similar course in the south. In April 1437, the Estates of Languedoc, meeting at Béziers in the King's presence, were persuaded to re-establish the *aides* there as well. In theory this was for three years only, but the King treated it as open-ended. When in 1439 the Estates called for a written undertaking that the *aides* would be abolished after the expiry of the three years, the answer from his ministers was that 'the King's needs are so great and so obvious that he cannot at present agree'. On top of the *aides*, regular *tailles* were levied in Languedoc as they were in Languedoil. In theory, they too were authorised by the Estates, but in practice the assemblies were left with little choice, for the King's ministers made it clear that he would impose them without consent if they were not volunteered. Over the following years meetings of the Estates of Languedoc became less frequent and their freedom of action more limited. As a result, the contribution of Languedoc to the King's revenues rose inexorably, until it was paying nearly half the *tailles* of the whole kingdom.

The disappearance of the central financial records makes it impossible to quantify the overall results. But they must have been impressive. Old debts began to be repaid. The range and scale of military operations increased. From 1437, Charles VII was able to deploy more and larger field armies. Between 1438 and 1440, his war treasurers were maintaining forty-two permanent garrisons in the Île-de-France and the Caux.[13]

The first fruits of the new system came in August 1437 with a major French offensive from the Loire into the Paris area. The objective was to eliminate the ring of English fortresses which were strangling the capital. In three months, they conquered all but one of the English strongholds south of Paris. Montargis, Château-Landon and Nemours, the three English strongholds in the Gâtinais were besieged, while the main body of the French army penetrated north and laid siege to Montereau. This town with its mighty fortress at the confluence of the Seine and the Yonne, was the key to the English positions in the region. The French were joined there by troops raised in Champagne. More than 4,500 men were engaged at the height of the siege. A powerful bastide was built against the main gate of the town. Pontoon bridges were constructed across the two watercourses. Bombards reduced parts of the fortress to ruins.

At Rouen, the Duke of York struggled to raise an army to intervene, but distance, shortage of money and the competing needs of Normandy combined to frustrate him. The fortresses of the Gâtinais were abandoned to their fate, while efforts were concentrated on rescuing Montereau. The Duke told a correspondent in September that he could attend to nothing else. It was an ill-starred enterprise. A small force was raised to fight its way through the siege lines under the command of Lord Scales and reinforce the garrison. They were attacked on the road by French troops from Chartres. Many of them were killed or captured, and the rest dispersed. A full-scale relief operation was supposed to follow, but it was never a realistic option. York's councillors were opposed to the whole idea and eventually vetoed it on the ground that the Duke's commission had expired and his authority was at an end. Château-Landon, Nemours and Montereau all surrendered in the course of October 1437. Charles was determined to show that in the aftermath of the treaty of Arras this was no longer a civil war but a war of nations. The English in the garrison of Montereau were treated as prisoners of war and received safe-conducts back to Normandy. But the native French among them, who were probably subjects of the Duke of Burgundy, were all hanged as traitors. Only the onset of winter and shortage of funds stopped the French King from marching at once against Meaux and Creil. In the Gâtinais, François de Surienne's garrison at Montargis held out as the solitary outpost of English power.[14]

The Duke of York was succeeded as lieutenant in Normandy by the Earl of Warwick. Warwick had been reluctant to go. He had important interests and great estates to manage in England, and at the age of fifty-five declared that he was 'full far from the ease of my years and from the continual labour of my person at sieges and daily occupation in the war'. He was still owed nearly £14,000, an enormous sum, for past service. Before taking on the lieutenancy he submitted a number of demands to the council about his terms of service, his powers, the forces that he would command and the settlement of his arrears. Negotiations on these points continued well into July, and logistical problems then caused further delay. As a result, it was not until 8 November 1437 that

Warwick landed at Honfleur, accompanied by Robert Willoughby and an expeditionary army of just over 2,000 men.[15]

Warwick arrived in the midst of a new military crisis. Four days before his ship entered Honfleur, Jean de Croÿ had laid siege to Le Crotoy with an army of nearly 1,300 men supported by a fleet and an artillery train. A bastide was being built outside the gate of the town and blockships were being sunk in the entrance of the harbour. Philip the Good was on his way to direct the siege in person. Le Crotoy was England's sole remaining fortress in Picardy and its only usable harbour between Calais and the Seine. Warwick took charge of a major relief operation. A field army was raised very quickly from nearly every garrison in Normandy. Plausible estimates put its strength at about 2,000 men. At about the beginning of December 1437, Talbot took command of this force and moved north with his usual speed. He forded the Somme at Blanchetaque and began to waste the country behind the Burgundian siege lines. The Burgundians were taken by surprise and panicked. Their urban levies fled in disorder. The men-at-arms defied their officers and withdrew from the siege, burning their bastide as they left and leaving much of their artillery behind them. From England a fleet of seven large ships arrived in the mouth of the Somme, laden with men and supplies. They scattered the Burgundian squadron lying off the town and forced an entry into the town. The English returned in triumph to Normandy, laden with booty, including Philip the Good's personal carriage. Warwick's lieutenancy had begun on a high note.[16]

It did not continue that way. Like his predecessor, the Earl was hamstrung throughout his time in Normandy by shortage of money and men. Most of Richard of York's army had returned with him to England leaving Warwick with his own, much smaller army. The permanent establishment in Normandy had a nominal strength of about 4,500 men, but desertion had reached alarming levels and the real figure was substantially lower. The Earl had been ordered to carry out a general survey of the Norman garrisons and report the numbers available for field service to the council in England so that reinforcements could be sent to him the following year. In the event, however, the available manpower was diverted to another theatre. Cardinal Beaufort had ambitious plans for his nephew Edmund, who was being groomed to take over the Duke of Bedford's appanage in Alençon, Maine and Anjou. In March 1438, Edmund was raised to the peerage as Earl of Dorset and given an independent command as 'captain-general and governor' of Maine and Anjou and captain of Alençon. He was given his own army of 1,700 men, funded from the Cardinal's loans. These decisions were made without consulting Warwick or waiting for his report on Normandy's manpower needs. The result was that he received no reinforcements from England in 1438, the first time that this had happened since Henry VI's accession.[17]

A week before Christmas 1437, the Estates of Normandy met in the chapel of the Archbishop's palace at Rouen to review the finances of the duchy. Judging by its duration (eleven days) it was a difficult meeting. The assembly was finally persuaded to grant an unusually large *aide* of 300,000 *livres* to cover about three-quarters of the cost of the army in Normandy, upon Warwick promising that the rest would be paid from English revenues. The result was disappointing. Disease, famine and war damage combined to make much of the Norman *aide* uncollectable. The English revenues which Warwick had promised did not exist. The Duke of Bedford's attempt in June 1434 to put the subsidies for the French war on a more formal and regular basis had failed. After the fall of Paris, the English council had come up with another scheme. This envisaged that in addition to paying the advances of expeditionary armies, the English Exchequer would be charged with the wages of 400 men-at-arms and 1,200 on the permanent establishment. The new scheme was no more successful than the old. The first year's subsidy was diverted to the defence of Calais in June 1436, and none of the subsequent payments was ever made. Instead, the council reverted to the older practice of making ad hoc payments whenever the pressure of events forced their hand and the money could be found. Both the Duke of York and the Earl of Warwick had arrived in France with chests of cash to pay off the arrears of the Norman garrisons. But to keep the arrears from building up again, the Treasurer of Normandy had to rely on shipments of cash sent at unpredictable intervals from England. In the four years after the death of the Duke of Bedford, a total of just over £53,000 reached the Norman Treasury from England, an average of about £13,000 a year. But the average concealed wild fluctuations, and payments fell off sharply after June 1437. Nothing was received from England during the whole sixteen months of Warwick's lieutenancy.[18]

In the summer of 1438, the harvest failed across northern France for the second year in succession. By July wholesale grain prices in the Rouen market stood at ten times their normal level. Widespread famine was followed by an epidemic of smallpox. Natural disaster combined with the government's insolvency to produce an accelerating breakdown of discipline in the Norman garrisons. We have a graphic account of conditions around Tancarville in May 1438. The captain of the fortress reported that taxes could not be collected, food could not be found and men were absconding every day to support themselves by looting. Similar reports came in from the captains of the major garrisons at Pontoise and Pont-de-l'Arche. Rural brigandage rose to unprecedented levels. In Rouen, the rhythm of executions on the Place du Marché quickened. A serious plot was discovered in August 1438 to deliver the city to the enemy. Repression was tightened.[19]

Edmund Beaufort, the newly elevated Earl of Dorset, landed at Cherbourg at about the end of May 1438 with the army that might have been used to reinforce Warwick. He marched directly into Maine. The English position in Maine had progressively declined since the death of the Duke of Bedford. In 1438 they were confined to Le Mans and four other garrisoned towns. The region suffered from continual raids by the French garrisons on its southern and eastern marches. Much of the open country had been lost to French partisans and depopulated by the competing demands of both sides for *patis*. Dorset was a competent soldier, but his appearance in the region did very little to improve things. From Alençon he marched down the valley of the Sarthe and captured two garrisoned French castles north of Le Mans, at Saint-Aignan and La Guierche. After two months, when reports began to arrive of a French counterattack, he abandoned the campaign and withdrew to his castle at Harcourt in Normandy, leaving the bulk of his army cantoned around Alençon and Le Mans. Within a few months La Guierche had been lost again, 'by misgoverance' according to an English chronicler. The Grand Conseil protested against this diversion of troops to a marginal theatre, which they claimed had cost them territory in more important places. The Duke of Gloucester blamed the Cardinal, with good reason.[20]

Against this difficult background, Warwick was condemned to watch impotently as the English military position in Normandy continued to deteriorate. In June 1438, Talbot invaded the Caux once more and captured some of the outlying forts protecting Dieppe. But there was no attack on Dieppe itself. An attempt to recapture Harfleur failed with the loss of all eight of the English ships employed to blockade the town from the sea. Meanwhile, further east, the French were consolidating their gains around Paris.

In November 1438, the English lost Dreux and Montargis within a few days of each other. In both cases the town was sold to the enemy by its captain. Dreux was, after Evreux, the principal fortress of the south-eastern march of Normandy. According to a French captain it was 'impregnable except by treachery or dereliction of duty by the watch'. Yet it was captured at night with the connivance of Guillaume Broulart, the only native Frenchman to command an English fortress. Like other Frenchmen in English service, Broulart had links with neighbouring families in the French obedience and was worried about his future. His reward was a large cash bribe, a rich marriage for his daughter and the prospect of a better career in French service. At Montargis, François de Surienne withstood a siege of nearly two months before giving up hope of relief and selling out to the Bastard of Orléans in December 1437. He remained in occupation for some months while Charles VII struggled to raise the money. The English always hoped that he would dishonour the terms of surrender. They kept his garrison reinforced and resupplied and assumed responsibility for their wages. But when the French King finally came up with the money in November 1438, Surienne opened his gates and left. He was offered a career in French service, but unlike Broulart he continued to serve the English. When, shortly before Christmas, the castle of Saint-Germain-en-Laye outside Paris was betrayed to Talbot for money, the one bright moment in a dismal year for English arms, François de Surienne was installed as its captain.[21]

The reoccupation of Saint-Germain-en-Laye was the last notable event of Warwick's lieutenancy. He had been appointed for a term of eighteen months, and his commission expired in January 1439. Like the Duke of York, he agreed to stay on until a successor could be found. But he was by now a sick man and was not destined to see England again. He died at Rouen on 30 April 1439. His body was brought back to England, where the magnificent Beauchamp Chapel at St Mary's Warwick was built to accommodate his tomb.[22]

Financial penury and defeat on the ground rekindled the English council's interest in a negotiated peace but did nothing to shift the unrealistic positions which they had adopted at Arras. They never came to terms with the weakness of their political position. They were convinced that Charles VII was a puppet in the hands of his Angevin councillors, and blamed them for the failure of the Congress. They pinned their hopes on a change of regime at the French court. The Duke of Gloucester declared that it was a matter of 'common fame and report' that neither Charles VII nor the Dauphin Louis had the mental capacity to govern and that a regency of some kind would sooner or later be imposed on them. This idea was misconceived, but it was almost certainly shared by Henry VI's other councillors. Viewed from England it seemed plausible. There had, after all, been four palace revolutions in France in less than a decade, each of which had resulted in the forcible replacement of ministers in whom Charles had apparently had confidence. But it was never plausible to think that a different French ministry might concede the issues of sovereignty and homage, which were fundamental to the identity of the French state and had been articles of faith with successive French Kings for decades, regardless of who their advisers were.[23]

In 1437 Henry VI's councillors reverted to an earlier scheme to engineer a palace revolution in France with the aid of the Duke of Orléans. Charles of Orléans himself was probably the council's main source of information about what was happening at the French King's court. But he deceived both himself and his captors about the extent of his political influence in France. Orléans was an increasingly embittered figure. He did not want to die in captivity, like the late Duke of Bourbon. He believed that the French King's councillors were obstructing his release, preferring to leave him languishing in an English prison than to see him take his rightful place as the chief among them. The Angevin ministers at the French court had many enemies and Orléans was certainly in touch with some of them.

The gradual restoration of the government's finances had brought a more assertive style to the business of government and with it a growing distance between Charles VII and the court nobility. They had done well by the indigence of the King in his first decade, but were the main losers when the flow of grants of land, pensions and collusive mortgages was reduced to a trickle. In December 1438, an ordinance was issued revoking most royal grants since 1418, a serious blow to those who had flourished under the indulgent regimes of Louvet and La Trémoille. Like each successive dominant faction at the court of Charles VII, the regime of Charles of Anjou provoked jealousies and faction-fighting among those who perceived themselves to be excluded from power and the status and rewards that came with it. Some of the French King's old councillors who had been influential in La Trémoille's time bitterly resented their relegation to the wings after his fall. Their leader was the Duke of Bourbon, who had fallen from favour after the Congress of Arras. The Dukes of Bourbon were royal princes, descendants of Louis IX, but they suffered from the poverty of their mountainous and infertile appanage, which was never capable of supporting their high status and even higher pretensions. They had been dependent for at least three generations on grants from the Crown, which made the loss of royal favour painful. Duke Charles, the 'new Absalom' of the Burgundian chronicler Georges Chastellain, was an impetuous man of passionate and enduring hatreds, with an instinct for violent solutions. The Duke of Alençon, his closest ally, burned with anger at what he saw as the King's ingratitude for his service in the field with Joan of Arc and had already come to regard Charles of Anjou as his mortal enemy.[24]

The malcontents were well placed to challenge the King's government. By putting an end to the war between France and Burgundy, the treaty of Arras had cast large numbers of unemployed soldiery onto the crowded market for military manpower. They formed armed bands, which coalesced into large freelance armies. Their numbers were swollen by mobs of displaced peasants and the unemployed of the cities. The notorious Castilian brigand Rodrigo de Villandrando had several thousand mounted men at his back, most of whom had been intermittently employed before 1435 by Charles VII's ministers against the eastern domains of the house of Burgundy. Another brigand army, reported to be 3,000 to 4,000 strong, was recruited from French garrison troops who had been operating against the Burgundians in Picardy and the Laonnais. When they were expelled from these regions by Richemont in 1436, they migrated into the Cambrésis and Hainaut, and then poured into Champagne under a trio of captains, Antoine de Chabannes and two bastards of the house of Bourbon, Guy and Alexander. Charles VII's ministers counted at least twelve of these irregular armies. In northern France they received the name of '*écorcheurs*', after the skinners who did the dirtiest work in the butcheries of French cities and were often regarded as scarcely human.

The *écorcheurs* were a serious threat to the political stability of the Valois monarchy, because behind them stood prominent noblemen, who protected the leading captains and had a measure of control over their operations. The Duke of Bourbon was the most significant of the *écorcheurs'* princely patrons. He was associated with Rodrigo de Villandrando, who had married his bastard half-sister; with Guy and Alexander bastards of Bourbon, his half-brothers, who commanded two of the larger bands; and with the Chabannes brothers, Jacques and Antoine. Jacques de Chabannes commanded a contingent of Rodrigo de Villandrando's army. He was also the Duke's seneschal for the Bourbonnais, and controlled on Bourbon's behalf the garrisons of most of the principal French fortresses around Paris, including Vincennes, Pont-de-Charenton, Saint-Cloud, Corbeil and Brie-Comte-Robert.[25]

Bourbon and Alençon saw Charles of Orléans as the figurehead of a coalition against the King's ministers. Everyone knew that Henry V's will forbade the release of Charles of Orléans except as part of an overall peace. To get him out of the clutches of his captors, there would have to be a general settlement with England. The malcontents found an ally in the Bastard of Orléans, who was the guardian of his half-brother's interests, and had his own differences with the King's Angevin ministers. At the beginning of 1437, he approached John V of Brittany with a proposal to broker a peace between England and France. The plan, as it developed, was that the Dukes of Brittany and Orléans should offer themselves as joint mediators at a fresh peace conference. The idea appealed to John V. He sent his private secretary and a herald to England in April to put it to the English council. In May 1437 John presided at a meeting at Vannes attended by the Bastard of Orléans and the Dukes of Bourbon and Alençon. They endorsed the proposal for a peace conference. They planned to hold it at Cherbourg, a venue which was convenient for everyone except Charles VII.[26]

In October 1437, the Duke of Brittany's proposals were considered at a great council gathered in Henry VI's presence in his father's palace by the Thames at Sheen. Chancellor Stafford opened the proceedings by posing three questions. How was England to respond to the deteriorating relations between Pope Eugenius IV and the Council of Basel, which threatened a schism in the Church and the election of a French-backed antipope? How were they to arrive at reasonable terms of peace with France, now that the hopes invested in the Congress of Arras had been dashed? And what was to be done about England's dire financial position? The assembly agreed that the Duke of Orléans should be taken to Cherbourg to participate in the Duke of Brittany's peace conference. Lord Cobham, the Duke's current custodian, was ordered to bring him to Sheen the following week to discuss the details. The financial review which followed made it clear how urgent the task of peacemaking had become. The position was so bad that England could hardly afford to participate in a diplomatic conference, let alone continue the war. Disposable revenue was at its lowest level of the reign to date. With wool exports close to zero as a result of the trade war with Burgundy, customs revenues had plumbed new lows. The most recent Parliamentary tax, a single lay subsidy granted in January 1437, had been entirely pledged to creditors as security for their loans. Without cancelling the assignments in their favour, the Treasurer reported, he could not even pay the cost of transporting the Duke of Orléans under guard to Cherbourg. Charles had to be asked to find the money himself from his war-torn estates in France.[27]

In fact, the peace project was already doomed, although the men gathered at Sheen did not know it. Charles VII soon discovered the Duke of Bourbon's plot against his councillors and pre-empted it. In Languedoc, where he had been presiding over the Estates, he gathered an army before Bourbon was ready. He invaded the Bourbonnais and then made for the Loire. The Duke of Bourbon was obliged to make a humiliating submission in August. Rodrigo de Villandrando fled the realm, and Bourbon's other *écorcheur* clients were redeployed against the English. Charles VII's ministers suspected the Duke of Brittany of being involved in the plot, which inevitably discredited him as a peacemaker. The English council did their best to keep the peace project alive. In March 1438 they sent the treasurer of the royal household Sir John Popham to France to negotiate the preliminaries with the Earl of Warwick, the Duke of Brittany and the Bastard of Orléans. Popham spent six exhausting months passing to and fro between Rouen, Cherbourg and Brittany. Negotiations finally broke down in September 1438. Charles VII's ministers refused to take part in any negotiations under the Duke of Orléans's auspices until they had sent their own agents to discuss the matter with him directly. Experience had taught them to be sceptical of proposals involving desperate prisoners in England.[28]

That autumn, the Breton peace plan was replaced by another, this time promoted by the Duke of Burgundy. Like John V, Philip desperately needed peace. The garrisons that he was keeping under arms to contain the English at Calais and Le Crotoy were dead weight in his accounts. Discontent with the trade war was rising in Holland and

Brabant. The foreign merchant community in Bruges was threatening to quit Flanders and boycott its trade if the stand-off between Burgundy and England continued. Conscious of his cool relations with Charles VII, Philip had been building alliances with the leading noblemen of France. He too saw Orléans as an important ally.

In November 1438, Philip finally took Lannoy's advice and offered himself as mediator to broker a permanent peace. He approached the court of France himself, but knowing how much he was hated in England, he arranged for the Duchess of Burgundy, Isabella of Portugal, to front the talks with the ministers of Henry VI. She sent a personal emissary to Westminster to propose that she and Cardinal Beaufort should jointly preside at a fresh peace conference under Burgundian auspices. Beaufort and Isabella were well matched. The Cardinal was a major influence on English policy and by instinct a peacemaker, while Isabella was a Lancastrian, the granddaughter of John of Gaunt, the Cardinal's niece and an old friend from the days when he had been a regular visitor to the Burgundian court. In January 1439 Beaufort and Archbishop Kemp settled the preliminaries with Charles VII's representatives in the Duchess's presence at a meeting outside Calais. They agreed that the peace conference would open on 8 May 1439 either at Cherbourg, the venue previously agreed with John V, or somewhere near Calais. Charles of Orléans was to be brought to the conference and allowed to participate, although for the moment his role was left undefined.[29]

The new project faced opposition in both countries. In England, the Duke of Gloucester professed to have no idea what was the point of more peace talks. They only wasted money that might have been better spent on prosecuting the war. From the French side, there was an ominous silence which is likely to have reflected divisions among the King's councillors. A sizeable body of opinion thought that Charles VII would do better to prosecute the war than to horse-trade with the enemy. The issue came to a head at the beginning of April 1439 when the King was at Riom in Auvergne, and his council was considering the membership of the French delegation. Most of the soldiers on the council were opposed to the peace process. The Duke of Bourbon, now that his plans for an armed rising had collapsed, spoke against it. So did his associates Jacques de Chabannes and Marshal Lafayette. Richemont was not present but shared their view. He had been pressing for some time for a major offensive against the remaining

English fortresses on the approaches to Paris. The outcome was a decision which conceded something to both sides of the argument. It was decided to go ahead with the peace conference, but at the same time to increase the pressure on the English around Paris by mounting a major offensive against either Meaux or Creil. It was Meaux that they eventually selected as the target.[30]

The arrangements which Kemp and Beaufort had negotiated at Calais were approved by a great council at Westminster in February 1439. The instructions of the English ambassadors took longer to prepare. They were considered over several days at the end of May 1439 at another great council in the Black Prince's old manor at Kennington. A delegation from the Grand Conseil, including Bishop Cauchon, Jean Rinel and Sir William Oldhall crossed the Channel to be there. The documents which emerged were surprisingly lacking in realism considering the collective experience that went into their drafting and the desperation of the English to achieve a negotiated exit from the war. The new idea was a partition of the country between Henry VI and Charles VII, with each of them calling himself King of France and each being sovereign in the lands under his own control. The divisions of Merovingian France and the partition of the country under the successors of Charlemagne were cited as historical precedents for this arrangement. The English instructions envisaged dividing France at the Loire, which made sense strategically but not politically. It would have required the French King to surrender all that he had gained since the siege of Orléans. Much thought was devoted to the problem of the exiled French landowners of Normandy, which had given rise to so much difficulty at Arras. The English had little to offer to this politically important constituency. The ambassadors were authorised to concede that they might recover their lands if they were in the English Crown's hands. But otherwise, they would have to make whatever deal they could negotiate with the current occupiers. There is little doubt that Beaufort believed in this vision. If the French would not accept it, the instructions required him to lecture them on the evils of war in terms which he must have drafted himself. They must realise, he was to tell them,

Either this war must ever endure and never have end ... [or] if it shall have end it must have end by one of two ways, that is to say either by fine force so that one of them destroy and subdue wholly that other ... [or] it must end by good appointment and accord, the which is the goodly ending thereof.

In spite of his long experience of dealing with the French, Beaufort always underestimated the strength of the French government's commitment to the unity of the realm and the sovereignty of their King over its entire territory. Beaufort was given a separate, personal authority to cut through any deadlock, and the ambassadors were informed that the King had privately told him his views. His secret instructions have not survived, but it is clear that he was not empowered to make the kind of concessions that might have broken the deadlock. Archbishop Kemp told the conference at Calais what he had already told the conference at Arras: the English 'had not come to uncrown their King'. If it proved impossible to make peace on these terms, the English ambassadors were instructed to report back to the King and his council in England and ask for further instructions. If even these did not break the impasse, then they were to suggest the longest truce that could be negotiated, up to fifty years if possible. In a revealing observation, the council added that to make the truce more secure, it would be desirable to eliminate the fortresses that each side held in the territory of the other. The proposal was to exchange the English-held enclaves of Creil, Meaux and Saint-Germain-en-Laye for French ones in Normandy at Dieppe, Harfleur and Mont-Saint-Michel. It was a transparent hint that their territorial ambitions were now limited to retaining Normandy and presumably Gascony and Calais.[31]

The conference opened two months late on 6 July 1439 under lowering skies in the windswept coastal plain between Calais and Guines. Isabella brought with her a group of her husband's councillors including his Chancellor Nicolas Rolin and Hughes de Lannoy. They were lodged at Gravelines along with the French delegation. Cardinal Beaufort and the English were lodged at Calais. Philip the Good followed the proceedings from the discreet distance of the abbey of St Bertin at Saint-Omer. The conference had been planned on a lavish scale. Plenary sessions were held every three or four days, separated by pauses for internal discussion and informal exchanges between the delegations and the mediators. On session days, the mediators and the delegates would ride out from their bases in a carefully choreographed order towards an improvised town of tenting and timber which had been constructed for the occasion about a mile south of the ruins of the fort of Oye. It was divided into separate sectors for the mediators, the delegations and a corps of some 600 soldiers charged to maintain security. Two large timber lodges had been built for Cardinal

Beaufort and Isabella. Beaufort's was especially magnificent. It was a spacious hall hung with scarlet cloth and rich tapestries, where the Cardinal stored large stocks of wine and entertained lavishly. Between the mediators' lodges stood the great pavilion where Cardinal Beaufort and Isabella of Portugal presided over the plenary sessions from gilded thrones hung with gold cloth.

The leaders of the French delegation were Charles VII's Chancellor Regnault de Chartres, the Count of Vendôme and the Bastard of Orléans, who had recently become Count of Dunois, the title by which he is known to history. The English had sent a large delegation headed by Archbishop Kemp. He was supported by an imposing group of peers, bishops and officials, a contingent from the Grand Conseil at Rouen, a corps of lawyers, and two secretaries, the King's diplomatic secretary Thomas Beckington (who kept the official record) and the combative French secretary Jean Rinel. Most of the leading members of the English delegation had been at Arras. Beaufort, although not technically a member of the English delegation, in practice acted as its chairman in spite of his status as a mediator. Charles of Orléans had been brought to Calais and was held under secure guard in the castle. The English hoped that he would persuade their adversaries to soften their traditional negotiating positions. As the conference proceeded the Duke took an increasingly prominent part in it and was eventually co-opted by Beaufort and Isabella of Portugal as an additional mediator.[32]

Seven formal sessions of the conference were held between 6 and 29 July 1439, in the course of which the opening position of the English unravelled. By the end of the second session, both sides had adopted positions from which they refused to shift. The French insisted, as they had always done, that there could be no peace unless the English King abandoned his claim to the Crown of France, and that any territory which they held in France must be held as a vassal of Charles VII. The English declared that as far as they were concerned their King's title was not up for debate. It followed that there could be no question of his settling for vassal status. On the evening of the second session, Henry Beaufort took wine and spices with the Duchess in her lodge. The Cardinal told her that he could not envisage any circumstances in which the English would agree to do homage to a rival for territory that they occupied in France. If the French insisted, he said, negotiations would break down. The time had come for the English to deploy Charles of Orléans. The third session was given over to discussions between Charles, Isabella and the French delegation. The English were terrified that an attempt might be made to carry their prisoner away. This session, therefore, had to be held in a great tent outside Milkgate, the fortified gate on the east side of Calais, watched from a distance by a large body of English soldiers. Beckington's journal records the Duke telling Isabella as they entered the tent that he would 'die for peace', but otherwise we are dependent on the brief minutes made by the French delegation. These record only that the discussions were lengthy and covered 'several openings' that might lead to agreement. What is clear is that Charles of Orléans failed to persuade the French ambassadors to change their position on any major point of principle.[33]

On 18 July 1439, Beaufort reported to the English delegation on the current prospects for agreement. He was very pessimistic. The Duchess, he said, had explored the issues with Regnault de Chartres and his colleagues, and was satisfied that there was no room for movement on title to the Crown or on homage. As matters stood, therefore, there would be no peace. The only alternative was a long truce. The Duchess put forward a proposal for a truce of fifteen, twenty or thirty years, which had been drafted for her by Nicolas Rolin. The rest of July was passed in argument about the exact terms of such a truce. As Isabella conceived it, the object was to defer the whole issue of sovereignty for the duration of the truce, leaving Henry VI free to reassert his claims if no permanent peace had been made by the time it expired. In the meantime, Henry VI must refrain from calling himself King of France, allow the Norman exiles to return to their estates and release Charles of Orléans without ransom. This left open the contentious question of what territory the English would be allowed to occupy while the truce was in force, which was the main bone of contention at the next plenary session. The delegations reassembled in the presence of the mediators on 22 July, a cold, blustery day with gusts of high wind and bursts of torrential rain which leaked through the tent roof onto the heads of the participants. It was an ill-tempered occasion. Each side was asked for its response to the Duchess's proposals. The French gave them a cautious welcome but were not prepared to agree to the English remaining in occupation of the whole of Normandy. They insisted that they must withdraw from all but two of the seven Norman *bailliages* and abandon the *pays de conquête*. The English dismissed this out of hand and demanded the inclusion not just of Normandy and the *pays de conquête* but the whole of western France. The Duchess broke down in tears of frustration, but 'whether of anger or pain I know not' wrote Thomas Beckington in his journal. Would the English accept the truce on the terms proposed even if agreement could be reached on territory, the Duchess asked them. Their reply was that they had no instructions on the point. Neither, as it turned out, did the French. Shortly after this, it was reported that the French delegation had given up and were packing their bags.[34]

Regnault de Chartres and his colleagues were persuaded to unpack them while the English considered their next step. On 27 July, Cardinal Beaufort called for the conference to be adjourned while Archbishop Kemp and his colleagues returned to England for further instructions. The French, who needed to confer with their own government, agreed to an adjournment of six weeks, until 11 September. Before the delegations dispersed, the Duchess fixed a final session for 29 July. Isabella spent the whole of that day in conclave with Charles of Orléans and the French delegation, trying to make the proposed truce more palatable to the English. There was no prospect of their agreeing to abandon most of Normandy, and the problem of the exiled Norman landowners had not gone away. Isabella pressed the French to be more realistic, and at the end of the day they backed down. Isabella and the Duke of Orléans produced a joint memorandum, which the French accepted in principle and the Cardinal said that he would recommend to the English King and his council. In its final form, it proposed that during the truce the English should retain everything that they currently held in Normandy and Aquitaine with their 'appurtenances and appendages', but would lose the *pays de conquête*, including the counties of Maine and Perche and possibly the French Vexin with its major fortress at Pontoise. The document took up the English proposal of an exchange of fortresses. The French would deliver up the principal places which they had conquered in the Caux, but not Mont-Saint-Michel which had never been in English hands. The English for their part would abandon their fortresses in the Île-de-France, Creil, Meaux and Saint-Germain-en-Laye. The Norman exiles would be restored to their estates in the duchy, except for a limited number of strategic fortresses which the English authorities would be allowed to retain and garrison. The returning exiles would not be required to do homage for their land to the English King, but neither would they be allowed to serve Charles VII in arms while they held land in Normandy. Finally, there was a clause inserted at Beaufort's insistence that the arrangement would be terminable by either side at any time on a year's notice. It was a complicated but ingenious compromise. The Duchess handed the document to both delegations and called on them to obtain their government's instructions. The French delegation left Gravelines on 30 July. On 5 August 1439, Archbishop Kemp and five other members of the English delegation boarded a ship bound for England to report to the King. The rest of the English embassy remained at Calais with the Cardinal, kicking their heels until Kemp's return. Life in Calais, wrote Beckington to a friend, was insufferably dull.[35]

On 20 July 1439, shortly before the adjournment of the conference, Richemont laid siege to Meaux with about 5,000 men. His army was unusual in that nearly two-thirds of it had been drawn from the ranks of freelance companies of *écorcheurs*. The companies had been engaged since the previous year on both sides of a vicious regional war being fought out between the partisans of Réné of Anjou and Antoine Count of Vaudémont for control of the duchies of Lorraine and Bar. After the discordant council meeting at Riom in April 1439, the officers of the King and the Duke of Bourbon had been sent to the region to put an end to this destructive conflict which pitted French soldiers against each other. They recalled the companies to the Île-de-France and placed them under Richemont's orders at Corbeil, the muster point designated for the army of Meaux. It was the first stage of a determined effort on the part of Charles VII's government to tame the *écorcheurs* by incorporating them in the King's army at regular wages and then deploying them against the English. The policy was only partly successful. The freelance captains were not disposed to leave Lorraine without payment, and Réné's lieutenants had to buy off the mercenaries of both sides at considerable cost. Even then, some of them preferred the prospect of looting Alsace, Burgundy or Auvergne to what seemed likely to be a difficult siege in the service of Charles VII. It was not until mid-July that Richemont had the numbers at Corbeil to attack Meaux.[36]

Meaux was one of the strongest fortresses in France. It comprised two walled enclosures on opposite sides of the Marne. The city itself stood on the north bank, defended by an ancient circuit of walls most of which dated from Roman times, and by the old castle of the counts of Champagne overlooking the river at its western end. But the place owed its strength to the immense fortified suburb on the opposite side of the river known as the Marché. The Marché occupied a tight bend in the river, which flowed beneath its walls on three sides while the fourth, to the south, was protected by a canal cut across the bend. A stone bridge joined the two enclosures. The garrison, at over 500 men, was among the largest in France. It was completely surrounded by hostile territory, and was too large to be supplied by local foraging. This meant that its supplies had to be brought in by regular convoys from Normandy, a logistical nightmare involving long trains of laden wagons escorted across the Île-de-France by more than a thousand men each time. The last such convoy had arrived in September 1438, ten months earlier, and stores must have been low when Richemont arrived. In 1439, the captain of Meaux was the Norfolk knight Sir William Chamberlain, a cousin and protégé of Sir John Fastolf. He had been away for several months, recruiting troops in England. In his absence, the command was taken by the captain of the town Sir Thomas Everingham and the *bailli*, John Bastard of Thian. John of Thian, the real energy behind the defence, was a French professional soldier who had begun his career as a *routier* in the service of John the Fearless before entering English service after his murder. He had been knighted by Henry V in 1422 for his role in the original English siege of Meaux. When Richemont arrived with his army, he established his headquarters in the village of Chauconin, two miles away, close to the road by which any relief force could be expected to come. Over the following days, his troops occupied the suburban villages and monasteries and built seven timber bastides, isolating both the city and the Marché. A formidable line of batteries was drawn up at close range on the north bank of the river, opposite the walls and gates of the city.[37]

Although the Constable's plans had been the talk of Paris since May, his appearance outside Meaux caught the English by surprise. The government of Normandy was in disarray. The Earl of Warwick had not yet been replaced. The Duke of Gloucester wanted the job, but was kept out of it by Cardinal Beaufort, who was pushing the claims of his nephew, John Beaufort Earl of Somerset. The result was political paralysis. The English council avoided making a choice between these two powerful princes by putting the government of Normandy temporarily in the hands of a commission of twelve men, of whom Somerset was one. The others included the Chancellor Louis of

Luxembourg and the principal English commanders in France, Talbot, Scales, Fauconberg and Dorset. In point of form, Somerset had no more power than the others. But because of his exalted rank and his connections in England he had the dominant voice in practice. He was wholly unsuited for this role. John Beaufort had been captured at the battle of Baugé in March 1421 at the age of seventeen and had passed almost all his adult life in French prisons. The years of captivity had left their mark on him. He was released, broken in health, financially ruined, and devoid of military experience late in 1438 after years of complex and protracted negotiations. Thomas Basin, who had probably met him, drew an unattractive portrait: proud, arrogant, vain, incapable and impervious to advice. This judgement is echoed by a well-informed English observer, who remarked on his domineering manner and irascible temper.

The Norman commission had a difficult task which would have challenged abler men than the Earl of Somerset. The expeditionary army for that year was small and late. Just under 1,000 men indented to go to Normandy in April 1439 but did not sail until the end of July. There was no money available in Rouen or at Westminster. The expeditionary army, together with a larger army which sailed for Gascony which sailed at about the same time, had to be financed by controversial sales of Crown lands to the Cardinal. The Norman garrisons were at a low ebb, perhaps no more than 2,500 men in all, and had been denuded of troops to create a field army. They had not been paid for months. In October 1439 the financial officers at Rouen were reporting a deficit of 90,000 *livres* on the garrison accounts. A whole quarter's wages were outstanding. Six months later the deficit had more than doubled.[38]

Sir John Talbot was responsible for organising the relief of Meaux. He had to take considerable risks. He withdrew as many men as he dared from the Norman garrisons. He pressed ex-soldiers living on the land into service. He was joined by Sir William Chamberlain, the captain of Meaux, who had just returned from England with fresh recruits. All of these forces converged on Pontoise, which served as the forward base for the operation. Outside Meaux, Richemont ordered an assault on 12 August in the hope of taking it before the English army arrived. The walls of the town had been reduced to rubble in several places and were seized with little difficulty. The Bastard of Thian, who was taken prisoner in the assault, was summarily executed along with other native French prisoners. The French poured into the city and ran through the streets towards the Marché. But before they could reach it, the defenders broke the bridge over the Marne and retreated into the fortress. Several attempts were made to storm the Marché across the breach. All of them were beaten back. Richemont tried negotiation before the garrison discovered that relief was on its way. But the defenders discovered the truth from a Gascon soldier in French service and abruptly broke off the talks.[39]

Richemont's army substantially outnumbered the relief force. But he was unwilling to risk a pitched battle outside Meaux in which he was liable to be attacked in the rear by the garrison of the Marché. So he blockaded the north end of the bridge, abandoned his siege lines and withdrew the whole of his army behind the walls of the city, apart from the men serving in the bastides. When the English appeared outside the walls on 14 August, they found the siege lines deserted and the enemy massed on the walls of the old town. The English captains challenged Richemont to a battle, which he naturally declined. This left them with a difficult dilemma. They did not have the strength to carry the walls of the city against several thousand defenders, or the time to starve them out. The army of relief comprised most of the English troops in France, leaving Normandy dangerously exposed in their rear. The men had only a few days' rations. The English captains considered occupying Crépy-en-Valois, twenty miles away, and turning it into a supply base, but Richemont pre-empted them by sending one of his officers with a detachment of men to defend it. This left the English with no alternative but to reinforce and resupply the Marché, and then return to Normandy. They moved south of the Marne and stormed the bastide which the French had built on that side. Then they approached the canal with boats made from leather stretched over timber frames. Sir William Chamberlain was able to enter the fortress across the narrow stretch of water with 500 men, together with their equipment and supplies and a number of artillery pieces captured in the abandoned French siege lines. On 18 August the main body of the English army withdrew to Pontoise, leaving two of the seven French bastides in flames.[40]

After their departure, the French rebuilt the two bastides and resumed the siege. Substantial reinforcements were brought up from the Loire by the King himself. They were not needed, for just five days after Talbot's withdrawal, Chamberlain decided that the Marché could not be held. Although his stores were now full and a fresh relief operation was planned, on about 23 August he entered into a conditional surrender agreement with the Constable. He undertook to open his gates on 15 September unless he was relieved by then. The most likely explanation is that his garrison mutinied when they found themselves once more surrounded by the enemy. At Calais, Beaufort was stupefied. Meaux was one of the fortresses that he had hoped to exchange for Dieppe or Harfleur. At Pontoise, Talbot was aghast. He set about building a second army of relief by the deadline, a remarkable logistical challenge. He very nearly succeeded. The expeditionary army from England had landed at Honfleur just as Chamberlain was giving up the fight. The men were directed straight to Pontoise to join the new army of relief. More men were pulled out of Norman garrisons. The whole force set out for Meaux on about 13 September. When 15 September came, their troops were just a day's march away. They got messages through to the Marché, urging Chamberlain to hold out. But Chamberlain insisted on honouring his agreement. The English arrived on the following day to find the French royal standard floating above the walls. Chamberlain and his garrison were released to return to Rouen under safe-conduct. He was arrested for treason as soon as he arrived, but an official enquiry exonerated him and he went on to hold a number of important military commands and diplomatic appointments.[41]

Archbishop Kemp arrived back in England on 8 August 1439 with the deputation from the conference at Calais. A few days later, they reported to the King and the council at Windsor castle. Kemp and his colleagues brought with them the joint proposal of Isabella of Portugal and Charles of Orléans, a memorandum of advice from the ambassadors in Calais and another which seems to record the advice of the Grand Conseil at Rouen. Neither memorandum made a formal recommendation, but their authors' reasoning left little doubt about their views. The ambassadors at Calais reluctantly recommended the mediators' proposal. They had serious misgivings about it, but the fact had to be faced that neither England nor Normandy could afford to continue the war.

The fullest statement of the problem, however, was due to the Rouen councillors. They took a different view. Their analysis pitilessly exposed the English dilemma. Normandy, they pointed out, was exhausted and impoverished by war, famine and depopulation. Across the duchy, as much as half the rural population had abandoned the land, while the loss of the Channel ports had seriously damaged the commerce of the towns. Taxes could no longer be collected. The war treasurer was unable to repair or supply the fortresses or pay their garrisons. Military discipline was breaking down. Some of the garrisons were effectively on strike. Others lacked the competence or enthusiasm to fight even when they were paid. By comparison, Charles VII's armies had become immeasurably more effective. They had recovered twenty-two dioceses in France since 1429. It was only a matter of time before Normandy went the same way. The lesson was clear. Either Normandy must be defended with the revenues of England or it would be lost. The councillors at Rouen had had this argument out with their English counterparts many times. They doubted whether English taxpayers were either able or willing to bear the burden. At the same time, they felt unable to recommend the mediators' proposal, because it would only lead to more war with the same result. If Henry VI abandoned the use of his title for thirty years, it would probably be impossible for him to resume it at the end of that period. Psychologically and politically, it would be dead. Without the title there would be no legal basis for his authority in the occupied provinces of France. He would be subject to the prerogative powers of the Valois King. If he resisted, Charles VII would use it as an occasion for renewing the war at a moment of his own choosing. The return of the Norman exiles would be a disaster. It would mean dispossessing loyal vassals of the English King and transferring large areas of Normandy into the hands of the likes of the dukes of Alençon, the counts of Eu and the lords of Harcourt, who were firm partisans of the French King. The restoration of the francophile bishops would leave them free to preach against the English administration. In short, the terms would signal to the world that Henry VI was unable to defend Normandy, and would lose him what support he still had there. The Rouen councillors found it hard to believe that something better could not be negotiated.[42]

Archbishop Kemp struggled to defend the mediators' proposal in the face of a hostile gathering. Predictably, the opposition was led by the Earl of Gloucester. He launched a root and branch attack on the whole idea of a negotiated peace. It involved making concessions which betrayed the legacy of Henry V. Gloucester believed that the Duke of Orléans, who had had such a prominent role in drawing up the mediators' proposal, was a natural enemy of England. He argued that the talks had simply provided the French with a screen behind which they had been able to attack Meaux. As for the mediators' proposal, it was an 'infamy'. 'I would never agree me thereto ... and of the same disposition I am yet and will be while I live.' The council advised the King to reject the proposal. They recorded their reasons in a document. They were very similar to those of the Grand Conseil. The council was not prepared to abandon a claim to the French Crown which had been used by successive English Kings to justify a century of war. If Henry did that, even temporarily, the right would have disappeared by the time that the truce came to an end. But the main consideration which influenced them was the destruction of Henry V's land settlement in Normandy which would follow if the French exiles were allowed to return. This was a sensitive point for this group of men, many of whom had themselves inherited or been granted Norman estates. The mediators' plan, they said, would 'withdraw the heart and courage' of the English. It is unlikely that many of them saw the issue in the same terms as the Duke of Gloucester. He regarded it as a simple question of peace or war. The real problem had been pointed out by the Rouen councillors. Peace was absolutely necessary, but the mediators' proposals were practically unworkable and likely to lead to more war. Yet nothing else was on offer.

At the conclusion of the debate, the King withdrew with a small group of councillors to the royal manor of King's Langley. Here, they drew up fresh instructions for the ambassadors at Calais. The terms demanded by the French 'seem unto the King right unreasonable', they declared. The ambassadors were to try to negotiate them away. If they could not, the English government was willing to make limited concessions. It would be content with a truce which allowed it to retain Normandy, provided that that included Mont-Saint-Michel. The Norman exiles could be allowed to return to their former domains, provided that they compensated the existing occupiers. They would consider releasing Charles of Orléans, but only on parole in order to enable him to persuade the French King to make peace on more acceptable terms. On the critical question of sovereignty, however, there were to be no concessions. On no account would Henry abandon even temporarily his title as King of France.[43]

When Kemp and his colleagues returned to Calais, Beaufort took one look at the new instructions and observed that the conference was doomed. In fact, the scope for compromise was never tested. On 11 September 1439, the date appointed for the resumption of negotiations, the French delegation did not appear. Instead, a copy was produced of a letter which Charles VII had sent to Isabella of Portugal and Charles of Orléans. The French King told them that he needed more time to consult his council and the princes of his family about the mediators' proposals. He had summoned the Estates-General to meet in Paris on 25 September and would give his answer after that. The English delegates regarded this as a subterfuge, designed to give the French time to overrun Meaux and the remaining English garrisons of the Île-de-France. Their suspicions were probably unfounded. Large representative assemblies were the traditional way in which the French monarchy had always rallied support for major decisions in the course of the war. But there was in any event nothing that they could do about it. On 15 September 1439, the three mediators, the Duchess, Beaufort and the Duke of Orléans, met and agreed to adjourn the conference until the following April.[44]

The occasion was not entirely wasted. The English and Burgundian teams remained at Calais and Saint-Omer for another fortnight to complete the settlement of their trade wars. At the end of September, a commercial treaty was agreed which resolved most of the issues between them for an initial period of three years. The boycott of English cloth in Flanders remained in place, for protectionist rather than political reasons, but the wool trade resumed and cloth was allowed to be freely exported from England to Philip's other domains. The grateful Members of Flanders made a gift of 6,000 *saluts* to the Duchess of Burgundy and 12,000 to Cardinal Beaufort personally. The commercial treaty did not put an end to the formal state of war between England and Burgundy, but in practice it ruled out the resumption of fighting. It was followed in 1442 by a long-term truce which remained in force until the end of the Anglo-French wars. Philip had finally achieved his ambition to shelter his domains from the Anglo-French war without engaging too closely with either belligerent. The more restrictive provisions of the Partition Acts, including the ban on credit sales, were for practical purposes repealed in January 1442. Two years later, enforcement of the rest was abandoned under pressure from the Staple merchants. Even they had come to recognise that their attempt to manipulate the wool market had been a damaging mistake.[45]

Beaufort and Kemp returned to England at the beginning of October 1439. The King, who was at Windsor, came to London and received them at Kennington on 9 October. The whole of the following day was given over to a discussion of the negotiations with France. Selected councillors were present, but not the full council and not the Duke of Gloucester. The negotiations at Oye had failed, but things were not the same as they had been. The English government had been pushed into some important concessions. For practical purposes their territorial ambitions were now limited to the retention of Aquitaine, Normandy and Calais free of the sovereignty of the King of France. They had privately reconciled themselves to the loss of Maine and their few surviving strongholds in the Île-de-France and Picardy. They clung to the title of King of France to save face and indulge their King, but without any expectation of making it a reality. Charles of Orléans had assumed growing importance during the three months that he had passed in Calais, and his status as a mediator had in the end been acknowledged by both sides. Privately, the English now accepted that he would have to be released if progress was to be made towards a negotiated peace. At Kennington, the council decided to concede the point.[46]

The council knew that Charles VII was facing domestic opposition from parts of the nobility. They believed that the failure to find a solution at Calais was due to powerful men at the French court, who were deliberately raising demands which they knew that the English could not accept. The only solution was to release Charles of Orléans so that he could influence the critical decisions in France. This plan was based on a very limited understanding of the political situation in France. Like all of the English councillors' plans to use the Duke of Orléans, it over-estimated his influence and underestimated the competence of the French King. The Duke was brought to London to await the King's final decision, and the terms of his release were negotiated with him there. Charles's ransom was fixed at 100,000 English nobles (£33,300 sterling), equivalent to 200,000 *écus* of France. In addition, he was to pay 20,000 nobles (£6,666) for the cost of his keep in England over the past quarter of a century. Before the Duke was released, he would have to pay the first 40,000 nobles in cash and provide guarantees for the rest, backed by bonds from the French King and nine prominent French magnates. Once released, he was to have a year in which to bring about a permanent peace between England

and France. If he succeeded, the whole ransom would be cancelled and any instalments received would be repaid. If not, then he must return to captivity in England until the ransom had been fully paid. On 22 October 1439, Henry VI declared that his ambassadors would return to Calais in April to resume the peace negotiations.[47]

The decision to release the Duke of Orléans was extremely controversial in England. It was contrary to the terms of Henry V's will, and for many of those who had served and revered him it seemed a betrayal of his memory. Even the council acknowledged that there had 'grown and spread in [the] people a noise and grouching' against it. The spokesman for the grouchers, naturally enough, was the Duke of Gloucester. The dispute opened the final chapter in his long vendetta against Henry Beaufort. Parliament opened in November 1439. The peace process was eventually discussed in January 1440, after the Christmas recess. The government was expecting trouble, and had transferred the sittings to Reading, far away from Gloucester's London allies. When the new session opened, Gloucester launched a blistering attack on the Cardinal from his seat in the Lords. He recounted all of his familiar grievances going back to the beginning of the reign but concentrating on the negotiations with France over the past five years. Gloucester alleged that Beaufort and Archbishop Kemp had taken control of the King and directed his foreign policy. He, Gloucester, had been pushed aside and prevented from playing the part to which his status as the senior royal prince and heir apparent to the throne entitled him. His many offers to take command in France had been spurned by the Cardinal's influence 'in preferring other[s] of his singular affection'. Gloucester was not just referring to Beaufort's shameless promotion of his nephews. He claimed that other outstanding figures who did not belong to the Cardinal's favoured circle, like the Duke of York and the Earl of Huntingdon, had been pushed into the shadows for the same reason. This had allowed Beaufort to conduct a succession of wasteful and pointless negotiations with France that never had any prospect of success owing to the cunning and deceitful ways of the French. The result, Gloucester thought, had been the destruction of the Anglo-Burgundian alliance, the loss of Meaux and much of northern France, and the expenditure of huge sums on diplomatic show which would have been better spent on war. Beaufort, he complained, was now proposing to resume the negotiations in the spring and to release the Duke of Orléans unilaterally.[48]

It looked as if the Duke of Gloucester was seeking to impeach the Cardinal before the Parliamentary peers. The King was sufficiently concerned to commission a rebuttal. The council issued a 'plain declaration', drafted by Adam Moleyns. The release of the Duke of Orléans, they said, had been ordered on the personal authority of the King. What 'he had done in the said matter he hath done of himself of his own advice and courage . . . moved and stirred by God and of reason'. Some of his reasons were said to be too sensitive to be publicly disclosed. This probably referred to the council's covert dealings with Charles VII's domestic opponents. But the council made no secret of their hope that Charles of Orléans might break the impasse which had so far frustrated the peace negotiations. They did not mince their words. England had won many battles, captured many notable prisoners and conquered many places. But the war was lost. France was 'so ample, so great and so mighty' that it was unlikely ever to be conquered by force of arms. There were too many walled cities and towns, too many garrisoned castles, too many impassable rivers. Normandy, which was substantially all that was left to the English in the north, was ruined and in the long run indefensible. In the past six or seven years, parts of the duchy were said to have lost nine-tenths of their population. Those who remained would willingly throw off the King's government if they could. Only the presence of the English garrisons was holding them down. This could not continue. The cost was beyond England's resources. In the past thirty months alone, the council claimed to have spent half a million marks (£333,000) on war, but they had still been unable to prevent the loss of some major fortresses. With a schism now opening up between the Pope and the Council of Basel, peace between lay princes was a moral duty which the King could not evade. Henry, they said, was determined to bring an end to a war that had now endured for a hundred years and had shed so much Christian blood for so little purpose.[49]

In the end, the King's ministers defeated their domestic opponents with ease. Beaufort was not even called upon to answer the charges against him, and the Duke's bitter denunciation of his rival had no impact on the government's policy. It did, however, mark a turning point in the political fortunes of Beaufort himself. He was now an old man. He had been an active participant in national and international politics for forty years. For all his doubts about England's war, he had failed to bring it to an end. Over the following months and years, his influence waned. He appeared less often in council. His peace policy was pursued by his successors. Pre-eminent among them was Beaufort's real political heir, William Pole Earl of Suffolk.

The French Estates-General had been summoned to Paris for 25 September 1439. In the end an outbreak of plague in the capital made it necessary to change the venue to Orléans. The assembly opened there a month late in the great hall of the ducal castle. It was one of the fullest gatherings of its kind for many years. In addition to the principal noblemen of France, it included the representatives of the absent princes: Philip the Good, John V of Brittany and Charles of Orléans. The opening session was the occasion for a public exhibition of the power of the Angevin caucus around the King. Charles VII entered the hall side by side with Yolande of Anjou. She and her son Charles of Anjou and their allies stood out among the circle of princes standing around the throne. The King himself cut a poor figure by comparison. He appears to have been going through one of his periodical bouts of depression. Jean Juvénal complained that except at the opening and closing sessions he was invisible, hiding away in his private apartments and refusing to receive anyone but his intimates, as if the proceedings were not really his concern.

The Chancellor Regnault de Chartres opened the proceedings with a report on the negotiations with England. Copies of the mediators' proposals were distributed. The question before the assembly was whether to continue with negotiations on that basis in the spring, or to abandon them and prosecute the war to a conclusion. After the Chancellor's address, the delegates discussed the proposals in the absence of the King for a week. At the end of that time opinions were divided and no firm conclusion had been reached. So two teams of advocates were appointed to present the case for each side. The Count of Vendôme and the Bishop of Poitiers spoke for continuing the negotiations on the basis of the mediators' proposals, while Marshal Lafayette and the Count of Dunois spoke for prosecuting the war. When they were done, the consensus was that the peace conference should resume but in the meantime the King should keep up the pressure on the English on the marches of Normandy. As in earlier assemblies, the dominant theme was the collapse of public order in much of France, the indiscipline of the King's troops and the ravages of the freelance companies. According to Jean Juvénal, who was present throughout, the general sentiment was that the loss of Normandy was a grievous price but worth paying for peace. Many of the participants must have agreed with him that the war now had 'no rhyme or reason'. His view of the mediators' proposals was surprisingly similar to that of Henry VI's Norman councillors: putting Henry VI's French title into abeyance for thirty years would be a tacit admission of its lack of substance and a moral victory for France. Why not grasp it with both hands? Charles VII's private views are not recorded. But at the last moment he deferred a final decision until a further meeting of the Estates-General, to be held at Bourges in February 1440. His explanation was that although the northern provinces were well represented at Orléans, Languedoc was not. In particular the young Dauphin Louis was not present. This was probably not the whole truth. Sentiment on the French King's council was running strongly against the resumption of the peace conference. They did not want to see the mediators' compromise publicly endorsed by the Estates-General.[50]

One reason was that they were planning a major offensive against English positions in Maine and Lower Normandy. The *écorcheurs* who had supplied the main strength of the army of Meaux were still in arms at the King's pay. Richemont concentrated them at Angers, and then led them north to join the regular French forces stationed on the march of Maine. The outcome was an unhappy story. In November 1439 the combined army entered Maine in four columns, led by Richemont himself and three prominent commanders in the region: Jean de Bueil, the Duke of Alençon and the Marshal André de Laval lord of Lohéac. Sainte-Suzanne, one of the principal English fortresses of the region, was captured by escalade with the connivance of the English captain of the watch. This man had been Alençon's prisoner of war and had been promised his release in return for delivering up the fortress. The abandoned ruins of Pontorson and Saint-James de Beuvron were reoccupied without resistance. On 30 November, the columns joined up outside Avranches, the great English fortress-town guarding the approaches to the Cotentin and Mont-Saint-Michel. The siege of Avranches lasted for three weeks until 23 December. On that date an English army fought its way through to the beleaguered city under the command of Sir John Talbot and Edmund Beaufort Earl of Dorset. They had stripped the Norman garrisons to the bone to manage this, but the risk paid off. Emerging from the southern gates of the town, the English fell upon the main French encampment. The

French army was about five times the size of the English one. But it was spread out along their extensive siege lines, and a large part of it was stranded north of the river Sée on the other side of the town. Richemont rapidly drew up the men who were at hand in battle order. His *écorcheur* captains, however, fled the field, leaving him to face the English with a handful of men. Richemont was forced to flee in his turn, abandoning large stores of foodstuffs and most of his artillery to the enemy.[51]

The delegates summoned to Bourges gathered in the city in the course of February 1440 for the adjourned meeting of the Estates-General. But the assembly never opened. Over the winter, the peace process was overtaken by the aristocratic rebellion known as the 'Praguerie', after the Hussite rising in Prague which had become a byword for the breakdown of civil society. Once again, the main object of the rebellion was to bring down the King's Angevin ministers. Once again, the leading spirit was the Duke of Bourbon. The immediate occasion for the rising was an ordinance against the companies of *écorcheurs*, which had been debated in the Estates and was proclaimed by the council on 2 November 1439. This ambitious measure was directly targeted against the noble patrons of the freelance companies, and in particular against the Duke of Bourbon who was the greatest of them all. It sought to put an end to the companies' depredations by taking them permanently into royal service and promising them regular pay. It made the recruitment of troops a royal monopoly, reserving the appointment of their captains to the King alone. The nobility were permitted to employ garrisons to defend their own castles, but their companies were no longer to operate beyond their walls. At the same time, the ordinance sought to make taxation a royal monopoly by forbidding the nobility to interfere with the collection of royal taxes or to impose taxes of their own in their domains.

The Duke of Bourbon had sat in the meeting of the royal council which approved the ordinance, but he was already building another coalition to challenge the ministers who had devised it. The Duke of Alençon, Marshal Lafayette and Jacques de Chabannes, old allies of Bourbon's, joined the plot. So did Bourbon's cousin the Count of Vendôme. Dunois was won over to their cause by suggestions that Charles VII's ministers were obstructing the release of his half-brother. Georges de la Trémoille, an old enemy of the house of Anjou, still resenting the coup which had displaced him in 1433, sent a secret message of support. The Duke of Brittany was not an active participant but was certainly a sympathiser. As for Philip the Good, his position was enigmatic, as he no doubt intended it to be. He was certainly in touch with the plotters during the period when Bourbon was building his coalition, and probably expressed his sympathy just as the Duke of Brittany had done.[52]

Bourbon's first idea was to kidnap the King and murder his councillors while they were staying at Angers in November 1439. This crude plan proved to be impractical. Security around the King was too tight. A better one was hatched in February 1440 when Bourbon met his allies in the castle of Blois, the headquarters of the house of Orléans. They proposed to take a leaf out of John the Fearless's book. They would put pressure on the King with a combination of military force, appeals to the towns and promises to reduce taxation. The military force would be recruited from the companies of *écorcheurs* who were now encamped near Angers after the debacle of Avranches. All of this was noisy and hard to conceal from the government. The meeting at Blois was interrupted by the arrival of Richemont, Poton de Saintrailles and Raoul de Gaucourt, who had been sent by the King to reason with them. They got nowhere. The Duke of Bourbon responded with a stream of abuse. Dunois threatened the Constable with arrest.[53]

Undeterred by the leakage of their plans, the rebels managed shortly afterwards to recruit the Dauphin Louis to their cause. The future Louis XI was then sixteen years old. He was quite unlike his father: unkempt, big-mouthed and rather coarse. Louis had never got on with his moody and reclusive father. He was frustrated by the tutelage of Charles's servants. He particularly resented the fact that the Dauphiné, the traditional appanage of the heir to the throne, was still in the King's hands and he himself derived no income from it. In 1440 the young Dauphin was serving a political apprenticeship as his father's lieutenant in Languedoc. But he had recently been sent into Poitou to enforce the ordinance against the *écorcheurs*. From gamekeeper, Louis turned poacher. Towards the end of February, he met the Duke of Alençon at Niort. Alençon dangled before him the prospect of supplanting his father. Charles would be treated as incapable of governing and Louis installed as regent in his place. Louis was easily seduced. He dismissed the Count of La Marche, the tutor whom the King had assigned to guide him, and a number of other members of his household whom he regarded as his father's spies, and joined the plotters. His participation was a significant boost to their cause. Letters were drafted in his name appealing for support. He was expected to win over the more reluctant captains of the army and many towns struggling under the rising burden of taxation.[54]

The fighting began in March 1440. The rebels successfully drew to their banner most of the companies of *écorcheurs*. They concentrated their strength in two centres. Bourbon established his headquarters in the fortress-town of Loches in Touraine. He had with him the companies of the Chabannes brothers, the two bastards of Bourbon and a number of lesser captains. The Dauphin was at Niort with the Duke of Alençon and his troops and the *routier* companies of La Trémoille's old ally Jean de la Roche.

Charles VII was on his way to preside over the Estates-General at Bourges when he learned of these events. He was accompanied by Prégent de Coëtivy Admiral of France and Pierre de Brézé, both close associates of Charles of Anjou. There were very few troops with them, only the King's personal bodyguard and the retinues of his companions. But it was essential to nip the rebellion in the bud before it spread any further. So, abandoning his plans, Charles turned south and marched on Loches. Some of Bourbon's freelance companies were encountered on the road and put to flight. Bourbon himself fled to his domains in Auvergne, leaving Pierre d'Amboise to hold the town against the King. At Loches, the King was joined by the Constable with his large retinue of Bretons. Leaving part of their army to contain the rebels in Loches, Charles and Richemont invaded Poitou, which was emerging as the epicentre of the rebellion.

At Poitiers, where he celebrated Easter, the King received the news that Alençon and the Dauphin, accompanied by Jean de la Roche, were advancing towards him. They had already occupied the castle of Saint-Maixent, standing over the road to Niort. Other rebel detachments had occupied La Trémoille's town of Melle, probably with the connivance of his officers. Several other places in Poitou had fallen to them. Charles VII, by now equipped with an artillery train and reinforced by troops raised in Anjou and Poitou, marched on Melle. He recaptured it without difficulty, and then moved on to Saint-Maixent. Alençon, Jean de la Roche and the Dauphin slipped out of the town before the King's army appeared, leaving their men to hold out as long as they could.

After ten days of bombardment, Saint-Maixent surrendered to the King's mercy. Charles's mercy was selective. The Duke of Alençon's companies had served in royal garrisons on the marches of Maine for years. They were spared, on swearing an oath never to take up arms against him again. But Jean de la Roche's men were regarded as freebooters, and their captains were summarily beheaded. The three leaders took refuge in Alençon's town of Niort. But they did not give much for their chances of holding out there, and shortly fled to join the Duke of Bourbon in Auvergne.[55]

Echoes of these events reached Henry VI's council in England during the early summer of 1440. It was not easy to know how to react. The rebel leaders were unpromising allies for the English. The only firm supporter of the peace process among them was the Count of Vendôme, and he took a marginal part in the rebellion. Bourbon and Lafayette believed in prosecuting the war to the end. Dunois's instincts were the same, although qualified in his case by his concern for the interests of his half-brother in England. The English had little to offer the plotters. The only English troops in a position to intervene quickly in support of them were those of the Earl of Huntingdon, Henry VI's lieutenant in Gascony. Huntingdon was in fact approached by agents of Alençon and Jean de la Roche in April, after the fall of Saint-Maixent, but it was too late. The Earl was only interested if the rebels were in a position to cede territory to him, and by then they hardly had any to cede. But although the Praguerie was not a military opportunity for the English, it was a political opportunity which generated much excitement at Westminster. It reignited the debate about the release of the Duke of Orléans. As France subsided into anarchy, the government's deal with Charles of Orléans seemed ever more promising. The council had the Duke brought to Westminster on 8 May to finalise the arrangements. Only the difficulty in raising the first instalment of the ransom and finding security for the rest now stood in the way of his release.[56]

The resumption of the peace conference had been fixed for 15 April, or at the latest 1 May 1440. Philip the Good and Isabella of Portugal arrived in early April at his pleasure palace at Hesdin, some fifty miles south of Calais, which became their base throughout the following months. Neither of the Duchess's two co-mediators, Beaufort and Charles of Orléans, appeared. The only French ambassador whose presence is recorded was the Chancellor Regnault de Chartres, who arrived at Saint-Omer early in May. The Count of Dunois had broken with the leaders of the Praguerie and made his peace with the King, claiming (not very plausibly) to have been deceived about its objectives. He arrived shortly afterwards as his half-brother's representative. Henry VI was represented by a new delegation led by William Wells Bishop of Rochester, a political lightweight with no diplomatic experience and no instructions to discuss either a peace or a long truce until Charles of Orléans was present. The English were dragging their feet until Charles could return to France to join in the power struggle in progress there.[57]

The delegations never met face to face. The English remained at Calais and the French at Saint-Omer, while the Duchess laboriously negotiated with each in turn by messenger from Hesdin. The tent city outside Oye was deserted. The discussions revolved entirely around the arrangements for the Duke of Orléans's release. It was Philip the Good who made the running. He proposed a formal alliance to put an end to the vendetta provoked by the murder of their two fathers. It was to be sealed by a marriage between Charles of Orléans and Philip's fourteen-year-old niece, Marie of Cleves. It was Philip too who made it possible to pay the first instalment of the ransom. A complicated transaction was agreed. The prisoner ceded to Philip all his domains in Picardy, northern Champagne and Hainaut, including the barony of Coucy and the counties of Soissons and Fère-en-Tardenois, for 85,000 *écus*, which Philip agreed to transfer to England to satisfy the 40,000 nobles due on his release. Philip would then settle these domains on Marie of Cleves as her dowry, plus 15,000 *écus* in cash. The money was raised by borrowing from the towns of Flanders and Artois, from his kinsmen and allies in the Low Countries, and from the bankers of Bruges.[58]

In England, the long debate about the Duke of Orléans's release was finally drawing to a close. In May 1440, the council made it clear that they intended to go ahead with it as soon as the money was assured. At the beginning of June, Humphrey Duke of Gloucester submitted a formal protest which he asked to be enrolled in the Chancery records. Gloucester's protest was written against the background of the anarchy which seemed to be engulfing Valois France. He shared the exaggerated view of Charles VII's weakness that had become common currency at Westminster. He believed that if the Duke of Orléans was freed, he would probably become regent and effective ruler of Valois

France. But unlike the other councillors, he thought that an Orléans regency would put England in mortal danger. The Duke, he wrote, was a Valois, whose interests were bound up with the fortunes of the dynasty. If he became Regent of France, he was more likely to unite the warring lords of France against England than to make peace on English terms. His allies in the south-west, the Counts of Armagnac and Foix and the lord of Albret, would be deployed against the English King's possessions in Gascony. He might even join forces with the Duke of Burgundy to expel the English from Normandy. It was not as if the ransom amounted to much. It would make hardly a dent in the financial deficit of Normandy. In England itself, there would be a terrible retribution against the men responsible for this act, once the King's domains in France were lost beyond recall:

> I never was, am, nor never shall be consenting, counselling nor agreeing to his deliverance nor elargissment ... otherwise than is expressed in my said Lord my brother's last will, or else [in return for] so great good whereby my Lord's both realms and subjects be increased and eased.

Gloucester's protest fell on deaf ears. On 2 July 1440, the terms agreed with the Duke of Orléans were formally drawn up and sealed in the King's presence in the palace of Westminster.[59]

In France, the speed and vigour with which Charles VII suppressed the Praguerie did much to undermine the rationale for Orléans's release. The King was obviously not the political nonentity that the English had supposed. By the end of April 1440, the rebellion had been extinguished at its centre in Poitou, and its leaders had taken refuge with the Duke of Bourbon in central France. But Bourbon's subjects there were lukewarm in their support for his cause. His principal towns, including Clermont and Montferrand, declared against him. The Estates of Auvergne assembled on its own initiative and voted a subsidy to the King to aid the suppression of the revolt. Charles VII, whose army had by now swollen to some 2,800 men, marched into the Bourbonnais, taking one garrisoned castle after another. As the rebels' position grew more precarious, the Duke of Bourbon's noble supporters and the companies of *écorcheurs* on whom they had counted melted away. The rebel leaders began to look for a way out. At first, they hoped to negotiate a compromise. The Dauphin took the lead. But the King refused to bargain with his son or to accept anything less than his unconditional submission. The

Duke of Alençon was the first openly to break ranks. He submitted to the King at the end of June. The final act was played out in the middle of July in the small town of Cusset in northern Auvergne. The Dauphin and the Duke of Bourbon submitted and were pardoned, together with their allies. Some captains of *écorcheurs*, like the Chabannes brothers, were included in the informal amnesty which followed. Others were not. When Alexander Bastard of Bourbon came before the King in Champagne in the following year, he was arrested and after a summary trial was tied up in a bag and drowned in the river Aube. As for the Dauphin, he was dismissed as lieutenant in Languedoc and deprived of his own household, thus placing him under the direct tutelage of his father. It was a humiliation which the young prince never forgot.[60]

On 28 October 1440, Charles of Orléans was brought into Westminster Abbey to attend Mass and to swear on the sacrament to abide by the undertakings that he had given to his English captors. He promised never to bear arms against the King of England and to work unsparingly to bring about a permanent peace with France. Henry VI and much of the peerage were present to witness the occasion. The Duke of Gloucester entered the abbey with the rest but stormed out theatrically as the Mass began and made for the Thames where his barge was moored. Six days later, the first instalment of the ransom was paid into the English Treasury by a syndicate of Florentine bankers on behalf of the Duke of Burgundy, and the bonds of Orléans's guarantors in France were delivered to Henry VI's agents to secure the balance when it became due. The Duke was formally released from captivity and placed in the custody of Garter King of Arms to be escorted to Calais. On 26 November, Charles married Marie of Cleves at Saint-Omer, and was received into the Order of the Golden Fleece at a special chapter of the knights. As soon as the formalities of his release had been completed, the English King authorised his ambassadors at Calais to fix a fresh date for the next session of the peace conference. A date of 1 May 1441 was agreed. By then, the English hoped that Orléans would have brought about a change of mood at his cousin's court. The Duke himself was characteristically optimistic. He told the crowds who greeted him as he passed through the towns of northern France that he had come to make peace. He was privy to the secret thoughts of Henry VI, he said.[61]

*

On 8 August 1440 Edmund Beaufort Earl of Dorset and Sir John Talbot appeared outside the walls of Harfleur. The town had been a serious threat to the English government in Normandy ever since its capture by the French at the end of 1435. The siege of the place was to be the main military operation of the year. Harfleur had a garrison of 270 men, the largest in the French King's service, in addition to another forty men based in the walled town of Montivilliers seven miles to the north. The captain of the town was Jean d'Estouteville lord of Torcy, the man who had deserted the English cause in 1424 on the eve of the battle of Verneuil. The English dug trenches around the walls and fortified their siege lines with watchtowers at regular intervals. Artillery had been taken from several fortresses of the march and assembled at Rouen or Cherbourg before being carried to the siege on barges. The Earl of Somerset commanded a field army to guard against the approach of a relief force and protect the marches of the duchy against opportunistic French raids. The troops participating in these operations came from almost every garrison in Normandy. A flotilla of ships sealed off the town from the sea. At Plymouth, more ships were being made ready to join them.[62]

The French made a determined attempt to save Harfleur. The principal royal officer in the region was Charles of Artois Count of Eu, Charles VII's lieutenant in the Caux and the Beauvaisis. He controlled a number of garrisons, including those of Beauvais and Dieppe, but did not have the strength to attempt a relief on his own. Instead, the operation was directed by the King's ministers from the Loire. An army several thousand strong was mustered at Orléans. Men were withdrawn from French garrisons as far away as the march of Gascony to swell its numbers. A heavy *taille* was imposed in Languedoil to finance it. Early in September 1440, Charles VII arrived at Orléans to confer with his principal captains. They decided to create two task forces. The larger force, commanded by Raoul de Gaucourt and the Count of Dunois, was to join forces with the Count of Eu before attacking the English siege lines from the north. They passed through Paris and made their base at Abbeville on the Somme. The other task force was placed under the command of Poton de Saintrailles and the Angevin captain Pierre de Brézé. They were ordered to create a diversion on the southern march of Normandy in the hope of drawing off the Earl of Somerset's field army. The English were well informed about these movements. Dorset operated an efficient intelligence service. He had spies in Picardy watching the progress of the relief force. Messages passing between Abbeville and Harfleur were regularly intercepted and read.[63]

Early in October 1440 the French army of relief moved south from Abbeville and entered the Caux. At Montivilliers, a short distance north of Harfleur, they divided their forces. One group, under the Count of Eu, embarked on boats collected at Chef de Caux to make their way round the coast and reinforce the garrison of Harfleur. The other, under Dunois, made straight for the English siege lines. Both groups failed. The Count of Eu's flotilla tried to reach the town by passing along the shore inside the ring of English ships, but most of them grounded on the sandbanks of the Seine. The men waded ashore some distance from the town. They were cornered by Talbot and driven off. On 14 October Dunois's column approached Talbot's sector of the English lines carrying timber pontoons to bridge the trenches. They launched an assault but found that their pontoons were too short. Within half an hour they had been put to flight. Inside the town, the garrison was running low on food. The captains of the relief army gathered at Montivilliers towards the end of October to review the situation. By now their own supplies were close to exhaustion. They decided that there was no option but to withdraw into Picardy. The garrison, seeing them marching off, opened negotiations with the besiegers. On 28 October they surrendered.[64]

The capture of Harfleur was a famous event in England, where control of the Channel ports had always had more resonance with the public than the wider territorial ambitions of the Crown. The town, as one of John Paston's correspondents observed, was a 'great jewel to all England and in especial to our country'. Its capture enabled the English to complete the pacification of the Caux. But victory came at a price. At the high point of the operation, more than 3,000 men had been engaged, either in the siege lines or in the Earl of Somerset's field army, about half of the entire English forces in Normandy. The garrisons had been stripped of men to make up the numbers, leaving the marches of Normandy dangerously exposed at a time when French troops were active on all fronts. The Earl of Somerset responded to each scare as it arose. Reinforcements were sent to Pontoise, Mantes, Vernon and Avranches, all of which were at one time or another thought to be threatened. But Somerset could not be everywhere at once, and the blow fell elsewhere. In early October 1440, Poton de

Saintrailles and Pierre de Brézé came up the valley of the Eure from Orléans with between 2,000 and 3,000 men. Brézé laid siege to Conches-en-Ouche. The place was in a poor state of repair and half its garrison was away at the siege of Harfleur. Many of the rest had been given leave of absence. The defenders surrendered after a few days in return for their lives. Poton passed down the valley and reoccupied the town of Louviers, which was undefended.[65]

These were serious losses. The French rapidly repaired the walls of Conches, which became a base for damaging raids around the frontier fortresses of Evreux and Verneuil. In a remarkably short time, they recut the ditches of Louviers and began to rebuild the walls and gates from the debris of the old ramparts which were still lying on the ground by the ditches. In the following year they built a fort on the left bank of the Seine at Saint-Pierre-du-Vauvray, thus cutting the route along the Seine valley upstream of Rouen. These incidents spread panic across Lancastrian Normandy. The gravity of the situation can be measured by the efforts made to expel the three garrisons over the following months. The most experienced commanders in the theatre, Talbot, Fauconberg and Scales, gathered an army of 2,400 men at Pont-Audemer at the end of November. Many of them had had to be recruited from the riff-raff of freelance English soldiery living on the land. They spent six months prowling around Louviers without actually attacking it or attempting a siege, while their strength was gradually wasted by desertions. Meanwhile, the French poured men into the region. Charles VII himself, accompanied by Charles of Anjou and the Dauphin, came to Chartres to direct the defence of Louviers and Conches from a distance. The English made no impression on either place. In the spring of 1441, they built a fort on an island off Elbeuf, at the confluence of the Seine and the Eure, to prevent the new French garrisons from penetrating into Upper Normandy. Then they abandoned the campaign.[66]

Many of the problems of Normandy in these months were due to the void of authority at the heart of the English administration. Two years after the death of the Earl of Warwick he had still not been replaced. After six months of government by a temporary commission, there had been a review of the situation at Westminster in November 1439 during the Parliamentary session. A delegation from the Grand Conseil led by Pierre Cauchon arrived in England for the occasion.

Gloucester once again put himself forward for the job. This time Beaufort, weakened by the failure of his diplomacy, was unable to stop the council offering it to him. But without Beaufort's money, it proved impossible to raise an army consistent with Gloucester's status. He insisted on a delay until the summer, while funds were found and troops recruited. In the meantime, John Beaufort Earl of Somerset, who had been the Cardinal's candidate, served as acting lieutenant, ostensibly until Gloucester's arrival. The whole issue was overtaken by the row over the release of the Duke of Orléans. The government needed a representative in France who would cooperate with the peace process at what was expected to be a critical point. Gloucester was obviously unsuitable for that role. Somerset was anathema to Gloucester and equally unsuitable for other reasons. Eventually, Henry VI's ministers turned to the Duke of York, the only candidate with the necessary status who was acceptable to all sides. On 2 July 1440, he was nominated for the second time as lieutenant in Normandy, for a term of five years. However, although the Earl of Somerset returned to England in early November 1440, the Duke of York delayed his departure for several months while he haggled with the council about the terms of his appointment. Normandy was left leaderless.[67]

Richard of York regarded the lieutenancy as a poisoned chalice. It put him in the eye of the political storm provoked by the peace policy. It made him responsible for the defence of a duchy which was already well on the way to being lost. He would have to incur large personal commitments to his staff and military retinue, on behalf of a government with a long history of default. He took advice from experienced Normandy hands, including Sir John Fastolf and Sir William Oldhall, and set out his terms. They were exacting. He was to be paid an annual fee of 36,000 *francs* (£4,000) from Norman revenues to cover the cost of his household and personal staff, more than any of his predecessors except for the Duke of Bedford. In addition to the initial costs of the annual expeditionary armies from England, which had always been met from English revenues, York was to have an allowance of £20,000 a year for the defence of Normandy, secured by assignments from English revenues. On top of that, there was to be a supplementary allowance for any 'great war or laying of great sieges'. He was to be supplied with six 'great guns of divers sorts', twelve lighter pieces and fourteen professional gunners, together with gunstones and saltpetre which were known to be in short supply in Normandy. If Dieppe was besieged, he was to be provided with ships to blockade it and an extra 2,000 armed men to man them. The Duke insisted that he must have the authority to deal with the long-standing problems of the Norman duchy. He must have complete control of the revenues of Normandy. He must be entitled to nominate his own council, to appoint captains and to dismiss those who did not perform their duties even if they had tenure for life or fixed terms. York's financial terms were agreed, and he seems to have received some kind of assurance that his other demands would be met too. He reserved the right to throw up his appointment and return to England if they were not. The new lieutenant was well aware of the scale of the challenge facing him. He demanded an assurance that if he did his duty he would not be blamed if the duchy was lost, 'be it by battle, rebellion of the people or otherwise'.[68]

The promises made to the Duke of York represented a significant increase in the burden of the war on English revenues. But he was fortunate in his timing. Although Norman revenues continued to decline, 1440 and 1441 were years of recovery for those of England. In February 1440, Parliament had voted one and a half standard subsidies. The end of the trade wars with the Burgundian Low Countries was marked by a brief spike in exports of both raw wool and finished cloth, which generated the largest customs receipts of the reign. At the same time, the King's ministers put an end to the system under which the revenues of the Duchy of Lancaster were reserved to the payment of his father's debts, thus opening an important new revenue stream. The first instalment of the Duke of Orléans's ransom brought a welcome additional windfall. These receipts made possible a significant increase in the size of the annual expeditionary army from England. Richard of York's army was to be 3,200 strong, including two earls and four bannerets. This was later increased to 3,600. In the event it was larger still, because a shortfall in the number of men-at-arms had to be made good by recruiting three archers for every missing knight or squire. The recruitment of these men depended heavily on the Duke's wealth and station. Most of the army was raised by captains who were his retainers in England or were notable figures in the counties where he was a great lord. It is unlikely that anyone else, apart from the King, could have raised such a force at this stage of the war. Unfortunately, although his lieutenancy formally began on 1 September 1440, the recruiting of his army took several months. As an interim measure, it was decided that an advance guard of 800 men would sail for the Seine in September. But the departure of York himself with the rest of his army was repeatedly deferred until the following June.[69]

In the meantime, the French resolved upon a major offensive against the few remaining English fortresses around Paris. With the government of Normandy rudderless and the Duke of York delayed in England, the opportunity was too good to miss. Between January and April 1441, Charles VII was in Champagne with Charles of Anjou and the Constable, operating against the companies of *écorcheurs* who were still defying the ordinance of 1439. He had a large army with him. Their numbers were swollen by the companies of *écorcheurs* themselves, many of whom submitted to him and were taken into his service at pay. On 28 April 1441 the King presided at an important council meeting at Laon. It was attended by Charles of Anjou, the Chancellor, the military officers of the Crown and several of his leading captains. The meeting came at a critical moment. The peace conference on the march of Calais was due to reopen three days later on 1 May. The French delegates were either waiting at Saint-Omer or on their way there. At the last moment it was decided to revoke their powers and to invade the valley of the Oise instead. There would be a better time to pursue peace, when fresh conquests had boosted the King's bargaining power. The new plan was to capture Creil and Pontoise, the last remaining English fortresses of the Oise valley, and then invade Normandy itself. This would finally liberate Paris from the loose siege which it had endured for more than a decade. But the King had higher hopes for the campaign. He thought that it might even mark the final expulsion of the English from Normandy. Fresh troops were summoned to join his army at Compiègne. On 19 May 1441, Charles VII laid siege to Creil.[70]

The Grand Conseil regarded Creil as one of the most important fortresses of France. Situated on an island in the Oise and defended by fortified bridges on either side, it commanded the northern approach to Pontoise and the French Vexin. Sixty miles away at Pont-de-l'Arche, Talbot struggled to raise an army of relief. At Westminster Henry VI and his councillors were receiving cries of alarm. The Duke of York's fleet had been lying idle in the Solent since March and almost all of his troops were ready. He should have sailed by the beginning of April. But in spite of the urgency York seemed to be in no hurry.

A certain testiness entered into the council's correspondence with him. The King, they told him, 'prayeth him heartily to shape him in all commodious haste to the other [side] of the sea'. The French army was receiving reinforcements all the time and Creil was in danger of being lost. 'By his speedy coming shall well success,' the council wrote. By the time that the Duke of York received this missive, Creil had fallen. The French invested it from both sides of the river. Their bombards rapidly opened up several breaches. On 24 May, the fifth day of the siege, they assaulted the walls on the western side. After an hour of fierce fighting on the rubble, its captain, the Warwickshire knight Sir William Peyto, surrendered in return for the lives of his garrison. From Senlis, where he had established his headquarters, Charles VII called for reinforcements of infantry, crossbowmen and artillery from the northern towns. On 6 June, his army appeared outside Pontoise, which was now the last remaining English fortress on the approaches to Paris.[71]

From Rouen, the Grand Conseil dispatched an assessment of the situation to Westminster. The French army, they reported, was large, well equipped and in excellent spirits. They had repeatedly warned the English council of imminent catastrophe. The response had been a succession of promises that first the Duke of Gloucester and then the Duke of York would shortly be with them. None of them had been honoured. Promises from Westminster were no longer believed at Rouen. Discipline had collapsed. Even the charismatic Talbot was having difficulty in getting his orders obeyed. In the meantime, the government of Normandy had been left 'like a ship tossed upon the sea by the changing winds, with no captain, no helmsman, no rudder, no anchor and no sails'. Corroboration of this grim picture reached Westminster at about the same time from François de Surienne, the Aragonese mercenary in English service. He had seen which way the wind was blowing for months. He abandoned Saint-Germain-en-Laye, selling out to the French while he could still get a good price. Returning to Normandy, he found a smell of rot in the air. The Norman treasury was bankrupt. Men called up to serve in the field were still being paid, but the rest had received nothing for over a year. His own garrison troops at Longny in Perche were deserting to eke out a living in the towns. Everywhere, Englishmen who had put down roots in Normandy were worried about their future. They no longer believed in victory. They were more worried about the prospect of peace. They had heard

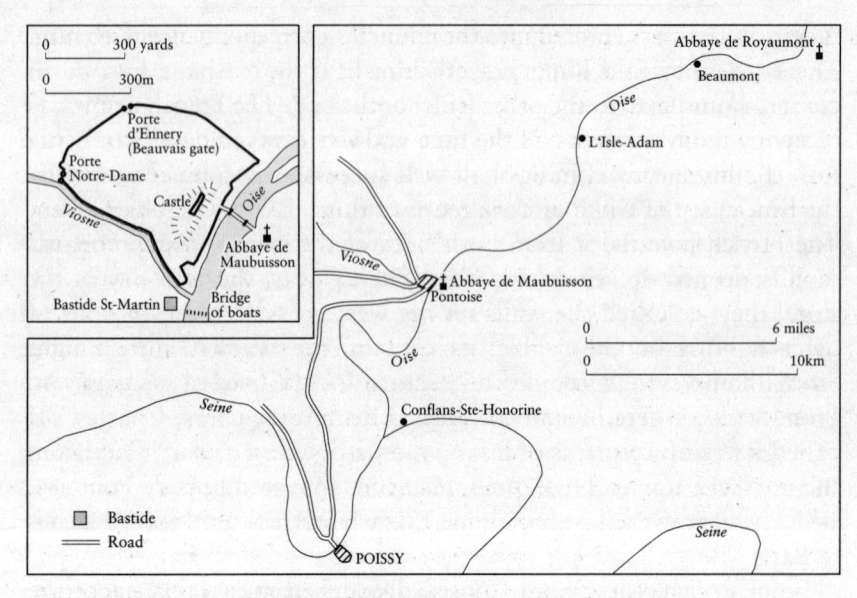

11 The siege of Pontoise, June–November 1441

rumours that the old pre-conquest proprietors might be allowed to return. If so, what would become of them?[72]

Pontoise was a densely populated town on the west bank of the Oise seventeen miles north-west of Paris. The town was a natural fortress, defended by the Oise on the east, by the broad waterway of the Viosne to the south and by a deep ditch on the west and north. A stone bridge of twelve arches, defended at each end by powerful fortified gateways, carried the Roman road from Paris to Rouen into the town. Towering 150 feet over the Oise from the centre of the town was a long spur of rock with its own walls, on which stood the old royal castle. The English had carried out extensive repairs. They had installed artillery around the citadel and greatly increased the size of its garrison. But Pontoise had serious weaknesses in spite of its strong position. The walls dated from the twelfth century, and like all town walls of that era they were vulnerable to artillery. The French had garrisons downstream at Conflans-Sainte-Honorine and Poissy, which meant that the English garrison had to be laboriously supplied by escorted overland convoys.[73]

The French were never able to invest Pontoise completely. To do that they would have had to divide their forces into three parts separated by the Oise and the Viosne and risk seeing them surprised and defeated in detail. Most of their army was stationed on the east bank of the Oise opposite the head of the bridge. Their artillery rapidly destroyed three arches of the bridge and wrecked the fortified gate at its eastern end. After two days of assaults the gateway was captured and garrisoned on 12 June 1441. Charles VII established his headquarters in the walled abbey of Maubuisson, a royal foundation for Cistercian nuns half a mile from the town. Downstream of the walls, Charles of Anjou and the Admiral Prégent de Coëtivy had a pontoon bridge built over the Oise, which enabled them to occupy the suburban abbey of St Martin on the opposite bank. They fortified the monastic buildings with ramparts, ditches and artillery and garrisoned it with several hundred men. The north-west side of the town was never invested. The fortified Beauvais gate remained open and uncovered throughout. Charles VII was under severe financial pressure and after six months in the field was struggling to keep his army together. His freelance companies would desert him without hesitation if their pay stopped. The siege proved to be a test of the government's growing authority to impose taxes at will. A *taille* of 100,000 *livres* was imposed on the Lyonnais and the Loire provinces. Local *tailles* were imposed on Paris and the cities of Champagne, Picardy and the Île-de-France. Forced loans were levied on churchmen and civil servants.[74]

Sir John Talbot was thirty miles away at Vernon on the Seine, trying to raise a field army from the garrisons of Normandy, freelance soldiers at large, and landowners owing military service. Remarkably in the circumstances, he was able to raise no fewer than 3,300 men from these sources, an unprecedented achievement that must have left many sectors of the march almost defenceless. Between 22 and 24 June, Talbot, Fauconberg and Scales led this force towards Pontoise with a convoy of supplies and munitions. In the French camp, there was a debate about whether to intercept them. The Constable would have concentrated his men by the bastide Saint-Martin and offered battle. He believed that victory was assured. But all the old French fears of battle against the English on open ground returned to haunt Charles's other councillors. They remembered Agincourt and Verneuil only too well. At the last moment Charles VII ordered Richemont to avoid a pitched battle at all costs. The English entered the town by the Beauvais gate without opposition. Scales stayed in Pontoise with part of this force and took command of the defence, while Talbot withdrew into Normandy taking the sick and wounded with him.[75]

The Duke of York finally sailed from the Solent at the end of June 1441. He landed at Harfleur with just over 3,000 men. As soon as they had disembarked from the ships, the Duke marched to Rouen. On 13 July he joined forces with Talbot at Juziers, a small village on the banks of the Seine between Mantes and Meulan. The combined army must have been about 6,000 strong, the largest English army to take the field in France since 1429. They moved out of Juziers on 15 July and entered Pontoise by the Beauvais gate with another convoy of supplies. The Duke of York assumed nominal command, but it was Talbot who directed operations. His strategy was to try to force Charles VII to a decisive battle which might finally turn the fortunes of the war. The French commanders were equally determined to avoid one. They remained on the east side of the river and guarded all the crossings of the Oise from Conflans-Sainte-Honorine to Creil to keep the English on the west side.[76]

On the night of 20 July 1441, Talbot and York marched unseen fifteen miles up the valley of the Oise, carrying light boats. In the early hours of the morning, they crossed the river opposite the abbey of Royaumont under the noses of the French commanders in the sector, who had failed to post sentries. By the time that the alarm was sounded, the whole English army had crossed and begun to march down the east side. At the abbey of Maubuisson, the French captains panicked. The gatehouse at the end of the bridge of Pontoise was abandoned. As much of the artillery as could be moved in time was taken to safety in the bastide Saint-Martin. Charles VII fled across the pontoon bridge making for the Seine and shut himself in the walled Dominican abbey outside Poissy, while the Duke of York occupied his headquarters at Maubuisson. The English repaired the stone bridge and reoccupied the gatehouse, opening up access to the town from the east bank. Then, after three days, they crossed the Oise in pursuit of the French King. Talbot devised an ambitious plan to trap him. He proposed to cross the Seine with part of the army at Mantes and surprise Charles at Poissy, while Richard of York occupied Conflans-Saint-Honorine to block his escape by the north. Talbot carried out his part of this operation. The King fled from his quarters in the abbey so quickly that his bed was still warm when the English burst in. But the Duke of York failed to hold Conflans. His supply system had collapsed. The land had been stripped bare for miles around by the armies of either side. His men were starving. When Talbot entered Poissy, he found that the Duke had left for Rouen, taking with him all the men that he had brought from England. Charles VII escaped with most of his own army to Saint-Denis. By the end of July, the only troops at Pontoise were Scales's garrison in the town and the French troops holding the bastide at Saint-Martin.[77]

In the middle of August 1441, Charles VII held a council of war at Saint-Denis. Morale had fallen after the early triumphs of the campaign. Desertion was becoming a problem. Some important contingents had left the army. Talbot had just brought another supply convoy into Pontoise and replaced Scales's garrison with fresh men under Lord Clinton. In the streets of Paris people were openly mocking the King for his undignified flight from Poissy. Charles felt the pressure of opinion just a year after the Praguerie. In the third week of August his army returned to Pontoise. The batteries of bombards opened up again. But the town remained open on the west and north, and Talbot continued to bring in escorted convoys of supplies.

By mid-September it was clear that Pontoise could not be starved out. It would have to be taken by assault or not at all. On 16 September the French stormed the church of Notre-Dame, a parish church standing on high ground outside the walls at the south-west corner of the town, which had been incorporated into the defences. From the tower of the church, they were able to see inside the city and direct the fire of their artillery. Three days later, at midday on the 19th, a general assault was launched from three points at once. One force attacked the south-east corner of the walls, by the confluence of the Oise and the Viosne. Another launched their assault from barges moored in the Viosne. A third was directed against the Beauvais gate on the west. After four hours of hand-to-hand fighting the French poured over the walls and into the town. The most reliable estimate of the casualties suggests that the English lost at least 500 killed. More than 300 were captured, including Lord Clinton. Many of the prisoners were pulled out of hiding places in the town on the day after the assault. Captured in a town taken by assault, they were at the mercy of the assailants. Some of them were summarily put to death where they were found. The rest were paraded through the streets of Paris in rags without coverings for their heads or shoes for their feet, bound together with chains two by two, before being taken off to their captors' castles until they could find a ransom. Some were not worth the cost of keeping them. They were obscurely killed in cellars or taken to the Place de Grève to be drowned in the Seine in front of a crowd of onlookers.[78]

Talbot had taken even greater risks to supply Pontoise than he had the year before to besiege Harfleur. As in 1440, there was a price to be paid. Garrisons stripped of their numbers to man field armies were unable to maintain the same level of sentries and watches. Tired men fought badly. The large French garrison at Conches was directed by the Angevin nobleman and royal councillor Pierre de Brézé and his brother-in-law, the soldier of fortune Robert de Flocques. They took advantage of the preoccupations of the English at Pontoise to attack enemy garrisons in southern Normandy. In June they captured the walled town of Beaumont-le-Roger in the valley of the Risle and the nearby castle of Beaumesnil. In the post-mortem which followed, the loss of Beaumesnil, like that of Conches itself, was put down to too many absentees.

Lord Fauconberg, who had a prominent role at Pontoise, was captain of the cathedral city of Evreux. It had one of the largest garrisons of the region, but he is likely to have drawn heavily on it for the siege. On 15 September, four days before the assault which delivered Pontoise to the French, Robert de Flocques came over the walls of Evreux. The citizens, like those of other Norman towns, were divided. The patriciate and the municipal officers were generally loyal to their English rulers. But there was a well-organised group of French partisans in Evreux. A local fisherman had guided Robert de Flocques's men across the waterways protecting the northern ramparts. When the alarm went up, the garrison tried to seal off that sector of the city with a barrier of upturned carts, but they were rapidly put to flight. The small number of casualties on either side (five men killed) suggests that they hardly put up a fight. The loss of Evreux was a serious blow for the English, opening up a great salient in the south-east of Normandy extending to the Seine. The lifetime association of these two soldiers is commemorated today in the beautiful stained-glass window which they commissioned for Evreux cathedral to mark the final expulsion of the English from Normandy. They can be seen kneeling together in prayer at the foot of the window beside images of Charles VII and the Dauphin Louis.[79]

In November 1441, the council at Westminster received Jean Rinel with a report from the Duke of York on the catastrophic course of events since his arrival in France. The councillors devoted several sessions to its implications. They were scathing about the losses of territory, which they attributed to the negligence of the garrison commanders. They threatened condign punishment for any who were found to have been at fault. Most of the Duke of York's men were now returning to England after their six months of indentured service, leaving him with only about 3,500 men in Normandy. The council calculated that, with an allowance from English revenues equivalent to 120,000 *livres* a year and Norman revenues of 340,000 *livres*, the Duke should have been able to support an establishment of 6,200 men. They questioned whether he should continue to be paid his allowance when he had little more than half that number still on his payroll. In fact, the councillors were using outdated estimates of Norman revenues. The true figure was probably no more than a quarter of what they were assuming, and that had to cover the civil administration as well.

The council ordered Sir John Popham to accompany Rinel back to Rouen and convey their views to York and Talbot. These views must have been extremely unwelcome to both men. They were told to concentrate on the defence of the Norman ports and Le Crotoy and to take no risks with their security. This looks like a criticism of Talbot's policy of withdrawing men from the garrisons for field service. It was a response to English priorities. Control of the Channel was an issue on which the Parliamentary Commons were increasingly vocal. It was also a vital interest of the City of London and the Staplers of Calais, who were emerging as the government's chief creditors. But, seen from Rouen, the council's apparent preference for a purely defensive policy concentrating on the Channel coast must have seemed unrealistic. It would have reversed two decades of military doctrine, which was based on the flexible employment of garrison troops. It would also have involved diverting resources away from the eastern and southern marches of Normandy, where the main threat from the French came. The Westminster councillors, however, were increasingly resistant to considerations like these. They were no longer confident that Normandy could be defended and were already asking themselves what could be salvaged from the wreckage.[80]

In the summer of 1441, the English political world was rocked by a scandal which silenced the only notable voice to support the old war aims of Henry V. In July, several members of the Duke of Gloucester's household were arrested and charged before an ecclesiastical court with heresy, sorcery and necromancy. Some of them implicated Humphrey's wife, Eleanor Cobham. Eleanor's interest in necromancy and magic was well known. It seems that from April 1440, which was the high point of the row over the release of the Duke of Orléans, she had encouraged her servants to use the black arts to forecast the time of the King's death, when as the wife of the heir presumptive she would become Queen. The accused were said to have made a figure of the King and to have invoked devils and used spells to predict that he would die of melancholia in May or June 1441. They also predicted that the lords of the council who controlled the King would be beheaded for their presumption. In a world which believed in the power of Satan and his ministers to determine the fate of men, predicting the death of the King and his ministers was tantamount to wishing it. Eleanor fled to sanctuary at Westminster Abbey. She was eventually removed and convicted of sorcery before an ecclesiastical tribunal presided over by Archbishop Chichele. One of her associates was executed at Tyburn as a traitor and another burned at Smithfield as a witch. As for Eleanor herself, her marriage was annulled and she was sentenced to a humiliating public penance in the streets of London. Although she was never brought before a secular court, she was imprisoned for life by order of the council, initially in Kenilworth castle and then on the Isle of Man. The case against her was not fabricated. She admitted some of the charges. But the timing of the trials, the public theatre which accompanied them, her humiliation in the London stronghold of her husband, and the involvement of the council and the royal household at nearly every stage, all suggest that this was a political trial whose real target was Gloucester himself. After this, Humphrey was a broken man. 'He waxed then strange each day unto the King,' wrote a contemporary. Apart from occasional attendance at council meetings, he withdrew from public life. The incident crippled domestic opposition to the peace process, which had always been associated with the Duke and his friends. There was no other champion with the status or the eloquence to fight for their cause.[81]

Ironically, at the time of Gloucester's political destruction, events were vindicating his objections to the release of the Duke of Orléans. The Duke never enjoyed any real influence at the French court. The French King was suspicious of the terms on which he had recovered his liberty and disapproved of his new-found friendship with the Duke of

Burgundy. He initially refused to receive his cousin in public audience, insisting upon a private meeting without attendants, which the Duke rejected as a slight upon his dignity. Orléans does not appear to have attended the council until 1444. His relations with the King's ministers were so poor that within six months of his release he was convinced that they were trying to poison him. The problem about the idea of using him to change the basic lines of French foreign policy was that it depended on the support of declared opponents of the dominant group in the French government. They were all men who had either participated in the Praguerie or supported it from a distance. The Duke of Orléans could never have acquired any influence through these men, short of a successful *coup d'état*. As a result, in the eighteen months following his release, he found himself steadily drawn into the plots of more experienced and ruthless politicians bent on an aristocratic *putsch*.[82]

The chief supporters of Charles of Orléans's efforts to make peace were John V of Brittany and Philip the Good, the two territorial princes who had most to gain from an end to the Anglo-French war. In February and March 1441, John V presided at a conference in the castle of Nantes, attended by Charles himself and the Duke of Alençon, at which yet another scheme was hatched for John V and Philip the Good to act as joint mediators. The idea was canvassed with the French King by John's representatives. But it was immediately overtaken by the French King's decision to postpone the peace conference at Calais and invade the Oise valley. Another conference, at Rennes in August 1441, was attended in addition by Dunois and Vendôme and by Garter King of Arms, the senior English royal herald. There was no doubt about the conspiratorial character of these meetings. Their object was to remove the French King's current councillors. The participants undertook to give each other mutual support in the event that the councillors responded by attacking them. They concerted their plans with the English at Westminster and their officers at Rouen. John V asked for and received assurances from the Duke of York that he would step in with military support in the event that the plot led to the invasion of his duchy. The Duke of Alençon curried favour with Richard of York by passing on the names of French fifth columnists in English garrisons, who were promptly arrested.[83]

Charles VII declined to participate in any peace initiative until after Pontoise had fallen. It was not until October that he agreed that the peace conference would finally reopen on 1 May 1442 in what was now regarded as the traditional place between Calais and Gravelines. In preparation for the occasion, Philip the Good and Charles of Orléans met at Hesdin at the end of October 1441. They decided to summon all the leading territorial princes of France to a gathering at Nevers in the new year at which the two of them would preside as the senior Valois princes after the King and the Dauphin. There were to be three main items on the agenda at Nevers. The first was the growing estrangement between the King and the princes, who believed that they were being excluded from the influence at court to which their rank entitled them. The second item was the state of the kingdom, and in particular the high levels of taxation and the continuing depredations of the freelance companies of *écorcheurs*, most of whom were now in the service of the King. The third was the peace process, now that the conferences outside Calais were due to resume in May. The King was invited to consent to the gathering and to attend it himself. He did consent, but understandably preferred to send his Chancellor Regnault de Chartres to represent him rather than attend in person. The princes' object was obvious. It was to force their way into the King's inner counsels and take over the conduct of the negotiations with England. Charles VII had no intention of submitting to this scheme.[84]

The princes' conference opened at Nevers on 28 January 1442. Apart from the Dukes of Burgundy and Orléans, it was attended by the Dukes of Bourbon and Alençon and the Counts of Vendôme, Nevers, Eu and Dunois. Most of these men had been active or passive supporters of the Praguerie two years before. The Duke of Brittany was daily expected, but in the end was represented by his eldest son Francis Count of Montfort. It was an awkward occasion, for Charles VII remained forty miles away at Bourges and discussions with him had to be laboriously conducted by exchanges of ambassadors and written memoranda. The King also made it clear that he was in a hurry because he was imminently expected with his army on the march of Gascony.

Ultimately, the assembly achieved nothing other than to advertise the differences between the King and his leading subjects. The princes protested against their poor representation on the King's council and in the major offices of state. They called for a more deliberative style of government, in which important decisions were not made in small cabals of two or three people. They pressed for a more prominent role for the Estates-General. They objected to the high current levels of taxation. In addition, some of them had particular grievances of their own. The King brushed all of these criticisms aside. He had always chosen his counsellors from the most 'notable' men of his realm, he said. He was unapologetic about taxation, simply replying that it was necessary. The princes' demand for closer consultation with the Estates-General provoked a vigorous discussion in the King's council. The prevailing view was that these assemblies simply provided a forum in which the nobility could marshal opposition to the King among the clergy and the towns. He might as well, they said, abandon the government to the three estates.

Charles VII was uncompromising on the peace process. He blamed the English for its failure to date. They had repeatedly rejected reasonable offers. He detailed their various defaults, not entirely accurately. But the main point which he made was unanswerable. Further negotiations were unlikely to succeed. His predecessors had built the monarchy as the ultimate embodiment of a single national identity. He had no intention of betraying their legacy by allowing the English to hold any territory in France, except as a fief of the Crown and in return for homage. He could not believe that the princes would wish him to. Yet, as he reminded them, Beaufort and Kemp had made it perfectly clear in 1439 that the English King would never accept this.

Shortly after the assembly at Nevers, Charles VII put an end to the peace process in its current form. He declared his intention of putting off the reopening of the peace conference from 1 May 1442 until 25 October in order to accommodate his campaign plans in the southwest. When he returned from the march of Gascony, he proposed to invade Normandy and expected to recover the whole duchy. The reopening of the conference, repeatedly deferred by one side or the other since August 1439, was finally abandoned. Charles VII's remarks to the princes at Nevers about the uselessness of negotiations with the English were no doubt reported back to the English by the Duke of Orléans, who remained in touch with them throughout. Isabella of Portugal gave up her efforts at mediation shortly afterwards. Only John V of Brittany thought it worth trying to breathe life into the negotiations. He suggested a meeting under his own auspices on the marches of Brittany. But John died at the end of August 1442 and the project died with him.[85]

*

In February 1442, as the princes were arguing with the French King at Nevers, Sir John Talbot returned to England for the first time in seven years to press the case for sending another expeditionary army to Normandy. Talbot was received as a hero in England and raised to the peerage as Earl of Shrewsbury. But the enthusiasm which greeted him masked a deeper weariness with the war. The generation that had fought with Henry V was dying off. The King's lack of interest in the war was obvious. It was going badly, and people assumed that a peace would soon follow. Ambitious young men no longer looked to France for opportunity as their fathers had done. In spite of the council's misgivings about offensive operations in Normandy, Talbot was eventually commissioned to recruit an expeditionary army of 2,500 men for six months' service in France. But it was necessary to scrape the barrel to find them. There were few men-at-arms, and only one in eight of the archers was mounted. Funding was even more problematic. Parliament voted a single standard subsidy in March but made it clear that the deployment of a war fleet to suppress French commerce raiding in the Channel had first call on the proceeds. In the end the wages of Talbot's army were funded partly by loans from Cardinal Beaufort and partly by diverting the quarterly payments of the Duke of York's salary. The sequel largely vindicated the council's concerns.[86]

When Talbot landed at Harfleur on 15 June 1442, he was met by the Duke of York's military advisers Sir William Oldhall and Sir Andrew Ogard. They brought a report on the situation in Normandy and proposals for the deployment of the new army. It was agreed that the first task must be to re-establish the English position on the south-eastern march, by recovering Louviers, Conches and Evreux. Talbot marched straight to Pont-de-l'Arche, where he joined forces with Fauconberg, the English commander of the sector. Fauconberg had 1,200 men under his command, most of whom had been recruited from men 'living on the land'. The combined force, between 3,000 and 4,000 strong but of very variable quality, marched on Conches. The castle had lost some of its earlier importance since the French recovered Evreux, which was a better base. But Talbot and Fauconberg spent six weeks besieging it, before finally buying out the French garrison on about 9 September.

It proved difficult to follow up this success. Dunois, the French commander on this front, was perhaps the only French soldier who matched Talbot's tactical skills. His movements were hampered by the smaller size of his army and the current military orthodoxy that a French army should on no account risk a pitched battle with the English. But he hovered over the region, falling upon other English garrisons at unpredictable moments. Robert de Flocques, another formidable opponent, now based at Evreux, harassed the English lines of supply and attacked isolated detachments, inflicting heavy casualties. Talbot was short of time. The council at Westminster wanted to see Dieppe recovered, and he could not count on the men he had brought from England once their indentures expired at the beginning of December. As a result, he was forced to give up the idea of attacking Louviers and Evreux, and to withdraw westward. His withdrawal left Verneuil and Gallardon, the two remaining English garrisons of the south-eastern march, dangerously exposed. Within days of his departure, the keep of Gallardon, which had been captured by François de Surienne in a bold *coup de main* earlier in the year, sold out to Dunois. Verneuil seemed likely to be next.[87]

The troops assigned to the attack on Dieppe had been ordered to gather at the Benedictine abbey of Jumièges by the banks of the Seine west of Rouen. Talbot met them there in October 1442. In addition to the survivors of his expeditionary army, 600 men were withdrawn from garrisons, making about 2,500 men altogether. At the end of October, the first companies of Talbot's army reached Dieppe and began to build a large timber bastide on a hill east of the walls called Le Polet, overlooking the entrance to the harbour. Here Talbot sited four large bombards. Another, smaller, bastide was built on the west side of the town. Off the coast, the harbour was blockaded by a small naval squadron. This was probably the flotilla of five ships mobilised at Southampton by the Hampshire knight Sir Stephen Popham. It was a formidable force for the siege of a small port which had lost much of its population since it became a frontier town. It shortly became clear how much the strategic position of the French had gained from the capture of the eastern marches of Normandy over the past fifteen months. With the Seine upstream of Mantes and the whole of the Oise valley now under French control, the Count of Dunois was able to lead 800 to 1,000 men directly from the Beauce over the bridge at Meulan and into the Beauvaisis and the Caux. Their arrival at Dieppe on 29 November transformed the situation of the town. It coincided with a mutiny among the troops of the English expeditionary army, who had reached the end of their six months and refused to serve any longer. Talbot had no option but to withdraw to Rouen, leaving Sir William Peyto, the former captain of Creil, to hold the bastide at Le Polet with 500 men until the siege could be resumed in the following year. In the event, it never did resume. Talbot's expeditionary army returned to England at the end of 1442, leaving only about 3,000 English troops in Normandy, enough to maintain minimum garrison strengths, but not enough to allow troops to be withdrawn for any major operation.[88]

Lancastrian rule in Normandy was visibly crumbling. While Talbot was preoccupied with Dieppe, the French captured another fortress which was to prove an even sharper thorn in the side of the English occupiers. Granville was a large rock projecting into the bay of Mont-Saint-Michel some fifteen miles north of Avranches. It was accessible at low tide from Mont-Saint-Michel and the garrison of the mount had for many years launched regular raids across the sands into the region around. To defend it against these raids Lord Scales, the English lieutenant in Lower Normandy, had built a fortress on the rock. A small town and harbour grew up at its base. A garrison of forty men was installed under the command of his bastard son. In the autumn of 1442, the captain received intelligence that Louis d'Estouteville, the veteran French commander on the mount, was having scaling ladders made for a coup against Granville. Nevertheless, on the night of 8 November 1442 when Estouteville's men came over the walls, the garrison was taken by surprise. The attackers had suborned an English soldier who told them when and where to strike. The castle was swiftly captured and occupied. This conquest gave the garrison of Mont-Saint-Michel a secure base in the Cotentin, which was easy to supply across the bay. From Granville they were able to loot and ransom the whole of the peninsula. In the following year, Scales besieged the place with some 800 men for two months without success. As a result of this failure, he was obliged to double the garrison strengths in the surrounding region. The classic weapons of attack in this war of ambushes were surprise, ladders and bribery. They were cheap, while static defence was immensely costly in both men and money.[89]

The Duke of York never recovered from the disasters of his first six months, which not only weakened him militarily but lost him the confidence of the council in England. They never really understood the scale of his problems. He had inherited an intractable legacy of deficits, indiscipline and maladministration from his predecessors which hung like a ball and chain around his feet. One of his first encounters after his arrival was with the herald William Bruges, Garter King of Arms, who had been travelling through Normandy on diplomatic business and was appalled by what he had seen. The new lieutenant's first priority, the herald told him, must be to address the 'injustice reigning in the King's domains and the vices and sins of the people of our nation'. William Worcester, Sir John Fastolf's secretary and business manager, accompanied his master to the duchy in 1441. His impressions were very similar to Garter's. He was shocked by the bullying, brutality, looting and cattle rustling that officers of the garrisons allowed to go unpunished and unremedied. He was convinced that it was driving the peasantry of Normandy into the arms of the French. The root cause of the problem was the inability of the Norman treasury to pay regular wages. York had brought nearly £3,200 in coin with him in 1441 to pay off their arrears. But although there was some increase in the flow of money from England in his time, the payments fell a long way short of what he had been promised when taking on the job, and the arrears soon began to build up again.

To every well-advised man [wrote Worcester], it is easy to understand that . . . men of solde and of arms . . . may be duly paid of their wages by the month, as John Regent of France paid, or by quarter . . . and that such payments be made content without delay or need of long and great pursuit . . . whereby your soldiers shall not have cause to oppress and charge your obeissants and your people, in taking their victuals without paying therefor, which great part of them in default of due payment hath been accustomed.

Worcester thought that the situation sharply deteriorated during the lieutenancy of the Duke of York. His assessment is borne out by the rising tide of rural brigandage in these years, especially in Lower Normandy where a high proportion of the English garrison troops were stationed.[90]

The Duke of York did what he could to improve discipline in the garrisons. He encouraged complaints against the troops. He took steps to stop the long-standing practice of captains treating their offices as financial perks, farming out the work to deputies and living in England on the profits, 'not labouring nor employing their persons in the King's service, nor no thing done for the well of his conquest'. York toured the duchy personally dealing with disputes. Observing the situation from Lille, the chronicler Jean de Waurin thought that he governed

Normandy well and attributed the criticisms from England to envy. Yet if York's government was more effective than its predecessors, there was no mistaking its increasingly alien character. The Duke refashioned the Grand Conseil, which had hitherto consisted mainly of native Frenchmen, filling it with English captains like Oldhall and Fastolf. They were reinforced by professional administrators brought over from England. By the end of 1442, there were only two French councillors left, Pierre Cauchon and Louis of Luxembourg, both of whom were dead by the end of the following year. Louis of Luxembourg's position as Chancellor was left vacant for two years and then filled by an English knight, Sir Thomas Hoo. Just as the generation of Henry V was passing in England, so a generation of French servants of the Lancastrian regime, formed in the service of John the Fearless during the civil wars, was disappearing in France.[91]

CHAPTER XII

The King's Peace, 1442–1448

Gascony had been a backwater for most of Henry VI's reign. The logistical difficulties of operating south of the Loire and the concentration of England's resources in the north had made it a marginal factor in the calculations of politicians at Westminster. The figures prepared for Parliament by Treasurer Cromwell in 1433 showed that the English Treasury spent only £3,400 a year on the defence of the duchy, representing the cost of the Seneschal's personal retinue and the garrison of Fronsac. This was barely a third of the cost to English revenues of Calais, let alone all of Normandy. The duchy's local revenues had suffered from war damage, the vicissitudes of the wine trade and assignments in favour of noblemen whose support had to be purchased. In the 1430s they fluctuated around £750 sterling a year. This had to pay for the ordinary civil administration and the important garrison of Langon which defended the approach to Bordeaux by the Garonne. There was little or nothing left for field operations or the defence of the marches. For these, the council at Bordeaux depended on the goodwill of the Gascon nobility and the towns, who were left to fund the defence of their own places. Gascony was not like Normandy. It was not a conquered land but an inheritance of the English Kings, who had held it for nearly three centuries. Force of tradition and fear of Valois France with its centralising tendencies and high levels of taxation generated a large measure of unforced loyalty. But the maintenance of that loyalty called for the continual exercise of internal diplomacy and deft political management. Political management had its limits. It could only work for as long as men believed that the duchy would survive.[1]

In the 1430s the area under English rule was limited to two blocks of territory (*Map VI*). A northern block around Bordeaux comprised the Médoc north of the city, the area east and south of it, and a thin strip of territory along the right bank of the Gironde and the lower Dordogne including the towns of Blaye, Bourg, Libourne and Saint-Émilion and the fortress of Fronsac. Further south, towards the Pyrenees, a second centre of English rule comprised the city of Bayonne, together with the territory known as the Terre de Labourt lying south of it, and the Adour valley to the east, including the important towns of Saint-Sever and Dax. A narrow ribbon of bleak, windswept coastal land connected the two regions. The duchy was always vulnerable to invasion, for it had no natural defences from the east. The river valleys provided broad highways from Languedoc and the Massif Central into the heart of English territory. During the early 1420s, the highly competent Seneschal Sir John Radcliffe had conquered the area around Bazas and extended the limits of English rule up the valley of the Garonne as far as Marmande and the Dordogne beyond Bergerac. He 'hath brought by his labour in knighthood to his sovereign lord's obeisance within the duchy of Guyenne many diverse cities, towns and fortresses', the Duke of Bedford wrote when recommending his election to the Order of the Garter. Yet Radcliffe's achievement owed very little to the government at Westminster, which had starved Gascony of money and men for many years. In the spring of 1425, he declared that he could no longer take responsibility for the defence of the duchy in these conditions and asked in vain to be relieved of his office.[2]

English Gascony owed its survival to the preoccupations of Charles VII's ministers in the north and the ambiguous position of the three great territorial lords whose domains bordered on the duchy, the Counts of Foix and Armagnac and the lords of Albret. They were all in the allegiance of the King of France and in an earlier generation, they had been the animating spirits of the French wars on the Gascon march. But they had regional interests and extensive networks of allies and clients on both sides of the march. They maintained close contacts with the administration in Bordeaux, some of whose members accepted retainers from them. Without the active military support of the French King, these men had little to gain and much to lose by fighting the English. It depleted their revenues and distracted them from other political priorities without bringing them significant territorial gains. The Counts of Foix had hedged their bets for many years. The current Count's younger brother, Gaston Captal de Buch, was the largest landowner of the Bordelais and remained a firm English partisan to the end. Béarn, the westernmost of the Count's domains, had close commercial links with English Gascony and continued to supply mercenaries to the English Seneschals as it had done for two centuries. In the course of 1424 and 1425, Radcliffe had concluded local truces with all three French magnates of the march. They were fragile, as truces tended to be in a region where private war was endemic. However, despite sporadic outbreaks of localised violence, Radcliffe's truces had largely insulated Guyenne from events in the rest of France.[3]

These arrangements broke down at the end of the 1430s with the rise of the *écorcheurs* and the renascence of the Valois monarchy. After the treaty of Arras, Charles VII turned his attention to operations on the Gascon march, as a way of clearing the *écorcheurs* from politically sensitive regions such as the Loire valley and the marches of Burgundy. In 1437 the Castilian freelance captain Rodrigo de Villandrando appeared with his companies in the south-west. The English King's council in Bordeaux patched up a truce with him. But they were sufficiently concerned to send the Chancellor of Guyenne, Bernard Angevin, to England to discuss the security of the duchy with Henry VI's ministers. In the spring of 1438, while Angevin was in England, there was a much more damaging incursion. Poton de Saintrailles's companies, which had been operating in Touraine, followed Villandrando south. The French King offered both of them regular pay and placed them under the overall command of Charles II lord of Albret, perhaps the closest of the great southern feudatories to the French court.

Albret saw in the bands of *écorcheurs* an opportunity to recover the extensive domains in the Bazadais and the lower valley of the Garonne which he had lost to Sir John Radcliffe a decade and a half earlier. Rodrigo and Poton entered the duchy by the north in May 1438 and joined forces outside Bordeaux. Their combined strength was reported to be about 14,000 men. A number of smaller companies which had been operating in Languedoc were directed to invade the valley of the Adour from the south at the same time. The defence was weak and uncoordinated in both theatres. Gascony had been without a Seneschal ever since the spring of 1435, when Radcliffe had been recalled to take part in the Congress of Arras. In Bordeaux, the government's coffers were empty. The Constable had to borrow money from English merchants in the city, and when that was exhausted he was reduced to persuading men to serve for IOUs redeemable in England. The invaders, however, had their own difficulties. They had no artillery and were unable to undertake any major siege. They conquered only three places of any consequence: Bazas, the principal fortress of the eastern march, which they captured by escalade; Tartas in the southern Landes; and Tonneins near the confluence of the Lot and the Garonne. By September the invaders had exhausted the available supplies of food and loot and were forced to withdraw into Languedoc, leaving garrisons in all three towns and in a number of smaller places of the Bordelais. The French campaign achieved little of real strategic importance. But it had been extremely destructive, especially in the Médoc and Entre-Deux-Mers. Several hundred men of Bordeaux had lost their lives in an ill-advised sortie. Wine exports, the lifeblood of the local economy, fell to a little over 4,000 tons in 1438, less than half the usual quantity. The region took two decades to recover from the destruction of vines and buildings.[4]

The invasion was a shock for Henry VI's councillors at Westminster. The defence of Guyenne suddenly took on a significance that it had not had for many years. A great council met in the King's presence at Eltham Palace on 24 February 1439 to decide what to do. It was evidently a contentious meeting, for the discussion occupied at least four days spread over a month. The Duke of Gloucester, who held a large portfolio of valuable lordships in Guyenne and had recently been balked in his attempt to take the lieutenancy in Normandy for himself, seems to have been behind the pressure for resources to be diverted from Normandy to Guyenne. It was decided to send his closest political ally, John Holland Earl of Huntingdon, to Bordeaux as lieutenant for six years. Huntingdon was the first lieutenant to be appointed for the duchy since the reign of Henry IV. His expedition was an expensive commitment. He was to be accompanied by 2,300 men, the largest English army to serve in Gascony since the departure of the Duke of Clarence in 1413. Moreover, it had to be paid at the traditional Guyenne rates, which were half as much again as the rates paid in the north. The new army sailed from Plymouth in July 1439 in a requisitioned fleet of more than a hundred large ships and moored in the Gironde on 2 August.[5]

The Earl of Huntingdon's term as lieutenant began well. Over the winter after his arrival, he cleared the garrisons that Charles of Albret had left in the Garonne valley and recaptured Bazas. In the summer of 1440, he turned his attention to Tartas. Tartas was a walled town on the river Adour which had once belonged to the lord of Albret and had been reoccupied by his troops in 1438. Huntingdon collected a considerable force with which to besiege it. He assigned 500 men from his own army to the operation. Another 3,600 men and an artillery train were raised and funded by the provincial Estates of the Landes for a limited period of six months. No sooner had these arrangements been made, than he learned that he had been recalled to England only a year into his six-year term. The decision had been made at Westminster in the spring. The reasons were probably financial. The King's ministers had recently decided to send the Duke of York to Normandy. They could not afford to maintain large armies simultaneously in both theatres. As a result, Huntingdon had to leave for England in August 1440, taking most of his army with him. He left behind him Sir Thomas Rempston, a veteran of the Norman march, whom he appointed as Seneschal. The Earl retained the title and powers of lieutenant for a year after his departure and endeavoured to exercise them from England. Perhaps he expected to go back. But he never did, and effective power in Gascony remained with Rempston. It was he who laid siege to Tartas on 31 August 1440.[6]

The timing of Huntingdon's recall was unfortunate, for the siege of Tartas was to generate the next crisis in the duchy's affairs. Charles of Albret was determined to hold the town but was unable to match the forces at Rempston's disposal. In October 1440 he gathered his clients and vassals and joined forces with the son of the Count of Armagnac to launch a devastating raid into the Chalosse region south of the Adour, in the hope of drawing off the besieging army. Rempston refused to be diverted. However, he was facing pressures of his own. The men supplied by the Estates of the Landes were only available for six months, which would expire in February 1441. The walls of Tartas had so far resisted everything that had been thrown at them. The town's stores were reported to be nowhere near to exhaustion.

In January 1441, Rempston and Albret arrived at a complicated compromise. They agreed that Tartas and the whole of the surrounding *vicomté* would be vested in Albret's fourth son, who was still a child, and occupied by an English garrison. The young man would be required to swear an oath of allegiance to Henry VI and would be brought up in the English allegiance by Gascon noblemen of unquestionable loyalty. The Albrets were proposing to do what the Counts of Foix had done since the early years of the century, namely divide their assets between different branches of their family, one accepting French allegiance, the other English. Meanwhile, their lands were to be protected by a twenty-year truce. But there was a proviso. The agreement would fall away and Tartas and its region remain in the lord of Albret's hands if Charles VII or the Dauphin Louis appeared outside the town with the stronger army at a *journée* to be held in three months' time. The agreement was a serious threat to Charles VII and his ministers. If it was performed according to its terms, it would deprive them of the aid of their most dependable ally in the south-west and reinforce English control over much of southern Gascony. Albret had no desire to break with Charles VII. The Tartas agreement was an astute piece of blackmail designed to force the King to intervene in force on the Gascon march for the first time in a generation. The original deadline for the *journée* of Tartas proved impossible for the French King. It was equally problematic for Rempston, who had only a handful of troops once the men of the Landes had left. The *journée* was postponed at least once before it was finally fixed for 1 May 1442. Albret extracted a written undertaking from Charles VII that he would be there in person at the head of a large army.[7]

For Henry VI's ministers this happened at the worst possible time. With some 8,000 English troops in Normandy, they were not in a position to reinforce the southern duchy. Instead, they hoped to shore up their position on the Gascon march by recruiting the Count of Armagnac as an ally. The vast Armagnac domains and the Counts' extensive network of clients and retainers in the region enabled them to recruit large forces in Languedoc and Gascony. The current Count, John IV, had been estranged from the court of France for years. The English believed that they could persuade him to do homage to Henry VI for his lands in Gascony while maintaining his allegiance to Charles VII in Languedoc. They hoped to add secret clauses which would presumably have committed him to come to the aid of the Bordeaux government if it was threatened. As a bait, they dangled in front of him the prospect of a dazzling marriage between the English King and one of his daughters. This scheme seems to have originated with the Dukes of Brittany, Orléans and Alençon. It was part of their plan to pressure the French King into making peace. But John IV was a poor instrument for such an ambitious scheme. Weak and vacillating, he did not have the same political influence or military skills as his father, the former dictator of Paris. In the event, his ambassadors did not reach England until April 1442. By then Charles VII had already set out for Gascony.[8]

In Bordeaux, Sir Thomas Rempston played for time. Knowing that Charles VII had been delayed by his arguments with the princes at Nevers, he managed to negotiate a further postponement of the *journée* to midsummer, 24 June 1442. Meanwhile, having heard nothing from England, he sent Sir Edward Hull, the acting Constable of Bordeaux, back with a dramatic warning of imminent disaster and a renewed appeal for troops. But Hull did not reach Plymouth until the second week of June and by that time, Charles VII had entered Toulouse. The nobility of Languedoc had gathered there in force to meet him. They were joined by large bands of *écorcheurs* commanded by Poton de Saintrailles, La Hire and Antoine de Chabannes. The total strength of the army was estimated at between 10,000 and 16,000 men, far more than was needed to relieve Tartas. The ultimate objectives were obviously Bordeaux and Bayonne. A Carmelite friar in the pay of the council at Bordeaux watched the scene and reported on the numbers. Without large reinforcements, the English duchy seemed to be threatened with extinction. Urgent letters were sent to Westminster. The council there panicked and finally decided to send reinforcements. The King's diplomatic secretary Thomas Beckington and the courtier Sir Robert Roos had been charged with negotiating the alliance with the Count of Armagnac. They were waiting at Plymouth for a passage to Bordeaux when a messenger arrived post-haste from London with a reassuring message for the council in Bordeaux, announcing that a powerful relief force would soon be on its way. Some companies were hastily recruited. The mayor of Bayonne, Sir Philip Chetwind, who was in England, was commissioned to return urgently to his city with 500 archers. Edward Hull was ordered back to Bordeaux with another company. But this was only an interim measure. No one at Westminster had any idea how or when the larger army which they had promised could be recruited or paid.[9]

On 11 June 1442, Charles VII marched out of Toulouse, accompanied by the Dauphin Louis, Charles of Anjou, Richemont and Charles of Albret. On 24 June, the date appointed for the *journée*, the King's host appeared outside Tartas. His army was drawn up in battle order beneath the walls. It was a symbolic gesture, for there was no English army to challenge them. Tartas was bound to surrender if the King had the stronger force and Rempston was in no position to beat him on numbers. He had only between 1,000 and 1,500 troops, mostly recruited locally. He stayed at a prudent distance, behind the walls of the fortress-town of Saint-Sever fifteen miles away. Tartas surrendered on the evening of 24 June. On the following day, the French arrived outside Saint-Sever. After a brief siege the place was taken by assault. The town suffered all the horrors of a *'ville prise'*. More than 800 of Rempston's men died in the fighting. Rempston himself was captured. Much of the population of the town was slaughtered. Reports reaching the government in England put the total death toll at about 4,000. From Saint-Sever, the French army moved twenty-five miles downstream to the episcopal city of Dax. The town was reputed to be the strongest in the region. There, on about 10 July, they set up their artillery and began to batter the walls.[10]

On 16 July 1442, the ship carrying Beckington and Roos arrived at Bordeaux. The two envoys were appalled by what they found. Writing to the King in England, they declared that Bordeaux was

> at our first coming ... as sorrowful a town and as greatly dismayed and discouraged as any might be in the earth, as people desolate and cast out of all comfort of any succour to be had from your said majesty against your enemies that ben in this country in great puissance.

The city was buzzing with rumours. The two ambassadors had Henry VI's letters promising relief translated into Gascon and the Archbishop read them out in the cathedral in a 'good and right stirring' sermon. The King's promise was well received. But it was far from clear that the reinforcements would reach Bordeaux in time. The French were making rapid progress. The ambassadors reported on the fall of Saint-Sever and the opening days of the siege of Dax. The enemy had begun to construct three bastides outside Dax and were erecting batteries before the walls. There was a large, fortified enclosure out of range of the town's guns, from which deep trenches were being dug towards the town. Once these works were complete, they reported, the French King planned to leave 3,000 to 4,000 men to maintain the siege and then to advance on Bayonne with the rest of his army. From there, he would march on Bordeaux. Meanwhile, the lord of Pons, the principal baron of Saintonge, was advancing down the river Isle with another French army and was only a day and a half's march from Bordeaux. The citizens were building defensive boulevards outside their gates and arming them with artillery. The government was falling apart. The Seneschal was a prisoner. The Constable was still in England. Most of the English troops left behind by the Earl of

Huntingdon had been killed or captured at Saint-Sever. The council at Bordeaux was leaderless, incompetent and corrupt.

The message bearing this gloomy report was taken to England by Pey Berland, the saintly Archbishop of Bordeaux. Berland came with a list of the Gascons' demands. They needed substantial reinforcements soon. A permanent force of at least 4,400 men would be needed to garrison thirteen towns of the duchy. Bordeaux alone needed 2,000 men. These demands, which would have created a second Normandy in the south-west, were well beyond the military and financial capacity of England. Perhaps conscious of this, Beckington and Roos wrote privately to Treasurer Cromwell to warn him that Archbishop Berland was a simple man who must be 'well groped and thoroughly examined'. A fortnight later, another report was carried back to England, sewn into the hem of a pilgrim's cloak, with the news that Dax had submitted on 3 August. The citadel was surrendered by its captain, an Englishman called James Harsage, who did homage to the French King and entered his service. The French were already marching on Bayonne, which was expected to fall within a week.[11]

In fact, by the time that this second report was written, the worst was over. The French had their own problems. Their army had not been paid since leaving Toulouse. Its supply train was inadequate for such a large host, and the food supplies in the Landes were rapidly exhausted. At the end of July 1442, a large part of the army had deserted and left to plunder Languedoc. Charles VII was forced to abandon the plan to besiege Bayonne. Instead, he withdrew north with the rest of his forces to the Garonne, where he hoped to be able to replenish his stores and reorganise his army. At the end of August, he established his headquarters at Agen. As soon as he had left the Adour valley, the loyalist nobility of the Landes and Chalosse launched a counterattack with the support of the men of Bayonne. A group of Gascons in French uniforms surprised one of the gates of Dax on 24 August, killing the porters and taking back the town. Three days later the citadel, which had a garrison of only thirty men, was taken by assault by a force from Bayonne. Most of its defenders were killed. The French captain was among the prisoners, together with James Harsage, who was arrested and charged with treason. At Saint-Sever the townsmen rose up and expelled their French garrison as soon as they heard the news.[12]

At Westminster, the council finally found a commander for the army of relief. It was John Beaufort, Earl of Somerset. The choice was not ideal, but it was necessary, for his uncle the Cardinal was the only possible source of funding. However, no decision had yet been made about the timing or the strength of the expedition when the Archbishop of Bordeaux arrived in England in the middle of August 1442. On 21 August he reported the dire situation of the duchy to a small group of councillors at Sheen. They included Cardinal Beaufort, the Duke of Gloucester and the Earls of Suffolk and Huntingdon. Over the following days, the council reassembled several times to decide what to do. The cupboard was bare. Cash receipts at the Exchequer since March stood at a mere £5,500. Almost all of the Parliamentary subsidy granted in March had been assigned away as security for advances made to the Duke of York and very little could be borrowed against the remainder. Beaufort declared that he would lend cash if he had it, 'but he said he had it not'. He offered to lend £4,000 worth of plate which could be pledged or coined. The councillors present put their hands into their chests and committed another £1,000 in addition to Beaufort's plate. An appeal to 'the mightiest men in every shire of England', the third such appeal in a year, brought in another £1,000. When, in September 1442 Sir Edward Hull finally sailed with his small company to Gascony, he brought with him a letter promising that Somerset would lead 'a noble puissance of men of war to pass into our said duchy, which with God's mercy shall be there in all possible haste'.[13]

Sir Edward Hull reached Bordeaux in October 1442. He found that the French army had already overrun most of the Bazadais and advanced up the Garonne valley, occupying Langon and threatening the city itself. The defence of Bordeaux was in the hands of Sir Robert Roos, who had been elected 'Regent', in effect acting Seneschal, by the Estates of the Bordelais. Roos had come to Bordeaux as a diplomat, but he was also an experienced soldier who had fought with Henry V at Harfleur and served for many years in Normandy. He took to his task with great energy. The fate of Bordeaux turned on control of the valley of the Garonne, by which any army besieging the city would have to be supplied. The English still held two powerful pinch-points on the Garonne, at Saint-Macaire and La Réole, from which they were able to stop the traffic of the river. Roos mustered the men of Bordeaux and the retinues of the leading noblemen of the Bordelais. They were joined by the company which Hull had brought from England and by the crews of his ships, who were promptly pressed into service. From these forces, Roos was able to put garrisons into the remaining castles of the Garonne and to build up a field force in Bordeaux. On 26 October, he and Hull took the field with 400 English troops and 1,000 Gascons to expel a French company which had established itself in the small town of Saint-Loubès on the Dordogne, just twelve miles from Bordeaux. A fortnight later, another field force recovered Langon.[14]

The final act was played out at La Réole. The castle of La Réole was one of the most powerful fortresses of Guyenne, built by that great master of fortification Richard Coeur-de-Lion for the purpose of defending Bordeaux and the lower Garonne from invasion from the Toulousain. But it was vulnerable to attack from inside the town, parts of which overlooked its walls and provided ideal platforms for artillery. The French army arrived outside its walls in early October. On the 8th, they captured the town by assault and began to besiege the castle. The castle was defended by a garrison of 140 men commanded by an English squire, George Swillington. In the seventh week of the siege the French succeeded in getting their artillery into the town. The bombardment began on 24 November. Projectiles of up to 800 pounds were hurled against the castle walls. The garrison's stores were by now close to exhaustion. On 7 December, Swillington surrendered in return for a safe-conduct to Bordeaux for himself and his men. It was a defeat, but a fertile one. Their dogged defence, which had lasted two months, saved Bordeaux. In the final weeks of the siege, the French army had begun to suffer serious hardship. An arsonist set fire to the King's lodgings in the town, forcing him to flee in his nightshirt. The weather deteriorated. The autumn and winter were among the coldest in living memory. Large snowdrifts covered the region and made foraging impossible. Supplies had to be brought in at irregular intervals by barge from Toulouse, over a hundred miles away. Famine and sickness took their toll. One of the victims was La Hire, who died, probably of dysentery, in December. On the day after the surrender of the castle, the rivers of the south-west began to freeze over, and barge traffic stopped completely. Shortly before Christmas, Charles VII abandoned the campaign and withdrew to Montauban.[15]

Bordeaux had survived, but the French campaign in Gascony was the beginning of the end for the English duchy. The loss of territory was serious. Most of the southern Landes, the Bazadais, and the Garonne valley above Langon had been lost, together with much of the lower valleys of the Dordogne and the Isle. The duchy had been reduced to this extremity before, in the 1340s, in the 1370s and again in the opening years of the fifteenth century. On each occasion it had enjoyed at least a partial recovery. What made recovery difficult to envisage this time was the abandonment of the English cause by much of the Gascon nobility. In areas overrun by Charles VII, families like the Gontauts of Biron in southern Périgord or the Grammonts of the Chalosse and the Garonne valley, hastened to make their peace with the dominant power. Even in regions which remained under the control of Bordeaux, some major families like the Lamothes of Roquetaillade, who had been in English allegiance for generations, submitted to Charles VII because they could no longer be confident that the English duchy would endure. Bérard de Lamothe was well rewarded for his defection. He received a pension of 1,000 *livres* a year from the French King. His brother Jean de Lamothe lord of Castelnau followed his example a year later. Many of the Gascon noblemen who had answered Sir Thomas Rempston's call to join him at Tartas and Saint-Sever submitted when the Adour valley was overrun. Their path was eased by generous cash grants and pensions from the French King.[16]

Relations between the Bordeaux government and the three great feudatories of the south-west never recovered. After years in which they had maintained an awkward, undeclared neutrality, they now came down firmly on the side of the Valois and remained there. The truce with Charles of Albret had been destroyed when the French relieved Tartas. The Count of Foix had brought his army to join Charles VII outside Saint-Sever. After its recapture by the English, he returned to capture the town once again. The Count of Armagnac got cold feet about a marriage alliance with Henry VI when the French King began to conquer large parts of Gascony and no army arrived from England. He engaged in a long and evasive correspondence with the English envoys in Bordeaux. They finally gave up in January 1443 and returned empty-handed to England. The Count's intrigues were by now an open secret. When, a year later, John IV was arrested on Charles VII's orders in his castle at L'Isle-Jourdain, the incriminating correspondence was found in his chests. The Count was destined to pass the next two years incarcerated in the royal fortress of Carcassonne.[17]

At Westminster the council was divided by bitter arguments about priorities. Normandy or Gascony? The debate rumbled on into the new year while nothing was done for either theatre. The only reinforcements recruited in this period were the retinue of the Devon magnate

Sir William Bonville, who was appointed as Seneschal of Aquitaine in December 1442 to relieve Robert Roos. He indented to lead a handful of men-at-arms and 600 archers to the duchy, but they had to wait until the worst of the winter gales were over and did not sail until March. One of his ships, carrying eight men-at-arms and 230 archers, foundered with all hands in the Bay of Biscay, so that fewer than 400 men made it to the duchy. It was still unclear whether they were the advance guard of a great army to follow.[18]

On 6 February 1443 the council met in the King's presence in his private chamber at Westminster. There was general agreement that Normandy and Gascony were both badly in need of reinforcement. There was some discussion about whether the government's finances would support two expeditionary armies. Treasurer Cromwell said that he would look into it. But he also voiced the growing weariness at Westminster with the intractable problems of defending Normandy. 'The money that was last spent in Normandy, he wot not what it availeth, neither he wot not in whom default is.' If, as Cromwell later confirmed, the government's borrowing capacity would only run to one expeditionary army, the next question was which theatre should have priority. At Beaufort's suggestion the choice was referred to the lay lords 'the which have their feet in that matter'.

Over the following days, intelligence arrived from France which sharpened the dilemma. Four days after the meeting at Westminster, Beckington returned to England, followed a few days later by Roos. In the last few days of February, they briefed the council in the King's presence at Sheen. The King's officers in Bordeaux had received detailed intelligence of Charles VII's intentions from a spy in his entourage at Montauban. According to this source Charles had passed the Christmas and New Year festivities planning a fresh offensive in the spring along the Garonne and the Adour valleys. A council of war had met to prepare for a campaign whose ultimate objectives were the capture of Bordeaux and Bayonne. Representatives of the King of Castile were reported to have arrived at Montauban to discuss the provision of a Castilian fleet to blockade both cities from the sea. From the Duke of York's councillors at Rouen came less specific intelligence of uncertain provenance, suggesting that the French were also planning a major offensive in lower Normandy, directed against Avranches. Other reports pointed to an attempt on Rouen with the connivance of plotters within the walls.[19]

Beaufort's suggestion that the lay councillors should decide where to intervene was disingenuous. Everyone knew that nothing could be done without his support and his funding. The old nepotist was determined that whatever its destination any expeditionary army must be commanded by John Beaufort Earl of Somerset. In the end, Henry VI's ministers decided to leave the strategic decision to Somerset himself. He was invited, in effect, to write his own orders. Somerset, whose health had always been delicate, was unwell and attended none of the critical council meetings. So Adam Moleyns, then clerk of the council, was charged to negotiate the terms of his commission with him. The outcome was a set of articles listing the Earl's demands, with the King's responses noted in the margin. Somerset wanted a 'sufficient puissance of men', by which he meant at least 1,000 men-at-arms and 3,000 archers; an artillery train complete with specialised gun crews; and prefabricated pontoons for bridging rivers. He wanted the powers of a royal lieutenant, with complete freedom to deploy his army without reference to the Duke of York 'where as him shall think best and most necessary after his own conceit'. He was not to be 'maunded or countermaunded' by any authority whatever, whether in England or France. All of these conditions were agreed.

It was only at the end of March 1443 that anything like a strategic plan emerged. It was explained in the instructions of Garter King of Arms, who was sent to Normandy to break the news to Richard of York. 'It seemed full behoveful and necessary,' York was to be told, 'that the manner of the conduct of the war be changed.' After disembarking his army in Normandy, Somerset planned to march south into Maine and Anjou and then to cross the Loire. There, he would fight a 'most cruel and mortal war'. The object was to draw French forces away from the Gascon march and bring them to battle somewhere in Anjou or Poitou. At the same time, by operating between Normandy and Guyenne the army would shield York's vulnerable garrisons from the armies of Charles VII in the south-west. The herald was to explain that none of this would prejudice York's authority as lieutenant, because although Somerset's authority extended to all of France, his army would operate 'in other places than be now in the King's obeisance and in the which my said lord of York cometh not'. In spite of Garter's emollient message, it was clear to York that he was being sidelined. He would not receive the usual annual reinforcements in 1443, or even the allowance due to him for the troops already in

Normandy. To rub in the point, Somerset demanded and was granted promotion to the rank of Duke, so that York would not outrank him. He was formally invested with his new dignity at a Garter feast at Westminster in April.[20]

The official explanation for Somerset's adventure was that a confrontation with the French in the field was necessary to force the French King back to the negotiating table with terms that the English could accept. As Somerset himself pointed out in the articles setting out his terms, a 'sufficient puissance of men' was the essential condition for a successful negotiation. But it must have struck many people at the time that the real purpose of his expeditionary army was to advance the territorial ambitions of his family. Neither of the Beaufort brothers, Edmund Earl of Dorset and John Duke of Somerset, had a substantial endowment in England. Edmund had done well in Normandy, where he had accumulated a significant portfolio of property. John's position was more difficult, for he had had to pay a heavy ransom to purchase his freedom. Maine and Anjou had recently been granted to Edmund. However, the grant had not yet been registered and as part of the deal with John it was now cancelled and both territories were diverted to him. Edmund was compensated by being raised to the rank of marquess. Against this background Somerset's strategy looked suspiciously like an attempt to take possession of his new appanage. For the second time in five years the defence of Normandy was sacrificed to the promotion of the Cardinal's family. Henry Beaufort had been present at the main council meetings and ruthlessly exploited his hold over the government's finances. He lent £21,666 on very limited security to cover three-quarters of the advances due to his nephew's army and half the shipping costs.[21]

The Earl of Suffolk and Adam Moleyns were now the driving force behind English attempts to make peace with France. Suffolk's concern to bring the war to an end was well known. Moleyns was a civil lawyer, like most of the workhorses of English diplomacy, with a 'thirst for peace' if we are to believe the epitaph incised on his tomb. He was a protégé of Cardinal Beaufort who had recently joined the council after serving for six years as its clerk. He was also a man of profound culture who impressed many of his contemporaries in England and abroad. The papal diplomat Aeneas Silvius Piccolomini thought that he was the best latinist that England had produced since the twelfth century. After the final collapse in Normandy, it suited the enemies of these men to claim that they had acted alone with the connivance of a clique of self-interested cronies. But this was very far from the truth. The peace policy had its opponents, but by now the problems of the war were widely understood. Suffolk's views had the support of the King and were endorsed by almost everyone actively involved in government as well as by most of the Parliamentary peerage.[22]

In France, the initiative was taken once again by the Duke of Orléans and the new Duke of Brittany, Francis de Montfort. Charles of Orléans had learned wisdom after his first, clumsy re-entry into French politics. He had repaired his relations with Charles VII and distanced himself from the rebellious cabals of the princes. The King received him at Limoges in May 1442 as he was on his way to the *journée* of Tartas. There was a carefully stage-managed and very public reconciliation between the two men, followed by generous grants towards the cost of the Duke's ransom and an annuity from the royal treasury. As a result, the Duke acquired a measure of influence which he had not previously enjoyed, but he also became politically and to some extent financially dependent on the King. As for Francis de Montfort, he was still an unknown quantity. He had hardly been involved in his father's government and had very little experience of public affairs. At the outset of his reign he allowed himself to be guided by his father's old councillors and proposed to continue his father's ambiguous policy of navigating a path between England and France without wholly committing himself to either. In December 1442, the Duke of Orléans came to Rennes and persuaded Francis to pick up the threads of John V's earlier attempts to broker a peace. Francis's principal herald, Brittany, arrived in England in February 1443 with proposals for yet another peace conference under Breton auspices.[23]

It was left to the Duke of Orléans to win round Charles VII. The French King entered Poitiers on 25 May 1443. Shortly afterwards the Duke arrived in the city for discussions. The King was wary of the Duke of Brittany's role in the peace process. But he did not take ultimate victory for granted, as some of his councillors did, and he was genuinely worried about the threat from Somerset's army. So he authorised Charles and Francis to pursue the matter. At the beginning of June Francis appointed his younger brother Gilles to lead an embassy to the English court. Gilles's instructions were to convey the French King's agreement to the new peace conference, to offer Francis's services as mediator, and to agree the preliminaries. He was also authorised to tell Henry VI that the new Duke intended at a suitable moment to adhere to the treaty of Troyes, as his father had done.[24]

The Duke of Somerset's expedition was expected to boost England's diplomatic bargaining power. But it began badly and continued worse. Recruitment was difficult. Somerset commanded little respect among the nobility, and they did not sign up. The four barons and eight bannerets that he had planned to recruit were reduced to a single banneret and there were only six belted knights instead of thirty. There were long delays at Portsmouth, due mainly to shipping and recruitment problems and to fraud and desertion at the musters. These were common problems for major expeditionary armies, but the council was not inclined to make allowances. They were impatient of the delay and irritated at the difference between Somerset's promises and his performance. Some of them were already beginning to wonder whether they had made the right decisions in the spring. 'The King', they wrote, 'marveleth greatly and not without cause the long abode of his said cousin on this side of the sea.' Somerset eventually sailed from the Solent at the beginning of August 1443 with 4,550 men.

The army disembarked in the great open bay of La Hougue on the north coast of the Cotentin. A week later, he established his headquarters at Avranches, of which he was the titular captain. He was joined there by troops drawn from the heavily garrisoned fortresses of the south-west of which he or his brother Edmund were captains. There were also volunteers, including the company of the captain of Bayeux Matthew Gough, perhaps the closest in spirit to the French *écorcheur* captains. With these additions to his strength, Somerset's army must have numbered between 5,500 and 6,000 men. He lost no time in making himself unpopular with both the population of the Cotentin and the administration in Rouen. He commandeered the services of local officials. He levied a cartage tax and requisitioned at least 120 carts on his own authority. These high-handed acts provoked howls of protest and eventually led to the appointment of a commission of enquiry. The commission's report, which ran to eighty-seven pages, related in detail innumerable acts of extortion and violence for which Somerset's army was held responsible.[25]

By the time that Somerset arrived in Normandy, the intelligence which had informed his strategy in the spring was out of date. The

French King was no longer in the south-west. He had moved north to Saumur on the Loire, and most of his forces were now stationed on the marches of Normandy. The Dauphin Louis and the Count of Dunois were on the northern march with a field force of about 1,600 men. Marshal Laval was on the march of Maine with the garrisons of the west. The captain of Evreux Robert de Flocques, who had taken temporary command of the Beauce sector, had collected a large field force and was poised to invade Lower Normandy from the south-east. Somerset's claim that by crossing the Loire his army would serve as the shield of Normandy was now meaningless. This was brought home to the English when, in the second week of August, the Dauphin and Dunois arrived at Dieppe with about 900 men. The council at Rouen had had some warning of what was afoot and had sent reinforcements. But the English siege works at Le Polet were swiftly captured. Supported by seamen from the town, Dunois's troops attacked the English bastide on 15 August. They threw improvised timber pontoons across the ditches and assaulted the walls from ladders. The defenders were overwhelmed and most of them were killed. The prisoners included the captain, William Peyto. Some sixty native Normans were found in the place. Some had been fighting with the garrison. Others were merchants and carters bringing in food and other supplies. They were all hanged without distinction.[26]

It was unclear what Somerset intended to do now. The Norman chronicler Thomas Basin remarked on the Duke's obsessive secretiveness. Not even his own captains knew what was in his mind. When they asked him, he would scowl and say that if the shirt on his back knew his plans he would burn it. Somerset did not lack professional advice. His captains included experienced professional soldiers like Sir Thomas Kyriel and Matthew Gough. But he declined to consult them. It seems to have been his own idea to make first for Anjou. In the second week of September, he appeared without warning outside Angers. He installed himself with the captains of his army in the suburban abbey of St Nicholas, south of the walls, looted the area around, and imposed *pâtis* on unwalled places along the Loire. Panic spread through the region as far as Tours. But Somerset had no siege artillery and made no attempt to attack the town. His position at St Nicholas soon became untenable. One night, a cannonball fired from the town walls killed a man sitting next to him at dinner. After three days, Somerset broke his camp and marched north again.

In late September, Somerset arrived outside Pouancé, the great fortress of the Duke of Alençon on the march of Brittany and Maine. Here he was joined by his baggage train, which had been proceeding laboriously down the Breton march from Avranches under escort. There was a great quantity of artillery from England, but it consisted entirely of field pieces collected in anticipation of a pitched battle. There were no bombards or other siege guns. Somerset presumably hoped that a siege of Pouancé would draw the French army into battle. Richemont took the bait. He marched to Château-Gontier where he joined up with troops from the borders of Maine under Marshal Laval and Jean de Bueil. There, he suffered a serious reverse. Matthew Gough took some 1,500 troops from Somerset's army and fell on the French encampment without warning in the middle of the night, massacring many of the men and dispersing the rest. This coup ensured that Somerset encountered no organised resistance for the rest of his campaign. But it made little difference to the outcome.[27]

After two or three weeks sitting outside Pouancé, the Duke of Somerset folded his tents and sloped away under cover of darkness, heading north to La Guerche on the Breton march. The old fortress of La Guerche had no strategic value. Its walls had not been maintained for many years and its citadel had been partly dismantled. Somerset occupied it without difficulty and began to waste the surrounding region. This pointless exercise provoked a major diplomatic incident. The town was situated on the Breton side of the border. The Duke of Brittany was furious at the attack on his duchy by an ally. He had to be restrained by his councillors from raising an army and making war on the Duke of Somerset. Instead, he had to buy Somerset out for 20,000 *saluts*. He instructed his ambassadors in England to protest in the strongest terms. The English ministers, who were learning about the incident for the first time from the Bretons, were embarrassed. Henry VI apologised to Francis and sent a message to Somerset peremptorily ordering him to compensate the Duke and refrain from any further acts of war against his territory. By the time that Somerset received this letter he had left the Breton march and regrouped his forces outside Le Mans. From here he marched on Beaumont-le-Vicomte, the principal French garrison town of eastern Maine, which surrendered after a short siege in December. This proved to be the only significant gain of the whole campaign. By the end of 1443 Somerset had returned to Normandy, and in January he sailed back to England, leaving his army behind. The men had been paid in advance for six months' service, which expired in January, but no arrangements had been made to pay for their continued service after that. In their commander's absence, the army broke up. Many of them took to brigandage in Lower Normandy.[28]

Somerset returned to a glacial reception in England. He was accused on all sides of having wasted his army and the great sums that it had cost, and of alienating England's only continental ally. Henry VI, who had supported his claim to an independent command, was outraged and banished him from court. The Exchequer pursued him and his heirs for years for an account of how he had spent the large sums of money paid to him. The Duke shortly retired to his castle at Corfe in Dorset where he died on 27 May 1444, reportedly by his own hand. He preferred, according to the chronicler who recorded this rumour, 'to cut short his grief rather than pass his life in misery under the shadow of such a disgrace'. His tomb of marble and alabaster, with a handsome effigy in full plate armour still stands on the south side of the choir in Wimborne Minster.[29]

Gilles de Bretagne had arrived in England in August 1443. Francis could not have chosen an ambassador more agreeable to his hosts. Gilles and Henry were cousins through their mothers. As a child Gilles had spent two years in the royal household and had formed a strong bond with the young King. Yet his embassy was the origin of many of the problems between England and Brittany over the following years. The Breton prince was ambitious, conceited and inept. He had no conception of the delicate balancing act which had enabled Brittany to stay out of the war under John V, and which his elder brother hoped to continue. He was determined to exploit his connections with Henry VI and his court to promote himself. The English King encouraged this ambition without ever thinking through the implications. He told Gilles that he 'always loved and admired him and always would, for his close kinship, and the great virtues and noble manners that had marked him out ever since they lived together as children'. He awarded him an annuity of 2,000 nobles a year. For his part Gilles offered to swear a personal oath of allegiance to the English King and declared that it would be his pleasure to serve him in peace and war in whatever ways he might command, even if it cost him his assets in France, provided that Henry granted him a suitable alternative endowment in England. In a letter issued under his own signet, the English King agreed to participate in a new peace conference and accepted Francis's offer of mediation. The Bretons left in the middle of December 1443, accompanied by the senior English herald, Garter King of Arms, bearing the King's consent. Yet Gilles's embassy very nearly wrecked the peace process which it was intended to promote. Charles VII was outraged by reports of the affectionate exchanges between him and the English King, which reinforced his instinctive distrust of Breton mediation. He declared that Gilles' years of living among the English had made him more English than French and accused him of having treasonably made use of his embassy to give aid and comfort to the enemy. He ordered the confiscation of all Gilles's assets in France.[30]

The events of the summer of 1443 shocked Henry VI's ministers and forced them into a fundamental reassessment of their position. The destruction of the bastide of Dieppe and the humiliating outcome of Somerset's expedition left the Duke of York facing superior French armies on several fronts with few troops on his payroll and no prospect of substantial reinforcement. Breton mediation had no chance of success after the debacle of Gilles de Bretagne's embassy. The sense of panic and demoralisation at Westminster was palpable. The time had come to get an agreement with France on whatever terms might be available, before worse disasters befell them. The council resolved to dispense with mediation and the formality of a peace conference. Instead, they would negotiate directly with Charles VII. The moment was captured by the poet John Lydgate, ever sensitive to the mood of his patrons, who saw the ghost of Henry V finally vanishing from men's minds:

> His title of France and of Normandy
> Died in his conquest . . .
> God grant us all, now after his decease
> To send us grace atween each party,
> By love and charity to live in perfect peace.[31]

In January 1444 Charles of Orléans's herald arrived in England with a letter from the French King inviting Henry VI to nominate an embassy to deal directly with his councillors. Compiègne was proposed as the venue. More controversially, Charles VII asked that the Earl of Suffolk, whose support of the peace process was well-known in France, should lead it. The English council met to consider this unusual request in the King's private chamber at Westminster on 1 February. Suffolk was reluctant. He pointed out that having spent two years as a prisoner of the Count of Dunois in France he knew many of the principals on the French side personally. He was also close to the Duke of Orléans, with whom he had often discussed the issues during the Duke's captivity in England. If large concessions had to be made to the French, his own role was likely to be misrepresented. Rumours that he would conduct the negotiations were already circulating in London and had aroused unfavourable comment. But the King insisted, and Suffolk submitted. He imposed two conditions. He must have 'sad and circumspect' men with him to share the responsibility, and letters exonerating him in advance from any charge of misconduct that might subsequently be made against him. The sad and circumspect men were Adam Moleyns, Sir Robert Roos, who would speak for Gascon interests, Richard Andrew, who had recently taken over as the King's diplomatic secretary, and a rising household squire called John Wenlock, who had been on earlier confidential missions in France. These were among Henry's most trusted household servants. They were to be joined from Normandy by Sir Thomas Hoo, Henry's French Chancellor. The Earl of Suffolk was very obviously the leading member of this group. The others were told to do nothing without his personal approval. Their instructions were to agree a permanent peace or, failing that, a truce. In either case, it was hoped to seal the deal by a marriage between Henry VI and a French princess. To accomplish their task, they were given what Suffolk later called 'as large power as any was given to any ambassador among other convocations and treaties'.[32]

Suffolk and his colleagues sailed for France at the end of February 1444. To the irritation of the French, they did not go to Calais, where a French escort was waiting to take them to Compiègne. Instead, they landed at Harfleur to assess the situation in Normandy before meeting the French councillors. In the middle of March Suffolk was closeted with the Duke of York at Rouen. Seen from the Norman capital, the situation was menacing. A month earlier, Charles VII had issued a declaration from Angers that he would take command in person of a great army to invade Normandy in the spring if the negotiations failed. In addition to men withdrawn from garrisons and noblemen summoned to the army, the French King had taken thirteen freelance captains with nearly 4,000 men onto his payroll. All of these troops had been directed to concentrate at Pontoise on the eastern edge of the duchy. Altogether, they were reported to be 18,000 strong. The figure was probably exaggerated, but Normandy would have been almost defenceless in the face of a host half as strong. According to Suffolk's statements six years later, when he was on trial for his life, desertion and wastage had reduced the Norman garrison establishment to just 1,500 men. Most of the fortresses had empty storerooms. Few of them had artillery. The unpaid remnants of the Duke of Somerset's army were roaming through Lower Normandy killing, looting and exacting *pâtis*. The English authorities at Rouen told Suffolk that unless a peace or truce was made soon Lancastrian Normandy would be extinguished. The atmosphere of impending crisis hung over the English ambassadors throughout their mission.[33]

In the event, negotiations opened at Vendôme on 8 and 9 April 1444. Once the preliminaries had been settled, the discussions were adjourned and the diplomats reassembled at Tours a week later on the 16th. The French Chancellor Regnault de Chartres, who was to have led the negotiations on their side, had died of a heart attack a few days before the opening. He was replaced by Pierre de Brézé, a rising power at the French court who was reputed to be the most seductive speaker of his day. 'His voice softened and conquered the mighty,' was what the Burgundian chronicler Georges Chastellain said about him. He was supported by the Duke of Orléans and the Count of Vendôme. In the background was a papal legate, none other than the anglophile Piero da Monte, who had passed much of the 1430s as Eugenius IV's representative in England. On the morning of 17 April, the English delegation travelled downriver in barges from Tours to Charles VII's castle at Montils, where they were received by the King and presented their credentials. The main lines of an agreement emerged over the next fortnight. The mood was convivial. The English ambassadors were accommodated in Charles of Orléans's castle at Blois in the intervals between negotiating sessions. There were jousts and feasts. For many of those present, it was a meeting of friends.[34]

The friendship of these men, however, was personal and skin-deep, whereas their differences were enduring and profound. The French were in a strong position and in no mood to make concessions. Negotiations for a permanent peace quickly broke down over the perennial questions of territory and sovereignty. For the first time, the English came ready to abandon their King's title to the Crown of France in return for an acceptable territorial settlement, but their territorial demands were exorbitant. They wanted to be confirmed in possession of everything that the Kings of England had held by inheritance before Edward III proclaimed himself King of France in 1340. They considered that this meant Normandy and Guyenne as they had been held by Henry II in the twelfth century, and Ponthieu, which Edward II had inherited from his mother at the beginning of the fourteenth. But they were not prepared to do homage for them, as every King of England had done before 1340. They envisaged that they would be held as autonomous territories independent of the French Kingdom. The French took their stand on the terms of the successive treaties of the thirteenth and early fourteenth centuries in which the English had renounced Normandy, abandoned Ponthieu and accepted the loss of much that earlier Kings of England had once possessed in Guyenne. Piero da Monte supported the English territorial claims, but he was not well briefed on the complex history and the French brusquely rejected all of his interventions. They were willing, they said, to concede Gascony, Quercy and Périgord to which they added, perhaps illogically, Calais and Guines, which the English Kings had only ever held by conquest. Normandy was a striking omission from this list. Influential voices were urging Charles VII to remember that the duchy had been part of the 'true demesne' of the Kings of France since its conquest from King John of England at the beginning of the thirteenth century. Perhaps Charles would have sacrificed Normandy if there had been agreement about the English King's tenure. We cannot know, for the English were immovably opposed to doing homage. Charles was no more willing than his predecessors to compromise the unity of his realm by allowing the English to hold any territory in France except as fiefs of his Crown.[35]

The alternative to a permanent peace was a truce which allowed both sides to remain in possession of what they currently occupied but left their claims unresolved. The French were prepared to consider a truce but only if it was short. They wanted to hold the threat of conquest over England's head until a permanent peace was finally agreed on terms that they could accept. So they refused to grant the truce of fifteen years or more which had been discussed outside Calais in 1439. It must be a mere interval for further negotiation. This was what was finally agreed. The English knew how fragile truces could be, especially short ones, but were in no position to insist. They looked for security in a marriage alliance. Charles VII was unwilling to offer one of his own daughters. He did not care to provide the house of Lancaster with another link to the French royal line to burnish their hereditary claims to the Crown. The preferred candidate was the Queen's niece Margaret of Anjou, the fifteen-year-old daughter of Réné of Anjou. The English were attracted by this proposal. They saw in the match a chance to make allies of the Angevin clan which dominated the French King's council and had hitherto been among their most persistent enemies. Margaret was brought before the English ambassadors by her mother in the midst of the negotiations and met with their approval. Her father, crippled by the ransom promised to the Duke of Burgundy and with much of his domains in Italy and Lorraine in the hands of his enemies, could not afford a Queen's dowry. But the English wanted the match enough to accept her with a modest 20,000 *francs* in cash plus her grandmother's worthless claim to the kingdom of Majorca.

On 24 May 1444, Margaret of Anjou was betrothed to the English King at a ceremony in the abbey church of St Martin of Tours. The Earl of Suffolk stood in as proxy for Henry. Piero da Monte officiated. Charles VII was present. A crowd of noblemen, officials and courtiers was packed into the choir of the old Romanesque church. Four days after the ceremony, on 28 May, the truce was formally sealed. It was to apply to the whole territory of both kingdoms and the seas about them for an initial period of just twenty-two months, ending on 1 April 1446. In itself the truce resolved nothing. The difficult questions of territory, tenure and sovereignty all remained unanswered. The claims of the exiled Norman landowners were not even broached. It was agreed that the pause in the fighting would be used to negotiate a permanent peace in which all of these questions would have to be addressed. A French embassy armed with large powers would visit England to discuss them.[36]

In November 1444 another English embassy, also led by the Earl of Suffolk, left for France to bring Margaret of Anjou back to England. It was an impressive affair. Apart from Suffolk himself, John Talbot Earl of Shrewsbury accompanied the cavalcade together with five barons, seventeen knights, 65 squires, 215 yeomen and a large number of wives, clerks and servants. Seventy ships were required to carry their baggage and retinues. The cost, at nearly £7,000, was equivalent to a minor military campaign. The French court was then at Nancy in Lorraine. It was there that the marriage was celebrated in March 1445, Suffolk once again standing in as proxy for the King. On 9 April 1445, Margaret and her retinue arrived at Portsmouth. Five days later Henry VI was at Southampton to welcome the wife that he had never met. The marriage service was performed again on 22 April in the presence of both spouses at Titchfield Abbey in Hampshire. Margaret became Queen not only of England, but in her husband's eyes of France also. Henry marked the event by having the gold ring which he had worn at his coronation in Paris refashioned into a wedding ring. On 29 May 1445 the Queen was escorted through the streets of London from Tower Hill to Westminster with the traditional theatrical tableaux, pageants, speeches, singing choirs, noisy crowds and lavish distributions of wine. She was crowned in Westminster Abbey on the following morning.[37]

Across northern France, reports of the negotiations at Tours had generated high expectations. An immense procession for peace wound its way through the streets of Paris behind the clergy, carrying portable reliquaries on their shoulders with the most famous relics of the city's churches. When eventually the truce was proclaimed to the sound of the trumpet at markets and cross-roads, there was a spontaneous outburst of joy. People assumed that it marked the end of their troubles. The roads were suddenly filled with travellers, and the suburban vineyards and vegetable plots with men clearing the weeds of years. The Seine and the roads of the Beauce were reopened to traffic and the markets of Rouen were filled with produce after a pinched decade. The Lendit fair, traditionally held each June in the open plain north of Paris, was held that year for the first time since 1426, albeit within the walls of Saint-Denis and with a military guard. The Porte Saint-Martin in northern Paris, which had been walled up ever since the attack on the city by Joan of Arc in 1429, was reopened. 'In the year of grace 1444, God relieved our sufferings,' ran the legend on a tapestry commissioned by the canons of Beauvais, which hung above the nave of their cathedral until the nineteenth century.[38]

In reality, three decades of war had left a legacy which could not be extinguished by mere seals on a treaty. Valois France was full of unemployed soldiers with no way of making a living except by violence. Once the truce came into force, the companies of *écorcheurs* could no longer be redeployed against the English at the King's wages as they had been since 1439. It was necessary to revert to the older practice of finding employment for them beyond the frontiers of France. This had never been more than a temporary palliative, for when their employment ended the troops invariably returned. But there was no alternative. 'We have decided that to suppress the pillaging during the truce it is sensible, in fact necessary, to find a way to expel these soldiers living on the land of our kingdom,' the King declared. As soon as the truce with England was sealed, he began to organise two large-scale campaigns, one in Switzerland and the other in Lorraine.

In Switzerland, the opportunity had arisen from the attempt of the two Habsburg Dukes of Austria to reassert their authority over the Swiss cantons. The attempt had provoked a civil war between their only Swiss ally, the city of Zurich, and a confederation of the other cantons. In April 1444, Zurich was besieged by the armies of the confederation. The French King had been allied to the Habsburgs since 1430 and had received several appeals for help over the years, which he had always turned down on account of other calls on his resources. When, just after the conclusion of the truce of Tours, an ambassador arrived with another appeal for military support from Frederick III, King of Germany and Duke of Austria, Charles VII and his councillors seized their chance. They proposed to intervene with an army drawn almost entirely from the companies of *écorcheurs* and footloose English soldiery from Normandy, and to place it under the command of the 21-year-old Dauphin. A second army was intended to suppress resistance to the house of Anjou in the duchies of Bar and Lorraine, and especially in the Imperial free city of Metz, which the Dukes of Lorraine had been trying for years to incorporate into their territory. It would include a number of companies of *écorcheurs* but was to be recruited mainly in the traditional way from royal garrisons and the military retinues of the nobility.[39]

The Swiss expedition was the first to leave. The Dauphin established his headquarters at Langres in eastern Champagne towards the end of July 1444. In practice the recruitment of the army and the direction of its day-to-day operations were delegated to the experienced Angevin captain Jean de Bueil. Well-informed correspondents of the city of Strasbourg who accompanied the army counted 140 captains, including some of the most notorious *écorcheur* leaders of the past decade: Antoine de Chabannes, once Bourbon's principal captain; Jean de Salazar, Villandrando's old deputy, who had been fighting on the march of Gascony with the remnants of his companies; John Bastard of Armagnac, another southern *routier*; Jean de Blanchefort, the former captain of Breteuil and terror of Picardy. They were reported to have 23,000 mounted men at their backs, about half of them actual combatants. They included companies of French, Bretons and Gascons, Castilians, Italians and Scots and the usual mobs of hucksters and hangers-on. Six weeks into the campaign, they were joined by the companies of the French captain and *bailli* of Evreux, Robert de Flocques, and the Welsh captain of Bayeux Matthew Gough, old enemies who had made their way together across northern France with their followers, 'like brothers in arms' wrote a chronicler. Robert de Flocques's company was drawn mainly from Picardy, the Île-de-France and the marches of Normandy. Matthew Gough's 1,500-strong English contingent had been raised in Lower Normandy, mainly among the men abandoned in the Cotentin by the Duke of Somerset in January. Some of them, including Gough himself, were being paid from the French King's war treasury.[40]

The whole horde left Langres on 5 August 1444. They made their way across the imperial county of Burgundy and into Alsace and the Swiss Jura, leaving a trail of burned-out villages, looted churches and mutilated corpses in their wake. Their first objective was the rich city of Basel, where the Council of the Church was sitting. On 26 August 1444, at Sint Jakob on the river Birs just east of Basel, they wiped out the much smaller army of the Swiss confederation which had been sent to confront them. After that, however, the difficulties began to mount. They were unable to penetrate into the city, by force, guile or negotiation. Their Austrian allies, who had not reckoned on such destructive assistance, became increasingly hostile. The terrain was difficult for cavalry. The Swiss, who knew the ground better, abandoned the siege of Zurich and began to concentrate formidable forces against the invaders. Finally, the Dauphin resolved to abandon the Habsburg cause. In September 1444, he retreated to the town of Ensisheim in Alsace where he opened negotiations with the towns of the Swiss confederation. There was a cease-fire, followed at the end of October by a treaty of peace under which the brigand army undertook to evacuate the confederation's territory. The great tide of military flotsam flowed back into Alsace, where they found themselves winter quarters. In October, the Dauphin was wounded in the knee by an arrow and abandoned his army to join his father in Lorraine. For some five months, his army was left to waste the rich region of Alsace until in February 1445, the Dauphin finally agreed with the representatives of Frederick III to leave the region.[41]

Charles VII opened his own campaign in July 1444, a few days after the Dauphin. The King was accompanied by his brothers-in-law Réné and Charles of Anjou, and by Réné's son John Duke of Calabria. In addition to the retinues of the officers of the Crown and the leading members of the royal council, they were followed by many of the men who had served on the marches of Normandy as well as freelance captains like Poton de Saintrailles. Passing through Langres a fortnight after Louis had left it, Charles based himself at Nancy, the capital of Lorraine. Toul and Verdun, which had been French protectorates for half a century, submitted readily enough. Épinal submitted reluctantly, protesting that they found it strange to be treated as a subject city 'like Paris'. The main centre of resistance was Metz, which had never accepted French 'protection' and was resisting incorporation into Réné of Anjou's duchy. In the middle of September, the French army laid siege to the city. The inhabitants defended it with ferocity. At the end of February 1445, after a siege of more than five months, the French King entered into a treaty by which the citizens in effect bought him off. In April 1445, Charles VII withdrew to France with his army.[42]

Neither campaign did anything to address the longer-term problem of unemployed soldiery. Where were they to go now? The captain of Isenheim, writing to the city of Strasbourg, reported the plans of the Dauphin's companies of *écorcheurs*. If a permanent peace was made between England and France, they intended to leave for Italy at Easter to find employment there. If not, they would return to France hoping for employment in the renewed war with England but ready to support themselves by looting if need be. With no permanent peace in sight, the first companies of the Dauphin's army had already begun to drift back to France when negotiations began for the evacuation of Alsace. The main body followed them homeward in March 1445.[43]

Matthew Gough and his men were among the first to withdraw from the Dauphin's army. They were back in Lower Normandy in February 1445. There, they resumed their old ways, doing serious damage across the region. The disorder threatened to destroy what little remained of the English government's goodwill among the Norman population. From Rouen, the Duke of York and his council issued ordinances directing the *baillis* to arrest all soldiers found living off the land. He threatened dire punishment for those caught looting. Accompanied by members of his council, the lieutenant toured Lower Normandy in March and again in May, to punish infractions. None of these measures had much effect. In June, the Grand Conseil resorted to more radical steps. All troops who had returned to Lower Normandy from Switzerland and Lorraine and were on the ordinary garrison establishment were ordered to return to their bases. Those living off the land with no garrison to return to were told to muster before the lieutenant at Écouché, near Argentan, on 25 July. There, some 600 of them who were judged fit for service were conscripted and assigned to garrisons. The rest were escorted to Cherbourg or Barfleur and put on ships bound for England. A special session of the Estates of Normandy was summoned to Argentan to vote funds to pay for this exercise.[44]

These measures were only partially effective, for with the mounting arrears of pay, discipline broke down even among those on the garrison establishment. The garrisons of François de Surienne at Longny and Verneuil and the important garrison at Mantes on the Seine disguised themselves with masks and raided along the roads to Paris and Orléans, plundering travellers, looting homes and cutting throats. The garrisons of the northern march followed their example and took to brigandage along the roads from Paris to the Somme, even taking other English soldiers for ransom. The large garrisons of Domfront and Avranches spread terror across much of Lower Normandy while the garrison of Le Mans raided into Brittany and Touraine, seizing men and cattle in defiance of the truce. Some English captains, like Sir Roger Camoys, abandoned garrison service altogether and turned their companies into freelance bands operating for their own account. These problems were never resolved. The truce commissioners of each side met for nearly two months in the spring of 1446 at Evreux and Louviers. Long lists of infractions were produced. The conference got nowhere. Charles VII hinted that the English commissioners were dragging their feet and he was probably right. Their difficulty was that the Norman administration could not afford to pay the garrisons. It was therefore forced to turn a blind eye to their operations in Valois France. The alternative would have been mass desertion followed by the looting of Normandy. Another conference, near Mantes in December of that year, accomplished little more.[45]

The French ministers had a more intractable problem, with many more soldiers on their hands and nowhere to send them, but they also had a more radical and ultimately more successful solution. At some time between February and April 1445, they unveiled a new scheme which had been in preparation for some time. It was approved in its final form at a great council in the castle of Sarry near Châlons in Champagne. The text of the ordinance has been lost, but its contents are known from other sources. It provided for the incorporation of selected *écorcheurs* into tactical units of six mounted men which came to be known as *'lances'*. The *lance* was an integrated unit of different arms of a kind which had been familiar in English armies since the fourteenth century. But its make-up reflected the growing importance of cavalry in French tactical doctrine. Each *lance* consisted of a cavalryman in full armour, supported by two lightly armoured bowmen, a *coutillier* armed with an axe or a short sword, and two pages who were not usually combatants. Companies, which became known as *compagnies d'ordonnance*, were each to be formed of 100 *lances*, or 400 combatants, commanded by a captain appointed by the Constable. The King proposed to retain and pay twenty such companies, or 2,000 *lances*, 1,500 of them in Languedoil and 500 in Languedoc, in addition to the troops of the royal household and those stationed in garrisons on the marches of Normandy and Guyenne.

Detailed arrangements for implementing the scheme were announced in a further ordinance issued from Louppy-le-Château in Lorraine on 26 May 1445. The *compagnies d'ordonnance* would not be concentrated in places where they could threaten the government or the people around them. Instead, they were to be dispersed across the kingdom, one company to each place, and brought together only when they were needed. The cost of these arrangements was high, which was the main reason for the misgivings expressed by some of Charles's advisers. The solution adopted was to impose the cost on the provinces in which the companies were quartered. A precise tariff was laid down: for each *lance*, one *livre* per month plus specified quantities of wine, wheat, meat, oil, salt, eggs, cheese and lard; for every twelve horses, specified quantities of fodder and straw. Commissioners were empowered to nominate the places where the companies were to be quartered and to assess the obligations in cash and kind of the province. In practice contributions in kind were soon phased out, to be replaced by cash payments at a standard rate of 30 *francs* per *lance* per month and an extra *franc* for the captain. As time went on, the relationship between the government's demands and the numbers of men cantoned became largely fictional. The provincial assessments developed into a permanent tax, in effect a *taille* for the upkeep of a standing army.[46]

The plan delivered less than it promised, but even so the delivery was impressive. At least twenty-four companies can be identified during 1445, although most of them were below the regulation strength. Altogether, Charles's ministers were able to raise about 1,800 *lances*, or 7,200 combatants. Most of the captains who commanded *compagnies d'ordonnance* were not themselves *écorcheurs*. They were men whom the government had learned to rely on: prominent noblemen, royal councillors or established captains with a record of royal service. A few, like Poton de Saintrailles and Robert de Flocques, occupied the nether world between freebooters and royal servants. Four were foreign: an Italian, a Castilian and two Scots, whose companies were probably drawn from their fellow countrymen. A number of these men would enjoy long careers in royal service extending into the next reign and in some cases into the 1470s. The new scheme did not incorporate by any means all of the *écorcheurs* who had returned from Switzerland and Lorraine. About half of them and the great majority of their captains were not taken on. They included some famous names. Jean de Salazar and the Bastard of Armagnac, for example, were rejected. Both of them had operated mainly in Languedoc and returned there. Antoine de Chabannes, who was also rejected, complained to the King that he had been deprived of his livelihood and began to dress ostentatiously in black to mark his vexation. The rejected captains and their men were paid off. They received letters of remission pardoning their past misdeeds and threats of punishment if they resumed their former activities. Perhaps surprisingly, few of them did. The French scheme was better conceived and better enforced than the efforts of the English in Normandy, mainly because it was better funded by a richer state. Contemporaries agreed that the level of internal disorder sharply declined and that Valois France began its slow recovery from the years of insecurity and destruction.[47]

In England the reception of the truce of Tours was muted. The Earl of Suffolk told Parliament that it was 'the greatest universal well that ever came to the King or to his subjects'. Henry VI was delighted and raised him to the rank of Marquess. There was an effusive vote of thanks from both houses of Parliament recording his knightly courage, wisdom, providence and discretion. Yet beyond the political class, the truce and the royal marriage were not popular. There was a widespread feeling that Henry had sold himself too cheaply. The London chronicler's later verdict that Margaret of Anjou was 'a dear marriage for England' was widely shared at the time.

THE KING'S PEACE, 1442–1448

The records of the court of King's Bench, which tried cases of seditious speech, are not necessarily a representative sample of opinion, but doubts about the King's capacity to govern are a theme of growing importance from 1444 onwards. Henry was regarded as a vacant idiot, a king in name alone. Many people must have agreed with the Reading man who was sentenced to death that year for comparing him unfavourably to Charles VII and saying that it would have been worth £100,000 to England if he had never been born. The London draper who observed that Henry had the face of a child and was not 'steadfast of wit' probably echoed the street wisdom of London, where the Duke of Gloucester was still regarded as the true heir of Henry V. That was certainly the view of the porter of Gloucester castle, who thought that the Duke of Gloucester should have been King. Nothing good had happened since Margaret of Anjou's arrival in England, this man thought. He wished the King hanged and the Queen drowned. 'If the commons were well advised,' another declared, 'they should arise and destroy him and all his counsel that is about him.' Within five years, the truce would be regarded across the land as the source of all England's misfortunes and its authors as traitors.[48]

In fact, the English government had had no choice but to agree to a truce. It brought a temporary respite from what would otherwise have been a disastrous defeat in Normandy. The main problem was that it was too short. Whenever difficulties were encountered in the negotiations for a permanent peace, it was necessary to negotiate an extension. This meant that the English had to deal with complex and intractable issues under the pressure of a succession of deadlines, with the threat to Normandy still hanging over them. Henry VI was naïve enough to think that his marriage would generate enough goodwill to avoid this problem. Perhaps Suffolk believed that too. But they had misread their antagonists. The atmosphere was certainly more courteous. But Charles VII and his advisers had no intention of making unnecessary concessions. Their attitude to the marriage was more calculating than Henry's. They believed that placed at the heart of the English court Margaret, whose strong personality may already have been noticed in her family, would be an effective advocate for peace on French terms.[49]

To negotiate from strength the English would have had to reinforce Normandy and repair and resupply its castles. Suffolk himself made the point forcefully to the Duke of York when passing through Rouen with the Queen in March 1445, and again when reporting on his mission to Parliament two months later. His warning fell on deaf ears. Unlike France, which took advantage of the truce to create a new army, the English did nothing to rebuild their strength. Talbot had been due to cross to France with 400 men at the time that the truce was agreed, but the expedition was immediately cancelled. No further troops were sent to Normandy for the next four years. The nominal establishment of the Norman garrisons was reduced to just over 2,500 men, about half of what had been thought necessary in the 1430s. There was no field force. The castles and town walls had not been properly maintained for years. The towns, which were responsible for the upkeep of their walls and the keeping of watches, were reluctant to spend money in a time of truce. The war treasurers at Rouen had no money to spend. The truth was that Suffolk's advice, although sound, was never realistic. The truce had been necessary because England could not afford to defend Normandy. The Lancastrian government in Rouen had been dependent on English revenues for more than a decade. Up to 1442, the English Exchequer had been paying out more than £30,000 a year for the defence of the duchy. But in that year the flow of cash across the Channel began to dry up, and during the truce it stopped completely. The administration at Rouen was left to manage on local revenues. The Norman Estates continued to vote subsidies, in diminishing amounts, but they were becoming more difficult to collect. Much of what the collectors were able to remit to Rouen was spent on reducing the accumulated burden of debt and getting rid of freelance soldiery. In addition, the Norman treasury had to meet the considerable cost of paying compensation to French frontier garrisons for lost *pâtis*, which was one of the terms of the truce. Charles VII and his ministers were well aware of all this. As Suffolk later pointed out, 'the French party knowen every day our poverty, our debility, improvidence, non-resistance, non-power and every mishap that followeth among us'.[50]

Apart from a general war-weariness, the underlying causes of this debility were to be found in the conditions in England: economic recession, a prolonged crisis at the Exchequer and societal breakdown. The 1440s saw the beginning of a slump which would last until the end of the century. Agricultural prices and production declined. In town and country alike, rents fell to levels not seen for many years. There was a sharp fall in English wool and cloth exports. The Commons responded to the truce by reducing the burden of direct taxation. In the six years from 1443 to 1448, they voted only two full subsidies, both of which were earmarked for other purposes than the defence of Normandy. Revenues from the customs, the royal demesne and the duchies of Lancaster and Cornwall were all in decline, and much of the yield was diverted at source to satisfy old debts. At the same time other demands on the Crown's resources rose inexorably. The new Queen had to be given her own household, and much of the revenues of the duchies of Lancaster and Cornwall were assigned to fund it. The King's new foundations at Eton College and King's College Cambridge, which were closer to his heart than any other enterprise, consumed much of the rest. The cost of Henry VI's household and his improvident grants to well-placed courtiers increased year by year. In the summer of 1446 government debts were dishonoured on a large scale. The cautious Marmaduke Lumley Bishop of Carlisle succeeded Ralph Butler (now Lord Sudeley) as Treasurer in December of that year. For the next three years he struggled to control the spiralling public debt and bring order to its management. Nevertheless, the financial statement which he presented to the Commons in 1449 showed that accumulated debt stood at £372,000, equivalent to more than five times total revenues.[51]

The breakdown of law and order in much of England had deeper roots. Disputes among the magnates and gentry over land and local office were endemic in late medieval England. What had contained them in the past was a functioning court system which ultimately depended on the knowledge that behind it stood the authority and power of the Crown. Pressure on the system tended to rise in wartime, when the King's government was preoccupied elsewhere, but it had rarely failed completely or for long periods. The two decades which followed Henry VI's majority, however, saw a collapse of the court system in the counties. Henry did not inspire respect. He rarely travelled outside the home counties. He had a long record of indulging lawlessness with profligate pardons. In the absence of impartial and effective courts, landowners looked instead for what was universally known as 'good lordship'. They offered their support to a great magnate and wore his livery badge to proclaim their allegiance. In return, they received the protection of his other clients, which enabled them to occupy disputed land by force and obstruct redress in the courts. In the absence of effective monarchy, the magnates protected their interests by mustering small armies, procuring compliant sheriffs, manipulating

Parliamentary elections, intimidating justices, and arranging partisan juries for their friends' causes.

The situation in East Anglia is illuminated by the accidental survival of the Paston Letters, a cache of over a thousand letters between members of the Paston family and their agents, allies, patrons and friends over more than half a century. The letters reveal the division of Norfolk and Suffolk into rival parties, the eruption of their quarrels into violence and the insidious connection between local and national politics. In the 1440s, East Anglia was dominated by the Duke of Suffolk and his allies, who maintained their power by large-scale racketeering. 'While the world is as it is,' wrote Margaret Paston to her husband John in 1449, 'ye can never live in peace without ye have his good lordship.' Similar stories could be told about the vendettas of Grey of Ruthin and Fanhope in Bedfordshire, of Talbot and Berkeley in the West Country, of Bonville and Courtenay in Devon and Cornwall, of Northumberland and Archbishop Kemp in Yorkshire, and of Cromwell and Tailboys in Lincolnshire. In most of these cases, one side was able to prevail by influence at the centre. They either sat on the King's council or had the ear of someone else who did. Unlike the Kings of France, English Kings did not have a corps of salaried officials to enforce the law and maintain order in the counties. They depended on the nobility and gentry to serve as an intermediate layer of government. The resort of members of this class to force and crime to defend their interests therefore led rapidly to anarchy and social disintegration.[52]

The impact of mounting disorder in England on English fortunes in France was indirect but important. Men whose interests were threatened in England were unwilling to fight in France. The desire to win royal favour, or at least not to lose it, had always been a significant factor in the recruitment of armies, especially in a time of defeat when the material rewards were poor. With the declining prestige of the Crown and the increasingly obvious incapacity of the King, this was no longer as important. The Earl of Warwick and the Duke of York had both had to be pressured into accepting office as lieutenant of Normandy. When, in June 1449, the council discussed the pressing need to reinforce Normandy and Guyenne, a sizable contingent of councillors including two former treasurers, Sudeley and Cromwell, thought that the problem of public order at home had to be addressed before they could contemplate sending another major expedition overseas. The same point was repeatedly made over the following years by those such as the Duke of York who blamed the loss of Normandy on the chaos overtaking England under Suffolk's ministry. As the Commons pointed out in 1449,

> The honour, wealth and prosperity of every prince reigning on his people standeth most principally upon conservation of his peace, keeping of justice and due execution of his laws, without which no realm may long endure in quiet nor prosperity.[53]

The truce of Tours brought Suffolk to the pinnacle of his power. A generation of older men was disappearing from the scene. Archbishop Chichele was dead. Cardinal Beaufort retired to the rooms prepared for him at Christchurch Canterbury and followed Chichele to the grave in 1447. Humphrey of Gloucester was discredited. The nobles and bishops who had added ballast to the council's deliberations gradually ceased to attend, with a handful of exceptions such as Kemp and Cromwell whose participation in decision-making was sporadic at best. After a brief return to conciliar government between 1441 and 1443, most decisions were once again being made by a tight circle of household officers in which Suffolk was the pre-eminent figure. He had the ear of the King as no one else did. He established a rapport with the Queen, who must have found his culture and fluent French a welcome change from the crudeness of some of her husband's other courtiers. Suffolk's intellect and force of personality swept away the doubts of others. Apart from Moleyns, Sudeley and Treasurer Lumley, the government's most prominent figures were William Ayscough Bishop of Salisbury, Humphrey Earl of Stafford and his brother-in-law John Viscount Beaumont. Ayscough had been the King's confessor and was believed to have a hold over him second only to Suffolk's. He had been with Suffolk at Tours and officiated at the King's marriage at Titchfield. Humphrey Earl of Stafford was a rich and diligent mediocrity with a long career in royal service. He had fought briefly in France under Henry V and again in the coronation expedition of 1430–2. He held valuable estates in Normandy. But he had also become a convinced advocate of peace. His growing influence at the centre was marked by his promotion to be Duke of Buckingham in September 1444. Beaumont was an important landowner in Maine but had no experience of fighting in Normandy and no obvious abilities. Like many others who reached positions of influence and power, he owed his influence and much of his wealth to his loyalty and his friendship with the King, in whose household he had spent part of his childhood.[54]

In their dealings with France, these men had a weak hand and they played it badly. For three years after the agreement at Tours, attempts to agree a permanent peace were overshadowed by a dispute about Maine. The county of Maine was important to the English. It served as a buffer zone between Lower Normandy and the western provinces of Valois France. It was also a valuable source of war profits for a small but influential group of English captains and settlers, some of whom had powerful allies in England. For Charles VII, Maine was important for different reasons. It bordered on the Breton march at a time when the alliance of Brittany was emerging as a great strategic prize. It mattered, too, to his principal councillor Charles of Anjou, to whom the county had been assigned in a partition of the domains of the house of Anjou. The prospect of recovering this old possession of their house had been a large part of the Angevin princes' reasons for supporting the marriage alliance with Henry VI. In private conversation with the Earl of Suffolk at Montils during the negotiation of the truce, Charles VII told him that he wanted Maine ceded to Charles of Anjou regardless of the outcome of negotiations for a permanent peace. He tried to make this a condition of the truce. Suffolk refused to agree. He refused again when Charles VII pressed him the following year at Nancy. But he may have given the French King informal assurances on the point. Suffolk was too candid to be a good negotiator. The congenial atmosphere of Montils and Tours must have encouraged some common assumptions between those on either side with a shared interest in ending the war, who grew closer to each other in the six weeks that they were together.[55]

The 'great embassy' (as the French came to call it) which was to open the negotiations for a permanent peace arrived in England on 3 July 1445. Its spokesman was Jacques Juvénal des Ursins, a scion of the famous family of churchmen and civil servants, who had recently succeeded Regnault de Chartres as Archbishop of Reims. His fellow ambassadors were an able and varied group. The political head of the mission was Bertrand de Beauveau lord of Précigny, one of Charles VII's closest and most influential advisers. Louis de Bourbon Count of Vendôme was the senior layman, and a veteran of such occasions. Étienne Chevalier, best known as the patron of the painter Jean Fouquet and the sitter for one of his greatest portraits, was a career civil servant and currently one of the King's secretaries. Guillaume Cousinot, the nephew of Charles of Orléans's old Chancellor, was the author of a notable chronicle of his times and was destined to become Charles VII's principal expert on English affairs. These men were joined in England by separate embassies sent to defend their own interests by the Dukes of Anjou, Brittany and Alençon, and the King of Castile. On 14 July they were escorted by the English councillors over London Bridge in a cavalcade in which precedence assigned to every man his place, to be received at the city gate by the Mayor and corporation and the London guilds drawn up in their liveries.[56]

On the following morning the ambassadors were taken to the palace of Westminster to present their credentials to the King. They had two audiences with Henry, on 15 and 16 July in the palace of Westminster, at which formal speeches were made, greetings exchanged and credentials read out. It was the first time that influential figures in the French government had met the English King. Reading between the lines of their report, they were not impressed. Henry received them seated on a raised throne, with a tapestry back showing the arms of France being presented to Henry V. Chancellor Stafford, the Marquess of Suffolk and Archbishop Kemp (recently made a Cardinal) stood on the King's right, and the Duke of Gloucester on his left. Whenever anything was said, the King would look to each side in turn for reassurance, with a fixed grin on his face. When the Chancellor advanced into the room to deliver his formal welcome in Latin, Henry rose from his throne and interrupted him to say that his words did not sound friendly enough, before approaching the ambassadors and greeting each one of them personally, doffing his cap and patting them on the back, all the while crying *'Saint Jean, grand merci!'* The audiences appeared to have been stage-managed by Suffolk, who was very obviously in charge. Adam Moleyns, who had been appointed as Keeper of the Privy Seal, was perennially in the background. If the King was effusive in his declarations of affection for Charles VII, they were even more so. Suffolk told the French ambassadors that there was no one whom his master loved more, as Henry kept saying *'Saint Jean, oui!'* in the background. Coming into the antechamber where the Frenchmen were gathering for their second audience, Suffolk repeated the message 'three or four times'. He himself, he added, was at the French King's service against all but Henry VI.[57]

The working sessions of the conference were conducted on the English side by a committee of Suffolk, Kemp and Treasurer Sudeley. The French for their part nominated the Archbishop of Reims, the Count of Vendôme and the lord of Précigny as their own negotiating committee. The six men met in the Dominican convent of Blackfriars, the usual seat of the council, over three days, 19–21 July 1445. Their discussions were almost entirely devoted to the territorial question. Suffolk tried to cut through the tortuous system of piecemeal concessions which had prolonged earlier diplomatic conferences. He wanted both sides to proceed directly to their best offer. The French repeated the offer of Gascony, Périgord and Quercy which they had made at Tours, all to be held as fiefs of the King of France. They were eventually persuaded to add Limousin and then Saintonge as well. This would have reconstituted the duchy of Aquitaine as it had stood in the 1360s at the high point of Edward III's reign, with the important exception of Poitou. It was, they said, as much as their instructions would allow them to concede. For their part, the English insisted on retaining Normandy and were not prepared to shift from their position that their French domains should be held in full sovereignty, without homage. By the end of 21 July, it was clear that agreement on territory was within reach but agreement on tenure was not.

At this point Bertrand de Précigny proposed that the outstanding issues should be resolved by the two Kings personally at a summit meeting. The English reflected on this suggestion. Henry's ministers had misgivings about it. It is not difficult to imagine what they were. At a personal meeting between the two Kings Henry was likely to give too much away too easily to his older and more worldly and intelligent uncle. 'Great princes should never meet if they wish to remain friends,' wrote Philippe de Commynes. On 30 July Henry VI received the French ambassadors in the hall of the Bishop of London's palace at Fulham to explain the delay in responding. Chancellor Stafford spoke on the King's behalf. The King, he said, was overjoyed at the prospect of meeting Charles VII in person. But it was a significant step. It would require careful thought and further reflection. They would have an answer in due course.[58]

Henry VI had made it all too obvious that he was desperate for a permanent peace and was counting on the goodwill of the King of France to get it. The French ambassadors can hardly have failed to notice. Behind the unctuous courtesies of the diplomats lay the realities of power politics. The first year of the truce had passed while the French King campaigned in Lorraine. It now had little more than seven months to run. The English needed an extension. But the French were not willing to relieve the pressure on them without some significant concession. Bertrand de Précigny told the King at Fulham that they would agree to an extension only if Henry accepted their proposal for a summit meeting. He also raised the sensitive question of Maine. If the English wanted to retain Charles VII's goodwill, they would have to cede it irrespective of the outcome of the peace process. In the end the English King conceded both points. It was Henry who insisted on attending the summit meeting. As Chancellor Stafford later told Parliament in his presence, he was moved to agree by Almighty God, 'without that any of the lords or other of your subjects of this your realm in any way have stirred or moved you so to do'. It was Henry, too, who insisted on the surrender of Maine. Suffolk later protested that he had done everything by Henry's personal authority. According to a later French record of the occasion, which there is no reason to doubt, Adam Moleyns gave Bertrand de Précigny an oral undertaking that the King would surrender Maine to the officers of Charles VII and Charles of Anjou by 1 October 1445.

On 11 August, Moleyns was charged with the task of negotiating an extension of the truce with the French ambassadors. The parties agreed that the two Kings would meet on the march of Normandy in the summer of 1446. Moleyns asked for an extension of the truce of at least a year, to 1 April 1447, in order to leave time to prepare for war if the summit failed. He got just seven months, until 1 November 1446. It was as much as the French ambassadors were authorised to agree. For anything longer, they said, one of Henry's councillors would have to accompany them back to France to ask Charles VII himself. On 13 August, that was what they agreed to do. Moleyns himself was directed to accompany the ambassadors back to France. His first task was to see to the surrender of Maine by the deadline. Having given the French King what he wanted, he was then to extract a longer extension of the truce.[59]

In July 1445, while the 'great embassy' was in England, there was another palace revolution at the court of Charles VII, although this time it was directed by the King himself. Charles of Anjou's decade in power had aroused the kind of jealousies and antagonisms that were endemic in the enclosed world of royal courts. The ambitious and smooth-talking Pierre de Brézé persuaded the King that his principal chamberlain was plotting another Praguerie with the Constable and the Count of Saint-Pol. This allegation was probably untrue. But it persuaded the King to banish all three men from his court together with many of their allies on the council. Pierre de Brézé emerged as the King's chief minister. Angevin influence was not wholly eliminated. Pierre de Brézé was himself a protégé of the house of Anjou. So was Bertrand de Précigny, one of the ambassadors to England, whose influence over the King was second only to Brézé's. The new men in power were just as committed to the truce of Tours and the recovery of Maine as their predecessors. But Charles of Anjou's successors had fewer personal reasons to accommodate Henry VI and his ministers. This made for a more difficult relationship, which was severely tested by the coming crisis over Maine.[60]

Adam Moleyns left for France at the end of August 1445 but he failed to surrender Maine. It is not clear why, but the most likely explanation is resistance in Normandy. The Duke of York and the Grand Conseil, who had had no warning of what was afoot, cannot have welcomed such a sudden reversal of long-standing English policy. The abandonment of Maine was also likely to provoke opposition in England when it became known. Parliament had been prorogued while the 'great embassy' was in England and was due to reconvene at Westminster on 20 October. Henry VI's ministers decided that it would be prudent to obtain the Lords' advice on the peace proposals and the fate of Maine. The Duke of York, who had not attended earlier sessions of this Parliament, was recalled to England to participate.

In October, Moleyns arrived empty-handed at the French court at Montils, full of apologies for the delay in surrendering Maine. It was not his master's fault, he explained. Henry was not an entirely free agent. Parliament had to be consulted. Charles VII did not, it is true, understand the relations between the Crown and Parliament in England, which had no equivalent in France. His response was to refuse to discuss the extension of the truce. Instead, he sent Guillaume Cousinot back to England, accompanied by one of his household officers, Jean Havart, to negotiate directly with Henry VI and his advisers, or indeed with Parliament if the decision lay with them. Cousinot's instructions were to insist that one way or the other Maine had to be surrendered. At the same time the French King wrote to Margaret of Anjou, calling on her to exercise all her influence over her husband to ensure that the cession of the county went through.[61]

Moleyns returned to England at the beginning of November 1445, accompanied by Cousinot and Havart. The record is silent, perhaps deliberately, about the discussion that must have occurred in Parliament about current negotiations with France. All that is known for certain is that the Lords approved of the proposed summit meeting with the French King, which Henry later announced 'by the authority of Parliament'. Were they told about the plan to surrender Maine? The probability is that they were. A number of peers must already have known about it, including the Duke of York. The inference from the subsequent course of events is that they declined to support it. What is clear is that Henry VI was determined to go ahead anyway. The Queen worked on him to stiffen his resolve. By his own account she urged him 'several times' to accept the French demands 'out of regard for her father and uncle'. As soon as Parliament was prorogued for Christmas, he did accept them. On 19 December Cousinot and his colleague agreed to extend the truce to 1 April 1447. On the same day, Henry VI gave him a letter under his own hand, formally confirming 'in good faith and upon his word as a King' that he would attend the summit not later than 1 November 1446. Three days later, on 22 December, he gave him another letter under his hand, promising to deliver up Maine by 30 April 1446. He hoped, he wrote, that this would ease the path to a permanent peace. The first of these undertakings was published in the new year, but the second was kept secret. Suffolk later claimed that the decision was Henry's own. That was probably the truth.[62]

Parliament was dissolved on 9 April 1446. Four days later, on the 13th, Richard of York was reappointed as lieutenant in Normandy. But York never took up his appointment. Over the following months he fell out with the governing caucus at Westminster. He was criticised by those such as Adam Moleyns and Ralph Lord Cromwell who believed that he had mismanaged the affairs of Normandy and wasted the men and money made available to him. Moleyns, now Bishop of Chichester and an increasingly powerful figure, had examined the accounts of the Norman government while he was in France and pronounced that 'the said duke is cause of the loss and destruction of Normandy'. In the autumn of 1446, Moleyns made himself the spokesman of a group of Norman captains who alleged that York had embezzled their pay. The Duke responded by bringing members of the Rouen council to

England to rebut the charges and accusing Moleyns of having bribed the captains who made them. Suffolk eventually prevailed on the King to revoke York's appointment as lieutenant. On Christmas Eve 1446 Edmund Beaufort Marquess of Dorset was appointed in his place. These decisions left Normandy rudderless once more, for the new lieutenant did not arrive until April 1448. There was a hiatus of a years and a half between the departure of Richard of York and the arrival of Edmund Beaufort, in which there was no political leadership at Rouen. Henry VI's Chancellor in Normandy, Sir Thomas Hoo, did his best to keep the government going with the support of an interim council. But Hoo and his colleagues did not have the authority in Normandy or the political weight at Westminster to address the increasingly pressing problems of the duchy.[63]

As Normandy slid into chaos and England into bankruptcy Brittany, Henry VI's only continental ally, abandoned him. Like the business of Maine, the dispute with Brittany was a gratuitous folly of the English government, for which the King himself was at least partly responsible. It arose out of the widening rift between the Duke of Brittany and his younger brother Gilles. Before his death the previous Duke, John V, had endowed his younger son with the domains of the house of Montfort in Anjou, comprising the valuable lordship of Ingrande and the fortress of Champtoceaux guarding the approach to Brittany by the Loire valley. Gilles had never been able to make good his right to these domains. John V had bought them from the notorious ex-Marshal Gilles de Retz, who had been executed for pederasty and murder in 1440. Gilles de Retz's heir, the Admiral of France Prégent de Coëtivy, challenged the sale and succeeded in having his rights recognised by the Duke of Anjou. Gilles's claims were finally extinguished in September 1443, when his effusive declarations of loyalty to Henry VI resulted in the confiscation by Charles VII of all his assets outside Brittany including his claims to the territories in Anjou. Gilles called on his brother to replace it with land in the duchy. An appanage in Brittany, he argued, would not be vulnerable to confiscation by the French King on account of his English sympathies. He regarded himself, he said, as a subject of Henry VI, not Charles VII.[64]

Henry VI aggressively took Gilles's part in this family dispute, and Gilles responded by entering into a closer alliance with the English. He hired a company of indigenous Norman troops and joined forces with Matthew Gough in the Cotentin. The two of them mounted joint raids along the march of Brittany and Maine. He made contact with Henry VI and prominent people at his court and in July 1445 sent a messenger to England with a letter reminding Henry VI of his unqualified devotion to the English cause. He invited him as his sovereign to vindicate his rights against his brother and offered to put all his castles in Brittany at his disposal. This meant the castles which he held in right of his wife, including four major fortresses in eastern Brittany, as well as Saint-Malo and Moncontour which he held as captain for the Duke. This extraordinary missive never reached the English King. It was intercepted and laid before the Duke of Brittany. Confronted by the document, Gilles at first denied that it was his, and then admitted it and made an abject submission to his brother. He promised to have no further dealings with the English without Francis's leave. Gilles was promptly removed from the captaincies of Saint-Malo and Moncontour. From England, Suffolk raised the stakes. In November 1445, his herald arrived at the ducal court at Nantes bearing a letter from Henry VI conceived in the most undiplomatic terms. It defended Gilles's joint military operations with the English garrisons in Normandy and called on Francis to satisfy his brother's demands for a personal appanage in Brittany. Henry authorised his representatives at Rouen to open discussions with Gilles about the possibility of endowing him with land in England if this came to nothing. Meanwhile, the council at Rouen detached a company of two dozen English archers from the garrison of Avranches and sent them to serve as Gilles's garrison and personal bodyguard at Le Guildo, the Breton prince's favourite residence on the estuary of the river Arguenon in northern Brittany.[65]

England's militant support of Gilles de Bretagne served only to drive his brother into the arms of the King of France. Duke Francis had already abandoned his declared intention of acceding to the treaty of Troyes. He had attended the ceremonies at the conclusion of the truce of Tours, in which he was named as an ally of France. In March 1446, he travelled to Chinon and did homage to Charles VII for his duchy. In the following month, he had an explosive interview with his brother. Francis refused once again to endow him with land in Brittany and Gilles walked out. Not long afterwards, Gilles was heard threatening to claim his patrimony from his brother at the head of 5,000 or 6,000 Englishmen. Francis took fright. He returned to the French court in

June and met Charles VII at the castle of Razilly outside Chinon. He appealed to him for support against his brother's English allies. The French King directed Prégent de Coëtivy to lay siege to Le Guildo. Francis for his part authorised Prégent to arrest his brother.

At Rouen, the Norman Chancellor Sir Thomas Hoo, had seen this coming. He warned Gilles to take refuge in Normandy under English protection while he still could. Le Guildo, he pointed out, was a pleasure palace, and not fit to withstand a siege. 'Here, you will be the most feared man that ever came out of Brittany,' he wrote, 'and we will put ourselves at your service and help you with all our power.' On 25 June 1446, the garrison of Avranches, who had detected unusual troop movements, sent a messenger with another warning that Gilles was about to be attacked and should leave at once. It was too late. On the following day, 26 June, Prégent de Coëtivy arrived outside the gate of Le Guildo at the head of 400 mounted men. He demanded admittance in the King's name. The gates were opened. His men took possession of the castle, looted its contents and carried the young prince off to Dinan, where he was delivered to his brother's jailers.

The affair divided Brittany. Many noblemen believed that it was indecent for the Duke to proceed like this against a brother. The Estates, which was specially summoned to Redon at the beginning of August to convict him of treason, refused to do it. But Francis was unbending. After being imprisoned in various ducal castles, Gilles was confined under guard at his wife's castle at Châteaubriand. It was the end of the century-long alliance of England and the house of Montfort. For most of that time, it is true, they had never been more than nominal allies, but this had at least ensured that they did not become enemies.[66]

Henry VI and his ministers had painted themselves into a corner. They could not afford to restart the war. But they were not willing to surrender Normandy or to hold it as a fief of the French Crown, which ruled out a permanent peace. The King had secretly promised to surrender Maine, but the secret would be out once he tried to implement his promise, and then there would be anger and resistance both in England and Normandy. The only escape from these dilemmas was to play for time, which is what he did. The deadline for the surrender of Maine, 30 April 1446, came and went. The deadline for the summit meeting was 1 November, but by July nothing had been done to prepare for it. In July 1446, Adam Moleyns left for France with the courtier John Sutton Lord Dudley, ostensibly to agree the venue and the logistical arrangements for the summit meeting, but in fact to ask for yet another postponement. Charles VII gave them a chilly reception. He complained about the breakdown of discipline by English garrisons, which had mounted plundering raids into the Île de France and the Loire provinces. Many of these raids had been launched from Maine. The French King refused to agree to the postponement of the summit meeting until the county had been surrendered. Cousinot and Havart, the two agents who had procured Henry VI's undertaking in December, were sent back to England to get some assurance that it would be honoured. They were at Westminster for much of December. But they were unable to break the deadlock. It fell to Moleyns and Dudley to return with them to France in a final attempt to postpone the summit and extend the truce before it expired at the beginning of April.[67]

During the autumn of 1446, the plan to abandon Maine became public knowledge. The disclosure revived bitter old controversies about the peace process that had seemed to have died with the disgrace of the Duke of Gloucester. Gloucester himself no longer had any influence in government, but his views were well known and his status as heir presumptive to the Crown made him a natural focus of loyalty for those who objected to the direction of English policy. They may even have included the Duke of York. York was not an opponent of the peace process, as Gloucester was, but he had built up a large and valuable appanage in Normandy and was completely committed to the survival of the Lancastrian regime there. He cannot have approved of the surrender of Maine. Accusing fingers were pointed at the Earl of Suffolk. He was said to have authorised the surrender of Maine without the King's authority and even to have recommended the abandonment of Normandy. Hostility to both Gloucester and York mounted among Suffolk's allies. Rumour quickly displaced fact in this poisonous atmosphere. There were reports of treasonable activity among Gloucester's supporters, of plots in his household at Greenwich and of plans to raise an army in Wales. Henry VI was persuaded by those around him that the Duke was plotting to kill him and take the throne.[68]

At some point the government decided to get rid of the Duke of Gloucester. Suffolk was believed to have been the main mover, but he was certainly not the only one. On 14 December 1446, the day on which negotiations with Cousinot and Havart at Westminster broke down, writs were issued for a new Parliament to meet on 10 February 1447. All the surrounding circumstances suggest that it was specially called to try the King's uncle. Unusually, all the justices of King's Bench and Common Pleas were ordered to suspend their sittings and attend. The venue was originally to be Cambridge, far away from the mobs of London, where Gloucester was popular. It was later changed to Winchester and then to Bury St Edmunds. Charges of treason were prepared against the Duke, although there can be little doubt that the real ground of complaint was his role as a focus of opposition to the peace process and the surrender of Maine. The London chronicler observed, voicing the conventional sentiment in the capital, that 'Them that were governors and had promised the duchy of Anjou and the earldom of Maine caused the destruction of this noble man, for they dread him that he would have impeached that deliverance.'[69]

When Parliament opened in the refectory of St Edmund's abbey at Bury, the Duke of Gloucester was absent. It was necessary to send him a further summons. On 18 February 1447, eight days into the session, Gloucester approached the town with a mounted escort of about eighty men. He was met on the road by two officers of the royal household with a message from the King inviting him to go straight to his lodgings in the hospital of St Saviour outside Northgate. That evening, as the Duke was finishing his dinner there, John Viscount Beaumont, the Steward of the royal household, entered with Edmund Beaufort Marquess of Dorset, Humphrey Stafford Duke of Buckingham, Richard Neville Earl of Salisbury and Ralph Butler Lord Sudeley, all loyal allies of the Earl of Suffolk. Beaumont arrested Humphrey for treason and ordered him to be detained under guard in his quarters. His retainers were told to leave the building. Later that evening thirty-two of them were arrested in their lodgings. Three days later, twenty-eight more dependents and members of the Duke's household staff were arrested. All of these men were taken under escort to separate prisons in different parts of England.

Five days after his arrest, on 23 February 1447, the Duke of Gloucester was found dead in his lodgings. Gloucester's death was never explained. 'How he died God knoweth, to whom nothing is hid,' wrote the London chronicler. The Duke's health had not been good. The shock of arrest might well have provoked a heart attack which killed him. But his death was too convenient for the governing clique.

It avoided a state trial at which Gloucester, an eloquent man with many friends, would have defended himself with vigour. In the eyes of the public, Gloucester was murdered. The council put his body, apparently uninjured, on public display, but the rumours persisted. Humphrey's surviving servants who were still at liberty were eventually allowed to carry the body to St Albans abbey for burial in the vault that he had prepared for himself in his lifetime. But eight of his closest associates were charged with treason. It was alleged that they had conspired to depose the King and put Gloucester on the throne in his place. They were convicted in London in July and sentenced to be drawn, hanged and quartered. Even Suffolk had qualms about this act of judicial murder. A sullen crowd gathered at Tyburn to watch the first five executions, but Suffolk produced charters of pardon in the middle of the barbarous ceremony just as the executioner was about to eviscerate them.[70]

Adam Moleyns and John Dudley arrived at Tours in the middle of February 1447 to negotiate another extension of the truce. By then it had just six weeks to run. They encountered what Charles VII called 'certain difficulties'. The French King was furious about the failure to deliver Maine. On 22 and 23 February 1447 two linked agreements were sealed. One postponed the summit meeting to a date to be agreed, not later than 1 November 1447. The other extended the truce until 1 January 1448. The purpose of the postponement was to enable another 'great' embassy to travel to England, led by the Count of Dunois and Bertrand de Précigny. Their task was to see to the surrender of Maine before the final arrangements were made for the summit meeting. They were accompanied by the perennial diplomatic technicians Cousinot and Havart, and a crowd of clerks and servants, some of whom had joined the party just to satisfy their curiosity about a country which had loomed so large in recent French history but of which they knew next to nothing.[71]

The French ambassadors arrived at Westminster in the middle of June 1447 in the midst of the continuing row over the promise to surrender Maine. All the antagonisms at the heart of the English government were exposed. Three weeks earlier Suffolk had had to appear at a tense meeting of the council to explain the underhand way in which negotiations over Maine had been conducted. The King, who was largely responsible, presided. Most of those who were emerging as Suffolk's leading critics were present, including the Duke of York,

Cardinal Kemp and Ralph Cromwell. Suffolk stopped short of openly blaming Henry. But he claimed to have acted 'prudently and loyally' towards the Crown and the kingdom. In effect he was saying that he had done nothing behind the King's back. Edmund Beaufort Marquess of Dorset, who had inherited Maine from his brother, was not present, but he had his own objections to its surrender. Behind the scenes he was pressing for compensation. This proved to be another source of dispute. Dorset's claims were contested by others, including the Duke of York, who pointed out that the grant of Maine to him had expressly reserved the King's right to take it back as part of the terms of peace with France.[72]

The French ambassadors had no interest in the divisions within the English government. They were only concerned to hold Henry VI to his promises. They wanted firm guarantees that Maine would be surrendered, and soon. There was a difficult meeting of the council on 27 July, attended by all the principal protagonists, followed by another on the next day at which Dunois himself was present. The outcome was an English climbdown. Maine would be surrendered within three months, by 1 November 1447. The King appointed two commissioners, Matthew Gough and Fulk Eyton, the captain of Caudebec, to effect the transfer on behalf of the Marquess of Dorset. They were also charged to agree with their French opposite numbers a reasonable measure of compensation for the dispossessed English settlers. A copy of their commission was handed to Dunois. The French ambassadors were satisfied. They agreed to put off the summit to the following spring. Henry VI solemnly promised to cross the Channel by 1 May 1448 at the latest. The truce was extended too, but only to the same date. These disputes left the King and his ministers bruised. Two days later the Duke of York was appointed lieutenant in Ireland for a term of ten years. Contemporaries believed that the object was to get him out of the way. The rumour in London was that those close to the King had told him that he was being 'exiled into Ireland for his rebellion'.[73]

If Suffolk thought that the latest agreement had settled the business of Maine, he underestimated the strength of feeling in England and the obstructiveness of his opponents in Normandy. Maine was a settler society. The number of settlers was smaller than it was in Normandy, but they were a powerful and belligerent group. They had fought to conquer and defend Maine and were now destined to lose everything. 'If you had been well and loyally advised and warned of the consequences,' they wrote in a petition subsequently addressed to the King, 'you would never have authorised such a thing.' Behind the scenes, the Marquess of Dorset actively fomented resistance. Henry VI's commissioners Gough and Eyton were both professional soldiers who had made their careers in Normandy and must have sympathised with the objectors. On 23 September 1447, they arrived in Le Mans to perform their distasteful task. They were confronted by Osbern Mundeford and Sir Richard Frogenhall. Mundeford was royal *bailli* of Maine and the Marquess of Dorset's captain of Le Mans and Beaumont-le-Vicomte. He had served in Maine for at least fifteen years. Frogenhall was Dorset's chamberlain and the administrator of his domains in France. The two men refused to surrender the county. Their excuse was that the commissions contained no formal discharge for themselves, either from Dorset or from the King. Technically, they were right. The King's commissions had been poorly drafted and there was no commission from Dorset. From Eltham, where he received the commissioners' report, Henry VI sent his letters of discharge to Gough and Eyton and a furious letter to Dorset ordering him to send them his own discharge at once. The Duke of York later accused Dorset of deliberately dragging things out in order to get the King to agree to his steep demands for compensation. If so, his resistance paid off. Henry was forced to buy Dorset's cooperation with an annual income of £10,000 for life, secured on the tax revenues of the *bailliages* of Caen and the Cotentin. This was far more than the revenues that he could have drawn from Maine.[74]

In early October 1447, John Lord Dudley arrived at the French court at Bourges, accompanied by Walter Hart Bishop of Norwich. Both men were on their way to other courts, to Rome in the case of Hart and to Castile in that of Dudley. But they had been instructed to stop on their way in order to negotiate yet another extension of the timetable for the summit meeting and the truce. They arrived at a difficult moment, a few days after the news of the events at Le Mans. Their reception must have been frosty. On 15 October, they succeeded in getting the summit meeting postponed by a year to 1 November 1448. The negotiations for an extension of the truce went less well. The French were willing to extend it by a year to 1 January 1449, but only on condition that Maine was surrendered by 1 November, as agreed in July. That was only two weeks away.[75]

On 31 October 1447 Cousinot and Havart arrived at Le Mans to attend the much delayed handover of Maine. Gough and Eyton were not there. Instead, they found themselves facing Nicholas Molyneux the Master of the Norman Chambre des Comptes, and two other commissioners appointed in the English King's name by the Grand Conseil in Rouen. The Rouen council had never approved of the decision to abandon Maine and they were not inclined to ease the process. The new commissioners' instructions were to insist on an agreement about compensation for the dispossessed settlers. They interpreted this as meaning that the compensation must be paid or secured before the county was transferred. This could not be done, as they must have known. The deadline for the surrender was on the following day. The next morning, there was a crowded public meeting in the chapter house of the cathedral. About 500 people were present, including the Bishop, lawyers and officials, several dozen English and French landowners and a crowd of townsmen. In addition, Sir John Fastolf had organised an action group of absentee landowners in England, who were represented by attorneys. The French commissioners repeatedly summoned the English to honour Henry VI's promise. The English replied that compensation would have to be settled first. Cousinot protested that there was nothing about that in the agreements between the two monarchs. The English King's commissions were perfectly clear in requiring the county to be delivered up to them that very day. The English refused. On that note, the meeting broke up. Cousinot and Havart left empty-handed to report to their master at Bourges. Charles VII complained angrily to Henry VI and the Grand Conseil about the 'subterfuges, pretences and deceits' of the English officers at Le Mans. He thought that Gough, Eyton and Molyneux were in league with them and suggested, probably rightly, that the real problem was the opposition of professional soldiers and administrators to the whole peace process.[76]

The result of the breakdown of talks at Le Mans was that the extension of the truce negotiated at Bourges fell away, leaving only two months before it expired. There was a scramble to sort out the question of compensation in time. In December 1447 Matthew Gough travelled to Tours, where the French court had moved. There had been no time to get a proper diplomatic procuration or instructions, and Gough himself was probably not the most welcome ambassador. But Pierre de Brézé was instructed to negotiate with him, supported by

Dunois and Bertrand de Précigny. On 30 December they reached a provisional agreement. Charles VII authorised his commissioners to agree the terms of compensation with Gough and Eyton. The deadline for surrendering Maine and the expiry of the truce were both put off to 15 January 1448. Unfortunately, Eyton was not present at Tours. Gough undertook that his fellow commissioner would ratify the agreement within four days. But when Eyton was told about the agreement he refused to do so. He wanted a longer extension. Charles VII's patience was exhausted. He gave them until 20 January and in the meantime ordered the mobilisation of an army to occupy Maine by force. Troops were recruited from the French garrisons on the marches of Maine. The *compagnies d'ordonnance* were summoned. Artillery was collected and carts requisitioned to carry it. The Berry Herald reckoned the army's total strength at between 6,000 and 7,000 men.

There was a flurry of diplomatic activity as the English played for more time. From Rouen, Henry VI's Chancellor Sir Thomas Hoo urged patience on the French, protesting that Maine was about to be delivered. At Westminster, Moleyns was despatched post-haste to France to urge the French ministers to calm down. Pierre de Brézé, accompanied by Cousinot and Havart, visited Rouen twice to discuss the crisis with the Grand Conseil. All that was achieved was the postponement of the French ultimatum until 10 February.[77]

Early on 13 February 1448, Pierre de Brézé, the Count of Dunois and Prégent de Coëtivy arrived outside Le Mans at the head of the advance guard of the French army. The city had been made ready for a siege. The garrison had been reinforced by a large number of freelance troops recently expelled from Normandy. Barriers had been erected in front of the gates, behind which stood densely packed formations of armed men. The French captains summoned Mundeford, Gough and Eyton to surrender the city in accordance with the agreement of the two monarchs. Back came a stream of abuse (*'langaiges bien estranges'*). That afternoon the French commanders had a conference with the three English captains across the barrier. The Englishmen read out a letter which they claimed to have received from Henry VI, announcing that Adam Moleyns was on his way and ordering them not to surrender Le Mans until Moleyns had been able to discuss the matter with Charles VII. Dunois and Pierre de Brézé declared that they would wait for a week while they conferred with the King at Montils. An attempt to set up a further conference for the following day ended abruptly when the English troops began to advance on the French commissioners and threatened to attack them. A few days later, the English captains prepared a formal protest, which they read out on the bridge over the moat of the citadel. Henry VI, they claimed, had not agreed to renounce his sovereignty over Maine. He had merely agreed to surrender it in the cause of peace. Any cession of the county must therefore be conditional on peace subsequently being made. If the war restarted, the English King must be at liberty to resume possession.[78]

The news of the French advance on Le Mans reached Westminster in about the middle of February 1448 and provoked immediate alarm. There was now no truce in force. Henry's ministers feared that a full-scale invasion of Normandy was imminent. Edmund Beaufort was in the final stages of recruiting his army before leaving for Rouen to take up his lieutenancy. Its strength was trebled overnight, from 1,000 men to 3,200. A desperate struggle followed to find the extra 2,200 men in time. A 'mighty siege' had been laid before Le Mans, Henry VI declared. 'Sharp war' was being daily waged against his subjects in France. Meanwhile, Adam Moleyns, accompanied by Sir Robert Roos, came before Charles VII in the imposing castle of the Counts of Vendôme at Lavardin, overlooking the river Loir forty miles from Le Mans. The castle had been appointed as the advance base of the French army. The signs of approaching war were all around. The main body of the army was encamped in the fields around the walls. The King had all his principal advisers with him.

Between 11 and 15 March a series of agreements were made. Le Mans would be surrendered to the representatives of the house of Anjou by 27 March, followed by all the other walled places of the English in Maine except for Fresnay-le-Vicomte, the great fortress guarding the route into Alençon by the valley of the Sarthe. All English landowners in the county were required to surrender their lands and leave, in exchange for compensation equal to ten years' revenue. But the compensation was effectively capped by a provision that it was to be funded from the sums payable to Charles VII under the truce of Tours as compensation for *pâtis* lost by French garrisons on the Norman march. A fresh truce was agreed for a period of two years to 1 April 1450. Moleyns appears to have argued for a conditional surrender along the lines suggested by the protest of the captains at Le Mans. But it was hardly a realistic idea. The most that he could get was an agreement that if the truce expired without a permanent peace, the French King would pay a sum of 24,000 *livres* to Henry VI for the county. Mundeford's garrison at Le Mans did not wait for the appointed day. They opened their gates at ten o'clock on the night of 15 March, as soon as the agreement was brought to them from Lavardin. On the next morning, they marched out north towards Normandy. Within a few weeks the whole of Maine was in French hands. Edmund Beaufort's reinforcements were stood down. Suffolk's credit with the King rose even higher. In June he was made a Duke.[79]

The army raised by Charles VII for the siege of Le Mans was the first test of the military reforms inaugurated in the spring of 1445. Another milestone was passed at the end of April 1448, six weeks after the truce of Lavardin had been sealed. The *compagnies d'ordonnance* were formations of cavalry with infantry support. For dedicated infantry, the French had traditionally relied on the contingents of the towns, which were irregular in numbers and quality. On 28 April the King presided at an enlarged meeting of his council at Montils, which approved an ordinance establishing the *francs-archers*. The ordinance was declared to be necessary to prepare for an invasion of Normandy if the truce of Lavardin failed or expired without a permanent peace. Accordingly, every parish in the land was required to nominate and equip a bowman available to be summoned to the King's wars. In practice, many rural villages were too poor to comply, and regional quotas had to be drawn up by officials. A *franc-archer* was required to have a stringed bow or crossbow, a sword and dagger, a heavy steel helmet, and a padded jacket with steel platelets. He was to practise his art on feast days. He was paid only once he had been called up, but the real attraction of the job was that every *franc-archer* was entitled to a certificate exempting him from direct taxation. There seems to have been little difficulty in finding men willing to serve on these terms. In the early years of the new ordinance, there were about 8,000 *franc-archer*s, serving in companies about 200 to 300 strong. Taken with the *compagnies d'ordonnance*, the King's household troops and the garrisons, Charles VII would now be in a position to field an army of between 15,000 and 20,000 men, about three times the largest force which England could muster in this period. According to information reaching the council at Rouen, all of them had orders to be available for service within fifteen days of any summons.[80]

At the same time there was a dramatic expansion of the French artillery arm. The men mainly responsible for this development were the two Bureau brothers, Jean and Gaspard. They had begun their careers as administrators, initially in the service of the Dukes of Burgundy and then in that of the English regency. They had a lifelong interest in artillery. Jean had directed the artillery at the siege of Soissons in 1414 and both brothers had fought in the English army at the battle of the Herrings in 1429. When Paris fell, they transferred their allegiance to Charles VII and rose rapidly in his service. Jean became a royal councillor in 1437 and Treasurer of France in 1440, but he continued to concern himself with artillery. Between 1437 and 1441, he directed the artillery at the sieges of Montereau, Meaux, Creil and Pontoise, in all of which bombards played a critical role. Gaspard became acting Master of the King's Artillery when the holder of the office fell ill in 1441 and succeeded him as Master in 1444. He remained in post until his death in 1469.

During the long period when the Bureau brothers were responsible for the French Kings' artillery, the English advantage in artillery was entirely eroded. To some extent this was due to technical improvements in the manufacture of guns. Only one of them is likely to have been introduced before the end of the English wars, but it was the most important. By the mid-1440s, cannons were being cast in one piece instead of being assembled from wrought-iron staves, and projectiles of cast iron were beginning to appear, instead of cut stone. These changes enabled the gunfounders to achieve a tighter fit of the projectile in the barrel, resulting in greater range and impact. They also enabled the guns to be fired more frequently, without the long periods for cooling down that had been required by earlier models. Smaller field pieces of this period, such as culverins, which had always been made of cast iron, were improved at the same time, achieving greater size, range, accuracy and penetration. There is no evidence that either of the Bureau brothers were technicians. The changes are more likely to have been due to the gunfounders themselves. What the Bureaus contributed was an impressive financial and logistical administration, a notable increase in the quantity of artillery of all calibres available to French armies, and considerable skill in the siting of guns and the design of field works.[81]

The creation of a standing army, an infantry reserve and an expanded artillery arm was expensive. They were made possible by the restoration of relative peace in the French countryside and a further turn of the fiscal screw. The successes of French arms and the defeat of the Praguerie put Charles VII in a strong position to override the vested interests that for decades had stood in the way of efficient public finance. The periodic *tailles* became larger and more frequent. From 1443 officials embarked on a vast programme of work to reverse decades of historic encroachments on the lands and rights of the royal demesne under cover of the wars. The quality of the government's financial information was improved. The treasurers and the *généraux des finances* who oversaw the collection of taxes met each year in the King's presence to report on revenues from all sources and charges on those revenues. The loss of the government's financial records makes it difficult to measure the results. But the nominal value of the *tailles* in the five years from 1445 to 1449 rose to an average of more than 500,000 *livres* a year on top of the sums imposed for the upkeep of the *compagnies d'ordonnance*. This was half as much again as the sums imposed in the previous decade. Charles VII's total receipts including the *aides*, the *gabelle* and the revenues of his demesne must have been at least twice that. It is clear even from the fragmentary information available that the French King received a considerable boost to his revenues at a time when the English government's financial administration was disintegrating and its revenues were at their nadir.[82]

The new lieutenant of Normandy landed at Cherbourg early in April 1448, sixteen months after his appointment. To mark his status, Edmund Beaufort had been promoted in the peerage, taking his dead brother's title of Duke of Somerset. He was accompanied to France by Lords Talbot and Fauconberg, several other experienced captains and 1,000 archers to fill gaps in the garrisons. Thomas Basin, now Bishop of Lisieux, met him shortly after his arrival. The new lieutenant struck this astute observer as a handsome man of imposing presence, 'reasonably courteous', well-meaning and friendly, and keen to make a good impression, but marred by a consuming appetite for riches. Somerset made his ceremonial entry into Rouen on 8 May. He was received at the cathedral with much pomp. The church was magnificently decorated. The triptychs on every side altar were opened as if for a feast day. The monuments of the Duke of Bedford and Charles V were uncovered. Speeches of welcome were delivered in Somerset's honour. Over the following weeks there were banquets, presentations and bonfires in the streets.[83]

The Duke of Somerset arrived in a duchy racked by fear and insecurity. In some of the richer districts the first signs of economic recovery were visible after four years of relative peace. But the general picture was bleak. The frontier areas still bore the marks of the fighting before 1444. The pay of the English garrisons was almost everywhere in arrears. Discipline in many regions had broken down as garrison troops supported themselves by levying *pâtis* on friend and foe alike. The situation was aggravated by the scourge of freelance soldiers 'living off the land' who were still present in large numbers, especially in Lower Normandy. Somerset was later accused of aggravating the problem by pocketing part of the money assigned to the wages of the troops. The real problem, however, was not the lieutenant's appetite for money but the decline of the Norman revenues. One of Somerset's first acts was to preside over the Estates of Normandy, which met at Rouen in May 1448. It granted a subsidy of 90,000 *livres*, less than half the usual level, declaring that the 'general poverty of the country was so great that it was impossible for them to bear any more'. Unless they had a few years' relief from the constant demands for taxes, they complained, more people would abandon the land and migrate to other regions and the yield of the *aides* would decline even further. Garrison numbers, they said, would just have to be reduced unless money could be found for them in England. Somerset did what he could to improve the situation. He tightened up the collection of the *aides*. He instituted an inquiry into official corruption and mismanagement. He made a determined attempt to suppress the violence of garrison troops. But the only effective means of dealing with the freelances was to incorporate them in garrisons and pay them, which put yet further pressure on the government's finances. There was nothing that Somerset could do to address the fundamental problem that Normandy could no longer afford to support a large permanent military establishment from its own resources. He had been promised £20,000 a year from English revenues if war broke out, but by that time it would be too late. No provision was made for building up Normandy's defences in advance.[84]

In February 1449, Reginald Boulers Abbot of Gloucester, a member of both the Westminster and Rouen councils, offered a grim assessment of the situation in a statement to Parliament. Flanked by the Chancellor of Normandy Sir Thomas Hoo, he warned the assembly that the French military reforms had greatly increased Charles VII's strength. Their border garrisons, he reported, had been reinforced. Large enemy field forces prowled along the marches. None of the castles and walled towns on the English side were properly manned or supplied. Their artillery was deficient where it existed at all. Almost all of them were indefensible for want of repairs. With fourteen months of the truce to run, the time to take the defences of Normandy in hand was now. As matters stood, if war were to break out Normandy was 'in no wise of itself sufficient to make resistance against the great puissance of the adversaries'.[85]

CHAPTER XIII

The Death of Lancastrian Normandy, 1449–1450

After struggling for four years to prolong the truce, it was the English who repudiated it. In the early hours of 24 March 1449, François de Surienne, the Aragonese mercenary in English service, captured the fortress-town of Fougères on the Breton march. Some 600 men came over the walls at two o'clock in the morning, overcame the garrison, who were asleep, and took over the town, looting every building and doing 'every evil that man can conceive'. A large permanent garrison was installed in the citadel. Fougères was the principal Breton fortress of the northern march. It was also one of the richest and most populous towns of Brittany. It had an expanding cloth industry, boosted by skilled migration from Normandy. It had become one of the main entrepots for trade between Lancastrian Normandy and Valois France. Exaggerated reports reaching the French court put the value of the loot at two million *livres*.[1]

The capture of Fougères was the culmination of more than two years of tension between England and Brittany, which had begun with the arrest of Gilles de Bretagne in June 1446. Ever since that event, the English government had been engaged in an obsessive campaign to get him released. The drivers of this policy were the King and the Duke of Suffolk. Henry was moved by personal affection for the Breton prince. Suffolk's motives were more overtly political. He believed that if Gilles were at liberty, he would be able to challenge the francophile policy of his elder brother and bring Brittany back to the benevolent neutrality of the two previous dukes. Suffolk had always had a naïve faith in the ability of well-placed friends in France to turn the tide in England's favour. He had made the same mistake with Charles of Orléans. His illusions about Gilles were encouraged by the Breton prince's former intimates and household servants, many of whom had taken refuge in England after his arrest, some in Suffolk's own household. Yet Gilles de Bretagne was an even less promising champion than Charles of Orléans had been. Francis faced no serious domestic challenges in Brittany. He was in the process of settling the feud with the Penthièvres which had destabilised the government of his father and grandfather. Gilles had friends in Brittany but no political following. Undeterred, the English claimed him as a vassal of Henry VI and protested energetically against his imprisonment. Charles VII for his part became ever more suspicious of Gilles. In June 1448, he sent his First Chamberlain Pierre de Brézé to the Breton court to press the Duke not to release him except on the most stringent conditions. It may have been because of these representations that Gilles, who had hitherto been held in honourable captivity in one of his wife's castles, was transferred to the custody of a mortal enemy and confined in a dungeon of the remote castle of La Hardouinaie west of Rennes.[2]

Behind this dispute lay a bitter contest between England and France for the allegiance of Brittany. The English refused to accept that with the progressive decline of their power in France Brittany had passed out of their sphere of influence into that of their enemy. In August 1448, there had been a conference on the march of Normandy at Louviers, one of a series intended to resolve issues between England and France about breaches of the truce. The question of Brittany's status was argued out inconclusively between Adam Moleyns and Guillaume Cousinot, the leaders of their respective teams. Moleyns contended that Bretons were subjects of Henry VI and that disputes between them were internal matters, not covered by the truce. Cousinot and the Duke of Brittany's representative declared that Francis was a vassal of Charles VII who wished to live under French protection. The same arguments were rehearsed, equally inconclusively, at the next conference in November. As Cousinot later wrote in a letter to the Count of Foix, the English were determined to vindicate their claim that Brittany was not part of Valois France, by force if necessary, and this was not something that Charles VII could ever have conceded. Among the princely states of France, Brittany was a military power second only to Burgundy. The homage of Brittany was just as fundamental to the French King's concept of territorial unity as that of Normandy and Guyenne. It 'touches the King more closely than almost any other which can arise in this realm,' his diplomats declared.[3]

Fougères was situated in one of the most sensitive parts of the Breton march (*Map IV*). The surrender of Maine had altered the military geography of western France. It left the narrow region between the valleys of the Selune and Couesnon in the north as the only common border between Brittany and Lancastrian Normandy. The English had always sought to maintain a menacing military presence here to remind the Dukes of Brittany of their obligations as allies and vassals. The region had been contested for years between the English garrisons at Avranches and Domfront and the French garrisons of Mont-Saint-Michel, La Gravelle and Laval. In 1447, this rivalry hotted up. Sir Roger Camoys and his freelance companies reoccupied the ruins of Saint-James, the old fortress on the river Beuvron twelve miles south of Avranches, which had been briefly occupied by the English in the mid-1420s and then dismantled. Camoys's men rebuilt the walls. Many of the English military refugees forced out of Maine in the following year came to join him there. They were taken onto the payroll of the war treasurer at Rouen. Others were hired by the Duke of Somerset for his own account and lodged in his castle at Mortain, which was in the process of being refortified. The Bretons regarded the reconstruction of border fortresses like these as a threat. The French claimed that it was a breach of the truce. They protested loudly and persistently.[4]

Although the facts took some time to emerge, it became clear that the attack on Fougères had been planned and authorised at the highest level in England. François de Surienne was no ordinary mercenary captain. He was a Knight of the Garter, an influential figure at Westminster, and close to several of Henry VI's English councillors including Suffolk. He enjoyed a pension from the English Exchequer and held land in Hampshire together with the keepership of Porchester castle. In Normandy, he was a member of the Grand Conseil and captain of Verneuil, the principal English garrison of the south-eastern march. Suffolk had been planning since 1446 to force the issue with the Duke of Brittany by capturing a significant border fortress in Brittany and trading it against the release of Gilles de Bretagne. He had first raised the subject with François de Surienne's deputy Jean Rousselet, suggesting several possible targets, including Fougères, Vitré, or possibly Laval. François de Surienne thought Fougères the most promising, and possibly the most lucrative. One of his men, sent to spy out its defences, reported that its capture would be risky but feasible. When Surienne visited England in the autumn of 1447 for his installation as a Knight of the Garter, he discussed the matter with Suffolk and Somerset. The minister assured him that there would be no breach of the truce. The coup, he said, would be directed only at the Duke of Brittany, not at the

King of France. He arranged for Surienne to use Sir John Fastolf's castle at Condé-sur-Noireau as a base. He promised that he would be relieved if he was besieged and offered him a handsome reward for success. Surienne agreed to go ahead, but it took him more than a year after returning to Normandy to launch the attack. There were periodic fears that the plot might have been betrayed. Somerset's more experienced councillors in Rouen worried about the diplomatic fallout. The attack was set up and then cancelled at least once. In England, Suffolk pressed for action. When the plot finally succeeded he wrote personally to Surienne to express his satisfaction. The Duke of Somerset and Sir John Talbot both wrote adding their own congratulations. There was some suggestion at the time that at least part of the loot may even have ended up in the Norman lieutenant's hands. 'Ask the Duke of Somerset what his take was,' urged Sir John Fastolf when recriminations had begun to fly in England.[5]

The Duke of Brittany was at Rennes when Fougères fell. He was roused from his bed to receive the news, and briefly lost his head. Crying 'We are lost!' he called for his horses and fled through the night to Vannes with just three companions. The captain of Rennes was dispatched to François de Surienne with an offer to release Gilles de Bretagne and pay 50,000 écus ('*un bon pot de vin*') for the surrender of the town. This offer would have given Suffolk all that he wanted, but François de Surienne had his own agenda. 'I have authority to take,' he replied, 'not to restore.' Francis soon recovered his balance, largely through the support of Charles VII. The French King received the news of the capture of Fougères in the saddle as he was leaving the castle of Montils for Bourges. He promptly cancelled his plans and made for Razilly near Chinon where his council assembled to consider the implications. Hot on his heels came three emissaries from Duke Francis who had come to appeal for help. The Duke, they reported, had no confidence in the military capacity of the Breton nobility after so many years of peace. He believed that a relatively small English army would be enough to overcome their resistance. The French King promised to make their master's cause his own. In the meantime, Prégent de Coëtivy and the Marshal André de Laval were ordered to raise a task force of 1,200 men to reinforce the duchy's defences.[6]

The laws of war required the victim to summon a trucebreaker to make good his breach. Only if he refused was it legitimate to exercise a right of reprisal. With an eye to opinion among his own nobility, Charles VII resolved to observe the forms. If the war was to be reopened, it must be understood throughout France that it was the fault of the English. He sent Guillaume Cousinot to Rouen at the head of a small delegation to demand the immediate restitution of Fougères and compensation for the looting. Cousinot was followed by a herald of the Duke of Brittany with the same demand. Somerset gave the same answer to both of them. He disavowed François de Surienne who, he said untruthfully, had not acted by his authority. In any event, it was a matter between the English King and his Breton vassal and no concern of the King of France. Given the scale of the operation and François de Surienne's known standing at Rouen and Westminster, this answer was received with incredulity when the French emissaries returned with their report. Charles VII's suspicions were confirmed by the interrogation of members of Surienne's garrison at Fougères who had recently been captured during a raid. They revealed that the Duke of Somerset had been closely concerned with the preparation of the coup. Reinforcements were at that moment reported to be making for Fougères from almost every English garrison in Normandy.[7]

The truce commissioners were due to meet on 15 May 1449 to deal with the allegation of breach. The French King wrote to the Duke of Somerset telling him that he expected the English delegation to be ready with an explanation. The meeting never happened. It was overtaken by the first incidents in an undeclared war. The initiative was taken by Robert de Flocques, Pierre de Brézé's brother Jean, and the French garrisons of Evreux and Louviers. On 21 April Robert de Flocques tried to seize the walled town of Mantes on the Seine. Mantes had a large English garrison and its inhabitants, according to a French chronicler, were 'more fiercely anti-French than the English'. The attack was foiled by the alertness of its lieutenant-captain. But Flocques had better fortune three weeks later at Pont-de-l'Arche, a walled town at the confluence of the Seine and the Eure. It controlled an important fortified bridge which was a critical part of the forward defences of Rouen. It was also the venue for the forthcoming conference of the truce commissioners. The English commissioners, Lord Fauconberg, Sir Thomas Hoo and Abbot Boulers had already arrived, but the French failed to appear. Instead, early the next morning two of Robert de Flocques's men approached the fortified gatehouse at the north end of the bridge with a laden cart. They bribed the gatekeeper to admit them, and then overpowered and killed him along with an English soldier who came to investigate the noise. Then they penetrated the town and opened the Louviers gate to let in 400 or 500 men crying 'St Yves for Brittany!' The citadel was taken. The rest of the town followed, except for some towers where the garrison held out for a day or two before surrendering. Hoo and Boulers had left the night before, but Fauconberg was still in the town and was taken prisoner. The coup does not seem to have been sanctioned by the French King. Its authors claimed to be exercising a right of reprisal on behalf of the Duke of Brittany. A few hours after the town had fallen, two heralds arrived from Rouen to ask in whose name the invaders were acting. They replied that they were soldiers of the Duke of Brittany and sent out a Breton-speaker to do the talking.[8]

The Duke of Somerset was at Rouen, where the Estates of the four *bailliages* of Upper Normandy and the Eure valley had opened on 8 May 1449. The first reports of the fall of Pont-de-l'Arche were brought by refugees from the town at about seven o'clock in the morning. Somerset flew into a towering rage. He accused the first bearer of bad news of lying and threatened him with imprisonment. Then, when it became all too obvious that he was telling the truth, he ran through the castle summoning his slumbering officers and councillors from their beds. He railed against the French with such violence that his wife hid her French doctor in a cauldron for fear that he would be murdered. Somerset's first instinct was to march on Pont-de-l'Arche at once. But that idea was quickly abandoned. Robert de Flocques's men in the town were unlikely to be surprised as the English had been. And Somerset was tied to Rouen by the fear that if he left, the city would rise up and expel his garrison. Meanwhile the fighting had begun to spread. The castle of Conches near Evreux was captured. On the northern march, Gerberoy fell to a surprise attack by the French captain of the Beauvaisis. On the march of Brittany, those long-standing bones of contention Saint-James de Beuvron and Mortain were both captured in the course of June by the French troops of Prégent de Coëtivy, who had been sent to support the Duke of Brittany in the spring. On the march of Gascony, French partisans acting in the name of the Duke of Brittany seized Cognac and some smaller places. In spite of their earlier warning that they could do no more, the Estates of Normandy responded to the crisis with a generous new grant of 188,000 *livres*, in four instalments spread over a year. But only the first instalment was ever collected. The collection of the rest was rapidly overtaken by events.[9]

Over the next two months a dense succession of messages and embassies passed between Rouen and the court of France. The delayed conference between the truce commissioners opened on 15 June 1449 at Louviers and continued for the next four weeks. The negotiations were conducted under the shadow of increasingly obvious preparations for war. At Rennes the Estates of Brittany had gathered to discuss the current crisis in the presence of the Duke. Dunois and Bertrand de Précigny attended on behalf of Charles VII. On 17 June, Francis sealed a military alliance with the French King. He promised to be ready to take the field against the English in person at the end of July if Fougères had not by then been restored. At Rouen, the Duke of Somerset must by now have understood the peril in which he stood, but he showed no sign of allowing it to influence his actions. His truce commissioners at Louviers stuck to their line that the capture of Fougères had been unauthorised. They claimed with a wealth of mendacious detail that Somerset had rebuked François de Surienne for his temerity but could do nothing to expel him from the town. In the parish church of the village of Venables on the Seine, to which the negotiations had moved, the discussions descended into repetitious speeches reiterating the incompatible positions of each side. The English professed to be willing to restore Fougères, but only if the French first restored Pont-de-l'Arche, Gerberoy and Conches and released Lord Fauconberg. They were unwilling, and probably unable, to restore the loot, which had already been distributed. They also insisted that the Duke of Brittany freed Gilles de Bretagne.

The final sessions were held in the Cistercian abbey of Bonport, on the banks of the Eure outside Pont-de-l'Arche. On 4 July, when no agreement had been reached, the French delegation made their final offer and issued an ultimatum. By 25 July, Fougères must be restored and compensation paid for the looting. The French were willing to restore Pont-de-l'Arche, Conches and Gerberoy and to release Fauconberg, but only once that had been done. They refused to contemplate the release of Gilles de Bretagne, observing that he was a vassal of the Duke of Brittany who had been justly imprisoned for his treachery. If the English did not comply with these demands, the French commissioners said, Charles VII would regard the truce as repudiated.[10]

THE DEATH OF LANCASTRIAN NORMANDY, 1449–1450

On 20 July 1449, five days before the expiry of the French ultimatum, Robert de Flocques attacked Verneuil. Verneuil was the key English fortress of the south-east march, defended by a powerful circuit of walls and a modern citadel dominated by its keep, the famous Tour Grise. Its captain was François de Surienne, who was at Fougères. The place was defended by his nephew Jean with a garrison of more than 120 men, almost all of them French. Robert de Flocques advanced on the town through the forest of Conches. His men got in through an opening pierced in the walls to accommodate two water mills, with the connivance of the miller. Some of the garrison fled through the gates and made for François de Surienne's other castle at Longny. The rest retreated into the citadel, accompanied by the mayor and a handful of loyalists. The citadel was protected by its own moat, but the French opened the sluices and drained it, and then came over the walls from ladders. On the following day, the Count of Dunois entered the town with several hundred more men. By the evening, only the Tour Grise was holding out. This time there could be no doubt that Robert de Flocques was acting with Charles VII's authority.[11]

The French court had moved to the castle of Les Roches-Tranchelion, high above the valley of the Vienne in Touraine. An enlarged meeting of the King's council gathered there on 31 July 1449. Charles VII needed to act quickly. If the war was to be reopened, it had to happen before Somerset could be reinforced from England. The King knew what advice he wanted to receive and duly got it. It was decided to proceed by force of arms against the remaining English domains in France. Two representatives of the Duke of Somerset were still in the castle after spending more than a fortnight trying to stave off the worst. At the conclusion of the meeting, they were summoned into the hall to hear a long recitation of the dismal course of the negotiations since March. They began to respond with their own version of events but were silenced by the French Chancellor. It was too late for speeches, he said. The truce was at an end.[12]

The row about breaches of the truce might perhaps have been resolved if that had been all there was to it. But there were deeper antagonisms in the background which made compromise difficult. The French profoundly distrusted the Duke of Somerset, with reason. Jean de Waurin thought that Somerset had behaved as if he wanted to lose Normandy. Many people in England thought so too. An anonymous soldier in France whose bitter complaints were preserved among Sir

John Fastolf's papers, thought that Somerset should have accepted the French final offer. But we do not know, any more than he did, how much discretion Somerset really had. His truce commissioners claimed that for all his extensive powers as lieutenant, his instructions left him little leeway. This may well have been true. He was constantly obliged to refer major issues back to the Duke of Suffolk in England. Suffolk unquestionably bore the main responsibility for what had happened. The capture of Fougères was his project. The misjudgement that the King of France could be kept out of the dispute with Brittany was his misjudgement. As for Gilles de Bretagne, he remained in prison until 1450, when he was murdered by his jailers, probably on the instructions of his brother. He died, as Fastolf's secretary William Worcester told another English King, 'for his great truth and love he had to your royaumeward'.[13]

The council in England took some time to appreciate the gravity of the situation in Normandy. At the time of the capture of Fougères, their attention was fixed on Scotland, not France. The nineteen-year-old Scottish King, James II, known to the French as 'Fire-face' from the large red birthmark that disfigured one side of his face, was an astute, aggressive politician who was quick to see the implications of events in France for his country. He had recently taken the government of Scotland out of the hands of the uneasy consortium of noblemen who had dominated Scotland since his father's assassination. In the previous summer he had sent an embassy to Charles VII headed by his Chancellor Sir William Crichton to renew the auld alliance. In the meantime, he had allowed the truce on the border to lapse. The Douglases had mounted several major raids into the north of England. Viewed from Westminster, the situation was grave enough for Henry VI, who was notoriously averse to long journeys, to go north as far as Durham. But if his presence was expected to inspire his northern subjects, it failed. A large punitive expedition which entered Scotland in October 1448 under the command of the Earl of Northumberland suffered a humiliating defeat on the banks of Sark Water. Two months later the instrument renewing the auld alliance was sealed by Crichton and his fellow ambassadors at Tours. Tension on the Scottish border continued through the winter, and in May and June 1449 there was a fresh bout of open warfare. The English responded with two powerful raids into Scotland.

Dunbar and Dumfries were burned. The Scots retaliated by entering Northumberland and burning Alnwick and Warkworth. The truce was not reinstated on the border until July.[14]

The news of the fall of Pont-de-l'Arche was brought to Westminster by two heralds sent post-haste from Rouen. The council immediately decided to send 1,300 men to reinforce the Duke of Somerset. It was hoped that they would be ready to sail for Normandy by the end of June. It took much longer to persuade the Parliamentary Commons. They had heard the sombre warning of Abbot Boulers about the state of Normandy's defences with no obvious sign of alarm. When they voted a half-subsidy at the beginning of April, it was assigned to the King's more pressing debts and the defence of Calais, the Scottish march, Le Crotoy and the Channel. There was nothing for Normandy. By 16 June, when Parliament reconvened at Winchester after the Whitsun break, it was clear that England and France were moving towards war. The Duke of Somerset had written pressing for more men. But the Commons dug their heels in. They proposed that the King should raise the money by revoking the many improvident grants that he had made to his friends since his majority, something which Henry refused point blank to do. Behind the scenes, a vigorous debate was in progress in the council. Not everyone recognised the need to reinforce Normandy, even now. Those who did fell to arguing about a new form of taxation which might prove more palatable to the Commons than the traditional tenth and fifteenth. It was not until July that the Commons, with ill-grace and loudly protesting the poverty of the country, agreed to grant another half-subsidy in the usual form.[15]

Sir John Fastolf, now a bitter old man living in retirement in Norfolk, inspired a memorandum for the council outlining how the war might still be won. After thirty-two years in Normandy, he protested, England could not possibly betray the Englishmen who had settled there or the loyal French who had sustained their rule. Fastolf envisaged an army of 30,000 men operating in the north and another of 10,000 in Gascony. Separate task forces were to clear the French from the Norman marches, reconquer Picardy and the Beauvaisis, carry the boundary of Lancastrian France to the Loire and occupy Brittany. The idea that England could have recruited or paid such an army was fanciful, but there were flashes of realism even in this fantastic scheme. Fastolf pointed out that the defensive strategy followed for the past fifteen years in Normandy was bound to fail because it exposed the population to war damage on a scale which was certain to alienate them from English rule. It was necessary to carry the war to the enemy. This would require overwhelming force and could not be done on the cheap. The problem, as he saw it, was that the English no longer had the stomach for the war. All around him, 'mean-spirited faint-hearts' were complaining about its burdens. 'Why can't we stay in England and abandon continental domains,' he imagined them saying, 'then we can live in peace.'[16]

The accumulating signs of war-weariness were obvious to everyone. A general appeal for loans produced little over £3,300, most of which came from Henry VI's councillors. No money reached Normandy from England until the end of July, when just £1,750 was found to sustain the English administration in the greatest crisis of its existence. As if to mock Fastolf's project for an army of 30,000, it was proving hard to find even the additional 1,300 men that the council had already promised. At the end of July 1449, a month after the date originally envisaged, Sir William Peyto sailed from Portsmouth with less than half of them. Another 400 men followed at the end of September under the command of the Earl of Oxford's brother Sir Robert Vere. Most of these men were intended to reinforce the garrisons. The English assumed that the war would be fought in the traditional way: a campaign of attrition with a succession of slow-moving sieges. They were wholly unprepared for the speed and scale of the collapse which followed.[17]

Overall command of the French armies had been given to the Count of Dunois. Initially, the forces at his disposal were quite modest. Two armies were to launch a coordinated invasion of Normandy. Dunois himself, with about 3,300 men, was to invade the south-east from his base at Verneuil. A second army of about 1,800 men raised mainly in Picardy was to make for Rouen through the Caux under the command of the Counts of Eu and Saint-Pol. Two more armies would follow as soon as they were ready. One, commanded by the Duke of Alençon, was to invade his own duchy and enter Lower Normandy by the south-west. He was assigned about 1,200 troops who had responded to the French King's summons, and gathered more from the garrisons of Maine and the Vendômois as he marched north. The other, much larger army, under the Duke of Brittany and his uncle Arthur de Richemont, was to invade the Avranchin and the Cotentin. They would comprise the

THE DEATH OF LANCASTRIAN NORMANDY, 1449–1450

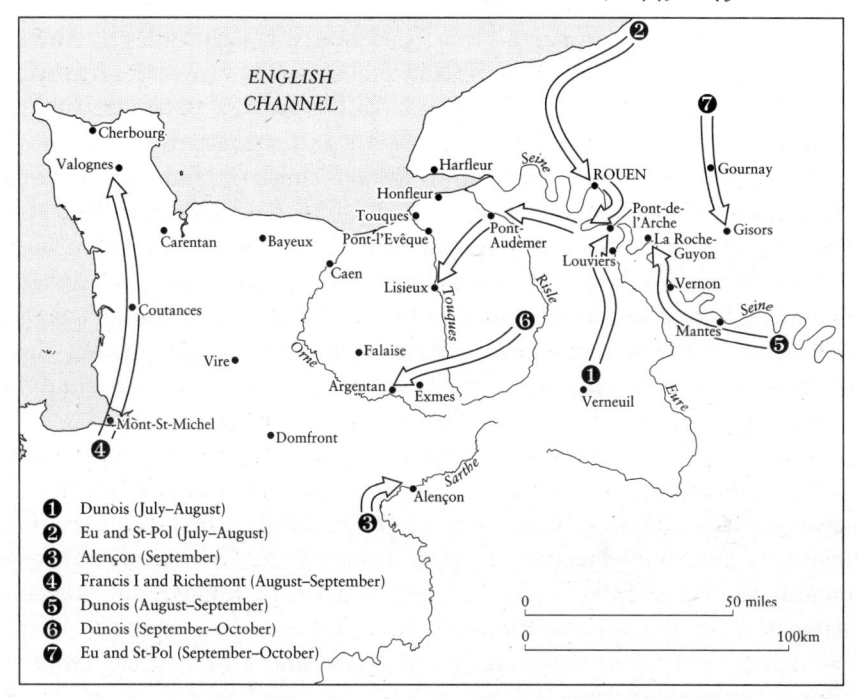

❶ Dunois (July–August)
❷ Eu and St-Pol (July–August)
❸ Alençon (September)
❹ Francis I and Richemont (August–September)
❺ Dunois (August–September)
❻ Dunois (September–October)
❼ Eu and St-Pol (September–October)

12 The French invasion of Normandy, July–October 1449

1,200 French troops already operating on the Breton march in support of the Duke and some 6,000 Bretons who had yet to be recruited. Dunois's calculation was that by attacking from several directions at once, he would make it impossible for the English to concentrate their own forces. The strength of the English forces in Normandy at this stage is not known but given the small number of reinforcements received from England in the last six years, there were probably no more than about 3,000 to 4,000 English troops in the whole duchy, distributed between some forty royal garrisons and perhaps a dozen private ones. The only significant concentration was at Rouen. As the campaign continued, the strength of the French armies tended to increase with new arrivals from the more distant provinces, while the English forces were progressively wasted by casualties, capture and desertion.[18]

On the day after the fall of Verneuil the Duke of Somerset ordered Talbot to take 1,500 men, the largest field force that could be raised, to recover the town and relieve the men still holding out in the Tour Grise. Talbot left Rouen at once, but it took him ten days to collect his forces. On 31 July 1449, he reached Breteuil, eight miles north of Verneuil. Dunois called off an assault on the Tour Grise and advanced towards him with about 2,500 men. Talbot was unwilling to make a stand at Breteuil. He withdrew north and arrayed his men in a stronger position across the road to Rouen, south of Harcourt. Dense forest protected his rear and thick hedges his flanks. A row of carts punctuated by artillery was placed in front of his lines. Dunois and his army approached and dug themselves in a short distance away. However, neither side was prepared to risk leaving the protection of their prepared positions. When dawn broke the next morning, the English lines were empty. Talbot had withdrawn to Harcourt under cover of darkness. He had decided not to chance his only field army in a pitched battle, even in a prepared position. Shortly afterwards, Talbot abruptly abandoned his field operations and hurried back to Rouen. The Counts of Eu and Saint-Pol had begun their advance on the city. They hoped to enter it with the connivance of a group of men within the walls. Talbot's men reached Rouen on 4 August, only just in time to forestall them. Left to fend for themselves, the men in the Tour Grise of Verneuil held out for another two and a half weeks before finally surrendering on 22 August.[19]

Once their plan to get into Rouen was frustrated, the Counts of Eu and Saint-Pol crossed the Seine at Pont-de-l'Arche, where they joined forces with Dunois on 8 August. There, they paused to consider their next move. Their combined forces were now more than 5,000 strong. The whole of south-eastern Normandy was in their hands, apart from a handful of small privately held castles. They decided to expand the area under their control westward to the valley of the Touques. Their first objective was Pont-Audemer, which commanded the only feasible crossing of the river Risle. In Rouen castle the Duke of Somerset presided at a council of war. All the captains in and around Rouen were present, along with the principal officers of the Norman administration. The general sentiment was that Pont-Audemer was indefensible. Its ancient walls dated from the twelfth century and in places had collapsed, leaving large gaps to be defended by timber palisades. They thought that its fixed defences should be demolished and the town abandoned. Fulk Eyton, who was captain of both Caudebec and Pont-Audemer, disagreed. He persuaded the meeting that if the garrison was reinforced the wet moat and the marshes and watercourses around the town could be successfully defended. It was decided to send Eyton to hold the town along with Osbern Mundeford, the Treasurer of Normandy and effectively Somerset's deputy. Some 400 men were made available to them. But there were to be no more field operations like Talbot's march to Breteuil. Every garrison would be left to defend itself as best it could until substantial further forces could arrive from England.

This strategy was much criticised after the event. The experienced French captain Jean de Bueil, who took part in the campaign, thought that Talbot and Somerset should have bet Normandy on a pitched battle with all their strength. In the first few days of the campaign they had the numbers to defeat each of the French armies in detail. 'If they had lost,' he wrote, 'at least they would have lost with honour.' The alternative was inevitable defeat, as each English garrison was picked off one after the other. The same criticism was made in England. In hindsight, the critics were right. Nothing could have been worse than the actual outcome. But Somerset and Talbot were both able soldiers without the benefit of hindsight. With their small, scattered forces and the constant threat of popular risings in the towns, they took what was probably the only reasonable course.

Pierre de Brézé and Robert de Flocques arrived outside Pont-Audemer with the advance guard of the French army on the evening on 10 August 1449, only to find that Eyton and Mundeford had entered the town a few hours before them. The French immediately launched a bold night-time attack on the palisades. They had already made several breaches when Mundeford, roused from his bed by the noise, arrived on the scene and succeeded in pushing the invaders back. Two days later, on 12 August, the rest of the French army arrived. A rocket was fired at a tower which set fire to some straw stored inside. The fire spread to the neighbouring buildings and through the town. Seizing their opportunity, the French launched an assault from two points and carried the palisades on both. The citizens fled for the churches, the garrison to the dilapidated citadel. The French began to assault the citadel. Initially, Mundeford would not contemplate a negotiated surrender. But he changed his mind after his men started to desert en masse, jumping into the Risle and surrendering to the French on the other side. The defence lost all coherence as different groups of defenders lost contact with each other, some fighting their own battles against overwhelming odds, others fleeing into the fields or surrendering. Dunois and a herald entered the castle from a ladder under safe-conduct and sat down with Mundeford in an upper chamber, while Eyton carried on the fight from one of the towers. Mundeford later alleged that he had reached agreement with Dunois on a collective ransom for the entire garrison. But it seems that the castle was overwhelmed before the talks had been completed. Eyton and Mundeford were both taken prisoner, together with almost all of their men.[20]

At Rouen, Somerset struggled to keep up with a fast-moving situation. He tried to establish a new line of defence along the river Touques and the hills of the pays d'Auge. Instructions were prepared for the garrisons at Touques, Pont-l'Evêque and Lisieux, the three main walled towns of the region. In the chaotic state of the country, it took the messenger three days to get there, only to find that Pont-l'Evêque and Lisieux had already opened their gates without a fight. The garrison of Pont-l'Evêque had abandoned the place, demolishing its walls as they left. At Lisieux, the decision to surrender had been driven by the Bishop, the chronicler Thomas Basin, a member of Somerset's council who quickly transferred his allegiance to Charles VII and would shortly be admitted to his council. The same calculation was being made across western Normandy. Within a day of the surrender of Lisieux, sixteen walled towns of the surrounding region had sent in their submissions. The whole of the territory east of the river Risle was now in French hands except for Bernay, whose resistance was short-lived.[21]

Shortly after the surrender of Lisieux, the captains of the French army gathered in the town in the presence of the Bishop. The French advance to the Touques had divided Lancastrian Normandy in two: Upper Normandy and the Seine valley were now cut off from the Cotentin and the duchy of Alençon, where some of the largest English garrisons were stationed. The question for the French captains at Lisieux was whether to continue their westward advance and complete the conquest of Lower Normandy or to withdraw to the Seine. The leaders of the army had received messages from many towns of western Normandy promising to rise up against the English as soon as they approached. According to Basin's account the decisive voice was his own. He pointed out that the towns of western Normandy were among the strongest and best defended in the duchy. Places like Caen and Falaise would not be easy to take. Even if the towns were captured, they had powerful citadels which could hold out independently for a long time. The country around had suffered severe war damage. It was incapable of feeding the French army, which would risk starvation if a siege lasted any length of time. The outcome was a decision to return to the Seine valley. The Seine was the political heart of Normandy. The river was the spine of the English defensive system and the key to the communications of the whole region. Charles VII had just entered Chartres with substantial additional forces. Two of the captains present at Lisieux were sent to report their advice to him. The King readily accepted the suggested strategy. He was already making for the Seine by the valley of the Eure.[22]

In the last week of August 1449 Dunois's army began methodically to eliminate the English garrisoned fortresses of the Seine valley between Paris and Rouen. On 24 August he appeared outside Mantes at the eastern limit of the territory under English control. The story of Mantes spoke volumes about the state of Lancastrian Normandy in its last days. It had an English garrison of over 160 men commanded by the Somerset knight Thomas of Saint-Barbe. He was determined to defend the town, but his hand was forced by the inhabitants. They had traditionally been among the most loyal in Normandy and only three months before had stoutly resisted the attack by Robert de Flocques. But the fate of Verneuil and Pont-Audemer had changed the mood. They were afraid of losing everything in an assault. The town council had already made contact with Charles VII. They had been assured that they would be pardoned for their past loyalty to Henry VI and that their charters would be respected. On the day after Dunois's arrival, there was a general meeting of the citizens. Nearly 300 householders attended. The mayor reported that the French were on their way with a powerful artillery train. The meeting resolved to surrender. There was not a single dissenting voice. The citizens occupied one of the quarters of the town, seized a gate, and barricaded all the alleyways leading from the citadel. Then they let in the French. On 26 August, the garrison surrendered in return for the right to leave.

Fifteen miles downstream, Vernon was already under siege. Its garrison was commanded by John Butler, brother of the Irish Earl of Ormond. He too resolved to defend the town. He sent Dunois an old key to the gates that no longer worked to make his point. But, like Thomas of Saint-Barbe, he found the townsmen determined to surrender. A plot to open the gates was suppressed and its leaders executed. But the garrison had no stomach for a fight on two sides. All they wanted were sealed letters certifying that the loss of the town was none of their doing. The gates were opened to the French on 29 August.

The fortress of La Roche-Guyon with its great circular keep and its powerful clifftop position on the opposite bank of the river was commanded by a Welsh squire, John Edward. He could probably have held out. But he was married to a French woman with extensive property and social connections in Normandy. Edward entered into a conditional surrender agreement shortly after the arrival of the French army, undertaking to surrender in fifteen days unless relieved. The Duke of Somerset was outraged. He was in no position to relieve La Roche-Guyon, but he sent a small group of soldiers to arrest Edward and take over its defence. Edward refused to admit them and surrendered on the appointed day. He dismissed his garrison, did homage to Charles VII for his wife's lands and continued to serve as captain of La Roche-Guyon for its former French proprietors. Others would follow the same course. The only remaining fortress on the Seine above Rouen was now Château-Gaillard, and that was shortly blockaded by French troops.[23]

Gunpowder artillery had so far played only a limited part in the campaign, owing to the logistical difficulty of moving the larger pieces overland. The Tour Grise of Verneuil had been battered with mangonels and other mechanical stone-throwers, one of the last recorded appearances of these clumsy machines whose basic design had remained almost unchanged since Roman times. Dunois's army had had only a few small bombards at Pont-Audemer and Lisieux. But his operations in the Seine valley unlocked the river for the French and made it possible to deploy guns on a larger scale. In Paris, a powerful artillery train had been in preparation for several weeks which could now be brought downriver by barge into the heart of Normandy.[24]

At the end of August 1449 Charles VII arrived at Louviers after a triumphal progress through the towns of south-eastern Normandy in which the crowds had received him with acclamation. Here, he established his headquarters for the next six weeks. A council of war was held shortly after his arrival. The strength of the French forces had increased since the beginning of the campaign. With the troops gathered around the King, there were now about 11,000 men under arms. It was decided that Dunois would mop up the surviving enclaves of resistance south of the Seine, while the Counts of Eu and Saint-Pol crossed the river and opened a fresh offensive against the

English fortresses of the northern march. The only serious resistance encountered by either army was at the Duke of Somerset's castle at Harcourt, where Sir Richard Frogenhall's garrison held Dunois at bay for a fortnight until the arrival of the artillery forced them to surrender. Everywhere else, walled places surrendered as soon as the French armies appeared.[25]

While these operations were under way, south-western Normandy came under sustained attack from several directions at once. The Duke of Brittany launched his campaign from Dinan at the beginning of September 1449. Effective command was exercised by Richemont. At Mont-Saint-Michel the Bretons joined forces with a large contingent of French troops led by the Marshal André de Laval and Prégent de Coëtivy. The Duke's brother was sent to lay siege to Fougères, while the main body of the army crossed the sands at low tide to Granville. From here, they invaded the Cotentin peninsula. The pattern of the rest of Normandy was repeated. The English garrisons were caught between the enemy outside and the frightened and rebellious townsmen within. Coutances, Saint-Lô, Carentan and Valognes, all strongly garrisoned towns, surrendered without striking a blow, in some cases after a nominal siege of two or three days. The smaller castles were overrun with ease. Many of them were found abandoned.[26]

The duchy of Alençon was the best defended region of Lancastrian Normandy. Its fortresses had been better maintained and garrisoned than those of any other border area. But they fell like dominoes to the Duke of Alençon when he returned to reclaim them in September. At Alençon itself, which had one of the largest garrisons of the region, the citizens opened the gates to him as soon as he began to prepare his siege lines. The garrison took refuge in the citadel and opened negotiations for its surrender. A third line of attack was opened at the beginning of October, when Dunois advanced to the river Orne and captured Exmes and Argentan. The citizens of Argentan opened their gates like those of Alençon. The garrison fled to the citadel, but they were scarcely inside it before the French artillery blew a hole in the walls big enough for a cart to pass. The French poured in. 'In all the history books of every age ...' wrote Guillaume Cousinot to the Count of Foix, 'you will not find any other prince who has conquered so much or taken so many places in so short a time ... Believe me, I was there. I saw it with my own eyes.'[27]

*

The French invasion of Normandy set off a slow-burning political crisis in England. The Duke of Suffolk retained the affection of the King, but his grip on power weakened as the disaster unfolded across the Channel. In the streets, anger was mounting. The London lawyer Robert Bale, who lived through these years, blamed Suffolk for everything and thought that most of his fellow citizens did too. The Duke, 'having then about the King all the rule and the governance of this land was wonder[ful]ly in the common voice of the people noised and dislandered to be the mean and cause of the said hurts and loss by the said Frenchmen.' On 11 September a great council met at Sheen. It was exceptionally well attended. Reports from Normandy reached England with a delay of at least a week, depending on the weather in the Channel. The men gathered at Sheen must have known about the fall of Pont-Audemer and Lisieux and the opening of Dunois's offensive in the Seine valley. The assembly advised that an expeditionary army of 3,000 men should be sent to France. This would bring the total strength of the English army in Normandy to about 7,000, which might make it possible for Somerset to challenge the French in the field. Twelve captains were found who agreed to recruit them. They were expected to muster at Portsmouth in October and reach Normandy by the end of that month.

The timetable was critical, but unrealistic. It took much longer than six weeks to requisition the necessary shipping. There was no money to pay either the shipmasters or the soldiers' advances. None of the twelve captains were men of any real substance, and none were rich enough to recruit men on their own credit. Treasurer Lumley's cautious attempt to rebuild the King's finances had depended on the continuance of the truce. At his wits' end to find money for the new army, he resigned, exhausted, on 17 September, leaving just £480 cash in the Treasury. The only hope now was more Parliamentary taxation. On 23 September, writs were issued for a new Parliament, barely two months after the dissolution of the last one. Meanwhile, commissioners were appointed to raise loans from prominent men in the counties on the security of the subsidy which it was hoped to obtain. 'Subtle and strange means' were used to induce them to lend, according to Robert Bale. Whatever those means were, they yielded promises of £12,250, a respectable sum in the circumstances, in addition to substantial loans from Cardinal Beaufort's executors. But it was not until November that any of this money came in and recruitment could begin.[28]

THE DEATH OF LANCASTRIAN NORMANDY, 1449-1450

On 9 October 1449 Charles VII appeared before Rouen. Inside the city, Talbot took command of the defence. He had at least 1,000 men who had been there since the beginning of the campaign. In addition, there were several hundred soldiers from the defeated garrisons of Normandy who had found their way there after the surrender of their strongholds. Rouen was a strong city. It was enclosed by nearly four miles of walls, pierced by five fortified gates and protected by a deep dry ditch. There were two strongpoints, the old citadel of Philip Augustus by the northern rampart and the still incomplete royal palace in the south-west corner of the walls. A long fortified bridge of stone connected the city to the opposite bank of the Seine, ending on the south side in a powerful barbican with its own garrison. On the heights of Ste Catherine east of the city, the fortified abbey also had its own garrison. It had taken Henry V nearly six months to starve Rouen out in 1418–19. Dunois did not have that long. It was late in the season. The weather was foul. He needed to take the city before an army arrived from England. He was counting on the citizens to open their gates as they had done in so many smaller towns.

There had already been some contact between the French King's officers and prominent citizens of Rouen. A delegation had come before Charles VII while he was still at Louviers, promising to admit his troops if they arrived outside in sufficient strength. Few of the inhabitants were willing to sustain a siege or run the risks of an assault for the sake of a regime which was unable to protect them and seemed to have no future. They called on the Duke of Somerset to surrender. Somerset rejected their demand out of hand and showed every sign of intending to fight. Dissent among the inhabitants was firmly repressed, and a number of people who had plotted with the French were executed on Talbot's orders. When two French royal heralds advanced to the gate bearing a summons to surrender, they were received at the barriers by Talbot himself. He took the document, tore it up in the heralds' faces and threw it in the mud at their feet, before telling them to get lost if they valued their lives. Charles VII withdrew to Pont-de-l'Arche, leaving the conduct of operations to his commanders. Dunois drew up his men in the plain outside the walls, hoping to provoke either a rising inside the city or else a pitched battle with the defenders in which he would have an overwhelming superiority of numbers. They stood in battle array for two days in the pouring rain as the fields were churned up into a sea of mud. Then they too withdrew to Pont-de-l'Arche.[29]

On 16 October the French army returned. The commanders had succeeded in making contact with sympathisers in the city. The plotters had a carefully laid plan to deliver up the Porte Saint-Hilaire, the fortified gate that gave onto the Paris road on the east side of the city. A major operation was mounted to take advantage of their help. Some 4,000 French troops appeared in the early afternoon before the Porte Saint-Hilaire and the Porte Beauvoisine. Many noblemen came forward to be knighted before the walls, including the Count of Nevers, the soldier-diplomat Guillaume Cousinot and the Scottish soldier of fortune William Monypenny. The men in the city succeeded in taking possession of the gateway. Dunois's men approached with ladders. About thirty of them came over the walls. But the alarm had gone up and Talbot arrived on the scene with a large force of soldiers. He recovered the gate and drove the invaders back into the ditch. The attempt had failed.[30]

That evening, another delegation from the city came before Charles VII at Pont-de-l'Arche, apparently on their own initiative. They asked for a cease-fire to allow for negotiations. The French King was as anxious to avoid a bloody assault as they were. He wanted the city intact and the citizens on his side. He agreed a two-day cease-fire and suggested a conference at the river port of Saint-Ouen, half-way between Rouen and Pont-de-l'Arche. Inside the city, the citizens were organising themselves under the leadership of the Archbishop, Raoul Roussel. Roussel, a native Norman from the Cotentin, had up to now been a loyal partisan of the English regime. He was an active member of the Grand Conseil. He had been one of the more prominent judges of Joan of Arc. He had undertaken frequent administrative and diplomatic missions for the English. But, like Thomas Basin, who was now with Charles VII at Pont-de-l'Arche, he regarded the Lancastrian cause as lost. His main concern now was to spare his city a destructive siege.

On the following morning, 17 October, Roussel presided at an assembly of the citizens. There was almost universal resentment of Somerset's attempt to defend Rouen and a determination to find a way of surrendering without a fight. After the meeting the leaders went before the lieutenant in a body. They said that the city was as good as lost. No supplies had reached them for the last six weeks. Between 800 and 1,000 Rouennais had already taken up arms and were ready to take over the city. The rest were arming themselves. Somerset dithered. He tried to play for time. Finally, he agreed to let them send a delegation to meet the French King's councillors.

The fifty-strong delegation, led by the Archbishop, appeared the next day, 18 October, at Saint-Ouen. Two representatives of the Duke of Somerset were present, but they were only observers with no authority to agree anything. The French Chancellor, Guillaume Juvénal des Ursins, was waiting for them. With him were Pierre de Brézé, Guillaume Cousinot and the Count of Dunois. The citizens opened by demanding a truce of six months to consult Henry VI in England. This was peremptorily refused. The rest of the discussion was about the terms of submission. On the French side, Dunois took the lead. After much talking, the French conceded all the citizens' demands: letters of remission for their past loyalty to Henry VI, confirmation of their charters and liberties and a safe-conduct for the English garrison to leave. All this must be ratified by the citizen body and accepted by the Duke of Somerset. Dunois gave them two days.

The Archbishop returned to Rouen to report to a packed public meeting in the town hall. He advised them to submit to the French. They would not be offered such favourable terms again. The citizens agreed with enthusiasm. The Duke of Somerset's representatives, who were present, walked out. Later that evening, the English in the city withdrew to the castle, the palace and the bridge barbican and prepared to hold out. The citizens sent a messenger to Pont-de-l'Arche to ask the King to send troops to the city with all possible speed. The following day, 19 October, was a Sunday. At seven o'clock in the morning, the Duke of Somerset received a delegation of citizens at the palace. It was led by the Archbishop's representative. He brought with him two notaries to record the proceedings. The churchman called on the lieutenant to surrender the city in accordance with the terms offered at Saint-Ouen. 'I would rather die,' Somerset replied. 'What are you afraid of?' he asked them. 'Your walls are sound. Your enemies have been repulsed. You still hold the forts. The enemy army has not returned.' It was too late for argument. The great bell of the Tour de l'Horloge was ringing to call the citizens to arms. The townsmen were already filling the streets. They took over the walls and gates and blockaded the English in their three redoubts. Several English soldiers who were found at large were lynched. The Porte Martainville on the east side of the city was opened. Dunois's troops, who were standing outside, poured in. Towards the end of the day, Charles VII appeared from Pont-de-l'Arche with the rest of his army.

The Duke of Somerset's position was hopeless now. His men were divided between the three strongpoints still in English hands in the city and the abbey of Ste Catherine outside. The palace had not been made ready for a siege. Its storerooms were empty. On the Sunday afternoon, Somerset sent a message to the Count of Dunois accepting the terms offered at Saint-Ouen and promising to surrender all four redoubts. This put Dunois in a quandary. He had given the English until ten o'clock the next morning to accept his terms. The deadline had not yet expired, but he had obtained possession of the city without their cooperation. He was not inclined to let them go free now that he had them at his mercy. So he ignored Somerset's proposal and prepared to storm the English strongholds. The garrison of Ste Catherine surrendered as soon as the French brought up their artillery. The small English force in the bridge barbican followed suit that evening. The next morning, Somerset sent some of his officers before Charles VII himself. They repeated the offer to surrender and invoked the terms offered at Saint-Ouen. The King replied that he would honour any promise to hold the offer open. But he said that he had made no such promise and knew of none by Dunois. Meanwhile, the French were digging trenches around the palace. Artillery was brought up to the meadows of the Seine beneath its walls. On 22 October, the bombardment began. Inside the building, Somerset resolved to endure the bombardment for a day, so that he could at least say that he had tried to defend the place before surrendering. On the following morning, he agreed to negotiate.

The Duke of Somerset, flanked by his Chancellor Sir Thomas Hoo and the *bailli* of Rouen Sir Henry Redford, were escorted to the abbey of Ste Catherine, where Charles VII had established his headquarters. They were brought into a large, richly hung chamber where the King, Réné and Charles of Anjou, the Count of Dunois and a crowd of French noblemen and courtiers were waiting for them. The King declared a truce, which was extended a day at a time while negotiations continued in Rouen between the English and a committee of French councillors. The talks extended over a whole week. The French played a hard game. The issue was the meaning of the terms offered at Saint-Ouen. Had Dunois promised to hold them open until 20 October, even if by then the city was no longer theirs to surrender? The Chancellor Guillaume

Juvénal, who had been at Saint-Ouen and had consulted his colleagues, reported that Dunois's offer was conditional on Somerset delivering up the city. Somerset had not done this. The citizens had done it without his consent. The terms were therefore no longer on the table. If Somerset wanted his garrison released, he would have to surrender not just the two surviving redoubts in Rouen but other garrisoned towns of Normandy. The French negotiators demanded possession of all the walled towns of the Seine valley between Rouen and the sea.

The terms, which were finally agreed after much horse-trading on 29 October, were only marginally better for the English than that. Rouen castle was to be surrendered the next day and the palace in four days, together with all artillery, equipment and personal armour inside them. Somerset had to undertake in addition to procure the surrender of Caudebec and Tancarville in the Seine valley, Honfleur in the estuary and Arques in the northern Caux. The English were able, after much argument, to retain Harfleur, which was needed as a landing place for the army of relief assembling in England. But they had to surrender the town of Montivilliers which commanded the roads north of it. A collective ransom of 50,000 gold *saluts* (£8,333) was to be paid within a year for the entire garrison. Eight prominent hostages were to be given to secure the performance of these terms, including Sir John Talbot, Sir Henry Redford and Sir Richard Frogenhall.[31]

In the eyes of people in England and many in Normandy, the terms of surrender were an embarrassing humiliation. The Duke of York, who would later act as their spokesmen, called them 'fraudulent and inordinate'. Somerset, he said, had boxed himself in by allowing the Archbishop to negotiate a deal with the French which he had no right to offer. He had abandoned the city to the enemy, withdrawing to the palace which could not be defended. Worst of all, he had agreed to surrender five major fortresses none of which (except Caudebec) was in any immediate danger, and had allowed his leading captains to be detained as hostages. All this had been agreed simply 'for the [release] and deliverance of him, his children and goods, which might not nor hath not be done nor seen, by law, reason or chronicle or by course of any lieutenant [even if] he had be[en] a prisoner'. Not even the Dukes of Orléans, Bourbon and Alençon when they were prisoners of war, had sunk so low.[32]

Somerset left for Harfleur under safe-conduct on 4 November 1449, accompanied by the rest of the English troops in Rouen. On the afternoon of 10 November 1449, Charles VII made his ceremonial entry through the Porte Beauvoisine in the northern quarter of the city, where Henry V had made his own entry thirty years before. A long procession of princes and counts, officers of state, captains and officials, and cohorts of liveried soldiers, pages and grooms, made their way to the cathedral through streets decked with damask cloth embroidered with the fleurs-de-lys and filled with cheering crowds. The Duchess of Somerset and the English hostages watched the show from an upper window opposite the cathedral. 'It was a fine thing to see,' wrote Charles VII's official historiographer, 'never in the memory of man has there been such a fine army and such a joyful company . . . so many lords, barons, knights and squires.' English rule may have lasted thirty years, but the message was that it had always lacked legitimacy. The King was returning to his own.[33]

The remaining English captains in northern France were thinking about their own future. When the Count of Eu arrived outside Le Crotoy with an army at the beginning of November 1449, he found that the lieutenant-captain, John Coppledyke, had already agreed to give up the place to the Duke of Burgundy. Coppledyke could have fought on. He had recently been resupplied from England, and 130 men had been added to his garrison. He does not seem to have been bribed. But he plainly had his own view about the sustainability of the English presence in the Somme estuary once Normandy had been lost.

Gisors was the principal English fortress of the northern march of Normandy. It had been strongly reinforced with men transferred from places already overrun by the French. But in early October, as the prospects for holding Rouen were clouding over, its captain Sir Richard Merbury sold Gisors to the French without even being besieged. Merbury was one of the most experienced captains in English service. He had been in France since 1417, becoming trencherman to the Duke of Bedford and holding a long succession of important commands. Like John Edward at La Roche-Guyon, he had put down roots in Normandy. He was a substantial landowner in the Cotentin and the Norman Vexin. He had married a woman from an influential Norman family with important local property interests of her own. Merbury had suffered badly by the breakdown of the truce. Most of his lands had been overrun by the French. His two sons, who had also settled in France, had been taken prisoner at Pont-Audemer. He had nothing to return to in England. So he agreed to do homage to

Charles VII in return for the release of his sons, the confirmation of his and his wife's property rights, and a cash payment. The French took possession of Gisors on 29 October. Merbury was subsequently naturalised in France. He became Charles VII's captain of Saint-Germain-en-Laye and then a royal chamberlain and *bailli* of Troyes. One of his sons also entered French service and became captain of a *compagnie d'ordonnance*.[34]

At the opposite end of Normandy, at Fougères, a very different kind of man, François de Surienne, also had reason the rue the day that the truce broke down. He had lost everything, including his castle at Longny, betrayed by his own son-in-law, who took a bribe from the French and entered their service. Surienne had been blockaded in Fougères since early September with a garrison of 400 men, less than half the number that he reckoned he needed. He was haemorrhaging men as troops drafted in from other English garrisons were recalled to defend their bases. Even his own company were beginning to abandon him. The Duke of Suffolk had promised that he would be relieved within six weeks if he was besieged, and one of Surienne's officers was in England pressing for action. Suffolk instructed Sir Robert Vere, who sailed for Honfleur at the end of September with 400 men, to go to his aid. But Vere's force was too small. He got no closer than Caen. When the Duke of Brittany arrived with reinforcements and an artillery train, the fate of the fortress was sealed. Surienne, always a mercenary at heart, had a record of selling out to the French when things got difficult. He had done it at Montargis in 1437, at Saint-Germain-en-Laye in 1441 and at Gallardon in 1442. His chance came when an epidemic took hold in the besieging army, and Francis could no longer hold his army together. On 5 November 1449, the day after Somerset had left Rouen with his defeated army, Fougères was sold to the Duke of Brittany for 10,000 *écus* and a safe-conduct out for Surienne and his men. His unusual career had a characteristically unusual ending. He renounced his Order of the Garter and returned the insignia to Henry VI. Then he took service with Philip the Good, intrigued with Charles VII's domestic enemies and finally switched sides to become *bailli* of Chartres under Louis XI. He died in 1462.[35]

From Harfleur the Duke of Somerset took ship for Caen across the estuary and there set up a temporary government in what remained of Lancastrian Normandy. Sir Thomas Hoo and Sir Fulk Eyton were given the distasteful task of arranging the surrender of the five fortresses ceded under the terms agreed at Rouen. The surrender went smoothly except at Honfleur, the only one of the ceded places south of the Seine. Honfleur had strong modern walls and a garrison of some 300 men commanded by the Derbyshire squire Richard Curson. The council at Westminster had written to him in the King's name ordering him to 'retard' the surrender of the town for as long as he could. Curson complied and refused to open the gates for Somerset's officers. As a result, Talbot and the other hostages in the French King's hands were retained as prisoners of war.[36]

Château-Gaillard and Harfleur were now the only remaining English fortresses north of the Seine. They did not hold out for long. The garrison of Château-Gaillard, forty miles upstream of Rouen, had been reinforced in August by the Bastard of Somerset with troops from his half-brother's own retinue. However, the fall of the Norman capital made its continued defence impossible and pointless anyway. It surrendered within days. Harfleur was besieged on 8 December shortly after Somerset had left it. The defence was commanded by Sir Thomas Everingham, who had conducted the defence of Meaux in 1439. The port had strong fixed defences and a very large garrison, comprising the permanent establishment, several hundred military refugees from other English castles and many volunteers. Nonetheless, it was an unequal fight. The besiegers dug deep trenches around the walls and deployed about 10,000 troops to man them. With the whole of the Seine valley now under their control, they were able to bring in a powerful artillery train including sixteen large bombards directed by the brothers Bureau. Twenty-five French ships blockaded the harbour mouth. After little more than a fortnight, Everingham asked for terms, and on Christmas Day he entered into a conditional surrender agreement. On New Year's Day, the first town to be conquered in France by Henry V opened its gates to the French. The cross of St George was taken down and replaced by the French royal arms, to loud cheering from the soldiers gathered beneath the walls. The garrison was evacuated by sea. Some rejoined the lieutenant at Caen. Others made for England.[37]

Parliament opened at Westminster on 6 November 1449. The occasion was overshadowed by the plague that was raging in Westminster and the news of the surrender of Rouen, which arrived that evening. The Chancellor told them that they had been summoned to deal with 'difficult and urgent' business. The most difficult and urgent was the dispatch of the army of the 3,000 men which had been planned in September before the latest disasters. A week after the opening, the council decided to increase its strength to 4,000, and appointed Sir Thomas Kyriel to command it. Kyriel was an experienced soldier who had been a successful commander on the northern march of Normandy in the early 1430s. He was related by marriage to the Beauforts, which may be why he was chosen. But he was a quarrelsome man with a record of falling out with his troops, and he had been absent from Normandy for six years when he was selected to lead the last expeditionary army to operate there.

The latest plan was for Kyriel to sail with his army from Portsmouth immediately after Christmas. But the timing was critically dependent on finance. The government managed to borrow enough to pay the first advance due to Kyriel's men on the sealing of their indentures. But they were unable to raise the money for the second advance, which was due on embarkation, or the wages due to the shipmasters and their crews. The council was counting on getting a fresh Parliamentary subsidy early in the session. But with the stream of terrible news arriving from Normandy and growing criticism of the King's ministers, the Commons were in no mood to throw good money after bad. They returned to the demands first aired in the Winchester Parliament the previous July that the King should fund the war by revoking ('resuming') past grants of land and pensions. This was to become an issue of growing importance in the years to come. Henry VI had been a profligate dispenser of largesse. As Abbot Wheathampstead of St Albans remarked, he was apt to ask not what a man deserved but what it was fitting for a King to give. Since his majority, he had alienated Crown lands and demesne revenues to people outside his own family on a scale unprecedented in English history. The fact that many of the recipients were the very people who were thought to have misconducted the war emboldened the Commons to call for the cancellation of these grants before they would vote any new taxes.[38]

The suppressed anger broke out into the open on 28 November 1449, when an attempt was made to murder Suffolk's most prominent opponent Ralph Lord Cromwell as he emerged from the Star Chamber in the palace of Westminster. The perpetrators were a gang of thugs employed by William Tailboys, a notorious criminal who was known to be one of Suffolk's enforcers in East Anglia. The Commons responded with demands for Tailboys's impeachment. Adam Moleyns saw the trouble coming. He begged in vain to be allowed to resign as Keeper of Henry VI's privy seal and retire, pleading infirmity and failing eyesight. When Parliament was prorogued for Christmas, the members returned to their homes spreading anger through the country as they went. It was widely believed that the councillors had corruptly sold Normandy to the King of France to line their own pockets. 'Suffolk Normandy hath sold', declared one of the many verses, pamphlets and handbills circulating in the streets of London.[39]

Pressure on Henry's ministers mounted as troops assigned to Kyriel's army began to arrive at Portsmouth and found no one there to pay them. Some of them took to roaming through Hampshire looting the country. In desperation, the government borrowed £5,000 from Cardinal Beaufort's executors and another £1,600 from the Treasurer Lord Saye. Several thousand pounds more were raised by pledging the King's and the Queen's jewels. Adam Moleyns was commissioned in the new year to go to Portsmouth to calm the temper of the soldiers and seamen and pay them something on account. He took rooms in God's House, the hospital by the town quay. When the seamen and soldiers realised that they were only to receive a part-payment, there were angry protests. In the early hours of 10 January 1450, a mob made its way to God's House led by one Cuthbert Colville, a squire of the royal household and the captain of one of the companies of the army, who had previously served under the Duke of York in Normandy. They dragged Moleyns out of the building and into a nearby field, where they hacked off his head. Before he died, he was said to have denounced the Duke of Suffolk 'and others' as the real traitors. According to reports reaching the court, the crowd loudly abused the King and called for the Duke of York to return with an army from Ireland to take power.

Reports of the murder of Moleyns and his supposed accusation against the Duke of Suffolk spread rapidly across the south of England and provoked a series of localised outbreaks of violence. Ex-soldiers were prominent among the leaders. In Kent, mobs sacked religious houses and planned to take over Dover castle. In East Anglia, where Suffolk was the largest landowner, there were plots to raise an army to depose the King. The rebels had lists of councillors whom they wanted to see beheaded. The Duke of Suffolk, Treasurer Saye and Bishop Ayscough appeared prominently in everyone's list. Handbills and doggerel verses were seen in windows and on doors claiming that the King was a cipher in their hands. At Westminster a certain Nicholas Jakes, a servant of one of the Duke of Gloucester's squires, planned to kill the King's councillors and take over the government. He was denounced and arrested before anything was done, and the other risings were quickly suppressed. The ringleaders were hanged at Tyburn.[40]

Parliament reconvened at Westminster on 22 January 1450 in an atmosphere of crisis and incipient violence. Weapons had been issued to the grooms and pages of the royal household. Outside the palace of Westminster the streets were full of the armed retainers of the magnates. In London, guards were put on all the gates and mounted patrols passed through the streets. Soldiers who had been at Harfleur at its fall were beginning to arrive in England to pour oil on the fire with their own tales of betrayal and incompetence. In the home counties and East Anglia the disorder continued through the Parliamentary session.

Seated among the Lords, the Duke of Suffolk knew that the protests were directed mainly against him, and that the rebels' grievances were shared by many of the Commons meeting across the way in the refectory of Westminster Abbey. On the opening day of the new session he stood up to make a statement. He had heard, he said, what Adam Moleyns was supposed to have said before he was killed. He knew about the 'odious and horrible language' directed against him. He angrily rejected the accusation of treason in language whose intensity shines through the lapidary record of the clerks who wrote up the Parliament roll. His father had died at Harfleur in 1415, he said, and his elder brother at Agincourt. He had lost two more brothers at Jargeau and had himself been taken prisoner there. He had fought for the King in France for seventeen years and had been a Knight of the Garter for thirty. To his dying day he would protest that he had always been loyal to the Crown. He called on his accusers to bring charges against him so that he might defend himself. The Commons deliberated about this for four days. Then, on 26 January, they called for Suffolk to be arrested and committed to the Tower. The Lords consulted the judges. They gave it as their opinion that nothing so far alleged against Suffolk justified his committal. The Commons responded with more extreme allegations. Suffolk, they said, had plotted with Charles VII against his own country. He had even fortified his castle at Wallingford in Norfolk and made it ready to support a French invasion. On 28 January, the minister was committed to the Tower. 'Now is the fox driven to hole,' crowed the London mobs. Three days later, Archbishop Stafford, Henry VI's long-serving Chancellor, resigned.[41]

On 7 February 1450, the Commons brought a bill of impeachment charging the Duke of Suffolk with treason. They alleged that while Dunois and the other French ambassadors had been in England in 1447, he had received them in his London house, where they had planned a French invasion of England with a view to deposing Henry VI and awarding the Crown to Suffolk's daughter-in-law Margaret Beaufort. He was said to have engineered the release of Charles of Orléans so that he would encourage Charles VII to invade Normandy. He had treacherously brought about the surrender of Maine. He had passed state secrets to the French to help them defeat the English in diplomacy and war. He had taken bribes from them to delay the passage of English armies to the continent. He had openly boasted of his influence with the French King and his councillors. Most of this was absurd. But it fairly reflected the intense public pressure to find scapegoats in the aftermath of the humiliations in Normandy. A month later, the Commons brought in a second bill of impeachment with supplementary articles alleging a miscellaneous collection of offences. These were essentially political rather than criminal. They charged the minister with incompetence and with corruptly abusing his influence for his personal gain and that of his favoured friends.

On 9 March, Suffolk was transferred from the Tower to a gentler captivity in the palace of Westminster in order to be on hand to hear the charges against him. Four days later he robustly defended himself, article by article. Much of his defence could not be heard above the continual heckling. But his main point was clear enough. The decisions which were being held against him had been made collectively by the whole council and not just by him. He mentioned Adam Moleyns in particular, on whom he blamed the whole affair of Maine. These observations may not have convinced everyone, but it was undoubtedly true that other people must have given their tacit consent. 'So great things could not be done nor brought about,' said Suffolk, 'unless that other persons had done their part and be privy thereto as well as he.' As he pointed out, the real cause of the defeats in Normandy was that it was weak. The subtext, too obvious to be mentioned, was that the fault was Parliament's for failing to heed his warnings about the need to build up Normandy's defences and provide the King with the means to hold it.[42]

In the ordinary course, the articles of impeachment would have been tried in the Lords. They were embarrassed. Suffolk had been foolish but not criminal. The 'others' who had gone along with his decisions included many of those sitting there on the benches of the Lords. All of them knew that the King was as much the author of the peace policy and the surrender of Maine as Suffolk was. However, the Commons had to be appeased if the King was to get a grant of taxation, and the mood in the country at large had reached a pitch of fury which would have made it dangerous to throw the charges out. A way out was found, which was negotiated with Suffolk himself. On 17 March the King summoned the Lords into his private chamber overlooking the palace courtyard and had Suffolk brought in. The new Chancellor, Cardinal Kemp, announced that the King proposed to put a halt to the proceedings and deal with the matter himself, 'not by way of judgment, for he is not in place of judgment', but according to his 'rule and governance'. Henry dismissed the first bill of impeachment with its extravagant allegations of treason. As to the charges of corruption and incompetence in the second bill, he announced that Suffolk would be banished from England for five years. That evening, the Duke was released from custody.

The news provoked an immediate outburst of violence in London. A mob of some 2,000 men gathered outside Suffolk's mansion threatening to lynch him. Several of his servants were manhandled. But the crowd was balked of its prey, for the Duke had already made his escape and was on his way to his manor at Easthorpe in Suffolk. For many Londoners, however, the real target was the King. 'By this town, by this town, for this array the King shall lose his crown,' a vintner's servant chanted as he tried to raise a riot in protest against Suffolk's escape. He was summarily convicted by a special commission sitting at Guildhall and hanged at Tyburn. But London was becoming too hot for the royal court. On 30 March Parliament was prorogued for Easter and ordered to reassemble on 29 April at Leicester, a smaller town, far from the London mob, with close connections to the house of Lancaster.[43]

In the wars of Henry VI, this session of Parliament had a place very like that of the Good Parliament of 1376 in the last years of Edward III. Both were moments for anger, recrimination and self-doubt, the prelude to a descent into civil war. On both occasions, the Commons bitterly resented the humiliation of losing territory, although they had not been willing to make the sacrifices necessary to defend it. The main consequence of the fight over the fate of the Duke of Suffolk was to delay the sailing of Sir Thomas Kyriel's army at Portsmouth. Until they were paid the second instalment of their advances, they would not embark. Henry's councillors pressed the Commons with mounting desperation for a subsidy against which they could borrow. Some of the younger courtiers threatened to make the Commons sit on until they granted one. But the Commons were unmoved. They believed that the King's poverty was due to the greed of his servants and the persistent diversion of his revenues into their pockets. 'So poor a King was never seen,' declared the handbills, 'nor richer lords.' The Commons declared that there would be no subsidy until the King agreed to an act of resumption recalling past grants. As a result, Kyriel was not able to sail until the two half-subsidies voted by the previous Parliament had come in. Collection of those did not begin until November 1449. Cash dribbled slowly in over the next three months. The troops finally received their money on 9 March. By that time their numbers had been diminished by desertions. Of the 3,500 men who had enlisted, some 3,000 finally embarked on the ships. Kyriel's fleet sailed out of the Solent for Normandy five months later than planned.[44]

Much had changed during those five months. Rouen, the Seine valley and the whole of Upper Normandy were now in French hands. In Lower Normandy, everything east of the valley of the Dives had been lost except for Honfleur. When the Duke of Somerset withdrew to Caen at the beginning of January 1450, the territory under his effective control was limited to the narrow region between the valleys of the Dives and the Vire in south-western Normandy, roughly corresponding to the western part of the modern *département* of Calvados. The main concentrations of English in this region were at Caen and Bayeux, both populous cities, and Falaise and Vire, which were military towns dependent mainly on their garrisons. In addition, English garrisons were holding out in isolated fortresses which were now surrounded by French-held territory. In the Cotentin, the English held only three places after the invasion of the region by the Duke of Brittany the previous autumn: Cherbourg, Saint-Sauveur-le-Vicomte and Bricquebec. On the marches of Brittany and Maine the English clung to three border fortresses at Avranches, Domfront and Fresnay-le-Vicomte.

THE DEATH OF LANCASTRIAN NORMANDY, 1449-1450

At Caen, the Duke of Somerset presided over the wreckage of the English government of Normandy. The financial administration, which had been under severe pressure even before the French invasion, had ceased to exist with the fall of Rouen. The Estates of Lower Normandy had met, for the last time under English rule, in late October 1449, probably at Caen. The assembly went through the motions of granting an *aide* of 110,000 *livres*, but very little of it can have been collected. As the French overran each region, they took over the local administration, collecting arrears of taxes voted to the English and imposing new ones of their own. In addition to his own retinue and the remaining garrisons, Somerset had at his disposal Sir Robert Vere's company of 400 men, who had arrived the previous October and had been sitting idle in Caen ever since. There were about 2,000 military refugees from garrisons which had been overrun by the French. In addition, there were many Englishmen who had fled to the dwindling remnant of Lancastrian France, like field mice fleeing from the reaper. They included men who had been employed in private garrisons, former soldiers living on the land, and able-bodied settlers. Well-informed French estimates based on the numbers counted when English strongholds surrendered, suggest that there may have been about 4,000 troops available to the Duke of Somerset in the final months of his lieutenancy. By drawing on these sources it was possible to put an army of up to 2,000 men into the field for short periods. But the one attempt to relieve a besieged town, at Bellême in December, had to be abandoned when it became clear that the relief force would be heavily outnumbered by the besiegers. When, in January 1450, the Count of Dunois laid siege to Honfleur, the English were obliged to stand impotently by without being able to intervene. The garrison entered into a conditional surrender agreement in the hope that the delay would allow time for Kyriel to come to their rescue. But no relief army appeared. Honfleur opened its gates on 18 February 1450 and the garrison marched out under safe-conduct to join the Duke of Somerset at Caen. This left Cherbourg as the only seaport still in English hands.[45]

Even the most inspired leadership could not have saved Lancastrian Normandy in these conditions. But the direction of affairs was not inspired. Somerset himself, once a respected military commander, had gone to pieces since the debacle at Rouen and took almost no personal part in the defence of the territory under his control. Sir John Talbot, who had directed the defence of Upper Normandy, was a prisoner. The leading spirit behind the English defence in the final months was the resourceful and determined captain of Bayeux, Matthew Gough. He was probably the best-known Welsh soldier in France, already celebrated by the bards of his native land. The French, who called him 'Matago', regarded Gough as a mere freebooter. But he was the only soldier apart from Talbot whose role in these events received unstinting praise in England when it was all over. He 'excelled every other squire engaged in the war for courage, toughness, loyalty and generosity' according to William Worcester. Gough, however, found few followers to share his enthusiasm. For most of these demoralised men the only question was whether they could sell their strongholds for their lives and enough money to cover their arrears of pay.[46]

The French King undertook no significant military operation for a month after the surrender of Honfleur. After keeping large forces in the field for more than six months, Charles's finances were under strain. There had been a crushing increase in the burden of taxation during the campaign, with heavy *tailles* throughout France. The King had borrowed large sums from his officers and servants and from the towns, and by February 1450 had already anticipated the whole of the current year's tax revenues. In the new year part of his army had been assigned to other theatres, and part had been paid off. Charles VII spent much of February at the abbey of Grestain in the meadows of the Seine near Honfleur preparing to relaunch his campaign in the spring. A fresh offensive was planned against the remaining territory under English control from two sides at once. The Picards and the *francs-archers* were recalled to join a new army to attack from the east. The Marshal André de Laval lord of Lohéac and the Admiral Prégent de Coëtivy were directed to join forces with the Duke of Brittany to attack from the south-west. These projects were interrupted by the arrival of Kyriel's fleet, which entered Cherbourg harbour on 15 March 1450.[47]

The French were caught off-guard by Kyriel's appearance. The Picards and *francs-archers* had not yet arrived. The Bretons were not ready. Arthur de Richemont and Marshal Laval were at Messac south of Rennes, where the first contingents of the Breton army were still mustering. Charles VII was at Alençon, where he had gone to oversee the siege of Fresnay-le-Vicomte, the last English garrison to hold out on the march of Maine. Dunois's whereabouts are uncertain. It was necessary to improvise an army to confront Sir Thomas Kyriel. The task was given to the Duke of Bourbon's son John Count of Clermont. John was twenty-four years old and this was his first recorded campaign. He was assigned some capable and experienced lieutenants, including Pierre de Brézé, Robert de Flocques and Prégent de Coëtivy, but he would not have been chosen if anyone else of sufficient rank had been available. A force of just 2,000 mounted men was placed under his command, a pitifully small army for such an important operation. Richemont and Laval were summoned urgently to join them from Brittany with every extra man that they could find.[48]

Kyriel's orders were to proceed straight to Caen to join the Duke of Somerset. However, the English *bailli* of Cotentin, Sir Bertrand Entwhistle, persuaded him to undertake the siege of Valognes first. Entwhistle was a major landowner in the area, and his advice may not have been wholly disinterested. Kyriel was strongly criticised in England for accepting it. But there were sound reasons for the decision. Cherbourg was now the only port by which men and supplies could reach Normandy from England. Eleven miles south of the port, Valognes was the hub of the road system of the northern Cotentin and an important part of Cherbourg's forward defences. The problem about the decision to besiege it was that it delayed the junction of Kyriel and Somerset and exposed both of them to defeat in detail. Somerset resolved upon a high-risk change of strategy. He withdrew 1,800 men from the garrisons of Caen, Bayeux and Vire, placed them under the command of Matthew Gough and sent them to join Kyriel outside Valognes. This involved staking everything on the success of Kyriel's operations, but it also posed a serious challenge to the French, who at this stage were short of men. The Count of Clermont was instructed at all costs to stop Gough's contingents from joining forces with Kyriel's army. He arrived on the scene too late to do that. The two English captains met outside Valognes early in April. Their numbers were swollen by fresh arrivals from the remaining English garrisons of the Cotentin. Shortly, their total strength stood at between 6,000 and 7,000 men, the largest English field army to operate in Normandy for nearly a decade and substantially larger than any force that the French were able to throw against it. It did not take Clermont long to decide that the English were too strong and too well dug in to be attacked outside Valognes. Instead, he occupied Carentan, another major road hub twenty miles south and waited for reinforcements. He was joined by about 1,000 men from the French garrisons of the

Cotentin, bringing his strength up to about 3,000. Meanwhile Arthur de Richemont and Marshal Laval had advanced to Dol in northern Brittany with another 2,000 men, the largest number that they had been able to gather in the time available.[49]

Valognes surrendered to Kyriel and Gough on about 10 April 1450. Its garrison negotiated a deal which allowed them a safe-conduct out of the town to join Clermont at Carentan. On 12 April, the English army set out eastward to join Somerset at Caen. They avoided the concentration of French troops at Carentan by marching along the coast through the *bocage* and tidal sands (*Map 12*). Behind the walls of Carentan, the French captains were arguing about strategy. The question was whether to intercept the English army on the coast road or allow them to pass east into the Bessin and challenge them there. Clermont and Brézé were against confronting them in the *bocage*. Its soft ground and lacework of rivulets and hedgerows were poor terrain for cavalry but ideal for the English archers. Prégent de Coëtivy wanted to remain on the defensive and avoid confronting the English until Richemont and Laval had arrived with reinforcements. They were still at least a day's march away, at Coutances. The more aggressive captains wanted to attack the English columns at the earliest opportunity. They were supported by local men who were afraid that unless they were stopped the English would waste the Cotentin. Clermont insisted on his own plan. But the decision was poorly received. When on 14 April, an ill-organised band of local men tried to challenge the English as they crossed the fords of the Vire, the pressure to intervene became irresistible, and some companies were sent to support them. The outcome did much to vindicate the original decision. There was a brief and murderous fight by the fords as the tide rose. The attackers were driven off, and the English pressed on eastward to rejoin the Bayeux road, shadowed by Clermont's mounted scouts. That evening the French leaders held another council of war. They resolved to cut the English off at Vieux-Pont, where the valley of the Aure narrows and an old stone bridge crossed the river on the road to Bayeux. Richemont and Laval had by now reached Saint-Lô. A pursuivant was ordered to ride through the night with letters urging them to join forces with the main army on the following day at the village of Trévières, a short distance from Vieux-Pont.[50]

On the afternoon of 14 April 1450, the English army halted their march and encamped outside the village of Formigny, about two miles

THE DEATH OF LANCASTRIAN NORMANDY, 1449-1450

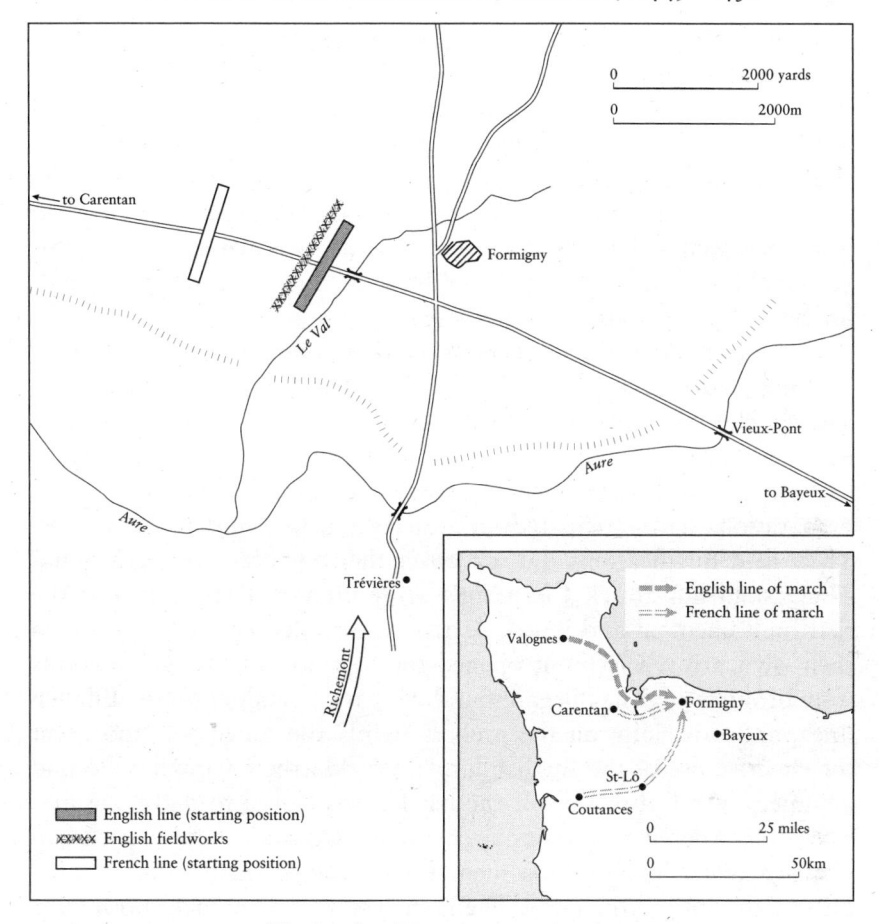

13 The battle of Formigny, 15 April 1450

short of the bridge. Kyriel and Gough decided to wait there for Clermont to arrive and then give battle. They had twice Clermont's numbers and expected to have the advantage of the defensive. They knew nothing about the army of Richemont and Laval. Gough left for Bayeux, ten miles away, to get what reinforcements he could find there and returned later with some extra men from the garrison. Meanwhile, the English constructed field fortifications across the route by which Clermont was expected to arrive. Clermont left Carentan before dawn on the next morning, 15 April. He had his whole army with him, about 3,000 men.

Formigny is about fifteen miles from Carentan. At about eight o'clock in the morning, the French approached the village and the English

693

army came into sight. They were drawn up dismounted in a line across the road. Gough's men-at-arms were on the left wing and Kyriel's on the right, with the archers massed at intervals along the line. In front of them was a line of trenches and potholes, protected by sharpened stakes. Their rear was protected by a stream known as Le Val and by the dense gardens and orchards of Formigny. The French army halted just out of longbow range and drew up their own men in battle array. For three hours, from about nine o'clock to midday, they stood in their lines waiting for Richemont and Laval to appear.

At about midday, the banners of the Bretons were seen coming over the ridge which marked the line of the river Aure to the south. The English cheered, thinking that these were friends. As the realisation dawned that they were enemies, the cheering turned to horror. They had more men than both enemy armies combined. But none of their preparations had anticipated an attack from two directions at once. Their field fortifications did not cover their exposed southern flank. They could not attack Clermont's army without being taken in the rear by Richemont and Laval. As the Bretons dismounted to draw up their own array, Clermont opened the fighting. Two large culverins were brought up. They began to inflict heavy casualties on the English lines, and especially on the archers, while the range was too great for effective use of the English longbows. Matthew Gough, who had assumed overall direction of the battle, was forced to make the first move. He ordered 500 to 600 archers forward against the French gun emplacements. Some of the men-at-arms joined them. There was a bitter fight around the guns. The French were driven back. Both guns were captured and hauled back to the English lines. Writing after the battle, Prégent de Coëtivy thought that this was the moment when the English should have attacked Clermont's army with all their strength. The French would probably have been overwhelmed before Richemont could intervene. But the moment passed and the opportunity was lost.

Shortly after the capture of the guns, the Bretons began to advance from the south. The English captains tried to retreat towards the village of Formigny, while wheeling their whole line round to face the new threat. This exceptionally difficult manoeuvre involved abandoning the protection of their field works, thus leaving themselves temporarily unprotected on both sides. The French seized the moment. Pierre de Brézé led a cavalry charge against the English lines from the west. His men recovered the guns and brought them back to their lines. The

THE DEATH OF LANCASTRIAN NORMANDY, 1449–1450

whole of Clermont's army then advanced against the English on foot. Richemont, watching the spectacle from a windmill south of Formigny, ordered his cavalry forward. The heavily armoured horsemen charged into the English lines, throwing the English to the ground and seizing the bridge over Le Val, thus dividing the English army in two. The rest of the Breton army dismounted and threw itself against the flank of Matthew Gough's division. The English line disintegrated in minutes. According to the Welsh bard Lewis Glyn Cothi, Gough was pulled out of the melée by his countryman Gwilym Gwent of Pengelly and led off the field. He and Robert Vere decided that all was lost and fled towards Bayeux on horseback. Several hundred English men-at-arms ran for their horses and followed them. Pierre de Brézé and his company rode round the mass of men to cut off the retreat of the rest. They were trapped. About 1,200 of them were captured. Of these, forty-three were reckoned to be noblemen, with armorial surcoats that identified them as worth a ransom. They included Sir Thomas Kyriel himself and several of the captains who had accompanied him from England. Those who were not worth taking were butchered, including almost all the archers. In the closing moments of the battle, the local peasantry joined in, killing every Englishman they found alive without mercy. By two o'clock, it was all over. When the heralds passed through the field to do the usual body count, they found 3,774 English dead. Fourteen vast burial pits were dug in the following days to receive them. It was a decisive defeat. The English had lost 5,000 men killed or captured out of an army of rather more than 6,000. Almost all of Kyriel's expeditionary force had been destroyed. Nearly half the troops that the Duke of Somerset had had in garrison before Kyriel's arrival were lost too.[51]

Parliament reopened after the Easter recess on 29 April 1450 at Leicester. The battle of Formigny had been fought a fortnight before, and the first news was beginning to come in. The sense of impending catastrophe was palpable. There were reports that an attack on Calais would be launched within days, that the French were about to invade England and that a general rebellion was imminent in the counties. The magnates arrived in town with large armed and mounted retinues, ready for the worst. The Earl of Devon alone came with 300 men and the Earl of Warwick with 400. The King's councillors decided at the outset to bend before the gale. To get a fresh grant of taxation, the

King agreed to an act of resumption revoking royal grants going back to the beginning of the reign, with certain exceptions. In return, the Commons granted a subsidy at the beginning of June, but it was an ungenerous one. It was a progressive income tax on wages and revenues from land, the latest attempt to escape from the antiquated assessment of 1334. Its estimated yield was only £10,000, less than a third of the value of a standard subsidy. Even that could not be collected until commissioners had made individual assessments across the country. This would take some time.[52]

Meanwhile, the pent-up anger of the past nine months exploded into revolution. The first victim was the Duke of Suffolk, whose supposed treasonable dealings with the French were widely believed to be the source of all of the current disasters. On 30 April 1450, Suffolk boarded a ship at Ipswich for Calais on his way to exile in the domains of the Duke of Burgundy. Off the Kent coast, his ship was intercepted by the *Nicholas de la Tour*. The *Nicholas* was a London ship, part of a squadron requisitioned to patrol the Channel against a French invasion. It was filled with pressed crewmen and archers. The master ordered Suffolk to come on board. 'Welcome, traitor', they said as he boarded. Next day, Suffolk was brought before a drumhead court. He pleaded the King's safe-conduct. They replied that they 'knew nothing of this King but well knew of the crown of England, and the crown of England was the community of the realm'. Suffolk was summarily condemned to death. They put him down the side into the ship's boat and hacked off his head against the gunwale with a rusty sword. His head and body were dumped on Dover beach.[53]

The murder of the Duke of Suffolk sparked off a rising in Kent which spread over the following weeks across much of southern England. It began in the Rochester area in the middle of May. Over the next fortnight much of Kent rose as Suffolk's funeral cortege passed from Canterbury to Rochester and London, before reaching its resting place in the family chapel at Wingfield church in Suffolk. By the beginning of June, the local disorders in Kent had coalesced into an organised movement involving several thousand men. They found a leader in Jack Cade, a 'subtle man' according to a London chronicler, who adopted the alias 'John Mortimer' and called himself 'Captain of Kent'. Contemporaries believed him to be a low-born Irishman, but very little is reliably known about his origins. Following, perhaps consciously, the example of the Peasants' Revolt of 1381, Cade led his growing horde in a march on London. But his rebellion was very different from the Peasants' Revolt. It was not only, or even mainly, a social movement. It was a political movement, inspired by hatred of the King's ministers, anger and humiliation at the loss of Normandy, and insecurity arising from the perceived threat of invasion. Its followers included people of every rank except the highest.[54]

In London, the city authorities fortified and manned their gates. Sir John Fastolf hired a company of soldiers and quartered them in his house in Southwark. At Leicester, Parliament was hastily adjourned on 6 June and nine peers were commissioned to suppress the revolt. It was already too late. On 11 June, several thousand armed Kentishmen gathered on Blackheath. They built a fortified encampment, protected against cavalry with trenches and rows of sharpened stakes in the ground – a standard English battlefield technique which they had probably learned from ex-soldiers in their ranks. A delegation of bishops and lay magnates was sent out from London to meet them. They promised that their grievances would be addressed and urged them to disperse. Cade produced a list of their complaints and demands. Some of these were of purely local significance. Some were incoherent. Three stood out. First, the King had been persuaded to tax his subjects unnecessarily because his demesne revenues had been appropriated by his ministers. He must therefore revoke all grants from his demesne so that he might rule 'like a King royal'. Cade was apparently unaware that this had already been conceded in principle at Leicester. Second, the King must dismiss all of Suffolk's allies at court and in government who had lost him Normandy and Maine, 'the which ben openly known traitors'. Third, they believed that the 'good Duke of Gloucester', whose myth was growing year by year, had been murdered by the King's ministers and demanded that those responsible should be brought to trial and punished.

Underlying all these complaints was the popular instinct that the King's councillors lacked legitimacy. They were not princes of his blood with the independence of mind that came from their high status, but low fellows exploiting the King's incapacity and motivated by personal ambition and greed. As a result, they said, Henry's 'merchandise is lost, his commons destroyed, the sea is lost, France is lost, himself so poor that he may not pay for his meat nor drink; [and] he oweth more than ever did King in England'. The rebels urged Henry to take advice from the Dukes of Exeter, Buckingham and Norfolk, but above all from 'the high and mighty prince the Duke of York, exiled from our sovereign lord's person by the noising of the false traitor the Duke of Suffolk and his affinity'. York's name was on the lips of the rebels everywhere. His emergence as a focus of opposition was perhaps inevitable. He was heir presumptive to the childless Henry VI. He was no friend of the Duke of Suffolk and his party. His term as lieutenant in Normandy had not been a success, but it was golden in comparison with what followed. York's absence as lieutenant in Ireland since the autumn of 1448 was providential. It meant that he had no responsibility, even indirect, for the debacle in Normandy.[55]

The government resolved upon a show of force. On 18 June 1450 the King came to Blackheath with an army drawn from the retinues of a large number of lords. They brought field artillery with them. But they found that their prey had vanished. Cade had withdrawn overnight rather than face unequal odds against professional soldiers. But while the King and the lords settled into Humphrey Duke of Gloucester's old palace at Greenwich, their own army mutinied. Many of the lords' retainers sympathised with the Kentishmen. They too called for the heads of traitors, naming Treasurer Saye, Bishop Ayscough and Abbot Boulers among others. That evening the Duke of Buckingham appeared before the King to tell him that he could no longer rely on his army. The King tried to appease the mutineers. He appointed a special commission to try unspecified 'treasons'. Of the various 'traitors' named, only Lord Saye was at hand. Henry had him arrested and put in the Tower, mainly for his own protection. But when he returned by river to Westminster that night and ordered Saye's release, the Constable of the Tower, Henry Holland Duke of Exeter, refused to comply. Frightened by the haemorrhaging of support, the King fled from the capital, accompanied by the lords and courtiers about him and a group of officials and judges. They made for the Midlands and shut themselves in Kenilworth castle, one of the strongest places in England.[56]

In Henry's absence, the government lost what little control of the situation it ever had. The rebellion spread across southern and eastern England. Anger against the King's government merged with local grievances. There were serious outbreaks of rioting in Wiltshire, a cloth-producing region suffering from the depression of the trade and traditionally a major centre of Lollardy. Bishop Ayscough of Salisbury had fled from London to his diocese with the enormous sum of £3,000 in cash. As he travelled across southern England, his baggage was plundered and his manor houses trashed. He decided to make for safety at Sherborne castle in Dorset. The rebels caught up with him in the Wiltshire village of Edington. He was saying Mass in the chapel of the Augustinian house there when some 600 men converged on the village from across the region. They dragged him out and bludgeoned him to death in a nearby field. At Gloucester a mob invaded the abbey searching for Abbot Boulers, whom they accused of having sold Normandy to the French. They sacked the abbey and plundered Boulers's manor at Wyreyard. Fortunately for the Abbot he was away, or he would have met the same fate as Ayscough.

Organised opposition to the rebellion in London collapsed. Cade and his horde returned to Blackheath and occupied Southwark, while a second rebel army formed in Essex and marched to Mile End. On 3 July, the Kentishmen captured the gatehouse at the south end of London Bridge and poured into London. A special judicial commission was sitting at Guildhall under the chairmanship of Thomas Lord Scales and the Mayor of London to examine treasons, felonies and acts of rebellion in London. Under the pressure of Cade's mob, the judges turned it into a tribunal for eliminating old allies and clients of the Duke of Suffolk. The chief victim was Lord Saye. He was brought from the Tower and tried on various trumped-up charges of treason, including the murder of the Duke of Gloucester. Saye was summarily convicted. As soon as the verdict was pronounced, the mob seized him from the custody of the court's officers and hauled him to Cheapside, where they beheaded him in the street and mutilated his body.[57]

On 5 July 1450, the Londoners recovered control of their city. Cade and his men were in the habit of withdrawing at the end of each day to quarters that they had appropriated in Southwark. A group of aldermen with an improvised army occupied London Bridge. They were supported by royal troops commanded by Lord Scales. There was a battle on the bridge which began at nine o'clock in the evening and continued until dawn. Cade's men were successfully ejected. On the following day, the authorities opened negotiations with the rebels. They promised them a free pardon and persuaded them to disperse and return to their homes. Many pardons were issued but Cade's followers might have learned from the past how little they were worth. Once the Kentishmen had dispersed, the rebellion was suppressed with great brutality. Cade's pardon was repudiated on the ground that it had been issued to him under a false name. A price was put on his head. He was eventually tracked down at Heathfield in Sussex and died of injuries received during his capture. His body was taken to London, where it was ritually beheaded at Newgate and quartered at Tyburn.[58]

Cade's rebellion paralysed England just as the last outposts of English power in Normandy were falling to the French. Within a few days of the battle of Formigny, the joint offensive began which Charles VII and the Duke of Brittany had been planning since February. The Duke of Brittany crossed the river Selune and laid siege to Avranches on 1 May 1450, while the Counts of Dunois and Clermont advanced on Bayeux. By June, the arrival of fresh troops had brought Charles VII's army to 17,000 men. With reports reaching them of chaos and incipient civil war in England, few English garrisons had the stomach for a fight. A handful fought on without hope until their walls had been battered to ruins by French or Breton artillery, and then made the best deal they could to save their lives. At Avranches they held out for a fortnight. But such cases were rare. At Tombelaine, the island fortress in the bay of Saint-Malo was reputed to be impregnable, but the garrison surrendered as soon as the besiegers approached. Saint-Sauveur, with 200 men in its garrison, promptly opened its gates when the besiegers appeared outside, even though they had no artillery. Bricquebec abandoned the fight without any siege at all. Some places had captains who were prisoners of war and were persuaded to order their garrisons to surrender as part of the terms for their own release. Osbern Mundeford, who had been captured at Pont-Audemer, persuaded his brother-in-law, who deputised for him at Fresnay, to surrender the place to the French. Sir Henry Norbury, who had been captured at Formigny, did the same at Vire. At Valognes the English lieutenant-captain, a squire called Thomas Chiswall, did homage to Charles VII and was naturalised in France, like John Edward and Richard Merbury. Chiswall can have had few roots in England. He had served in English garrisons in Normandy all his adult life. He took service with the French garrison of Mont-Saint-Michel, where a quarter of a century before he had served among the English besiegers. Nothing illustrated the inner rottenness of the Lancastrian regime by 1450 so well as these tales of frightened men who saw no point in risking their lives any longer.[59]

THE DEATH OF LANCASTRIAN NORMANDY, 1449–1450

The Duke of Somerset was condemned to see the remaining English positions in Lower Normandy crumble before his eyes in the space of a few weeks. Bayeux and Caen had large communities of English settlers. Both were filled with armed and able-bodied men who had fled there from the surrounding district or from other garrison towns. Bayeux was besieged by the Count of Dunois at the end of April 1450. The city was weak. The walls dated from Gallo-Roman times and its citadel from the tenth century. The citizens had prevented Matthew Gough from demolishing the suburbs, with the result that the besiegers were able to come close to the walls under cover. Gough vigorously defended his town with some 500 men, but the outcome was decided by artillery. The Bureau brothers set to work. Within two weeks, the bombards had brought down the walls at several points. On 16 May, Gough agreed to surrender the town in three days. The terms were harsh, some indication of how close the place had been to falling. Some 900 Englishmen were counted in the town after its fall, plus 300 or 400 wives and many children. Those who were prepared to swear allegiance to Charles VII within two months were allowed to stay and to keep their houses and movable property. The rest had to leave. The sight of the column of English refugees passing through the gates moved even hardened French soldiers to pity. They had to leave everything behind them except for ten *écus* for each man-at-arms, five for the others, the clothes they stood up in and the personal jewellery of the women. They were required to leave France via Cherbourg for England or the Channel Islands, without entering any other place in English allegiance. As an act of indulgence, women of gentle birth were allowed to take a horse, and carts were provided for the more 'notable' commoners. The rest had to walk, carrying their small children on their shoulders or in slings round their necks and dragging the older ones after them. They left Normandy weeping, according to the contemporary Norman chronicler Robert Blondel, 'as if it was their native country and England a place of exile'. For many of them, it was.[60]

Caen, the principal commercial town of the region, was stronger than Bayeux. Its walls had been rebuilt in the previous century and a good deal of money had been spent on them in the 1430s. The normal population of about 7,500 must have risen to at least 10,000 or 11,000 as a result of the influx of refugees. By French reckonings, between 3,000 and 4,000 of these were English. On 5 June 1450 the French army began to arrive outside the walls, and within a few days the town was invested on all sides. The news reached Westminster in about the third week of June at the worse possible moment. London was in chaos. A large rebel army was encamped on Blackheath. The council's thoughts were a long way from Normandy. The only person with a plan was Sir John Fastolf, who had recently been admitted to the council. He pressed the case for sending an expeditionary army to Caen. He thought that it would be necessary to find at least 3,000 men immediately to hold the present position in Lower Normandy. A larger army would follow under the leadership of a commander 'of noble and great estate, having knowledge and experience of the wars' to recover lost territory. A powerful train of field artillery would be required. Ships would have to be requisitioned to bring in supplies by sea. All of this was fantasy. There was no possibility of recruiting or funding either the smaller or the larger army. Caen was already coming to the end of its resistance when the court fled from London and the project was abandoned.[61]

In the closing days of the siege Somerset hatched a desperate scheme to kidnap the French King and some of his principal lieutenants, including the Count of Dunois and Jean Bureau, and carry them off to Cherbourg. The task was to be accomplished by a sortie party of 500 men, while another 1,000 men created a diversion by attacking the French artillery, spiking the guns and blowing up the powder stores. Four Scots serving in the French army were suborned and persuaded to guide the two sorties to their targets in return for a bribe of 4,000 *écus* and £50 sterling. They included Robert Cunningham, captain of one of the Scottish *compagnies d'ordonnance*, and his deputy Robert Campbell. The scheme came to nothing, and we would know nothing about it but for the fact that the Scottish plotters were denounced some years later and the ringleaders condemned to death.

By 23 June 1450, all the boulevards which the English had constructed outside the gates of Caen had been captured by the French. Twenty-two large bombards and six smaller ones were pounding the walls from the French lines. One tower had been destroyed by gunfire. Another on the west side of the town opposite the Abbaye aux Hommes had been brought down by mines, together with a large section of the walls. Dunois ordered a general assault through the breach. Once the French had taken possession of the breach, the Duke of Somerset asked Dunois for a truce for negotiations. Both men were ready to do a deal. Somerset's priority was to save his skin and that of the men around him. Dunois wanted to take Caen intact. Even if the town fell, he was by no means confident of being able to take the citadel. Planted on rock and powerfully built with an imposing keep, four massive towers and deep ditches, it could have held out for a long time.

Agreement was reached on the following day, 24 June. Caen was to be surrendered on 1 July unless a relieving army appeared on that date. The delay was too short to allow for relief, but perhaps long enough to save Somerset's honour. As at Bayeux, those residents of whatever nation who wished to stay were allowed to do so and retain their property on swearing allegiance to Charles VII. The others were given three months to leave for England with their horses, personal weapons and what property they could carry. The French commanders were anxious to see the English leave as soon as possible and offered them carts for their baggage and shipping for the sea passage from the port of Caen at Ouistreham. The Duke and Duchess of Somerset and their children left the town as soon as the formal surrender had been accomplished. They made for Ouistreham at the head of a long column of English refugees and an escort of French soldiers and then took ship for England.[62]

The fall of Caen left just three garrisoned places in English hands: Cherbourg, Falaise and Domfront. The dominant factor in Charles VII's plans now was money. His army had been consuming cash fast and by the time Caen fell the war treasurers had very little left. Standing his army down until a future campaign would be a considerable risk. In spite of the chaos reigning in England, the French King could not rule out the possibility that the three surviving castles might become the bases of another expeditionary army from England. In this extremity, he turned to his *argentier*, Jacques Coeur. Jacques Coeur was regarded by contemporaries as the Crassus of his age. Some of them believed that he had funded the entire Norman campaign personally. He was certainly extravagant and showy, as his fine urban palace at Bourges and castle on the Cher at Ainay-le-Viel still testify. He had been a prominent figure in Charles's victory parade at Rouen, wearing the same scarlet jacket and fur trimming as the Count of Dunois. But like many medieval businessmen, Jacques Coeur had feet of clay. A detailed enquiry into his affairs after his disgrace in 1453 revealed a variety of unsuccessful business ventures and a lifestyle funded mainly by moneylending and corruption. But he was at the height of his influence and fame when he advanced the money for the final stage of the Normandy campaign. Not all of it was Coeur's own. Some of it had been borrowed from Italian merchants and prominent noblemen at court and lent on, while some was the King's own money that was being lent back to him.[63]

The French King divided his army in two. Poton de Saintrailles was given the task of reducing Falaise and Domfront, while Richemont was charged with the conquest of Cherbourg. Falaise and Domfront were old border fortresses, built by the twelfth-century Kings of England, but they were still formidable in spite of their age and they were strongly garrisoned. Domfront in particular had been refortified by Henry V in a major campaign of works between 1418 and 1421, and continually strengthened during the two decades that Thomas Lord Scales had been its captain. Morale was low, however, and neither place offered much resistance. Poton arrived outside Falaise on 6 July 1450, followed by Jean Bureau's artillery train and its escort of *francs-archers*. The garrison launched a sortie against them as they approached the fortress but were beaten back. Once the bombards had been set up they opened negotiations. Sir John Talbot, who was captain of Falaise, appears to have bought his release from captivity by authorising his lieutenants in the fortress to surrender. The King arrived with a crowd of noblemen to be present when Falaise opened its gates on 21 July. The fortress had held out for just five days. Domfront lasted a little longer. It withstood several assaults, and finally surrendered at the beginning of August after a siege of ten days.[64]

Cherbourg was one of the strongest fortresses of western France. Its harbour was an enclosed lagoon entered by a narrow passage dominated from the west by the great citadel rebuilt by Charles the Bad, King of Navarre in the 1360s. With its massive keep, its cavernous stores, its wedge-shaped curtain wall of sixteen towers, its stone outworks and the sea serving as an unbridgeable moat, the castle was regarded as invulnerable to assault. It had taken six months for a large English army and fleet to starve it out in 1418. The captain of Cherbourg was the Yorkshire squire Thomas Gower. He was a veteran of the Norman wars who had served continuously in France for at least twenty-six years, ten of them at Cherbourg. He was one of many English soldiers who had put down roots in France, acquiring extensive property in the Cotentin and marrying a French wife. In 1450 Gower's normal garrison of 120 was swollen by refugees to about 1,000 men.

Richemont arrived before Cherbourg early in July, accompanied by both Marshals of France, the Admiral Prégent de Coëtivy, Pierre de Brézé and the Count of Clermont. They had about 4,000 men with them as well as a horde of conscripted labourers and craftsmen. But in spite of the large numbers deployed and the elaborate network of trenches around the castle, the siege was an artillery battle. Gaspard Bureau arrived with the artillery train at the end of July. His bombards were set up along the strands of the harbour. A battery was installed on a rock on the seaward side encased in waterproof greased leather against the tide which submerged it twice a day. It brought down a tower and a section of wall with its first shot. The castle, which had been better supplied with artillery than most English fortresses, fought back, raking the trenches with lead and stone pellets. Prégent de Coëtivy was killed by cannon fire and the *bailli* of Troyes by a culverin.[65]

In England attempts to save the last corner of Normandy still in English hands began within days of the commencement of the siege. From Kenilworth castle, Henry VI's ministers ordered the urgent recruitment of troops and began to importune the richer ecclesiastical corporations for loans. The King hurried south to preside over a great council in the abbey of St Albans on 24 July. There is no record of the discussion, but the fate of Lancastrian Normandy must have been top of the agenda. The council appears to have approved a project to relieve Cherbourg. A ship with reinforcements and supplies left England a few days later. But the recruitment of larger forces proved more difficult, and the requisitioning of shipping did not begin until 14 August. Cherbourg had already surrendered before the requisitioning officers could even begin their work.

The story of its surrender reveals much about the mood of the English in their last days in Normandy. Thomas Gower could probably have held out for longer than the cash reserves of the French war treasurers. In early August Charles VII sent Jacques Coeur to Cherbourg to negotiate an early capitulation. Coeur offered Gower a large bribe and the release of his son Richard, a prisoner of war whom Coeur had purchased from his captors for the purpose. Gower had been a conspicuously loyal officer. But he decided that the time had come to look after his own interests and those of his men. By 8 August, he had reached agreement with Jacques Coeur. Once the French King had approved the terms, Gower and Richemont sealed the document on 12 August, and the fortress was surrendered that very day. The cost of this transaction to the French treasury was 40,000 *écus* (about £6,700). Of this, some was spent on shipping to hurry the garrison and English community of Cherbourg home (back to their 'miserable huts' in England, wrote the Norman propagandist Robert Blondel). Some was spent on procuring the release of English garrison troops who had been taken prisoner, so as to use them as bargaining counters. A sum of 2,000 *écus* was distributed among the garrison to buy their acquiescence. Some went into Gower's chests. In addition, his son Richard was released. The whole cost was advanced by Coeur himself. The English were allowed to leave with their movable property and, unusually, to sell their lands to anyone that they could find to buy them. It must have been a buyers' market. Gower himself gave his land away to the abbey of Notre-Dame du Voeu outside the town in return for prayers for himself and his friends, living and dead. The first reports of his surrender reached London on 19 August, probably with the returning garrison. John Paston's London agent wrote to him with the news. 'We have not now a foot of land in Normandy,' he complained.[66]

The speed and completeness of the collapse of what had once been the most efficient military machine in Europe provoked much reflection on both sides of the Channel. Looking back over the campaign, Sir John Fastolf attributed the 'unmanly disseising' of the English to neglect of the manning and victualling of the Norman garrisons. This was certainly part of the explanation. But far more significant was the fact that the English army was outclassed by the new army of the King of France, not just in numbers but in quality. This had been well understood by the English council at Rouen but not by the government at Westminster. The French King's senior herald identified the main factors at work: the discipline and equipment not just of the *compagnies d'ordonnance* and the *francs-archers* but of the military retinues of the nobility which were increasingly modelled on them; the scale on which the French armies were supported by artillery from bombards to culverins; the impressive logistical support which kept the army fed and supplied in the field; and the restoration of a functioning tax system which made it possible to afford these things. The soldier-chronicler Jean de Waurin, who was well informed about English politics, reproduced this catalogue, but added another factor: the collapse of law and order in England, and the rancour and jealousies which had divided the English nobility and paralysed Henry VI's government. But if these factors explained the feebleness of the English military response, it was William Worcester who put his finger on the fundamental problem of the English occupation in its last years. It was the wholesale desertion of the English cause by the indigenous population of Normandy, who refused to fight for them. This was a particularly important factor in the towns. Their motives were the mirror image of those which had led them to surrender to Henry V between 1417 and 1420. The English could no longer offer them security against the French or even against their own garrisons.[67]

Sir John Talbot left Normandy to participate in the Roman Jubilee proclaimed for the year 1450. This was probably another of the terms of his release, intended to keep him out of the way until the completion of the French conquest. Of the eight hostages given for the performance of Somerset's agreement at Rouen, Talbot did best. Three others seem to have been released at an early stage on terms which are not recorded. The other four were assigned to a syndicate comprising Jacques Coeur, Dunois and Pierre de Brézé, probably in partial repayment of their loans to the King. They were eventually ransomed for large amounts, in some cases after long and tortuous negotiations. George Neville, the thirteen-year-old heir of Lord Bergavenny and potentially the richest of the hostages, suffered the harshest fate. He was assigned to Jacques Coeur and auctioned off as part of the merchant's bankrupt effects after the collapse of his business empire. The successful bidder, Jean de Bueil, drove a hard bargain, and Neville did not recover his freedom until 1467. These men paid a high price for the English government's decision to 'retard' the surrender of Honfleur.[68]

Thirty years of English occupation left a mark on Normandy which took many years to efface. Old controversies obstinately refused to die. The French King's decision in February 1450 to have the case of Joan of Arc reopened stirred many old ghosts. Charles VII had been silent about Joan since her execution, mainly out of embarrassment that the turning point of his fortunes should have been due to a woman whom the Church had condemned as a sorcerer and a heretic. The issue had to be addressed once final victory was in his grasp. As Guillaume Bouillé, the Paris theologian whom Charles commissioned to conduct a preliminary investigation, pointed out, Joan had in reality been condemned for what she had done to support his recovery of his kingdom. The King's silence, he said, stained his honour and discredited his achievement. Cardinal d'Estouteville, the papal legate in France, who conducted another preliminary enquiry two years later, made much the same point. Joan's mother and brothers demanded justice against her judges. There were many others who would have preferred to forget the whole episode. The University of Paris and the cathedral chapter of Rouen, now pillars of the Valois monarchy, had been among the main drivers of Joan's conviction. Some of her judges were still alive. When, after the lengthy preliminaries, a full-scale inquiry into the earlier proceedings opened in 1455, many of those who had participated in the trial gave evidence. Almost all of them claimed that it had been rigged by the English and resorted to convenient lapses of memory when it came to their own role. The outcome was as inevitable as the original condemnation. On 7 July 1456, the articles against Joan were quashed on the ground of procedural irregularity and her confession declared to have been obtained under duress.[69]

Thomas Basin, the Bishop of Lisieux, wrote that nothing but force had ever kept the Normans in subjection and that they returned to their 'natural' and 'ancient' allegiance as soon as they were able to. But Basin's own career demonstrated that this was too simple an explanation. In the heyday of Lancastrian Normandy, in the 1420s, English rule had been generally accepted by the Normans. Much of the landowning nobility and most of the urban oligarchies had actively supported it. Many Frenchmen found that an equivocal past came back to haunt them after 1450. Basin himself was one of them. Archbishop Roussel, who had played such a prominent role in the surrender of Rouen, was another. The municipal officer who presided at the submission of Caen apologised for the tardiness of the town in returning to its true allegiance, which he attributed to English oppression. Yet he himself had served as lieutenant of the English *bailli* for sixteen years. In general, there was no purge of public officers after the French conquest of Normandy. The administrators in Rouen, the *vicomtes* who collected local revenues, the councillors and magistrates of the major towns, the judges, jailers and executioners, passed seamlessly into the service of the Valois monarchy. But many scars remained. There were plenty of Normans who had done well by English patronage. They feared for their future under the new regime.[70]

Most Rouennais had probably been glad enough to be rid of the English in 1450, but over the next few years their enthusiasm for the Valois monarchy waned as they came up against its centralising tendencies and significantly higher levels of taxation. The government of Normandy was placed in the hands of the Constable Arthur de Richemont and the Count of Dunois. With them came carpetbaggers like Pierre de Brézé, who owed his opportunities to royal favour and over the years made a fortune from royal office and speculation in land. Like other major towns in Normandy and elsewhere in France, Rouen gradually lost its autonomy as its municipality was absorbed into the expanding web of royal authority. After years as a capital, it became just another provincial city governed from the Loire valley. Charles VII abolished many of the provincial institutions which the English had established in Normandy, including the local audit offices and, for a time, the University of Caen. Others, like the Estates and the Échiquier (the appeal court) were hemmed in with restrictions on their independence and powers. These things offended the provincial patriotism which had always been strong in Normandy. By the time of the Estates-General of Tours in 1484, some Normans had forgotten the difficulties of the English occupation and had begun to look back on it with rose-tinted spectacles. The delegation of Rouen told the assembly that the English had never looted the duchy or killed or ransomed its inhabitants but had continually striven to protect it from the horrors of war. According to the house chronicler of the Dukes of Alençon, writing at about the same time, a significant body of opinion in Normandy still looked upon the Kings of England as the rightful heirs of William the Conqueror.[71]

The most dramatic changes occurred in the countryside, where the Lancastrian land settlement was reversed with extremely disruptive results. Charles VII's edict of Compiègne of 1429 entitled the previous owners to take back their former land free of all claims by intervening purchasers or mortgagees. They were authorised to claim arrears of rent without limit of time and to require property to be put back in the condition it had been in when its owner had been dispossessed. In reissuing the edict in October 1450, the King acknowledged that its application in Normandy after thirty years of English rule had been widely resisted and was criticised by jurists as unjust. But Charles had incurred obligations to the Norman exiles and insisted that it must be applied. Indeed, he ordained that it was to prevail even over the terms which he had himself granted to towns on their surrender. The ordinance was an invitation to violence and litigation on a scale which quickly overwhelmed the courts. The old nobility who returned with the armies were usually able to expel the existing occupiers of their old lands by force. Smaller landowners were less well placed and often encountered difficulty in recovering their estates. Land values had sunk, sometimes below the cost of litigating. Tenants were scarce and had no cash to pay up arrears of rent, especially if they had already been paying it to their English landlords. It was pointless to pursue them. Many disputes ended in compromise. But even those who succeeded in recovering their property found it diminished by war damage and emigration. Settlements were abandoned. Buildings were in ruins. At Tancarville, Guillaume d'Harcourt returned to find his castle dilapidated and his revenues drastically diminished since the Greys of Heton had taken it over in 1419. The Greys had only managed to extract about 60 per cent of the pre-war yield of the domain, even before the revolt of the Caux in 1435. Since then, revenues had fallen much further, in the worst cases to barely a sixth of their original level. Louis d'Estouteville reclaimed his father's domains after a quarter of a century in command of Mont-Saint-Michel, only to find them charged with debts incurred while they were occupied by the Dukes of Bedford and Somerset. Many returning landowners must have had similar stories to tell.[72]

A handful of English settlers in Normandy chose to stay behind, swearing allegiance to Charles VII and fortifying their title with royal grants. Some of them were men of substance, like Richard Merbury and John Edward who had become naturalised and merged with the indigenous nobility. Many more were humble men like Thomas Bourton, who took a lease on a house in Caen on the very day that the town was surrendered to the French; or Oliver Martin, one of the marshals of Somerset's army at Caen, who had served in Normandy for at least twenty-four years and forfeited his assets in England by refusing to leave; or men who had married locally like Thomas Chiswall, the lieutenant at Valognes, whom we have seen joining the French garrison of Mont-Saint-Michel; or John Fermen, a former retainer of Matthew Gough who had settled at Sainte-Suzanne and found alternative employment in the household of the Duke of Alençon.[73]

The great majority of English settlers in Normandy left for England. Their wretched fate was brought home to Londoners when the refugees from Normandy began to pour through the streets. They were bitter against the King's ministers. The first groups, from Bayeux, appeared in June. The men of Caen shortly joined them. They 'came out of Normandy in great necessity as starving beggars', said their captain. Some seem to have joined Jack Cade's mobs. Others wandered aimlessly about the city for want of money or any home to go to, coalescing into angry mobs. On 21 July 1450 they invaded the Franciscan church by Newgate where Lord Saye had been buried after his execution. They took down his coat of arms from the pillar by the grave and reversed it, the traditional ritual for dishonouring the absent and the dead. They roamed through the streets looking for buildings displaying the Duke of Suffolk's arms so that they could pull them down and deface them. On 28 July, they crowded round the palace of Westminster, blockading the King inside and preventing him from leaving to celebrate the feast of the Assumption at his new foundation at Eton. The Duke of Somerset eventually returned to England at the head of a column of demoralised soldiers from Caen on 1 August. A few days later the civilians of Caen followed, men, women and children dragging carts through Cheapside filled with armour, bedding and furniture 'in right poor array, piteous to see', wrote the lawyer Robert Bale. The council distributed alms covering fifteen days' subsistence in the hope that they would go away. They paid for the burial of one poor wretch who collapsed and died in Fleet Street. The city corporation believed that it was sitting on a powder keg. When the annual St Bartholomew fair opened on 25 August they had 300 armed and mounted men standing by.[74]

Most of the refugees from Normandy had had to abandon a country in which they had expected to spend the rest of their lives. They had built houses for themselves in France. They had married locally and established families. The richer of them had commissioned monuments in local churches, like Fulk Eyton, captain of Caudebec, who paid an English craftsman for a stained-glass window in the newly built church of Caudebec, showing St George and the Virgin, with St Catherine and St Michael, surmounted by his arms and motto: *'Je m'y oblige'* ('It is my duty'). It is still there. At a less conspicuous social level, others had held minor offices in the Norman administration with good salaries (when they were paid) or else had received modest grants of land. Their lives in Normandy had often been hard but offered a route to a higher income and status than they could ever have enjoyed in England.

After their return, their fortunes varied widely. Thomas Gower, the last defender of Cherbourg, had made money from ransoms and piracy off the Norman coast and must have remitted a fair amount of it back to England before he was expelled. He returned with his French wife and family, acquired a valuable manor in Clapham, a tenement in Southwark and property in Lambeth and Chingford, before embarking on a long and flourishing career of lawlessness. He was more fortunate than most. After surviving for more than a quarter of a century in the murderous wars of France, Matthew Gough was killed shortly after his return in the battle with Cade's rebels on London Bridge. Sir Robert James, Gough's lieutenant at Bayeux, had served in Normandy since 1417 and lost everything when the town fell. He returned penniless. Oliver Catesby, who defended Domfront at the end, was taken prisoner during the siege and returned ruined to die of 'grief of heart' in dire poverty at Westminster. Those who had married French women found that their wives were viewed with suspicion in England. A petition which appears to have been presented in Parliament in November 1450, complained that they 'be but as spies' and ought not to be allowed to enter or leave the country without a visa. These cases were more typical than Gower's.[75]

The soldiers and settlers of Maine had a particular grievance. The sums earmarked to compensate them had been diverted by the Duke of Somerset to other expenditure. None of them had received a penny except for Somerset himself and the King's friend Viscount Beaumont. Many of them were humble soldiers who had received small grants of land in Maine as a reward for their service at the battle of Verneuil. Others had bought property there or married local women who had their own inheritance. Some had laid out all their funds on improvements. These men had lost not just assets but status. They had gone to Maine, they said in their petition to the King, 'to have the means of living better and keeping up a respectable position in your service', but were now reduced to beggary. They wanted compensation out of the fortunes of those who had 'wickedly and disloyally' advised the King to surrender the county. A note on the petition records its rejection. Many of the petitioners, it asserted, had either stayed in France and pledged their allegiance to the King's enemies, or else returned to England where they had died in poverty or had taken to crime and ended up in prison or on the gallows.[76]

The French officers and supporters of the Lancastrian regime were a special case. More than 200 Frenchmen from the northern provinces are known to have migrated to England in the ten years after the fall of Normandy. There must in fact have been many more, for we only know about the minority who took out letters of denization or appear in the tax records. Most of them were servants or small craftsmen who probably came with the households of grander figures. A few had been too closely associated with the Lancastrian regime to have any future in Valois France. This applied particularly to the men who been involved in the negotiations with Charles VII over the capture of Fougères, a difficult role that branded them as traitors and deceivers in the eyes of the French King's councillors. The soldier turned lawyer Jean Lenfant had been president of the Échiquier, the duchy's highest court, and the bearer of many dishonest excuses between April and July 1450. He lost all his property in the French reconquest and arrived with his family in England without a penny to his name. Louis Gallet had been an officer of the Châtelet and an *échevin* of Paris in the Duke of Bedford's time, before moving to Rouen when Paris fell and eventually joining the Grand Conseil. He had the misfortune to be a known friend of François de Surienne, and to have been at Charles VII's court when the news of the capture of Fougères arrived. Gallet seems to have begun by trying to make his way under the new regime at Rouen, for he assisted the French official enquiry into the Fougères incident in the autumn of 1449. But within three years he too had left to settle in London. At least three members of the Grand Conseil's secretariat followed him on the well-beaten path to England, along with a small number of indigenous Normans who had made careers fighting in English armies. Some of these exiles lived in England on pensions from the English Exchequer. A few of them, like Henry VI's French secretary Gervase le Vulre, enjoyed some influence about the court. Gallet provided introductions to the emissaries of French malcontents plotting against Charles VII. Le Vulre was important enough for the Commons to petition for his removal from the King's household.[77]

The returning English soldiers and settlers, now several thousand strong, were becoming a serious threat to public order not only in London but in East Anglia and much of southern England, where sporadic outbreaks of violence continued throughout the autumn of 1450. These came with clamorous demands for action against the Duke of Somerset and the surviving cronies of the Duke of Suffolk. The court and the peerage set about filling the void of authority left by the increasingly obvious incompetence of the King and the fall of the Duke of Suffolk. Faced with chaos and bankruptcy at home and the mounting fear that Guyenne and Calais would be the next to fall, another great council, the second in a month, met on 24 and 25 August at Westminster. It was probably this body that endorsed the choice of the Duke of Somerset as Suffolk's successor. In the eyes of the political establishment there was much to be said for him in spite of his failure in Normandy and his unpopularity at home. As a Beaufort, he was close to the royal line, but unlike the Duke of York was not seen as an alternative King. Unlike the Duke of Suffolk, he was not a great territorial magnate presenting a threat to the regional interests of other peers. Unlike the young and unstable Duke of Exeter, he was not suspected of sympathy with the rebels. Within a few weeks of his return Somerset was admitted to the council and made Constable of England.[78]

On 5 September 1450, writs were issued for a new Parliament less than three months after the dissolution of the last one. Two days later, the Duke of York returned from Ireland and landed in north Wales with a large military retinue. The government viewed his return with foreboding. They were frightened by the support for him among the rebels and in some sections of the political community. His Chamberlain Sir William Oldhall was believed to have been plotting with supporters in England to put him on the throne. York himself believed that he was in danger of being indicted for treason and that the King's officers in north Wales had orders to arrest him as soon as he landed. The most plausible reason for the Duke's return was the one that he gave himself. It was dangerous in fifteenth-century England to allow allegations of treason to fester unchallenged. York wanted to confront them head-on. 'I have been informed,' he wrote to the King, 'that diverse language hath been said of me to your most excellent estate, which should sound to my dishonour and reproach.' In his reply, the King did not deny it. However, if that was York's original object, he soon became the main focus of a broader opposition to the government. He had not expected to see the Duke of Somerset ensconced at the heart of government, a man whom he despised and who had supplanted him as lieutenant in Normandy only to preside over the loss of the whole duchy. He had himself lost heavily by the French reconquest. He resented the government's failure to pay the huge accumulated arrears owing to him from his time as lieutenant in Normandy and Ireland, at a time when most of the debts owed to Somerset had been paid promptly and in full.

During his march across England, the Duke of York was joined by armed tenants from his domains on the Welsh marches and by friends in the West Country. By the time he entered London on 27 September for an audience with the King, he had some 3,000 armed men at his back. A few days after this he wrote to the King what amounted to a manifesto, copies of which were distributed far and wide. He called for reform of the government, the repair of the legal system, the re-establishment of order in the counties and the punishment of unspecified 'misrulers'. York offered himself as Henry's instrument for carrying out these policies. It was an overt bid for power. The King and those around him were intimidated by York's armed entourage and by reports that his allies in the country were gathering their own armed retinues. An emollient reply was sent. The King did not accept York's offer of his services. He had no intention, he said, of ruling through a single adviser in future. He would govern through a 'sad and substantial council', broader than hitherto, which would include York himself. This reply, which was probably drafted by Chancellor Kemp, was cleverly framed and may have appeased some people who would otherwise have joined the Duke of York. Meanwhile Henry's household officers began to muster their own retainers in preparation for the opening of Parliament and what seemed likely to be a violent showdown with the government's opponents.[79]

Parliament opened at Westminster on 6 November 1450 in an atmosphere of high excitement. 'The people stood in great dread and doubt,' reported Robert Bale. The government banned public discussion of, or 'meddling' with, the business of Parliament. The officers of the city corporation tried to disarm York's followers at the city gates, as crowds of men forced their way in with swords, daggers, billhooks and axes. The magnates were divided between supporters and opponents of the Duke of York. Many of them had come with large armed retinues which they quartered in their city mansions. The London mobs reflected the divisions of the peers. Broadsheets were nailed to walls and doors. Gangs roamed the streets putting up York's arms while rival gangs pulled them down again. At Westminster, the Commons showed their own sympathies by electing Sir William Oldhall, York's right-hand man, as their Speaker. They turned at once to recrimination against the King's advisers. On the first day of business, they presented a petition for the rehabilitation of the Duke of Gloucester. They recited his valiant deeds under Henry V and his years of service to Henry VI.

They called for him to be posthumously acquitted of the charges of treason made at the Bury Parliament of 1447. There was a move to impeach those believed to have been responsible for his murder.[80]

The Duke of York was not present during the opening days of the Parliament. He had withdrawn to his castle at Ludlow on the Welsh marches to gather his strength. When eventually he appeared, he made sure to do it to maximum effect. He entered the city of London on 23 November with his entire retinue at his back and a naked sword carried upright before him. He received a tumultuous welcome from the Londoners who filled the streets and crowded round his cavalcade. The ambassador of the Teutonic Order, who watched the spectacle, reported that it took York four hours to pass the length of Cheapside. His ally, the Duke of Norfolk, followed the next day escorted by a 'great people' in armour-plated jackets with six trumpeters leading the way. The Duke of York issued another manifesto in which he was more specific about the 'misrulers' whom he wanted to see brought to book. It was the men responsible for the collapse of law and order in England, the diversion of the King's revenues, the loss of Normandy and Maine and, indirectly, the risings in England. It was the shady diplomats whose treasonable dealings with the court of France were said to have led to the conquest of the Île-de-France, Normandy, Maine and Anjou. He called for a commission of knights and judges to identify the guilty men and prosecute them.

Taking their cue from the Duke of York, the Commons drew up another petition, this time for the exclusion from court of a list of twenty-nine objectionable persons. Most of them were associates of the Duke of Suffolk or had been involved in the affairs of France and Normandy or had for one reason or another been targets of Jack Cade's rebels earlier in the year. The Duke of Somerset and the Duchess of Suffolk headed the list, which also included Sir Thomas Hoo the former Chancellor of Normandy, Lord Hastings former Chamberlain of Normandy, Abbot Boulers and Lord Dudley. The charge against Somerset, and presumably against Hoo and Chamberlain, was that they had betrayed Normandy. Henry VI's answer was that he knew of no reason to remove them but would suspend them for a year while the allegations against them were considered.[81]

It may have been this answer that provoked the explosion of mob violence which began on 30 November 1450 and continued for most of the following week. An angry crowd invaded Westminster Hall protesting that nothing was being done against the Duke of Somerset and other 'traitors'. On 1 December a mob of about a thousand men tried to kill the Duke. They invaded his lodgings in the Dominican convent at Ludgate. He managed to escape by the river and take refuge in the Tower. But his possessions were looted and the convent was trashed. It was later alleged that the attack had been organised by Sir William Oldhall and there is reason to believe that it was. On the following day the mob passed through the city of London attacking and looting the houses of real or imagined 'traitors' including Hoo and Hastings. A show of force and an exemplary execution put an end to the disorders over the following days. In hindsight, however, these can be seen as the opening moments of the civil war that was destined to destroy the house of Lancaster. The irony of Englishmen tearing each other apart in a time of war was not lost on those who watched the King in December 1450 as he rode through the streets of London to suppress the riots with his household troops and the armed retinues of the lords. It would have been 'a gay and glorious sight', one of them observed, 'if it had been in France and not in England'.[82]

CHAPTER XIV

Gascony and Beyond, 1450–1453

The collapse of the truce of Tours came as a shock in Gascony. The administration in Bordeaux had had no warning of the attack on Fougères and was surprised by the reprisals on the march of Saintonge which followed. Returning from a visit to Bordeaux, the captain of Cognac had no idea that it was in enemy hands until he was arrested outside his own gates. Militarily, the region was even more vulnerable than Normandy. There were hardly any English troops. No significant assistance, whether in money or men, had reached Bordeaux since the arrival of Sir William Bonville as Seneschal six years before. Bonville, although nominally still in post, had taken advantage of the truce to return to England in the winter of 1445–6 and, although apparently intending to return, he never did. In his absence, the dominant figure in the Bordeaux government was the mayor of Bordeaux, Sir Gadifer Shorthose. Shorthose was getting on in years in 1449. He had arrived in the south-west as a young man in 1413, probably in the army of the Duke of Clarence, and had spent the rest of his life there. After a period serving as a soldier of fortune in central France, he had become Mayor of Bordeaux in 1433, a royal appointment which he had held ever since. In addition, he was a power in the Dordogne valley, where he was captain of Bergerac and lord of Biron. Shorthose had done well to stabilise the region after the disasters of 1442, but he had no influence at Westminster and limited authority over the Gascon nobility on whom the defence of the duchy ultimately depended. When the truce failed, the council in Bordeaux could count on only a small number of noble families with strong traditional ties to the Kings of England; and on the maritime cities of Bordeaux and Bayonne, both of which enjoyed a privileged position and important commercial links with England. But the obvious inability of the English government to defend its Gascon territories had lost them the support of many Gascons, especially in the towns of the interior. Few were willing to risk their lives or fortunes for what seemed to be a dying regime. The French ministers knew this. They had partisans and spies in the Bordelais who kept them well informed about conditions there.[1]

Charles VII's lieutenant in the south-west was Gaston IV Count of Foix. He had everything to gain from the failure of the truce. It enabled him to expand his territory at the expense of the English at a low point in their fortunes. When the French King declared war, Gaston lost no time in launching an offensive against the few remaining English strongholds south of the Adour. There was very little resistance. At the end of July 1449 Gaston laid siege to the Pyrenean fortress of Mauléon in Soule, the southernmost outpost of English Gascony. Situated close to the borders of France, Castile and Navarre, Mauléon had once been described by a Speaker of the House of Commons as the 'key to three kingdoms'. It belonged to a long-standing partisan of the English, Louis de Beaumont, hereditary Alferez (or standard-bearer) of Navarre. The council in Bordeaux rushed reinforcements to the fortress, but after a short siege Beaumont transferred his allegiance to the French and surrendered the place to the Count of Foix. His defection brought over the nobility of the entire region. John lord of Luxe, whose family had been vassals of the English Kings for generations, appeared before the Count of Foix at the head of several hundred men to swear allegiance to Charles VII. They arrived dramatically with the upright red cross of England on their tunics and left wearing the white cross of France. From Soule, Gaston de Foix moved into the terre de Labourt and laid siege to the fortress of La Guiche on the Adour, part of the outer defences of Bayonne. La Guiche's Gascon garrison put up a more spirited fight than Mauléon, and there was a serious attempt to relieve the place from Bayonne. But La Guiche also surrendered in December 1449. This event led, like the fall of Mauléon, to mass defections in the surrounding region. Fifteen castles submitted to the Count of Foix in the aftermath of the fall of La Guiche, leaving Bayonne surrounded by hostile territory.[2]

At the end of the year, the Estates of Guyenne sent a delegation to Westminster, headed by Pey du Tasta, the dean of the collegiate church of Saint-Seurin of Bordeaux. It was the latest of a succession of Gascon embassies sent to press the English government for action. The council needed no reminding of Gascony's weakness, but the tremendous effort required to raise Sir Thomas Kyriel's army for Normandy ruled out any attempt to send help there as well. It was not until after Kyriel's army had been wiped out at Formigny, that any steps were taken to rescue the duchy. The plan slowly took shape over the following weeks. In its final form it involved the recruitment of an army of 3,000 men, nine-tenths of them archers. Most of them were expected to be found among the unruly and unemployed soldiery who had returned penniless from Normandy during the summer of 1450. The idea was to reinforce Gascony, while getting these men away from the politically explosive atmosphere of London and southeastern England. The command of the expedition was given to Richard Woodville Lord Rivers, who was nominated as Seneschal of Guyenne for a term of five years. Woodville had a colourful past and an even more colourful future. He was a Northamptonshire gentleman with a moderately distinguished record of service in Normandy under the Duke of Bedford. Returning to England after the Duke's death, he had shocked the courts of England and Burgundy by secretly marrying Bedford's young widow Jacquetta of Luxembourg, a lady far above his station, without the King's licence. This earned him a fine of £1,000, but it made him rich and sealed his social ascent. In 1448 he had been raised to the peerage as Lord Rivers.[3]

Rivers's army was supposed to sail from Plymouth by the end of September 1450, and if he had been able to stick to the timetable his presence might have made a considerable difference. However, his plans were overtaken by a succession of political disasters in England. The collapse of the administration during Cade's rebellion was followed by several months in which the government's energies and those of Rivers himself were absorbed by its suppression. At the same time the old contest for local influence between Courtenay and Bonville in Devon had reduced to anarchy much of the region where Rivers's army was due to muster. Recruitment of the troops did not begin until September 1450 and continued fitfully over the following months. As always, the abiding problem was want of money to pay them. The income tax voted by Parliament in June was a failure. The cumbersome process of assessment was delayed by administrative chaos at the centre and the breakdown of order in the counties. Even in regions which had been assessed, there was widespread opposition to the rates, which were thought to bear too hard on the poorer taxpayers. The government had counted on an early grant of taxation in the Parliament which opened in November. But its hopes were dashed by the uproar provoked by the loss of Normandy, the ferment surrounding the Duke of York's bid for power and the demands of the Commons for an act of resumption. No subsidy had been voted by the time that Parliament was prorogued for Christmas on 18 December. Instead, the Commons simply reconfirmed the subsidy of June at slightly softer rates and urged greater diligence in its collection. By that time, the English duchy of Guyenne had already begun to crumble.[4]

When Cherbourg fell, Charles VII paid off most of the army which had fought in Normandy. At the beginning of September 1450, while processions of thanksgiving and celebration were being organised across France, the King presided over a great council at Tours to review the future course of the war. Charles's dilemma was one which had troubled his predecessors ever since the disaster at Crécy a century before: whether to risk a war on two fronts simultaneously. Although the whole of Normandy had been reconquered, his ministers continued to live in fear of a fresh English descent on the Norman coast. To contain this risk, they were obliged to put 4,400 men into the Norman garrisons, not far short of the garrison establishment which the English had maintained at the height of their fortunes. The French King's commissioners told the Estates of Normandy at the end of 1450 that they expected to spend 400,000 *livres* a year on garrisoning the province. The outcome of the assembly of Tours was a decision to send a modest army, between 2,000 and 3,000 strong, to test the northern defences of Gascony. John Count of Penthièvre and Poton de Saintrailles were put in command of this force. They were supported by an artillery train directed by Jean Bureau and by locally recruited troops raised by Arnaud-Amanieu lord of Orval, a younger son of the lord of Albret. A financial official, Jean le Boursier, was given the task of organising a fleet to blockade Bordeaux and Bayonne.[5]

The campaign opened in mid-September 1450 and lasted barely six weeks. It confirmed what was already suspected, that the English duchy was almost defenceless. Bergerac was the principal English town of the Dordogne. Its important stone bridge marked the eastern limit of English power. Neither the bridge nor the town was well fortified. Gadifer Shorthose shut himself in the town and put up a brief defence but abandoned it as soon as Bureau began to site his guns. The French army swept down the Dordogne valley beyond Sainte-Foy-la-Grande. Everywhere, the townsmen opened their gates. The French encountered no resistance until they reached Gensac, the only garrisoned fortress in the region, which was carried by assault. From Gensac, the French army split up into a number of different forces which fanned out in all directions sweeping up undefended places. The largest group, commanded by Orval himself, headed south, crossed the Garonne and reoccupied the city of Bazas, traditionally an Albret stronghold. From there, they lunged down the Garonne with about 500 men and appeared without warning outside Bordeaux at the end of October.

Inside the city, Shorthose resolved to attack them. He had gathered around him what remained of the loyal nobility of the Bordelais and the Landes. He also had the remnants of Bonville's company of archers and some soldiers recently arrived in the port with the annual wine fleet from England. On 1 November 1450, the whole force marched out of the city under Shorthose's command, accompanied by a citizen militia commanded by his Gascon deputy. The two armies met near the suburban hamlet of Le Haillan in the Médoc north of the city. Although they greatly outnumbered the French, the Anglo-Gascons advanced in poor order and were routed by Orval's more disciplined companies. Shorthose fled the scene on horseback, leaving the unmounted citizen militia to be slaughtered in the pursuit. After the fight, the heralds counted some 2,000 Gascon dead on the field. Over the following days, the wounded and the dead were collected and brought into the city in carts. Crowds gathered at the gates to watch the scene. The *'male journade'*, as it became known, had a disastrous impact on the morale of the defenders of Bordeaux, which would show in the following year. From Bazas, where they had withdrawn after the battle, Orval and his fellow captains reported to the King that Guyenne would be even easier to conquer than Normandy. With another 1,200 men they thought they could complete the job over the winter.[6]

The first reports of the French offensive were brought to Westminster in early November 1450 by the crews of ships trading from Bordeaux, but the full extent of the rout did not become apparent until the new year. Its political impact was muted, because by then the Duke of York's star was in decline. His limitations as a party leader were becoming increasingly obvious. Richard of York was a proud and aloof man, headstrong, abrasive and without judgement. His role in raising an army to overawe the court and encouraging mob violence in London had lost him many allies among the lords, who closed ranks against him. Parliament, which was his main political platform, had been prorogued for Christmas. Opposition to the government moved to the fields and streets. In January 1451 there was a fresh rising in Kent. The man believed to be responsible was one of York's household retainers called Stephen Christmas, who had spread reports that Henry planned to lay waste the county in revenge for Cade's rebellion. The rising was brutally suppressed by the King with the aid of Somerset, Talbot and Exeter. At the sessions of the peace at Canterbury and Rochester many were condemned for treason for 'having more favour unto the Duke of York than unto the King'. More than a hundred men were drawn, hanged and quartered.[7]

The second session of Parliament opened just as the revolt in Kent was catching fire. It was almost entirely taken up with the Commons' continuing obsession with the resumption of royal grants. The earlier statute had been emasculated by exceptions and had achieved little. The Commons were pressing for a new and more watertight one. The King's ministers could not fight two battles at once. They resolved to compromise with the Commons. They conceded a tighter statute of resumption and then set about consolidating the power of the governing group around the Duke of Somerset. Several of the twenty-nine courtiers denounced by the Commons as creatures of the Duke of Suffolk and his friends were tried in Parliament or in the London courts in the early months of 1451 and exonerated. The 'sad and substantial council' which the King had promised York in October was quietly forgotten. The Duke of York himself was excluded. The Commons were resentful and truculent. Shortly after Easter, they were recalled for a third session in the hope that they would grant fresh taxes now that the dispute over resumption had abated. But the session came to an abrupt end when Thomas Young, a retainer of the Duke of York who sat for Bristol, moved a petition that York should be recognised as heir presumptive to the throne. The King and his ministers were not prepared to concede so much status to their most prominent opponent. The Commons for their part declined to proceed with any other business until they had received satisfaction on Young's petition. The King responded by dissolving Parliament and sending Young to the Tower, along with several other officers and councillors of the Duke. No financial support was forthcoming. This left Rivers and his captains stranded.[8]

The embarkation of an army was a difficult moment in the life of a medieval port. The streets were crammed with bored, impatient soldiers, waiting for their advances. They were joined by crowds of seamen, purveyors, thieves and prostitutes. Horses and cattle for the passage had to be accommodated and fed. Stores piled up in barrels on the quaysides. Over the winter of 1450–1 men gathered at Plymouth for the army of Gascony. Their advances could not be paid. The ships were assembling in the port but there was no money for their masters or crews. The shipmasters began to sail away. The soldiers took to looting the surrounding villages. The government was able to borrow small sums on the security of future tax receipts, but significant amounts did not start to come in to the Treasury until well into the summer. Embarkation was put off to the end of February 1451, then to March, April and May and finally to 23 June. Meanwhile, the council in Bordeaux was becoming increasingly alarmed. Bidau de Ville, a Gascon squire frequently employed as an agent to deal with the government at Westminster, arrived in England in February 1451 with another urgent appeal for help. A month later he was complaining that he could not even get an answer to his letters.[9]

Bidau de Ville was still in England when Charles VII summoned another great council to meet at Tours at the end of March 1451. Active preparations for the invasion of Gascony had by this time been in progress for several weeks. The coffers of the war treasurers were filling up again, after the great financial exertions in Normandy. A *taille* of 120,000 *livres* had been imposed on Languedoil and another of the same amount on Languedoc. Jean le Boursier had recently returned from Castile. He had failed to obtain the services of a war fleet to blockade the Gironde. But the Castilian King, John II, had allowed him to hire six carracks in the ports of northern Castile with some 600 soldiers on board. Another six large vessels were hired in La Rochelle. Jean Bureau supplied a galley and other oared vessels. French spies were active around the Gironde. Arnaud-Amanieu d'Orval reported that there were no signs in the Bordelais that reinforcements were expected from England. The captain of Dieppe had ships cruising along the south coast of England looking for signs of a fleet of transports. Jacques Coeur's agents were picking up gossip in English towns. From these sources the French ministers probably learned about the disorder in England and the problems of Lord Rivers's army.[10]

The great council at Tours approved the plans for an immediate invasion of Guyenne. They hoped to complete the conquest before

Rivers's army could get there. The strategy was the same as in Normandy – to attack from several directions at once in order to stretch the thin English defences to breaking point. The Count of Dunois was put in command of 4,600 men available at short notice from the *compagnies d'ordonnance* and the *francs-archers*. The retinues of the nobility of the centre and north would take longer to recruit, and were expected to join them in the course of the campaign. Dunois himself intended to advance directly on Bordeaux from the north through the open plain of Saintonge. A second army, operating independently, would be recruited in Languedoc and advance down the valley of the Garonne under the command of the Count of Armagnac. A third would attack from the south across the Landes under the lord of Albret and the Count of Foix. At the height of the campaign, Dunois expected to have about 20,000 men under arms divided between the three fronts. An elaborate commissariat was created to supply the army by sea.[11]

According to Dunois's intelligence, Sir Gadifer Shorthose had only about 2,500 men with which to meet these threats. Apart from about 200 to 300 English archers, they were all Gascons recruited from the citizenry of Bordeaux or retained by the few noblemen whom he could still count on. They were concentrated in the critical region around Bordeaux. The defence of this region depended on the network of waterways east of the city: the lower reaches of the Dordogne and the Garonne and the broad estuary of the Gironde into which both rivers flowed (*Map VI*). On the north side of the Gironde and the Dordogne stood a line of English strongholds comprising the walled towns of Blaye, Bourg, Libourne and Castillon, and the fortress of Fronsac outside Libourne. All of these places were accessible by boat from Bordeaux, enabling troops and supplies to be transferred easily between them. The system had proved its worth in 1406–7 when Louis of Orléans had adopted the direct line of attack across Saintonge but had been stopped at the water's edge.

Shorthose established his headquarters at Blaye. He had with him the leading Gascon noblemen and about 800 men. In addition, five large armed merchant ships had been requisitioned in Bordeaux to hold off the French fleet in the Gironde. Further south, in the valley of the Garonne, Gascon garrisons guarded the river approaches to Bordeaux at Rions and Saint-Macaire. In the south, however, the duchy was completely exposed. The river Adour had traditionally been its main line of defence, but almost all the principal fortresses and crossings of the river except Dax were now in French hands. The English commander in this sector was George Swillington, the squire whose resolute defence of La Réole had saved Bordeaux in 1442. Since then, he had prospered mightily by the defections of the Gascon nobility, building up a large portfolio of confiscated property, joining the royal council at Bordeaux and becoming one of the most influential figures in the duchy. In 1451, Swillington was mayor of Bayonne and captain of Dax. Dunois reported to the King, probably on the basis of prisoner interrogations, that the English plan was to delay the French for up to four months, long enough for Rivers's army to reach them from England. But the odds were heavily stacked against them. French morale was high. They had an overwhelming superiority of numbers, a much larger fleet and Jean Bureau's powerful artillery train.[12]

Dunois opened his campaign in April 1451. His army mustered at Tours and appeared outside the castle of Montguyon in Saintonge on about 28 April. Montguyon, the only significant garrisoned fortress held by the Anglo-Gascons beyond the Gironde towns, stood across Dunois's line of supply, and could not be left intact in his rear. The captain held out for a week before opening his gates and withdrawing with his men to join Shorthose's forces on the Gironde. The first French troops, commanded by Charles of Anjou, had already reached Blaye. Dunois joined them with the main body of his army on 15 May. Almost immediately, the English lost control of the vital waterway. Jean le Boursier's French fleet bore down on Shorthose's five ships anchored off Blaye. After a bloody fight the English ships were forced to withdraw upstream into the Garonne with the enemy in pursuit, until they reached safety in Bordeaux.

The French ships returned to blockade Blaye from the river, while their army dug trenches around the town on the landward side. Within a week, Bureau's artillery had reduced the walls and gates of Blaye to rubble. On the night of 22 May, the French assaulted the town at dusk. The Anglo-Gascons were thrown back with heavy losses and the French took possession of the streets. Shorthose withdrew into the citadel with his garrison. He quickly decided that with the citadel subject to bombardment from the town and cut off from Bordeaux by Le Boursier's ships, further resistance was hopeless. He opened negotiations on the following morning, 23 May. He had very little to bargain with and the terms were correspondingly tough. The garrison were promised their lives, but all of them had to surrender as prisoners of war, including Shorthose himself, his deputy, and all the Gascon noblemen who were with him. None of them was to be ransomed or paroled unless he agreed to deliver up his own strongholds to Dunois's officers and undertook not to fight for the King of England before September. The citadel of Blaye opened its gates to the French that very day.[13]

The fall of Blaye led to the rapid collapse of the whole of the defensive line east of Bordeaux. The principal English officer in the duchy had been taken prisoner along with a third of his forces. Bordeaux, without its mayor or his deputy, was leaderless. Some of the Gascon lords who had surrendered at Blaye resolved to switch sides. Pierre de Montferrand, Soudan de la Trau, had married an illegitimate daughter of the Duke of Bedford and had been among the firmest pillars of the English duchy. Captured at Blaye, he bought his freedom and escaped a ransom by swearing allegiance to Charles VII and promising to surrender five of his castles, 'not knowing how else to save his lands and lordships, just like many other nobles', as he put it when excusing himself later to Henry VI. Bourg, at the confluence of the Dordogne and the Garonne where Louis of Orléans had come to grief in 1407, surrendered after a perfunctory resistance at the end of May. Pierre de Montferrand's cousin Bérard, who was in command there, seems to have had his hand forced by the townsfolk, whose terror mounted as they watched the artillery being set up and the trenches getting closer. He was allowed to withdraw with his entire garrison to Bordeaux. Bourg opened its gates as soon as he had left. Libourne and Saint-Émilion, neither of which had a professional garrison, surrendered as soon as the French heralds appeared before the gates. At Fronsac, reputedly the strongest fortress in Gascony, the garrison clung to the hope that Rivers's army might still appear in time to save them. On 5 June they sealed a conditional surrender agreement providing for the place to be delivered up to the French if no army of relief had reached them by 23 June.[14]

The Count of Dunois established his headquarters at Bourg, and his army remained on the right bank of the Dordogne and the Gironde. It was left to the two other French armies to roll up the English duchy from the south. The lord of Albret and the Count of Foix advanced to the Adour and laid siege to Dax at the end of May. By the end of the first week of June, the Adour had been blocked downstream, the stores were nearly exhausted and the walls of Dax had been breached in several places. It was only a matter of time before the place fell.

Meanwhile, the Count of Armagnac was sweeping through the valley of the Garonne encountering no resistance. Duras and Sauveterre-de-Guyenne surrendered in quick succession. In the second week of June Armagnac laid siege to Saint-Macaire and Rions, the last walled places still in Anglo-Gascon hands before Bordeaux.[15]

Inside Bordeaux, the royal council lost control to the leading citizens and the Gascon noblemen in the city. They were preparing to give up the fight. The main movers were Gaston de Grailly Captal de Buch, the richest and most influential landowner of the Bordelais; Bertrand IV de Montferrand, the head of a powerful family whose domains were concentrated in Saintonge and the valley of the Isle; and Gaillard de Durfort lord of Duras, a prominent landowner of the Garonne valley and the Médoc. These men represented families which had supported the English regime through thick and thin for generations. All of them had lost everything they possessed to the advancing French except for their mansions in the city. There were also newer men: Pey Berland the Archbishop of Bordeaux, and Bernard Angevin the rich and ambitious president of the duchy's appeal court. Gadifer Shorthose, who had been paroled by the French, came to join them. He had probably earned his release by secretly promising to throw in his lot with his French captors. These men constituted themselves as the Estates of Guyenne. They resolved to negotiate a surrender which would preserve as much as possible of the privileged position which they had enjoyed under English rule. The initial approach was made by the Captal. He obtained a safe-conduct to visit the Count of Foix, who was his nephew, in the siege lines outside Dax. The Count referred him to Dunois. Negotiations were opened in Bordeaux. A Gascon negotiating committee was formed, led by the Archbishop and Bertrand de Montferrand, while in the background the English duchy was collapsing about their ears. Their opposite numbers were Poton de Saintrailles and Jean Bureau, who took their instructions from Dunois. He was prepared to make substantial concessions to avoid what might have been a long siege.

Terms were finally sealed on 12 June. Bordeaux agreed to surrender to the Count of Dunois on 23 June, the same day as Fronsac, unless by then they had been relieved by Lord Rivers. The negotiators agreed to procure the provisional surrender of four places that were still holding out, Rions, Saint-Macaire and Blagnac in the Garonne valley and Castillon on the Dordogne. These places were to open their gates at once but would be restored to the English if Bordeaux was relieved. Those who were unwilling to swear allegiance to Charles VII were to have six months to arrange their affairs and leave for England with whatever movable goods they could carry. English royal grants would be recognised. The customs of the duchy as they had grown up over three centuries of English rule would be observed. Bordeaux would retain all of the extensive privileges against royal taxation which it had hitherto enjoyed.

By now few people can have expected Rivers's army to appear, but the customary rituals were observed. On 23 June the French army stood in battle array outside the walls of Bordeaux from dawn to dusk. As the sun went down, an English herald climbed onto the walls and cried out, 'Relief for Bordeaux from England?' No answer came. A similar ceremony was played out at Fronsac. Dax had already agreed to surrender on the same terms as Bordeaux and opened its gates to the French a fortnight later.[16]

On 30 June 1451, a week after his officers had taken possession of Bordeaux, the Count of Dunois made his formal entry into the city. It was a theatrical demonstration of French power in a city which had been part of the inheritance of the Kings of England for so long. Between eighty and a hundred ships gathered at Blaye to carry the ranking dignitaries and some 7,000 troops across the Gironde. They formed up in the suburb of the Chartrons north of the walls. Outside the Porte Saint-Germain, a herald summoned the *jurats* (or councillors), who appeared carrying the keys of the city. These were presented to Dunois. He passed them to Jean Bureau, who had been nominated as mayor by the conquerors. The procession passed through the narrow streets of the city to the cathedral in the baking sun. A corps of liveried archers came first, followed by the Lombard mercenary Teodoro di Valperga, who acted as chief marshal. Then came the Marshals of France with their retinues, the Counts of Armagnac and Nevers at the head of several hundred dismounted men-at-arms who had been at the siege of Rions, followed by the officials and judges of the new order. Behind them the heralds and trumpeters, wearing the armorial tunics of their masters, gave way to the great seal of the King of France, carried on a bed of velvet in an open coffer on the saddle of a white horse, richly caparisoned in blue and velvet spangled with fleurs-delys. The Chancellor of France Guillaume Juvénal des Ursins followed behind. Poton de Saintrailles and his nephew came next, carrying

Charles VII's banner, followed by the solitary figure of the Count of Dunois in full plate armour, mounted on a white charger. The Counts of Angoulême, Clermont, Vendôme and Castres with their liveried pages took up the rear with the remaining troops. In front of the cathedral, they were received by the Archbishop and the canons with the relics of their church, and by the leading citizens and nobles of the Bordelais.[17]

Dunois's triumph was not entirely complete, for Bayonne, the duchy's second city, had refused to be bound by the treaty with Bordeaux. Bayonne had always enjoyed a greater degree of autonomy than other Gascon towns and showed every sign of intending to hold out. In addition to the armed citizens, the Bayonnais had the English company of George Swillington and a large band of Navarrese mercenaries under the command of Jean de Beaumont, a prince of the cadet branch of the royal house of Navarre. The continuing resistance of the city posed a serious problem for the French because the danger of intervention by a seaborne army from England was not yet over. Eighty-one large transports were lying in Plymouth harbour ready to embark Rivers's army. Some 3,000 men were waiting by the shore for their advances. Payments to the seamen finally began on 18 July, but the money for the men was not found until 9 August, when some £26,000 was paid out. Finding these sums had required a good deal of barrel-scraping. Some of the cash had been raised by selling the King's jewels. The rest was advanced by the treasurers of the income tax and the taxes on the Church.[18]

Within a week of the money being released the Gascon expedition was cancelled. The reason seems to have been a sudden panic about the security of Calais. Charles VII had recently asked the Duke of Burgundy to mount an attack on Calais in order to draw English forces away from other theatres. It seems likely that the English council, which had plenty of informants in Flanders, had picked up reports of this approach, because early in August, they suddenly decided that an attack on the town was imminent. A thousand men were raised in London by the mayor and the Staple merchants. They sailed from Sandwich at once. Ralph Lord Sudeley and Sir John Stourton were directed to follow them with another 1,150 men. Many of those sent to Calais must have been taken from Rivers's army. Certainly nothing more is heard of the expedition to Gascony. Rivers's fleet never left Plymouth, and some months later he too was redirected to Calais.

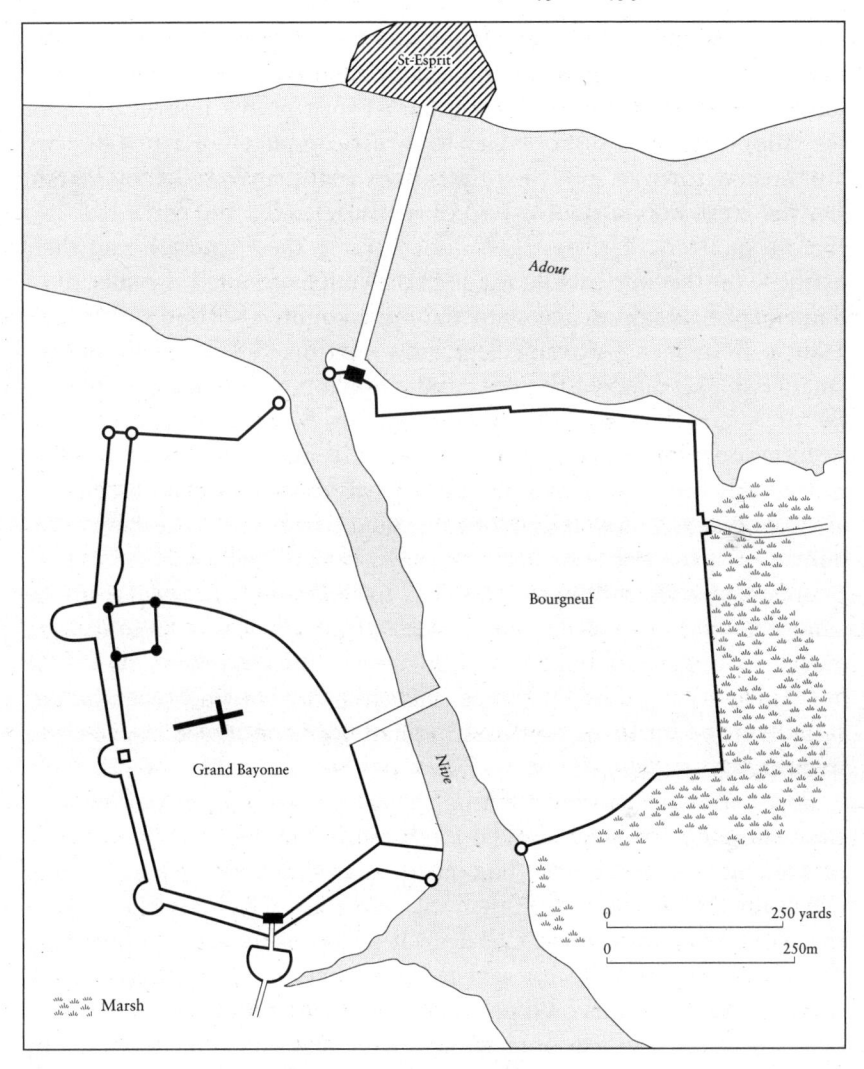

14 The siege of Bayonne, August 1451

In fact, the panic had been unnecessary. Philip the Good's relations with England at this stage were difficult, but he had no desire to see the power of Charles VII installed on his borders. He replied to Charles VII's appeal with a curt refusal.[19]

On 6 August 1451, the Count of Dunois and Gaston de Foix arrived before Bayonne with some 4,400 men and an artillery train directed by Gaspard Bureau. They were shortly joined by more troops under the lord of Albret. Bayonne was situated on the south side of the Adour at its confluence with the river Nive. A long timber bridge joined the town to the suburb of Saint-Esprit on the opposite side of the Adour. It was a difficult city to invest completely. East of the city lay the new town, a suburb with its own walls, surrounded by marsh. On the west side, a double line of walls defended the cathedral and the old quarters. The besiegers concentrated their strength and their artillery on the west, while the lord of Albret occupied the suburb of Saint-Esprit, blocking access to the open country beyond the bridge. Jean le Boursier's Castilian fleet, now reinforced with a number of smaller ships, occupied the river and closed off the opening to the sea. By 18 August, the courage of the besiegers had failed. They opened negotiations with the French captains. Agreement was finally reached in the early hours of the 20th. The city was made to pay an indemnity of 40,000 *écus* (later reduced by the King to 20,000). The Bayonnais agreed to surrender their Navarrese and other foreign mercenaries as prisoners of war. Swillington's English troops were only saved from the same fate because the Bayonnais were afraid that their large trading stocks in England would be seized to pay their ransoms. With the surrender of Bayonne, the entire English duchy was in French hands. It had existed for three centuries but had been conquered in just three months.[20]

For many of those watching, Dunois's grandiose entries into Bordeaux and Bayonne marked a traumatic change. The small group of men at Bordeaux who had negotiated the surrender agreement exemplified the dilemmas of their age and class. They were faced with the choice of submission to Charles VII or the loss of all their domains. Two days after putting his seal to the surrender treaty, Bertrand de Montferrand made his own personal agreement with Dunois, in which he reserved the right to fight with Lord Rivers's army if it arrived by 23 June but promised to swear allegiance to Charles VII if it did not. Prominent councillors of the French King were already circling round Gaillard de Durfort's choicer properties when he finally did homage to Charles VII after three months of agonising. It must have seemed an obvious choice, but not everyone made it. Gaston de Grailly, Captal de Buch, and his son Jean de Grailly Viscount of Castillon were both Knights of the Garter. Jean also held an English peerage as Earl of Kendal. They negotiated a complicated agreement with Dunois under which the lands of both men were sold to the Count of Foix for 15,000 *écus*. They were then settled on Jean's three-year-old son, who was placed in the Count's household to be brought up as a loyal Frenchman. Gaston and Jean had been great figures at Bordeaux, but left Gascony to settle in Aragon. The same choice was made by many humbler men. Some of Jean de Grailly's councillors abandoned their own Gascon lands to follow him to Aragon.[21]

Others left for England. At any one time there were usually many Gascons in England on political, legal or commercial business. These men were trapped when the duchy fell to the French. An English royal proclamation announced that anyone returning from England to Gascony or trying to trade with the region would be regarded as a traitor. They were eventually required to appear in person before the council to explain their intentions and apply for licences. Pey du Tasta had been in England as a delegate of the Estates of Guyenne since 1449 and had been detained there ever since, waiting for assurances from the council about its plans for the duchy. He joined the King's council as an expert on Gascon affairs and never returned home. A number of Gascon merchants, mainly in the wine trade, did the same, managing their businesses from London. A few Englishmen in the duchy faced the same dilemma the other way round. The most notable defector was Gadifer Shorthose. After nearly forty years in south-western France, he probably had nothing to go back to in England. He stayed behind and submitted to Charles VII. He accepted a pension from the French Treasury and was released from his parole without ransom in recognition of his role in the surrender of Bordeaux. The Yorkshireman Robert Rokeley, who had been captain of the castle of Lesparre in the Médoc at the time of the French conquest and was still peacefully in possession a year later, had probably made the same decision.[22]

The conquest of Guyenne was not as traumatic for the English as the loss of Normandy. Although the Kings of England had held Guyenne for much longer, their English subjects had never settled there in great numbers. They did not maintain a large military establishment in Gascony, as they did in Normandy. Nor did the defence of Gascony have the same implications for the security of England itself.

The main source of tension during the winter of 1451–2 was the perceived threat to Calais. The English council had called the threat too early in the summer. But once the campaign in Gascony was over, it was real enough. From Saint-Maixent, the Florentine ambassador

Angelo Acciaiuoli reported to the Council of Ten in November on his audiences with Charles VII in the vast and uncomfortable castle of Villedieu nearby. The French King, he said, was already making detailed plans for the siege of Calais. The talk at his court was of a campaign on a vast scale to be opened in March. Artillery was being assembled. Ships were being hired in Castile, the Low Countries and the Hanse ports of Germany. Travelling across France from Lyon to Poitou, Acciaiuoli saw soldiers on the move everywhere.[23]

These preparations did not pass unnoticed in England. The council received regular reports from friends and spies on the continent. From these sources, they learned that after the false alarm of the previous year the King of France was preparing to invade the pale of Calais 'with as great a puissance as any was assembled in France for many years and devices of war as any man hath seen'. The English believed that a successful attack on the town would be followed by a full-scale invasion across the Channel. Along the south and east coasts local men were being arrayed for coastguard duty and warning beacons were being built on hilltops. At one point, Henry VI's ministers even proposed to send an army to Calais under the nominal command of the King himself. But Charles VII was probably right when he remarked to Acciaiuoli that Henry himself would gladly have given up Calais for the sake of peace if it was left to him. Henry's problem, he added, was that he was too frightened of his own people.[24]

Henry had good reason to be frightened, for the Duke of York seized the opportunity of the rising chaos to make a second bid for power. In the autumn of 1451, York had 2,000 men under arms in the Welsh marches. His allies in the West Country, led by the Earl of Devon, were arming. Appeals for support had been sent out to other allies in East Anglia and the Midlands. 'What are we to say of the state of England,' wrote one of Bishop Beckington's correspondents, 'its people and its rulers divided and the land threatened with invasion by the French, the Scots and other nations.' In February 1452, Richard of York advanced on London, gathering support as he went. He issued a manifesto addressed to the principal towns of England, which was calculated to exploit the current mood of shame and fear.

I suppose it is well known unto you, as well by experience as by common language said and reported throughout all Christendom, what land, what worship, honour and manhood was ascribed of all nations unto the people of this realm whilst the kingdom's sovereign lord stood possessed of his lordship in the realm of France and duchy of Normandy; and what derogation, loss of merchandise, lesion of honour and villainy is said and reported unto the English nation for loss of the same, [especially] unto the Duke of Somerset when he had the commandance and charge thereof. The which loss hath caused and encouraged the King's enemies for to conquer and get Gascony and Guyenne and now daily they make their advance for to lay siege unto Calais ... and so for to come into the land with great puissance.

He declared his intention of unseating the Duke of Somerset, 'seeing that the said Duke ever prevaileth and ruleth about the King's person'. He called on his followers to join him with 'as many goodly and likely men as ye may make to execute the intent abovesaid'.[25]

The Duke of York's second attempt to unseat Henry VI's ministers failed like the first. The government had resolved not to call Parliament in the current mood of the country, in spite of its desperate need for money. At a great council held at Westminster in January 1452, the peerage closed ranks, as they had done the year before. The Londoners had been York's strongest allies in 1450, but in 1452 the city corporation complied with a royal command to close their gates against him. The Duke crossed the Thames at Kingston and passed into Kent, where he expected to find mass support. But Kent, after the tumults and repression of 1450, was quiescent. The King had assembled a large army from the county levies and the retainers and followers of loyal peers. At the beginning of March, they encamped on Blackheath, and from there advanced to Welling, barring York's road to the capital. York's army approached as far as Dartford, five miles away, where they stopped and were arrayed in battle order. A delegation from the King's army crossed to the opposing lines to negotiate. The Duke of York presented them with his articles of accusation against the Duke of Somerset. They were mainly directed to Somerset's conduct of the war. York held him personally responsible for the loss of Normandy which, he said, had alone made possible the French conquest of Gascony. He accused Somerset of having obtained full compensation for his own losses in Maine while embezzling the funds intended to compensate others. Turning to the current situation, he denounced Somerset's recent appointment as captain of Calais. Somerset's real design, York suggested, was to sell Calais to the Duke of Burgundy, just as he had sold Normandy to the King of France.

The Duke of York put his case very high, but the outcome was an embarrassing climb-down. The charges against the Duke of Somerset were referred to a commission of arbitrators packed with Somerset's allies, which never made an award. York himself was obliged to swear a humiliating public oath at St Paul's cathedral in London, acknowledging the error of his ways. He was then banished to his estates. Most of his followers were pardoned, but not before they had endured show trials and, in some cases, long periods of imprisonment. The unrest provoked by York's rebellion persisted for the remainder of the year, surfacing in plots and occasional local risings, all of which were firmly put down. The Duke of Somerset was already securely in control when two developments in the war with France relieved the pressure on him. One was the abandonment by the French King of his plans for an attack on Calais and the lifting of the threat of invasion. The other, a more dramatic and unexpected turn of events, was the recovery of much of Gascony.[26]

Charles VII had been drawn, like so many French rulers before and after him, by the lure of Italy. During the wars with England, the once powerful position of France in the Italian peninsula had collapsed. The princes of the house of Anjou had been expelled from Naples by the Aragonese. Genoa, for years a French protectorate, had shaken free. Fortuitously, tensions between the leading Italian states opened up fresh opportunities for French intervention in Italy at the very moment that Charles VII had completed the conquest of the English territories in France. In February 1452, the French King had concluded a military alliance with Florence and Milan, old enemies who had been thrown together by the aggressive expansion of the Republic of Venice in the east and the Aragonese kingdom of Naples in the south. In May, just three months after the treaty had been sealed, Charles was called on to honour it when war broke out between the two allies and Venice. Over the summer months, he began to concentrate his forces at Lyon with a view to invading Savoy and northern Italy. Plans to besiege Calais were first deferred and then shelved. The sudden lifting of the threat allowed the English to reassign the forces assembled for its defence. Towards the end of June 1452, the council decided to send Sir John Talbot to Gascony with an army of 5,000 men to reconquer Gascony. That old freebooter Sir Roger Camoys was directed to accompany him as the new Seneschal.[27]

The inspiration for the last military campaign of the Hundred Years War came from the small group of Gascon exiles gathered around Pey du Tasta in London. Some of them had arrived in England with Pey as part of his delegation. They were joined after the fall of Bordeaux by others who arrived in England with every intention of returning to their homes with an English army. In the spring of 1452, these men made contact with prominent Gascon noblemen, including the Captal de Buch and his son in Aragon and Pierre de Montferrand in Bordeaux, who pledged their support for a campaign of reconquest. At some point, a delegation of unnamed Gascons travelled to England to add their own voices to those of the London-based exiles.[28]

We cannot know how widely shared the attitude of these conspirators was, but they could not have succeeded as well as they did without a large measure of support in Gascony. The Gascons had a strong sense of regional identity, reinforced by political and commercial links with England which had endured for centuries. Their attitudes to England were practical rather than emotional. The attraction of English rule was that it was distant and weak, which allowed them a high degree of autonomy. The English government in the duchy had never been more than marginally English. The principal officers were Englishmen, but their councillors, judges and officials were all native Gascons. The French government which succeeded it looked more like an occupying power than the English had ever done. The Count of Clermont was Charles VII's lieutenant in Guyenne and the young Breton knight Olivier de Coëtivy became Seneschal. Jean Bureau was appointed mayor of Bordeaux and Jean le Boursier mayor of Bayonne. All of these men had been prominent commanders in the French reconquest and were very obviously northerners. They were insensitive and brash. During their frequent absences, their work was done by younger men of the same kind.

It was harder for the French to accommodate Gascon particularism than it had been for the English. The ideology of the French reconquest depended on an exalted view of the unifying role of the Crown. The Norman bishop and sometime royal councillor Thomas Basin thought that Charles's ministers 'resented the independence of the Gascons and covertly sought to reduce them to the same state of servitude as other provinces'. There was some force in this view. The French tried to bully the saintly and popular Pey Berland Archbishop of Bordeaux into resigning his see, and when eventually he did resign he was replaced by an Auvergnat with a long career in royal service in Paris. The garrisons, which had previously been overwhelmingly Gascon, were neither large nor numerous, but they were now French. Apart from duties on wine, taxation had previously depended on the consent of the Estates and had generally been low. In the rest of France, however, the government now imposed *aides* and *tailles* by executive order and had come to regard this as a prerogative of the Crown. Charles VII was determined that the same principle must apply to Gascony. The tax burden rose significantly. When a delegation of the Estates of the duchy appeared at the French court to protest, they were sent packing. Many Gascons must have felt like Bernard Georges of Bordeaux, one of the lesser conspirators who was later arrested by the French. He told his interrogators that he had joined the rebellion because 'did not want to be French', but it was clear that he had no emotional attachment to the English either. When asked why he had not migrated to England like some of his fellow citizens, he replied that he did not want to live in England and would not like the beer.[29]

At sixty-five, Talbot was an old man by the standards of the time. He had lost much of the energy and skill which had once marked him out from other English captains. French soldiers noticed that he was no longer comfortable on a war-horse and rode a small hackney on campaign. They thought him 'aged and worn out'. But Talbot was at the height of his reputation in England. His aggressive instincts in Normandy stood out by comparison with the flaccid generalship of the Duke of Somerset. In the eyes of the popular pamphleteers and handbill writers he was still 'Talbot our good dog'. His army was expected to be ready within three weeks of his appointment, by 17 July. This was thought to be realistic because most of the men who were to take part were already under arms. Talbot himself, who indented for 3,000 men, had been engaged since March to defend the seas around Calais against the French. He already had a fleet of requisitioned ships based in the ports of Kent and the Thames estuary, and a large complement of seamen and soldiers to man them. Gervase Clifton, the Treasurer of Calais, and Sir Edward Hull, still nominally Constable of Bordeaux, each indented for another 1,000 men. At least some of their companies are likely to have been withdrawn from the garrison of Calais and from men assigned to the defence of Jersey. The rest were drawn to Talbot's banner by his reputation, something which no other English captain could have achieved at the time. In the parlous state of English public finance, unusual arrangements had to be made for funding these men's wages. Talbot and his fellow captains agreed to serve for the first three months for a lump sum fee which was a small fraction of the remuneration normally payable. They probably expected to recoup themselves by taxing the Gascons when they got there.[30]

The destination of Talbot's army was kept secret for as long as possible. It was coyly described as being intended for the keeping of the sea and the defence of 'our land'. But it became increasingly obvious that Gascony was the destination. A large number of grants of offices, lands and revenue in Gascony were made to Gascon supporters in London or Bordeaux in the expectation that the duchy's English administration would shortly be restored. The mask finally dropped on 1 September, when Talbot was appointed as the King's lieutenant in Gascony. In the event the new lieutenant's embarkation was delayed by the need for additional shipping for the long passage around Finistère and across the Bay of Biscay. His fleet of about a hundred ships did not sail until the end of September. But the secret was maintained to the end, The French only learned about the expedition a few days before it sailed, and they believed that its destination was Normandy. Arthur de Richemont, the governor of the province, responded to the news by taking command in the Cotentin and Lower Normandy while the Count of Dunois, based at Dieppe, was given responsibility for the Caux. Artillery was released from the arsenal in Paris and brought downriver to Rouen. Meanwhile there were very few French troops in Gascony. The only recorded garrisons were at Bordeaux, Bayonne and Dax. Poton de Saintrailles at Bordeaux had just seventy men. The Count of Clermont had a personal retinue of sixty to eighty bowmen.[31]

The arrival of Talbot's fleet in the Gironde on 20 October 1452 took the French completely by surprise. The English landed in the Médoc north of Bordeaux. The Count of Clermont, who was staying nearby, was very nearly captured and had to flee across the river to Bourg leaving his baggage behind him. On the night of 21 October, the English arrived outside the walls of Bordeaux and made their way along the strand between the walls and the river. Pierre de Montferrand had assembled about 300 citizens in the Salnières quarter in the south of the city. They seized one of the river gates, the Porte de Beyssac, and broke it open to let in the English. The French woke up to find the enemy in possession of the whole city. The *bailli* Olivier de Coëtivy was arrested in his lodgings. Most of the garrison was captured.[32]

Charles VII was in Forez with his army, heading for Lyon. He received the news on about 27 October in the fortified priory of

Pommiers, where he was preparing to meet the Duke of Savoy. His council was hurriedly convened. They were shocked and angry. The King declared that he would not rest until Guyenne had been reconquered and the men responsible for this breach of faith punished. The Marshal Philippe de Culant and Arnaud-Amanieu d'Orval were ordered to take 2,400 men of the *compagnies d'ordonnance* and make at once for the Gironde to garrison the walled places around Bordeaux, pending the arrival of a much larger army in the spring. They were too late. Within three days of occupying Bordeaux, Talbot had moved out of the city and begun his advance up the Garonne. Rions was occupied on 25 October, Saint-Macaire on 2 November and Langon two days later on the 4th. Within a short time, the English were in possession of most of the Bordelais. In December, Gervase Clifton moved into the lower valley of the Dordogne with 400 men, occupying Libourne, Saint-Émilion and Castillon on Christmas Day (*Map VI*).[33]

In spite of these spectacular successes, Talbot faced serious problems, strategic and financial. He had not succeeded in taking the vital fortresses on the east side of the Gironde. The Count of Clermont was firmly ensconced in Bourg and had garrisoned Blaye and Fronsac. He was strongly reinforced in February when Philippe de Culant and Arnaud-Amanieu d'Orval finally arrived with their troops. From the Gironde towns, the French were able to block access to Bordeaux from the sea and the movement of troops and supplies by water between Bordeaux and the castles of the Dordogne. Talbot made no attempt to reoccupy any of the towns in the south of the duchy, in the Landes and the Adour valley. With much of his army already tied down in garrisons, he was unwilling to spread himself too thinly. The awful warning of Normandy must have haunted him. He kept about 3,800 men, three-quarters of his army, in the field. They were joined by the Gascon retainers of the great anglophile lords of the Bordelais who had previously submitted to Charles VII. Pierre de Montferrand Soudan de la Trau summoned his followers and urged his extensive network of allies and clients to do the same. The Captal de Buch, now getting on in years, stayed in Aragon, but his son Jean de Grailly, Viscount of Castillon and Earl of Kendal, returned to Gascony and joined the English army with his followers. Some families were divided. Gaillard de Durfort, the head of his house, was with the conspirators in Bordeaux when the English arrived and put his great fortress of Blanquefort in the Médoc at their disposal.

But his uncle, Aimeric de Durfort, held his castle at Duras against him and fought in the ranks of the French. Even with the support of the Gascon lords of the Bordelais, Talbot's numbers were far short of what he would need to confront the inevitable French counterattack in the spring. He also needed to find a way of paying his army if it was to be prevented from disintegrating and looting the Gascons. Shortly after his arrival, Talbot summoned the Estates of Gascony to Bordeaux and persuaded them to grant him an *aide*. But he lacked the administrative machinery to collect it outside Bordeaux itself. That left him with the wine customs, traditionally the main source of Gascon revenues. They held up quite well by the poor standards of recent years but covered barely a third of the cost of the army. Talbot and his fellow captains were obliged to borrow on their own credit to pay their troops.[34]

At Westminster, the council was acutely aware of Talbot's weakness. In December 1452 they decided to send another army to Gascony in the spring. They sent commissioners into the counties to borrow the money to pay for it. Reports of Talbot's initial success aroused much enthusiasm among both recruits and lenders. By the end of January, nearly £8,000 had been raised, and Talbot's son John Viscount Lisle had indented to serve as captain of the new army, with 2,420 men. They finally sailed from Plymouth early in April 1453. Their arrival in Gascony towards the end of that month brought the total strength of Talbot's army to over 7,300 men, the largest English army to fight in Gascony for more than a century. It enabled Talbot to besiege and capture Fronsac and to close his grip on the lower valley of the Dordogne.[35]

The Parliament which opened at Reading on 6 March 1453 was one of the most compliant of Henry's reign. Having seen off the challenge from the Duke of York, suppressed the revolts in the counties and fought the first successful campaign in France for twenty years, the government was in a self-confident mood. In the first session, which lasted until the end of the month, the Commons voted a full standard subsidy and increased the rate of the wool duty. They also agreed in principle to an ambitious government scheme to conscript up to 20,000 archers for service at the expense of the counties. This scheme, if it had been implemented, would have given England an army comparable in size to France's new army. However, by the time that Parliament reassembled at Westminster after the Easter recess the government had become nervous about the threat to Talbot's position in Gascony and had decided that a third army would have to be sent there urgently. The council could not wait for the details of the levy of archers to be agreed and the necessary notice to be given to the counties. So, after much negotiation, the levy was deferred for two years, until 1455, in return for a further half-subsidy. But these arrangements were not agreed until the beginning of July. The council set about borrowing against the new tax as soon as it had been granted. Letters were sent to potential lenders in insistent terms. Some of those who declined were summoned before the council to explain themselves. By 16 July over £10,000 had been borrowed, more than enough to pay the advances of the new army. By 25 July, indentures had been sealed for 2,200 men, but it had been necessary to scrape the barrel to find them. The designated captain, William Fiennes Lord Saye, was a young man in his mid-twenties with no known military experience.[36]

The delay proved to be fatal. By the time that Lord Saye and his companions had sealed their indentures, the long-awaited French counterattack in the south-west had begun. It opened at the beginning of June 1453. The plan of campaign was similar to the one adopted in 1451. The main offensive was conducted by the two marshals, André de Laval and Philippe de Culant. They came down the Dordogne valley with between 6,000 and 7,000 men. They were accompanied by Jean and Gaspard Bureau and their artillery and by some 700 pioneers. The three great southern feudatories, Foix, Armagnac and Albret, came up from the south with nearly 3,000 more, including the company of the Italian captain Teodoro de Valperga. The King himself advanced from the north, through Saintonge. A fourth force, under the Count of Clermont, had been based on the east shore of the Gironde since the winter. The Count crossed the waterway into the Médoc with some 2,000 men and began systematically to lay waste to the land north of Bordeaux. Between them the four armies came to more than 12,000 men. A fleet of ships requisitioned in Normandy, Brittany and Flanders was assembling at La Rochelle to blockade the Gironde.[37]

Talbot's only hope in the face of the gathering strength of the enemy was to defeat the separate enemy armies in detail before they could join forces. His problem was the Count of Clermont's army in the Médoc. Clermont's strength doubled when he was joined in the third week of June by the Counts of Foix and Armagnac and the lord of Albret. Their combined forces, about 4,000 strong, represented a serious threat to

Bordeaux. Talbot was reluctant to leave the capital uncovered and was under strong pressure from its inhabitants to remain in the city with his army. On 21 June, he tried to confront Clermont's army in the Médoc but then, with uncharacteristic hesitation, backed off rather than risk a battle. This enterprise cost him several hundred casualties, as the unmounted English archers retreated across the marshes to Bordeaux pursued by French cavalrymen.[38]

On 14 July 1453, the French began two major sieges on the same day. Clermont and the three Gascon lords invested the castle of Castelnau-de-Médoc, some twenty miles north of Bordeaux. At the opposite end of the theatre, the French Marshals laid siege to Castillon with the army of the Dordogne. Talbot decided to attack the Marshals' army outside Castillon, although it was further away and substantially larger than the Count of Clermont's. His intelligence may have been faulty. But it would have been characteristic of him to attack the larger army whose defeat would have a bigger impact on the campaign. The decision aroused strong protests from the men of Bordeaux, but Talbot was unmoved. The Seneschal Sir Roger Camoys was left in command in the city with 1,650 English troops. The rest formed the kernel of Talbot's field army. He made up the numbers by calling on his Gascon allies and stripping troops from the other towns and castles under his control. On the morning of 16 July he marched out of Bordeaux, heading for Castillon. French estimates, which are broadly in line with English records, put Talbot's strength at 6,000 to 7,000 men, about the same as the army of the French Marshals. At least 1,500 of them were Gascons fighting under his two leading Gascon allies Pierre de Montferrand and Jean de Grailly. The rest were English.[39]

Castillon had belonged to the Graillys for two centuries. It was a small walled town on the north bank of the Dordogne dominated from its eastern end by a large and ancient fortress, the last traces of which were swept away at the beginning of the nineteenth century. In July 1453 it was defended by an English garrison commanded by Gervase Clifton. But before that it had not been garrisoned for many years and its defences were in bad repair. Part of the walls had recently collapsed. Castillon was the first of three places on the river which the French had to capture if their artillery was to be brought by water before Bordeaux. The French captains were expecting an attempt to relieve the town. In accordance with a system developed by the Bureau brothers, their pioneers had prepared a large fortified enclosure in the plain east of the town, out of artillery range from the walls and protected by deep trenches, field works and artillery. Talbot sent out scouts to reconnoitre their positions during the night. Remarkably, they did not notice these works.

On 17 July, the Anglo-Gascon army appeared on the heights above Castillon at about nine o'clock in the morning with banners flying. The French had already begun to withdraw into their fortified enclosure and were forming up behind the trenches in battle array. Descending the wooded slopes onto the plain around the town, the English fell on the walled enclosure of the priory of St Florent. The priory was occupied by the *francs-archers* of Anjou and Berry. They had not seen the Anglo-Gascons' approach and fled in disorder towards the fortified enclosure. It was dry and hot. The movements of both armies had raised a haze of dust over the plain. Talbot, seeing the mass of men moving east in the opaque sunlight believed that he had the whole French army on the run. He gathered his cavalry, about 1,000 men, and charged the fleeing men on horseback, leaving the infantry and archers to follow on foot. The horsemen cut down several hundred of them before realising that they were riding straight into the heavily defended French field fortifications, of whose existence they had been unaware.

Reaching the timber barriers at the entrance to the fortified enclosure, Talbot resolved to fight his way in. He halted and ordered his men to dismount, while he himself commanded the battle from his horse, a prominent and exposed figure. His cavalry was now separated from the infantry and archers, who were still some distance away. The men around him were heavily outnumbered by the French inside the enclosure. There was no time to array them in formation. One of his lieutenants, Sir Thomas Everingham, urged him to withdraw and regroup so as to attack with his entire army. But Talbot was possessed by the *élan* of the attack. The English rushed the opening on foot, crying 'Talbot!' and 'St George!' They were met by a hail of enfilading gunfire from culverins sited along the edge of the enclosure. Firing into the flank of the dense crowd of men, each discharge from a single weapon could kill or disable five or six of them. When the survivors reached the opening, there was a disorderly hand-to-hand fight lasting about an hour. The English were pushed back. At the critical moment the Breton cavalry, some 300 mounted men who were being held in reserve, completed the rout. The standards of the King

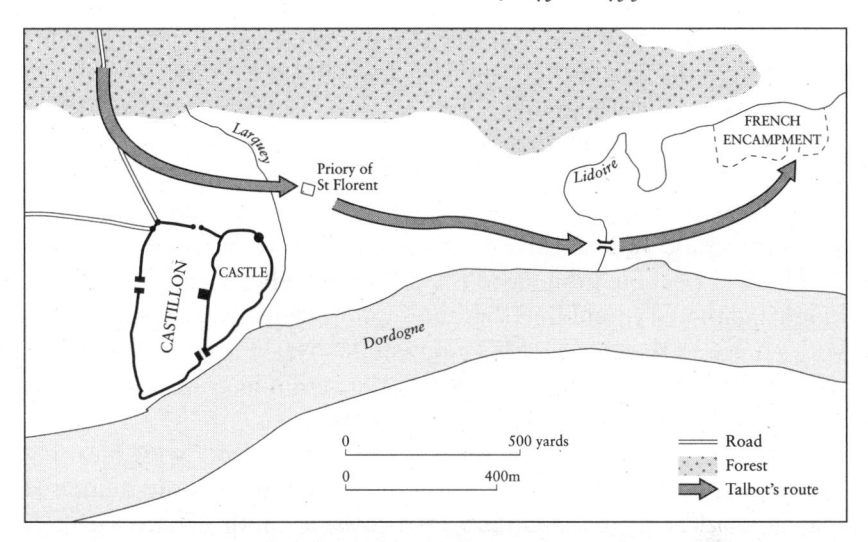

15 The battle of Castillon, 17 July 1453

of England and St George and the personal standard of Talbot himself were seen to fall. Talbot's horse was shot by a culverin and rolled over on top of him. Like many commanders, he preferred to wear a light brigandine of leather or canvas with metal platelets rather than heavy and constricting plate armour, but in close fighting it offered little protection. He was hacked to death as he lay pinned to the ground. His men turned and fled the field. The infantry and archers, who were coming up behind, joined the headlong flight. The French artillery opened up against the fleeing men. Most of the fugitives made it into Castillon. Some threw themselves into the river, where many of them drowned. Others fled to Saint-Émilion six miles away, pursued by the victorious French. Between 300 and 400 men were killed in the battle or the pursuit, including thirty knights. Apart from Talbot himself, his son Viscount Lisle and his fellow captain Sir Edward Hull were among the dead.

On the following day, the French brought their siege artillery up to the walls of Castillon. After three days of bombardment, the town surrendered on 20 July. Clifton's garrison of about 150 men were taken prisoner along with some 1,500 men who had taken refuge in the town after the battle. They included most of the leading Gascon noblemen in Talbot's army. Among the leaders, only Pierre de Montferrand succeeded in escaping and making his way back to Bordeaux.

'So died this renowned and legendary English captain who had for so long been the greatest scourge and chief enemy of France,' wrote the French official historiographer. The Anglo-Gascons owed their defeat to Talbot's reckless aggression and poor field intelligence. He had failed to identify and locate the French field works, allowed his army to be divided in two and then fought the battle in a confined space where he could not effectively deploy his men. It was surely Talbot that his old rival Sir John Fastolf had in mind when he told the young knights gathered round him that the captain who advanced cautiously with an eye to the safety of his companions was a better soldier than the 'hardy man that suddenly, without discretion or good advisement, advanceth him in the field to be held courageous'.

Talbot's herald went through the battlefield on the following morning to find his master. His corpse was still there, but so badly mutilated that he could only be identified by a missing tooth. The scavengers who attended every battlefield had already taken the armour from his body. His throat-piece was found and sent as a trophy to Charles VII. His brigandine ended up in the military museum which Charles VIII established in the castle of Amboise at the end of the century, where for years it was displayed alongside the supposed sword of Sir Lancelot, the axe of Bertrand du Guesclin and some armour of Joan of Arc. His sword was found centuries later in the river, engraved with the words *'Sum Talboti pro vincere inimico meo'* ('I am Talbot's, to vanquish mine enemies'). Talbot's body was buried on the field. A small oratory marked the spot until the Revolution. But he did not lie there long. In 1493, his body was exhumed by his grandson and brought back to England to be reinterred in accordance with the directions in his will beneath the crude stone effigy which can still be seen in the parish church at Whitchurch in Shropshire.[40]

The French followed up their victory immediately. The English garrisons of Libourne and Saint-Émilion, which had been depleted to reinforce Talbot's army, withdrew after the battle, leaving the Marshals' army to reoccupy both towns without opposition. Shortly afterwards, they laid siege to Fronsac, the only garrisoned fortress remaining to the English on the Dordogne. The other French forces in the region converged on the ring of walled places around Bordeaux. The Count of Clermont took the surrender of Castelnau-de-Médoc on 20 July, the same day as the fall of Castillon. His next task was to free up the passage of the Garonne so as to enable French armies to besiege Bordeaux and receive supplies and artillery by water. He laid siege to Gaillard de Durfort's fortress of Blanquefort, which stood at the edge of a vast marsh that gradually merged with the waters of the Garonne a short distance north of Bordeaux. The Count of Foix and the lord of Albret attacked the walled places still held by the English upstream of the city. The river towns of Saint-Macaire and Langon and the nearby fortress of Villandraut were captured in quick succession. In the Dordogne valley, the Marshals left a detachment of their army to maintain the siege of Fronsac, which surrendered a few days later. Meanwhile they crossed the Dordogne and approached the Gascon capital through the vineyards of Entre-Deux-Mers. They finally established themselves around Lormont just north of the city on the opposite bank of the Garonne. There, they set about building a powerful bastide at the water's edge. The French fleet left La Rochelle and entered the Gironde, mooring off Lormont under the protection of the bastide. From Angoulême, where he had established his headquarters, Charles VII announced his intention of marching to the Gironde by the end of July. On 1 August 1453, the French army laid siege to Bordeaux.[41]

The defence was directed by Sir Roger Camoys. As soon as he heard the news of the fall of Castillon, he prevailed on the royal council in the Château de l'Ombrière to summon the Estates of Guyenne. The Estates, which by now represented only Bordeaux, gathered in the cathedral. They nominated Camoys as their governor and cried out 'pitiably' that they would rather die than be subject to the Crown of France. Camoys was pessimistic about the chances and did not hide the fact. Bordeaux was a well-defended city. Its fourteenth-century walls had a circuit of four miles. It had direct access to the river, which at that point was nearly 700 yards wide. These things made it difficult to surround. But, as Camoys pointed out, the French had an overwhelming superiority of men and guns. The English troops in the city were reluctant to risk their lives without pay, and the council's coffers were empty. The Estates responded by imposing a *taille* on the city. More than two dozen prominent figures, led by the Archbishop, entered into personal bonds to secure the English army's wages while it was being collected. Once the refugees from the battlefield and the outlying garrisons had found their way back to Bordeaux, Camoys had more than 3,200 men under his command. In addition, there were still two important outlying garrisons on the Garonne. Rions, twenty miles upstream of Bordeaux, was defended by 130 English troops and Cadillac, three miles further, by 460. These places were critically important to the defence of Bordeaux, because they impeded the flow of French supplies and artillery. Cadillac was besieged by the Count of Foix but was defended with ferocity by its Gascon captain. Downstream of Bordeaux, the same strategic purpose was served by the castle of Blanquefort, where Gaillard de Durfort's Gascon garrison was still holding out against the army of the Count of Clermont. Meanwhile, messengers left Bordeaux for England with reports of the peril in which Bordeaux stood and urgent calls for reinforcements.[42]

The first reports of the battle of Castillon and the death of Talbot reached Westminster in about the middle of August 1453. The news was brought to the royal manor of Clarendon near Salisbury, where Henry VI was staying. It seems to have been this which provoked the sudden crisis in the King's health that followed. Henry was 'smitten with a frenzy' and lost his reason. Over the following days and weeks he would stare blankly ahead for hours, unable to speak or understand what was said to him. He had to be spoon-fed and carried everywhere by his attendants. For some weeks the King's condition was concealed from his subjects in the hope that he would recover. Day-to-day business continued to be handled by the King's councillors in his name as it always had been. For a time, they were able to keep up the illusion that nothing untoward had happened.[43]

The army of Lord Saye, nearly 2,200 strong, was by now ready, but the fleet to carry it was not. Frantic efforts were made to find ships. Meanwhile, a replacement had to be found for Talbot. The sailing date was put off to the end of August and then to 7 September. On 12 September, the command was transferred from Lord Saye to William Lord Bonville, a much more experienced captain who was appointed Seneschal of Guyenne for the second time and commissioned to leave for Gascony at once with a 'notable fellowship'.[44]

Almost immediately, fresh difficulties crowded in, provoked by the political crisis in England. It soon became clear that the King's illness was more than a passing episode. Some arrangement would have to be made for the government while he was incapacitated. The Duke of York was the heir apparent, and if he wanted the regency his claim would be difficult to resist. Suddenly, the position of the Duke of Somerset and his allies, apparently so secure in the summer, seemed to fall apart. As the void of authority became more obvious,

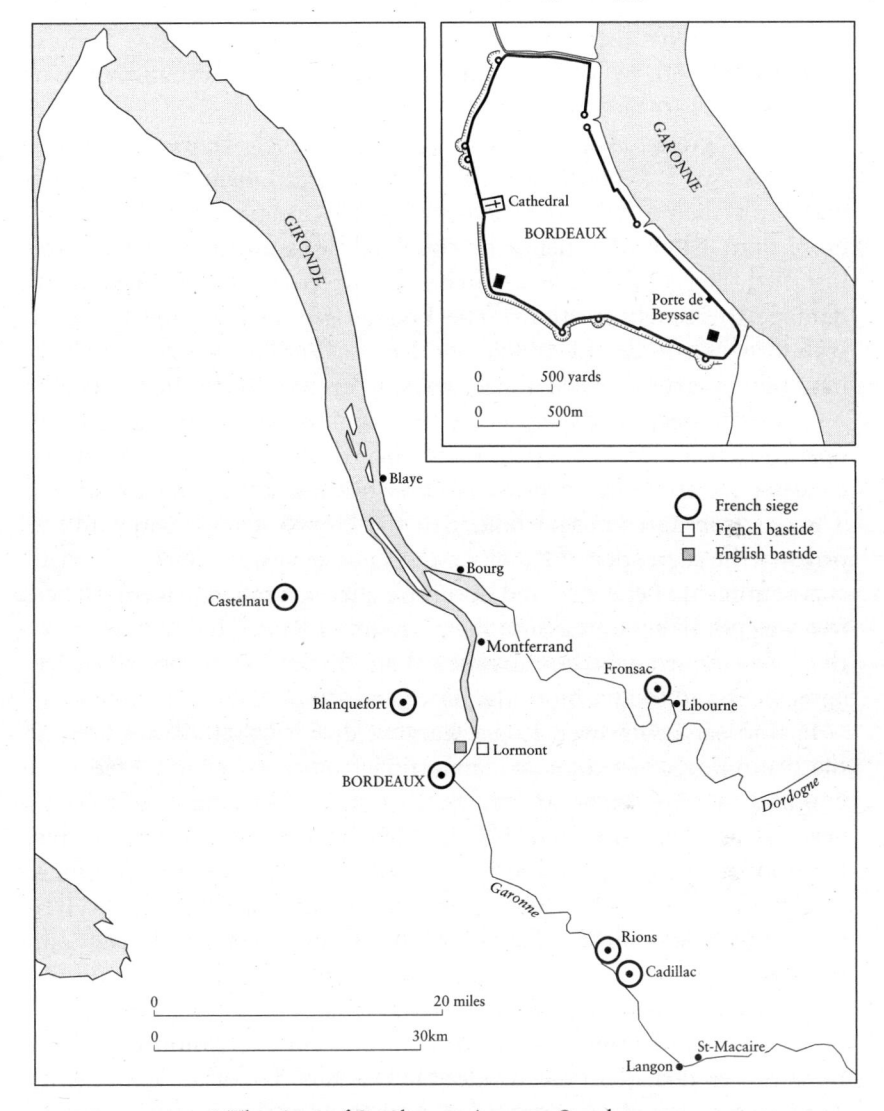

16 The siege of Bordeaux, August–October 1453

public order deteriorated. Bonville himself was Somerset's chief ally in the West Country and could not be spared. His troops would be needed in England. The stream of orders to shipmasters and mustering and requisitioning officers abruptly stopped. By mid-September, the expedition had been cancelled. Bordeaux was left to defend itself as best it could.[45]

On 13 August 1453, Charles VII arrived at the massive fortress of Montferrand by the Garonne a short distance downstream of Bordeaux, where he established his headquarters. The siege had by now been in progress for nearly a fortnight. The French were encountering fierce resistance. Opposite the French bastide at Lormont, the English had built their own bastide, armed with cannon and manned by more than a hundred men. Camoys sited guns on the city gates and installed them in the ships moored in the river. They did considerable damage to French positions. The French siege was inhibited by the stubborn resistance of Cadillac and Rions. Cadillac was continuously battered by artillery and the town was eventually taken by assault on 28 September. The garrison withdrew into the citadel and shortly opened negotiations with the French. Charles VII was in no mood for concessions after the fortress had resisted his troops for six weeks. The garrison agreed to surrender to the French King's mercy and to procure the surrender of Rions on the same terms. Its Gascon captain was summarily beheaded and his entire garrison taken prisoner. Their fate was not likely to reassure the garrison of Rions. Baldwin Fulford, the Devon squire who commanded there, refused to be bound by the agreement and fought on to the bitter end.[46]

In Bordeaux, however, Roger Camoys decided that all was lost. At the beginning of October, a deputation from the city, escorted by a hundred mounted men, arrived at the castle of Montferrand to open negotiations with the French King. Charles was initially implacable. He told them that he would accept nothing less than unconditional surrender. Camoys's loyalties were split. His first duty as he conceived it was to extricate his English troops from the impending disaster and get them back to England. The negotiations opened at Lormont on 5 October. Camoys led the delegation from Bordeaux. The French Chancellor Guillaume Juvénal des Ursins and the Admiral Jean de Bueil represented the French side. On the first day of the conference, Camoys negotiated a separate deal on behalf of the English garrison. He agreed to surrender the English bastide opposite Lormont and to deliver up all French prisoners of war without ransom by the following day. In return the English troops were to be allowed to evacuate the city and sail back to England in the English ships at Bordeaux, taking with them their artillery and all their movable property. It was an inglorious transaction that left the citizens of Bordeaux in the lurch. The only concession that Camoys made to them was to hold off surrendering the English bastide while they negotiated the best deal they could with the French King's representatives. Camoys did what he could for them, but it was not much, for they had little to bargain with once he had announced his intention to leave. The men of Bordeaux were willing to submit to the King. They declared that their repudiation of the earlier submission had been entirely the work of a treacherous minority, a convenient fiction. They asked for an amnesty and were willing to pay for it with a heavy indemnity. But Juvénal was adamant that they could expect no mercy. The Gascon ringleaders must be treated as traitors and would have to be surrendered to French justice. He produced a list of twenty marked men, headed by Pierre de Montferrand and Gaillard de Durfort.[47]

The city's bargaining position diminished with each passing day. Its food supplies were nearly exhausted. People were beginning to starve. Jean Bureau had surveyed the walls on the landward side and reported that he was confident of being able to reduce them rapidly to ruins with his guns. On 8 October, the French fleet arrived from La Rochelle and succeeded in capturing the armed ships which the English had moored in the river. On the following day the Anglo-Gascon delegates came before the French King in the castle of Montferrand to ask for terms. Charles dismissed them without a word while he consulted his councillors. By this time, however, his captains had their own problems. Dysentery, the classic disease of siege armies, was spreading in the French encampments. It was taking a heavy toll in the army and an even bigger one in the fleet. The councillors thought that limited concessions should be made for a quick agreement. A compromise was agreed and sealed later that day. Bordeaux agreed to pay an indemnity of 100,000 *écus*. There would be a general amnesty, with twenty exceptions for the ringleaders of the revolt of 1452. The exceptions, who were to be nominated in due course by the King, would have their lives spared but would be banished from the realm and forfeit all their lands. Up to forty more Gascons who were unwilling to submit to the French King were to be allowed to go into exile. They would be entitled to take their movable property with them and were given a month in which to sell up their land. As for the English garrison, Camoys's agreement with Jean de Bueil was confirmed and it was agreed that his men would have safe-conducts for England. On these terms the city was to be surrendered on 16 October. When the document was brought back to Bordeaux, many of the citizens thought that their delegates had conceded too much. There were acrimonious disputes which continued for several days. Camoys lost patience and proceeded to surrender the bastide north of the walls to the French on 14 October while the men of Bordeaux were still arguing among themselves. With the loss of the bastide the hopelessness of their position became obvious even to the die-hards. They missed the deadline of 16 October, but finally surrendered on the 19th. The occasion was marked more perfunctorily than it had been in 1451. The King stayed away. The city formally surrendered all its privileges into the hands of his representatives. His arms were nailed to the walls above the main gates. The Count of Clermont produced the names of the twenty men who were to be excluded from the amnesty, headed as usual by Pierre de Montferrand and Gaillard de Durfort. On the day after the French entered Bordeaux, Rions and Blanquefort, which had held out throughout the siege, surrendered. Over the following days, the English army embarked on their ships and sailed away.[48]

Some hundreds of Gascons emigrated rather than submit to Charles VII. England was the usual destination, but some left for Italy, Brittany or the kingdoms of the Iberian peninsula. Some families split up, like the Montferrands. Pierre de Montferrand and his uncle François de Montferrand, who were among the twenty proscribed men, came to England, while François's sons, who left voluntarily, established themselves in Navarre. Some of the Gascon refugees left with the returning army of Roger Camoys. More left over the following years, as they were released after being captured at Castillon or Cadillac, or as the deteriorating situation of Gascony persuaded them that they would be better off elsewhere. They settled, for the most part, in London or in the southern counties. The great majority were noblemen or merchants or members of their households. These were the classes who had lost most by the extinction of the English regime. Many of them arrived penniless. They subsisted in England on royal grants of money or, occasionally, land. A few entered royal service, like the veteran conspirator Pey du Tasta. Many more set up businesses in England, generally in the wine trade. Some took shares in ships or trading ventures. Over the next eight years, some 200 licences were issued to Gascons in England to trade to various destinations in wine, grain, vegetables, horses and other commodities. They were quickly assimilated. Most of them learned English and anglicised their names. Only the grandest of them, who had once been lords of great domains in the south-west, ever returned to France, generally after the death of Charles VII when it became easier to negotiate a pardon and restitution of their property.[49]

Bordeaux was able to get the indemnity reduced from 100,000 to 30,000 *écus* when the larger sum proved to be uncollectable. But it lost most of the liberties that it had been allowed to retain on its first surrender in 1451. Economically, the city and its region suffered grievously by the severance of the connection with England. The annual wine fleets came to an end. Individual sailings continued, but they required a licence from the English government, and from time to time were forbidden by the French. After April 1455 shipments out of Gascony were also subject to heavy French export taxes. The result was a prolonged decline of the trade. Volumes dropped to less than half the previous levels and never entirely recovered. Prices fell. The English found alternative sources of wine in Castile, Portugal and Greece, but the Gascons found it harder to reach different markets in an age when wine could not be carried for long distances overland. Petitions to the Crown for relief late in the century alleged that Saint-Émilion had lost nine-tenths of its population and Libourne two-thirds.[50]

The French reconquest led to a major redistribution of land in Gascony. The Gascon domains formerly held by Englishmen and those of the twenty men excluded from the amnesty were confiscated and redistributed among the King's councillors and local supporters. Gascon families who had abandoned the English dynasty years earlier and had seen their lands confiscated by the English King's officers returned to claim them back under the terms of the edict of Compiègne. Some of the Bordeaux government's officers, both English and Gascon, were said to have abused their offices to occupy other men's lands and were now faced with claims for restitution. For every genuine claim, there were others which were doubtful or fabricated. Many of the new landowners were northerners. Captains like Antoine de Chabannes, whose family came from the Limousin, and the Coëtivy family from Brittany did well. A large class of lesser figures, soldiers and administrators, established themselves in the region with royal grants of land. They included an important group of Scottish soldiers of fortune: Robin Petilow, the captain of a Scottish company, John Bron of Coulton, John Ross and Patrick Abercrombie. Most of these intruders into the closed world of south-western society left little trace.

They eventually moved elsewhere or their lines died out. The great winners were the prolific and cunning lords of Albret, who picked up many of the best morsels of property left by the departing Gascon exiles. Over the next half-century they pursued a policy of territorial aggrandisement based on strategic marriages, the careful cultivation of royal favour and the judicious use of local influence and force, which would shortly make them the dominant power in Gascony. Their descendants became Kings of Navarre and finally Kings of France.[51]

The wars of France were over. The wars of England were about to begin. Yet it was some time before this was understood in either country. In France there were periodic invasion scares over the following years. Reports of ships assembling in ports of southern England sent troops scurrying to the coast and townsmen to the repair of their walls. There were hunts for English fifth columnists who were supposed to be suborning local men and preparing the way for landings. In England, the royal chancery continued to treat Gascony as an English possession. The chancery rolls which recorded the English King's transactions with his Gascon officials and subjects were kept up until 1468. Henry VI and Edward IV continued to make appointments to ghost offices in a Gascon administration which no longer existed, and grants of land and revenues which they no longer possessed. The beneficiaries were invariably Gascon exiles in England who counted on returning to the duchy one day to take up their lands and places. The pension awarded to Gaillard de Durfort was expressed to endure 'into the time that he be restored to his said lordships in the duchy of Guyenne or otherwise recompensed'.[52]

The chances of this ever happening were limited by the political turmoil which engulfed England once the King's disability became known. The disasters at Castillon and Bordeaux destroyed what remained of the Duke of Somerset's reputation. His enemies were circling round him. Prominent among them were the captains and settlers who had lost out in Normandy. Sir John Fastolf collected materials to show that Somerset had been responsible for the disaster and to help bring him and his allies to book. The council put off the political reckoning for as long as they could, but in November 1453 the crisis broke. Richard of York's ally John Mowbray Duke of Norfolk delivered a 'bill' to the council which owed much to Fastolf and is written in the hand of his secretary. Norfolk complained of the 'great dishonours and losses that been come to this full noble realm of England'. He demanded a commission of inquiry into the loss of France and accused Somerset of treason. A lesser man, he declared, would have been beheaded for surrendering castles that had never been besieged.

On 23 November 1453 the council bent before the storm. Somerset was arrested and committed to the Tower. After repeated prorogations, Parliament finally reassembled at Westminster in February 1454 to settle the arrangements for a regency. The position was complicated by the birth of an heir, Edward, to Henry and Queen Margaret the previous autumn. The rival claimants to the government were the Duke of York, no longer the heir presumptive to the throne but still Henry's closest male relative of full age, and the Queen as guardian of her infant son. If Margaret had prevailed, the Duke of Somerset, would certainly have returned to power. This was probably the main reason, apart from Margaret's sex and French origin, why at the end of March 1454 the Lords nominated the Duke of York as 'Protector of England' for as long as the King's incapacity lasted.[53]

In the event it lasted just nine months. Shortly after Christmas 1454, Henry VI partially recovered his wits. But if the King's illness had been a misfortune, his recovery was a disaster. It was enough to put an end to the Duke of York's protectorate, but not enough to enable Henry to resume even the limited measure of control that he had exercised before. Henry was destined to pass in and out of coherence for the rest of his life, weak in mind and will even when he was well. The Queen, who had conceived a deep loathing for the Duke of York, was almost certainly behind the decision in February 1455 to dismiss him and his allies from the council. The Duke of Somerset was released from the Tower, restored to his former position and declared to be innocent of all that had been alleged against him. His tenure was brief. The Duke of York took up arms for the third time in five years. The great majority of the peerage continued to support the King as they had done before.

This time, however, York's prospects were transformed by the outbreak of open war between the two great northern dynasties of Neville and Percy, which brought the Neville clan into his camp. The head of the house, Richard Neville Earl of Salisbury, was York's brother-in-law. He was the warden of the west march towards Scotland and the possessor of vast estates in Yorkshire and the south Midlands.

His eldest son Richard had married the heiress of the Beauchamps, acquiring the title of Earl of Warwick and their even larger estates in southern England and Wales. Unlike the Duke of York, Richard Earl of Warwick was a politician and propagandist of genius. In May 1455, York and the Neville Earls defeated the King's army in a brief skirmish in the streets of St Albans. The Duke of Somerset took refuge in a nearby house but was forced out and hacked to death in the street. His principal baronial ally, Henry Percy Earl of Northumberland, met the same fate. The Yorkists seized power. Leadership of the Lancastrian party passed to Margaret of Anjou, 'a great and strong-laboured woman', as one of Sir John Fastolf's correspondents described her, 'for she spareth no pain to [pur]sue her things to an intent and conclusion to her power'.[54]

Apart from an interval of three months the Duke of York was the effective ruler of England for two and a half years from the beginning of 1454 to the summer of 1456. For the next five years after that, England was effectively without a government, as the King and Queen wandered about the Midlands, rarely visiting Westminster, while the Queen's allies contested power with the Duke of York and the Neville Earls in the council chamber and then on the field of battle.

The shadow of the war with France loomed large over these events. Richard of York had never been close to Humphrey Duke of Gloucester, but his fierce criticisms of the governments of Suffolk and Somerset meant that he came to be regarded as Humphrey's political heir. York himself sedulously encouraged this idea. The men around the Queen were dismissed as the direct heirs of those who had undermined the war effort, 'suffering all the old possessions that the King had in France and Normandy, Anjou and Maine, Gascony and Guyenne, won and gotten by his father of most noble memory and other his noble progenitors to be shamefully lost or sold'. He adopted as his own the myth of the 'good Duke Humphrey', claiming that his ambition to restore England's fortunes had been frustrated by these same men ever since they had established their power over an inert King by murdering that 'noble, worthy and Christian prince'.[55]

The days of the great continental armies were gone, but there were incidents at sea to remind the English that they were still at war with a power that now controlled the whole Atlantic coast of France. In Norfolk, enemy ships were seen cruising off Yarmouth and Cromer, making their way up the creeks and rivers and dropping landing parties to take prisoners for ransom. Writing to her husband in London, Margaret Paston reported that 'The said enemies ben so bold that they come up to the land ... as homely as they were Englishmen.' Pierre de Brézé, the Grand Sénéchal of Normandy, was one of a number of men who bought shares in privateering ships operating against English shipping in the Channel. In August 1457, together with Robert de Flocques and Charles Desmarais, he organised the most ambitious coastal raid of the period. On the morning of 28 August, a large fleet collected in all the main ports of Normandy, landed between 1,600 and 1,800 men near Sandwich and then forced its way into the harbour. They remained there for three days before being driven back to their ships by an improvised force under Sir Thomas Kyriel. But they took away several captured merchant ships, great quantities of spoil and many prisoners. It was the most damaging raid on the English coast for eighty years.[56]

Henry VI was a passive spectator of events that passed over his head. The Kings of England had never achieved the sacral status that kept Charles VI on his throne through his years of raving incoherence or Charles VII at the lowest point of his fortunes. The logical outcome in a society whose institutions depended critically on the personal role of the King, was Henry's deposition. The Duke of York finally resolved to take this step in October 1460, claiming the throne for himself. He never sat on it, for on 30 December 1460, he was defeated and killed by the Queen's allies at Wakefield Bridge in Yorkshire. His severed head was impaled on a spike over the city gate of York with a paper crown pinned to the skull. His cause triumphed only after his death, in the more skilful hands of his son Edward Earl of March. Edward proclaimed himself King Edward IV at Westminster with the support of most of his father's allies. The rights of Edward III's second son Lionel Duke of Clarence were declared to have descended by inheritance to himself. All three Lancastrians since Henry Bolingbroke's coup of 1399 were said to have usurped the throne and to have been no true kings.

No one doubted that Edward IV's real title to rule was force. On Palm Sunday, 29 March 1461, he decisively defeated the Lancastrian army at Towton in Yorkshire. Almost all the Lancastrian leaders were slain in the battle or captured and beheaded afterwards. Margaret of Anjou fled with her son to Scotland and finally, in 1463, to her native France. The last of her English allies were slaughtered at two engagements at

Hedgeley Moor and Hexham in 1464. Henry VI himself remained at liberty in England for another year, sheltered by loyal friends among the northern gentry. He was finally caught in a wood by the river Ribble in Lancashire, attended by just two chaplains and a squire. His captors took him to London, paraded him through the streets with his legs tied beneath the belly of his horse, and then shut him in the Tower. The house of Lancaster, which had seemed immovably secure on the death of Henry V in 1422, had been destroyed in a single generation.

Few things symbolised the emptiness of Henry VI's kingship more aptly than the pathetic story of his 'readeption' and death. In 1469, the Earl of Warwick ('the Kingmaker') broke with Edward IV, the King that he had made. They fell out ostensibly over foreign policy, in fact because of differences over Warwick's future role in government. Over the next two years, the government of England changed hands three times. Between October 1470 and April 1471, the Earl of Warwick controlled London and the government. Henry VI was brought out of the Tower and reinstated on the throne. In the graphic words of the Burgundian chronicler Georges Chastellain, the Earl ruled through Henry, a 'stuffed woolsack lifted by the ears ... pushed about as in a game of blind man's buff'. When Edward IV finally recovered power in April 1471, Henry is supposed to have told him, 'My cousin of York, you are most welcome for I know that in your hands my life will be safe.'[57] He was wrong. The only thing that kept him safe was that his death would have passed his titles and the leadership of the Lancastrian party to the young Prince Edward, who was still at large. He would have presented a much more dangerous challenge to the victorious Yorkists. Henry's fate was sealed by the defeat of two Lancastrian armies and the death in battle of both Warwick and Edward. On the night of 21 May 1471, he was discreetly murdered in the Tower of London. The customary hypocrisies were observed. He lay in state in St Paul's, where his body was reported to have bled onto the marble pavement.

The expulsion of the English from France marked a revolution in the internal politics of the French kingdom as well as in those of England. For more than a century, every successful English invasion had depended on the political divisions of France. Edward III had invaded with the support of dissidents in Normandy and Flanders. Henry V had entered the country through the great breach opened up by the civil wars between Armagnac and Burgundy. The Dukes of Burgundy, Brittany and Bourbon and the Counts of Armagnac and Foix had been able to conserve their political autonomy in large part because of the threat that they would make common cause with England. The princes behind the Praguerie of 1440 and the cabal at Nevers in 1442 had all to a greater or lesser degree depended for their bargaining power on the same implicit threat. The constraint was still there, as long as a fresh English descent on France seemed to be a real possibility.

For some years, the threat that the English would return hung over the French government. In the south-west, they embarked on an ambitious programme of fortification against the appearance of another Talbot. The vulnerability of a region where the Kings of England had ruled for so long was brought home to them within a year of the battle of Castillon when Pierre de Montferrand, the chief author of the plot which had delivered Bordeaux to Talbot in 1452, returned to the city. He came ostensibly to wind up his affairs, but in fact to organise a fresh rebellion. The plan was to raise an army of 4,000 to 5,000 men to capture Bayonne. Montferrand's plans were betrayed and he was arrested. Taken under guard to Poitiers, he confessed everything and was condemned to death. His body was butchered into six pieces, which were exhibited at the city gates as a warning to others. That year, two modern fortresses began to rise from the ground at Bordeaux, the Château Trompette and the Château du Hâ, designed to repel an attack from outside and to control the city within. In the south of the duchy, on the Adour, major works of refortification were undertaken at Bayonne, Dax and Saint-Sever. As late as 1485 Charles VIII supported the repair of the walls of Bourg because the town was thought to be in danger of capture by the English.[58]

John V Count of Armagnac had succeeded to the domains and ambitions of his family on the death of his father in 1450. He made no secret of his resentment when English Gascony was absorbed into the royal demesne. He openly expressed his satisfaction when Talbot recovered Bordeaux in 1452. He joined the French campaign of 1453 with obvious reluctance and was visibly dismayed to learn of Talbot's defeat and death. This, rather than the Count's incestuous marriage to his sister or his meddling with the cathedral chapter of Auch, was probably the real reason for the King's confiscation of his domains in 1455. Charles's fears were probably justified. The Count fled over the Pyrenees into Aragon, and from there appealed for help to the English government, promising to deploy his network of vassals and clients in support of a fresh English invasion of Guyenne.[59]

The Duke of Alençon, another princely malcontent, was Armagnac's brother-in-law. He had returned to his duchy in the reconquest of 1449–50, but never recovered his family's former influence. His debts were great, his revenues diminished by war damage and his means inadequate to support his grandiose way of life. Towards the end of 1452 there had been a showdown between Alençon and Charles VII. Alençon asked, not for the first time, for his war service over twenty years to be properly rewarded. Charles, who had never trusted the Duke's impulsive personality, refused. His councillors, he said, were firmly opposed to any more largesse in his direction. The Duke returned to his domains and opened negotiation with Talbot in Bordeaux. The go-between was a professional soldier in Talbot's company called Jack Hay. He had been the English lieutenant at Alençon at the time of its surrender to the Duke in 1449 and counted himself a friend. These discussions came to an abrupt end when the English withdrew from Gascony. But in 1455 the Duke renewed contact with Jack Hay who was then serving under Earl Rivers in the garrison of Calais. Rivers and Hay put him in touch with Louis Gallet, one of the most prominent Norman exiles in England, and through him with the Duke of York, then the dominant figure in the English government. Another channel of communication was found in a herald of the Duke of Exeter, who travelled regularly to France to deal with outstanding disputes about ransoms and takings at sea. Over a period of a year, Alençon sent three successive missions to England to urge the English council to invade western France. The plan was for the English to land an army of 10,000 men at Granville in the Cotentin to take possession of Alençon's castles and defend his duchy, while another 40,000 men invaded Normandy across the Channel. Alençon told them that Normandy had been denuded of troops to support other theatres. The Normans, he said, were oppressed with the burden of royal taxation and would welcome the English back with open arms. His terms were exorbitant and some of the English council were sceptical. But the Duke of York was prepared to back the idea, albeit with smaller forces. In the spring of 1456, one of Alençon's emissaries got cold feet and betrayed the plot to the French King's officers in Rouen. Alençon was arrested. When his various agents and messengers were rounded up and interrogated in the Bastille the whole story came out. It was widely believed in France that Alençon's schemes were the tip of an iceberg. Other prominent noblemen were thought to be involved, including the Duke of Burgundy.[60]

In hindsight, all of these plots seem doomed, but that was not at all obvious to Charles VII and his councillors. When Alençon's conspiracy came to light, troops which had been withdrawn from Normandy were hurriedly sent back to defend the coast against an English invasion. The *francs-archers* were mobilised throughout France. The duchy of Alençon was occupied by French troops, who took over all of its principal fortresses, just as they had in the domains of the Count of Armagnac the year before. The principal Norman ports, Dieppe, Harfleur and Honfleur, were warned to expect an English descent at any time. Writing to the King of Scotland early in the following year, Charles VII explained his strategic quandary. The English still had partisans in Normandy and the Gascons were known to be at heart entirely favourable to them. The threat from England, he said, had forced on him an extremely expensive policy of static defence. Normandy was only six hours by sea from England and was obviously vulnerable. But the English could land anywhere. He had to guard the entire coast of France from Picardy to the Pyrenees. The financial implications were crippling. Although Normandy was the richest province in France, its revenues fell short of the cost of defending its coasts by 100,000 *livres* a year. In Gascony he had to maintain large garrisons commanded by his most senior commanders, at a cost ten times the revenues of the province. Between these two provinces, Brittany, Poitou and Saintonge all lived in constant fear of invasion.[61]

Charles VII's biggest fear was that the Duke of Burgundy would become involved. Relations between France and Burgundy deteriorated rapidly in the 1450s. When, in 1456, the Dauphin Louis finally broke with his father and was given asylum in Brabant by Philip the Good, they sank to a new low. Philip was as troubled as the Duke of Alençon and the Count of Armagnac about the growing power of the French King now that the English had been evicted from France. An alliance with England was an obvious defensive measure. Philip and his advisers were belatedly discovering the wisdom of Hughes de Lannoy's advice at the time of the treaty of Arras. The great appanaged princes of France needed the English presence if they were to defend themselves against an expansive monarchy.

Charles VII was confident that England would not ally with Burgundy while his niece had any influence over its government. But he was less sanguine about the attitude of the Duke of York and his followers. Given the family relationship between the Queen of England and the French royal house, it was natural to expect that if her enemies came to power they would turn to Burgundy for support. The exiled Dauphin, who espoused his father's enemies on principle, declared his support of the house of York. Philip the Good allowed him to send a small contingent to England which fought under Louis's banner at the battle of Towton. As Antoine de Croÿ, Philip's chief councillor, explained to the Milanese ambassador, a Lancastrian victory in England would present a serious threat to the house of Burgundy. Margaret of Anjou could be expected to cede Calais to her uncle in return for peace. That would be the signal for Charles VII to invade Flanders and Artois and settle old scores with the house of Burgundy.[62]

When Louis XI ascended the throne of France on the death of his father in July 1461, he came to power with a programme. Calculating, unscrupulous and amoral, Louis intended to curtail the autonomy of the appanaged princes whose figurehead he had once been. In particular he was determined to absorb the most powerful of the princely states, Burgundy and Brittany, into the centralised model to which the French state had aspired since the beginning of the thirteenth century. Louis's attack on the autonomy of the princes threatened to revive an older dynamic which had made them the natural allies of England. Fears of English intervention had real substance once Edward IV had seized the throne and defeated his domestic enemies. Louis was prepared to pay a high price to neutralise him. In October 1463, he did a deal with Edward under which he agreed to drop his support for Margaret of Anjou and Prince Edward, in return for a reciprocal promise from Edward IV not to give aid to Louis's own internal enemies. In a secret side-agreement, he even promised to abandon the 'auld alliance' and, if need be, to support an English conquest of Scotland.[63]

The War of the Common Weal was launched in March 1465 by a formidable coalition of princes, including the Dukes of Burgundy, Brittany and Bourbon and the heir of the house of Anjou. They rose against Louis XI in the name of the 'common weal', by which they meant an end to oppressive levels of taxation and the dismissal of the King's low-born advisers in favour of the princes of the King's blood. It was the programme of John the Fearless in 1417 and the

Praguerie in 1440. The figurehead of the rebellion was the King's unstable younger brother Charles of France Duke of Berry. Its real instigator, however, was Charles Count of Charolais, the heir of the ailing Duke of Burgundy. He invaded France with a large army and confronted Louis XI in battle at Montlhéry, south of Paris. The French King was forced to make humiliating concessions to the princes and to grant Normandy as an appanage to his brother. Louis accused the princes of opening up France to an English invasion and hinted that they had a secret understanding with Edward IV. Suspicion turned to certainty when documents fell into Louis's hands suggesting that his brother Charles had bought English support with a promise to restore Guyenne to them. It is not clear what documents these were. There is no trace of such an agreement in the English records. But Louis's conviction that Edward IV was about to intervene in the civil war was certainly genuine. If Edward had done, the result might have been disastrous for Louis. When he seized Normandy from his brother within three months of having granted it, he gave that as his reason.[64]

Not long after the end of the War of the Common Weal, the nightmare of a coalition between the English and the French princes became a reality. In June 1467, Charles of Charolais ('the Rash') succeeded his father as Duke of Burgundy. France and Burgundy were now both ruled by determined men intent on settling permanently in their own favour the tense and distrustful relationship between the French Crown and the house of Burgundy which had subsisted for sixty years. Charles the Rash set about rebuilding the coalition of 1465 with English support. The allies agreed to divide up France between them. The English were to take everything which belonged to the French royal demesne including Normandy and Guyenne. Francis II of Brittany was promised an army of 3,000 English archers to defend it against the French King. In July 1468, as these negotiations were being concluded, Charles of Burgundy married Edward IV's sister Margaret of York in the Flemish town of Damme amid ceremonies of unparalleled splendour. 'I heard never of the like to it, save King Arthur's court,' wrote John Paston, who was present in Margaret's suite.[65]

These events marked, on the face of it, a re-creation of the alliance of England, Burgundy and Brittany celebrated at Amiens in 1423. But like so many earlier dissident princes of France, Charles the Rash had no interest in reviving the empire of the Angevin, Plantagenet and Lancastrian Kings of England. He only ever intended to use the

English alliance as a way of bringing pressure to bear on Louis XI. The same was probably true of the Duke of Brittany. Nevertheless, Edward IV had high hopes of his network of alliances. His Chancellor told Parliament in May 1468 that its object was to

[di]minish and lesse[n] the power of his old and ancient adversary of France, the French King, whereby his said highness [Edward IV] should move the lightlier and rather ... recover and enjoy the title and possession of the said realm of France, his duchies and lordships of Normandy, Gascony and Guyenne.

The English King declared his intention of crossing the sea in person and joining forces with the Dukes of Brittany and Burgundy in the field. They had impressed upon him 'daily' that England had never had such a good opportunity to reverse the defeats of the previous generation.

It is unlikely that Edward seriously thought that he would be able to make good Henry V's claim to the Crown of France, but there is little doubt that he hoped to recover Normandy and Guyenne. This was a popular policy in England, where control of the Norman coast was regarded as part of the defence of England. The Commons granted two standard subsidies to support it. The sequel, however, was a sobering lesson in strategic realities. Louis XI knocked out both of England's continental allies before Edward IV was able to organise his own campaign. By the time the English army was ready in September 1468, Louis had already invaded Brittany, the weak link in the alliance, and forced Francis II to submit and pull out. A month later, the French King settled his differences with Charles the Rash in a treaty sealed at Péronne. The affair was resolved without reference to the princes' dangerous English ally.[66]

The renewed civil war in England between 1469 and 1471 presented Louis XI and Charles the Rash with fresh dilemmas and fresh opportunities. The new wars of the Roses were in one sense a revival of the old issues between Lancaster and York which had followed the loss of Normandy and Guyenne. In another they were surrogate wars fought by the two principal continental powers through their English clients. Louis XI threw himself behind the Lancastrian cause. In July 1470 he presided at a theatrical reconciliation at Angers between those old adversaries Warwick and Margaret of Anjou. Warwick's successful campaign to wrest power back from Edward IV later that year was launched from France with French ships and French money. He had been promised the Imperial territories of the House of Burgundy as England's share of the spoils. As for Charles the Rash, with French troops massing on his borders, he had no choice but to support the house of York. Edward IV's invasion of England to recover his throne in the following year was launched from Zeeland with Burgundian ships, troops and money.[67]

If there was a moment when both sides recognised that the great series of wars between England and France was over, it came in 1475 with a campaign and a treaty. Once Edward IV was securely re-established on his throne, he turned on Louis XI, who had tried so hard to unseat him. The tumults of 1470 and 1471, he told Parliament in October 1472, had been provoked by the 'subtle and crafty enterprises of Louis, the King's adversary in France'. He was the 'principal ground, root and provoker of the King's said let and trouble'. These statements were part of a remarkable survey of English foreign policy. Unusually, it was circulated to members of the two Houses in writing and has survived in the muniments of Canterbury cathedral. Edward presented Parliament with a strategic vision which dated back to the opening years of the war under Edward III. It involved an alliance with the autonomous principalities on the western seaboard of France: Flanders, Brittany and Guyenne. The power of the French appanaged princes, he said, had put them on a collision course with the French Crown. Tensions had come to a head since the accession of Louis XI. 'How that he hath dealt with the Dukes of Burgundy and Brittany, also with his own brother, divers other princes and lords in like case it is notoire.' Edward reasserted the claim of the English Kings to the Crown of France and reminded his audience of the past glories of England's warriors. But the heart of his case was that England could best protect itself by acquiring allies in France and diminishing the power of the French King in his own realm. If the French territorial princes were left to their fate, Louis XI might reduce them to submission and become even more powerful and dangerous than he already was. By comparison the recovery of Normandy and Guyenne would give England and her allies control of the Channel and the western seaboard of Europe, making an invasion of England logistically impossible and piratical cruises along the trade lanes exceptionally difficult. The English King drew a direct link between the loss of Normandy and Guyenne between 1449 and 1453 and the subsequent outbreak of civil war in England. Henry VI 'notwithstanding his simpleness of wit, stood ever in glory and honour while the war was continued by yonder and, that left, successively all fell to decay'. The Croyland chronicle, which was probably the work of one of Edward's councillors, reported that Edward's statement of his war aims was received by both Houses with the 'highest praise'. The Commons responded with an unusually generous grant of taxation.[68]

When, in 1475, Edward IV invaded France, the ostensible purpose was once again to partition the country. Charles the Rash was to hold all his existing French fiefs plus Tournai, Champagne and Bar in full sovereignty. This would have realised the long-standing ambition of the house of Burgundy to emancipate itself from feudal dependence on the French Crown and join up his dispersed territories. Edward would take the rest as King of France. Ostensibly, these were the old war aims of Henry V. But Edward IV had learned caution since his earlier bargains with Charles the Rash. His real objective was more modest. He wanted a durable peace with France on terms that would secure England against invasion and would not shame him in his subjects' eyes. Shortly before the invasion force was due to sail, the senior English royal herald, Garter King of Arms, was sent to France to deliver the English King's formal defiance and call on Louis XI to surrender the kingdom of France. But in a private audience with Louis XI immediately afterwards, Garter told him that once his master had salved his honour by landing with his army in France he would welcome proposals for a permanent peace.[69]

On 4 July 1475 Edward IV landed at Calais with his army. He told a Milanese diplomat that it was 20,000 strong, and it may well have approached that number. Philippe de Commynes, who was with the French King, thought that it was the largest English army that had ever crossed the Channel. With the instinct which rarely deserted him, Louis XI decided to buy off the English before the coalition was able to open a joint offensive. The English King's instructions to his ambassadors show that Louis's instinct was sound. Edward's main concern was to extract the largest possible financial indemnity for leaving France and to secure a long truce with a mutual promise that neither he nor Louis would support the other's domestic enemies. The two Kings met at Picquigny on the Somme, a short distance from Amiens, on 29 August 1475. There, they sealed the instruments which marked the end of the campaign. A seven-year truce was proclaimed. Edward agreed to leave France as soon as he had received the sum of 75,000 *écus*. He was also to have a pension from French revenues of 50,000 *écus* a year. Finally, Margaret of Anjou, who was still a prisoner in England, was to be released and allowed to return to France in return for a ransom of 50,000 *écus*. The Duke of Burgundy was furious. He summoned the Milanese ambassador in the middle of the night to tell him that if Edward had persisted 'they would certainly have achieved their ends and won more fame and honour than ever princes enjoyed'. This was a fantasy. But it was clear that Charles now had no choice but to make his own deal with the French King on the best terms he could get. A fortnight after the treaty of Picquigny, Louis and Charles the Rash concluded a nine-year truce and non-aggression pact. Francis II of Brittany made his own submission a month later, formally renouncing his alliance with the English. The treaty of Picquigny inaugurated a period of more than seventy years, for most of which the English Kings were pensioners of the French Crown. By the time that these payments finally ceased on the death of Henry VIII in 1547, they had received more than three million *écus*.[70]

The Gascon exiles were among the first to realise the significance of what had happened at Picquigny. Gaillard de Durfort had had a successful career in English service since his flight from Bordeaux in 1453. He became a Yorkist partisan and was elected to the Order of the Garter when Edward IV came to the throne. He had played a prominent part in negotiating the alliance with both Francis II and Charles the Rash and had commanded the English archers in Breton service. Gaillard had counted on the recovery of Guyenne. When Edward began to build his coalition in 1472, he obtained the King's confirmation of his rights to his Gascon property. However, after the treaty of 1475, he realised that Edward IV had abandoned any thought of recovering the old domains of the English Kings in the south-west. Gaillard turned to Louis XI. He negotiated a pardon and was restored to some of his confiscated estates in south-western France. This step automatically entailed his expulsion from the Order of the Garter, but Edward IV retained enough affection for him to leave his name inscribed above his stall instead of having it effaced in accordance with tradition. Gaillard died in 1481 as he had begun, a Gascon nobleman in Gascony.[71]

The treaty of Picquigny marked the end of the ancient alliance between England and the dissident princes of France. The result was to transform the dynamic of French politics. Over the following years, the princes' old autonomy was extinguished, just as Edward IV had predicted in his address to Parliament. After a succession of humiliating defeats at the hands of the Swiss confederation, Charles the Rash was killed at the battle of Nancy in 1477, to the unconcealed delight of Louis XI. The duchy of Burgundy and the Burgundian lands in Picardy were invaded and annexed by the French King. Flanders, Artois, the imperial county of Burgundy and the German territories of the Dukes eventually fell by the fortunes of marriage and war to Maximillian Habsburg, Archduke of Austria and later Holy Roman Emperor, marking the beginning of two centuries of rivalry between France and the Habsburg Emperors. Flanders was finally, and as it turned out permanently, detached from the kingdom of France.

The last notable aristocratic rising of the old, familiar kind was the so-called *'guerre folle'* of 1487-8, which pitted a coalition of the Dukes of Brittany and Orléans, the lord of Albret and the Count of Foix, supported by Maximillian, against the regents governing France in the name of the teenage King Charles VIII. For the last time, Francis II appealed for help to England. A company of English volunteers responded to the call. Henry VII, as yet barely secure on his throne, toyed with the idea of intervening but in the end did nothing. When Francis II died in 1488 leaving no male heirs, Brittany was overrun by a French army and the heiress, Francis's daughter Anne, was more or less forcibly married to two French kings in succession. In the following century, Brittany was finally incorporated into the political and administrative structure of the French kingdom.

The houses of Armagnac, Anjou, Alençon and Bourbon all became extinct in the male line in the next generation and their appanages reverted to the Crown. The house of Orléans merged with the Crown when the line of Charles VI was extinguished in 1498 and the son of Charles of Orléans (the prisoner of Agincourt) succeeded to the throne. A series of spectacular treason trials, starting with John II of Alençon, reminded the nobility that they no longer had the same political freedom as their forebears in matters of state.

The consolidation of the monarchy's authority made it all but impossible to mount another aristocratic coup on the model of the Praguerie or the League of the Common Weal. When the Constable, Charles of Bourbon-Montpensier, tried in 1523 to raise a princely rebellion and partition France in alliance with the King of England and the German Emperor, he attracted very little aristocratic support. The rising was snuffed out before it had even begun. Reflecting on these changes in the middle of the sixteenth century, an experienced French soldier and diplomat observed that the princely houses who had once moved men to rebellion 'are now extinct and their lands and duchies absorbed by the Crown, so that there is not a man left in France who dares to persuade soldiers to take the field against the King'. Foreign governments took note. As Henry VIII wearily complained to the Imperial ambassador, it was 'useless to count upon the rebellion and support of the people of France, for they have never been known to rise'.[72]

The claims of the English dynasty retained a vestigial existence long after their realisation became impossible. Henry VII intervened several times in France. He entered into a treaty of mutual defence with Anne of Brittany and sent several thousand men to defend her duchy between 1489 and 1491, in the forlorn hope of preventing its annexation by France. He intervened in Flanders in 1489 and again in 1492 to help the Archduke Maximillian to resist French offensives in the Low Countries. On all of these occasions Henry invoked the old Plantagenet claim to the Crown of France. When Henry VII entered France himself with an army in 1492, his indentures with his captains recited that they were to 'pass the sea and make his arrival within his realm of France for the recovering of his right there'. But Henry VII was a realist. Statements like these were intended partly as propaganda to rally support for war taxation among his own subjects. They were also a bargaining counter in the negotiated peace that was always his main object. His actions show that he wanted to be bought off with money and the promise of peace, like Edward IV in 1475. The treaty of Étaples (1492) achieved both things, ushering in a long period when war with France would be the exception rather than the rule. Henry VII's minister Edmund Dudley warned his master that aggressive continental wars were expensive and served no interest of England. 'The beginning seemeth a great pleasure,' he said, 'but the way out is very narrow to come honourably out thereof.'[73]

Henry VIII was the last English King to take the old dynastic and territorial claims at face value. He succeeded his father in 1509 at the age of eighteen, ambitious, anxious to make an impression and sensitive to a public mood which remained instinctively hostile to France. Henry's own francophobe instincts were already well developed at his accession. Yet romanticism and propaganda counted for more than law or power in Henry's revival of these ancient disputes. Early in his reign he commissioned a life of Henry V in English, based on early fifteenth-century sources, and a few years later an English translation of Froissart's chronicle by John Bourchier Lord Berners, which remains one of the most attractive versions of this literary masterpiece.

Henry VIII's first military move against France took up the issue where it had been left by Talbot in 1453. In 1512, he resolved upon an ambitious plan to land an army of 6,000 men in Castile and invade Gascony over the Pyrenees in conjunction with a Castilian army raised by his ally Ferdinand of Aragon. 'Now is the time prophesied, now is the very season,' wrote a royal propagandist, 'that the red rose shall wear the crown of France.' The venture was a fiasco. The army landed in Castile in the summer of that year, but as a result of disputes with Ferdinand it got no further. Henry VIII invaded France three times over the next decade. In 1513, he invaded in alliance with the Emperor Maximillian and captured Tournai, something which Edward III had tried but failed to do in 1340. He occupied the town for six years, ostensibly as King of France, before surrendering it back to Francis I. After an unsuccessful invasion attempt in 1522, another English army commanded by the Duke of Suffolk entered Picardy in the following year in support of the abortive rising of the Constable of Bourbon. Suffolk marched on Paris, penetrating as far as the Oise at Pont-Sainte-Maxence. Henry VIII had high expectations of this expedition. He told Sir Thomas More that he expected the French to submit to him in the same way as the English had submitted to his father after the battle of Bosworth. He 'trusted in God to be their governor'. It was an expensive illusion, as even he eventually recognised. In 1525, when Francis I was defeated and captured by an imperial army at Pavia in northern Italy, Henry called on the Emperor Charles V to ensure that his claims to the French Crown, or at least to Normandy and Guyenne, were secured by the terms of the French King's release. His request was ignored and the claim was never pressed again.[74]

The result of these attempts was repeated humiliation and a disastrous loss of money and lives which went far to vindicate Edmund Dudley's gloomy view of continental wars. In the Parliament of 1523, which refused to grant a subsidy for war, Henry's future minister Thomas Cromwell delivered a shrewd analysis of Henry's strategic dilemma. It was impossible, he said, to ape the ambitions of Henry V a hundred years later, when the condition of France was so different, and it was pointless to capture 'ungracious dogholes' like Tournai. Some of Henry's councillors privately shared Cromwell's views, but it was dangerous for men to speak their mind too openly in Tudor England. Most of them kept their opinions to themselves. One who did not was Archbishop Warham of Canterbury. Writing to the King in 1525, he reported on the difficulty that he had encountered in trying to persuade the men of Kent to contribute to the 'Amicable Grant', a forced loan intended to fund another invasion of France. Henry's friends, said Warham, were telling him confidentially that the King 'should not attempt to win France, the winning whereof should be more chargeful to England than profitable, and the keeping thereof much more chargeful than the winning'.[75]

Henry VIII invaded France for the last time in 1544 in alliance with the Emperor Charles V, but this time the objective was different. The King rejected Charles's plan to march on Paris in favour of the more limited strategy of consolidating English control of the Channel and providing a forward defence against invasion. It was essentially the strategy proposed in 1436 by the author of the *Libel of English Policy*. Henry had lost interest in his ancestors' duchy of Guyenne, and at one point even tried to swap England's claims to Guyenne for Charles V's claims to the walled towns of the Somme. The invasion of 1544 resulted in the capture of Boulogne. Henry VIII took its surrender in person, riding through the gates, 'the sword born naked before him ... like a noble and valiant conqueror'. The town was occupied for the next six years by a garrison more than twice the size of any that the English had ever maintained at Calais. Better, the King told the Spanish ambassador, to 'take two or three frontier places than to have burnt Paris'. The notion that England's wall against invasion lay in continental Europe would become one of the axioms of English foreign policy from the sixteenth century to the twentieth. But in the late middle ages, long before England became a military and economic power on a European scale, it made little sense and proved to be financially ruinous. The main consequence in the 1540s was that the Channel ports assumed greater importance in French strategic calculations. The French King Henry II bought back Boulogne in 1550 and began to take a renewed interest in the recovery of Calais.[76]

Calais had enjoyed a remarkable immunity from attack since the Burgundian ventures of the 1430s. There had been several French projects for retaking it, all of which had been abandoned in the face of the formidable challenge of penetrating the ring of marsh and floodwater and maintaining a blockade from the sea. Towards the end of his reign Louis XI confessed to the English royal councillor Lord Hastings that he had no interest in the place and had turned down every proposal to recover it that had been made to him. For the English, Calais was the last reminder of the triumphs of Edward III, a source of prestige but no longer of power. Its commercial importance had dwindled with the decline of the wool trade. Customs duties on wool passing through the Staplers' hands no longer covered the cost of its defence after the 1520s. The English government had to fund the garrison's wages and the considerable cost of modernising its fourteenth-century defences from other revenues. Yet in spite of all this expenditure, the town was vulnerable. The ramparts were not designed to resist modern artillery. Parts of them were in serious disrepair. The castle, which should have been the strongest part of the defences, was 'more apt to give the enemy an entry to the town than to defend the town or itself', the Privy Council ruefully observed in 1556.[77]

In November 1557 Henry II finally resolved upon its recapture. The designated commander, François de Lorraine Duke of Guise, had excellent and up-to-date intelligence on the state of the defences, of which he made good use. Decades of immunity had made the garrison complacent. In spite of the increasingly obvious signs of a military build-up in north-western France no action was taken either by Lord Wentworth, the commander in Calais, or by the council in England until it was too late. The French army appeared on the heights of Sangatte on New Year's Eve and launched its attack on New Year's Day 1558. Wentworth, who was concerned about the town's supply of fresh water, refused to allow the sluices at Newenham Bridge to be opened until the following day. As a result, the French were able to overwhelm the fort at Newenham and close them again before the plain had flooded. They seized the Rysbank Tower on the mole dominating the harbour entrance, thus closing the harbour to any relief force from England and allowing artillery to be sited directly opposite the weakest part of the castle. The defenders of both of these vital outworks withdrew into the town without firing a shot. When, on the night of 5 January, the French took the castle by storm, they had the town at their mercy. The garrison refused to fight on and Wentworth surrendered on the 7th. Guines held out for two more weeks before a mutiny in the garrison forced its captain to surrender. With the rest of the pale in French hands, the garrison of Hammes gave up and fled into Flanders. The loss of Calais was a grave blow to the prestige of England and the morale of its people. Addressing the first Parliament of Elizabeth I a year later, the Lord Keeper said that the Crown had not suffered any 'greater loss in honour strength and treasure than to lose that place'. At the time, however, Parliament received the news with weary indifference. More realistic perhaps than the Queen's ministers, they responded to proposals to recapture it by observing that the times were bad, the cost would be very great, and 'if the French have taken Calais, they have taken nothing from the English, but only recovered what was theirs'.[78]

All that now remained of the legacy of Edward III and Henry V was the title Rex Franciae, which had first been adopted as part of the royal style by Edward III in 1340. It had become an empty formula but proved to be the most durable of Edward's acts. For a time, the English claim continued to provoke literary and diplomatic polemic. Louis XI took an obsessive interest in the issue. The treatise which he commissioned to support the French position, probably from the veteran diplomat Guillaume Cousinot, was one of the earliest books to be printed in France and was regularly reprinted up to the middle of the sixteenth century. In England there was less interest in the merits of the claim, and pragmatic reasons for regarding it as a pipedream. When Henry VIII met Francis I at the Field of Cloth of Gold in 1520, during an interval of close relations between the two monarchs, a good-humoured altercation was provoked by the reading of the articles of agreement, in which the title appeared. It was 'a title given to me which is good for nothing', Henry declared.[79]

The Kings and Queens of England continued to call themselves Kings and Queens of France in their official style for nearly three centuries longer, even in treaties and diplomatic correspondence with France. No one made an issue of it until the revolutionary wars of the late eighteenth century. During the abortive peace negotiations between Britain and France in 1797, the republican government of France insisted that the practice must stop. In vain did the British plenipotentiary Lord Malmesbury riposte that the title meant nothing and that none of the former Kings of France had objected. Its use, the French delegates insisted, was offensive to a republican regime which had abolished the monarchy. Reporting on the negotiations to the

House of Commons, William Pitt unconsciously echoed the words of Henry VIII in 1520. The title, he said, was a 'harmless feather at most'. Yet even now, not everyone agreed. One member rose to remind the House of the glorious deeds of their ancestors, of the great victories of Edward III and of the treaty that he had been able to impose on France at Brétigny at the height of his power:

No ancient dignity which for so many centuries had shed lustre on the English crown, ought to be considered as a mere slight, unsubstantial ornament. It was bound up indissolubly with the honour of the nation. If we suffered that feather to be plucked, he feared that three other feathers, which were nearly connected with the crown, and were gallantly won in the same glorious wars by which we first asserted the claim of our monarchs to that harmless feather, would soon follow; the crown, and the throne itself, would hardly be secure. A great nation can never safely be disgraced.[80]

George III, for one, was not convinced. When, in 1801, the Act of Union with Ireland empowered him to modify his royal title, he took the opportunity to drop the Crown of France from his style and the fleurs-de-lys from his arms. With Napoleon in power in France and Louis XVIII living in exile in England, these symbols of an ancient war had become an embarrassment.

CHAPTER XV

The Reckoning

Writing in the early 1490s, that worldly cynic Philippe de Commynes, practised diplomat and counsellor of kings and princes, observed that

God never created man or beast in the world without creating his opposite to keep him on his toes and prevent him from getting above himself... Thus to the Kingdom of France he has given the English, and to the English the Scots.[1]

A century and a half of war had emphasised old differences and generated new ones. The war left England physically unscathed but inflicted serious physical damage on France which took many years to mend. It promoted national antagonisms which eventually faded, and self-conscious national identities which persisted. While it lasted, it preserved the autonomy of Scotland and the princely states of France which but for the war would probably have been extinguished earlier. It formed the institutions of both England and France in ways which influenced much of their subsequent history.

England was already the most centralised state in Europe when the war began in the 1330s. The King's authority extended to the whole realm. His courts penetrated almost everywhere. Parliament represented every part of England. War brought the state closer to everyone. The growing preponderance of archers meant that English armies were recruited across a wide social spectrum and in every part of the country. The requisitioning of ships, the collection of taxes, the commissions of array, the beacons on hilltops and proclamations in market squares were all part of the daily experience of the whole population. A web of rumour united disparate communities. The records of indictments and convictions in the criminal courts and pardons issued from the royal chancery reveal a nation intensely interested in politics and possessed by strong prejudices and powerful common instincts, especially in the towns, but not only there. The omnipresence of the state made people conscious of its ambitions and also of its failings. They were brought together by the triumphs of

Edward III and Henry V, but also by common grievances, many of them arising from the hardships of war and the bitterness of ultimate defeat.

The English did not regard themselves as aggressors. They saw their country as an island defended by the sea against a hostile continent. At the end of the thirteenth century, Robert of Gloucester's verse chronicle in middle English had declared that England was 'a well good land, of all other lands the best. Set at the end of the world in the west, the sea girding it about ... it fears no foe except who comes by treachery.'[2] There was in fact only one point at which England was at serious risk of invasion, in 1386 when French armies massing by the coast of Flanders provoked panic across the land. Yet the English always felt insecure. They lived in constant fear of invasion from Scotland, although Scottish raids, for all their brutality, never penetrated far south of Durham. The memory of the coastal raids on Southampton in 1338, Rye in 1377 and Plymouth in 1403 lived on long after the danger had passed and the damage had been made good. Piracy and commerce raiding at sea barely affected the course of the war but had an immense impact on public opinion. The defence of Calais was a popular cause, like that of Cherbourg and Brest in the 1390s and Boulogne in the 1540s, because these fortresses in France were regarded as bastions of England, the first line of defence against invasion.

The country's separation from the rest of the known world was emotional as well as physical. The English thought of themselves as belonging to a distinct culture, which they defined mainly by contrasting it with stereotypes of their neighbours: the 'wild' inhabitants of the Celtic fringe of Scotland, Wales and Ireland; and the powerful, vindictive, proud, deceitful, effeminate and cowardly French. The distinctiveness of England was the theme of the two most popular English histories of the age, Ranulph Higden's *Polychronicon*, translated into English in 1387, and the numerous versions of the middle English *Brut*, the London chronicle which traced England's origins back to the mythical Brutus the Trojan. It is not unusual for people to believe in the superiority of their own culture. Noel de Fribois, one of Charles VII's private secretaries, accused his own countrymen of much the same vice. But objective outsiders thought that it was carried further in England, and there is much literary and anecdotal evidence to support their view. They were 'great lovers of themselves', a well-travelled Venetian diplomat reported at the end of the fifteenth century. They thought that there was 'no other world but England'.[3]

Language was the badge of identity. As the English delegate Thomas Polton told the Council of Constance in 1417, it was 'by divine and human law the authentic sign and very essence of nationhood'. Middle English, the language of all but a small minority of English people, was spoken nowhere outside the British Isles, even as a second language. Charles the Rash, Duke of Burgundy, was the only continental prince of this period who is known to have spoken some English. The language had no international currency, as French, Occitan and even the various forms of low German did. As early as 1295 Edward I had tried to rally support for war with France by accusing its Kings of planning to eradicate the English language. This accusation was regularly repeated in official propaganda over the next century and a half. Already the language of popular literature and political propaganda, English was in the process of displacing Latin as the language of law and government and French as the language of polite discourse. Edward III's mother-tongue was French; Henry IV's was English. The change owed much to political sentiment against the background of war. Henry V consciously sought to identify nation with language and adopted English in almost all his communications with his subjects. His example was infectious. When in 1422 the Brewers' Guild of London decided to change the language of their proceedings to English, they cited Henry's practice among their reasons.

Anglo-Norman French, the insular dialect which had once been the common language of the nobility, the gentry and the patriciate of the larger towns, was a dying language. It progressively diverged from the 'standard' French of Paris, which was a vigorous, living language spoken by a larger and more varied population with a wider range of experience. Chaucer's Madame Eglantine spoke the French of Stratford-at-Bow, 'for French of Paris was to her unknow'. The poet was mocking her, but he knew that his readers would share the joke. When the diplomats of Richard II and Henry V refused to speak French at diplomatic conferences, they were making a political point, but their complaint that they could not understand the language's subtleties may well have been right. In the fifteenth century, a knowledge of French was still the sign of a gentleman, but it was a foreign language and not their own. It was generally the French of Paris that they spoke, and they had to learn it. They spoke and wrote English at home.[4]

Among the political and military class, resentment of France was driven less by hatred than by distrust of French elites, with which they actually had much in common. The French were regarded as a tricky people who could not be relied upon to observe any truce or treaty that they made. Their failure to honour the one-sided treaties imposed on them under the duress of civil war, at Brétigny in 1360 and Troyes in 1420, was constantly cited against them. But resentment of France was not confined to those who were directly involved in diplomacy and war. There was force in Froissart's complaint that in England's volatile political world, elites were constrained by popular feelings which were more aggressive than their own. He was not the only one who thought so. 'As you well know,' the Duke of Berry wrote to his brother after the coup which placed Henry IV on the throne, 'Lancaster governs by the will of the English people, and the English people like nothing better than war.'[5]

England's long history of popular xenophobia was probably at its most virulent in the fifteenth century. The Czech traveller Leo of Rozmital, who toured Europe in the 1460s, was only briefly in England, but it was long enough to find the English officious and hostile. Behind a mask of courtesy, he thought them treacherous and antagonistic. Traditionally, hostility to foreigners was London-led. The main targets were the foreign business communities settled in the city and the immigrant artisans concentrated in the neighbouring borough of Southwark across the river. Commercial malpractice, espionage, religious heterodoxy, loose morals and various kinds of anti-social behaviour were among the charges laid against them by London mobs and the Parliamentary Commons alike. These ancient animosities were themselves unrelated to the war, but the war aggravated and broadened them. It was no coincidence that London was the scene of such intense elation after England's victories and anger after defeat. The Black Prince after Poitiers and Henry V after Agincourt had been received there with extravagant adulation which readily turned to fury in the time of their less fortunate successors. It was in this intensely political city, with its densely packed population, its volatile mobs and its proximity to the centre of government, that Humphrey Duke of Gloucester found the most vocal supporters for his aggressive war policy, and Richard Duke of York for his attack on the government after the loss of Normandy. London led the way, but it was not alone. The Kent mobs who broke into the city in 1450, the

Portsmouth mutineers who murdered Adam Moleyns, the Wiltshire villagers who lynched William Ayscough and the Gloucester rioters who pillaged Reginald Boulers's abbey, were all moved by the same impulses. The conquests of Edward III and Henry V became a benchmark against which the achievements of later kings were measured. A myth of invincibility and betrayal grew up, which never acknowledged the limits to what military operations alone could achieve. Half a century after the loss of Normandy, the scholar Robert Gaguin, who came to England twice with French embassies, was taken aback by the 'envious hatred' that he encountered there. He reported that Englishmen were still teaching archery to their sons by setting up a target and saying, 'Go on, son, learn how to strike and kill a Frenchman.'[6]

For most Frenchmen, the war was a much more bitter and direct experience than it was for the English. The fate of townspeople slaughtered in the streets of a *ville prise*, or defeated infantry and camp-followers cut down by horsemen in their thousands as they fled the field, or peasants and merchants killed or kidnapped by freelance brigands in open country, these things touched even a world inured to violence. Peasants and townsmen took brutal revenge against soldiers whom they caught unawares or alone. In the fourteenth century, the victims' hatred of their oppressors had commonly been directed against fighting men in general and reflected class antagonisms as much as national ones. This became the orthodoxy of contemporary moralists, who condemned the entire knightly class without necessarily singling out the English. But in the fifteenth century 'enemy' became synonymous with 'English'. The presence in northern France after 1417 of a standing English army and a network of permanent English garrisons inevitably underlined the national character of these antagonisms. The classic stereotype of the brawny, blond, heavy-drinking and hard-swearing monoglot English brute had its origins in older literature but came into its own in these years. Like all caricature, it was exaggerated but recognisable. But if caricature often has an element of affection, the polemical literature of the fifteenth century had none. In a treatise presented to Charles VII shortly after the expulsion of the English from Normandy and Gascony, the English were characterised as treacherous, mendacious, cruel, greedy, regicidal and given to every vice of the flesh. Another pamphleteer reckoned that more than two million French lives had been lost in the wars, not to speak of those who suffered from abduction, rape and arson. 'And all this has come about by the pride of this wretched generation of Englishmen.' They were 'ravenous wolves, proud, pompous, hypocrites, unconscionable liars, tyrants and persecutors of Christian souls, who lap up human blood like birds of prey'.[7]

The English left France scarred by the four decades of war which followed Henry V's invasion of 1415. The payroll strength of armies on both sides seems small. There were never more than 15,000 English soldiers at any one time on the English payroll in France. The armies of Charles VII were never more than 20,000 strong and usually smaller. But figures like these give a misleading idea of the scale of military activity. The actual strength of armies was at least twice as great when armed pages, servants and auxiliaries are included. In addition, there were important garrisons and freelance companies in contested territory which lived on the population around them and did not appear on any payroll. The impact of all these disparate forces was magnified by the general breakdown of public order which followed their passage, as local men took up arms and were driven by poverty and unemployment to banditry or swelled the numbers of the companies of *routiers* and *écorcheurs*.

Every traveller who passed through northern France remarked on the scale of war damage. Jean de Bueil described riding through a landscape wrecked by war: the land desolate and abandoned, the inhabitants few and poor, peasant houses that looked like the lairs of wild animals, and the occasional gentlemen living in modest castles and fortified manors with ancient, crumbling walls and freezing halls. In his powerful allegorical poem *Testament of War*, written in about 1480, Jean Molinet imagined War leaving his legacy of high taxation in the towns and physical destruction in the country:

> Je laisse aux abbaies grandes
> Cloistres rompus, dortoirs gastés,
> Greniers sans bled, troncqs sans offrandes
> Celiers sans vins, fours sans pastés.
> ...
> Je laisse au pouvre plat payz
> Chasteaux brisiés, hostieux brullés,
> Terre sans blef, gens extrahis,
> Bergers battus et affolés,

Marchands meurdris et mutilés,
Et corbaux crians a tout lés
Famine dessoubs les gibbés.*

Thomas Basin's famous description of northern France as a sea of brambles in which abandoned animals were the only sign of life, is often dismissed as hyperbole. But it was true of the worst affected regions: Picardy, the Beauvaisis, the Île-de-France, northern and western Champagne and the marches of Normandy. Sir John Fortescue, the Lancastrian Chief Justice who fled to France with Margaret of Anjou in 1463, travelled through these regions and remarked on the ill-dressed, undernourished peasants and the barren ground that he saw everywhere. 'Verily,' he said, 'they liven in the most extreme poverty and misery, and yet dwellen they in the most fertile realm of the world.'[8]

It was not simply physical violence which destroyed these regions, but the depopulation which followed and made recovery so difficult. Jean Juvénal des Ursins was exaggerating when he told the Estates-General of Blois in 1433 that France had lost nine-tenths of its population. Only in a small number of the most heavily damaged regions did depopulation approach that level. But he put his finger on the deadly combination of war, famine and disease which lay behind France's demographic catastrophe. The pamphleteer's figure of two million deaths was a guess, but a plausible one if indirect casualties are included. War provoked famine by destroying crops and barns, looting draft animals, and stopping the movement of grain and other foodstuffs. It increased mortality, especially among children, through poverty, exposure, malnutrition and the transmission of disease. Above all, it provoked large-scale migration away from the war zones. Initially, the crowds of displaced country folk fled to nearby castles and walled towns, which offered a temporary refuge. But towns and villages had limited shelter to offer and no subsistence or employment for strangers. People returned to their homes when the danger had passed, but each time in smaller numbers. The landscape slowly changed, as the countryside emptied out. The suburbs of walled towns

---

* 'To the great abbeys I bequeathe the wrecked cloisters, ruined dormitories, barns without wheat, chests without offerings, cellars without wine and ovens without loaves ... To the miserable open country I bequeathe the demolished castles, burned out guest houses, lands without grain or cultivators, shepherds beaten insane, merchants murdered or mutilated, crows croaking everywhere and famine under the shadow of the gallows.'

were demolished to deprive an enemy of cover. Outlying farmsteads were abandoned in favour of village houses clustered together for safety. Eventually, families gave up, abandoned the land and moved away. The governors of the hospital of St John in Saint-Omer, which received many refugees, summarised the mechanics of destruction in a petition of 1434. The town, they said, was

> full of poor people with no idea how to earn a living, some from the town itself, some from the Île-de-France, Normandy, Picardy and other parts of this realm destroyed by the wars. They include many children and people ill from cold and hunger or suffering from exhaustion or wounds inflicted by the enemy.

Many of the displaced thousands from Picardy, Normandy and Maine migrated south of the Loire. Others made for Brittany or Flanders, islands of relative peace in spite of sporadic irruptions of fighting.[9]

While England and Burgundy were allies, Artois and the Boulonnais had been largely sheltered from the war. But their experience after 1435 showed how rapidly a region could be destroyed. It was invaded by the French in the summer of 1435, by the army of Humphrey Duke of Gloucester in 1436, repeatedly by the garrison of Calais in the following years, and then by the *écorcheurs* for nearly a decade. The tax records of the town of Étaples, which was attacked by the French in 1435, reveal that it lost a quarter of its population in a matter of months. The canons of St Vaast in Arras informed Philip the Good in the following year that freelance companies and English raiders had reduced their agricultural revenues to next to nothing, as their tenants had all deserted their holdings. In districts within raiding distance of Calais or Le Crotoy, many villages were abandoned, some of them never to rise again. The story of Artois and the Boulonnais was repeated across much of northern France.[10]

Josas was one of the three archdeaconries of the diocese of Paris. It covered a large area south-west of the capital on either side of the Roman road to Chartres, comprising some 200 parishes. The region was fought over by the armies of Armagnac and Burgundy before 1420, by the armies of the English lieutenants and the Bastard of Orléans during the two decades of English occupation, by the companies of *écorcheurs* in the 1430s and 1440s, and by the confederates of the War of the Common Weal in 1465. Between 1458 and 1470 the archdeacon's vicar on his tours faithfully recorded the after-effects of war. The picture of devastation recorded in his notes is confirmed by other sources. The barony of Chevreuse was a microcosm of the fate of much of the region. The castle, which stood over the Roman road, was one of the principal strongholds of the region. It had been occupied by an English garrison in the 1430s. All around it, manors, churches, barns and mills lay burned out and ruinous. Parish churches, where the population had run for shelter as the soldiers approached, were found gutted by fire, the bells taken away and the sacristies looted. The land around had reverted to forest and scrub. When the Celestine house of Paris let out their estate at Châteaufort, a survey of the village included six habitable houses, seven more which were roofless and forty-five which had left no sign of their existence except for the trace of their foundations on the ground. Some thirty villages were not recorded by the archdeacon's vicar because they no longer existed. Others had only two or three households remaining. Many had no priest, or a priest who had abandoned his office, usually for want of revenues. Very few parishes were able to meet the cost of repairing the parish church. Monastic buildings were abandoned. At Gif near Palaiseau, only half the abbey church was still standing. The abbess was still there, a solitary survivor living among the ruins. Another solitary head of house, the abbot of La Roche, subsisted by selling off the abbey's bible and chalice and finally the tiles from the roof. The Cistercian abbey of Vaux-de-Cernay had once been among the most flourishing of the Île-de-France. By 1463, the country around it had become a wasteland into which no one ventured. A single aged monk, with a beard reaching to his waist, had been left to look after the buildings. He survived on a dole of bread and beans supplied by the dame de Chevreuse. Her own position was parlous enough. Chevreuse had lost nine-tenths of its population. Its lords had been unable to collect their rents or enforce their seigneurial rights for many years. They survived by selling rentcharges secured on their worthless domains and then defaulting. They struggled on until 1543 when they finally sold up. Their fate was common enough. Out of sixty-five parishes with lay lords, fifty-two were sold between 1400 and 1550. Some of them changed hands two or three times, or in one case eleven times. The sales were commonly made at low prices to purchasers belonging to groups which had profited by the wars: successful soldiers and lawyers, royal officers, money changers. Even they could not always make their investment pay. Eight years after the sale of the barony of Chevreuse, the courtier who bought it was himself sold up by the Bishop of Paris for non-payment of dues.[11]

Maine was continuously fought over until the province was restored to the house of Anjou in 1448, and in some districts even after that. Right up to the end of the fifteenth century, leases and acts of sale in the county contain frequent references to the depopulation of villages and the ruinous state of buildings, vines and gardens. At Le Mans, the provincial capital, part of the palace of the counts was reported to be a gutted shell with the roofs beginning to fall through and the gardens abandoned. When the barony of Tucé was recovered by Charles of Maine in 1453, the act which recorded the fact declared that the whole barony was a wasteland. The forest had spread over the arable land. The buildings were burned out or collapsed. Much of the population had migrated to Brittany, Anjou or Touraine, where some of them had died in abject poverty. Only a few had returned. The description could be matched in many other lordships and villages across the county. The small town of Solesmes, clustered round its Benedictine priory, was reported in 1497 to have been populated by rich merchants and adorned with grand houses before the wars, but now to be inhabited only by beggars. The surviving accounting records suggest that half a century after the departure of the English the estate revenues of these places had still not recovered.[12]

Recovery from war damage was patchy and slow. Buildings, vines and draft animals represented substantial capital investments which would take years to replace. But the most significant obstacle to recovery was reforestation. 'The forests came to France with the English' was a familiar saying among the peasants of Saintonge.[13] In regions such as the Île-de-France and the Beauvaisis which were fought over for long periods, the cultivated area retreated to islands of security around the walled towns and castles. The forest, which had been in retreat for two centuries before the wars, advanced to fill the void left by abandoned farms and smallholdings. In an age without central registers or cadastres, those who had migrated to other regions returned to find the landmarks gone and the boundaries of their land obliterated by trees and scrub. Roads and paths disappeared beneath a featureless landscape. Bringing the land back into cultivation was tough work and extremely labour-intensive. Trees and bushes had to be cut down and the roots grubbed up by hard digging and ploughing, generally with wooden tools. It took decades to re-create viable farms.

THE RECKONING

In the years following the truce of Tours and the suppression of the *écorcheurs*, the main engine of economic recovery was a dramatically rising birth rate, accompanied by a decline of child mortality and powerful tides of internal migration towards the more fertile war zones where the emptiness of the landscape created opportunities for the footloose and landless. The movement was encouraged by the greater landowners, who abandoned their seigneurial rights and reduced their rents to attract colonists. Fresh outbreaks of civil war and epidemic disease scarcely dented the upward trend.

We can trace the process in miniature at Sepeaux, a small village of the Gâtinais, whose older inhabitants gave evidence to an inquiry commissioned in 1494 by the cathedral chapter of Sens. Sepeaux had once been a prosperous village. At the beginning of the fifteenth century, the villagers cultivated an area of about 4,000 *arpents* (about 5,000 acres or 2,000 hectares). They also operated three forges using iron ore which they extracted from open cast mines. Their problems began during the civil wars following the murder of Louis of Orléans in 1407, when the region was violently contested between Armagnac and Burgundy. The village was finally abandoned in about 1427, when it became uninhabitable as a result of François de Surienne's occupation of Montargis. The English left Montargis in 1438 but were succeeded by roving bands of *écorcheurs*, which were worse. Most of the inhabitants fled into the forest where they lived on wild fruit and trapped animals before vanishing without trace. Some took refuge at Joigny and other walled places of the district. In a few years, trees grew up among the houses. The nave of the church collapsed. The fields were invaded by scrub and marsh. Sepeaux's recovery began in 1450, when one of the original inhabitants returned with his family from Joigny, together with two other families from other parts of France. A fourth family joined them in 1453. They cleared about twenty or thirty *arpents* (25–37 acres or 10–15 hectares). In 1454, a parish priest was nominated, who lived on the charity of the settlers and slept in the church tower. Some of the new settlers gave up the struggle and left, but by the 1460s there were twelve families at Sepeaux. The turning point of the village's fortunes came when the lordship was bought by Jean de Surienne, François's nephew, who had settled in Burgundy. He brought in colonists to drain the marsh and clear the forest in return for grants of land. The population began to grow rapidly. Only a handful of families were native to Sepeaux or its district. Most were migrants, mainly from Burgundy and the Nivernais, Limousin, Touraine, Anjou and Brittany. By the end of the century much of the old cultivated area had been reclaimed. It had taken fifty years.[14]

Cities served as catalysts for the recovery of the countryside. Their walls had saved them from the worst of the war damage. They were generally the first places to be repopulated. They provided capital, local and wholesale markets and manpower. Paris was the most striking example. The city enjoyed a precocious economic revival in the middle years of the century. The reopening in 1440 of gates which had been walled up for a decade was an important moment. The capture of Pontoise from the English in September 1441 was another. The lawyers, officials, merchants and craftsmen and the teachers at the university began to return. Over the next sixty years it is estimated that the population of Paris doubled, eventually exceeding the level in the medieval city's golden age around 1400. Turnover at the fairs of Lendit and Saint-Germain rose more than threefold in the 1450s and 1460s, as the city recovered its regional and national reach. Land values were perhaps the most telling economic indicators. The shops on the Pont au Change, more than half of which were unlet in 1440, began to fill up. Rents rose fivefold in the decade after the truce of Tours. The gaps in the streets filled up as derelict and demolished houses were rebuilt.

The Parisian boom accelerated the recovery of the Île-de-France, one of the most war-damaged regions of the country. The lead was taken by the great churches of Paris with their immense holdings of land and their access to capital. The chapter of Notre-Dame and the Benedictines of Saint-Denis and Saint-Germain-des-Prés were active improvers. Their efforts were seconded in the latter part of the period by rich professionals with money to buy the social prestige that came with the ownership and improvement of land. As early as 1465 Philippe de Commynes, serving in the Burgundian army in the War of the Common Weal, thought that he had never seen a city surrounded by such beautiful and productive landscapes. Except in the most marginal and heavily wooded areas, the deserted villages were repopulated, barns and mills rebuilt, vines replanted. By 1500 the forest and scrub had been pushed back and the cultivated area had returned to something like its original extent. The pull of Paris extended well beyond the Île-de-France into Champagne, Burgundy and the Beauce, which by 1500 had largely recovered the prosperity of a century earlier.[15]

For its size, Paris was unique, but the dynamic of its expansion was by no means exceptional. Lyon, which had been at the centre of a war zone since 1417, experienced a spectacular economic ascent in the half-century after the wars. The trade routes between Italy and the Low Countries, which had shifted east into the Rhine valley during the wars, reverted to the older passages of the Rhône and the Saône. Lyon's four annual fairs recovered the business lost to Geneva. The city's population, which had fallen by about a third during the wars, had recovered by the end of the century. The expansion of Lyon opened up fresh markets for the mainly grain-growing region around. The rural population rose rapidly. Their prosperity was written in the landscape, dotted with new barns and mills.[16]

Rouen experienced a similar renaissance. The city had lost a large part of its population in the 1430s and 1440s. Its severance from its natural markets to the north and east after the campaigns had hit the inhabitants hard. Once the city was in the same hands as Paris, after 1449, it was able to resume its traditional function as an entrepot for the distribution across western France of grain and wine from the basins of the Seine, the Marne and the Yonne, and fish, salt and raw wool brought in by sea. Already one of the major textile cities of France, Rouen became once again an important centre of trade with the Low Countries and northern Europe and, after the treaty of Picquigny, with England. The population in 1500 surpassed its thirteenth-century peak. Many of the smaller towns, especially in upper Normandy, enjoyed a rebirth which was almost as dramatic. By the end of the fifteenth century, Dieppe's population had increased by nearly half and it had become Normandy's leading commercial seaport. The urban revival in Normandy contributed to a remarkable restoration of the Norman countryside. By the beginning of the sixteenth century, the population of rural Normandy had risen sharply. Land values and agricultural revenues were rising and the cultivated area was not far short of what it had been in the early fourteenth century, before the age of the great wars and epidemics.[17]

Opening the Estates-General of Tours in 1484, the Chancellor of France, Guillaume de Rochefort, declared that for the beauty of its countryside and fertility of its soil France surpassed every country of the world. 'Where else do we find such rich pasturage, such a variety of fish, such fine flocks of animals? Who can produce wheat and wine to match ours? Is there any land so rich in everything to satisfy the needs of mankind?' As if in answer to Sir John Fortescue's observations two decades earlier, he compared the economic fortunes of France favourably to those of England. This was rhetoric, but it must have sounded plausible to the highly critical audience in front of him. When, in 1508, the courtier-bishop Claude de Seyssel wrote his tract in praise of Louis XII, he made the same point as Chancellor Rochefort. A third of the land, he thought, had been abandoned during the wars and restored to cultivation since they had ended. If France was populous and rich, he argued, the evidence was to be found in the current building boom. Throughout the realm men were putting up great buildings, public and private, with gilded finials, elaborate roofs and painted walls. Building was a metaphor for resurgence. The last three decades had seen an explosion of building activity after the long dearth. In Paris, the Hôtel de Sens and the Hôtel de Cluny, both of which were completed in the 1490s, were the first aristocratic mansions to be built in the city since the reconstruction of the Hôtel d'Artois by John the Fearless at the outset of the civil wars. No fewer than forty-three Parisian churches were built or rebuilt in this period. The fifteen that survive today include some of the great masterpieces of flamboyant gothic: Saint-Séverin, Saint-Gervais, Saint-Germain l'Auxerrois, Saint-Étienne-du-Mont, Saint-Merri and the tower of Saint-Jacques. Victor Hugo set *The Hunchback of Notre-Dame* in 1482, the year in which he imagined that medieval Paris had come closest to harmonious perfection, a fleeting moment before the coldness of the classical age and the vandalism of the Revolution took their toll. Fifty years after the English left, Rouen too had marked its new wealth in a building boom, creating the towers of the cathedral, the church of Saint-Maclou and the Palais de Justice, and transforming the harsh military capital of the Duke of Bedford into the ideal city of Turner and Pugin.[18]

England's experience of the war was very different. The only significant military operations on English soil were the rare Scottish raids into the northern counties and even rarer French seaborne landings on the south coast. 'If the whole of England were put up for sale, it would not fetch a hundredth part of the damage the English have done to France,' declared a pamphleteer writing in about 1420. The difference was reflected in the built landscape. There was no equivalent in England of the dense network of garrisoned castles in Normandy, the Île-de-

France or the march of Gascony. A French herald, who had probably visited England, claimed in the 1450s that the country's characteristic noble residence was a manor house, not a castle, and that for every proper castle in England there were fifty in France. His figures may have been suspect, but his impression was right. At least half of the 1,500 or so castles built in England since the Norman conquest had been abandoned by 1300 and allowed to fall into ruin. Many of the rest were no longer surveyed or maintained in defensible condition. No one troubled to repair them at the onset of the war with France. Very few new castles were built for defence in the fourteenth century and none in the fifteenth. The many fine castles put up in the fifteenth century were designed for status, comfort and display. They had thin walls, large windows and no provision for a garrison. Their crenellations and gatehouses were more decorative than functional. Fewer than half of English towns important enough to have royal charters were walled, and many of the rest had walls built for prestige rather than defence. Leo of Rozmital was surprised to find that even important places like Salisbury and Poole were unwalled.[19]

Did the wars enrich England? Many contemporary Frenchmen thought so. Thomas Basin believed that the English had extracted 'immeasurable riches' from France. To him it seemed obvious that England's prosperity was the mirror image of France's ruin. The English looted France. They received grants of land in Normandy which had been confiscated from their French owners. They levied *pâtis*. They plundered captured towns. They took valuable prisoners, from whom they exacted large ransoms. Some English captains made fortunes which they brought back to England and spent on conspicuous consumption or invested, usually in land and buildings. Their expenditure brought money into the English economy, indirectly benefiting many who had never set foot in France. Henry of Grosmont Earl of Derby was reported to have paid for the entire cost of building the Savoy palace in the Strand from the ransoms of the battle of Auberoche in 1345, while Thomas Walsingham thought that the loot of Calais later that year could be found in every well-to-do home in England. These stories tended to grow in the telling. But the great mounted raids of the fourteenth century undoubtedly offered ideal conditions for gains of this sort. The English were on the offensive throughout. Their tactical and technical superiority on the battlefield was at its height.

When the antiquary John Leland toured England in the 1530s, the wars were still a powerful memory. People pointed out great castles and palaces said to have been built with the spoils of France. In some cases, this was a fable, fondly repeated by credulous proprietors. But it is clear that there was a boom in the construction of grand aristocratic houses by successful soldiers who had made money in France. Wealth was a route to status and building was a public assertion of status. The County Durham knight Sir William Bowes, who crossed to Normandy with Henry V in 1417, returned in about 1423 with at least two prisoners. Leland was told that he 'waxed rich and, coming home, augmented his land and fame'. He marked his fame in stone by building Streatlam castle, the only notable new mansion commissioned in the north-east in the fifteenth century. The Herefordshire knight Sir Roland Lenthall fought at Agincourt and 'took many prisoners there, by the which prey he began the new building and manor place at Hampton'. In about 1425, Sir Walter Hungerford, future Treasurer of England and founder of his family's fortunes, greatly enlarged his show castle at Farleigh on the river Frome in Somerset. Part of Hungerford's great wealth was derived from royal service in England and judicious marriages. But his greatest accession of riches came from war profits. His retinue had taken at least eight valuable prisoners at Agincourt, and he was handsomely endowed with Norman lands by Henry V. Ampthill castle, 'standing stately on an hill' with its prominent gatehouse and nine towers, was built by Sir John Cornwall, 'of such spoils, it is said, that he won in France'. Sir John was a man of modest gentry origins who became a great figure through riches won in the wars of Henry IV and Henry V. He received 21,375 *écus* (about £3,600) as his share of the payment made to buy off the army of the Duke of Clarence in 1412. Three years later, he captured the Count of Vendôme and several other valuable prisoners at Agincourt. He also carried on a lucrative trade in other people's prisoners.[20]

Yet these visible signs of wealth were deceptive. The striking thing about the stately residences of successful English soldiers is that they were almost all built on fortunes made before 1425. The Agincourt campaign was the last great mounted raid in the style of Edward III and the Black Prince. Conditions were more difficult later. English captains did not rush home with their spoils like the victors of Agincourt or their fourteenth-century forebears. They were based in France, where they were engaged in a permanent military occupation. Occupation brought fewer occasions for profit and very large costs. The profits, such as they were, tended to be retained in France and brought little benefit to England. The biggest sources of wealth for English captains in France in this period were grants of land in Normandy and Maine. But these came with military obligations which consumed much of the revenue, and the land itself could not be sold without permission, which was sparingly granted. Ransoms were more likely to be remitted to England than revenues from land, but the occasions for exacting them were rarer. The golden ransoms of Agincourt continued to be collected for thirty years after the battle. The Duke of Bedford's share (presumably a third) of the ransoms of Cravant in 1423 was reported to be 160,000 *saluts* (about £27,000 sterling). The ransoms of Verneuil in the following year were certainly larger. The Duke of Alençon alone fetched 200,000 *écus* (about £33,000). After Verneuil, however, there were few pitched battles and the English lost most of them. From 1429, they were generally on the defensive. Few men brought fortunes home in these conditions.[21]

One man who did was Sir John Fastolf, whose war profits are unusually well documented. Fastolf was the Grand Master of the Duke of Bedford's household, and later a councillor of the Duke of York. His war service made him one of the richest men in England. His gains from prisoners taken at Verneuil were worth 20,000 marks (£13,667). He commanded some of the principal garrisons of Alençon and Maine. These garrisons were essentially large, mounted raiding forces which conducted a persistent guerrilla war against the Angevin garrisons of the southern march for nearly two decades. They were also, unusually for garrisons in English-occupied territory, allowed to impose *pâtis* on the inhabitants of Maine. When he left France for the last time in 1445, Fastolf held a Norman barony, ten Norman castles, fifteen manors and an inn at Rouen. Much of this property was still in his hands when it was lost in the final debacle of 1449–50, although by that time Fastolf had already remitted large sums to England.

Fastolf husbanded his gains carefully. He employed accountants, receivers, bankers and business managers. He deposited funds with Italian banking houses in Paris and Bruges, with prominent London merchants, and with the abbey of St Benet Hulme in Norfolk. He acquired more than thirty estates in England. He laid out nearly £14,000 on the purchase of property in East Anglia and Southwark, including Caister castle in Norfolk and a fine town house by the

Thames near London Bridge. He spent another £9,500 on building works, mostly in rebuilding Caister. He adorned his homes with precious tapestries of Arras and filled his chests with jewellery and plate. This was conspicuous wealth, almost all of it derived from gains of war made in France after 1420. Fastolf had begun his career with very little, but his income in 1445 was nearly £1,500 a year, more than that of most Parliamentary peers. It is not surprising that he became a fierce foe of the Duke of Somerset and a firm Yorkist in the civil wars of the 1450s.

Like many old soldiers, in his final years Fastolf worried about his salvation. 'The hand of God's punishing hath grievously touched me,' he wrote in the final months of his life. When he died, a childless, embittered and tight-fisted old man, in December 1459, he was buried beside his wife in the south choir-aisle which he had added to the abbey church of St Benet Hulme. He had planned to leave his fortune to endow a college of priests at Caister to pray for him, for Henry IV and Henry V, for his patrons the Dukes of Clarence, Exeter and Bedford, for the 'good estate and prosperity' of Henry VI, and for a long list of friends and kinsmen who had served with him in France, most of whom had died there. In the event, the old man's wishes were frustrated by the machinations of his enemies. His estate, much depleted by the cost of litigation, was eventually diverted to create the founding endowment of Magdalen College, Oxford. The old warrior had had no interest in education. But perhaps there was something fitting about the ultimate fate of his riches. If the college of Caister had ever been created, it would have been dissolved with the other chantry foundations during the Reformation, whereas this rough professional soldier is still remembered at Magdalen for his unwitting support of scholarship.[22]

How typical was Fastolf? He had uncommon advantages, including the patronage of the Duke of Bedford, who generously endowed him with land in Normandy and Maine and appointed him to commands in the most active theatres of the war. The best-documented case after Fastolf's was that of the Danish adventurer Sir Andrew Ogard. He was born Anders Gyldenstierne, becoming naturalised in England as Andrew Ogard, after his birthplace at Aagaard in western Denmark. It is no accident that Ogard, like Fastolf, had been a household officer of the Duke of Bedford and owed his opportunities in large measure to the Regent's favour. Ogard entered English service in about 1422 and made a considerable fortune over the next quarter-century, mainly in Maine. He ended up as captain of Caen, where he performed his duties through deputies, taking a turn for himself and (it was alleged) embezzling part of the garrison's wages. He must have transferred some of his gains to England, for he bought land in Hertfordshire and Norfolk. He built himself a grand house at Stanstead Abbots, with three courtyards and a chapel served by four chaplains and a dozen clerks and choristers. Most of his fortune, however, appears to have stayed in France. At the time of the French reconquest, Ogard held offices and land in Normandy which had once yielded £1,000 a year. There was also 7,000 marks (£4,666) in gold in a chest in the house of his deputy at Caen, where it was presumably lost in 1450. Beneath the great heights at which Fastolf and Ogard operated, there were others who acquired agreeable but unspectacular fortunes in France, like Fastolf's friend Sir Henry Inglose, who invaded France with the Duke of Clarence in 1412 and then with Henry V in 1415 and 1417. Like so many others of his kind, Inglose is found investing large sums in land in England in the 1420s.[23]

Fortunes like those of Fastolf, Ogard and Inglose were highly visible, but they were only part of the picture. Many of their English contemporaries were ruined by the war. Their fate was more obscure and easily overlooked by men like Thomas Basin. Yet it was an increasingly common fate in the last two decades of Lancastrian France, when the fortunes of war had turned and the government was bankrupt. The captains who retained companies to fight in France assumed personal responsibility for their wages, which they were not always able to recover from the Exchequer. Some of the greatest names, like the Earl of Warwick and the Duke of York, lost heavily when they were forced to write off debts owed to them by the King. Lesser men without influence at the centre came off worse.

Ransoms, so often cited as a source of wealth, were more significant as a source of impoverishment. There can be little doubt that in Henry VI's time English soldiers collectively paid out much more in ransoms than they received. Several hundred men were captured with the Beaufort brothers and John Holland at Baugé in 1421. In 1429 at least 400 Englishmen were taken at Patay with Talbot, Scales and Fauconberg; more than 100 with Fauconberg at Pont-de-l'Arche in 1449; over 1,200 with Kyriel at Formigny in 1450; and some 2,000 after the battle of Castillon. Garrisons which surrendered too late or succumbed to an assault were liable to be taken prisoner en masse. For every noble pile built in England from the profits of war, there were others whose owners were forced to sell or mortgage them to pay ransoms. The East Anglia knight Sir John Knyvet did three tours of duty in France and was captured in two of them. He was forced to sell Knyvet Hall in Cambridgeshire to pay the first ransom and mortgaged his ancestral home at Mendlesham in Suffolk to pay the second.

The system bore particularly hard on men of high military standing but small landed endowments. Sir Thomas Rempston was one of the most prominent English captains of the age but one of the poorest knights in Nottinghamshire. He was captured at the battle of Patay in 1429 and by his own account was held for seven years in a 'hard and straight prison' before being released for a ransom of 18,000 *écus* (£2,000). This was a crushing burden for a man whose income was only £60 a year from English lands plus the uncertain yield of his Norman lordships at Gacé and Bellencombre. He was captured again at Saint-Sever in 1442 and held for at least four years. The second ransom is likely to have been higher for he was then serving as acting Seneschal of Gascony. By 1451 he was free but had lost his Norman lands in the reconquest while disposals had reduced the worth of his English lands to £20 a year, not even enough to support his status as a knight. The petitions to the King from indigent soldiers record countless cases of men like Rempston. They were men of modest rank and fortune, who had been ruined by ransom payments consuming most or all of their assets and often much of their family's as well. Most of these documents date from after the final collapse of Lancastrian Normandy. They are a melancholy reminder that most Englishmen who became landowners in Normandy lost everything in 1450.[24]

The fortunes and misfortunes of war lay behind many individual stories of social ascent or ruin. But it is not possible to translate the stories of a few thousand individuals into an assessment of the economic impact of the war on England as a whole. The war was a significant drag on the English economy. Taxation hit levels which were historically high by English standards. Over the whole of its 120-year course, about £8.25 million in war taxation was collected, an average of about £70,000 a year.[25] Great quantities of silver left England in the pockets of the troops, to be spent or lost in France. Productive resources were diverted on a large scale into fighting. At any one time between 5,000 and 40,000 soldiers (including pages, varlets and hangers-on) were serving in France. To carry them to France, ships were requisitioned and large numbers of seamen were pressed to man them, at considerable cost to England's overseas trade. Measured against a total population of between 2 and 2.5 million, of whom perhaps a third were able-bodied adult males, the war must have consumed up to a tenth of the available manpower at times of peak demand, which is comparable to the proportion conscripted in the Second World War. At a time of labour shortage and high wages, this represented a substantial economic burden. The fact that recruitment was often concentrated in a limited geographical area associated with a great captain must have created pockets of severe economic disruption.

The most significant economic cost of the war to England was probably due to the disruption of its export trades. England was dependent on exports, mainly of wool, cloth and tin, to a degree unmatched in Europe except by the Low Countries. The English government tightly regulated the wool trade throughout the war, partly in order to use it as a diplomatic weapon against Flanders and the principalities of the Low Countries, and partly to generate monopoly profits from a commodity which was essential to the textile industries of Italy and northern Europe. Edward III effectively nationalised the trade between 1337 and 1342 and used it to fund his early campaigns in France. From 1343 onwards, the English government operated a staple system under which wool exports were compulsorily channelled through a designated staple port, generally Calais, and a privileged cartel of staple merchants. The controlled wool market and mint at Calais were an important element in English war finance until well into the sixteenth century. The main victims of this system were the industrial consumers of continental Europe. But it must also have depressed the prices paid to growers. Ultimately, it contributed to the slow demise of the trade, as wool was diverted to feed an indigenous textile industry which was more lightly taxed and regulated.

The trade wars, which affected both raw wool and finished cloth, added to the economic burden. Valois France was closed to direct English exports for the best part of 120 years. Castile, an important market for English cloth, was closed during the 1370s and 1380s when England was at war with the Trastámaran Kings, and again in the reign of Henry V when Castile boycotted English goods in support of its French ally. The breach with the house of Burgundy in 1435 resulted in a ban on trade with England throughout the Burgundian Low Countries until 1440, and another between 1447 and 1452. Although the ban was widely evaded, it had a serious impact on cloth exports to Flanders, Holland and Brabant. Trade with the Baltic, another major market, was badly disrupted in these years, since much of it was conducted through the great entrepots of Middelburg, Bergen op Zoom and Antwerp. Even allies and neutrals periodically broke off commercial relations in reprisal for English naval operations which often degenerated into piracy. Trade with the Hanse towns was suspended for this reason from 1447 until the 1470s.[26]

It is unlikely that England was better off for having fought a long, costly and ultimately unsuccessful war in France. In reality, however, this kind of profit and loss account is meaningful only in an age like our own in which material welfare is the proper concern of the state, and resources expended on avoidable wars are by definition diverted from more worthwhile alternatives. Pity and charity were Christian duties in the middle ages, as they have always been, but material welfare in a broader sense was not the collective concern of human societies that it later became. This explains much that seems strange about the attitude of medieval people to war. War was not a catastrophic exception to the orderly course of life. It was a natural feature of human affairs. At the end of the fourteenth century the civil lawyer Honoré Bovet, whose work was widely read by lawyers, heralds and soldiers, condemned the view of 'simple fellows' that war was necessarily an evil. Antipathies, rivalries and conflicts were unavoidable, he argued, and war was a natural and inevitable mode of dispute resolution between sovereigns who acknowledged no superior. It was 'good and virtuous, for war by its very nature seeks nothing other than to set wrong right and to turn discord to peace in accordance with Scripture'. Bovet acknowledged that in war many evil things are done, but they never came from the nature of war, only from its abuse.

The spilling of Christian blood was sinful if it could be avoided, as the Church never ceased to proclaim. But what was avoidable was very much a question of social and moral values. Justice meant the vindication of legal and territorial claims. Victory signified God's sanction of those claims. In an address to Edward IV, which was probably delivered in the Parliament in 1472, the English King was enjoined to emulate the 'invincible manhood, the undeceived truth and immortal fame' of his ancestor Edward III, whose victories had shown that his cause was God's. 'Like it your good grace for to be advertised,' the document declared, 'how that every Christian man is bounden to revenge God's quarrels, in especial lords and knights which are sworn thereto.' There are few better insights into this mentality than Jean de Bueil's autobiographical novel *Le Jouvencel*, written in the mid-1460s after a military career extending over four decades. Men fight over trifles, he wrote, for none will willingly give up his rights. War reduced most soldiers to indigence in the end, but they fought on regardless because of their faith in God, their hope of better fortune and their 'high ambition and lust for honour and the praise of the world'. The quest for justice, the pursuit of honour, and the exercise of martial skills were values worth pursuing for their own sake. They defined nobility, but were admired by the world, even among those who were not noble. *Honi soit qui mal y pense*.[27]

The justice of war was a question much debated in the middle ages by the theologians and lawyers responsible for the first precocious essays in international law. Just war theorists were broadly agreed on the essential criteria for a just war. It must be fought by a sovereign for a specific purpose, which must be objectively justified and pursued in good faith, not for some collateral object. Most of these criteria, however, were far too general in their formulation and debatable in their application to operate as rules of law. They had little influence beyond the world of scholars. The one exception was the criterion known to canonists as *auctoritas*. Only a sovereign could authorise a just war. This principle had enormous implications, not just for scholars but for governments, judges and soldiers. It was the criterion by which public war was distinguished from mere criminal violence. For the soldier who was captured it marked the difference between being ransomed or hanged. *Auctoritas* became for practical purposes the badge of *the* just war. In the eyes of soldiers and statesmen, a just war was a war fought by sovereign authority. The rest was just organised criminality. The civil lawyers, who had never been happy with the vagueness of the theological criteria of justice, tended to agree. According to John of Legnano, the fourteenth century Italian civilian whose treatise on war set the academic standard, 'War is licit whenever it is sanctioned by legally constituted authority.'[28]

If law did little to limit the occasions for war, it did even less to moderate its savagery. Chivalric literature portrayed a world in which the violence of war was moderated by courtesy, generosity and Christian sentiment. Magnanimity in victory and mercy to the weak were an essential part of this ideal. Yet attempts to control the way in which war was fought had little impact. Honoré Bovet had something to say about this too, which bore the same imprint of pragmatic realism as the rest of his treatise. A knight, he thought, was bound to respect the 'ordinances of worthy chivalry and the ancient custom of noble warriors who upheld justice, the widow, the orphan and the poor'. But he was the first to acknowledge that in practice chivalry did little to civilise the conduct of war. The Black Prince, Bertrand du Guesclin, Henry V and Sir John Talbot were the epitome of chivalry in the eyes of all Europe, but their campaigns were among the most brutal of the entire war. 'It is their custom to pillage, rob and kill,' remarked the Paris chronicler impassively; 'they call it the laws and customs of war.' Contemporaries would have seen no contradiction. War was the pursuit of justice. Retribution against those who had refused to acknowledge the justice of a sovereign's claim was a normal incident of war. Once banners were unfurled, ransom or quarter was a choice of the captor, not a right of the prisoner. As for non-combatants, the laws of war offered them no protection at all except in theory for clergy, pilgrims, ambassadors and heralds. Bovet accepted that the destruction of a country's means of subsistence was a legitimate operation of war. In practice, he observed, 'the man who does not know how to set places on fire, to rob churches and usurp their rights and imprison the priests is not fit to carry on war'.[29]

The pursuit of honour mattered to men of gentle birth, both English and French, who went to war. It was the basis of the code of practice that governed the treatment of prisoners. It contributed to the discipline of armies and the sense of solidarity which is fundamental to the spirit of fighting men. It promoted military skills, especially horsemanship and weapon-handling. It moved them to deeds of astonishing and sometimes pointless courage. Flight from the field of battle was explicitly forbidden in the statutes of some orders of chivalry, and implicitly in others. Sir John Fastolf was criticised for fleeing the field at Patay and the Prince of Orange was disgraced for doing the same at Anthon, whereas Sir Lewis Robesart was held up as a model for the hopeless stand which cost him his life at Conty. Otherwise, however, the contribution of chivalry to military life was purely decorative. It became part of the manners of princely courts, where courtesy and display were highly prized and well rewarded. In an age of paid, professional armies and codes of military discipline, the practical relevance of this aristocratic code of conduct tended to decline. Writing at the end of the fourteenth century, Jean Froissart had hinted at this when he observed that the old ideal of gentility in war was still honoured by noblemen, but not by the base fellows who now filled the ranks of armies. Half a century later, William Worcester said much the same. Noblemen, he thought, were 'naturally piteous'. The problem, he lamented, was that except at the level of command, war was no longer conducted by noblemen but by professionals.[30]

In the fifteenth century all Europe was torn apart by war: civil wars, regional and international conflicts, and organised brigandage. The imagery and values of war coloured the outlook of people to a degree which today is hard to imagine. In a war zone they lived under the perpetual threat of sudden death and destruction. The life of townspeople was framed by fortified and guarded gates, walls and watch duty, that of country folk by the towers of parish churches and the garrisoned castles within reach of their fields, where they took refuge as the church bells warned of the approach of soldiers. The book-cupboards of literate laymen were filled with treatises on chivalry and the art and history of war. They read romantic fiction celebrating war, from the Arthurian legend of Sir Gawain and other mythical heroes to the real life of *Le Jouvencel*, which was written as its author tells us, 'for the glory of God and the instruction of warriors'. Battle scenes were a staple of painting in manuscripts and on church walls, in tapestries and stained glass. In Italy equestrian statues of armoured warriors made their first appearance in public places since the eclipse of the Roman world. In churches across England (and at one time in France too) the imposing marble and alabaster tombs and incised brasses of the nobility and gentry marked the status of the dead by showing them in full plate armour, while proud inscriptions recorded their martial deeds. Sir John Cressy, who died in 1445, is declared on his tomb at Dodford in Northamptonshire to have been captain of Lisieux, Orbec and Pont-l'Evêque before following Matthew Gough to Lorraine and dying there. In the church at Tideswell, the incised letters on the tomb of the Derbyshire knight Sir Sampson Meverell tell us that he passed years in the service of the great Earl of Salisbury and fought in eleven 'great battles' in the Duke of Bedford's time. Sir Thomas Hungerford may have seen war as a young man, but throughout his mature years he was an administrator and estate manager who never swung an axe in anger. Yet after his death in 1397 his more famous son had him buried in the chapel of Farleigh castle in a carved tomb showing him in full armour, beneath a wall-painting of St George slaying the dragon and a stained-glass image of his helmeted head.[31]

War created the state and the state created the nation. France was a monarchy with strong authoritarian aspirations, a pervasive bureaucracy and a powerful central judiciary. But unlike England it was fragmented by regional differences, legal, linguistic and economic, which had for many years frustrated the attempts of its Kings to extend their authority over the whole realm. The crises generated by the long war with England weakened these barriers, ushering in a more powerful state.

Taxation was the critical test. By the end of the thirteenth century, most west European states had outgrown the constricting framework of feudal obligation on which the recruitment of armies had once been based. Governments deployed large and increasingly professional armies whose soldiers received money wages. As a result, the cost of war increased exponentially. A proper framework of public finance was required, based on secure and predictable tax revenues. The late middle ages developed an elaborate theory of royal sovereignty, which was due mainly to civil and canon lawyers but became conventional among many people who had never read a law book. The King had an obligation to act for the common profit, and to declare a state of emergency if the collective welfare of his subjects was threatened. In this case, the property rights of his subjects must yield to the collective needs of the community, and the King was entitled to levy taxes. The authoritarian implications of this principle were constrained by conventional notions of legitimacy. Everyone agreed that the King could not act like a tyrant, and that the characteristic feature of tyranny was the arbitrary will of one man. 'What could be more intolerable,' asked Jean Gerson, the most highly regarded philosopher of his day, 'than that the opinion of one man should arbitrarily determine the direction of public affairs?' The King's right to tax was therefore subject to another principle, which the canonists adapted from Roman law. What affects all must be approved by all ('*Quod omnes tangit ab omnibus approbetur*'). Philippe de Commynes was no lawyer, but he took it for granted that there was 'no King or ruler on earth with power to levy a single penny in taxation without the consent of those who have to pay it, for otherwise it is mere tyranny and brute force'.[32]

The principle was conventional and political theorists continued to pay lip-service to it. But it had been largely discarded in France by the time Commynes wrote those words at the end of the fifteenth century. The Kings of France never succeeded in creating representative institutions whose consent would bind the whole realm. The result was that Kings who were politically strong enough dispensed with consent and imposed taxes by decree. Charles V did this after 1369, but felt sufficiently guilty about it to order the abolition of war taxes on his deathbed in 1380. Nevertheless, the ministers of Charles VI's minority reimposed them and the system endured until the civil wars of the early fifteenth century destroyed it. His son had to start again. The main problem was provincial particularism. Charles VII made at least six attempts to convene the Estates-General of the whole realm, only one of which succeeded, at Chinon in 1428 during the crisis provoked by the English siege of Orléans. Even then, the representatives of Languedoc protested at being made to go to Chinon. The deputies of Rouergue were present but declined to participate because, they said, they had their own assemblies for Rouergue and were not accustomed to confer with others. They added that they had their own problems with public order and English raids and preferred to reserve their taxes for those. Frenchmen had multiple identities, as subjects of the French King but also as inhabitants of a region, a province, a town or a parish. Most of them thought about tax and defence in local and not national terms. They were suspicious of national or even regional assemblies, identifying the whole concept of representation as an instrument of royal power. Even when representatives attended with full powers, as they usually did in the 1420s and 1430s, their grants were in practice only the prelude to a wearying round of local negotiations, without which the tax would have been difficult to collect. The results were long delays and large concessions that reduced their yield.[33]

The outcome was the same under Charles VII as it had been under his father and grandfather. Unable to fund the war from consensual taxes, he dispensed with consent as soon as he was strong enough to do so. There was little overt resistance while the war lasted. The rates remained unchanged. People grew accustomed to the *aides* and came to accept them as a necessary addition to the King's demesne revenue. As sales taxes they were collected from sellers and were less visible. The *tailles* were more controversial. They were direct taxes, payable in cash, at rates in the discretion of the King which relentlessly increased. The process of collection could be brutal. Their successful use by Charles VII was a turning point in the history of the French state. The principle of permanent taxation imposed and varied by royal ordinance was too valuable to the King to be abandoned even after the war had ended.

Philippe de Commynes reckoned Charles VII's revenues at the end of his life at 1,800,000 *livres* a year, which was roughly equivalent to his father's income in the 1380s. Of this, 97 per cent came from taxation. Nearly 60 per cent was generated by the *taille* alone. After a brief period of experimentation, Louis XI taxed his subjects by royal ordinance even more heavily than his father. At the time of his death in 1483 he enjoyed a peacetime revenue of 4,700,000 *livres* a year, almost all of it from taxation. The *taille* accounted for more than four-fifths of receipts. 'I am privileged to levy whatever I like from my subjects,' Philippe de Commynes imagined him saying although, ever loyal to the memory of his royal master, he attributed the sentiment to his officials.

When the Estates-General met at Tours in 1484, at the outset of Charles VIII's minority, there was an angry reaction against these policies and a serious attempt to change them. There were calls for a reduction in the size of the army and the cessation of the *taille* and the *gabelle*, which were said to be unwarranted in time of peace. The Estates-General should be summoned every two years and taxes should not be reimposed without their consent. In his closing speech the Chancellor went so far as to call the assembly of Tours the most famous meeting of the Estates-General ever, but its attempt at fiscal reform was stillborn. The government temporarily cut the size of the standing army and lightened the tax burden. But the demands of the Estates-General for a veto over taxation and a fuller role in government fell on deaf ears. When the Estates-General granted less than the King's ministers had demanded and limited it to the current year and the next, the government collected the full amount anyway and imposed fresh *tailles* without consent when the two years expired. Several royal councillors were persuaded that such gatherings subverted the proper authority of the King. Like Charles VII in 1442, they declared that anyone who advised the King to summon another was committing a crime against God, the King and the public interest.[34]

These developments brought an immense and permanent accretion of power to the French monarchy. Charles VII's revenues at the time of the final campaign in Normandy were about four times those of the King of England in a good year. They enabled him to maintain a standing army of 8,000 men in the *compagnies d'ordonnance*, in addition to the permanent reserve of 8,000 *francs-archers*. Louis XI doubled both numbers.[35] For the first time, the King of France had a crushing preponderance of armed force within his realm. Only the largest coalitions of French princes could now hope to challenge him by force, and then only with the assistance of external powers. This is what happened in the War of the Common Weal in 1465, when a coalition led by Louis XI's brother Charles joined forces with the Duke of Burgundy. Their promise to abolish war taxes was calculated not just to win support for their cause within France, but to cripple the revived monarchy and reduce it to its condition of forty years before. But even the League of the Common Weal was not strong enough to achieve more than a draw in military terms. Politically, it was a failure.

As a result, France emerged from the wars with a large and permanent military establishment which committed the country to a system of permanent taxation of indefinite duration. The Kings were constrained only by their conscience and the diminishing risk of rebellion. Moderate levels of taxation, Claude de Seyssel told Francis I in 1519, were desirable because they accorded with his duty to God and his concern for the wellbeing of his subjects, not because of any constitutional requirement for their approval. He thought that these moral constraints were enough. Sir John Fortescue's view was more perceptive. Writing in France under Louis XI, he cited Aristotle's dictum that it was better to be ruled by the best of men than the best of laws but pointed out that Kings were not always the best of men. Fortescue thought that the difference between taxation by consent and by royal ordinance was fundamental. It marked the difference between the unfettered royal power of the Kings of France (*dominium regale*) and the more limited 'political monarchy' of England (*dominium politicum et regale*). France too had once been a political monarchy before the wars, when the Estates had performed a function comparable to the English Parliament, but those days were over. Like many English political writers since, Fortescue thought that this was due to the authoritarian traditions of the civil law derived from the Roman imperial codes. He regarded it as alien to the English common law. If the Kings of England had been able to govern with a 'power entirely regal', he wrote, they too would have been able to change the laws and tax their subjects at will as the Kings of France did. 'This is the sort of government to which the civil laws refer when they say that, "What pleases the prince is law".' Fortescue did not welcome this kind of government, and most of his compatriots shared his view.[36]

These differences accounted in large part for the different political destinies of England and France in the following centuries. The roots of the absolute monarchy of seventeenth- and eighteenth-century France lay in the methods needed to defeat the English in the fifteenth. The decisive factor in determining the course of the Hundred Years War had been the ability of the two major belligerents to impose and collect taxes. The wars resulted in the virtual elimination of the French Estates as taxing authorities, the emasculation of the smaller provincial estates and the creation of an increasingly authoritarian system of government. In England, the Kings' need for money to fund their wars in France had the opposite effect. The war reinforced the role of Parliament and the Kings' dependence on it. Even the Tudors, with their strong authoritarian instincts, were unable to reverse the central role which Parliament had acquired in authorising taxation. With control of the purse came political authority. The role of the English Parliament intensified political activity in the communities represented there: the gentry of the shires, royal officials, clients and councillors of the nobility and the oligarchies of the towns. It dispersed political power among a relatively large and coherent political community, forcing a more consensual style of government on the English Crown.

The received opinion in France about the politics of England was that they were inherently unstable and unduly impeded the exercise of royal authority. The French Chancellor Guillaume de Rochefort told the Estates-General of 1484 that they had only to look over the Channel to see how fortunate they were by comparison with their neighbours. The fact that three English Kings had usurped the throne within a century seemed to speak for itself. On the contrary, argued Louis XI's councillor Philippe de Commynes, who knew England well, there was no country in the world where public affairs were better or more peacefully conducted. Commynes rejected the idea common among French royal propagandists of his day that the King of France was the mystical embodiment of the nation whose sacral status justified the exercise of absolute power. Kings were just 'men like us'. He was the first prominent Frenchman in a line that led to Voltaire and de Tocqueville to identify the English Parliament as a significant source of strength for English governments. Taking his cue from the speeches at Tours in 1484, Commynes argued that the Kings of England were 'stronger and better served' for having a representative assembly whose obligation to sustain the state was accepted and whose consent to taxation was decisive. The need for Parliamentary consent imposed delays and sometimes operated as a restraint on the King's ambitions. But it stood for a more deliberative style of government which ensured that when the King embarked on a war or some other great enterprise, he had the willing support of his people.[37]

The price which the English Kings paid for this advantage was a severe constraint on their foreign policy. After the wars with England were over, France returned to the career of conquest in Italy and the Empire which had characterised its history before the 1330s. France was the first major European power to establish a standing army funded by permanent taxation and to deploy it in support of foreign conquests. Other states, notably Burgundy, the Swiss Confederation, Spain and Austria, quickly followed suit. The sixteenth century was to be the first age of European standing armies. England was unique among the major European powers in being without one until the time of Oliver Cromwell, and even Cromwell's army was much smaller than the immense hosts deployed by the continental powers. Standing forces and discretionary taxation enabled the major European states to conduct a persistently aggressive foreign policy. The principalities of fragmented Italy, Germany and the Rhineland, which could not deploy resources on the same scale, became prizes for which these powers contended with ever larger and more expensive professional armies.

England might have been another prize had events turned out differently. The Spanish Armada of 1588 was the gravest external threat that England had faced since the abortive French invasion project of 1386. Spain deployed nearly 80,000 professional soldiers against England in 1588, 19,000 on the ships and 60,000 waiting in Flanders to cross the sea. This was more than four times the strength of the French army gathered by the coast of Flanders two centuries before. Leaving aside the inexperienced volunteers of the trained bands, England had fewer than 6,000 professional soldiers available to confront them in 1588, much the same as in 1386. The crippling cost of warfare would ultimately bankrupt all the leading states of Europe, and in France would provoke a revolution. The English Kings stood outside this movement, not by choice but because of the difficulty of raising taxes on the scale that had become normal in much of continental Europe. It was not until the reigns of William III and Queen Anne at the outset of the eighteenth century that England, aided by a growing maritime empire, a rapidly expanding economy and an exponential increase in the tax take, once again played the decisive role in European politics that it had played under Edward III and Henry V.[38]

What enabled the Kings of France to assert their authority in this way was a developed ideology of kingship which was the direct result of the war. All governments depend for their survival on a large measure of tacit acceptance. This was especially true of medieval governments, which never enjoyed a monopoly of organised force and presided over subsistence economies with only thin surpluses available to be taxed. They depended on a collective sense that their authority was legitimate. What conferred that legitimacy in France was the war and the role of the King in fighting it. In the 1350s and again in the 1420s, France had come close to disintegration as the English challenged the Valois monarchy in alliance with powerful regional interests. The monarchy was the agent of recovery on both occasions. The Kings were sacred beings, anointed by God, historic pillars of His Church, a unifying force profoundly identified with the soil and people of France. These were ancient ideas, but until the fifteenth century, they had little resonance beyond the administrative and ecclesiastical elites about the monarch. Their survival and penetration into the population at large was a response to external threats: the challenge to the legitimacy of the royal line in the aftermath of the murder of John the Fearless, the breaking of the association of King and country by the importation of a foreign dynasty, the prospect of dismemberment of the national territory by the Duke of Bedford, and the horrifying level of organised violence which afflicted most of the country. A nascent sense of national solidarity eventually enabled Charles VII to overcome these threats. Without it, he could not have imposed the *tailles* and the *compagnies d'ordonnance* on every region of his kingdom, including those which were far away from a war zone.

Closely associated with the myths of sacral kingship was the idea of the descent of the French people from imagined common ancestors and a common allegiance to an unbroken royal line extending back to a remote past. Christine de Pisan believed that the Kings of France were descended in a direct line from Clovis and opened her eulogy of Charles V by invoking the 'memory of the august descent of the noble Kings of France from which he issued'. Addressing the Estates-General of Tours in 1484, Charles VIII's Chancellor restated what had emerged during the wars as the doctrine of the French monarchy. Reviewing an idealised version of French history from its mythical foundation by the Trojans, he declared that France owed its existence as a nation to the continuity of the royal dynasty, and the solidarity of Frenchmen united by a common allegiance to the royal line and the common consciousness of a heroic past. Joan of Arc's recorded statements suggest an elevated, almost mystical conception of France, identifying the nation with the dynasty that she believed had ruled it by the grace of God from time immemorial. What complex layers of meaning lay behind Joan's words to Charles VII at their first meeting at Chinon, 'You are the true heir of France.'[39]

Charles VII was an intensely image-conscious ruler. The poet, diplomat and sometime royal secretary Alain Chartier, the official historiographer Jean Chartier of Saint-Denis, the sober chronicler Gilles le Bouvier Berry Herald, the prolix and didactic lawyer-bishop Jean Juvénal des Ursins and the historian and propagandist Noel de Fribois were all royal officials. Others, like the passionately anglophobic Norman writer Robert Blondel, although never employed by the King, were actively patronised by him. All of them in their different ways had the same story to tell: the wounds of the civil wars healed, Frenchmen reconciled, hardship overcome and national destiny realised by divine providence through the agency of the King. The works of these men were read by a limited circle of cultivated officials, clerics and noblemen. But their convictions had other ways of reaching a wider audience. The King was a visible presence. He travelled widely with a great entourage of liveried guards, heralds, trumpeters and minstrels. He marked his arrival with grandiose entries into the cities of his realm. He announced great events in circulars sent to all the main walled towns and read out at street corners by liveried messengers, sergeants and heralds. He ordered processions at times of anxiety, and more at times of victory. Beneath the veneer of public worship, these occasions were in reality celebrations of the monarchy itself. The annual commemoration of the conquest of Normandy, celebrated by royal order in every cathedral of France on the anniversary of the surrender of Cherbourg, was known as the 'feast of the King'. Across France, the feast was regularly observed until the end of the century and in some places long afterwards. The message was amplified by sermons in parish churches, by itinerant *jongleurs* singing their pieces outside, and by public theatre staged in towns like Orléans and Compiègne to commemorate the sieges which they had survived.[40]

When, in the early 1480s, William Caxton translated and printed the *Book of the Ordre of Chyvalry* by the Spanish seer Ramon Lull, he added an epilogue of his own. It was an elegiac lament for the decline of England as a military power.

O ye knights of England, where is the custom and usage of noble chivalry that was used in tho[se] days. What do ye now but go to the *bains* and play at dice? And some, not well advised, use not honest and good rule against all order of knighthood. Leave this, leave it and read the noble volumes of *saint grail*, of Lancelot, of Galahad, of Tristan, of Perys Forest, of Percival, of Gawain and many mo[re]. There shall ye see manhood, courtesy and gentleness. And look in later days of the noble acts sith the conquest, as in King Richard days *Coeur de Lion*, Edward the first and the third and his noble sons, Sir Robert Knolles, Sir John Hawkwood, Sir John Chandos, Sir Walter Mauny. Read Froissart. And also, behold that victorious and noble King Harry the fifth and the captains under him, his noble brethren, the Earl of Salisbury Montagu and many other whose names shine gloriously by the virtuous noblesse and acts that they did in the honour of the order of chivalry.[41]

When the last remnants of Sir John Talbot's army sailed for England from Bordeaux in October 1453, it was far from clear to contemporaries that this era had passed. It was not until the nineteenth century, when 'Hundred Years War' was coined as a phrase by the French historian Jules Michelet, that people began to perceive the essential unity of the period which began with the French forfeiture of Guyenne in 1337 and ended with the final expulsion of the English from the duchy in 1453. Michelet's phrase was born of hindsight. Yet it expressed the truth that later wars between England and France were fundamentally different. Before 1453, England's insular identity had been a literary conceit. Politically, England had not been an island when Edward III came to the throne in 1327. It had been the heart of a European polity that embraced parts of western France. But for these facts, England's Kings would have had no reason to involve themselves in a continental war and France would have had no interest in fighting them. It was because England was a continental power that Edward III passed most of his adult life at war with France and tried to make his son Count of Flanders; that John of Gaunt fought a three-year war for the Crown of Castile; that Henry V tried and almost succeeded in becoming King of France; that Humphrey Duke of Gloucester tried to make himself ruler of Hainaut and Holland. It was the expulsion of the Plantagenet Kings from their continental possessions at the end of the Hundred Years War that made England a political island for the first time since the Norman conquest four centuries earlier. As Henry VIII eventually discovered, the growing disparity of wealth and power between the English and continental monarchies after 1453 made a revival of the dynasty's old European ambitions unrealistic. The historic rivalry of England and France which had dominated European politics in the late middle ages gave way to a world in which Italy, central Europe and the Low Countries, and the European empires in Asia and the Americas were the focus of international tensions.

Defeat proved to be as decisive for the future of England as victory was for that of France. If Henry V and the Duke of Bedford had achieved their ambition of uniting France and England under the house of Lancaster, as the treaty of Troyes envisaged, England's subsequent history would have been very different. In an age when the state was not readily distinguished from the person of the monarch, the concept of the dual monarchy would sooner or later have broken down. This was what Parliament had perceived when Edward III proclaimed himself King of France at Ghent in 1340, and again when the treaty of Troyes was laid before it in 1420. England would of necessity have remained a continental power, but in a very particular sense. It would have become a subordinate part of a continental empire whose centre of gravity would inevitably have moved eastward towards its richer and more populous French territory, until the resulting tensions became intolerable. As it was, the outcome vindicated the prediction of Charles VII's councillor Jean Juvénal des Ursins after the Congress of Arras. 'France will be France and England will be England,' he had declared, 'separate and incompatible countries, in the nature of things too immense to be united in one body.'[42]

General Maps

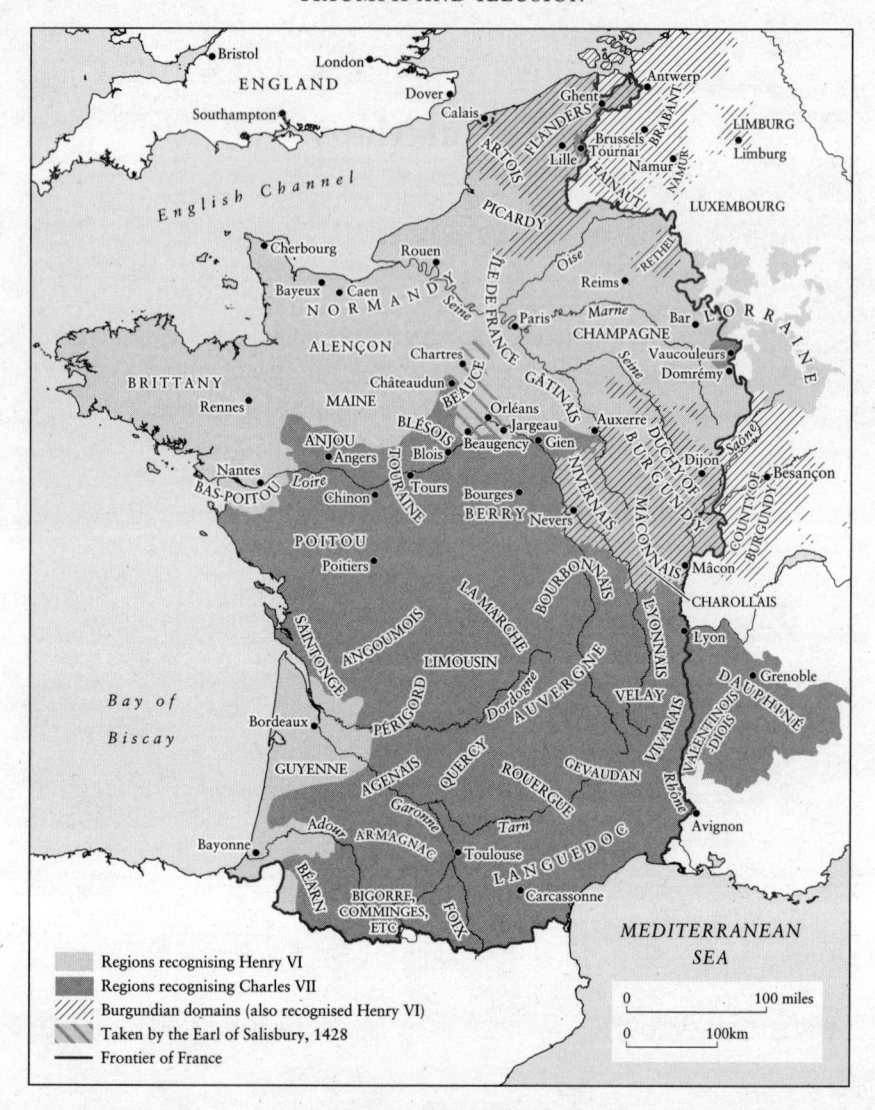

I France (April 1429)

II (*opposite*) Normandy and the *pays de conquête*

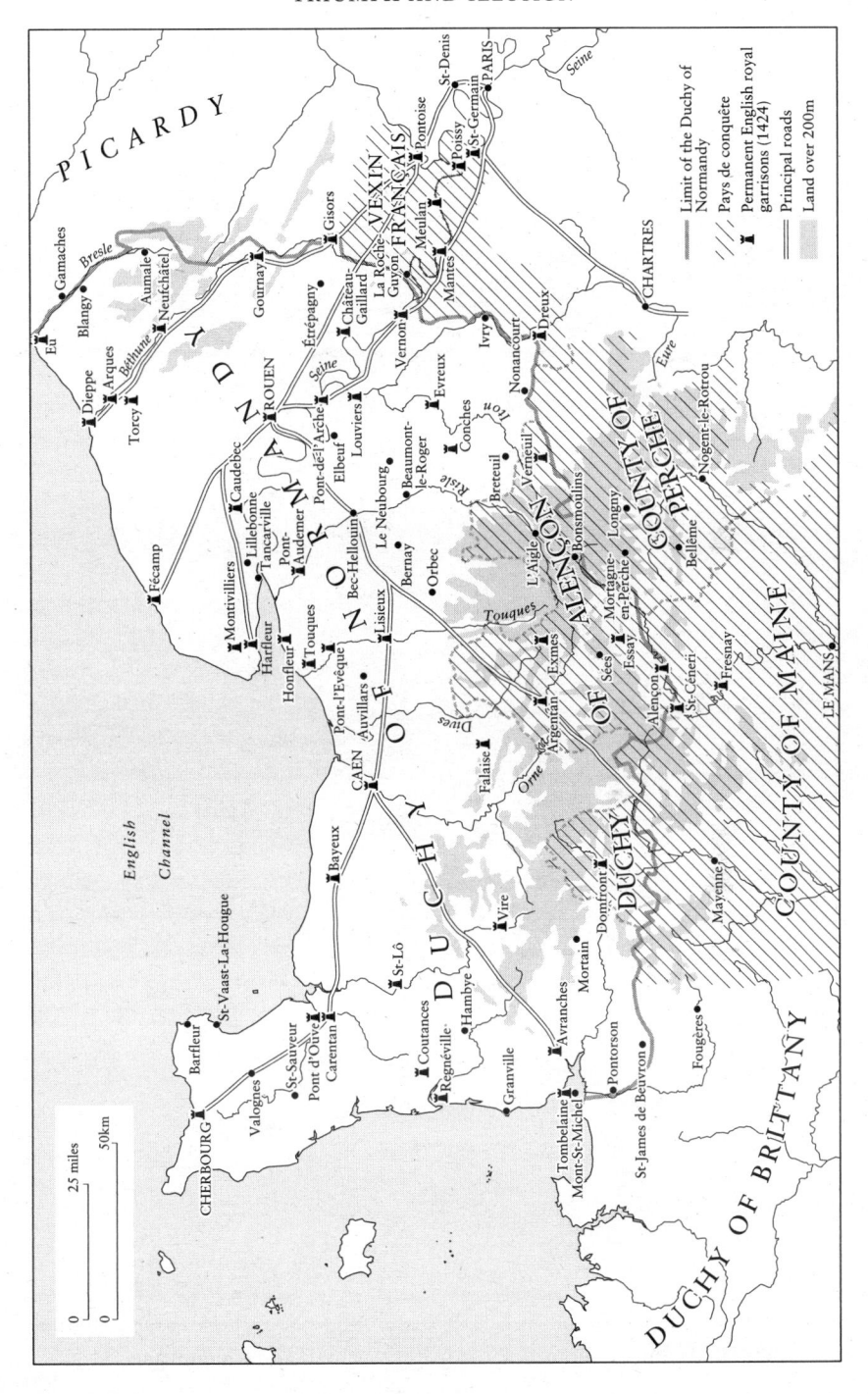

TRIUMPH AND ILLUSION

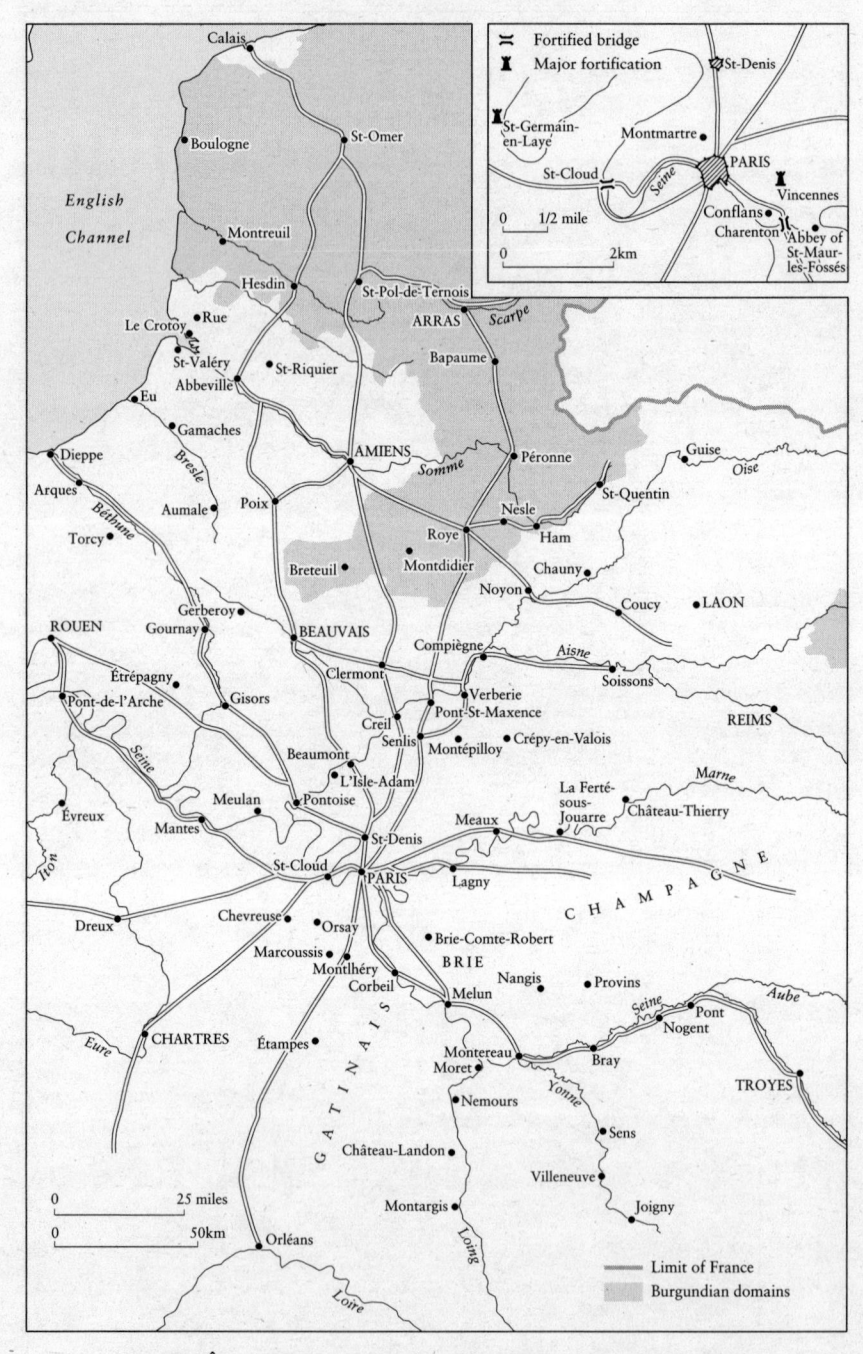

III The Île-de-France, Picardy, the Gâtinais and Champagne

IV Maine and its marches

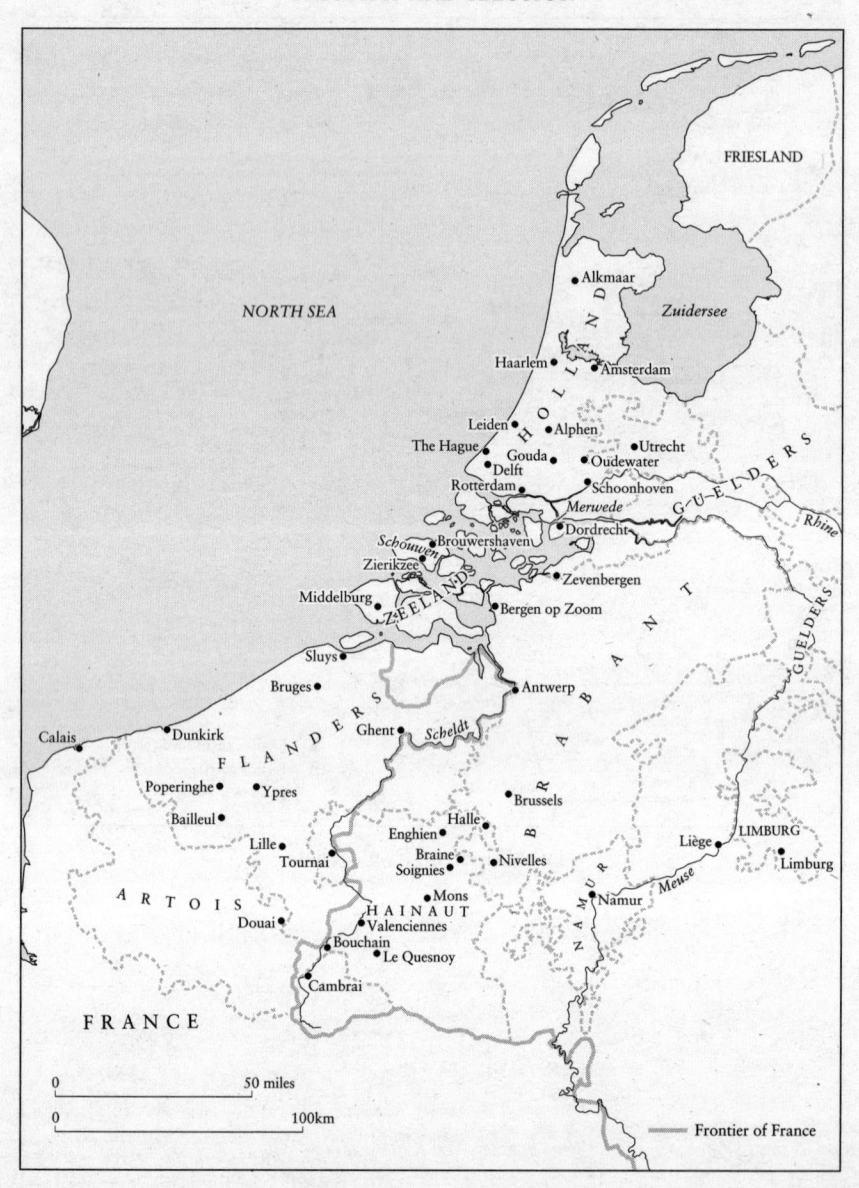

V The Low Countries

TRIUMPH AND ILLUSION

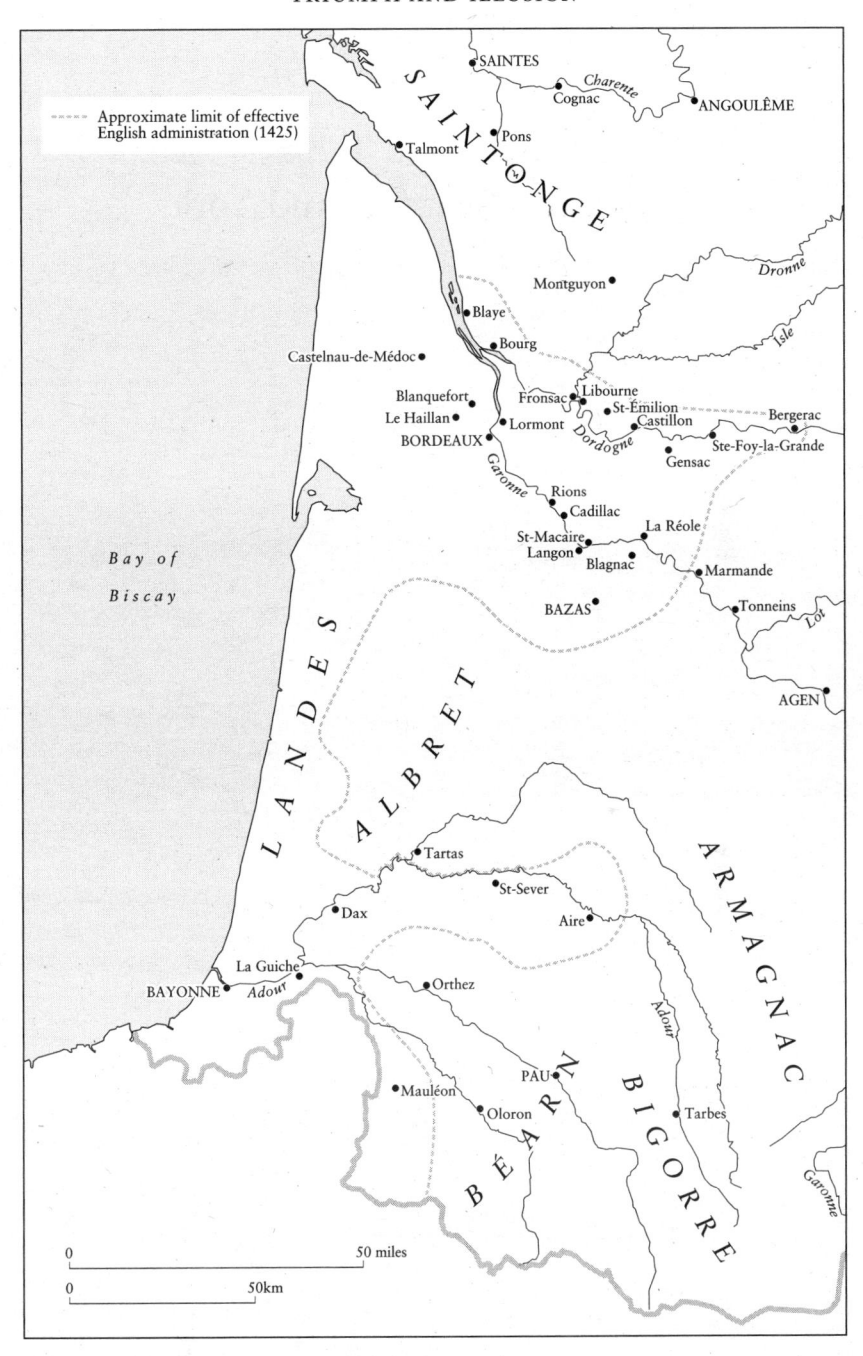

Approximate limit of effective English administration (1425)

VI Gascony

Genealogical Tables:
Lancaster, Beaufort and York

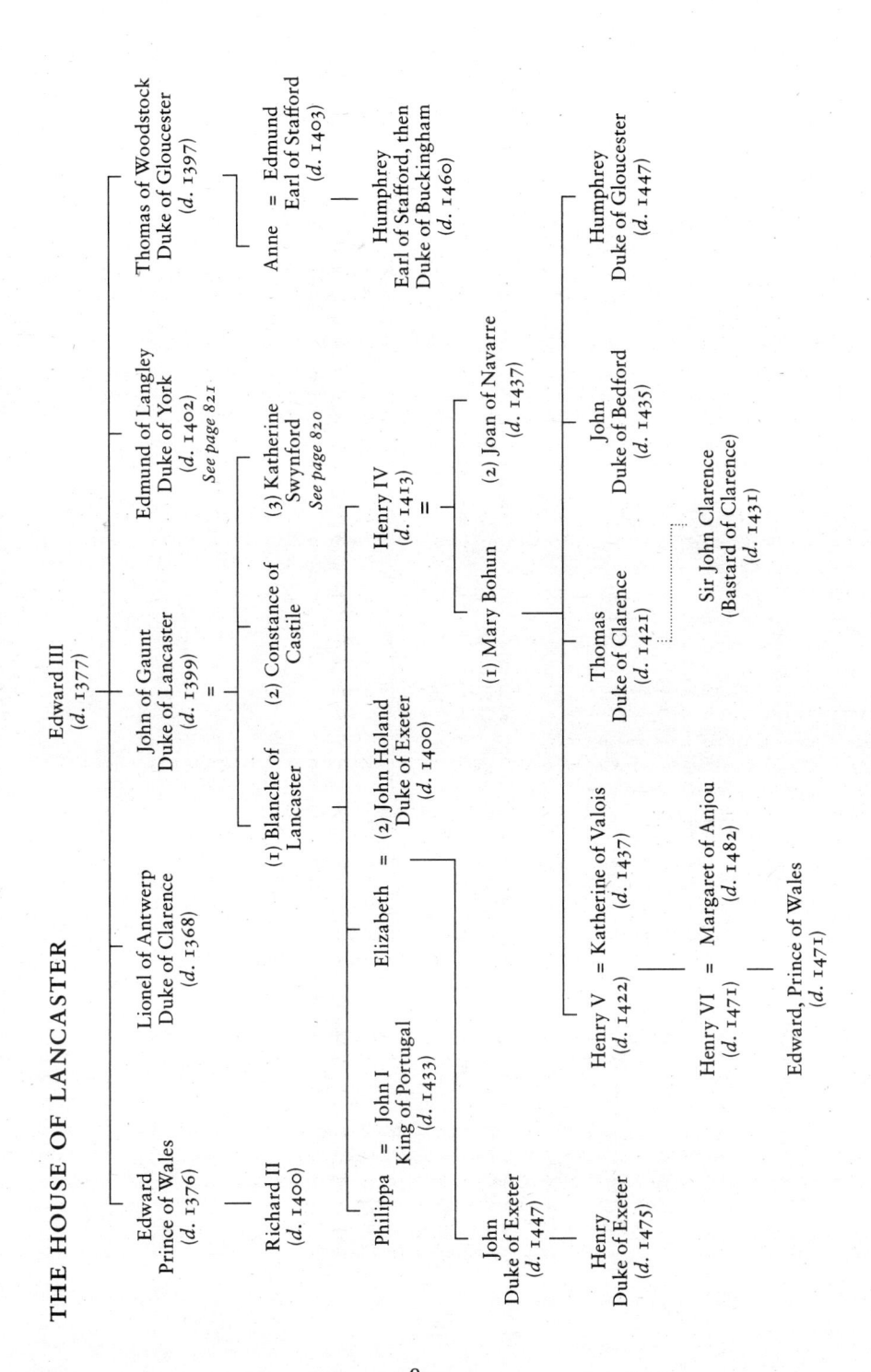

THE HOUSE OF LANCASTER

Edward III (d. 1377)
- Edward, Prince of Wales (d. 1376)
  - Richard II (d. 1400)
- Lionel of Antwerp, Duke of Clarence (d. 1368)
- John of Gaunt, Duke of Lancaster (d. 1399)
  = (1) Blanche of Lancaster
  = (2) Constance of Castile
  = (3) Katherine Swynford (See page 820)
  - Philippa = John I, King of Portugal (d. 1433)
  - Elizabeth = (2) John Holand, Duke of Exeter (d. 1400)
    - John, Duke of Exeter (d. 1447)
    - Henry, Duke of Exeter (d. 1475)
  - Henry IV (d. 1413)
    = (1) Mary Bohun
    = (2) Joan of Navarre (d. 1437)
    - Henry V (d. 1422) = Katherine of Valois (d. 1437)
      - Henry VI (d. 1471) = Margaret of Anjou (d. 1482)
        - Edward, Prince of Wales (d. 1471)
    - Thomas, Duke of Clarence (d. 1421)
      - Sir John Clarence (Bastard of Clarence) (d. 1431)
    - John, Duke of Bedford (d. 1435)
    - Humphrey, Duke of Gloucester (d. 1447)
- Edmund of Langley, Duke of York (d. 1402) (See page 821)
- Thomas of Woodstock, Duke of Gloucester (d. 1397)
  - Anne = Edmund, Earl of Stafford (d. 1403)
    - Humphrey, Earl of Stafford, then Duke of Buckingham (d. 1460)

THE BEAUFORT FAMILY

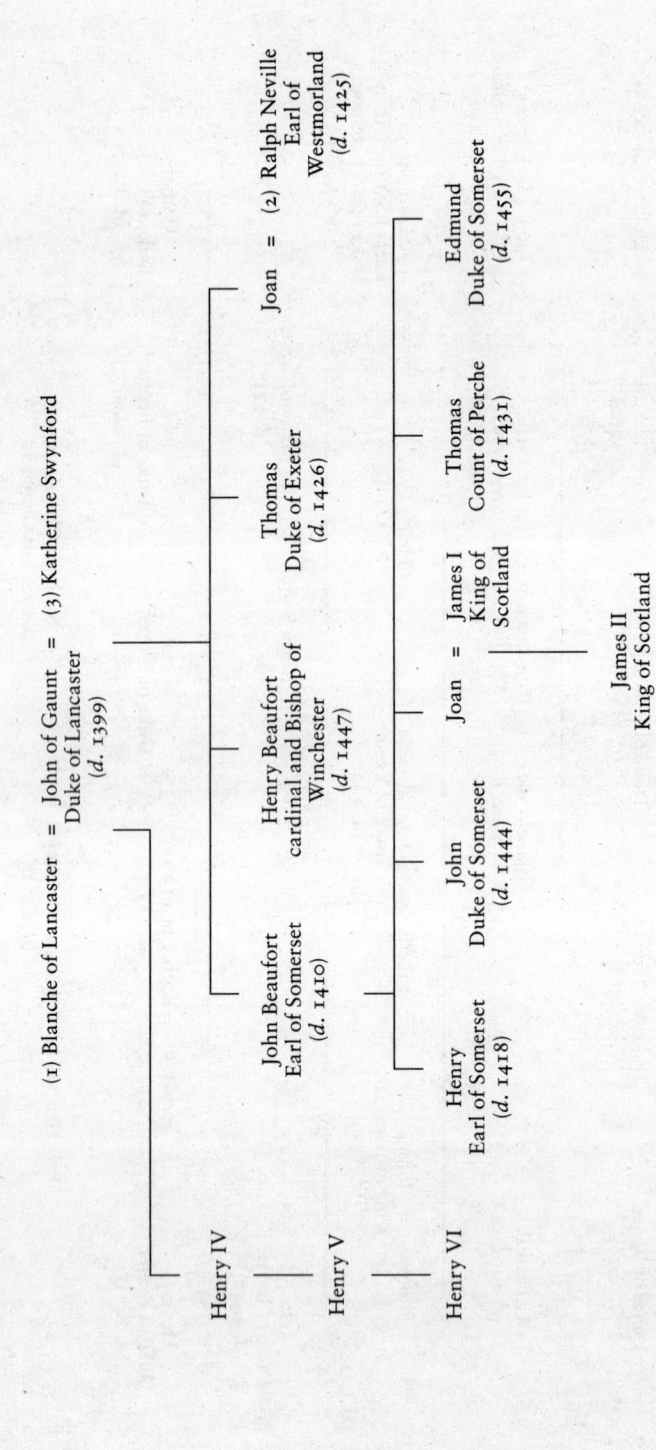

```
(1) Blanche of Lancaster = John of Gaunt = (3) Katherine Swynford    Joan = (2) Ralph Neville
                           Duke of Lancaster                                    Earl of
                           (d. 1399)                                            Westmorland
                                                                                (d. 1425)
        ┌──────────────┬─────────────────┬──────────────────┬──────────┐
        │              │                 │                  │          │
Henry IV    John Beaufort    Henry Beaufort    Thomas            Joan
            Earl of Somerset  cardinal and      Duke of Exeter
            (d. 1410)         Bishop of         (d. 1426)
                              Winchester
                              (d. 1447)
        ┌──────┬──────┐
        │      │      │
Henry V   Henry    John         Joan = James I
          Earl of  Duke of             King of
          Somerset Somerset            Scotland
          (d. 1418) (d. 1444)
                        │                    │
                    ┌───┴───┐            James II
                    │       │            King of Scotland
Henry VI        Thomas    Edmund
                Count of  Duke of Somerset
                Perche    (d. 1455)
                (d. 1431)
```

THE HOUSE OF YORK

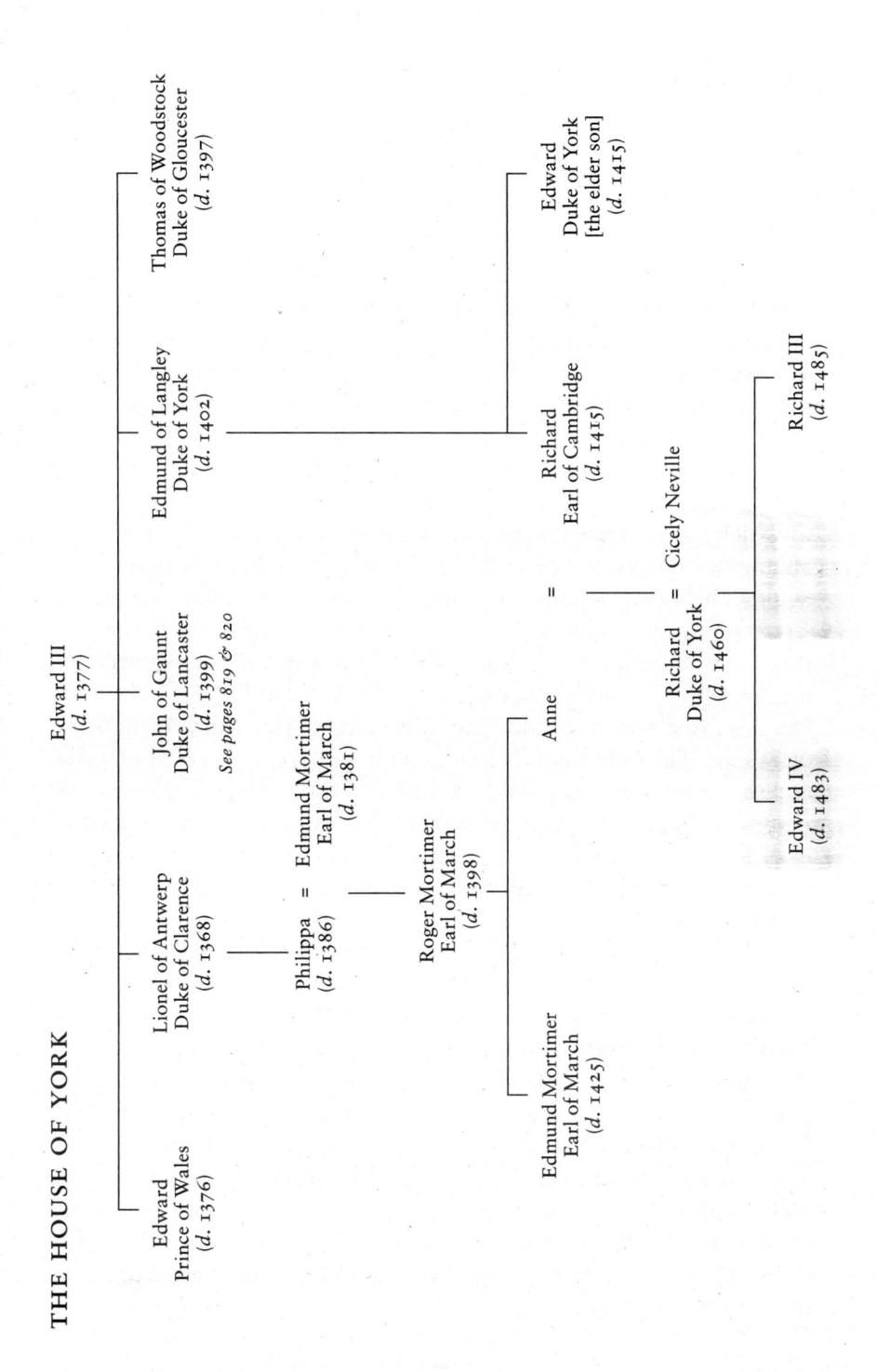

```
Edward III
(d. 1377)
 ├── Edward Prince of Wales (d. 1376)
 ├── Lionel of Antwerp Duke of Clarence (d. 1368)
 │     └── Philippa (d. 1386) = Edmund Mortimer Earl of March (d. 1381)
 │           └── Roger Mortimer Earl of March (d. 1398)
 │                 ├── Edmund Mortimer Earl of March (d. 1425)
 │                 └── Anne = Richard Earl of Cambridge (d. 1415)
 ├── John of Gaunt Duke of Lancaster (d. 1399)  See pages 819 & 820
 ├── Edmund of Langley Duke of York (d. 1402)
 │     ├── Edward Duke of York [the elder son] (d. 1415)
 │     └── Richard Earl of Cambridge (d. 1415) = Anne
 │           └── Richard Duke of York (d. 1460) = Cicely Neville
 │                 ├── Edward IV (d. 1483)
 │                 └── Richard III (d. 1485)
 └── Thomas of Woodstock Duke of Gloucester (d. 1397)
```

Note on Money

The fifteenth century was an age of unstable monetary values, partly because of volatile changes in the value of silver, which was the standard against which they were generally reckoned; and partly because of the policies of competitive coinage devaluation practised by many rulers. This is therefore a complicated subject, which is addressed here only so far as it assists in understanding the text.

It is necessary to distinguish between money of account, the units in which values were commonly expressed for accounting purposes, and money of payment, i.e. the coin in which payments were actually made. The English pound sterling was the most stable currency in western Europe, and where currency equivalents are given in the text, it is usually in pounds sterling. The pound was a money of account, divided into 20*s* (shillings), each of 12*d* (pence). In England, the mark was also used as a unit of account. It was worth two-thirds of a pound, or 13*s* 4*d*. The only English coin in widespread use as a unit of value, and then only for larger transactions, was the noble, a gold coin first minted in 1344. The weight of gold in the coin was regularly changed in order to maintain a constant relationship with the silver standard used for sterling values. A noble was worth a third of a pound, or 6*s* 8*d*.

In France the standard unit of account in both Valois and Lancastrian regions was the *livre tournois*, or pound of Tours. All references in the text to *livres* are to *livres tournois*. The *livre parisis*, or pound of Paris (worth four-fifths of a *livre tournois*) had been widely used in the fourteenth century but almost disappears in the fifteenth. Like the pound sterling, the *livre* was a silver standard, divided into 20 shillings (*sous*), each of 12 pence (*deniers*). Unlike the pound sterling, its silver value changed from time to time. Broadly speaking, a pound sterling was worth four *livres* in 1400, six *livres* from 1422 and nine *livres* from 1425. Thereafter, the silver value of the *livre* remained roughly stable, apart from a brief period in the late 1430s, when it fell to eleven *livres* to the pound sterling.

NOTE ON MONEY

In French documents, values were often expressed in coin. The standard coins in use for this purpose were the *franc* and the *écu*. The *franc* was a silver coin first minted in 1360, which was conventionally worth one *livre*. It was devalued in line with the *livre* in 1422 and 1425. The *écu* was a gold coin originally minted by Louis IX in the thirteenth century but modified several times since then. In the fifteenth century, references to it are almost always to the *écu à la couronne* (so-called because it showed a crown over the fleurs-de-lys of France), first minted in 1385. Its value remained stable at 3s 4d sterling, or six to the pound. The English authorities in France issued their own gold coin, the *salut*, which was minted in Rouen and Paris from 1421. The *salut* maintained a fixed relationship with the *livre*, at one and a half *livres* to the *salut*. Imitations of this highly regarded coin were also minted by both Charles VII and Philip the Good.

Accounting records are an important source for the Burgundian domains, but they are difficult to use for its financial history because they were kept in multiple coinages and units of account, mostly of fluctuating value. The duchy of Burgundy used the *livre tournois* as its money of account and the county of Artois the *livre parisis*. Flemish units of value began to diverge from those of the rest of France under John the Fearless. From 1424, Flanders used the *livre de Flandre* of 40 *gros* (shillings) as its money of account. It was worth about a tenth more than the *livre tournois*. The German territories of the house of Burgundy used a bewildering variety of local and foreign coins.

The value of money is notoriously difficult to assess and modern equivalents are generally misleading. Incomes were more stable than prices and are a better guide. In the fifteenth century, most English stipendiary parish priests enjoyed an annual income between £5 and £10. At £9 a year, the entitlement of an archer in permanent service was roughly comparable. The average income of a knight, judging by the income tax returns of 1436, was about £60 a year. The average Parliamentary peer declared a taxable income from land and annuities of about £865 in that year, which was enough to support a household of several dozen retainers and domestic servants. The richest man in England, Richard Duke of York, claimed to be worth £3,230 a year. As a very rough guide, values expressed in sterling may be multiplied by 3,000 to arrive at an approximate modern (2022) equivalent.

Abbreviations

ABSHF	Société de l'Histoire de France, Annuaire-Bulletin
AC	Archives Communales/Municipales
AD	Archives Départmentales
AHG	Archives historiques . . . de la Gironde
AHP	Archives historiques du Poitou
AN	Archives Nationales (Paris)
ARA	Algemeen Rijkarchief (Brussels)
BIHR	Bulletin of the Institute for Historical Research
BHP	Comité Historique et Scientifique, Bulletin Historique et Philologique
BEC	Bibliothèque de l'École des Chartes
BL	British Library (London)
BN	Bibliothèque Nationale (Paris)
CCR	Calendar of Close Rolls
CFR	Calendar of Fine Rolls
CPR	Calendar of Patent Rolls
EHR	English Historical Review
ESFDB	European State Finance Database
GEC	Complete Peerage (Cockayne)
HoC	History of Parliament. The House of Commons
HMC	Historical Manuscripts Commission
L&P	Letters and Papers . . . Henry the Sixth . . .
ODNB	Oxford Dictionary of National Biography
PPC	Proceedings and Ordinances of the Privy Council
PRO	National Archives [Public Record Office] (London)
RDP	Reports from the Lords Committees . . . touching the Dignity of a Peer
VCH	The Victoria History of the Counties of England

References

Printed sources (Bibliography, Sections B and C) are cited by title alone or by author/editor and title. Secondary works and unpublished theses are cited by author alone or by author and date.

References marked with an asterisk * are to the documentary notes or appendices of the work cited.

PREFACE

1. Lydgate, *The Fall of Princes*, Book IX, ll. 1210–11, ed. H. Bergen (1924), 953.
2. Marc Bloch, *L'étrange défaite* (Folio, 1990), 198.

CHAPTER 1: *Crises of Succession, 1422*

1. *Giesey (1960), 200–1; Monstrelet, *Chron.*, iv, 123–4; *Journ. B. Paris*, 180; Juvénal, *Hist.*, 397 (wax); Grandeau (1970), 143–7, 153–4, 156–7.
2. *Grands traités*, 106 (art. 12).
3. *Parl. Rolls*, x, 77 [2]; Chartier, *Chron.*, i, 29–30; Lafaurie, *Monnaies*, i, no. 449.
4. *Strong, 99; *Parl. Rolls*, x, 15–16 [14]; Monstrelet, *Chron.*, iv, 110; Thomas Walsingham, *The St Albans Chronicle*, ed. J. Taylor, W. R. Childs and L. Watkiss, ii (2011), 776. My reference at Sumption, iv, 767 to the arrangements for England, based on Pseudo-Elmham, *Vita*, 332–3, is, as I now think, mistaken.
5. Chastellain, 'Chron.', i, 331–2; Monstrelet, *Chron.*, iv, 112.
6. *Rec. doc. monnaies*, ii, 333; Fauquembergue, *Journ.*, ii, 67–75, 72–5; *Journ. B. Paris*, 180; AD Côte d'Or B1622, fol. 62vo–63 (D. Burgundy), *Ord.*, ix, 267–9 (ordinance of 1407).
7. Le Fèvre, *Chron.*, ii, 61–2; *Brut*, ii, 497 (Douglas); *PPC*, iv, 225; *Cron. Norm.*, 81; *Journ. B. Paris*, 320; Basin, *Hist.*, i, 88–90.
8. *Foed.*, x, 253; *Parl. Rolls*, x, 15 (13); Roskell (1953), 195–7; *CCR 1422–9*, 43–4.
9. Hoccleve, *Selections*, 88–90; Titus Livius Forojuliensis, *Vita Henrici Quinti*, ed. T. Hearne (1716); Hardyng, *Chron.*, 391; Pius II, *Comm.*, ii, 535.
10. Harriss (1988), 3–4, 27, 37–8; *Reg. Jurade*, ii, 257, 329.
11. Harriss (1988), 107–11, 123, 394–5, 401–6, 411–12; Vespasiano, *Vite*, 291–2; *L&P*, ii, 450 (Humphrey). Syndicate: see, e.g. PRO SC8/144/7180 (Sept. 1431).
12. *Coll. doc. Angleterre*, 232–3; *Chrimes, 102–3. For *tutela*, see Roskell (1953), 206–7.
13. *Cartul. Hainaut*, iv, 78–9, 85–6, 94–9, 109–12, 199–201, 271, 310–11, 318, 580, 592, 599; *Groot Charterboek*, iv, 521–30, 545–8, 549; Dynter, *Chron.*, iii, 345–8, 357–8, 363–4, 388–9, 414–15; Monstrelet, *Chron.*, iii, 280, iv, 26–8; Chastellain, 'Chron.', i, 170, 211. And see *Algemene geschiedenis Nederlanden*, iii, 230–2; Janse, 115–38, 163–91; Gysels, 416–25. Role of Henry V: *Foed.*, x, 67–8; PRO E403/649, m. 3 (2 May).

14. 'Avis du chancelier Rolin', 131-2; *Löher (1865-7), i, 47.
15. PPC, iii, 6-7.
16. Parl. Rolls, x, 13 [5], 23-4 [22-33], 26 [26], 61 [1], 347-9 [24-7].* Chrimes, 102-3; PPC, iii, 13-18, 233-4 (quotation); Foed., x, 261. On the councillors, Griffiths (1981), 22-3; Harriss (1988), 118-21.
17. J. Smyth, Lives of the Berkeleys, ed. J. Maclean, ii (1883), 6.
18. Froissart, Chron., vii, 321 (St-Pol); *Kingsford (1912), 745 (Hardyng). Vendettas: E. Powell, Kingship, Law and Society. Criminal Justice in the Reign of Henry V (1989), 266-7; Griffiths (1981), 128-47; Carpenter (1992), 372, 377-88; Bellamy, 7-9, 27-9 and passim.
19. Foed., x, 113-15 (£15,066 demesne revenues, May 1421), Somerville, i, 187, 188 (£6,400 Duchy of Lancaster, average, 1413-22); Ormrod (2013), 208 (Table 1) (£45,800 customs, 1421-2). The statement omits the cost of household, works, artillery, ships, diplomacy and arrears. The household alone consumed £24,389 between 1 Oct. 1421 and 31 Aug. 1422: PRO E101/407/7.
20. Somerville, i, 199-205, 207-8; Roskell (1954), 113-20. Arrears: Stratford (2013), 157, 165, 168-9; PRO E364/66, m. 1d (Clitheroe, Curteys); Parl. Rolls, x, 172-3 [34]. Calais: Rot. Parl., iv, 159 (May 1421); £12,557 paid since then to the Treasurer of Calais seems not to have been spent on arrears, PRO E364/59, mm. 3-3d (Bokeland); PPC, iii, 55-6. Cf. Sumption, iv, 730, and see Fig. 1.2 in Ormrod (1999)[2], 35.
21. Ormrod (1999)[1], 161 (Table 8.2); Ormrod, The Reign of Edward III (1990), 207 (Table 4); Ormrod (2013), 187, 208 (Table 1); Parl. Rolls, xi, 107 [24]; ESFDB [http://www.esfdb.org/table.aspx?resourceid=11771]; Parl. Rolls, x, 21-2 [19]; R. Schofield, 'The geographical distribution of wealth in England, 1334-1649', Econ. H. R., 2nd series, xviii (1965), 483-510.
22. Parl. Rolls, ix, 137 [10], 233-4 [9]; 272-8 [17], x, 104-5 [26], 237-8 [20], 294-5 [17], 385-6 [23]; Fortescue, Governance, 118. Lenders: Kleineke, 6, 22-3; Barron (1970), App. XLV; Steel, 193, 251, 252-3, 260. Interest: McFarlane (1947), 59-68.
23. Ormrod (2013), 207-15; Parl. Rolls, ix, 233-4 [8-9]. Overall reduction estimated from the receipt rolls in Ramsay, i, 321, ii, 266.
24. Childs, 46, 48-50.
25. Bell, Curry, et al., 38, 41-2.
26. Bell, Curry, et al., 58-61, 75-7, 83-4, 96-9, 273; Curry (1985), i, 103-8, i, App. I; Curry (1994)[2], 46-7; Bogner, 29-31; HoC 1422-61, i, 333-41; S. M. Wright, 8-10; Acheson, 39, 41-2; Payling (1991), 73-7; Carpenter (1992), 59-73, 85; PPC, v, 90-1 ('beeth few . . .'); Worcester, Boke of Noblesse, 77; Upton, De studio militari, 257-8. Agincourt: Powicke (1969), 374.
27. Bell, Curry, et al., 92-4, 113-14, 129; HoC 1386-1421; HoC 1422-61, i, 327-31; Roskell (1954), 93-4. Sir John Tyrrell (Speaker, 1427, 1431, 1437) served in France in 1417 and 1431: HoC 1386-1421, iv, 684, 685.
28. Inv. AC Amiens, ii, 42.
29. Comptes état Bourg., i, p. xli-xlii.
30. Schnerb (1988), 215-19; Schnerb (2002), 55-62, 64-7; Lobanov (2015)[1], 302-6, 399-409 (App. C).
31. BL MS Cotton Caligula DV, fol. 65.
32. Henry V: Sumption, iv, 751-2, 761; Monstrelet, Chron., iv, 110; PPC, iii, 247-8; *Dickinson, 218 (1435). Minority: PPC, iv, 95-6 (1431). Rolin: 'Avis du Chancelier Rolin', 119 (1435).
33. Favier (1974), 104 (Louvre); Journ. B. Paris, 193, 202 (Isabelle); Paravicini and Schnerb, 413-15 (H. d'Artois). H. de Bretagne: Guillebert de Metz, 'Description'

194; *Félibien, iii, 75–6. Dance of Death: *Journ. B. Paris*, 203; Leroux, *Paris et ses historiens*, 293–317.
34. Favier (1974), 54–61; *Journ. B. Paris*, 192; *Comptes Domaine*, i, 37–40, 83–8; Le Roy Ladurie and Couperie, Table 1. Trades: Thompson (1991), 220 n.82; *Doc. Paris*, 351–2; *Doc. industrie et commerce*, ii (1900), 216–17; *Ord.*, xiii, 146–8 (wine). Les Halles: Lombard-Jourdan, 87–8.
35. *Champion (1906), 156 (quotation); Thompson (1991), 133–6, 138–9; Favier (1974), 112–13; V. Weiss, 23, 68.
36. *Journ. B. Paris*, 262; Thompson (1991), 173–5; *Foed.*, x, 432 (Bedford).
37. Rowe (1932–3) (genealogy); Thompson (1991), 133–6, 214–17; Thompson (1988), 56; *Journ. B. Paris*, 214, 256, 279. Plot: *ib.*, 182–3; Monstrelet, *Chron.*, iv, 135; 'Chron. Cordeliers', BN Fr. 23018, fol. 432.
38. Fourquin, 316–17; *Journ. B. Paris*, 175, 192, 200–1, 209.
39. *Journ. B. Paris*, 193 (quotation); Fauquembergue, *Journ.*, ii, 138; Boulet, 475, 523. I am grateful to M. Boulet for supplying me with a copy of his valuable thesis.
40. Rowe (1934), 210–11; Boulet, 473–6, 515–23. Luxembourgs: Fenin, *Mém.*, 67; Le Fèvre, *Chron.*, ii, 9; AN P2298, pp. 769–73 (Treasurer); Fauquembergue, *Journ.*, ii, 159; *Fasti*, ii, 125–6; *L&P*, ii, 535. Cauchon: Favier (2010), Ch. 6–8; Guillemain; AN PP110, p 161 (G. Conseil); Boulet, 332, 475. Rinel: Bossuat (1956), 135–41; Contamine (2009)[1].
41. *Grands traités*, 109 (art. 18); Fauquembergue, *Journ.*, ii, 72–5. Institutions: Rowe (1934), 216–18; Curry (1998)[1], 97–101; Allmand (1983), 129–45; *English suits*, 5–8; Boulet, 450–5.
42. Miller (1991), iii, 566; Cailleux (2003); Massey (1994), 272–5, 281–6; Allmand (1983), 83–5, 89–105; AN Coll. Lenoir xxi, 227ff and *passim*.
43. Curry (1985), ii, App. II and BN Fr. 4485, pp. 147–8, 176–276, recording garrison strengths in Normandy in Sept. 1423. Personal retinues, see below. Revenue: BN Fr. 4484, fols. 21vo–31; Fr. 26047/335.
44. 'Extr. Journ. Trésor', 472–83; *L&P*, ii, 532–40; BN Fr. 4484, fols. 9vo–34vo.
45. Basin, *Hist.*, i, 84–8. Estates-General: *L&P*, ii, 32–7; BN Fr. 26047/362; 'Doc. assemblée d'états', 361–9. Le Crotoy: *Inv. AC Amiens*, ii, 25, iv, 100, 103; Lediu, 360–1, 388–9, 391, 406–7. Champagne: BN Fr. 4484, fols. 9–10vo, 18, 19–19vo; BN Fr. 7626, fols. 412–413vo; Boutiot (1870–80), ii, 473–4; Rowe (1927), 436–8. Paris: Favier, *Contribuables*, 5. Suffolk: *Desplanques, 73. Salaries: Fauquembergue, *Journ.*, ii, 75–6, 106, 121, 137–8, 149–50, 177–8, 181–2, 194–5, 224–5, 228, 364–7; Boulet, 272–6, 293–8.
46. Héraut Berry, *Description*, 47–8; Rey, *Le domaine du Roi* (1965), 81–9, 97–9; Bois, 61–2, 95 (graphique 7), 117–21, 290–3, 295–9; Mollat (1952), 25–51; Allmand (1983), 155–63; Le Cacheux, lxi–xcviii; Cailleux (2006), 247, 258 (figs 2, 3). Dieppe: Lardin (2005), 180 (Table 1); Mollat (1979), 137. Note the increases in trade-related taxes, i.e. the sales tax and the *gabelle*: BN Fr. 4485, pp. 26–48 (14 months, 1423–5); BN Fr. 4488, pp. 31–48 (12 months, 1428–9). Cf. receipts of the Vicomté de l'Eau of Rouen: *Beaurepaire (1856)[2], 422–77.
47. Doucet (1926)[1], 286–96; BN Fr. 26048/481 (Oct. 1425) (quotation). Figures are annualised from PRO E364/61, mm. 2d–4d (Alington); BN Fr. 4485, p. 145 and *passim* for defence costs; BN Fr. 4488, p. 199. Assemblies: Rowe (1931)[2], 556–9; Rowe (1927), 441–5, 451–4, 456–7. *Guet*: Baume (1998), 276–7, 279; Chave, 148.
48. The fundamental work is the unpublished thesis of Anne Curry (1985), see for this para. ii, App. III; Curry, (1994)[2], 54. Bastille: *Nichols; Thompson (1991), 93–4; *L&P*, ii, 538, 539. Rouen: 'Paiements et quittances', nos. 678; *Cron. Norm.*, 48; Cochon, *Chron.*, 344; Massey (1994), 271–2; Curry (1994)[2], 54–8. Harfleur: BN Fr.

4485, pp. 361; BL Add. Chart. 323; BN Fr. 26048/543, 546, 26049/611. Honfleur: BN Fr. 4485, pp. 151–2; BL Add. Chart. 323, 3582.
49. Curry (1985), i, 209, 344–58, ii, App. II (total adjusted to include garrisons for which no record survives, on the assumption that the strength was the same as from 29 Sept. 1423, as recorded in BN Fr. 4485); Curry (2014). Indigenous troops: Bell, Curry, et al., 249–59; Newhall (1940), 113–22. Garrisons outside Normandy: BN Fr. 32510, fol. 368; *L&P*, ii, 538–9; Thompson (1991), 93–4 (Bastille).
50. Baume (1988), 393–5. Tancarville: *La Roque, iv, 1473–4; Massey (1987), 339–44, 356.
51. Personal retinues: BN Fr. 4485, pp. 147–8, 149, 307 (Bedford, Suffolk, Salisbury); BN Clair. 139/13, 112 (Warwick); BN Fr. 26062/3085, 26063/3212, 26064/3421 (York). The greater noblemen appear to have been expected to support their military retinues from their Norman endowments. Their war wages were paid from public revenues for some operations only, and generally only up to a specified limit. As a result, they are not fully recorded in the accounting documents. Land grants: Wylie and Waugh, iii, 74–5, 240–1; *CCR 1422–9*, 449–50; Curry (1985), 185–7. Living on the land: Curry (1996), 216–20; Curry (1985), ii, 178; Bossuat (1936), 291–2. Towns: Curry (1988)[1], 254–5. Noble service: Curry (1985), ii, App. IX; Curry (1988)[1], 242–4; Allmand (1983), 192–3.
52. Curry (1985), i, 168–71; Ratcliffe, 8, 11–12, 15, 19–20, 21, 23–4. Negotiations, 1423: Monstrelet, *Chron.*, iv, 133–4; PRO E101/322/3; PRO E 28/39; E403/658, m. 13.
53. Pay rates: Curry (1985), i, 211 (compare BN Fr. 26287/73 for building rates in 1435). 1422–3 crisis: *Chéruel, ii, 85–91; *L&P*, ii, 34–5.
54. *Rowe (1931)[1], 201–8. Curry (1999); Allmand (2000); Newhall (1924), 222–8, 230–6; Baume (1998), 277–8; *Roles normands*, no 653; *PPC*, ii, 351 (quotation). Controllers: Curry (1985), i, 245. Certificates: BN Fr. 4485, p. 134. Inspections: Baume (1998), 276–7. Contemporary opinion: *Journ. B. Paris*, 83; *Chron. R. St-Denys*, v, 556; Juvénal, *Écrits*, i, 312–17, 408.
55. Warner (1998), 146–53; *Desplanques (1867), 72 (joke). Council: Boulet, 475. Character: Waurin, *Cron.*, iii, 247–8. Profits, gifts: *Doc. Paris*, 249–50; AN JJ172/269, 578, JJ173/293, 299; *English Suits*, 128, 141–2, 148–9; Sauval, iii, 317.
56. Castor (2000), 83–5; *ODNB*, xliv, 732–3; *GEC*, xii, 443–7; Massey (1987), 12–13, 14, 78–9, 116 (endowment).
57. Clarence: *CPR 1408–13*, 41; BL Add. Chart. 66, 1403. Harfleur: PRO E101/46/24, m. 3, E101/44/30 (2), m. 7, E101/47/39, E101/50/26; PRO E36, p. 34. Bastille: PRO E364/74, m. 7d. Memoranda: *L&P*, ii, 575–97, 718–30. Bedford's service: BN PO 1101 (Fastolf)/2; *L&P*, ii, 414, 535; Boulet, 332, 475; Massey (1987), 27, 99–100. His last surviving muster is in March 1438: BN Fr. 25774/1309, 1310. Wealth: McFarlane (1957)[1], 104–7. Views: Worcester, *Boke of Noblesse*, 41.
58. Willoughby: *ODNB*, lix, 423–4; Thompson (1991), 135. His company: Livius, *Vita*, 32; PRO E403/666, mm. 3–4 (29 May). Oldhall: Roskell (1961), 89–91; *English suits*, 298–9; Worcester, *Itin.*, 355. Rempston: Payling (1991), 59–62; *HoC 1386–1421*, iv, 192–4; *ODNB*, xlvi, 459–61. Scales: PRO E101/51/2, m. 12; PRO C76/104, m. 18; BN Fr. n.a. 1482/18; *ODNB*, xlix, 175–6. Scales was born in 1399: *Cal. Inq. P. M.*, xxi, nos. 260, 672.
59. Worcester, *Boke of Noblesse*, 29, cf. 76–7; Bueil, *Jouvencel*, ii, 20–1.
60. Worcester, *Itin.*, 361. For the individuals named: *ib.*, 358; Roskell (1961), 89–91; *HoC 1486–1421*, iii, 536; *HoC 1422–61*, iii, 921, v, 16–17, 722–3; Virgoe (1990–92), 5–6; Castor (2000), 97, 145; Moreton and Richmond, 40–1.
61. Fortescue, *Governance*, 138; Vale (1981), 104–15; Loades (2013), 66–8; Loades (2018), 25–7. Barded horses: Harbinson, 188–95.

62. Bueil, *Jouvencel*, ii, 100; Buttin, esp. 101–7, 110–25; Harbinson, esp. 143–53, 158–60, 196–7; Vale (1981), 115–19, 128; Capwell, 26–8, 37 (armourers).
63. Inventories at PRO E101/51/27, E101/52/3 (1428); *L&P*, ii, 565–73 (1435). Range: Salamagne (1993)[1], 89–97. On the Michelettes: Smith and Brown, 68–78. On field artillery, Vale (1981), 134–7. The fullest information about such weapons comes from Burgundian sources: see J. Garnier, 239–44; Smith and De Vries, Chap. 3, esp. 204–19, 230–36. For France, Dubled. For Gascony, Vale (1976), 59–63. Tactics: Bueil, *Jouvencel*, ii, 41.
64. Allmand (1982); A. King; Bell, Curry, et al., 196–202; Rogers, 247–52. Rouen ordnance office: 'Extr. Journ. Trésor', 473 (10) (Jan. 1423); BN Fr. 25769/529, 25770/632 (Sept. 1431).
65. *Grands traités*, 106–8 (arts. 13–16); Paris: *Journ. B. Paris*, 182–3; Thompson (1991), 151.
66. Cailleux (2003), 266–8, 274–6; Allmand (1983), 68–9, 79–80, 102–4, 120; Curry (2009), 210–11; Boüard, 54–5; Thompson (1991), 216–17; Boulet, 83–4, 258 (*baillis*). Swearing: *Proc. N.*, i, 406, 407–8; Rickard, 173–7. Language: Rickard, 174–5; *Actes Chanc. Henri VI*, ii, 18–21; *Chron. Mont-St-M.*, i, 227. Approved usage: *Rowe (1931)[1], 205 (para 12); cf. *Doc. Paris*, 304.
67. Chartier, *Poetical Works*, 419; *Quad. Invect.*, 15–16; Chartier, *Chron.*, ii, 31; *Houtard, 494–5 (quotation); Jouet (1969), 42–3. Hangings: Chartier, *Chron.*, i, 52 (Ramefort, 1425); *Journ. B. Paris*, 335 (Montereau, 1437); *PPC*, v, 384 (Meaux, 1439).
68. Allmand (1983), 171–86; Rowe (1931)[2] (esp. table at 556–7); Beaurepaire (1859)[2].
69. *Rôles normands*, no. 1001; Jouet (1969), 79–83, 115–16, 130, 149; M. R. Evans, 110, 114; Sumption, iv, 612 (my final comment at 828 n.37 is overstated).
70. *Actes Chanc. Henri VI*, i, 291–4, 337, ii, 11, 212–15; *Rôles normands*, no. 272; Ambühl (2013), 88–97; Jouet (1969), 25–6, 43–7, 79–81; Basin, *Hist.*, i, 106–8. Treason: Digest, ¶ xlviii.4.1; Cuttler (1981)[1], 4–5, 7–9, 21–3, 26, 28; Gauvard (1991), 832–5, 840–1.
71. Allmand (1983), 216–17; Cochon, *Chron.*, 310, 312–14; *Gut (1982), 144.
72. Bouteillier: Roger (1978), 299–307; Monstrelet, *Chron.*, iii, 299–300. Jolivet: Le Roy, i, 328–30; Huynes, ii, 99–100; *Chron. Mont-St-M.*, i, 88–91, 93–7; *Rôles normands*, nos. 346, 1376; *Denifle (1897–9), i, 75–6; BN Fr. 4485, pp. 154, 172, 349, 352–3, 358–9; Rowe (1934), 213; Labory, 522–3, 525–7. Le Sage: Rowe (1927), 123–8; *Rôles normands*, no. 1376; BN Fr. 4485, pp. 155, 172–3, 349, 365; BN PO 2604 (Le Sage)/34, 36. His English grants: PRO C76/115, m. 4; *Parl. Rolls*, xi, 115 (28); *PPC*, iv, 175; *CPR 1429–1436*, 594; *CPR 1436–1441*, 122–3, 369.
73. Juvénal, *Écrits*, i, 430; Worcester, *Boke of Noblesse*, 7.

CHAPTER II: *The Kingdom of Bourges, 1422–1424*

1. Proclaimed: AN KK53, 153, 153vo; Monstrelet, *Chron.*, iv, 130. Coinage: Lafaurie, *Monnaies*, i, 95–100. Pope: *Choix de pieces inédites relatives au règne de Charles VI*, ed. L. Douët-d'Arcq, i, (1863), 447–9. 'Dauphin': *Proc. N.*, iv, 13; Thomassin, *Reg. Delphinal*, 224; *Plancher, iv, PJ no. 58.
2. See the remarkable summary of Chastellain, 'Chron.', ii, 178–89; cf., less objectively, Henri Baude, in *Vallet (1853), 8–9; Fenin, *Mém.*, 222.
3. Chastellain, 'Chron.', vii, 324 n.1; *Hallopeau, li, 324–5.
4. Gaussin, 98, 106; Beaucourt, i, 68, 411–18, 431, ii, 65–9; *Cosneau, 507–8 (blank warrants); 'Geste des nobles', 190, 199 ('scandalous'). Cadart: E. Wickersheimer,

Dictionnaire biographique des médecins en France au moyen age (1936), i, 374–5; Inv. AD Côte d'Or, v, 200 (B11901); La Marche, *Mém.*, i, 211 n.

5. Le Maçon: Juvénal, *Hist.*, 335; *Beaucourt, ii, 653–8; Gaussin, 120. Gouge: *Beaucourt, ii, 654. Regnault: *Fasti*, iii, 200–1; Fauquembergue, *Journ.*, i, 151; Juvénal, *Hist.*, 355; *Journ. B. Paris*, 89.
6. *Lettres de Jean V*, iii, no. 1630; cf. Fenin, *Mém.*, 195; Juvénal, *Écrits*, i, 454, 462; Gaussin, 88–90, 90–1, 122.
7. Grandmaison, 'Nouv. Docs',14.
8. R. Dion, *Le val de Loire* (1934); Sumption, iv, 740–1.
9. Le Crotoy: Sumption, iv, 726, 735, 741, 743, 746, 756, 758, 759; BN Fr. n.a. 7625, fol. 246 (lieutenancy); Monstrelet, *Chron.*, iv, 130–1, 142–3; 'Chron. Cordeliers', BN Fr. 23018, fols. 436–436vo; 'Extr. Journ. Trésor', 475–6 (no. 29); Le Fevre, *Chron.*, ii, 72–3. Guise, Poton: *Chron. Martiniane*, 2–3; Waurin, *Cron.*, iii, 86 (quotation); 'Chron. Cordeliers', BN Fr. 23018, fols. 447vo–448. Its satellites: Monstrelet, *Chron.*, iv, 132–3, 164, 179–80, 181. La Hire: Bueil, *Jouvencel*, ii, 60, 271; *Luce (1886), 94–5, 119–27, 138–40, 156–7; Monstrelet, *Chron.*, iv, 132–3; Fenin, *Mém.*, 209–11; Raoulet, 'Chron.', 175–6, 178.
10. Nivernais: Leguai (1969), 326–7; Sumption, iv, 762–5; Flamare, 151–2; BN Fr. 32510, fol. 365 (La Charité); *Gall. Reg.*, v, no. 20501 (St-Pierre-le-M.). Mâconnais, Charolais: Sumption, iv, 617–18; Déniau, 341–412; Leguai (1969), 333. 1422 campaign: BN Fr. 32510, fol. 365vo, Fr. 32511, fol. 35vo (commanders); *Caillet (1909)[2], 328–9. Dauphiné companies, *Reg. Lyon*, ii, 14–15.
11. De Loré: Angot, ii, 717–19; Cagny, *Chron.*, 185. Mont-St-M.: *Chron. Mont-St-M.*, i, 22; BN Fr. 32510, fol. 365; Beaune (1985), 194–6; Laporte, *Millénaire monastique*, iii, 251–70 (roads). English dispositions: Curry (1985), ii, 22, and App. III.
12. Loiseleur in 'Comptes dépenses' 49 (his estimate of the cost of the Queen's household, based on the known figure for 1413, is likely to be too high); *Avis à Yolande d'Aragon*, paras. 12, 15, 100; Chartier, *Quad. Invect.*, 64.
13. *Rec. doc. monnaies*, ii, 315–16; Dieudonné, 265–7; Sumption, iv, 535, 539, 620, 681.
14. Clermont: *Grandmaison, 10–13; *Beaucourt, i, 458–60; Thomas (1889)[1], 307–8. Bourges: Thomas (1878), 125–6. Selles: Grandmaison, 'Nouv. docs', 14–15; *Thomas (1889)[1], 60–2; Beaucourt, ii, 580, 583, 631. An earlier grant of 1,000,000 l.t., at Selles in March 1424, was expressed to include the tax granted at Bourges: Thomas (1878), 157 n.1.
15. Collection: Thomas (1878), 156–7, 160–2. Lyon: Caillet (1909)[2], 29–31, 36–40; Déniau, 418–19. Héron: Contamine (1972), 241. Alienations: Beaucourt, ii, 634–6; *Rec. doc. Poitou*, vii, 405–12 (Niort).
16. *La Roque, iii, 495–6, iv, 1681–6; BN Fr. 18949, pp. 643, 645; BM Add. Chart. 13537; *Chron. Mont-St-M.*, i, 206–8, 266–9.
17. *Rég. Tournai*, ii, 118–20; Bueil, *Jouvencel*, i, 95–6.
18. Contamine (1972), 248–50; Ditcham (1978), 34–6, 51, 58–60, 68, 76–8, 84, 87–8 (Touraine); *Lecoy (1875), i, 521 n.1; *Quicherat (1879), 211.
19. Billot, 49–61, 196–200; *Rég. Dunois*, 15–18.
20. Contamine (1972), 242–5, 255–62, 371–2, 630; *Houtard, 514 (4,000 men); Chartier, *Quad. Invect.*, 72; Héraut Berry, *Description*, 51–2; Basin, *Hist.*, i, 92.
21. *Foed.*, x, 163 (Henry V); Chartier, *Quad. Invect.*, 72–3; Héraut Berry, *Chron.*, 111; *Beaucourt, iii, 493–4; Pulgar, *Claros Varones de Castilla*, ed. R. B. Tate (1971), 35; Beaucourt, i, 342 (mission to Italy); Basin, *Hist.*, i, 92.
22. Sumption, iv, 634, 676–7, 707, 720. The Scots numbered *ca.* 4,000 at Cravant in July 1423: Waurin, *Cron.*, iii, 69.

23. Garrison: BN Fr. 25766/816, 26044/5763. Capture: 'Geste des nobles', 189; Monstrelet, *Chron.*, iv, 134, 139; BN Fr. 26047/207 (execution of alleged traitor). On Garencières: Gonzales, App., 246–7. Siege: Waurin, *Cron.*, iii, 37–8; Monstrelet, *Chron.*, iv, 136; BN Clair. 219/6; 'Extr. Journ. Trésor', 475–6 (nos. 10, 29).
24. Relief army: *Preuves Bretagne*, ii, cols. 1124–5; BN Fr. 32510, fol. 365; *Beaucourt, iii, 492; 'Geste des nobles', 189–90; *Journ. B. Paris*, 184–5; Waurin, *Cron.*, iii, 16–17; Monstrelet, *Chron.*, iv, 137–42 (English and French captains present are listed in the English text of the capitulation in Gregory, 'Chron.', 150). Finance: *Beaucourt, iii, 492; 'Geste des nobles', 189–90; *Preuves Bretagne*, ii, cols. 1124 (payments to Tanneguy). English response: *Foed. Supp.*, App. C, 149 (no. 236); *Chéruel (1840), 119–22; 'Extr. Journ. Trésor', 472–3 (no. 4); Fauquembergue, *Journ.*, ii, 89–91.
25. La Marche, *Mém.*, i, 240; Chastellain, 'Chron.', ii, 9–10. Exploratory talks: Morosini, *Chron.*, ii, 223; *Plancher, iv, PJ no. 20; AD Côte d'Or 1623, fols. 114vo–115.
26. AD Côte d'Or B1622, fols. 62vo–63, 65; AD Nord B1935, fols. 42vo–43; Gruel, *Chron.*, 26–7; *Inv. AC Nord*, i, 293. On Richemont: Sumption, iv, 712.
27. Touchard, 157–74; Pius II, *Comm.*, i, 225–6; Pocquet (1957), 278–9; Kerhervé (1987), i, 160–9, 312–13, ii, 613–15, 620–4, and generally Chaps II, III, V.
28. Blondel, 'Reduct. Norm.', 17–18; *Plancher, iv, PJ no. 60 (Malestroit). Marriages: Fauquembergue, *Journ.*, ii, 79; *Preuves Bretagne*, ii, cols. 1125–8; *Inv. AC Nord*, i, 293; *Plancher, iii, PJ no. 311, 313. Breton embassy: Fauquembergue, *Journ.*, ii, 88–9.
29. BN Coll. Bourgogne 70, fols. 4–4vo (partly printed in Valat, xlii, 65–72, and more selectively in Beaucourt, ii, 319–25); *Plancher, iv, PJ, no. 29; *Baud (1971), 65–7.
30. *Baud (1971), 68–9; *Beaucourt, iii, 491–2; *Inv. Titres Nevers*, 628–32. Chalon conference: AD Côte d'Or B1623, fols. 213–213vo; Waurin, *Cron.*, iii, 43.
31. Plancher, iv, 69–71; *Preuves Bretagne*, ii, cols. 1135–6, 1173–4; *Foed.*, x, 280–1; *Inv. AD Nord*, i, 224–5 (B297); AD Côte d'Or B1622, fols. 120, 121, 139vo (gifts); *L&P*, ii, 530; Monstrelet, *Chron.*, iv, 147; *Journ. B. Paris*, 185.
32. Sumption, iv, 712–14, 759–60; Vale (1970), 92–4; *Foed.*, x, 271–9; *L&P*, i, 1–10.
33. BN Coll. Doat 214, fols. 34–41vo; Flourac, 87–8; Vignaux, 359; PRO E101/188/6 (47), (52), E101/189/3 (52); Flourac, 252–66; BN Coll. Doat 214, fols. 33vo–34. Negotiations with Dauphin: *Vignaux, 364–9; BN PO 1172 (de Foix)/24 (5 Jan., should be Feb. 1425); *Vaissète, x, cols. 2050–55.
34. Bourbon: Sumption, iv, 711–12. Orléans: Champion (1969), 180–1, 669; PRO E364/63, m. 7; E403/663, m. 4 (in London); *Foed.*, x, 264–5, 290–1.
35. *Lettres de Jean V*, iii, no. 1557.
36. *Cartul. Hainaut*, iv, 306–7, 318–19, 328, 335–8, 345–6, 349, 387; 'Chron. Cordeliers', BN Fr. 23018, fol. 436vo ('*environ Noël*'); *Foed.*, x, 279. The first document in which Humphrey assumes her titles dates from March 1423.
37. *Cartul. Hainaut*, iv, 340–4, 354–6; Dynter, *Chron.*, iii, 451.
38. AD Côte d'Or B11880 (depredations); C. A. J. Armstrong (1965), 85–101; Bossuat (1936), 76–7.
39. La Marche, *Mém.*, i, 240 (quotation). Revenues: *Arnould, 206–8.
40. Le Crotoy: BN Fr. 26046/71; BN Fr. 4485, pp. 329–32; BL Add. Chart. 6818; BN Fr. 25767/15, 16, 19 ('commissioner for the siege of Le Crotoy'). On Butler: AN Coll. Lenoir iii, 248; *Gall. Reg.*, ii, no. 5877; BN Fr. n.a. 1482/16; *ODNB*, vi, 750–1; Bogner (1997), 126–7. Paris chronicler: *Journ. B. Paris*, 190. Guise: *Cartul. Hainaut*, iv, 309–10; Hirschauer, ii, 20.
41. Waurin, *Cron.*, iii, 35–42; Monstrelet, *Chron.*, iv, 156, 157; Le Fèvre, *Chron.*, ii, 79–80; 'Chron. Cordeliers', BN Fr. 23018, fol. 439. Urban contingents: *Ledieu,

388. Ships: BN Fr. 26046/61; *Bréard, 169–71. Artillery: BN Fr. 4485, pp. 334–5; *Huguet, 422–4.
42. Héraut Berry, *Chron.*, 110; *Chron. R. St-Denys*, vi, 460–2 (misdated); *Journ. B. Paris*, 190; Waurin, *Cron.*, iii, 29–31; Basset, *Chron.*, 204; 'Chron. Cordeliers', BN Fr. 23018, fol. 438; Fauquembergue, *Journ.*, ii, 98–9; Le Fèvre, *Chron.*, ii, 75; *Preuves Bretagne*, ii, col. 1125.
43. Passy: Basset, *Chron.*, 204; Armstrong (1976), 46–7. Ivry: Basset, *Chron.*, 204; AN Coll. Lenoir xiii, 255; *Actes Chanc. Henri VI*, i, 76–9; *Quicherat (1879), 272; *Journ. B. Paris*, 191; BN Fr. 4485, p. 306–10 (Rambouillet, Rochefort). Ivry fell before Feb. 1423: Beaurepaire (1859)[2], 16–17. On La Paillière: *Chron. Pucelle*, 222. Orsay: Waurin, *Cron.*, iii, 33–5; Le Fèvre, *Chron.*, ii, 75–6; *Journ. B. Paris*, 186. Montaiguillon: Waurin, *Cron.*, iii, 31–2, 62; Héraut Berry, *Chron.*, 110; Juvénal, *Hist.*, 391. Strain: BM Add. Chart. 6818 (Rouen); BN Fr. 25767/16 (Harfleur); ordinary establishments in BN Fr. 4485, pp. 213, 218; and see Curry (1985), ii, 165; Beaurepaire (1859)[2], 19–20.
44. Héraut Berry, *Chron.*, 110–11; Martial, *Vigiles*, 50–1. Pay: *Stuart, 141–3, 398–9.
45. Héraut Berry, *Chron.*, 110–11; 'Livre des trahisons', 168–9. Dates: Déniau, 484 (occupation, 23 May); *Chastellux, 391 (recapture); AD Côte d'Or B11942/41 (siege reported to Philip at Bruges, 3 July). Mailly: *Quantin (1882), 30. On La Baume: BN Coll. Bourgogne 29, fol. 57; AN JJ 172/37; *English Suits*, 149 (Waurin, *Cron.*, iii, 42–60 is not reliable on his role).
46. Truce: AD Côte d'Or 1623, fol. 213–213vo; Waurin, *Cron.*, iii, 43. Relief army (Burgundian): BN Coll. Bourgogne 29, fols. 129 (messengers), 238; AD Côte d'Or B1623, fols. 216–217; Waurin, *Cron.*, iii, 62; 'Livre des trahisons', 169. Relief army (English): PRO E403/661, mm. 14, 15 (17 July); E101/51/7, 8; E 28/39; *PPC*, iii, 87; *CPR 1422–9*, 124. The Duke of Exeter was sick and his company went without him: *ib.*; *PPC*, iii, 113. John Mowbray Earl Marshal (480 men) and Robert Willoughby (160 men) who commanded contingents of the expeditionary army, were among those at Montaiguillon in late June: Waurin, *Cron.*, iii, 62; Héraut Berry, *Chron.*, 110. Sir Thomas Rempston, Sir William Oldhall and Sir Gilbert Halsall, who were also at Montaiguillon and Cravant, had all come over with Mowbray: PRO C76/106, mm. 16, 14, 13. Garrisons: *L&P*, ii, 385. Scales (for his presence, Héraut Berry, *Chron.*, 112) was captain of Verneuil and Sir Thomas Burgh of Dreux and Vernon: BN Fr. 1482/18, Fr. 26044/5765–6, Fr. 26046/76.
47. Héraut Berry, *Chron.*, 111–12; *Inv. AD Nord*, iii, 146 (numbers). Supplies *Chastellux, 391–2; Waurin, *Cron.*, iii, 61, 68.
48. BN Fr. 4485, pp. 324–6 (Suffolk's dates of service); Monstrelet, *Chron.*, iv, 159–60; Waurin, *Cron.*, iii, 62–6. Numbers: *Quantin (1882), 29; Monstrelet gives equal numbers of archers and men-at-arms. English archers are assumed to bear the standard ratio to men-at-arms of 3:1. The proportion of archers in armies recruited in the duchy of Burgundy was usually much smaller. Artillery: *J. Garnier, 67–8.
49. Suffolk's report to the council, written on 1 Aug., survives only in Belleforest, ii, fol. 1069vo; Toulongeon's report to Philip of the same date is at *Quantin (1882), 29–31; Waurin, *Cron.*, iii, 66–70 is the work an eye-witness. Cf. Monstrelet, *Chron.*, iv, 161; Basset, *Chron.*, 205–7; Héraut Berry, *Chron.*, 112; *Chron. Pucelle*, 213–14; Bueil, *Jouvencel*, ii, 63. Topography: O. Chardon, *Histoire de la ville d'Auxerre*, i (1834), 256n; Mesqui (1986), 137 (Fig. 135).
50. Belleforest, ii, fol. 1069vo; *Quantin (1882), 30 (Mailly); Waurin, *Cron.*, iii, 68–9; *L&P*, ii, 385; *Chron. Pucelle*, 213–14; Monstrelet, *Chron.*, iv, 161–2; *Journ. B. Paris*, 187–8; Fauquembergue, *Journ.*, ii, 105–6. Darnley: Beaucourt, iii, 511–12.

51. *Beaucourt, 493–4 (quotation); *Preuves Bretagne*, ii, col. 1125 (recruitment); Cagny, *Chron.*, 129.
52. Fauquembergue, *Journ.*, ii, 107; *Journ. B. Paris*, 189; Basset, *Chron.*, 207. Salisbury, Suffolk: AN PP 110, fols. 69vo, 71vo; BN Fr. n.a. 7626, fol. 187; *Gall. Reg.*, ii, no. 6577. Fastolf: *Rôles normands*, Supp., no. 1359; *Foed. Supp.*, App. D, 150. Ivry: Monstrelet, *Chron.*, iv, 172; BN PO 3050 (Willeby)/2.
53. Culant's army: BN Fr. 32510, fols. 35, 365vo; MS Arsenal 4522, fol. 16vo; Héraut Berry, *Chron.*, 114–15; Bazin, 119. On Borno: Beaucourt, i, 342 n.5; Louis XI, *Cat. Actes Dauphiné*, i, no. 346 (his origins). La Bussière: *Quantin (1882), 30; Bazin, 119; Monstrelet, *Chron.*, iv, 165; Waurin, *Cron.*, iii, 74–5; Héraut Berry, *Chron.*, 113–14; *Chron. Pucelle*, 221; 'Geste des nobles', 192; *Houtard, 495–6. Date: AD Côte d'Or B11800 (muster for *journée*). Ransom: AD Nord B1931, fols. 105vo–106, 114vo–115. The footings of a large castle (90 metres across) can be seen north of the village of St-Leger-sous-La Bussière (Saône-et-Loire).
54. *Itin. Philippe*, 34; AD Côte d'Or 1623, fol. 209–214, 218–218vo, 220–223vo, 239vo; BN Coll. Bourgogne 29, fol. 44; *Flamare, i, 208–9. Suffolk, Glasdale: BN Fr. 4485, pp. 324–6 (Suffolk's dates of service); BN Fr. 25767/45; *Rôles normands*, no. 1359. On Glasdale: Worcester, *Itin.*, 2; PRO E101/51/2, m. 10; BN PO 1338 (Glasdale)/3; *Reg. Chichele*, ii, 394.
55. *Beaucourt, iii, 494–5; Bossuat (1936), 19–20, 33–4, 35, 38, 48–50. On Gressart and Surienne: *ib.*, 1–19, 42–6. Quotation: Bueil, *Jouvencel*, ii, 80.
56. *Chron. Mont-St-M.*, 126–7; BN Fr. 26046/94 (feudal summons); Harcourt's report at *Caillet (1909)[1], 570–1; *Chron. Pucelle*, 214–18 (Alençon Herald); Chartier, *Chron.*, i, 33–7; Basset, *Chron.*, 208–9; Cagny, *Chron.*, 129–31. Scots: Bower, *Scottichron.*, viii, 294.
57. Chartier, *Chron.*, i, 37–8; *Chron. Pucelle*, 218–19; Monstrelet, *Chron.*, iv, 172; Waurin, *Cron.*, iii, 84–5; *Chéruel (1840), ii, 134 (*arrière-ban*). Reinforcements: BN Fr. 26265/121, BN Fr. n.a. 21289/69; BN PO 3050 (Willeby)/2 (companies at Ivry). Chapel: *La Roque, iii, 496.
58. Monstrelet, *Chron.*, iv, 154–5; Waurin, *Cron.*, iii, 31–3.
59. Monstrelet, *Chron.*, iv, 166–70.
60. AN JJ172/241; *Rec. doc. Picardie*, 95; 'Livre des trahisons', 172–6; Monstrelet, *Chron.*, iv, 133, 164–5, 172–4, 181; Waurin, *Cron.*, iii, 73–4, 85–6; 'Chron. Cordeliers', BN Fr. 23018, fol. 440–440vo, 445; 'Notices et extraits' (Bougenot), 50–1; Fenin, *Mém.*, 209–10, 212–13. The last recorded incident of the campaign was the conditional surrender of Oisy (Aisne), before 22 Jan. 1424: AD Nord B17637.

CHAPTER III: *The New Army of Scotland, 1423–1424*

1. *Beaucourt, iii, 490–1; *Houtard, 496; Raoulet, 'Chron.', 186; Quicherat (1879), 24–5, *211–12. Taxes: *Thomas (1889)[1], 60. Visconti: *Codex Italiae Diplomaticus*, ed. J. C. Lunig, i (1725), cols. 443–4, 439–48.
2. Sumption, iv, 679, 701, 707–8, 709, 732–3; *Beaucourt, i, 336 n.2.
3. Quotations: Bower, *Scottichron.*, viii, 114; 'Dethe of the Kynge of Scotis', 24–5. Douglases: M. Brown (1998), 101–2, 104–5; *Exch. R. Scotland*, iii, 515 (Edinburgh castle).
4. *Rot. Scot.*, ii, 228, 229.
5. *Foed.*, x, 123–5.
6. *Beaucourt, iii, 490–1; *Houtard, 496. Fleet: BN Fr. 32511, fol. 37; *AHP*, ii, 291–7.

7. *Beaucourt, iii, 490–1; *Cartul. Orbestier*, 430–3; *Houtard, 496. On Cranach: Sumption, iv, 633; Watt, 118–22.
8. Balfour-Melville, 92–4; *Rot. Scot.*, ii, 232, 233, 234, 235, 238; *Foed.*, x, 266–7, 286, 294–6; *Cal. Doc. Scot.*, iv, no. 927; *Issues*, 381; James I, *Kingis Quair*, 14.
9. Boece, *Vitae*, 33; *Foed.*, x, 298–300. Political background: Brown (1992), 23–5.
10. AD Côte d'Or B11886 (ransom); AN J677/20 (embassy).
11. AN J677/20, J680/71. Fleet: *Cartul. Orbestier*, 430; *L&P*, ii, 15–24; AN J183/141. On Sir Walter: Bower, *Scottichron.*, viii, 134; Brown (1992), 29–34.
12. Fleet: AN J183/141. The first ships had reached La Rochelle by 15 Feb.: *ib.* Douglas was at Edinburgh on 6 Feb. 1424 (*Liber S. Marie de Melros*, ed. C. Innes [1837], ii, no. 507) and at La Rochelle on 7 March (*Liber Pluscard.*, 359; *Rég. Poitiers*, i, 181). Marriage: Harriss (1988), 132. Negotiations: *Foed.*, x, 322–3, 329–32; *Liber Pluscard.*, i, 369; Balfour-Melville, 102–3.
13. *L&P*, ii, 444; *Parl. Rolls*, x, 81 [10]; Ratcliffe, 159 n.2 (ransom); Neville, Ch. 6 (marches).
14. Montaiguillon: Monstrelet, *Chron.*, iv, 155, 174; Waurin, *Cron.*, iii, 33; Basset, *Chron.*, 207; *Rôles normands*, no. 1359. Compiègne: Basset, *Chron.*, 209; Fenin, *Mém.*, 209–11; Monstrelet, *Chron.*, iv, 174; *Journ. B. Paris*, 192. Date: *Carolus-Barré (1930), 61 n.3; Carolus-Barré (1988), 385. Creil: 'Geste des nobles', 194–5.
15. *Rég. Tournai*, ii, 81–9.
16. *PPC*, iii, 135, 138. Indentures were signed for 568 men, not including the retinue of Gloucester himself: PRO E404/40 (148, 149, 154–156, 158, 160, 162, 165, 166); PRO E101/71/2 (804, 805); Basset, *Chron.*, 209; Monstrelet, *Chron.*, iv, 176; Fenin, *Mém.*, 211. Towns: Flammermont, 239.
17. Fauquembergue, *Journ.*, ii, 122–3; Monstrelet, *Chron.*, iv, 176–8; Waurin, *Cron.*, iii, 90–2; *Ledieu 389–92; Basset, *Chron.*, 209–10; AN JJ175/203 (analysis in Armstrong [1976], 46–8); *Carolus-Barré (1930), 184–5.
18. Amiens conference: *Itin. Philippe*, 37; Fauquembergue, *Journ.*, ii, 121, 122, 123–4, 125–6; 'Chron. Cordeliers', BN Fr. 23018, fols. 446vo–447. Bedford left Abbeville for Amiens on 4 March: *Ledieu, 389–92. Champagne: Chartier, *Chron.*, i, 38; BN Fr. n.a. 7626, fol. 266–269vo. Guise: Monstrelet, *Chron.*, iv, 179–80, 204; Waurin, *Cron.*, iii, 94, 95–6; *L&P*, ii, 29–31. Date: BN Fr. 4485, pp. 280–1.
19. *Liber Pluscard.*, i, 359; Héraut Berry, *Chron.*, 114; 'Geste des nobles', 195; BN Fr. 20684, pp. 541, 542; *Houtard, 499–500; *Rég. Poitiers*, i, 181. Touraine: AN X1a 8604, fol. 65; J680/70; *Chron. Pucelle*, 221–2; AC Tours reg. CC22, 96vo–97.
20. *Delachenal (1885), 347 n.1 (general summons); *La Roque, iv, 1684–5; 'Chron. Cordeliers', BN Fr. 23018, fols. 447vo–448; 'Notices et extraits' (Bougenot), 50; Monstrelet, *Chron.*, iv, 181–3; *Caillet (1909)[2], 342–3 (Bourges conference). Spy: AN Coll. Lenoir xiii, 251.
21. Lecoy (1875), i, 42 n.5.
22. AD Côte d'Or B1622, fol. 191; AN KK244, fols. 63vo–64; *Preuves Bretagne*, ii, col. 1164. Richemont and Bedford: Gruel, *Chron.*, 27.
23. 'Geste des nobles', 195; AN KK244, fol. 77, 63vo–64; AC Tours reg. CC21 fol. 92; *Preuves Bretagne*, ii, col. 1164. Protocol: *Lettres de Jean V*, iii, no. 1588.
24. Guise: BN Fr. 4485, pp. 280–2. Mâconnais: BN Coll. Bourgogne 29, fol. 44. Rethelois: 'Chron. Cordeliers', BN Fr. 23018, fol. 448. Sézanne: *Luce (1886), 118–19, 133–5; 'Geste des nobles', 195–6; Chartier, *Chron.*, i, 38. On Sézanne: Jarry, *La vie politique de Louis de France, duc d'Orléans* (1889), 182. Eustache de Conflans, captain of Sézanne, was based at Mont-Aimé: *L&P*, ii, 56. Nesles: *Arch. Reims, Statuts*, i, 576–7n. Nangis: *Journ. B. Paris*, 193.

25. *Journ. B. Paris*, 194; 'Chron. Cordeliers', BN Fr. 23018, fol. 447; Cochon, *Chron.*, 293; 'Chron. Rouennaise', 348; *Actes Chanc. Henri VI*, i, 156; BN Fr. 4485, pp. 256–7, 283–91, 403–4, 429–30; BL Add. Chart. 309 (order to retake Gaillon). La Paillière's role: Héraut Berry, *Chron.*, 115.
26. Expeditionary force: *PPC*, iii, 135; PRO E101/71/2 (805–11); E403/666, mm. 3–4, 5 (29 May, 5 June). Cauchon: PRO E364/57, m. 7 (Brewster). Feudal service: BN Fr. 26047/256, 257.
27. *Itin. Philippe*, 39. Arbitration: *Cartul. Hainaut*, iv, 368, 380–1, 384–9, 391–2; 'Chron. Cordeliers', BN Fr. 23018, fols. 446vo–447. Humphrey's army: *Coventry Leet Book*, 84. His preparations were known in Holland in early July: *Groot Charterboek*, iv, 728. D. Brabant: Dynter, *Chron.*, iii, 437.
28. Strategy: Plancher, iv, 87–8; Cosneau, 78–9. Ivry: BN Fr. 4485, pp. 292–4. Contacts with Dauphin: AD Côte d'Or B1625, fols. 149vo, 155vo; *Baud (1971), 73–5. English complaints: *Desplanques, 73 (a forgery, but based partly on fact).
29. *L&P*, ii, 24–8. Sézanne: *Luce (1886), 118–19; Monstrelet, *Chron.*, iv, 185–6; 'Geste des nobles', 195–6. Gaillon: BN Fr. 4485, p. 291; Monstrelet, *Chron.*, iv, 186; Héraut Berry, *Chron.*, 115; 'Chron. Cordeliers', BN Fr. 23018, fol. 448vo (date). Ivry: Monstrelet, *Chron.*, iv, 186; *Journ. B. Paris*, 194. Date of the *journée*: *Actes Chanc. Henri VI*, i, 103; BN Fr. 4485, pp. 295, 412; Le Fèvre, *Chron.*, ii, 84.
30. Garrisons: BN Fr. 4485, pp. 295–306. Analysis in Curry (1985), App. II, XB. (I have added Verneuil, whose garrison's whereabouts are not recorded in the Receiver-General's account.) Militias: 'Geste des nobles', 197–8. L'Isle-Adam: Waurin, *Cron.*, iii, 100, 107–8; Héraut Berry, *Chron.*, 116. Bedford movements: BN Fr. 4485, p. 358; Waurin, *Cron.*, iii, 100–1; Monstrelet, *Chron.*, iv, 189; *Journ. B. Paris*, 194–5; 'Geste des nobles', 197.
31. Héraut Berry, *Chron.*, 115–16; Basin, *Hist.*, i, 92; Raoulet, 'Chron.', 183–4. Berry: *Chron. Pucelle*, 222; Raoulet, 'Chron.', 183–4.
32. Withdrawal from Berry: see preceding note. Châteaudun: AC Tours reg. BB2 (4 Aug. 1424); Augis, 118; Héraut Berry, *Chron.*, 115–16; Waurin, *Cron.*, iii, 101–2. Dauphin: Raoulet, 'Chron.', 188.
33. 'Chron. Cordeliers', BN Fr. 23018, fol. 451; Monstrelet, *Chron.*, iv, 190; Waurin, *Cron.*, iii, 104–6; *Journ. B. Paris*, 195–6; Héraut Berry, *Chron.*, 116; Chartier, *Chron.*, i, 41, 184–5; AC Tours reg. CC21 fol. 95 (9 Aug.). Alençon's domains: Chartier, *Chron.*, i, 41; *Chron. Pucelle*, 223; Cagny, *Chron.*, 133. Verneuil garrison: Curry (1985), i, 217.
34. Waurin, *Cron.*, iii, 106; 'Chron. Cordeliers', BN Fr. 23018, fol. 451.
35. Waurin, *Cron.*, iii, 106–9; Héraut Berry, *Chron.*, 116; Monstrelet, *Chron.*, iv, 192.
36. *Journ. B. Paris*, 197; *Chron. Pucelle*, 223–4; *Liber Pluscard.*, i, 359–60; Basset, *Chron.*, 214. Coulonces: *Chron. Pucelle*, 215.
37. Lorraine: *Luce (1886), 322–3. Picardy: Fenin, *Mém.*, 216–18; Monstrelet, *Chron.*, iv, 187–8. Normandy: AN JJ 173/315 ('waiting'); *Actes Chanc. Henri VI*, i, 153–7, 161–3, ii, 324, 338, 351, 355. Estouteville: AN 172/600 (confusing Jean with his father Guillaume); Anselme, viii, 87; *Journ. B. Paris*, 196; Waurin, *Cron.*, iii, 120–1; Fenin, *Mém.*, 222. Mites: *Actes Chanc. Henri VI*, ii, 44–5, 47–53. On him, Lefèvre-Pontalis (1896), 9–13.
38. Waurin, *Cron.*, iii, 109, 110–11; Héraut Berry, *Chron.*, 117. Bueil, *Jouvencel*, ii, 63–4, records the starting positions of the Dauphinist cavalry; cf. Basin, *Hist.*, i, 90–2.
39. Waurin, *Cron.*, iii, 110, 112; Worcester, *Itin.*, 335; *English Suits*, 104, 308–9 (Tilleman).

40. This reconstruction is based mainly on Waurin, *Cron.*, iii, 111–16 and Bueil, *Jouvencel*, ii, 62–3, both of whom were present on the English and Dauphinist side respectively; and, where consistent with these, on *Chron. Pucelle*, 224–5 and *Brut*, ii, 465–7. Bedford's brief report to Rempston and John of Luxembourg after the battle is at Newhall (1924), 319–20. Late but generally well informed are Héraut Berry, *Chron.*, 117–18, and Basin, *Hist.*, i, 92–8, and, for the Scottish tradition, *Liber Pluscard.*, i, 361–2. Jean de Saane: *Cron. Norm.*, 73. Flight of English: *Actes Chanc. Henri VI*, i, 97–9, 104–6, 124–7, 173–6, 237–9; **Chron. Mont-St-M.*, i, 142–4; AN JJ 173/25. Burne Ch. XII and M. K. Jones (2002) offer alternative reconstructions.
41. Worcester, *Boke of Noblesse*, 19, 32; Newhall (1924), 319–20 (Bedford's report); Waurin, *Cron.*, iii, 116–17, 119–20; *Liber Pluscard.*, i, 360; *L&P*, ii, 394–5; Basin, *Hist.*, i, 96; *Brut*, ii, 565; Bower, *Scottichron.*, viii, 126.
42. 'Chron. Cordeliers', BN Fr. 23018, fol. 451vo; Waurin, *Cron.*, iii, 117, 119, 120–2, 186–7; *Brut*, ii, 565; Roye, 'Chron.', 192–3. Alençon: Waurin, *Cron.*, iii, 122, 186–7; Chartier, *Chron.*, i, 57, 81; *Lettres de Jean V*, iii, no. 1706. Land grants: AN Coll. Lenoir xxi, 265, 273, 305–6, 313, 314–17, 329, 331–3, 337, 341–3, 349, 353, 359–60, 369–70, 373, 375, 377, 379, 383, 387, 389–91.
43. BN Fr. 25767/89; Waurin, *Cron.*, iii, 122; *Actes Chanc. Henri VI*, i, 238. Scots: Anselme, vi, 225, ix, 404–5. Narbonne: Anselme, vii, 766. Dauphiné: Thomassin, *Reg. Delphinal*, 222–3; Deschamps. Ossuary: *Cron. Norm.*, 73–4.
44. Waurin, *Cron.*, iii, 122; *Journ. B. Paris*, 200; Fauquembergue, *Journ.*, ii, 142–3; *Parl. Rolls*, xi, 83 [17].
45. BN Fr. 20684, p. 542; *Preuves Bretagne*, ii, 1164; 'Comptes dépenses', 164–5; *Houtard, 514; M. Brown (1998), 230–3.
46. Louis XI, *Cat. Actes Dauphiné*, i, no. 346n; 'Comptes dépenses', 180, 188; *Houtard, 514; Beaucourt, ii, 485–6.
47. Plans: BN Fr. 4485, pp. 307–310; BL Add. Chart. 170 (for the Paris assembly, see Beaurepaire (1859)[2], 24–5; *L&P*, ii, 32–7); **Chron. Mont-St-M.*, i, 147–9. Grant of Maine and Anjou: AN JJ173, fol. 315. Norman garrisons: BN Fr. 4491, fols. 46–87, Fr. 4488, pp. 227–315 (analyses in Curry [1985], ii, App. II). The total is very approximate, because of the number of garrisons let to captains at a fixed fee, so that their payroll strength is not recorded. Glasdale: AN K62/18 (20), cf. Curry (1985), ii, App. III. Expeditionary army: Fauquembergue, *Journ.*, ii, 146. Warwick: *PPC*, iii, 207–8; *CPR 1422–9*, 361; **Chron. Mont-St-M.*, i, 254; BN Fr. 26050/799.
48. *Extr. Rég. Tournai*, ii, 106. Tardenois: 'Chron. Cordeliers', BN Fr. 23018, fol. 449; Monstrelet, *Chron.*, iv, 186–7. Paris area: BN Fr. 4485, pp. 307–10; *Journ. B. Paris*, 205; Monstrelet, *Chron.*, iv, 245. Guise: *Luce (1886), 323–8; Monstrelet, *Chron.*, iv, 199–205, 229–30. La Hire: *Luce, 119–27; BN Fr. n.a. 7626, fols. 368–369, 477; *L&P*, ii, 56–7.
49. *Itin. Philippe*, 41. Messengers: AD Cote d'Or B1625, fol.178. Nivernais: BN Coll. Bourgogne 29, fol. 77. Mâconnais: AD Côte d'Or B1628, fol. 142vo; BN Coll. Bourgogne 29, fol. 129; Bazin, 124–7; *J. Garnier, 93–4; Waurin, *Cron.*, iii, 70–2. Bourbon's lieutenancy: *Titres Bourbon*, no. 5217.
50. *Plancher, iv, PJ no. 37; *Morosini, *Chron.*, iv, 332–6; Baud (1971), 35–8, 43–5, 50–2, *92–102.
51. Mont-Aimé: 'Chron. Cordeliers', BN Fr. 23018, fols. 466–466vo, 473–473vo; Luce (1886), 177; *Cab. Hist.*, i, 63–5; Waurin, *Cron.*, iii, 214–16; Monstrelet, *Chron.*, iv, 270; BN Fr. 4484, fols. 36–44 (last musters at the siege taken on 24 April 1427). On its connection with Vitry: Luce (1886), 138–9, 156–7. Vertus: BN Fr. 7627, fols. 18–20vo; Fr. 32510, fols. 368vo, 369–369vo; Fr. 4484, fols. 36–37.

REFERENCES TO PAGES 145–158

52. Fauquembergue, *Journ.*, ii, 144. Plots: Fenin, *Mém.*, 188; Monstrelet, *Chron.*, iv, 187–8; Lefèvre-Pontalis (1896), 21. D. Lorraine: *Luce (1886), 322–3; BN Fr. 26047/342–4. Taxes: BN Fr. 26047/342–4; *L&P*, i, 22–3.
53. *Chron. Mont-St-M.*, i, 88–92, 116–17, 149–54, 195–8, 210–11; Gout, i, 33–4, ii, 514, 520–87; Cintré, 32–4, 100–1; *La Roque, iv, 1684–5. Burdet: CCR 1413–16, 448, 500; *CPR* 1413–19, 111; Basset, *Chron.*, 341–2. Water: *Gr. Rôles Échiquiers*, 212–13. Defenders: *Chron. Mont-St-M.*, i, 110–12, 114; *Rôles normands*, no. 99; *Preuves Bretagne*, ii, 1143–4.
54. *Chron. Mont-St-M.*, i, 24–5, 27–8, *114–15, 138–41, 149–50, 160–1, 163–6, 170–1, 174–9, 181–2, 193, 204–5, 259–60. Tombelaine: Gout, i, 74–5; BN Fr. 25766/794; Fr. 4485, pp. 182–3, 317–18; BN Fr. 4491, fol. 48vo. Supplies: *Chron. Pucelle*, 219; Roncière, ii, 248.
55. Sumption, iv, 685–7, 760; *Triger (1886), 138–43; Bouton, 45 and n.4; Broussillon, iii, 214–16. Coulonces: Angot, ii, 80, 812; *Extr. rég. dons*, 12, 15; Chartier, *Chron.*, i, 39; *Chron. Mont-St-M.*, i, 229–31.
56. BN Fr. 4485, pp. 141–2, 319–23, 266, 270, 272–3; Basset, *Chron.*, 215–16; Triger (1901), 9–26 (Beaumont); AN JJ173/98 (Montfort).

CHAPTER IV: *Jacqueline of Bavaria, 1424–1428*

1. *L&P*, ii, 397, 399; *Cartul. Hainaut*, iv, 417–18; *Coventry Leet Book*, 84 (quote); Barron (1970), App. XLVI (no. 19).
2. *Chartul. U. Paris*, iv, no. 2248. Critics of Burgundy: *Desplanques, 71, 72, 73; *Plancher, iv, PJ no. 59; Fenin, *Mém.*, 239; Monstrelet, *Chron.*, iv, 259.
3. *L&P*, ii, 398–400; *Cartul. Hainaut*, iv, 415, 418, 420; Monstrelet, *Chron.*, iv, 206–8; Dynter, *Chron.*, iii, 437–9.
4. *Rég. Tournai*, ii, 109–10, 122–4; *L&P*, ii, 399; *Cartul. Hainaut*, iv, 419; Monstrelet, *Chron.*, iv, 210–11.
5. *Cartul. Hainaut*, iv, 406–7, 409–10, 420, 422–6, 437–9, 441–3; 'Codex Tegernseer', 16; Monstrelet, *Chron.*, iv, 135–6; Dynter, *Chron.*, iii, 440–1.
6. *L&P*, ii, 409–11; Dynter, *Chron.*, iii, 443–4; Monstrelet, *Chron.*, iv, 212–13, 225–6; Fenin, *Mém.*, 230–1; BN Coll. Bourgogne 29, fol. 241. On Peter of Luxembourg, Smedt, 22–3. War wages: AD Nord B1931, fols. 65–65vo.
7. Dynter, *Chron.*, iii, 445–9; Monstrelet, *Chron.*, iv, 226–9; Fenin, *Mém.*, 231–2; *Cartul. Hainaut*, iv, 451; Le Fèvre, *Chron.*, ii, 93–5.
8. Monstrelet, *Chron.*, iv, 213–25, 244; Le Fèvre, *Chron.*, ii, 106–7; *Itin. Philippe*, 45–6. Philip's preparations: BN Coll. Bourgogne 29, fol. 243; AD Nord B1931, fol. 57vo, 107, 112, 113, 152, 160, 182–94; B1933, fols. 189vo–190.
9. 'Chron. Pays-Bas', 387–8; Monstrelet, *Chron.*, iv, 230–1; Waurin, *Cron.*, iii, 187–9; Le Fèvre, *Chron.*, ii, 106. Dates: BN Fr. 4491, fol. 18; *Partic. Curieuses*, i, 112. Health: Gilbert Kymer, 'Dietario de sanitatis', ed. T. Hearne, *Liber Niger Scaccarii* (1774), ii, 550–9.
10. *Plancher, iv, PJ no. 46; AD Côte d'Or B11942/46; Le Fèvre, *Chron.*, ii, 109–10.
11. Dynter, *Chron.*, iii, 454–6, 448–9; Waurin, *Cron.*, iii, 168–9; Monstrelet, *Chron.*, iv, 234; Le Fèvre, *Chron.*, ii, 106; *Partic. Curieuses*, i, 104–7, 111, 112–13. Philip's offer: see next note.
12. Conference: *Cartul. Hainaut*, iv, 382 (quotation), 463–4, 477–80; *Rec. Ord. Pays-Bas*, iii, no. 2; Dynter, *Chron.*, iii, 456; Monstrelet, *Chron.*, iv, 234–5; Waurin, *Cron.*, iii, 179–81; Le Fèvre, *Chron.*, ii, 107–8. Jacqueline's fall: 'Codex Tegernseer', 20–1; Monstrelet, *Chron.*, iv, 235–40; Waurin, *Cron.*, iii, 181–4; *Cartul. Hainaut*, iv, 481–4; Boone, 79, 83–5; AD Nord B933, fol. 49.

13. Gruel, *Chron.*, 32; *Chron. Pucelle*, 231, 232.
14. *Rég. Tournai*, 106; *Chron. Pucelle*, 231-2; Gruel, *Chron.*, 34-5; *Preuves Bretagne*, ii, 1148-9; *Cosneau (1886), 500-1.
15. *Lecoy (1875), i, 43 n.1; *Chron. Pucelle*, 232-3; Gruel, *Chron.*, 34-5.
16. Plancher, iv, 95, 97-8; Monstrelet, *Chron.*, iv, 211-12; *Chron. Pucelle*, 229; Héraut Berry, *Chron.*, 120-1. Attendance: *Lettres de Jean V*, iii, nos. 1594-6; *Itin. Philippe*, 43.
17. *Baud (1971), 86-91.
18. *Plancher, iv, PJ no. 98.
19. *Lettres du Connétable*, 1-2; Héraut Berry, *Chron.*, 121; *Beaucourt, ii, 81-2, 84 n.2, 653; *Cosneau (1886), 89 n.3; 503-4; *Godefroy, *Hist. Charles VII*, 792-4; Gruel, *Chron.*, 36; 'Lettres inéd. du Connétable', 332-4.
20. *Lettres du Connétable*, 2-3; *Lettres de Jean V*, iii, no. 1630, v, no. 2671; *Rég. Lyon*, ii, 135; Héraut Berry, *Chron.*, 121-2; Gruel, *Chron.*, 37-8; Beaucourt, ii, 91-5. Retainer: *Preuves Bretagne*, ii, col. 1164. Frotier: Anselme, viii, 480.
21. *Lettres du Connétable*, 3; *Caillet (1909)[2], 349; Beaucourt, ii, 96-7, *97; 'Lettres inéd. du Connétable', 333-4; AC Tours BB3, fols. 35-37; *Plancher, iv, PJ no. 58 (p. lxiii); *Cosneau (1886), 507-9. The Dauphin was at Vierzon by 4 June: *Ord.*, xiii, 103-4.
22. Beaucourt, ii, 99-102; Héraut Berry, *Chron.*, 122; *Chron. Mont-St-M.*, i, 208-10, 223-4; *Cosneau (1886), 509-10. Frotier: *La Roque, iv, 1428-9; BN Clair. 33/2487.
23. Mont-St-M.: *Chron. Mont-St-M.*, i, 181-2, 184-95, 203; BN Fr. 4491, fol. 17vo. Maine: Basset, *Chron.*, 216; *Charles, 201; *Planchenault (1925), 30; *L&P*, ii, 38-41, 41 n.1; AN K62/14; BN Fr. 4491, fol. 26vo, 35; BL Add. Chart. 327; BN Fr. 26048/433 (artillery). La Chartre: AC Tours reg. BB3, fol. 15, reg. CC22, fols. 97vo-98, 116, 117-117vo, 118-118vo, reg. CC23, fol. 96; *Livre Mirac. Ste-Catherine*, nos. 101-2, 104.
24. *Chron. Pucelle*, 219-20. Date: *Chron. Mont-St-M.*, i, 172-3, 184, 199, 201-5, 260.
25. Basset, *Chron.*, 216-18; *Planchenault (1925), 29-30. English expeditionary army: PRO E403/671, mm. 9-10 (13 June) (1,396 men); BN Fr. n.a. 7626, fol. 390. Of the five appointed leaders of the expeditionary army, at least three, Sir John Popham (120 men), Sir Lancelot de Lisle (160 men) and Sir John Grey (160 men), served in Maine, in addition to at least one other captain, Sir Reginald Grey (80 men): see *CPR 1422-9*, 299; Basset, *Chron.*, *loc. cit.*; and, for Sir Reginald, PRO E403/669, m. 18 (2 Mar.). Artillery: BN Fr. 26048/433.
26. *Preuves Bretagne*, ii, col. 1164; AN K62/20 (C. Foix). Girard: BN Fr. 32510, fol. 65vo. English at Le Mans: BN Fr. 20684, p. 545; Fr. n.a. 3642/759. Dates: *Chron. St Vincent*, cited in *Charles, 182 n.6; BN Fr. 4491, fol. 33vo.
27. Siege: Waurin, *Cron.*, iii, 191-2; Le Fèvre, *Chron.*, ii, 115-16; *Chron. Pucelle*, 227. Summons: BL MS Lansdowne 285, fols. 152vo-153. Powder: *Planchenault (1925), 30. Capitulation: *Gr. Chron. London*, 134-5; *Chron St Vincent*, cited in *Charles, 182 n.6 (date). Relief army: *Preuves Bretagne*, ii, col. 1164; 'Lettres inéd. du Connétable', 334-5; AC Tours reg. CC22, fol. 98vo; Héraut Berry, *Chron.*, 122.
28. Basset, *Chron.*, 218; *Desplanques, 65, 72; BN Fr. 4491, fols. 29, 35; *Chron. Pucelle*, 228; Chartier, *Chron.*, i, 45-6; Planchenault (1925), 30. Dates: AD Seine-Mar. 100J4/6; BN Fr. 4491, fol. 35.
29. *Preuves Bretagne*, ii, cols. 1164-5; BN Fr. 20684, p. 542 (Stewart's archers); *Beaucourt, iii, 501; BN Fr. 32510, fol. 66; *Cosneau (1886), 513-14, 516. St Julien: BN Coll. Bourgogne 29, fol. 240 (the only record of this event).

30. Basset, *Chron.*, 218; *Chron. Pucelle*, 228–9; **Chron. Mont-St-M.*, i, 213–14; Planchenault (1925), 30–1; BN Fr. 4491, fol. 26vo. On its captains: Angot, ii, 80, 669, 812. Dates: AD Côte d'Or B11942/46, BN Fr. 4491, fol. 35.
31. BN Clair. 206/18; *Chéruel, ii, 136–7; BN Fr. 4491, fol. 26vo; Basset, *Chron.*, 218–19; *Chron. Pucelle*, 230–1; Chartier, *Chron.*, i, 46–7. D'Avaugour: Planchenault (1925), 188; *Chron. Pucelle*, 230; Basset, *Chron.*, 188, 197, 218 (wrongly calling him Jean). His family: R. Couffon, 'Quelques notes sur les seigneurs d'Avaugour', *Bulletin et Mémoires de la Société d'Émulation des Côtes-du-Nord*, lxv (1933), 127–9.
32. French garrisons: BN Fr. 32510, fols. 58vo, 59vo, 66 (Craon, La Flèche, Château du Loir, Durtal, Baugé, Briollais, Le Lude, Château-Gontier); *Cosneau (1886), 514 (Sablé); BN Fr. 25710/51 and 'Comptes Droniou', 359 (no. 129) (Craon); BN Fr.20684, p. 546 (Laval); Raoulet, 'Chron.', 190 and AC Tours CC22, fol. 127vo (Vendome). Cf. Bueil, *Jouvencel*, ii, 271; *Planchenault (1938), 57–60; Basin, *Hist.*, i, 102–4; Le Mené, 228–45. English garrisons: Basset, *Chron.*, 216–20 (Beaumont-le-Vicomte, Sillé-le-Guillaume, Le Mans, Ste-Suzanne, St-Calais, Château-l'Ermitage, Guécélard, Malicorne, L'Isle-sous-Brûlon, Louplande, Montsûrs, La Suze-sur-Sarthe, La Chartre-sur-le-Loir, La Ferté-Bernard; Château-du-Loir, Mayet, Le Lude, Mondoubleau, St-Laurent-des-Mortiers).
33. War damage: Cintré, 121–4. Administration: Coll. Arms MS Arundel 26, fols. 59–63; *Rec. doc. monnaies*, ii, 361; *L&P*, ii, 549–56. On Popham: 'Doc inéd Maine', 259–60; *HoC 1422–61*, vi, 200–1. Land grants: Massey (1987), 79–80, 100–1, 112; *L&P*, ii, 550–1, 687–90. Finance: *Planchenault (1925), 317–27; *L&P*, ii, 549–52, 727; AN KK324, analysed by Luce (1878)[1]; *L&P*, ii, 549–52.
34. *Ord.*, xiii, 117–19; Gaussin, 105, 110, 111–12, 116–17, 189–90. Giac: Contamine (1994), 144–50; *Chron. Pucelle*, 237. Gouge: Beaucourt, ii, 110. Champeaux: 'Geste des nobles', 189–90.
35. Taxes: *Rég. Lyon*, ii, 145–6; *Thomas (1878), 215–17; *Thomas (1889)[2], i, 313–14; Beaucourt, ii, 587. Grants: Beaucourt, i, 119–20. Councillors: *Beaucourt, iii, 501; *Chron. Pucelle*, 237.
36. *Beaucourt, iii, 501–2; Gruel, *Chron.*, 47 (numbers – add companies of other Gascon lords); *Cosneau (1886), 513–14, 516; *Stuart, 141–2; 'Geste des nobles', 198–9; AC Tours reg. BB4, fols. 7vo–23, 24, 26; reg. CC22, fol. 99; reg. CC24, fols. 96, 97, 98, 98vo, 99.
37. Garrisons: Tringant, 'Comm.', 270–1; Basin, *Hist.*, i, 102–4; Le Mené, 228–45; AC Tours reg. CC22, fols. 114–114vo; AN KK269, fol. 52vo; Le Mené, 230–52. Coinage: Lafaurie, *Monnaies*, i, nos. 465–6; Dieudonné (1912), 266–7.
38. Embassies: *Beaucourt, ii, 105–6; 'Lettres inéd. du Connétable', 334–5; Héraut Berry, *Chron.*, 122–3. Saumur: Gruel, *Chron.*, 40–2; *Preuves Bretagne*, ii, cols. 1180–2; *Beaucourt, ii, 114 n.2, iii, 504–6; Héraut Berry, *Chron.*, 123–4. Dowry: *Preuves Bretagne*, ii, cols. 1149–51 (background, see Reynaud, 42–3).
39. *Preuves Bretagne*, ii, cols. 1183–4; Le Fèvre, *Chron.*, ii, 117; *Plancher, iv, PJ no. 48.
40. Sea war: *PPC*, iii, 181; PRO E101/71/2 (821); Touchard, 117. Penthièvre: *Foed.*, x, 354–5; *Preuves Bretagne*, ii, 1195. Raids: Monstrelet, *Chron.*, iv, 284–5 (wrongly assigned to 1428); *Chron. Pucelle*, 237, 239–40; Basset, *Chron.*, 219. Pontorson had been garrisoned in 1422 (PRO E364/61, m. 2d [Alington]), and St-James in 1418 (PRO C64/9, m. 40d). Neither is recorded among the garrisons at pay in 1423–5 (BN Fr. 4485, pp. 176–259). Topography of Pontorson: BN Cartes et Plans GE F Carte–7306 (plan of 1616).

41. *Lettres de Jean V*, iii, no. 1670; Gruel, *Chron.*, 43; Gregory, 'Chron.', 161; *Gr. Chron. London*, 149; *Chron. Pucelle*, 237; *Cosneau (1886), 517–18; Monstrelet, *Chron.*, iv, 286–7.
42. Gascons: Beaucourt, ii, 121–2; *Inv. AC Albi*, CC181. Others: Lecoy (1875), i, 50–1; *Daumet (1898), 225–31.
43. *Plancher, iv, PJ no. 60; Gruel, *Chron.*, 45–6. Cf. 'Geste des nobles', 199–200.
44. *Plancher, iv, PJ nos. 48, 51, 54 (dated 2 Oct. '1414', for 1425: see AD Côte d'Or B11921), 58; *Houtard, 523–4; Fenin, *Mém.*, 227; Vaudrey; Lefèvre-Pontalis (1895)[2], 438–40; Bartier, 105–6.
45. Prevenier & Blockmans, 391–2; Kerling, 29–30, 35–6, 39–40.
46. Jansen, 58–82.
47. *Groot Charterboek*, iv, 522, 546–7, 729–30; 'Codex Tegernseer', 17; *Plancher, iv, PJ no. 22.
48. Initial appeal: ARA CC21800, fols. 42vo, 44vo; *Cartul. Hainaut*, iv, 446. Rising: 'Codex Tegernseer', 18–19; *Bronnen Holland*, i, no. 1079–83, 1089, 1093–5, 1099–1101; *Stadsrek. Leiden*, ii, 12; Beke, *Cron.*, 371–2; *Groot Charterboek*, iv, 746–8; Dynter, *Chron.*, iii, 442–4. Uitkerke: AD Nord B1931, fols. 60–1, 67 (on him, see Smedt, 9–10). Burgundian troops: AD Nord B1933, fol. 108vo.
49. *Riemsdijk, 66–82; Dynter, *Chron.*, iii, 466–7.
50. Monstrelet, *Chron.*, iv, 240–2; Fenin, *Mém.*, 241–2; AD Nord B1931, fol. 112vo–113. Dates and participants: BN Fr. n.a. 7626, fols. 394, 396, 398, 400–401vo, 402; BN Fr. 4491, fol. 18vo.
51. 'Codex Tegernseer', 21–2; Monstrelet, *Chron.*, iv, 248–9; *Rapport Dijon*, 115; 'Chron. Hollande', 271. Dates: *Bronnen Holland*, i, no. 1110; ARA CC21801, fol. 10.
52. Ports: AD Nord B1933, fol. 49. Expedition: *Itin. Philippe*, 50; AD Nord B1931, fols. 162–162vo, 167; B1933, fols. 62vo, 77, 189; AD Côte d'Or B11942/46; 'Chron. Cordeliers', BN Fr. 23018, fol. 466. Campaign: *Bronnen Holland*, i, 1113–19, 1155 (identifies the members of the Hook confederacy in April 1427); *Groot Charterboek*, iv, 794; *Handelingen*, i, no. 210E, 213, 225; 'Codex Tegernseer', 19, 22, 25; Dixmude, *Merkw. Gebeurtenissen.*, 116.
53. Kerling, 65–6, 71–2, 74–7, 143–56, 201, 202–3, 207–8; Van der Wee, ii, 45–6; Nightingale (1995), 391; Nightingale (1996), 101–2; Barron, 102 (fig. 5.5); E. Carus-Wilson, 147–54; A. F. Sutton, *The Mercery of London* (2005), 139, 157–9, 239–41; Munro (1977), 235, 238–43.
54. *Brut*, ii, 432; Gregory, 'Chron.', 157–8; *Chrons. London*, 77, 79–81; PPC, iii, 167; Rhymer, 55–6.
55. PPC, iii, 182 ('heaviness'); *Parl. Rolls*, x, 213 [1], 237 [19], 262 [34]; *Chrons. London*, 81–2; Gregory, 'Chron.', 158.
56. *Handelingen*, i, nos. 210–11. Fitzwalter: GEC, v, 482–4; Dugdale, i, 222–3; CPR 1422–1429, 211; *Hunger (1925), 70–2; 'Doc. inéd. Maine' (1889), 250–4 (Maine); *Cal. Inq. P. M.*, xxiii, no. 714.
57. Reports: *Handelingen*, i, nos. 210–11. Butler: BL Add. Chart. 514; BN Fr. 4491, fols. 19vo, 20. Riots: *Chrons. London*, 77, 82–4; Gregory, 'Chron.', 159–60; *Brut*, ii, 432, 567–8. Loan: PPC, iii, 179.
58. *Chrons. London*, 84; *L&P*, ii, 65–7; BN Fr. n.a. 7626, fols. 459–460vo; *Journ. B. Paris*, 212; *Foed.*, x, 359; CCR 1422–9, 261–2; Gregory, 'Chron.', 160.
59. Philip wrote two reports in similar terms on the same date, to John of Lorraine (AD Côte d'Or B11942/49) and to the Council in Dijon on 19 Jan. (AD Côte d'Or B11942/48, partially printed in *Rapport Dijon*, 116–17). 'Livre des trahisons', 179–83 is based on an eye-witness account. Cf. *Itin. Philippe*, 50; Monstrelet, *Chron.*, iv, 252–3. Sailing date: see *Handelingen*, i, no. 222. Bedford's information:

ARA CC21801, fol. 16vo. Burgundian reinforcements: AD Nord 1933, fols. 70, 173-174vo, 191vo, 192; B1935, fol. 136.

60. *PPC*, iii, 247-8.
61. *Parl. Rolls*, x, 284 [1]; Gregory, 'Chron.', 160; *Cartul. Hainaut*, iv, 539-41; *Paston Letters*, i, 6; *PPC*, iii, 181-7.
62. *Parl. Rolls*, x, 287-92 [12-14]; *Chrons. London*, 78-94; *PPC*, iii, 195-6; Harriss (1988), 155.
63. *Parl. Rolls*, x, 104-5 [26], 237-8 [20], 294-5 [17], 385-6 [23]; *Chrons. London*, 78-94; *PPC*, iii, 195-6; Harriss (1988), App. I (nos. 11-13); Steele, 169; *Reg. Chichele*, iii, 177 (Bedford's threat). Reports: *Issues*, 395; *Foed.*, x, 353; PRO E403/675, m. 3 (11 May). Trade: *England's Export Trade*, 123, 138; Ormrod (1999)[1], 160-2; *Bronnen Engeland*, i, no. 1003; *Daumet (1898), 226; *Handelingen*, i, nos. 243, 259-60; *Foed.*, x, 360.
64. Warwick's army: PRO 403/675, m. 12 (26 July). Borrowing: Barron (1970), App. XLVI (no. 21); Steele, 170; Kleineke, 14, 15, 17, 22.
65. Troops: PRO E403/675, mm. 12, 15 (26 July, 30 Aug.); E403/677, mm. 11, 17 (16 Dec., 14 Mar.). Economies: PRO E364/62, mm. 1-1d (Bokeland); Ratcliffe, 132; Steele, 170. Scottish ransom: PRO E28/47 (25 July 1426); *PPC*, iii, 242-3. Arrears: *ib.*, iii, 259-65.
66. *Parl. Rolls*, x, 298 [24]; *PPC*, iii, 241. Holland: *Itin. Philippe*, 54; *Groot Charterboek*, iv, 837-9, 841; *Bronnen Holland*, i, 1134, 1137; Beke, *Cron.*, 388; 'Livre des trahisons', 189-92; Waurin, *Cron.*, iii, 204-5; Monstrelet, *Chron.*, iv, 254-5.
67. AC Tours reg. BB23, fols. 87vo-88; *Desplanques, 66-7, 69; *Rég. Tournai*, ii, 227.
68. *Desplanques, 57-74; *Lettres de Jean V*, iii, no. 1709; *Plancher, iv, PJ no. 59.
69. AC Tours reg. CC23, fols. 87vo-88, 96vo; AC Tours reg. BB4, fols. 4vo, 54, 7vo-8vo, 17 (partial text in Beaucourt, ii, 589-90); BN Fr. 26050/810-11 (appointment of ambassadors).
70. *Plancher, iv, PJ no. 54. Toulongeon: *Baud (1971), 96; *Desplanques, 69.
71. Ambassadors: *Rég. Tournai*, ii, 224, 227. Border war: *PPC*, iii, 207-8; PRO E403/675, mm. 12. 15 (26 July, 30 Aug.). BN PO 3047 (Warwick)/2; *Lettres de Jean V*, iii, 199, v, 78; Cintré, 125-30.
72. AC Tours reg. CC23, fols. 96-97, 99; *Plancher, iv, PJ nos. 53, 61. On the agreements of 1417: Sumption, iv, 544-5.
73. *Desplanques, 64; *Plancher, iv, PJ no. 57; *Rég. Tournai*, ii, 233; *Itin. Philippe*, 60-1. Geneva: AD Côte d'Or B11929 (26 Mar. 1427).
74. *Chron. Mont-St-M.*, i, 253-7; Gruel, *Chron.*, 52-7; Basset, *Chron.*, 220; Waurin, *Cron.*, iii, 233-4; *Chron. Pucelle*, 253-4; *L&P*, ii, 68-75. Artillery: *Cosneau (1886), 527; *Chron. Mont-St-M.*, i, 263-4. Location of Richemont: BN Fr. n.a. 1482/47 (at Malicorne); BN Fr. 26084, pp. 548-50; cf. Basset, *Chron.*, 220-1; *Chron. Pucelle*, 241-3. And John V: Gruel, *Chron.*, 56. Boussac: Chastellain, 'Chron.', ii, 118.
75. Bedford's movements: PRO E403/677, m. 18 (14 Mar.); *Brut*, ii, 243-4; *Chrons. London*, 131; 'Chron. Cordeliers', BN Fr. 23018, fol. 473vo; *Journ. B. Paris*, 213-14. Brittany: Gruel, *Chron.*, 56-7; *Preuves Bretagne*, ii, cols. 1198-9, 1200-2; *Foed.*, x, 378, 385; Knowlson, 136-7.
76. *Fornier, ii, 298-305.
77. *Preuves Bretagne*, ii, cols. 1200-4; *Daumet (1898), 232.
78. Dynter, *Chron.*, iii, 480-1; *Cartul. Hainaut*, iv, 587-90, 604-5, 602-10, 638; *Partic. Curieuses*, ii, 50, 53-4, 304-5, 307-8, 310; *Actes États Généraux*, i, 1-7; 'Chron. Cordeliers', BN Fr. 23018, fols. 475vo-476.

79. *Dagboek Gent*, i, 58–9; *Cartul. Hainaut*, iv, 579–82, 596–8; *Algemene geschiedenis Nederlanden* [D], iii, 247–8; Vaughan (1970), 44–5, 47–8.
80. *Cartul. Hainaut*, iv, 579–82, 598–9, 624, 638; *Löher (1865–7), 235; PRO E404/43 (337) (Montfoort); PRO E404/43 (337–9) (Alnwick embassy). Arras conference: *Itin. Philippe*, 62; Le Fèvre, *Chron.*, ii, 134; *Journ. B. Paris*, 214–15 (26 May). Loan: *PPC*, iii, 271–4, 276–7, 296; *Foed.*, x, 374–5.
81. *Cartul. Hainaut*, iv, 622–5; *CCR 1422–9*, 340–1; *PPC*, iii, 274; Gregory, 'Chron.', 161; Waurin, *Cron.*, iii, 239; Monstrelet, *Chron.*, iv, 258–9.
82. *Cartul. Hainaut*, vi, 96; Le Fèvre, *Chron.*, ii, 134; *Stadsrek. Leiden*, ii, 237; *Löher (1865–7), 231–5 (Grenier's instructions).
83. *Itin. Philippe*, 65; 'Livre des trahisons', 195; Beke, *Cron.*, 420–1; Paviot (1995))[1], 68–9.
84. *Parl. Rolls*, x, 331 [13]; 347–9 [24–27]; 'Chron. Mon. S. Albani', 19; Monstrelet, *Chron.*, iv, 259; PRO E403/683, m. 11 (5 Dec.); *PPC*, iii, 296.
85. Dynter, *Chron.*, iii, 487–9; AD Nord B1938, fol. 129vo–130.
86. 'Livre des trahisons', 180; Lydgate, *Minor Poems*, 608–13 (ll. 123–4); Common Council Journal, cited by Sharpe, i, 271; *Cal. Letter Books K*, 68; 'Chron. Mon. S. Albani', 20; Lydgate, *Minor Poems*, 608–13 (ll. 123–4); *Parl. Rolls*, x, 331 [13].
87. *Cartul. Hainaut*, iv, 917–22; *Algemene geschiedenis Nederlanden* [D], iii, 249–51.

CHAPTER V: *The Road to Orléans, 1427–1429*

1. *Les La Trémoille*, i, 215–18; Gruel, *Chron.*, 48–9; *Chron. Pucelle*, 239; Chartier, *Chron.*, i, 54; Héraut Berry, *Chron.*, 124.
2. Court: *Avis à Yolande d'Aragon*, para. 86 (quote); Giac: *Chron. Pucelle*, 238; Raoulet, 'Chron.', 190; *Lettres du Connétable*, 12–14; Gruel, *Chron.*, 49–50. Gouge: Beaucourt, ii, 146–8; Juvénal, *Écrits*, i, 485.
3. Chalençon: *Cosneau (1886), 526. Le Camus: Beaucourt, ii, 140 n.1; Gaussin, 126; Anselme, viii, 488; Héraut Berry, *Chron.*, 125 (quote); Chartier, *Chron.*, i, 54. His murder: *Chron. Pucelle*, 247–8; Gruel, *Chron.*, 53–4; *Chron. Pucelle*, 248; AN X2a 21, fol. 76vo.
4. Gruel, *Chron.*, 54. On La Trémoille: *Les La Trémoille*, i, 155, 156; Gaussin, 126; Monstrelet, *Chron.*, iii, 161–2; Juvénal, *Hist.*, 555; 'Geste des nobles', 201; Vissière, 17–26. Jonvelle: Smedt, 24–5.
5. *Les La Trémoille*, i, 134, 136–44, 147–51, 159, 171–3, 177–82, 217; Beaucourt, ii, 145–6, 293 and nn.2, 3; Juvénal, *Écrits*, i, 78; 'Geste des nobles', 201.
6. 'Geste des nobles', 201; Monstrelet, *Chron.*, v, 73; Cagny, *Chron.*, 187; Commynes, *Mém.*, i, 236–7.
7. *PPC*, iv, 223 (high point). Paris area: *Journ. B. Paris*, 209, 373; Fourquin, 316. Laval: Basset, *Chron.*, 222–3; *Chron. Pucelle*, 254; 'Comptes Droniou', 356 (no. 103).
8. Waurin, *Cron.*, iii, 216; Basset, *Chron.*, 221; BN Fr. 4484, fol. 45vo. The English held Château-Landon and Nemours: BN Fr. 4484, fols. 154vo–155; Waurin, *Cron.*, iii, 284; Héraut Berry, *Chron.*, 126.
9. Charles's status: M. K. Jones (2000); Keen (1965), 160–1; Pius II, *Comm.*, i, 380; *L&P*, ii, 459; *Strong, 92 (art. 15). Negotiations: Champion (1969), 182–7; *Escouchy, *Chron.*, iii, 78–9 (Orléans's complaint in 1442); *Villaret, 134–6; *Samaran (1907), 368; *PPC*, iii, 255–6; *Flamare, i, 328–9; BN Fr. n.a. 3655/340 (at Canterbury); *Foed.*, x, 556. In 1433, Charles declared that he had acknowledged Henry VI as his King 'often': *Foed.*, x, 556.
10. Numbers: PRO E403/677, mm. 11, 17 (16 Dec., 14 Mar.) (Bedford's escort); BN Fr. 4484, fols. 74–75 (indigenous troops). In March 1427, Warwick had 2,400 men at

Pontorson and in Maine (*Chron. Mont-St-M., i, 253–5) and Salisbury had 1,600 in Champagne (BN Fr. 4484, fols. 36–37). These are nominal strengths. Numbers actually mustered may have fallen short. Assuming residual garrison strengths of at least 1,000 men in all occupied regions combined, the number of English troops in France before Bedford's return may be estimated at about 5,000. Salisbury: Waurin, Cron., iii, 239. Suffolk: BN Fr. 26049/724; Fr. 4484, fols. 45vo–47. Vendome: BN Fr. 4484, fols. 175vo; Lettres du Connétable, 20–1; BN Fr. 4484, fols. 11vo–12, 13, 177vo; Inv. AC Amiens, ii, 43. Montargis: Gruel, Chron., 39; Preuves Bretagne, ii, col. 1183.

11. *Villaret (1893), 125–7; BN Fr. 4484, fols. 47–65vo, 66–66vo; Journ. B. Paris, 217–18. Truce: BN Fr. 20379, fol. 45; BN Fr. 25986/11; BL Add. Chart. 334; Compte armée, 69.

12. Monstrelet, Chron., iv, 271–2; Chron. Pucelle, 243–4; Raoulet, 'Chron.', 191–2; Ord., xiii, 152–3.

13. Gruel, Chron., 57–8; Raoulet, 'Chron.', 192; 'Geste des nobles', 201–2; Monstrelet, Chron., iv, 272–3; Waurin, Cron., iii, 217–19; *Daumet (1898), 232. Gaucourt: Champion (1969), 183; Gaussin, 116. Kennedy: Scots Peerage, ii, 450–1. Noble retinues: *Flamare, i, 328 (Clermont).

14. *Beaucourt, iii, 512; Raoulet, 'Chron.', 192–3; Chron. Pucelle, 246–7; Gruel, Chron., 58–9; Monstrelet, Chron., iv, 273–5; Waurin, Cron., iii, 219–21; Basset, Chron., 225; Journ. B. Paris, 221. Forest: Maury, 111–14.

15. *Beaucourt, ii, 512–13; Lettres du Connétable, 20–1; BN Fr. 26050, p. 771; Ord., xiii, 167.

16. *Chron. Mont-St-M., i, 208–10, 223–4 (dismissal of John of Orléans as captain of Mont-St-M., Aug. 1425); Gaussin, 122; BN Fr. 20380, fol. 10.

17. Chartier, Livre de l'espérance, 7 (quotation); Titres Bourbon, ii, nos. 5304, 5306–7; Beaucourt, ii, 149–51; Leguai (1962), 123–5; Escouchy, Chron., i, 63–4; Thaumassière, i, 119.

18. Maine: Gruel, Chron., 59–60; Chron. Pucelle, 248–9. BN Fr. 26050/774; Fr. 25768/260; Fr. 21289/80; Curry (1985), ii, clxx. Poitou: Beaucourt, ii, 151–3, 156–61, 164; Gruel, Chron., 62–3; Cosneau (1886), 149–52, 154–6, *533; Leguai (1962), 125–7; *Caillet (1909)[2], 392–3.

19. 'Geste des nobles', 202 (Nogent-le-Rotrou, Nogent-le-Roi, Rochefort, Châteauneuf-en-Thymerais, Béthencourt); BN Fr. 26050/801 (Rambouillet); BN Fr. 26050/834 (Farcheville, Malesherbes); AN K63/20 (Conches). Defensive measures: BL Add. Chart. 3618 (Dreux), BN Fr. 4484, fols. 139–139vo (Chartres); ib. fols. 130vo–136 and Fr. 26050/873, 884, 888, 889, 894, 896 (Seine). Warwick: BN Fr. 26050/799, 801, 834; Fr. 25768/262. Suffolk: BL Add. Chart. 3618.

20. Le Lude: *Planchenault (1933), 149–52; BN 20684, pp. 548–50; Basset, Chron., 221; Chron. Pucelle, 241–3, 250; Tringant, 'Comm.', 273–5; Chron. Pucelle, 250. La Ferté: English Suits, 220–30; Fauquembergue, Journ., ii, 348–50; 'Geste des nobles', 202; 'Doc. inéd. Maine', 259–60; Actes Chanc. Henri VI, ii, 359.

21. Basset, Chron., 223–4; Chron. Pucelle, 251–2; 'Geste des nobles', 202–3; Raoulet, 'Chron.', 194–6; Journ. B. Paris, 225–6; Héraut Berry, Chron., 127–8; English Suits, 206–7. On Gough: Basset, Chron., 207; Gall. Reg., i, no. 4737.

22. Salisbury's mission: Gregory, 'Chron.', 161; PPC, iii, 274; CCR 1422–9, 340–1; Waurin, Cron., iii, 239. Parliament: Parl. Rolls, x, 284 [4]; Chron. Mon. S. Albani, i, 22; Monstrelet, Chron., iv, 259 (Salisbury and Gloucester). Expeditions: Foed., x, 392–4; PPC, iii, 295.

23. Taxes: Parl. Rolls, x, 329–31 [12, 13]; Jurkowski et al., 86. Loans: Brut, ii, 453. Customs: https://www.esfdb.org/table.aspx?resourceid=11405; https://www.esfdb.org/table.aspx?resource eid=11461. Hungerford's measures: Harriss (1988), 171–2.

24. PRO E101/71/2 (826–853B), E101/71/3 (854/868B); PRO E364/64, m. 3–3d (Salisbury); *PPC*, iii, 322; BN Fr. 4488, p. 689. Radcliffe: *PPC*, iii, 303–4 (he was still in England in 1429: PRO E404/45[140]).
25. *CPR* 1422–9, 471; BN Fr. 4484, fol. 106. Equipment: *Foed.*, x, 392–4; PRO E101/51/27, mm. 2, 3; E101/52/3; E403/686, m. 5; *CPR* 1422–9, 499; and see Spencer, 183–5.
26. *L&P*, ii, 76–84; *Itin. Philippe*, 69; *Boucher (1892), 216–18, 278–9; AN KK648/14; BN Fr. 4484, fols. 106, 107vo–108; *Inv. AC Abbeville*, 63–4.
27. BN PO 994 (Dernele); *Acts Parl. Scotland*, ii, 26–8; *Inv. doc. Écosse*, 41; *Exch. R. Scotland*, iv, 485; Bower, *Scottichron.*, viii, 246–8. Passage: *Les La Trémoille*, i, 137, 178. Oration: Chartier, *Oeuvres latines*, 213. Leighton: *Inv. doc. Écosse*, 39–40. Ogilvy: 'Comptes dépenses', 182, 197.
28. *Daumet (1898), 232–5.
29. Gruel, *Chron.*, 63–6; *Chron. Pucelle*, 250–1; 'Mém. Nobiliaire', 337; Cosneau (1886), 159–60.
30. *Les La Trémoille*, i, 136–43, 177–81; BN Fr. 20684, pp. 565–6; Gruel, *Chron.*, 66; Le Baud, *Hist.*, 475. Bretons: *Preuves Bretagne*, ii, col. 1206.
31. *Cosneau (1886), 534–6; *Titres Bourbon*, ii, nos. 5327–8; *Thomas (1878), 218–19; Gruel, *Chron.*, 66–7.
32. *Rec. doc. Poitou*, viii, pp. ii–iii, viii–xix, xxi–xxxvii, xxxviii–xlii. On La Roche: *ib.*, lxiv–lxviii, 8–20, 33–6, 266–73, 294–6, 309–12, and Clément-Simon (1895))[1].
33. PRO E403/686, m,. 10, 11 (19 July); *Inv. AC Amiens*, iv, 120. Paris Conference: Monstrelet, *Chron.*, iv, 293–4; Basset, *Chron.*, 225; 'Notices et extraits' (Bougenot), 55; BN Fr. 4484, fol. 106–106vo; *PPC*, iv, 223. Truce: *Chron. Pucelle*, 269–70.
34. 'Chron. Cordeliers', BN Fr. 23018, fol. 481; Monstrelet, *Chron.*, iv, 294, 296–7; *Chron. Pucelle*, 256–9; Waurin, *Cron.*, iii, 242–3; Basset, *Chron.*, 225; *Coll. gén. doc.*, 236–7; Chartier, *Chron.*, i, 66; BN Clair. 180/84, 85, 87 (pause); *L&P*, ii, 79–84 (Estates).
35. *Chron. Pucelle*, 257, 259; *Coll. gén. doc.*, 236–7; Chartier, *Chron.*, i, 66.
36. Beaucourt, ii, 170–3, *514–15; *Les La Trémoille*, i, 141–2; Cosneau (1886), 163–4.
37. *Chron. Pucelle*, 258–60; Basset, *Chron.*, 225; PRO E364/64, m. 3 (Salisbury); Waurin, *Cron.*, iii, 241; Héraut Berry, *Chron.*, 129–30; *Journ. siège*, 2.
38. Topography: Dubois, 117–239; Michaud-Fréjaville (1980); Debal. Defenders: *Journ. siège*, 6, 7; *Chron. Pucelle*, 260, 261; 'Comptes dépenses', 162–6 (numbers). Bastard, taille: AC Orleans, CC653, fol. 26, 26vo. Stocks: Villaret, 136–9.
39. Numbers: *L&P*, i, 417–21; PRO E364/64, m. 3 (Salisbury). Add 1,038 from Normandy (*Compte armée*, 87–107), plus Suffolk's company of 400, mustered late Aug./early Sept. (BN Clair. 180/84) but not recorded in Surreau's account beginning 1 Oct., and 592 from outside Normandy (BN Fr. 4484, fols. 106–129); *Chron. Pucelle*, 260 (urban contingents). Porteriau: *ib.* and *Journ. siège*, 4, *142–3.
40. *Journ. siège*, 4–5, 9; *Chron. Pucelle*, 260–4.
41. Monstrelet, *Chron.*, iv, 299–300; Waurin, *Cron.*, iii, 246–9; Basset, *Chron.*, 226; Brut, ii, 500. Dates: *Journ. siège*, 9–10; *Cal. Inq. P. M.*, xxiii, no. 262. Will: *Reg. Chichele*, ii, 392–3, 396–7.
42. Basset, *Chron.*, 226; *Journ. siège*, 7–12, 32, 37, 51; *Chron. Pucelle*, 263; 'Comptes dépenses', 164–5, 168–70; *Boucher (1892), 286.
43. *PPC*, iii, 322–3; BN Fr. 4488, p. 689; *Compte armée*, 115, 117, 132, 136, 138, 139; Chéruel, ii, 137; *Boucher (1892), 286–8; BN Fr. 4488, pp. 692–6.
44. AD Nord B1938, fols. 224vo, 225, 233, 233vo, 234; BN Coll. Bourgogne 29, fol. 182.
45. Regrouping: *Journ. siège*, 13; *Journ. B. Paris*, 230; *L&P*, ii, 87–9; BN Fr. 4484, pp. 621–2, 624–5, 637; *Compte armée*, 86–204; *Boucher (1892), 286–8. Burgundian

REFERENCES TO PAGES 242–255

army: AD Nord B1938, fol. 225vo; B1647, fol. 79; *Chron. Pucelle*, 270; *Journ. siège*, 70. Orléans's status: Monstrelet, *Chron.*, iv, 317–18 (*'n'estoient point de la guerre'*). Burgundians at siege: *Chron. Pucelle*, 260, 265; BN Fr. 4484, fols. 128vo–129.

46. Basin, *Hist.*, ii, 198; *Cent nouvelles*, 54–9; Taylor (2021), 329–32, 329–32; Woodcock.
47. *Boucher (1892), 253–4; *Chron. Pucelle*, 265; *Journ. siège*, 15–16; *Boucher (1892), 231–2; BN Fr. 4488, pp. 652–4, 669–72. Bourges: Sumption, iv, 313.
48. *Journ. siège*, 13–20; *Boucher (1892), 241–2, 246, 257–8; BN Fr. 4488, pp. 630–1, 638–9, 652–3, 698–9; *Compte armée*, 132, 136, 138; *Chron. Pucelle*, 265–6.
49. *Chron. Pucelle*, 265–6; *Journ. siège*, 20, 22, 23, 24, 26, 54–5, 60, 65, 67, 68, 74, 82; Chartier, *Chron.*, i, 63; Morosini, *Chron.*, iii, 16. Topography: Dubois, 241–72.
50. *Journ. siège*, 23, 34, 36, 46–7; Monstrelet, *Chron.*, iv, 301; Thomassin, *Rég.* Delphinal, 229; Morosini, *Chron.*, iii, 16 (Giustiniani); 'Compte armée', 130–45. Finance: Beaucourt, ii, 174 n.3; Compte dépenses', 147–60.
51. *Journ. siège*, 21–33, 27, 55–6, 58. Topography: Dubois, 188–93.
52. *Journ. B. Paris*, 230, 234; BN Fr. 4488, pp. 652–4, 661–2, 664–6, 669–70, 671–2, 673 (wages); *Boucher (1892), 226–7, 245–6, 248–52; *Journ. siège*, 26–7.
53. *Journ. siège*, 36–44, *169–70; *Chron. Pucelle*, 265–9; *Journ. B. Paris*, 230–3; Basset, *Chron.*, 227–8; Monstrelet, *Chron.*, iv, 310–14; Waurin, *Cron.*, iii, 253–9; Monstrelet, *Chron.*, iv, 311–14; Cagny, *Chron.*, 137–9; Héraut Berry, *Chron.*, 130–2; *Brut*, ii, 435. Date of departure, cash: BN Fr. 4488, pp. 664–5, 673. Stewart: Bower, *Scottichron.*, viii, 294; E. Cust, *Some account of the Stuarts of Aubigny in France* (1891); Ditcham (1978), 227 (Masses).
54. Blame: *Journ. siège*, 50–2; Héraut Berry, *Chron.*, 131. Troops: 'Comptes dépenses', 162–8, 187–92, 197. Finance: Bouillé, 99; 'Comptes dépenses', 162–98; *Proc. N.*, iv, 60.
55. Waurin, *Cron.*, iii, 253; *Leroux de Lincy, 62–3; AN KK269, fols. 52vo–53 (Blois); Pius II, *Comm.*, i, 381; Basin, *Hist.*, i, 6–8.
56. *Journ. siège*, 52, 65, *397–8; Pius II, *Comm.*, i, 380–1; *Chron. Pucelle*, 270; Chartier, *Chron.*, i, 65. Date: *Journ. siège*, 69–70, *281 (35 days to 17 April).
57. *Journ. B. Paris*, 233; Monstrelet, *Chron.*, iv, 317–19; Morosini, *Chron.*, iii, 18–22; Waurin, *Cron.*, iii, 266–70; Chartier, *Chron.*, i, 65; *Chron. Pucelle*, 270; *Journ. siège*, 69–70, *217, 280. Sully: *Chron. Pucelle*, 308–9.
58. Bedford, summons: BN Fr. 4488, pp. 627, 628, 631–2, 646, 714; *Boucher (1892), 288–93; *Compte armée*, 193–204. Finance: Beaurepaire (1859)[2], 29–37, *168–71; Luce (1878)[2], 303–5; *Boucher (1874), 22–3, 105–6.
59. *Journ. siège*, 57–8, 60, 68, 69, 72; Monstrelet, *Chron.*, iv, 319–20; Dubois, 188–93, 255–61. Bedford's plans: *PPC*, iii, 322; BN Fr. 4488, pp. 644, 660.
60. *Proc. N.*, i, 290.

CHAPTER VI: *Joan of Arc: Domrémy to Reims, 1429*

1. Pius II, *Comm.*, i, 387; *Proc. Q.*, iii, 392 (quotation); *Brut*, ii, 439 (written in 1430); 'Réponse d'un clerc parisien', 173–4; *Proc. C.*, i, 5–9, 260.
2. *Proc. C.*, i, 40, 41, 46, 65, 126, 181; *Proc. N.*, i, 259–60, 261, 389–90; Luce (1886), pp. xxiii–xxv.
3. Schnerb (1993), 3–24; Lacaze (1981), 147–52; Lecoy (1875), i, 70–1, *ii, 217–19 (Réné's homage).
4. Luce (1886), lxi–lxii, clviii–clix, *184, 191–2, 195–7, 198, 202, 205, 211–12, 217–19, 222–5, 226–8, 234, 249, 317–18; Champion (1906), 14–22; Toureille (2013), 999–1000. Gargrave: BN Fr. 4484, fols.149–151vo. John of Luxembourg:

'Chron. Cordeliers', BN Fr. 23018, fol. 480vo; BN Fr. 4484, 73vo–105, 160–161vo. On Gargrave: Curry & Ambühl, 191, 207, 209, 213, 226, 322 n.692, 366 nn. 1003, 1004.

5. Luce (1886), pp. lxiii–lxv, lxxi–lxxiv, lxxx–lxxxviii, *93, 97–100, 107, 142, 192, 198, 202, 211, 222, 225, 234, 275–9, 316–18; *Proc. N.*, i, 258, 290, 296, 298; *Proc. C.*, i, 46, 48, 50–1, 63–4, 128–9, 163; *Nouv. Recherches*, 15.
6. *Proc. N.*, i, 208, 368, 378, v, 145–7, 253–4, 262, 263, 264, 271, 283, 305, 308, 309, 327–30, 362, 368, 387, 390–1, 399, 403–4, v, 120, 145–7; *Proc. C.*, i, 41; *Chron. Pucelle*, 231, 285, 295; Perceval de Boulainvilliers in *Proc. Q.*, v, 120; Greffier de La Rochelle, 'Rel.', 337.
7. *Proc. C.*, i, 47–9, 63, 67, 71–5, 75, 83–4, 85, 87, 88–9, 91–2, 123–5, 126–7, 161–6, 176–8. On expectations and hallucinations: P. C. Fletcher and C. D. Frith, 'Perceiving is Believing: a Bayesian approach to explaining the positive symptoms of schizophrenia', *Nature Reviews Neuroscience*, x (2008), 48–58. Reputation: Luce (1886), cxcvii–cxcviii; *Proc. C.*, i, 49; *Proc. N.*, i, 290, 296.
8. Sin: *Proc. C.*, i, 170. Saviours: see, for example, Gerson, *De puella aurelianensi* (*Oeuvres*, ix, 665); and Pierre de Versailles in *Thes. novus anecd.*, i, 1723–37, and Coville, 220–2.
9. Vauchez (1982), 160–4; Vauchez (1987), 239–64, 280–1; Vauchez (1990), 580–6; Blumenfeld-Kosinski, 323–4.
10. Bloch, 51–86; Krynen (1993), 345–76; Beaune (1985), 77–206; Beaune (2004), 92–7, 109–11, 230–2; Lewis (1968), 81–4; M. Reeves, *The Influence of Prophecy in the Later Middle Ages. A Study in Joachimism* (1969), 300–2, 320–31, 341–3; Pisan, *Ditié*, 31 (ll. 121–8); Vauchez (1987), esp. 230–5; Martin de Bois-Gautier, 'De venerabili vidua ac virgine Maria de Mailliaco', para. iv. 30, *Acta Sanctorum*, March, iii (1668), 743; Luce (1886), ccxxx–ccxxxv.
11. *Journ. B. Paris*, 236, 236, 259–60, 271–2; 'Notices et extraits' (Bougenot), 65; Gélu, *De la venue de Jeanne*, 157 (para. 125). Cf. 'Chron. Tournai', 406; Monstrelet, *Chron.*, iv, 434–5; *Arch. Reims, Statuts*, i, 604–5n; *Proc. C.*, i, 104–5, 116 ('Go home').
12. Morosini, *Chron.*, iii, 38–40, 126; *Journ. siège*, 235, 236, 238; *Journ. B. Paris*, 233–5, 235–6, 237; Basin, *Hist. (Q.)*, iv, 103–4; Monstrelet, *Chron.*, iv, 335, 341; Pius II, *Comm.*, i, 381; Pisan, *Ditié*, 34 (ll. 241–8); Fraioli (1982), 194–6; Beaune (2004), 104–11. Charles VII's circle: Simon de Phares, *Rec.*, i, 22–3, 579, ii, 272–3, 274–6, 282–3; Vale (1974), 43–4; Chastellain, 'Chron.', i, 337–40; Louis XI, *Lettres*, ix, 317–20; *Proc. N.*, i, 293, 296, 410–12, 470–1 (Bréhal's *Recollectio*); *Proc. C.*, i, 66–7; *Proc. N.*, i, 369; Thomassin, *Rég. Delphinal*, 224.
13. *Proc. C.*, i, 48–50; *Proc. N.*, i, 296, 297–8, 299, 305–6. Bertrand de Poulengy, one of the witnesses in 1456 (*ib.*, 305), must be mistaken in placing the first interview with Baudricourt in May 1428.
14. *Proc. C.*, i, 49–50; *Proc. N.*, i, 266, 289–90, 296, 298, 306, 371, 400; Luce (1886), cxcvii–cc, *234, 236–7, 237 n.1.
15. *Proc. N.*, i, 317, 329; *Proc. C.*, i, 51, 76, 206.
16. *Proc. C.*, i, 51; *Proc. N.*, i, 399–400; *Proc. Q.*, v, 118–19; *Chron. Pucelle*, 273. Diplomat: Jouffroy, 'Oratio', 137–8. Date: see Greffier de La Rochelle, 'Rel.', 336; *Proc. C.*, ii, 55 n.3. Charles's secretary Alain Chartier (*Oeuvres latines*, 327) and Perceval de Boulainvilliers (*Proc. Q.*, v, 118–19) recorded in private letters written within a few weeks of the event that the investigation occurred first, but this is not consistent with Joan's evidence at trial (*Proc. C.*, i, 51) that she was received on the day of her arrival, nor with the late but clear and circumstantial account of the order

REFERENCES TO PAGES 264-277

of events in 1456 by Raoul de Gaucourt (*Proc. N.*, i, 326) and the Duke of Alençon (*ib.*, i, 381-2).

17. *Proc. C.*, i, 51-2, 76; *Proc. N.*, i, 326, 389-90, 475 (my translation omits 'and son of a King', words not found in BL Stowe 84 but added in other MSS to support the later myth that Joan told Charles a 'secret' known only to him, namely that he was Charles VI's legitimate son); *Chron. Pucelle*, 273; Basin, *Hist.*, i, 130-2 (derived from Dunois). Date: see *Proc. C.*, ii, 55 n.3. Clothing: Greffier de La Rochelle, 'Rel.', 336-7.
18. Chartier, *Oeuvres latines*, 327; *Proc. N.*, i, 326, 362, 369, 376-7, 380-8. Alençon and astrology: *Proc. Alençon*, 85-6, 96.
19. *Fornier, ii, 313-16, 317-18.
20. Prophets: Vauchez (1990). Investigation: *Proc. N.*, i, 381-2, 389, 400, 476; *Fornier, ii, 313-14; *Fornier, ii, 314; *Proc. Q.*, iii, 411-21 (*De quadam puella*, which was probably the response of Henry of Gorckum, can be dated from internal evidence to March/April 1429); Gerson, *De puella aurelianensi* (*Oeuvres*, ix, 661-5) was completed five days after the relief of Orléans but based on information supplied and questions raised before.
21. *Proc. N.*, i, 328-9, 471-2. Criteria: *Proc. Q.*, iii, 391; Gerson, *De distinction verarum revelationum a falsis* (*Oeuvres*, iii, 36-56). War: Pius II, *Comm.*, i, 382. Dress: *Proc. C.*, i, 1, 67, 75, 94-5, 153, 205, 206, 210, 391. Experts: *Proc. Q.*, iii, 419-20 (*De quadam puella*); Gerson, *De puella aurelianensi* (*Oeuvres*, ix, 664, 664-5).
22. *Proc. Q.*, iii, 391; *Proc. N.*, i, 328-9, 367-8, 374-5, 471-3, 476; *Proc. C.*, i, 71, 72, 73, 93; *Chron. Pucelle*, 275-7; Thomassin, *Rég. Delphinal*, 224-5; 'Documents relatifs à Jeanne d'Arc', 365-9; Tobin (1990); Contamine (1992)[2], 47-51.
23. *Proc. Q.*, iii, 391-2; *Proc. N.*, i, 375 (*scripta*)
24. *Proc. C.*, i, 221-2; *Proc. N.*, i, 368; *Journ. siège*, 74, 79; *Journ. B. Paris*, 237.
25. *Proc. C.*, i, 76, 116-18, 133-40, 417-18; *Proc. N.*, i, 317-18, 382, 476; *Chron. Pucelle*, 277.
26. *Proc. C.*, i, 76-7, 78, 172-4; *Proc. N.*, i, 325, 333, 390-1, 476-7; *Proc. Q.*, v, 107-8, 265, 267; 'Compte dépenses', 207-8; 'Documents relatifs à Jeanne d'Arc'; Contamine, Bouzy & Hélary, 1057-62.
27. *Proc. C.*, i, 48, 77-8, 115; *Proc. N.*, i, 378, 381, 387-8, 400.
28. *Proc. C.*, i, 221-2, 262; Chartier, *Chron.*, i, 75-6.
29. *Journ. siège*, 72-3, 75; *Proc. N.*, i, 317-18, 382, 391-2; *Boucher (1874), 30, 107; *Chron. Pucelle*, 277; 'Chron. Tournai', 409. Escort force: 'Comptes dépenses', 192-5, 196-9 records payments for 448 men withdrawn from garrisons, 1,158 men from other companies, and 14 companies for whom no strengths are given. My calculation (i) omits the company of Florent d'Illiers from Châteaudun, which proceeded directly to Orléans and only joined the army on its return on 3-4 May; and (ii) assumes that where the strength of companies is not specified in the pay records, it bore the same proportion to pay as it did for other companies whose strength is recorded. Since all served for the same period, this depends on the ratio of bowmen to men-at-arms.
30. *Journ. siège*, 74, *260-1; *Proc. N.*, i, 318, 371, 373-4, 391, 473, 477.
31. *Proc. N.*, i, 318-19, 371; *Journ. siège*, 74-7.
32. *Proc. N.*, i, 319, 331-2, 477-8; *Chron. Pucelle*, 286-7; *Journ. siège*, 79-80; Cagny, *Chron.*, 142-3.
33. *Chron. Pucelle*, 287; *Journ. siège*, 81; *Proc. N.*, i, 391, 478, 479.
34. *Chron. Pucelle*, 288-9; *Journ. siège*, 81-2; *Proc. N.*, i, 363-4, 372, 392-3, 407-9, 478-80.
35. Chartier, *Chron.*, i, 73-5; *Journ. siège*, 82-3; *Proc. N.*, i, 393-4.
36. *Proc. C.*, i, 79; *Proc. N.*, i, 372, 480-2; *Journ. siège*, 83-4; *Chron. Pucelle*, 290-1.

847

37. *Journ. siège*, 84-9; *Proc. N.*, i, 320-1, 331-2, 364-5, 372-3, 394-5, 482-4; Cagny, *Chron.*, 146-7; Monstrelet, *Chron.*, iv, 321-2; Waurin, *Cron.*, iii, 276; *Beaucourt, iii, 516-17; *Journ. B. Paris*, 237.
38. *Proc. N.*, i, 321; *Journ. siège*, 89-90; *Proc. N.*, i, 321; Monstrelet, *Chron.*, iv, 322-3; Waurin, *Cron.*, iii, 277-8, 279.
39. *PPC*, iv, 223 (quotation); *Proc. N.*, i, 320; Cochon, *Chron.*, 301; 'Chron. Cordeliers', BN Fr. 23018, fol. 484; 'Chron. Tournai', 412. Cf. *Proc. N.*,i, 331.
40. *Correspondance de Napoléon 1er*, xvii (1865), 549; *Proc. N.*, i, 331, 472.
41. Bossuat (1956), 135; Gerson, *De puella aurelianensis* (*Oeuvres*, ix, 664); Gélu, *De la venue de Jeanne*, 154 (para.124). Brittany: BN Fr. 8267, fol. 142; Windecke, *Denkw.*, 252-3; Cosneau (1886), 166. Circulars: *Proc. Q.*, v, 100-4.
42. 'Chron. Tournai', 412-13; Windecke, *Denkw.*, 252; *Proc. N.*, i, 373; *Chron. Pucelle*, 298-9; *Journ. siège*, 93-4; *Beaucourt, iii, 516-17; *Proc. N.*, i, 321. Coronation: Bloch, 217-21; *Proc. N.*, i, 322-3; Pius II, *Comm.*, i, 384.
43. *Proc. N.*, i, 322-3; *Journ. siège*, 93-4; *Chron. Pucelle*, 300; *Proc. N.*, i, 322-4.
44. *Proc. N.*, i, 322-3, 373; *Chron. Pucelle*, 299-300; *Journ. siège*, 94; cf. Cagny, *Chron.*, 148-9.
45. *Chron. Pucelle*, 298, 300; 'Compte dépenses', 196-205; *Proc. Q.*, v, 106-11; *Proc. N.*, i, 325, 383 (giving numbers); *Journ. siège*, 94-5; 'Compte dépenses', 199-205; Cagny, *Chron.*, 172. Alençon's ransom: *Chron. Pucelle*, 249-50; *Preuves Bretagne*, ii, cols. 1213-17, 1220-2.
46. Waurin, *Cron.*, iii, 278; *Chron. Pucelle*, 296, 297; Monstrelet, *Chron.*, iv, 331, 334.
47. *Chron. Pucelle*, 297; Waurin, *Cron.*, iii, 278-9, 283-4, 287. Recruitment: *Lefèvre-Pontalis (1894)[1], 96; *L&P*, i, 95-8; BN Fr. 4488, p. 721. *Baillis*: BN PO 468 (Burgh)/4. Garrison troops: BN Fr. 4488, pp. 478-86, 495, 528-9, 718. Indigenous nobility: *PPC*, iii, 349-51; *Foed.*, x, 432-3; *Chron. Pucelle*, 297; Curry (1982), 98-9.
48. *PPC*, iii, 322-3, 326. Delegation: BN PO 477 (Le Bouteiller)/10; 1023 (Doulé en Normandie)/14; BN Fr. 4488, pp. 625-6, 629-30, 654.
49. Raynaud, *Ann. Eccl.*, xxviii, 48-9 (1427, ¶1-3); Waurin, *Cron.*, ii, 325-6 (misdated 1421). Background: Bezold, i and ii; Holmes (1973), 722-3. Plan: Lannoy, *Oeuvres*, 228 n.4, 229-30 (relating to discussions between Beaufort and Philip in March 1428: *Itin. Philippe*, 68). Beaufort in England: Gregory, 'Chron.', 162; *Brut*, ii, 436; 'Chron. S. Albani', 26; *Reg. Langley*, iii, 128-47 (bull).
50. *PPC*, iii, 330-6; *Holmes (1973), 738 n.4.
51. *Chron. Pucelle*, 299, 301-2; *Journ. siège*, 96-100; Monstrelet, *Chron.*, iv, 325-6; Héraut Berry, *Chron.*, 137-8; *Proc. N.*, i, 383-5; *Proc. C.*, i, 79; Cagny, *Chron.*, 150-1. Artillery: accounts of Orléans in *Journ. siège*, 286, 311-15, 323, 370, and *Villaret, 145-53. Ex-nun: HMC, *Rep.*, iii, 279.
52. Waurin, *Cron.*, iii, 283-5, 288. Scales was in the army that left Janville on 17 June: *Chron. Pucelle*, 306. Talbot: 'Notices et extraits' (Bougenot), 59. Radcliffe: CPR 1422-9, 552.
53. *Journ. siège*, 100-1; Waurin, *Cron.*, iii, 296.
54. *Proc. N.*, i, 386; *Journ. siège*, 101-2; Gruel, *Chron.*, 69-72; *Chron. Pucelle*, 304-5.
55. Waurin, *Cron.*, iii, 282-3, 284-5, 288-90, 294-5; *Journ. siège*, 101; Cagny, *Chron.*, 152-3; *Villaret, 153-9. Topography: Mesqui (1982). On Gethin and Gough: H. T. Evans, 46-7, 48-52, 54-63.
56. Waurin, *Cron.*, iii, 290-9; 'Notices et extraits' (Bougenot), 59-60 (letter of Jacques de la Marche); *Journ. siège*, 101-2, 103; Gruel, *Chron.*, 72-3; Cagny, *Chron.*, 154; *Chron. Pucelle*, 305, 306.
57. Eye-witness accounts: on the English side, Waurin, *Cron.*, iii, 299-304, 306; on the French side, Alençon and lord of Termes (*Proc. N.*, i, 385-7, 404), Jacques de la

Marche ('Notices et extraits' [Bougenot], 60-2) and Gruel, (*Chron.*, 73-4). Cf. *Journ. siège*, 104-5; Cagny, *Chron.*, 154-5; Bueil, *Jouvencel*, ii, 279-80; *Chron. Pucelle*, 307-8. Talbot's release: Pollard (1983), 17-18. Rempston captivity: *Parl. Rolls*, xi, 179-80 [16]; Payling (1991), 60-1. 'Fugitive': *English Suits*, 264; Curry & Ambühl, 31-2; McFarlane (1957)[2], 200 and n.5; Shakespeare, *Henry VI Part I*, Act IV. Sc. 1.
58. *Journ. siège*, 105; *Chron. Pucelle*, 307-8, 309-10; Morosini, *Chron.*, iii, 60-6, 78-80, 134; *Proc. Q.*, v, 122-3; *Journ. B. Paris*, 238-9; *Bull. Acad. Delphinal*, ii (1847), 460; 'Notices et extraits' (Bougenot), 61.
59. *Journ. B. Paris*, 239; Monstrelet, *Chron.*, iv, 332-4; BN Fr. 4488, pp. 477-529, 728, 752, 756-7; Curry (1985), i, 235-9; Beaurepaire (1859)[1], 228-9.
60. *PPC*, iii, 337-51; *CPR 1422-9*, 552, 554; *Foed.*, x, 417-18, 423-4; BN Fr. 4488, p. 198 (crusaders' numbers); Raynald, *Ann. Eccl.*, xxviii, 74-6 (1429, ¶ 16-17), with wrong dates, see *Cal. Pap. R. Letters*, vii, 38-9; Martin V, 'Pol. Korr.', no. 348. Crusade funding: Holmes (1973), 742-6.
61. *Chron. Pucelle*, 312; Cagny, *Chron.*, 156, 157; Chartier, *Chron.*, i, 90.
62. *Chron. Pucelle*, 308-9, 313; *Journ. siège*, 105-6; Cagny, *Chron.*, 156-7; Chartier, *Chron.*, i, 89-90; Gruel, *Chron.*, 74.
63. ARA CC21803, fol. 21vo; AD Côte d'Or B1643, fols. 65vo-66; BN Coll. Bourgogne 21, fol. 68; *ib.*, 29, fols. 37, 40, 116, 310vo; AD Nord B1942, fols. 5-5vo; *Champion (1906), 137; *L&P*, ii, 101-11.
64. *Chron. Pucelle*, 309, 310-11, 312, 316-17; Cagny, *Chron.*, 157; Chartier, *Chron.*, i, 87; *Proc. N.*, i, 400-1. Border fortresses: *ib.*, 310 (Bonny); AN X1a 9199, fol. 292 (Châtillon-sur-Loire).
65. BN Coll. Bourgogne 29, fols. 37, 109; AD Côte d'Or B1643, fol. 66-66vo; Auxerre: *Chron. Pucelle*, 313; Monstrelet, *Chron.*, iv, 336; *Journ. siège*, 108-9.
66. *Chron. Pucelle*, 314; Waurin, *Cron.*, iii, 312-13. Burgundian readiness: BN Coll. Bourgogne 29, fols. 40, 310vo.
67. Boutiot, ii, 120-1, 482, 487-8, 498-505; *Chron. Pucelle*, 314-19; *Arch. Reims, Statuts*, i, 597-9n, 601-2n; *Gall. Reg.*, vi, nos. 22522, 22718, 22718bis; Roserot, ii, 1036; *Proc. C.*, i, 98; *Proc. N.*, i, 323-4, 401-2; *Proc. Q.*, v, 130; BN Fr. n.a. 7627, fol. 204. Agreement: *Ord.*, xiii, 142-4. Dissent: *Rég délib. Troyes*, 62, 63.
68. *Journ. B. Paris*, 239, 240-1, 242; *Proc. Q.*, v, 130; Monstrelet, *Chron.*, iv, 337; *Chron. Pucelle*, 319-20; *Foed.*, x, 432; AN X1a 4796, fol. 209 (processions).
69. *Foed.*, x, 432-3; Monstrelet, *Chron.*, iv, 333; 'Chron. Cordeliers', BN Fr. 23018, fol. 485. English troops: *Inv. AC Amiens*, iv, 125; PRO E403/689, m. 14 (14 July); *L&P*, ii, 120-1. Norman troops: BN Fr. 4488, pp. 541-3, 666, 677.
70. *Journ. B. Paris*, 239-41; 'Chron. Cordeliers', BN Fr. 23018, fol. 485; *Foed.*, x, 433.
71. AD Nord B1942, fol. 12vo; 'Chron. Cordeliers', BN Fr. 23018, fol. 485vo; *Rég. délib. Reims*, 135; Monstrelet, *Chron.*, iv, 338; *Jadart, 84-6; *Arch. Reims, Statuts*, i, 601-2n.
72. *Chron. Pucelle*, 320-1; Waurin, *Cron.*, iii, 316-17; Cagny, *Chron.*, 159; *Arch. Reims, Statuts*, i, 596-608, 602n. Reims churchmen opposed to the dual monarchy: BN Fr. n.a. 7627, fol. 204; *Rég. Délib. Reims*, 132. Châtillon at Ch.-Thierry: BN Fr. 26048/451.
73. *Chron. Pucelle*, 321-3; *Proc. Q.*, v, 127-9, 130; *Proc. C.*, i, 89, 101-2, 178-9; Cagny, *Chron.*, 159. Family etc.: *Proc. Q.*, v, 266; *Proc. N.*, i, 255, 279, 467. On the *ordines*: Jackson, 34-6.
74. Pisan, *Ditié*, 28-9 (ll. 33-40); *Proc. Q.*, iv, 288; *Proc. C.*, i, 221; 'Chron. Cordeliers', BN Fr. 23018, fol. 486; Fauquembergue, *Journ.*, ii, 315; *Journ. B. Paris*, 254, 274, 281.

75. Monstrelet, *Chron.*, iv, 339–40; *Journ. siège*, 114–15; *Chron. Pucelle*, 320–1, 324; Cagny, *Chron.*, 160–1; *Proc. N.*, i, 324–5; *Arch. Reims, Statuts*, i, 602–3n (Lagny, Meaux). Administration: *Gall. Reg.*, iv, no. 15126, vi, nos. 22486, 22523, 22964. Réné: see also Héraut Berry, *Chron.*, 140; Lecoy (1875), i, 72–4, *ii, 219–20.

CHAPTER VII: *Joan of Arc: Reims to Rouen, 1429–1431*

1. AD Côte d'Or B1942, fol. 77vo; *Proc. Q.*, v, 130, 140; Pius II, *Comm.*, i, 385; *Guichenon, iv, 296–7 (referring back to earlier exchanges). La Fère conference: 'Chron. Cordeliers', BN Fr. 23018, fol. 487. On La Fère: N. Le Long, *Histoire ecclésiastique et civile du diocèse de Laon* (1783) 548–9.
2. Cagny, *Chron.*, 160; *Proc. C.*, i, 105; *Proc. Q.*, v, 126–7, 139–40.
3. *Inv. AC Amiens*, iv, 125; Waurin, *Cron.*, iii, 309–10; *Journ. B. Paris*, 241, 242; Fauquembergue, *Journ.*, ii, 316–17; BN Fr. 4488, pp. 541–3, 661, 677–8 (English at Pontoise). Burgundians: *Champion (1906), 137; AD Nord B1942 (*compte d'armées*), fols. 11–11vo. Meaux: Monstrelet, *Chron.*, iv, 334; AD Nord B1942 (*compte d'armées*), fols. 8–10vo.
4. *Chron. Pucelle*, 325; *Rég. délib. Reims*, 136, 137; Cagny, *Chron.*, 160–1; Fauquembergue, *Journ.*, ii, 317; 'Chron. Cordeliers', BN Fr. 23018, fol. 487.
5. *Chron. Pucelle*, 324–6; Monstrelet, *Chron.*, iv, 340–4; Cagny, *Chron.*, 161; Héraut Berry, *Chron.*, 139.
6. Waurin, *Cron.*, iii, 324–9; Monstrelet, *Chron.*, iv, 344–7; *Journ. siège*, 118–24; *Chron. Pucelle*, 326–7, 327–31; Le Fèvre, *Chron.*, ii, 147–9; Cagny, *Chron.*, 161–3; Héraut Berry, *Chron.*, 139; *Livre des trahisons*, 198–9. Castle of Montépilloy: Harmand.
7. Retreat: *Chron. Pucelle*, 331; Cagny, *Chron.*, 163–4; Héraut Berry, *Chron.*, 139–40. Advance into N. France: 'Chron. Cordeliers', BN Fr. 23018, fol. 487, 489vo; *Chron. Pucelle*, 327; Juvénal, *Écrits*, i, 312–13; Cagny, *Chron.*, 164; *Sorel (1889), 114 n.1, 115 n.1, 325–7; *Mestre, 212. Senlis's sympathies: Sumption, iv, 556–7; Flammermont, 236, 238–9.
8. Cagny, *Chron.*, 164; Monstrelet, *Chron.*, iv, 352, 353–4; 'Chron. Cordeliers', BN Fr. 23018, fols. 487, 489vo, 490; *PPC*, iv, 223 (Bedford quotation); 'Chron. Tournai', 414; Juvénal, *Écrits*, i, 321.
9. *Chron. Pucelle*, 335; *Journ. B. Paris*, 242, 243, 244 n.1, 253–4; Fauquembergue, *Journ.*, ii, 318; *Journ. B. Paris*.
10. Alençon: *Chron. Pucelle*, 334; BN Fr. 4488, p. 734; *L&P*, ii, 204–10 (esp. 206). On Bonsmoulins: Chave, 146–7. Eure: 'Chron. Cordeliers', BN Fr. 23018, p. 489vo; BN Fr. 4488, pp. 753, 755, 756; BL Add. Chart. 359; *L&P*, ii, 132 (Conches). N. march: Monstrelet, *Chron.*, iv, 350, 367; Cochon, *Chron.*, 302–3; *Actes Chanc. Henri VI*, ii, 168–9, 176–8, 296–8. On Rambures: Anselme, viii, 67; *Ledru, ii, 167–8; AN J172/515. Warwick: *La Roque, iv, 1439–40. Garrisons: Curry (1985), ii, App. II. Raids: BN Fr. 26055/1768–9, 1836.
11. Relief of Evreux: 'Chron. Cordeliers', BN Fr. 23018, p. 489vo; *Chron. Pucelle*, 332; Cagny, *Chron.*, 165; Monstrelet, *Chron.*, iv, 353; *Chron. Mont-St-M.*, i, 291 (Bedford was in Rouen by 24 Aug.: BN Fr. 4488, p. 758). N. march: BN PO 65 (Angleterre)/11, 13; BN Fr. 4488, p. 299. SE march: BN Clair. 206/12; BN Fr. 4488, pp. 478–80.
12. Waurin, *Cron.*, iii, 335–6.
13. Monstrelet, *Chron.*, iv, 348–9; 'Chron. Cordeliers', BN Fr. 23018, fol. 490; *Plancher, iv, PJ no. 70.

14. Cagny, *Chron.*, 165–6; Waurin, *Cron.*, iii, 338; *Journ. B. Paris*, 243; Monstrelet, *Chron.*, iv, 354; AD Nord B1942, fols. 77, 120 (venue changed). Date: *Proc. C.*, i, 226.
15. Conference: BN Fr. 4488, pp. 626–7, 656. Recruitment: *L&P*, ii, 112–19. Finance: *ib.* 141–2; Fauquembergue, *Journ.*, ii, 321–2; Fourquin, 325.
16. AD Nord B301 (summary in Beaucourt, ii, 410). Side-agreement: 'Délib. Beauvais', 161, 164; *Champion (1906), 152; *Proc. Q.*, v, 174–5.
17. Cagny, *Chron.*, 166. Defences: Avinain.
18. Fauquembergue, *Journ.*, ii, 318–20; BN Fr. n.a. 7627, fols. 206–206vo (proscriptions); *Journ. B. Paris*, 243–4, 246. Armed citizens: G. L. Thompson (1991), 101–4.
19. *Chron. Pucelle*, 332–4; *Journ. siège*, 126–8; Chartier, *Chron.*, i, 107–9; *Journ. B. Paris*, 244–6, 244 n.1; Waurin, *Cron.*, iii, 339–41; Cagny, *Chron.*, 166–8.
20. Cagny, *Chron.*, 168–9; *Journ. siège*, 128–9.
21. Burgundian/French contacts: Héraut Berry, *Chron.*, 141; AD Nord B1942, fol. 77 (payment for two missions to Charles, 17 Sept.). Government of north: BN Fr. 21405, p. 102 (commission); Monstrelet, *Chron.*, iv, 375, 376–7; *Chron. Pucelle*, 335–6. Withdrawal: Cagny, *Chron.*, 170; Monstrelet, *Chron.*, iv, 358. Cease-fire: AD Nord B301 (summary in Beaucourt, ii, 411).
22. *Chron. Pucelle*, 335–6; Chartier, *Chron.*, i, 112. Troops: BN Fr. 4488, pp. 667–8, 679; AD Nord B1942 (*compte d'armées*), fols. 11–17; BN Fr. n.a. 1482/55, 65 (dispersal).
23. Chartier, *Chron.*, i, 127–8; Héraut Berry, *Chron.*, 141, 146–7, 163, 171; Monstrelet, *Chron.*, iv, 379–80, 385–6, 398–9, 428; Chastellain, 'Chron.', ii, 33–4, 70–1; *Rég. délib. Reims*, 141, 163, 171; *Champion (1906), 153, 165; *Rég. délib. Troyes*, 74, 179–81; Bazin, 160–4. Chaumont: *Claudon, 190–4. Bassigny, Gargrave: *Luce (1886), 184, 191, 205, 249; Héraut Berry, *Chron.*, 147; BN Coll. Bourgogne 29, fols. 101, 154; BN Fr. 4484, fols. 43vo, 149–152vo, 153. French and Scots: *Arch. Reims, Statuts*, i, 601n, 604n.; *Rég. délib. Reims*, 196–7; *Reg. Délib. Troyes*, 63; *Champion (1906), 183–4; *Flammermont, 284–5 (Laon).
24. *Beaucourt, iii, 518; *Flammermont, 287–9; Juvénal, *Écrits*, i, 321–2; Chastellain, 'Chron.', ii, 27–8; Monstrelet, *Chron.*, iv, 363–4, v, 74; Waurin, *Cron.*, iii, 343, 375–6; *Journ. B. Paris*, 247–8; Guenée (1963), 53–5. Beauvais: Juvénal, *Écrits*, i, 310–12, 315, 317; *Ord.*, xiii, 52–4; *Flammermont, 287–8; *Actes Chanc. Henri VI*, 177, AN JJ175/354; Monstrelet, *Chron.*, iv, 368–70, v, 12–13; BN Fr. 26052/1243; BN Clair. 208/9; BN Fr. n.a. 1482/66, 67; *L&P*, ii, 544 (payment of English); 'Délib. Beauvais', 162–4, 166–7, 170–8, 190–3, 196–7, 199, 204, 214, 227, 228, 229, 233, 236; AN JJ171/129 (Kyriel's lieutenant).
25. *Ord.*, xiv, 102–5.
26. Departure: Monstrelet, *Chron.*, iv, 358; Cagny, *Chron.*, 169–70; *Proc. C.*, i, 170–1. Mission: *Proc. C.*, i, 52, 83, 105–6, 128–9, 140–1, 160–1; *Arch. Reims, Statuts*, i, 598n. Fame: Morosini, *Chron.*, iii, 229–33; *Proc. Q.*, v, 150–3. Critics: *Proc. C.*, i, 103–6, 264–6; *Arch. Reims, Statuts*, i, 604–5n.
27. Cagny, *Chron.*, 170–1; Héraut Berry, *Chron.*, 142.
28. Héraut Berry, *Chron.*, 142; *Proc. N.*, i, 330, 484–5; *Proc. Q.*, v, 147, 148, 356–7; Cagny, *Chron.*, 172.
29. Fauquembergue, *Journ.*, ii, 325–6; *Journ. B. Paris*, 247; Monstrelet, *Chron.*, iv, 359–60, 361; Waurin, *Cron.*, iii, 343–4. Montdidier conference: *Guichenon, iv, 297; 'Délib. Beauvais', 163, 164–5; Héraut Berry, *Chron.*, 141. Escort: AD Nord B1942 (*compte d'armées*), fols. 8vo–10.
30. *Proc. Q.*, v, 174–5; *Champion (1906), 142, 148–50, 152, 218–19; 'Délib. Beauvais', 161, 164; 'Chron. Cordeliers', BN Fr. 23018, fols. 494vo–495; Chartier, *Chron.*, i, 125.

31. Coronation plan: *Foed.*, x, 432–3. Agreement: Fauquembergue, *Journ.*, ii, 327; AN X1a 8605, fols.14–14vo; BN Mélanges Colbert 380/534 (town and *vicomté* of Paris); Monstrelet, *Chron.*, iv, 362; Waurin, *Cron.*, iii, 344–5; *Journ. B. Paris*, 247–8. Garrison: AD Nord 1942 (*compte d'armées*), fols. 18–19. Duration: Murphy (2012)[1], 154–9.
32. St-Denis conference: Fauquembergue, *Journ.*, ii, 326–8; Guichenon, iv, 296–7; *L&P*, ii, 126–7; *Champion (1906), 151. Library: Stratford (1987), 340.
33. *Brut*, ii, 436–7, 451, 454–5; Gregory, 'Chron.', 164–70. French councillors: BN Fr. n.a. 1482/53, 54; Le Cacheux, 157–9.
34. *Champion (1906), 142–6. On Lannoy: P. Bonenfant, *Du meurtre de Montereau au traité de Troyes* (1958), 75–7, 157, 172, *224.
35. Army: PRO E403/691, m. 14 (2 Jan.); *PPC*, iv, 8; *CPR 1429–36*, 41–2; PRO SC8/96/4753 (petition). Diplomacy: *PPC*, iv, 9, 12–14; PRO E404/46 (167).
36. *PPC*, iv, 10–11. Finance: http://www.esfdb.org/table.aspx?resourceid=11771 (customs); Ratcliffe, 125, and Harriss (1988), 197 (arrears). Taxes: 'Chron. Mon. S. Albani', i, 43; *Parl. Rolls*, x, 378–9 [11], 380–1 [14], 385–6 [23]; *Reg. Chichele*, iii, 211–13.
37. Laval: *Chron. Pucelle*, 337; Basset, *Chron.*, 222–3; BN Fr. 4488, pp. 541–2; Angot, i, 341–2 (date). Estates: *L&P*, ii, 131–2. Étrépagny: BL Add. Chart. 11726; Monstrelet, *Chron.*, iv, 367–8, 370; Cochon, *Chron.*, 304. Torcy: Cochon, *Chron.*, 307; Monstrelet, *Chron.*, iv, 351; Waurin, *Cron.*, iii, 343–4. Verneuil: Cochon, *Chron.*, 307–8; Morosini, *Chron.*, iii, 220–3. Fastolf: BN Fr. 4488, pp. 541–2. Verneuil was recovered by 6 Dec.: BN Fr. 25768/440.
38. Cochon, *Chron.*, 308; Monstrelet, *Chron.*, iv, 372; Basin, *Hist.*, i, 150; *Cartul. Louviers*, ii², 126; H. Guibert, 52–4, 55–7; AN Coll. Lenoir iv, 205 (forfeitures). Topography: H. Guibert, 13–18; BN Cartes et Plans GE D–16856. Population: H. Guibert, 18 (1,017 households in 1414, at a coefficient of 4). Bernay, Beaumont: BN Fr. n.a. 1482/71. Ch.-Gaillard: Cochon, *Chron.*, 308–9; Héraut Berry, *Chron.*, 146, 430; Monstrelet, *Chron.*, iv, 350–1; Morosini, *Chron.*, iii, 264–6; *Actes Chanc. Henri VI*, ii, 157–60; Curry (1985), ii, p. ix (garrison).
39. Evreux: BN Fr. 25769/462; Curry (1985), ii, p. ix for its establishment. Clarence: PRO E403/691, mm. 14–15 (2 Jan.). Torcy: Monstrelet, *Chron.*, iv, 368; BN Fr. 26052/1241 (date). Ch.-Gaillard: BN Fr. n.a. 1482/74, 75; BN Fr. 26053/1297.
40. Mantes: BL Add. Chart. 379. Dreux, Melun: BN Fr. n.a. 3642/771. Rouen: *Chron. Pucelle*, 338–9; Héraut Berry, *Chron.*, 142; Morosini, *Chron.*, iii, 223–4. Falaise: *L&P*, 119. Gournay, Gisors: PRO E404/50 (343). Paris: *Doc. Paris*, 301–310; *Journ. B. Paris*, 251–3; Fauquembergue, *Journ.*, ii, 336–7; 'Chron. Cordeliers', BN Fr. 23018, fols.496vo–497; Morosini, *Chron.*, iii, 274.
41. Bell, Curry, et al., 249–53; Newhall (1940), 113–22. Fastolf: A. R. Smith (1995), 138.
42. Le Fèvre, *Chron.*, ii, 210–12; Chastellain, 'Chron.', iii, 7, 9–13, 21; Armstrong (1965), 367. Sens: S.-A. Tarbé des Sablons, 'Détails historiques sur le bailliage de Sens', in B.-L. Pelée de Chenouteau, *Conférence de la coutume de Sens* (1787), 537–621 at 595; Héraut Berry, *Chron.*, 428. Bets hedged: *Guichenon, iv, 296; AD Nord B1942, fols. 129vo–130; AD Nord B301.
43. *PPC*, iv, 18; PRO E404/46 (179); E403/691, m. 18 (23 Feb.); BL Add. Chart. 7959; *Lobanov (2015)[2], 314–17.
44. Beaufort: 'Chron. Mon. S. Albani', i, 48–9; AD Nord B1942 (*compte d'armées*), fols. 5vo–6; *Foed.*, x, 454–5. Preparations: *Foed.*, x, 449, 450, 451–2; *CPR 1429–36*, 43–4 (indentures sealed from 18 Feb.: Ratcliffe, 47–9, 51–6, 58–60); *Brut*, ii, 438; Gregory, 'Chron.', 171; Monstrelet, *Chron.*, iv, 378 (Péronne). Borrowings: *CPR*

1429–31, 49–51, 60–2; Steel, 174–5 (cash receipts to be increased by £8,333, the amount of Beaufort's loan to pay the Duke of Burgundy). Rolin: *Baud (1992), 254.
45. 'Chron. Cordeliers', BN Fr. 23018, fol. 496; Morosini, *Chron.*, iii, 274; *Journ. B. Paris*, 251; Monstrelet, *Chron.*, iv, 365–7; Cochon, *Chron.*, 309; Bazin, 154–8. Melun: Héraut Berry, *Chron.*, 428–9; Monstrelet, *Chron.*, iv, 378; Chartier, *Chron.*, i, 125–7. Date: *Proc. C.*, i, 141.
46. English army: *L&P*, ii, 140–1; Gregory, 'Chron.', 171; Monstrelet, *Chron.*, iv, 389; PRO E404/46/187–287 (analysed by Ratcliffe, 47–65); Curry (2003), 32–5; PRO E364/69, mm. 17–18 (Hampton) (artillery). Burgundian army: AD Nord B1942 (*compte d'armées*), fols. 25–29, 54–54vo. Verses: *Religious Lyrics*, nos. 130, 131 (quotation: no. 131, ll. 50–2).
47. *Foed.*, x, 456–7; Rowe (1934), 223–8, 232–4; *PPC*, iv, 29, 36, 84, 95; Boulet, 322–3, 325, 330–3, 473–6. Warwick: *ODNB*, iv, 592–5; Sumption, iv, 367, 370–3, 558, 583, 587, 601, 635–7, 640, 645, 661–2, 753, 759, 765–6; 'Elmham', *Vita et Gesta Henrici Quinti*, ed. T. Hearne (1727), 213 (quote). Morgan: Sumption, iv, 387, 401, 423, 494–6, 516, 550, 596–8, 601, 714. Alnwick: *ODNB*, i, 889–90; Hayes, 362. Tiptoft: *ODNB*, liv, 832–3; Sumption, iv, 516–17, 541–2. Stafford: *ODNB*, lii, 55–7. Norman towns: Curry (1985), ii, App. VIII. Lordships: BL Add. Chart. 374.
48. *Champion (1906), 144–5, 155–60; *L&P*, ii, 157, 166.
49. *Itin. Philippe*, 84; Champion (1906), 36–7, 152, 153; AD Nord B1942 (*compte d'armées*), fols. 11–11vo; 'Chron. Cordeliers', BN Fr. 23018, fol. 497–497vo; Monstrelet, *Chron.*, iv, 379, 397. English contingent: *PPC*, iv, 72; PRO C76/112, m. 14; *Lobanov (2015)[2], 316 (numbers).
50. Beaucourt, ii, 265–6; *Rég. Tournai*, ii, 347–51; Juvénal, *Écrits*, i, 323–4 (north); Vaissète, ix, 1104.
51. *Proc. Q.*, v, 156–62; Cagny, *Chron.*, 172–3; Chartier, *Chron.*, i, 120. Letters: *Proc. Q.*, v, 160–2; *Proc. C.*, i, 141, 150–1; Monstrelet, *Chron.*, iv, 384–5; *Musée des Arch. Dep.*, 306; *Sorel (1889), 145 n.3. Italians: Champion (1906), 38 n.2.
52. Héraut Berry, *Chron.*, 142–3; Chastellain, 'Chron.', ii, 37–8; *Sorel (1889), 145 n.3; Monstrelet, *Chron.*, iv, 382–3; 'Chron. Cordeliers', BN Fr. 23018, fol. 497vo.
53. Héraut Berry, *Chron.*, 143–4. Date: *Sorel (1889), 145 n.3; Carolus-Barré (1982)[1], 17.
54. Arch. Reims, *Statuts*, i, 604n; *Champion (1906), 217–19; Monstrelet, *Chron.*, iv, 376–8, 382–3, 404–5; *Flammermont, 281–2; *Carolus-Barré (1981), 316–26, esp. 319 (para. 550); Lépinois (1863), 488. Numbers: Carolus-Barré (1982))[1], 23; *Sorel (1889), 333–7. Topography: Sorel (1889), 162–9. Barbican: 'Chron. Cordeliers', BN Fr. 23018, fol. 498.
55. Monstrelet, *Chron.*, iv, 382–4, 397.
56. *Proc. C.*, i, 110–11; *Proc. Q.*, v, 166–7 and *Champion (1906), 170 (Philip's report, originally written same evening); *ib.*, v, 176–7 (Flavy's later account); *Proc. C.*, i, 112–13 (Joan's account); Monstrelet, *Chron.*, iv, 386–9 (present but an eye-witness only at the end); Fauquembergue, *Journ.*, ii, 342–3 (John of Luxembourg's account). Cf. Le Fèvre, *Chron.*, ii, 179–80; Cagny, *Chron.*, 174–6; 'Chron. Cordeliers', BN Fr. 23018, fols. 498–498vo.
57. *Proc. Q.*, v, 177; *Sorel (1889), 355–6, 359, 360; *Champion (1906), 174–80 (artillery); Monstrelet, *Chron.*, iii, 390–1; Chastellain, 'Chron.', ii, 52–3, 55–6.
58. English: Monstrelet, *Chron.*, iv, 396–7 (1,000 archers, the most plausible figure); Le Fèvre, *Chron.*, ii, 181–2 (2,000 combattants); 'Chron. Cordeliers', BN Fr. 23018, fol. 498, 500 (4,000 men). French: *Champion (1906), 51 n.2, 181, 219; Crépy: 'Chron. Cordeliers', BN Fr. 23018, fol. 499vo; *Sorel (1889), 333–4, 335–6.

59. Monstrelet, *Chron.*, iv, 396–7; 'Chron. Cordeliers', BN Fr. 23018, fol. 164; *Champion (1906), 171, 175–6; *Carolus-Barré (1981), 319–25. Date: 'Docs siège de Compiègne', 28.
60. Marches of Burgundy: Bazin, 154–63; Bossuat (1936), 136–7; Denis, 'Journ.', 200; 'Processus guerrae Anthonis', 311–14, 315–16, 317–20, 323–33; Thomassin, *Reg. Delphinal*, 243–5; Monstrelet, *Chron.*, iv, 406–8; Héraut Berry, *Chron.*, 247–8; Déniau, 550–5, 557–61; *Protokollbücher*, i, 31–3, 39. Namur: Loncin; 'Chron. Cordeliers', BN Fr. 23018, fol. 499; Monstrelet, *Chron.*, iv, 392–5.
61. Overstretched: *Champion (1906), 172; AD Nord B1942 (*compte d'armées*), fols. 30–42; *Rec. Ord. Pays-Bas*, i, 21–2. Subsidy: *L&P*, ii, 157, 166–7; AD Nord B1942 (*compte d'armées*), fols. 5vo–6; BN Fr. 20327, fol. 150.
62. Dynter, *Chron.*, iii, 498, 500–3; 'Chron. Cordeliers', BN Fr. 23018, fol. 500vo; Monstrelet, *Chron.*, iv, 399–401; Le Fèvre, *Chron.*, ii, 182–3; *Itin. Philippe.*, 86–7. Background: Vaughan (1970), 52.
63. 'Chron. Cordeliers', BN Fr. 23018, fol. 500vo–501; Monstrelet, *Chron.*, iv, 402–4, 409, 411–12, 415–16; Le Fèvre, *Chron.*, ii, 183; *Sorel (1889), 341–2. Burgundian army: AD Nord B1941/55943; AD Nord 1942 (*compte d'armées*), fols. 43–49; *Champion (1906), 173–4. St-Ladre (name): *L&P*, ii, 177. Golden Fleece: Smedt, 38, 43, 23–4.
64. Héraut Berry, *Chron.*, 144–5; Monstrelet, *Chron.*, iv, 404–5, 409–19, 420–1; *Champion (1906), 51 n.2, 176–7, 181; *Sorel (1889), 342–3; 'Chron. Cordeliers', BN Fr. 23018, fol. 502vo–503vo; 'Livre des trahisons', 202; Le Fèvre, *Chron.*, 184–6; *L&P*, ii, 177; Morosini, *Chron.*, iii, 322; *Sorel (1889), 343. Bombards: AD Nord B1942 (*compte d'armées*), fols. 84vo–85.
65. *L&P*, ii, 159, 161, 168–79; *Itin. Philippe*, 88; Monstrelet, *Chron.*, iv, 419–21; 'Chron. Cordeliers', BN Fr. 23018, fol. 503vo; Morosini, *Chron.*, iii, 322–30; Le Fèvre, *Chron.*, ii, 186–7; Chastellain, 'Chron.', ii, 108 (curse).
66. *L&P*, ii, 156–81. Payments: AD Nord B1942 (*compte d'armées*), fols. 6–6vo, 85vo.
67. Monstrelet, *Chron.*, iv, 420–8; 'Chron. Cordeliers', BN Fr. 23018, fol. 504–504vo; Le Fèvre, *Chron.*, ii, 192–7; Chastellain, 'Chron.', ii, 130–42; *Itin. Philippe*, 88–91. English reinforcements: Monstrelet, *Chron.*, iv, 427–8; *PPC*, iv, 72; Le Fèvre, *Chron.*, ii, 194–5; Lannoy, *Oeuvres*, 457–8. Thomas Beaufort: BL Add. Chart. 11671, 11672; BN Fr. 20327, fol. 150. Amiens: *Inv. AC Amiens*, iv, 130; AD Nord B1942, fols. 85vo–86; *Itin. Philippe*, 88–91.
68. *Proc. C.*, i, 107, 155–6; Journel, 51.
69. Ambühl (2017)[1], 1048–59; *Proc. C.*, i, 8–9, 433, ii, 403, iii, 5; *Basin, *Hist. (Q.)*, iv, 103–4; *Journ. B. Paris*, 259, 270–1. On the University: Denifle and Chatelain, 4–9.
70. Monstrelet, *Chron.*, iv, 443–4; *Proc. N.*, i, 418.
71. *Proc. C.*, i, 9–10; *Proc. Q.*, v, 178–81, 191–2, 194–5; Beaurepaire (1859)[2], 40–1; BN Fr. 20327, fol. 150 (Beaufort).
72. *Proc. C.*, i, 14–15, 42, 87, 107, 143–5, 153, 161; 'Chron. Cordeliers', BN Fr. 23018, fol. 498vo; *Proc. N.*, i, 181–2, 197, 201, 206, 219, 222, 231, 239, 348, 349, 351, 356–7, 405, 418, 419, 420, 430–1, 445, 468; *Rég. Tournai*, ii, 336; PRO E101/408/9 (escort to Rouen); Beaune (2004), 456.
73. Cauchon: *Proc. C.*, i, 22, 25. Le Maistre: *Proc. C.*, i, 27–32, 118–20; *Proc. N.*, i, 419, 430–1, 441. Estivet: *Proc. N.*, i, 349, 351, 438. Assessors: *Proc. C.*, i, 21, 32. For the full list, see *ib.*, ii, 383–425, and Beaurepaire (1890). English involvement: *Proc. Q.*, 196–201, 202–9; *Proc. N.*, i, 503–7; *Proc. C.*, ii, 392, 404, 421. On Duremort: Boulet, 332. On Hatton: Otway-Ruthven, 154, 169. Chaplains: Emden, i, 360–1, 1514–15 (John Carpenter and Richard Praty).
74. *Proc. C.*, i, 1–3, iii, 61–2, 69–73; Poirey, 95–6.

75. *Proc. C.*, i, 22–4, 24–6, 29, 36–7; *Proc. N.*, i, 293, 301–3, 462–3.
76. *Proc. C.*, i, 32, 109–10, 121, 129, 142, 154, 164, 181; *Proc. N.*, i, 416–18, 423.
77. *Proc. C.*, i, 32–142 *passim*, 189–90; *Proc. N.*, i, 419, 421, 432. Advocates: Poirey, 101.
78. *Proc. C.*, i, 184–289.
79. *Proc. C.*, i, 289–327, 352–74.
80. *Proc. C.*, i, 327–52; *Proc. N.*, i, 420–1, 437–8. Tricks: Poirey, 100. Grosse Tour: Lardin (2012), 63.
81. *Proc. C.*, i, 354–8, 374–85.
82. *Proc. C.*, i, 385–94; *Proc. N.*, i, 202, 225, 227, 231–2, 352, 353, 358, 361, 425, 433–4, 466.
83. *Proc. C.*, i, 395–9, 399–411; *Proc. N.*, i, 206–7, 209–10, 426–7, 434, 439, 455–6.
84. *Proc. C.*, i, 408–14; *Proc. N.*, i, 199, 202, 205, 218, 242, 352, 435, 449–50, 456; *Doc. et recherches*, i, 38; Fauquembergue, *Journ.*, iii, 13–14; Basin, *Hist.*, i, 160.
85. *Proc. C.*, i, 416–30; Monstrelet, *Chron.*, iv, 442–7; *Journ. B. Paris*, 270–2.
86. *'Notices et extraits' (Viriville), 116; *Journ. B. Paris*, 354; 'Chron. St-Thiébault', [Calmet v]; *Proc. Q.*, v, 331–41 *Journ. B. Paris*, 354–5; Lecoy (1871).
87. *Fornier, ii, 320; *Proc. N.*, i, 503–7; 'Notices et extraits' (Bougenot), 65.

CHAPTER VIII: *The Parting of Friends, 1431–1434*

1. *Journ. B. Paris*, 254, 255; Cochon, *Chron.*, 310.
2. Laonnais: 'Chron. Cordeliers', BN Fr. 20318, fols. 498vo–499, 501, 502, 505vo; cf. *Champion (1906), 159. Lagny: *Journ. B. Paris*, 263; *Foed. Supp.* D 153 (reoccupations). Magic: A. Coville, *Jean Petit* (1932), 311–16.
3. *Journ. B. Paris*, 251, 253, 255; Fauquembergue, *Journ.*, ii, 351–2. La Chasse: BL Add. Chart. 3667; BN Fr. 26053/1380. Sweeps: Monstrelet, *Chron.*, iv, 405.
4. Torcy, Aumale: Monstrelet, *Chron.*, iv, 368, 370; Cochon, *Chron.*, 311; PRO C76/119, m. 12 (Rambures). Ch.-Gaillard: BN PO 65 (Angleterre)/13. Henry VI: 'Chron. S. Albani', i, 52; *Inv. AC Abbeville*, 64; Cochon, *Chron.*, 312–13.
5. Monstrelet, *Chron.*, iv, 405; *Champion (1906), 192–3; *Flammermont, 283–4. Paris: *Journ. B. Paris*, 260, 261–3, 264; Fauquembergue, *Journ.*, iii, 2–3; BL Add. Chart. 3678–3681.
6. Departures: 'Chron. S. Albani', i, 56 (Clarence was in England in July 1431, *CPR 1429–36*, 122). Finance: Ratcliffe, 66–9; BN Fr. 26054/1495, 1535, 1536; *Sharpe, iii, 372–4. Parliament: *PPC*, iv, 67–8; *CCR 1429–35*, 99–101.
7. Finance: *Parl. Rolls*, x, 444 [1], 447–51 [13–15], xi, 11, 53–4 [11, 50]; Jurkowski et al., 88–9; *Reg. Chichele*, iii, 216–28. Economies: *PPC*, iv, 79–80. Borrowing: Steel, 174–6; Harriss (1988), 206–7. Recruitment: PRO E403/696, mm. 13–14 (20 Feb.), m. 17 (8 Mar.), E403/696, m. 18 (16 Mar.), m. 19 (18 Mar.), E403/698, m. 10 (18 July), m. 12 (13 Aug.).
8. Sailing: Gregory, 'Chron.', 172. Louviers (1430): BN Fr. n.a. 1482/92; BN Fr. 26053/1374; BN Fr. 26054/1625. Louviers (1431): *Cartul. Louviers*, ii², 77–81, 88–90, 102–4, 109–11, 113–14, 116; BN Fr. 25769/523, 528, 530, 530bis, 535, 538, 540–542bis; BN Fr. 26053/1401, 1413, 1419, 1423, Fr. 26054/1625. *H. Guibert, 62–5, 81; BN Clair. 1122/55 (additional defenders); *Journ. B. Paris*, 270; Basin, *Hist.*, i, 170–2; Chartier, *Chron.*, i, 162–3. Numbers: BL Add. Chart. 1020 (1,200 men under Willoughby); PRO E403/696, m. 19 (18 Mar.) (2,156 men 'lately come from England'); AN K63/13 (24); BN PO 1257 (Fulman)/2; BN Fr. 25295, fol. 875; BN Fr. 25770/618, 620, 628, 685. Artillery, labourers: *Cartul. Louviers*, ii², 84–7,

90-2, 93-4, 105-6, 112-13, 118, 119-20. Pontoons: BN Coll. Moreau 1431, fol. 220. Release of La Hire (1432): *Caillet (1909)[2], 412; *Cab. Hist.*, v2, 116.
9. *Cartul. Louviers*, ii², 114, 119, 120-1, 140-4; *H. Guibert, 80-1. Diversions: Anselme, vii, 71; *Livre Rouge*, 328-9; BN Fr. 26054/1595; BN Fr. n.a. 1482/109. Milly: Héraut Berry, *Chron.*, 152-3, 434-5; Monstrelet, *Chron.*, iv, 434-5; *Journ. B. Paris*, 272; Gregory, 'Chron.', 172-3.
10. Beaune, 'Doc. Inéd.', 17.
11. Héraut Berry, *Chron.*, 146-7, 430-1; Monstrelet, *Chron.*, iv, 385-6, 454 (quotation); *Rég. délib. Troyes*, 74-5; Plancher, iv, 142-3; Belotte, 108-9; BN Coll. Bourgogne 29, fol. 149 (Bar-sur-Seine). English at Chappes: Canat, *Doc. inéd.*, 306; AN X1a 4796, fols. 298vo, 301vo.
12. *Les La Trémoille*, i, 190-1; Bossuat (1936), 133-6, 138-40, 142; Bazin, 165-7; Canat, *Doc. inéd.*, 309-18; Quicherat (1879), 57-61; *Plancher, iv, PJ no. 75.
13. Monstrelet, *Chron.*, iv, 455-6; *Itin. Philippe*, 92; Schnerb (1993), 39-40, *153-4. Corbie: AD Nord B1942, fol. 74vo; Chastellain, 'Chron.', ii, 200-1; *Plancher, iv, PJ no. 75. Dying words: Chastellain, 'Chron.', ii, 43.
14. Monstrelet, *Chron.*, iv, 453-4, 459-65; Le Fèvre, *Chron.*, ii, 259, 261-2; Héraut Berry, *Chron.*, 147-50, 431; Vigneulles, *Chron.*, ii, 224; 'Chron. St-Thiébault', cols. lvi-lvii; *Chauvelays, 277-80; *L&P*, ii, 530; Schnerb (1993), 40-2, 89-94, *135-6, 138, 154, 155.
15. *Plancher, iv, PJ nos. 76-6; AD Nord B1942, fols. 131vo-132; Monstrelet, *Chron.*, v, 8-11.
16. BN Fr. n.a. 7627, fols. 378-400vo; AD Côte d'Or B1647, fols. 82-82vo; Boutiot, ii, 528 (date); *Plancher, iv, PJ nos. 79, 90, 91, 95; *L&P*, ii, 196-202; *Rég. délib. Troyes*, 284.
17. Use of freelances: *L&P*, ii, 253; BN Fr. n.a. 7627, fol. 435. 'English service': e.g. Monstrelet, *Chron.*, iv, 41-2, v, 26-7. Raids: Monstrelet, *Chron.*, v, 62-3, 70; Le Fèvre, *Chron.*, ii, 280-3; *Chastellux, 402; Bossuat (1936), 134-5, 185-7; Bazin, 169-72, 177-8. Forte-Épice: BN Coll. Bourgogne 29, fols. 26, 144, 330vo; AD Nord B1948, fol. 337vo-341vo; AD Côte d'Or B1651, fol. 78-78vo, 79-79vo.
18. *Coll. doc. Angleterre*, 239-48; Waurin, *Cron.*, iv, 3-8; Monstrelet, *Chron.*, v, 1-4; *Brut*, ii, 458-61; *Journ. B. Paris*, 274-6; Fauquembergue, *Journ.*, iii, 25-6; G. L. Thompson (1991), 199-204, *243-6. William's fate: Le Fèvre, *Chron.*, ii, 264.
19. Lebigue, 322-37, *343-60; Waurin, *Cron.*, iv, 9-11; Monstrelet, *Chron.*, v, 4-6; *Journ. B. Paris*, 277-8; Chartier, *Chron.*, i, 131; Martial, *Poésies*, i, 128-9; *Brut*, ii, 461; Basin, *Hist.*, i, 178. Music: C. Wright, *Music and Ceremony at Notre Dame of Paris, 500-1550* (1989), 206-17. Philip's disapproval: Isabelle of Portugal, *Corr.*, no 28 [5].
20. *Journ. B. Paris*, 274, 278; *Brut*, ii, 461; Fauquembergue, *Journ.*, iii, 29; BN Fr. n.a. 7627, fol. 324-335 (letter); Monstrelet, *Chron.*, v, 6. Lords: PPC, iv, 113, 127.
21. *Coll. doc. Angleterre*, 244-8; Gregory, 'Chron.', 173-5; *Gr. Chron. London*, 168.
22. Harriss (1988), 214; *L&P*, ii, 450 (Gloucester's statement in 1440).
23. Harriss (1988), 214-16, 217-18; *Sharpe, iii, 374-5; *Parl. Rolls*, xi, 17-18 [17].
24. *Parl. Rolls*, xi, 13-17 [14-16]; Foed., x, 516-19; Harriss (1988), 221-2.
25. AN PP 2398, pp. 935-7; *Coll. doc. Angleterre*, 248-9, 250-1.
26. Numbers: *L&P*, ii, 205-6 (3,600 in garrisons); Foed. Supp. D, 391, Joubert, *Docs. Maine* (1889), 261-3 (1,200 in Willoughby's field army). Bedford's military household numbered 'at least' 800 (*L&P*, ii, 542), but some of these may have served in Willoughby's force. Reorganisation: Newhall (1940), 124-30; Curry (1985), i, 240-4, 254, 256, 265-6, 267-70 (Prof. Curry regards this as a new system introduced in 1434); Foed. Supp. D, 391; 'Doc. inéd. Maine', 261-3; *L&P*, ii, 257-8. Regional

captains: BN Fr. 26055/1724 (Rouen and south march towards Beauce, Jan. 1432), Fr. 26056/1965 (north march of Normandy and Picardy, Dec. 1432), *Foed. Supp. D*, 404 (between Seine, Loire and the sea, May 1433); BN Fr. 26056/1905 (Caen, Cotentin and Alençon, Sept. 1432), *Foed. Supp. D*, 403-4 (north march of Normandy and Picardy, April 1433).

27. Allmand (1983), 177; Rowe (1931)[2], 557; *L&P*, ii, 547-9, 559-65. Comparison with 1429: BN Fr. 4488, pp. 17-56.
28. *PPC*, iv, 93-4; *Foed.*, x, 568-9; *Foed. Supp. D*, 404-5; PRO E403/703, m. 15 (21 July); BN Fr. n.a. 1482/122; *PPC*, iv, 163,187. Wage arrears: Fauquembergue, *Journ.*, ii, 364-7, 369-71, iii, 3-4, 36-7, 75-9. Review: Boulet, 503-13; AN Coll. Lenoir xxi, 282-6, xxii, 217-18.
29. Ratcliffe, 40-1, 46-65, 66, 72, 76-9. To these totals, add £19,632 for loans advanced by Beaufort in France but repaid in England: Harriss (1988), 403 (nos. 15, 17, 20-2). Cash transfers: PRO E403/696, m. 10 (16 Nov.), m. 17 (8 Mar.); E403/698, m. 10 (18 Jul.); E404/306, 340; E403/709, m. 7 (26 May); *PPC*, iv, 108, 112-13.
30. 'Chron. Mon. S. Albani', i, 55; *Parl. Rolls*, xi, 8 [4], 11, 53-4 [11, 50]; Steel, 459-60; *PPC*, iv, 93-4. John of L.: *PPC*, iv, 44; PRO E403/691, m. 22 (12 Apr.); E101/52/35. St-Pol: PRO E101/52/35; BN Fr. 20327, fol. 150. Cf. PRO E404/49 (9); *Foed. Supp. D*, 402.
31. *Parl. Rolls*, x, 425-30 [59-66]; Lloyd (1977), 260-3; Power, 79-90; Munro (1970), 225-36; Munro (1972), 95-8; *Cartul. Estaple*, i, 569 (quote); *Hanserecesse*, i, 133-6. Bullion problem: Spufford, 96-100; Munro (1970), 228-32. Exports: *England's Export Trade*, 123. Revenues: https://www.esfdb.org/Table.aspx?resourceid=11404 and graphically in Ormrod (1999)[1], 162 (Fig. 8.3).
32. Parlement: *Rec. doc. Poitou*, viii, pp. xxii-xxiii and xxiii n.1. Lannoy: *Champion (1906), 146-7.
33. *Notice Arch. Hallay-Coëtquen*, 51-60, esp. 52-5; Cagny, *Chron.*, 181; Monstrelet, *Chron.*, v, 11. On Alençon: Waurin, *Cron.*, iii, 186; *Proc. Alençon*, 116, 122-3, 150-1.
34. Pouancé: Cagny, *Chron.*, 184-5. Numbers: 'Comptes Guinot', 61, 66, 80, 81, 83-5 (nos. 252, 306, 442, 452-3, 476-524). Agreements with English: *ib.*, 60, 66, 71, 79, 80, 81, 82 (nos. 250, 303, 349, 437, 440-1, 446-8, 450, 474); 'Comptes Guinot', 63, 72, 86-7 (nos. 271, 277-8, 358, 535-6). Grant: *Preuves Bretagne*, ii, 1247-8; *Lettres de Jean V*, iv, no. 2002. Bonsmoulins army: BN Fr. 26055/1689, 1691; Fr. 26285/331; 'Comptes Guinot', 81, 84, 85, 86 (nos. 451-5, 514-16, 522, 531); BN Fr. 26056/1994. French intervention: Chartier, *Chron.*, i, 157-8; Cagny, *Chron.*, 184; *Cosneau (1886), 538-8; 'Comptes Guinot', 66, 67, 74 (nos. 302, 304, 308, 310, 312, 377, 380); BN PO 1292 (Gaucourt)/34; *Lettres de Jean V*, iv, nos. 2259, 2389; 'Comptes Guinot', 69 (no. 332). For La Trémoille and Craon, see Angot, i, 808; *Joubert (1888), 332-41.
35. 'Comptes Guinot', 57, 72, 82, 85 (no. 177, 358, 461, 466, 469-70, 472, 519-20); *Preuves Bretagne*, ii, cols. 1248-50; Gruel, *Chron.*, 79; *Lettres de Jean V*, iv, nos. 2000, 2015.
36. 'Comptes Guinot', 57 (no. 177) (Yolande at Chinon). Charles of Anjou: Beaucourt, ii, 267; Gaussin, 105; *Bueil, *Jouvencel*, ii, 310; Bourdigné, *Chron.*, ii, 170-1; Chastellain, 'Chron.', ii, 162.
37. *Monstrelet, *Chron.*, v, 12-15; *Chéruel, ii, 94-7; *Coll. doc. Angleterre*, 250; *Beaurepaire (1856))[1], 321-6, 330-9; BN PO 2604 (Saenne)/4; *Doc. Rouen*, 224-5; BN Fr. 26055/1758; *L&P*, ii, 202-3.
38. Siege: BN Fr. n.a. 1482/18; BN Clair. 207/101, 111-20; 'Doc. inéd. Maine', 261-3. Beaumont: Monstrelet, *Chron.*, v, 100-2; Cagny, *Chron.*, 185-7; Héraut Berry, *Chron.*, 436-7; Bueil, *Jouvencel*, i, 141-50; Tringant, 'Comm.', 285-7. Willoughby

recalled: BN Fr. 26056/1863. St-Evroul: BN Fr. 26056/1862; *Foed. Supp. D*, 401.
L'Aigle: *Chron. Mont-St-M.*, ii, 7–9; *Foed. Supp D*, 402; BN Fr. 26057/2155.
Séez: BN Fr. 26280/67. Sillé, remaining garrisons: *L&P*, ii, 549–52. Caen: Chartier, *Chron.*, i, 150–3.

39. Monstrelet, *Chron.*, v, 21–5; Héraut Berry, *Chron.*, 433–4; *Journ. B. Paris*, 282–3; 'Lettres Chartres', 7–11. Chartres' politics: Billot, 47–8. Burgundian garrison: *Plancher, iv, PJ no. 91. Raids: *Foed. Supp. D*, 407; BN Fr. n.a. 3642/778. Mantes: AC Mantes CC25; BN Fr. 26057/2107.

40. Paris: *Coll. doc. Angleterre*, 248–9. Lagny: BN Fr. n.a. 1482/116; Monstrelet, *Chron.*, v, 27–8; Waurin, *Cron.*, iv, 26–7; *Journ. B. Paris*, 283–4; Anselme, vii, 11. L'Isle-Adam left Paris after 3 May: Fauquembergue, *Journ.*, iii, 57.

41. Monstrelet, *Chron.*, v, 28–30. Garrison: Héraut Berry, *Chron.*, 435. Ambroise: 'Délib. Beauvais', 209.

42. 'Délib. Beauvais', 210–11.

43. Desertions: Monstrelet, *Chron.*, v, 28–9. Reinforcement: BN Fr. 26055/1844, 1849; Fr. 26056/1855, 1863. Finance: *Parl. Rolls*, xi, 11–13 [11–12]; Harriss (1988), 220–1. Indentures: PRO E403/703, mm. 13, 14 (19 July).

44. Boussac: 'Délib. Beauvais', 209–10. 2 June: BN Fr. 26055/1844, 26056/1863. Bedford: *Curry & Ambühl, 375.

45. *Les La Trémoille*, i, 143–4; Monstrelet, *Chron.*, v, 32–5; Waurin, *Cron.*, iv, 28–31; Héraut Berry, *Chron.*, 154, 435–6; *Journ. B. Paris*, 285–6; Fauquembergue, *Journ.*, iii, 63. Hungerford: CPR 1429–36, 218; PRO E403/703, m. 13. Cash: PRO E403/703, mm. 14–15 (19 July); BN Fr. n.a. 1482/122.

46. Fauquembergue, *Journ.*, iii, 74–5; *Journ. B. Paris*, 286–90; Fourquin, 335; *Foed.*, x, 534–5.

47. Sigonio, 'Vita', 482; Raynald, *Ann. Eccl.*, xxviii, 97 (An. 1431, ¶ 14). On Albergati: Flavio Biondo, *Italia Illustrata*, vi. 64, ed. J. A. White, i (2005), 338; Vespasiano, *Vite*, 75–7; Taverne, *Journ.*, 40, 41; Raynald, *Ann. Eccl.*, xxviii, 61–3 (An. 1428, ¶ 2–4); Morosini, *Chron.*, iii, 344–6.

48. Ferguson, 120–30, 133–5; Raynald, *Ann. Eccl.*, xxviii, 82 (An. 1430, ¶ 4); Juvénal, *Écrits*, ii, 56.

49. PPC, iv, 91–7; *Parl. Rolls*, x, 453 [18] undated, but after the appointment of councillors to go to France (probably early Feb. 1431), and before the grant of Parliamentary authority to negotiate with Charles VII (first half of March). Departures: PRO E403/696, m. 17 (8 Mar.) (Beaufort, Alnwick, Cromwell); *PPC*, iv, 83–4 (Tiptoft).

50. Beaucourt, ii, 420 (Charles VII's letter of 22 April to Amadeus); *Plancher, iv, PJ nos. 29 (misdated), 81, 102 (pp. cxxiii–cxxiv), 103; *L&P*, ii, 251. Lille: AD Nord B1942, fols. 119, 128, 136.

51. Valois (1909)[1], i, 110–60

52. Allmand (1965)[2], 4–7; Mansi, *Conc.*, xxix, cols. 634–7; Valois (1909)[1], i, 153–4, 230–1; Toussaint (1942), 22; *Conc. Basiliensis*, v, 76, 396.

53. *Zellfelder, 248–52, 312–13, 316–23; *Plancher, iv, PJ no. 102 (pp. cxx, cxxiv); Bekynton, *Corr.*, ii, 61–6 (quote); John of Segovia, *Hist.*, i, 412–14; Stouff, 'Contribution', 101–2; Schofield (1961), 172–4, 176, 178–85, 193–4; Schofield (1966), 30.

54. Helmrath, 181–5; Toussaint (1942)[2], 73–6, *245–8; *Conc. Basiliensis*, ii, 250, 453, 479, 482.

55. *Plancher, iv, PJ nos. 29 (misdated), 99, 102 (pp. cxx, cxxiv), 105, 112 (misdated); Fauquembergue, *Journ.*, iii, 42–4; *L&P*, ii, 251–2; Monstrelet, *Chron.*, iv, 405; *Journ. B. Paris*, 260; AD Nord B1945, fols. 57vo, 58–58vo (secretary); *L&P*, ii, 252.

56. BN Fr. Coll. Bourgogne 29, fol. 76; BN Coll. Bourgogne 21, fol. 72; AD Côte d'Or B1649, fol. 90; *Plancher, iv, PJ nos. 102 (pp. cxix–cxxii) (misdated), 105; *Conc. Basiliensis*, i,262–3, ii, 144, 146, 149.
57. Representation: *Foed.*, x, 514, 524–5; Héraut Berry, *Chron.*, 151–2; 'Comptes Guinot', 71, 73 (nos. 353–5, 369); *Conc. Basiliensis*, ii, 309. Langdon: *ODNB*, xxxii, 475–6. Bromflete: PRO C64/10, m. 41, C64/12, m. 40, C76/104, mm. 8, 9. Beckington: Emden, i, 156–9. Fastolf: *Foed.*, x, 527–8, 530–1. Debate: Héraut Berry, *Chron.*, 50–2; *L&P*, ii, 252–3, 259–60; *Plancher, iv, PJ no. 102 (pp. cxxiii–cxxiv), 105; *Schneider, 164. Paris: *Journ. B. Paris*, 290.
58. *L&P*, ii, 253–5; *Plancher, iv, PJ nos. 107, 109, 111 (pp. cxxxxiv–cxxxv); *Journ. B. Paris*, 294–5; John of Segovia, *Hist.*, i, 405; *Conc. Basiliensis*, ii, 479, 482. Abbey (Barbeau): *Gall. Christ.*, xii, 239.
59. *PPC*, iv, 224; 'Comptes Guinot', 76 (no. 399) ('*pour le traité de paix génèralle*'). It had been arranged before Bedford left Paris on 5 Feb. 1433: Fauquembergue, *Journ.*, iii, 84; PRO E403/709, m. 1 (25 Apr.) (copies of truces taken to Calais).
60. Non-payment: PRO E364/69, mm. 2–2d (Bokeland). Warwick: PRO E101/188/2 (15). Mutiny: *Brut*, ii, 502, 570; PRO C76/115, m. 11; *Huguet, 437. Bedford: PRO C76/111, m. 1.
61. *PPC*, iv,141, 143–5, 146, 162–3, 242–3; PRO E403/706, m. 17 (2 Mar.); E403/709, m. 2 (6 May); *CPR 1429–36*, 278.
62. *Foed.*, x, 548–9; *PPC*, iv, 158–9. Kemp's letter of 19 May to the English delegates at Basel lists councillors present: Schofield (1961), 185. Ships: PRO E404/49 (156). Luxembourgs: AD Côte d'Or B11898 (undated, *ca.* June 1433). Godart: 'Comptes Guinot', 76 (no. 399).
63. St-Valéry: 'Délib. Beauvais', 203–4, 209–10; Monstrelet, *Chron.*, v, 56–7. Le Crotoy: *PPC*, iv, 163. Relief: AD Nord B17640; Monstrelet, *Chron.*, v, 70–1. Finance: PRO E404/50 (326, 356), E404/52 (397); *PPC*, iv, 162, 167, 242–3.
64. *PPC*, iv, 163–4, 224–5; *CCR 1429–35*, 244; *Brut*, ii, 467.
65. *Parl. Rolls*, xi, 77–8 [10–11], 83–4 [17].
66. Griffiths (1981), 42–3; *PPC*, iv, 108; PRO E404/49 (169) (expenditure); Harriss (1988), 232–3.
67. *Parl. Rolls*, xi, 78 [11], 102–13 [24–5]; Fortescue, *Governance*, 120.
68. *L&P*, ii, 220, 242–3, 246–7; *PPC*, iv, 178; 'Comptes Guinot', 75 (no. 392); *PPC*, iv, 178. On Cusack: *Preuves Bretagne*, ii, col. 1235; BL MS Harley 782, fol. 74vo (Agincourt); *Plancher, iv, PJ no. 116; Monstrelet, *Chron.*, v, 55–8; Armstrong (1965), 97–8.
69. Instructions: *L&P*, ii, 233; AD Côte d'Or B11898 (undated, *ca.* June 1433). St-Valéry: *L&P*, ii, 257–8; Monstrelet, *Chron.*, v, 70–1; *Huguet, 426, 428–30, 431, 433.
70. *L&P*, ii, 218–30 (quotation at 225–6), 238–51; *PPC*, iv, 225–6. Lannoy left Westminster on 9 July: AD Côte d'Or B11898 (letter of Gloucester to Philip, 9 July 1433).
71. Previous interventions: *L&P*, ii, 243–4; *Foed.*, x, 556; *Samaran (1907), 369; *L&P*, ii, 232. Suffolk: *ODNB*, xliv, 733–4; L. E. James, 231–4, 239–40; Castor (2000), 85–93; Watts (1996), 160–1; *PPC*, iv, 108, 124, 182; Pearsall, 148–50; Champion (1969), 222, 671; BN Coll. Moreau 705, fol. 145. French contacts: *Foed.*, x, 537, 556.
72. *Foed.*, x, 556–61; *PPC*, iv, 260–1.
73. *Foed.*, x, 561–3; *Plancher, iv, PJ no. 111 (p. cxxxv); *L&P*, ii, 144–5.
74. Bueil, *Jouvencel*, 151–3; Tringant, 'Comm.', ii, 288–9; Quicherat (1879), 78–84; Héraut Berry, *Chron.*, 156–7; Monstrelet, *Chron.*, v, 73–4; Chartier, *Chron.*, i, 170–1. La Hire: 'Doc. inéd. La Hire', 41.
75. Beaucourt, iii, 41–3.

REFERENCES TO PAGES 426–437

76. *Foed.*, x, 561–3; *Plancher, PJ nos. 111 (pp. cxxxv–cxxxvii), 113 (pp. cxxxviii, cxxxix).
77. *Macrae, 422.
78. *PPC*, iv, 178, 191–3; Bower, *Scottichron.*, viii, 286–90 (wrongly attributing the English offers to Scrope); *Liber Pluscard.*, i, 378–9.
79. *Parl. Rolls*, xi, 88–9 [20]; *Reg. Chichele*, iii, 247–52; *Rec. Convoc.*, v, 331–6; Steel, 441, 460; *PPC*, iv, 225 (quotation).
80. *Parl. Rolls*, xi, 83–7 [17–18]; *PPC*, iv, 227–8.
81. *PPC*, iv, 210–16. Commissioners: *CPR 1429–36*, 353–5.
82. Bedford's scheme: *L&P*, ii, 540–63; *PPC*, iv, 226–33. Half-yearly payments: *Foed.*, x, 590. A permanent force of 400 men-at-arms and 1,200 archers would have cost about £18,000 a year. The revenues of Bedford's appanage in Anjou, Maine and Alençon were estimated in 1431 at 40,000 *francs* a year (*Foed.*, x, 457), and his other appanage revenues at 12,773 *l.t.* in 1433 (*L&P*, ii, 555–9), making a total of *ca.* 53,000 *l.t.*, or *ca.* £5,900. The revenue of the duchy trustees was *ca.* £5,000 a year (Somerville, i, 201–2). Pressure on revenue: *L&P*, ii, 551–3, 555–6; Somerville, i, 206–7; Steel, 441, 460. Funding of Bedford's army: Harriss (1988), 245; *PPC*, iv, 233–9, 244–54; *Foed.*, x, 591–2.

CHAPTER IX: *The Congress of Arras, 1433–1435*

1. Monstrelet, *Chron.*, v, 62–3.
2. Governorship: AN K63/24 (3, 4, 5). Huntingdon: PRO E403/709, mm. 2, 3, 7 (6, 14, 26 May). Burgundian movements: AD Nord B1948, fols. 116, 336–337vo–338; Le Fèvre, *Chron.*, ii, 273–4. Artillery: AD Nord B1948, fols. 363–388vo; J. Garnier, 65–7, 98–105. English movements: *Flamare, ii, 55–6. Arundel (860 men): *Foed. Supp. D*, 404, 405. Huntingdon (1,340 men): PRO E403/709, m. 2 (6 July). Burgundian service of Gressart: AD Côte d'Or B11805; B1651, fol. 125vo. Bourc de Jardre: Héraut Berry, *Chron.*, 154–5. Talbot: PRO E403/709, m. 10 (18 July). E403/712, m. 9 (13 Feb.); E403/715, m. 1 (26 Apr.); *PPC*, iv, 167; Gregory, 'Chron.', 177. Montereau: Fauquembergue, *Journ.*, iii, 43. Nemours: Waurin, *Cron.*, iii, 283–4; Monstrelet, *Chron.*, v, 292. Ch.-Landon: BN Fr. 4484, fols. 154vo–155; Monstrelet, *Chron.*, v, 292. Provins: AD Nord B1948, fol. 123vo; *Journ. B. Paris*, 288–9. Plan: Flamare, ii, 56; *L&P*, ii, 427–9.
3. Héraut Berry, *Chron.*, 154–6; *Bossuat (1936), 412–13; AN JJ 186/12 (*échelleur*); *Chrons. London*, 136; Cagny, *Chron.*, 255. *Flamare, ii, 55 (date of capture).
4. Arundel: *Flamare, ii, 55–6, 60. Philip: Monstrelet, *Chron.*, v, 64–6, 69–70; Le Fèvre, *Chron.*, ii, 274, 275–283; Bossuat (1936), 208 n.3; *Itin. Philippe*, 110; AD Nord B1948, fols. 123vo, 128vo, 165vo, 256–256vo, 258vo (Pacy); *ib.*, fols. 130–132, 134vo, 236vo–237, 342–357vo (Avallon); *ib.*, fols. 90–91, 137, 358–358vo (Chablis, etc.); *ib.*, fols. 127vo, 136, 281 (Pierre-Perthuis); *ib.*, fol. 237 (Cravant); Belotte, 112–14. Huntingdon, Talbot: *Foed. Supp. D*, 405–6; *Chrons. London*, 136.
5. Army: 'Doc. inéd. Maine', 264–6. Artillery: Caen, Coll. Mancel, 1/38. Feudal summons: BN Fr. 25771/792, Fr. 26057/2155, 2222; PO 1374/Gourde, 5, 2. Bonsmoulins: *Foed. Supp. D*, 405–6; BN Fr. 26057/2166. St-Céneri, Sillé: *Cosneau, 545–6; 'Doc. inéd. Maine', 264–6; BN Fr. 26057/2227; Chartier, *Chron.*, i, 164–9; Gruel, *Chron.*, 82–6; Héraut Berry, *Chron.*, 159–60; *Bueil, *Jouvencel*, ii, 317–18; AN JJ175/360; AD Seine-Mar. 100J29/44, 38/31. Mantes region: BN Fr. 26057/2227, Fr. 26058/2278, 2336, Fr. 25771/817–825, 851–853, 858, 860.
6. *Journ. B. Paris*, 296–8; *Doc. Paris*, 348–53; Beaucourt, ii, 49 n.2 (Boussac); *Coll. doc. Angleterre*, 238–9 (pamphlet).

7. Talbot: PRO E403/712, m. 9 (13 Feb.); Gregory, 'Chron.', 177. *Inv. AC Amiens*, ii, 52–3, iv, 142; *Inv. AD Nord*, viii, 843. On Desmarais: Basin, *Hist.*, i, 212; Monstrelet, *Chron.*, iv, 433, v, 85; BN Fr. 26055/1768, 1769, 1836.
8. Talbot: BN PO 2787 (Talbot)/9; BN Fr. 25771/894. Oise: Basin, *Hist.*, i, 210; Monstrelet, *Chron.*, v, 91–2; *Journ. B. Paris*, 298, 299; *Chron. Martiniane*, 18–21; *Chrons. London*, 136; *Douet-d'Arcq, 128–9 (Beaumont); *Mathon, 668–9 (Creil). Reinforcements: *CPR 1429–36*, 359. Somme: Monstrelet, *Chron.*, iv, 87–8, 93–4; *Inv. AC Amiens*, ii, 54, iv, 140, 142.
9. Gruel, *Chron.*, 87–8, 89–90; Monstrelet, *Chron.*, v, 91–5; Héraut Berry, *Chron.*, 162; *Preuves Bretagne*, ii, col. 1267 (1,400 men); AD Nord B1951, fols. 60vo, 70vo; B1954, fol. 38vo; *Inv. AC Amiens*, ii, 54, iv, 142. Poton: BN Fr. 32510, fol. 374vo; *Rég. délib. Reims*, 243, 260.
10. Burgundian demands: *Plancher, iv, nos. 113 (p. cxxxix), 114; PRO E403/715, m. 9 (14 June); E404/51 (301). Peace: *Dickinson, 210; *PPC*, v, 254–5; Chaplais, *Dipl. Practice*, 135–8.
11. *Rec. Ord. Pays-Bas*, i, 33–8; *England's Export Trade*, 138. Background: Munro (1970), 225–37; Munro (1972), 7–8, 68–9, 93–108.
12. Bedford: AN JJ175/327. Conditions: H. H. Lamb, *Climate, present past and future*, ii (1977), 457–9; Fourquin, 326–7; *Journ. B. Paris*, 295, 298–301; *Cron. Norm.*, 81.
13. Chartier, *Chron.*, i, 175, 176–7; Basin, *Hist.*, i, 198–202; Monstrelet, *Chron.*, v, 104–5; *Journ. B. Paris*, 300, 302; *Chron. Mont-St-M.*, ii, 42, 47–9, 67–8; *Cron. Norm.*, 80–1; AD Seine-Mar. 100J29/95–6. On Venables: BN Fr. 4488, p. 542; Fr. 25769/459; Fr. 25770/709; *Chron. Mont-St-M.*, ii, 41; 'Comptes Guinot', 99, 103 (nos. 122–3, 148).
14. *Chron. Mont-St-M.*, ii, 50–60, 63–4, 251–3; Cagny, *Chron.*, 189–91; Basin, *Hist.*, i, 202–4; Chartier, *Chron.*, i, 172–3; Monstrelet, *Chron.*, v, 113–14.
15. *Chron. Mont-St-M.*, i, 34–5, 43–4, *ii, 62–4; Cagny, *Chron.*, 191–2; BN Fr. 26058/2301 (assault); BN PO 2659 (Scales)/5 (St-Jean).
16. Men living on the land: BN PO 2623 (Salvain)/32; BN Fr. 25772/935; Fr. 26059/2546; BN Clair. 219/51; BN Fr. 26059/2489, 2585. St-Jean: BN Fr. 26060/2668; BNPO 2659/Scales 5. Mentality: *L&P*, ii, 577, 585; Curry (1985), ii, App. IX; Bell, Curry, et al., 248–50; Harmand (1975), 235–6; Curry (2014), 9–10; BN Fr. 26066/3869, 3934 (Rouen); Goulay, 49–51 (counter-insurgency).
17. Harmand (1975), 227–8; BL Add. Chart. 3895 (Harcourt); 'Devis'; R. Jones (1999), 113. Rouen: R. Jones (1994), i, 215–33.
18. Lusignan: *Conc. Basiliensis*, iii, 77, 83, 88–9, 113; Héraut Berry, *Chron.*, 160. English embassy: *Plancher, iv, PJ no. 114; Chaplais, *Dipl. Practice*, 137–8; PRO C76/116, mm. 12, 10, 9, 2.
19. John of Segovia, *Hist.*, i, 726, 771–2; *Conc. Basiliensis*, iii, 232, 272–3, 290; *PPC*, iv, 297–8. On Talaru: Müller (1990), i, 94–142.
20. Helmrath, 202–10; Müller (1990), ii, 800–5, 808–15; *Schneider, 153–4.
21. Germany: Herbomez; F. von Löher (1866), 353–66. Castile: Daumet (1898), 80–6. Scotland: BN Fr. 17330, fol. 129vo–132; Bower, *Scottichron.*, viii, 249; *Bochaca, 48–9.
22. *Itin. Philippe*, 125–6; AD Nord B1951, fols. 60vo, 70vo; Gruel, *Chron.*, 90–2; *Cosneau (1886), 547–51; Monstrelet, *Chron.*, v, 95–6; *Inv. AC Amiens*, ii, 54–6, iv, 140–1.
23. Leguai (1962), 135–8; Bossuat (1936), 215–18, 220; Bazin, 202–4; *Arcelin, 127–30; Déniau, 582–9; *Flamare, ii, 113–28; *Plancher, iv, PJ no. 118; Monstrelet, *Chron.*, v, 106.

24. Monstrelet, *Chron.*, v, 106–9; Le Fèvre, *Chron.*, ii, 303–4; *Cosneau (1886), 552–3 (evidence given to an inquiry, Jan. 1449). Terms: *Plancher, iv, PJ no. 117; *Cosneau (1886), 552–4; *Dickinson, 213.
25. *Foed.*, x, 609, 625; *Dickinson, 221–4; *Schneider, 170.
26. *Dickinson, 215; *Schneider, 86; AD Nord B1954, fols. 44vo–45; *Parl. Rolls*, xi, 164 [1].
27. AD Nord B1954, fols. 45vo, 211vo; *Schneider, 123–3; Dickinson, 34–49, *209–14.
28. *Dickinson, 214–16; *Schneider, 90, 102–3, 123–4; *L&P*, ii, 575; *Foed.*, x, 611–13, 616.
29. *Dickinson, 216–18, at 216; *Foed.*, x, 616; *Samaran (1907), 370–2; *L&P*, ii, 431–3. For the sequence of instructions: Dickinson, 33–4.
30. *Schneider, 123; *Beaucourt, ii, 307n; Héraut Berry, *Chron.*, 164–5, 166.
31. Monstrelet, *Chron.*, v, 117, 119–23, 127–9; Waurin, *Cron.*, iv, 58–65. Date: AD Nord B1954, fols. 49vo–50, 75; *Inv. AC Amiens*, ii, 60, 61; Juvénal, *Écrits*, i, 198; Héraut Berry, *Chron.*, 183–4; Gruel, *Chron.*, 108–9; *Chrons. London*, 136–7; *Coll. doc. Angleterre*, 252–3. Date of death: *Cal. Inq. P. M.*, xxiv, no. 462.
32. BN Fr. 26060/2657 (Verneuil); BN Fr. 26059/2542 (Eure); Chartier, 'Chron. Lat.', 228–9; *Journ. B. Paris*, 305–6; Héraut Berry, *Chron.*, 164–7; Monstrelet, *Chron.*, v, 126; Fauquembergue, *Journ.*, iii, 155–6.
33. *Dickinson, 213–14; Curry (1985), i, 266–70, ii, App. III.
34. Philip: *Journ. B. Paris*, 304–5; Monstrelet, *Chron.*, v, 116. English troops: BN Fr. 25772/944, 954bis, 963; *Bournon (1893), 252 (Talbot); BN Fr. 26059/2546. Indigenous troops: *Foed.*, x, 610; Monstrelet, *Chron.*, v, 125–6; PRO E403/719, mm. 6, 12 (14 June, 19 July); E404/51 (323, 324). Finance: Ratcliffe, 100; *PPC*, iv, 294–5; PRO E403/719, m. 6 (14 June), E404/51/323, 324.
35. Expedition: PRO E101/71/3 (880–2); E404/51 (306–10, 312, 320); E403/719, mm. 6–7, 11, 13, 14 (15 June, 19, 20 July); CPR 1429–36, 475, 476. Borrowing: Harriss (1988), 246–7, 404.
36. *Thes. nov. anecd.*, i, cols. 1784–6; *Grands traités*, 119–23; 'Doc. Croÿ', 71–3.
37. J. Lestocquoy, 'Étapes du developpement urbain d'Arras', *Revue Belge de philologie et d'histoire*, xxiii (1944), 163–85; Clauzel, 19–24; Bocquet, 46–8, 50–6, 58; Monstrelet, *Chron.*, iii, 31; *Inv. Chartes d'Arras*, 223–7; Denifle (1897–9), i, nos. 23, 25, 933.
38. Taverne, *Journ.*, 3–6, 9–10; *Conc. Basiliensis*, iii, 397; *Dickinson, 85–6, 224–5; Le Fèvre, *Chron.*, ii, 306–7.
39. M. Decaluwé, 'Albergati's diplomacy: communication of friendship between Eugene IV and the Council of Basel', *Revue d'Histoire Ecclésiastique*, ciii (2008), 85–118; *Dickinson, 90, 91, 224–5; Taverne, *Journ.*, 40; Pius II, *Comm.*, i, 389; *Schneider, 157–8.
40. Taverne, *Journ.*, 11–12, 21–4, 27–30,; *Dickinson, 225–6; *Schneider, 82–3; Waurin, *Cron.*, iv, 74; Le Fèvre, *Chron.*, ii, 307–9, 311; Monstrelet, *Chron.*, v, 132–6.
41. Monstrelet, *Chron.*, v, 132–3, 150–1; Dickinson, 13–14, 17–18, 53–4, *230–1. Milan: *Taverne, *Journ.*, 110; Brittany: 'Comptes Bretagne', 109 (no. 74). Portugal: *Paviot (1995)[2], no. 180A. Liège, Paris: Taverne, *Journ.*, 56–7, 63–8.
42. AD Nord B1954, fol. 44–44vo; Taverne, *Journ.*, 7, 10, 14, 23–4, 25, 33–5, 37–8, 39–40, 110; Chartier, *Chron.*, i, 207–8.
43. Taverne, *Journ.*, 9, 40, 43, 46; *Schneider, 92, 94–5, 96, 97, 99–100, 139, 143, 144, 146, 148.
44. Jean de Montreuil, *Opera*, ed. N. Grévy, O. Ornato and G. Ouy, ii (1975), 266; *Schneider, 117, 118, 140, 150; Germain, 'Liber', 51.
45. *Schneider, 96, 98, 99–100, 101–2, 119–21, 140–1; *L&P*, i, 51–2.

46. *L&P*, i, 53–5; *Schneider, 100–2, 139–40.
47. *Schneider, 104–5.
48. Monstrelet, *Chron.*, v, 143–4.
49. *Cosneau (1886), 553–4; Gruel, *Chron.*, 102–3. Isabelle: Vaughan (1970), 167–8; *Cartul. Hainaut*, v, 339.
50. Taverne, *Journ.*, 53–4; *Schneider, 185–208; 'Avis du Chancelier Rolin'. Authorship: Dickinson, 241–4.
51. *Schneider, 106–8, 143–4.
52. *Schneider, 89–91, 92, 144; Taverne, *Journ.*, 55–6; Monstrelet, *Chron.*, v, 144–5.
53. *Schneider, 113–14; *L&P*, ii, 444–5.
54. *Schneider, 109–18, 144–8, 166–7; Pius II, *Comm.*, i, 389.
55. Taverne, *Journ.*, 61–6; Chaplais, *Dipl. Practice*, 636–52.
56. Taverne, *Journ.*, 66, 68; *Schneider, 119, 167–70; *Dickinson, 228–9; *Vet. Script.*, viii, cols. 864–8; Isabelle of Portugal, *Corr.*, no 28; *Livre des trahisons*, 210.
57. Commynes, *Mém.*, Lib. III.8 (p. 209); *L&P*, ii, 575–6; Bossuat (1954), 141 (37 volumes). Martel: *G. P. Cuttino, 'Another memorandum book of Elias Joneston', *EHR*, lxiii (1948), 90, 96.
58. Taverne, *Journ.*, 75–6; *Schneider, 163–73.
59. *Grands traités*, 119–51; Taverne, *Journ.*, 79–83; Monstrelet, *Chron.*, v, 182–3. Bourbon: *Beaucourt, iii, 68 n.3 (Jean Louvet's memorandum).
60. Oaths: Taverne, *Journ.*, 82; Le Fèvre, *Chron.*, ii, 326; Monstrelet, *Chron.*, v, 270–1, 342–3, 376–87, 391–6, 454–5. Réné: Escouchy, *Chron.*, i, 44–5. Saxony: *J. Hansen, *Westfalen und Rheinland im 15. Jahrhundert*, i (1888), 279. Disputes: *Plancher, iv, PJ nos. 139, 141; *Escouchy, *Chron.*, iii, 105–12; Basin, *Hist.*, ii, 246; Vaughan (1970), 113–22, 346–54, 392–5. Warnings: *Schneider, 197; Waurin, *Cron.*, iv, 129–30.
61. *Cal. Inq. P. M.*, xxiv, no. 520; *Royal Wills*, 271–2; *Cron. Norm.*, 81. Tomb: A. W. Deville, *Tombeaux de la Cathédrale de Rouen* (1833), 166–71; Hall, *Chron.*, 178 (I can find no French source for this story).

CHAPTER X: *The Hinge of Fortune, 1435–1436*

1. Pius II, *Comm.*, i, 48; *Reg. Lacy*, ii, 15–16; *Paviot (1995)[2], nos. 184–5; *Chrons. London*, 139; *Brut*, ii, 503–4; *Hist. Poems*, 86.
2. *Vet. Script.*, viii, cols. 864–8; Le Fèvre, *Chron.*, ii, 362–4; Waurin, *Cron.*, iv, 96–8; Monstrelet, *Chron.*, v, 190–3. The heralds left Arras on 29 Sept. and returned to Hesdin on 14 Nov.: AD Nord B1957, fols. 118vo–119. This suggests that the council meeting occurred shortly before the opening of Parliament on 10 Oct. and that the heralds were detained in England until early Nov., i. e. for the first three weeks of the Parliamentary session.
3. *Parl. Rolls*, xi, 164–5 [1–2], 188 [26], 189–90 [28]; 'Programme d'un gouvernement constitutional', 229–30; Monstrelet, *Chron.*, v, 192, 193–4; Le Fèvre, *Chron.*, ii, 363–4, 377; Waurin, *Cron.*, iv, 98–9.
4. *L&P*, ii, 577–85; *Parl. Rolls*, xi, 168–71 [10]; *Foed.*, x, 624.
5. Chartier, 'Chron. Lat.', 229–30; Héraut Berry, *Chron.*, 167–70; Monstrelet, *Chron.*, v, 126–7, 187; BN Fr. 32510, fol. 375vo. On Rieux: Sumption, iv, 685, 686–7; 'Comptes Guinot', 76 (no. 401). Siege: BN PO 3021 (Villiers)/31.
6. Taverne, *Journ.*, 84–5; Gruel, *Chron.*, 104–5; Monstrelet, *Chron.*, v, 186–7; Chartier, 'Chron. Lat.', 230–4; Chartier, *Chron.*, i, 181–3; Héraut Berry, *Chron.*, 170–1; *Journ. B. Paris*, 307–8.

7. Monstrelet, *Chron.*, v, 187; *Protokollbücher*, i, 65–6, 67–9; Taverne, *Journ.*, 88–9; Chartier, *Chron.*, i, 184; BN Clair. 179/51 (Willoughby).
8. *Dickinson, 219; HMC, *Rep.*, iii, 279; PRO E404/52 (206); E101/323/1; E364/69, m. 3; Chartier, *Chron.*, i, 181–2; *Foed. Supp. D.*, 412–13. Rouen: Goulay, 43. French build-up: Taverne, *Journ.*, 57–9, *101–2; Monstrelet, *Chron.*, v, 146–8, 199–200; BN Fr. 3645bis/1359 (La Hire).
9. *Coll. Bastard*, p. xvii (with date); Monstrelet, *Chron.*, v, 200–1; *Cron. Norm.*, 89–90; Héraut Berry, *Chron.*, 174–5; Cagny, *Chron.*, 212; *Lettres de rois*, ii, 439 (artillery). English garrison: Curry (1985), ii, x. Piracy: PRO C81/1367/40–42.
10. Bekynton, *Corr.*, i, 289–95; Basin, *Hist.*, i, 214–16; *Cron. Norm.*, 81, 84; Héraut Berry, *Chron.*, 175; Monstrelet, *Chron.*, v, 104, 201, 203; Basin, *Hist.*, v, 214–16; Chartier, *Chron.*, i, 173–4; Gruel, *Chron.*, 126 (3,000 men). Garrisons: Massey (1987), 55–6, App. I, IV; *Deck, 274 (Eu); AN K64/1 (24) (Arques, Eu); Curry (1985), i, 407–26. Arming peasants: BN Fr. 25772/958, 26059/2554; *L&P*, ii, pp. xlv–xlviii.
11. PRO E101/192/6 (Suffolk); Monstrelet, *Chron.*, v, 201–2 (for 'Monsieur Vilers', read Montivilliers); Basin, *Hist.*, i, 216; *L&P*, i, 424; *Foed. Supp. D*, 416; *Lettres de rois*, ii, 439; BN Fr. 26060/2726 (Rouen).
12. Upper Normandy: *Chrons. London*, 140–1. Lower: BN Fr. n.a. 3654/332; *Cron. Norm.*, 84–5; Monstrelet, *Chron.*, v, 202–3; *Chrons. London*, 139–40; *Coll. Bastard*, 85–6 (with wrong dates); *L&P*, i, 424, 510–12; *Chron. Mont-St-M.*, ii, 74, 75, 76–77, 94–5; 'Répertoire Lenoir', no. 304; Basin, *Hist.*, i, 204–6; CPR 1429–36, 533; cf. Jouet (1969), 131–40.
13. Pulpit: *L&P*, ii, xlv–xlvii; BL Add. Chart. 124. Estates: *Lettres de rois*, ii, 423–8. Tax: Beaurepaire (1859)[2], 46–8 (1434); BN Fr. 3642/790 (1435). Gisors: BL Add. Chart. 135; AD Seine-Mar. 100J38/37; *Inv. AC Amiens*, iv, 149; Monstrelet, *Chron.*, v, 231; Gruel, *Chron.*, 123–4; Goulay, 46; *Chrons. London*, 140–1 ('so much treason').
14. *Lettres de rois*, ii, 423, 431–2, 437, 438 (quotation), 439. French agents: BN Fr. 17330, fols. 120vo, 124vo–125vo, 128vo, 129vo–132, 137–139vo.
15. Suffolk: CPR 1429–36, 590. York: *Johnson, 226–7; *Lettres de rois*, ii, 428–31; PPC, v, 7 (term); *Chrons. London*, 141. Companions: PRO E403/721, m. 14 (20 Feb.), E403/723, mm. 4, 6 (10, 24 May).
16. PRO E403/721, mm. 6, 8, 15 (29 Nov., 12 Dec., 1 Mar.); CPR 1429–36, 525, 526, 533; *Lettres de rois*, ii, 428–31; CPR 1429–36, 595; *Foed.*, x, 642–4. E. Beaufort: PRO E404/52 (196); PPC, v, 15.
17. Louis of Luxembourg: PRO E30/443; PRO E403/721, m. 17 (26 Mar.); E403/723, m. 6 (24 May). Finance: *Parl. Rolls*, xi, 166–8 [9], 174–9 [12–14]; CFR 1430–37, 269–71, 309–10; Gray (1934), 612; Ormrod (1999)[1], 160–2 (Figs. 8.1–8.3); Steel, 208–9; Harriss (1988), 404 (nos. 30–33); *Foed.*, x, 631; PRO E404/52 (199); Barron (1970), 611, 624; PPC, iv, 312–29.
18. BN Fr. n.a. 8606/51; BN Fr. 25772/1052–7; BN PO 530 (Brouillard)/15; *Foed. Supp. D*, 417. Norbury: CPR 1429–36, 525; *Chrons. London*, 140; PRO E403/721, m. 12 (16 Dec.) (numbers).
19. *Cron. Norm.*, 84–5; BN Fr. 25772/1050; Basin, *Hist.*, i, 216–20. Topography: see the Magin plan (early eighteenth cent.), https://gallica.bnf.fr/ark:/12148. btv1b85918211.
20. Caux: BN Fr. n.a. 3654/332; Basin, *Hist.*, i, 224–6; *Chrons. London*, 140; *Cron. Norm.*, 85–6; Masselin, *Journ.*, 560–2. Cotentin: Basin, *Hist.*, i, 204–6; 'Livre des trahisons', 215–16; *Chron. Mont-St-M.*, ii, 243; 'Répertoire Lenoir', no. 304; Jouet (1969), 137–9.
21. *Cron. Norm.*, 85; Basin, *Hist.*, i, 222–4; Chartier, *Chron.*, i, 174–5; Bois (1981), 300–4; Lardin (2002), 35; AN Coll. Lenoir, iv, 169 ('total destruction'), cf. *ib.* xiii, 263–4;

REFERENCES TO PAGES 494–504

Fortescue, *Governance*, 141; Masselin, *Journ.*, 560–74. Dieppe: *Inv. AC Abbeville*, 80–1. Hospitals: Denifle (1897–9), i, nos. 184–6. Tax records: BN Fr. 26067/4059, 26074/5372; Allmand (1983), 170.

22. Rouen, Ry: Monstrelet, *Chron.*, v, 204–5, 281–2, 297–8 (referring to the same incident); *Chrons. London*, 140; 'Délib. Beauvais', 251–2. Eu: *Coll. Bastard*, 85. Its garrison: BN Fr. 25772/938, 1022 (changes are recorded up to 2 March).
23. Meulan: *Journ. B. Paris*, 310, 311; Fauquembergue, *Journ.*, iii, 166, 189–92; BN Fr. 26060/2764, 2789; *Foed. Supp. D*, 418; BN PO 2487 (Rigmayden)/3. Officers, Parlement: Fauquembergue, *Journ.*, iii, 168–9, 188–92 (for the 'normal' complement at this time, see Boulet, 352–4, 503).
24. Garrisons: *Journ. B. Paris*, 313; BN PO 530 (Brouillart)/15; AN X1a 4798, fol. 8vo (arrears). Cash subsidies: Burney, Chap. III (App.). Corbeil: Héraut Berry, *Chron.*, 175–6; *Journ. B. Paris*, 311; Chartier, *Chron.*, i, 177. Charenton: AN X1a 4798, fol. 53; Fauquembergue, *Journ.*, iii, 178. Parisians: *ib.*, iii, 177, 180–2, 185–6, 187. On La Haye: Ambühl (2017)[2], 267–75.
25. Basin, *Hist.*, i, 226–8. Vincennes: Héraut Berry, *Chron.*, 176, 437; Chartier, *Chron.*, i, 178–9; *Titres Bourbon*, ii, nos. 5510. Pontoise: Chartier, *Chron.*, i, 217–18; Monstrelet, *Chron.*, v, 205, 216; Gruel, *Chron.*, 112–13; AD Nord B1957, fols. 126, 150 (Burgundian troops). Poissy: Gruel, *Chron.*, 117 (in French hands by 12 April). St-Germain: BN Fr. 25772/946 (muster, 28 May). Richemont: BN Fr. 2861, fols. 213–15; Gruel, *Chron.*, 111. Pardon: *Félibien, iii, 558–9.
26. Fauquembergue, *Journ.*, iii, 188–92; *Journ. B. Paris*, 312, 319; AN X1a 8605, fol. 33 (ordinance); Grassoreille, 191; Gruel, *Chron.*, 113.
27. Advance guard: CPR 1429–36, 526, 533; *Lettres de rois*, ii, 435–6, 438–9; PRO E403/721, m. 16 (10 Mar.); Monstrelet, *Chron.*, v, 218. Invasion scare: CPR 1429–36, 519–24; Doig (1998), 272, 273; Doig (1995)[2], 97; *White and Black Books*, 7; *Foed.*, x, 629–30; PPC, iv, 308–15; *Rot. Scot.*, ii, 294. Expedition: PRO E403/721, m. 14 (20 Feb.); PPC, iv, 316.
28. Conciliation: CPR 1429–36, 527; PPC, iv, 331–2; Monstrelet, *Chron.*, v, 210, 377–8. Calais: *Schneider, 197–8, 204; *Potvin, 127–38; AD Nord 10401, fol. 29; Waurin, *Cron.*, iv, 127–33; Monstrelet, *Chron.*, v, 212–14; Thielemans (1966), 78–9, *437–8; *Doig (1995)[1], 410–11.
29. PRO E28/57 (20 May 1436); E404/52 (226, 227, 322, 347, 352, 356, 370); CPR 1429–36, 533; CPR 1436–41, 314; *Brut*, ii, 574.
30. Gruel, *Chron.*, 112–13; Monstrelet, *Chron.*, v, 217–18; Basin, *Hist.*, i, 228–30; Chartier, *Chron.*, i, 224. On Sanguin: *Journ. B. Paris*, 239 n.2. On Lallier: Fauquembergue, *Journ.*, iii, 190. On de Landes: *Journ. B. Paris*, 322 n.1. On de Belloy: *ib.*, 315 n.2, 321 n.3.
31. Chartier, *Chron.*, i, 220–2, 223; *Journ. B. Paris*, 313–14 (confused); Héraut Berry, *Chron.*, 176–7; Gruel, *Chron.*, 113–16; Cagny, *Chron.*, 213–14; Fauquembergue, *Journ.*, iii, 194.
32. Gruel, *Chron.*, 116–19; Monstrelet, *Chron.*, v, 218–20; Héraut Berry, *Chron.*, 177–8; *Journ. B. Paris*, 314–15; Fauquembergue, *Journ.*, iii, 193; Chartier, *Chron.*, i, 225–6; Cagny, *Chron.*, 216. Forest: Maury, 101–2.
33. Fauquembergue, *Journ.*, iii, 193–4; Monstrelet, *Chron.*, v, 220–1; *Journ. B. Paris*, 315–19; Héraut Berry, *Chron.*, 178–9; Chartier, *Chron.*, i, 226–8; Cagny, *Chron.*, 216–17; AN X1a 4798, fol. 53 (Morhier).
34. Bossuat (1963), 33; Allmand (1983), 142–8; *Curry (1998)[2], 118–19.
35. Rinel: *Foed.*, x, 552, 678–9; Otway-Ruthven, 92 and n.3; BN Fr. 26067/4116, 4117. Calot: CPR 1429–36, 193; CPR 1441–46, 257, 328 (my translation from the original roll); Otway-Ruthven, 94–5. Le Vulre: *ib.*, 95–102. Morhier: Roger (1980), 103–7,

*146. Others: PRO E404/59 (160, 166); E404/62 (28, 198); E404/63 (87); E404/64 (21, 254); E404/65 (20), 142; E404/67 (137–139, 171); E404/68 (54, 70); *CPR 1441–46*, 159. Luxembourg: *PPC*, v, 28; *CCR 1435–41*, 337; *Fasti*, ii, 125; PRO E404/54 (112); E403/729, mm. 7–8 (5 Dec.); *Gall. Christ.*, xi, col. 56 (will).

36. Officers: *Gall. Reg.*, iv, nos. 16504–5, 16533, 16546, 16548, 16607–12; Favier (1974), 420–1. *Grands corps*: *Tessereau, i, 47; *Ord.*, xiii, 218, 226, 229–30; *Journ. B. Paris*, 328.

37. Parlement: Delachenal (1891). Ch. des Comptes: Jassemin, 3–4, 9. King: *Journ. B. Paris*, 338, 344, 361.

38. Resistance: *Journ. B. Paris*, 330–2; Cagny, *Chron.*, 230–3; Gruel, *Chron.*, 130–1, *255; Monstrelet, *Chron.*, v, 279–80. Land: *Ord.*, xiii, 223–5; *Inv. livres couleur*, no. 547. Legal wall: Bossuat (1950), 54–8.

39. *Journ. B. Paris*, 323–4, 337, 338–40, 341–2; Chartier, *Chron.*, i, 229, 245–8; Gruel, *Chron.*, 144–5, 147–9; *Chron. Martiniane*, 16; Fourquin, 329–40; Baulant, 537; Favier (1974), 56–8, 60–1, 269–70, 299.

40. *Handelingen*, i, no. 612D, 613D; Le Fèvre, *Chron.*, ii, 374–81; Monstrelet, *Chron.*, v, 214–15; *Doig (1995)[1], 412; *Handelingen*, i, nos. 620D, 622, 623D; *Hanserecesse*, i, 471–2; Dixmude, *Merkw. Gebeurtenissen*, 147; 'Laetste deel', 49.

41. Sommé, 198–9. The Estates of Burgundy made a small grant (8,000 *livres*) in March reserved to buying off the depredations of Perrinet Gressart: *Fréminville, 220–3.

42. *Doig (1995)[1], 410–11, 412; Vlietinck, 92–3; *Foed.*, x, 636–9; *Brut*, ii, 574. Offer of service: *Brut*, ii, 574–5; *PPC*, iv, 352c. This appears to be the meaning of their offer and it is what happened: see PRO E403/723, mm. 13–14 (29 Aug.). The reference in the council minute to Parliament must be to the great council. Army: PRO E403/723, mm. 13–14 (29 Aug.); Doig (1995)[2] 95; Doig (1998), 273. Finance: *Brut*, ii, 574–5; Steele, 209; PRO E401/747 (17 Apr.–23 May); *Foed.*, x, 649–50.

43. Colvin, i, 423–56; Dillon; AD Nord B1957, fols. 315vo–316 (plans).

44. Monstrelet, *Chron.*, v, 203–4; *Thielemans (1966), 438; PRO E101/193/5. Repairs: Brown, Colvin and Taylor, i, 437 (sea walls); *Brut*, ii, 573–4. Artillery: PRO E404/52 (219, 225, 372). Garrison: *Parl. Rolls*, xi, 168–71 [10]; PRO E404/52 (17, 20, 32, 34, 35, 187, 222, 394); E101/71/3 (883–90); E403/721, m. 8–9 (12 Dec.); AD Nord B1957, fol. 163vo–164, 456vo (Beaufort's arrival); *Hist. Poems*, 80–1 (townsmen); Doig (1998), 274 ('dragons').

45. Delay: Sommé, 199. Croÿ: AD Nord B1957, fols. 164, 165vo–166, 460vo–462vo. Raids: *Brut*, ii, 575–6; Gregory, 'Chron.', 178; Waurin, *Cron.*, iv, 147–8, 150–6; Monstrelet, *Chron.*, v, 231–2, 235–8; Budt, 'Chron.', 248; *Hist. Poems*, 84. Garter: *Foed.*, x, 640.

46. Army: Dixmude, *Merkw. Gebeurtenissen*, 147; *Thielemans (1950), 291; *Hist. Poems*, 84; Monstrelet, *Chron.*, 246; Gruel, *Chron.*, 125–6. Numbers: AD Nord B1957, fols. 460vo–474; AD Côte d'Or B1659, fols. 177–181. Fleet: Paviot (1995)[1], 73–8; *Paviot (1995)[2], nos. 186, 190; *Hanserecesse*, i, 502–3; *Memorialen Rosa*, i, no. 397, and cf. no. 440. Artillery: Sommé, 202–6; *J. Garnier, 151–7, 158–9, 163–5; AD Nord B1957, fols. 388vo–394vo (Burgundy guns).

47. Invasion: *Brut*, ii, 576, 577. Le Crotoy: *Inv. AC Amiens*, ii, 67–8; *Huguet, 452–3; Monstrelet, *Chron.*, v, 260–2; 'Livre des trahisons', 213. Gloucester: *Doig (1995)[1], 412–14; *Cal. Letter Books K*, 205; *Foed.*, x, 647–8.

48. *Brut*, ii, 576–8; *Doig (1995)[1], 414; Monstrelet, *Chron.*, ii, 241–5; Schnerb (2018), 171–2.

49. *Brut*, ii, 578–9; Monstrelet, *Chron.*, 247; Waurin, *Cron.*, 169–70. Hammes: Colvin, i, 454. Guines: PRO E404/62 (214); *PPC*, v, 293.

50. *Brut*, ii, 578; Dixmude, *Merkw. Gebeurtenissen*, 150; Monstrelet, *Chron.*, v, 246–7; *Hist. Poems*, 81, 89; *Thielemans (1950), 291–2.

51. Monstrelet, *Chron.*, v, 245–6, 248–50; *Brut*, ii, 578–9; *Hist. Poems*, 81. Bastides: Sommé, 206–7. Bombards: AD Nord B1957, fols. 388vo–394vo.

52. Waurin, *Cron.*, iv, 170–1; Monstrelet, *Chron.*, v, 250–2, 266; *Brut*, ii, 579–80; Paviot (1995)[1], 75–6, 77–8; AD Nord B1957, fols. 237vo, 430–448.

53. Doig (1995)[1], 414; *Hist. poems*, 88; CCR 1435–41, 66; *Dits de cronike*, 321. Council: Gregory, 'Chron.', 178; *Foed.*, x, 649–50. Final preparations: *Cal. Letter Books K*, 206–7; CPR 1429–36, 611–12; *Brut*, ii, 581; *Thielemans (1950), 292, 294. Sermons: *Reg. Lacy*, ii, 15–17; *Reg. Spofford*, 215–16.

54. AD Nord B1957, fol. 317; Monstrelet, *Chron.*, v, 250, 253; *Brut*, ii, 469–70; *Doig (1995)[1], 415 (attributes leadership to Radcliffe); *Hist. Poems*, 80, 82–3. Le Crotoy: Monstrelet, *Chron.*, v, 262; *Huguet, 452–3.

55. *Thielemans (1950), 292–5; Monstrelet, *Chron.*, v, 254–8; Waurin, *Cron.*, iv, 182–4, 192–5; *Brut*, ii, 581; *Hist. Poems*, 83; AD Nord B1957, fols. 479vo–480.

56. *Foed.*, x, 652–3; *Brut*, ii, 505; AD Nord B1957, fols. 178vo, 180–180vo.

57. *Groot Charterboek*, iv, 1083; Monstrelet, *Chron.*, v, 258–9, 260, 268; Schnerb (2018), 172; AD Nord B1957, fols. 313–313vo; Canat, *Doc. inéd.*, 375. Letter to Bourbon: *Thielemans (1950) (on the addressee, see Leguai [1962]W, 151).

58. 'Short Engl. Chron.', 62; Waurin, *Cron.*, iv, 201–6; Monstrelet, *Chron.*, v, 263–5; *Dits de cronike*, 321–6; 'Laetste deel', 46–7; Dixmude, *Merkw. Gebeurtenissen*, 151–3; *Brut*, ii, 470; *Handelingen*, i, nos. 639–40; *Memorialen Rosa*, i, nos. 414, 440–1; Paviot (1995)[1], 81–2; 'Documents gantois', 253–7. Indentures: PRO E101/71/3 (893–7).

59. *Hist. Poems*, 78–89; *Brut*, ii, 582–4, 600–1; cf. 582; R. Weiss (1957), 222–7; *Libelle*, i, 29–30, 42, 43, 55, 57–8 (ll. 5–7, 554–85, 819, 1150–56, 1092–7); Sobecki, 104–26.

60. Sobecki, 103; *Parl. Rolls*, xi, 203–4, 209–10 [11–12, 18]; Holmes (1961), 207–9.

61. *Libelle*, 30 (l. 36); PPC, iv, 352d; Richmond (1964), 290; *Soper Accounts*, 54–5, 247–52.

62. CPR 1429–36, 509–10, 511–12, 515, 603; *Parl. Rolls*, xi, 189–90 [28]. Unlicensed privateers: Appleby, 91–2; Kingsford (1925), 87–98; Bower, *Scottichron.*, viii, 248–50; *Parl. Rolls*, xi, 212–13 [24].

63. Boycott: *Foed.*, x, 654–5; *Libelle*, 6 (ll. 93–5). Ghent: *Hanserecesse*, ii, 45; 'Laetste deel', 56; 'Documents gantois', 257–8; Waurin, *Cron.*, iv, 196; Monstrelet, *Chron.*, v, 266–7. Bruges: *Inv. Arch. Bruges*, v, 136–69; 'Laetste deel', 76–80; *Merkw. Gebeurtenissen*, 153–9, 162–3; Dumolyn, 158–71, 215–95.

64. Van der Wee, ii, 49–55, 67–9, 73–7, 314–16; Munro (1972), 69, 103–6; *Bronnen Engeland*, ii, nos. 63, 1076, 1079–80, 1082, 1090–94, 1097, 1102–3, 1106–9, 1111, 1113; *Bronnen Holland*, ii^2, no. 85d; *Memorialen Rosa*, i, no. 444; Kerling, 48–50, 84–5; Holmes (1961), 196–7; *Dits de cronike*, 316–17; *England's Export Trade*, 60, 92–4, 138; Munro (1972), 108–10. Pressure: ARA CC32491, fol. 91.

65. 'Programme d'un gouvernement constitutional', 225–32, 237–8, 248–50.

66. Lecoy (1875), i, 115–28; *Inv. AC Amiens*, ii, 67–8; *Huguet, 230–99, 452–3, 456–70, 473–83; Monstrelet, *Chron.*, v, 260–2, 308–16, 353–4; 'Livre des trahisons', 213; Héraut Berry, *Chron.*, 194–6; *Chrons. London*, 144–5.

67. *Scottichron.*, viii, 250, 296, 378n; *Brut*, ii, 470, 505; *Rot. Scot.*, ii, 294–5; Balfour-Melville, 230–1. Berwick garrison: *Cal. Doc. Scot.*, v, no. 1030.

68. BN Fr. 17330, fols. 137–139vo, 141–142vo, 143vo–144; *Scottichron.*, viii, 250.

CHAPTER XI: *The King's War, 1436–1442*

1. Piero da Monte, *Briefsammlung*, no. 53; *Three Books of Polydore Vergil's English History*, ed. H. Ellis (1844), 70. For reasons which will become clear in this and

the following chapters, I do not accept the now widely held view put forward by Watts (1996) and Carpenter (1997) that Henry VI was a vacant and purely nominal participant in the making of English policy.

2. *PPC*, iv, 134, 287–8. Council meetings: PRO C81/1545 (55); *Cal. Letter Books K*, 206; Watts (1996), 129–30. Grants: Griffiths (1981), 329–33; Watts (1996), 132–3, 135–40.
3. *Lettres de rois*, ii, 430–1; *PPC*, v, 71, vi, 312–15; Watts (1996), 128–34, 140–51; Griffiths (1981), 232–4, 278–80.
4. Watts (1996), 158–66; L. E. James, 12–14.
5. Henry: Monstrelet, *Chron.*, v, 192; *Proc., Alençon*, 123; *Gr. Chron.*, 149; *CPR 1452–61*, 247. Kemp: *L&P*, ii, 442, 446.
6. Juvénal, *Écrits*, i, 221–3; *L&P*, ii, 446.
7. York: Cagny, *Chron.*, 222–3; BN Fr. 26061/2977; *Chrons. London*, 141; *L&P*, ii, 289–94. Creil: *Journ. B. Paris*, 323–4; Cagny, *Chron.*, 217–19; Gruel, *Chron.*, 125; Chartier, *Chron.*, i, 228–9; Monstrelet, *Chron.*, v, 229. Talbot: BL Add. Chart. 3781; AN Coll. Lenoir, xxvi, 293–4.
8. M. K. Jones (1989)[2], 106–7; *Vicomté d'Orbec*, 11–12, 198–201; McFarlane (1957)[1], 104; Massey (1987), 149, 355–9; Plaisse (1961), 324–34; Allmand (1968), 474–5.
9. Caux: Monstrelet, *Chron.*, v, 271–2; AN Coll. Lenoir xxvi, no. 25397; AN K64/12, 19; BN Fr. 26063/2317, 3236, 3256. Vexin: BN Fr. 26063/3234–5. Demolitions: *PPC*, iv, 97; R. Jones (1994), i, 282–5. In Alençon: BN Fr. 26055/1728, 26057/1918; AD Seine-Mar. 100J, 38/24; Chave, 144–6. In Upper Normandy: BN Fr. 26054/1606; Fr. 26061/2998, 3065, 26062/3129, 3162–3, 26063/2317, 3236, 3256; AN Coll. Lenoir xix, no. 19676, xxviii, no. 30352; BL Add. Chart. 1191.
10. Pontoise: Chartier, *Chron.*, i, 233–5; *Journ. B. Paris*, 329; Waurin, *Cron.*, iv, 207–8; Héraut Berry, *Chron.*, 179; Cagny, *Chron.*, 230–1. Fécamp: Cagny, *Chron.*, 226–7; Monstrelet, *Chron.*, v, 297–8; BN Fr. 26062/3030. Tancarville: AN K81/16; BN Fr. 26063/3255, 3257, 3263, 3306–8, 3312, 3314, 3388; Fr. 26064/2477; BL Add. Chart. 137; AN Coll. Lenoir iv, 401; *Cron. Norm.*, 86; Héraut Berry, *Chron.*, 187; *Chrons. London*, 143; Curry (1985), i, 198. Desertions: BN Fr. n.a. 1482/144.
11. Discipline: BN 26061/2921. Strength: PRO E404/53 (324), E404/54 (104). Finance: Beaurepaire (1859)[2], 61–3. Resignation: *PPC*, v, 6, 7; *Chrons. London*, 144.
12. Thomas (1878), 169–70, 200–5; Thomas (1889)[1], 68–84; Thomas (1892), 12–14; *Les La Trémoille*, i, 165–8, 177–82, 198, 210.
13. Estates-Gen.: Thomas (1878), 206; Thomas (1889)[1], 82–7; Thomas (1878), 207–8; Beaucourt, ii, 600. *Tailles*: Beaucourt, iii, 436, 472–5; *Monstrelet, *Chron.*, vi, 39. Institutions: *Ord.*, xiii, 211–15; Beaucourt, iii, 477–83; Gilles, 197–8. Languedoc: *Vaissète, x, cols. 2127–8; 2150 (art. XVII); Gilles, 50–8; Spont (1890), 495; Dupont-Ferrier (1930–2), ii, 50; F. Garnier, 304–5, 307–10. Debts: Beaucourt, iii, 477. Garrisons: BN Fr. 32510, fols. 383–385.
14. Monstrelet, *Chron.*, v, 292–5; *Journ. B. Paris*, 333–5; Cagny, *Chron.*, 238–44; Héraut Berry, *Chron.*, 182–6; Gruel, *Chron.*, 135–7, *260–1; *Beaucourt, iii, 522–6; *Chrons. London*, 143. French numbers: BN Fr. 32510, fols. 381vo (assuming one varlet for each man-at-arms). Relief: BN Fr. n.a. 1482/148 (Scales); *Cosneau (1886), 562–3; *Chrons. London*, 143. Meaux, Creil: *Inv. AC Amiens*, ii, 72; BL Add. Chart. 3828.
15. *PPC*, v, 15, 16–17, 22, 28–31, 40–1; *L&P*, ii, pp. lxvi–lxxi; *Foed.*, x, 674–5; *Chrons. London*, 143–4. Numbers: PRO E403/727, mm. 9, 12 (17, 25 June).
16. *Huguet, 456–71, 474–82; *Inv. AC Amiens*, ii, 72; Monstrelet, *Chron.*, v, 309–16; Héraut Berry, *Chron.*, 194–6; *Chrons. London*, 144–5; BL Add. Chart. 3830;

Waurin, *Cron.*, iv, 230–41. Blockade squadron: Paviot (1995)[1], 84–5. Relief fleet: PRO E403/729, m. 8 (7 Dec.); E404/54 (151).
17. Strengths: *ca.* 3,500 garrison troops (Curry [1985], ii, xii, xix), plus the personal retinues of the principal captains, Talbot, Scales and Fauconberg, and the returning garrisons of Montereau and the Gâtinais. Survey: *PPC*, v, 70. Beaufort: PRO E404/54 (175, 179–80, 182); BL Add. Ms. 11542, fol. 90; BN Fr. 26064/3589 (Alençon); Gregory, 'Chron.', 181; Newhall (1940), 148–50.
18. Estates: *Foed. Supp.*, D, 432; Beaurepaire (1859)[2], 65–6. English subsidies: PRO E404/52 (352, 370); BN Fr. 26062/3164; Burney, Chap III (App.).
19. Famine: Monstrelet, *Chron.*, v, 319–20, 339–40; Cagny, *Chron.*, 252; *Journ. B. Paris*, 338–9, 340, 342–3, 342 n.3; Bois (1976), 303; Fourquin, 330–1, 335; Lardin (2002), 36–8. Discipline: BN Fr. 26064/3477, 3541, 3558; *Statutes*, ii, 314–15 (desertion). Brigandage, plot: Goulay, 43–6.
20. PRO E403/731, m. 6 (28 May); *Chrons. London*, 145; Héraut Berry, *Chron.*, 197–8; AC Tours, CC27, fol. 53–56vo; BL Add. Chart. 1183; *L&P*, ii, 449–50. Depopulation: Bouton, 74–81.
21. Caux: BN Fr. 25774/1322, 1348–9; Fr. n.a. 1482/149; Monstrelet, *Chron.*, v, 340–1. Harfleur: BN Fr. 25774/1391, 1393; Monstrelet, *Chron.*, v, 346–7; *Chrons. London*, 145; Héraut Berry, *Chron.*, 198. Dreux: Cagny, *Chron.*, 250–2, 255–6; Chartier, *Chron.*, i, 235–6; *Journ. B. Paris*, 342; BM Add. Chart. 11663 (indigenous troops); BN Fr. 26065/3608–9 (date). 'Impregnable': Bossuat (1936), 305 n.3, citing AN X1a 4801, fol. 359vo. Montargis: Cagny, *Chron.*, 247–8, 250, 255. English support: BN Fr. 25774/1300, 26063/3394; BN Clair. 185/22, 201/24. St-Germain: *Journ. B. Paris*, 343–4; Cagny, *Chron.*, 256–7; BN PO 2738 (Surienne)/5; BN Clair. 201/25, 27.
22. *Brut*, ii, 473–4, 507; *Cal. Inq. P. M.*, xxv, nos. 261–92 (date). Chapel: Saul (2009), 122–4. The tomb inscription refers to a 'longe siknes'.
23. *Foed.*, x, 765.
24. Ch. of Orléans: Beaucourt, iii, 42 n.1, 87–8, 89–90. Grants revoked: *Ord.*, xiii, 293–5. Bourbons: Beaucourt, iii, 41–2; Leguai (1962), 155–9; M. Rey, *Les finances royales sous Charles VI. Les causes du déficit* (1965), 590–2. Alençon: Chastellain, 'Chron.', ii, 164; *Proc. Alençon*, 116, 122, 150–1.
25. Quicherat (1879), 41–84, 103–9, *307–9; Chartier, *Chron.*, i, 215–17, ii, 12–13; Monstrelet, *Chron.*, v, 199, 316–19; Héraut Berry, *Chron.*, 181–2; Gruel, *Chron.*, 147; Cosneau (1886), 237–8; Plaisse (1984), Chap. II; Fréminville, Chap. II; Leguai (1962), 155–7, 159, 160; *Escouchy, *Chron.*, iii, 5–6. Paris fortresses: *ib.*, 19; Maupoint, 'Journ.', 26; *Cosneau (1886), 573–7.
26. BL Add. Chart. 3793, 4400; *Foed.*, x, 663–4, 665, 707; *PPC*, v, 52–4, 64–5; Cagny, *Chron.*, 233.
27. *PPC*, v, 64–5, 67–8. Finance: Steel, 450–1 (Table C6); *England's Export Trade*, 123; Ormrod (1999)[1], 160, 162 (Figs. 8.1, 8.3); *Parl. Rolls*, xi, 216–18 [28].
28. Cagny, *Chron.*, 233–5; Leguai (1962), 157–60; Beaucourt, iii, 45–8; PRO E101/323/5, 6 (Popham).
29. AD Nord B1969, fol. 156; BN Clair. 53/4029; *Foed.*, x, 716; 'Doc. negotiations', 85–9. Background: Thielemans (1966), 115–17. Foreign merchants: *Inv. Arch. Bruges*, v, 190–1, 199.
30. *Foed.*, x, 718–19; 'Doc. negotiations', 89–96; *L&P*, ii, 445; Gruel, *Chron.*, 143–4, 148–9; *Escouchy, *Chron.*, iii, 5–6.
31. *Foed.*, x, 718–19, 724–8, 732–3. Great council: 'Doc. negotiations', 94–5. Rouen delegation: BN Fr. 20884/72, 73. Kemp statement: 'Doc. negotiations', 123.
32. *PPC*, v, 337, 340–4, 346–9; 'Doc. negotiations', 112–14, 135, 138–9; Thielemans (1966), 125; *Itin. Philippe*, 190–2; *Foed.*, x, 728–30; PRO E404/55 (297) (Ch. of

Orléans); *L&P*, ii, 448; *Lettres de rois*, ii, 457. Dunois: *Godefroy, *Hist.*, 805–6 (he was already using the title in June 1439, *PPC*, v, 336).

33. 'Doc. negotiations', 117–19; *PPC*, v, 363–4.
34. *PPC*, v, 336–70, 373–4, 375, 377; 'Doc. negotiations', 120–1, 122–4, 126–8; *Plancher, iv, PJ no. 132.
35. *PPC*, v, 376–7, 381, 383, 395–6; 'Doc. negotiations', 124–5, 129–30, 135–9; Bekynton, *Corr.*, i, 103–4.
36. Gruel, *Chron.*, 145–6; *Schnerb (1993), 113–14. Army: BN Fr, 32510, fols. 383–385 (analysis in Contamine [1972], 262–72). Lorraine war: Tuetey, i, 62–71, 99–114; *Chron. Martiniane*, 37–8; *Rec. doc. Lorraine*, i, 141–6, 149–50; Monstrelet, *Chron.*, v, 336–9, 387; *Calmet, vii, cols. clxii–clxiii; *Chron. Martiniane*, 28–34; *Rec. doc. Lorraine*, i, 149–50; Héraut Berry, *Chron.*, 198–9; 'Chron. St-Thiébault', col. lxxxvii; *Quicherat (1879), 324–5.
37. Monstrelet, *Chron.*, v, 387–8; Héraut Berry, *Chron.*, 199–201; Gruel, *Chron.*, 146–7. Topography: Wilmart, 371 (map). Convoy: BN Fr. 26063/3566 (Sept. 1438). Defenders: BL Add. Chart. 129; BN Clair. 150/4. Chamberlain: *Paston Letters*, ii, 185, 213, iii, 123; PRO E403/734, mm. 6, 11 (21 May, 17 July). Thian: Monstrelet, *Chron.*, iii, 150, 255, 281, 386, iv, 92, v, 126, 184; 'Chron. Cordeliers', in Monstrelet, *Chron.*, vi, 251, 315; *Gall. Reg.*, iv, no. 15127.
38. Talk: *Journ. B. Paris*, 347. Lieutenancy: *L&P*, ii, 449; BL Add. MS 11542, fols. 78–78vo; Monstrelet, *Chron.*, v, 389; Gruel, *Chron.*, 151; Héraut Berry, *Chron.*, 208. On Somerset: *Foed.*, x, 697–8; Basin, *Hist.*, i, 280–2; 'Hist. Croyland', 518. Forces: PRO E404/55 (186); E403/734, mm. 5, 11 (21 May, 17 July); Curry (1985), ii, App. II (2,825 men at 30 Sept. 1439, including some of the expeditionary force of August 1439); AN K65/1 (30, 33). Finance: Harriss (1988), 288–91; Beaurepaire (1859)[2], 68–9, 70–1, 72.
39. Army of relief: BL Add. Chart. 12031; BN Fr. 26066/3832, 26067/4055; Héraut Berry, *Chron.*, 201. Siege: *PPC*, v, 384; Gruel, *Chron.*, 147, 150–1, 152; Monstrelet, *Chron.*, v, 388, 390; Héraut Berry, *Chron.*, 201.
40. *PPC*, v, 385, 386; Gruel, *Chron.*, 151–4; Héraut Berry, *Chron.*, 201–4; Monstrelet, *Chron.*, v, 388–90; Waurin, *Cron.*, iv, 257–9; Chartier, *Chron.*, i, 249–50.
41. *PPC*, v, 387, 403; Héraut Berry, *Chron.*, 437–8; *Journ. B. Paris*, 347–8; Monstrelet, *Chron.*, v, 390. Second relief force: BL Add. Chart. 568; AD Seine-Mar. 100J39/11.
42. PRO E364/73, m. 1 (Abp. York); 'Doc. negotiations', 140–9 (the original of 147–9, at BN Fr. n.a. 6215, comes from the seventeenth-century Colbert collection and is likely to have come from the Norman archives).
43. *PPC*, v, 388–95.
44. *PPC*, v, 395–7, 399; *Beaucourt, iii, 526–7; *Lettres de rois*, ii, 457–60.
45. Thielemans (1966), 138, *443–53; *Inv. Arch. Bruges*, v, 189–90; *Foed.*, xi, 24–6; *Parl. Rolls*, xi, 382–4 [38]; *PPC*, v, 216–19, 222; Munro (1970), 242–3.
46. PRO E364/73, m. 1 (Abp. York); *PPC*, v, 406–7.
47. *L&P*, ii, 447, 457–8; AN 65/15 (5, 6, 7); Charles d'Orléans, *Poésies*, i, 143–4 (*Ballade* LXXXIX); *Foed.*, x, 776–86 (formalising earlier agreement). The first of the bonds required as security for the second instalment were executed in Dec.1439: *Cosneau (1886), 581–2; *Mon. hist.*, nos. 2168–70. 22 Oct.: *Lettres de rois*, ii, 456–61.
48. *L&P*, ii, 440–51; *Parl. Rolls*, xi, 247 [1]
49. *L&P*, ii, 451–60. Moleyns: PRO E404/56 (177).
50. Héraut Berry, *Chron.*, 204–8; Juvénal, *Écrits*, i, 301, 322–3, 325, 421–3, 427, 522–3, 524, ii, 165; *Ord.*, xiii, 306; *Inv. AC Amiens*, ii, 76; *Beaucourt, iii, 528.
51. Héraut Berry, *Chron.*, 209–12, 213, 214; Chartier, *Chron.*, i, 250–1, 252–3; *Proc. Alençon*, 35–6, 103, 110; Gruel, *Chron.*, 156; Bueil, *Jouvencel*, ii, 227; *Chron. Mont-*

St-M., i, 39–40, *ii, 121–2, 125; 'Notices et extraits (Viriville)', 112; AD Seine-Mar. 100J39/16, 17. English army: AN Coll. Lenoir xxvi, 347; BN Fr. 26066/3910.

52. Ord., xiii, 306–13; Leguai (1962), 151–2, 165; *Preuves Bretagne*, ii, cols. 1327–8; Héraut Berry, *Chron.*, 213–14; Chartier, *Chron.*, i, 253–4; *Chron. Martiniane*, 40; *Escouchy, *Chron.*, iii, 8; Thielemans (1966), 137–8; *Titres Bourbon*, ii, no. 5615.
53. *Beaucourt, iii, 529; Gruel, *Chron.*, 157; Héraut Berry, *Chron.*, 212–13; *Escouchy, *Chron.*, iii, 7–11.
54. *Thibaudeau, ii, 468–70; *Escouchy, *Chron.*, iii, 7, 11; *Inv. AC Narbonne*, AA (Annexes), 391–3; *Beaucourt, iii, 529–31; *Duclos, iv, 16; *Chron. Martiniane*, 40; Chartier, *Chron.*, i, 253–4. Date: *Louis XI, *Lettres*, i, 170, 178–80. On Louis: M. Thibault, 458–62; *Escouchy, *Chron.*, iii, 23.
55. *Escouchy, *Chron.*, iii, 9, 11–14; *Duclos, iv, 16; Héraut Berry, *Chron.*, 215–17; Chartier, *Chron.*, i, 254–8; Gruel, *Chron.*, 157–9; *Chron. Martiniane*, 40–1; Favreau (1971), 289–93.
56. Echoes: BL Add. MS 11542, fol. 27; BL Add. Chart. 3897; PRO C76/122, mm. 32, 26, 25, 18, 11, 9. Huntingdon: *Escouchy, *Chron.*, iii, 13. Westminster: *Foed.*, x, 765; PRO E403/739, m. 8 (21 June); Champion (1969), 672.
57. *Foed.*, x, 763, 767–8; *Itin. Philippe*, 196–8; Gruel, *Chron.*, 159; PRO E364/74, m. 4d (Bp. Rochester); *Monstrelet, *Chron.*, vi, 29–30 (wrongly stating that the English were not represented). Dunois: *Escouchy, *Chron.*, iii, 8–9; BN PO 2653 (Saveuses)/7; AD Nord B1969, fol. 181.
58. Conference: Thielemans (1966), 135 and n.128. Philip and Ch. of Orléans: Monstrelet, *Chron.*, v, 435–6; AN K66/2–10; *Plancher, iv, PJ no. 134; Champion (1969), 312 n.1; Thielemans (1966), 136–7.
59. *Foed.*, x, 764–7, 776–86.
60. *Escouchy, *Chron.*, iii, 15–27; Héraut Berry, *Chron.*, 218–28. Bastard of Bourbon: Monstrelet, *Chron.*, v, 458.
61. *Foed.*, x, 819–23, 826–7; *Mon. hist.*, no. 2198; *Paston Letters*, ii, 21–2; PRO E404/57 (110, 190) (release); Monstrelet, *Chron.*, v, 437–41, 443–4, vi, 30; *Arch. Reims, Statuts*, i, 605; *Journ. B. Paris*, 357.
62. BN Clair. 166/31, 201/78; BN Fr. 32510, fol. 384vo; *Foed. Supp.* D, 452–5, 456, 457–8, 459–61, 498; Monstrelet, *Chron.*, v, 418–19; *Gruel, *Chron.*, 266–8. Artillery: L&P, ii, 308–9; BN PO 1929 (Merbury)/15; BN PO 1202 (Forsted)/7; BN PO 2085 (Mustel-en-Normandie)/11; BN PO 1383 (Gower)/10; BN Fr. 26067/4169. Ships: BN Fr. 26067/4164, 26427/108; PRO E101/53/30 (1, 2, 4). Labourers: BN Fr. 26067/4103.
63. Héraut Berry, *Chron.*, 229–30; *Journ. B. Paris*, 354–5; Basin, *Hist.*, i, 252–4; *Inv. AC Abbeville*, 77. Taille: *Journ. B. Paris*, 354, 355; Thomas (1879), i, 199–200. Count of Eu: AN K65/15 (8). Spies: L&P, ii, 313–16; BN Fr. 26067/4133, 4136, 4137.
64. BN Fr. 26067/4133, 4136–7; Monstrelet, *Chron.*, v, 419–24; Chartier, *Chron.*, i, 259–60; Héraut Berry, *Chron.*, 229–30; *Cron. Norm.*, 86–8; *Paston Letters*, ii, 22. Dates: BN Fr. 26067/4145 (assault), Fr. 26068/4395 (surrender).
65. *Paston Letters*, ii, 22. Garrisons: Curry (1985), ii, clxxiii–clxxiv. Pontoise: AN Coll. Lenoir xxvii, 27; BN PO 2787 (Talbot)/38. Vernon: BN Fr. n.a. 21289/158. Avranches: *Inv. AD Manche*, ii, 142. Eure: *Foed. Supp.* D, 467–8; Héraut Berry, *Chron.*, 229 ('800 *lances et les archers*'); Chartier, *Chron.*, ii, 7–8; BN PO 1167 (Flocques)/34, 42. Conches garrison: BN Clair. 144/109; BN Lat. n.a. 2385/78; BN Fr. 26068/437.
66. Raids: Chartier, *Chron.*, ii, 7; *Cron. Norm.*, 91–2; Basin, *Hist.*, i, 252–4; BN Fr. n.a. 7629, 86–92. St-P. du V.: BN Fr. 26068/4335. Panic: e.g. AC Lisieux, CC12, fols. 7, 13vo, 15. Siege: BN Fr. 25711/135; BN Fr. 25775/1502, 25776/1514, 1517, 1620; BN Fr. 26067/4170, 26068/4228, 4244, 4299; BN PO 1363 (Goth)/19, PO 444

(de Boudeville)/2; BL Add. Chart. 453, 1196, 1201, 1494, 3910–12, 3916, 6947–9, 8006–7; *Ord.*, xiii, 351–4; Héraut Berry, *Chron.*, 230.
67. PRO E404/56 (46); BL Add. MSS 11542, fols. 81–81vo; BN PO 1091 (Eyton)/3. Cf. *L&P*, ii, 586, 604–5; *Foed.*, x, 786–7.
68. *L&P*, ii, 585–91. For evidence of agreement, PRO E404/57 (263).
69. Finance: Steel, 214–18; *Parl. Rolls*, xi, 250–3 [12, 13]; *England's Export Trade*, 123, 138; Ormrod (1999)[1], 162 (Fig. 8.3); Harriss (1988), 307–8; Somerville, i, 215 n.2. Army: PRO E404/57 (130); E403/740, m. 10 (16 Jan.); E101/53/33; PRO E403/740, m. 10; Johnson, 36.
70. Champagne: Héraut Berry, *Chron.*, 230–1; Chartier, *Chron.*, ii, 12; Monstrelet, *Chron.*, v, 457–8, 461–7. Laon: BN Fr. n.a. 7005 (text in part in Beaucourt, iii, 197 n.2, and from another version in *Foed. Supp. D*, 81–2); *Foed.*, x, 847. Oise: *Caillet (1909)[2], 468; *Beaucourt, iii, 532–3; Monstrelet, *Chron.*, vi, 5–6; Héraut Berry, *Chron.*, 232; *Journ. B. Paris*, 359.
71. Creil: *L&P*, ii, 606; BL Add. Chart. 1201; BN Fr. 26068/4294, 4346, 4348, 4351, 25776/1520–3; BN PO 1965 (Gouel)/3, 2602 (Le Sac)/9; *CPR 1436–41*, 539; PRO E403/740, mm. 13, 15 (19, 24 Feb.); *PPC*, v, 146–7; Gregory, 'Chron.', 183; Chartier, *Chron.*, 15–17; *Journ. B. Paris*, 359–60 (dates); Héraut Berry, *Chron.*, 232; Monstrelet, *Chron.*, vi, 6. Peyto's garrison: BN Fr. 26066/3921; BL Add. Chart. 129; BN Clair. 187/112. Pontoise: *Cosneau (1886), 584; *Inv. AC Amiens*, ii, 79; Monstrelet, *Chron.*, vi, 7–8; Gruel, *Chron.*, 164.
72. *L&P*, ii, 603–7. Surienne: Gruel, *Chron.*, 161, *248; Maupoint, 'Journ.', 26. Morale: *PPC*, v, 147–50.
73. Topography: Poirier and Manceau. Defence: AN K65/1 (31) (repairs in 1439–40); BN PO 2787 (Talbot)/35; Curry (1985), ii, xviii–xix. French garrisons: BN Fr. 26066/800.
74. Monstrelet, *Chron.*, vi, 6–7, 10–11; Héraut Berry, *Chron.*, 233–4; Gruel, *Chron.*, 165–7; Chartier, *Chron.*, ii, 20–2; *Caillet (1909)[2], 468 (taille); *Journ. B. Paris*, 360–1; Beaucourt, iii, 182.
75. Monstrelet, *Chron.*, vi, 9–10, 11, 12–13; Héraut Berry, *Chron.*, 234–5; Gruel, *Chron.*, 167; Chartier, *Chron.*, ii, 22–3. English army: Curry (1985), ii, clxvii. Feudal service: AN Coll. Lenoir xvi, 197.
76. Landing: *HMC, Rep.*, viii, 634; PRO E101/53/33 (numbers); *Brut*, ii, 477; *L&P*, i, 193. Advance to Poitiers: *Foed. Supp. D*, 470–1; BN PO 1363 (Goth)/20; BN Fr. 25776/1528–9; Fr. 26068/4340; Gruel, *Chron.*, 168; Basin, *Hist.*, i, 264–6.
77. Monstrelet, *Chron.*, vi, 13–18; Héraut Berry, *Chron.*, 235–7, 438–9; Gruel, *Chron.*, 168–71; Chartier, *Chron.*, ii, 23–5; Basin, *Hist.*, i, 266–70.
78. *Marchegay (1866), 471–3; Monstrelet, *Chron.*, vi, 18–24; Héraut Berry, *Chron.*, 237–42; Gruel, *Chron.*, 171; Chartier, *Chron.*, ii, 25–7; Basin, *Hist.*, i, 270–4; *Journ. B. Paris*, 362–3. Supply convoys: July: BN Fr. 26068/4335, 4340–1; BN PO 1011 (Don)/3, 2602 (Le Sac)/10. August: *Foed. Supp. D*, 472–3, 473, 474; *Mon. hist.*, no. 2222.
79. Beaumont, Beaumesnil: Chartier, *Chron.*, ii, 17–18; BN Fr. 26068/4371. Evreux: Héraut Berry, *Chron.*, i, 242–3; Basin, *Hist.*, i, 276–8; Chartier, *Chron.*, ii, 32; *Cron. Norm.*, 93–4; *Journ. B. Paris*, 362; Plaisse (1984), 116–17; *Plaisse (1978), 267–71; Callias Bey et al., 144, 153.
80. *PPC*, v, 157–8, 164–5, 171–2, 178. They appear to have used figures from Bedford's budget of 1433 (*L&P*, ii, 547–9, 559–65), but the Estates granted only 30,000 l.t. in 1441 and domain revenues had been hit by war and territorial losses. For establishment strengths in Normandy: Curry (1985), i, 201 (Table V).
81. Griffiths (1968–9); Hardyng, *Chron.*, 400 (quotation).
82. Monstrelet, *Chron.*, v, 453, 470; Gaussin, 122.

83. *Lettres de Jean V*, v, no. 2472; *Preuves Bretagne*, ii, cols. 1327-8, 1346-8; *Champollion-Figeac, i, 339-40; *L&P*, i, 189-92.
84. *Foed. Supp. D*, 474-5, 477; BN Fr. 26068/4406, on the abortive conference at Mantes (Sept. 1441); *Escouchy, *Chron.*, iii, 29-41, 63; Monstrelet, *Chron.*, vi, 25-6; *Itin. Philippe*, 206 (date).
85. *Escouchy, *Chron.*, iii, 41-91; Monstrelet, *Chron.*, vi, 27-50; *M. K. Jones (1983), 344-58 (art. 5).
86. Talbot: BN PO 2787 (Talbot)/51, 42; *RDP*, v, 287-8. Army: PRO E404/58 (131); E101/54/11; E403/746, m. 7. Finance: *Parl. Rolls*, xi, 326-9, 373-5 [5, 30]; Harriss (1988), 326; Johnson, 55-6; Steel, 321-2.
87. Talbot: *Foed. Supp. D*, 490-1. Fauconberg: BN Fr. 7628, fols. 517-531vo. Pont-de-l'Arche: AN K67/12 (59, 76, 78); BN Fr. 25776/1574. Conches: *Foed. Supp. D*, 496-7, 497-8. Flocques: Héraut Berry, *Chron.*, 249-50; Monstrelet, *Chron.*, vi, 57-9; *Cron. Norm.*, 93-4; *Foed. Supp. D*, 495. Gallardon: *L&P*, ii, 331-2; Bossuat (1936), 277-80.
88. BN Fr. 25776/739, 1589-91; BL Add. Chart. 144; Chartier, *Chron.*, ii, 36-8; Monstrelet, *Chron.*, ii, 60-1; Waurin, *Cron.*, iv, 372-3; *Chrons. London*, 150. Ships: *ib.*, 150; PRO E404/58 (170); E101/53/38. Small bastide: BN Fr. 25776/1617, 26070/4735, 26071/4733. Peyto's garrison: BN Fr. 25776/1570. Remaining troops: Curry (1985), i, 201 (Table V).
89. *Ord.*, xiii, 439-62; *Chron. Mont-St-M.*, i, 43, *ii, 129-30, 145, 160-5; Héraut Berry, *Chron.*, 257-8; *Chrons. London*, 151-2. Garrison strengths: Curry (1985), ii, xxii (App. III).
90. *L&P*, i, 192-3; Worcester, *Boke of Noblesse*, 71-3. Finance: PRO E404/57 (168, 260); Burney, Chap. III (App.); Johnson, 55-64. Brigandage: Goulay, 46-8.
91. Curry (1985), i, 304-5, 345-9; Johnson, 39; *L&P*, ii, 371-3, 590; Waurin, *Cron.*, iv, 349; *Foed.*, x, 13-14 (list of councillors in Sept. 1442 – the Bishop of Bayeux was Italian); *GEC*, vi, 562 (Hoo).

CHAPTER XII: *The King's Peace, 1442-1448*

1. *Parl. Rolls*, xi, 108; Vale (1970), 236 (Table 5). Expenses: for the 1430s, see PRO E364/70, mm. 8-9d (Colles), E364/75, mm. 4-5d. Langon: PRO E364/71, mm. 1, 6 (Colles).
2. *Gr. Chron. London*, 131-2; *Jurades Bergerac*, i, 223-5, 228, 235; *AHG*, xvi, 102-4; PRO E364/67, m. 4-4d (Angevin), E101/188/6 (6), E28/42 (16); Vale (1970), 96-8; *PPC*, iii, 170. Bazadais: Héraut Berry, *Chron.*, 107; *Foed.*, x, 806-7.
3. *AHG*, xvi, 307-13, esp. 309; *Ord.*, xvi, 388-92; Sumption, iv, 138-40; *Flourac, 290-5. Truces: Vale (1970), 188-91, 193-6; Samaran (1907), 61-3. For the position in 1438: *Foed.*, x, 543, 673-4; *Flourac, 290-5.
4. Villandrando: PRO E364/75, m. 4-5d (Colles); PRO E101/192/9 (25) (Jan. 1438); PRO E101/192/9 (4, 6) (background, see Quicherat [1879], 145-51). Campaign of 1438: Vaissète, ix, 1129-32, *x, cols. 2142-4; BN Coll. Doat 217, fols. 48-50 (Albret's commission); Monstrelet, *Chron.*, v, 354-6; Bernis, 'Chron.', 457-8; 'Petite chron.', 65; *Coll. doc. Angleterre*, 258 (Tartas, numbers); *Quicherat (1879), 172-84, 313-16. Pay: BN PO 2356 (Poton Saintrailles)/15, 2608 (Saintrailles)/2. Bazas: *Foed.*, x, 806-7; PRO 01/192/8, fol. 22vo. Tonneins: PRO E101/191/9 (21). South: *Leseur, *Hist.*, ii, 288-90; *Foed.*, x, 704-5; Courteault, 52-8. Bordeaux funding: PRO 101/191/9 (21-23). Destruction: *AHG*, iii, 447; PRO C61129, m. 10; Boutruche (1963), 428-9; M. K. James, 56 (App. 3). Revenues: PRO E101/192/8, fols. 8vo-26vo.

5. *Chrons. London*, 145 (cf. Henry VI's itinerary in Wolffe [1981], 362); *PPC*, v, 108; PRO C61/129, mm. 16, 14; E403/734, m. 5 (19 May); E101/53/22, 23; 'Petite chron.', 65–6. Gloucester's lands: Vale (1970), 99–103. His support is apparent from his later recriminations: *L&P*, ii, 448; *Foed.*, x, 765–6.
6. Campaigns: PRO E28/65 (47); 'Petite chron.', 65–6; PRO C61/130, m. 20; *Coll. doc. Angleterre*, 258–9; *Foed.*, x, 850 (confirming the year). Recall: *Foed.*, x, 765; PRO C61/130, mm. 15, 14, 13, 11, 8. Rempston: Vale (1970), 23.
7. *Coll. doc. Angleterre*, 258–9; *Comptes Riscle*, 6 (the editors wrongly suggest a date in 1441); AD Pyr.-Atl. E229/12 (agreement); *Escouchy, *Chron.*, iii, 45; Monstrelet, *Chron.*, vi, 25.
8. Samaran (1907), 72–8, *373–4; Bekynton, *Corr.*, ii, 206; *PPC*, v, 161. Armagnac embassy: PRO C76/123, m. 7; PRO E364/76, m. 1 (Pury), E403/745, m. 4.
9. Rempston: Monstrelet, *Chron.*, vi, 51; PRO E101/193/9 (6). Charles VII: Vaissète, ix, 1143–4; Gruel, *Chron.*, 173; Monstrelet, *Chron.*, vi, 51–2; Bekynton, *Corr.*, ii, 178, 180, 181. Reports: 'Compte Bordeaux', nos 51, 54. English reinforcements: PRO C76/124, m. 1; *Foed.*, xi, 7–8; Bekynton, *Corr.*, ii, 181, 188, 216, 219; *PPC*, v, 193, 206.
10. Monstrelet, *Chron.*, vi, 51–4, 55; Gruel, *Chron.*, 173–7; Héraut Berry, *Chron.*, 247–9, 251–3; *Chron. Mont-St-M.*, i, 42; *L&P*, ii, 465. Bekynton, *Corr.*, ii, 196.
11. Bekynton, *Corr.*, ii, 186–93, 196–7, 246; *Fasti*, xiii, 208.
12. Charles VII: itinerary in Beaucourt, iii, 244 n.4; Vaissète, ix, 1145; Gruel, *Chron.*, 179–80; Monstrelet, *Chron.*, vi, 56. Counterattack: Bekynton, *Corr.*, ii, 246–7; Héraut Berry, *Chron.*, 257.
13. Council: PRO E404/58 (172, 173); *PPC*, v, 197–9. Loans: Steel, 218–19; *PPC*, v, 199; *PPC*, v, 201, 202; *L&P*, ii, 465–6; Kleineke, 22. Hull: Bekynton, *Corr.*, ii, 216–17.
14. Bekynton, *Corr.*, ii, 215–16, 197–8, 200, 205–6, 219, 223, 224, 244–5. On Roos: PRO E101/44/30, m. 19 (1415), E101/51/2, m. 1 (1417), E101/53/33, m. 2 (1441); AN K64/12/7 (1437).
15. Bekynton, *Corr.*, ii, 206, 228, 247–8; PRO E364/84, m. 3–4d (Hull); Héraut Berry, *Chron.*, 256–9; Monstrelet, *Chron.*, vi, 56–7; 'Petite chron.', 66.
16. Vale (1970), 206–15; Vale (1969), 120–1.
17. Albret: Héraut Berry, *Chron.*, 257; Bernis, 'Chron.', 460. Armagnac: Bekynton, *Corr.*, ii, 193–5, 198–202, 206–12, 220, 224–7, 230–1, 241, 243; Héraut Berry, *Chron.*, 264–6, 439–40; Monstrelet, *Chron.*, vi, 82–3; Escouchy, *Chron.*, i, 61–7; Samaran (1907), 93–8.
18. PRO E101/71/4 (914); Bekynton, *Corr.*, v, 239; *PPC*, v, 233; *CPR 1441–6*, 424.
19. *PPC*, v, 223–4, 229, 415–17, 240, 259–60, 261–2; Bekynton, *Corr.*, ii, 240–1, 244. Cash receipts: Steel, 219–20.
20. *PPC*, v, 226–7, 233, 234–5, 236, 237, 251–6, 259–64; *M. K. Jones (1983), 344–58, esp. arts. 5, 6, 7, 8, 11, 14–15; E101/71/4 (916) (numbers); PRO E101/71/4 (916); Johnson, 56–7; PRO E101/71/4 (916) (rates). Investiture: *English Chron.*, 64.
21. Explanation: *M. K. Jones (1983), 346 (art. 5). Property: M. K. Jones (1983), 342–3 *344–58 (art. 22); BN Fr. n.a. 3642/804; *PPC*, v, 252, 255. Cardinal: Harriss (1988), 338–40, 406. Advances: PRO E403/747, m. 15 (6 Apr.), E403/749, mm. 12, 20–1 (6, 26 July). Shipping costs: PRO E101/54/4, E403/749, mm. 11, 12, 14–15, 17 (6 July).
22. Thielemans (1966), 146; *Foed.*, xi, 13–14; Moleyns: *ODNB*, xxxviii, 536–7; *Giles's Chron.*, iv, 33; R. Weiss (1967), 80–3.
23. Champion (1969), 337–8, 674; Saint-Paul, *Chron.*, 56–7; PRO E403/747, m. 13 (9 Mar.) (herald).
24. Beaucourt, iii, 265; *PPC*, vi, 11–12; *Preuves Bretagne*, ii, cols. 1360, 1371; *PPC*, vi, 17, 22.

25. Numbers: PRO E403/749, m. 12 (6 July); *Brut*, ii, 484; *PPC*, v, 303-4, 409-14; *CPR 1441-6*, 202. In Normandy: AN K68/19; *Foed. Supp. D*, 506; *Inventaire Surreau*, 93; Gruel, *Chron.*, 182; *Chron. Mont-St-M.*, ii, 157-8; AN Coll. Lenoir, ix, 286. Inquiry: BN Fr. 23189, fol. 17; M. K. Jones (1988), 462-3. Somerset's captaincies: M. K. Jones (1983), 363. Carts: *Chron. Mont-St-M.*, ii, 157-8.
26. *Ord.*, xiii, 372, 378, 384, 386, 388; Chartier, *Chron.*, ii, 38-42; *Inv. AC Amiens*, iv, 166, 169; Monstrelet, *Chron.*, vi, 60-1, 67, 77-80; Héraut Berry, *Chron.*, 263-4; BN Fr. 26071/4844, 4847; AD Seine-Mar. 100J27/10, 31/3 (reinforcements); Waurin, *Cron.*, iv, 379-84; Basin, *Hist.*, i, 286-8.
27. Basin, *Hist.*, i, 280-2; Artillery: *M. K. Jones (1983), 344-58, esp. art. 8; PRO E403/747, m. 14 (2 Apr.); *CPR 1441-6*, 199. Ch.-Gontier: Gruel, *Chron.*, 181-2; Héraut Berry, *Chron.*, 263-4; Le Baud, *Comp.*, 511; Bourdigné, *Chron.*, ii, 191. Panic: BN Fr. 32511, fol. 85 (distribution of artillery to Loire towns); AC Tours BB8, fols. 260, 275.
28. La Guerche: Le Baud, *Comp.*, 511-12; M. K. Jones (1983), 177-8; *PPC*, vi, 13-18. End of campaign: AC Tours BB18, fol. 269; *Foed. Supp. D*, 505-6; *L&P*, ii, 347-9; Monstrelet, *Chron.*, vi, 67; BL Add. MS 11542, fol. 29; Benet, 'Chron.', 190. Brigandage: PRO E404/60 (253); BN PO 2411 (Queniret)/5.
29. Basin, *Hist.*, i, 284; Héraut Berry, *Chron.*, 264; Benet, 'Chron.', 190; *Giles's Chron.*, iv, 31; *English Chron.*, 64; *Cal. Inq. P. M.*, xxvi, no. 178; 'Hist. Croyland', 519 (suicide). Exchequer: M. K. Jones (1983), 182-5; M. K. Jones (1988), 465-7.
30. *PPC*, iv, 128, 150-1, 181; *Preuves Bretagne*, ii, cols. 1327, 1361; *Foed.*, xi, 48-9, 52; *PPC*, vi, 9-11, 13-16, 20-1.
31. *Preuves Bretagne*, ii, col. 1362; Lydgate, 'A praise of peace' (ll. 180-4), *Minor Poems*, ii, 791.
32. *L&P*, i, 67-9; *PPC*, vi, 32-5 (misdated); *Foed.*, xi, 53, 60-1, 62-3; HMC, *Rep.*, iii, 280. On Wenlock: *HoC 1422-61*, 417-21.
33. Suffolk: PRO E101/324/9, 10; *L&P*, i, 67-9. French preparations: BN Fr. 24031/16; Beaucourt, iv, 387-8; *L&P*, i, 119, 243-4; HMC, *Rep.*, iii, 279. Somerset's army: PRO BN PO 2411 (Queniret)/5.
34. Oxford, Bodleian, MS Digby 196, fol. 155vo. Regnault: *Journ. B. Paris*, 372. On Brézé: Gruel, *Chron.*, 182-3; *Escouchy, *Chron.*, iii, 318; Chastellain, 'Chron.', iii, 347-8; cf. La Marche, *Mém.*, ii, 56. On Da Monte's role: Raynald, *Ann. Eccl.*, xxviii, 415-17 (An. 1444, ¶ 5); *Auctarium Chart. U. Paris*, ii, 521 n.1; *L&P*, i, 133-5.
35. *L&P*, i, 131-5, 151-2. Influential voices: Juvénal, *Écrits*, i, 393-5.
36. *Grands traités*, 154-71; Basin, *Hist.*, i, 290-6; *Lecoy (1875), i, 236-7, ii, 254-7; *L&P*, ii, 356-60; *Parl. Rolls*, xi, 411-12 [19].
37. *L&P*, i, 443-64; PRO E404/61 (32, 264); *Calmet, vi (Preuves), cols. clxx-clxxi; *Brut*, ii, 488-9; Benet, 'Chron.', 190-1; *Foed.*, xi, 76; *Brut*, ii, 488-9, 510; Kipling.
38. *Journ. B. Paris*, 372-4; Maupoint, 'Journ.', 30-1; Basin, *Hist.*, ii, 8-10; Escouchy, *Chron.*, i, 5-8; *Inv. livres couleur*, nos. 606, 607; C. L. Doyen, *Histoire de la ville de Beauvais*, i (1842), 90.
39. *Tuetey, i, 307-8n, ii, 151; Héraut Berry, *Chron.*, 267.
40. Tuetey, i, 151, 160-1, 371, *ii, 133, 140, 509-10, 516-17; *Frankfurts Reichskorr.*, ii, no. 79; Bueil, *Jouvencel*, i, 93 n.7, ii, 152-3; Tringant, 'Comm.', 294; Escouchy, *Chron.*, i, 11-12, 13-16; *Journ. B. Paris*, 374-5; *Parl. Rolls*, xii, 103-4 [46]; BN Fr. 32511, fol. 82vo, 84, 85 (French payments). On Blanchefort: 'Délib. Beauvais', 183, 192, 200, 204, 233-6; *Inv. AC Amiens*, ii, 49, 53, 54, iv, 134, 139; Monstrelet, *Chron.*, v, 38-9.

41. *Tuetey, i, 177–97, 217–30, 236–9, 278–95, 309–24, 327–8, *ii, 301–80, 507–8, 519–20; *Escouchy, *Chron.*, iii, 19–21, 92–4; *Frankfurts Reichscorr.*, ii, no. 94; *Eidg. Abschiede*, ii, 181–2, 807–11; *Königshoven, *Chron.*, 955–6, 1016.
42. BN Fr. 32511, fols. 80–85ᵛᵒ. John of Anjou: *Calmet, vi (Preuves), cols. clxxi–clxxiii; Marot, 119–35. 'Like Paris': Duhamel, 94.
43. Tuetey, i, 330–5, *ii, 32–9, 520–1.
44. Gough: AC Lisieux, CC17, fol. 144. Men living on the land: AD Calvados, F1378/3; AN K68/12 (14); BN Fr. n.a. 1482/169; BN Fr. 26073/5158, 5164, 5167, 5264, 5270, 5299; BL Add. Chart. 8019; BL Add. Chart. 4006, 6973; *Beaurepaire (1859)[2], 189–92; *Chron. Mont-St-M.*, ii, 184–5.
45. Garrisons: Basin, *Hist.*, ii, 52–6; Burney, 202–4; PRO E28/60 (N. march); BN Fr. 26076/5689 (Domfront). Le Mans: Héraut Berry, *Chron.*, 294–5; Chartier, *Chron.*, ii, 79–80; *Escouchy, *Chron.*, iii, 158–60; BL Add. Chart. 4015. Camoys: BN Fr. 25778/1804, 26076/5716, 26077/5804; BL MS Egerton Charters 207. Conferences: *L&P*, i, 171–7; *Cartul. Louviers*, ii², 159–60; AN J647/20.
46. *Vaissète, xii, cols. 9–12; *Cosneau (1886), 609–12; Escouchy, *Chron.*, i, 51–60; Basin, *Hist.*, ii, 16–18. Cash payments: BN Fr. 21427/10, 38; Thomas (1879), i, 152–62; Solon, 93–4.
47. Contamine (1972), 278–94, 399–404, 411–16, 596–7. Payment: BN Fr. 21427/10; Basin, *Hist.*, ii, 18–20; *Cosneau (1886), 614–16. Contemporary opinion: Escouchy, *Chron.*, 59; Chastellain, 'Chron.', ii, 184–5; 'Livre des trahisons', 218; Germain, *Liber*, 66; *Chron. Martiniane*, 57 (Chabannes).
48. HMC, *Rep.*, iii, 279–80; *RDP*, v, 251; *Parl. Rolls*, xi, 410, 411–12 [18, 19]; *Brut*, ii, 511. Public criticism: I. M. W. Harvey (1991), 33–4; Virgoe (1964), xv–xvi.
49. Lecoy (1875), ii, 258–9.
50. Suffolk's warning: *Parl. Rolls*, xi, 412 [19]. Troops: PRO E404/60 (126); Curry (1985), i, 201 (Table V), 310, 315–18, 328–9, ii, xiii, xx (App. II). Repairs: 'Doc. negotiations', 141; BL Add. Chart. 12658. Finance: Harriss (1986), 143–52; Beaurepaire (1859)[2], 83–100; Allmand (1983), 182–6; Curry (1988)[2], 151–3; HMC, *Rep.*, iii, 180 (quotation).
51. Jurkowski et al., 96–100; Harriss (1986), 152–66; *Parl. Rolls*, xii, 106–7 [53].
52. See, generally, Griffiths (1981), Ch. 7, 20. *Paston Letters*, i, 236 (quote).
53. Myers (1938), 399, 402–4; *Parl. Rolls*, xii, 147 [56], and cf. [55].
54. Watts (1996), 242–3; Griffiths (1981), 284–6; Baldwin, 190–2. Ayscough: *ODNB*, i, 524–5. Stafford: Rawcliffe, 19–21, 109, 114–15. Beaumont: *ODNB*, iv, 663–5. On Suffolk's relations with the Queen: Dunn, 133–8.
55. Value of Maine: McFarlane (1957)[1], 104; Massey (1987), 355–9; *Denifle (1897–9), i, 107–15. Ch. of Anjou: Lecoy (1875), i, 131–2, *ii, 258–9; HMC, *Rep.*, iii, 280.
56. *Foed.*, xi, 86–7; *L&P*, i, 89–91, 97–102, 155–7. On Précigny: *Escouchy, *Chron.*, iii, 318.
57. *L&P*, i, 103–23, 157–9.
58. *L&P*, i, 128–48. Commynes, *Mém.*, i, 131.
59. Henry VI: *L&P*, i, 145; *Parl. Rolls*, xi, 471 [23]; *Foed.*, xi, 172–4. Moleyns: BN Fr. 18442, fol. 173; BN Coll. Moreau 706, fol. 237–239ᵛᵒ; *Foed.*, xi, 97–100, 101–3; BN Fr. 18442, fol. 173; Héraut Berry, *Chron.*, 275.
60. Gruel, *Chron.*, 187; Escouchy, *Chron.*, i, 68–9; Beaucourt, iii, 291–3, iv, 101–4. Cf Gaussin, 105, 110 for disappearances from council.
61. *Parl. Rolls*, xi, 398 [11]; BN Fr. 26067/4117 (York's return); *L&P*, i, 161–2, 166–7; *Foed.*, xi, 101–3; *Lecoy (1875), 258–9.
62. *Foed.*, xi, 108–14, 122, 172–4; *L&P*, ii, 639–42.

REFERENCES TO PAGES 640–654

63. BN Fr. 26075/5486 (reappointment); *John Vale's Book*, 180–2; Whethamstede, *Reg.*, i, 160; Basin, *Hist.*, ii, 64–6; PRO E404/63 (11) (Mqs. Dorset). Hoo: BN Fr. n.a. 1482/179; Curry (1985), 324–30.
64. La Borderie, iv, 315; *Cartul. Rays*, i, 203–10, 228–36, 256–7; *Preuves Bretagne*, ii, cols. 1362, 1380, 1407–8; Le Baud, *Comp.*, 513.
65. *Preuves Bretagne*, ii, 1380–1, 1382, 1386–8, 1391–2, 1398, 1400–1; PRO E403/759, m. 6 (16 Nov.) (herald); Le Baud, *Comp.*, 513–14. Gilles's fortresses: La Borderie iv, 319.
66. Lecoy (1875), ii, 256; *Grands traités*, 163; *Preuves Bretagne*, ii, 1373, 1399–1404, 1407–8; *Cartul. Rays*, i, 227–8; Le Baud, *Comp.*, 513–14; Gruel, *Chron.*, 191–3; Héraut Berry, *Chron.*, 277; Escouchy, *Chron.*, i, 97–8.
67. *Foed.*, xi, 138–9, 152–3; Chaplais, *Dipl. Practice*, 810; *Escouchy, *Chron.*, iii, 158–61; BN Clair. 307, pp. 57–61.
68. *Foed.*, xi, 172–4; HMC, *Rep.*, iii, 280. York: Johnson, 47–8, 70; Massey (1987), 170–1. Appanage: Baume (1991), 39–40, 41–3. Gloucester: Whethamstede, *Reg.*, i, 178–9; *English Chron.*, 65–6; Benet, 'Chron.', 192; *Foed.*, xi, 178–9.
69. *English Chron.*, 65. Cf. *Parl. Rolls*, xii, 104 [47]; *Rot. Parl.*, v, 226, 335; CCR 1441–7, 417–18, 453–5, 465–6; PRO C81/1370/41 (venues); *Brut*, ii, 513.
70. *English Chron.* (Davies), 116–18; *Brut*, ii, 512–13; Gregory, 'Chron.', 188; *English Chron.*, 65–6; Benet, 'Chron.', 192–3; Bale, 'Chron.', 121–2; *Chrons. London*, 157–8.
71. *Foed.*, xi, 151–5, 160–2, 163–8; PRO E30/509. Curiosity: BN Fr. 32511, fol. 114vo.
72. Benet, 'Chron.', 193; *Foed.*, xi, 172–4, 175–6; *Paston Letters (G)*, i, 107–8; *L&P*, ii, 684–5.
73. Embassy: *L&P*, ii, 638–43, 693, 696–9, 700–2; *Foed.*, xi, 182–4, xi, 193 (reciting truce). Council, attendance: M. K. Jones (1983), 199. York: PRO E101/71/4 (920, 921); Gregory, 'Chron.', 189, 195. Cf. *Kingsford (1913), 360–1.
74. *L&P*, ii, 598–603, 692–6, 704–10. Compensation: *Paston Letters (G)*, i, 107–8; BN Fr. 26077/5834; BL Add. MSS 11509, fols.20–20vo. On Mundeford: *ODNB*, xxxix, 746–7.
75. *Foed.*, xi, 189–91, 193 (reciting extension); *L&P*, ii, 714–15 (art. 5). Ambassadors' other missions: PRO E101/323/14, 15.
76. *L&P*, ii, 361–8, 634–92.
77. *L&P*, i, 198–206, ii, 710–17; *Escouchy, *Chron.*, iii, 175–8, 181–3; *Planchenault (1923), 198–202; Héraut Berry, *Chron.*, 282; *Foed.*, xi, 196–7.
78. *Escouchy, *Chron.*, iii, 183–92; Héraut Berry, *Chron.*, 281–2; *Foed.*, xi, 204–6.
79. Panic: *L&P*, i, 482–3; E403/769, m. 14 (20 Feb.). Embassy: *L&P*, i, 204, 207–8, ii, 717–18; Héraut Berry, *Chron.*, 282; *Foed.*, xi, 198–204, 206–11. Le Mans: Chronicle of St Vincent du Mans, cited in *Planchenault (1923), 195 n.3; Héraut Berry, *Chron.*, 282–3. Troops stood down: PRO E404/64 (146). Dukedom: *RDP*, v, 259–60.
80. *Ord.*, xiv, 1–5; Contamine (1972), 305, 313–15; Bonnault, 14; *Parl. Rolls*, xii, 54 [17].
81. Dubled, 557–60, 567–8, 578–80; Borrelli, iii, 358–63; Hall, 115, 118–22; 'Recouvrement', 372–4; Chartier, *Chron.*, ii, 178
82. *Ord.*, xiii, 372–7, 414–20, 428–30, 444–52, 516–18; *Doc. admin. financière*, xiv-xvi, 13–16; Borrelli, iii, 579–80; Beaucourt, iii, 472, iv, 431.
83. Basin, *Hist.*, ii, 66; PRO C76/130, mm. 14, 8; BL Add. MS 11509, fols. 39vo–40; PRO E404/64 (117); *CPR* 1446–52, 130–1. Reception: Beaurepaire (1859)[2], 99; M. K. Jones (1983), 218–19.

84. M. K. Jones (1989)[2], 116–18; M. K. Jones (1983), 209–10, 213–14, 222–5; *Paston Letters (G)*, i, 105. Finance: Beaurepaire (1859)[2], 98–9; *Parl. Rolls*, xii, 55 [17]; PRO E404/63 (11).
85. *Parl. Rolls*, xii, 54–5 [17] (the date is fixed by Boulers's statement that the truce had fourteen months to run).

CHAPTER XIII: *The Death of Lancastrian Normandy, 1449–1450*

1. Blondel, 'Reduct. Norm.', 7–9; Héraut Berry, *Chron.*, 288; Chartier, *Chron.*, ii, 60–3; 'Recouvrement', 239–40; Basin, *Hist.*, ii, 70–4; *Preuves Bretagne*, ii, cols. 1467, 1475.
2. *Basin, *Hist. (Q)*, iv, 320–1; *Preuves Bretagne*, ii, cols. 1397–8, 1412–27, 1438–9, 1478 (para. 18); *L&P*, i, 280–1.
3. *Preuves Bretagne*, ii, cols. 1430–6, 1439–41; *L&P*, i, 263; *Beaucourt, v, 439.
4. *Chron. Mont-St-M.*, i, 262, ii, 209; *Escouchy, *Chron.*, iii, 132–3; BL Add. MS 11509, fol. 107 (military refugees); Beaucourt, iv, 311 (Mortain); *L&P*, i, 211–14.
5. *L&P*, i, 275–91; *Basin, *Hist. (Q)*, iv, 293–310, 312–14, 338–41. Loot: BL Add. MS 11509, fols. 70vo, 82–82vo; *L&P*, ii, 718.
6. Blondel, 'Reduct. Norm.', 22–5; *Escouchy, *Chron.*, iii, 250–1; *Basin, *Hist. (Q)*, iv, 326; *L&P*, i, 296; 'Recouvrement', 242–4; *Preuves Bretagne*, ii, col. 1485; Héraut Berry, *Chron.*, 288; Chartier, *Chron.*, ii, 61–2.
7. *Preuves Bretagne*, ii, cols. 1467, 1485, 1487; Escouchy, *Chron.*, i, 160–2, *iii, 231–3; BL Add. MS 11508, fols. 46, 49.
8. *Preuves Bretagne*, ii, cols. 1456, 1475, 1476–7; BL Add. MS 11509, fols. 24; Blondel, 'Reduct. Norm.', 84 (quote); Escouchy, *Chron.*, i, 163–6, *iii, 365–6; Héraut Berry, *Chron.*, 290–2; Chartier, *Chron.*, ii, 69–71; 'Recouvrement', 245–50; Blondel, 'Reduct. Norm.', 26–30, 33; *Cron. Norm.*, 102–5; Basin, *Hist.*, ii, 82–6.
9. Estates: BN Fr. n.a. 1482/191, 192; BL Add. Chart. 4064; BN Fr. 6200/119. Attacks: Basin, *Hist.*, ii, 82–4; Blondel, 'Reduct. Norm.', 30–7, 80–2; Héraut Berry, *Chron.*, 292–3, 298–9; Chartier, *Chron.*, ii, 74–5; *Beaucourt, v, 439; Gruel, *Chron.*, 197–8; Escouchy, *Chron.*, i, 173.
10. *Preuves Bretagne*, ii, cols. 1451–10, 1474, 1492–7, 1501–6; Escouchy, *Chron.*, i, 162–3. Division of loot: *Basin, *Hist. (Q)*, iv, 325.
11. *Beaucourt, v, 439–40; Héraut Berry, *Chron.*, 295–6; Chartier, *Chron.*, ii, 80–2; 'Recouvrement', 257–9; Blondel, 'Reduct. Norm.', 55–9.
12. *Escouchy, *Chron.*, iii, 245–51.
13. Waurin, *Cron.*, v, 127; *L&P*, ii, 719–20; *Preuves Bretagne*, ii, cols. 1466, 1451–4; *Escouchy, *Chron.*, iii, 249–50; Worcester, *Boke of Noblesse*, 5.
14. Border: *CPR 1446–52*, 228; *PPC*, vi, 65–6; *Cal. Doc. Scot.*, v, no. 1059; Bale, 'Chron.', 123–4; *Auchinleck Chron.*, 18–19, 27, 39; *Foed.*, xi, 232. 'Auld alliance': BN Lat. 10187/10; AN J678/28, J1039; 'Rôles de dépenses', 127–9.
15. *Parl. Rolls*, xii, 45–7 [11, 13]; PRO E404/65 (126, 130); E403/773, mm. 15–16 (7 Apr.); *Myers (1978), 82; Myers (1938), 402–4; Bale, 'Chron.', 125.
16. *L&P*, ii, 723–30.
17. Subsidy: PRO E403/775, m. 9 (29 July) (subsidy). Loans: PRO E401/810, mm. 12–13 (21–29 July); E404/65 (221, 223, 249); *PPC*, v, 86–7; *CPR 1446–52*, 268. Recruitment: BL Add. MS 11509, fol. 61vo; PRO E101/54/11; E404/65 (225), E404/66 (12–22, 27).
18. Dunois: *Ord.*, xiv, 59–61; *Vallet de Viriville (1862–3), iii, 167n. Eure: Héraut Berry, *Chron.*, 296; Chartier, *Chron.*, ii, 83, 85–6 (2,500 men at Evreux on 8 Aug. and 800 men under Florent d'Illiers at Verneuil on the same date). Picardy, Caux: Blondel, 'Reduct. Norm.', 70; *Beaucourt, iv, 440–1; Héraut Berry, *Chron.*, 297; Escouchy,

Chron., i, 188–9, 190. Alençon: Chartier, *Chron.*, ii, 174–5; 'Recouvrement', 263. Brittany: Héraut Berry, *Chron.*, 304–5; Chartier, *Chron.*, ii, 122–3.
19. BL Add. MS 11509, fol. 76vo (Talbot's movements); *Beaucourt, v, 440–1; Héraut Berry, *Chron.*, 296–7; Chartier, *Chron.*, ii, 82–3, 92, 93; 'Recouvrement', 260–1; Blondel, 'Reduct. Norm.', 61–5; Basin, *Hist.*, ii, 88–90; Escouchy, *Chron.*, i, 190 (attempt on Rouen).
20. *Beaucourt, v, 441–2; Basin, *Hist.*, ii, 92–4; *Escouchy, *Chron.*, iii, 354–8; Blondel, 'Reduct. Norm.', 69–5; Héraut Berry, *Chron.*, 297–8; Chartier, *Chron.*, ii, 86–7; Basin, *Hist.*, ii, 94; BL Add. MS 11509, fols. 76vo–77; Bueil, *Jouvencel*, ii, 147–8; *Paston Letters (G)*, i, 105.
21. BN Fr. 26079/6146; *Beaucourt, v, 442; *L&P*, ii, 620–1; Blondel, 'Reduct. Norm.', 76–9; Basin, *Hist.*, ii, 96–104; 'Recouvrement', 266–7; *Ord.*, xiv, 61–4; Héraut Berry, *Chron.*, 299–300. Basin French councillor: *Basin, *Hist. (Q)*, iv, 191–2.
22. Basin, *Hist.*, ii, 104–10. Chartres: AC Mantes BB5, fol. 27.
23. AC Mantes BB5, fols. 27–28vo; *Beaucourt, v, 442–4; Héraut Berry, *Chron.*, 301–2, 305–6; Chartier, *Chron.*, ii, 95–101, 103–8, 116–19 (calling him John Howell); Blondel, 'Reduct. Norm.', 85–7, 89–91, 95; BN Fr. 20585, fol. 32 (Vernon); 'Recouvrement', 277; BL Add. Chart. 4069.
24. Basin, *Hist.*, ii, 90–4; AC Mantes BB5, fols. 27vo–28.
25. Héraut Berry, *Chron.*, 303, 311–13; Chartier, *Chron.*, ii, 116, 119–21, 177; *Beaucourt, v, 442–3; Blondel, 'Reduct. Norm.', 91–2; Escouchy, *Chron.*, i, 197; 'Recouvrement', 271–2, 290–1.
26. *Preuves Bretagne*, ii, col. 1513; *Beaucourt, v, 443, 444; Héraut Berry, *Chron.*, 304–5; Chartier, *Chron.*, 122–6; *Chron. Mont-St-M.*, i, 47–52, *226; Escouchy, *Chron.*, i, 199–204; Blondel, 'Reduct. Norm.', 97–122.
27. Chave, 149–55; Héraut Berry, *Chron.*, 306, 308–9; Chartier, *Chron.*, ii, 121, 126–7, 131–2; Escouchy, *Chron.*, i, 206, 209–10; *Beaucourt, v, 443–4.
28. Suffolk: Watts (1996), 242–6; Bale, 'Chron.', 125. Council: PRO E403/773, m. 8 (29 July); Benet, 'Chron.', 196. Army: PRO E404/66 (12–22, 28); E101/71/3 (924–7); *CPR 1446–52*, 317; *CPR 1446–52*, 317–18. Lumley: Harriss (1986), 169. Parliament: *CCR 1447–54*, 160–2. Loans: *CPR 1446–52*, 297–9; Bale, 'Chron.', 126; Griffiths (1981), 391, 399 n.81; Steel, 233; PRO E403/777, mm. 3–4 (7 Nov.).
29. *Beaucourt, v, 444; AN Coll. Lenoir xxviii, 205 (defeated garrisons); Escouchy, *Chron.*, i, 211–14, *iii, 383 (contact with French); Basin, *Hist.*, ii, 116; Héraut Berry, *Chron.*, 313–14; Chartier, *Chron.*, ii, 137–40; Blondel, 'Reduct. Norm.', 130–33; 'Annales angl.', 765; 'Recouvrement', 292–3; Topography: see plan in Sumption, iv, 585.
30. Héraut Berry, *Chron.*, 314–16; Chartier, *Chron.*, ii, 140–3; Blondel, 'Reduct. Norm.', 133–8; Basin, *Hist.*, ii, 116–18; Waurin, *Cron.*, v, 140–1; 'Recouvrement', 293–6; Escouchy, *Chron.*, i, 214–17, *iii, 385 (Monypenny).
31. Héraut Berry, *Chron.*, 316–21; Beaurepaire (1880–3), 351–4; Chartier, *Chron.*, ii, 144–57; *Siège de Rouen*, 4–14; BN Fr. 4054, fols. 140vo, 150vo–151; Escouchy, *Chron.*, i, 219–20, *iii, 358–64; Basin, *Hist.*, ii, 118–24; Blondel. 'Reduct. Norm.', 143–52. On Roussel: *Fasti*, ii, 127–9; *Proc. C*, ii, 422.
32. *Paston Letters (G)*, i, 105–6.
33. Héraut Berry, *Chron.*, 322–8; Chartier, *Chron.*, ii, 60–71, 158–9; Blondel, 'Reduct. Norm.', 156–63; 'Recouvrement', 309–20.
34. Le Crotoy: Huguet, 364–71; PRO C76/132, m. 7; E403/777, m. 1 (1 Oct.) (reinforcement). Gisors: BL Add. MS 11509, fols. 5vo, 10vo–11; Héraut Berry, *Chron.*, 310–1; Chartier, *Chron.*, ii, 135–6, 159; Escouchy, *Chron.*, i, 210; BN Clair. 152/80. On Merbury: PRO E101/50/1, m. 1 (service in 1421); AN JJ162/362, 175/225, 231 and

BN Fr. 26284/250 (lands); *Gall. Reg.*, vi, no. 22527. His son: Escouchy, *Chron.*, i, 210, *iii, 380, 387; BN Clair. 123/539,

35. Chartier, *Chron.*, ii, 102–3, 172–4; *Escouchy, *Chron.*, iii, 374; *L&P*, i, 291–6; *Basin, *Hist. (Q)*, iv, 306; *Chron. Mont-St-M.*, i, 52–3; Héraut Berry *Chron.*, 329–30; Blondel, 'Reduct. Norm.', 155–6; Gruel, *Chron.*, 200–1; Bossuat (1936), 345 (payment, but I have not found the source for this), 346–75.

36. Héraut Berry, *Chron.*, 322–3; Chartier, *Chron.*, i, 171–2, 188. 'Retard': *Paston Letters (G)*, i, 106.

37. Ch.-Gaillard: BL Add. MS 11509, fol. 5vo, 11; 'Recouvrement', 322; Héraut Berry, *Chron.*, 309–10, 330. On the Bastard of Somerset: Marshall, 111–12. Harfleur: Héraut Berry, *Chron.*, 328–9; Chartier, *Chron.*, ii, 176–80; Blondel, 'Reduct. Norm.', 163–5; 'Recouvrement', 322–4.

38. Expedition: 'Annales angl.', 765; PRO E404/66 (92), E28.79 (63). Numbers: PRO E403/777, mm. 3–4. On Kyriel: *HoC 1422–61*, v, 138–40; Marshall, 138–9, 290–4. Advances: PRO E403/777, mm. 3–4 (7 Nov.). Resumption: *Parl. Rolls*, xii, 77; Whethamstede, *Reg.*, i, 248–9; Wolffe (1958), 593.

39. Parliament: *Parl. Rolls*, xii, 147–9 [56]; 'Annales angl.', 766. On Tailboys: Virgoe (1964), 321–5. Moleyns: *Foed.*, xi, 255–6.

40. Troops: Bale, 'Chron.', 128. Loans: Steel, 233; PRO E403/777, m. 6 (11 Dec.); *Foed.*, xi, 259; Virgoe (1964), 187–8. Anger: *Giles's Chron.*, iv, 38; *Political Poems*, ii, 230 (quote). Moleyns: Benet, 'Chron.', 196; *English Chron.*, 67; 'Annales angl.', 766; Aeneas Silvius Piccolomini, 'De Europa', in *Opera* (1551), 443; *John Vale's Book*, 186–7. Plots: I. M. W. Harvey (1991), 64–7; Virgoe (1964), *192–3, 195–201, 199–201. Handbills etc: *Political Poems*, ii, 221–42.

41. Tensions: PRO PSO1/17 (876, 879); Bale, 'Chron.', 127; City of London Journal, cited in Virgoe (1964), 194. Parlt: *Parl. Rolls*, xii, 83, 92–4 [10, 14–17]; *Political Poems*, ii, 224 ('fox').

42. *Parl. Rolls*, xii, 94–5 [18–49]; HMC, *Rep.*, iii, 179–80; 'Annales angl.', 766.

43. *Parl. Rolls*, xii, 83–4, 105–6 [11, 50–2]; 'Annales angl.', 767; Benet, 'Chron.', 198; Bale, 'Chron.', 129; *CPR 1446–52*, 320; *L&P*, i, 515–16; Virgoe (1964), 202.

44. Tax: Gascoigne, *Loci*, 189–90; *Political Poems*, ii, 230; *Parl. Rolls*, xii, 43 [8], 47 [13]; PRO E401/814 (19 Nov. ff.) (substantial receipts in Feb. and early March). Army: PRO E403/777, mm. 3–4, 12, 13–14 (7 Nov., 9 Mar.); E28/79 (63).

45. Héraut Berry, *Chron.*, 331–3; Chartier, *Chron.*, ii, 174–6, 188–9; 'Recouvrement', 327–8; *Chron. Mont-St-M.*, i, 55. Finance: BN Fr. 26079/6185; BN Fr. 6200/119; *Hunger (1912), PJ nos. 38, 45–7.

46. Blondel, 'Reduct. Norm.', 230–1; *L&P*, ii, 630–1.

47. Beaucourt, v, 338, 341–2; BN Fr. 6200/119; *Caillet (1909)[2], 501; *Cosneau (1886), 626–8; 'Doc. Prégent de Coëtivy', 54–5. Kyriel: BN Fr. n.a. 7630, fols. 255–1577vo.

48. *Chron. Mont-St-M.*, ii, 225–6; Héraut Berry, *Chron.*, 333; Chartier, *Chron.*, ii, 189–90; *Triger (1886), 168–9; Escouchy, *Chron.*, i, 278–9, 285; Basin, *Hist.*, ii, 136–8; Blondel, 'Reduct. Norm.', 176–7.

49. *Chron. Mont-St-M.*, i, 56, *ii, 225–6; Héraut Berry, *Chron.*, 333–4; Chartier, *Chron.*, ii, 191–2; Escouchy, *Chron.*, i, 276–8, 285; Basin, *Hist.*, ii, 136; Blondel, 'Reduct. Norm.', 171–7. On Entwhistle: *Chron. Mont-St-M.*, i, *20, 49, 169–70; Allmand (1983), 66–8. Criticisms: *L&P*, ii, 595. Clermont's numbers: Callu-Turiaf, 'Documents', 278. Richemont: Escouchy, *Chron.*, i, 279–80; Gruel, *Chron.*, 203–4; Chartier *Chron.*, ii, 195 (his numbers).

50. Callu-Turiaf, 'Documents', 277–8; *Chron. Mont-St-M.êe*, i, 56; Héraut Berry, *Chron.*, 335; Chartier, *Chron.*, ii, 193; Blondel, 'Reduct. Norm.', 177–81; Gruel, *Chron.*, 204–5.

51. Older accounts must be revised in the light of documents published in 1966 by Callu-Turiaf, 'Documents', 278–80 (Coëtivy's report, written on the evening of the battle, and Charles VII's summary of Clermont's and Richemont's reports, now lost save for fragments at *Delisle (1867), i, 273 n.2); *Preuves Bretagne*, ii, col. 1521 (Coëtivy's shorter report in a private letter); Héraut Berry, *Chron.*, 335–8; Chartier, *Chron.*, ii, 193–200; Escouchy, *Chron.*, i, 282–6; Gruel, *Chron.*, 205–8; Basin, *Hist.*, ii, 138–42; Blondel, 'Reduct. Norm.', 186–92; 'Recouvrement', 333–8; H. T. Evans, 60.
52. *Parl. Rolls*, xii, 83–7, 106–45 [11–12, 53]; *Paston Letters*, ii, 35–7; *CPR 1446–52*, 583; Virgoe (1982), 129.
53. *Paston Letters*, ii, 35–6; *Virgoe (1965), 501–2. Cf. Bale, 'Chron.', 129; *English Chron.*, 71; Gregory, 'Chron.', 189–90; Benet, 'Chron.', 198; *Brut*, ii, 517. On the Nicholas: *CPR 1446–52*, 380, 470.
54. I. M. W. Harvey (1991), 75–80; *English Chron.*, 67–8.
55. *I. M. W. Harvey (1991), 186–91; *John Vale's Book*, 186–7.
56. Bale, 'Chron.', 131–2; Gregory, 'Chron.', 190–1; Benet, 'Chron.', 199; *English Chron.*, 68; 'Short English Chron.', 67; I. M. W. Harvey (1991), 84–6; Barron (1970), 485–93.
57. Ayscough: I. M. W. Harvey (1991), 121–5; Benet, 'Chron.', 199; *English Chron.*, 67. Gloucester: *Kingsford (1913), 355–6; London: Bale, 'Chron.', 132–3; Gregory, 'Chron.', 191–3; Benet, 'Chron.', 199–201; *English Chron.*, 69–70; 'Short English Chron.', 67–8; I. M. W. Harvey (1991), 91–3; Barron (1970), 493–518.
58. Gregory, 'Chron.', 193–4; Bale, 'Chron.', 133–4; Benet, 'Chron.', 201–2; 'Short English Chron.', 68; I. M. W. Harvey (1991), 95–100; Barron (1970), 522–30.
59. Gruel, *Chron.*, 208–10; *Preuves Bretagne*, ii, cols. 1445–6, 1520; 'Recouvrement', 340, 347, 350; Escouchy, *Chron.*, i, 278, 291–2, 311–12 (omits *ca.* 6,000 *francs-archers*); Chartier, *Chron.*, ii, 190, 201–4, 211–13, 215–17; Cosneau (1886), 635–6; Héraut Berry, *Chron.*, 338–42; *L&P*, ii, 626. On Chiswall: BN Clair. 152, p. 3779 (with correct version of his name); BN Fr. 25767/100, 2576, 7/139, 25769/470, 570, 25772/1041, 25774/1251, 25777/1758, 25778/1809; *Chron. Mont-St-M.*, i, 307; Poli (Preuves), nos. 1283, 1342, 1356. Cf. Contamine (1972), 313–14.
60. Héraut Berry, *Chron.*, 339–40; Chartier, *Chron.*, ii, 202, 204–11; Blondel, 'Reduct. Norm.', 228–30; Gregory, 'Chron.', 193. Defences: Neveux (1996), 45–7, 186.
61. *L&P*, ii, 595–7, 631–2; Chartier, *Chron.*, ii, 214–16, 219; Basin, *Hist.*, ii, 144, 148; Héraut Berry, *Chron.*, 342–4. 1430s works: R. Jones (1994), i, 179–80, 246–55, ii, 48–9. Population: J.-M. Laurence, 'La population de Caen, XIe–XVe siècles', *Annales de Normandie*, xlix (1999), 115 at 129–32.
62. Sortie plan: *Contamine (2015)[1], 44; *Valois (1888), 267; *L&P*, i, 334–6, 346–51. Fall of town: Héraut Berry, *Chron.*, 344–8; Chartier, *Chron.*, ii, 214–22; *L&P*, ii, 631–2; Escouchy, *Chron.*, i, 306–13; Basin, *Hist.*, ii, 142–8; Blondel, 'Reduct. Norm.', 233–9, 242–4. Terms: *Hunger (1912), PJ nos. 40–1. Mines, artillery: *Cosneau (1886), 636–7; *Hunger (1912), PJ no. 34–5, 43.
63. Escouchy, *Chron.*, i, 281, 286; Chastellain, *Oeuvres*, vii 92; Chartier, *Chron.*, ii, 167; Basin, *Hist.*, ii, 150–4; Dauvet, *Journ.*, 11, 20; Beaucourt, v, 429; Mollat (1988), Ch. 9.
64. Héraut Berry, *Chron.*, 348–51; Chartier, *Chron.*, ii, 223–8; Blondel, 'Reduct. Norm.', 248–52; *L&P*, ii, 633, 735–42. Defences of Domfront: Chave, 149–50.
65. *Cosneau (1886), 637–9; Héraut Berry, *Chron.*, 351–2; Chartier, *Chron.*, ii, 231–3; Gruel, *Chron.*, 213–14; 'Recouvrement', 361, 365–6; Blondel, 'Reduct. Norm.', 252, 254–9. Topography: Plaisse (1989), 23–45. Gower: *HoC 1422–61*, iv, 617–19. Lands: *Escouchy, *Chron.*, iii, 368. Garrison: Curry (1985), ii, p. xiv.

66. Rescue effort: PRO E404/67 (115, 201); *CPR 1446-52*, 388; *L&P*, i, 520-1; Benet, 'Chron.', 202. Surrender: *Cosneau (1886), 640-2; Delisle (1875), 213-17; *Paston Letters*, ii, 42. Gower's gift: Masson, 53.
67. Worcester, *Boke of Noblesse*, 48, 74 (cf. *L&P*, ii, 718-22); Héraut Berry, *Chron.*, 354-7; Waurin, *Cron.*, v, 162.
68. Ambühl (2019), 194-9.
69. *Doc. et recherches*, iii, 33-5, 67-9, iv, 28; *Proc. N.*, iii, 605-12; Vale (1974), 60-9.
70. Basin, *Hist.*, ii, 106; Désert, 108.
71. Boüard, 53; Prosser, 81-8, 128-45; *Allmand (1981), 155-7; *L&P*, i, 342; Masselin, *Journ.*, 554; 'Chronique des ducs d'Alençon', in *Proc. Alençon*, 206-7.
72. E. of Compiègne: *Ord.*, xiv, 102-6; Allmand (1976), 348-53, (1981), 151-2, *159 n.36; Prosser, 27-59. War losses: Massey (1987), 339-44; Deville, 205-7; Morandière, 381-2.
73. Allmand (1983), 80 n.119; BN Fr. 25767/218 (Martin); *CPR 1446-52*, 419; *Proc. Alençon*, 35-6, 103, 110 (Fermen).
74. PRO E404/66 (205), E404/67 (23, 32, 55), E28/80 (83); Bale, 'Chron.', 134-5; Benet, 'Chron.', 202. Caen: McFarlane (1973), 27.
75. Caudebec: M. Callias Bey et al., 280, 281, 284. Gower: *HoC 1422-61*, iv, 618-19. Gough: Gregory, 'Chron.', 193. James: PRO E101/51/2, m. 40; *CPR 1446-52*, 470. Catesby: *L&P*, ii, 633. Petition: Curry (2009), 212-13.
76. BL Add. MS 11509, fols. 20-20vo, 21vo-22; *Letters of Margaret of Anjou*, 119; M. K. Jones (1983), 214-16; *L&P*, ii, 598-603; cf. Marshall, 153.
77. Lenfant: *Escouchy, *Chron.*, iii, 200-1, 216-18, 232, 235, 237, 238, 244, 248; *Preuves Bretagne*, ii, 1461; *L&P*, i, 243; PRO E403/786, m. 1 (28 Oct.). Gallet: Favier (1974), 421; Allmand (1983), 145; *Basin, *Hist. (Q)*, iv, 341, 345; *L&P*, i, 249-50; PRO E404/67 (137); *Proc. Alençon*, 120-1, 131. Le Vulre: *Parl. Rolls*, xii, 185 [16]. Others: PRO E404/67 (138); PRO E403/779, m. 1 (16 Apr.); E404/67 (139).
78. *Parl. Rolls*, xii, 54-5 [17]; *Paston Letters*, ii, 41; *Foed.*, xi, 276. Public order: I. M. W. Harvey (1991), 120-1, 129-30, 133-51.
79. Writs: *CCR 1447-54*, 225-7. D. York: Johnson, 78; *Griffiths (1975), 203; *John Vale's Book*, 185-7, 189-90. For the sequence of York's 'bills' and Henry VI's replies, *ib.*, 186; Johnson, 104-5; Hicks (1999); I. M. W. Harvey (1991), 116-17; *Paston Letters*, ii, 47, 49-51, 55; Bale, 'Chron.', 137.
80. Bale, 'Chron.', 136-7; Benet, 'Chron.', 203; *Hanserecesse*, iii, 506-9, 511; *Parl. Rolls*, xii, 207-8).
81. Bale, 'Chron.', 137; *John Vale's Book*, 187-8; *Parl. Rolls*, xii, 184-6 [16]; *Kingsford (1913), 372; Johnson, 88-9; I. M. W. Harvey (1991), 91-2, 165.
82. Bale, 'Chron.', 137-8; Benet, 'Chron.', 203-4; Gregory, 'Chron.', 195-6 (quotation). Oldhall: *Kempe, 140-4.

CHAPTER XIV: *Gascony and Beyond, 1450–1453*

1. Cognac: Chartier, *Chron.*, ii, 74-5. Bonville: *CPR 1446-52*, 89, 138, 187, 191-2, 298, 380. Shorthose: PRO C61/124, m. 15; C61/125, m. 15; C61/134, m. 8; C61/132, m. 7; Tarneau, 'Chron.', 228. Spies: *Escouchy, *Chron.*, iii, 387; BN Fr. 32511, fol. 143.
2. Héraut Berry, *Chron.*, 306-8, 330-1; Chartier, *Chron.*, ii, 127-30, 186-7; Leseur, *Hist.*, i, 46-104, *52 n.2; PRO C61/140, m. 9; *Foed.*, xi, 243-4. Speaker: *Parl. Rolls*, viii, 354 [57]. Reinforcements: PRO E364/91, mm. 12-14 (Hull).

3. *Cartul. St-Seurin*, xxvii; Vale (1970), 141; PRO E403/779, m. 6 (12 June); E403/784, m. 14 (9 Aug.); C61/138, mm. 14, 12; Bale, 'Chron.', 157; *CPR 1446–52*, 389. Woodville: *ODNB*, lx, 227–8.
4. *CPR 1446–52*, 385, 389; PRO E404/67 (19); C61/138, mm. 15, 14, 13, 12, 11, 10, 9 (letters of protection). Anarchy: Cherry, 126–32; Storey (1966), 88–90. Tax: *Parl. Rolls*, xii, 173–5 [7]; *CCR 1447–54*, 252–3; *CFR 1445–52*, 207–8, 223–5; Virgoe (1982), 131–2, esp. 132 n.45; *Harrod, 75–6; Jurkowski et al., 102–3.
5. Normandy: Escouchy, *Chron.*, i, 317–18; BN Fr. 26080/6304–6, 6319; Boüard, 53. Penthièvre, Poton: Héraut Berry, *Chron.*, 353, 357–8; Chartier, *Chron.*, ii, 240–1; Escouchy, *Chron.*, i, 318, 322, *iii, 372. Le Boursier: BN PO 474 (Boursier); *Daumet (1898), 245–8.
6. Chartier, *Chron.*, ii, 241–3; PRO E364/91, mm. 12–14 (Hull); *Ord.*, xiv, 109–14; C61/138, m. 8 (grant to Louis Despoy); Escouchy, *Chron.*, i, 322–4; Héraut Berry, *Chron.*, 358–60; Chartier, *Chron.*, ii, 246–8; *AHG*, iii, 462.
7. News: *Hanserecesse*, iii, 511. Kent: I. M. W. Harvey (1991), 95; Gregory, 'Chron.', 196–7; Benet, 'Chron.', 205.
8. I. M. W. Harvey (1991), 95–6, 97–8; 'Annales angl.', 770; Benet, 'Chron.', 204–5; *Chrons. London* (Nicolas), 137; Kempe, 140.
9. Plymouth: Benet, 'Chron.', 205; *CPR 1446–52*, 414, 437, 438, 439, 444, 456–7, 472, 478, 515; Bale, 'Chron.', 157; PRO E159/230 (Hilary), m. 23d (riots). Borrowing: PRO E404/69 (68); Virgoe (1982), 132. Bidau: PRO E404/67 (135).
10. Fleet: *Daumet (1898), 239–48; Delisle, 'Lettre', 379–80; Leseur, *Hist.*, i, 213. Tailles: Thomas (1879), i, 270–1; BN Fr. 26080/6335. Intelligence: Escouchy, *Chron.*, i, 324; Beaucourt, v, 40 n.1; BN Fr. 32511, fol. 142vo–143; Delisle, 'Lettre', 379.
11. Armies: Héraut Berry, *Chron.*, 373–4; Chartier, *Chron.*, ii, 249, 305–9; Héraut Berry, *Chron.*, 360; Leseur, *Hist.*, i, 113; Delisle, 'Lettre', 379–80. Armagnac, Albret: BN Doat 218, fol. 176–177vo; Fr. 5909, fol. 181–181vo.
12. *Delisle, 'Lettre', 378; Chartier, *Chron.*, ii, 186, 254–5. Swillington: PRO C61/132, mm. 11, 5, C61/133, m. 5; E364/91, mm. 12–14 (Hull).
13. Héraut Berry, *Chron.*, 360–3; Chartier, *Chron.*, ii, 249–59; Delisle, 'Lettre', 378; Escouchy, *Chron.*, i, 329–34; PRO C61/139, m. 1 (bombardment).
14. Chartier, *Chron.*, ii, 259–64, 267–75, iii, 49; Héraut Berry, *Chron.*, 363, 363–4, 365; *Ord.*, xiv, 155–7, 166–7; Escouchy, *Chron.*, i, 335. Soudan: Chartier, *Chron.*, ii, 256, 259–61, C61/139, m. 1 (quotation); PRO C61/137, m. 2 (marriage).
15. Chartier, *Chron.*, ii, 265–6, 268; *Gebelin, 406; Héraut Berry, *Chron.*, 364; Leseur, *Hist.*, i, 115–21; *Ord.*, xiv, 134–7; *AHG*, x, 185.
16. Escouchy, *Chron.*, i, 337–9; Chartier, *Chron.*, ii, 266, 276–9, 304; Héraut Berry, 366–8; *Ord.*, xiv, 139–45, 158–61. On Angevin: Boutruche (1963), 374. On Berland: *Fasti*, xiii, 203–13.
17. *Gebelin, 406–9; Héraut Berry, *Chron.*, 368–73; Escouchy, *Chron.*, i, 356–60.
18. Bayonne: *Escouchy, *Chron.*, iii, 399; 'Anales de Vizcaya', 180. Ships: E101/54/14. Finance: Vale (1970), 138–41, 234 (Table 3). Jewels: *CPR 1446–52*, 455–6; Steel, 237–8.
19. Calais: BL Add. MS 48031, fol. 28vo (the Milanese ambassador [*Dispatches*, i, 33] seems to have misunderstood the position); Bale, 'Chron.', 138; *CPR 1446–52*, 480; *PPC*, vi, 112–13; PRO C76/133, m. 6; E404/67 (220); E159/231 (Easter), m. 2; E101/195/1; BL Add. MS 48031, fol. 28vo.
20. Héraut Berry, *Chron.*, 375–83; Chartier, *Chron.*, ii, 313–23; Escouchy, *Chron.*, i, 361–7, *iii, 397–400.

21. Montferrand: *Ord.*, xiv, 137-9. Durfort: *Doc. Durfort*, ii, nos. 1565, 1567-9, 1577. Graillys: Chartier, *Chron.*, ii, 291-8; Courteault, 154-5; PRO C61/138, mm. 3, 2. On them: *Reg. Garter*, i, 135 (as Count of Longueville and Earl of Kendal); *GEC*, vii, 108-9.
22. PRO C61/138, mm. 6, 5, 4; C61/140, mm. 9, 8, 7, 6, 2; C61/141, mm. 6, 5, 2. Pey du Tasta: PRO E404/67 (121); C61/139, m. 5; C61/140, m. 8; C61/141, m. 1; *CPR 1452-61*, 152; *Cartul. St-Seurin*, xxvii. Shorthose: PRO C61/139, m. 6; BN Fr. 32511, fol. 154; *Ord.*, xiv, 143 (art. 24). Rokeley: Ribadieu, 259, 261.
23. *Dispatches*, i, 33. Cf. *Carteggi (Francia)*, i, 18, 28 (to the D. of Milan). Villedieu: Beaucourt, v, 76.
24. *PPC*, vi, 119; *CPR 1446-52*, 477, 480, 512-13, 537, 540; *Paston Letters*, ii, 79; *L&P*, ii, 477-8; *Dispatches*, i, 33.
25. Benet, 'Chron.', 205; Bekynton, *Corr.*, i, 266-7; *Orig. Letters*, Ser. I, i, 11; *PPC*, vi, 90-2; Johnson, 100, 108-10; Cherry, 131-2; Storey (1966), 90-2.
26. PRO E28/82 (9) (great council); *CPR 1446-52*, 512-13; *Kingsford (1913), 297-8, 373; Benet, 'Chron.', 206-7; *Six Town Chrons.*, 107; *English Chron.*, 71; *Giles's Chron.*, iv, 43; *Paston Letters (G)*, i, 103-8; CCR 1447-54, 327, 334; *John Vale's Book*, 193-4; 'Hist. Croyland', 529; Johnson, 115-915-19. Captain of Calais: PRO C76/134, m. 17 (21 Sept.).
27. Ilardi, 131-7; Beaucourt, v, 161-72. Talbot: PRO E404/68 (138, 144, 145, 149, 156); E403/788, mm. 4, 5 (14, 18 July). Camoys: PRO C61/139, m. 3.
28. PRO C61/138, mm. 3, 2; *AHG*, xii, 343; BN Fr. 6963, fol. 27; Chartier, *Chron.*, ii, 330-1; Basin, *Hist.*, ii, 184; Vale (1970), 129-31.
29. *Gall. Reg.*, iii, nos. 13394, 13462; Chartier, *Chron.*, ii, 305, 322; Basin, *Hist.*, ii, 176-84; *Fasti*, xiii, 210-11, 218 (Archbishop); BN Fr. 6963, fols. 26, 28 (Bernard Georges).
30. Talbot: *Political Poems*, ii, 222; Chartier, *Chron.*, iii, 5. Company: *CPR 1452-61*, 78, 108; PRO E404/68 (138, 144, 145, 149, 156); E403/788, mm. 4, 5 (14, 18 July); *PPC*, vi, 120. Jersey: PRO E404/68 (138); *Ancient Petitions (I. de la Manche)*, 89-90. Clifton's company mustered at Dover (*CPR 1452-61*, 583-4) and embarked at Plymouth, suggesting that they came from Calais. The three captains were paid advances of £3,300 (£666 per 1,000 men): PRO E403/788, mm. 4, 5 (14, 18 July).
31. Grants: PRO C61/138, mm. 5, 3-1, C61/139, mm. 8-6. Seneschal: PRO C61/139, m. 6. Delay: PRO E403/788, m. 6 (4 Aug); Benet, 'Chron.', 208. Normandy: BL Add. Chart. 12422; BN Fr. 20437, fol. 22; BN Fr. 20683, fol. 46; BN Fr. 20683, fol. 47; *Bernus, 340-1; *Cosneau (1886), 645-6. Gascony: Escouchy, *Chron.*, i, 415; Vale (1969), 125.
32. Invasion: BN Fr. 6963, fols. 26-26vo; *AHG*, xii, 343; Héraut Berry, *Chron.*, 385-6; Chartier, *Chron.*, ii, 331-2; *Marchegay (1877), 9-10. Clermont: Escouchy, *Chron.*, i, 414-15; Dates: PRO 364/92, mm. 10-11 (Hull).
33. Charles VII: *Bueil, *Jouvencel*, ii, 372; Louis XI, *Lettres*, i, 57-8; Escouchy, *Chron.*, ii, 30-1; Héraut Berry, *Chron.*, 386; Chartier, *Chron.*, ii, 332. English expand: Vale (1970), 240 (Table 9) (garrison dates); Héraut Berry, *Chron.*, 386-7; Chartier, *Chron.*, ii, 332-3. Dates: PRO E364/92, mm. 10-11 (Hull); *CPR 1452-61*, 78.
34. French troops: Escouchy, *Chron.*, i, 415; *Gall. Reg.*, iii, nos. 13578, 13631; Leseur, *Hist.*, ii, 6; Chartier, *Chron.*, ii, 333-4 (Fronsac). Anglo-Gascons: PRO C61/139, m. 1; *Beaucourt, v, 463; *Doc. Durfort*, ii, nos. 1465, 1467, 1577-9; BN Fr. 32511, fol. 165vo. Finance: PRO E101/193/14 (51), 15 (27); E364/92, m. 10 (Hull); *CPR 1452-61*, 78, 108.

35. *CPR 1452–61*, 52–3 (for date, see Kleineke, 29), 59; *L&P*, ii, 479–80; PRO E403/791, mm. 14–16 (5 Mar.); C61/139, mm. 4, 3; PRO E364/89, m. 6 (Bowman); Benet, 'Chron.', 209; Héraut Berry, *Chron.*, 387. Finance: Kleineke, 22.
36. Parliament: *CCR 1447–54*, 394–5; *Parl. Rolls*, xii, 230–1, 232–4, 236, 241, 247–8 [7, 9, 11, 15, 19–20]; Steel, 272–4; *CPR 1452–61*, 78, 108. Borrowing: Vale (1970), 148–51, 234 (Table 3); *L&P*, ii, 482–1, 487–8; Steel, 274. Army: PRO E404/69 (198–206); E101/71/4 (933). On Saye: GEC, xi, 482–3.
37. Chartier, *Chron.*, ii, 334, iii, 1–3; Tringant, 'Comm.', 295–6; Escouchy, *Chron.*, ii, 72; BN Fr. 26081/6589; AHG, xii, 343; BN Fr. 26081/6589; Beaucourt, 'Trois documents', 154–5. Southern feudatories: AD Pyr.-Atl. E68/5; *Leseur, *Hist.*, ii, 328–40. The distribution of forces is confused by the official historiographer of Foix, Guillaume Leseur, *Hist.*, ii, 8–12, who places Clermont and Culant with the Count of Foix from the outset.
38. AHG, xii, 343; Leseur, *Hist.*, ii, 8–9; Escouchy, *Chron.*, ii, 35; Beaucourt, 'Trois documents', 154–5; Leseur, *Hist.*, ii, 9–12.
39. Sieges: Héraut Berry, *Chron.*, 393; *Beaucourt, v, 463; Chartier, *Chron.*, iii, 1–2. Talbot: Escouchy, *Chron.*, ii, 35; *Beaucourt, v, 463. 7,240 English troops had come with Talbot or Lisle to Gascony. Allowing for losses of *ca.* 500 in the Médoc (Leseur, *Hist.*, ii, 11) and 930 stationed in garrisons in the Bordelais and Dordogne (Vale [1970], 240), Talbot had *ca.* 5,800 English troops in Bordeaux on the morning of 16 July of whom *ca.* 4,160 participated in the Castillon campaign. If he withdrew half of the 930 garrison troops, a reasonable guess, he would have had 4,600 English at Castillon and between 1,400 and 2,400 Gascons. Camoys: PRO C61/139, m. 3; *Rec. Privilèges Bordeaux*, 181.
40. *Beaucourt, v, 463–4; Beaucourt, 'Trois documents', 155–6; Favreau, *Poitiers*, 139–40; Héraut Berry, *Chron.*, 388–92; Chartier, *Chron.*, iii, 3–8; Basin, *Hist.*, ii, 190–200; Escouchy, *Chron.*, ii, 36–43 (implausibly suggesting two separate attacks on the opening). Fastolf: Worcester, *Boke of Noblesse*, 64–5. Armour, burial: Taylor (2021), 332–3. Topography: Drouyn, ii, 89–90, 98–105; *Foed.*, xi, 11. Burial: ODNB, liii, 704.
41. Beaucourt, 'Trois documents', 156, 158–9; Chartier, *Chron.*, iii, 9–10, 12–13, 16; Héraut Berry, *Chron.*, 393–6; Tringant, 'Comm.', 296; AN JJ182/14 (date of fall of Castelnau). Blanquefort topography: Boutruche (1963), endmap 1.
42. Héraut Berry, *Chron.*, 393–4; Chartier, *Chron.*, iii, 11–12; *Beaucourt, v, 464. Outlying garrisons: *Rec. Privilèges Bordeaux*, 177–82; PRO E101/193/14 (48) (Rions).
43. Bale, 'Chron.', 140; Giles's *Chron.*, iv, 44; 'Annales angl.', 771; *Paston Letters (G)*, ii, 295–6; *Parl. Rolls*, xii, 258–9 [12].
44. PRO C61/140, m. 9; E403/793, mm. 13, 18 (23 July, 4 Aug.); E28/83 (55); *L&P*, ii, 483–4, 489–90, 492; *CPR 1452–61*, 123, 124–5; PPC, vi, 151, 153–4, 155–7. Delay: PRO E28/83 (28 Aug.).
45. R. A. Griffiths, 'Local rivalries and national politics: the Percys, the Nevilles and the Duke of Exeter, 1452–1454', *Speculum*, xliii (1968), 593–606.
46. Héraut Berry, *Chron.*, 395–6; Chartier, *Chron.*, iii, 14–17; Escouchy, *Chron.*, ii, 64–7, 77–8; *Beaucourt, v, 467; *Rec. Privilèges Bordeaux*, 181.
47. Escouchy, *Chron.*, ii, 70, 72–4; *Ord.*, xiv, 271n. Garrison agreement: *Rec. Privilèges Bordeaux*, 183–5.
48. Héraut Berry, *Chron.*, 396, 397, 398; Escouchy, *Chron.*, ii, 70–2, 74–6, 79; *Rec. Privilèges Bordeaux*, 30–3; *Doc. Durfort*, ii, no. 1579; *Beaucourt, v, 467.
49. Peyrègne, Durfort: *Doc. Durfort*, ii, no. 1580.
50. *Rec. Privilèges Bordeaux*, 34–41; M. K. James, 43–50; Boutruche (1963), 412; Boutruche (1966), 21, 23.

51. *AHG*, ix, 491; Boutruche (1963), 416, 417–19; Hubrecht, 72–3; Harris, 26–8.
52. Invasion scares: e.g. summer of 1454, see BN Fr. 25712/282, 285. In 1470: AN Coll. Lenoir xxv, 127, 151; Boüard, 55–7, *59–60; *Doc. Durfort*, ii, nos. 1578–9. Chancery: PRO C61/141, m. 1, C61/143, mm. 11, 10, 9, 2, C61/144, m. 4, 3, 1.
53. *Paston Letters (G)*, ii, 190–2, 297–8; Benet, 'Chron.', 210–11; *Parl. Rolls*, xii, 259–64 [34–40]. Fastolf's role: Richmond (2008), 92 n.63; Curry & Ambühl, 33–5, 43.
54. *Paston Letters*, iii, 162.
55. *English Chron.*, 83, 84.
56. Norfolk: *Paston Letters*, i, 237–8. Sandwich: Contamine (2003), 312–17; Héraut Berry, *Chron.*, 406–11; Chastellain, 'Chron.', iii, 347–53; Benet, 'Chron.', 218; *Brut*, ii, 524–5; *English Chron.*, 75; *CPR 1452–61*, 400–10, 413.
57. Chastellain 'Chron.', v, 490; *Waurin, *Cron.* (Dupont), iii, 211.
58. Plots: BN Fr. 6963, fol. 27vo; Chartier, *Chron.*, iii, 49–50; Ribadieu, 378–81. Fortification: Chartier, *Chron.*, iii, 47; *Rec. Privilèges Bordeaux*, 59–60; Drouyn, ii, 458–61; Harris, 110–12; *AHG*, xxxi, 278–9.
59. *Mém. pairs*, 780–205, esp. 796, 801–2 (articles of accusation, 1460); *Proc. Alençon*, 91, 124–5. Background: Samaran (1907), 114–30.
60. *Proc. Alençon*, 10, 26–37, 43, 46, 48–63, 65–103, 110, 113–32, *205–6; Chartier, *Chron.*, iii, 91–111; *Carteggi (Francia)*, i, 356. On Hay: *L&P*, ii, 623–4.
61. *Carteggi (Francia)*, i, 360, 364–5; BN Fr. 14371, fols. 191vo–192 (Norman ports); *L&P*, i, 332–51, esp. 341–4; *Contamine (2015)[1], 44–5; Solon, 102 (cost of Norman garrisons).
62. *Carteggi (Francia)*, i, 379; Basin, *Hist.*, ii, 256–8; *Cal. S. P. Milan*, i, no. 73; *Dispatches*, ii, 215–17.
63. *Foed.*, xi, 508–9; Calmette & Périnelle, 45–6, 54; *Scofield, ii, 469–70.
64. *Ord.*, xvi, 308–9; *Dépêches Milanais*, iii, 284, iv, 106–7.
65. *Paston Letters*, i, 538–9 (quotation).
66. *Parl. Rolls*, xiii, 362–4 [27–9] (quotation). Brittany: *Preuves Bretagne*, iii, cols. 167–82, 183–5; Pocquet (1929), 104–43. Burgundy: Bittmann, i, 289–301; Vaughan (1973), 53–8.
67. Calmette & Périnelle, 107–34; Ross (1974), 160; Vaughan (1973), 71.
68. *Lit. Cant.*, iii, 274–85; 'Hist. Croyland', 557–8. Distribution: *Parl. Rolls*, xiv, 14 [8].
69. *Foed.*, xi, 804–14; Commynes, *Mém.*, i, 262–3.
70. Army: *Carteggi (Borgogna)*, ii, 14, 15; *Foed.*, xii, 14–15; Commynes, *Mém.*, i, 260. English records, which are incomplete, account for 11,451 men: Barnard; Lander (1972), 91–6. Campaign: *Carteggi (Borgogna)*, i, 537–8, ii, 20–1; Commynes, *Mém.*, i, 266; Louis XI, *Lettres*, v, 368–70; Scofield, ii, 124. Treaties: *Foed.*, xii, 14–22; *Carteggi (Borgogna)*, ii, 36–8, 45–6, 72, 74; *Commynes, *Mém. (LdF)* iii, 409–44. Pension: Giry-Deloison (1993–4).
71. *Reg. Garter*, i. 176, ii, 199–202; *Doc. Durfort*, ii, nos. 1622, 1636–8. On his career: *ib.*, ii, nos. 1631, 1652–3; *Foed.*, xi, 761, xii, 12; Scofield, ii, 90–4, 100–1, 151.
72. Pocquet (1929), 283–97; Gunn (1986), 609–20; R. Beccarie de Fourquevaux, *Instructions sur le faict de la guerre* (1548), fol. 9vo (reflexion); *Letters & Papers Henry VIII*, xix, no. 730.
73. *Foed.*, xii, 355–8, 362–72, 377, 438–9, 442–3, 456–7, 490–504; Currin (2000), 384–412; Giry-Deloison, 48–9; Edmund Dudley, *The Tree of Commonwealth*, ed. D. M. Brodie (1948), 50.
74. Francophobia: *Cal. S.P. Venice*, i, no. 942, ii, no. 11; *Letters & Papers Henry VIII*, i, no. 264. Literature: *The First English Life of Henry the Fifth*, ed. C. L. Kingsford (1911); *The Chronicle of Froissart translated out of French by Sir John Bourchier*

Lord Berners, ed. W. P. Ker, 6 vols (1901–3). Invasions: Murphy (2015); C. S. L. Davies (1998)[2]; Gunn (1987); C. S. L. Davies (1995), 129. More: *Letters & Papers, Henry VIII*, iii, no. 2555.
75. R. B. Merriman, *Life and Letters of Thomas Cromwell*, (1902), i, 30–44; *Orig. Letters*, 3rd series, i, 369–75.
76. Scarisbrick, 445–8; *Letters & Papers, Henry VIII*, xvii, no. 468, xix¹, no. 730; Hall, *Chron.*, 862; Colvin, iii, 383–93; Grummitt (2008), 54–6. Murphy (2019), 171, 174–5, 201–4.
77. Louis XI, *Lettres*, ix, 52; Colvin, iii, 359–61; Grummitt (2008), 129–40.
78. Potter (1983), 483–507; Grummitt (2008), 165–86; Rose, 153–70; *Proceedings in the Parliaments of Elizabeth I*, i, ed. T. E. Hartley (1981), 36–7; *Cal. S. P. Venice*, vi, no. 1164.
79. Taylor, *Debating the Hundred Years War*, 1–49; Louis XI, *Lettres*, vii, 31–3, 112–14, viii, 275–7, x, 218–19; *Cal. S. P. Venice*, iii, no. 60 (Field of Cloth of Gold).
80. *Parliamentary History of England*, xxxiii (1818), cols. 917, 925–6, 1009, 1021.

CHAPTER XV: *The Reckoning*

1. Commynes, *Mém.*, Lib. V.18 (p. 400).
2. Robert of Gloucester, *Metrical Chronicle*, ed. W. A. Wright, i (1887), 1 (ll. 1–5).
3. Coleman, 71–8; Fribois, *Abrégé*, 191; *Relation of England*, 20–1, 23–4.
4. Mansi, *Conc.*, xxvii, col. 1066; *Foed.*, i, 827; *Book of London English*, 16; Sumption, iii, 806–7, iv, 371, 374, 601. Charles the Rash: Vaughan (1973), 163.
5. Froissart, *Chron.*, i, 214, 311–12, 337–8; *O. Cartellieri, *Philipp der Kühne* (1910), 152.
6. Rozmital, *Travels*, 61–2; *O. Cartellieri, *Philipp der Kühne* (1910), 152; Ormrod, Lambert et al., 60–1, 240–5; Waurin, *Cron.*, iii, 96–7; Gaguin, *Épistole et orationes*, ed. L. Thuasne (1903), i, 86–7.
7. N. Wright (1988), 80–95; Gauvard (1991), 535–40, 543–51, 556–7; Roch, 53–6; Sumption, ii, 328–31. Hatred: Rickard, 163–79; Contamine (2009)[3], 207–14; Doudet, 84–8; Pons, *L'honneur de la couronne*, 68 (*Pour ce que plusieurs*); Fribois, *Abrégé*, 134–5, 173–5.
8. Bueil, *Jouvencel*, i, 19; Molinet, 'Le Testament de la Guerre', quoted in P. Champion, *Histoire Poétique du XVᵉ siècle*, ii (1923), 343–4; Basin, *Hist.*, i, 84–8; Fortescue, *Governance*, 114–15.
9. Juvénal, *Écrits*, i, 58; Bocquet, 66–7. Migration: e.g. *Gr. Chron.*, ii, 255; Puiseux (1866), 38–9; Wolff (1954), 81–2; Boutruche (1947), 151–4.
10. Bocquet, 56–60.
11. *Visites archidiaconales*, esp. nos. 25, 36, 74–9, 120, 144, 261, 312, 347, 400, 410, 470, 527, 617, 650, 685–5, 688, 693, 718, 722, 727, 729, 749, 887, 913, 976, 1110, 1220; A. Moutié, *Chevreuse*, ii (1875), 431–40, 443–66, 494–6; *Cartulaire de l'abbaye de Notre-Dame des Vaux-de-Cernay*, ed. L. Merlet, ii (1858), 148–9; Bézard, 46–9, 64–79; Fourquin (1964), 465–83.
12. Bouton, 63–6.
13. Petit-Dutaillis (1911), 126.
14. Dupâquier et al., 371–409. Seigneurial inducements: Bézard, 92–8, 115–30; Fourquin, 377–86; Plaisse (1961), 329–31, 337–9, 361–8; Leguai (1969), 400–9; Boutruche (1935), 22–37, 124–43. Sepeaux: Quantin (1866), 6–20. On Jean de Surienne: Bossuat (1936), 360.
15. Fourquin (1964), 273–7, 430–56; Commynes, *Mém.*, Lib. I.8 (p. 53); Billot, 58–61; Botton & Offredo-Sarrot; Guilbert.

16. Kleinclausz, i, 319–22, 348–54; R. Gascon, *Grand commerce et vie urbaine au XVIe siècle. Lyon et ses marchands* (1971), 47–9; Lorcin, 231–47, 399–411, 458.
17. Mollat (1952), Ch. II–VI; Mollat (1979), 159; Bottin (1995), 313–14; Bois (1981), 65–6, 309–28; Plaisse (1961), 337–43.
18. Masselin, *Journ.*, 39; Seyssel, *Les Louenges du roi Loiys XII (1508)*, ed. P. Eichel-Lojkine and L.Vissière (2009), 216, 232; A. Bos, *Les églises flamboyantes de Paris, XVe–XVIe siècles* (2003), 27.
19. *Après la Destruction de Troie la Grant* (ca. 1419–20), cited in Contamine (2009)[3], 207; *Débat des hérauts d'armes*, 42; M. W. Thompson, 4–7, 71–102; Pounds, 249–72; Turner, 91; Rozmital, *Travels*, 61, 62.
20. Basin, *Hist.*, i, 291; Leland, *Itin.*, i, 102–3, 138, ii, 9, 72; Emery, i, 138–9, ii, 205–6, 544, iii, 553–7. Bowes: *ODNB*, vi, 945–6. Lenthall: *N. H. Nicolas, *History of the Battle of Agincourt*, 3rd. ed. (1833), 381. Hungerford: Roskell (1956), 303–5, 314, 315, 316–17. Cornwall: *VCH Bedford*, iii, 270; Reeves (1981), 156–7, 169–73; M. K. Jones (1991), 225.
21. Worcester, *Boke of Noblesse*, 19; *Lettres de Jean V*, iii, no. 1706.
22. Smith (1982), 6 (Table 1); McFarlane (1957)[1], 92–104; Richmond (1996), 213–16, 235–8; *Paston Letters (G)*, iii, 147–60, 163–6 (quotation at 159).
23. Worcester, *Itin.*, 46–8; *HoC 1422–61*, v, 702–8; Hunger (1925), 81–2; Massey (1987), 104–5. Whittingham was Ogard's deputy in the last year of Lancastrian Normandy: *L&P*, i, 501, 513, ii, 631. Inglose: Moreton and Richmond, 40–1.
24. Baugé: *C. Compayré, *Études historiques ... sur l'Albigeois* (1844), 266; Patay: Cagny, *Chron.*, 155. Pont-de-l'Arche, Formigny: Chartier, *Chron.*, ii, 71, 198; Castillon: *Beaucourt, v, 464. Knyvet: *HoC 1386–1421*, iii, 536–7. Rempston: Payling (1991), 59–62. Petitions: M. K. Jones (1991), 222–4; Ambühl (2013), 213, 225–6.
25. McFarlane (1962), 142–3.
26. Childs, 40–53; Munro (1972), 113–20, 133–46; Lloyd (1991), 180–234.
27. Bovet, *L'arbre des batailles*, 199–200; Westminster Abbey Muniments 12235, cited in Morgan, 873; Bueil, *Jouvencel*, i, 20–1, 27.
28. Contamine (1982)[2], 10–13, 17–18; Keen (1965), Ch. V.
29. Bovet, *L'Arbre des batailles*, 319–22, 476–7; *Journ. B. Paris*, 288–9. Keen (1965), 104–8; Taylor (2013), 177–230; Kaeuper, Ch. 6.
30. Froissart, *Chron.*, i, 214; Worcester, *Boke of Noblesse*, 73.
31. Bueil, *Jouvencel*, i, 18; Kemp, 196.
32. Scordia, 133–64, 199–215, 355–7; Post, *Studies in Medieval Legal Thought* (1964), 15–24, 108–68, 310–32, 447–8; M. V. Clarke, *Medieval Representation and Consent* (1936), 247–316; Strayer, 294–8; Y. Congar, 'Quod omnes tangit ab omnibus tractari et approbari debet', *Revue historique du droit français et étranger*, xxxv (1958), 210–59, esp. 230–9, 242–3; Lewis (1962), 8; Lewis (1968), 361–2, 364–6; Commynes, *Mém.*, Lib. V.19 (p. 408).
33. Lewis (1962), 8–11, 14; Major, 25–47.
34. Lassalmonie, 15, 60, 609–14, 673–6; Major, 50–8; Commynes, *Mém.*, Lib. V.19 (pp. 409–11); Masselin, *Journ.*, 350–489 (esp. 422), 518–91, 594–6, 671–80. Army cuts: Contamine (1972), 286, 307.
35. Contamine (1972), 282, 285–6, 305–6.
36. Claude de Seyssel, *La monarchie de France*, ed. J. Poujol (1961), 110–11, 163–4; Fortescue, *De Laudibus*, 22–4, 80–90; Fortescue, *Governance*, 113–14, 116–18.
37. Masselin, *Journ.*, 36–8; Commynes, *Mém.*, Prol., IV.1, V.19 (pp. 1, 244–5, 408–13, 417–19).

38. P. Williams, *The Later Tudors, 1547–1603* (1995), 535–6 (Armada); P. K. O'Brien and P. A. Hunt, 'England, 1485–1815', *The Rise of the Fiscal State in Europe, c. 1200–1815* (1999), 54–8.
39. Krynen (1981), 213–58; Beaune (1985), esp. Ch. I, IV, VII, X, XI; Pisan, *Livre des fais et bonnes meurs du sage roi Charles V*, ed. S. Solente, i (1936), 12; Masselin, *Journ.*, 36–66, 642–8; *Proc. N.*, i, 390.
40. Beaucourt, v, 52–3 (processions). Commemoration: *L&P*, i, 307–9; Waurin, *Cron.*, v, 162; Contamine (2009)[2], 350–1; Taylor (2021), 330–1.
41. Lull, *Book of the Ordre of Chyvalry*, ed. A. T. P. Byles (1926), 122–3.
42. Juvénal, *Écrits*, i, 270.

Bibliography

A MANUSCRIPTS

Brussels: Algemeen Rijksarchief
CC21800–6: Council of Flanders, accounts [1423–36]
CC32491–3: Bruges, general accounts [1436–40]

Caen: Archives Départementales du Calvados
F/1260–F/1649: Collection Danquin

Caen: Musée des Beaux Arts
Collection Mancel

Dijon: Archives Départementales de la Côte-d'Or
Série B: Chambre des Comptes de Bourgogne
   1622–65: Accounts of the Receivers-General and Treasurers [1422–38]
   11799–810: War, musters and reviews [1422–47]
   11880: War, general [1420–44]
   11884–7: Ransoms
   11897–908: Diplomatic documents (France) [1419–56]
   11921: Diplomatic documents (Brittany) [1341–1442]
   11929: Diplomatic documents (Savoy) [1420–34]
   11942: Council and Chambre des Comptes (Dijon), correspondence [1350–1597]

Lille: Archives Départementales du Nord
Série B: Chambre des Comptes de Lille
   297–308: Diplomatic documents (England) [1424–49]
   1927–76: Accounts of Receivers-General and supporting documents [1422–42]
   17636–53: Lettres reçues et dépêchées [1423–35]

Lisieux: Archives Communales
CC1–16, 19–23: Comptes [1423–48]

London: British Library
Additional Charters
Additional Manuscripts
   11509: Account of Receiver-General of Normandy, 1448–9 (fragment)

11542: Collection Joursanvault (France and Normandy)
48031: Formulary, late 15th cent
Cotton MSS:
Caligula D V: War, English possessions in France (badly damaged by fire)
Egerton Charters
Lansdowne Manuscripts
285: *Sir John Paston's Great Book*

London: College of Arms
MS Arundel 26, fols. 55–63: Fastolf papers

London: The National Archives [Public Record Office]
Chancery
C61/119–144 Gascon rolls [1422–68]
C64/9–17 Norman rolls [1418–22]
C76/106–159 Treaty (formerly French) rolls [1422–76]
C81 Chancery warrants
  C81/583–669 Writs of Privy Seal [1422–55]
  C81/1085–1164 Bills of Privy Seal [1422–55]
  C81/1366–71 Warrants under the signet [1431–56]
  C81/1544–6 Warrants of the Council [1422–71]

Exchequer
E28/38–85: Council and Privy Seal [1422–54]
E30/441–519, 1350, 1503, 1599, 1627: Diplomatic documents, Exchequer [1432–49]
E101: Accounts various
  E101/51/1–E101/55/2: Army, navy and ordnance [1422–61]
  E101/71/2–E101/71/4: Indentures of war [1422–53]
  E101/188/14–194/10: English possessions in France [1422–54]
  E101/322/1–E101/324/20: *Nuncii* [messengers and diplomatic agents] [1422–52]
  E101/407/13–E101/410/16: Wardrobe and household [1422–55]
E159: *Brevia directa baronibus*
E364/57–116: Enrolled accounts, foreign [1422–83]
E401/703–842: Receipt rolls [1422–55]
E403/658–847: Issue rolls [1422–78]
E404/39–71: Warrants for issue [1422–61]
Privy Seal Office
PSO1/5–19 Signet and Privy Seal Warrants [1423–54]
Special Collections
SC8 Ancient Petitions

Mantes: Archives Municipales
BB4–5: Délibérations [1440–56]
CC23–30: Comptes [1422–51]

Orléans: Archives Communales
CC652–3: Comptes [1424–8]

BIBLIOGRAPHY

Oxford: Bodleian Library
MS Digby 196, fols. 155vo–156: Narrative of the Earl of Suffolk's embassy to France, 16 April–28 May 1444

Paris: Archives Nationales
Série J Trésor des Chartes
Série JJ Trésor des Chartes, Régistres
    JJ172–5: Henry VI [1422–34]
    JJ176–192: Charles VII [1441–61]
Série K Monuments historiques
    62–72: Cartons des Rois [1422–83]
Série KK Monuments historiques, Régistres (comptes)
    50–3: Charles VII
    55–6: Marie d'Anjou
    243–4: Yolande of Aragon, Chambre aux deniers [1419–27, 1431–8]
    269: Charles of Orléans
    324: Duke of Bedford, sealing fees (Anjou and Maine) [1433–4]
    648: Collection Monteil (États Provinciaux)
Série P Chambre des Comptes
    2298: Mémoriaux H, J, K [1412–49]
Série PP Chambre des Comptes
    110: Table chronologique des Mémoriaux [1404–1516]
Série X Parlement
    X^{1a}: Parlement civil
    Parlement de Paris:
        4793–806: Plaidoiries (matinées) [1420–60]
        8603–5: Actes royaux [1418–62]
    Parlement de Poitiers:
        9190–203: Arrêts et jugés [1418–36]
    X^{2a}: Parlement criminel
        18–26: Arrêts [1423–55]
Collection Dom Lenoir

Paris: Bibliothèque Nationale
Collection de Bourgogne
    21: Chambre des Comptes de Dijon, Abstracts of Dom Sallazard
    29: Extraits divers
    70: Chartes et pièces diverses
Collection Clairambault:
    1–227: Titres scellés
    307: Actes, pièces, montres, documents et extraits
Collection de Languedoc (Doat):
    214–19: Houses of Foix, Armagnac, Albret [1423–56]
Collection Moreau:
    704–7: Collection de Bréquigny, Pièces rélatives à l'histoire de France tirées des archives et bibliothèques d'Angleterre, Pièces historiques [1417–80]
    1431: Ordonnances [1380–1591]
Manuscrits français

2861, fols. 213–15: Letters patent for Arthur, Count of Richemont (1436)
4054: Angleterre. Lettres et pieces originales sur les querelles de la France et l'Angleterre
4484: War Treasurer's account, Lancastrian France (André d'Esparnon, 1427–8)
4485, 4488, 4491: Accounts of Receiver-General, Lancastrian Normandy (Pierre Surreau, 1423–6, 1428–9)
5909: Formulary, Charles VII and Louis VI
6200: États provinciaux
6963, fols. 26–9: Papiers Le Grand, pièces originales, confession of Bernard Georges
8267: Recueil de pièces concernant l'histoire de Bretagne
14371: Chancery formulary, late 15th century
17330, fols. 119–148vo: Ambassade de Regnault Girard en Écosse (fragment) [1434–6]
18442: Affaires d'état [1445–90]
18949: Histoire du Mont Saint-Michel composée par un religieux bénédictins de l'abbaye royale du Mont Saint-Michel [ca. 1750]
20327, fols. 149, 150: Collection de Gaignières, Cardinal Beaufort
20366–419: Collection de Gaignières, maisons royales de France
20437: Letters, saec. XIV–XVI
20579–85: Chambres des Comptes, taxation
20683: Chambre des Comptes, comptes originaux
20684, pp. 541–74: Chambre des Comptes (War Treasurers' accounts, extracts)
20878–89: Collection de Gaignières, Archevêques et Evêques de France
21405: Mémoriaux de la Chambre des Comptes (extracts)
21425–8: Collection Gaignières, Impositions et aides pour la guerre
23018: Chronique des Cordeliers [extracts from this important chronicle are published by Quicherat in 'Documents nouveaux' and Champion (1906)]
23189: Normandy [1410–48]
24031: Collection de Gaignières, Auvergne, impositions [1442–1539]
25710–2: Chartes royales [1418–66]
25767–78: Musters and reviews [1422–61]
26046–82: Chambre des Comptes, Quittances et pièces diverses [1422–54]
26263–99: Collection Villevieille, Titres originaux
26309–484: Collection Blondeau de Charnage
26485–29545: Pièces originales [cited as PO 1–3061]
32510–1: Chambre des Comptes (War Treasurers' and other accounts, extracts, transcriptions)

Manuscrits français, Nouvelles acquisitions
1482: Mandements, quittances et pieces diverses (Normandy, 1419–49)
3639–42, 3645bis: Collection de Bastard d'Estang, pièces originales
3653–5: Inventaire Aubron
7005: Collection de Brienne, Mélanges (affaires des rois de France et d'Angleterre)
7626–30: Portefeuilles de Fontanieu (transcriptions) [1422–55]
8605–7: Cabinet des Titres, musters and reviews [1410–69]
21289: Chambre des Comptes, chartes et pièces originales, Normandie [1305–99]

Manuscrits latins, Nouvelles acquisitions
2320: Chambre des Comptes (mandements royaux, quittances)
2385–6: Pièces diverses

Mélanges de Colbert
380: Actes des rois d'Angleterre [1338–1480]

Pièces originales: see Ms. Fr. 26485–29545

BIBLIOGRAPHY

Pau: Archives Départementales des Pyrennées-Atlantiques
Série E (Titres de famille)
13–236: Albret

Rouen: Archives Départmentales de la Seine Maritime
100J Collection Danquin

Tours: Archives Municipales
BB reg. 2–8: Régistres de délibérations [1422–50]
CC reg. 20–9: Comptes Urbains [1422–45]

B PRINTED RECORD SOURCES

Actes de la Chancellerie d'Henri VI concernant la Normandie sous la domination anglaise (1422–1435), ed. P. Le Cacheux, 2 vols (1907–8)
'Actes concernant les états provinciaux [de Normandie]', ed. F Blanchet and M. Nortier, *Cahiers Léopold Delisle*, xv, fascs 3–4 (1966), 21–42
Actes des États Généraux des Anciens Pays-Bas, ed. J. Cuvelier, i (1948) [all published]
Acts of the Parliaments of Scotland, ed. T. Thomson and C. Innes, 12 vols (1814–75)
'Advis à Isabelle de Bavière. Mémoire politique addressé à cette reine vers 1434', ed. A. Vallet de Viriville, *BEC*, xxvii (1866), 129–57
'Analyses et fragments tires des archives municipales de Tours', *Le Cabinet Historique*, v (2) (1859), 102–21
'Ancient indictments in the King's Bench referring to Kent, 1450–1452', ed. R. Virgoe, *Documents Illustrative of Medieval Kentish Society*, ed. F. R. H. Du Boulay (1964), 214–65
'*Ancient Petitions of the Chancery and the Exchequer' ayant trait aux Îles de la Manche conservées au 'Public Record Office' à Londres* (1902)
Archives historiques du Département de la Gironde, 59 vols (1859–1936) [cited as AHG]
Archives historiques du Poitou, 69 vols (1872–2015) [cited as AHP]
Archives historiques de la Saintonge et de l'Aunis, 50 vols (1874–1967)
Archives legislatives de la ville de Reims. Seconde partie: statuts, ed. P. Varin, 3 vols (1844–52)
'Archives municipales de Mantes: analyse des régistres des comptes de 1381 à 1450', ed. V.-E. Graves, *BHP* (1896), 306–31
Arnold, Richard, *The Customs of London*, ed. F. Douce (1811)
Auctarium chartularii Universitatis Parisiensis, ed. H. Denifle, E. Chatelain, et al., 6 vols (1894–1964)
'Avis du chancelier Rolin pour le paix d'Arras', ed. P. Noirot, *Bulletin d'histoire, de littérature et d'art du diocèse de Dijon*, xxiii (1905), 116–35

Baronius, C., Raynaldus, O. and Laderchius, J., *Annales ecclesiastici*, 37 vols (1864–83)
Beaucourt, G. du Fresne de, 'Trois documents inédits sur la seconde campagne de Guyenne (1453)', *ABSHF*, cxxiv (1864)[2], 154–9
Beaune, C. (ed.), 'Un document inédit sur Jeanne d'Arc. La lettre d'Henri VI, roi d'Angleterre au duc Charles de Lorraine', *Mémoires de la Société des Sciences et Lettres de Loir-et-Cher*, lxv (2010), 17–20

BIBLIOGRAPHY

Beaurepaire, F. de, 'Sources de l'histoire du moyen age à la Bibliothèque de la ville de Rouen. Analyse des pièces antérieures à 1500', *Cahiers Léopold Delisle*, xiv, fasc. 2 (1965), 41–70, xvi, fascs 3–4 (1967), 7–54

Bekynton, Thomas, *Official Correspondence of Thomas Bekynton, secretary to King Henry VI and bishop of Bath and Wells*, ed. G. Williams, 2 vols (1872)

Blanchet, F., 'Sources de l'histoire de la Normandie aux Archives Nationales, Série KK', *Cahiers Léopold Delisle*, xv, fascs 3–4 (1966), 1–19

Book of London English, 1384–1425, ed. R. W. Chambers and M. Daunt (1931)

Bronnen voor de geschiedenis der dagvaarten van de Staten en steden van Holland voor 1544, ed. W. Prevenier, J. G. Smit et al., 6 vols (1987–2011) [all published]

Bronnen tot de geschiedenis van den handel met Engeland, Schotland en Ierland, ed. H. J. Smit, 2 vols (1928)

Cabinet Historique (Le), 27 vols (1854–83)

Calendar of Close Rolls, 45 vols (1892–1954) [cited as CCR]

'Calendar of Diplomatic Documents, formerly in the Treasury of the Receipt of the Exchequer, Chapter House, Westminster', *Annual Report of the Deputy Keeper of the Public Records*, xlv (1885), 283–380; xlvii (1887), 561–619

Calendar of Documents relating to Scotland, ed. J. Bain, 5 vols (1881–1988)

Calendar of Entries in the Papal Registers relating to Great Britain and Ireland. Papal Letters, ed. W. H. Bliss, C. Johnson et al., 19 vols (1894–1998)

Calendar of Fine Rolls, 22 vols (1911–63) [cited as CFR]

'Calendar of French Rolls', *Annual Report of the Deputy Keeper of the Public Records*, xlviii (1887), 221–450

Calendar of Inquisitions Post Mortem, 26 vols (1904–2010)

Calendar of Letter Books of the City of London, ed. R. R. Sharpe, 11 vols (1899–1912)

Calendar of Patent Rolls, 70 vols (1891–1982) [cited as CPR]

Calendar of Scottish Supplications to Rome, 1418–1422, ed. E. R. Lindsay, A. I. Dunlop et al., 4 vols (1934–83)

Calendar of State Papers and Manuscripts existing in the Archives and Collections of Milan, ed. A. B. Hinds, i (1912) [all published]

Calendar of State Papers and Manuscripts relating to English Affairs existing in the Archives and Collections of Venice and in other Libraries of Northern Italy, ed. R. and H. F. Brown and A. B. Hinds, 38 vols (1864–1947)

Callu-Turiaf, F., 'Nouveaux documents sur la bataille de Formigny', *BEC*, cxxiv (1966), 273–80

Canat, M. (ed.), *Documents inédits pour servir à l'histoire de Bourgogne* (1863)

Carteggi diplomatici fra Milano Sforzesca e la Francia, ed. E. Pontieri, i (1978)

Carteggi diplomatici fra Milano Sforzesca e la Borgogna, ed. E. Sestan, 2 vols (1985–7)

Cartulaire de l'ancienne Estaple de Bruges, ed. L. Gilliodts-van Severen, 4 vols (1904–6)

Cartulaire des comtes de Hainaut, ed. L. Devillers, 6 vols (1881–96)

Cartulaire de l'église collégiale Saint-Seurin de Bordeaux, ed. J.-A. Brutails (1897)

Cartulaire de Louviers, ed. T. Bonnin, 5 vols in 6 (1870–83)

Cartulaire de l'abbaye d'Orbestier (Vendée), ed. L. de la Boutetière, *AHP*, vi (1877)

Cartulaire des sires de Rays (1160–1449), ed. R. Blanchard, 2 vols, *AHP*, xxviii, xxx (1898–9)

Catalogue analytique des archives de M. le baron de Joursanvault, 2 vols (1838)

Catalogue générale des manuscrits des bibliothèques publiques de France
i–ii, *Rouen*, ed. H. Omont, 2 vols (1886–8)
xliv, *Caen (Collection Mancel)*, ed. R.-N. Sauvage (1911)

BIBLIOGRAPHY

Chaplais, P., *English Medieval Diplomatic Practice*, i: *Documents and Interpretation* (1982)
Chartularium Henrici V et Henrici VI regum Angliae, ed. H. Barckhausen, *AHG*, xvi (1878)
Chartularium Universitatis Pariensis, ed. H. Denifle and E. Chatelain, 4 vols (1889–97)
Collection Danquin. Inventaire analytique, ed. M.-C. de la Conte (1996)
Collection générale des documents français qui se trouvent en Angleterre, ed. J. Delpit (1847)
Collections de Bastard d'Estang à la Bibliothèque Nationale. Catalogue analytique, ed. L. Delisle (1885)
'Complainte sur les misères de Paris en 1435', ed. L. Auvray, *Bulletin de la Société de l'Histoire de Paris*, xviii (1891), 84–7
'Complainte des Normans envoyée au roy nostre sire', ed. P. Le Verdier, *Bulletin de la Société de l'Histoire de Normandie*, Années 1887–90 (1890), 77–87
Compte de l'armée anglaise au siège d'Orléans, 1428–1429, ed. L. Jarry (1892)
'Compte du trésorier de la ville de Bordeaux pour 1442 (fév.–août)', *BHP* (1961), 179–215
Comptes consulaires de la ville de Riscle de 1441 à 1507, ed. P. Parfouru and J. de Carsalade du Pont, 2 vols (1886–92)
'Comptes d'Auffroy Guinot, trésorier et receveur général de Bretagne, 1430–1436', ed. M. Jones, *Journal des Savants* (2010), 17–109, 265–306
Comptes de l'archevêché de Bordeaux, ed. L. Drouyn, 2 vols, *AHG*, xxi, xxii (1871–2)
'Comptes de Jean Droniou, trésorier et receveur général de Bretagne, 1420–1429', ed. M. Jones, *Bulletin de la Société Archéologique de Finistère*, cxli (2013), 295–373
Comptes des consuls de Montréal-du-Gers, ed. A Breuils, *AHG*, xxix (1894), 283–355, xxxii (1897), 1–85
'Comptes des dépenses faites par Charles VII pour secourir Orléans pendant le siège de 1428', ed. J. Loiseleur, *Mémoires de la Société Archéologique de l'Orléanais*, xi (1868), 1–209, 537–8
Comptes du domaine de la Ville de Paris, ed. A Vidier, L. Le Grand, P. Dupreux and J. Monicat, 2 vols (1948–58)
'Comptes du duché de Bretagne', ed. B. A. Pocquet du Haut-Jussé, *BEC*, lxxvii (1916), 88–110
Comptes généraux de l'état bourguignon entre 1416 et 1420, ed. M. Mollat, 3 vols and index (1965–76)
Concilium Basiliensis. Studien und Dokumente zur Geschichte des Concils von Basel, ed. J. Haller, 8 vols (1896–1936)
Cotton manuscrit Galba B. 1, ed. L. Gilliodts-van Severen (1896)
Coventry Leet Book or Mayor's Register, ed. M. D. Harris (1907–13)

Dagboek van Gent van 1447 tot 1470, ed. V. Fris (1901–4)
Dauvet, Jean, *Les affaires de Jacques Coeur. Journal du Procureur Dauvet. Procès-verbaux de sequester et d'adjudication*, ed. A.-M. Yvon-Briand, Y. Lanhers and C. Marinesco (1952)
['Délibérations de l'Hôtel de Ville de Beauvais'] 'Beauvais dans l'angoisse pendant la seconde partie de la guerre de Cent Ans. Extraits des délibérations de l'Hôtel de Ville de Beauvais (1402–1445)', ed. V. Leblond, *Memoires de la Société Académique d'Archéologie, Sciences et Arts du Departement de l'Oise*, xxvii (1932), 93–363
Delisle, L., 'Lettre du bâtard d'Orléans acquise par le Musée Condé', *Comptes rendus des séances de l'Académie des Inscriptions et Belles-Lettres* (1899), 375–94
Dépêches des ambassadeurs Milanais en France sous Louis XI et François Sforza, ed. B. Mandrot and C. Samaran, 4 vols (1916–23)

'Devis pour la construction d'une maison-forte à Elbeuf-sur-Seine pendant l'occupation anglaise du quinzième siècle', ed. M. L. Régnier, *Société de l'histoire de Normandie. Mélanges*, vi (1906), 333–50

Dispatches with Related Documents of Milanese Ambassadors in France and Burgundy, 1450–1483, ed. P. M. Kendall and V. Ilardi, 3 vols, 1970–81

'Doc. Croÿ': see Thielemans, M. R. (1959) [B]

'Doc. negotiations': see 'Documents relating to the Anglo-French negotiations of 1439'

Doc. Paris: see Longnon, A. [B]

Doc. Rouen: see Le Cacheux, P. [B]

Documents et recherches relatifs à Jeanne la Pucelle, i, *La minute française des interrogatoires de Jeanne la Pucelle*; ii, *Instrument public des sentences portées les 24 et 30 mai 1431 par Pierre Cauchon et Jean le Maitre contre Jeanne la Pucelle*; iii, *La rehabilitation de Jeanne la Pucelle. L'Enquête ordonnée par Charles VII en 1450 et le codicille de Guillaume Bouillé*; iv, *La rehabilitation de Jeanne la Pucelle. L'enquête du cardinal d'Estouteville en 1452*; v, *La rehabilitation de Jeanne la Pucelle. La redaction épiscopale du procès de 1455–1456*; ed. P. Doncoeur and Y. Lanhers, 5 vols (1952–61)

'Documents gantois concernant la levée du siège de Calais en 1436', ed. V. Fris, *Mélanges Paul Frédéricq* (1904), 245–58

'Document inédit sur une assemblée d'états convoquée à Amiens en 1424', ed. L. Demaison, *Travaux de l'Academie de Reims*, lxxiii (1882–3), 351–69

'Documents inédits pour servir à l'histoire de la guerre de Cent Ans dans le Maine de 1424 à 1452', ed. A. Joubert, *Revue historique et archéologique du Maine*, xxvi (1889), 243–85

'Documents inédits sur La Hire, Chabanne et autres capitaines du xve siècle', ed. A. Vallet de Viriville, *Bulletin de la Société de l'Histoire de France*, 2e série, ii, (1859–60), 9–14, 36–45

'Documents inédits sur le siège de Compiègne en 1430', ed. A. Fons-Mélicocq, *La Picardie. Revue littéraire et scientifique*, iii (1857), 21–9

'Documents manuscrits de la Bibliothèque Nationale de France concernant Saint-Lô, spécialement au xve siècle', ed. M. Nortier, *Revue de la Manche*, xlviii, fasc. 194 (2006), 3–34

'Documents nouveaux sur Jeanne d'Arc. Supplément aux témoignages contemporains sur Jeanne d'Arc', ed. J. Quicherat, *Revue Historique*, xix (1882), 60–83

Documents relatifs à l'administration financière en France de Charles VII à François Ier (1443–1523), ed. G. Jacqueton (1891)

'Documents relatifs à la biographie de Jean, bâtard d'Orléans, Comte de Dunois et de Longueville', ed. A. Vallet de Viriville. *Le Cabinet Historique*, iii (1857), 105–20

Documents relatifs à l'histoire de l'industrie et du commerce en France, ed. G. Fagniez, 2 vols (1898–1900)

'Documents relatifs à Jeanne d'Arc et à son époque exraits d'un manuscrit du xve siècle de la ville de Berne', ed. C. de Roche and G. Wissler, *Festschrift Louis Gauchat* (1926), 329–76

'Documents relatifs à Prégent de Coëtivy, seigneur de Taillebourg et Admiral de France, tires du chartrier de Thouars', ed. P. Marchegay, *Archives Historiques de la Saintonge et de l'Aunis*, vi (1879), 23–88

'Documents rélatifs au siège d'Orléans et à la délivrance de Beaugency et de Jargeau', ed. L. Dumuys, *Bulletin de la Société Archéologique de l'Orléanais*, ix (1887), 32–7

'Documents relating to the Anglo-French negotiations of 1439', ed. C. T. Allmand, *Camden Miscellany*, xxiv (Royal Historical Society, Camden Fourth Series, ix) (1972), 79–149

Documents sur la maison de Durfort, ed. N. de la Peña (1977)

BIBLIOGRAPHY

'Documents sur les États Généraux de Poitiers de 1424 et 1425', ed. R. Lacour, *AHP*, xlviii (1934), 91–117
Documents sur la ville de Millau, ed. J. Artières (1930)

Eidgenössischen Abschiede: Amtliche Sammlung der ältern eidgenössischen Abschiede, ed. G. M. non Knonau, J. K. Krütli, A. P. Segesser et al., 8 vols (1839–86)
England's Export Trade, ed. E. M. Carus-Wilson and O. Coleman (1963)
English suits before the Parlement de Paris, 1420–1436, ed. C. T. Allmand and C. A. J. Armstrong (1982)
Exchequer Rolls of Scotland, ed. J. Stuart et al., 23 vols (1878–1908)
Extrait du régistre des dons, confiscations, maintenues et autres actes faits dans le duché de Normandie pendant les années 1418, 1419 et 1420 par Henry V roi d'Angleterre, ed. C. Vautier (1828)
'Extraits du Journal du Trésor, 1423–1424', ed. G. Ritter, *BEC*, lxxiii (1912), 470–89

Favier, J. (ed.), *Les contribuables parisiens à la fin de la guerre de Cent ans. Les rôles d'impot de 1421, 1423 et 1438* (1970)
Favreau, R. (ed.), *Poitiers à la fin de la guerre de cent ans. L'apport des sources financières avec l'édition des comptes de 1448–1455, AHP*, lxxi (2022)
Foedera, conventiones, literae et acta publica, ed. T. Rymer, 20 vols (1727–9), and Supplement in C. P. Cooper, *Report on Rymer's Foedera*, Appendices A–E, 6 vols (1869)
Frankfurts Reichscorrespondenz von 1376–1519, ed. J. Janssen, 2 vols in 3 (1863–72)
Frondeville, H. de (ed.), *I. La vicomté d'Orbec pendant l'occupation anglaise (1417–1449), II. Compte de Jean de Muet, vicomte d'Orbec pour la Saint-Michel 1444* (1936)

Gallia Christiana, 16 vols, ed. D. de Sainte-Marthe, F. Hodin et al. (1716–1865)
Gallia Regia, ou état des officiers royaux des baillages et des sénéchaussés de 1328 à 1515, ed. G. Dupont-Ferrier, 7 vols (1942–65)
Gascogne dans les régistres du Trésor des Chartes, ed. C. Samaran (1966)
Grandmaison, C. de, 'Nouveaux documents sur les États-Généraux du xve siècle', *Bulletin de la Société Archéologique de Touraine*, iv (1879), 139–55
Grands traités de la guerre de Cent Ans, ed. E. Cosneau (1889)
Groot Charterboek der Graaven van Holland en Heeren van Vriesland, ed. F. van Mieris, 4 vols (1753–6)

Handelingen van de Leden en van de Staten van Vlaanderen. Regering van Filips de Goede (10 september 1419–15 juni 1467), ed. W. P. Blockmans, 3 vols (1990–2006)
Hanserecesse von 1431–1476, ed. G. von der Ropp, 7 vols (1876–92)
Historical Manuscripts Commission, *Reports* (1874–)

Inventaire analytique des livres de couleur et bannières du Châtelet de Paris, ed. A. Tuetey (1899)
Inventaire analytique des ordonnances enregistrées au Parlement de Paris jusqu'à la mort de Louis XII, ed. H. Stein (1908)
Inventaire des archives des chambres des comptes, ed. L. P. Gachard, 7 vols (1837–1995)
Inventaire des archives de la ville de Bruges. Inventaire des Chartes, ed. L. Gilliodts-van Severen, 9 vols (1871–82)
Inventaire chronologique des chartes de la ville d'Arras, ed. A. Guesnon (1890)
Inventaire chronologique des documents relatifs a l'histoire d'Écosse conservés aux Archives du Royaume à Paris, ed. A. Teulet (1839)

BIBLIOGRAPHY

Inventaire des documents normands de la Collection Villevieille de la Bibliothèque Nationale, ed. M. Nortier (1987)
Inventaire de Pierre Surreau, receveur-général de Normandie, ed. J. Félix (1892)
'Inventaire des rôles de fouage de d'aide', ed. M. Nortier, 6 series, *Cahiers Léopold Delisle*, xix (1970), xx. 1-2 (1971), xxii (1973), xxv (1976), xxx (1981), xxxix (1990)
Inventaire des sceaux de la Collection Clairambault à la Bibliothèque Nationale, ed. G. Demay, 2 vols (1885-6)
Inventaire des sceaux de la Collection des Pièces Originales du Cabinet des Titres à la Bibliothèque Nationale, J. Roman, i (1909)
Inventaire des titres de Nevers, ed. M. de Marolles (1873)
Inventaire-sommaire des Archives Communales antérieures à 1790
  Ville d'Abbeville, ed. A. Ledieu (1902)
  Ville d'Albi, ed. E. Jolibois (1869)
  Ville d'Amiens, ed. G. Durand, 7 vols (1891-1925)
  Ville de Narbonne, ed. G. Mouynès, 4 vols (1871-7)
Inventaire-sommaire des Archives Départementales antérieures à 1790
  Basses-Pyrennées, ed. P. Raymond, 6 vols (1863-76)
  Côte d'Or. Archives civiles. Série B: Chambre des Comptes de Bourgogne, ed. C. Rossignol and J. Garnier, 5 vols (1863-78)
  Manche, Série A, ed. N. Dubosv and P. Le Cacheux, 2 vols (1865-1925)
  Nord. Archives civiles, Série B: Chambre des Comptes de Lille, ed. Dehaisnes, J. Finot, A. Desplanque et al., 9 vols (1899-1913)
Isabelle of Portugal, Duchess of Burgundy, *La correspondence d'Isabelle de Portugal, duchesse de Bourgogne (1430-1471)*, ed. M. Sommé (2009)
Issues of the Exchequer, ed. F. Devon (1837)
Itinéraires de Philippe le Bon, duc de Bourgogne (1419-1467) et de Charles, comte de Charolais (1433-1467), ed. H. Vander Linden (1940)

Jurades de la ville de Bergerac, 14 vols, ed. G. Charrier (1892-1941)

Lafaurie, J., *Les Monnaies des rois de France*, 2 vols (1951-6)
Languedoc et le Rouergue dans le Trésor des Chartes, ed. Y. Dossat, A.-M. Lemasson and P. Wolff (1983)
Larson, A., 'English Embassies during the Hundred Years War', *EHR*, lv (1940), 423-3
*Le Cacheux, P., *Rouen au temps de Jeanne d'Arc et pendant l'occupation anglaise* (1931)
Leroux de Lincy, A. (ed.), 'La bibliothèque de Charles d'Orléans à son château de Blois n 1427', *BEC*, v (1844), 59-82
Les La Trémoille pendant cinq siècles, i, *Guy VI et Georges, 1343-1446* (1890)
Letters and Papers, Foreign and Domestic, Henry VIII, ed. J. S. Brewer, J. Gairdner and R. H. Brodie, 21 vols in 28 (1864-1920)
Letters and Papers illustrative of the wars of the English in France during the reign of Henry the Sixth, King of England, ed. J. Stephenson, 2 vols (1861-4) [cited as *L&P*]
Letters of Queen Margaret of Anjou and Bishop Bekington and others, ed. C. Monro (1863)
'Lettre sur la bataille de Castillon en Périgord, 19 juillet 1453', *BEC*, viii (1846), 245-7
Lettres du Connétable de Richemont, ed. G. du Fresne de Beaucourt (1883) [extr. *Revue d'histoire nobiliaire et d'archéologie héraldique*, i (1882)]
'Lettres inédites du Connétable Arthur de Richemont et autres grands personnages aux conseillers et habitats de la ville de Lyon', ed. J.-P. Gauthier, *Revue du Lyonnais*, no. 219 (1859), 323-43

BIBLIOGRAPHY

Lettres et mandements de Jean V, duc de Bretagne, ed. R. Blanchard, 5 vols (1889–95)
'Lettres des rois de France, des reines, princes et hauts personnages du royaume aux évêques, chapitre, gouverneurs, baillis, maire, échevins habitants et commune de Chartres', ed. L. Merlet, *Mémoirs de la Société Archéologique de l'Orléanais*, iii (1855)
Lettres de rois, reines et autres personnages des cours de France et d'Angleterre, ed. L.-A. Champollion-Figeac, 2 vols (1839–43)
Literae Cantuarienses, ed. J. B. Sheppard, 3 vols (1887–9)
Livre Rouge d'Eu, 1154–1454, ed. A. Legris (1911)
Longnon, A., *Paris pendant la domination anglaise (1420–1436). Documents extraits des Registres de la Chancellerie de France* (1878)
Louis XI, *Catalogue des actes du Dauphin Louis II, devenu le roi de France Louis XI relatifs à l'administration du Dauphiné*, ed. E. Pilot de Thorey, 3 vols (1899–1911)
Louis XI, *Lettres de Louis XI, roi de France*, ed. E. Charavay, 11 vols (1883–1909)
Luce, S., 'Quittances de Georges de la Tremoille et d'Etienne de Vignolles dit Lahire', *BEC*, xx, (1859), 510–12
Luce, S., 'Deux documents inédits rélatifs à frère Richard et à Jeanne d'Arc', *La France pendant la guerre de Cent Ans. Épisodes historiques et vie privée aux xive et xve siècles*, ii (1893), 195–206

Mansi, G. D. (ed.), *Sacrorum conciliorum nova et amplissima collectio*, 31 vols (1759–98)
Marot, P., 'Expédition de Charles VII à Metz (1444–1445). Documents inédits', *BEC*, cii (1941), 109–55
Martin V., 'Die politische Korrespondenz Martins V nach den Brevenregister', ed. K. A. Fink, *Quellen und Forschungen aus Italienischen Archiven und Bibliotheken*, xxvi (1935–6), 172–245
Masselin, Jean, *Journal des États-Généraux de France tenus à Tours en 1484 sous le règne de Charles VIII*, ed. A. Bernier (1835)
Mémoires concernant les pairs de France avec les preuves [ed. A. Lancelot] (1720)
Mémoires et consultations en faveur de Jeanne d'Arc par les juges du procès de rehabilitation, ed. P. Lanéry d'Arc (1889)
Mémoires pour servir à l'histoire de France et de Bourgogne, ed. G. Aubrée, 2 vols (1729)
Memorialen van het Hof (den Raad) van Holland, Zeeland en West-Friesland van den Secretaris Jan Rosa, 4 vols (1929–88)
Memorials of London and London Life in the XIIIth, XIVth and XVth centuries, ed. H. T. Riley (1868)
Mémoriaux de la Chambre des Comptes de Normandie (XIVe–XVIIe siècles), ed. B. Paris, 11 vols (2009–in progress)
Mirot, L. and Deprez, E., 'Les ambassades anglaises pendant la guerre de Cent ans. Catalogue chronologique (1327–1450)', *BEC*, lix (1898), 530–77, lx (1899), 177–214, lxi (1900), 20–58 [for corrections, see Larson, A.]
Monte, Piero da, *Piero da Monte, ein gelehrter und päpstlicher Beamter des 15 Jahrhunderts. Seine Briefsammlung*, ed. J. Haller (1941)
Monuments historiques. Cartons des rois, ed. J. Tardif (1866)
Morice, P.-H., *Mémoires pour servir de preuves à l'histoire ecclesiastique et civile de Bretagne*, 3 vols (1742–6)
Musée des Archives Départementales (1878)

Négociations diplomatiques de la France avec la Toscane, ed. G. Canestrini and A. Desjardins, 6 vols (1859–86)

Nortier, M., 'Les sources de l'histoire de la Normandie au département des manuscrits de la Bibliothèque Nationale de Paris. Le fonds des nouvelles acquisitions françaises. Ms. 1482: Pièces relatives à l'occupation anglaise', *Cahiers Léopold Delisle*, xvi, fascs 3–4 (1967), 55–92

Nortier, M., *Les sources de l'histoire de la Normandie au département des manuscrits de la Bibliothèque Nationale de Paris. Le fonds des nouvelles acquisitions latines* (1959)

Notice des archives de Monsieur le Marquis de Hallay-Coëtquen, ed. A. Vallet de Viriville (1851)

'Notices et extraits de chartes et de manuscrits appartenant au British Museum de Londres', ed. A. Vallet de Viriville, *BEC*, viii (1847), 110–47

'Notices et extraits de manuscrits intéressant l'histoire de France conservés à la Bibliothèque Impériale de Vienne (XIIIe–XVIe siècles)', ed. E.-S. Bougenot, *BHP* (1892), 4–65

Nouvelles recherches sur la famille de Jeanne d'Arc. Enquêtes inédites, ed. G de Bouteiller and G de Braux (1879)

Ordonnances des rois de France de la troisième race, ed. D. Secousse et al., 21 vols (1729–1849)

Original Letters illustrative of English History, ed. H. Ellis, 11 vols in 3 series (1825–46)

Parliament Rolls of Medieval England, ed. C. Given-Wilson et al., 16 vols (2005)

Particularités curieuses sur Jacqueline de Bavière, comtesse de Hainaut, A. Decourtrai and L. Devillers, 2 vols (1838–79)

Paston Letters, 1422–1509, ed. J. Gairdner, 6 vols (1904) [all references to *Paston Letters (G)* are to supplementary documents printed in this edition].

Paston Letters and Papers of the Fifteenth Century, ed. N. Davis, R. Beadle and C. Richmond, 3 vols (1971–2005) [Unless otherwise stated, other references are to this edition]

Pays de la Loire moyenne dans le Trésor des chartes. Berry, Blésois, Chartrain, Orléanais, Touraine, 1350–1502 (Archives nationales, JJ 80–235), ed. B. Chevalier (1993)

Potvin, C. (ed.), 'Hughes de Lannoy, 1384–1456', *Compte-rendu des séances de la Commission Royale d'Histoire*, 4e série, vi (1879), 117–38

Preuves Bretagne: see Morice, P.-H.

'Private indentures for life service in peace and war, 1278–1476', ed. M. Jones and S. Walker, *Camden Miscellany*, xxxii (Royal Historical Society, Camden Fifth Series, iii) (1994), 1–190

Proceedings and Ordinances of the Privy Council of England, ed. N. H. Nicolas, 7 vols (1834–7)

Procès de condamnation et de réhabilitation de Jeanne d'Arc, dite Pucelle, ed. J. Quicherat, 5 vols (1841–9) [cited as *Proc. Q.*]

Procès de condamnation de Jeanne d'Arc, ed. P. Tisset and Y. Lanhers, 3 vols (1960–71) [cited as *Proc. C.*]

Procès en nullité de la condamnation de Jeanne d'Arc, ed. P. Duparc, 5 vols (1977–88) [cited as *Proc. N.*]

Procès politiques au temps de Charles VII et de Louis XI. Alençon, ed. J. Blanchard (2018)

'Programme d'un governement constitutional en Belgique au xve siècle', ed. J. Kervyn de Lettenhove, *Bulletin de l'Académie Royale de Belgique*, 2e série, xiv (1862), 218–50

Protokollbücher des Ordens vom Goldenenflies, ed. S. Dünnebeil, 4 vols (2002–16)

Quelques actes normands des XIVe, XVe et XVIe siècles, ed. V. Hunger, 3 vols (1909–11)

Rapport . . . sur les différentes séries de documents concernant l'histoire de la Belgique qui sont conservées dans les archives de l'ancienne chambres des comptes de Flandre à Lille, ed. L. F. Gachard (1841)
Rapport . . . sur les documents concernant l'histoire de la Belgique qui existent dans les dépots littéraires de Dijon et de Paris, i, *Archives de Dijon*, ed. L. F. Gachard (1843)
Raynald, O.: see Baronius, C.
Records of Convocation, ed. G. Bray, 20 vols (2005–6)
Recueil des documents concernant le Poitou contenus dans les régistres de la Chancellerie de France, ed. P. Guerin and L. Célier, 14 vols, *AHP*, xi, xiii, xvii, xix, xxi, xxiv, xxvi, xxix, xxxii, xxxv, xxxviii, xli, l, lvi (1881–1958)
Recueil de documents sur l'histoire de Lorraine, ed. H. Lepage, i (1855)
Recueil de documents inédits concernant la Picardie, ed. V. de Beauvillé, 5 vols (1860–82)
Recueil de documents relatifs à l'histoire des monnaies frappées par les rois de France depuis Philippe II jusqu'à François I, ed. F. de Saulcy, 4 vols (1879–92)
Receuil des ordonnances des Pays-Bas, Première série: 1381–1506. Deuxième section (Ordonnances de Philippe le Bon), i, *Ordonnances générales de Philippe le Bon, 1430–1467*; ii, *Ordonnances de Philippe le Bon pour les duchés de Brabant et de Limbourg et les pays d'Outre-Meuse, 1430–1467*; iii, *Ordonnances de Philippe le Bon pour le comté de Hainaut, 1425–1467*, ed. P. Godding and J.-M. Cauchies, 3 vols (2005–13)
Recueil des privilèges accordés à la ville de Bordeaux par Charles VII et Louis XI, ed. M. Gouron (1938)
Register of Edmund Lacy, Bishop of Exeter, 1420–1455. Registrum Commune, ed. G. R. Dunstan, 5 vols (1963–72)
Register of Henry Chichele, Archbishop of Canterbury, 1414–1443, ed. E. F. Jacob, 4 vols (1943–7)
Register of the Most Noble Order of the Garter, ed. J. Anstis, 2 vols (1724)
Register of Thomas Langley Bishop of Durham, 1406–1437, ed. R. L. Storey, 6 vols (1956–70)
Régistre de délibérations du Conseil de Ville de Reims (1422–1436), ed. S. Guilbert (1990–1)
Régistre de délibérations du Conseil de Ville de Troyes (1429–1433), ed. A. Roserot (1886)
Régistre et minutes des notaires du Comté de Dunois, ed. L. Merlet (1886)
Régistres consulaires de la ville de Lyon, ed. M.-C. Guigue, 2 vols (1882–1926)
Régistres de deliberations du corps de ville de Poitiers, ed. R. Favreau, 4 vols, *AHP*, lxvi–lxix (2014–15)
Régistres de la Jurade, 7 vols, *Archives municipales de Bordeaux*, iii–iv, vi–x (1873–1913)
[*Régistres de Tournai*] *Extraits analytiques des anciens régistres des consaux de la ville de Tournai*, ed. H. Vandenbroeck, 2 vols (1861–3)
Registrum Thome Spofford Episcopi Herefordensis, ed. A. T. Bannister (1919)
'Répertoire des documents copiés ou analysés par dom Lenoir concernant la region de Vire et ses principaux familles, 1271–1724', ed. E. Taverson, *Répertoire Périodique de Documentation Normande*, 2e série, no. 1 (1984)
Répertoire sommaire des documents manuscrits de l'histoire de Bretagne antérieurs à 1789 conservés dans les dépôts publics de Paris, i, *Bibliothèque Nationale et Archives Nationales*, ed. H. du Halgouet (1914) [all published]

Reports from the Lords Committees . . . touching the Dignity of a Peer, 5 vols (1820–9) [cited as *RDP*]

'Rôles de dépenses du temps de Charles VII (1450–51)', ed. G. du Fresne de Beaucourt, *ABSHF*, ii, (1864), 123–53

Rôles normands et français et autres pièces tirées des Archives de Londres par Bréquigny, Memoires de la Société des Antiquaires de Normandie, xxiii. 1 (1858)

Rose, S. (ed.), *The Navy of the Lancastrian Kings. Accounts and Inventories of William Soper, Keeper of the King's Ships, 1422–1427* (1982)

Rotuli Parliamentorum, ed. J. Strachey et al., 7 vols (1767–1832)

Rotuli Scotiae, ed. D. Macpherson et al., 2 vols (1814)

[*Royal Wills*] *A Collection of all the Wills . . . of the Kings and Queens of England, Princes and Princesses of Wales and every Branch of the Blood Royal*, ed. J. Nichols (1780)

Samaran, C., 'Chanteurs ambulants et propagande politique sous Louis XI', *BEC*, c (1939), 233–4

Select Documents of English Constitutional History, 1307–1485, ed. S. B. Chrimes and A. L. Brown (1961)

Sir John Paston's 'Grete Boke'. A Descriptive Catalogue with an Introduction, of British Library MS Lansdowne 285 (1984)

Soper Accounts: see Rose S., *The Navy of the Lancastrian Kings*

Stadsrekeningen van Leiden (1390–1434), ed. A. Meerkamp van Embden, 2 vols (1913–14)

Statutes of the Realm, ed. A. Luders, T. E. Tomlins et al., 11 vols (1810–28)

Stouff, L., 'Contribution à l'histoire de la Bourgogne du concile de Bâle. Textes inédits extraits des archives de la Chambre des Comptes de Dijon, 1433', *Publications de l'Université de Dijon*, i, *Mélanges* (1928), 83–133

Taylor, C. (ed.), *Joan of Arc. La Pucelle. Selected sources translated and annotated* (2006)

'Texte restitué de deux diplomes de Charles VII relatifs à la Pucelle', ed. A. Vallet de Viriville, *BEC*, xv (1854), 271–9

Thesaurus novus anecdotorum, ed. E. Martène and U. Durand, 5 vols (1717)

Thielemans, M. R. (ed.), 'Les Croÿ, conseillers des ducs de Bourgogne. Documents extraits de leurs archives familiales', *Bulletin de la Commission Royale d'Histoire*, cxxiv (1959), 1–141

Titres de la maison ducale de Bourbon, ed. A. Huillard-Bréholles, 2 vols (1867–74)

Verdier, M. L. (ed.), 'Quelques rôles relatifs à la garnison du château d'Arques', *Mélanges de la Société de l'histoire de Normandie*, xii, (1933), 97–111

Veterum scriptorum et monumentorum historicorum, dogmaticorum moralium amplissima collectio, ed. E. Martène and U. Durand, 9 vols (1724–33)

Views of the Hosts of Alien Merchants, 1440–1444, ed. H. Bradley (2012)

Vicomté d'Orbec: see Frondeville, H. de

Visites archidiaconales de Josas, ed. J.-M. Alliot (1902)

White and Black Books of the Cinque Ports, 1432–1955, ed. F. Hull (1966)

BIBLIOGRAPHY

C NARRATIVE AND LITERARY SOURCES

Asterisks * mark editions having important documentary notes or appendices

'Anales breves de Vizcaya', ed. S. Aguirre Gandarias, *La dos primeras cronicas de Vizcaya* (1986), 107-96

Annales rerum anglicarum [attributed to William Worcester], in *Letters and Papers*, ii (1864), 743-93

Auchinleck Chronicle, ed. T. Thomson (1819)

'Avis à Yolande d'Aragon: un miroir au prince du temps de Charles VII', ed. J.-P. Boudet and E. Sené, *Cahiers de recherches médiévales et humanistes*, no. 24 (2012), 51-84

Bale, Robert, 'Chronicle', *Six Town Chronicles*, 114-53

Basin, Thomas, *Apologie ou plaidoyer pour moi-même*, ed. C. Samaran (1974)

Basin, Thomas, *Histoire des règnes de Charles VII et de Louis XI*, ed. J. Quicherat, 4 vols (1855-9) [all references to *Hist. (Q.)* are to the minor works and documents printed in vol. iv of this edition]

Basin, Thomas, *Histoire de Charles VII*, ed. C. Samaran, 2 vols (1933-44) [all references to the History are to this edition]

Basset, Peter, and Hanson, Christopher, *De actis armorum conquestus regni francie*, ed. A. Curry and R. Ambühl, *A Soldiers' Chronicle of the Hundred Years War* (2022) [cited as Basset, *Chron.*]

Beke, Johannes de [Continuator], *Croniken van den stichte van Utrecht ende van Hollant*, ed. H. Bruch (1982)

Benet, John, 'Chronicle for the years 1400 to 1462', ed. G. L. and M. A. Harriss, *Camden Miscellany*, xxxii (Royal Historical Society, Camden Fourth Series, ix) (1972), 151-252

Bernis, Michel de, 'Chronique des comtes de Foix', ed. H. Biu, 'Du panegyrique à l'histoire: l'archiviste Michel de Bernis, chroniqueur des comtes de Foix (1445)', *BEC*, clx (2002), 385-473

Blacman, John, *Henry the Sixth*, ed. M. R. James (1919)

Blondel, Robert, 'Reductio Normannie', ed. A. Héron, *Oeuvres*, ii (1893)

Boece, Hector, *Murthlacensium et Aberdonensium Episcoporum Vitae*, ed. J. Moir (1894)

Boke of Noblesse: see Worcester, William

Bouchart, Alain, *Grandes chroniques de Bretagne*, ed. M.-L. Auger and G. Jeanneau, 3 vols (1986-8)

Bourdigné, Jean, *Chroniques d'Anjou*, ed. V. Godard-Faultrier, 2 vols (1842)

Bouvier, Gilles le, *Les Chroniques du Roi Charles VII*, ed. H. Courteault and L. Célier (1979)

Bouvier, Gilles le, *Le livre de la description des pays*, ed. E.-T. Hamy (1908)

[Bouvier, Gilles le]: see 'Recouvrement de Normandie', ed. J. Stevenson (1863)

Bovet, Honoré, *L'arbre des batailles*, ed. R. Richter-Bergmeier (2017)

Bower, Walter, *Scotichronicon*, ed. D. E. R. Watt, 9 vols (1989-98)

[*Breviarium historiale*], L. Delisle, 'Un nouveau témoignage relative à la mission de Jeanne d'Arc', *BEC*, xlvi (1885), 649-68

Brut, or the Chronicles of England, ed. F. W. D. Brie (1906-8)

Budt, Adrian de, 'Chronique', *Chroniques ... Belgique*, i, 211-717

Bueil, Jean de, *Le Jouvencel*, ed. W. Lecestre, 2 vols (1877-9)

Cagny, Perceval de, *Chroniques*, ed. H. Moranvillé (1902)

Calot, Laurent, 'Document relatif à l'entrée du roi d'Angleterre Henri VI à Paris en 1431', ed. M. Floran, *Revue des Études Historiques* (1909), 411-15
Capgrave, John, *Liber de Illustribus Henricis*, ed. F. C. Hingeston (1858)
Cent nouvelles (Les), ed. F. P. Sweetser (1966)
Chartier, Alain, *Le livre de l'espérance*, ed. F. Rouy (1989)
Chartier, Alain, *Oeuvres latines*, ed. P. Bourgain-Hemeryck (1977)
Chartier, Alain, *Poetical Works*, ed. J. C. Laidlaw (1974)
Chartier, Alain, *Le Quadrilecte Invectif*, ed. F. Bouchet (2011)
*Chartier, Jean, *Chronique de Charles VII*, ed. A. Vallet de Viriville, 3 vols (1858)
Chartier, Jean, *La chronique latine inédite de Jean Chartier (1422-1450)*, ed. C. Samaran, *ABSHF* (1926), Part 2, 183-273
*Chastellain, Georges, 'Chronique', *Oeuvres*, ed. J. Kervyn de Lettenhove, vols i-v (1863-4)
Christine de Pisan: see Pisan, Christine de
Chronicle of London from 1089 to 1483, ed. N. H. Nicolas and E. Tyrell (1827)
Chronicles of London, ed. C. L. Kingsford (1905)
'Chronicon rerum gestarum in monasterio Sancti Albani', ed. H. T. Riley, in Amundesham, John, *Annales Monasterii S. Albani*, i, (1870), 3-69
'Chronique de doyen de S. Thiébault de Metz', in A. Calmet, *Histoire ecclésiastique et civile de Lorraine*, v (1745), *Preuves*, pp. vi-cxvii
Chronique Martiniane, ed. P. Champion (1907)
Chronique du Mont-Saint-Michel (1343-1468), ed. S. Luce, 2 vols (1879-1883)
Chronique de la Pucelle, ed. A. Vallet de Viriville (1859)
Chronique du Religieux de Saint-Denys, ed. L. Bellaguet, 6 vols (1839-52)
'Chronique Rouennaise, 1371-1434', ed. C. R. de Beaurepaire, in Cochon, *Chronique normande*, 316-56
['Chronique de Tournai'] 'Chronique des Pays-Bas, de France, d'Angleterre et de Tournai', *Corpus Chronicorum Flandriae*, iii, 110-569
'Chroniques des pays de Hollande, Zellande et aussi en partie de Haynnau', ed. F. de Reiffenberg, *Compte-rendu des séances de la Commission Royale d'Histoire*, xii (1847), 250-72
Chroniques relatives à l'histoire de la Belgique sous la domination des ducs de Bourgogne, ed. J. Kervyn de Lettenhove, 3 vols (1870-6)
Cochon, Pierre, *Chronique normande*, ed. C. R. de Beaurepaire (1870)
['Codex Tegernseer'], ed. F. von Löher, 'Beiträge', 12-28
Commynes, Philippe de, *Mémoires*, ed. D. Godefroy and N. Lenglet du Fresnoy, 4 vols (1747) [All references to Commynes (LdF) are to the documents printed in vols ii-iv of this edition]
Commynes, Philippe de, *Mémoires*, ed. J. Blanchard (2007) [all references to the text are to this edition]
'Complainte sur les misères de Paris composée en 1435', ed. L. Auvray, *Bulletin de la Société de l'Histoire de Paris*, xviii (1891), 84-7
Corpus chronicorum Flandriae, ed. J. J. de Smet, 4 vols (1837-65)
Cronicques de Normendie (1223-1453), ed. A. Hellot (1881)

Denis, Jehan, 'Journal de Jehan Denis, bourgeois de Macon ... 1430-1438', *Documents inédits pour servir à l'histoire de Bourgogne*, ed. M. Canat (1863), 195-493
'Dethe of the Kynge of Scotis', ed. L. M. Matheson, *Death and Dissent*, 1-59
'Deux chansons normandes sur le siege d'Orléans et la mort de Salisbury' ed. L. Jarry, *Bulletin de la Société Archéologique et Historique de l'Orléanais*, x (1893), 359-70

BIBLIOGRAPHY

Dits de cronike ende genealogie van den Prinsen ende graven van het Foreeste van Buc dat heet Vlaenderlant van 863 tot 1436 [attributed to Jan van Dixmude], ed. J.-J. Lambin (1839)
Dixmude, Olivier van, *Merkwaerdige gebeurtenissen vooral in Vlaenderen en Brabant van 1377 tot 1443*, ed. J.-J. Lambin (1835)
Dynter, Edmond de, *Chronique des ducs de Brabant*, ed. P. F. X. de Ram, 3 vols (1854–60)

*English Chronicle of the Reigns of Richard II, Henry IV, Henry V and Henry VI, ed. J. G. Davies (1856)
English Chronicle, 1377–1461, ed. W. Marx (2003) [all references to the text are to this edition]
Escouchy, Mathieu de, *Chronique*, ed. G. du Fresne de Beaucourt, 3 vols (1863–4)
Esquerrier et Miègeville, Arnaud, *Chroniques romanes des comtes de Foix composées au xve siècle*, ed. H. Courteault and F. Pasquier (1893)

Fauquembergue, Clément de, *Journal de Clément de Fauquembergue, Greffier du Parlement de Paris, 1417–1435*, ed. A. Tuetey, 3 vols (1903–15)
Fenin, Pierre, *Mémoires*, ed. L. M. E. Dupont (1837)
Fortescue, Sir John, *The Governance of England*, ed. C. Plummer (1885)
Fortescue, Sir John, *De Laudibus Legum Anglie*, ed. S. B. Chrimes (1942)
Fribois, Noël de, *Abrégé des croniques de France*, ed. K. Daly (2006)
Froissart, Jean, *Chroniques*, ed. S. Luce, G. Reynaud et al., 15 vols (1869–1975)

Gairdner, J., *Three Fifteenth-century English Chronicles* (1880)
Gascoigne, Thomas, *Loci e Libro Veritatum*, ed. J. E. Thorold Rogers (1881)
Gélu, Jacques, *De la venue de Jeanne. Un traité scolastique en faveur de Jeanne d'Arc*, ed. O. Hanne (2012)
Germain, Jean, 'Liber de virtutibus Philippi, Burgundiae et Brabantiae ducis', *Chroniques . . . Belgique*, iii, 1–115
Gerson, Jean, *Oeuvres complètes*, ed. P. Glorieux, 10 vols (1960–73)
'Geste des nobles françois', in *Chronique de la Pucelle*, ed. A. Vallet de Viriville (1859), 87–204
[*Giles's Chronicle*]: *Chronicon Angliae de regnis trium regum Lancastriensium Henrici IV, Henrici V et Henrici VI*, ed. J. A. Giles (1848)
*Godefroy, D. (ed.), *Histoire de Charles VII, Roi de France* (1661)
Great Chronicle of London, ed. A. H. Thomas and I. D. Thornley (1938)
[Greffier de La Rochelle], 'Relation inédite sur Jeanne d'Arc', ed. J. Quicherat, *Revue Historique*, iv (1877), 327–44
Gregory, William, 'Chronicle', ed. J. Gairdner, *Historical Collections*, 55–239
Gruel, Guillaume, *Chronique d'Arthur de Richemont, Connétable de France, Duc de Bretagne (1393–1458)*, ed. A. Le Vavasseur (1890)
Guillebert de Metz, 'Description de la ville de Paris sous Charles VI', ed. A. Leroux de Lincy, *Paris et ses historiens aux xive et xve siècles* (1867), 117–511

Hall, Edward, *Chronicle*, ed. E. Ellis (1809)
Hardyng, John, *Chronicle*, ed. H. Ellis (1812)
Héraut Berry: see Bouvier, Gilles le
'Historiae Croylandensis Continuatio', ed. W. Fulman, *Rerum Anglicarum Scriptorum Veterum*, i, (1684), 451–546
Historical Collections of a Citizen of London, ed. J. Gairdner (1876)

BIBLIOGRAPHY

Historical Poems of the XIVth and XVth Centuries, ed. R. H. Robbins (1959)
Hoccleve, Thomas, *Selections from Hoccleve*, ed. M. C. Seymour (1981)

James I, King of Scotland, *Kingis Quair, together with a Ballad of Good Counsel*,
 ed. W. W. Skeat (1911)
John Vale's Book: see Vale, John
Jouffroy, Jean, 'Ad Pium Papam II de Philippo duce Burgundiae oratio', *Chroniques . . . Belgique*, iii, 137–8.
Journal d'un Bourgeois de Paris, 1405–1449, ed. A. Tuetey (1881)
*Journal du siège d'Orléans, 1428–1429, ed. P. Charpentier and C. Cuissard (1896)
Juvénal des Ursins, Jean, *Écrits politiques*, ed. P. S. Lewis, 3 vols (1978–92)
Juvénal des Ursins, Jean, *Histoire de Charles VI, roi de France*, ed. D. Godefroy (1653)

*Königshoven, Jacob von, *Elsässische und Strasburgische Chronicke*, ed. J. Schiltern
 (1698)

'Laetste deel der kronyk van Jan van Dixmude' [attributed to Jan van Dixmude], *Corpus Chronicorum Flandriae*, iii, 30–109
La Marche, Olivier de, *Mémoires*, ed. H. Beaune and J. d'Arbaumont, 4 vols (1883–8)
Lannoy, Ghillebert de, *Oeuvres*, ed. C. Potvin (1878)
Le Baud, Pierre, *Histoire de Bretagne*, ed. P. d'Hosier (1638)
Le Baud, Pierre, *Compillation des croniques et ystoires des Bretons. Transcription du manuscrit 941 de la Bibliothêque municipale d'Angers*, ed. K. Abélard (2018)
Le Fèvre, Jean le, *Chronique de Jean Le Fèvre, Seigneur de Saint-Rémy*, ed. F. Morand, 2 vols (1876–81)
Leland, *Itinerary*, ed. L. Toulmin Smith, 5 vols (1906–10)
Leroux de Lincy, A., *Paris et ses historiens aux xive et xve siècles* (1867)
Leseur, Guillaume, *Histoire de Gaston IV, comte de Foix*, ed. H. Courteault, 2 vols (1893–5)
Libelle of Englyshe Polycye. A poem on the use of seapower, 1436, ed. G. Warner (1926)
Liber Pluscardensis, ed. J. H. Skene, 2 vols (1877–80)
Livre des miracles de Sainte-Catherine-de-Fierbois (1375–1470), ed. Y. Chauvin, *AHP*, lx (1976)
'Livre des trahisons de France envers la maison de Bourgogne', *Chroniques . . . Belgique*, ii, 1–258
Lydgate, John, *Minor Poems*, ed. H. N. MacCracken, 2 vols (1911–34)

Martial d'Auvergne, *Les poesies. Les vigiles de la mort du roi Charles VII*, 2 vols (1724)
Matheson, L. M., *Death and Dissent. Two Fifteenth-Century Chronicles* (1991)
Maupoint, Jean, 'Journal Parisien de Jean Maupoint, prieur de Sainte-Catherine-dela-Couture (1437–1469)', *Memoires de la Société de l'histoire de Paris*, iv (1877), 1–114
'Mémoire nobiliaire et clivages politiques. Le témoignage d'une courte chronique chevalaresque (1403–1442)', ed. N. Pons, *Journal des Savants* (2002), 299–348
Mistere du siège d'Orléans, ed. V. L. Hamblin (2002)
Monstrelet, Enguerrand de, *Chronique*, ed. L. Douet-d'Arcq, 6 vols (1857–62)
Monumenta Conciliorum Generalium seculi decimi quinti. Scriptores, ed. F. Palacky, E. Birk and R. Beer, 4 vols (1857–1935)
Morosini, Antonio, *Chronique*, ed. G. Lefèvre-Pontalis and L. Dorez, 3 vols, 1898–1902

Orléans, Charles d', *Poésies*, ed. P. Champion (1966)

BIBLIOGRAPHY

'Petite chronique de Guyenne jusqu'à l'an 1442', ed. G. Lefèvre-Pontalis, *BEC*, xlvii (1886), 53–79

Phares, Simon de, *Le recueil des plus célèbre astrologues*, ed. J.-P. Boudet, 2 vols (1997–9)

Pisan, Christine de, *Le livre du corps de policie*, ed. A. J. Kennedy (1998)

Pius II, *Commentarii rerum memorabilium que temporis suis contingerunt*, ed. A. van Heck, 2 vols (1984)

Political Poems and Songs, ed. T. Wright, 2 vols (1859–61)

Pons, N. (ed.), '*L'honneur de la couronne de France*'. *Quatre libelles contre les anglais (vers 1418–vers 1429)* (1990)

'Processus super insultu guerrae Anthonis', ed. U. Chevalier, *Choix de documents historiques inédits sur le Dauphiné (Collection de cartulaires dauphinois*, vii) (1874), 300–38

Raoulet, Jean, 'Chronique', ed. A. Vallet de Viriville, in *Chronique de Charles VII*, iii (1858), 142–99

'Recouvrement de Normandie' [attributed to Gilles le Bouvier, Berry Herald], ed. J. Stevenson, *Narratives of the Expulsion of the English from Normandy, MCCCCXLIX–MCCCCL* (1863), 239–376

Relation or rather a true account of the Island of England, tr. C. A., Sneyd (1847)

'Relation du passage de Charles VII à Limoges en 1438', ed. C.-N. Allou, *Mémoires de la Société Royale des Antiquaires de France*, xi (1835), 357–73

Religious Lyrics of the XVth Century, ed. C. Brown (1939)

['Réponse d'un clerc parisien'], 'Un nouveau témoignage sur Jeanne d'Arc. Réponse d'un clerc parisien à l'apologie de la Pucelle par Gerson', *ABSHF* (1906), 161–79

Roye, Gilles de, 'Chronique', *Chroniques . . . Belgique*, i, 167–210

Rozmital, Leo of, *The Travels of Leo of Rozmital*, ed. tr. M. Letts (1957)

Saint-Paul, Jean de, *Chronique de Bretagne*, ed. A. de la Borderie (1881)

Segovia, John of, *Historia gestorum generalis synodi Basiliensis*, ed. E. Birk and R. Beer, 3 vols, *Monumenta conciliorum generalium saeculi decimi quinti. Scriptores*, II–IV (1873–1935)

'Short English Chronicle', ed. J. Gairdner, *Three Fifteenth-century English Chronicles*, 1–80

Siège de Rouen par le roi Charles VII en 1449, ed. A Pottier (1841) [reissued in *Revue Retrospective Normande. Documents Inédits pour servir à l'histoire de Rouen et de la Normandie* (1842)]

Sigonio, Carlo, 'Vita Beati Nicolai Cardinalis Albergati', *Acta Sanctorum*, May, ii (1866), 475–88

Six Town Chronicles of England, ed. R. Flenley (1911)

'Supplément aux témoignages contemporains sur Jeanne d'Arc. Chroniques relatives à l'histoire de Belgique sous la domination des ducs de Bourgogne', ed. J. Quicherat, *Revue Historique*, xix (1882), 60–83

Tarneau, Gérard, 'Chronique et journal de Gérard Tarneau, notaire de Pierrebuffière, 1423–1438', *Chartes, chroniques et mémoriaux pour servir à l'histoire de la Marche et du Limousin*, ed. A. Leroux and A. J. B. Bosvieux (1886), 203–37

Taverne, Antoine de la, *Journal de la paix d'Arras (1435)*, ed. A. Bossuat (1936)

Taylor, C. (ed.), *Debating the Hundred Years War* (2006)

Thomassin, Mathieu, *Régistre Delphinal*, ed. K. Daly (2018)

Tringant, Louis, 'Commentaire du "Jouvencel"', Jean de Bueil, *Le Jouvencel*, ii, 265–99

BIBLIOGRAPHY

Upton, Nicholas, *De Studio Militari*, ed. E. Bysshe (1654)

Vale, John, *The Politics of Fifteenth-century England. John Vale's Book*, ed. M. L. Kekewich, C. Richmond et al. (1995)
Vespasiano da Bisticci, *Vite di Uomini Illustre del Secolo XV*, ed. P. d'Ancona and E. Aeschlimann (1951)
Vigneulles, Philippe de, *Chronique*, ed. C. Bruneau, 3 vols (1927–32)

*Waurin, Jean de, *Anchiennes cronicques d'Engleterre*, ed. L. M. E. Dupont, 3 vols (1858–63) [cited as *Cron.* (Dupont); all references to this edition are to the documentary appendix]
Waurin, Jean de, *Recueil des croniques et anchiennes istories de la Grant Bretaigne à present nommé Engleterre, 1399–1422, 1422–1431*, ed. E. L. C. P. Hardy, 5 vols (1864–91) [all references to the text are to this edition]
Whethamstede, John, *Registrum Abbatiae Johannis Whethamstede Abbatis Monasterii Sancti Albani*, ed. H. T. Riley, 2 vols (1872–3)
Windecke, Eberhard, *Denkwürdigkeiten zur Geschichte des Zeitalters Kaiser Sigmunds*, ed. W. Altmann (1893)
Windecke, Eberhard, *Les sources allemandes de l'histoire de Jeanne d'Arc. Eberhard Windecke*, ed. G. Lefèvre-Pontalis (1903)
[Worcester, William], *The Boke of Noblesse*, ed. J. G. Nichols (1860)
Worcester, William, *Itineraries*, ed. J. H. Harvey (1969)

D SELECTED SECONDARY WORKS

Asterisks * mark works having important documentary notes and appendices

Acheson, E., *A Gentry Community. Leicestershire in the Fifteenth Century* (1992)
Algemene geschiedenis der Nederlanden, ed. J. A. van Houtte et al., 13 vols (1949–58)
Allmand, C. T., 'The collection of Dom Lenoir and the English occupation of Normandy in the fifteenth century', *Archives*, vi (1964), 202–10
Allmand, C. T., 'Alan Kirketon: a clerical royal councillor in Normandy during the English occupation in the fifteenth century', *Journal of Ecclesiastical History*, xv (1965)[1], 33–9
Allmand, C. T., 'Normandy and the Council of Basel', *Speculum*, xl (1965)[2], 1–14
Allmand, C. T., 'A note on denization in fifteenth-century England', *Medievalia et Humanistica*, xvii (1966), 127–8
Allmand, C. T., 'The Anglo-French negotiations, 1439', *Bulletin of the Institute of Historical Research*, xl (1967), 1–33
Allmand, C. T., 'The Lancastrian land settlement in Normandy, 1417–50', *Economic History Review*, xxi (1968), 461–79
Allmand, C. T., 'La Normandie devant l'opinion anglaise à la fin de la guerre de Cent Ans', *BEC*, cxxviii (1970), 345–68
Allmand, C. T., 'The aftermath of war in fifteenth-century France', *History*, lxi (1976), 344–357
Allmand, C. T., 'Local reaction to the French reconquest of Normandy: the case of Rouen', *The Crown and local communities in England and France in the Fifteenth Century*, ed. J. R. L. Highfield and R. Jeffs (1981), 146–61

BIBLIOGRAPHY

Allmand, C. T., 'L'artillerie de l'armée anglaise et son organisation à l'époque de Jeanne d'Arc', *Jeanne d'Arc. Une époque. Un rayonnement. Colloque d'histoire médiévale, Orléans, octobre 1979* (1982), 73–83

Allmand, C. T., *Lancastrian Normandy, 1415–1450. The history of a medieval occupation* (1983)

Allmand, C. T., *The Hundred Years War. England and France at War, c.1300–c.1450* (1988)

Allmand, C. T., 'Changing views of the soldier in late medieval France', *Guerre et société en France, en Angleterre et en Bourgogne, xive–xve siècle*, ed. P. Contamine, C. Giry-Deloison and M. Keen (1991), 171–88

Allmand, C. T., 'The English and the Church in Lancastrian Normandy', *England and Normandy in the Middle Ages*, ed. D. Bates and A. Curry (1994), 287–97

Allmand, C. T., 'Le traité d'Arras en 1435: une perspective anglaise', *Arras et la diplomatie européenne, XVe–XVIe siècles*, ed. D. Clauzel, C. Giry-Deloison and C. Leduc (1999), 101–8

Allmand, C. T., 'Le problème de la desertion en France, en Angleterre et en Bourgogne à la fin du moyen age', *Guerre, pouvoir et noblesse au moyen age. Mélanges en l'honneur de Philippe Contamine* (2000), ed. J. Paviot and J. Verger, 31–41

Allmand, C. T., and Keen, M., 'History and the literature of war: the *Boke of Noblesse* of William Worcester', *War, Government and Power in Late Medieval France*, ed. C. Allmand (2000), 92–105

Allmand, C. T., 'National reconciliation in France at the end of the Hundred Tears War', *Journal of Medieval Military History*, v (2008), 149–64

Ambühl, R. *Prisoners of war in the Hundred Years War. Ransom culture in the late midle ages* (2013)

Ambühl, R., 'Joan of Arc as *prisonnière de guerre*', *EHR* cxxxii (2017)[1], 1045–76

Ambühl, R., 'Le maître et son prisonnier de guerre: droit romain contre droit coutumier', *Autour d'Azincourt: une société face à la guerre (v. 1370–v. 1420)*, ed. A. Marchandisse and B. Schnerb (2017)[2], 265–82

Ambühl, R., '"Il ne voudroit faire chose qui fust à deshonneur": Charles VII à la conquête de Rouen (1449)', *La guerre en Normandie (XIe–XVe)*, ed. A. Curry and V. Gazeau (2018), 283–95

Ambühl, R., 'Hostages and the laws of war: the surrender of the castle and palace of Rouen', *Medieval Hostageship, c. 700–c.1500: hostage, captive, prisoner of war, guarantee, peacemaker*, ed. M. Bennett and K. Weikert (2019), 187–206

Angot, A., *Dictionnaire historique, topographique et biographique de la Mayenne*, 5 vols (1900–10)

Anselme de la Vierge Marie [Pierre de Guibours], *Histoire généalogique et chronologique de la maison royale de France*, 3rd edn, 9 vols (1726–33)

Appleby, J. C., 'Devon privateering from early times to 1668', *The New Maritime History of Devon*, ed. M. Duffy et al., i (1992), 90–7

*Arcelin, A., 'Histoire du château de la Roche de Solutré', *Annales de l'Académie de Mâcon*, 2e série, ii (1880), 106–57

Armstrong, C. A. J., 'La Toison d'Or et la loi des armes', *Publications du Centre des Études Bourguignonnes*, v (1963), 71–7

Armstrong, C. A. J., 'La double monarchie France – Angleterre et la maison de Bourgogne (1420–1435): le déclin d'une alliance', *Annales de de Bourgogne*, xxxvii (1965), 81–112

Armstrong, C. A. J., 'La politique matrimoniale des ducs de Bourgogne de la maison de Valois', *Annales de Bourgogne*, xl (1968), 5–58, 89–193

BIBLIOGRAPHY

Armstrong, C. A. J., 'Sir John Fastolf and the law of arms', *War, Literature and Politics in the Late Middle Ages*, ed. C. T. Allmand (1976), 46–56
*Arnould, M. A., 'Une estimation des revenus et des dépenses de Philippe le Bon en 1445', *Acta Historica Bruxellensia*, iii (1974), 131–219
Ascoli, G., *La Grande-Bretagne devant l'opinion française depuis la guerre de cent ans jusqu'à la fin du XVIe siècle* (1927)
Askins, W., 'The brothers Orléans and their keepers', *Charles d'Orléans in England*, ed. M.-J. Arn (2000), 27–45
Atlas historique des villes de France (1982–in progress)
Augis, J., 'La bataille de Verneuil (jeudi 17 août 1424) vue de Châteaudun', *Bulletin de la Société Dunoise*, xvi (1932–5), 116–21
Autrand, F., 'Rétablir l'état: l'année 1454 au Parlement', *La réconstruction après la guerre de Cent Ans (Actes du 104e Congrès National des Sociétés Savantes, Bordeaux, 1979)* (1981)[1], i, 7–23
Autrand, F., *Naissance d'un grand corps de l'état. Les gens du Parlement de Paris* (1981)[2]
Avinain, J., Paris. 'Découverte d'une section de l'enceinte de Charles V', *Archéologia*, no. 543 (May 2016), 34–9

*Baldwin, J. F., *The King's Council in England during the Middle Ages* (1913)
Balfour-Melville, E. W. M., *James I, King of Scots* (1936)
*Barbé, L. A., *Margaret of Scotland and the Dauphin Louis. An historical study* (1917)
Barbey, F., *Louis de Chalon, prince d'Orange, seigneur d'Orbe, Echallans, Grandson, etc. (1390–1463)* (1926)
Barker, J., *Conquest. The English Kingdom of France, 1417–1450* (2009)[1]
Barker, J., 'The foe within: treason in Lancastrian Normandy', *Soldiers, Nobles and Gentlemen. Essays in honour of Maurice Keen*, ed. P. Coss and C. Tyerman (2009)[2], 305–20
*Barnard, F. P., *Edward IV's French Expedition of 1475. The Leaders and their Badges* (1925)
Barron, C. M. (1970): see E: Unpublished Theses.
Barron, C. M., 'Introduction', *England and the Low Countries in the Late Middle Ages* (1995), 1–28
Barron, C. M., *London in the Middle Ages. Government and People, 1200–1500* (2004)
Bartier, J., *Légistes et gens de finances au xve siècle. Les conseillers des Ducs de Bourgogne Philippe le Bon et Charles le Téméraire* (1952)
*Baud, H., *Amadée VIII et la guerre de cent ans* (1971)
*Baud, H., 'La correspondance entre le roi Charles VII et le duc Amadée VIII pendant la gerre de cent ans', *Amadée VIII–Felix V premier duc de Savoie et Pape (1383–1451)*, ed. B. Andenmatten and A. Paravicini Bagliani (1992), 247–57
Baulant, M., 'Le prix des grains à Paris de 431 à 1788', *Annales. Economies, sociétés, civilisations*, xxiii (1968), 520–40
Baume, A. J. L. (1978): see E: Unpublished Theses
Baume, A. J. L.,'Les operations militaires anglaises pour expulser les companies françaises du pays de Caux et du Vexin normand, 1436–1437', *La 'France Anglaise' au moyen age (Actes du 111e Congrès National des Sociétés Savantes, Poitiers, 1986)* (1988), 393–400
Baume, A. J. L., 'L'organisation militaire des seigneuries du duc d'York, 1443–1449', *Cahiers Léopold Delisle*, xl (1991), 37–44
Baume, A. J. L., 'Gisors et la Normandie anglaise, 1419–1449', *Cahiers de la Société Historique et Géographique du Bassin de l'Epte*, no. 40 (1997), 47–54

BIBLIOGRAPHY

Baume, A. J. L., 'Soldats et paysans en Normandie', *Le monde rurale en Normandie: Actes du XXXIIe Congrès des sociétés historiques et archéologiques de Normandie, Gisors, 2–5 octobre 1997, Annales de Normandie, Série des Congrès des sociétés historiques et archéologiques de Normandie*, iii (1998), 275–82

Baume, A. J. L., 'Une bataille, ses acteurs et ses historiens. Gerberoy et la Normandie lancastrienne (1435)', *Cahiers de la Société Historique et Géographique du Bassin de l'Epte*, no. 65–6 (2011)

Bazin, J.-L., *La Bourgogne de la mort de Philippe le Hardi au traité d'Arras, 1404–1435* (1897)

Beauchesne, A. de, 'Jean des Vaux, capitaine de Mayenne pendant la guerre de cent ans', *Revue historique et archéologique du Maine*, lxxiii (1913), 225–72

*Beaucourt, G. du Fresne de, *Histoire de Charles VII*, 6 vols (1881–91)

Beaune, C., *Naissance de la nation France* (1985)

Beaune, C., *Jeanne d'Arc* (2004)

Beaurepaire, C. R. de, 'Notes sur la prise du château de Rouen par Ricarville en 1432', *Précis analytique des travaux de l'Académie des Sciences, Belles-Lettres et Arts de Rouen*, lviii (1856)[1], 306–29

*Beaurepaire, C.R. de, *De la Vicomté de l'Eau de Rouen et de ses coutumes au XIIIe et au XIVe siècles* (1856)[2]

Beaurepaire, C. R. de, 'De l'administration de la Normandie sous la domination anglaise aux années 1424, 1425 et 1429 d'après trois comptes de la recette générale de Normandie, conservés à la Bibliothèque Impériale', *Mémoires de la Société des Antiquaires de Normandie*, 3e série, xxiv (1859)[1], 170–230

Beaurepaire, C. R. de, *Les états de Normandie sous la domination anglaise* (1859)[2]

Beaurepaire, C. R. de, *Recherches sur le procès de condamnation de Jeanne d'Arc* (1869)

Beaurepaire, C. R. de, *Fondations pieuses du duc de Bedford à Rouen* (1873), 343–86

*Beaurepaire, C. R. de, ['Deux épisodes de l'histoire rouennaise'], *Bulletin de la Société des Antiquaires de Normandie* (1880–3), 325–54

Beaurepaire, C. R. de, *Notes sur les juges et assesseurs du procès de condamnation de Jeanne d'Arc* (1890)

*Beauvillé, V. de, *Histoire de la ville de Montdidier*, 3 vols (1857)

Bell, A. R., Curry, A., King, A., Simpkin, D., *The Soldier in Later Medieval England* (2013)

Bellamy, J. G., *Crime and public order in England in the Later Middle Ages* (1973)

Belleforest, F. de, *Les grandes annales et histoire générale de la France*, 2 vols (1579)

Bellis, J., *The Hundred Years War in Literature* (2016)

Belon, M.-J. and Balme, F., *Jean Bréhal, Grand Inquisiteur de France et la rehabilitation de Jeanne d'Arc*, (1893)

Belotte, O., 'Les opérations militaires dans la vallée de la Seine aux confins de la Bourgogne et de la Champagne de 1429 à 1435', *Cahiers d'histoire militaires*, no 3 (1970), 101–16

Beltz, G. F., *Memorials of the Order of the Garter* (1841)

Benet, J., *Jean d'Anjou, duc de Calabria et de Lorraine (1426–1470)* (1997)

Bennett, H. S., *The Pastons and their England. Studies in an Age of Transition* (1968)

Bennett, M., 'The Plantagenet Empire as "Enterprise Zone": war and business networks, c. 1400–50', *The Plantagenet Empire, 1259–1453*, ed. P. Crooks, D. Green and W. M. Ormrod (2016), 335–58

Bennett, M., 'Last men standing: Lancashire soldiers in the wars in France', *The Fifteenth Century*, xviii, *Rulers, regions and retinues. Essays presented to A. J. Pollard*, ed. L. Clark and P. W. Fleming (2020), 151–64

BIBLIOGRAPHY

Berland, J.-M., 'Les statuts de réforme du prieuré de la Réole (vers 1472) et la restauration des bâtiments conventuels', *La réconstruction après la guerre de Cent Ans (Actes du 104ᵉ Congrès National des Sociétés Savantes, Bordeaux, 1979)* (1981), i, 143–52

Bernard, G. W., *War, Taxation and Rebellion in Early Tudor England. Henry VIII, Wolsey and the Amicable Grant of 1525* (1986)

*Bernus, P., 'Le rôle politique de Pierre de Brézé au cours des dix dernières années du règne de Charles VII (1451–1461)', *BEC*, lxix (1908), 303–47

Bézard, Y., *La vie rurale dans le sud de la région parisienne de 1450 à 1560* (1929)

Bezold, F. von, *König Sigmund und die Reichskriege gegen die Hussiten*, 3 vols (1872–7)

Billot, C., *Chartres à la fin du moyen age* (1987)

Bittmann, K., *Ludwig XI und Karl der Kühne. Die Memoiren des Philippe de Commynes als historische Quelle*, 2 vols (1964)

Bloch, M., *Les rois thaumaturges* (1961)

Blockmans, W. and Prevenier, W., *The Promised Lands. The Low Countries under Burgundian Rule, 1369–1530*, tr. E. Fackelman (1999)

Blok, P., 'Philips de Goede en de hollandsche steden in 1436', *Mededeelingen der Konincklijke Akademie van Wetenschappen, afdeeling Letterkunde*, lviii, B (1924), 33–51

Blumenfeld-Kosinski, R., 'The strange case of Ermine de Reims: a medieval woman between demons and saints', *Speculum*, lxxxv (2010), 321–56

*Bochaca, M., 'Navigation entre la France et l'Écosse d'après le recit de l'ambassade de Regnault Girard auprès de Jacques 1ᵉʳ Stuart (1434–1436)', *Annales de Bretagne*, cxix (4) (2012), 35–53

Bogner, G. (1997): see E: Unpublished Theses

Bocquet, A., *Recherches sur la population rurale de l'Artois et du Boulonnais* (1969)

Bogner, G., 'The English Knights of 1434: a Prosopographical Approach', *Medieval Prosopography*, xxv (2004), 178–203

Bogner, G., '"Military" knighthood in the Lancastrian era: the case of Sir John Montgomery', *Journal of Military History*, vii (2009), 104–26

Bois, G., *Crise du feodalisme*, 2nd edn (1981)

Boissonade, P., 'Une étape capitale de la mission de Jeanne d'Arc', *Revue des questions historiques*, 3ᵉ série, xvii (1930), 12–67

Bolton, J. L., 'How Sir Thomas Rempston paid his ransom: or, the mistakes of an Italian banker', *The Fifteenth Century*, vii, *Conflicts, Consequences and the Crown in the Late Middle Ages*, ed. L. Clark (2007), 101–18

Bonnault d'Houet, X. de, *Les francs archers de Compiègne, 1448–1524* (1897)

Boone, M., 'Jacqueline of Bavaria in September 1425, a lonely princess in Ghent', *Tant d'Emprises – So Many Undertakings. Essays in Honour of Anne F. Sutton, The Ricardian*, xiii (2003), 75–85

Booth, P., 'Men behaving badly? The west march towards Scotland and the Percy–Neville feud', *The Fifteenth Century*, iii, *Authority and Subversion*, ed. L. Clark (2003), 95–116

Bord, P., 'Au lendemain d'Azincourt. Jean, bâtard d'Orléans (1403–1468), l'enjeu de la captivité du duc Charles', *Autour d'Azincourt: une société face à la guerre (v. 1370–v. 1420)*, ed. A. Marchandisse et B. Schnerb (2017), 237–50

Bordeaux, M., *Aspects économiques de la vie de l'église aux 14ᵉ et 15ᵉ siècle* (1969)

Borrelli de Serres, L.-L. de, *Recherches sur divers services publics du xiiiᵉ au xviiᵉ siècle*, 3 vols (1895–1909)

*Bossuat, A., *Perrinet Gressart et François de Surienne, agents d'Angleterre* (1936)

Bossuat, A., 'L'idée de la nation et la jurisprudence du Parlement de Paris au XVe siècle', *Revue historique*, cciv (1950), 54–61

Bossuat, A., 'Les prisonniers de guerre au xve siècle: la rançon de Guillaume seigneur de Châteauvillain', *Annales de Bourgogne*, xxiii (1951)[1], 7–35

Bossuat, A., 'Les prisonniers de guerre au xve siècle: la rançon de Jean seigneur de Rodemack', *Annales de l'Est*, 5e série, iii (1951)[2], 145–62

Bossuat, A., 'Le rétablissement de la paix sociale sous le règne de Charles VII', *Moyen Age*, lx (1954), 137–62

Bossuat, A., 'La littérature de propagande au XVe siècle: le mémoire de Jean de Rinel, secrétaire du roi d'Angleterre contre le duc de Bourgogne (1435)', *Cahiers d'Histoire publiés par les universités de Clermont–Lyon–Grenoble*, i (1956), 129–46

Bossuat, A., 'Une famille parisienne pendant l'occupation Anglaise au XVe siècle', *Bulletin de la Société de l'Histoire de Paris*, lxxxvii–lxxxviii (1960-1), 77–96

Bossuat, A., 'La formule "Le roi est empereur en son royaume". Son employ au XVe siècle devant le Parlement de Paris', *Revue d'histoire de droit français et étranger*, 4e série, xxxix (1961), 371–81

Bossuat, A., 'Le Parlement de Paris pendant l'occupation anglaise', *Revue Historique*, ccxxix (1963), 19–40

Bottin, G., 'Démographie historique et histoire domaniale: le fouage à Dieppe au XVe siècle', *Cahiers Léopold Delisle*, xliv (1995), 309–21

Botton, I. de and Offredo-Sarrot, M., 'Ruines et réconstruction agraires dans le commanderies du grand prieuré de France', *La réconstruction après la guerre de Cent Ans (Actes du 104e Congrès National des Sociétés Savantes, Bordeaux, 1979)* (1981), i, 79–122

*Boüard, M. de, 'Normands et anglais au lendemain de la guerre de Cent Ans', *Mélanges d'histoire normandes dédiés en hommage à M. Réné Jouanne. Numéro spécial du 'Pays Bas-Normand'* (1970), 49–60

*Boucher de Molandon, R., *Première expédition de Jeanne d'Arc. Le ravitaillement d'Orléans* (1874)

*Boucher de Molandon and Adalbert de Beaucorps, R., *L'armée anglaise vaincue par Jeanne d'Arc sous les murs d'Orléans* (1892)

Boudier, A., 'Charles Desmarets, corsaire dieppois', *Revue Historique*, cxxxvii (1921), 32–49

Bouillé, A. de, *Un conseiller de Charles VII, le maréchal de la Fayette, 1380–1463* (1955)

Boulay, F. R. H. du, *The Lordship of Canterbury: an Essay on Medieval Society* (1966)

Boulet (2010): see E: Unpublished Theses

Bouly de Lesdin, A.-M., 'Le Vexin français sous la domination anglaise (1419–1449)', *Mémoires de la Société Historique et Archéologique de Pontoise, du Val d'Oise et du Vexin*, lxii (1969), 55–69

Bourdeaut, A., 'Gilles de Bretagne – Entre la France et l'Angleterre – Les causes et les auteurs du drame', *Memoires de la Société d'Histoire et d'Archéologie de Bretagne*, i (1920), 53–145

Bournon, F., *La Bastille* (1893)

Boursier, A., *Histoire de la ville et châtellenie de Creil* (1883)

Boutiot, T., *Histoire de la ville de Troyes et de la Champagne méridionale*, 5 vols (1870–80)

Bouton, A., *Le Maine. Histoire économique et sociale, XIVe, XVe et XVIe siècles* (1970)

Boutruche, R., 'Les courants de peuplement dans l'Entre-Deux-Mers', *Annales d'Histoire Economique et Sociale*, vii (1935), 13–37, 124–54

Boutruche, R.,'La devastation des campagnes pendant la guerre de Cent Ans et le réconstruction de la France', *Mélanges 1945*, iii, *Études historiques (Publications de la Faculté des Lettres de Strasbourg*, cvi) (1947), 127–63

Boutruche, R., *La crise d'une société. Seigneurs et paysans du Bordelais pendant la guerre de Cent ans* (1963)

Boutruche, R. (ed.), *Bordeaux de 1453 à 1715* (1966)

Bouzy, O., 'Jeanne d'Arc, les signes au roi et les entrevues de Chinon', *Guerre, pouvoir et noblesse au moyen age. Mélanges en l'honneur de Philippe Contamine* (2000), ed. J. Paviot and J. Verger, 131–8

Braun, P., 'Les lendemains de la conquête de la Réole par Charles VII', *La 'France Anglaise' au moyen age (Actes du 111ᵉ Congrès National des Sociétés Savantes, Poitiers, 1986)* (1988), 269–83

*Bréard, C., *Le Crotoy et les armements maritimes des xivᵉ et xvᵉ siècles. Étude historique* (1902)

Bridbury, A. R., 'The Hundred Years' War: costs and profits', *Trade, Government and Economy in Pre-industrial England. Essays Presented to F. J. Fisher*, ed. D. C. Coleman and A. H. John (1976), 80–95

Brill, R., 'The English preparations before the Treaty of Arras: a new interpretation of Sir John Fastolf's "Report", September, 1435', *Studies in medieval and Renaissance history*, vii (1970), 211–247

Britnell, R. H., 'The economic context', *The Wars of the Roses*, ed. A. J. Pollard (1995), 41–64

*Broussillon, B. de, *La maison de Laval, 1020–1605*, 5 vols (1895–1903)

Brown, M. (1992): see E: Unpublished Theses

Brown, M., *The Stewart Dynasty in Scotland. James I* (1994)

Brown, M., *The Black Douglases. War and Lordship in Late Medieval Scotland, 1300–1455* (1998)

Brown, M., 'French alliance or English peace? Scotland and the last phase of the Hundred Years War, 1415–53', *The Fifteenth Century, vii, Conflicts, Consequences and the Crown in the Late Middle Ages*, ed. L. Clark (2007), 81–99

Brown, M., 'The Plantagenet Empire and the insular world: retrospect and prospect', *The Plantagenet Empire, 1259–1453*, ed. P. Crooks, D. Green and W. M. Ormrod (2016), 384–402

Burne, A. H., *The Agincourt War. A military history of the latter part of the Hundred Years War from 1369 to 1453* (1956)

Burney, E. M.: see E: Unpublished Theses

Buttin, F., 'La lance et l'arrêt de cuirasse', *Archaeologia*, lxxxxix (1965), 77–178

Butterfield, A., *The Familiar Enemy. Chaucer, Language and Nation in the Hundred Years War* (2009)

*Caillet, L., 'La bataille de La Brécinière, dite de La Gravelle', *Revue des Questions Historiques*, lxxxvi (1909)[1], 566–71

*Caillet, L., *Étude sur les relations de la commune de Lyon avec Charles VII et Louis XI (1417–1483)* (1909)[2]

*Caillet, L., *Les préliminaires du congrès d'Arras d'après un document lyonnais* (1909)[3]

Cailleux, P., 'La presence anglaise dans la capitale normande: quelques aspects des relations entre Anglais et Rouennais', *La Normandie et l'Angleterre au Moyen Age*, ed. P. Bouet and V. Gazeau (2003), 265–76

Cailleux, P., 'Le marché immobilier rouennais au XVᵉ siècle', *Les villes normandes au moyen age. Renaissance, essor, crise*, ed. P. Bouet and F. Neveux (2006), 241–65

BIBLIOGRAPHY

Callias Bey, M., Chaussé, V., Gatouillat, F. and Hérold, M., *Les vitraux de Haute-Normandie* (2001)

*Calmet, A., *Histoire de Lorraine*, n.e., 7 vols (1745–57)

Calmette, J and Déprez, E., *La France et l'Angleterre en conflit* (1937)

*Calmette, J. and Périnelle, G., *Louis XI et l'Angleterre (1461–1483)* (1930)

Capwell, T., *Armour of the English Knight, 1400–1450* (2015)

*Carolus-Barré, L., *Étude sur la bourgeoisie au moyen age. Une famille de tabellions royaux. Les de Kerromp* (1930)

*Carolus-Barré, L., 'État de la ville de Compiègne au lendemain de la guerre de Cent Ans d'après un mémoire de 1448', *La réconstruction après la guerre de Cent Ans (Actes du 104e Congrès National des Sociétés Savantes, Bordeaux, 1979)* (1981), i, 253–330

*Carolus-Barré, L., 'Le siège de Compiège et la délivrance de la ville', *Bulletin de la Société Historique de Compiègne*, xxviii (1982)[1], 15–62

Carolus-Barré, L., 'Deux "capitaines" italiens, compagnons de guerre de Jeanne d'Arc. Barthélémy Barette (*Baretta*), Théaude de Valpergue (*Valperga*)', *Bulletin de la Société Historique de Compiègne*, xxviii (1982)[2], 81–118

*Carolus-Barré, L., 'Compiègne et la guerre, 1414–1430', *La 'France Anglaise' au moyen age (Actes du 111e Congrès National des Sociétés Savantes, Poitiers, 1986)* (1988), 383–92

Caron, M. T., *La noblesse dans le duché de Bourgogne* (1987)

Carpenter, C., *Locality and Polity. A Study of Warwickshire Landed Society, 1401–1499* (1992)

Carpenter, C., *The Wars of the Roses. Politics and the Constitution in England, c. 1437–1509* (1997)

Cartellieri, O., 'Philippe le Bon et le roi de France en 1430 et 1431', *Annales de Bourgogne*, i (1929), 78–83

Carr, A. D., 'Welshmen and the Hundred Years War', *Welsh History Review*, iv (1968–9), 21–46

Carus-Wilson, *Medieval Merchant Venturers* (1954)

Castor, H., *The King, the Crown and the Duchy of Lancaster. Public Authority and Private Power, 1399–1461* (2000)

Castor, H., *Blood and Roses. The Paston Family in the Fifteenth Century* (2004)

Challet, V., '"*Tuchins*" and "*Brigands de Bois*": peasant communities and self-defence movements in Normandy during the Hundred Years War', *The Fifteenth Century*, ix, ed. L. Clark (2010), 85–100

*Champion, P., *Guillaume de Flavy, capitaine de Compiègne* (1906)

*Champion, P., 'Ballade du sacre de Reims (17 juillet 1429)', *Le Moyen Age*, xxii (1909), 370–7

Champion, P., *Louis XI*, 2 vols (1927)

Champion, P., *Vie de Charles d'Orléans (1394–1465)*, 2nd edn (1969)

*Champollion-Figeac, A., *Louis et Charles d'Orléans. Leur influence sur les arts, la literature et l'esprit de leur siècle*, 2 vols (1844)

Chaplais, P., 'The Chancery of Guyenne, 1289–1453', *Studies presented to Sir Hilary Jenkinson*, ed. J. Conway Davies (1957), 61–95

Chaplais, P., 'The Court of Sovereignty of Guyenne (Edward III–Henry VI) and its antecedents', *Documenting the Past. Essays in Medieval History Presented to George Peddy Cuttino*, ed. J. S. Hamilton and P. J. Bradley (1989), 137–53

Charbonnier, P. 'La réconstruction en Auvergne', *La réconstruction après la guerre de Cent Ans (Actes du 104e Congrès National des Sociétés Savantes, Bordeaux, 1979)* (1981), i, 37–50

BIBLIOGRAPHY

*Charles, R., 'L'invasion anglaise dans le Maine de 1417 à 1428', *Revue historique et archéologique du Maine*, xxv (1889), 62–103, 167–208, 305–27

*Chastellux, H. P.-C. de, *Histoire généalogique de la maison de Chastellux* (1869)

Chauvelays, J. de la, 'Les armées des trois premiers ducs de Bourgogne de la maison de Valois', *Mems. Acad. Sci. Arts et Belles-Lettres de Dijon* (1880), 19–335

Chave, I., *Les châteaux de l'appanage d'Alençon (1350–1450)* (2003)

Cherry, M., 'The struggle for power in mid-fifteenth-century Devonshire', *Patronage, the Crown and the Provinces in Later Medieval England*, ed. R. A. Griffiths (1981), 123–44

*Chéruel, A., *Histoire de Rouen sous la domination anglaise au quinzième siècle*, 2 vols (1840)

Chevalier, B., *Tours, Ville Royale* (1975)

Chevalier, B., 'Les écossais dans les armées de Charles VII jusqu'à la bataille de Verneuil', *Jeanne d'Arc. Une époque. Un rayonnement. Colloque d'histoire médiévale, Orléans octobre 1979* (1982), 85–94

Childs, W. R., *Anglo-Castilian Trade in the Later Middle Ages* (1978)

Cintré, R., *Les marches de Bretagne au moyen age* (1992)

*Chrimes, S. B., 'The pretensions of the duke of Gloucester in 1422', *EHR*, xlv (1930), 101–3

*Claudon, F., *Histoire de Langres et de ses institutions municipales jusqu'au commencement du XVIe siècle* (1955)

Clauzel D., 'Quand Arras était au cœur de la diplomatie Eurpéenne', *Arras et la diplomatie européenne, XVe–XVIe siècles*, ed. D. Clauzel, C. Giry-Deloison and C. Leduc (1999), 11–25

*Clément, P., *Jacques Coeur et Charles VII*, 2 vols (1853)

Clément-Simon, G., *Une page ignorée de l'histoire de Tulle. La prise de Tulle par Jean de la Roche, capitaine de routiers, le jour de la Fête-Dieu (30 mai) 1426* (1895)[1]

Clément-Simon, G., 'Un capitaine de routiers sous Charles VII. Jean de la Roche', *Revue des Questions Historiques*, lviii (1895)[2], 41–65

Cockshaw, P., *Le personnel de la chancellerie de Bourgogne-Flandre sous les ducs de Bourgogne de la maison de Valois (1384–1477)* (1982)

Cockshaw, P., *Prosopographie des secrétaires de la cour de Bourgogne (1384–1477)* (2006)

Cokayne, G. E., *The Complete Peerage*, ed. V. Gibbs et al., 12 vols (1910–59) [cited as GEC]

Coleman, J., *English Literature in History, 1350–1400. Medieval Readers and Writers* (1981)

*Collard, F., '"Et est ce tout notoire encores a present audit pays": le crime, la mémoire du crime et l'histoire du meurtre de Gilles de Bretagne au procès su maréchal de Gié', *Le Prince, l'argent, les hommes au moyen age. Mélanges offerts à Jean Kerhervé*, ed. J.-C. Cassard, Y. Coativy, A. Gallicé and D. Le Page (2008), 133–43

Collin, A., 'Le Pont des Tourelles à Orléans, 1120–1760', *Memoires de la Société Archéologique et Historique de l'Orléanais*, xxvi (1895)

Collins, H. E. L., *The Order of the Garter, 1348–1461. Chivalry and politics in late medieval England* (2000)[1]

Collins, H. E. L., 'Sir John Fastolf, Lord John Talbot and the dispute over Patay: ambition and chivalry in the fifteenth century', *War and Society in Medieval and Early Modern Britain*, ed. D. Dunn (2000)[2], 114–40

Colvin, H. M. (ed.), *The History of the King's Works*, 6 vols (1963–82)

Contamine, P., 'The French nobility and the war', *The Hundred Years War*, ed. K. Fowler (1971), 135–62

Contamine, P., *Guerre, état et société à la fin du moyen age. Étude sur les armées des rois de France, 1337–1494* (1972)

Contamine, P., *L'Oriflamme de St.-Denis aux xive et xve siècles* (1975)

Contamine, P., *La vie quotidienne pendant la guerre de Cent ans* (1976)

*Contamine, P., 'Rançons et butins dans la Normandie anglaise, 1424–1444', *La guerre et la paix au moyen age (Actes du 101e Congrès national des sociétés savantes, Lille 1976)* (1978)[1], 241–70

Contamine, P., 'Les fortifications urbaines en France à la fin du moyen age: aspects financiers et économiques', *Revue historique*, cclx (1978)[2], 23–47

Contamine, P., *La guerre au moyen age* (1980)

Contamine, P., 'L'action et la personne de Jeanne d'Arc. Remarques sur l'attitude des princes à son égard', *Bulletin de la Société de l'Histoire de Compiègne*, xxviii (1982)[1], 63–80

Contamine, P., 'La théologie de la guerre à la fin du moyen age: la guerre de Cent Ans, fut-elle une guerre juste?', *Jeanne d'Arc. Une époque. Un rayonnement. Colloque d'histoire médiévale, Orléans octobre 1979* (1982)[2], 9–21

Contamine, P., 'La "France anglaise" au XVe siècle. Mirage ou réalité?', *Des pouvoirs en France 1300/1500* (1992)[1], 99–108

Contamine, P., 'Mythe et histoire. Jeanne d'Arc, 1429', *Razo*, xii (1992)[2], 41–54

Contamine, P., 'Charles VII, les français et la paix, 1420–1445', *Comptes-rendu des séances de l'Académie des Inscriptions et Belles-Lettres* (1993), 9–23

Contamine, P., 'The Norman "nation" and the French "nation" in the fourteenth and fifteenth Centuries', *England and Normandy in the Middle Ages*, ed. D. Bates and A. Curry (1994), 215–34

Contamine, P., *La noblesse au royaume de France de Philippe le Bel à Louis XII. Essai de synthèse* (1997)[1]

Contamine, P., 'Les rencontres au sommet dans la France du XVe siècle', *Spannungsfeld von Recht und Ritual: soziale Kommunikation in Mittelalter und früher Neuzeit*, ed. H. Duchhardt (1997)[2], 273–89

Contamine, P., 'France et Bourgogne. L'historiographie du XVe et la paix d'Arras (1435)', *Arras et la diplomatie européenne, XVe–XVIe siècles*, ed. D. Clauzel, C. Giry-Deloison and C. Leduc (1999)[1], 81–100

Contamine, P., 'Le recouvrement par Charles VII de son pays et duché de Normandie (15 mai 1449–12 août 1450)', *La Normandie au XVe siècle. Art et histoire* (1999)[2], 17–23

Contamine, P., 'Lever l'impôt en terre de guerre: rançons, appatis, souffrances de guerre dans la France des XIVe et XVe siècles', *L'Impôt au moyen age. L'Impôt public et le prélèvement seigneurial, fin XIIe – début XVIe siècle*, i (2002), 11–39

*Contamine, P., 'A l'abordage! Pierre de Brézé, Grand Sénéchal de Normandie et la guerre de course', *La Normandie et l'Angleterre au Moyen Age*, ed. P. Bouet and V. Gazeau (2003), 307–58

Contamine, P., 'Charles VII, roi de France, et ses favoris: l'exemple de Pierre, sire de Giac (†1427)', *Der Fall des Günstlings: Hofparteien in Europa vom 13. bis zum 17. Jahrhundert*, ed. J. Hirschbiegel and W. Paravicini (2004), 139–162

Contamine, P., 'Serments Bretons (8–15 septembre 1427)', *Le Prince, l'argent, les hommes au moyen age. Mélanges offerts à Jean Kerhervé* (2008), 123–32

Contamine, P., 'Maitre Jean de Rinel (vers 1380–1449), notaire et secrétaire de Charles VI, puis de Henry [VI] pour son royaume de France, l'une des "plumes" de "l'union des deux couronnes"', *Annales de Normandie*, xxxv (2009)[1], 115–34

BIBLIOGRAPHY

Contamine, P., 'Rendre graces, prier, faire mémoire: la "fête du roi", 14 octobre de l'année 1450 puis 12 août de l'année 1451 et les années postérieures', *Bulletin de la Société Nationale des Antiquaires de France* (2009)[2], 338–53

Contamine, P., 'Les Anglais, "anciens et mortels ennemis" des rois de France et de leur royaume et des Français pendant la guèrre de cent ans', *Revista de história das ideias*, xxx (2009)[3], 201–18

Contamine, P., 'Yolande d'Aragon et Jeanne d'Arc: l'improbable rencontre de deux parcours politiques', *Femmes de pouvoir, femmes politiques durant les derniers siècles du moyen age et au cours de la première Renaissance*, ed. E. Bousmar, J. Dumont, A. Marchandisse and B. Schnerb (2012), 11–30

Contamine, P., 'Après le bücher. La campagne de propagande de la royauté franco-anglaise au sujet de Jeanne d'Arc en juin 1431', *Epistolaire politique*, i, *Gouverner par les lettres*, ed. B. Dumézil and L. Vissière (2014), 215–25

*Contamine, P., 'Entre fiction et frictions: les rapports diplomatiques de la France de Charles VII avec l'Écosse de Jacques II Stewart à la fin de la guerre de Cent Ans (1449–1457)', *Cahiers d'archéologie et d'histoire du Berry*, no. 205 (2015)[1], 33–45

Contamine, P., 'Jean, comte de Dunois et de Longueville (1403?–1468), ou l'honneur d'être bâtard', *La bâtardise et l'exercise du pouvoir en Europe du XIIIe au début du XVIe siècle*, ed. E. Bousmar, A. Marchandisse, C. Masson and B. Schnerb (*Revue du Nord*, Hors série, no. 31) (2015)[2], 285–311

Contamine, P., *Charles VII. Une vie, une politique* (2017)

Contamine, P. and Autrand, F., 'Réforme de l'état et prise de pouvoir dans le royaume de France d'après deux traités du XVe siècle', *Groupe de recherches Les Pouvoirs, XIIIe–XIVe siècles, Lettre II* (1984), 10–25

Contamine, P., Bouzy, O. and Hélary, X., *Jeanne d'Arc. Histoire et dictionnaire* (2012)

Cosneau, E., *Le Connétable de Richemont (Artur de Bretagne) (1393–1458)* (1886)

Courteault, H., *Gaston IV, comte de Foix, vicomte souverain de Béarn, prince de Navarre* (1895)

Coville, A., 'Pierre de Versailles (1380?–1446)', *BEC*, xciii (1932), 208–66

Currin, J. M., 'Henry VII and the treaty of Redon (1489): Plantagenet ambitions and early Tudor foreign policy', *History*, lxxxi (1996), 343–58

Currin, J. M., 'Persuasions to peace. The Luxembourg–Marigny–Gaguin embassy and the state of Anglo-French relations, 1489–90', *EHR*, cxiii (1998), 882–904

Currin, J. M., '"The King's army into partes of Bretaigne". Henry VII and the Breton wars, 1489–1491', *War in History*, vii (2000), 379–412

Currin, J. M., '"To traffic with war"? Henry VII and the French campaign of 1492', *The English Experience in France, c. 1450–1558*, ed. D. Grummitt (2002), 106–131

Curry, A., 'The first English standing army? Military organisation in Lancastrian Normandy, 1420–50', in *Patronage, Pedigree and Power in Later Medieval England*, ed. C. Ross (1979), 193–214

Curry, A., 'L'effet de la libération sur l'armée anglaise: les problèmes de l'organisation militaire en Normandie de 1429 à 1435', *Jeanne d'Arc. Une époque. Un rayonnement. Colloque d'histoire médiévale, Orléans octobre 1979* (1982), 95–106

Curry, A. (1985): see E: Unpublished Theses

Curry, A., 'The impact of war and occupation on urban life in Normandy, 1417–1450', *French Hist.*, i (1987), 157–81

Curry, A., 'Le service féodale en Normandie pendant l'occupation anglaise (1417–1450)', *La 'France Anglaise' au moyen age (Actes du 111e Congrès National des Sociétés Savantes, Poitiers, 1986)* (1988)[1], 233–57

BIBLIOGRAPHY

Curry, A., 'Towns at war. Relations between the towns of Normandy and their English rulers, 1417–1450', *Towns and Townspeople in the 15th century*, ed. J. A. F. Thompson (1988)[2], 148–72

Curry, A., 'The nationality of English men-at-arms serving in English armies in Normandy and the *Pays de Conquête*, 1415–1450: a preliminary survey', *Reading Medieval Studies*, xviii (1992), 135–63

Curry, A., 'Lancastrian Normandy: the jewel in the Crown?', *England and Normandy in the Middle Ages*, ed. D. Bates and A. Curry (1994)[1], 235–52

Curry, A., 'English armies in the fifteenth century', *Arms, Armies and Fortifications in the Hundred Years War*, ed. A. Curry and M. Hughes (1994)[2], 39–68

Curry, A., 'Les *"gens vivans sur le païs"* pendant l'occupation anglaise de la Normandie', *La guerre, la violence et les gens au moyen age*, i, *Guerre et violence*, ed. P. Contamine and O. Guyotjeannin (1996), i, 209–21

Curry, A., 'L'administration financière de la Normandie anglaise: continuité ou changement?', *La France des principautés. Les chambres des comptes, xive et xve siècles*, ed. P. Contamine and O. Mattéoni (1998)[1], 83–103

*Curry, A., 'La Chambre des Comptes de Normandie sous l'occupation anglaise, 1417–1450', *Les Chambres des Comptes en France aux XIVe et XVe siècles*, ed. P. Contamine and O. Mattéoni (1998)[2], 91–125

*Curry, A., 'The organisation of field armies in Lancastrian Normandy', *Armies, Chivalry and Warfare in Medieval Britain and France*, ed. M. Strickland (1998)[3], 207–31

Curry, A., 'L'occupation anglaise du xve siècle: la discipline militaire et le problème des gens vivans sur le pais', *La Normandie dans la Guerre de Cent Ans, 1346–1450*, ed. J.-Y. Marin (1999), 47–9

Curry, A., 'Bourgeois et soldats dans la ville de Mantes pendant l'occupation anglaise de 1419 à 1449', *Guerre, pouvoir et noblesse au moyen age. Mélanges en l'honneur de Philippe Contamine*, ed. J. Paviot and J. Verger (2000)[1], 175–84

Curry, A., 'Isolated or integrated? The English soldier in Lancastrian Normandy', in *Courts and Regions of Medieval Europe* ed. S. R. Jones, R. Marks and A. J. Minnis (2000)[2], 191–210

Curry, A., 'The loss of Lancastrian Normandy: an administrative nightmare?', *The English Experience in France, c. 1450–1558*, ed. D. Grummitt (2002), 24–45

Curry, A., 'The "coronation expedition" and Henry VI's court in France, 1430 to 1432', *The Lancastrian Court. Proceedings of the 2001 Harlaxton Symposium*, ed. J. Stratford (2003), 29–52

Curry, A., 'Soldiers' wives in the Hundred Years War', *Soldiers, Nobles and Gentlemen. Essays in honour of Maurice Keen*, ed. P. Coss and C. Tyerman (2009), 198–214

Curry, A., 'Guns and Goddams. Was there a military revolution in Lancastrian Normandy, 1415–50', *Journal of Medieval Military History*, viii (2010), 171–88

Curry, A., 'Les anglais face au procès', *De l'hérétique à la sainte. Les procès de Jeanne d'Arc revisités*, ed. F. Neveux (2012), 69–87

Curry, A., 'John Duke of Bedford's arrangements for the defence of Normandy in October 1434: College of Arms MS Arundel 48, 274r–276r', *Annales de Normandie*, lxii (2012), 235–51

Curry, A., 'Concilier les ambitions militaires et les intérêts civils: l'occupation anglaise de la Normandie (1417–1450)', *Revue du Nord*, xcv (2013), 967–76

Curry, A., 'English war captains in the Hundred Years War' (2014), [https://eprints.soton.ac.uk/388755/1/curry_Engl_war_captains.doc]

Curry, A., 'Les soldats anglais en garnison en Normandie', *Bulletin de la Société des Antiquaires de Normandie*, lxxxiv (2015), 139–67

BIBLIOGRAPHY

Curry, A., 'The *baillis* of Lancastrian Normandy: English men wearing French hats', *The Plantagenet Empire, 1259–1453*, ed. P. Crooks, D. Green and W. M. Ormrod (2016)[1], 359–370

Curry, A., 'Representing war and conquest, 1415–1429: the evidence of College of Arms Manuscript M9', *Representing War and Violence, 1250–1600*, ed. J. Bellis and L. Slater (2016)[2], 139–58

Curry, A., 'The garrison establishment in Lancastrian Normandy', *Military Communities in Late Medieval England. Essays in Honour of Andrew Ayton*, ed. G. P. Baker, C. L. Lambert and D. Simpkin (2018), 237–69

Curry, A., 'Southern England and campaigns to France, 1415–1453', *The Fifteenth Century*, xviii, *Rulers, regions and retinues. Essays presented to A. J. Pollard*, ed. L. Clark and P. W. Fleming (2020), 133–49

*Curry, A., and Ambühl, R., *A Soldiers' Chronicle of the Hundred Years War* (2021)

Cuttler, S. H., *The Law of Treason and Treason Trials in Later Medieval France* (1981)[1]

Daly, K, 'War, history and memory in the Dauphiné in the fifteenth century: two accounts of the battle of Anthon (1430)', *The Fifteenth Century*, viii, *Rule, Redemption and Representation in Late Medieval England and France*, ed. L. Clark (2008), 29–46

*Daumet, G., *Étude sur l'alliance de la France et la Castille au xive et au xve siècles* (1898)

*Daumet, G., *Calais sous la domination anglaise* (1902)

Davies, C. S. L., 'The English people and war in the early sixteenth century', *Britain and the Netherlands*, vi, ed. A. C. Duke and C. A. Tamse (1977), 1–19

Davies, C. S. L., 'Roi de France et Roi d'Angleterre: the English claims to France (1453–1558)', *L'Angleterre et les pays bourguignons: relations et comparaisons (XVe–XVIe s.)*, ed. J.-M. Cauchies (1995), 123–32

Davies, C. S. L., 'Henry VIII and Henry V: the wars in France', *The End of the Middle Ages. England in the Fifteenth and Sixteenth Centuries*, ed. J. L. Watts (1998)[1], 235–62

Davies, C. S. L., 'Tournai and the English Crown, 1513–1519', *Historical Journal*, xli (1998)[2], 1–26

Debal, J., 'La topographie de l'enceinte fortifiée d'Orléans au temps de Jeanne d'Arc', *Jeanne d'Arc. Une époque. Un rayonnement. Colloque d'histoire médiévale, Orléans octobre 1979* (1982), 23–41

Deck, S., *La ville d'Eu, son histoire, ses institutions (1151–1475)* (1924)

*Delachenal, R., 'Les gentilshommes dauphinois à la bataille de Verneuil', *Bulletin Académique Delphinale*, xx (1885), 347–58

Delachenal, R., 'Une clause de la paix d'Arras: les parlementaires bourguignons dans le Parlement de Charles VII', *Bulletin de la Société de l'histoire de Paris et de l'Île de France*, xviii (1891), 76–83

Delaruelle, E., Labande, E.-R., and Ourliac, P., *L'église au temps du Grand Schisme et de la crise conciliaire (1378–1449)* (1962)

*Delisle, L., *Histoire du château et des sires de Saint-Sauveur-le-Vicomte* (1867)

*Delisle, L., 'Jacques Cœur à Cherbourg', *Mémoires de la Société Nationale Académique de Cherbourg* (1875), 212–7

*Déniau, J., *La commune de Lyon et la guerre bourguignonne, 1417–1435* (1934)

*Denifle, H., *La guerre de Cent ans et les désolations des églises, monastères et hôpitaux en France*, 2 vols (1897–9)

Denifle, H., and Chatelain, E., 'Le procès de Jeanne d'Arc et l'université de Paris', *Mémoires de la Société de l'Histoire de Paris*, xxiv (1897), 1–32

BIBLIOGRAPHY

Desama, C., 'La première entrevue de Jeanne d'Arc et de Charles VII à Chinon (mars 1429)', *Analecta Bollandiana*, lxxxiv (1966)[1], 113–26

Desama, C., 'Jeanne d'Arc et Charles VII: l'entrevue du signe (mars–avril 1429)', *Revue de l'histoire des religions*, clxx (1966)[2], 29–46

Desama, C., 'Jeanne d'Arc et la diplomatie de Charles VII: l'ambassade française auprès de Philippe le Bon en 1429', *Annales de Bourgogne*, xl (1968), 290–9

Deschamps, P., 'Un monument aux morts du quinzième siècle: la Vierge au manteau de l'église de Laval en Dauphiné', *Bulletin monumental*, cxviii (1960), 123–31

Désert, G. (ed.), *Histoire de Caen* (1981)

*Desplanques, A., *Projet d'assassinat de Philippe le Bon par les anglais (1424–1426)* (1867)

Deville, J. A., *Histoire du château et des sires de Tancarville* (1834)

De Vries, K., *Joan of Arc. A Military Leader* (1999)

*Dickinson, J. G., *The Congress of Arras, 1435* (1955)

Dictionnaire d'histoire et de géographie ecclesiastiques, 32 vols (1912–in progress)

Dieudonné, A., 'La monnaie royale depuis la réforme de Charles V jusqu'à la restauration monétaire par Charles VII, spécialement dans ses rapports avec l'histoire politique', *BEC*, lxxii (1911), 473–99, lxxiii (1912), 263–82

Dillon, H. A., 'Calais and the Pale', *Archaeologia*, liii (1893), 289–388

Ditcham, B. G. H. (1978): see E: Unpublished Theses

Ditcham, B. G. H., '"Mutton guzzlers and wine bags": foreign soldiers and native reactions in fifteenth century France', *Power, Culture and Religion in France, c. 1350–c. 1550*, ed. C. Allmand (1989), 1–13

Ditchburn, D., 'Anglo-Scottish relations in the later middle ages: the other side of the coin', *The Plantagenet Empire, 1259–1453*, ed. P. Crooks, D. Green and W. M. Ormrod (2016), 310–34

Dodu, G., 'Le roi de Bourges', *Revue Historique*, clix (1928), 38–78

*Dognon, P., *Les institutions politiques et administratives du pays de Languedoc du XIIIe siècle aux guerres de religion* (1895)

*Doig, J. A., 'A new source for the siege of Calais in 1436', *EHR*, cx (1995)[1], 404–16

Doig, J. A., 'Propaganda, public opinion and the siege of Calais in 1436', *Crown, Government and People in the Fifteenth Century*, ed. R. Archer (1995)[2], 79–106

Doig, J. A., 'Political propaganda and royal proclamations in late medieval England', *Historical Research*, lxxi (1998), 253–80

*Dondaine, A., 'Le frère prêcheur Jean Dupuy Eveque de Cahors et son témoignage sur Jeanne d'Arc', *Archivum Fratrum Praedicatorum*, xii (1942), 118–84, xxxviii (1968), 31–41

Doucet, R., 'Les finances anglaises en France à la fin de la guerre de Cent Ans', *Le Moyen Age*, 2e série, xxvi (1926)[1], 265–332

Doucet, R., 'Livre tournois et livre sterling pendant l'occupation anglaise sous Charles VI et Charles VII' *Revue Numismatique*, 4e série, xxix (1926)[2], 102–5

Doudet, E., 'De l'allié à l'ennemi: la représentation des anglais dans les œuvres politiques de George Chastelain, indicière de la cour de Bourgogne', *Images de la guerre de cent ans: actes du colloque de Rouen (23, 24 et 25 mai 2000)* (2002), ed. J. Maurice, D. Couty and M. Guéré-Laferté (2002),81–94

*Douet-d'Arcq, L., *Recherches historiques et critiques sur les anciens comtes de Beaumont-sur-Oise* (1855)

Dousset, F., *La commune de Pontoise au moyen age* (1989)

Drouyn, L., *La Guyenne militaire*, 3 vols (1865)

BIBLIOGRAPHY

Dubled, H., 'L'artillerie royale française à l'époque de Charles VII et au début du règne de Louis XI (1437–1469): les frères Bureau', *Sciences et techniques de l'armement: Mémorial de l'artillerie française*, l (1976), 555–637

Dubois, F. N. A., *Histoire du siège d'Orléans*, ed. P. Charpentier (1894)

*Duclos, C. P., *Histoire de Louis XI*, 4 vols (1745–6)

Dugdale, W., *The Baronage of England*, 2 vols (1675–6)

Duhamel, L., *Négociations de Charles VII et de Louis XI avec les évêques de Metz pour la châtellenie d'Epinal* (1867)

Dumolyn, J., *De Brugse Opstand van 1436–1438* (1997)

Dunham, W. H., 'Notes from the Parliament at Winchester, 1449', *Speculum*, xvii (1942), 402–15

Dunn, D., 'Margaret of Anjou, Queen Consort of Henry VI: a reassessment of her role, 1445–53', *Crown, Government and People in the Fifteenth Century*, ed. R. Archer (1995), 107–43

Dupâquier, J., Biraben, J.-N., Étienne, R. et al., *Histoire de la population française*, i, *Des origines à la Renaissance* (1988)

Duparc, P., 'La délivrance d'Orléans et la mission de Jeanne d'Arc', *Jeanne d'Arc. Une époque. Un rayonnement. Colloque d'histoire médiévale, Orléans octobre 1979* (1982), 153–8

Dupont, A., 'Pour ou contre de roi d'Angleterre. Les titulaires de fiefs à la date du 2 avril 1426 dans les sergenteries de Saint-Lô, Le Hommet, Sainte-Marie-du-Mont, La Haye-du-Puits et Sainte-Mère-Église dépendant de la vicomté de Carentan', *Bulletin de la Société des Antiquaires de Normandie*, liv (1957–8), 35–42

Dupont-Ferrier, G., *Études sur les institutions financières de la France à la fin du moyen age*, 2 vols (1930–32)

Dupont-Ferrier, G., *Nouvelles études sur les institutions financières de la France à la fin du moyen age* (1933)[1]

Dupont-Ferrier, G., 'Le personnel de la Cour ou Chambre des Aides de Paris des origines à 1483', *ABSHF* (1931), 219–56; (1932), 191–297; (1933)[2], 167–269

Dupont-Ferrier, G., 'Le personnel de la Cour du Trésor', *ABSHF* (1935), 185–298; (1936–7), 175–241

Dupont-Ferrier, G., *Les origines et le premier siècle de la Cour du Trésor* (1936)

Dyer, C., *Standards of Living in the Later Middle Ages. Social Change in England, c. 1200–1520* (1989)

Edwards, J. G., 'The second continuation of the Crowland Chronicle', *Bulletin of the Institute of Historical Research*, xxxix (1966), 117–29

Emden, A. B., *A Biographical Register of the University of Oxford to A.D. 1500*, 3 vols (1957)

Emery, A., *Greater Medieval Houses of England and Wales*, 3 vols (1996–2006)

Evans, H. T., *Wales and the Wars of the Roses* (1915)

Evans, M. R., 'Brigandage and resistance in Lancastrian Normandy: a study of the remission evidence', *Reading Medieval Studies*, xviii (1992), 103–34

Fasti ecclesiae gallicanae. Répertoire prosopographique des évêques, dignitaires et chanoines des diocèses de France de 1200 à 1500 (1996–in progress)

Fauchon, J., 'Notes pour servir à l'histoire de Robert Jolivet', *Revue de l'Avranchin et du pays de Granville*, lxvii (1989), 137–60

Favier, J., *Paris au XVe siècle* (1974)

BIBLIOGRAPHY

Favier, J., '"Occupation ou connivence?" Les anglais à Paris (1420–1436)', *Guerre, pouvoir et noblesse au moyen age. Mélanges en l'honneur de Philippe Contamine* (2000), ed. J. Paviot and J. Verger, 238–60

Favier, J., *Pierre Cauchon. Comment on devient le juge de Jeanne d'Arc* (2010)

Favreau, R., 'La Praguerie en Poitou', *BEC*, cxxix (1971), 277–301

Favreau, R., *La ville de Poitiers à la fin du moyen age* (1978)

*Félibien, M., *Histoire de la ville de Paris*, 5 vols (1725)

Ferguson, J., *English Diplomacy, 1422–1461* (1972)

Fiasson, D., 'Un chien couché au pied du roi d'Angleterre? Robert Jolivet, abbé du Mont Saint-Michel (1411–1444), *Annales de Normandie*, lxiv (2014), 47–72

Fiasson, D., 'Ravitaillement, communications et financement de la garnison du Mont Saint-Michel (1417–1450)', *La guerre en Normandie (XIe–XVe)*, ed. A. Curry and V. Gazeau (2018), 217–29

Fichet de Clairfontaine, F., 'Les fortifications du Mont-Saint-Michel durant la guerre de Cent Ans', *La Normandie dans la guerre de Cent Ans, 1435–1450*, ed. J.-Y. Marin (1999), 121–5

Fizelier, J. Le, 'Un épisode de la guerre des anglais dans le Maine. La bataille de La Brossinière, septembre 1423', *Revue Historique et archéologique du Maine*, i (1876), 28–42

*Flamare, H. de, *Le Nivernais pendant la guerre de Cent Ans. Le xve siècle*, 2 vols (1913–25)

*Flammermont, J., 'Histoire de Senlis pendant la guerre de Cent Ans', *Memoires de la Société de l'Histoire de Paris*, v (1878), 180–298

*Flourac, L., *Jean Ier, Comte de Foix, vicomte souverain de Béarn* (1884)

*Fornier, M., *Histoire Générale des Alpes Maritimes ou Cottiènes et particulière de leur métropolitaine Ambrun*, ed. P. Guillaume, 3 vols (1890–2)

Fournier, G., *Le château dans la France médiévale* (1978)

Fourquin, G., *Les campagnes de la région parisienne à la fin du moyen age* (1964)

Fraioli, D., 'L'image de Jeanne d'Arc. Que doit-elle au milieu littéraire et religieux de son temps', *Jeanne d'Arc. Une époque. Un rayonnement. Colloque d'histoire médiévale, Orléans octobre 1979* (1982), 191–6

Fraioli, D., *Joan of Arc. The early debate* (2000)

*Fréminville, J. de, *Les écorcheurs en Bourgogne (1435–1445)* (1887)

*Fréville, E. de, *Mémoire sur le commerce maritime de Rouen* (1857)

Frondeville, H. de, 'La région de la Basse-Seine pendant la guerre de Cent Ans', *BHP* (1955–6), 319–37

Gardelles, J., *Les châteaux du moyen age dans la France du sud-ouest* (1972)

Garnier, F., *Un consulat et ses finances. Millau (1187–1461)* (2006)

*Garnier, J., *L'artillerie des ducs de Bourgogne d'après les documents conservés aux archives de la Cote d'Or* (1895)

Gasté, A., *Les insurrections populaires en Basse-Normandie au XVe siècle pendant l'occupation anglaise et la question d'Olivier Basselin* (1889)

Gaussin, R., 'Les conseillers de Charles VII, 1418–1461', *Francia*, x (1982), 67–127

Gauvard, C., 'Résistants et collaborateurs pendant la guerre de Cent Ans: le témoignage des lettres de rémission', *La 'France Anglaise' au moyen age (Actes du 111e Congrès National des Sociétés Savantes, Poitiers, 1986)* (1988), 123–38

Gauvard, C., *'De grace especial'. Crime, état et société en France à la fin du moyen age* (1991)

*Gebelin, F.,'Recit de l'entrée de Dunois à Bordeaux en 1451', *Mélanges d'Histoire Offerts à M. Charles Bémont* (1913), 403–10

Genet, J.-P., 'Le roi de France anglais et la nation française au XVe siècle', *Identité régionale et conscience nationale en France et en Allemagne du Moyen Age à l'époque modern*, ed. R. Babel and J.-M. Moeglin (1997), 39–58

Genet, J.-P., 'La Normandie vue par les historiens et les politiques anglais au XVe siècle', *La Normandie et l'Angleterre au Moyen Age*, ed. P. Bouet and V. Gazeau (2003), 277–306

Giesey, R. E., *The Royal Funeral Ceremony in Renaissance France* (1960)

Giesey, R. E., *Le rôle méconnu de la Loi Salique. La succession royale, xive–xvie siècles* (2007)

Gilles, H., *Les états du Languedoc au XVe siècle* (1965)

Giry-Deloison, C., 'Money and early Tudor dipomacy. The English pensioners of the French Kings (1475–1547)', *Medieval History*, iii (1993–4), 128–46

Giry-Deloison, C., 'France and England at peace, 1475–1513', *The Contending Kingdoms: France and England, 1420–1700*, ed. G. Richardson (2008), 43–60

Glénisson, J. and Deodato de Silva, V., 'La pratique et le rituel de la reddition aux XIVe et XVe siècles', *Jeanne d'Arc. Une époque. Un rayonnement. Colloque d'histoire médiévale, Orléans octobre 1979* (1982), 113–22

Gonzalez, E., *Un prince en son hôtel. Les serviteurs des ducs d'Orléans au xve siècle* (2004) [with prosopographical appendix on CD-ROM]

Goodman, A., *The Wars of the Roses. Military Activity and English Society, 1452–97* (1981)

Goodman, A. and Tuck, A. (eds), *War and Border Societies in the Middle Ages* (1992)

Goulay, D., 'La résistance à l'occupation anglaise en Haute-Normandie (1435–1444)', *Annales de Normandie*, xxxvi (1986), 37–55, 91–104

Gout, P., *Le Mont-Saint-Michel*, 2 vols (1910)

Grandeau, Y., 'La mort et les obsèques de Charles VI', *Bulletin philologique et historique du Comité des travaux historiques et scientifiques* (1970), 134–86

Grassoreille, G., 'Histoire politique du Chapitre de Notre-Dame pendant la domination anglaise', *Memoires de la Société de l'histoire de Paris et de l'Île de France*, ix (1882), 109–92

Gray, H. L., 'Incomes from land in England in 1436', *EHR*, xlix (1934), 607–39

Green, D., *The Hundred Years War. A People's History* (2014)

Griffiths, R. A., 'The trial of Eleanor Cobham: an episode in the fall of Duke Humphrey of Gloucester', *Bulletin of the John Rylands Library*, li (1968–9), 381–99

Administration. Studies Presented to S. B. Chrimes (1974), 69–86

*Griffiths, R. A., 'Richard Duke of York's intentions in 1450 and the origins of the Wars of the Roses', *Journal of Medieval History*, i (1975), 187–209

Griffiths, R. A., *The reign of King Henry VI. The exercise of royal authority, 1422–1461* (1981)

*Griffiths, R. A., 'The King's council and the first protectorate of the Duke of York, 1453–1454', *EHR*, xcix (1984), 67–82

*Griffiths, R. A., 'Richard Duke of York and the crisis of Henry VI's household in 1450–1: some further evidence', *Journal of Medieval History*, xxxviii (2012), 244–56

Grondeux, A., 'La présence anglaise en France: les anglais dans la vallée de la Seine sous la régence du Duc de Bedford (1422–1435)', *Journal des Savants*, no 1–2 (1993), 89–109

Grummitt, D., 'Introduction: war, diplomacy and cultural exchange', *The English Experience in France, c. 1450–1558*, ed. D. Grummitt (2002)[1], 1–23

Grummitt, D., '"One of the mooste pryncipall treasours belonging to his realme of Englande": Calais and the crown, c. 1450–1558', *The English Experience in France, c. 1450–1558*, ed. D. Grummitt (2002)[2], 46–62

BIBLIOGRAPHY

Grummitt, D., 'Deconstructing Cade's rebellion: discourse and politics in the mid-fifteenth century', *The Fifteenth Century*, vi, *Identity and Insurgency in the Late Middle Ages*, ed. L. Clark (2006), 107–22

Grummitt, D., *The Calais Garrison. War and Military Service in England, 1436–1558* (2008)

Grummitt, D., 'Changing perceptions of the soldier in late medieval England', *The Fifteenth Century*, x, *Parliament, Personalities and Power*, ed. L. S. Clark (2011), 189–202

Guenée, B., *Tribunaux et gens de justice dans le bailliage de Senlis à la fin du moyen age (vers 1380–vers 1550)* (1963)

Guenée, B., 'État et nation en France au moyen age', *Revue Historique*, ccxxxvii (1967), 17–30

Guibert, H., *Louviers pendant la guerre de cent ans* (1895)

Guilbert, S., 'La réconstruction dans les campagnes champenoises après la guerre de Cent Ans', *La réconstruction après la guerre de Cent Ans (Actes du 104e Congrès National des Sociétés Savantes, Bordeaux, 1979)* (1981), i, 123–42

*Guichenon, S., *Histoire généalogique de la maison de Savoie*, n.e., 4 vols (1778–80)

Guillemain, B., 'Une carrière: Pierre Cauchon', *Jeanne d'Arc. Une époque. Un rayonnement. Colloque d'histoire médiévale, Orléans octobre 1979* (1982), 217–25

Guillon, F., *Étude historique sur le journal du siège d'Orléans qui fut mis devant Orléans par les anglais en 1428–1429* (1913)

*Guillot, R., *Le procès de Jacques Cœur (1451–1457)* (n.d.)

*Guillot, R., *La chute de Jacques Cœur. Une affaire d'état au XVe siècle* (2008)

Gunn, S. J., 'The Duke of Suffolk's march on Paris in 1523', *EHR*, ci (1986), 596–634

Gunn, S. J., 'The French wars of Henry VIII', *The Origins of War in Early Modern Europe*, ed. J. Black (1987), 28–51

*Gut, C., 'Quelques letters de rémission inédites (1422–1425)', *Bulletin de la Société archéologique, historique et géographique de Creil*, no. 76 (1972), 21–31

*Gut, C., 'Deux nouvelles lettres de rémission rélatives à Creil', *Bulletin de la Société archéologique, historique et géographique de Creil*, no. 88 (1975), 1–12

*Gut, C., 'Actes de la chancellerie royale rélatifs à Senlis (1420–1435), *Société d'Histoire et d'archéologie de Senlis. Comptes rendus et mémoires* (1978), 25–57

*Gut. C., 'Scènes de la vie journalière à Compiègne et aux environs (1420–1435) d'après les lettres de rémission', *Bulletin de la Société Historique de Compiègne*, xxviii (1982), 133–76

*Gut, C., 'Clermont et le Clermontois à l'époque de Jeanne d'Arc d'après les lettres de rémission', *Autour du donjon de Clermont. Actes du colloque de Clermont (10–11 octobre 1987)* (1989)

*Gut, C., 'Les pays de l'Oise sous la domination anglaise (1420–1435) d'après les régistres de la Chancellerie de France', *La guerre, la violence et les gens au moyen age*, ii, *Guerre et gens*, ed. P. Contamine and O. Guyotjeannin (1996), ii, 141–314

Gysels, G., 'Le départ de Jacqueline de Bavière de la cour de Brabant (11 avril 1420)', *Mélanges d'Histoire offerts à Leon van de Essen* (1947), 413–27

Haegeman, M., *De Anglofilie in het Graafschap Vlaanderen tussen 1379 en 1435. Politieke en economisch aspecten* (1988)

Hall, B. S., *Weapons and Warfare in Renaissance Europe. Gunpowder, Technology and Tactics* (1997)

Hallopeau, L.-A., 'Essai sur l'histoire des comtes et ducs de Vendôme de la maison de Bourbon', *Bulletin de la Société archéologique, scientifieque et littéraire du Vendômois*, l (1911), 181–232, li (1912), 312–33, lii (1913), 311–30

Harbinson, M., 'The lance in the fifteenth century: How French cavalry overcame the English defensive system in the latter part of the Hundred Years War', *Journal of Medieval Military History*, xvii (2019), 141–200

Hardy, D., 'The 1444–5 expedition of the Dauphin Louis to the upper Rhine in geopolirical perspective', *Journal of Medieval History*, xxxviii (2012), 358–87

*Hardy, M., 'La mission de Jeanne d'Arc prêchée à Périgueux en 1429', *Bulletin de la Société Archéologique du Périgord* (1887), 50–55

Harmand, J., 'Un document de 1435 concernant Houdan et la fin de l'occupation anglaise dans l'ouest de l'Île de France', *Bulletin de la Société nationale des Antiquaires de France* (1975), 205–47

Harmand, J., 'Le château de Montépilloy', *Bulletin Monumentale*, cxxxvii (1979), 93–140

Harris, R., *Valois Guyenne* (1994)

Harriss, G. L., 'Aids, loans and benevolences', *Historical Journal*, vi (1963), 1–19

Harriss, G. L., Marmaduke Lumley and the Exchequer crisis of 1446–9, *Aspects of Late Medieval Government and Society. Essays presented to J. R. Lander*, ed. J. G. Rowe (1986), 143–78

Harriss, G. L., *Cardinal Beaufort. A study of Lancastrian Ascendency and Decline* (1988)

Harriss, G. L., *Shaping the Nation. England 1360–1461* (2005)

*Harrod, H. D., 'A defence of the liberties of Cheshire, 1450', *Archaeologia*, lvii, 71–86

*Harvey, I. M. W., *Jack Cade's Rebellion of 1450* (1991)

Harvey, I. M. W., 'Was there popular politics in fifteenth-century England?', *The McFarlane Legacy. Studies in Late Medieval Politics and Society*, ed. R. H. Britnell and A. J. Pollard (1995), 155–74

Harvey, M., *England, Rome and the Papacy, 1417–1464* (1993)

Hatcher, J., *Plague, Population and the English Economy, 1348–1530* (1977)

Hatcher, J., 'The great slump of the mid-fifteenth century', *Progress and Problems in Medieval England. Essays in Honour of Edward Miller*, ed. R. Britnell and J. Hatcher (1996), 237–72

Hayes, R. C. E.: see E: Unpublished Theses

Hayez, M., 'Un exemple de culture historique au XVe siècle: La geste des nobles francois', *Mélanges d'Archéologie et d'Histoire publiés par l'École Française de Rome* (1963), 127–78

Heers, J., *Jacques Coeur* (1997)

Helmrath, J., *Das Basler Konzil, 1431–1449* (1987)

Herbomez, A. d', 'Le traité de 1430 entre Charles VII et le duc d'Autriche', *Revue des questions historiques*, xxxi (1882), 409–37

Hicks, M., 'Counting the cost of war: the Moleyns ransom and the Hungerford land-sales', *Southern History*, viii (1986), 11–35

Hicks, M., 'From megaphone to microscope. The correspondence of Richard Duke of York with Henry VI revisited', *Journal of Medieval History*, xxv (1999), 243–56

Hicks, M., *The Wars of the Roses* (2010)

Higounet-Nadal, A., *Périgueux aux xive et xve siècles. Étude de démographie historique* (1978)

Hirschauer, C., *Les états d'Artois de leurs origines à l'occupation française, 1340–1640*, 2 vols (1923)

History of Parliament. The House of Commons, 1386–1421, ed. J. S. Roskell, L. Clark, and C. Rawlcliffe, 4 vols (1992)

History of Parliament. The House of Commons, 1422–1461, ed. L. Clark, 7 vols (2020)

BIBLIOGRAPHY

Hobbins, D., 'Jean Gerson's authentic tract on Joan of Arc: *Super facto puellae et credulitate sibi praestanda*' (14 May 1429)', *Medieval Studies*, lxvii (2005), 95–155
Holmes, G., 'The Libel of English Policy', *EHR*, lxxvi (1961), 193–216
*Holmes, G., 'Cardinal Beaufort and the crusade aganst the Hussites', *EHR*, lxxxviii (1973), 721–50
*Houtard, M., *Les Tournaisiens et le Roi de Bourges* (1908)
Hubrecht, G., 'Juridictions et compétences en Guyenne recouvrée', *Annales de la Faculté de Droit de l'Université de Bordeaux, Série juridique*, iii (1952), 63–79
*Huguet, A., *Aspects de la guerre de Cent ans en Picardie maritime* (1941–4)
Huillard-Bréhollès, 'La rançon du duc Jean 1er, 1415-1436', *Mémoires présentés à l'Académie des Inscriptions et Belles Lettres*, 1ere série, viii (2) (1874), 37–91
Huizinga, J. H., 'L'état bourguignon, ses rapports avec la France et les origines d'une nationalité néerlandaise', *Le Moyen Age*, xl (1930), 171–93; xli (1931), 11–35
Huizinga, J. H., 'La physionomie morale de Philippe le Bon', *Annales de Bourgogne*, iv (1932), 101–39
*Hunger, V., *Le siège et la prise de Caen par Charles VII en 1450* (1912)
*Hunger, V., *L'abbaye fortifiée de Saint-Pierre-sur-Dive pendant la guerre de Cent Ans* (1914)
Hunger, V., *Les capitaines de Vire aux XIVe et XVe siècles* (1925)
Hunger, V., *Le château de Vire (1350-1500)*, (1927)
Hunger, V., *Les vicomtes de Vire aux XIVe et XVe siècles. Notices biographiques* (1931)
Huynes, J., *Histoire générale de l'abbaye du Mont-St.-Michel au peril de la mer*, ed. E. R. de Beaurepaire, 2 vols (1872–3)

Ilardi, V., 'The Italian League, Francesco Sforza and Charles VII (1454–1461)', *Studies in the Renaissance*, vi (1959), 129–66

Jackson, R. A., *Vive le Roi! A History of the French Coronation from Charles V to Charles X* (1984)
Jacob, E. F. *The Fifteenth Century* (1961)
Jacob, E. F., *Archbishop Henry Chichele* (1967)
*Jadart, H., *Jeanne d'Arc à Reims. Ses relations avec Reims, ses lettres aux rémois* (1887)
James, L. E.: see E: Unpublished Theses
James, M. K., *Studies in the Medieval Wine Trade* (1971)
Jamieson, N., 'The recruitment of northerners for service in English armies in France, 1415–50', *Trade, Devotion and Governance. Papers in Later Medieval History*, ed. D. J. Clayton, R. G. Davies and P. McNiven (1994), 102–15
Janse, A., *Een pion voor een dame. Jacoba van Beieren (1401–1436)* (2009)
Jansen, H. P. H., *Hoekse en Kabeljauwsebtwisten* (1966)
Jassemin, H., *La Chambre des Comptes de Paris au xve siècle* (1933)
Johnson, P. A., *Duke Richard of York, 1411–1460* (1988)
Johnston, C. E., 'Sir William Oldhall', *EHR*, xxv (1910), 715–22
Jones, M., 'The defence of medieval Brittany: a survey of the establishment of fortified town, castles and frontiers from the gallo-roman period to the end of the middle ages', *Archeological Journal*, cxxxviii (1981), 149–204
Jones, M., '"Bons bretons et bons francoys": the language and meaning of treason in later medieval France', *Transactions of the Royal Historical Society*, 5th series, xxxii (1982), 91–112
Jones, M., '*Membra disjecta* of the Breton *Chambre des Comptes* in the late middle ages: treasures revisited and rediscovered', *War, Government and Power in Late Medieval France*, ed. C. Allmand (2000), 208–20

Jones, M., 'Sur les pas du connétable de Richemont: quelques sources financières inédites', *Le Prince, l'argent, les hommes au moyen age. Mélanges offerts à Jean Kerhervé* (2008), 271–81

Jones, M. K., 'John Beaufort, Duke of Somerset, and the French expedition of 1443', *Patronage, the Crown and the Provinces in Later Medieval England*, ed. R. A. Griffiths (1981), 79–102

Jones, M. K. (1983): see E: Unpublished Theses

Jones, M. K., 'L'imposition illégale de taxes en "Normandie anglaise". Une enquête gouvernementale en 1446', *La 'France Anglaise' au moyen age (Actes du 111e Congrès National des Sociétés Savantes, Poitiers, 1986)* (1988), 461–9

Jones, M. K., 'Somerset, York and the Wars of the Roses', *EHR*, civ (1989)[1], 285–307

Jones, M. K., 'War on the frontier: the Lancastrian land settlement in eastern Normandy, 1435–1450', *Nottingham Medieval Studies*, xxxiii (1989)[2], 104–21

Jones, M. K., 'Ransom brokerage in the fifteenth century', *Guerre et société en France, en Angleterre et en Bourgogne, xive–xve siècle*, ed. P. Contamine, C. Giry-Deloison and M. Keen (1991), 221–35

Jones, M. K., 'The relief of Avranches (1439): an English feat of arms at the end of the Hundred Years War', *England in the Fifteenth Century. Proceedings of the Harlaxton Symposium*, iv, ed. N. Rogers (1994), 42–55

Jones, M. K., 'Gardez mon corps, sauver ma terre' – Immunity from war and the lands of a captive knight: the siege of Orléans (1428–29) revisited', *Charles d'Orléans in England*, ed. M.-J. Arn (2000), 9–26

Jones, M. K., 'The battle of Verneuil (17 August 1423). Towards a history of courage', *War in History*, ix (2002), 377–412

Jones, R. (1994): see E: Unpublished Theses

Jones, R., 'Les fortifications municipales de Lisieux dans les chroniques et dans les comptes (première moitié du XVe siècle)', *La guerre, la violence et les gens au moyen age*, i, *Guerre et violence*, ed. P. Contamine and O. Guyotjeannin (1996), 235–44

Jones, R., 'Les fortifications dans la Normandie des Lancastres, 1417–1450', *La Normandie dans la guerre de Cent Ans, 1435–1450*, ed. J.-Y. Marin (1999), 111–15

Jones, R. W., and Coss, P., *A Companion to Chivalry* (2019)

Joret, C, *La bataille de Formigny* (1903)

Joubert, A., 'Les négociations relatives à l'évacuation du Maine par les anglais (1444–1448)', *Revue historique et archéologique du Maine*, viii (1880), 221–40

Joubert, A., *Histoire de la baronnie de Craon de 1382 à 1626* (1888)

Jouet, R., *La résistance à l'occupation anglaise en Basse-Normandie (1418–1450)* (1969)

Jouet, R., 'La fidelité à la France à l'épreuve de l'occupation anglaise (1417–1450)', *La Normandie dans la guerre de Cent Ans, 1435–1450*, ed. J.-Y. Marin (1999), 51–3

Journel, C., 'La captivité de Jeanne d'Arc à Beaurevoir', *Mémoires de la Société Académique de Saint-Quentin*, x (1929), 43–73

Judd, A., *The Life of Thomas Bekynton* (1961)

Jurkowski, M., Smith, C. L., and Crook, D., *Lay Taxes in England and Wales, 1188–1688* (1998)

Kaeuper, R., *Medieval Chivalry* (2016)

Keen, M. H., 'Brotherhood in arms', *History*, xlvii (1962), 1–17

Keen, M. H., *The Laws of War in the Late Middle Ages* (1965)

Keen, M. H., *Chivalry* (1984)

Keen, M. H., 'The end of the Hundred Years War: Lancastrian France and Lancastrian England', *England and her Neighbours, 1066–1453. Essays in Honour of Pierre Chaplais*, ed. M. Jones and M. Vale (1989), 297–311

BIBLIOGRAPHY

Keen, M. H., *Origins of the English Gentleman* (2002)
Keen, M. H. and Daniel, M. J., 'English diplomacy and the sack of Fougères in 1449', *History*, lix (1974), 375–91
Kemp, B., 'English church monuments during the period of the hundred years war', *Arms, Armies and Fortifications in the Hundred Years War*, ed. A. Curry and M. Hughes (1994), 195–211
*Kempe, A. J., *Historical Notices of the Collegiate Church or Royal Free Chapel and Sanctuary of St. Mart-le-Grand* (1825)
Kerhervé, J., *L'État Breton aux xive et xve siècles. Les ducs, l'argent et les hommes*, 2 vols (1987)
Kerhervé, J., 'Entre conscience nationale et identité régionale dans la Bretagne de la fin du moyen age', *Identité régionale et conscience nationale en France et en Allemagne du moyen age à l'époque moderne*, ed. R. Babel and J.-M. Moeglin (1997), 219–43
Kerling, N. J. M., *Commercial Relations of Holland and Zeeland with England from the Late 13th Century to the Close of the Middle Ages* (1954)
King, A., 'Gunners, aides and archers: the personnel of the English ordnance companies in Normandy in the fifteenth century', *Journal of Medieval Military History*, ix (2011), 65–75
*Kingsford, C. L., 'The first version of Hardyng's Chronicle', *EHR*, xxvii (1912), 462–82, 740–54
*Kingsford, C. L., *English historical literature in the fifteenth century* (1913)
Kingsford, C. L., 'An historical collection of the fifteenth century', *EHR*, xxix (1914), 505–15
Kingsford, C. L., *Prejudice and Promise in Fifteenth-Century England* (1925)
Kipling, G., '"Grace in this Lyf and aftirwarde Glorie": Margaret of Anjou's royal entry into London', *Research Opportunities in Renaissance Drama*, xxix (1986–7), 77–84
Kirby, J. L., 'The issues of the Lancastrian Exchequer and Lord Cromwell's estimates of 1433', *Bulletin of the Institute Historical Research*, xxiv (1951), 121–51
Kleinclausz, A., *Histoire de Lyon*, 3 vols (1939–52)
Kleineke, H., 'The commission de mutuo faciendo in the reign of Henry VI', *EHR*, cxvi (2001), 1–30
Kleinert, C., *Philibert de Montjeu, ca. 1374–1439. Ein Bischof im Zeitalter der Reformkonzilien und des Hundertjährigen Krieges* (2004)
Knowlson, G. A., *Jean V, duc de Bretagne, et l'Angleterre (1339–1442)* (1964)
Kosto, A. J., *Hostages in the Middle Ages* (2012)
Krynen, J., *Idéal du prince et pouvoir royal en France à la fin du moyen age (1380–1440). Étude de la littérature politique du temps* (1981)
Krynen, J., '"Naturel". Essai sur l'argument de la nature dans la pensée politique francaise à la fin du moyen age', *Journal des Savants* (1982), 169–90
Krynen, J., 'Réflexion sur les idées politiques aux États généraux de Tours de 1484', *Revue historique de droit français et étranger*, lxii (1984), 183–204
Krynen, J., *L'Empire du roi. Idées et croyances en France, xiiie–xve siècle* (1993)

La Borderie, A. le Moyne de, *Histoire de Bretagne*, 6 vols (1905–14)
*Labory, G., 'Une généalogie des rois de France se terminant à Henri VI roi "de France" et d'Angleterre', *Saint-Denis et la Royauté. Études offertes à Bernard Guenée*, ed. F. Autrand, C. Gauvard and J.-M. Moeglin (1999), 521–36
Lacaze, Y., 'Philippe le Bon et le problème hussite: un projet de croisade Bourguignon en 1428–9', *Revue Historique*, ccxli (1969), 69–98
Lacaze, Y., 'Aux origines de la paix d'Arras (1435). Amadée VIII de Savoie, médiateur entre France et Bourgogne', *Revue d'histoire diplomatique*, lxxxvii (1973), 232–76

BIBLIOGRAPHY

Lacaze, Y., 'Philippe le Bon et l'Empire: bilan d'un règne', *Francia*, ix (1981), 133–75; x (1982), 167–227

Laidlaw, J., 'Alain Chartier and the Arts of Crisis Management, 1417–1429', *War, Government and Power in Late Medieval France*, ed. C. Allmand (2000), 37–53

Lair, J., *Essai historique et topographique sur la bataille de Formigny (15 April 1450)* (1903)

Lambert, C., 'Naval service and the Cinque Ports, 1322–1453', *Military Communities in Late Medieval England. Essays in Honour of Andrew Ayton*, ed. G. P. Baker, C. L. Lambert and D. Simpkin (2018), 211–36

La Martinière, J. de, 'Un grand chancelier de Bretagne. Jean de Malestroit, Evêque de Saint-Brieuc (1405–1419) et de Nantes (1419–1443)', *Mémoires de la Société Historique et Archéologique de Bretagne*, i (1920), 9–52

Lander, J. R., *Conflict and Stability in Fifteenth-century England* (1969)

Lander, J. R., 'The Hundred Years War and Edward IV's 1475 campaign in France', *Tudor Men and Institutions: Studies in English Law and Government*, ed. A. J. Slavin (1972), 70–100

Lapierre, A., *La guerre de Cent ans dans l'Argonne et le Rethelois* (1900)

Laporte, J. (ed.), *Millénaire monastique du Mont Saint-Michel*, 5 vols (1967–1993)

Lardin, P., 'L'hôtel archépiscopal de Rouen à l'époque de Louis de Luxembourg (1437–1443)', *Images de la guerre de cent ans: actes du colloque de Rouen (23, 24 et 25 mai 2000)* (2002), ed. J. Maurice, D. Couty and M. Guéré-Laferté (2002), 27–45

Lardin, P., 'L'activité du port de Dieppe à travers la comptabilité de l'archevêque de Rouen', *Ports maritimes et ports fluviaux au moyen age. Actes du XXXVe Congrès de la Société des historiens médiévistes de l'enseignement supérieur public (La Rochelle, 2004)* (2005), 171–82

Lardin, P., 'Les transformations de la ville de Dieppe pendant la guerre de Cent Ans', *Les villes normandes au moyen age. Renaissance, essor, crise*, ed. P. Bouet and F. Neveux (2006), 75–107

Lardin, P., 'Le château de Rouen au moment du procès de Jeanne d'Arc', *De l'hérétique à la sainte. Les procès de Jeanne d'Arc revisités*, ed. F. Neveux (2012), 49–67

*La Roque, G.-A. de, *Histoire généalogique de la maison de Harcourt*, 4 vols (1662)

Lassalmonie, J.-F., *La boîte à l'enchanteur. Politique financière de Louis XI* (2002)

*Lebigue, J.-B., 'L'ordo du sacre d'Henri VI à Notre-Dame de Paris (16 décembre 1431)', *Notre-Dame de Paris, 1163–2013*, ed. C. Giraud (2013), 319–63

Le Breton, C., *L'Avranchin pendant la guerre de Cent ans* (1879)

Lecoy de la Marche, A., 'Une fausse Jeanne d'Arc', *Revue des Questions Historiques*, x (1871), 562–82

*Lecoy de la Marche, *Le Roi Réné. Sa vie, son administration, ses travaux artistiques et littéraires*, 2 vols (1875)

*Ledieu, A., 'Documents inédits sur le siège du Crotoy en 1423', *Bulletin Mensuel de la Société d'Histoire et d'Archéologie du Vimeu*, i (1905), 339–43, 356–62, 370–5, 388–93, 406–10

*Ledru, A., *Histoire de la maison de Mailly*, 2 vols (1893)

Lefèvre-Pontalis, G., 'Un detail du siège de Paris par Jeanne d'Arc', *BEC*, xlvi (1885), 5–15

Lefèvre-Pontalis, G., 'La panique anglaise en mai 1429', *Moyen Age*, vii (1894)[1], 81–96

Lefèvre-Pontalis, G., 'La fausse Jeanne d'Arc', *Le Moyen Age* (1895)[1], 97–112, 121–36

Lefèvre-Pontalis, G., 'Épisodes de l'invasion anglaise. La guerre de partisans dans la haute Normandie (1424–1429)', *BEC* liv (1893), 475–521; lv (1894)[2], 259–305; lvi (1895)[2], 433–508; lvii (1896), 5–54

BIBLIOGRAPHY

Lefèvre-Pontalis, G., 'Le siège de Meulan en 1423', *Commission des antiquités et des arts du département de Seine-et-Oise*, xxiii (1903), 54–68

Leguai, A., 'Le problème des rançons au XVe siècle: la captivité de Jean Ier, duc de Bourbon', *Cahiers de l'Histoire*, vi (1961), 42–58

Leguai, A., *Les ducs de Bourbon pendant la crise monarchique du XVe siècle* (1962)

Leguai, A., *De la seigneurie à l'état. Le Bourbonnais pendant la guerre de Cent ans* (1969)

Leguai, A. 'Les révoltes rurales dans le royaume de France du milieu du XIVe siècle à la fin du moyen age', *Le Moyen Age*, lxxxviii (1982), 49–76

Leguai, A., 'La "France Bourguignonne" dans le conflit entre la "France française" at la "France anglaise" (1420–1435)', *La 'France Anglaise' au moyen age (Actes du 111e Congrès National des Sociétés Savantes, Poitiers, 1986)* (1988), 41–52

Le Mené, M., *Les campagnes angevines à la fin du moyen age* (1982)

Lemercier, F.-X., 'Falaise pendant l'occupation anglaise', *Les villes normandes au moyen age. Renaissance, essor, crise*, ed. P. Bouet and F. Neveux (2006), 125–38

Lennel, F., *Histoire de Calais*, 3 vols (1908–1913)

Léost, D., 'Le château de Rouen pendant la guerre de Cent Ans', *La Normandie dans la guerre de Cent Ans, 1435–1450*, ed. J.-Y. Marin (1999), 127–9

Lepingard, E., 'Les effets à Saint-Lô de la conquête de la Normandie par les anglais, 1418–1437', *Notices, mémoires et documents publiés par la Société d'Agriculture, d'Archéologie et d'Histoire Naturelle du département de la Manche*, ix (1890), 164–8

Lepingard, E., 'Trois patriotes Saint Lois, 1417–1448', *Notices, mémoires et documents publiés par la Société d'Agriculture, d'Archéologie et d'Histoire Naturelle du département de la Manche*, x (1892), 54–8

Lepingard, E., 'Les Biote, 1418–1473', *Notices, mémoires et documents publiés par la Société d'Agriculture, d'Archéol. et d'Histoire Naturelle du département de la Manche*, xvi (1898), 137–46

Lépinois, H. de, 'Notes et extraits des archives communales de Compiègne', *BEC*, xxiv (1863), 471–99; xxv (1864), 124–61

Le Roy, T., *Les curieuses recherches du Mont-Sainct-Michel*, ed. E. R. de Beaurepaire, 2 vols (1878)

Le Roy Ladurie, E. and Couperie, P., 'Le mouvement des loyers parisiens de la fin du moyen age au XVIIIe siècle', *Annales. Économies – sociétés – civilisations*, xxv (1970), 1002–23

Lespinasse, R. de, *Le Nivernais et les comtes de Nevers*, 3 vols (1909–14)

*Lesquier, J., 'La reddition de 1449', *Études Lexoviennes*, i (1915), 19–50

Lesquier, J., 'L'administration et les finances de Lisieux de 1423 à 1448', *Études Lexoviennes*, ii (1919), 37–175

Lewis, P. S., 'The failure of the French medieval Estates', *Past & Present*, xxiii (1962), 3–24

Lewis, P. S., 'France in the fifteenth century: society and sovereignty', *Europe in the Late Middle Ages*, ed. J. R. Hale, J. R. L. Highfield and B. Smalley (1965)[1], 466–94

Lewis, P. S., 'Jean Juvenel des Ursins and the common literary attitude towards tyranny in fifteenth century France', *Medium Aevum*, xxxiv (1965)[2], 103–21

Lewis, P. S., 'War propaganda and historiography in fifteenth century France and England', *Transactions of the Royal Historical Society*, 5th series, xv (1965)[3], 1–21

Lewis, P. S., *Later Medieval France. The Polity* (1968)

Lewis, P. S., 'La "France Anglaise" vué de la France française', *La 'France Anglaise' au moyen age (Actes du 111e Congrès National des Sociétés Savantes, Poitiers, 1986)* (1988), 31–9

Leyte, G., *Domaine et domanialité publique dans la France médiévale (XIIe–XVe siècles)* (1996)
Little, R. G., *The Parlement of Poitiers. War, Government and Politics in France, 1418–1436* (1984)
Lloyd, T. H., *The Movement of Wool Prices in Medieval England* (1973)
Lloyd, T. H., *The English Wool Trade in the Middle Ages* (1977)
Lloyd, T. H., *England and the German Hanse, 1157–1611. A study of their trade and commercial diplomacy* (1991)
Loades, M., *The Longbow* (2013)
Loades, M., *The Crossbow* (2018)
Lobanov, A. (2015)[1]: see E: Unpublished Theses
*Lobanov, A., 'The indenture of Philip the Good Duke of Burgundy and the Lancastrian Kingdom of France', *EHR*, cxxx (2015)[2], 302–17
*Löher, E. von, 'Beiträge zur Geschichte der Jacobäa von Bayern', *Abhandlungen der Historischen Classe der Königlich Bayerischen Akademie der Wissenschaften*, x (1865–7), I–III, 205–336
Löher, E. von, *Jacobäa von Bayern und ihre Zeit*, 2 vols (1862–9)
Löher, F. von, 'Kaiser Sigismund und Herzog Philipp von Burgund', *Münchner historisches Jahrbuch der Historischen Classe der Königlich Akademie der Wissenschaften* (1866), 305–419
Lombard-Jourdan, A., *Les Halles de Paris et leur quartier (1137–1969)* (2009)
Loncin, T., 'La guerre namuroise (1429–1431): un épisode de la rivalité Liège–Bourgogne au XVe siècle', *Bulletin de l'Institut Archéologique Liègeois*, cvi (1994), 139–63
London, H. S., *The Life of William Bruges, the First Garter King of Arms* (1970)
Longnon, A., 'Les limites de la France et l'étendue de la domination anglaise à l'époque de la mission de Jeanne d'Arc', *Revue des questions historiques*, xviii (1875), 444–546
Lorcin, M.-T., *Les campagnes de la region Lyonnaise aux XIVe et XVe siècles* (1974)
Lovatt, R., 'John Blacman: biographer of Henry VI', *The Writing of History in the Middle Ages. Essays Presented to Richard William Southern*, ed. R. H. C. Davies and J. M. Wallace-Hadrill (1981), 415–44
Luce, S., 'Le Maine sous la domination anglaise en 1433 et 1434', *Revue des Questions Historiques* (1878)[1], 226–41
*Luce, S., 'Le trésor anglais à Paris en 1431 et le procès de Jeanne d'Arc', *Memoires de la Société de l'Histoire de Paris*, v (1878)[2], 299–307
*Luce, S., *Jeanne d'Arc à Domrémy. Recherches critiques sur les origines de la mission de la Pucelle, accompagnées de pièces justificatives* (1886)
*Luce, S., *Philippe le Cat. Un complot contre les anglais à Cherbourg à l'époque de la mission de Jeanne d'Arc* (1887)
Luce, S., 'Louis d'Estouteville et la defense du Mont-Saint-Michel', *La France pendant la guerre de Cent Ans. Episodes historiques et vie privée aux xive et xve siècles*, ii (1893), 217–79
Lunt, W. E., *Financial Relations of the Papacy with England*, 2 vols (1939–62)

McCracken, H. N., 'An English friend of Charles of Orléans', *Publications of the Modern Language Association of America*, xxvi (1911), 141–80
*Macrae, C., 'The English Council and Scotland in 1430', *EHR*, liv (1939), 415–26
Maddern, P. C., *Violence and Social Order. East Anglia, 1422–1442* (1992)
Major, J. R., *Representative Institutions in Renaissance France, 1421–1559* (1960)
Malloué, B., 'La bastille de Saint-Jean-le-Thomas pendant la guerre de cent ans', *Revue de l'Avranchin*, xx (1922–3), 369–86

Mandrot, B. de, 'Jean de Bourgogne, duc de Brabant, comte de Nevers et le procès de sa succession', *Revue des questions historique*, xciii (1907), 1–45
*Marchegay, P., 'L'assaut de Pontoise (19 septembre 1441)', *Revue des Sociétés Savantes*, 4ᵉ série, iv (1866), 470–3
*Marchegay, P., 'La rançon d'Olivier de Coëtivy, seigneur de Taillebourg et sénéchal de Guyenne', *BEC*, xxxviii (1877), 5–48
Marshall, A.,: see E: Unpublished Theses
Martinière, J. de la, 'Frère Richard et Jeanne d'Arc à Orléans, mars-juillet 1430', *Le Moyen Age*, xliv (1934), 189–98
Masson d'Autume, M. de, *Cherbourg pendant la guerre de Cent ans* (1948)
Massey, R., 'The land settlement in Lancastrian Normandy', *Property and Politics: Essays in Later Medeival English History*, ed. A. Pollard (1984), 76–96
Massey, R. (1987): see E: Unpublished Theses
Massey, R., 'Lancastrian Rouen: military service and property holding, 1419–49', *England and Normandy in the Middle Ages*, ed. D. Bates and A. Curry (1994), 269–86
*Mathon, M., 'Notice historique sur la ville de Creil et sur son ancien château', *Mémoires de la Société académique de l'Oise*, iv (1859), 590–682
Maurer, H. E., *Margaret of Anjou. Queenship and Power in Late Medieval England* (2003)
Maury, A., 'Les forêts de la France dans l'antiquité et au moyen age; nouveaux essais sur leur topographie, leur histoire et la législation qui les régissait', *Mémoires présentés à l'Académie des Inscriptions et Belles Lettres*, 2ᵉ série, iv(1) (1860), 1–265
McCullough, D. and Jones, E. D., 'Lancastrian politics, the French war and the rise of the popular element', *Speculum*, lviii (1983), 95–138
McFarlane, K. B., 'Bastard Feudalism', *BIHR*, xx (1945), 161–80
McFarlane, K. B., 'Loans to the Lancastrian Kings. The problem of Inducement', *Cambridge Historical Journal*, ix (1947), 51–68
McFarlane, K. B., 'At the deathbed of Cardinal Beaufort', *Studies in Medieval History presented to Frederick Maurice Powicke*, ed. R. W. Hunt, W. A. Pantin and R. W. Southern (1948), 405–28
McFarlane, K. B., 'The investment of Sir John Fastolf's profits of war', *Transactions of the Royal Historical Society*, 5th ser., vii (1957)[1], 91–116
McFarlane, K. B., 'William Worcester: a preliminary survey', *Studies Presented to Sir Hilary Jenkinson*, ed. J. Conway Davies (1957)[2], 196–221
McFarlane, K. B., 'War, the Economy and Social Change: England and the Hundred Years War', *Past & Present*, xxii (1962), 3–15
McFarlane, K. B., 'A Business Partnership in War and Administration, 1421–1445', *EHR*, lxxviii (1963), 290–308
McFarlane, K. B., *Lancastrian Kings and Lollard Knights* (1972)
McFarlane, K. B., *The Nobility of Later Medieval England* (1973)
McFarlane, K. B., *Collected Essays* (1981)
McKenna, J. W., 'Henry VI of England and the dual monarchy: aspects of royal political propaganda, 1422–1432', *Journal of the Warburg & Courtauld Insts.*, xxviii (1965), 145–62
Meekings, C. A. F., 'Thomas Kerver's Case, 1444', *EHR*, xc (1975), 331–46
*Menard, L., *Histoire civile, ecclesiastique et littéraire de la ville de Nismes*, 7 vols (1744–58)
*Menard, V., *Histoire réligieuse, civile et militaire de Saint-James de Beuvron* (1897)
Merindol, C. de, 'Saint Michel et la monarchie française à la fin du moyen age dans le conflit franco-anglais', *La 'France Anglaise' au moyen age (Actes du 111ᵉ Congrès National des Sociétés Savantes, Poitiers, 1986)* (1988), 513–42

Mesqui, J. 'Les grandes heures du pont de Beaugency', *Revue générale des routes et des aerodromes* no. 589 (1982), 1–5
Mesqui, J., *Le pont en France avant le temps des ingénieurs* (1986)
Mesqui, J., *Châteaux et enceintes de la France médiévale*, 2 vols (1991–3)
Mesqui, J., 'Le château de Crépy-en-Valois, palais comtale, palais royale, palais féodale', *Bulletin Monumentale*, clii (1994), 257–312
Mesqui, J., *Châteaux forts et fortifications en France* (1997)
*Mestre, J.-B., *Guillaume de Flavy n'a pas trahi Jeanne d'Arc* (1934)
Michaud-Fréjaville, F., 'La forteresse d'Orléans (XIVe–XVe siècles)', *Le paysage urbain au moyen age. Actes des congrès de la Société des historiens médiévistes de l'enseignement supérieur public, 11e congrès* (1980), 61–78
Michaud-Fréjaville, F., 'Une cité face aux crises: les remparts de la fidelité, de Louis d'Orléans à Charles VII, d'après les comptes de forteresse de la ville d'Orléans (1391–1427)', *Jeanne d'Arc. Une époque. Un rayonnement. Colloque d'histoire médiévale, Orléans octobre 1979* (1982), 53–7
Michaud-Fréjaville, F., 'Jeanne d'Arc, *dux*, chef de guerre. Les points de vue des traités en faveur de la Pucelle', *Guerre, pouvoir et noblesse au moyen age. Mélanges en l'honneur de Philippe Contamine* (2000), ed. J. Paviot and J. Verger, 523–31
Michel, F., *Les Écossais en France. Les Français en Écosse*, 2 vols (1862)
Miller, E. (ed.), *The Agrarian History of England and Wales*, iii, *1348–1500* (1991)
Mirot, L., *Les d'Orgemont. Leur origine – leur fortune – le boiteux d'Orgemont* (1913)[1]
Mirot, L., 'Dom Bévy et les comptes des trésoriers des guerres. Essai de restitution d'un fonds disparu de la Chambre des Comptes', *BEC* lxxxvi (1925), 245–379
Mirot, L., 'Charles VII et ses conseillers, assassins présumés de Jean sand Peur', *Annales de Bourgogne*, xiv (1942), 197–210
Mitchell, R. J., *John Tiptoft (1427–1470)* (1938)
Mollat, M., *Le commerce maritime normand à la fin du moyen age* (1952)
Mollat, M., 'Recherches sur les finances des ducs Valois de Bourgogne', *Revue Historique*, ccix (1958), 285–321
Mollat, M. (ed.), *Histoire de Rouen* (1979)
Mollat, M., *Jacques Coeur ou l'esprit d'entreprise au XVe siècle* (1988)
Moore, T. K. and Bell, A. R., 'Financing the Hundred Years War', *Revisiting the Hundred Years War*, ed. A. Curry (2019), 57–84
Morandière, G. de la, *Histoire de la maison d'Estouteville en Normandie* (1903)
Moranvillé, H., 'Aide imposé par le roi d'Angleterre à Paris en 1423', *Bulletin de la Société de l'Histoire de Paris*, xxx (1903), 112–26
Moreton, C. and Richmond, C., 'Henry Inglose: a hard man to please', *The Fifteenth Century*, x, *Parliament, Personalities and Power. Papers presented to Linda S. Clarke*, ed. H. Kleineke (2011), 38–52
Morgan, D. A. L., 'The political after-life of Edward III: The apotheosis of a warmonger', *EHR*, cxii (1997), 856–81
Morice, P.-H. and Taillandier, C., *Histoire de Bretagne*, 2 vols (1750–56)
Müller, H., *Die Franzosen, Frankreich und das Basler Konzil (1431–1449)*, 2 vols (1990)
Müller, H., 'La division dans l'unité: Le Congrès d'Arras (1435) face à deux diplomaties ecclésiastiques', *Arras et la diplomatie européenne, XVe–XVIe siècles*, ed. D. Clauzel, C. Giry-Deloison and C. Leduc (1999), 109–30
Müller, H., 'Siège, rang et honneur: le querelle du préséance entre la Bretagne et la Bourgogne au concile de Bâle (1434), *Le Prince, l'argent, les hommes au moyen age. Mélanges offerts à Jean Kerhervé* (2008), 195–205

Munro, J. H. A., 'An economic aspect of the collapse of the Anglo-Burgundian alliance, 1428–1442', *EHR*, lxxxv (1970), 225–44

Munro, J. H. A., *Wool, Cloth and Gold. The Struggle for Bullion in Anglo-Burgundian Trade, 1340–1478* (1972)

Munro, J. H. A., 'Industrial protectionism in medieval Flanders: urban or national?', *The Medieval City*, ed. H. A. Miskimin, D. Herlihy and A. L. Udovitch (1977), 229–67

Murphy, N., 'Between France, England and Burgundy: Amiens under the Lancastrian dual monarchy', *French History*, xxvi (2012)[1], 143–63

Murphy, N., 'Henry VIII's French Crown. His royal entry into Tournai revisited', *Historical Research*, lxxxv (2012)[2], 617–31

Murphy, N., 'Henry VIII's first invasion of France: the Gascon expedition of 1512', *EHR*, cxxx (2015), 25–56

Murphy, N., *The Tudor Occupation of Boulogne. Conquest, Colonisation and Imperial Monarchy, 1544–1550* (2019)

Murphy, N. and Small, G., 'Town and crown in late 15th-century France: Rouen after the *Réduction*, c. 1449–1493', *La guerre en Normandie (XIe–XVe)*, ed. A. Curry and V. Gazeau (2018), 309–31

Myers, A. R., 'A parliamentary debate of the mid-fifteenth century', *Bulletin of the John Rylands Library*, xxii (1938), 388–404

Myers, A. R., 'The outbreak of war between England and Burgundy in February 1471', *BIHR*, xxxiii (1960), 114–15

Myers, A. R., 'A parliamentary debate of 1449', *BIHR*, li (1978), 78–83

Naegle, G., '"Qui desiderat pacem, preparat bellum". Guerre et paix chex Jean Juvénal des Ursins et Enea Silvio Piccolomini', *Frieden schaffen ind sich verteidigen im Spätmittelalter*, ed. G. Haegle (2012), 267–327

Nall, C., 'Perceptions of financial mismanagement and the English diagnosis of defeat', *The Fifteenth Century*, vii, *Conflicts, Consequences and the Crown in the Late Middle Ages*, ed. L. Clark (2007), 119–36

Neveux, F., *L'évêque Pierre Cauchon* (1987)

Neveux, F., *Bayeux et Lisieux. Villes episcopales de Normandie à la fin du moyen age* (1996)

Neveux, F., 'Le clergé normand pendant la guerre de Cent Ans', *La Normandie dans la guerre de Cent Ans, 1435–1450*, ed. J.-Y. Marin (1999), 55–8

Neveux, F., *La Normandie pendant la guerre de cent ans* (2008)

Neuville, D, 'Le Parlement royale à Poitiers (1418–36)', *Revue Historique*, vi (1878), 1–28, 272–314

Neuville, L. R. de, 'De la résistance à l'occupation anglaise dans le pays de Lisieux de 1424 à 1444', *Bulletin de la Société de Antiquaires de Normandie*, xvi (1892), 325–73

Neville, C. J., *Violence, Custom and Law. The Anglo-Scottish Border Lands in the Later Middle Ages* (1998)

Newhall, R. A., 'Discipline in an English army of the fifteenth century', *Military Historian and Economist*, ii (1917), 141–51

Newhall, R. A., 'The war finances of Henry V and the Duke of Bedford', *EHR*, xxxvi (1921), 172–98

Newhall, R. A., *The English Conquest of Normandy, 1416–1424* (1924)

Newhall, R. A., 'Henry V's policy of conciliation in Normandy, 1417–1422', *Anniversary Essays in Medieval History by Students of Charles Homer Haskins*, ed. C. H. Taylor and J. L. La Monte (1929), 205–29

*Newhall, R. A., 'Bedford's ordinance of the watch of September 1428', *EHR*, l (1935), 36–60

BIBLIOGRAPHY

Newhall, R. A., *Muster and Review. A problem of English Military Administration, 1420–1440* (1940)
*Nichols, J. G., 'An original appointment of Sir John Fastolf to be keeper of the Bastille of St. Anthony at Paris in 1421', *Archaeologia*, xliv (1873), 113–22
Nicholson, R., *Scotland. The Later Middle Ages* (1974)
Nicolle, D., *Orléans 1429. France turns the tide* (2001)
Nightingale, P., *A Medieval Mercantile Community. The Grocers' Company and the Politics and Trade of London, 1000–1485* (1995)
Nightingale, P., 'The growth of London in the medieval English economy', *Progress and Problems in Medieval England. Essays in Honour of Edward Miller*, ed. R. Britnell and J. Hatcher (1996), 89–106

O'Neill, B. H. St J., *Castles and Cannon. A study of Early Artillery Fortifications in England* (1960)
Orgeval, Le Barrois d', *La justice militaire sous l'ancien régime. Le tribunal de la Connétablie de France du xive siècle à 1790* (1918)
Ormrod, W. M., 'Finance and trade under Richard II', *Richard II. The Art of Kingship*, ed. A. Goodman and J. Gillespie (1999)[1], 155–86
Ormrod, W. M., 'England in the middle ages', *The Rise of the Fiscal State in Europe, c. 1200–1815*, ed. R. Bonney (1999)[2], 19–52
Ormrod, W. M., 'Henry V and the English taxpayer', *Henry V. New Interpretations*, ed. G. Dodd (2013), 187–216
Ormrod, W. M., Lambert, B. and Mackman, J., *Immigrant England, 1300–1550* (2019)
Otway-Ruthven, J., *The King's Secretary and the Signet Office in the XV Century* (1939)
Oxford Dictionary of National Biography, 60 vols (2004) [cited as ODNB]

Paravicini, W. and Schnerb, B. (ed.), *Paris, capital des ducs de Bourgogne* (2007)
Paviot, J., *La politique navale des ducs de Bourgogne, 1384–1482* (1995)[1]
Paviot, J., *Portugal et Bourgogne au XVe siècle (1384–1482)* (1995)[2]
Paviot, J., *Les ducs de Bourgogne, la croisade et l'orient (fin xive–xve siècle)* (2003)
Payling, S. J., *Political Society in Lancastrian England. The Greater Gentry of Nottinghamshire* (1991)
Payling, S. J., 'War and peace: military and administrative service amongs the English gentry in the reign of Henry VI', *Soldiers, Nobles and Gentlemen. Essays in honour of Maurice Keen*, ed. P. Coss and C. Tyerman (2009), 240–58
Pearsall, D., 'The literary milieu of Charles of Orléans and the Duke of Suffolk, and the authorship of the Fairfax Sequence', *Charles d'Orléans in England*, ed. M.-J. Arn (2000), 145–56
Pégeot, P., 'L'armement des ruraux et des bourgeois à la fin du moyen age. L'exemple de la region de Montbéliard', *Guerre et société en France, en Angleterre et en Bourgogne, xive–xve siècle*, ed. P. Contamine, C. Giry-Deloison and M. Keen (1991), 237–60
Perroy, E., *La guerre de cent ans* (1945)
Petit-Dutaillis, C., 'Un nouveau document sur l'église de France à la fin de la guerre de cent ans: le régistre des visites archidiaconales de Josas', *Revue Historique*, lxxxviii (1905), 296–316
Petit-Dutaillis, C., *Charles VII, Louis XI et les premières années de Charles VIII (1422–1492)* [*Histoire de France*, ed. E. Lavisse, iv.2] (1911)
Peyrègne, A., 'Les émigrés gascons en Angleterre, 1453–1485', *Annales du Midi*, lxvi (1954), 113–28

Peyronnet, G., 'Les complots de Louis d'Amboise contre Charles VII (1428–1431): un aspect de rivalité entre lignages fédaux en France au temps de Jeanne d'Arc', *BEC*, cxlii (1984), 115–35
Picot, G., *Histoire de États-Généraux*, 2ᵉ ed. (1888)
Pirenne, H., *Histoire de Belgique*, 4th ed, 6 vols (1947)
Plaisse, A., *La baronnie de Neubourg* (1961)
Plaisse, A., *Un chef de guerre du XVᵉ siècle. Robert de Flocques, bailli royale d'Evreux* (1984)
Plaisse, A., *La délivrance de Cherbourg et di Clos de Cotentin à la fin de la guerre de Cent Ans* (1989)
Plaisse, A. and S., *La vie municipale à Evreux pendant la guerre de Cent ans* (1978)
*Planchenault, R., 'La délivrance du Mans, janvier–mars 1448', *Revue historique et archéologique du Maine*, lxxix (1923), 185–202
*Planchenault, R., 'La conquête du Maine par les anglais: la campagne de 1424–1425', *Revue historique et archéologique du Maine*, 2ᵉ série, v (1925), 3–31
*Planchenault, R., 'La conquête du Maine par les anglais: les campagnes de Richemont', *Revue historique et archéologique du Maine*, 2ᵉ série, xiii (1933), 125–52
*Planchenault, R., 'La conquête du Maine par les anglais: la lutte des partisans (1427–1429), *Revue historique et archéologique du Maine*, 2ᵉ série, xvii (1937), 24–34, 160–72, xviii (1938), 47–60
*Plancher, U., *Histoire générale et particulière de Bourgogne*, 4 vols (1739–81)
Platt, C., *The Castle in Medieval England and Wales* (1982)
Pocquet du Haut-Jussé, B. A., *Les papes et les ducs de Bretagne*, 2 vols (1928)
Pocquet du Haut-Jussé, B. A., *François II duc de Bretagne et l'Angleterre (1458–1488)*, (1929)
*Pocquet du Haut-Jussé, B. A., 'Anne de Bourgogne et le testament de Bedford (1429)', *BEC*, xcv (1934)[1], 284–326
Pocquet du Haut-Jussé, B. A., 'Deux féodaux. Bourgogne et Bretagne (1363–1491)', *Revue des cours et des conférences* (1934)[2], 481–93, 595–612, (1935), 53–67, 164–71
Pocquet du Haut-Jussé, B. A., 'Le Connétable de Richemont, seigneur bourguignon', *Annales de Bourgogne*, vii (1935)[2], 309–36; viii (1936), 7–30, 106–38
Pocquet du Haut-Jussé, B. A., 'Le fief Breton', *Histoire des institutions française au moyen age*, i (1957), 267–88
Pocquet du Haut-Jussé, B. A., 'Une idée politique de Louis XI: la sujétion éclipse la vassalité', *Revue Historique*, ccxxvi (1961), 383–98
Poirey, S., 'La procédure d'inquisition et son application au procès de Jeanne d'Arc', *De l'hérétique à la sainte. Les procès de Jeanne d'Arc revisités*, ed. F. Neveux (2012), 91–110
Poirier, B. and Manceau, C., 'La ville fortifiée de Pontoise (Val d'Oise): bilan archéologique', *Bulletin archéologique du Vexin français et du Val d'Oise*, xl (2008), 47–85
*Poli, O. de, *Les défenseurs du Mont Saint-Michel* (1895)
Pollard, A. J., *John Talbot and the War in France, 1427–1453* (1983)
Pons, N., 'La guerre de Cent Ans vue par quelques polémistes français du XVᵉ siècle', *Guerre et société en France, en Angleterre et en Bourgogne, xivᵉ–xvᵉ siècle*, ed. P. Contamine, C. Giry-Deloison and M. Keen (1991), 143–69
Postan, M. M., 'Revisions in economic history: IX The fifteenth century', *Economic History Review*, ix (1939), 160–7
Postan, M. M., 'Some social consequences of the Hundred Years' War', *Economic History Review*, xii (1942), 1–12
Postan, M. M., 'The cost of the Hundred Years War', *Past & Present*, xxvii (1964), 34–53

Pot, J., *Histoire de Regnier Pot, conseiller des ducs de Bourgogne, 1362(?)–1432* (1929)
Potter, D., 'The Duc de Guise and the fall of Calais, 1557–1558', *EHR*, xcviii (1983), 481–512
Potter, D., 'Anglo-French relations: the aftermath of the Hundred Years War', *Journal of Franco-British Studies*, xxviii (1999–2000), 41–66
Pounds, N. J. G., *The medieval castle in England and Wales. A Social and Political History* (1990)
Power, E. E., 'The wool trade in the fifteenth century', *Studies in English Trade in the Fifteenth Century*, ed. E. Power and M. M. Postan (1933), 39–90
Powicke, M., *Military Obligation in Medieval England* (1962)
Powicke, M., 'Lancastrian captains', *Essays in Medieval History presented to Bertie Wilkinson*, ed. T. A. Sandquist and M. R. Powicke (1969), 371–82
*Prevenier, W., *De Leden en de Staten van Vlaanderen (1384–1405)* (1961)
Prevenier, W., and Blockmans, W., *The Burgundian Netherlands* (1986)
Probert, Y., 'Matthew Gough, 1390–1450', *Transactions of the Honourable Society of Cymmrodorion* (1961), Pt. II, 34–44.
Prosser, G. L. L.: see E: Unpublished Theses
Pugh, T. B., 'Richard Plantagenet (1411–60), Duke of York, as the King's Lieutenant in France and Ireland', *Aspects of Late Medieval Government and Society. Essays Presented to J. R. Lander* (1986), 107–41
Pugh, T. B., and Ross, C. D., 'The English baronage and the income tax of 1436', *Bulletin of the Institute of Historical Research*, xxvi (1953), 1–28
Puiseux, L., 'Des insurrections populaires en Normandie pendant l'occupation anglaise au xve siècle', *Mémoires de la Société des Antiquaires de Normandie*, xix (1851), 138–59
Puiseux, L., *L'émigration normande et la colonisation anglaise en Normandie au XVe siècle* (1866)

*Quantin, M., *Episodes de l'histoire du XVe siècle aux pays sénonais et gâtinais et au comté de Joigny, tirés des Archives du département de l'Yonne* (1866)
*Quantin, M., 'Episodes de l'histoire du XVe siècle', *Bulletin de la Société des sciences historiques et naturelles de l'Yonne*, xxxvi (1882), 21–31
Quicherat, J., *Aperçus nouveaux sur l'histoire de Jeanne d'Arc* (1850)
Quicherat, J., *Rodrigue de Villandrando, l'un des combattants pour l'indépendance française au quinzième siècle* (1879)

Ramsay, J. H., *Lancaster and York*, 2 vols (1892)
Ratcliffe, H. L.: see E: Unpublished Theses
Rawcliffe, C., *The Staffords, Earls of Stafford and Dukes of Buckingham, 1394–1521* (1978)
Reeves, A. C., 'Some of Humphrey Stafford's military indentures', *Nottingham Medieval Studies*, xvi (1972), 80–91
Reeves, A. C., *Lancastrian Englishmen* (1981)
Renouard, Y., *Bordeaux sous les rois d'Angleterre* (1965)
Resbecq, F. de F. de, 'Les rapports du gouvernement anglais et de la noblesse normande dans la vicomté de Valognes pendant l'occupation, 1418–1450', *Mémoires de la Société archéologique, artistique, littéraire et scientifique de l'arrondissement de Valognes*, ix (1907–12), 17–42
Reulos, M., 'L'indemnisation de l'abbaye du Mont Saint-Michel pour le dommages subis au cours de la guerre de Cent Ans', *Revue de l'Avranchin et du Pays de Granville*, lxxviii (2001), 233–53

Reynaud, M.-R., *Le temps des princes. Louis II et Louis III d'Anjou-Provence, 1384–1434* (2000)
Reynolds, C., 'English patrons and French artists in fifteenth-century Normandy', *England and Normandy in the Middle Ages*, ed. D. Bates and A. Curry (1994), 299–313
Reynolds, C., '"Les angloys de leur droite nature veullent touzjours guerreer": evidence for painting in Paris and Normandy, c. 1420–1450', *Power, Culture and Religion in France, c. 1350-c. 1550*, ed. C. Allmand (1989), 37–55
Rhymer, L., 'Humphrey Duke of Gloucester and the City of London', *The Fifteenth Century*, viii, *Rule, Redemption and Representation in Late Medieval England and France*, ed. L. Clark (2008), 47–58
Ribadieu, H., *Histoire de la conquête de la Guyenne par les français* (1866)
Richmond, C. (1963): see E: Unpublished Theses
Richmond, C., 'The keeping of the seas during the Hundred Years War, 1422–1440', *History*, xlix (1964), 283–98
Richmond, C.,'English naval power in the fifteenth century', *History*, lii (1967), 1–15
Richmond, C., *The Paston Family in the Fifteenth Century. Fastolf's Will* (1996)
Richmond, C., 'Sir John Fastolf, the Duke of Suffolk and the Pastons', *The Fifteenth Century*, viii, ed. L. Clark (2008), 73–104
Rickard, P., *Britain in Medieval French Literature, 1100–1500* (1956)
*Riemsdijk, T. van, *De opdracht van het ruwaardschap van Holland en Zeeland aan Philips van Bourgindië* (1905)
Rigaudière, A., 'Le financement des fortifications urbaines en France du milieu du xive siècle à la fin du xve siècle', *Revue historique*, cclxxiii (1985), 19–95
Rigault, J., 'Ravages de la guerre de cents ans. Les écorcheurs en Luxembourg et en Rethelois en 1445', *La réconstruction après la guerre de Cent Ans (Actes du 104e Congrès National des Sociétés Savantes, Bordeaux, 1979)*(1981), i, 153–60
*Rioult de Neuville, L., 'De la résistance à l'occupation anglaise dans le pays de Lisieux de 1424 à 1444', *Bulletin de la Société des Antiquaires de Normandie*, xvi (1892), 325–72
Roch, J.-L., 'Les guerres du peuple: autodéfense, révolte et pillage dans la guerre de cent ans', *Images de la guerre de cent ans: actes du colloque de Rouen (23, 24 et 15 main 2000) (2002)*, ed. J. Maurice, D. Couty and M. Guéré-Laferté (2002), 47–61
*Roger, J.-M., 'Guy Le Bouteillier', *La guerre et la paix au moyen age (Actes du 101e Congrès national des sociétés savantes, Lille 1976)* (1978), 271–329
*Roger, J.-M., 'Simon Morhier en Normandie', *BHP* (1980), 101–64
Rogers, C. J., 'The military revolutions of the Hundred Years' War', *Journal of Military History*, lvii (1993), 241–78
Rohr, Z. E., *Yolande of Aragon (1381–1442). Family and Power* (2016)
Roncière, C. de la, *Histoire de la marine française*, 6 vols (1899–1932)
Roosbroeck, R. van, Weerd, H. van de, Maeyer, R. de, Essen, L. van der et al. (eds), *Geschiedenis van Vlaanderen*, 6 vols (1936–49)
Rose, S., *Calais. An English Town in France* (2008)
Roserot, A., *Dictionnaire Historique de la Champagne Méridionale (Aube) des origins à 1790*, 4 vols (1942–8)
Roskell, J. S., 'The office and dignity of protector of England, with special reference to its origins', *EHR*, lxviii (1953), 193–233
Roskell, J. S., *The Commons in the Parliament of 1422* (1954)
Roskell, J. S., 'Sir Walter Hungerford', *Wiltshire Archaeological and Natural History Magazine*, lvi (1956), 301–41.
Roskell, J. S., 'Sir William Oldhall, Speaker in the Parliament of 1450–1', *Nottingham Medieval Studies*, v (1961), 87–112

Roskell, J. S., *The Commons and their Speakers in English Parliaments, 1376–1523* (1965)
Roskell, J. S., *Parliament and Politics in Late Medieval England*, 3 vols (1981–3)
Ross, C. D., *The Estates and Finances of Richard Beauchamp Earl of Warwick* (1956)
Ross, C. D., 'The estates and finances of Richard Duke of York', *Welsh History Review*, iii (1967), 299–302
Ross, C. D., *Edward IV* (1974)
Ross, J., 'Essex county society and the French war in the fifteenth century', *The Fifteenth Century*, vii, *Conflicts, Consequences and the Crown in the Late Middle Ages*, ed. L. Clark (2007), 53–80
Rowe, B. J. H., 'A contemporary account of the Hundred Years War from 1415 to 1429', *EHR*, xli (1926), 504–13
Rowe, B. J. H. (1927): see E: Unpublished Theses
*Rowe, B. J. H., 'Discipline in the Norman garrisons under Bedford, 1422–35', *EHR*, xlvi (1931)[1], 194–208
Rowe, B. J. H., 'The Estates of Normandy under the Duke of Bedford, 1422–1435', *EHR* xlvi (1931)[2], 551–78
Rowe, B. J. H., 'John Duke of Bedford and the Norman "Brigands"', *EHR*, xlvii (1932), 583–600
Rowe, B. J. H., 'King Henry VI's claim to France in picture and poem', *The Library*, 4th series, xiii (1932–3), 77–88
Rowe, B. J. H., 'The *Grand Conseil* under the Duke of Bedford, 1422–35', *Oxford Essays in Medieval History presented to Herbert Edward Salter* (1934), 207–34
Rowe, B. J. H., 'John, Duke of Bedford in "The Mirror for Magistrates", Tragedy 30', *Notes and Queries*, July 1975, 296–300

Sadourny, A., 'Occupants et occupés (1417–1449)', *La Normandie au XVe siècle. Art et histoire*, ed. 11–15 (1999), 11–15
Sadourny, A., 'Rouennais et anglais au temps de Jeanne d'Arc', *Images de Jeanne d'Arc*, ed. J. Maurice and D. Couty (2000), 29–34
Sadourny, A., 'Rouen au temps des procès de Jeanne d'Arc', *De l'hérétique à la sainte. Les procès de Jeanne d'Arc revisités*, ed. F. Neveux (2012), 39–48
Sadourny, M., 'L'occupation anglaise en Haute-Normandie d'après les comptes de l'archevêché de Rouen', *Revue des Sociétés Savantes de Haute-Normandie. Lettres et sciences humaines*, liii (1969), 27–35
Salamagne, A, 'L'attaque des places fortes au XVe siècle à l'exemple des guerres anglo- et franco-bourguignonnes', *Revue historique*, clxxxix (1993)[1], 65–113
Salamagne, A., 'A propos de l'adaptation de la fortification à l'artillerie vers les années 1400: quelques remarques sur les problèmes de vocabulaire, de typologie et de méthode', *Revue du Nord*, lxxv (1993)[2], 809–46
Samaran, C., *La maison d'Armagnac au XVe siècle* (1907)
Saul, N. *English Church Monuments in the Middle Ages. History and Representation* (2009)
Saul, N., 'Commemoration of the war dead in late medieval England', *Transactions of the Monumental Brass Society*, xix (2018), 383–415
*Sauval, H., *Histoire et recherche des antiquités de la ville de Paris*, 3 vols (1724)
Saygin, S., *Humphrey Duke of Gloucester (1390–1447) and the Italian Humanists* (2002)
Scarisbrick, J. J., *Henry VIII* (1968)
Scattergood, V. J., *Politics and Poetry in the Fifteenth Century* (1971)

BIBLIOGRAPHY

*Schneider, F., *Der Europäische Friendenskongress von Arras [1435] und die Friedenspolitik Papst Eugens IV under des Basler Konzils* (1919)
Schnerb, B. (1988): see E: Unpublished Theses
Schnerb, B., 'La bataille rangée dans la tactique des armées Bourguignonnes au début du XVe siècle: essai de synthèse', *Annales de Bourgogne*, lxi (1989), 5–32
*Schnerb, B., 'La preparation des operations militarires au début du XVe siècle: l'exemple d'un document prévisionnel bourguignon', *Guerre et société en France, en Angleterre et en Bourgogne, xive–xve siècle*, ed. P. Contamine, C. Giry-Deloison and M. Keen (1991), 189–96
Schnerb, B., *Bulgnéville (1431). L'état bourguignon prend pied en Lorraine* (1993)
Schnerb, B., *Enguerrand de Bournonville et les siens. Un lignage noble du Boulonnas aux XIVe et XVe siècles* (1997)
Schnerb, B., *Les Armagnacs et les Bourguignons. La maudite guerre* (1998)
Schnerb, B., 'L'honneur de la Maréchaussée.' Maréchal et maréchaux en Bourgogne des origines à la fin du xve siècle (2000)
Schnerb, B., 'Le recrutement sociale et géographique des armées des ducs de Bourgogne (1340–1477)', *Guerre, pouvoir, principauté*, ed. J.-M. Cauchies (2002), 53–67
Schnerb, B., 'Lourdin de Saligny et de la Motte-Saint-Jean (v. 1370–1446). Une carrière à la cour de Bourgogne', *Francia*, xxxi.1 (2004), 45–93
Schnerb, B., *La noblesse au service du prince. Les Saveuse: un hostel noble de Picardie au temps de l'état bourguignon (v. 1380–v. 1490)* (2018)
Schofield, A., 'The first English delegation to the Council of Basel', *Journal of Ecclesiatical History*, xii (1961), 167–96
Schofield, A., 'England, the Pope and the Council of Basel, 1435–1449', *Church History*, xxxiii (1964), 248–78
Schofield, A., 'The second English delegation to the Council of Basel', *Journal of Ecclesiatical History*, xvii (1966), 29–64
Schofield, A., 'England and the Council of Basel', *Annuarium Historiae Conciliorum*, v (1973), 1–117
*Scofield, C. L., *The Life and Reign of Edward the Fourth, King of England and of France and Lord of Ireland*, 2 vols (1923)
Scordia, L., *'Le roi doit vivre du sien'. La théorie de l'impôt en France, XIIIe–XVe siècle* (2006)
Scots Peerage (The), ed. J. Balfour Paul, 9 vols (1904–14)
Sepet, M., 'Observations critiques sur l'histoire de Jeanne d'Arc. La lettre de Perceval de Boulainvilliers', *BEC*, lxxvii (1916), 439–47
*Sharpe, R. R., *London and the Kingdom*, 3 vols (1894–5)
Simonneau, H., 'Le héraut bourguignon et la guerre à la fin du moyen age', *Revue du Nord*, xcv (2013), 915–44
Simpson, M. A., 'The campaign of Verneuil', *EHR*, xlix (1934), 93–100
Sinclair, A. F. J.: see E: Unpublished Theses
Smedt, R. de (ed.), *Les chevaliers de l'Ordre de la Toison d'Or au XVe siècle* (2000)
Smith, A. R. (1982): see E: Unpublished Theses
Smith, A. R., 'The greatest man of that age': the acquisition of Sir John Fastolf's East Anglian estates', *Rulers and Ruled in Late Medieval England. Essays presented to Gerald Harriss*, ed. R. Archer and S. Walker (1995), 137–53
Smith, R. D. and Brown, R. R., *Bombards. Mons Meg and her Sisters* (1989)
Smith, R. D. and De Vries, K., *The Artillery of the Dukes of Burgundy, 1363–1477* (2005)
Sobecki, S., *Last Words. The Public Self and the Social Author in Late Medieval England* (2019)

BIBLIOGRAPHY

Solon, P. D., 'Valois military administration on the Norman frontier, 1445-1461. A study in military reform', *Speculum*, li (1976), 91-111

Somerville, R., *History of the Duchy of Lancaster*, 2 vols (1953-70) [vol. 2 an unpublished typescript]

Sommé, M., 'L'armée bourguignonne au siège de Calais de 1436', *Guerre et société en France, en Angleterre et en Bourgogne, xive-xve siècle*, ed. P. Contamine, C. Giry-Deloison and M. Keen (1991), 197-219

*Sorel, A., *La prise de Jeanne d'Arc devant Compiègne et l'histoire des sièges de la même ville* (1889)

*Sorel, A., 'Dépenses du duc de Bourgogne au siège de Compiègne en mai 1430 lors de la prise de Jeanne d'Arc', *Bulletin de la Société Historique de Compiègne*, x (1901), 147-64

Soyer, J., 'La bataille de Patay: samedi 18 juin 1429', *Bulletin de la Société Archéologique et Historique de l'Orléanais*, xvi (1913), 416-24

Spencer, D., 'The provision of artillery for the 1428 expedition to France', *Journal of Medieval Military History*, xiii (2015), 179-92

*Spitzbarth, A.-B., *Ambassades et ambassadeurs de Philippe le Bon, troisième duc Valois de Bourgogne (1419-1467)* (2013)

Spont, A., 'La taille en Languedoc de 1450 à 1515', *Annales du Midi*, ii (1890), 365-84, 478-513

Spont, A., 'L'equivalent des aides en Languedoc de 1450 à 1515', *Annales du Midi*, iii (1891), 232-53

Spont, A., 'La gabelle du sel en Languedoc au XVe siècle', *Annales du Midi*, iii (1891), 427-81

Spufford, P., *Monetary problems and policies in the Burgundian Netherlands, 1433-1496* (1970)

Steel, A., *The Receipt of the Exchequer, 1377-1485* (1954)

Storey, R. L., *Thomas Langley and the Bishopric of Durham, 1406-1437* (1961)

Storey, R. L., *The End of the House of Lancaster* (1966)

Storey, R. L., 'The north of England', *Fifteenth Century England, 1399-1509*, ed. S. B. Chrimes, C. D. Ross, and R. A. Griffiths (1972), 129-44

Storey, R. L., 'The Wardens of the Marches of England towards Scotland, 1377-1489', *EHR*, lxxii (1957), 593-615

Stratford, J., 'The manuscripts of John Duke of Bedford: library and chapel', *England in the Fifteenth Century. Proceedings of the 1986 Harlaxton Symposium*, ed. D. Williams (1987), 329-50

Stratford, J., *The Bedford Inventories. The Worldly Goods of John, Duke of Bedford, Regent of France (1389-1435)* (1993)

Stratford, J., '"Par le special commandement du roi". Jewels and plate pledged for the Agincourt Expedition', *Henry V. New Interpretations*, ed. G. Dodd (2013), 157-70

Strayer, J., 'Defence of the realm and royal power in France', *Medieval Statecraft and the Perspectives of History. Essays by Joseph R. Strayer* (1971), 291-9

Strickland, M. and Hardy, R., *From Hastings to the Mary Rose. The Great Warbow* (2005)

Strohm, P., 'John Lydgate, Jacque of Holland and the poetics of complicity', *Medieval Literature and Historical Inquiry. Essays in Honour of Derek Pearsall*, ed. D. Aers (2000)

*Strong, P. and F., 'The last will and codicils of Henry V', *EHR*, xcvi (1981), 79-102

*Stuart, A., *Genealogical History of the Stewarts* (1798)

*Suárez Fernandez, *Navegación y comercio en el golfo de Vizcaya. Un estudio sobre la política marinera de la casa de Trastámara* (1959)

BIBLIOGRAPHY

Sumption, J., *The Hundred Years War*, i, *Trial by Battle* (1990), ii, *Trial by Fire* (1999), iii, *Divided Houses* (2009), iv, *Cursed Kings* (2015)
Swanson, N., 'Preaching crusade in fifteenth century England: instructions for the administration of the anti-Hussite Crusade of 1429 in the diocese of Canterbury', *Crusades*, xii (2013), 175–96

Taylor, C., 'War, propaganda and diplomacy in fifteenth-century France and England', *War, Government and Power in Late Medieval France*, ed. C. Allmand (2000)[1], 70–91
Taylor, C., 'Brittany and the French Crown: the legacy of the English attack upon Fougères (1449)', *The Medieval State. Essays presented to James Campbell*, ed. J. R. Maddicott and D. M. Palliser (2000)[2], 243–57
Taylor, C., *Chivalry and the Ideals of Knighthood in France during the Hundred Years War* (2013)
Taylor, C., 'John Talbot, John Fastolf and the death of chivalry', *People, Power and Identity in the Late Middle Ages. Essays in Memory of W. Mark Ormrod*, ed. G. Dodd, H. Lacey and A. Musson (2021), 324–40
*Tessereau, A., *Histoire chronologique de la Grande Chancellerie*, 2 cols (1676–1710)
Thaumassière, G. T. de la, *Histoire de Berry*, n.e., 2 vols (1865)
Thibaudeau, A. R. H., *Histoire de Poitou*, n.e., 3 vols (1839–40)
Thibault, J., 'Un prince territoriale au xve siècle. Dunois, bâtard d'Orléans', *Bulletin de la Société Archéologique et Historique de l'Orléanais*, n.s., xiv (1997), 3–46
Thibault, M., *La jeunesse de Louis XI, 1423–1445* (1907)
*Thielemans, M.-R., 'Lettre missive inédite de Philippe le Bon concernant le siège de Calais', *Bulletin de la Commission Royale d'Histoire*, cxv (1950), 285–96
*Thielemans, M.-R., *Bourgogne et Angleterre. Relations politiques et économiques entre les Pays-Bas Bourguignons et l'Angleterre, 1435–1467* (1966)
*Thomas, A., 'Les états généraux sous Charles VII. Étude chronologique d'après des documents inédits', *Le Cabinet Historique*, xxiv (1878), 118–28, 155–70, 200–21
*Thomas, A., *Les états provinciaux de la France centrale sous Charles VII*, 2 vols (1879)
*Thomas, A., 'Les états généraux sous Charles VII', *Revue Historique*, xl (1889)[1], 55–83
*Thomas, A., 'Le Midi et les états généraux sous Charles VII', *Annales du Midi*, i (1889)[2], 289–315; iv (1892), 1–24
*Thomas, A., 'Rodrigue de Villandrando en Rouergue', *Annales du Midi*, ii (1890), 209–32, 418–19
*Thomas, A., *Le Comté de la Marche et le Parlement de Poitiers (1418–1436)* (1910)
Thompson, G. L., 'Le regime anglo-bourguignonne à Paris: facteurs idéologiques', *La 'France Anglaise' au moyen age (Actes du 111e Congrès National des Sociétés Savantes, Poitiers, 1986)* (1988), 53–60
Thompson, G. L., '"Monseigneur Saint Denis", his abbey and his town under English occupation, 1420–1436', *Power, Culture and Religion in France, c. 1350–c. 1550'*, ed. C. Allmand (1989), 15–35
Thompson, G. L., *Paris and its People under English Rule. The Anglo-Burgundian Regime, 1420–1436* (1991)
Thompson, M. W., *The Decline of the Castle* (1987)
Thrupp, S. L., 'Aliens in and around London in the fifteenth century', *Studies in London History presented to Philip Edmund Jones*, ed. A. E. J. Hollaender and W. Kellaway (1969), 249–72

Tobin, M., 'Collection de textes prophétiques du XVe siècle: le manuscript 520 de la Bibliothèque de Tours', *Les textes prophétiques et la prophétie en occident (XIIe–XVIe siècle)*, ed. A Vauchez (1990), 127–33

Töth, P. de, *Il Beato Cardinale Nicolo Albergati e I suoi tempi, 1375–1444*, 2 vols (1934)

Touchard, H., *Le commerce maritime Breton à la fin du moyen age* (1967)

Toureille, V., *Vol et brigandage au moyen age* (2006)

Toureille, V., 'Deux Armagnacs au confins du royaume: Robert de Sarrebrück et Robert de Baudricourt', *Revue du Nord*, xcv (2013), 977–1001

Toureille, V., *Robert de Sarrebrück ou l'honneur d'un écorcheur (v. 1400–v. 1462)* (2014)

Toureille, V., 'Le siège de Dieppe (2 novembre 1442–15 août 1443): un épisode de la reconquête française de la Normandie', *La guerre en Normandie (XIe–XVe)*, ed. A. Curry and V. Gazeau (2018), 231–45

*Toussaint, J., 'Philippe le Bon et le Concile de Bâle (1431–1449)', *Bulletin de l'Académie Royale de Belgique*, cvii (1942), 1–126

Les relations diplomatiques de Philippe le Bon avec le Concile de Bâle (1431–1449) (1942)[2]

Tricard, J., 'Comparsonniers et réconstruction rurale dans le sud du Limousin au XVe siècle', *La réconstruction après la guerre de Cent Ans (Actes du 104e Congrès National des Sociétés Savantes, Bordeaux, 1979)*(1981), i, 51–62

Tricard, *Les campagnes limousines du XIVe au XVIe siècle. Originalité et limites d'une reconstruction rurale* (1996)

Triger, R., 'Un coup de main d'Ambroise de Loré en Basse-Normandie (1431)', *Revue historique et archéologique du Maine*, iii (1878), 279–303

*Triger, R., *Une forteresse du Maine pendant l'occupation anglaise. Fresnay-le-Vicomte de 1417 à 1450* (1886)

Triger, R., *Le château et la ville de Beaumont-le-Vicomte pendant l'invasion anglaise (1417–1450)* (1901)

Triger, R. and Beauchesne, A. de, 'Sainte-Suzanne', *Revue historique et archéologique du Maine*, lxi (1907), 45–85

Tuetey, A., *Les écorcheurs sous Charles VII. Episodes de l'histoire militaire de la France au XVe siècle d'après des documents inédits*, 2 vols (1874)

Turner, H. L., *Town Defences in England and Wales* (1970)

Tyrrell, J. M., *A History of the Estates of Poitou* (1968)

Vaissète: see Vic, C. de and Vaissète, J.

Valat, G., 'Nicolas Rolin, chancelier de Bourgogne', *Mémoires de la Société Éduenne*, xl (1912), 73–145; xli (1913), 1–73, xlii (1914), 53–148

Vale, M. G. A., 'The last years of English Gascony, 1451–3', *Transactions of the Royal Historical Society*, 5th series, xix (1969), 119–38

Vale, M. G. A., *English Gascony, 1399–1453* (1970)

Vale, M. G. A., 'Sir John Fastolf's "Report" of 1435: a new interpretation reconsidered', *Nottingham Medieval Studies*, xvii (1973), 78–84

Vale, M. G. A., *Charles VII* (1974)

Vale, M. G. A., 'New techniques and old ideals: the impact of artillery on war and chivalry at the end of the Hundred Years War', *War, Literature and Politics in the Late Middle Ages*, ed. C. T. Allmand (1976), 57–72

Vale, M. G. A., *War and Chivalry. Warfare and Aristocratic Culture* (1981)

Vale, M. G. A., 'Jeanne d'Arc et ses adversaires: Jeanne, victim d'une guerre civile?', *Jeanne d'Arc. Une époque. Un rayonnement. Colloque d'histoire médiévale, Orléans octobre 1979* (1982), 203—16

Vale, M. G. A., 'Cardinal Henry Beaufort and the "Albergati" portrait', *EHR*, cv (1990), 337–54
Vale, M. G. A., 'The war in Aquitaine', *Arms, Armies and Fortifications in the Hundred Years War*, ed. A. Curry and M. Hughes (1994), 69–82
Vale, M. G. A., *The ancient enemy. England, France and Europe from the Angevins to the Tudors* (2007)
*Vallet de Viriville, A., *Nouvelles recherches sur Henri Baude, poète et prosateur du XVe siècle* (1853)
Vallet de Viriville, A., *Histoire de Charles VII, roi de France, et de son époque, 1403–1461*, 3 vols (1862–3)
*Valois, N., *Le conseil du Roi aux xive, xve et xvie siècles* (1888)
Valois, N., 'Jeanne d'Arc et la prophétie de Marie Robine', *Mélanges Paul Fabre* (1902), 452–67
Valois, N., *Histoire de la Pragmatique Sanction de Bourges sous Charles VII* (1906)
Valois, N., *Le Pape et le Concile, 1418–1450*, 2 vols (1909)[1]
Valois, N., 'Conseils et predictions adressés à Charles VII par un certain Jean du Bois', *ABSHF*, xlvi (1909)[2], 206–38
Van der Wee, H., *The Growth of the Antwerp Market and the European Economy*, 3 vols (1963)
*Varenbergh, E., *Histoire des relations diplomatiques entre le comté de Flandre et l'Angleterre au moyen age* (1874)
Vauchez, A., 'Jeanne d'Arc et le prophétisme féminin des XIVe et XVe siècles', *Jeanne d'Arc. Une époque. Un rayonnement. Colloque d'histoire médiévale, Orléans octobre 1979* (1982), 159–79
Vauchez, A., *Les laics au moyen age. Pratiques et expériences réligieuses* (1987)
Vauchez, A., 'Les théologiens face au prophétisme à l'époque d'Avignon et du Grand Schisme', *Les textes prophétiques et la prophétie en occident*, ed. A Vauchez (1990), 287–98
Vaughan, R., *Philip the Good* (1970)
Vaughan, R., *Charles the Bold, the Last Valois Duke of Burgundy* (1973)
Vaultier, R., *Le folklore pendant la guerre de Cent ans d'après les lettres de rémission du Trésor des Chartes* (1965)
Vavasseur, A. Le, 'Étude critique sur la valeur historique de la chronique d'Arthur de Richemont', *BEC*, xlvii (1886), 525–65
*Vic, C. de and Vaissète, J., *Histoire générale de Languedoc*, n.e., 16 vols (1874–1905)
Vickers, K. H., *Humphrey, Duke of Gloucester. A Biography* (1907)
Victoria History of the Counties of England (1899–in progress)
*Vignaux, A., 'Une note diplomatique au XVe siècle – Charles VII, roi de France, et Jean Ier, comte de Foix', *Annales du Midi*, xii (1900), 355–69
*Villaret, A. F. de, *Campagnes des anglais dans l'Orléanais, la Beauce Chartrain et le Gâtinais (1421–1428). L'armée sous Warwick et Suffolk au siège de Montargis. Campagnes de Jeanne d'Arc sur la Loire postérieures au siège d'Orléans* (1893)
Virgoe, R. (1964): see E: Unpublished Theses
*Virgoe, R., 'The death of William de la Pole, Duke of Suffolk', *Bulletin of the John Rylands Library*, xlvii (1965), 489–502
Virgoe, R., 'The composition of the King's Council, 1437–61', *Bulletin of the Institute of Historical Research*, xliii (1970), 134–60
Virgoe, R., 'William Tailboys and Lord Cromwell: crime and politics in Lancastrian England', *Bulletin of the John Rylands Library*, lv (1973), 459–82
Virgoe, R., 'The Parliamentary subsidy of 1450', *Bulletin of the Institute of Historical Research*, lv (1982), 125–38

Virgoe, R., 'The earlier Knyvetts: the rise of a Norfolk gentry family', *Norfolk Archaeology*, xli (1990–92), 1–4, 249–77

Visser-Fuchs, L., *History as Pastime. Jean de Wavrin and his Collection of Chronicles of England* (2018)

Vissière, L., 'Georges de la Trémoille et la naissance du parti angevin', *Réné d'Anjou (1409–1480). Pouvoirs et gouvernement*, ed. J.-M. Matz and N.-Y. Tonnerre (2011), 15–30

Vlietinck, E., 'Les sièges de Calais et les villes de la côte flamande', *Annales de la Société d'Émulation de Bruges*, 5ᵉ série, iii (1890), 91–101

Vuitry, A., *Études sur le régime financier de la France avant la Révolution de 1789*, n.s., 2 vols (1878–83)

Waddington, C.-H., 'Note sur la dépopulation des campagnes gâtinaises pendant la guerre de cent ans et leur reconstitution économique', *Annales de la Société Historique et Archéologique du Gâtinais*, xxxix (1930), 164–78

Walsby, M., *The Counts of Laval. Culture, Patronage and Religion in Fifteenth- and Sixteenth-Century France* (2007)

Warner, M. W. (1991): see E: Unpublished Theses

Warner, M. W., 'Chivalry in action: Thomas Montagu and the war in France, 1417–1428', *Nottingham Medieval Studies*, xlii (1998), 146–73

Watt, D. E. R., *A Biographical Dictionary of Scottish Graduates to A.D. 1410* (1977)

Watts, J. L., 'The counsels of King Henry VI, c. 1435–1445', *EHR*, cvi (1991), 279–98

Watts, J. L., 'When did Henry VI's minority end?', *Trade, Devotion and Governance. Papers in Later Medieval English History*, ed. D. J. Clayton, R. G. Davies and P. McNiven (1994), 116–39

Watts, J. L., *Henry VI and the Politics of Kingship* (1996)

Watts, J. L., 'The pressure of the public on later medieval politics', *The Fifteenth Century*, iv, *Political Culture in Late Medieval Britain*, ed. L. Clark and C. Carpenter (2004), 159–80

Watts, J. L., 'The Plantagenet Empire and the continent; retrospect and prospect', *The Plantagenet Empire, 1259–1453*, ed. P. Crooks, D. Green and W. M. Ormrod (2016), 403–21

Waugh, W. T., 'Joan of Arc in English sources of the fifteenth century', *Historical Essays in Honour of James Tait*, ed. J. G. Edwards, V. H. Galbraith and E. F. Jacob (1933), 386–98

Weiss, R., 'Humphrey Duke of Gloucester and Tito Livio Frulovisi', *Fritz Saxl, 1890–1948. A volume of Memorial Essays from his Friends in England*, ed. D. J. Gordon (1957), 218–27

Weiss, R., *Humanism in England during the Fifteenth Century* (1967)

Weiss, V. (ed.), *La demeure médiévale à Paris. Répertoire sélectif des principaux hôtels* (2012)

Weske, D. B., *Convocation of the Clergy* (1937)

Whelan, M., 'Between Papacy and Empire: Cardinal Henry Beaufort, the House of Lancaster and the Hussite Crusades' *EHR*, cxxxiii (2018), 1–31

Williams, E. C., *My Lord of Bedford, 1389–1435* (1963)

Wilmart, M., *Meaux au moyen age. Une ville et ses hommes du xiiᵉ au xvᵉ siècle* (2013)

Wolff, P., *Commerces et marchands de Toulouse (vers 1350–vers 1450)* (1954)

Wolff, P., 'Le théologien Pierre Cauchon, de sinistre mémoire', *Economies et sociétés du moyen age. Mélanges offerts à Edouard Perroy* (1973), 553–70

Wolffe, B. P., 'Acts of resumption in the Lancastrian Parliaments, 1399–1456', *EHR*, lxxiii (1958), 583–613

Wolffe, B. P., *The Crown Lands, 1461–1536* (1970)
Wollfe, B. P., *The Royal Demesne in English History* (1971)
Wolffe, B. P., 'The personal rule of Henry VI', *Fifteenth Century England, 1399–1509. Studies in Politics and Society*, ed. S. B. Chrimes, C. D. Ross, and R. A. Griffiths (1972)
Wolffe, B. P., *Henry VI* (1981)
Woodcock, M., 'John Talbot, Terror of the French. A continuing tradition', *Notes and Queries*, li (2004), 249–51
Wright, N., 'The *Tree of Battles* of Honoré Bouvet', *War, Literature and Politics in the Late Middle Ages*, ed. C. T. Allmand (1976), 12–31
Wright, N., *Knights and Peasants. The Hundred Years War in the French Countryside* (1998)
Wright, S. M., *The Derbyshire Gentry in the Fifteenth Century* (1983)
Wylie, J. H. and Waugh, W. T., *The Reign of Henry V*, 3 vols (1914–29)

*Zellfelder, A., *England und das Basler Konzil* (1913)

E UNPUBLISHED THESES

Barron, C. M., 'The government of London and its relations with the Crown, 1400–1450 (University of London, 1970)
Baume, A. J. L., 'Des aspects militaires de l'occupation anglaise de la Normandie pendant la deuxième partie de la guerre de Cent Ans' (Paris, Sorbonne IV, 1978)
Bogner, G., 'Knighthood in Lancastrian England. A prosopographical approach' (Ohio University, 1997)
Boulet, V., '"Car France estoit leur vray heritage": le gouvernement du royaume français d'Henri VI (1422–1436)' (Université de Paris I, 2010)
Brown, M., 'Crown–magnate relations in the personal rule of James I of Scotland, 1424–1437' (University of St. Andrews, 1992)
Burney, E. M., 'The English Rule in Normandy, 1435–1450 (University of Oxford, 1958)

Curry, A., 'Military organisation in Lancastrian Normandy, 1422–1450' (CNAA, 1985)

Desama, C., 'Jeanne d'Arc de Vaucouleurs à Reims. Contribution à l'histoire de Jeanne d'Arc' (Université de Liège, 1964–5)
Ditcham, B. G. H., 'The employment of foreign mercenary troops in the French royal armies' (Edinburgh University, 1978)

Hayes, R. C. E., 'William Alnwick, Bishop of Norwich (1426–1437) and Lincoln (1437–1449)' (University of Bristol, 1989)

James, L. E., 'The Career and Political Influence of William de la Pole, 1st Duke of Suffolk, 1437–1450' (University of Oxford, 1979)
Jones, M. K., 'The Beaufort family and the war in France, 1421–1440' (University of Bristol, 1983)
Jones, R. L. C., 'The state of fortification in Lancastrian Normandy, 1417–50' (University of Oxford, 1994)

Lobanov, A., 'Anglo-Burgundian military cooperation, 1420–1435' (University of Southampton, 2015)

BIBLIOGRAPHY

Marshall, A., 'The role of English war captains in England and Normandy, 1436–1461' (University of Wales, 1974)

Massey, R. A., 'The Lancastrian Land Settlement in Normandy and Northern France, 1417–1450' (University of Liverpool, 1987)

Prosser, G. L. L., 'After the Reduction. Restructuring Norman political society and the Bien Public, 1450–65' (University of London, 1996)

Ratcliffe, H. L., 'The military expenditure of the English Crown, 1422–1435' (University of Oxford, 1979)

Richmond, C. F., 'Royal administration and the keeping of the seas, 1422–1485' (University of Oxford, 1963)

Rowe, B. J. H., 'John Duke of Bedford as Regent of France (1422–1435): his policy and administration in the north' (University of Oxford, 1927)

Schnerb, B. 'Aspects de l'organisation militaire dans le principautés bourguignonnes (v. 1315–v. 1420) (Université de Paris IV, 1988)

Sinclair, A. F. J., 'The Beauchamp Earls of Warwick in the Later Middle Ages' (University of London, 1986)

Smith, A. R., 'Aspects of the career of Sir John Fastolf (1380–1459)' (University of Oxford, 1982)

Virgoe, R., 'The Parliament of 1449–50' (University of London, 1964)

Warner, M. W., 'The Montague Earls of Salisbury, c. 1300–1428: a study of warfare, politics and political culture' (University College, London, 1991)

F DATABASES

European State Finance Database [http://www.le.ac.uk/hi/bon/ESFDB]

Gascon Rolls, 1317–1468 [http://www.gasconrolls.org]

Institut d'histoire du droit, Parlement civil (XVs); Parlement à Poitiers [http://www.ihd.cnrs.fr]

National Archives, Ancient Petitions [http://www.nationalarchives.gov.uk/documentsonline]

The Soldier in Later Medieval England [https://www.medievalsoldier.org]

Index

Abbeville, 313, 393, 575, 576
Abercrombie, Patrick, 753
Agen, Agenais, 71, 465, 605
Agincourt, battle (1415), 2, 5, 15
Ailly, Pierre d', 266
Ainay-le-Vieil, 703
Aiscough, William, Bishop of Salisbury, 633, 684, 698, 699, 779
Albany, Murdoch Stewart, Duke of, Governor of Scotland (d. 1425), 108–15, 140
Albany, Robert Stewart, Duke of, Governor of Scotland (d. 1420), 78, 108–10
Albergati, Niccolò, Bishop of Bologna, Cardinal (1426), 24, 405–14, 444, 449, 450, 457, 459–60, 462, 469–71, 475, 479
Albret, lords of, 598, 742, 754
Albret, Alain I (d. 1522), 768
Albret, Arnaud-Amanieu, lord of Orval (d. 1463), 721, 722
Albret, Charles II, lord of, Count of Dreux (d. 1471), 176, 209, 311, 327, 332, 573, 599–603, 608, 721, 725, 727, 732, 742, 747, 601, 602
Albret, Charles, viscount of Tartas (d. 1473), 601
Alençon, 37, 170, 224, 463, 542, 543, 673, 690
Alençon (duchy), 31, 38, 69, 148, 314, 340–1, 400, 435, 436, 465, 536, 541, 650, 670, 673, 761, 791
Alençon, house of, 168, 314, 709, 768
Alençon, John II, Duke of, 69, 73, 76, 127, 128, 132, 137, 148, 166, 264, 265, 269, 272, 284, 287, 288–92, 295, 305, 317, 318–19, 321, 327, 396–7, 400, 423, 435, 442, 443, 461, 465, 486, 546, 547, 560, 567–71, 573–4, 589–90, 602, 615, 635, 666, 673, 679, 710, 760–1, 768, 791
Alençon Herald, 104, 319
Alkmaar, 194, 203
Alnwick, 665

Alnwick, William, Bishop of Norwich, 204, 340, 370, 385, 406, 416
Alphen, battles (1425, 1426), 185, 195
Alsace, campaign (1444), 555, 624–5
Amadeus VIII, Duke of Savoy, *see* Savoy
Amboise, 128, 407, 457–8, 746
Amboise, lordship, 538
Amboise, Louis d', Viscount of Thouars, 231, 425
Amboise, Pierre d', lord of Chaumont, 570
Amiens, 119, 309, 312, 313, 358, 373, 393, 437, 447, 507, 766; Estates-General (1423), 34, 200; conference and treaty (1423), 86–8, 89, 90, 92, 94, 176, 200, 384, 673
Ampthill, castle, 790
Amsterdam, 184
Andrew, Richard, 632
Angers, 65, 122, 159, 163, 168, 169, 213, 227, 232, 233, 425, 442, 567, 569, 614, 618, 764
Angevin, Bernard, Chancellor of Guyenne, 599, 728
Angoulême, 747
Angoulême, John of Orléans, Count of, 412, 730
Anjou (duchy), 21, 62, 104, 121, 132, 134, 141–2, 165, 174, 198, 213, 216, 218, 223, 224, 227–8, 280, 425, 465, 490, 496, 537, 541–2, 570, 610, 611, 614, 640, 644, 650, 716, 744, 756, 784, 786; campaign (1432), 424, (1443), 614
Anjou, house of, 63, 121, 170, 171, 231, 254, 259, 305, 425–6, 568, 623, 638, 736, 768
Anjou, Charles of, Count of Maine, 398, 423, 424, 425, 435, 545, 546, 566, 570, 577, 580, 583, 603, 625, 634, 637, 678, 726
Anjou, John of, Duke of Calabria (1435) and Lorraine (1453), 625, 762
Anjou, Louis II, Duke of (d. 1417), 121

951

INDEX

Anjou, Louis III, Duke of (*d.* 1434), 121, 148, 179
Anjou, Margaret of, Queen of England, 621-2, 628, 629, 638-9, 756-8, 762, 764, 767, 781
Anjou, Marie of, Queen of France, 70, 198, 305, 425, 621
Anjou, Réné of, Duke of Lorraine, Bar and Anjou (*d.* 1480), 75, 133, 254-6, 262, 307, 311, 321, 381-3, 477, 527, 555, 621, 625, 635, 640
Anjou, Yolande of Aragon, Duchess of, 121-2, 159-64, 170, 172, 174, 175, 176, 198, 209, 210, 222, 254, 272, 305, 397, 398, 423, 424, 425, 461, 466
Anne, Queen of Great Britain (1702-14), 806
Ansières, Jean d', Bishop of Le Mans (1439-49), 167
Antwerp, 25, 181, 184, 526, 796
Aquinas, Thomas, St, 266
Aragon, Aragonese, 103, 733, 737, 740, 759
Arc, Jacques d', 253, 255, 305
Arc, Joan of, xii, xiii, 30, 54, 60, 212, 251, 252-3, 255-84, 287-8, 290, 292, 293, 295-7, 299-306, 309, 310, 311, 312, 313, 317, 318-21, 322, 326-7, 343-5, 347-9, 359-74, 379, 396, 546, 622, 676, 707-8, 746, 807
Arc, Pierre d', 348
archers, 20, 32, 38, 47-8, 78, 96, 98, 101, 104, 115, 120, 127, 132, 134-9, 189, 191, 227, 246-7, 286, 287, 291-2, 311, 336, 341, 382-3, 403, 419, 430, 445, 454, 492, 521, 528-9, 579, 592, 503, 609, 641, 653, 692, 694-5, 720, 725, 729, 741, 742, 743, 763, 767, 775
Ardevon, 147, 177, 553
Armagnac party, 23, 54, 56, 58, 62, 69, 165, 255, 259, 319, 332, 360, 364, 759, 782, 785
Armagnac, house, 81, 231, 364, 423, 505, 573, 768
Armagnac, Bernard, Count of (*d.* 1418), 57-8, 62, 63, 67, 68, 222
Armagnac, Bernard, Count of Pardiac, Castres (1429) and La Marche (1438), 68, 222
Armagnac, Jean de Lescun, Bastard of, 623, 628

Armagnac, Jean IV, Count of (*d.* 1450), 601, 602, 603, 608
Armagnac, Jean V, Count of (*d.* 1473), 601, 725, 728, 729, 742, 759-60, 761
Armoises, Claude des, 373
Arques, 37, 92, 486, 487, 494, 679
Arras, 106, 204, 315-17, 321, 356-7, 362, 420, 446, 449-50, 452, 455, 456, 482, 520, 782; Congress (1435), 458-75, 479, 480, 481, 487, 488, 490, 498, 508, 537, 544, 547, 550-1, 552, 599, 761, 809; Treaty (1435), 475-7, 483-4, 495, 508, 527, 540, 546
arrêt de cuirasse, 48
artillery, 52, 79, 92-3, 95, 96, 97, 105, 106, 119-20, 124, 126, 133, 143, 146, 148, 154, 157, 165, 166-8, 170, 178, 179, 184, 206, 213, 216-17, 220-1, 224, 227, 234, 237-9, 242, 243-4, 245, 251, 274, 278-80, 288, 290, 291, 297, 299-300, 307, 319-20, 327, 331, 339, 344, 347, 348-51, 356, 357, 358, 381, 383, 399, 402-4, 431, 434, 435, 443, 454, 459, 481, 482, 485, 487, 499, 502-3, 509, 512, 513-14, 515, 516-18, 528, 540, 541, 558, 568, 570, 571, 575, 578-9, 581-5, 593, 599-600, 601, 604, 607, 610, 614, 615, 619, 649, 652, 655, 668, 671, 672-3, 678, 679, 681, 682, 694-5, 698, 700-2, 704-5, 706, 721, 726-7, 731-2, 734, 739, 742, 743-5, 746-8, 750, 751, 772; Burgundian, 23, 513-14; English, 48-51, 227; French, 652
Artois, Bonne d', Countess of Nevers (1413), Duchess of Burgundy (1424), 68, 159, 195
Asti, 78, 101
Arundel, John Fitzalan, Earl of, 349, 352, 358, 385, 392, 399, 401-3, 431-8, 442, 443, 454-5
Aubervilliers, 317
Auberoche, battle (1345), 789
Aulon, Jean d', 270, 276, 278, 348
Aumale, 314-15, 333, 342, 375, 376
Aumale, Count of, *see* Harcourt
Austria, Dukes of, 623
Austria, Maximillian Habsburg, Archduke of, 768, 769
Auvergne, Estates (1440), 573
Auxerre, 94, 96, 297, 299, 381, 385, 433, 439, 449; proposed conference (1430),

952

INDEX

328, 329, 331–2, 337–8; conference (1432), 411–13
Avallon, captured by French (1431), 385; Burgundian siege (1433), 433–4
Avaugour, Guillaume d', 63, 165
Avaugour, Louis d', 170, 224
Aviz, Pedro de, Duke of Coimbra, 188
Avranches, 37, 69, 178–9, 199, 576, 609, 613, 615, 626, 641, 642, 658, 688; French siege (1423), 104–5, (1435), 442–3, (1439), 567–9, (1450), 700

Bagé, truce (1424), 161
Bailleul, English capture (1436), 521
Bale, Robert, 674, 711, 715
Balinghem, 415, 510; captured by Burgundians (1436), 515
Bar (duchy), 253–4, 307, 382–3, 527, 555, 623, 766
Bar, Louis of, Bishop of Châlons-sur-Marne, Cardinal-Duke of, 254
Bar-sur-Aube, 298
Bar-sur-Seine, 380
Barbazan, Arnaud-Guilhem de, Marshal of France (Valois), 334, 380–1, 382–3, 434
Barfleur, 626
Barham Down, 230, 294, 457
Barretta, Bartolomeo, 343
Basel, 624; Council of (1431–49), 374, 408–10, 411, 412, 414, 416, 444–7, 449, 459–60, 462, 464, 467, 565
Basin, Thomas, Bishop of Lisieux, 5–6, 34, 56, 77, 477, 492, 557, 614, 653, 670, 676, 722, 737, 789, 793
Baudricourt, Robert de, 255, 261–3, 382
Bauffrémont, Pierre de, lord of Charny, 321–2, 458
Baugé, battle (1421), 5, 7, 15, 43, 72, 78, 105, 137, 187, 221, 292, 332, 557, 793
Bavaria, John of, bishop-elect of Liège (1389–1418), Regent of Holland and Zeeland (1419–25), 10, 89, 182–3
Bavaria, Jacqueline of, Countess of Hainaut, Holland and Zeeland (d. 1436), 9–11, 89–90, 125, 150, 152–7, 181–5, 187, 189, 191, 192, 194, 202–8
Bavaria, William of, Count of Hainaut, Holland and Zeeland (d. 1417), 9, 181
Bayeux, 688, 691, 693, 695; *bailliage*, 56; French siege (1450), 700–1, 710–11, 712
Bayeux, Bishop of, *see* Castiglione

Bayonne, 598, 603, 604–5, 609, 718–19, 721, 726, 737, 739, 759; French siege (1451), 730–2
Bazas, Bazadais, 465, 599, 606, 607, 722
Béarn, Béarnais, 398, 598–9
Beaucaire, 165
Beaufort, Edmund, Count of Mortain (1427), Earl (1442) then Marquess (1443) of Dorset, Duke of Somerset (1448), Lieutenant in Normandy (1448–50), 315, 324, 335, 376, 378–9, 427, 444, 445, 490, 498, 499, 512–13, 514, 519, 541–2, 543, 557, 567, 575–6, 611, 640, 644, 646, 647, 650–1, 653–4, 658–65, 667–72, 674–82, 688–90, 691–2, 695, 701–3, 710, 711–14, 716–17, 723, 735–6, 738, 748, 754–6, 792
Beaufort, Henry, Bishop of Winchester, Chancellor of England (1424–6), Cardinal (1427), xi, 7–9, 11, 116, 156, 176, 186–9, 191–3, 200, 204, 286–7, 294–5, 302, 309, 317–18, 330–3, 337–8, 339–41, 342, 351, 370–3, 378, 383, 385–7, 389–90, 391, 403, 405, 406, 414, 416–17, 419, 420–1, 430, 452–3, 460, 469–73, 480, 484, 514, 517–18, 532, 533–4, 541, 543, 549–55, 556, 557, 559, 561–3, 564–6, 571, 578, 591, 606, 609–10, 633; loans to the Crown, 8–9, 17, 318, 337, 351, 361, 378, 415, 417, 428, 430, 456–7, 491, 510, 517–18, 592, 606, 674, 684
Beaufort, Joan, Queen of Scots, 113, 116, 228
Beaufort, John, Earl of Somerset (d. 1410), 7
Beaufort, John, Earl (1418) then Duke (1443) of Somerset (d. 1444), 457, 491, 556–7, 575–7, 578, 605–6, 610–11, 613–16, 624
Beaufort, Margaret, 686
Beaufort, Thomas, Duke of Exeter (d. 1426), 3, 7, 12, 40, 44, 45, 46–7, 113, 176
Beaufort, Thomas, Count of Perche (d. 1431), 3, 358, 378–9
Beaugency, 213, 234, 242, 246, 285, 289, 295–6; English siege (1428), 233–4; French siege (1429), 289–91
Beaujolais, 143
Beaulieu (Beaulieu-les-Fontaines), 349, 359
Beaumanoir, lord of: *see* Dinan, Jacques de

INDEX

Beaumesnil, captured by French (1441), 586
Beaumont, John, Viscount, 633–4, 644, 712
Beaumont, Jean de, Prior of the Hospitallers of Navarre, 730
Beaumont, Louis de, Alferez of Navarre, 719
Beaumont, Thomas, 497, 500–1
Beaumont-en-Argonne, 68
Beaumont-le-Roger, captured by French (1441), 586
Beaumont-le-Vicomte (Beaumont-sur-Sarthe), English siege (1443), 615
Beauquesne, 322
Beaurevoir, 359, 361–2
Beauvais, 312, 318, 322, 323–5, 328, 341, 379–80, 398, 402, 416, 439, 454, 575, 622
Beauvaisis, 312, 314, 323–4, 328, 342, 356–7, 359, 402, 403, 437, 447, 454, 484–6, 488, 514, 537, 575, 593, 661, 665, 781, 784
Beauveau, Bertrand de, lord of Précigny, 634, 636–8, 645, 649, 676
Beauvoir, Claude de, lord of Chastellux, 95, 99, 114
Beckington, Thomas, Bishop of Bath and Wells (1443), 412, 533, 552, 554, 555, 603–5, 609
Bedford, John of Lancaster, Duke of, Regent of France, 1, 3–6, 9, 13, 24, 25, 26, 27–36, 37, 38–45, 50, 55, 58, 73–4, 79–83, 85, 86–90, 92, 93–5, 100–1, 105–6, 118–19, 121–30, 132, 134–9, 141–2, 145, 151–6, 158, 165, 171, 172, 176, 180, 183–4, 186, 188, 189, 191, 193–5, 196, 197, 200, 204–7, 212, 213, 215–17, 221, 222, 225, 227, 231–3, 239–42, 245, 249–51, 268, 280, 281, 282, 285–7, 293–5, 300, 301–3, 306, 308–13, 315–18, 322, 328–30, 334, 335–6, 340–1, 363, 367, 376, 384, 385–6, 390–3, 395–7, 401–4, 407, 410–11, 414–22, 426, 428–30, 431, 433, 440, 441, 443, 452, 454, 469–70, 474, 478, 484, 499, 500, 532, 533, 542, 578, 598, 653, 680, 710, 720, 727, 791, 792, 799, 809
Bellême, 170, 689
Bellencombre, 794
Benoît, Guillaume, 195–6, 199
Bergen-op-Zoom, 526, 796

Bergerac, 718; French siege (1450), 721
Berghes, 521
Berkeley, James, Lord, 632
Berland, Pey, Archbishop of Bordeaux (1430–56), 605, 728, 737
Bernardini, Jacques, 506
Bernay, 133, 334, 670
Berners, John Bourchier, Lord, 770
Berry Herald, *see* Le Bouvier
Berry, Charles of France, Duke of (*d.* 1472), 763
Berry, John, Duke of (*d.* 1416), 62, 64, 211, 221, 229, 243, 272, 297, 342, 465, 744, 778
Berry, Jeanne de Boulogne, Duchess of, 211
Berry, Marie de, Duchess of Bourbon, 62
Berwick-on-Tweed, Scottish siege (1436), 426–7
Béthisy, 353
Beynes, captured by French (1432), 401
Béziers, 424; Estates-General of Languedoc (1437), 539
Biervliet, 509
Bigorre, 87
Billorel, Martin, 360
Biou, Pierrot de, 398–9
Biron, barony, *see* Gontaut, Shorthose
Bisset, Henry, 217, 219–20
Blackheath, 388, 697–8, 699, 702, 735, 788
Blagnac, 728
Blanchetaque, 454, 541
Blangy, captured by French (1429), 314–15
Blanquefort, 740, 748; French siege (1453), 747, 752
Blaye, 598, 725, 729, 740; French siege (1451), 726–7
Bléré, 538
Blois, 62, 213, 215, 234, 239, 242, 246, 248, 272–5, 278, 291, 423, 569, 619; Estates-General (1433), 781
Blois (county), 214
Blondel, Robert, 83, 701, 706, 807
Bohemia, 286, 295, 364, 408
Bonaparte, Napoleon, 281, 774
Bonneval, 75, 174
Bonsmoulins, captured by French (1429), 314; English siege (1432), 396–7, (1433), 435

954

INDEX

Bonville, William, Seneschal of Guyenne (1442–50), 608–9, 632, 718, 720, 722, 748–9

Bordeaux, 88, 226, 342, 597–8, 603, 604–5, 606–7, 609, 718, 719, 721, 732, 733, 737, 738, 739, 759, 760; French siege (1438), 599–600, (1450), 722, (1451), 725, 727–30; English capture (1452), 739–40, 745, 759; Estates of Gascony (1452), 741; French siege (1453), 740, 742, 743, 746–53

Bordeaux, Archbishop, *see* Berland, Gréelle

Borselen, Frank van, 208

Boschier, 487, 493

Bouchain, 152

Bouchet, Raoul du, 333

Bouchoir, battle (1430), 358

Bouillé, Guillaume, 707

Boulers, Reginald, Abbot of Gloucester, 654–5, 661, 665, 698, 699, 716, 779

Boulogne, 512, 513, 771, 776

Boulogne (county), 22, 520

Boulogne, Jeanne de, *see* Berry

Bourbon, house, 759, 768

Bourbon, Alexander, Bastard of, 546, 547, 574

Bourbon, Charles I, Count of Clermont (1424), Duke of (1434), 143, 160, 176, 197, 210, 222, 229, 239, 246, 246–8, 249, 269, 311–12, 321, 322, 324, 330, 344, 345–6, 381, 384–5, 423, 448–9, 457, 461, 462, 475, 476, 495, 520, 546–8, 549, 555, 568–71, 573–4, 590, 679

Bourbon, Charles III, Duke of, Constable of France (*d.* 1527), 768–9, 770

Bourbon, Guy Bastard of, 546, 547

Bourbon, Jacques de, Count of La Marche, 222, 231, 259, 332

Bourbon, Jean II de, Count of Vendôme (*d.* 1477), 650, 730

Bourbon, John I, Duke of (*d.* 1434), 88, 215, 217, 222, 231, 412–13, 545

Bourbon, John II, Count of Clermont, Duke of (1456), 762

Bourbon, Louis de, Count of Vendôme (*d.* 1446), 264, 311, 313, 322, 326, 344, 346, 350, 353–6, 457, 461, 482, 552, 566, 568, 571, 589, 590, 619, 634, 636, 790

Bourbon-Lancy, 197

Bourg, 598, 725, 739, 740, 759; captured by French (1451), 727

Bourg-en-Bresse, conference (1423), 85–6, 122, 160, 175

Bourges, 24, 62, 64, 65, 70, 80, 94, 96, 100, 103, 121, 164, 209, 219, 305, 327, 408, 423, 440, 590, 647, 648, 659, 703; siege (1412), 242; Estates-General (1423), 72, (1440), 567, 568, 570; captured by Richemont (1425), 164; captured by Clermont (1428), 229–30

Bourlémont, lords of, 253

Bournel, Guichard, 344–5

Bourton, Thomas, 710

Boussac, Jean de Brosse, Baron, Marshal of France (Valois), 200, 210, 222, 239, 272, 276, 313, 327, 350, 353, 355, 356, 358, 379, 398–9, 402–4, 437

Bouteiller, Guy le, 57–8

Bouvignes, 351

Bovet, Honoré, 796, 798

Bower, Walter, Abbot of Inchcolm, 248, 427

Bowes, William, 790

Bowet, William, 46–7

Brabant, John IV, Duke of (*d.* 1427), 10, 89–90, 124–5, 151–3, 155, 156–7, 183, 202–3, 207

Brabant, Philip I, Duke of (*d.* 1430), 351–2

Braine-le-Comte, besieged by D. of Gloucester (1425), 154–5

Brancepeth, 116

Bray-sur-Seine, 309–10, 434

Brest, 776

Bretagne, Gilles de, *see* Montfort

Breteuil, 447–7, 623, 668–9

Brézé, Pierre de, 425, 570, 575, 577, 586, 619, 637–8, 648, 649, 657, 660, 669, 677, 691, 692, 694, 695, 705, 707, 709, 757

Bricquebec, 688, 700

Bridget, St, of Sweden, 258

Bridlington, John of, 260

Brie-Comte-Robert, 411, 495, 510, 547

brigands, brigandage, 14, 38, 55–6, 66–8, 71, 77, 95, 96, 102–3, 117–18, 144–5, 224, 229, 255, 262–3, 350, 359, 376, 381, 385, 403, 424, 433–5, 440, 441–3, 454–5, 456, 477, 485, 509, 543, 546–7, 548, 555, 556, 566, 567–8, 569–70, 577, 579, 580, 583, 590, 595, 599, 603, 613,

955

INDEX

616, 618–19, 622–8, 630, 649, 654, 658, 779, 780, 782, 785, 799
Brimeu, David de, 308
Brimeu, Florimond, 514, 518
Brimeu, Jacques, 353
Brimeu, Jean de, 329, 519
Brittany (duchy), 18, 21, 82, 83–5, 86–7, 140, 159, 171, 229, 244, 332, 343, 493, 616–17, 626, 634, 640–2, 656–60, 762–3, 764, 765, 768–9, 782, 784, 786; Estates (1427), 200, 202, 223–4, (1449), 662, 664, 665; campaigns (1426–7), 176–9, 197–202, (1431), 396–8, (1443), 615, (1449), 673, 681
Brittany, Dukes of, *see* Montfort
Brittany Herald, 612
Bromflete, Henry, 412
Bron of Coulton, John, 753
Broulart, Guillaume, 544
Brouwerhaven, battle (1426), 190–1, 192
Bruges, 25, 90, 91, 155, 184, 244, 260, 326, 460, 509, 516, 518–19, 521, 525, 526, 549, 572, 791
Bruges, Franc of, 509, 516, 519, 521
Bruges, William, Garter King of Arms, 574, 589, 595, 610, 617
Brusac, Gauthier de, 171
Brussels, 11, 91, 153, 155, 202, 356, 508, 526
Brut, The, 776
Buchan, John Stewart, Earl of, 78–80, 94–6, 98–9, 101, 108, 109, 111, 112, 114, 120–1, 127–9, 131–2, 137, 138, 140, 159
Bucy, forest of, 291
Bueil, Jean de, 46, 48, 74, 99, 103, 239, 399–400, 424–5, 435, 567, 615, 623, 669, 707, 750–1, 780, 797
Bulgnéville, battle (1431), 383, 477
Burdet, Nicholas, 145–7, 165–6, 168
Bureau, Gaspard, Master of the King's Artillery (Valois), 652, 682, 701, 705, 731, 742, 743–4
Bureau, Jean, Treasurer of France (Valois), 652, 682, 701–2, 704, 721, 724, 726, 728–9, 737, 743–4, 751
Burgundy, house of, state, 10, 21–3, 64, 68, 81, 82, 84, 86, 89, 122, 151, 153, 157, 159, 162–3, 175, 180, 191, 211, 241, 254, 287, 296, 298, 302, 308–9, 316–17, 332, 351–2, 360, 381, 382, 406, 407, 426, 446, 448–50, 458, 467–8, 470–1, 477, 548–9, 562, 720, 762–3, 765, 766, 782, 785, 795–6, 805
Burgundy (duchy), 22–3, 27, 30, 56, 68–9, 82, 83, 84, 85, 86, 90, 94–5, 101, 102, 103, 158, 182, 183, 240, 241, 263, 296, 297, 326, 338, 339, 357, 382, 383, 384–5, 420, 447, 451, 458, 461, 509, 513–14, 516, 519, 520, 546, 555, 599, 768, 785–6, 786, 823; campaign (1422), 69, (1431), 381, 382, (1433), 431–6, (1444), 448
Burgundy (county), 23, 240, 509, 624
Burgundy, Anne of, Duchess of Bedford, 85, 93, 94, 303, 404, 419
Burgundy, Bonne, Duchess of, *see* Artois, Bonne d'
Burgundy, Charles ('the Rash'), Count of Charolais (1433), Duke of (1467, d. 1477), 763–8, 777, 803
Burgundy, John ('the Fearless'), Duke of (d. 1419), 2, 9, 10, 22, 24, 27, 33, 57, 61, 62, 63, 71, 91, 121, 122, 138, 162, 168, 214, 242, 302, 316, 325, 401, 410, 449, 475, 477, 499, 502, 538, 762, 788, 806, 823
Burgundy, Isabella of Portugal, Duchess of, 336, 466, 549, 466, 549, 551–5, 559, 562, 571–2, 591
Burgundy, Margaret of, dowager Countess of Hainaut, 152–3, 203
Burgundy, Margaret of, Countess of Richemont (1423), 82, 84–5
Burgundy, Michelle de Valois, Duchess of, 82
Burgundy, Philip ('the Good'), Duke of (d. 1467), 1, 2, 3–4, 22–4, 25, 27–8, 29–30, 43, 81–3, 85–7, 88–91, 95, 100–2, 103, 114, 118, 119, 121–6, 133, 143, 151–2, 155–60, 176, 180–5, 189, 190, 191, 195–6, 198–9, 203–8, 221, 227, 234, 240–1, 249–50, 283, 287, 294, 296, 297, 299, 301–3, 305, 308–9, 310, 315–18, 321–2, 327–30, 331, 336–8, 342, 344–6, 347, 348–52, 356–9, 360, 361, 382–4, 387, 393, 395, 405–9, 411–12, 419–21, 424, 431, 433–4, 439–40, 445, 446–50, 452, 456, 460–2, 466–9, 471–3, 475, 477, 479, 483, 495–6, 498–500, 505, 508–21, 524–7, 541, 548–9, 551, 569, 571–2, 574, 589–90, 730, 731, 761–2

956

INDEX

Bury St Edmunds, 644-5
Butler, John, 671
Butler, Ralph, Lord Sudeley (1441), Treasurer of England (1443-6), 92-4, 134, 188, 315, 372, 631, 644

Cabochian revolution and ordinance (1413), 26, 29, 30, 31
Cacherani, Borno dei, 101, 127, 140
Cadart, Jean, 63, 165
Cade, Jack, 696-700, 711, 712, 716, 720, 723
Cadillac, French siege (1453), 748, 750, 752
Cadzand, 521
Caen (town), 32, 50, 126, 400, 435, 487, 670, 681, 682, 688-9, 691-2, 701, 710, 793; University, 55, 709; battle (1434), 442; French siege (1450), 701-3, 708, 711
Caen (*bailliage, bailli*), 56, 74, 441, 647
Cagny, Perceval de, squire of the D. of Alençon, 284, 295
Caister, 791-2
Calais, xi, 11, 15, 21, 57, 126, 150, 152, 155, 166, 189, 194, 200, 231, 294, 295, 309, 332, 339, 341, 358, 375-6, 378, 379, 388, 389, 390, 413, 414, 416-17, 418-19, 423, 424, 426, 430, 431, 452-3, 455, 460, 467, 469, 479, 481, 484, 497, 498-9, 521, 522-3, 531, 532, 652, 548, 574, 597, 618, 620, 695, 696, 714, 730-1, 733-6, 738, 760, 762, 766, 771-3, 776, 782, 789; Staple, 17, 21, 395, 415, 491, 508, 523, 524, 562, 587, 730, 772, 795; Burgundian siege (1436), 508-20, 524-7, (1437), 527; conference (1439-42), 549-55, 559-63, 564, 572, 580, 589-90
Calot, Laurent, 504
Cambrai, 359, 410
Cambridge, 644; King's College, 631
Camoys, Roger, Seneschal of Guyenne (1453), 519, 626, 658, 736, 743, 747, 750-2
Camus (Le) de Beaulieu, *see* Vernet
Campbell, Robert, 702
Canterbury, 152, 215, 339-40, 517-18, 520, 531, 696, 723; Cathedral, 765; Christchurch, 633
Carentan, 673, 691-3
Carhaix, 69

Carrouges, Robert de, 133
Caruyer, 486, 491, 493
Castelnau-de-Médoc, 743, 746
Castiglione, Zenon de, Bishop of Bayeux, 445
Castile, King of, *see* John II
Castillon (Castillon-la-Bataille), 725, 728, 740; siege and battle (1453), 743-6
Castres, Count of, *see* Armagnac
Catesby, Oliver, 712
Catherine of France, Queen of England, 2, 109
Catherine of La Rochelle, 260, 326
Catherine, St, of Siena, 258
Cauchon, Pierre, Bishop of Beauvais (1420-32), then Lisieux (1432-42), 30-1, 124, 330-1, 332-3, 340, 359, 361-72, 374, 452, 503, 550, 577, 596
Caudebec, 487, 493, 494, 679, 711; battle (1436), 492
Caudray, Richard, 522
Caux, 375, 497, 514, 534-6, 539, 543, 554, 576, 593, 666, 710, 739; *bailliage*, 92; rebellion (1435), 442-3, 485-7, 491-4
Caxton, William, 808
Cecil, William, Lord Burghley, 522
Chabannes, Antoine de, 546, 547, 570, 574, 603, 623, 628, 753
Chabannes, Jacques de, 239, 547, 549, 568, 570, 574
Chablis, 385, 434
Chalençon, Louis de, 210
Chalon-sur-Saône, 86, 103, 143
Châlons-sur-Marne (Châlons-en-Champagne), 66, 68, 144, 254, 301, 304, 306, 327
Châlons-sur-Marne, Bishop, *see* Bar, Saarbrücken
Chalosse, 601, 605, 608
Chamberlain, William, 556-9
Chambéry, truce (1424), 143-4, 158
Chambre des Comptes (Normandy), 32, 503, 648
Chambre des Comptes (Paris), 27, 336, 370, 385, 474, 499-500, 505
Champeaux, Guillaume de, Bishop of Laon, 173
Champtoceaux, 640
Channel Islands, 701, 738
Chantepie, Pierre, 442

957

INDEX

Chappes, 323; French siege (1430-1), 380-1; Burgundian siege (1433), 434

Charles VI, King of France (1380-1422), 1, 2, 3, 28, 30, 58, 60, 70, 71, 79, 91, 211, 325, 438, 466, 471, 530, 757

Charles VII, Dauphin, then King of France (1422-61), 2, 23-4, 47, 51, 54, 60-4, 70, 71, 72, 75, 80, 81, 84, 85-6, 87-8, 92, 100, 112, 120, 121, 122, 127, 128, 142, 147, 159-65, 172, 174, 175-6, 180, 196, 202, 209-11, 212, 219, 220-1, 230, 239, 244, 248-9, 257, 260-70, 282-4, 289, 293, 295-7, 299-30, 301-2, 303, 304, 306, 307, 308-9, 311-13, 318-19, 321-2, 323, 325, 326, 329, 342-3, 345-6, 349-50, 366, 398, 423, 424-6, 445, 450, 453, 460, 476-7, 505-6, 527, 528-9, 538-9, 544-6, 548-9, 562, 563, 566-7, 569, 570-1, 572-4, 575, 577, 580-1, 583-5, 590-1, 602, 602-7, 608, 612, 617-21, 623, 625, 628, 634-6, 637-8, 663, 640, 641-3, 645, 648-50, 651, 653, 657, 659-60, 671-2, 675-80, 690-1, 703-6, 707-8, 721, 724-5, 733-4, 739-40, 742, 746, 747, 750, 752, 760-2, 779, 807-8

Charles VIII, King of France (1483-98), 746, 759, 768, 802

Charles ('the Rash'), Count of Charolais, Duke of Burgundy, *see* Burgundy

Chartier, Alain, 54, 70, 77, 180, 221, 228, 264, 807

Chartier, Jean, 461-2, 500, 807

Châtillon, Jean de, soldier, 303-4

Châtillon, Jean de, theologian, 368

Chartres, 75, 127, 217, 223, 236, 241-2, 250, 329, 436, 455, 482, 540, 577, 671, 681, 782; captured by French (1432), 400-1

Chartres, Regnault de, Archbishop of Reims, Chancellor of France (Valois, 1425-44), 64, 73, 109, 160, 172, 228, 266, 269, 274-5, 296, 299, 300, 305, 308, 310, 316-17, 322, 326, 328, 329-30, 344, 374, 384, 412, 423, 426, 447, 448, 457, 461, 464, 452, 552-5, 56, 585-6, 571-2, 590, 619

Chastellain, Georges, 61, 398, 546, 619, 658

Chastellux, *see* Beauvoir

Châtaubriand, 642

Châteaudun, 76, 127-8, 216, 223, 233, 423

Châteaufort, 783

Château-Gaillard, captured by French (1430), 334, 335; English siege (1431), 335, 342, 376; French siege (1449), 672, 682

Château-Gontier, 397, 615

Château-Landon, 220, 433, 539-40

Châteaurenard, 275

Château-Thierry, 304, 307, 311

Châtel, Tanneguy du, 63-4, 68, 79-80, 93, 100, 160, 161-3, 165

Chatelain, Adam, Bishop of Le Mans (1398-1438), 167, 224

Châtelier, Jacques du, Bishop of Paris, 495

Châtellerault, 222

Châtillon, Guillaume de, 304, 307

Châtillon, Jean de, 303, 368

Châtillon-sur-Marne, 303

Chaucer, Alice, Countess then Duchess of Suffolk, 422, 716

Chauconin, 556

Chaumont (town), 323

Chaumont (*bailliage*), 254

Chauvigny, 222

Cherbourg, 37, 147, 334, 487, 543, 547, 548, 549, 575, 626, 653, 688, 689, 690, 691, 701, 702, 703; French siege (1450), 704-6

Chetwind, Philip, 603

Chevalier, Etienne, 634

Chevreuse (castle, barony), 587, 783-4

Chichele, Henry, Archbishop of Canterbury, xiii, 12, 188, 330, 479, 588, 633

Chinon, 120, 159, 161, 180, 201, 217-18, 222-3, 229, 239, 243, 248-9, 252-3, 256, 258, 262-4, 267, 269, 270-1, 343, 365, 384, 398, 423, 425, 641; Estates-General (1425), 162, (1428), 233, 343, 801

Chiswall, Thomas, 710, 710

Choisy (Choisy-au-Bac), French siege (1430), 342, 344

Christmas, Stephen, 723

Clairoix, 346, 347, 349

Clamécy, Gilles de, 412, 496

Clarence, John, Bastard of, 332, 335, 336, 339, 376

Clarence, Lionel of Antwerp, Duke of (d. 1368), 489, 757

INDEX

Clarence, Thomas of Lancaster, Duke of (*d.* 1421), 5, 42, 44, 46, 78, 105, 137, 332, 600, 718, 790, 792, 793
Clarendon, 748
Clerkenwell, 352
Clermont (Auvergne), Estates-General (1421), 72
Clermont-en-Beauvaisis, 312, 323, 347, 356, 438; French siege (1430), 356-8
Clermont, Charles, Count of, *see* Bourbon
Cleves, duchy, 22
Clifton, Gervase, Treasurer of Calais, 738, 740, 743, 745
Clinton, John, Lord, 585
Cobham, Eleanor, *see* Gloucester
Cobham, Thomas Brooke, Lord, 547-8
Cochon, Pierre, 375
Cods, 181, 183
Coëtivy, family, 753
Coëtivy, Olivier de, 737, 739
Coëtivy, Prégent de, Admiral of France (1439), 93-4, 96, 105, 117, 231, 425, 570, 583, 640, 642, 649, 659, 661, 673, 690, 681-2, 694, 705
Coëtquis, Philippe de, Archbishop of Tours, 410
Cœur, Jacques, 703-4, 705-6, 707, 724
Cognac, captured by French (1449), 661, 718
Coiffy, 254
coinage, 33, 36, 55, 60, 70-1, 83, 174, 395, 822-3
Colette of Corbie, 259
Colville, Cuthbert, 684
Commynes, Philippe de, 212, 473, 636, 766, 775, 786, 800, 801, 802, 804-5
compagnies d'ordonnance, 627-8, 649, 651, 653, 702, 706, 725, 740, 803, 806
Compiègne, 317, 318, 322, 328, 338, 341, 358, 361, 438, 439, 447, 507, 580, 617-18; captured by French (1424), 117-18; English capture (1424), 118-19, 123; occupied by French (1429), 312-13; Anglo-Burgundian siege (1430), 252, 341-2, 344-57, 358, 375, 376, 391, 401, 406, 481, 508, 808; Edict of (1430), 325, 474, 506, 709, 753
Conches-en-Ouche, captured by French (1429), 314, (1440), 577, 586; English siege (1442), 592; captured by French (1449), 661, 662

Condé-sur-Noireau, 659
Conflans, Eustache de, 144
Conflans-Ste-Honorine, 582, 584
Constance, Council of, 8, 286, 408, 409, 446, 777
Conty, 358, 798
Convocation of Canterbury, 333, 428, 510
Coppledyke, John, 680
Corbeil, 205, 250, 251, 338, 414, 495, 507, 547, 555
Corbie, 309, 313, 356, 382
Corfe, 616
Cornwall, John, *see* Fanhope
Cotentin, rebellion (1434-5), 441-3
Coudun, 347, 351
Coulonces, lord of, *see* La Haye
crossbows, 23, 39-40, 47-7, 77, 78, 191, 229, 272, 278, 319, 461, 516, 581, 651
Coucy (castle, barony), 67, 572
Cousinot, Guillaume I, Chancellor of Orléans (*d. ca.* 1442), 215
Cousinot, Guillaume II (*d.* 1484), 635, 638, 639, 643-4, 645, 648, 649, 657, 660, 673, 676, 677, 773
Coutances, 673, 692
Cranach, John, 112
Craon, 170, 171, 397
Cravant, siege and battle (1423), xi, 94-100
Crécy, battle (1346), 721
Creil, 312, 313, 318, 322, 318, 332, 342, 346, 401, 438, 507, 540, 550, 551, 554, 584; captured by French (1424), 118; English capture (1424), 118-19; captured by French (1429), 313; English siege (1434), 438; French siege (1436), 534, (1441), 580-1, 652
Crépy-en-Valois, 311-12, 346, 375, 438, 558
Créqui, Jean de, 352-3
Cressy, John, 799
Crichton, William, Chancellor of Scotland, 664
Cromwell, Oliver, 45, 805
Cromwell, Ralph Lord, 390, 406, 416, 418-19, 427, 429, 491, 597, 605, 609, 632, 633, 639, 646, 683
Cromwell, Thomas, 770-1
Croÿ, Antoine de, 351, 458, 466, 499, 762
Croÿ, Jean de, 458, 471, 472, 499, 512, 513, 515, 519, 641
Croyland Chronicle, 766

INDEX

Cuffy, French siege (1424), 128
Culant, Louis de, Admiral of France (Valois), 101, 244, 248
Culant, Philippe de, Marshal of France (Valois), 740, 742
Cunningham, Robert, 702
Curson, Richard, 682
Cusack, Thomas, 419
customs, 15–16, 18, 193, 226, 332, 395, 491, 548, 579, 631, 772

Damme, 763
Damville, 130, 133
Dauphin of France, *see* Guyenne (Louis of), Charles VII, Louis XI
Dauphiné, 62, 68; Estates (1424), 138–9
Dax, 598, 726, 739, 759; French siege (1442), 604–5; captured by Gascons (1442), 605; French siege (1451), 727–9
Delft, treaty (1428), 208, 240
Desmarais, Charles, 437, 454, 484–6, 492, 494, 757
Devon, Thomas Courtenay, Earl of, 632, 695, 720, 734
Diepholt, Rudolph van, Prince-Bishop of Utrecht, 207
Dieppe, 35, 393, 426, 440, 486, 494, 534, 543, 551, 559, 575, 579, 593, 614, 617, 724, 739, 761; captured by French (1435), 484–5, 488; English siege (1442), 593–4
Dijon, 22, 91, 95, 96, 101, 103, 143, 297–8, 381, 382, 411, 520
Dinan, 200, 642, 673
Dinan, Bertrand de, lord of Châteaubriand, 199
Dinan, Jacques de, lord of Beaumanoir, 223
Dinteville, Jean de, *bailli* of Troyes, 298
Dixmude, Oliver van, 513
Dodford, 799
Dol-de-Bretagne, 179, 692
Domart, 67
Domfront, 37, 626, 658, 688, 703; French siege (1450), 704, 712
Domrémy, 253–7, 261, 305
Dordrecht, 182, 185, 199
Dorset, Earl, Marquess, *see* Beaufort
Douai, 157
Douglas, Archibald ('the Grim'), Earl of (d. 1400), 109–10

Douglas, Archibald, Earl of (d. 1424), 5, 78, 109–13, 115, 120–1, 127–9, 132, 136–8, 140
Douglas, Archibald, Earl of Wigtown (ca. 1419), and Douglas (1424, d. 1439)
Dourdan, 379
Dover, 124, 413, 423, 479, 684, 696
Dreux, 32, 37, 223, 335, 401, 444; captured by French (1438), 544
Dumbarton, 115
Duarte, King of Portugal (1433–8), 513
Dudley, Edmund, 769
Dudley, John Sutton, Lord, 642–3, 645, 647, 716
Dumfries, 664–5
Dunbar, 664–5
Dunkirk, 513, 521
Dunkirk, Roland of, 476
Dunois, Count of, *see* Orléans
Dunstaple, John, 387
Duras, 728, 741
Duremort, Gilles de, Abbot of Fécamp, 363
Durfort, Aimeric de, 741
Durfort, Gaillard de, lord of Duras, 728, 732, 740, 747, 748, 751, 752, 754, 767

Eastthorp, 687
écorcheurs, *see* brigands
Écouché, 626
Écouen, 481–2
Edington, 699
Edward, John, 672, 680, 700, 710
Edward I, King of England (1272–1307), 16, 427, 777
Edward II, King of England (1307–27), 16, 620
Edward III, King of England (1327–77), 12, 16, 19, 110, 152, 406, 427, 474, 481, 489, 523, 620, 636, 687, 757, 758, 765, 770, 772–4, 775–6, 777, 779, 790, 795, 797, 808–9
Edward IV, King of England (1461–83), 754, 757–8, 762–8, 796–7
Edward of Lancaster, Prince of Wales (d. 1471), 762
Edward, Prince of Wales ('the Black Prince'), 143, 550, 778, 790, 798
Elbeuf, 444, 577
Elizabeth I, Queen of England (1558–1603), 773
Eltham, palace, 188, 600, 647

960

INDEX

Ely, 504
Enghien, Gérard, lord of Havré, 153
Ensisheim, treaty (1444), 638
Entwhistle, Bertrand, 691
Épinal, 625
Erard, Guillaume, 370–1
Espailly, Jacques d' ('Forte-Épice'), 385
Estates-General of France (Lancastrian), (1420), 2, (1424), 34, 141–2
Estates-General of France (Valois), 590–1, 801, 804, (1421), 72, (1422), 80, (1423), 65, 71, 72, 173 (1425), 162–3, (1428), 230–1, 233–4, 243, 801, (1433), 781, (1439), 562, 566–7, 568, (1440), 567, 568, 570, (1484), 494, 709, 787–8, 802, 804, 807
Estates-General of Languedoc, 71, 539, (1425), 173, (1437), 539, (1438), 548, (1439), 539
Estates-General of Languedoil (Valois), 71, 537, 538–9, (1423), 72, 74, (1425), 173, (1426), 196–7, 209, (1435), 538, (1436), 538
Este, Niccolo, despot of Ferrara, 140
Estivet, Jean d', 363, 366–7
Estouteville, family, 57, 333
Estouteville, Guillaume, Cardinal, 708
Estouteville, Jean d', lord of Torcy, 129, 133, 575
Estouteville, Louis d', 73, 594, 710
Étampes, 80, 85
Étaples, 782; treaty (1492), 769
Eton College, 631, 711
Eugenius IV, Pope (1431–47), 405, 408, 450, 547, 619
Eu, 32, 37, 92, 486, 487, 494
Eu, Charles of Artois, Count of, 560, 575–6, 590, 666, 668, 672–3, 680
Everingham, Thomas, 556, 682, 744
Evreux, 130, 335, 400, 455, 577, 592–3, 626, 660; French siege (1429), 314–15, 317; captured by French (1440), 586
Exeter, Duke of, see Beaufort, Holland
Eyck, Jan van, 405
Eyton, Fulk, 492–3, 646–9, 668–70, 681, 711

Fages, Bouzon de, 217
Falaise, 37, 335, 441, 670, 688; French siege (1450), 703–4
Fanhope, John Cornwall, Lord, 632, 790

Farleigh, castle, 790, 800
Fastolf, John, xiii, 20, 44–5, 46, 58, 79, 94, 101, 119, 134, 137, 148–9, 165, 170, 171–2, 212, 222, 245–7, 275, 289–93, 334, 336, 340, 397, 412, 416, 441–3, 470, 473–4, 481, 490, 535, 556, 578, 595, 596, 648, 659, 663, 664, 665–6, 697, 702, 706, 746, 754–5, 756, 791–2, 793, 798
Fauconberg, see Neville
Fauquembergue, Clément de, Clerk of the Parlement, 306, 495
Fécamp, occupied by French (1435), 486, 534; English siege and French recapture (1437), 536
Ferdinand, King of Aragon (1479–1516), 770
Fère-en-Tardenois (castle, county), 142, 572
Fermen, John, 710
Ferrara, see Este
Ferrière, Guillaume de, 495
Field of Cloth of Gold (1520), 773
Fiennes, James, Lord Saye and Sele, Treasurer of England (1449–50, d. 1450), 684, 698, 699, 711, 748
Fiennes, William, Lord Saye and Sele (d. 1471), 742
Fitzhugh, Robert, Bishop of London, 445
Fitzwalter, Walter Lord, 187, 189–92
Flanders (county), Flemings, 16, 22–3, 84, 91, 95, 181, 185–6, 195, 199, 249, 287, 330, 389–90, 395, 431, 440, 461, 468, 479, 481, 484, 498–9, 508–9, 513, 515, 517, 518–19, 523, 524, 520, 521, 522–6, 549, 562, 572, 730, 742, 758, 762, 765, 768–9, 773, 776, 782, 795–6, 805, 823; Estates, 203
Flanders, Council of, 182–3, 188
Flavy, Guillaume, 345, 348–9, 353, 355, 455
Flocques, Robert de, 586, 593, 614, 624, 628, 660–1, 663, 669, 671, 691, 757
Florence, 405, 736
Fogo, John, Abbot of Melrose, 427
Foix, Gaston IV de Grailly, Count of (d. 1472), 81, 87–8, 167, 173, 176, 222, 232, 423, 461, 573, 598–9, 608, 657, 673, 719, 725, 727–8, 731, 732–3, 742–3, 747, 748, 759, 768
Foix, Jean I de Grailly Count of (d. 1436), 87

INDEX

Fontfroide, abbey, 138
Formigny, battle (1450), 692–5, 700, 720, 793
Forsted, William, 50
Fortescue, John, Chief Justice of King's Bench, 17, 47, 418, 493–4, 781, 788, 803–4
Foucault, Jean, 402
Fougères, 396, 442; English capture (1449), 656–64, 713; Breton siege (1449), 673, 681
Fouquet, Jean, 60, 634
Fowles, William, 112
franc archers, 651, 690, 704, 706, 725, 744, 761, 803
Francis I, King of France (1515–47), 770, 773, 803
Frederick III, King of the Romans (*sc.* Germany), Duke of Austria, 623–4
Fresnay-le-Vicomte, 37, 148, 650, 688; French siege (1450), 690, 700
Frétigny, Jean de, Bishop of Chartres, 401
Fribois, Noel de, 776, 807
Frogenhall, 647, 673, 679
Froissart, Jean, 77, 770, 778, 799, 809
Fronsac, 597–8, 725, 740; French siege (1451), 727, 729; English capture (1452), 741; French siege (1453), 746–7
Frotier, Pierre, 63, 164–5, 210
Fulford, Baldwin, 750
Fulham, 636–7

Gacé, 794
Gages, 222
Gaguin, Robert, 779
Gaillon, French capture (1424), 124; English siege (1424), 124, 126
Gallardon, 75–6, 80; English capture, French recapture (1442), 593, 681
Gallet, Louis, 713, 760
Garancières, Jean de, 79–80
Gargrave, Thomas, 254, 323, 381–3
Garter, Order of the, 293, 336, 478, 598, 681, 767
Garter King of Arms, *see* Bruges, Smert
Gaucourt, Raoul de, 218, 230, 233–4, 235–6, 264, 277, 321, 350–1, 397–8, 424–5, 569, 575
Gaunt, John of, *see* Lancaster
Gélu, Jacques, Archbishop of Tours, 201–2, 265, 282, 374

Gençay, 223
General Council of Scotland, (1423), 114, (1428), 228, (1433), 427
Geneva, 195, 197, 199, 787
Genoa, 78, 736
Gensac, 721–2
Geoffrey of Monmouth, 260
George III, King of Great Britain (1760–1820), 774
Georges, Bernard, 738
Gerberoy, battle (1435), 454, 455; French capture (1449), 661, 662
Germain, Jean, Bishop of Nevers, 463
Gerson, Jean, 266–7, 281, 800
Gethin, Richard, of Builth, 290–1
Ghent, 91, 158, 182–4, 337, 352, 389, 440, 508–9, 513, 516, 518–20, 521, 525, 809
Ghent, John of, 260–1
Giac, Pierre de, 172–3, 209–11, 221–2
Gien (town, county), 85, 94, 218–19, 263, 275, 295–7, 326
Gif, 783
Girard, Jean, 167, 218
Giovanni da Montalcino, 261
Gisors, 37, 315, 323, 335–6, 438; French occupation (1435), 488, (1450), 680–1
Giustiniani, Pancrazio, 244, 326
Glasdale, William, 102, 123, 141, 143, 165, 224–5, 238–9, 241–2, 245, 278–9
Glendower, Owen, 241
Gloucester, Humphrey of Lancaster, Duke of, 3, 6–7, 8, 9, 11, 12–13, 89–90, 116, 118, 119, 124–5, 150–7, 176, 181–9, 195, 204–8, 225, 227, 232, 240, 388–90, 403, 409, 412, 414, 416–18, 421, 422, 428–9, 469, 473, 479, 480–1, 498–9, 509–10, 511, 513, 514, 517–22, 523, 525, 531, 532–4, 543, 545, 549, 556, 560–1, 563–5, 572–3, 574, 578, 581, 587–8, 600, 606, 629, 633, 635, 643–5, 697, 699, 715, 757, 778, 782, 809
Gloucester, Eleanor (Cobham), Duchess of, 56, 207, 588
Gloucester Herald, 189, 191–3
Glyn Cothi, Lewis, 695
Godart, James, 416, 419
Golden Fleece, Order of the, 336–7, 350–1, 353, 450, 483–4, 574
Gontaut, lords of Biron, family, 608
Gouda, 181–2, 184–5, 203, 204, 207

962

INDEX

Gouge, Martin, Bishop of Clermont, Chancellor of France (1421–5), 63–4, 85, 122, 160, 163, 172, 210
Gough, Matthew, 224, 290–1, 333, 334, 613–15, 624–5, 640–1, 646–9, 690–5, 701, 712, 799
Gournay-en-Bray, 37, 315, 323, 325, 357, 379, 454
Gournay-sur-Marne, 376
Gower, Richard, 706
Gower, Thomas, 224, 704–6, 711–12
Grailly, Gaston de, Captal de Buch, 598, 728, 732, 737, 740
Grailly, Jean de, Viscount of Castillon, Earl of Kendal, 732–3, 740, 743
Grand Conseil, 29, 30–1, 32, 38, 40, 44, 93, 101, 124, 133, 141, 145, 227, 286, 293–4, 330, 340, 361, 363, 393, 401, 407, 411, 412, 416, 437, 441, 444, 456, 470, 474, 490, 495, 503, 536, 543, 550, 552, 559, 561, 577, 580, 581, 596, 626, 638, 648, 649, 658, 676, 713
Granville, 673, 760; French capture (1442), 594
Gravelines, 512–13, 519–21, 551, 555
great council (England), (1429), 286, (1434), 429, (1436), 509–10, (1435), 532, (1437), 547, (1439), 550, 600, (1445), 626–7, (1449), 674, (1450), 705, 713–14, (1452), 735
Gréelle, Baise de, Archbishop of Bordeaux (1456–67), 737
Greenwich, 643, 698
Grenier, Jean, 206
Grenoble, 138
Gressart, Pérrinet, 102–3, 128, 327, 342, 433
Grestain, abbey, 690
Grey of Heton, family, 38–9, 314, 491, 710
Grey of Ruthin, Edmund, Lord, 632
Grignaux, François de, 138
Grolée, Imbert de, Seneschal of Lyon, 350
Grosmont, Henry of, Earl of Derby (1337), Earl of Lancaster (1345), 789
Guelders, Arnold of Egmont, Duke of, 461
Guerre folle (1485–8), 768
Guesclin, Bertrand du, Constable of France, 82, 746, 798
Guines, 150, 152, 510, 515, 520, 620; French siege (1558), 772–3

Guise, 66–7, 74, 119; Anglo-Burgundian sieges (1423–4), 92, 101, 105–7, 118, 119–20, 123, 133, 137, 142, 145, 240
Guise, François de Lorraine, Duke of, 772
Guyenne, duchy, 21, 24, 65, 71, 332, 430, 464, 465, 470, 472, 473, 598–608, 620, 632, 714, 721–2, 724–33, 735, 736–54, 756, 759–60, 763–5, 767, 770, 771, 808; campaigns (1437), 599, (1438), 599–600, (1439–40), 600–2, (1442), 603–5, 607–8, (1451), 724–9, (1452–3), 739–52; Estates, 719, 733
Guyenne, Louis Duke of, Dauphin of France (*d.* 1415), 31, 82

Haarlem, 184; besieged by Hooks (1426), 195, 203
Hague, The, 10, 182–4
Hainaut, 10–11, 22, 89–91, 124–5 150–58, 181, 183–4, 186, 203, 546, 572, 809; campaign (1424–5), 152–5; Estates, 152, 153, 203
Hainaut, Count, Countess of, *see* Bavaria
Hakluyt, Richard, 522
Hall, Edward, 478
Halle, 153
Ham, French capture (1423), 106–7, (1434), 439, 447; truce (1434), 447–8
Hammes, 510, 515, 787
Harcourt (castle, county), 441, 444, 465, 543, 668, 673
Harcourt, family, 57, 314, 560
Harcourt, Christophe de, 448, 457, 461
Harcourt, Guillaume de, lord of Tancarville, 710
Harcourt, Jacques d', 66–7, 92–3, 105–6, 118, 314, 437
Harcourt, Jean de, Count of Aumale, 69, 122, 148
Hardyng, John, 14
Harfleur, 44, 50, 147, 534, 551, 559, 586, 592; siege (1415), 42, 43, 44, 418, 606, 618, 679, 681, 685, 761; sea battle (1416), 5, 42–3; French capture (1435), 486–7; English siege (1438), 543, (1440), 575–7; French siege (1449), 682, 685
Harling, Robert, 79
Harsage, James, 605
Hart, Walter, Bishop of Norwich, 647
Hastings, John, Lord, Chamberlain of Normandy, 716–17

963

INDEX

Hastings, William, Lord, 772
Hatton, William, 363
Havart, Jean, 638–9, 643–5, 648–9
Havré, lord of, *see* Enghien
Hay, Jack, 760
Heathfield, 700
Hedgeley Moor, battle (1464), 771–2
Heemstede, Jan van, 189, 191
Henry II, King of England (1154–89), 161, 620
Henry IV, King of England (1399–1413), 43, 117, 524, 600, 778, 790 806
Henry V, King of England (1413–22), xii, 2–3, 11, 12, 14, 16–18, 19–20, 24–5, 27, 30–3, 36, 41–4, 49, 51, 55, 57–8, 65–6, 69, 82, 87, 109–11, 119, 122, 148, 158, 193, 198, 214, 215, 242, 260–1, 330, 338–9, 340, 378, 396, 415, 421, 444, 451, 463, 465, 474, 530, 556, 560, 587, 592, 596, 606, 617, 629, 635, 675, 680, 704, 707, 715, 758–9, 766, 770, 773, 776, 777, 778, 779, 790, 792, 798, 809
Henry VI, King of England (1422–61, 1470–1), 2–3, 16–17, 19, 28, 57, 65, 90, 116, 176, 188, 251, 268, 280, 286, 303, 306–7, 322, 328, 329, 330–1, 331–2, 339, 369, 375–7, 365, 385–8, 375–7, 385–9, 390, 401, 406, 417–18, 420, 421, 423, 427, 443, 452, 464–5, 469–70, 472, 480, 503, 504, 520, 523, 530–4, 547, 551, 555, 559, 561, 563–5, 574, 581, 588, 591, 602, 604, 608, 612, 613, 615, 616–17, 618, 621–2, 628–9, 632–7, 639, 640–2, 643, 645–8, 650, 651, 656, 664, 674, 683, 684–5, 687–8, 698, 705, 711, 713–17, 723, 734, 735, 748, 755–8, 792
Henry VII, King of England (1485–1509), 530, 768–9
Henry VIII, King of England (1509–47), 767, 769–71, 773, 774, 809
Herrings, battle of the, *see* Rouvray-St-Denis
Hesdin, 155, 183, 294, 297, 382, 571–2, 590
Hexham, battle (1464), 757–8
Higden, Ranulph, 776
Holland, county, 9–11, 22, 89, 91, 119, 180–5, 187, 189–95, 199, 202–4, 206–8, 225, 240, 440, 446, 473, 514, 524–6, 548–9, 796, 809

Holland, Henry, Duke of Exeter (1447), 698
Holland, John, Earl of Huntingdon (1416), Duke of Exeter (1444), 11, 15, 349, 355, 357–8, 415, 431, 433–5, 452, 469, 514, 521, 522, 564, 571, 600–1, 606, 793
Honfleur, 37, 487, 541, 559, 679, 681, 682, 688, 761; French siege (1450), 689
Hoo, Thomas, Chancellor of France (Lancastrian, 1444–50), 596, 618, 640, 642, 649, 654–5, 660, 661, 678, 681, 716–17
Hooks, 181–5, 189, 207
Hoorn, Jan van, Admiral of Burgundy, 516–17
Houdan, 444; French capture (1432), 401, (1435), 455
Hugo, Victor, 788
Hull, Edward, Constable of Bordeaux (1442–53), 603, 606–7, 738, 745
Hungerford, Thomas (*d.* 1398), 799–800
Hungerford, Walter Lord, Treasurer of England (1426–32), 193, 226, 286, 416, 452, 522, 790
Hungerford, Walter junior, 292, 403–4
Hussites, 286–7, 294, 343, 409, 568
Hus, Jan, 286

Île-Bouchard, Catherine de, 211
Illiers, Florent d', 223, 230
Inglose, Henry, 793
Ingrande, 640
Inquisition, Holy Office of, 360
Ireland, Irish, 13, 15, 32, 44, 50, 241, 336, 378, 418, 430, 489, 646, 684, 698, 714, 774, 776
Isabelle of Bavaria, Queen of France, 2, 256, 261, 386
Isenheim, 625
Ivry (Ivry-la-Bataille), 82, 94, 101, 105, 119, 123–4; English siege (1424), 125–9, 132

Jacqueline of Bavaria, *see* Bavaria
Jakes, Nicholas, 685
James I, King of Scots (1406–37), 108–17, 139–40, 194, 228–9, 248, 256, 293, 332, 409, 426–7, 528
James II, King of Scots ('Fireface', 1437–60), 664, 761
James, Robert, 712

INDEX

Janville, 79–80, 242, 275, 285, 289–91, 293; English siege (1428), 232–3
Jardre, Le Bourc de, 433
Jargeau, 218–19, 234, 241–2; English capture (1428), 234; French siege (1429), 285, 287–9, 295, 622, 685
John ('the Fearless'), Duke of Burgundy, *see* Burgundy
John II, King of Castile (1406–54), 229, 724
John of Ghent, 260–1
Joigny, 785
Jolivet, Robert, Abbot of Mont St-Michel, 58, 165, 330, 332, 340, 370
Josas, achdeaconry of Paris, 782–4
Jumièges, abbey, 593
Juvénal des Ursins, Guillaume, Chancellor of France (Valois), 677, 678–9, 729, 750–1
Juvénal des Ursins, Jacques, Archbishop of Reims (1444), 634
Juvénal des Ursins, Jean II, Bishop of Beauvais (1432), then Laon (1444), Archbishop of Reims (1449), 58, 64, 210, 323, 325, 405, 533, 566–7, 781, 807, 809
Juziers, 584

Kemp, John, Archbishop of York (1426) and Canterbury (1452), Chancellor of England (1426–32), Cardinal (1439), 225, 287, 416, 452, 460, 462, 464, 469–73, 533–4, 549–52, 554–5, 559–61, 563–4, 591, 632–3, 635–6, 646, 687, 715
Kenilworth, 588, 698, 705
Kennedy, Hugh of Ardstynchar, 219, 230, 284, 402, 489
Kennington, 550, 563
Kijfhoek, Floris van, 182
Kingston, 735
Knyvet, John, 794
Kyriel, Thomas, 324, 357–8, 492, 614, 683–4, 688–95, 719–20, 757, 793

L'Aigle, 400
L'Archer, Jean, 502–3
L'Isle-Jourdain, 608
La Baume, Imbert Bastard of, 95, 99
La Brécinière, battle (1423), 104–5
La Bussière, 101–2, 143
La Chapelle, 317, 321

La Charité, 433; French capture (1422), 68; captured by Gressart (1423), 102–3, 128; French siege (1429), 327
La Chartre-sur-le-Loir, 165
La Chasse, occupied by French and recaptured (1430), 376
La Fère, 308, 310
La Ferté-Bernard, French capture (1425), 169–70; English siege (1425), 170; French capture (1427), 224
La Gravelle, 104, 658; English siege (1427), 222
La Guerche-sur-l'Aubois, 128; English occupation (1443), 615
La Guiche, French siege (1449), 719
La Guierche, English siege (1425), 166; English capture, French recapture (1438), 543
La Hardouinaie, 657
La Haye, Jean de, lord of Coulonces, 132, 136, 148, 169, 200, 496
La Hire, *see* Vignolles
La Hougue, 613
La Marche, Counts of, *see* Armagnac, Bourbon
La Marche, Olivier de, 81
La Paillière, Géraud de, 94, 101, 123–4, 128, 223, 230, 232, 334
La Réole, 726, French siege (1442), 606–7
La Roche-Guyon, French siege (1449) 672, 680
La Roche Solutré, Burgundian siege (1425), 143, (1435), 448
La Rochelle, 18, 85, 111–12, 115, 120, 228, 248, 423, 524, 724, 742, 747, 751
La Trémoille, Georges de, 180, 209, 211–12, 217, 221–2, 229, 230–1, 233–4, 264, 265, 269, 295–8, 305, 308, 310, 312, 327, 342, 374, 381, 385, 395–8, 424–5, 433, 538, 545, 568–9
La Trémoille, Jean de, lord of Jonvelle, 211, 296, 383–4
Lafayette, Gilbert Motier de, Marshal of France (Valois), 127–8, 137, 244, 246, 248, 448, 549, 566, 568, 571
Lagny, 307, 309, 436, 499, 507; submission to French (1429), 313, 322, 343–4, 350; English siege (1431), 375–6, (1432), 401–4, 414
Lallier, Michel de, 499–500, 502

INDEX

Lamothe, Bérard, lord of Roquetaillade, 608
Lamothe, Jean de, lord of Castelnau, 608
Lancaster, duchy, 15, 17, 415, 430, 456, 491, 510, 579
Lancaster, John of Gaunt, Duke of, xii, 7, 12, 16, 113, 549, 809
lance (weapon), 47–8, 271
lance (unit), 627
Landes, Pierre de, 500
Langdon, John, Bishop of Rochester, 412
Langenstein, Henry of, 258
Langley, Thomas, Bishop of Durham, Chancellor of England (1417–24), 6, 113, 489
Langon, 597; French capture, English recapture (1442), 606–7; English capture (1452), 754; French capture (1453), 747
Langres, 255, 323, 623–5
language, 54–5, 777
Laon, Laonnais, 93, 106, 307, 323, 341, 352, 375 447, 546, 580
Lauder, William, Bishop of Glasgow, Chancellor of Scotland, 113–15
Laval (Dauphiné), 139
Laval (Maine; town, barony), 104, 148, 170–1, 222, 658; English capture (1427), 213; French capture (1429), 333
Laval, Anne, Dame de, 213
Laval, André de, lord of Lohéac, Marshal of France (Valois), 213, 567, 659, 673, 690, 742, 567
Laval, Guy de, 270, 284–5, 305
Laval, Jeanne de, 333
Lavardin, truce (1448), 650–1
Le Boursier, Jean, 721, 724, 726, 732, 737
Le Bouvier, Gilles, Berry Herald, 77, 120, 168, 197, 210, 649, 807
Le Clerc, Jean, Chancellor of France (Lancastrian, 1420–4), 15
Le Crotoy, 19, 66, 73, 79, 138, 148, 362, 416, 454, 498, 524, 548, 587, 665, 782; English siege (1423–4), 34, 92–3, 94, 101, 105, 118–19; French siege (1436), 514, 518, (1437), 527, 541; French capture (1449), 680
Le Guildo, 641–2
Le Haillan, battle (1450), 722
Le Lude, French siege (1427), 224

Le Maçon, Robert, Chancellor of France (Valois; 1418, 1419–21), 63, 222, 230, 296
Le Maistre, Jean, 363, 371–2
Le Mans, 69, 148–9, 171, 373, 400, 442, 543, 615, 626, 784; English siege (1425), 166–9; French capture, English recapture (1428), 224–5; surrender to French (1447), 647–51
Le Mans, Bishops of, see Ansières, Chatelain
Le Neubourg (barony), 535
Le Puiset, English capture (1428), 232–3
Le Sage, Raoul, lord of St-Pierre, 58, 250, 340, 416
Le Vulre, Gervase, 504, 713
Legnano, John of, 797
Leicester, 192, 687, 695, 697
Leiden, 184, 190
Leighton, Henry, Bishop of Aberdeen, 228–9
Leland, John, 790
Lendit fairs, 212, 622, 786
Lenfant, Jean, 713
Lenthall, Roland, 790
Lesguisé, Jean, Bishop of Troyes, 300
Libel of English Policy, 522–3, 524–5, 771
Libourne, 598, 725, 753; French capture (1751), 727; English capture, French recapture (1752), 740, 746
Liège, prince-bishopric, 118, 351, 357
Lille, 22, 91, 158, 199, 204, 337, 381, 384, 387, 407, 520, 521, 595
Lillebonne, 491, 493
Limoges, Limousin, 424, 612
Linlithgow, 228
Lisieux, French capture (1449), 670–1, 672, 674
Lisieux, Bishop of, see Basin, Cauchon
Lisle, Viscount, see Talbot
Livius, Titus, of Ferrara, 60
Loches, 120, 159, 230, 283, 423, 425, 570
Lollardy, Lollards, 364, 409, 698
London, 6, 8, 19, 21, 48, 88, 89, 111–12, 114–15, 150, 185–9, 192, 205, 233, 247, 287, 330, 421, 423, 479, 480, 488, 499, 504, 511–12, 523, 563, 564, 587, 588, 603, 618, 622, 628, 629, 644–6, 674, 684–7, 696–700, 702, 706, 710–11, 713, 715–17, 720, 722, 723, 730, 733, 734, 735, 736–7, 739, 752,

966

INDEX

757, 758, 776, 778, 791; Brewers Guild, 777; Corporation, 17, 194, 208, 337–8, 377–8, 388, 437, 491; Franciscans, 711; Hospitallers, 532; London Bridge, 635, 712, 791–2; Mercers Guild, 185; St Paul's Cathedral, 238, 338, 428, 4229, 430, 736; Savoy Palace, 789

London, Bishop of, *see* Fitzhugh

longbows, 47, 191, 694

Longny, 581, 626, 663, 681

Longueval, Charles de, 133

Loré, Ambroise de, 69, 104, 168, 279, 322, 399, 400, 435, 442

Lormont, 747, 750

Lorraine (duchy), Lorrainers, 21, 31, 67, 144, 253–8, 262, 307, 364, 368, 373, 381–3, 477, 527, 555, 621, 623–8, 637, 799

Lorraine, Charles II, Duke of, 132, 145, 254, 258, 262, 381

Lorraine, Réné, Duke of, *see* Anjou

Louis the Pious, King of the Franks, 446

Louis IX, King of France (1214–70), 546, 823

Louis X, King of France (1314–16), 55

Louis XI, Dauphin, King of France (1461–83), 214, 478, 545, 567, 569–70, 586, 602, 603, 614, 681, 761–8, 772, 773, 802–3

Louvain, 151–2, 351–2

Louvet, Jean, 62–3, 64, 122, 160, 161–6, 172–3, 209–12, 221–2, 229, 425, 545

Louviers, 124, 592–3, 626, 657, 660, 661, 662, 672, 675; French capture (1429), 334, 335, 377, 391, 435; English siege (1430–1), 342, 378–80; French capture (1440), 576–7

Lull, Ramon, 808

Lumley, Marmaduke, Bishop of Carlisle, Treasurer of England (1446–9), 631, 633, 674

Lusignan, 159, 231, 538

Lusignan, Hughes de, Cardinal, 445, 459–60, 475

Luxe, John lord of, 719

Luxembourg, duchy, 22

Luxembourg, Jacquetta of, Duchess of Bedford, 419, 720

Luxembourg, John of, Count of Ligny, 30, 33, 35, 106–7, 117–19, 123, 133, 137, 145, 154, 200, 215, 255, 309, 330, 342, 246–8, 349, 352–3, 355–9, 361–2, 375–6, 383, 394, 416, 419, 447, 452, 471, 476–7

Luxembourg, Louis of, Bishop of Thérouanne (1415–36), Archbishop of Rouen (1436–43), Cardinal (1439), Chancellor of France (Lancastrian, 1424–43), 30, 33, 40, 241, 340, 369–70, 385, 414, 416–17, 419, 429–30, 452, 456, 490, 494–6, 499, 502–3, 596

Luxembourg, Peter of, Count of Conversano and St-Pol, lord of Enghien, 153–4, 419

Lydgate, John, xi, 187, 208, 617

Lyndwood, William, Keeper of the Privy Seal (1432), Bishop of St David's (1442), 378, 452

Lyon, Lyonnais, 62, 68, 73, 96, 100, 102, 103, 143, 160, 163, 173, 175, 210, 243, 248, 266, 350, 583, 736, 739, 787

Machet, Gérard, 261, 265–6, 301

Mâcon, Mâconnais, 22, 68–9, 86, 101–3, 120, 123, 141, 143–4, 151, 159–60, 175, 240, 280, 351, 381, 384–5, 449, 476

Maillé, Jeanne-Marie de, 59

Mailly, Jean de, Bishop of Noyon, 370

Mailly-la-Ville, 385, 434

Mailly-le-Château, 95, 99

Maine, county, 21, 31, 38, 56, 62, 69, 79, 104, 132, 134, 174, 189, 197, 198, 199, 212–13, 272, 280, 314, 327, 329, 333, 396, 398, 425–6, 430, 431, 470, 472, 490, 537–8, 554, 563, 571, 633, 666, 784, 791–3; campaigns (1424–5), 101, 103, 141–2, 147–9, 163, 165, 166–71, 187, 396 (1427), 223–5, (1432), 400, 403, (1433), 435–6, (1438), 541–3, (1440), 567–8, (1443), 610–11, 615–16, 651; ceded to French (1444–8), 634, 637–51, 657–8, 686–7, 697, 712, 716, 735, 756, 782

Majorca, kingdom, 621

Malestroit, Jean de, Bishop of Nantes, Chancellor of Brittany, 84, 180, 195–9, 396, 397, 440

Malet de Graville, Jean, Master of the Royal Archers (Valois), 219, 433

Malmesbury, James Harris, Earl of, 773–4

Man, Isle of, 588

INDEX

Mantes, 32, 37, 241, 285, 335, 401, 454–5, 482–3, 497, 507, 576, 584, 626, 660; French siege (1449), 671
Mar, Alexander Stewart, Earl of, 139–40
March, Edmund Mortimer, Earl of, 489, 757
Marck, Burgundian capture (1436), 510, 514–15
Marcoussis, 80
Margny, 346–8
Marmande, 598
Martin V, Pope (1417–31), 8, 10, 60, 207, 251, 286, 395, 330, 405, 408
Martin, Oliver, 710
Maubuisson (abbey), 583–4
Mauléon, French siege (1449), 719
Mauny, family, 57
Mauny, Walter, 808
Maxey, 255
Mayenne, 148, 166, 171, 400; English siege (1425), 169
Meaux, 307, 309, 313, 394, 507, 540, 551, 554; French siege (1439), 550, 555–9, 561–2, 564, 567, 652
Mechelen, 173, 352, 526
Mehun-sur-Yèvre, 60, 108, 159, 173, 196, 327
Melle, 231, 538, 570
Melun, 109, 153, 310, 329, 341, 350, 401, 411, 413, 436, 482; French capture (1430), 338–9, 343
Melun, viscounts of, 38, 57
Mendlesham, 794
Merbury, Richard, 680–1, 700, 710
Meslay-du-Maine, 333
Messac, 690
Metz, Lorrainers besiege (1429), 307; French siege (1444), 623, 625
Meulan (town, bridge), 335; 336, 593; French capture, English recapture (1423), 79–80, 132; French capture (1435), 483, 494; English siege (1435–6), 494
Meung, 213, 234, 238, 241–2, 246, 279, 285, 289; English capture (1428), 233; French siege (1429), 289–91
Meverell, Sampson, 799
Michael, St, 70, 372, 711
Michelet, Jules, 808
Middelburg, 181, 185, 526, 796
Middleton, John, 526

Milan, Milanese, 48, 78, 405, 461, 736, 762, 766–7
Milan, Filippo Maria Visconti, Duke of, 108
Mile End, 699
Milly, battle (1431), 379–80
Minors, William, 487
Mites, Richard, 133
Mitry, 404
Moleyns, Adam, Keeper of the Privy Seal (1444), Bishop of Chichester (1445), 450, 533, 565, 610, 611, 618, 633, 635, 637–40, 642–3, 645, 649–50, 657, 684–6, 779
Molyns, William, 278
Moncontour, 641
Mondoubleau, 216; French capture (1427), 220–1, 227
Mons, 153–4, 156–8, 203
Monstrelet, Enguerrand de, 87, 348, 352, 419, 480, 514
Montagu, John, Bastard of, 399–400
Montagu, Thomas, Earl of Salisbury, Count of Perche (d. 1428), 27, 39, 42–3, 44, 45, 46, 90, 93, 95–6, 98, 101, 102, 117, 119–20, 123, 126, 130, 136, 139, 142–5, 151, 165–70, 187, 197, 200, 205, 213, 215–16, 225–8, 230–4, 236–40, 280, 285, 399, 422, 431, 799, 808
Montaiguillon, English siege (1423–4), 93–6, 101, 105, 117
Mont-Aimé, 68, 144–5
Montargis, 275, 507, 785; English siege (1427), 216–21, 227, 229; English siege (1433), 433, 435; French siege (1437), 539–40, 544, 681
Montauban, 607, 609
Montbard, 82, 240–1
Montdidier, 22, 328–9, 476
Monte, Piero da, 530, 619–21
Montépilloy, 311–12, 315, 317
Montereau, 2, 61, 63, 85, 123, 160, 162, 310, 433, 471, 475, 477, 507; French siege (1437), 539–40, 652
Montferrand (Auvergne), 573
Montferrand (Gascony), 750–1
Montferrand, Bérard de, 727
Montferrand, Bertrand, lord of, 728, 732
Montferrand, François de, 752
Montferrand, Pierre de, Soudan de la Trau, 727, 737, 739, 740, 743, 745, 751–2, 759

968

INDEX

Montfoort, Louis van, 204–5
Montfort-l'Amaury, French capture (1432), 401
Montfort-le-Rotrou (Montfort-le-Gesnois), English capture (1424), 149
Montfort, Anne de, Duchess of Brittany (d. 1514), 768–9
Montfort, Arthur de, Count of Richemont, Constable of France (1425), Duke of Brittany (1457–8), 82, 84–5, 100, 119, 122, 124–5, 158–69, 172–5, 177–80, 195–7, 199–200, 209–11, 216–19, 221–3, 229–31, 234, 244, 289–90, 295–6, 394, 395–6, 398, 423–5, 435–6, 438–9, 447–9, 453, 457, 461, 466, 482, 496, 499–503, 507, 514, 520, 534, 536, 549–50, 555–9, 567–8, 569–70, 580, 603, 615, 627, 638, 666–7, 673, 690–5, 704–6, 709, 739
Montfort, Francis I de, Duke of Brittany, (d. 1450), 590, 612–13, 615–17, 640–2, 657–62, 666–7, 673, 681, 688, 690, 700
Montfort, Francis II de, Duke of Brittany (d. 1488), 763–4, 767–8
Montfort, Gilles de (Gilles de Bretagne), 612, 616–17, 640–2, 656–9, 662, 664
Montfort, John V de, Duke of Brittany (d. 1442), 25, 62, 64, 65, 83–5, 87–8, 121–3, 140, 151, 158–61, 163, 174–7, 179–81, 195–202, 221–3, 230–1, 282, 284, 332, 387, 395–8, 409, 416, 419, 423, 440, 461, 547–9, 566, 569, 589, 590–1, 616, 640
Montfort, Richard de, Count of Étampes, 177, 179, 200
Montgomery, John, 342, 344, 349, 486
Montigny-le-Roi, 254–5
Montils, 619, 634, 638, 649, 651, 659
Montivilliers, 486, 575–6, 679
Montjay, 376
Montlhéry, 80; battle (1465), 763
Montluçon, 222–3
Montluel, 160–2, 175
Montmartre, 317
Montrésor, 425
Montrichard, 538
Mont St-Michel, 49, 56, 69–70, 73–4, 103–4, 168, 170, 251, 423, 465, 551, 554, 561, 567, 594, 658, 673, 700, 710; English siege (1424–5), 141–2, 145–7, 165–6, (1435), 443
Monypenny, William, 676

More, Thomas, Chancellor of England (1529–32), 770
Morienval, 345
Morgan, Philip, Bishop of Ely, 113, 340
Morhier, Simon, Provost of Paris, 245, 401, 444, 502–3
Mortain, 658, 661
Morvilliers, Philippe de, First President of the Parlement of Paris, 416
Moulant, Philibert de, 298
Moulins, 197
Moulins-Engilbert, 159
Mouzon, 68
Mowbray, John de, Earl (1399) then Duke (1425) of Norfolk, Earl Marshal of England, 40, 150, 152–3, 754
Mundeford, Osbern, Treasurer of Normandy, 647, 649, 651, 669–70, 700
Murdrac, Henri, 147

Namur, county, 22, 91, 351, 357
Nancy, 381, 383, 621, 625, 634; battle (1477), 768
Nangis, 123, 310
Nantes, 65, 122–3, 124, 125, 160, 175, 397, 589, 641
Navarre, Navarrese, 461, 730, 732, 752
Navarre, Charles the Bad, King of, 704
Naples, 179, 445, 461, 736
Narbonne, Guillaume de Lara, Viscount of, 63, 127–8, 132, 136–8
Nemours, 289, 433, 507, 539–40
Nesles-en-Tardenois, 123, 142
Neufchâteau, 255–6
Neufchâtel, 37, 315, 383, 438
Neufmarché, 536
Nevers, Nivernais, 68, 101, 102, 128, 297, 410–11, 448–51, 457, 458, 475, 590–2, 603, 759
Nevers, Countess of, *see* Artois
Nevers, Charles, Count of (d. 1464), 676
Nevers, John of, Count of (1464–91), 438–9, 447–8
Nevers, Philip, Count of (d. 1415), 68
Neville, family, 116, 755–6
Neville, George, Lord Bergavenny (1476), 707
Neville, Richard, Earl of Salisbury (d. 1460), 331, 644

969

INDEX

Neville, Richard, Earl of Salisbury and Warwick ('the Kingmaker', d. 1471), 212, 756, 758, 764
Neville, William, Lord Fauconberg, 292, 490, 535, 557, 577, 583, 586, 592, 653, 660-2, 793
Newenham Bridge, 511, 514-16, 772
Nicholas de la Tour, 696
Niort, 73, 218, 569-71
Nivelles, 125, 151-2, 154
Nogent-sur-Seine, 93, 298, 318, 434
Nogent-le-Roi (Nogent-en-Bassigny), 232, 254-5
Nonancourt, 128-9
Norbury, Henry, 492, 497, 700
Normandy, duchy, 3, 20, 22, 29, 31-3, 35-9, 40-7, 49-50, 53-9, 69, 141-2, 391-2, 393, 429-30, 440-4, 455-6, 465, 470, 472, 474, 479-80, 488-91, 497, 503-4, 533-4, 534-5, 540-3, 550, 553-4, 556-7, 559-61, 565, 566-7, 577-82, 586-7, 594-6, 609, 618-19, 625-6, 629-30, 638, 639-40, 650, 653-5, 663-4, 688-90, 707-10, 787, 791-3, 807-8; Estates, 34, 36, 41, 141-2, 192, 233, 250-1, 283, 333, 361, 392, 542, 626, 654, 661-2, 721, 739, 761; campaigns (1423), 79-80, 93-4, (1424), 104-5, 120-1, 123-4, 125, 126-39, (1427-8), 223, (1429), 314-15, 333-6, (1430-1), 339, 342, 376-9, (1435-6), 482-3, 484-8, 491-4, (1436), 535-7, (1438), 543-4, (1539), 567-8, (1440), 575-7, 586, (1442), 592-4, (1443), 614, (1449-50), 660-2, 663, 665, 666-73, 675-82, 688, 690-5, 700-7
Northumberland, Henry Percy, Earl of, 664-5, 756
Noyelles, Baudot de, 346-8, 367, 519
Noyelles-sur-Mer, 92
Noyon, 342, 344, 347, 353, 356

Ogard, Andrew, 592, 792-3
Ogilvy, Patrick of Auchterhouse, 229, 248, 284
Oldhall, William, 45-6, 134, 224, 415, 426, 550, 578, 592, 596, 714-15, 717
Olivet, 273
Orange, Louis of Chalon-Arlay, Prince of, 157-8, 350, 798
Orléans (city), 288, 295, 391, 423, 538, 566, 575, 576-7, 808; English siege (1428-9), 213-15, 232-3, 234-51, 253, 256-7, 260, 263, 267-82, 283, 284, 286, 296, 298, 305-6, 307, 332-3, 341, 347, 401, 481
Orléans (duchy, dukes), 62, 78, 81, 214, 216, 342, 569, 571-5, 768
Orléans, Charles, Duke of (d. 1465), 61, 88, 123, 213-17, 232, 241, 248, 249, 326, 412-13, 422-4, 426, 453, 469, 472, 527, 545, 547-9, 552-4, 560-5, 578, 579, 588-602, 612, 617, 618, 619, 656-7, 686
Orléans, John Bastard of, Count of Dunois (1439), 64, 159, 218-21, 230, 235, 239, 246-7, 263, 270, 271-80, 283, 306, 311, 349-50, 373, 379, 400-1, 403, 422-3, 436, 455-6, 482-3, 499-502, 534, 544, 552, 782
Orléans, Louis Duke of (d. 1407), 27, 213-14, 376, 725, 727, 785
Orléans, Louis Duke of, later King of France (1483-98), 768
Orléans, Marie of Cleves, Duchess of, 572
Orsay, 93-4
Orval, lord of, *see* Albret
Orville, 482, 507
Ostrevant (county), 125
Oudewater, 185
Ouistreham, 703
Oye, 510-11; Burgundian capture (1436), 514-15, 517, 551, 572

Pacy, Burgundian siege (1433), 434-5
Pardiac, *see* Armagnac
Parentucelli, Tomasso (later Pope Nicholas V, 1447-55), 459-60
Paris, 21-2, 24, 25-9, 34, 37, 45, 50, 53, 57, 58-9, 61-2, 79-80, 90-1, 93-4, 100-1, 117-18, 124-6, 139, 141-2, 156, 200, 213, 227-8, 231-2, 249-50, 260, 285, 293, 301-4, 309, 310, 317, 322, 327-8, 329, 330, 336-7, 341, 360, 373, 375-7, 380, 385-8, 391, 401-2, 404, 413, 436-7, 452, 453, 456, 474, 505-9, 534, 580, 585, 622, 672, 786, 788; treaty of (1259), 464, (1496), 463; French siege (1429), 318-21, (1435), 481-4; French capture (1436), 494-7, 499-503; Parlement, 1, 4, 24, 27, 32, 91, 145, 293, 302, 306, 313, 461, 373-4, 385, 387, 388, 393, 408, 416, 461, 495-7,

970

INDEX

505–7; University, 30, 150, 151, 360, 363, 365, 368–70, 373–4, 408, 461, 708, 739, 770–1; Topography: Bastille, 37, 44, 235, 456, 495, 503–4, 760; Châtelet, 28; Fort St-Victor, 37; Les Halles, 26; Hôtel d'Arras, 27; Hôtel d'Artois, 25, 327; Hôtel de Cluny, 788; Hôtel de Sens, 788; Hôtel des Tournelles, 25, 27, 386; Hôtel St-Pol, 25; Louvre, 25; Notre Dame cathedral, 386, 786; Pont-au-Change, 386, 786; Pont Notre-Dame, 26; Porte St-Jacques, 501; Rue de l'Université, 27; Rue St-André des Arts, 27; Rue St-Antoine, 25; Rue St-Denis, 385–6; Rue St-Jacques, 501; Rue St-Martin, 502; St-Germain-des-Près, abbey, 786; St-Merri, 279

Parker, John, 227

Parlement of Paris, *see* Paris; First President, *see* Morvilliers

Parliament of England, 21, 775, 803–5, (1419), 18, (1420), 809, (1421), 15, 17, 18, (1422), 6, 12, 16, (1423), 2, (1425), 186–7, (1426), 189, 192–4, (1427), 205, 206–8, (1428), 225–6, (1429), 328–30, 333, 394–5, (1431), 378, 389, (1432), 390, 394, (1433), 417–19, 420–2, 597, (1434), 428–9, (1435), 450–1, 480, 481, 486, 488–9, (1437), 523, 448, (1439), 564–6, 577–8, (1440), 579, (1442), 592, (1445), 628–30, (1445–6), 638–9, (1446), 637, (1447), 644, (1449), 654–5, 665, (1449–50), 674, 682–8, 695–7, (1450–1), 712, 714–16, 720–1, 723, (1453–4), 741–2, 755, (1468), 764, (1472), 765–6, 767–8, 796–7, (1523), 770–1, (1559) 773

Parthenay, 223, 231, 234, 296

Partition Act, 394–5, 440, 562

Passy-en-Valois, English siege (1423), 93–4, 119

Paston, John, 576, 706, 763

Paston, Margaret, 632, 657

Patay, battle (1429), 291–3, 294, 295–6, 306, 311, 793, 794, 798

Pavia, battle (1525), 770

Paynel, Nicolas, lord of Bricqueville, 146–7

Pedro, *see* Aviz

Penthièvre, Olivier de Blois, Viscount of Limoges, Count of (d. 1433), 177, 231, 657

Penthièvre, Jean II de Blois, Viscount of Limoges, Count of (d. 1454), 176–7, 230, 657, 721

Pepys, Samuel, 523

Perche, county, 31, 32, 43, 69, 170, 223, 334, 554

Périgord, 71, 464–5, 620, 636

Péronne, 22, 338–9, 342; treaty (1468), 764

Perth, 114, 228, 427

Pesquerel, Jean, 270

Petilow, Robin, 753

Peyto, William, 581, 594, 614, 666

Philip ('the Good'), Duke of Burgundy, *see* Burgundy

Philip Augustus, King of France (1180–1223), 264, 321, 675

Piccolomini, Aeneas Sylvius, (later Pope Pius II, 1458–64), 7, 83, 214, 249, 252, 263, 283

Picquigny, treaty (1475), 766–7, 787

Pierrefonds, 342, 345, 352

Pierrone the Breton, 259, 360

Pisan, Christine de, 260, 306, 807

Pitt, William the Younger, 774

Pius II, Pope (1458–64), *see* Piccolomini

Plymouth, 375, 600, 603, 720, 724, 730, 741, 776

Portsmouth, 497, 613, 621–2, 666, 674, 683–4, 688, 778–9

Poissy, 32, 37, 79, 228, 306, 496, 501, 582, 584–5

Poitiers, 24, 62, 70, 164, 166, 168, 210–11, 266–9, 325, 374, 423, 442, 496, 505 Parlement, 210, 395; Estates (1424), 72, (1425), 173, (1435), 538, (1436), 538, 570, 612, 759

Poitou, county, 213, 465; campaigns (1427), 222–3, (1428–31), 231, 395–8, (1440), 569–70, 573

Pole, Alexander de la, 288

Pole, John de la, 103–4, 217, 219–20, 234

Pole, William de la, Earl (1415), Marquess (1444), Duke (1448) of Suffolk, Admiral of Normandy, 27, 35, 39, 42–4, 46, 93, 96, 99–100, 101–2, 125–6, 128, 130, 142, 150–1, 166, 168, 177–9, 195–6, 216–17, 220, 223, 239, 241–2, 279, 285, 287–8, 416, 420–3, 452–3, 460, 484, 486, 488–90, 532–3, 566, 606, 611–12, 617–21, 628–30, 632–7, 639–41, 43–5,

971

645–6, 651, 656, 658–9, 664, 674, 681, 683–8, 696–9, 711, 713–14, 716, 723
Polton, Thomas, 777
Pommiers, 739–40
Pons, Jacques, lord of, 604
Pont-Audemer, 56, 135, 577; French siege (1449), 668–70, 671, 672, 674, 700
Pont-de-Charenton, 37, 332, 547
Pont-de-l'Arche, 138, 335, 543, 580, 592, 662, 668, 675–8, 793; French capture (1449), 660–1, 662, 665
Pont-de-Veyle, 448
Pontefract, 112–14
Pont-l'Evêque (Beauvaisis), 356
Pont-l'Evêque (Normandy), 670, 799
Pontoise, 37, 285, 309, 315, 438, 484, 499, 500–1, 534, 543, 554, 557–9, 576; French capture (1436), 496, 497; English capture (1437), 536–7; French siege (1441), 580–6
Pontorson, 146, 177, 294, 567; Breton capture (1426), 177; English siege (1427), 199–200
Pont-Ste-Maxence, 312, 328, 342, 356, 507, 770; French occupation (1429), 313, (1430), 356; English capture (1434), 438; French capture (1435), 455
Ponts-de-Cé, 65, 168, 213, 216, 227–8, 424
Pont-sur-Seine, 434, 439
Poole, 789
Poperinghe, English capture (1436), 521
Popham, John, 171, 548, 597
Popham, Stephen, 593
Porcher, Robin and Jeanne, 76
Porchester, 658
Portugal, 461, 523, 753
Portugal, King of, see Duarte
Pouancé, Breton siege (1432), 396–7
Praemunire, statute of, 389–90
Prague, 286, 568
Praguerie (1440), 568–71
Provins, 307, 309–11; French capture (1433), 433
Pugin, A. W., 788

Quercy, 71, 464–5, 620, 636
Quiefdeville, Guillaume de, 229

Radcliffe, John, Seneschal of Aquitaine (1423–36), 226–7, 286, 289, 294, 302, 309, 452, 453, 511–12, 514, 598–99
Rambouillet, 401

Rambures, André de, 314, 376–7, 484
Raoulet, Jean, 68, 144
Razilly, 641–2, 659
Redford, Henry, 678–9
Reims, xii, 3, 60, 64, 93, 94, 111, 121, 123, 159, 257, 261–2, 263–4, 282, 282–3, 295–6, 299, 302–7; submits to French (1429), 304
Remon, Guillaume, 119
Rempston, Thomas, 45–6, 123, 137, 151, 177–8, 224, 245, 292, 601–4, 608, 794
Rennes, 69, 177, 179, 198, 201, 396, 398, 424, 589, 612, 657, 659, 662, 669, 690
Rethel, county, 123, 381, 431
Retz, Gilles de Laval, lord of, Marshal of France (Valois), 202, 223, 272, 305, 320, 373, 640
Ricarville, Guillaume, lord of, 398–9
Richard II, King of England (1377–99), 12, 406, 464, 524, 530, 777
Richard ('Brother Richard'), 299
Richemont, Arthur Count of, see Montfort
Rieux, Pierre de, Marshal of France (Valois), 438, 482, 484–7, 491–3
Rigmaiden, George, 456
Rinel, Jean, 30–1, 281, 285–6, 380, 441, 452, 471, 489, 504, 550, 552, 586–7
Riom, 72, 549, 555
Rions, 725, 729, 740, 747–8, 750, 752
Ripley, John, 496
Rivers, Richard Woodville, Lord, 720, 723–30, 732, 760
Robesart, Lewis, 358, 798
Robine, Marie (Marie of Avignon), 258, 268
Roche, Jean de la, see Rochechouart
Rochechouart, Jean de (Jean de la Roche), 231, 395, 397, 570–1
Rochefort, Guillaume de, Chancellor of France, 234, 787–8, 604
Rochester, 294–5, 696, 723
Rohan, Alain VIII, Vicomte de (d. 1429), 202
Rokeley, Robert, 733
Roland, Jeanette, 506
Rolin, Nicolas, Chancellor of Burgundy, 11, 25, 85, 89, 310, 338, 351, 411–12, 458, 460, 466–8, 471–2, 499, 551, 553
Roos, Robert, Seneschal of Guyenne (1442–3), 603–7, 609, 618, 650
Roos, Thomas Lord, 28

INDEX

Ross, John, 753
Rostrenen, Jean de, 199
Rotterdam, 184, 190, 523
Roubaix, John, lord of, 206
Rouen, 31–2, 35–6, 37, 41, 50, 55, 56–7, 92, 124, 126, 133, 139, 309, 315, 317, 330, 334–5, 335–6, 361, 362–3, 365, 369–73, 376–7, 379, 407, 408, 435, 441, 444, 470, 478, 484, 486–9, 492–4, 503–4, 534, 542–3, 544, 575, 618–19, 622, 629–30, 649, 653–4, 661–2, 667–8, 709, 787–8, 791; English siege (1419–20), 43, 45, 46, 51, 57, 242; French capture of castle (1432), 398–9, 400; French siege (1449), 675–9; Topography: castle, 31, 362, 675; defences, 675; Palais de Justice, 788; royal palace, 444, 675; St-Ouen, abbey, 369–70; St-Maclou, 788
Rouergue, 71, 801
Roussel, Raoul, Archbishop of Rouen (1443–52), 676, 708
Rousselet, Jean, 658
routiers, *see* brigands
Rouvray-St-Denis, battle (1429), 246–7
Royallieu, priory, 353–6
Royaumont, abbey, 584
Roxburgh, 426–7, 528
Roye, 22, 233, 145, 358, 476
Roye, Guy de, 484
Rozmital, Leo of, 778–9
Rue, 92, 454–5, 484
Ry, battle (1436), 494
Rye, 776

Saane, Jean de, 135
Saarbrücken, Joannes de, Bishop of Châlons-sur-Marne, 301
Saintonge, 465, 636, 761, 784
Saintrailles, Jean ('Poton') de, 67, 106–7, 117, 119–21, 134, 154, 230, 235–6, 248–50, 292, 310, 322, 353–6, 358, 379–80, 454–6, 467, 484, 488, 494, 569, 575, 576–7, 599, 603, 625, 628, 704, 721, 728, 729–30, 753
Salazar, Jean de, 623, 628
Salisbury, 789
Salisbury, Earl of, *see* Montagu, Neville
Salm, Counts of, 254
Sandwich, 302, 389, 517, 530, 757
Sangatte, 510, 515, 772
Sanguin, Guillaume, 499

Sark Water, battle (1448), 664
Sarrebrück, Robert de, lord of Commercy, 254, 255
Sarry, 626–7
Saumur, 167–9, 174–6, 180, 201, 248, 614
Sauveterre-de-Guyenne, 728
Saveuse, Philippe de, 303–4, 329, 338, 352
Savigny, abbey, 441
Savoy, 736
Savoy, Amadeus VIII, Duke of, 24, 81, 85–6, 95, 122, 143–4, 151, 159–61, 174–5, 194–9, 308, 316–17, 329, 338, 406, 425, 448, 739–40
Scales, Thomas, Lord, 45, 96, 105, 124, 126, 129, 165, 224, 241, 242, 279, 289, 292, 379, 396–7, 443, 492–4, 540, 557, 577, 583, 585, 594, 699, 704, 793
Schouwen, 189–90
Schoonhoven, 182, 185; Cod siege (1425), 183
Scrope, John Lord, of Masham, Treasurer of England (1432–3), 415, 418
Selles, Estates-General (1423), 65, 72, 74–5, 164, 284
Semur-en-Auxois, 411, 449
Seine-Port, 413, 424
Selden, John, 522–3
Senlis, 127, 313, 317–18, 322, 328, 345, 346, 350, 353, 482, 581
Sens, 329, 341, 434, 785; French capture (1429), 337
Sepeaux, 785–6
Sévérac, Amaury de, Marshal of France (Valois), 68–9, 73, 80, 96, 99, 222
Seyssel, Claude de, Bishop of Marseille, 788, 803
Sézanne, English siege (1424), 123, 126
Shakespeare, William, xii, 44, 293
Sheen, 547–8, 606, 609, 674
Sherborne, 699
Shorthose, Gadifer, 718, 721–2, 725–8, 733
siege warfare, 23, 50–53, 481
Sigismund, Holy Roman Emperor, 10, 408, 446
Sillé-le-Guillaume, 148, 400, 435–6
Sluys, 181, 184, 189, 509, 513, 517, 521
Smert, John, Garter King of Arms, 766
Soignies, 154–5
Soissons, 307–9, 341, 344–5, 347, 356, 484, 572, 652
Solesmes, 784

973

INDEX

Somerset, Earl of, Duke of, *see* Beaufort
Somerset, Eleanor Beauchamp, Duchess of, 680, 703
Southampton, 593, 622, 776
Southwark, 44, 188, 697, 699, 712, 778, 791; St Mary Overy, abbey, 116
Spanish Armada (1588), 805
St-Aignan, 243, 543
St Albans, 645, 705, 756
St-Antoine-de-Viennois, 138–9
St Benet Hulme, abbey, 791–2
St-Bris, 434
St-Céneri (St-Céneri-le-Gerei), captured by *routiers* (*ca.* 1429), 314; English siege (1432), 399, 400; English siege (1433), 435
St-Cloud, 322, 501, 507, 546
St-Denis-en-France, 1, 305, 326, 329–30, 386, 453, 585, 622; abbey, 1, 305, 386, 500, 786; French capture (1429), 317, 318–19, 321–2; English recapture (1429), 322, 326; French capture and withdrawal (1430), 338, 455, 456, 481–2; English capture (1435), 483–4; French capture (1436), 500–1
St-Denis-en-Val, 244
St-Dyé, 65
St-Émilion, 598, 753; French capture (1451), 727; English capture (1452), 740; French capture (1453), 745, 746;
St-Evroul, French capture (1432), 400
St-Florentin, French capture (1429), 298, 434–5
St-Germain, Waleran de, 106–7
St-Germain-en-Laye, 32, 37, 496, 551, 554; French capture (1436), 507; English capture (1438), 544; French capture (1441), 581
St-Jakob, 624
St-James-de-Beuvron, 197, 567, 658; English siege (1426), 177–9; French capture (1449), 661
St-Jean-le-Thomas, 443
St-Lô, 493, 673, 692
St-Macaire, 606, 725; French siege (1451), 728–9; English capture (1452), 740; French capture (1453), 747
St-Maixent, French capture from rebels (1440), 570–1, 733
St-Malo, 146–7, 166, 641
St-Maur-les-Fossés, abbey, 376

St-Mihiel, 262
St-Omer, 419–20, 513, 551, 562, 572, 574, 580, 782
St-Ouen, 676–9
St-Pierre-du-Vauvray, 577
St-Pierre-le-Moutier, 68
St-Pierre-sur-Dives, 441
St-Pol, John, Bastard of, 309, 394, 456, 482–3
St-Pol, Peter, Count of (*d.* 1433), *see* Luxembourg
St-Pol, Philip, Count of (*d.* 1430), 118, 153–5, 202, 351–2, 416, 419, 437–8, 452, 638, 666, 668, 672–3
St-Pol, Waleran of Luxembourg, Count of (*d.* 1415), 14
St-Quentin, 309, 313, 461
St-Sauveur-le-Vicomte, French capture (1450), 688, 700
St-Sever, 598; French siege (1442), 603–5, 608
St-Sigismond, 291
St-Valéry, 66–7; French capture, Anglo-Burgundian siege (1433), 416, 420, 431; French capture (1434), 437; Burgundian capture (1434), 438
Ste-Barbe, Thomas, 671
Ste-Catherine-de-Fierbois, 263, 270
Ste-Foy-la-Grande, 721
Ste-Suzanne, 171, 400, 710; English siege (1425), 168–9; French capture (1439), 567
Stafford, Humphrey, Earl of, Duke of Buckingham (1444), 340, 358, 376, 379–80, 385, 387, 496, 633, 644, 697, 698
Stafford, John, Bishop of Bath and Wells (1424–43), Archbishop of Canterbury (1443–52), Chancellor of England (1432–50), 193, 394, 416, 418, 450–1, 480, 547, 635–7, 686
Stafford, Robert, 224
Stanstead Abbots, 793
Stewart, John, of Darnley, 78, 99, 104, 120, 139, 168, 200, 218–19, 228, 244, 246–8, 529
Stewart, Margaret, of Scotland, Dauphine of France, 228, 248, 426, 528–9
Stewart, Walter, 114–15
Stewart, Walter, Earl of Atholl, 528
Stourton, John, 730
Strasbourg, 623, 625

INDEX

Streatlam, 720
Suffolk, Earl, Marquess, Duke of, *see* Pole
Suffolk, Charles Brandon, Duke of (*d.* 1545), 770
Sully-sur-Loire, 234, 250, 295, 342, 343, 425
Surienne, François de, 103, 433, 544, 581, 593, 626, 656, 658–60, 662–3, 681, 713
Surienne, Jean de, 785
Swillington, George, 607, 726, 730, 732
Switzerland, Swiss Confederation, xii, 623–4, 768, 805
Swynford, Katherine, Duchess of Lancaster, 7, 113

Tachov, battle (1427), 286
Tailboys, William, 646, 683–4
Talaru, Amadée, Archbishop of Lyon, 445
Talbot, John, Lord, Marshal of France (Lancastrian, 1436), Earl of Shrewsbury (1442), Lieutenant in Guyenne (1452–3), 212–13, 224–5, 241–2, 269, 272, 276, 279, 289–93, 433–5, 437–9, 447, 456–7, 482–4, 490, 492–4, 500, 506, 534–7, 541, 543–4, 557–9, 567, 575–7, 580–1, 583–7, 592–4, 621, 630, 632, 653, 659, 667–9, 675–6, 679, 682, 689–90, 704, 707, 623, 636, 738–46, 748, 759–60, 770, 793, 798, 808
Talbot, John, Viscount Lisle, 741, 745
Tancarville, 38–9, 465, 491, 534; English siege (1437), 536–7
Tarascon, 425
Tartas, French capture (1438), 600; English siege (1440), 600–2; French siege (1442), 603–4, 608
Tasta, Pey du, 719, 733, 736–7, 752
Taverne, Antoine de la, 471–2
taxation (Brittany), 83
taxation (Burgundy), 509–10, 512
taxation (England), 15–18, 193, 226, 332–3, 378, 394, 418–19, 427–8, 490–1, 630–1, 665, 695–6, 720, 794, 806
taxation (Normandy), 36, 171, 488, 560, 654, 708–9, 760
taxation (Lancastrian France), 22, 33–5, 173–4, 392–3
taxation (Valois France), 71–3, 75, 108, 164, 196–7, 343, 537–9, 568, 569–70, 583, 590–1, 627, 653, 690, 706, 738, 762, 780, 800–5

Teutonic Order, 716
Teylingen, 208
Thérouanne, 419, 520
Thian, John Bastard of, 556, 557–8
Thoisy, Jean, 315–16
Thouars, 231
Tideswell, 799
Tilleman, Henry, 134
Tiptoft, John, 204, 340, 406
Titchfield, abbey, 622, 633
Toison d'Or, King of Arms, 450–1, 479
Tombelaine, 147; French siege (1450), 700
Tonnerre, 385
Tonneins, 600
Torcy, 37; French capture (1429), 333, 375, 485; English siege (1430), 335, 336, 342, 376
Toul, 254, 262, 625
Toulongeon, Jean de, Marshal of Burgundy, 95–6, 98, 101–2, 143, 197
Toulongeon, Antoine de, Marshal of Burgundy, 102, 381–3
Toulouse, 70, 603, 607
Touques, 670
Touraine, duchy, 62, 74–5, 120, 179, 198, 424, 465, 599, 626, 784, 786
Touraine, John, Duke of (*d.* 1417), Dauphin of France, 9–10, 125
Tournai, Tournaisis, 66, 74, 118, 142, 766; English capture (1513), 770–1
Tournelle, Guillaume de la, *bailli* of the Mountains, 297
Tournus, 68–9
Tours, 104, 120, 127–9, 138, 163, 165, 174, 176, 196–7, 231, 233, 270, 282, 283, 423, 453–4, 494, 528, 619, 621, 645, 648–9, 721, 724–5, 726; truce (1444), 620–1, 622, 628, 633–4, 638, 641, 650, 664, 718, 785; Estates-General (1484), 494, 709, 787–8, 802, 805, 807
Tours, Archbishops, *see* Gélu, Coëtquis
Toury, 232
Towton, battle (1461), 757, 762
Trévières, 692
Troyes (city), 2, 24, 93, 102, 323; French siege (1429), 298–301, 303–4, 306
Troyes, treaty (1420), 2, 23–4, 25, 30, 31, 65, 85, 86, 87, 88, 109, 122, 155, 200, 214, 254, 256, 306–7, 315, 331, 387, 405, 407, 413, 450, 451, 458, 463, 466–8, 471, 475, 477, 503, 613, 641, 809

Troyes, Bishop, *see* Lesguisé
Tucé, 784
Turner, J. M. W., 788
Tyburn, 588, 645, 685, 687, 700

Uitkerke, Roland van, 183, 195
Upton, Nicholas, herald, 20
Utrecht, Prince-Bishop of, *see* Diepholt

Valenciennes, 152, 203
Valognes, 673; English siege (1450), 691–2; French capture (1450), 700
Valperga, Teodoro di, 127, 140, 239, 284, 322, 353, 729, 742
Vannes, 547, 659
Vaucouleurs, 144, 253, 255–6, 261–3, 270
Vaudémont, 382
Vaudémont, Antoine, Count of, 254, 381–2, 555
Vaudrey, Philibert de, 180
Vaudrey, Pierre de, 447
Vaux-de-Cernay, abbey, 783
Venables, 662
Venables, Richard, 441
Vendôme, 171, 176, 216, 218, 221, 224, 619
Vendôme, Count of, *see* Bourbon
Venette, 346–8, 356
Venice, 244, 405, 7335, 36
Verberie, 353–4
Verdun, 254, 256, 625
Vere, Robert, 666, 681, 689, 695
Vergil, Polydore, 530
Verly, Colard de, 74
Vernet, Jean du ('Le Camus de Beaulieu'), 210
Verneuil, 37, 216, 577, 593, 626, 658; battle (1424), xi, 133–41, 143, 146, 171, 214, 254, 284, 791; French capture (1429), 334, (1435), 455, (1449), 663, 668, 672
Vernon, 126, 228, 317, 576, 583; French siege (1449), 671–2
Vertus, 68; French capture, English siege (1426), 145
Vexin, 29, 31–2, 314, 534–5, 536, 554, 680
Vézélay, 385, 434
Vicques, 441
Vierzon, 73, 164
Vieux-Pont, 692

Vignolles, Amadoc de, 379, 438
Vignolles, Étienne de ('La Hire'), 67–8, 101, 106, 117–19, 121, 123, 134, 142, 144, 171, 217, 219–22, 225–6, 231, 234, 237, 240, 245, 247–9, 255, 273–4, 275–6, 278, 280, 289, 292, 306, 311–13, 315, 377–8, 380, 425, 438–9, 449, 455–7, 469, 486, 488, 495–6, 518, 605, 609
Villandrando, Rodrigo de, 230, 352, 382, 404–5, 425, 544–50, 601, 625
Villandraut, 749
Villars, Raymond de, 434
Ville, Bidau de, 726
Villedieu, 736
Villiers de, Jean de, lord of l'Île-Adam, Marshal of France (Lancastrian), 30, 34, 101, 105–6, 117, 123, 127, 142, 154, 303–4, 310, 323, 330, 337, 403, 434, 439, 453–4, 484, 485, 498, 502–3, 538
Vincennes, 3, 37, 286, 323, 377, 387, 509, 549; French capture (1436), 498
Vire, 38, 188, 489, 690, 693, 694, 702
Visconti, *see* Milan, Duke of
Vitré, 198, 660
Vitry-en-Perthois, 66, 68, 106, 142
Vliet, Jan van, 182

Wakefield Bridge, battle (1460), 759–60
Wales, 7, 13, 33, 51, 242–3, 482, 645, 716, 779
Wallier, Richard, 316
Wallingford, 688
Walsingham, Thomas, 792
Wancourt, Louis de, 417, 421
War of the Common Weal (1465), 765, 771, 785, 789, 806
Warham, William, Archbishop of Canterbury, 774
Warkworth, 666–7
Warwick, Richard Beauchamp, Earl of, Lieutenant in Normandy (1438–9), 40, 145, 194, 198–201, 214, 217–18, 220–1, 224–5, 315, 331, 340–1, 363–4, 366, 369, 372, 381, 386, 400, 415–16, 421–2, 533, 535, 542–6, 550, 558, 579, 632, 695, 793
Warwick, Earl of, *see* Neville
Waterhouse, Thomas, 442–3
Waurin, Jean de, 43, 130, 133–4, 136–7, 157, 195, 226, 290–1, 293, 335, 522, 598, 645, 665, 709

INDEX

Welling, 737
Wells, William, Bishop of Rochester, 573–4
Wenlock, John, 620
Wentworth, Thomas, Lord, 775
Westminster, 186–7, 189, 193, 195, 204, 207, 330, 332, 379, 384–5, 410, 418, 421, 430, 551, 573, 575, 716–18, 576, 590, 611, 613, 619–20, 624, 637, 648, 684–6, 687, 688, 700, 713, 714, 716, 717–19, 737, 744, 757, 760
Wheathamstead, John of, Abbot of St Albans, 685
Whitchurch, 748–9
William III, King of England (1689–1702), 809
William of Gévaudan ('William the Shepherd'), 260–1, 327–8, 380
Winchelsea, 333, 405, 416, 501
Winchester, 646, 667
Wingfield, 423, 698
Willoughby, Robert Lord, 27, 45–6, 47, 99, 105, 316, 325, 334–5, 380, 393, 398, 400–1, 404, 439–40, 458, 484, 486, 492, 497–8, 502–6, 542
Wimborne, 618
Windsor, 2, 6, 113, 561
Woodville, Richard, *see* Rivers

Worcester, William, 45, 46, 47, 537, 597, 666, 692, 709, 802
Wulpen, 524

Yker, Roger, 442–3
York, 114
York, Edmund Langley, Duke of (*d.* 1415), 491
York, Richard, Duke of (*d.* 1460), Lieutenant in Normandy (1436–7, 1441–6), Lieutenant in Ireland (1448–50), 40, 386, 491–2, 500–1, 536–9, 542–3, 546, 566, 580–3, 585–6, 588–9, 591–2, 594, 596–8, 603, 608, 612–13, 619–20, 627, 631–2, 634, 635, 640–2, 645, 648–9, 681, 686, 700, 722–5, 736–8, 744, 752, 757–61, 763–4, 781, 794, 796
Young, Thomas, 725
Ypres, 16, 511, 517, 521, 523, 528

Zeeland, county, 10, 11, 22, 90, 91, 181–6, 190–1, 193–4, 203–4, 208–9, 441, 448, 516, 526, 528, 767
Zevenbergen, 185; Cod siege (1427), 204
Zierikzee, 190
Zuiderzee, 204, 207
Zurich, siege (1444), 625–6

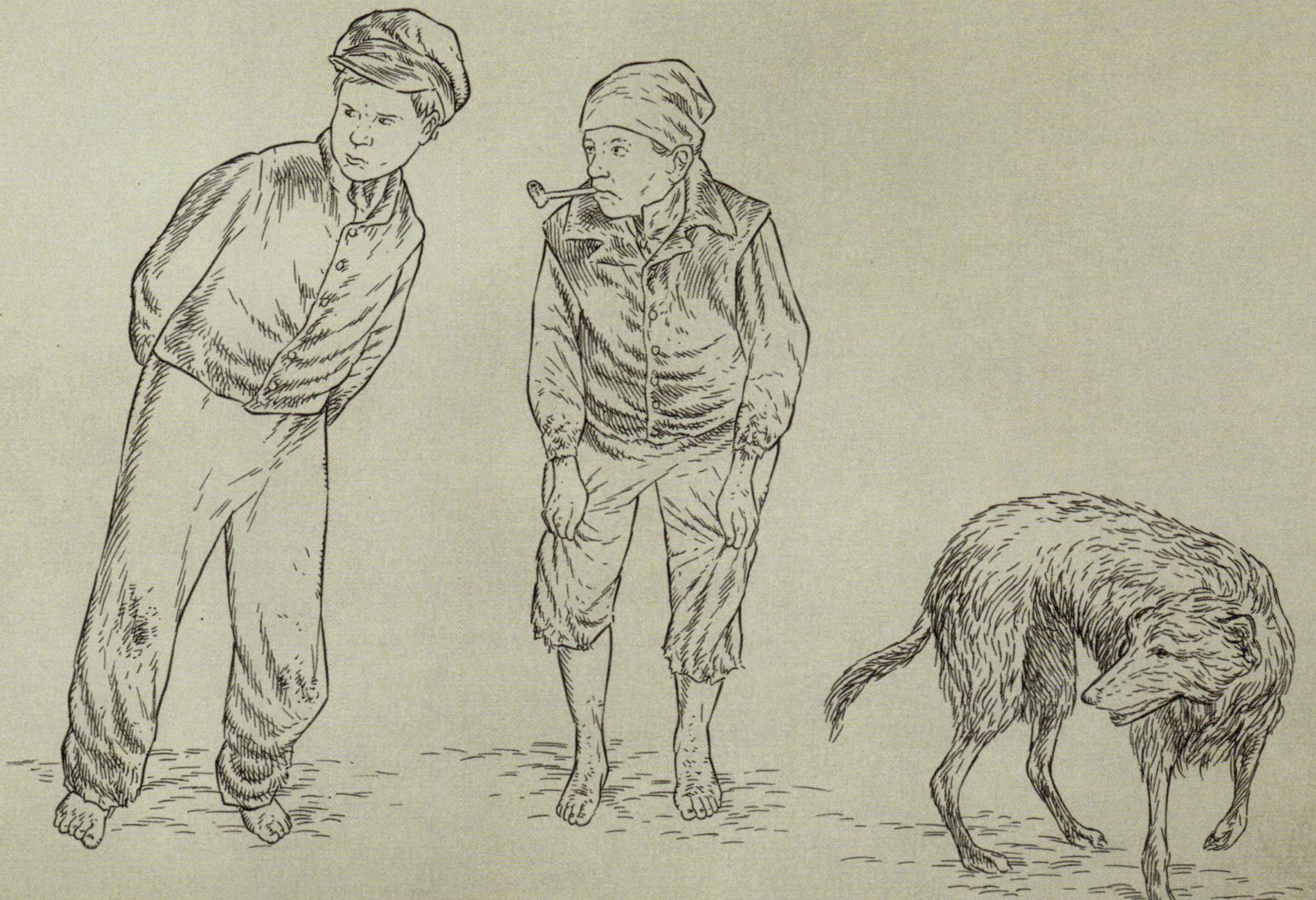

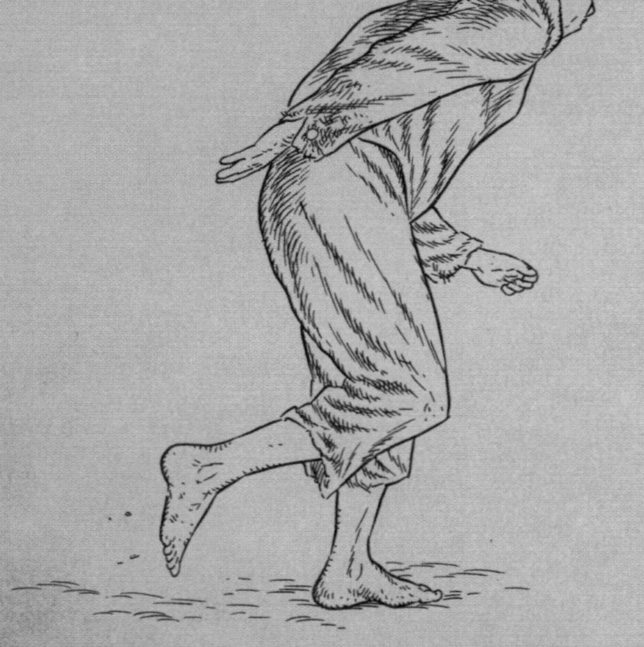

A–Z

OF

CONVICTS

IN

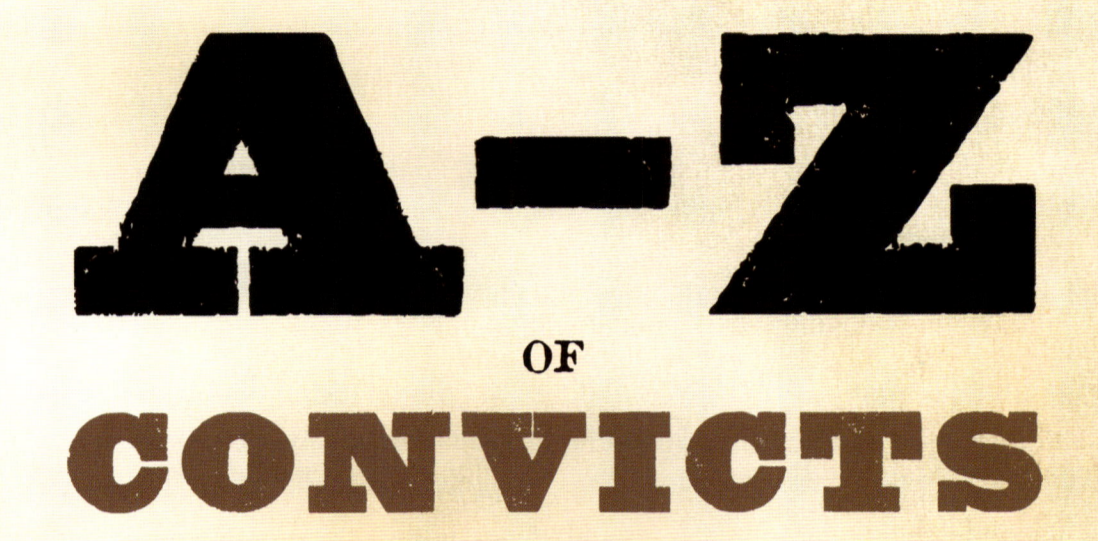

VAN DIEMEN'S LAND

WRITTEN AND
ILLUSTRATED BY

SIMON BARNARD

t

TEXT PUBLISHING MELBOURNE AUSTRALIA
TEXTPUBLISHING.COM.AU   SIMONBARNARD.COM.AU

INTRODUCTION

THE ISLAND OF VAN DIEMEN'S LAND WAS HOME TO ABORIGINES FOR AN estimated 40,000 years before Dutch explorer Abel Janszoon Tasman named it in 1642. In honouring the Governor-General of the Dutch East Indies, Anthony van Diemen, Tasman inadvertently bestowed a title that would resonate as a living hell for many of the convicts sentenced to transportation to this distant place.

Van Diemen's Land was established as a British penal colony, and the first convicts arrived in 1803. During the following 50 years, approximately 73,000 men, women and children were transported to Van Diemen's Land. Approximately 90 per cent of convicts were transported for theft. Standard sentences were seven- and 14-year terms. More serious crimes, such as arson and mutiny, could result in a life sentence.

In the early days of transportation, convicts were landed in New South Wales before being shipped to Van Diemen's Land. In 1812, convicts began to be transported directly to Van Diemen's Land from Britain. In that same year the two counties of Van Diemen's Land that had been controlled by district commanders were brought together under the command of a lieutenant-governor who was situated in Hobart Town. The lieutenant-governor was under the command of the governor of New South Wales until 1825, when Van Diemen's Land was proclaimed a separate colony.

Convicts made up a significant proportion of the Van Diemonian population and there were two systems for managing them. From 1803 until 1840, convicts were assigned to work for colonists under a system called the Assignment System. From 1840 until 1856, they worked at probation stations under the Probation System.

Both systems had their problems. Whether convicts should undergo severe punishment to deter potential criminals or be rehabilitated to take their place in colonial society was hotly debated. The Bigge inquiry of 1819 resulted in harsher punishments and stricter surveillance. Later, in 1837, the Molesworth Commission found that the treatment of convicts under the Assignment System amounted to slavery in many cases. The findings led to the introduction of the Probation System.

The authorities took great care to determine the skills of newly arrived convicts in order to place them in useful employment. Convict labour built bridges, roads, penal establishments, hospitals, courts and ships as well as houses, farms, chapels, cemeteries, schools and waterworks. But convicts also worked as overseers, police constables, signalmen, teachers, artists, clerks, maids, cooks, nurses and farmers.

Punishments for further crimes or misbehaviour were harsh. Serious offenders were executed. Others were sent to the notorious penal stations of Port Arthur, Sarah Island or Maria Island where conditions were often dismal and the work harrowing. Offending convicts could also have their sentences increased or be ordered to hard labour, floggings, time in leg irons or time imprisoned. In the 1840s, corporal punishment began to give way to psychological punishments such as solitary confinement.

For good behaviour, convicts were awarded a ticket-of-leave, which allowed them to possess property and to work for wages. For continued good conduct they were awarded a conditional pardon and then a free pardon. Some freed convicts returned to Britain or Ireland after completing their sentences or receiving a free pardon. But most stayed in Van Diemen's Land, in the new and growing society forged through their labours.

After a campaign by Van Diemonians, the transportation of convicts to Van Diemen's Land ended in 1853. The last vestige of the convict system, the penal station at Port Arthur, closed in 1877.

The illustrations of convicts in this book are based on contemporary records that detail their physical features such as height, hair colour and tattoos. Other illustrations are drawn from architectural plans, written descriptions and surviving artifacts.

ABSCONDER

An absconder, or 'bolter', was a convict who fled confinement. Some managed to start over with false identities; others tried their hand at bushranging or tried to make their way to other colonies by sea. Most were caught, and some died on the run. A convict could be charged with absconding after a 12-hour absence. In 1846 an *Absconding Act* was passed and offenders could be charged with felony and sentenced to a further 15 years.

Rewards

The government advertised rewards to encourage Van Diemonians to help bring absconders to justice. The standard reward was £2, and colonists were also offered land grants, while convicts could be rewarded with their freedom. The bushranger Matthew Brady was said to have retaliated by offering a reward of 20 gallons of rum for the capture of Lieutenant-Governor Arthur. In 1830, a *Harbouring Act* was passed. It allowed fines of up to £100 for assisting absconders.

Haversack

A bag to carry equipment was essential. But being caught with an escape kit could land you in big trouble. Brothers Phillip and Michael Flannagan were given 50 lashes and sent to Sarah Island for stealing two canvas bags and plotting an escape. Soon after arriving, however, they disappeared without trace.

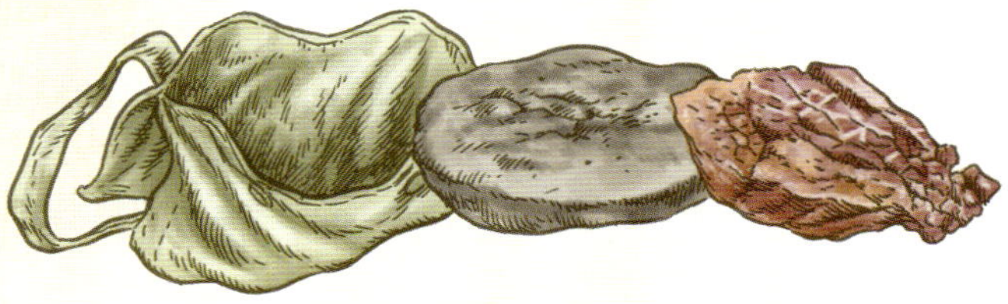

Food

Finding food was difficult for absconders. Plundering Aboriginal camps or purloining livestock was a way to stock up. James Goodwin and Thomas Connelly lived on mushrooms, grass roots and berries when their food ran out. Francis Oates was lucky to find a fish, but when his friend James Williamson ate it without him, Oates beat him to death with a stick. Nails could be fashioned into fishhooks and attached to bark or thread unpicked from government slops. The drowned body of absconder George Clay was found with several fishhooks wrapped around his neck.

Mary Ann Anderson

In January 1826, assigned convict Mary Ann Anderson threatened to knock her master's brains out with a fire poker. She was sent to the Cascades Female Factory, but her master requested she be returned to him as good servants were hard to find.

Clothes

Plain clothes enabled absconders to blend in with the public. Eleanor Philips was found disguised as a man three months after absconding. A spare pair of boots was invaluable. Blankets and greatcoats were also a huge comfort.

Fire

Convicts lit fires using tinder, typically dry straw or grass, which was ignited by striking a piece of steel against flint to produce sparks. Scorched pieces of clothing, known as charcloth, made ideal tinder in wet weather. Absconders also packed charcoal to use in campfires as it minimised conspicuous clouds of smoke.

Utensils

Vessels for carrying water and cooking were crucial. When Edward O'Hara absconded he managed to make off with a three-gallon kettle. Knives and axes were highly prized for cutting food and wood and also as weapons.

Alexander Pearce

Alexander Pearce was convicted of stealing six pairs of shoes and sentenced to seven years. He arrived in Van Diemen's Land in March 1820. In July 1822, he was sent to Sarah Island, but escaped with seven other convicts. In the inhospitable bush of the west coast, they ate boiled fern roots and leather from their kangaroo skin jackets before they set upon one of their own and murdered him. His heart, liver and flesh were rationed, but after a few days it was all gone. Two men fled, fearing for their lives, but the remaining five absconders struggled on. Soon they drew lots, and the man who drew the short straw said his prayers before submitting to the axe. Three more men were murdered and eaten, and only Pearce and Robert Greenhill remained. One night Pearce wrestled the axe from Greenhill and killed him. A week later, he made it to settled country, but two months later he was back in gaol. The authorities could not substantiate his ghastly tale and he was returned to Macquarie Harbour where, in November 1823, Thomas Cox convinced him to escape again. When Pearce eventually surrendered, a piece of flesh was found in his possession and a search uncovered Cox's remains. His body was horribly mutilated; the head and hands were lopped off, the torso was strung from a tree with the bowels, liver and heart wrenched out and strips of flesh sliced from the buttocks, thighs and calves. Pearce was found guilty of murder and executed in Hobart Town in July 1824.

ASSIGNMENT

Under the Assignment System convicts were assigned to work for the government and colonists. The convicts provided cheap labour for the construction of infrastructure, and it was hoped they would be reformed from their criminal ways. Masters had to supply their servants with food, clothes, blankets, comfortable lodgings and medicine. Many convicts were better off than free labourers in Britain. Others, however, were abused by their masters. In 1838, an inquiry headed by William Molesworth equated assignment with slavery, and the Assignment System was abolished and replaced with the Probation System.

BAKERY

A bakery or cookhouse was essential to all penal establishments. Bakeries were manned by convicts. Some had only one baker, but larger ones needed up to a dozen to provide the hundreds of loaves required every day. Bakers had to be trustworthy as they had access to stores. Food could be sold on the black market and flour was highly sought after because it could keep indefinitely. In March 1829, Richard Bruin spent three weeks in solitary confinement for stealing flour. James Woodward, chief baker at Sarah Island, absconded after stealing flour and disappeared without trace.

Ovens and Tools

Masonry ovens were made of fireproof brick. Heat radiated from a fire within the baking chamber, and loaves were lifted in and out of the oven with a peel. A rooker was used to shift hot coals, and ash was scraped into a bucket with a shovel and hoe.

Van Diemonian Bread

Bread was the most important item of food for convicts. Martin Cash sold his boots for a loaf and Joseph Clarke was transported for life for stealing bread. In September 1834, a *Bread Act* was introduced that specified that all loaves be weighed in the presence of the purchaser. Convict constable Bartholomew Gageiro was sold a loaf by Joseph Paterson that hadn't been weighed. Paterson was fined 5 shillings. Maintaining a decent standard of bread was difficult. Ingredients were often poor in quality and some bakers just weren't up to the task. In 1842, it was reported that the bread at the Hobart Town prisoners' barracks was so bad that convicts threw it to the dogs, preferring to go hungry.

William Cripps

William Cripps, a 23-year-old baker transported for stealing footwear, arrived in Hobart Town in February 1844. After gaining his ticket-of-leave in May 1850, he established a bakery in Sandy Bay with his wife Eliza Burchett. Cripps' baking expertise was passed on to his descendants, and his name has remained synonymous with baking.

Bread and Damper

Van Diemonian pastoralist Edward Abbot wrote the following recipe for bread. *Put a bushel of flour into a kneading trough. Mix a pint of yeast with a pint of tepid water. Make a well in the centre of the flour. Pour in the yeast mixture, gradually incorporating enough flour to make a thin batter. Mix well for a minute or two. Sprinkle batter with a little flour and cover with a thickly folded cloth to keep warm. Set it by the fire, ensuring there are no draughts. When the batter has risen, work in six ounces of salt and the remaining flour, adding more water if required, to form a soft dough and knead well. Form into loaves. Allow these to rise until doubled in bulk and place in a previously heated oven. Bake for approximately one hour for a four-pound loaf.*

Damper is the 'bread of the bush'. Flour, salt and water were mixed and shaped into a loaf and then cooked in the ashes of a campfire.

BED

Convicts slept in hammocks and beds made from wooden boards, though they often went without beds and slept on the ground. At times they were issued sturdy iron beds that could be neatly disassembled. Bedding was usually two blankets, a rug and a canvas mattress, called a palliasse, filled with wool, straw, sawdust or hair. The first duty of every convict each morning was to fold their bedding. Sometimes bedding was used to smother another convict to stop them witnessing a theft, and act known as 'blanketing'.

In July 1826, James Darcy, Richard Sutton, John Lomas and George Haycraft blanketed Peter Aylward and stole a knife, comb and cash. They received life sentences.

BLACKSMITH

A blacksmith's wares were an essential part of day-to-day life. The blacksmith shop at Port Arthur contained six forges where up to 37 men worked. They made and mended tools for their fellow convicts and produced an array of items such as bands, bars, bells, bolts, clamps, cleavers, cranes, hammers, hinges, hooks, keys, locks, latches, mauls and nails. Nailers had to produce a certain number of nails per week. In September 1834, Daniel Nightingale was given 25 lashes for not completing his quota.

Bellows
Working metal requires very high temperatures that could only be obtained by supplying additional air to the forge. Blacksmiths used two-chambered forge bellows to pump air into the fire. Working a lever drew air into the bottom chamber of the bellows, then forced it into the top chamber and out the nozzle.

Tools
Blacksmiths used tongs to hold hot metal. They were also equipped with a range of hammers, a vice and chisels. A large 'slack tub' held water to cool the hot metal.

Coal
Blacksmiths heated metal over a large hearth known as a forge. Coal was placed in the hearth and ignited. Inside the hearth, the coal transformed into burning coke. The blacksmith adjusted the amount of coal and the airflow from the bellows to get the temperature right. Blacksmiths at Sarah Island used 20 to 30 casks of coal every week.

Anvil
Blacksmiths beat the red-hot metal into shape against an anvil, an iron block with a smooth steel face, which was hardened so it didn't dent under the blows. In June 1824, John Clayton was charged with stealing an anvil. He narrowly avoided a death sentence, but received another seven-year term.

Grindstone
To sharpen a tool, its blunt edge was held against a large circular rotating stone. As the grindstone turned, it wore away the metal to produce a sharp edge.

John Barker
A skilled blacksmith could produce contraband items, so blacksmiths were closely monitored. John Barker, a watchmaker and gunsmith, was overseer of blacksmiths at Sarah Island. In January 1834, he ingeniously forged a tomahawk and two pistols from old gun barrels and scrap metal. Once armed, Barker and nine others seized the *Frederick* and sailed to Chile.

Nailed
Joseph Wilkes, a nailer, was sentenced to seven years' transportation in 1831 for stealing 69 pounds of iron. He committed many offences whilst serving in a blacksmith shop, including using the forge for his own use, refusing to work, not completing his quota, forging a knife and being suspected of forging a spear to catch fish.

Hit and Miss
Blacksmiths were entrusted to fit their fellow convicts with leg irons. In December 1824, William Yates copped 25 lashes for using a broken rivet that would have let the wearer slip his irons off. Another blacksmith had six months added to his sentence for removing his own leg irons twice in one week.

BRIDGE

In 1821 Governor Macquarie ordered that a bridge be built over the Macquarie River. The Ross Bridge was completed the following year. It was 75 metres long with 14 arches, and was made of stone buttresses topped with logs and covered with earth and gravel. By 1828, two of the central piers had partially collapsed and the bridge was in desperate need of repair. Six convicts were set to the task, but work stopped when their overseer was recalled to Hobart Town for failing to adequately supervise the work. The bridge finally collapsed in 1831 under the weight of a team of oxen. John Lee Archer, the colonial architect, designed a new bridge, but construction was delayed because of an argument about location. Brick kilns and a sandstone quarry were established but the convict crew spent most of their time working illegally for locals. Jorgen Jorgenson's report to Governor Arthur declared that corruption was rife and convicts had been supplying colonists with government property and working for goods and cash. Several convicts, including James Colbeck, were returned to Hobart Town for punishment. Colbeck was recalled in 1835 and work finally began in earnest. Under the direction of two talented convicts, Colbeck and Daniel Herbert, and overseen by Captain William Turner, the bridge was finally finished in just over a year.

Keystones

The keystone of each middle arch features a shield and crown flanked by military accompaniments. On the other keystones are a crowned lion (the symbol of Great Britain) clutching a lamb in its claws. This could be a reference to the treatment of convicts.

Daniel Herbert

Stonemason Daniel Herbert arrived in Hobart Town in December 1827 to serve a life sentence. In 1835, he was sent to work on the Ross Bridge, and he received a full pardon in 1842. Herbert was laid to rest in the Ross cemetery in a tomb carved by his own hand. It is thought that the 25th voussoir in the middle arch on the southern face bears his likeness.

Mail Service

The first regular overland mail service started in 1816. Convicts were permitted to send and receive mail, but all correspondence was inspected. In October 1833, Samuel Wilson received 10 days in solitary for sending letters without permission. In 1834 John Cox established a weekly passenger and parcel service. In that year 77,560 letters and 84,320 newspapers were sent from Hobart Town. When Cox died his wife took over the business. At the height of her career, she owned seven coaches and 150 horses.

Parapet

Each wall, or 'parapet', bears the name of the then governor, Lieutenant-Governor Arthur, and the year the bridge was completed. The northern parapet states that the distance to Launceston is 48 miles, while the southern parapet incorrectly says that Hobart Town is 69 miles away, five miles short.

James Colbeck

English stonemason James Colbeck worked on Buckingham Palace before falling destitute and resorting to burglary. He was sentenced to life and arrived in Van Diemen's Land in November 1828. He worked on the Ross Bridge for a daily wage of 1 shilling and received a conditional pardon for his service.

Mary Herbert

Mary Witherington arrived in Van Diemen's Land in January 1829 to serve 14 years for stealing blankets. In July 1835 she married Daniel Herbert. It is thought her likeness is carved into the 25th voussoir on the left arch on the northern face.

Voussoirs

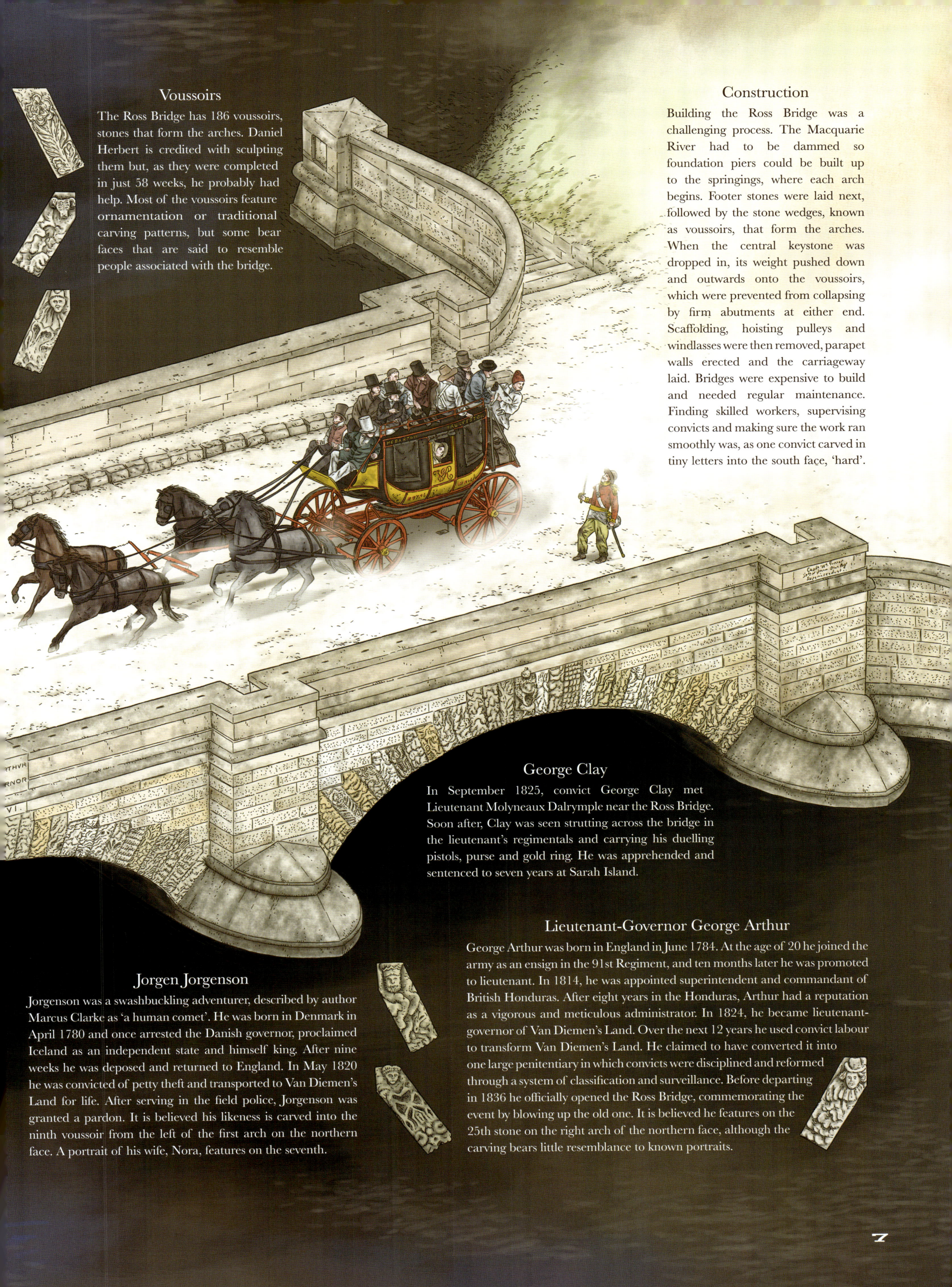

The Ross Bridge has 186 voussoirs, stones that form the arches. Daniel Herbert is credited with sculpting them but, as they were completed in just 58 weeks, he probably had help. Most of the voussoirs feature ornamentation or traditional carving patterns, but some bear faces that are said to resemble people associated with the bridge.

Construction

Building the Ross Bridge was a challenging process. The Macquarie River had to be dammed so foundation piers could be built up to the springings, where each arch begins. Footer stones were laid next, followed by the stone wedges, known as voussoirs, that form the arches. When the central keystone was dropped in, its weight pushed down and outwards onto the voussoirs, which were prevented from collapsing by firm abutments at either end. Scaffolding, hoisting pulleys and windlasses were then removed, parapet walls erected and the carriageway laid. Bridges were expensive to build and needed regular maintenance. Finding skilled workers, supervising convicts and making sure the work ran smoothly was, as one convict carved in tiny letters into the south face, 'hard'.

George Clay

In September 1825, convict George Clay met Lieutenant Molyneaux Dalrymple near the Ross Bridge. Soon after, Clay was seen strutting across the bridge in the lieutenant's regimentals and carrying his duelling pistols, purse and gold ring. He was apprehended and sentenced to seven years at Sarah Island.

Jorgen Jorgenson

Jorgenson was a swashbuckling adventurer, described by author Marcus Clarke as 'a human comet'. He was born in Denmark in April 1780 and once arrested the Danish governor, proclaimed Iceland as an independent state and himself king. After nine weeks he was deposed and returned to England. In May 1820 he was convicted of petty theft and transported to Van Diemen's Land for life. After serving in the field police, Jorgenson was granted a pardon. It is believed his likeness is carved into the ninth voussoir from the left of the first arch on the northern face. A portrait of his wife, Nora, features on the seventh.

Lieutenant-Governor George Arthur

George Arthur was born in England in June 1784. At the age of 20 he joined the army as an ensign in the 91st Regiment, and ten months later he was promoted to lieutenant. In 1814, he was appointed superintendent and commandant of British Honduras. After eight years in the Honduras, Arthur had a reputation as a vigorous and meticulous administrator. In 1824, he became lieutenant-governor of Van Diemen's Land. Over the next 12 years he used convict labour to transform Van Diemen's Land. He claimed to have converted it into one large penitentiary in which convicts were disciplined and reformed through a system of classification and surveillance. Before departing in 1836 he officially opened the Ross Bridge, commemorating the event by blowing up the old one. It is believed he features on the 25th stone on the right arch of the northern face, although the carving bears little resemblance to known portraits.

BUSHRANGER

During colonisation, some convicts were sent into the bush with guns and dogs to hunt for food for the struggling colony. Some decided to leave behind the hardships of penal servitude and remain at large. They survived by stealing and trading and became known as bushrangers. Most attempts to bring them to justice failed. In May 1814, Lieutenant-Governor Davey promised to pardon all who returned by December, excluding those guilty of murder. Many outlaws came in and had their slates wiped clean, but some then returned to the bush. The most effective way to bring bushrangers in was to offer rewards for their capture and to hand out penalties to anyone who helped them.

Clothing and Bedding

Kangaroo and possum skins were prized for their warmth, durability and ability to provide camouflage. Sixty possum skins sewn together made a 7-foot square blanket, which weighed about 8 pounds and was easily carried in a knapsack. John Frederick Mortlock sold one for the hefty price of £5. Bushrangers made and mended their own clothes, and needles and thread were greatly valued. When William Martin was apprehended in April 1815, he had needles, a thimble and kangaroo skins among his possessions. At the time of Michael Howe's death, he was clad entirely in kangaroo skins.

Disguises

Some bushrangers wore handkerchiefs around their faces or changed their facial hair. Others disguised themselves by smearing soot or charcoal over their faces. Despite committing raids with blackened faces, James Regan, James Atterall and Anthony Banks were later identified and executed.

Food and Drink

Flour, sugar, tea, tobacco and alcohol were highly sought after. Lamb and beef were procured from stolen livestock, and local game was often killed and eaten. Cooking utensils were also appropriated. When William Martin absconded in January 1815, he stole apples, a frying pan, a tin pot, a spoon and a knife. Alcohol was the downfall of many bushrangers. After a bout of drunkenness amongst his gang, Matthew Brady destroyed all the remaining liquor while the men slept. It was rumoured, however, that Brady forced his victims to drink hard liquor, leaving them too drunk to raise the alarm.

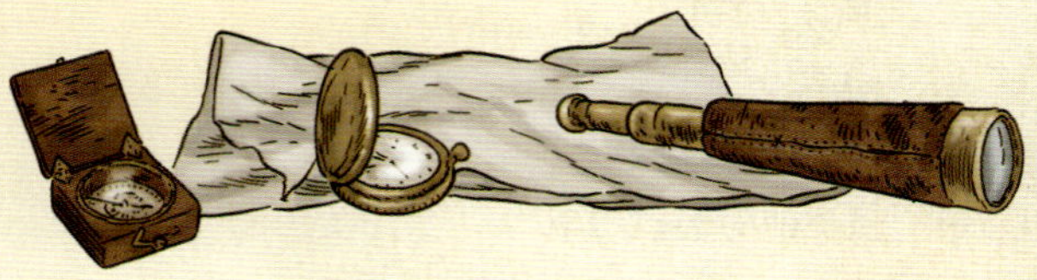

Prized Possessions

Being well informed meant a bushranger could keep one step ahead of the authorities. Telescopes, compasses, watches and newspapers were invaluable. Bushrangers stole weapons at every opportunity. It was not uncommon for one man to carry a rifle, two pistols and several knives. Gunpowder was carried in flasks and powder horns. Bushrangers carried food in knapsacks and hid supplies in hollow trees, logs, caves and huts.

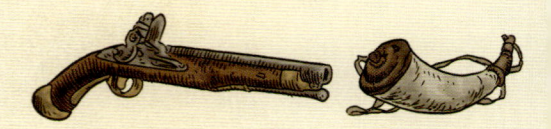

'Black Mary'

Mary Cockerill was called 'Black Mary'; her Aboriginal name is unknown. She was Michael Howe's companion from 1814 to 1817, and her bush skills were of great benefit to him. In 1817 a party of soldiers ambushed the pair and Mary was seized. She was put to work as a tracker and was instrumental in apprehending gang members. Mary died of pulmonic complications in the Colonial Hospital in 1819.

Michael Howe

Michael Howe was born in England in 1787. He was sentenced to seven years' transportation for highway robbery and arrived in Van Diemen's Land in 1812. By 1814, Howe was a member of James Whitehead's gang. In April 1815, a party led by Dennis McCarty tracked down the gang, and two colonists were killed in the ensuing shootout. Later, Whitehead was shot during a raid on McCarty's house, and Howe hacked off his leader's head with a penknife so that headhunters would not be able to claim a reward. In April 1817, a search party came across Howe and his Aboriginal companion, Black Mary. She was captured but Howe escaped. Howe then wrote to Lieutenant-Governor Sorrell requesting a pardon upon surrender. The governor agreed, on the condition that Howe divulge the names of his accomplices. The deal was struck, but Howe's information failed to bring about the capture of any bushrangers, and he returned to the bush. In October 1817, William Drew and George Watts decided to attempt to capture Howe and share the 100-guinea reward. Howe was collared but on the journey back to Hobart Town he stabbed Watts in the belly and shot Drew dead. In September 1818, Howe narrowly avoided capture by John McGill and Aboriginal tracker Musquito. In his haste Howe dropped a knapsack containing a small journal written in kangaroo blood on kangaroo skin; it listed flowers and vegetables he intended to grow and his dreams and nightmares. In October 1818, Robert Warburton, Thomas Worrall and William Pugh devised a plan to capture Howe. Pugh bludgeoned him to death with the butt of his gun. They cut off his head, buried his body in a shallow grave and set off for Hobart Town. Howe's head was hung from the gaol gates before being buried in the grounds.

Matthew Brady

Englishman Matthew Brady was sentenced to seven years' transportation for theft. He arrived in Van Diemen's Land in December 1820. In June 1824, he absconded in a whaleboat with 14 others and embarked on a bushranging career. The gang stole firearms and raided the home of Horatio Mason. During another raid, one of the gang drove a bayonet through a servant's chest. Some gang members were captured and executed, but the diminished group continued to carry out successful robberies. In October 1824, Brady was betrayed by a hut keeper called Thomas Kenton. Brady was wounded and captured, but he later escaped into the bush. The crimes continued, and colonists began deserting their farms for fear of attack. Lieutenant-Governor Arthur raised the reward offered from £10 to 50 guineas, with a conditional pardon for information, and a free pardon and passage to England for Brady's capture. After a violent arson attack on a farm, the reward was raised again, to 100 guineas or 300 acres of land or a ticket-of-leave and passage to England. In March, Brady caught up with Kenton and shot him through the head for his betrayal. A few days later, Brady was shot in the leg. He went into hiding until, wounded and unarmed, he surrendered to John Batman. He was shipped to Hobart Town and hanged in May 1826. Brady's Lookout and Brady's Sugarloaf were named after him.

Musquito

Musquito was born into the Gai-Mariagal tribe of coastal New South Wales and was known as Yerrangoulaga and Bush Muschetta. In 1805, he murdered an Aboriginal woman and was sent to Norfolk Island. Eight years later he was sent to Van Diemen's Land and employed as a tracker. In September 1818, he was promised repatriation to New South Wales in return for tracking Michael Howe. Musquito agreed, but the authorities broke their promise, and Musquito was arrested after fighting with a convict. He escaped and led his own native bushranging gang. His insider knowledge of guns, farms and fighting tactics made him a formidable opponent and he was nicknamed 'The Black Napoleon', 'The Terror of the Bush' and 'The Black Outlaw'. Musquito was captured in August 1824 after being tracked and wounded by a young Aboriginal tracker known as Tegg. Musquito was hanged in Hobart Town in February 1825.

Thomas Jeffries

Thomas Jeffries was born in England in 1791. After serving in the Navy and Army, he was arrested for robbing his friends and family and sentenced to life transportation. He arrived in Sydney in 1817. His time there was marked with escapes, one of which resulted in the cannibalisation of two of his fellow absconders. He was sent to Van Diemen's Land in 1821. In late 1825, he and two others took to the bush. They terrorised huts and homesteads throughout the north. In December, Jeffries' gang shot and wounded a man called Mr Tibbs, killed his servant and took Mrs Tibbs and her baby hostage. Mrs Tibbs was released but the baby was murdered. Soon after, the gang ran out of food and butchered one of its members. The men lived on his flesh for several days before discovering a search party of soldiers asleep in a hut. The gang fired on them and the soldiers fled. Jeffries and his gang were captured soon after. The *Colonial Times* reported that Jeffries had murdered eight people during a three-week killing spree. He was loathed throughout the land and was nearly lynched by an angry mob while being carted to Launceston gaol. Thomas Jeffries was executed in May 1826.

Martin Cash

Martin Cash was born in 1808 in Ireland. He was sentenced to seven years' transportation for shooting a man he caught embracing his mistress. Cash arrived in Sydney in February 1828. After earning his ticket-of-leave, he became involved in cattle duffing and fled to Van Diemen's Land with Eliza Clifford. In 1839, he was convicted of larceny and sentenced to another seven years. He escaped and reunited with Eliza, but he was recognised and sentenced to four years' hard labour at Port Arthur. Working in a stone-breaking gang, he met George Jones and Lawrence Kavanagh, and the three men escaped together on Boxing Day 1842. After a daring swim past the Eaglehawk Neck guard dogs, they began raiding huts and homesteads, earning a reputation for their charm and chivalry to women and children. Cash reunited again with Eliza, but he discovered that she had taken a new lover and resolved to forget her. The gang continued to elude the law until Kavanagh accidentally shot himself through the arm and decided to surrender. When Cash ventured into Hobart Town looking for Eliza, he was captured and sentenced to death. In gaol, he was besieged with gifts from the public. His death sentence was commuted to transportation for life and he was sent to Norfolk Island. After marrying Mary Bennett in March 1854, he returned to Van Diemen's Land and worked in the gardens in the Government Domain. He received a conditional pardon in May 1856 and died at his farm in Glenorchy in August 1877.

Catherine Henrys

Catherine Henrys is believed to have been born in Ireland in 1807. In October 1835, she was sentenced to life in Van Diemen's Land for stealing. Henrys garnered a reputation for absconding and became known as 'Jemmy the Rover'. Jemmy was a slang term for a smart, spruce character, and rover was a term for pirates and vagabonds. In July 1841, Henrys escaped, dressed in men's clothing, and found work as a timber splitter. She was captured a year later and sentenced to three years' hard labour, then sent to the Launceston female factory for assaulting a constable. Henrys cut the bars over her cell door with a sharpened spoon, scaled the factory wall and lowered herself down the other side using a blanket. She was recaptured seven months later and her cross-dressing, timber-splitting exploits became well known. After being granted a conditional pardon in 1850, Catherine Henrys travelled to Melbourne. She died there five years later.

CEMETERY

The first official burial ground in Van Diemen's Land was marked out in May 1804 a short distance from what would become Hobart Town. The earliest known gravestone is dated January 1810 and belongs to a seaman named James Batchelor who was buried at Taroona. Within twenty years, cemeteries were also located at Port Dalrymple, New Norfolk and Sorell. Port Arthur's chaplain, Reverend John Manton, thought nearby Opossum Island was an ideal place to inter the dead. The island's name was changed to Isle de Mort or, more commonly, the Isle of the Dead. It became the final resting place of most people who died at Port Arthur. Convicts towed the dead from Port Arthur to the island by boat. The first convict burial was in 1832, after convict John Hancock was crushed by a log. The last convict burial was probably in 1893. It is thought that the Isle of the Dead holds about 1000 bodies.

Shelter for Funeral Parties

Stonemasons

Thomas Pickering arrived in Van Diemen's Land in November 1842 to serve ten years for larceny. He ended up in Port Arthur in March 1856, by which time he was a skilled stonemason. It is thought that Pickering carved 19 headstones on the Isle of the Dead, 12 of which feature his trademark rope border, and four his autograph. Six other headstones bear the name of Thomas Sanders, a watch finisher serving seven years for housebreaking. John Johnson, a stonemason by trade, was convicted of highway robbery and sentenced to life. He arrived in Van Diemen's Land in October 1837 and worked on buildings such as Customs House and St John's Church before his death at Port Arthur in July 1861.

Gravediggers

John Barron was appointed gravedigger on the Isle of the Dead after arriving in Port Arthur in December 1856. He lived in a small cottage on the island and his provisions were rowed out to him twice a week. He grew flowers not vegetables, as he would not eat food cultivated in a cemetery. Barron received his ticket-of-leave in January 1874 and was replaced by Mark Jeffery. Jeffery was a convicted burglar and was regarded as a hard case. He baked his own bread and amused himself by making mats and brooms and even digging his own grave. If he required urgent attention, he lit a signal fire and a boat was dispatched to investigate. He reportedly lit the fire on several occasions only to inform the arriving officer that he was out of matches. When Port Arthur closed, Jeffrey was sent to Hobart Town. His memoirs, billed as a 'shilling shocker', became a bestseller.

Key to the Isle of the Dead

1. Reverend George Eastman, 1870
2. Three crewmen of the *Echo*, 1840
3. Christopher Meyers, overseer, 1844
4. Benjamin Horne, headmaster, 1843
5. Ann Gibbons, wife, 1838
6. Edward Cart, infant, 1838
7. Joseph Kerr, soldier, 1831
8. Andrew Burns, soldier, 1835
9. George Rogers, seaman, 1836
10. Detliff Wolfe, seaman, 1837
11. George Robinson, surgeon, 1877
12. Elizabeth Lowry, infant
13. James McDivitt, infant, 1840
14. Robert Young, soldier, 1840
15. William Gaynor, soldier, 1841
16. John Jameson, soldier, 1841
17. Robert Flowers, soldier, 1845
18. Daniel Gilmore, soldier, 1844
19. Joseph Ashworth, soldier, 1844
20. John Mullen, soldier, 1844
21. David Lowrey, soldier, 1845
22. John Leonard, overseer, 1845
23. Olive Edmonds, soldier, 1845
24. William Evans, soldier, 1846
25. Robert Acres, assistant superintendent, 1846
26. Eliza Aylett, 1869
27. Alexander Miller, 1845
28. Jannet Clark, infant, 1842
29. Henry Mitchell, infant, 1843 and Francis Mitchell, infant, 1841
30. Samuel Burrows, 1841
31. Footstone of John Strahan, constable, 1871
32. Footstone of Eliza Connolly, infant, 1873
33. Emma Johnson, 1873
34. John Sullivan, overseer, 1869
35. James Halkett, soldier, 1849
36. Footstone for Bridget Smith, 1867
37. John Simpson, soldier, 1847
38. Thomas Farrell, infant, 1845
39. Michael Bryan, soldier, 1846
40. Frances Tooze, infant, 1844
41. James Baxter, soldier, 1848
42. Thomas Bond, soldier, 1846
43. James Glass, soldier, 1846
44. George Staveley, 1870, Julia Staveley, infant, 1851, and Thomas Staveley, infant, with footstone, 1846
45. Sarah Harrison, infant, 1847
46. William Smith, soldier, 1856
47. William Doodie, constable, 1863
48. George Britton, convict, 1861
49. Christina Morley, footstone, 1861
50. Christina Morley, 1861
51. Marguerite Wilkie, infant, 1858
52. Harriet Chatfield, officer's wife, 1859
53. Frances Smith, 1853
54. Henry Burrows, child, 1853
55. George Whittington, infant, 1857 and Kezia Whittington, infant, 1859
56. John McArthur, 1857
57. John Strahan, constable, 1871
58. Eliza Connolly, infant, 1873
59. Redmond Matus, infant, 1853
60. Bridget Smith, 1867
61. Sarah Smith, child, 1860
62. Thomas Farrell, infant, 1854
63. Mary Reilley, infant, 1861
64. John O'Neil, infant, 1835
65. James McLoughlin, convict, 1868
66. Ada Huxtable, infant, 1862
67. Catherine Barnett, infant, 1857
68. Benjamin Goddard, infant, 1859
69. George Marshall, infant, 1875
70. John Aspinall, with footstone, 1869
71. Joseph Lee, ex-convict, 1869
72. William Chadwick, 1864
73. Henry Downer, ex-convict, 1866
74. James Smith, under keeper, 1867
75. John Livesay, ex-convict, 1858
76. Ferdinand Hauth, 1869
77. William Mansfield, convict, 1858
78. Michael Roach, convict, 1865
79. Patrick Howard, ex-convict, 1870
80. Charles Hunter, convict, 1868
81. John Owen, 1869
82. James Forbes, convict, 1866
83. James Goddard, infant, 1856
84. Henry Savery, 1842
85. John Johnson, convict, 1861
86. Edward Spicer, convict, 1854

Burying the Dead

Some contemporary sources describe deceased convicts being placed in rough wooden coffins, without even the shirt they died in. Others claim that bodies were dumped, coffinless, into mass graves and covered with lime. The Isle of the Dead was segregated. The northern end was reserved for the military and free persons, while the southern end was for convicts, who were laid to rest in unmarked graves. In time, attitudes changed and convicts were given headstones.

Gravedigger's Cottage

Henry Savery

Henry Savery was born in England in 1791 and worked as a newspaper editor. In October 1815, he married Eliza Elliot and soon found himself hopelessly in debt. He was sentenced to death in April 1825 for forging bills, but his sentence was later commuted to life transportation. In Hobart Town Savery worked as a clerk in the Colonial Secretary's Office, but when his wife arrived in October 1828 she found him in debt again. In despair, he tried to kill himself by cutting his throat. Eliza returned to England, and Savery was imprisoned for the debt. Whilst incarcerated, he wrote *The Hermit in Van Diemen's Land* under the pseudonym Simon Stukeley, for which he was sued for libel. He also wrote the first Australian novel, *Quintus Servinton*. In June 1832, Savery was granted a ticket-of-leave, but it was revoked following another libel suit. He was finally pardoned, but he soon fell back into debt and resorted to forgery once again. He was sent to Port Arthur where he died in February 1842. On the 150th anniversary of his death, the Fellowship of Australian Writers erected a memorial to Henry Savery carved in the shape of a broadsheet newspaper.

Robert Knopwood

Robert Knopwood was born in June 1763 and was ordained as a priest at the age of 25. He performed the first service in Van Diemen's Land in February 1804. Knopwood also served as magistrate but his reputation for kindness was at odds with the severity of the sentences he handed out. When bushranger Michael Howe surrendered in April 1817, he implicated Knopwood as a contact. Knopwood died in relative poverty in September 1838. His grave remained unmarked until a monument in his honour was erected at Rokeby.

David Collins

David Collins was born in England in March 1756. He followed his father into the military, and he married Maria Stuart in June 1777. In January 1788, he arrived in New South Wales with the First Fleet and later, back in London, wrote *An Account of the English Colony in New South Wales*. In 1802, Collins was appointed lieutenant-governor of Van Diemen's Land. Under-equipped and undermanned, he led the colony through the early years of unrest. He died unexpectedly in March 1810 and, after a large and expensive funeral, was interred in a brick vault inside two Huon pine coffins, one inside the other and one sealed with lead. There were rumours that the vault also held official documents and the corpse of his doctor. St David's Church was erected in Collins' honour. It later blew down in a gale, and St David's Cathedral was built nearby. In May 1838, a sandstone tomb was erected to commemorate his life. In 1925 the vault was accidentally discovered, Collins was exhumed and the rumours regarding the mysterious contents of the vault were laid to rest. Due to the preserving qualities of the Huon pine, the body had been perfectly preserved.

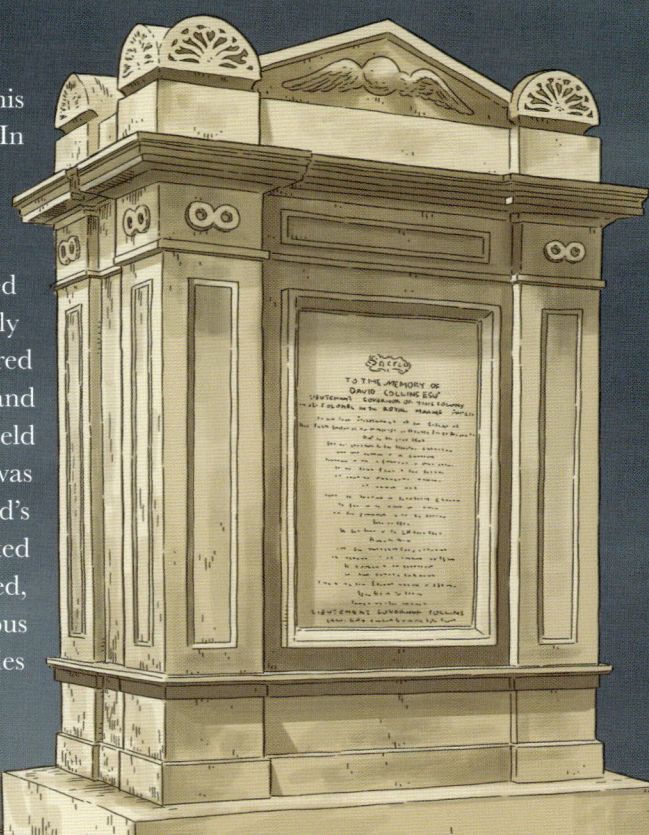

CHAPEL

In 1833 Trinity Chapel was built at the northern end of the Hobart Town prisoners' barracks. The unusual design, by architect John Lee Archer, incorporated cells beneath the chapel and the cruciform shape could seat 500 people in each arm. Convicts entered and exited the chapel through doors from the prisoners' barracks. Combining punishment and prayer was less than ideal, and just a year later plans for a new chapel began. 'Old Trinity' was closed to free inhabitants in 1845. In 1859, the nave and eastern transept were converted into courtrooms, which were used until 1983.

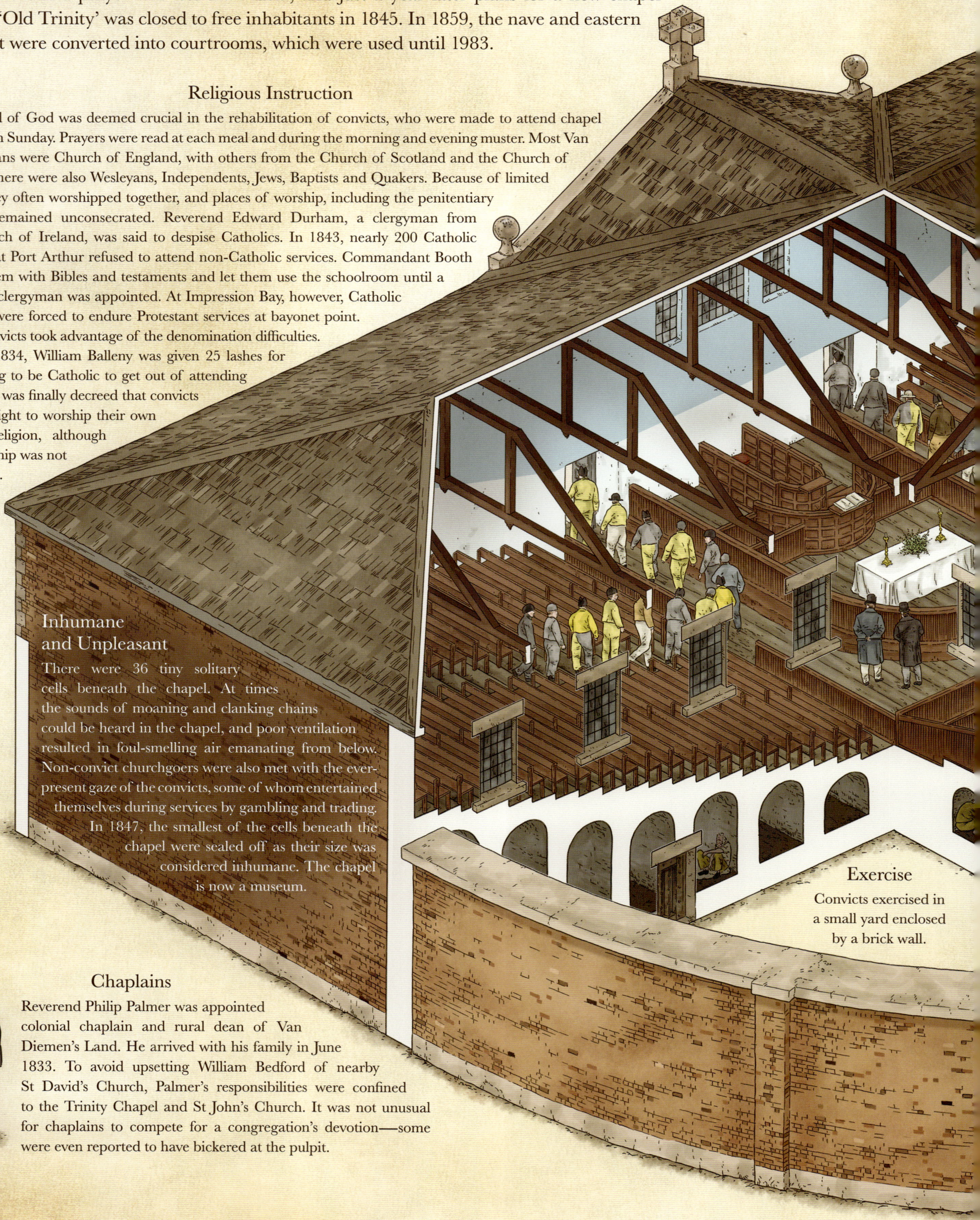

Religious Instruction

The word of God was deemed crucial in the rehabilitation of convicts, who were made to attend chapel twice each Sunday. Prayers were read at each meal and during the morning and evening muster. Most Van Diemonians were Church of England, with others from the Church of Scotland and the Church of Rome. There were also Wesleyans, Independents, Jews, Baptists and Quakers. Because of limited space, they often worshipped together, and places of worship, including the penitentiary chapel, remained unconsecrated. Reverend Edward Durham, a clergyman from the Church of Ireland, was said to despise Catholics. In 1843, nearly 200 Catholic convicts at Port Arthur refused to attend non-Catholic services. Commandant Booth issued them with Bibles and testaments and let them use the schoolroom until a Catholic clergyman was appointed. At Impression Bay, however, Catholic convicts were forced to endure Protestant services at bayonet point. Some convicts took advantage of the denomination difficulties. In May 1834, William Balleny was given 25 lashes for pretending to be Catholic to get out of attending service. It was finally decreed that convicts had the right to worship their own chosen religion, although non-worship was not an option.

Inhumane and Unpleasant

There were 36 tiny solitary cells beneath the chapel. At times the sounds of moaning and clanking chains could be heard in the chapel, and poor ventilation resulted in foul-smelling air emanating from below. Non-convict churchgoers were also met with the ever-present gaze of the convicts, some of whom entertained themselves during services by gambling and trading. In 1847, the smallest of the cells beneath the chapel were sealed off as their size was considered inhumane. The chapel is now a museum.

Exercise

Convicts exercised in a small yard enclosed by a brick wall.

Chaplains

Reverend Philip Palmer was appointed colonial chaplain and rural dean of Van Diemen's Land. He arrived with his family in June 1833. To avoid upsetting William Bedford of nearby St David's Church, Palmer's responsibilities were confined to the Trinity Chapel and St John's Church. It was not unusual for chaplains to compete for a congregation's devotion—some were even reported to have bickered at the pulpit.

Marriage

Although marriages were not officially permitted in the chapel, they did take place. The first occurred in November 1833. Convicts were encouraged to marry, but permission had to be obtained from the lieutenant-governor. When George Brown married Mary Ryan in January 1855 without approval, he was sentenced to nine months' hard labour. Not all marriages were entirely legitimate; it was suspected that many were a guise for 'licentious behaviour'. But marriage was one way for female convicts to improve their situation, and some married into wealth, security and ultimately freedom. A female convict assigned to her husband, however, had greater rights than a free married woman. A convict wife could lodge complaints about her husband and be reassigned if found to be abused.

William Derrincourt

William Derrincourt arrived in Van Diemen's Land in August 1840 to serve ten years for larceny. Confined to a cell below the Trinity Chapel, he claimed to have used his mess spoon as a knife, the metal hoops from his night-tub as a saw and the wooden staves as a pick to hack his way through the roof of his cell and into the chapel above. He escaped through the main entrance, but the clanking of his leg irons alerted a patrolling police constable and he was captured. Derrincourt's adventures were chronicled by Louis Beck in *Old Convict Days*, published in 1899.

The Clock

The world's oldest continuous clockmakers, Thwaites & Reed of London, built the dual-faced clock in 1828. It had to be wound by hand every six days. The clock was installed by convict watchmaker Richard Waters.

Coming and Going

Convicts entered and exited the chapel through two doors located in the southern wall that faced their barracks. The public entered via double doors in the nave.

Sinking Feeling

In June 1834, it was reported that the southern entrance was so muddy that congregants risked losing their boots and stockings in the quagmire.

COALMINE

Van Diemonian coal was of poor quality: in 1838 it sold for 11 shillings per ton, compared to 30 shillings per ton for the superior coal from New South Wales. Because it was cheap, the local coal was still in high demand for fuel, despite its troublesome tendency to spit out live embers.

Pillar and Stall

A shaft was sunk near the coal seam, and then convicts excavated tunnels or 'stalls' in all directions. The roof of each stall was supported by pillars of coal left standing. The man at the face of each tunnel hewed the coal, which was put into carts and pushed to the base of the shaft to be raised to the surface. During each eight-hour daytime shift, the miners sent up 40 carts of coal. When the coal was exhausted in a stall, the miners then worked backwards, extracting the pillars and removing the supporting timber beams, and the tunnel collapsed as they went.

Beasts of Burden

Four convicts were needed on each cart to haul the coal up the steep slopes inside the mine. Three men at the front, called donkeys, were fitted with leather harnesses. The fourth man, the putter, wore a thick pad inside his cap and 'putted' the cart with his head to stop it tipping over. Going downhill, the men rode on the cart and used a brake to guide it. In December 1839 James Jones was killed when a cart crashed into the one he was riding on.

In the Raw

The mines were very hot and stuffy. Many convicts reportedly worked naked and some went barefoot. William Derrincourt worked for a month with no shoes. But he claimed the pain in his feet was so unbearable it drove him to abscond.

Light

Lamps were used in the pitch-black mines. Candles gave better light, but they often went out due to a lack of oxygen and damp conditions. The heat from the lamps added to the stifling conditions.

Cart Rage

In July 1844, Thomas Smith and James Boyle were pushing a cart when they had an argument with overseer John Perry. Smith took a pickaxe and the men bludgeoned Perry to death. They were charged with murder and executed.

A Convict Colliery

Two convict surveyors, James Hughes and George Woodward, discovered coal on the Tasman Peninsula in August 1833. The discovery was welcomed: not only would the colony have its own cheap supply, but mining could occupy the most troublesome convicts with the kind of hard labour that pleased the authorities. In December 1833, a shaft was sunk to commence an underground mine. At 20 metres, no coal was found and water started to seep in. Digging continued, and coal was finally struck in April 1834. By 1838, the main shaft was at 45 metres and the workings stretched 150 metres in several directions. Fifty tonnes of coal were extracted each day, but water seeping into the mines was a constant problem. The only way to extract it was by winching it out in buckets, which could remove 450 litres of water an hour. In 1841 a steam engine was installed to extract the water, but the output of coal was slowing. In November 1847 expenditure for the mines was £6540 and revenue from the sale of the coal totalled just £3295. Inefficient management, equipment and buildings that were falling apart and discipline problems convinced the Convict Department to lease the mines to a private contractor. Production finally ended in 1877.

The Coalmines Barracks

In 1838, the coalmines barracks accommodated up to 170 convicts. The complex included a chapel, schoolroom, bakehouse, police office, guardhouse, a cottage for the surgeon, quarters and stables for the commanding officer and a small barracks for the military. The coalmines barracks were a 'punishment station'. Most convicts were there for reoffending. By 1847, the coalmines barracks had been redeveloped and could house more than 600 men.

Windlass

A windlass was used to raise and lower carts in the shaft. Convicts turned crank handles to rotate a horizontal barrel, winding rope around the barrel. The 'hooker on' was a convict who attached the carts of coal to the windlass rope at the base of the shaft. Convicts were raised and lowered in the same fashion.

Axe to Grind

In November 1845 John Harris asked George Gatehouse, the superintendent at the mines, for permission to sharpen his axe. They argued and a scuffle ensued in which Harris struck Gatehouse on his right arm with the axe. The blade was so blunt it barely made a scratch, and Harris avoided a charge of attempted murder.

Danger Below

In February 1840 Joseph Greaves fell to his death while being lowered into the mine. And in April 1841, Edward Branner was killed when another convict dropped his pick down the mineshaft.

Landing and Running Out

When a cart was hauled to the surface, the 'lander' guided it onto the railway before the 'runner out' ferried it to the screen where small pieces of coal, dirt and dust were removed. The coal was then carted to the jetty to be loaded onto ships. Each cart held about 90 kilograms of coal. A hundred tonnes could be loaded every seven hours.

Overseers

Joseph Lacey, an experienced miner who was transported for highway robbery, was appointed overseer in November 1833. In March 1838, he received a free pardon, and in 1840 he was sent to investigate a coal find in Recherche Bay. Another ex-coalminer, James Hurst, was appointed overseer. Hurst was also serving a sentence for highway robbery. He was pardoned in May 1844, and went on to lease the mines from the government.

William Thompson

William Thompson, a shoemaker, was transported for burglary. He arrived in Van Diemen's Land in September 1841 to serve a life sentence. He was then charged with absconding and larceny and sent to the coalmines for two years' hard labour in leg irons. Thompson received a ticket-of-leave in January 1852. He married Elizabeth Miller in April that year and they had seven children. In 1900, John Watt Beattie, a photographer and antiquarian, photographed Thompson and wrote about his experiences in two notebooks, which provided a valuable insight into convict life.

Unforgettable Horror

In February 1844 it was reported that the convicts did not have any cutlery to eat with or a single towel. Doctor Motherwell reported that meat rations were just skin and bone. Other visitors were equally appalled: Captain Charles Stanley described the men as having the 'worst possible countenances' and that the mines were infested with fleas, and Reverend Phibbs Fry claimed the scene was one of unforgettable horror.

Unnatural Crimes

In December 1845 Job Harris and William Collier were executed for committing an 'unnatural crime' on 19-year-old David Boyd. The *Colonial Times* deemed the details of the crime unfit for publication.

Buried Alive

Convicts dreaded being sent to the mines. Hard labour under ground in the damp and dark was severe punishment. Confining so many hardened criminals together worried the authorities, who feared they would learn from each other's vices and, under the cover of darkness, commit unnatural crimes. In 1834, four tiny cells were built at the base of the shaft for any offenders. They were unlit and poorly ventilated. Convicts likened the experience to being buried alive. In 1838, these cells were deemed inhumane and closed.

Dirty Work

At the end of each shift, the convicts returned to the station, undressed in the yard, and washed. Each man received an ounce (30 grams) of soap daily but, without hot water or baths, keeping clean was difficult. Every Sunday convicts were inspected and presented with a clean shirt.

COMMISSARIAT

A commissariat is a government-run storehouse that holds provisions and equipment. The Commissariat Department bought locally produced goods in order to supply military and penal establishments and the local colonists. Attached to the commissariat was the Ordnance Department who supplied goods imported from Britain or manufactured locally by convicts. Another branch of the commissariat was the Bond Store, where taxed goods such as liquor and tobacco were kept. These taxes were the main source of the colony's revenue.

Sneaking Suspicion

Stealing from the commissariat was a very serious crime and could lead to a death sentence. Even being suspected of theft could land you in trouble. William Williams was sent to Nottman's road gang for two years on suspicion of stealing from the commissariat. In January 1845, Thomas Lake was found with tobacco and charged with being an accessory to a raid on the commissariat. He was sentenced to six months' hard labour in chains.

The Launceston Commissariat

The Launceston commissariat was a rough store. In January 1806 it was robbed and the two perpetrators became the first people to be executed in Van Diemen's Land. When the acting commandant, Lieutenant-Colonel William Paterson, departed for New South Wales, he left the inhabitants with enough supplies to last five months on half rations. When he did not return for seven months, people took to the bush to hunt game. They included a group of absconders who formed the first gang of bushrangers. In desperation, the harbour master and four others made for Sydney but disappeared at sea. Lieutenant Thomas Laycock and four more men then set off for Hobart Town. They made the first overland journey through the uncharted territory in just nine days, but Hobart Town had similar problems and could offer little help.

By 1824, the colonial architect, David Lamb, reported that the Launceston commissariat was so dilapidated that it required wooden shores to prop it up. In 1825, he drew up plans for a new storehouse, which was completed in February 1829. The three-storey brick and bluestone building was regarded as the finest of its kind in the colony. When convict transportation ended, the commissariat was no longer needed. Part of the building was used by the Immigration Department to house newly arrived families. In 1860 the Volunteer Defence Force also moved in and eventually the military took control. It remains a military base to this day.

Under One Roof

Commissariats held a variety of goods such as sugar, pork, salt, soap, milk, rice, tea, pipes, vegetables, wheat, barley, rum, tobacco, trousers, wine, leg irons, beer, eggs, whale oil, lamps, cotton, candles, starch, water, axes, compasses, saws, handsaws, pit saws, rope, shovels, copper, spades, hoes, chalk, gimlets, awls, padlocks, bolts, brushes, pillows, hinges, shoes, ink, urine tubs, oars, horses, books, pots, whip cord, shirts, brass, towels, leather, adzes, turpentine, nails, linseed oil, boards, blankets, sewing needles, brooms, plough planes, steel, iron, soup ladles, scissors, jackets, trowels and glass. Everything was strictly itemised and scrupulously inspected, weighed, measured and accounted for.

Van Diemonian Meat

Meat was in high demand in the colony. By 1820, there were an estimated 28,838 cattle, 182,468 sheep and 1294 swine in Van Diemen's Land. In July 1820, sheep belonging to the Launceston commissariat were stolen, and Thomas Bailey was charged with the crime and sentenced to death. Despite Bailey's fate, another flock was stolen a few weeks later. Meat sold was scrupulously inspected, and in 1843 strict conditions were in force. It had to be from oxen at least three years old, cut into eight-pound pieces and packed with salt into tierces. A tierce was a wooden barrel that contained 336 pounds of salted beef. The salt was a preservative; meat had to keep for 12 months. Before it was eaten, it had to be soaked in freshwater for at least 24 hours to remove as much salt as possible. Convicts received the poorest cuts; the better quality portions ended up on the plates of their superiors.

Tricks of the Trade

In September 1816, William Maum, storekeeper at the Hobart Town commissariat, accepted a loan of £400 from Edward Lord, the colony's largest supplier of meat and grain. In return, Maum credited him for 800 bushels of grain that had not been delivered. Thomas Archer was in charge of the Launceston commissariat from 1813 to 1817 and is alleged to have used his position to amass a fortune.

Richard Dry

Richard Dry, an Irishman born in 1771, was convicted of a political charge during the Irish rebellion and transported to New South Wales in 1797. In 1807, he was appointed storekeeper at the Launceston commissariat, and in 1809 he married Anne Maughan and received a free pardon. When Dry retired in 1818, he was granted 300 acres of land and goods from the commissariat. He became a successful farmer and by 1827 he owned 12,000 acres. Dry died in 1843.

Weights and Measures

All goods were weighed and measured. In 1826, an Act was passed to standardise the system of units throughout the colony. Weights were to be in denominations of pounds, ounces and drams. Volume was measured in bushels, pecks, gallons, quarts, pints and gills. Inspectors armed with scales and the imperial standards performed spot checks. All approved units were imprinted with the King's mark and stamped S.W. for standard weight or S.M. for standard measure. In July 1837, William Bear was fined 5 shillings for having two short weights and unbalanced scales. In December he was fined again and his scales were destroyed.

In and Out

Commissariats were usually built near wharfs for ease of loading and unloading from vessels. A door on the northern wall of the Launceston commissariat faced the North Esk River and was fitted with a hoist to lift goods to the first and second floors. A large double door that faced St John Street was used to issue goods.

DISSIDENT

A dissident is a person who actively challenges the government or other institutions. Also known as rebels, radicals, objectors, martyrs and political prisoners, many dissidents were sentenced to transportation. Van Diemonians were often sympathetic to the dissidents' causes, and political prisoners frequently received good treatment, light punishments and, in some cases, an early release.

William Smith O'Brien

William Smith O'Brien, a well-educated parliamentarian, was born in Ireland in October 1803. He was the leader of Young Irelanders, a group that agitated for independence from Britain. For instigating an uprising in July 1848, he was charged with high treason and sentenced to be hanged, drawn and quartered. Petitions for clemency signed by 80,000 people led to his sentence being commuted to life transportation. He arrived in Van Diemen's Land in October 1849 and was sent to Port Arthur, where he was permitted to live in his own cottage. After receiving a full pardon in May 1856, O'Brien returned to Ireland. A statue was erected in his honour in Dublin, and his cottage still stands at Port Arthur.

DOG

Hunting dogs or 'kangaroo dogs' were very valuable because they were essential in supplying the early colonists with meat. In December 1806, Thomas Tombs received 300 lashes for absconding and stealing a dog. The Reverend Knopwood sent out search parties to recover his beloved dog Miss, and in January 1809 he paid the huge sum of £25 for a dog named Chance. Aborigines also adopted hunting dogs and ran large packs. Dog numbers soon grew out of control and a *Dog Act* was introduced in 1830. A licence was required to keep any dog over six months old, and dogs had to be collared. Despite Van Diemonians' affinity with canines, the term 'dog' was used as an insult. In May 1845, Joseph Gardiner murdered William Meade, whom he referred to as a 'bloody dog'. At his trial, the court was told that the term referred to a 'bad man who runs an innocent man into trouble'.

The Eaglehawk Neck Dog-Line

In January 1832 a military station was established at Eaglehawk Neck to prevent convicts on the run from Port Arthur escaping further. The tiny tract of land, just 400 metres long and 60 metres wide, connected the Forestier and Tasman peninsulas and was the only route overland. Dogs were placed as sentries across the isthmus to create what became known as the dog-line. It was hoped that the barking, biting sentinels would form an impassible barrier. The dogs were given ferocious names, and stories of their savagery soon circulated. They were known as the Lions.

George Hunt and Thomas Walker

George Hunt arrived in Van Diemen's Land in April 1825. In May 1832, he escaped from Port Arthur and attempted to cross Eaglehawk Neck disguised in a kangaroo skin. After nearly being shot by soldiers hunting game, he surrendered. Two months later, he managed to cross the Neck but was captured soon after. Hunt attempted to escape three more times and received a total of 625 lashes. Thomas Walker was another incessant absconder. In August 1833 he was apprehended at the Neck and, after bolting a second time on the same day, he was given 100 lashes and his sentence was extended by three years.

The Finer Things

Henry William St Pierre Bunbury of the 21st Regiment was stationed at Eaglehawk Neck in July 1835. He remarked that time was best spent gardening or hunting kangaroo rather than guarding and hunting marauding convicts. In his spare time he grew potatoes, cabbages and onions and whiled away the nights reading books. Not everyone stationed at the Neck found it so serene. Another member of the 21st was severely bitten by one of the dogs after daring to pass near it.

A Village

John Peyton Jones of the 63rd Regiment came up with the idea of placing guard dogs along the isthmus. By 1836 the military station had developed into a village with accommodation for officers, soldiers and a whaleboat crew. It had a guard house, commissariat, bake house, stable, garden and a school for the soldiers' children. In 1856, Matilda Murphy, the wife of Edward Murphy of the 12th Regiment, gave birth to a baby boy at the Neck. Eventually, the number of guards was decreased and the buildings fell into disrepair. It was closed in November 1873.

Lamps

In September 1832 Charles Corkham, who was serving a life sentence for stealing a handkerchief, was stationed at the Neck as a lamplighter. Lamps were lit at dusk using a wick on the end of a pole and were fuelled by whale oil. Keeping the lamps in good order was critical for security at the Neck. By 1834, nine lamps illuminated the isthmus at night. To increase the luminosity, seashells were spread across the track. The white surface reflected the light, creating better visibility.

Keeping a Look Out

Sentry boxes dotted the hills and beaches of Eaglehawk Neck. Huts were also stationed at intervals around the Tasman Peninsula and the shoreline was patrolled every night. In February 1838, Constable Thomas Dickinson saved a drowning man at Norfolk Bay. He was granted a conditional pardon in June, but the following year he was arrested for burglary and sentenced to 14 more years. In October 1834, Commandant Booth caught several guards asleep in a hut at Stony Point. They were dismissed.

Picturesque Pooches

The dog-line made such an impression on some sightseers that they were inspired to record the spectacle. In September 1842, Harden Melville portrayed the dogs as snarling, howling beasts. When Captain Charles Staniforth Hext sketched the dogs a few months later, he portrayed them as chubby puppies.

Rations

By 1850 dogs were on the same rations as convicts; one pound of meat and bread each day.

Pain in the Neck

A pass was required to cross the Neck. In 1848 James Calder and his surveying party were shocked when their official documents failed to gain them passage. When Calder stated he was mates with the lieutenant's superior officer, the party was permitted to cross.

Sea Sentries

To deter convicts from swimming to freedom, the authorities perpetrated rumours that sharks infested the waters of Van Diemen's Land. Offal was thrown into the water to attract sharks to the Neck, and dogs were stationed on platforms in Eaglehawk Bay. If a dog sighted a swimmer, it barked, alerting the guards. A convict rowed out to feed and tend the dogs each day. When William Derrincourt escaped from Port Arthur he covered his head with seaweed to elude the dogs. When a sudden swell carried away his disguise, the dogs spotted him and Derrincourt subsequently surrendered.

Cash and Co

In 1842, Martin Cash escaped from Port Arthur and swam past the dog-line under the cover of night. At the other side of Eaglehawk Bay, he battled his way through seaweed and arrived safely ashore. Cash hadn't eaten for five days and, after running into a party of soldiers, he gave himself up. On his return to Port Arthur he received 18 months' hard labour in irons. On Boxing Day 1842, Cash escaped with two other men. At the Neck they slipped into the water with their clothes bundled on their heads. But the clothes were washed away and the three convicts began their bushranging career completely naked. Outraged at the ease with which the men eluded the guard, Commandant Booth had three new stations established.

William Westwood

William Westwood arrived in New South Wales in July 1837. In September 1840, he absconded. He became known as Jacky Jacky and his polite demeanour and dandy appearance earned him the reputation as a gentleman bushranger. In March 1842, Westwood arrived in Hobart Town. On his third escape attempt from Port Arthur he swam past the Neck. He arrived safely on the other side and claimed that his two companions were eaten by sharks. But his freedom was short-lived and he was sent to Norfolk Island. Following severe treatment on the island, he led a rebellion in which one overseer and three constables were murdered. Westwood was hanged in October 1846, aged 26.

Maria Lord

In August 1802, Maria Riseley was charged with stealing from a dwelling house and sentenced to seven years' transportation. By December 1805, she was living in the first privately built house in Hobart Town with Edward Lord, a marine officer. Maria opened a store and they married in October 1808. Their business interests expanded and it was said Maria controlled over a third of all colonial resources, with monopolies in the wheat, meat and rum trades. Maria and Edward did not remain on good terms, however, and Edward returned to England. Maria relocated to Bothwell, where she died in July 1859.

EMANCIPIST

Ex-convicts were known as expirees, old hands, old lags and, more formally, emancipists. Approximately 35,000 convicts settled in Van Diemen's Land following their release. Governor Macquarie felt that 'a free man by pardon or emancipation, should be in all respects considered on a footing with every other man in the colony'. But the stigma of a convict past, commonly known as the 'convict stain', was still very real. When emancipists were granted the right to vote, the ruling class was appalled. Some emancipists concealed their convict pasts, but some, such as the prominent pastoralists William Field, Richard Dry, David Gibson and Mary Bowater, flourished despite their background.

ESCAPE CRAFT

In October 1803, the first convicts to escape Van Diemen's Land made off in a small sailboat. It is thought that a team of sealers captured them. The convicts were returned to New South Wales in 1804. In August 1814, the government schooner *Estramina* met with a vessel of 'very singular appearance' manned by 25 convicts who, after 100 kilometres at sea, had been forced to turn back. Investigations revealed that John Pascoe Fawkner, a shopkeeper, had supplied them with the well-stocked whaleboat. Fawkner was sentenced to 500 lashes and three years' transportation to New South Wales.

Some convicts built their own escape craft. In January 1827, George Clay, Steven Toole and William Humpage made a raft from two water casks, a night tub and part of a water closet. All three drowned. Other articles used in escape craft were cotton shirts, wattle branches, pitch, a washing tub, kelp and whale skin. When Matthew Brady bolted from Sarah Island with 14 others, they made sails from canvas mattresses. Commandant Booth amassed a dozen confiscated escape craft, which he proudly displayed on his verandah at Port Arthur.

Building Canoes

One Port Arthur absconder was said to have built a canoe in less than an hour. Commandant Booth offered to reduce his punishment if the claim could be substantiated. The convict built another boat in just 50 minutes and performed a successful trial run to the Isle of the Dead and back. Scipio Africanus, a convict born in the Cape of Good Hope, built a canoe with three other Port Arthur absconders. When it fell apart at sea, Scipio and one of the others drowned.

James Goodwin and Thomas Connelly

In March 1828, James Goodwin and Thomas Connelly absconded from Macquarie Harbour in a canoe carved from a Huon pine log. They paddled upstream, carrying their craft over obstacles and dragging it into the undergrowth to hide it from search parties, before taking to the bush. A month later they parted ways. Goodwin was apprehended within a week. His journey through uncharted wilderness was of great interest to the authorities, and in March 1833 he joined a surveying party to guide them through the area. Goodwin's Peak was named in his honour.

Maria Island Marauders

In November 1825, Thomas Bosworth and several others escaped from Maria Island. The gang paddled across five kilometres of open water to Prosser's Bay. A £10 reward was posted and they were all caught and executed in Hobart Town in January 1826. One report stated that their escape craft was a 'stringy bark canoe' that they had built themselves, but it is possible that the canoe belonged to Aborigines of the Tyreddeme group. In December 1826, another bark canoe was found hidden on the island. George Bailey was given 100 lashes and sent to Macquarie Harbour.

John Popjoy and Tom Morgan

In August 1829, the *Cyprus* was transporting convicts from Hobart Town to Sarah Island when convict mutineers seized the ship. Forty men, women and children were put ashore before the mutineers sailed away, leaving the castaways 80 kilometres from the nearest settlement. Two men, one a convict named John Popjoy, volunteered to make the perilous trek for help, but five days later they returned exhausted. Popjoy resolved to make a raft. Tom Morgan, another convict, had experience in making coracles. They cut wattle branches with penknives and made a four-metre frame, covered it with canvas and waterproofed it with boiled soap and rosin. Popjoy and Morgan paddled for two days before being picked up by a ship. The government sloop *Opossum* was despatched to rescue the castaways, and the two convicts were placed in Hobart Town gaol. Popjoy was granted a free pardon and returned to England and Morgan was appointed to work with government boats.

Coracles

Some convicts escaped in coracles, small boats constructed from branches lashed together with bark and covered with hide, tar or canvas.

Catamaran

Four of the first convicts to flee Sarah Island escaped on a catamaran. The double-hulled vessel fell to pieces, leaving them floating on the wreckage until they were rescued. In September 1843, four convicts from Port Arthur were believed to have drowned after they escaped on a catamaran that disintegrated during a gale.

Francis Jones and Robert Birch

In December 1836, while stationed at Point Puer, Francis Jones and Robert Birch launched a catamaran and attempted to row to freedom. The morning after, their craft was found floating offshore. It was two and a half metres long and made of cedar. The seams had been waterproofed and floats were fixed to each side. Three paddles were also recovered. Birch's floating body was found but Jones was never seen again.

Stowaways

James Heartzoke absconded in December 1849. He made it to San Francisco where he amassed a fortune in gold and dreamed about returning to England with a new identity to run for parliament. James Punt Borritt, an incessant absconder, stowed away on a merchant ship and nearly died from 'suffocation and want of food'. During the Victorian gold rush, the numbers of convict stowaways increased dramatically. Police resorted to smoking them out by burning sulphur below decks.

Silent Oars

Commandant Butler had his search parties wrap their oars in cloth so that they could sneak up on absconders. In September 1825, a party of soldiers heard sounds coming from the shoreline at Birch's Inlet. They rowed up silently and caught William Jarrett, Robert Burke and Morgan Edwards constructing a raft.

The Death of Constable George Rex

In October 1827, while making his rounds in the barracks on Small Island, a depot for the more hardened criminals on Sarah Island, Constable George Rex was ambushed and taken prisoner by a group of convicts. The other five officers were bound, gagged and left on the beach. The convicts dismantled the barracks for materials to make an escape raft. Doors, shelves and other bits and pieces were carried down to the water where convict John Williams began construction. The men clambered on but the raft would not hold their weight and, in frustration, Samuel Measures, James Reid and James Kirk set upon the constable and drowned him. At dawn the alarm was raised and the murderers were apprehended. Nine convicts were charged with participating in the murder of Constable Rex. In December 1827 they were hanged in front of a crowd of 600 in Hobart Town.

Islands of Ill Repute

When George Bass discovered and named Bass Strait in 1797, he also found seven marooned convicts. Some colonists believed the islands of Bass Strait were populated by escapees who became known as straitmen. It was claimed they lured ships onto the shore with false lights and then scavenged the wrecks.

21

FEMALE FACTORY

Penal establishments for women were known as female factories because they provided goods and labour for the colony. The first female factories were established following an increase in the number of female convicts transported to Van Diemen's Land. From the 1820s to the 1870s there were five major female factories in Van Diemen's Land, one of which was the Cascades Female Factory.

Classing the Convicts

Under the Assignment System, female convicts were classed according to their behaviour. A convict serving a punishment was placed in Third, or Crime, Class. After finishing her sentence she graduated to Second, or Probation, Class and then to First, or Assignable, Class and was ready to be sent to work for a colonist.

Chapel

The left half of the chapel was cordoned off for women in Crime Class. The other half was divided into an area for Probation Class near the pulpit and Assignable Class at the back.

Cascades Female Factory

In 1826, a rum distillery on the outskirts of Hobart Town was selected as the site for a new female factory. In December 1828, more than 100 women were transferred there. In less than a year, the number of female convicts doubled. Over the next 22 years, four more complexes were added. In 1832, a second complex, Yard Two, was built with a laundry and 100 solitary working cells. When Lieutenant-Governor Arthur visited, he saw unplastered walls, floors covered with bugs, and blankets black with fleas. Located in the gloom of Mount Wellington's shadow, the factory became notorious for its high death rate and appalling conditions and was nicknamed 'valley of the shadow of death'. But the female factory continued to expand and three more 'Yards' were built. By 1856, the number of women and children at the factory was declining and the buildings began to be used for other purposes, such as a female invalid depot, a male invalid depot, a boys reformatory, an insane asylum and a hospital. The doors were finally closed in 1900. Over half of the estimated 25,000 convict women transported to Australia arrived in Van Diemen's Land. The majority served time at the Cascades Female Factory. In 2010 the site was added to the World Heritage List.

The Daily Routine

In summer, a bell rang at 5.30 am to wake the women for muster. At 6 am they commenced work and at 8 am they ate breakfast. Chapel was at 8.30 am, followed by more work and dinner at noon. After dinner the women worked until sunset. Supper was served at 7.30 pm followed by prayers at 8 pm. The women's work was determined by their class. First Class worked as cooks and hospital attendants and in other day-to-day roles. Second Class sewed, made clothes and prepared linen, and Third Class did the laundry and wool work. Women confined in solitary cells unpicked old nautical ropes. The bulk of the work at the female factory was laundry. The people of Hobart Town were charged 1 shilling and 6 pence per dozen items and the money went towards running the factory.

Elizabeth Slater

Elizabeth Slater was sentenced to seven years for stealing. She arrived in Hobart Town in April 1834. In November she was sent to Crime Class for absenting her master's leave. The following year, Slater escaped through a hole in the wall to be reunited with her lover. She was punished with two weeks in a cell on bread and water, and her hair was cut off. More escapes followed, including a dangerous leap over the factory wall, and she was transferred to George Town. The change of address did not change her habits. Elizabeth Slater continued to escape before finally being awarded her freedom in March 1830.

Ellen Scott

Ellen Scott arrived in Van Diemen's Land in February 1830. For offences including stealing and absconding, she spent time in several female factories. In January 1833, she was charged with 'causing a violent illness to the infant child of her master' and was given the longest solitary confinement term possible and ordered to wear an iron collar. In May 1839 she assaulted Superintendent Hutchinson during a riot and was sentenced to two years' hard labour. An inquiry into female convict discipline denounced Scott as a member of the Flash Mob. Scott received her freedom in October 1847.

The Flash Mob

Factory women who refused to conform were known as the Flash Mob. They distinguished themselves with a showy style of dress. The Cascades Flash Mob was said to traffic in contraband goods, to intimidate other inmates and to instigate riots, assaults, escapes and unnatural crimes. During an inquiry in 1842, Grace Heinbury stated that after picking wool for an hour each day she spent her time singing, sewing and doing just as she pleased.

Superintendent and Matron

Reverend John Hutchinson and his wife Mary were appointed Superintendent and Matron in 1832 and stayed for 20 years. Their duties included reading scriptures twice daily, inspecting the facility, overseeing rations, teaching and keeping journals that detailed convicts' rations, behaviour and possessions.

Arrival

When a convict transport docked, the women were marched under guard to the Cascades in the early hours of the morning to avoid public scrutiny.

Mothers and Babies

When an assigned convict fell pregnant she was returned to the female factory. After giving birth she cared for her child in the nursery. After three months she was given another child to look after and, after six months, a third. When her baby was weaned at nine months, she was sent to Crime Class and the infant was put in the care of another convict. Mothers rarely saw their children again. When Lieutenant-Colonel Mundy visited the nursery, he saw babies in straw baskets, as well as wooden cribs. The infant mortality rate was high. In 1833, 40 of the 103 infants died.

23

GALLOWS

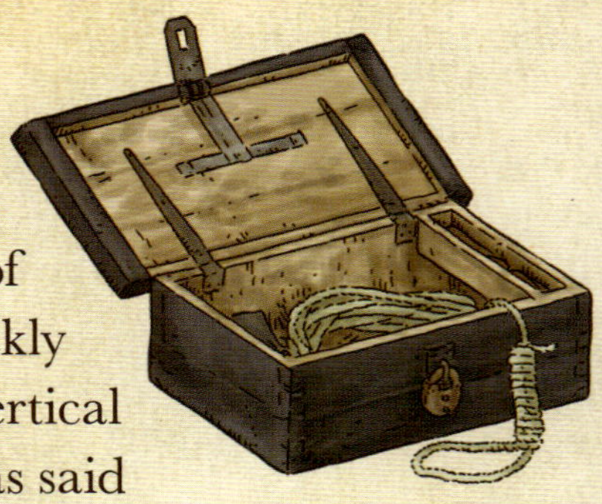

Convicts sentenced to death were hanged. A basic gallows consisted of an upright pole with a cross beam to which a rope was attached and a platform that could be quickly pulled away to create the drop. To hang several people at once, a longer beam was held up by two vertical poles. For a quick death, the rope had to be the right length for the victim's weight. Solomon Blay was said to hang all his victims at a drop of five feet regardless of their size, and, in June 1870, James Regan struggled on the rope for 15 minutes. The noose, or hangman's knot, was positioned behind the left ear and there were traditionally 13 coils in the knot. Execution equipment included rope, weights, straps, a notebook and a disguise. Some Van Diemonian hangmen concealed their identity with a hood or false beard and by smearing their face with burnt cork, but Solomon Blay chose to perform his duties barefaced.

Gallows Etiquette

In September 1826, 23 men were executed within just five days. One Sunday at 3 pm, eight of the condemned received a sermon. They prayed until 7 am the next day, when they were offered Holy Communion. At 8 am a death bell rang and javelin men and members of the military lined up to witness the event. Black coffins were carried in and the condemned men climbed the scaffold where the nooses and hoods were fitted. They were given a final three minutes in which to pray before they dropped to their deaths. Patrick Dunne prepared to meet his maker dressed in a long white robe and cap, and George Farquharson held a rose and part of an orange. John Conhope wore white with a nosegay stuck to his breast, and Mary MacLauchlan wore a white gown with a black ribbon around her waist. It was common practice for the condemned to sing, and sometimes the public joined in.

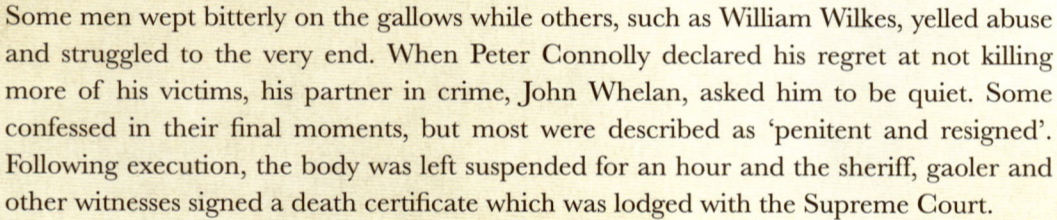

Some men wept bitterly on the gallows while others, such as William Wilkes, yelled abuse and struggled to the very end. When Peter Connolly declared his regret at not killing more of his victims, his partner in crime, John Whelan, asked him to be quiet. Some confessed in their final moments, but most were described as 'penitent and resigned'. Following execution, the body was left suspended for an hour and the sheriff, gaoler and other witnesses signed a death certificate which was lodged with the Supreme Court.

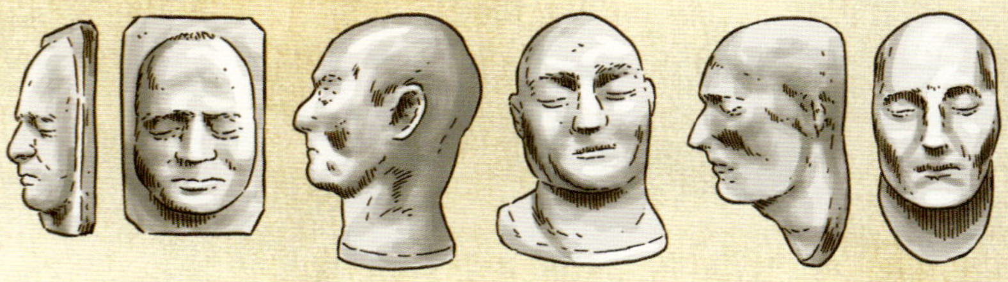

Researching Murderous Traits

The *Murder Act* of 1752 allowed the bodies of executed murderers to be dissected for research. When Patrick Minahan was sentenced to be hanged, anatomised and dissected in June 1841 he exclaimed, 'Yes, you may dissect my body, but thank God, you can't my soul'. Phrenology, the study of the human skull, was widely practised. It was believed that the shape of the skull determined personality type, intellect and human behaviour. Thomas Bock, a convict artist, was ordered to make portraits of the Brady Gang and Alexander Pearce post execution. Plaster casts, known as death masks, were made and skulls were preserved for further analysis.

Executions in Van Diemen's Land

Many transported convicts had received a reprieve from the British gallows and were considered lucky to set foot in Van Diemen's Land. But, for some, life in the colony proved fleeting. In 1806, the first men to be executed were Thomas England, a private of the New South Wales Corps, and a convict named James Keating. They had stolen pork from the commissariat. The first mass execution was held in April 1821 at Hobart Town when ten men were hanged. Initially, executions were held publicly, as the spectacle of seeing criminals swing was believed to be an excellent deterrent to others. In February 1825, however, three convicts mounted the scaffold at Sarah Island. They kicked their shoes off, laughed and whooped goodbye to their cheering comrades. The authorities were not amused and the gallows at Hobart Town were moved inside the Murray Street gaol. The tops of the scaffolding could still be seen above the wall, and that same month the public gathered outside the walls to watch nine men hang. Two of the condemned were Aboriginal men known as Musquito and Black Jack, the first Aboriginal people to be executed officially. Between 1826 and 1827, 103 Van Diemonians suffered the 'ultimate penalty'. Men were hanged for murder, sheep stealing, burglary, forgery, absconding, bushranging and 'unnatural crime'. In April 1830, Mary MacLauchlan was the first woman to be executed after being found guilty of infanticide. In February 1946, Frederick Thompson was the last man to be hanged in Tasmania, bringing the total number of executions to approximately 545. In 1963, the Hobart Town gallows were dismantled and in 1968 capital punishment was abolished. In 1991 the gallows were restored. They remain on display at the Penitentiary Chapel.

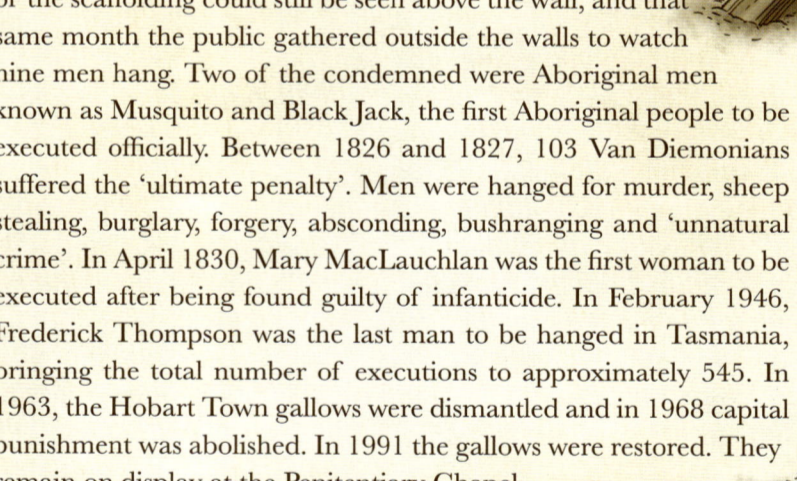

Gallows Humour

Gallows humour is joking and revelry among people who are facing a life-threatening situation. The gallows were referred to as 'the tree that bears fruit all year round', 'the sheriff's picture frame' and 'the morning drop'. The victim was called 'a gallows bird' and a 'hangdog'.

A Slant

To get relief from doing hard labour, some convicts spun stories or committed crimes in order to be removed from their current station. This was known as 'having a slant'. In February 1829, Daniel Brown and John Salmon killed Thomas Stopford with an axe to get a slant from Sarah Island to Hobart Town. At the time of their execution, the *Hobart Town Courier* reported that the men considered their punishment 'just'. It was also reported that Salmon had confessed to killing a man ten months earlier to get a slant to Pittwater. Once at Pittwater he was unable to produce a body and was ferried back to Sarah Island to receive 50 lashes.

Solomon Blay

Solomon Blay was born in 1816. In July 1836, he was sentenced to 14 years' transportation for forgery. During the voyage out he was flogged for insolence, and the ship's surgeon, James McTernan, described him as 'bad as can be'. In January 1840, Blay was caught trying to abscond and was sent to the Jerusalem chain gang. Blay was appointed executioner in August 1840. In April 1842, he was sentenced to life for burglary and went to Richmond gaol. He continued in his role as hangman and, when the need arose, was escorted to Hobart Town to perform his duties. Blay retired in August 1891. It is estimated he launched 205 people into the afterlife during his 50-year career. He died in August 1897, ironically after suffering a bout of dropsy.

William Bedford

In June 1822, William Bedford was appointed assistant military chaplain of Van Diemen's Land. One of his duties was to attend condemned men at their execution. This included taking a last confession, reading last rites and, in the case of the overcome George Lacy, carrying him to the gallows. Bedford said that 19 hangings out of 20 were for crimes committed under the influence of alcohol. When Reverend Philip Palmer arrived, he replaced Bedford as head of the church. This resulted in a succession of disagreements, which brought into question Bedford's trustworthiness and honesty.

GAOL

The first official gaol in Van Diemen's Land was constructed in August 1816. It was a small two-storey brick building in Murray Street, Hobart Town. The first gaol break was made by William Peck in March 1817. He was apprehended by Sergeant McCarthy of the 46th Regiment, who received a reward of five guineas. There were ten official gaols throughout Van Diemen's Land. Gaols housed convicts who were awaiting work placement, trial or punishment.

Women's Lavatory

Hot Spot
There was a stiflingly hot cell positioned between the two chimneys.

Break Out
In November 1849, six prisoners escaped by removing the lintel over a window, stacking bricks pulled from the lavatory against the wall, and clambering over it.

Men's Lavatory

Ward
When cells were added in 1835 the original four solitary cells were renovated into a sleeping ward.

Day Room
The first javelin men were housed in the one ward. After the gaol was enlarged the ward became a day room where convicts were put to work.

Richmond Gaol

In 1825, Lieutenant-Governor Arthur ordered a gaol be built at Richmond, 25 kilometres northeast of Hobart Town. Architect David Lambe designed a small sandstone building that was completed in 1827. Overcrowding was soon such a problem that inmates were forced to sleep in the passages and solitary cells. By 1835, eastern and western wings were added, allowing male and female inmates to be segregated. A cookhouse was also built and the number of solitary cells was increased to 16. In 1840 a four-metre stone wall was erected to enclose an exercise yard behind the gaol. The Richmond gaol was used continuously until 1928. In 1970, it was categorised as a historic site under the *National Parks and Wildlife Act*. Richmond gaol is the oldest intact gaol in Australia and is now a museum.

George Grover

George Grover arrived in Van Diemen's Land in August 1826, sentenced to 14 years for housebreaking. By 1829, he was serving as a flagellator at the Richmond gaol. During the following two years, he inflicted 4411 lashes on 129 men. After a drunken fracas with the local police magistrate, Grover himself received 25 lashes. In March 1832, he died after being pushed off the Richmond Bridge. Some people claim Grover's ghost still haunts the bridge, often accompanied by his dog.

Rations

Inmates received quarter of a pound of meat, half a pound of vegetables, 1 pound of bread, 2 ounces of flour, half an ounce of salt and half an ounce of soap per day.

Keeping up with the Gaol-keepers

The gaol-keeper lived on site. His duties included a daily inspection of each inmate as well as maintaining journals listing rations, punishments and correspondence. Reliable gaol-keepers were hard to come by. The first gaoler, William Speed, was appointed in February 1820 at a salary of £200. He was dismissed after being accused of embezzling the inmates' rations. Gaoler Randall Young was sacked following the escape of a prisoner. Samuel Whittaker, was sacked for being too lenient.

William Jemott suffered the humiliation of being locked up in his own gaol. George Wise was given the boot for various breaches of the rules including getting drunk and making off with prisoners' shoes. Richmond gaol's last gaol-keeper, Samuel McNeilly, was appointed in March 1851. When the gaol was proclaimed a watch house in December 1856 Samuel's services were no longer needed, and the 62-year-old was awarded a pension of £5, 9 shillings and 4 pence.

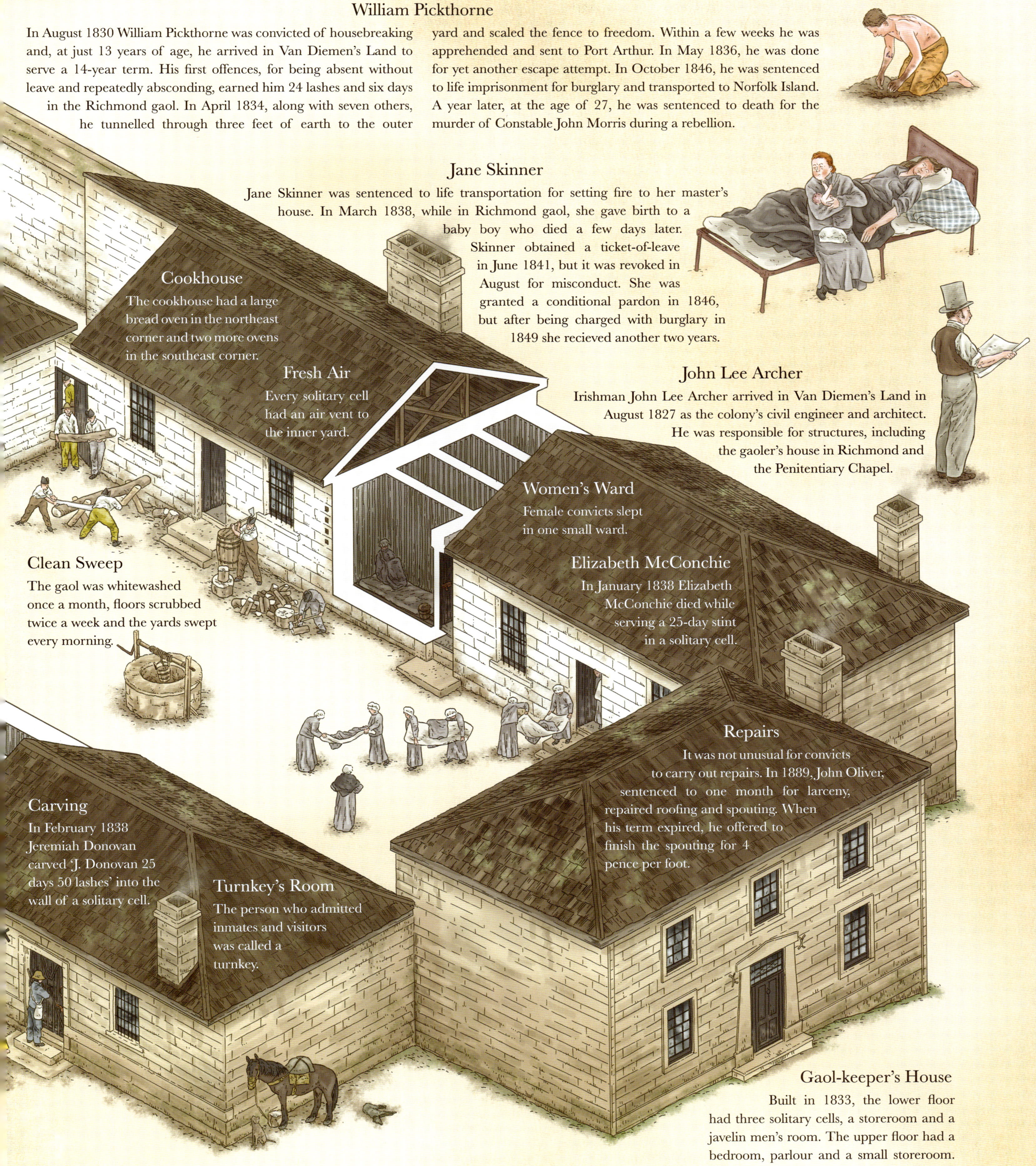

William Pickthorne
In August 1830 William Pickthorne was convicted of housebreaking and, at just 13 years of age, he arrived in Van Diemen's Land to serve a 14-year term. His first offences, for being absent without leave and repeatedly absconding, earned him 24 lashes and six days in the Richmond gaol. In April 1834, along with seven others, he tunnelled through three feet of earth to the outer yard and scaled the fence to freedom. Within a few weeks he was apprehended and sent to Port Arthur. In May 1836, he was done for yet another escape attempt. In October 1846, he was sentenced to life imprisonment for burglary and transported to Norfolk Island. A year later, at the age of 27, he was sentenced to death for the murder of Constable John Morris during a rebellion.

Jane Skinner
Jane Skinner was sentenced to life transportation for setting fire to her master's house. In March 1838, while in Richmond gaol, she gave birth to a baby boy who died a few days later. Skinner obtained a ticket-of-leave in June 1841, but it was revoked in August for misconduct. She was granted a conditional pardon in 1846, but after being charged with burglary in 1849 she recieved another two years.

Cookhouse
The cookhouse had a large bread oven in the northeast corner and two more ovens in the southeast corner.

Fresh Air
Every solitary cell had an air vent to the inner yard.

John Lee Archer
Irishman John Lee Archer arrived in Van Diemen's Land in August 1827 as the colony's civil engineer and architect. He was responsible for structures, including the gaoler's house in Richmond and the Penitentiary Chapel.

Women's Ward
Female convicts slept in one small ward.

Clean Sweep
The gaol was whitewashed once a month, floors scrubbed twice a week and the yards swept every morning.

Elizabeth McConchie
In January 1838 Elizabeth McConchie died while serving a 25-day stint in a solitary cell.

Repairs
It was not unusual for convicts to carry out repairs. In 1889, John Oliver, sentenced to one month for larceny, repaired roofing and spouting. When his term expired, he offered to finish the spouting for 4 pence per foot.

Carving
In February 1838 Jeremiah Donovan carved 'J. Donovan 25 days 50 lashes' into the wall of a solitary cell.

Turnkey's Room
The person who admitted inmates and visitors was called a turnkey.

Gaol-keeper's House
Built in 1833, the lower floor had three solitary cells, a storeroom and a javelin men's room. The upper floor had a bedroom, parlour and a small storeroom.

27

GHOST

The unfamiliar fauna of Van Diemen's Land along with superstition, Aboriginal folklore and the fear of an unknown country fuelled the imagination of some colonists. Charles Gould, son of John Gould the eminent ornithologist, suggested that strange creatures spotted in inland lakes were not bunyips as people thought, but inland seals. When convict Charles Smith drowned in Macquarie Harbour, his body, 'dreadfully disfigured by the fish', was recovered the following day. A few nights later, a sentry claimed to have seen Smith appear at the water's edge. Ghost sightings published in the Van Diemonian press were, however, usually reported in jest. In June 1829, the *Hobart Town Courier* stated that the demonic spirit infesting Van Diemen's Land was not of the supernatural variety but simply 'rum'.

GIBBET

The bodies of executed criminals were sometimes suspended from gibbets to deter others from criminal behaviour.

Gibbeted Van Diemonians

The first Van Diemonian to be gibbeted was a bushranger named John Brown. After being hanged and dissected, Brown's remains were gibbeted off Pinchgut Island in New South Wales. In May 1815, Denis McCarty carted the headless body of James Whitehead, the former leader of the Howe Gang, into Hobart Town where it was hung in chains off Hunter Island to greet incoming ships. In June, Richard McGuire, a bushranger from the same gang, was executed and gibbeted next to Whitehead's rotting corpse. One year later the bodies were moved to a point of land near the Queenborough Cemetery. The *Hobart Town Gazette* described the bodies as 'Objects of Disgust'. Others, however, believed them to be a beneficial beacon. In December 1818, Governor Macquarie congratulated Lieutenant-Governor Sorell on bringing Michael Howe to justice and regretted not being able to gibbet the corpse. When Judge Algernon Montagu ordered the execution of Francis Maxfield for the attempted murder of his overseer, Joseph Ellis, he stated his desire to have the body gibbeted at Port Arthur. Gibbeting was outlawed in 1834, but in the 1837 case of John McKey Van Diemonian authorities made an exception.

The Murder of Joseph Edward Wilson

In April 1837, Joseph Edward Wilson left Launceston to buy a boat in Hobart Town. Twenty kilometres into his journey he was bailed up, shot through the rib cage, beaten about the head and robbed. He died the next day. Several buttons, a broken firelock and a ramrod were found at the scene of the crime. The buttons matched Joseph's vest and the gun bits were identified as being from a fowling piece that belonged to John Lamb. Lamb shared a hut at Norfolk Plains with John McKey, a lifer who had been transported for assault and robbery. McKey was charged with the murder, found guilty and sentenced to be hanged and then gibbeted at the murder scene.

Gibbeting John McKey

On 5 May 1837 at 2 pm, John McKey's body arrived in Perth. It was placed in an iron casing and suspended from a seven-metre gibbet, 450 metres from the main road. A crowd gathered to view the proceedings. It was reported that two men positioned themselves below the gibbet and consoled themselves with rum. Rather than being reformed by the fate of their comrade, they committed numerous crimes on the journey back to Launceston and wound up in the police lock-up. Eight-year-old Henry Button, a future mayor and alderman, described McKey's blackened body swinging in the wind. Henry Reed, a successful merchant, philanthropist and fervent evangelist passed the body on a moonlight night and dismounted, fell to his knees at the foot of the gibbet and claimed to have 'had it out with hell' before crying out 'hallelujah' and riding on to a prayer meeting. Martin Cash remarked that, within a few weeks of McKey's body being displayed, locals were so disgusted by the thought of flies swarming on the body and flying into their dwellings that they lobbied to have it removed. In September, McKey's body was taken down and, after Doctor de Dassel and Dr Grant removed his head for phrenological examination, his remains were interred on the spot. McKey was the last man to be gibbeted in English history. Van Diemonians immortalised the end of an era by naming the area Gibbet Hill.

John Franklin

In 1837, John Franklin arrived in Hobart Town to relieve George Arthur as lieutenant governor. To satisfy the public's thirst for justice following the brutal murder of Joseph Edward Wilson, Franklin and his council approved the gibbeting of John McKey. Franklin was dismissed in 1843 after a dispute with Colonial Secretary John Montague. After returning to England, Franklin joined an Arctic expedition. He died after the ship was beset by pack ice.

GRAFFITI

Graffiti has long been a form of creative expression: a protest, declaration of love, indication of ownership or statement of presence. It has also been a long-standing source of irritation. The *Police Act* of 1833 stated that any person caught defacing any Van Diemonian wall, house or building would be fined 10 shillings. Francis McCallum was sentenced to nine months' hard labour in irons for defacing the walls of his sleeping ward.

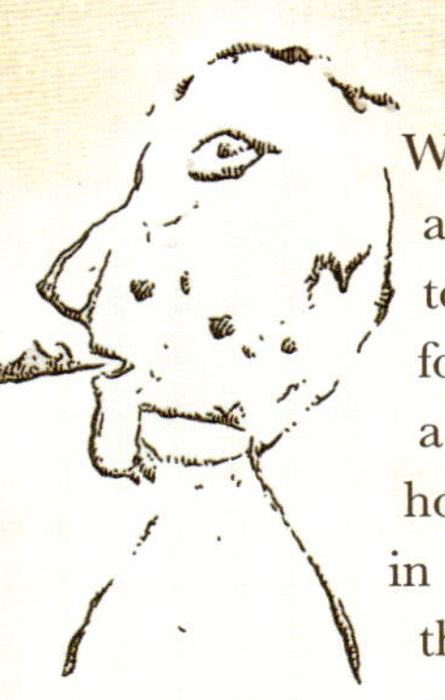

William Bray

William Bray was transported for burglary and arrived in Van Diemen's Land in March 1841 to serve 15 years. In February 1844, he was found enjoying a drink at a pub disguised as a soldier and was locked in the Bothwell watch house for five days. Bray immortalised his stay in solitary with various carvings including the date, his name, vocation and stomping ground, and his fondness for grog.

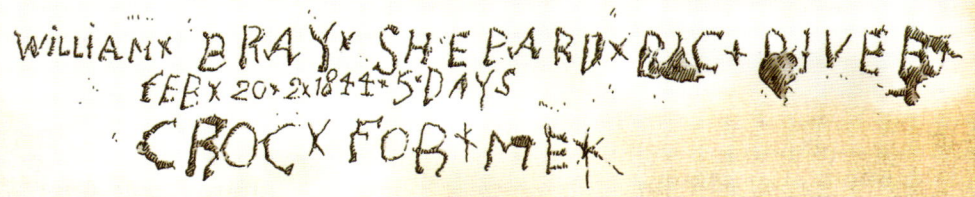

Thomas Lake

Thomas Lake arrived in Van Diemen's Land in March 1842 to serve a ten-year term. A year later he was arrested for burglary and he received a life sentence. While in Richmond gaol, he carved his name and place of birth (Writtle, Essex) on a window shutter. Alongside his inscription are two boats, images commonly used to represent voyages. Lake was caught trying to stow away on the *Providence* in September 1852.

Richard Waters

Richard Waters arrived in Van Diemen's Land in June 1821 to serve seven years. A watchmaker by trade, Waters installed the clock in the penitentiary chapel in August 1834. To mark his accomplishment he scratched his name and the date into one of the brass rope drums.

Words of Wisdom

A board in the Hobart Town prisoners' barracks read, 'May the Scotch thistle never grow, the rose of England never blow, the Harp of Ireland never play till I poor convict gets my liberty.' A beam at Woolmers Estate was inscribed, 'England expects that every man this day will do his duty.' The significance of these words, signalled by Admiral Nelson to his fleet before the Battle of Trafalgar, remains contestable. A stone on Sarah Island carries a simpler sentiment in the form of a naked woman.

HEALTH

Health checks were carried out on convicts prior to transportation. Preventing epidemics during the voyage was critical. Once in Van Diemen's Land convicts were inspected a second time before being permitted to land. They then received regular medical attention. However, misdiagnosis and maltreatment was common. In October 1831, the surgeon at Bridgewater were reported to have prescribed a dose of salts or the application of warm or cold water for symptoms as varied as swollen limbs, failing eyesight, skin irritation and festering wounds. Scurvy and dysentery were common diseases that were potentially fatal. Scurvy was caused by poor diet and could lead to loss of teeth and open, suppurating wounds. Dysentery resulted from unsanitary living conditions, and symptoms included diarrhoea, fever and abdominal pain. During the winter months convicts were more susceptible to pneumonia, bronchitis, tuberculosis and rheumatism. Deaths amongst the elderly were commonly attributed to heart disease, paralysis and 'old age'. Infants succumbed to convulsions, whooping cough and diarrhoea. Despite this, many convicts were healthier than persons living in Britain. The food was better, the climate more temperate and living conditions were cleaner and less crowded. By 1860 life expectancy was 44 years, compared to 41 in Britain.

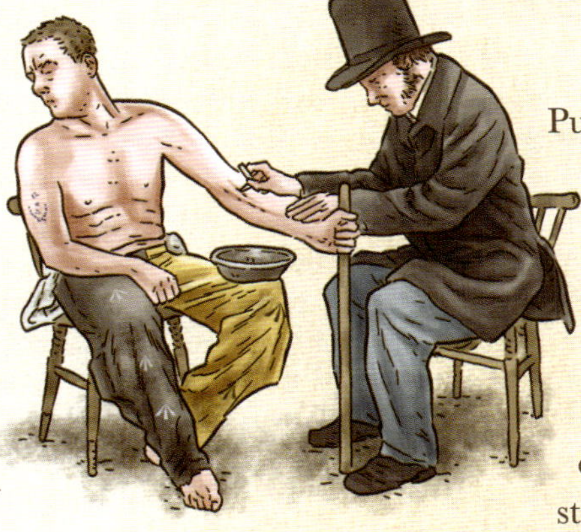

Treatment that Sucks

Purging the body of impurities was one of the primary remedies of mid-nineteenth century medicine. Bloodletting or phlebotomy was called 'breathing a vein'. It was accomplished by puncturing a blood vessel and letting the blood ooze out. It was believed that this stopped blood from stagnating in the body, and it was used to treat everything from cholera and convulsions to insanity and indigestion. Hirudotherapy, the use of leeches, was also widely practised to clean wounds and cleanse the body of impure blood. Up to 300 leeches a month were needed, so some convicts were appointed as leech gatherers.

Quacks

Quacks fraudulently provided treatment with no formal knowledge of medicine. After completing his seven-year sentence, John Gibbons established a medical practice in Launceston. He acted on a 'no cure, no payment' basis, and for a fee of £20, he attempted to cure Thomas Bishop's cancer using sulfuric acid. After 16 agonising days, Bishop was dead. Gibbons was sentenced to 18 months' hard labour.

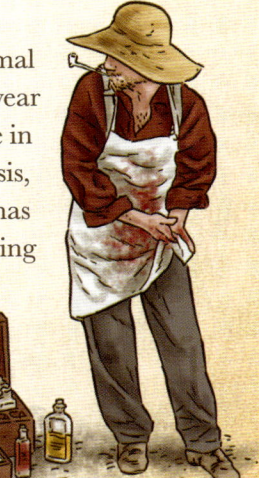

HOSPITAL

The first Van Diemonian hospital was a tent, erected in early 1803 at Sullivan's Cove. By 1818, it had been replaced by a house with two wards and two skillings at the rear. Another larger house was rented and the two buildings could accommodate up to 30 patients and 20 outpatients. In 1820, an official hospital was completed. It was known as the Colonial Hospital or Convict Hospital. Conditions were good; over the next decade the hospital mortality rate was lower than that of the British equivalent. By the 1830s, New Norfolk, Launceston, Port Arthur, Bothwell, Jericho, George Town, Richmond, Campbell Town, Norfolk Plains, Waterloo Point, Macquarie Harbour and Maria Island each had a hospital. Convicts were treated free of charge but assigned servants were charged 1 shilling per day, paid by their master. During the 1840s the number of convict hospitals increased.

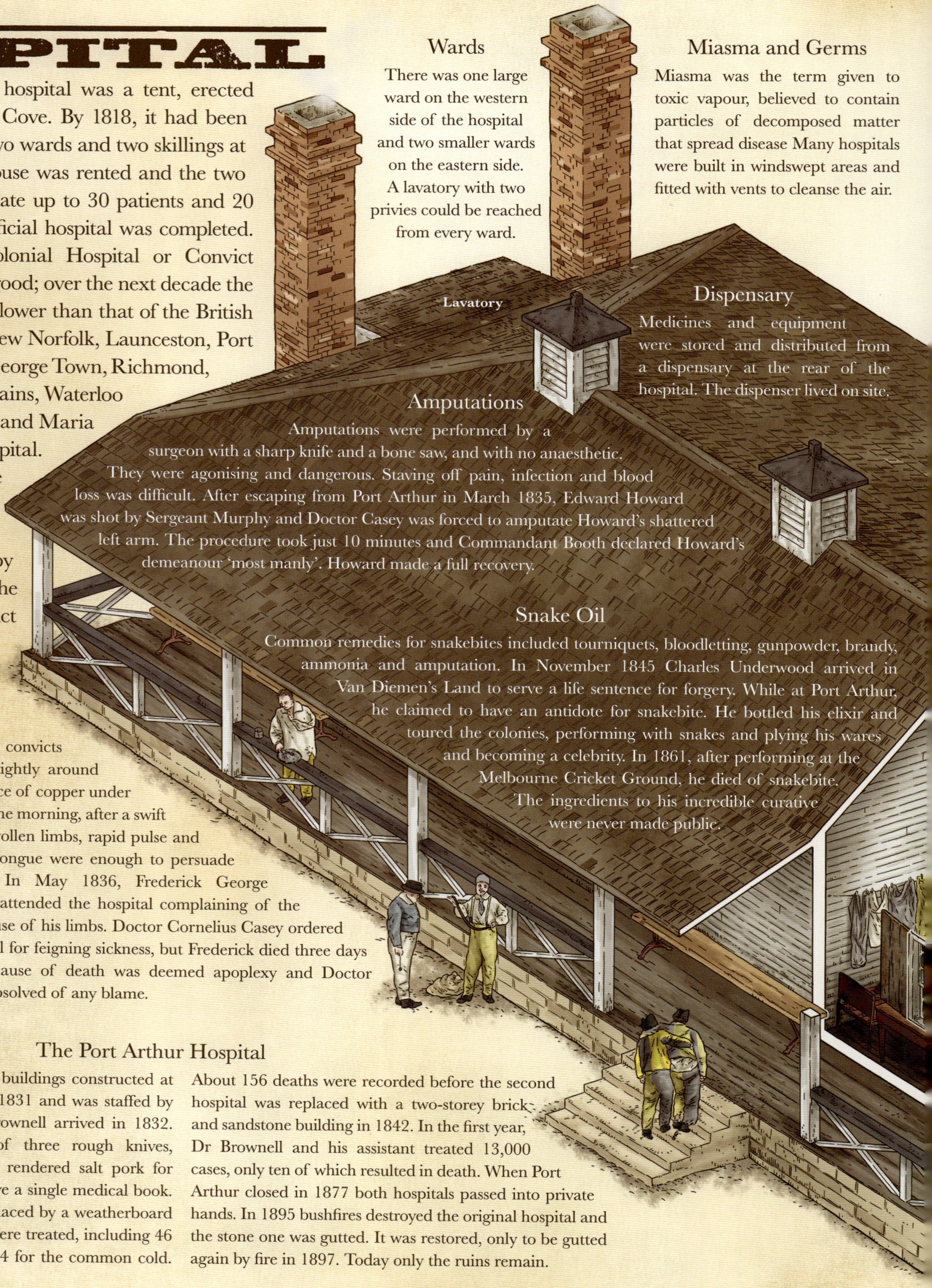

Wards
There was one large ward on the western side of the hospital and two smaller wards on the eastern side. A lavatory with two privies could be reached from every ward.

Miasma and Germs
Miasma was the term given to toxic vapour, believed to contain particles of decomposed matter that spread disease. Many hospitals were built in windswept areas and fitted with vents to cleanse the air.

Lavatory

Dispensary
Medicines and equipment were stored and distributed from a dispensary at the rear of the hospital. The dispenser lived on site.

Amputations
Amputations were performed by a surgeon with a sharp knife and a bone saw, and with no anaesthetic. They were agonising and dangerous. Staving off pain, infection and blood loss was difficult. After escaping from Port Arthur in March 1835, Edward Howard was shot by Sergeant Murphy and Doctor Casey was forced to amputate Howard's shattered left arm. The procedure took just 10 minutes and Commandant Booth declared Howard's demeanour 'most manly'. Howard made a full recovery.

Snake Oil
Common remedies for snakebites included tourniquets, bloodletting, gunpowder, brandy, ammonia and amputation. In November 1845 Charles Underwood arrived in Van Diemen's Land to serve a life sentence for forgery. While at Port Arthur, he claimed to have an antidote for snakebite. He bottled his elixir and toured the colonies, performing with snakes and plying his wares and becoming a celebrity. In 1861, after performing at the Melbourne Cricket Ground, he died of snakebite. The ingredients to his incredible curative were never made public.

Feigning Sickness
William Derrincourt stated that convicts feigned sickness by tying string tightly around the arm and placing a piece of copper under the tongue overnight. In the morning, after a swift elbow to the wall, the swollen limbs, rapid pulse and discoloured tongue were enough to persuade the doctor. In May 1836, Frederick George Hunniburn attended the hospital complaining of the loss of the use of his limbs. Doctor Cornelius Casey ordered him to a cell for feigning sickness, but Frederick died three days later. The cause of death was deemed apoplexy and Doctor Casey was absolved of any blame.

The Port Arthur Hospital
The hospital was one of the first buildings constructed at Port Arthur. It opened in March 1831 and was staffed by convicts until Doctor Thomas Brownell arrived in 1832. Medical instruments consisted of three rough knives, darning needles for sutures, and rendered salt pork for dressing wounds. Staff did not have a single medical book. Around 1832 the hospital was replaced by a weatherboard building. That year, 408 patients were treated, including 46 for scurvy, 45 for diarrhoea and 44 for the common cold. About 156 deaths were recorded before the second hospital was replaced with a two-storey brick and sandstone building in 1842. In the first year, Dr Brownell and his assistant treated 13,000 cases, only ten of which resulted in death. When Port Arthur closed in 1877 both hospitals passed into private hands. In 1895 bushfires destroyed the original hospital and the stone one was gutted. It was restored, only to be gutted again by fire in 1897. Today only the ruins remain.

James Backhouse and George Washington Walker
James Backhouse and George Washington Walker were English Quakers who embarked on a mission to the colonies in September 1831. They were in Van Diemen's Land from 1832 until 1834, investigating the conditions faced by convicts and Aborigines. Backhouse and Walker presented Lieutenant-Governor Arthur with eight reports on the penal stations of Sarah Island and Port Arthur: the conditions of road gangs, chain gangs, assigned servants and their masters; the Van Diemen's Land Company; and the Aboriginal establishment on Flinders Island. The reports contained recommendations for improving convict life. The men were acting as an independent committee of inquiry, but critics branded them as government spies. Extracts from their journals and letters were published along with information about Australian botany.

Thomas Brownell

Thomas Brownell was born in December 1800 in the Caribbean. In April 1830, he arrived in Hobart Town with his wife Elizabeth and their two children. Brownell was appointed medical officer at Maria Island Penal Station before being transferred to Port Arthur. He left after a year, defeated in his efforts to improve conditions. In July 1842 he was stabbed in the jaw by convict William Lanham but made a full recovery. The following year he returned to Maria Island with his wife and 11 children. In 1853 Brownell was appointed medical officer with the Immigration Department in Hobart Town, before returning to Port Arthur. He retired in 1857 and died in November 1871.

Head Wounds

In November 1842, James Harkness was found brutally murdered. Doctor Brownell counted ten wounds to his head.

Dead House

Autopsies were performed in the mortuary before the bodies were prepared for burial.

Cornelius Casey

Doctor Cornelius Casey, a 23-year-old Englishman, arrived in Van Diemen's Land in August 1833. He was appointed medical officer at Port Arthur in January 1834. In September 1835 he was praised after successfully stitching the head of James Stephens after another convict attacked him with an axe. In 1848 he was made medical officer to the gaol, watch house and police at Launceston, but trouble followed when he removed a female convict in labour from the gaol to the female factory. After a warning about his conduct he returned to private practice. He died in 1896.

Kitchen

The patients' food was prepared on site by convicts. In June 1822, Phillip Phillips was charged with repeated neglect of duty and embezzling food at the Colonial Hospital. He was dismissed and copped 50 lashes.

Thomas Davis

When Thomas Davis was sentenced to 75 lashes the punishment had to be remitted due to his poor health. Later he received 100 lashes. It took a month for him to recover.

George Fisher

Convicts were not permitted to leave hospital until officially discharged. When George Fisher walked out in 1871 he received a five-year term.

William Madams

Sixteen-year-old William Madams arrived in Van Diemen's Land in August 1839 to serve seven years. At Point Puer he complained of shortness of breath and severe swelling after being stung on the foot. He died at Port Arthur hospital. The autopsy report stated the cause of death as rheumatism. There was no mention of an insect or snake bite.

On Guard

The military and their families were treated at the hospital, but officers, civil servants and their families were attended to in their own houses.

HULK

Worn out vessels were transformed into floating prisons known as hulks as a cost effective way of alleviating congested prisons. The first Van Diemonian hulk was the 61-ton *Sophia*. She accommodated the Hobart Town boat crew and then later the town chain gang. The *Sophia* was used until the early 1840s. The second was the *Anson*, a 1742-ton 72-gun man-of-war that arrived in Hobart Town in October 1843 after a voyage of 126 days. The *Anson* was refitted to house newly arrived female convicts for six months probation. The first 370 women boarded the hulk in April 1844. By January the next year it was estimated that 600 women were on board. In manner and appearance they were reportedly a vast improvement on convicts in the other depots. However, they were in dire need of fresh air and exercise, having only been allowed on the upper deck for one hour twice a day. The six month probation on the *Anson* was devised to keep new arrivals free from the unsavoury influence of 'old hands', but the lieutenant-governor and the comptroller of convicts declared it a 'total failure' and claimed the *Anson* probationers reoffended at the same rate as other convict women. It was estimated that between April 1844 and August 1846, 531 of the 1141 probationers reoffended. In July 1849, the *Anson* was towed into Hobart Town, and in February 1851 her fittings were put up for auction.

Margaret Burke

Margaret Burke was transported for seven years for stealing clothes. She arrived in Van Diemen's Land in September 1849 at the age of 10 and was lodged in the *Anson*. In February 1854, she married Benjamin Collard with whom she would have three children. She gained her freedom in December 1855.

Security

The women on the *Anson* were divided into three classes according to their behaviour. They were segregated and lodged in wards on the three decks. Hatchways and portholes were fitted with bars to prevent escapes. The toilets, located at the bow, were securely boxed in. As the *Anson* was not required to sail, her masts were removed and sold. After 1844, the number of women on board at any one time never exceeded 400. In 1849, the *Anson* had 21 staff, including 11 female warders, lodged in the officers' quarters and the captain's 'great cabin'.

The Daily Routine

The women were woken by the ship's bell at sunrise. Their bedding was aired and the wards were cleaned. Between 8 am and 9 am they attended school, observed prayers and ate breakfast. The women then worked at various duties including washing, sewing and knitting. Dinner was at noon, followed by more work, an evening meal and prayers. They were mustered at 7 pm in winter and 8 pm in summer.

Recycled Timber

Timber from decommissioned ships was usually recycled. It was reported that in the chancel of St Matthew's Church in Rokeby, sat an elaborately carved chair made by Whitesides and Son from oak taken from the *Anson*.

Hard Labours

Mary Russell was transported for stealing two shirts and arrived at Hobart Town in September 1849 to serve a seven-year term. In May 1850, she absconded while assigned to the *Anson*'s assistant superintendent, Susannah Holditch. She was caught and sentenced to six months' hard labour. Eight months later, Russell gave birth to a stillborn child at the Cascades Female Factory. In September 1852, she had another baby, Elizabeth. In January 1855 Russell applied to marry Joseph Purcell, but as she had not gone six months without committing an offence, the application was refused. The couple married in April and in July Russell gave birth to William. After receiving her freedom in March 1857, she had two more sons.

Hiring Depots

The *Anson* operated as a hiring depot as well as a prison. Probationers could be hired out for private service. In 1847, there were also female hiring depots at Launceston and New Town, and male hiring depots at Fingal, Westbury, Oatlands, Jerusalem, Brown's River and New Norfolk.

Mooring

To keep her safely moored, the *Anson* had a series of iron swivels, shackles, chain cables and anchors.

Ruby Ring

In May 1848, Bridget Cashman, an *Anson* probationer, was charged with stealing a diamond and ruby ring and sentenced to six months' hard labour.

Rowe Your Boat

The *Anson* was moored six kilometres from Hobart Town. Convicts were rowed to and from the Risdon Ferry jetty by Thomas Rowe, boatman from 1844 to 1849, for 1 shilling a piece.

Matron and Superintendent

In 1843, Doctor Edmund Bowden, a qualified chemist and surgeon, and his wife Philippa, matron of Hanwell Asylum, were selected to run a new female penitentiary in Hobart Town. Their joint wage was £500 per year, with a further £300 allocated to Edmund to act as medical inspector. The penitentiary, however, was never built and the couple was appointed to run the *Anson*. In September 1847, Edmund died and Philippa succeeded him on a reduced salary of £400. Soon after, she applied for leave to visit her dying brother in England. But during her absence it was decided that the *Anson* be abandoned. In November 1850, the *Launceston Examiner* printed a long letter from Philippa Bowden in which she defended her administration of the *Anson*.

Deaths on Board

In May 1847, Mary Gilligan died aboard the *Anson*, followed the next month by Hannah Jones. Inquests returned verdicts of 'death by fever' and 'visitation from God'. The death rate on the *Anson* was quite low. Superintendent Bowden estimated that the number of sick never exceeded three per cent of the hulk's total population.

HUNTING

Convicts were among the first Europeans to hunt game in Van Diemen's Land. Native animals were an important source of food, but competition for hunting grounds was the main source of conflict between Aborigines and Europeans. By the 1830s hunting had also become a form of entertainment. Hunting parties pursued foxes and deer imported from mainland Australia.

Kangaroos

Kangaroos were a vital food source for early colonists and remained a popular staple for Van Diemonian cooks. 'Slippery Bob' was battered kangaroo brains fried in emu fat, while 'Pan Jam' was a dish of kangaroo tail with bacon and mushrooms. Sarah Crouch, the wife of the under sheriff, won a medal at the London Exhibition of 1862 for her 'Kangaroo Steamer'. Before long, the kangaroo population was in decline, and a *Kangaroo Hunting Act* was introduced in 1846.

Sealing

Seals were prized for their soft fur, and sealing was one of the earliest industries in Australia. Sealers herded groups of seals inland from the shoreline and shot, clubbed or lanced them to death. The seals were skinned and the pelts salted and stored in casks. The blubber was rendered into oil and shipped back to England. In 1810, Captain Hasselburgh discovered Macquarie Island while hunting for sealing grounds. Within 18 months, 120,000 fur seals were slaughtered there. By 1830 the seal population on Macquarie Island had been so diminished that sealing had all but ceased. Sealing was finally outlawed in 1923. By then, only one of the four seal species that once bred in Tasmania remained.

Thylacines

Van Diemonians were mystified by and terrified of the thylacine, calling it a tiger, wolf, hyena and panther. It was first described scientifically in April 1805 by Lieutenant-Colonel William Paterson, after one was fatally savaged by dogs at Port Dalrymple, and was officially classified *Thylacinus cynocephalus* in 1824. Well known Van Diemonians, including George Augustus Robinson, hunted thylacines with disregard. In April 1834 he recorded the finest hunt he'd ever seen when his dog Fly ran one down. Landowners insisted they were a threat to livestock and a bounty was introduced in 1830. Between 1888 and 1909 the government paid £1 for every dead adult thylacine and 10 shillings per pup. A total of 2184 bounties were claimed, although it was thought many more animals were slaughtered. In 1930 Wilf Batty killed the last known wild thylacine at Mawbanna. In 1933 a thylacine was sent to Hobart Zoo, but it died three years later. In that same year, the species was finally protected, but by then it was too late. The thylacine was declared extinct in 1986.

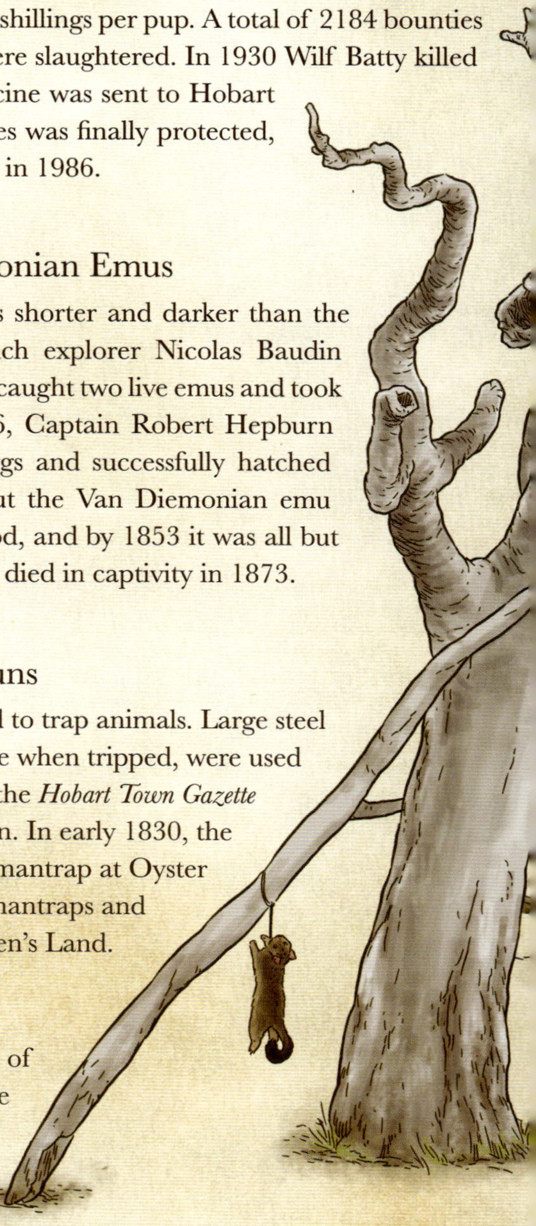

A Variety of Fare

Van Diemonians ate almost everything that came their way. Wombats and echidnas were roasted, wattlebirds and black swans were baked and parrots were made into dumplings. Sealers preserved mutton birds with salt for their long journeys. In 1864, a Van Diemonian pastoralist named Edward Abbot published Australia's first cookbook, to great acclaim.

Van Diemonian Emus

The Van Diemonian emu was shorter and darker than the mainland variety. When French explorer Nicolas Baudin visited King Island in 1802, he caught two live emus and took them back to France. In 1836, Captain Robert Hepburn found six large green emu eggs and successfully hatched them under his pet turkey. But the Van Diemonian emu was a convenient source of food, and by 1853 it was all but extinct. The last recorded emu died in captivity in 1873.

Snakes

In 1838, Lady Jane Franklin instigated a reward scheme in an attempt to eradicate snakes from Van Diemen's Land. After collecting nearly 14,000 snake heads and spending £700 she abandoned her plan.

Traps and Spring Guns

Steel traps and snares of wire, rope or twine were used to trap animals. Large steel traps known as mantraps and spring guns, rigged to fire when tripped, were used on people. In 1823, James Sharpe ran a warning in the *Hobart Town Gazette* that his Sandy Bay farm was fitted with a spring gun. In early 1830, the severed hand of an Aboriginal man was found in a mantrap at Oyster Bay. Despite being outlawed in England in 1827, mantraps and spring guns continued to be imported into Van Diemen's Land.

Tegg

Tegg was an accomplished Aboriginal tracker. In 1824, he accompanied Captain Innes in search of the Brady Gang. In 1825, Lieutenant-Governor Arthur promised him a boat made of pine if he tracked down Musquito, the Aboriginal resistance leader. Tegg, accompanied by two constables, found Musquito and shot him. When Tegg was presented with a boat made of stringybark, he took to the bush and swore he would kill any white men who came near him. Van Diemonians were in a panic; two colonists were reportedly murdered. Tegg returned and was paid his share of the reward money but never received the promised boat. It is thought that Tegg died in 1831.

HUT

The first convicts were housed in huts constructed of natural materials. They provided substantial secure shelter. Until the 1820s, convicts were allowed to build their own huts, known as 'skillings' or 'lean-tos', on plots of land of a quarter of an acre. Although these were not official land grants, convicts did what they pleased with the plots, even bequeathing them in their wills. Shepherds, farmers, sealers, hunters and emancipists also lived in huts. Some bushrangers built huts, camouflaging them in the bush. In 1826 Jorgen Jorgenson's roving party discovered one of Matthew Brady's huts south of the Great Lake. It was made from a hollow tree and was large enough to house 17 men. It had two doors, one of which seated a watchman and had a view commanding several miles. The hut was so well hidden that Jorgenson's party initially walked right past it.

Construction

The most rudimentary huts were called 'brush huts' or 'breakwinds'. David Burn, a Van Diemonian memoirist, said they were made of boughs and thatched with long grass. Slab huts were made by covering a basic wooden frame with large sheets of bark and timber. Log huts were built by placing logs on top of each other and interlocking them at the corners. They were weatherproofed with mud, daubing, sticks and rocks, or chinking, to seal joints and cracks. Wool was also used to seal gaps. A hut could be made in just two days and last for many years. Michael Howe's hut near the upper Shannon River remained largely undisturbed until 12 years after his death. In 1830 James Ross described it as a floor neatly paved with bark beneath a thatched roof. Thatched roofs were constructed with dry vegetation such as straw or grass. Shingles were pieces of timber, layered three deep to seal a roof.

The Shannon Hut

The Shannon hut, on the upper Shannon River, was originally built for stockmen. In 1822, it was home to an old shepherd named Dennis who sheltered absconders and bushrangers. In 1826, Jorgen Jorgenson visited it while attempting to map an overland stock route from Hobart Town to Circular Head.

Strange Friends

Some kangaroos were so successfully tamed that they would live with hunting dogs.

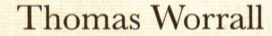

Thomas Worrall

Thomas Worrall arrived in Van Diemen's Land in September 1817 to serve a 14-year sentence. In October 1818, he was nearly shot while taking part in the killing of the bushranger Michael Howe at the Shannon hut. Worrall had traded with Howe, but a reward of 100 guineas and a free pardon with passage to England had proved irresistible. Worrall received a full pardon in January 1819, but in February 1833 he was convicted of burglary in New South Wales and given a seven-year sentence.

William Davis and Ralph Churton

William Davis and Ralph Churton were English convicts who remained in the colony after serving their sentences. In February 1822, they were arrested for stealing 106 sheep but they escaped into the bush. The Shannon hut provided an excellent hideout. Together with other convicts, including Alexander Pearce, they rustled sheep and sold them at Lovely Banks. In January 1823, after nearly a year at large, they were ambushed by the 48th Regiment. They were tried and executed in April 1823.

Sheep Stealing

In 1818, mutton was worth 6 pence per pound and sheep stealing was big business. The favoured technique was to break into the middle of a herd and drive off several hundred of the healthiest sheep. If the sheep weren't killed immediately, they were taken to a hidden stockyard where their brands were cut off or disguised. Some farmers lost 1000 head per year. Sheep stealing was such a problem in the colony that the *Sheep Stealing Act* imposed capital punishment for offenders.

Skins

In 1855, a variety of unique Van Diemonian skins were displayed in Paris. They included seal, emu, possum, platypus, quoll, wallaby, kangaroo, devil and thylacine.

35

INVALID STATION & INSANE ASYLUM

The term 'invalid' was used by Van Diemonian authorities to describe convicts who were incapable of earning a living due to age, illness or accident. After acquiring their freedom, many invalids were reduced to living on the streets. Many were cast back into penal establishments for vagrancy. In the 1820s, the number of invalids was on the rise, and in 1827 Lieutenant-Governor Arthur had them sent to New Norfolk where they were to be housed, given clothing and supplies and put to work. They lived in two leaking rooms. Their plight was described as miserable, wretched and hopeless. Lieutenant-Governor Arthur approved the building of a new establishment at New Norfolk, and architect John Lee Archer delivered the plans in December 1829. By October 1833, after a series of delays and the addition of an insane asylum, the complex was operating. In 1841 a new wing was completed, but the complex soon became severely overcrowded. Segregation of private patients from prisoners was not possible until 1859 when a 'gentleman's cottage' was constructed. Nearly nine years later an equivalent was built for women. The complex continued to grow, but it generated scandal and criticism well into the next century. It closed in 2001.

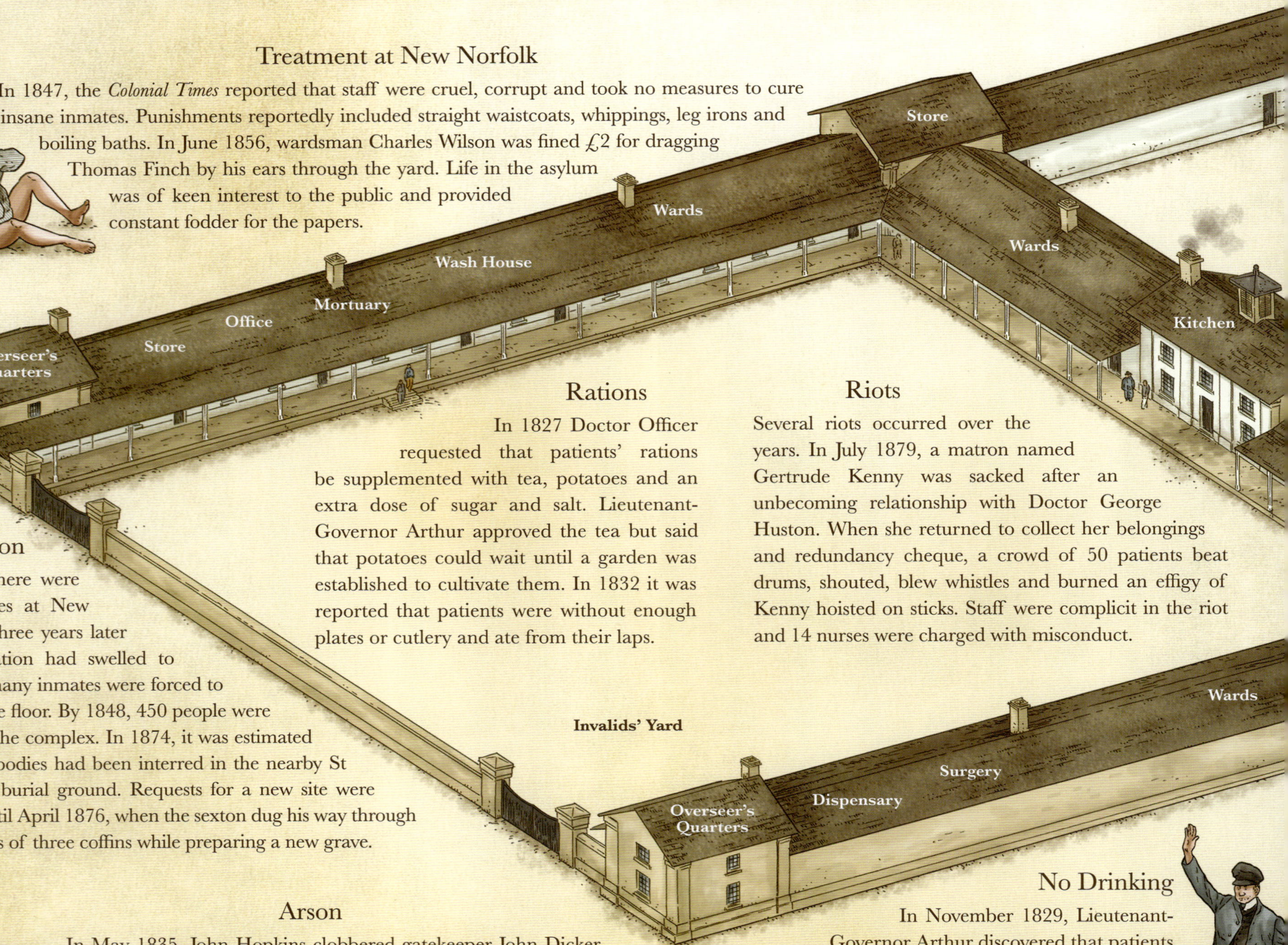

Treatment at New Norfolk
In 1847, the *Colonial Times* reported that staff were cruel, corrupt and took no measures to cure insane inmates. Punishments reportedly included straight waistcoats, whippings, leg irons and boiling baths. In June 1856, wardsman Charles Wilson was fined £2 for dragging Thomas Finch by his ears through the yard. Life in the asylum was of keen interest to the public and provided constant fodder for the papers.

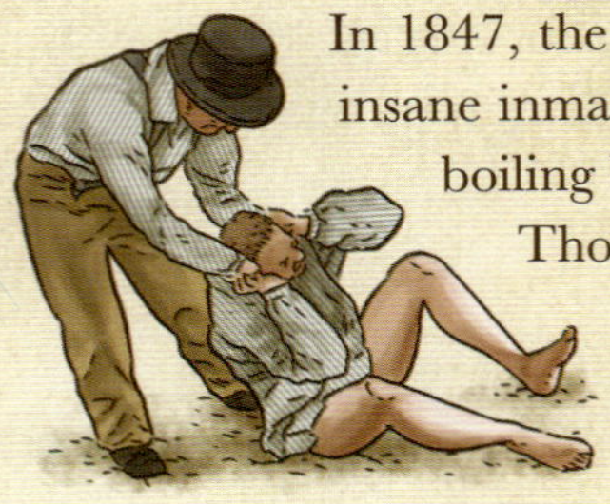

Population
In 1833, there were 109 inmates at New Norfolk. Three years later the population had swelled to 300, and many inmates were forced to sleep on the floor. By 1848, 450 people were housed in the complex. In 1874, it was estimated that 2000 bodies had been interred in the nearby St Matthew's burial ground. Requests for a new site were ignored until April 1876, when the sexton dug his way through the remains of three coffins while preparing a new grave.

Rations
In 1827 Doctor Officer requested that patients' rations be supplemented with tea, potatoes and an extra dose of sugar and salt. Lieutenant-Governor Arthur approved the tea but said that potatoes could wait until a garden was established to cultivate them. In 1832 it was reported that patients were without enough plates or cutlery and ate from their laps.

Riots
Several riots occurred over the years. In July 1879, a matron named Gertrude Kenny was sacked after an unbecoming relationship with Doctor George Huston. When she returned to collect her belongings and redundancy cheque, a crowd of 50 patients beat drums, shouted, blew whistles and burned an effigy of Kenny hoisted on sticks. Staff were complicit in the riot and 14 nurses were charged with misconduct.

Arson
In May 1835, John Hopkins clobbered gatekeeper John Dicker with an iron bar and attempted to escape. Following two more escape attempts he was ordered to Port Arthur but, before departing, he smuggled in flint and steel and set his cell on fire.

No Drinking
In November 1829, Lieutenant-Governor Arthur discovered that patients were working outside the complex to earn money to buy alcohol. He prohibited them from leaving and put them to work growing vegetables.

Problem Staff
Reliable staff were hard to find. After the first overseer was dismissed, Lieutenant-Governor Arthur appointed a lifer, Henry Harrington, but Harrington was soon caught swindling. His successor was a convict named William Pahle, who stole wine and made off with medicines. In 1832, Walter and Margaret MacQueen were appointed overseer and matron, but when their daughter was nearly killed by an inmate, Arthur dismissed them. Another lifer, John Dicker, was made gatekeeper in 1835. He was executed in March 1849 for attacking Constable Samuel Withers with a tomahawk.

Richard Lewis

In November 1832, Richard Lewis was sentenced to three months' imprisonment and hard labour for assaulting gatekeeper John Dicker. In October the following year, he was caught gambling and sent to a road gang for 12 months. A few weeks later he was charged with refusing to work. In May 1859, Lewis was charged with being insane and illegally at large. Clad in only a blanket he wept bitterly, claiming he possessed a horse that could jump nine yards, swim a river and catch a kangaroo and that the doctor had poisoned him in order to rob him. He was returned to New Norfolk and confined to the asylum.

Samuel Wade

In December 1847, Samuel Wade, an inmate and servant to the head keeper, James Deadman, obtained a gun. Wade shot Deadman through the arm and bolted. In Wade's cell were found four iron bars, two skeleton keys, a hammer and clothes stolen from the store. He was decreed insane, acquitted of all charges and returned to the asylum.

Travelling to New Norfolk

Lieutenant-Governor Arthur often visited New Norfolk. In 1827, he was appalled to see 12 of the first invalids arrive in an open boat. The men had endured three days and two nights exposed to the rain in inadequate clothing, and two of them had no bedding. Lieutenant-Governor Arthur ordered all inmates travel by cart.

Tender Care

In April 1834, assigned nurse Euphemia Kinghorn was sent to solitary for 24 hours for violent and outrageous conduct. When she was again charged with disorderly conduct three days later, she was sent back to the Cascades Female Factory for a six-month stint in Crime Class.

Quite Contrary

When the mood took her, Mary Campbell wandered into town to commit petty theft. In March 1836, she was caught in John Wiseman's parlour and charged with stealing a racing jacket and goods valued at 30 shillings.

Bolters

George Wright, John Hopkins, George Harrington and Joseph Green absconded in July 1846. The four convicts supported themselves by bushranging.

Robert Officer

Robert Officer served as surgeon during his voyage out, arriving in Hobart Town in March 1822. In October 1823, he married Jemima Patterson, with whom he would have 13 children. They moved to New Norfolk to take charge of the asylum and gaol. Officer entered politics in October 1853, was knighted in January 1869 and retired in April 1877. He died two years later, leaving an estate valued at £6200.

Accommodating Invalids

For many years, penal and non-penal invalid establishments were almost indistinguishable. As well as New Norfolk, there were invalid stations at Launceston, the Brickfields, the Cascades, Salt Water River, Wedge Bay, Impression Bay, Port Arthur and New Town. In the 1850s, the Crown agreed to assist the Colonial Government by paying the costs of most debilitated ex-convicts and those in lunatic asylums, hospitals and invalid depots who were 60 years of age and over when they arrived in Van Diemen's Land. By the 1890s, the New Norfolk insane asylum, known as the Hospital for the Insane, was the colony's only mental hospital. In the twentieth century it became the Mental Diseases Hospital, then Lachlan Park, and finally the Royal Derwent Hospital. The hospital was also known as Willow Court, after a willow tree planted by Lady Jane Franklin that was reputedly grown from a cutting of the tree on Napoleon Bonaparte's grave.

John Quigley

John Quigley was born in Ireland in 1819. He arrived in New South Wales in 1837 to serve seven years for theft. After committing numerous offences he was sentenced to life on Norfolk Island. In 1846, he fractured his skull during a fight, and it was thought that the injury permanently altered his state of mind. Quigley returned to Van Diemen's Land in 1849 and spent the next three years at the New Norfolk insane asylum. He was discharged on New Year's Day in 1852, and he embarked on a bushranging career which ended abruptly when he was shot in the thigh. At his trial in January 1856, the jury decided he was unable to comprehend the proceedings, of unsound mind and mute by the visitation of God. On the journey back to New Norfolk, Quigley tried to escape and reportedly confessed to feigning madness. The authorities were unable to agree on Quigley's mental state and after several more questionable episodes he was sent to Port Arthur. There he was kept in a purpose-built cell with an adjoining exercise yard that became known as Quigley's Cage. One visitor stated that he galloped wildly around and roared like a lion. When the station closed in 1877, Quigley was transferred to the asylum at the Cascades where he died in November 1883.

JUVENILE

Several thousand children were transported to Van Diemen's Land. Some were accompanying their convict parents, and others were transported for their own crimes. Finding a suitable place for convicted children within Van Diemonian society was difficult. By the early 1830s the number of convicted males between the ages of 10 and 18 years, juveniles, had increased. Lieutenant-Governor Arthur described them as 'entirely useless' and 'the dread of every family'. Juvenile convicts were viewed as a burden and suffered from abuse and corruption in adult penal establishments. Many remained separated from their families for the rest of their lives.

Walter Paisley

In 1832, Walter Paisley was convicted of burglary. The 15-year-old arrived in Van Diemen's Land to serve seven years. He was one of the first boys sent to Point Puer and was considered one of the most troublesome. His first offence was insubordination, for which he received seven days on bread and water in solitary confinement. He copped another seven days for reciting an obscene story. His other offences included plundering turnips, stealing and killing chickens and striking the schoolmaster. By 1838, he had committed 45 offences, and in 1839 he was sentenced to ten more years before receiving a conditional pardon in 1847. He did, however, master a trade. In October 1859, it was reported that 'the celebrated woodman Walter Paisley' lectured in Launceston. In 1872, a wooden dinghy he made was given to Dinah and John Wilson as a wedding gift. The dinghy still exists and is a testament to his fine workmanship.

Point Puer Boys' Establishment

In 1833, it was decided that boys boarding with adult prisoners in Hobart Town required a separate facility. A barracks was built on a point of land opposite Port Arthur. The area became known as Point Puer ('puer' is Latin for boy). It was the first exclusively juvenile penal institution within the British Empire. It had a strict regime of education, religious instruction and trades instruction. In 1843, the population peaked at about 800. Reports on the condition of the boys ranged from ragged and dirty to fit and well. Commandant William Champ declared Point Puer wretched, bleak, barren and utterly useless. Supplies had to be shipped in. Supervision was difficult, and the boys remained in contact with adult convicts. It was suggested that a new site be formed at Safety Cove, but it was never built. By the 1840s, fewer juveniles were being transported, and in 1849 the population of Point Puer had dropped to 162 and the gaol was closed. The remaining boys were transferred to the Cascades probation station.

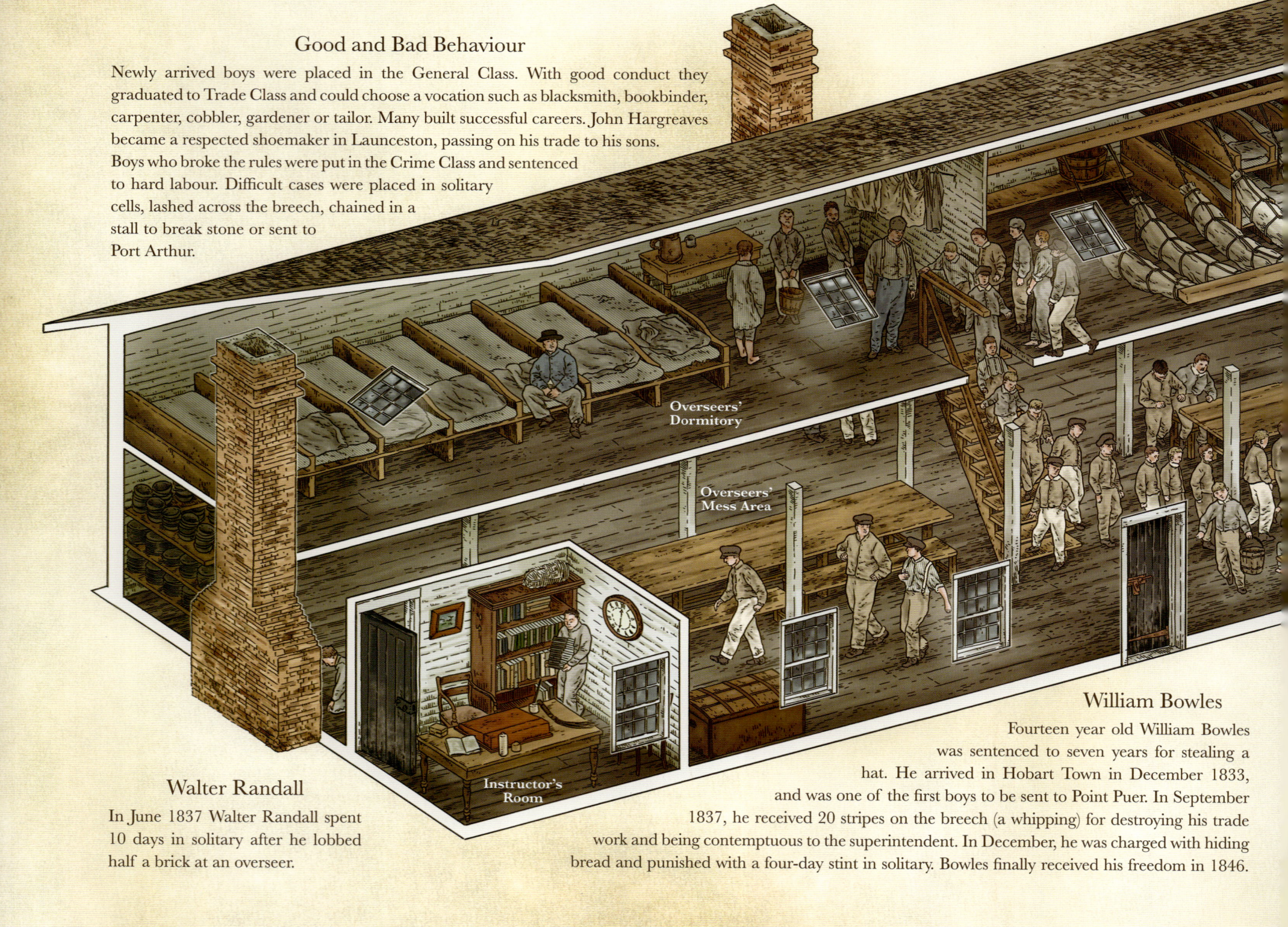

Good and Bad Behaviour

Newly arrived boys were placed in the General Class. With good conduct they graduated to Trade Class and could choose a vocation such as blacksmith, bookbinder, carpenter, cobbler, gardener or tailor. Many built successful careers. John Hargreaves became a respected shoemaker in Launceston, passing on his trade to his sons. Boys who broke the rules were put in the Crime Class and sentenced to hard labour. Difficult cases were placed in solitary cells, lashed across the breech, chained in a stall to break stone or sent to Port Arthur.

Overseers' Dormitory

Overseers' Mess Area

Instructor's Room

Walter Randall

In June 1837 Walter Randall spent 10 days in solitary after he lobbed half a brick at an overseer.

William Bowles

Fourteen year old William Bowles was sentenced to seven years for stealing a hat. He arrived in Hobart Town in December 1833, and was one of the first boys to be sent to Point Puer. In September 1837, he received 20 stripes on the breech (a whipping) for destroying his trade work and being contemptuous to the superintendent. In December, he was charged with hiding bread and punished with a four-day stint in solitary. Bowles finally received his freedom in 1846.

Leisure

An area along the coastline known as the Rocks was a hideout where the boys spent time fishing, catching crayfish, climbing, concealing little treasures or eating stolen food. One group used the Rocks as a place to worship. The boys played games with marbles and buttons. Buttons were a form of currency, used to obtain tobacco, food or other luxuries. The boys were searched regularly to prevent gambling and trafficking.

John Allen Manton

John Allen Manton was born in England in August 1807 and began preaching while still in his teens. He was the first chaplain at Port Arthur. Manton's duties included conducting lessons for the first batch of boys at Point Puer. He later established a Wesleyan school for boys in Campbell Town. He died in September 1864.

Uniform

The boys washed once a day in the sea, weather permitting. They were each issued a jacket and trousers of tanned sheepskin, a grey cloth waistcoat, a striped shirt, a leather or scotch cap and a pair of boots. In October 1836, however, Commandant Booth reported that three quarters of the boys were almost entirely naked and in desperate need of clothes.

Surveillance

A small military force and civil officers kept watch over the boys. Adult convicts from Port Arthur were appointed as overseers.

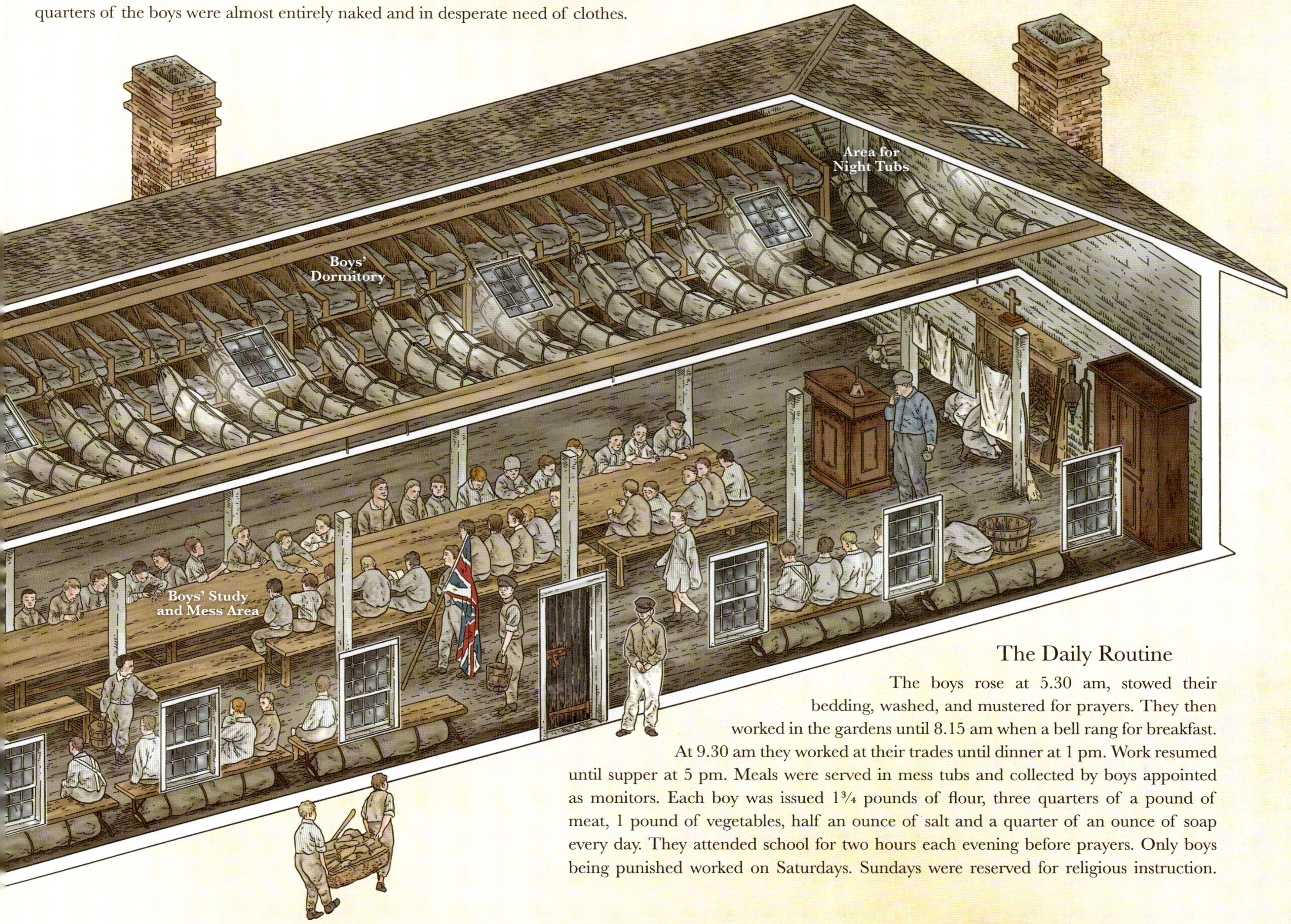

Boys' Dormitory

Area for Night Tubs

Boys' Study and Mess Area

The Daily Routine

The boys rose at 5.30 am, stowed their bedding, washed, and mustered for prayers. They then worked in the gardens until 8.15 am when a bell rang for breakfast. At 9.30 am they worked at their trades until dinner at 1 pm. Work resumed until supper at 5 pm. Meals were served in mess tubs and collected by boys appointed as monitors. Each boy was issued 1¾ pounds of flour, three quarters of a pound of meat, 1 pound of vegetables, half an ounce of salt and a quarter of an ounce of soap every day. They attended school for two hours each evening before prayers. Only boys being punished worked on Saturdays. Sundays were reserved for religious instruction.

Van Diemonian Orphanages

In 1826, it was estimated that 100 children were orphaned, destitute or neglected by immoral parents and in dire need of help. In 1833, the King's Orphan School was constructed at New Town and 325 children were taken in. It was run like a penal establishment. Children were mustered, inspected, punished, given religious instruction, school lessons and instruction in trades. When they turned 14 or 15 they were placed in employment. The King's Orphan School was plagued by mismanagement and a lack of funding. Reverend Thomas Beagley Naylor was hired to oversee the orphanage, but he resigned in 1839. His replacement, Reverend Thomas James Ewing, was accused of having relations with one of the girls. In 1843, there were 499 children at the school, 376 of whom were children of convicts. In 1848, a report stated that teachers were undertrained and underequipped, classes were overcrowded and that trades training was limited to tailoring, shoemaking and baking for boys and domestic work, knitting and needlework for girls. The King's Orphan School finally closed in 1879. The remaining children were sent to other institutions.

KILN

Bricks and lime were made in temporary kilns called clamps that were built from bricks or stone and daubed with clay. A fire was lit at the base and the hot air was sucked in through a vent. The first permanent kilns, scotch kilns, had three permanent walls and a fourth that was demolished to retrieve the fired bricks and rebuilt for next batch. In December 1842, convict William Flaherty had three months added to his sentence after he was caught cooking cakes and meat in a kiln.

Shipping Bricks
The first bricks arrived in 1803. By the next year they were being produced locally.

Making Lime
Lime was made from limestone or seashells from the beach and from Aboriginal middens. A lime kiln took one day to load, three to fire and two to cool. Lime was mixed with sand, or sometimes convicts' hair, to make mortar. It was also used to wash walls and fertilise plants. Lime is corrosive and can cause burns and blindness. Convicts made to carry lime sacks after being flogged suffered terribly.

Lashes for Bricks
In May 1823 George Clements and William Cooley got 100 and 50 lashes respectively for stealing 500 bricks.

Making Bricks
Clay was broken up with spades before being spread out and weathered. Convicts used their bare feet to mix in water until the clay had a doughy consistency. This process was called pugging. Brickmakers worked at a bench called a moulding stool. A lump of pugged clay, or a 'clot', was rolled in sand and shaped before being pressed into a wooden mould. The 'green bricks' were dried until they were ready for firing. Bricks had to be heated for three or four days at a temperature greater than 900°C. Brickmaking was smoky, dusty and laborious. In the 1840s, two brickmakers were expected to produce 7000 bricks a week.

Brick Marks
Bricks were branded with the broad arrow to mark them as government property. Bricks made for a specific purpose had initials such as E. D. for Engineers Department or R. E. for Royal Engineers. Tally marks recorded each convict's quota. Thumbprints were left when brickmakers pressed clots into the moulds. Other marks, such as paw prints, were purely accidental.

Bricks and Pebbles
Indomitable convicts were known as 'bricks' or 'pebbles'. Henry Roberts, when caught stealing brandy, stated that he was a brick and would not betray his accomplices. In May 1855 Elizabeth Douglas shook her fist in her mistress's face and declared she was a pebble and could take any punishment dished out. She received 12 months' gaol with hard labour.

LAW

Convicts who committed serious offences were sent to New South Wales to stand trial in the Supreme Court. The process was costly and time consuming. Magistrates who tried offenders in Van Diemen's Land had no legal authority to impose capital punishment or extend a convict's sentence. As a result punishments were often meted out with the lash, leg irons or a stint in the pillory or stocks. The system was impossible to manage fairly and was resented by colonists and convicts alike. Lawyers were mostly emancipated convicts. The first formally trained lawyer, Edward Cartwright, did not arrive until 1820.

In 1824 a Supreme Court was established in Van Diemen's Land, and Judge John Lewis Pedder was appointed chief justice for the colony. Juries were comprised of military officers until 1840 when civil juries replaced them. In 1825, Van Diemen's Land was granted administrative independence from New South Wales and acquired an executive council and a legislative council. Laws were known as 'general orders' and printed and distributed. Aboriginal laws and customs were disregarded. The presiding lieutenant governor was the Crown's sole representative and held almost absolute authority until 1855 when Tasmania, as it had become known, acquired responsible government.

Convicts were the first non-military people to police Van Diemen's Land. They worked as nightwatchmen, but robberies remained frequent, and in 1806 the watch was replaced with military patrols. In 1810, Governor Macquarie ordered a police force be established. Due to the sparse spread of settlements, rugged terrain and frequent attacks by Aborigines and bushrangers, an armed and mounted force of field police was formed in 1826. It was staffed by the best-behaved convicts and controlled by the government through a regime of punishment and reward. The government hoped that the freedom and power entrusted to convict constables would lead to their reformation. Free persons were generally not interested in police work due to the low pay. In 1828, the colony was divided into nine police districts. Field police in each district worked under the control of a local magistrate who reported to the chief police magistrate in Hobart Town. By 1835 the police force numbered 453, most of them convicts, and there was approximately one policeman for every 89 Van Diemonians. In 1857 an act was passed that transferred the control of police to local councils. By 1866, 21 municipal councils each had its own force, headed by the inspector of police. And in 1899, the *Police Regulation Act* was passed, amalgamating the forces into a single unit of 246 men.

LAWMAN

'Traps'

Police were initially paid in liquor at the rate of one quart per week. Drunkenness was so prevalent that the practice was discontinued. By 1827, the annual police wage was £10. This was not enough to live on, so many policemen had to earn extra cash. People complained that they weren't focusing on official duties. Although the pay was poor, convict constables were granted a ticket-of-leave or even a free pardon for exemplary service. Some, however, accepted bribes, stole property and bullied or entrapped Van Diemonians in order to acquire fines and rewards. The constabulary were known colloquially as 'traps'.

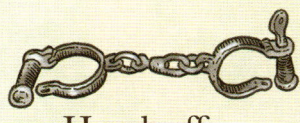

Handcuffs

Handcuffs were first mass-produced in 1780 by Hiatt and Co. The most common style was known as a D-Cuff. They could not be adjusted, allowing some convicts to slip their hands out while others bore the pain of the iron digging into their flesh. In later years handcuffs incorporated adjustable ratchets so they could be tightened and loosened.

Javelin Men

Javelin men were mostly well-behaved convicts or ex-convicts who worked in gaols to process and guard inmates. Javelin men took their name from the long pole they carried. It was fitted with an axe blade, spike and hook. They worked under the instruction that 'every prisoner wishes and is waiting for an opportunity to make his escape from gaol', and they could be called to duty at any time of the day or night.

Uniforms

In 1818 constables and overseers were supplied with a pair of duck trousers, a cotton shirt, a forage cap, two ounces of thread and 2½ yards of cloth in lieu of a jacket. In 1837, field police were issued blue cloaks, dress jackets, trousers, oilskin caps and ankle boots. Boots wore out very quickly. In 1853, constables in pursuit of bushrangers James Dalton and Andrew Kelly were incapable of performing their duties due to poor boots. A local magistrate ordered they be supplied with new ones.

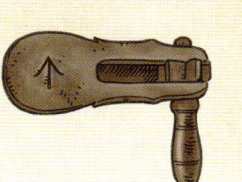

Alarm Rattle

Alarm rattles consisted of one or two blades held in a wooden frame. When swung by the handle, a rotating ratchet made the blades snap very loudly.

Truncheon

Police were armed with wooden truncheons that were painted blue with a crowned V. R. cypher carefully detailed in gold. V. R. stood for Victoria Regina and was the mark of Queen Victoria. Below the cypher were the letters V. D. L. for Van Diemen's Land. Lawmen also carried clubs made from wood or whale baleen.

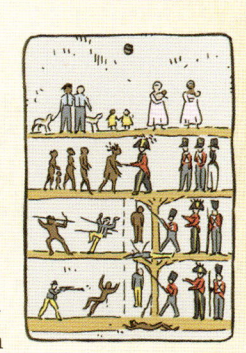

Proclamation Board

Following the increasing violence between colonists and Aborigines, illustrations depicting colonists and Aborigines embracing each other, as well as punishment for murder, were painted on pine boards and nailed to trees. Just what the Aborigines made of the pictures remains unknown, but equality was never achieved and capital punishment was never imposed on a European for the murder of an Aborigine.

Isaac Solomon

Isaac Solomon was born in London in 1787. He trafficked in stolen goods, primarily jewellery, and amassed considerable wealth. In April 1810, he was arrested for picking pockets and sentenced to life transportation, but he escaped from the prison hulk and resumed his life of crime. In April 1827 he was charged with theft and receiving but he fled to America. In his absence his wife, Ann, was transported for 14 years. She arrived in Hobart Town in June 1828 with her four young children. Upon hearing the news Solomon travelled to Van Diemen's Land under the assumed name of Slowman and opened a shop in Hobart Town. A petition to have his wife assigned to him was declined, but after Solomon paid a bond of £1000, Lieutenant-Governor Arthur relented. In 1829, warrants arrived from England and Solomon was arrested but he was released on £2000 bail. A vexed Lieutenant-Governor Arthur issued another warrant and transported Solomon back to England. He was sentenced to 14 years, and promptly returned to Van Diemen's Land, where he was sent to the Richmond gaol. Solomon, the basis for the character of Fagin in Charles Dickens' novel *Oliver Twist*, was ironically given the trusted position of javelin man. He received a conditional pardon in May 1840 and his free certificate four years later. He died in September 1850 leaving an estate of £70.

41

LEG IRONS

Convicts were fitted with leg irons—also known as shackles, fetters, chains, 'old wives' or irons—to impair movement. Irons made life miserable. Most weighed approximately two kilograms, some as much as 25 kilograms, yet convicts in irons still had to do manual labour. Convicts were responsible for keeping their irons in good condition, and when 'mustering irons' was called each set was carefully inspected. Convicts in 'flash mobs' took pride in keeping them spotless. William Thompson claimed his looked like polished silver. When irons were removed the change in weight left convicts walking with high clumsy steps. After many years in leg irons, some convicts were left crippled.

Gaiter
Gaiters were leather cuffs worn to reduce chafing from irons. Some had straps to hold up the basils. Shirts and even the lining from hats were used when gaiters weren't available.

Toerag
A rag was wrapped between the toes and around the foot as a makeshift sock.

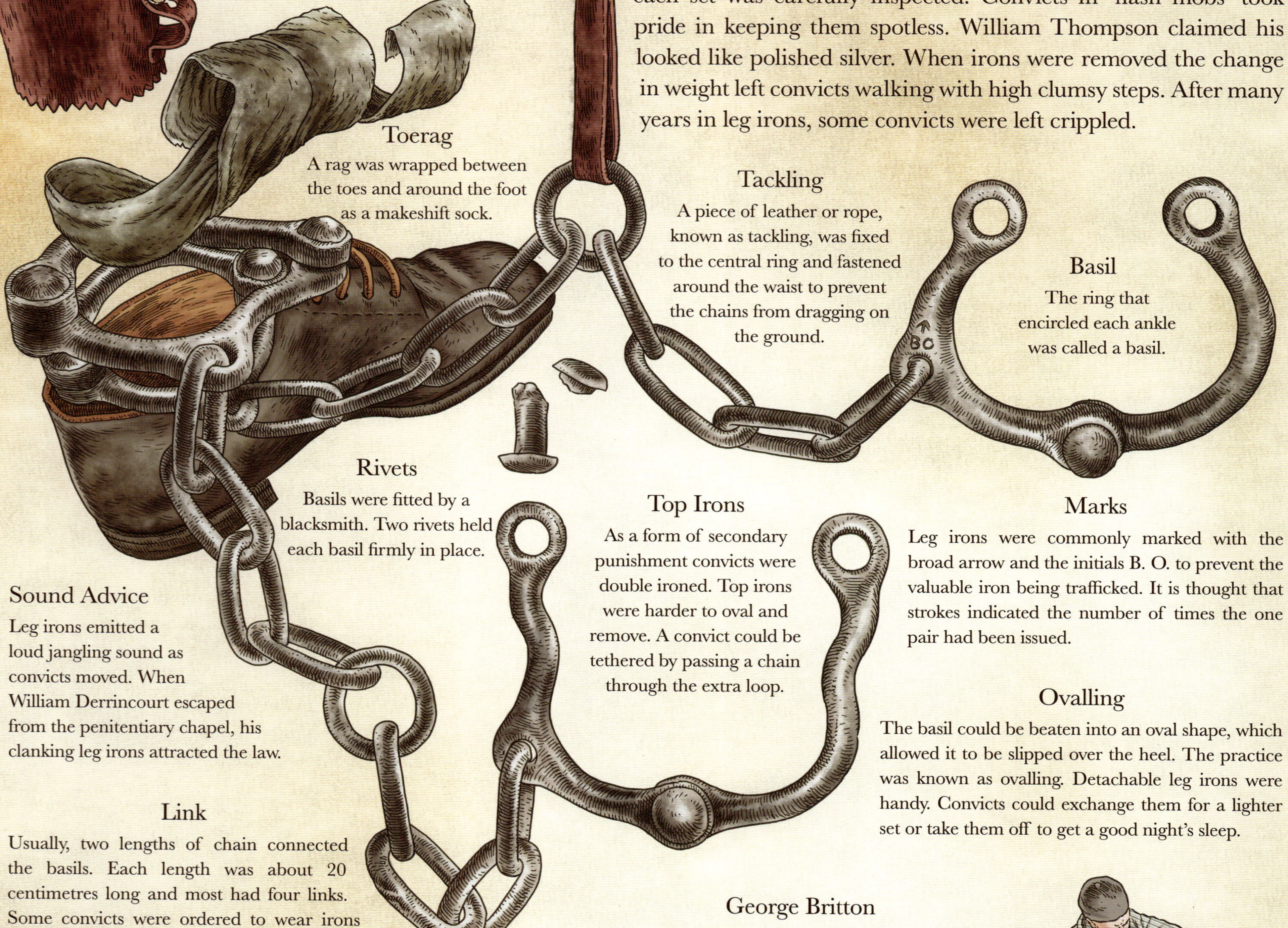

Tackling
A piece of leather or rope, known as tackling, was fixed to the central ring and fastened around the waist to prevent the chains from dragging on the ground.

Basil
The ring that encircled each ankle was called a basil.

Rivets
Basils were fitted by a blacksmith. Two rivets held each basil firmly in place.

Top Irons
As a form of secondary punishment convicts were double ironed. Top irons were harder to oval and remove. A convict could be tethered by passing a chain through the extra loop.

Marks
Leg irons were commonly marked with the broad arrow and the initials B. O. to prevent the valuable iron being trafficked. It is thought that strokes indicated the number of times the one pair had been issued.

Sound Advice
Leg irons emitted a loud jangling sound as convicts moved. When William Derrincourt escaped from the penitentiary chapel, his clanking leg irons attracted the law.

Ovalling
The basil could be beaten into an oval shape, which allowed it to be slipped over the heel. The practice was known as ovalling. Detachable leg irons were handy. Convicts could exchange them for a lighter set or take them off to get a good night's sleep.

Link
Usually, two lengths of chain connected the basils. Each length was about 20 centimetres long and most had four links. Some convicts were ordered to wear irons connected with just one link, which restricted their movement forcing them to shuffle. Some convicts were permitted to wear basils with no chains.

George Britton
George Britton arrived in Van Diemen's Land in December 1832 to serve seven years for stealing clothes. Britton was described as 'exceedingly bad', and he endured more than 16 years in leg irons.

Bribing the Blacksmith
A blacksmith could make a set of leg irons in about seven hours, but the vast majority of irons were imported from England. Irons were riveted on in a matter of minutes by blacksmiths, and removed by carefully striking the tops off the rivets. Some convicts bribed blacksmiths for favours. In 1834, William Leonard was caught making 'screw rivets' that could be removed by convicts. Blacksmith Henry Scarlett fitted irons so loosely that convicts were able to slip them off.

Log and Chain
It is unlikely that Van Diemonian convicts were subjected to the ball and chain. They were, however, sometimes chained to logs of wood. Nineteen year old George Wiggins, when bathing at Point Puer, got his irons, chain and log caught in kelp and he drowned.

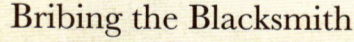

Most convicts worked from dawn till dusk, with time off on the weekend. Free time was spent working to earn cash, resting or enjoying various forms of entertainment.

LEISURE

Games of Chance
Although it was strictly forbidden, convicts gambled on games of chance like dice, cards and dominoes. In May 1844 John Glanville was given 36 lashes for making cards cut from the pages of a Bible.

Singing and Dancing
Song and dance empowered convicts by unifying them, celebrating their exploits and ridiculing authority. In June 1840 Ann Dixon and Dinah Baker were charged with dancing in a public house and received 14 days in solitary. In July 1843 James Doran copped 25 lashes for singing in his hut. Convict Francis MacNamara, known as Frank the Poet, was well known for contemptuous verse. He departed Van Diemen's Land with the words 'Land of lags and kangaroo, of possums and the scarce emu, the farmer's pride but the prisoner's hell, land of bums—fare-thee-well!'

Bare-knuckle Boxing
Bare-knuckle boxing, also known as pugilism and prizefighting, was popular with convicts. In April 1842, at the Jerusalem probation station, Charles Evans and Patrick Kelly decided to settle a disagreement by belting it out. A crowd of convicts gathered around as the two men fought for 45 minutes. In the final round Evans was struck under his right ear and after reeling, complaining of pain and experiencing several fits, he died. Kelly was charged with manslaughter and two other convicts, Patrick Norey and William Cutts, were charged with aiding and abetting. Bare-knuckle fighting was declared assault in 1882 and the sport died out.

Blood Sports
A cockfight is a contest between two roosters, held in a ring called a cockpit. In August 1831 John Williams was punished with a two-month stint on a chain gang for skipping a church service to attend a cockfight. In 1857 the *Licensing Act* permitted bull baiting, cockfighting and dog fighting within public houses.

LIQUOR

The most common alcoholic drink in Van Diemen's Land was rum. Convicts sometimes received a small rum ration to increase their stamina, mark a celebration or as a reward. In the early days, alcohol was more valuable than land. Publicans were forbidden to serve convicts, but liquor could be obtained from sly grog shops. When a large amount of rum arrived in 1807, almost the whole colony got drunk. Preventing convicts from frequenting taverns was extremely difficult. Jorgen Jorgenson noted that pubs were filled with convicts night and day and it was often dangerous to walk the streets, even in the daytime. In 1831, James Ross estimated that 100,000 gallons of liquor was consumed annually, five gallons for every man, woman and child. Between 1830 and 1836, 62 colonists, 36 convicts and 38 people of uncertain status died from alcohol-related incidents. By the 1850s there was one pub for every 127 Van Diemonians, and alcoholism was rife. Temperance societies failed to improve the situation despite massive public support as taxes on alcohol were a major source of government income.

Lieutenant-Governor Thomas Davey
Thomas Davey was born in England in 1758. At 21, he was commissioned as a second lieutenant in the Marines. He served in America and the West Indies and in 1787 was made a volunteer guard and accompanied the First Fleet to New South Wales. He was appointed lieutenant-governor of Van Diemen's Land in 1811. Davey soon earned a reputation for drunken behaviour. Edward Abbot claimed that he invented a particularly strong brew concocted from two pints of boiling water, one pint of rum and half a pint of brandy. It was called Blow My Skull. In 1814 Governor Macquarie of New South Wales recommend he be dismissed due to his 'lack of manners and morals'. With limited resources, however, Lieutenant-Governor Davey did manage to build a gaol, commence a church and initiate shipping and trade. But this did not impress his superiors and in 1816 he was dismissed. He died in relative poverty in May 1823.

LOVE TOKEN

Convicts sometimes smoothed the faces of coins and scratched messages into their surfaces to make love tokens, also known as leaden hearts. In July 1833, 21-year-old Joseph Budd left a love token. One face bore his name, date of birth and date of transportation and the other was inscribed, 'When this you see, remember me and bear me in your mind. Let all the world say what they will, don't prove to me unkind.'

43

MILITARY

In 1804, the Van Diemonian military amounted to just 50 personnel. The number peaked at approximately 2000 in 1845. Soldiers not only maintained civil law and order but also worked alongside convicts. Unlike convicts, however, they could not obtain a ticket-of-leave or pardon, and it could be decades before they returned to their homeland. Some bought their way out of military service and others deserted. Notorious deserter James Geary helped seize the military barracks at George Town, and a reward of 100 guineas was posted for his capture. Geary died a few weeks later from wounds received in a shootout with soldiers of the 46th Regiment. In 1826, military pensioners guarded convicts on the voyage out from England. Because they were not needed on the return journey, they were allotted land in outlying areas and served as field police or convict supervisors. In 1858, an Act of Parliament allowed the formation of volunteer corps. The first was formed in Hobart Town in 1859 and another in Launceston the following year. By the time British troops were withdrawn in 1870, 32 regiments had served in Van Diemen's Land. Following Federation in 1901, the Australian colonial corps merged to form the first federal army unit.

Cartridge Box
A leather box slung over the shoulder held ammunition cartridges, spare flints and leathers, and a tool for fixing muskets.

Red Coats
Soldiers were nicknamed redcoats. Regiments were identified by their coloured collars and cuffs.

Shako
Shakos were tall cylindrical hats made of felt and leather.

Plates and Plumes
The shako had a plate on the front and a coloured plume on top.

Shoulder Belt
Leather straps slung over the shoulders were used to carry equipment. A metal plate featuring the regiment's number was attached to the straps.

Trousers
White duck trousers were issued for summer; blue-grey for winter.

Backpack
Soldiers carried packs containing anything from a greatcoat to shaving gear.

Haversack
Rations were carried in a shoulder bag.

Shoes
Soldiers wore black leather boots and gaiters.

Barracks
In 1811, Governor Macquarie declared a hill southwest of Hobart Town the site for a formal barracks. The foundation stone was laid in August 1814, and by 1850 it incorporated quarters for the soldiers, subalterns and officers, a court for soldiers to play a game called fives, a taproom, guardhouse, gaol, hospital and a memorial for the 99th Regiment. Named after the Marquis of Anglesey, Anglesea Barracks is the oldest Australian army barracks still in military service.

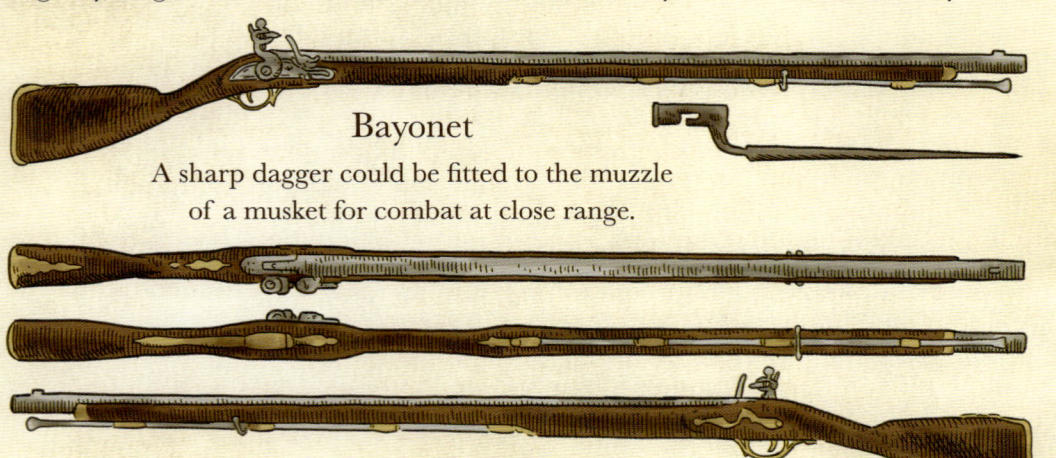

Bayonet
A sharp dagger could be fitted to the muzzle of a musket for combat at close range.

Water Canteen
Soldiers were issued wooden canteens which were carried on a leather strap. They were supplied by the Board of Ordnance and marked with B. O. and the broad arrow.

Firing the Brown Bess
Brown Bess was the nickname given to the British Army's Land Pattern Musket. When preparing to fire a Brown Bess, a soldier would first bite the end off a cartridge and place some of the gunpowder in the pan as a priming charge. The remaining powder was poured into the barrel, followed by the ball, and the empty paper cartridge was packed into the bottom of the barrel. If a soldier did not wish to fire immediately he could draw back the cock, which is where the expression 'going off half cocked' originated. If the powder was wet it might result in 'a flash in the pan'. If the flint was skinned or chipped, the soldier might be called a 'skin flint'. A Brown Bess could fire to a distance of roughly 275 metres, but they were considered accurate only to about 90 metres.

46th Regiment

In 1814, the 46th Regiment was called to eradicate the first large-scale bushranging outbreak. Initially the bushrangers had the upper hand, and roving parties of the 46th spent weeks clambering through the bush without success. After recruiting convict constables familiar with the terrain, the tables started to turn. In March 1817, the regiment found three bushrangers, William Elliot, James Parker and John Chapman, lying in ambush at Scantlings Plains. Elliot and Chapman were shot dead but Parker escaped. The heads of the dead bushrangers were hacked off and taken back to Hobart Town for identification. The next month, the infamous Michael Howe was very nearly taken. He managed to escape but Private Michael Sullivan caught his Aboriginal companion, Mary, and his hideouts were burned. When detachments of the 46th left Van Diemen's Land in June 1818, Lieutenant-Governor Sorell publicly commended them for bringing the Howe Gang to justice. The 46th had, however, been a pain in the governor's neck. At Port Dalrymple they were largely insubordinate drunks who committed acts of arson, including setting fire to their own barracks, and staged numerous burglaries.

Paying the Price

Soldiers were not paid in cash, as hard currency was in short supply and the paymaster in Sydney was not prepared to risk cash being lost at sea. Instead, they received commissariat notes. The pay for a private was just 6 pence a day but they also received rewards. In October 1825, Private William Moroney helped apprehend James McCabe and was entitled to share in a reward of 50 guineas. In the same year, Joseph Thompson of the 40th was shot dead by bushrangers. He paid the ultimate price.

Fur Coats

When a blunder in military supplies resulted in members of the 40th Regiment not being issued haversacks, knapsacks known as Derwent drums were fashioned from kangaroo skins. Some soldiers preferred to outfit their entire kit with skins, which were more suited to the climate. They wore possum-skin caps and jackets and trousers trimmed with fur, and they carried kangaroo skin cartridge boxes. In March 1821 a party of soldiers didn't recognise another party from Launceston. In the ensuing shootout Corporal John Deane was killed. The following year, serving convicts were officially banned from wearing any clothing fashioned from skins.

Lieutenant Colonel William Balfour

William Balfour joined the 40th Regiment at the age of 14. Within five years he had risen to lieutenant colonel, and in January 1825 he arrived in Sydney. Balfour travelled to Port Dalrymple, where he was appointed civil and military commandant. He was instrumental in cracking the Brady Gang and, when Edward Abbot replaced him, Lieutenant-Governor Arthur retained Balfour's services by dividing the colony into military districts, each under his command. In Hobart Town, Balfour improved regulations within the public stores and extended Anglesea Barracks. He retired in 1832.

48th Regiment

Members of the 48th Regiment sailed from New South Wales in March 1818. Their first job was to relocate the settlement of Port Dalrymple to George Town. As an incentive to speed up the move, Major Gilbert Cimitiere issued rum to the convicts. Consequently, the military had their rum ration cut. When replacement rum arrived, it was ordered to be sold to avoid a drunken frenzy. Members of the 48th were furious and threatened mutiny. Eventually the booze was doled out and the soldiers drank it peacefully. In October 1818, Private William Pugh received a reward of £50 for assisting in the slaughter of Michael Howe. Aside from bringing bushrangers to justice, the 48th also oversaw roadwork and inspected travellers to stamp out illegal trade. Soldiers from the 48th sailed to Sarah Island to form the first penal station. Life at the remote station was no picnic. Several soldiers perished in the bush, and in December 1823 Lieutenant Cuthbertson drowned. In April 1834, the 48th departed Van Diemen's Land for service in India.

Court Martial

Insubordinate soldiers risked severe punishment. Deserters faced up to 300 lashes or transportation. Soldiers lost their rations, were fined, sentenced to hard labour or executed.

Roast Boot

Rations frequently ran out. Soldiers resorted to hunting game and handouts from colonists whilst on patrol. When Lance Sergeant Justin McCarthy's men ran out of rations, they roasted their leather boots.

40th Regiment

The 40th Regiment arrived in Hobart Town in August 1823 and was faced with rising tensions between colonists and Aborigines. The regiment was sent into the bush to capture Aborigines, which resulted in many deaths. Lieutenant-Governor Arthur declared martial law, and in October 1830 he instigated the Black Line. More than 2200 men marched through the wilderness in an attempt to drive the Aborigines south. The march lasted six weeks, incurred costs of £30,000 and resulted in the capture of one boy and a man. The 40th also faced the second big bushranging outbreak in the 1820s. They fought bushrangers for several years but, with the death of Matthew Brady in May 1826, the threat diminished. In January 1830 residents of Hobart Town gathered to farewell them as they marched to the docks to travel to India.

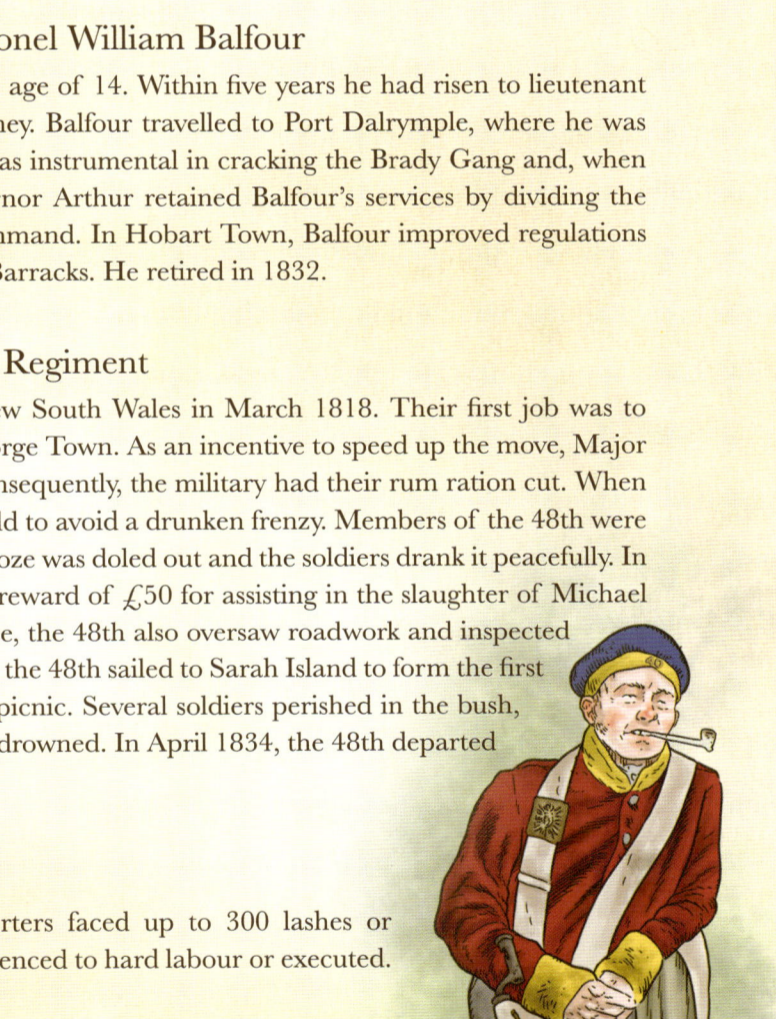

45

MONEY

In the early days, Van Diemen's Land faced a severe cash shortage. To get around the problem, Van Diemonians issued promissory notes, written contracts in which the issuer promised to pay a sum of money to the payee. Not all issuers were able to honour their promises, however, and forgery was rife. In March 1817, George Jackson received 50 lashes and 12 months on a chain gang for forging a note. Thomas Child was executed for forging £600 in treasury bills. In 1826, the *Sterling Money Act* was passed, and banks began printing their own notes. Currency tokens were minted in place of coins. After receiving his free certificate, Reuben Josephs rented the New Town Toll Gate and had tokens produced in his name.

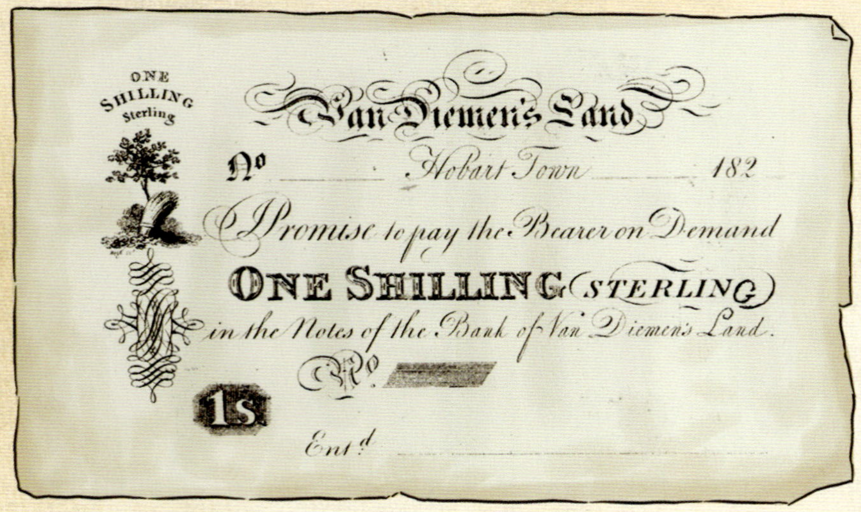

Thomas Bock

Thomas Bock, born in 1790, was an accomplished engraver. In 1817, he was awarded a silver medal by the Society of Arts, but in 1823, he was found guilty of administering drugs to bring about an abortion and was sentenced to 14 years' transportation. After arriving in Van Diemen's Land, he completed engravings for almanacks and businesses as well as several banknotes for the Van Diemen's Land Bank. He operated an art gallery in Hobart Town before receiving a free pardon in November 1832. Bock was the colony's first professional painter. He completed detailed portraits of colonists, Aborigines and condemned convicts and is the only known colonial artist to produce nudes and to experiment with photography. Bock died in March 1855.

Convict Wages

After 1816, colonists were required to pay their assigned servants wages. Men could earn £10 per year and women £2. Other convicts were allowed to seek employment outside of working hours. But under Lieutenant-Governor Arthur's rule, assigned servants were forbidden wages, though some convicts, such as those on ticket-of-leave, were permitted to earn money. Any new arrivals carrying cash had their money confiscated. In 1828, Arthur established the Convicts Savings Bank. Each convict's cash was compulsorily deposited and could only be obtained with his approval. Under the Probation System, convicts on a probation pass were permitted to work for wages. How much money convicts could bank, or were allowed to keep, was dependent on their behaviour. Troublemakers could lose their pass and their savings. By the late 1860s, convicts, excluding those serving life sentences, were entitled to a weekly wage of 6 pence. It was hoped that payments encouraged good behaviour, discouraged repeat offending and helped emancipated convicts become established in the colony.

NEWSPAPER

The first newspaper, the *Derwent Star and Van Diemen's Land Intelligencer*, was set up in 1810. It sold for 2 shillings and was produced fortnightly by government printer George Clarke. It lasted only two years. The next paper, the *Van Diemen's Land Gazette and General Advertiser*, began in 1814. It too was short-lived, and Clarke was dismissed and replaced by his assistant, newly arrived convict Andrew Bent. Newspapers were a source of local and foreign news, including weather, commerce, marriages, obituaries, remedies and advertisements. They also alerted the public to absconders and bushrangers, and posted rewards.

Andrew Bent

Andrew Bent was born in London in 1790. In October 1810, he was charged with burglary, and he arrived in Hobart Town in February 1812 to serve a life sentence. He was appointed government printer and began the *Hobart Town Gazette and Southern Reporter*, and in December 1818 he published Australia's first book of general literature, *Michael Howe, the Last and Worst of the Bushrangers of Van Diemen's Land*. On 1 January 1821, he retitled the paper the *Hobart Town Gazette and Van Diemen's Land Advertiser*, and in 1824 he bought the paper and declared freedom of the press. Lieutenant-Governor Arthur was not impressed. He fined Bent £500 and sent him to gaol. Bent continued to oppose the government so Arthur printed his own gazette and forced Bent to rename his paper. After another stint in gaol, Bent sold his now-named *Colonial Times* and moved to Sydney. After failing at numerous business ventures, Bent died in poverty in August 1851, leaving behind a large family.

Henry Melville

Henry Melville was born in 1799 and arrived in Hobart Town in 1827. In March 1830, he purchased the *Colonial Times* from Andrew Bent and later that year printed *Quintus Servinton*, the first Australian novel. In 1833, he began the first Australian monthly magazine, the *Hobart Town Magazine*. He also wrote *The Bushranger; or Norwood Vale*, the first play with an Australian theme to be published and staged in Australia. Melville was gaoled for 12 months and fined £200 for contempt of court after reporting on a cattle stealing case in his *Colonial Times*. While incarcerated, he completed *A History of the Island of Van Diemen's Land from the Year 1824 to 1835*, which was smuggled out and printed in England. Melville left Van Diemen's Land in 1849 and died in London in 1873.

The first convicts were managed by the lieutenant-governor, the colonial secretary and civil and military officers. In 1818, a formal Convict Department was formed. Detailed registers were kept listing each convict's physical description and criminal and personal history. Over time, the department was restructured. In 1827, the Office of the Muster Master was created to oversee the record-keeping. When the Probation System was introduced the Office of Registrar was formed, which was headed by the comptroller-general of convicts. The registers, known as the black books, make up the most all-encompassing account of persons living anywhere in the world during the 19th century.

OFFICE

Signing Off
In February 1832, Richard Williams, a clerk at the barracks, absconded. The following year another convict clerk drowned himself in the Derwent River.

Office Gateway
Two octagonal sandstone offices flanked the Campbell Street entrance to the Hobart Town prisoners' barracks. The office on the left was converted into quarters for the gaoler, complete with vegetable garden. The other remained the superintendent's office with a small outer office for the gatekeeper. Both buildings, and the gates, were demolished in 1963.

Knocker
The entrance to the Hobart Town prisoners' barracks featured a brass doorknocker in the shape of the head of Dionysus, Greek God of wine, ritual madness and ecstasy.

Gatekeeper
A trusted gatekeeper was crucial to maintain security and prevent contraband goods entering the barracks. James Cutmear recorded the comings and goings of convicts and inspected cells and dormitories.

Edward Cook
When Edward Cook, an ex-law-stationer, arrived in Van Diemen's Land in April 1825, Lieutenant-Governor Arthur ordered him to reorganise the black books. Cook worked up to 15 hours a day, writing out 12,305 entries. He was frequently charged with neglect of duty and being drunk, and later he claimed that the ordeal had ill effects upon his health. Cook died in April 1837 when he was crushed by a falling tree.

Convict Clerks
Educated convicts were often appointed as clerks. They were viewed by the authorities as a 'moral and Imperial menace of the worst type', as they could avoid hard labour and their stations held considerable influence. Some people suggested they should be banned from the colony once they gained their freedom. Lieutenant-Governor Arthur held little hope for their reformation believing they were lazy, dishonest and 'usually confirmed drunkards'. In March 1827, Douglas Gilchrist and Henry Cockerell, clerks at the Colonial Secretaries Office, were caught altering the sentence of Furniss Grass in the black books from life to seven years. They were sent to Maria Island to serve the rest of their sentences.

Josiah Spode, Muster Master
Josiah Spode was born in 1790 in England. He joined the Navy young and was made an officer in 1809. He moved to Hobart Town with his wife in 1821, and in 1827 he was appointed muster master. In 1831, he was promoted to principal superintendent of convicts. His duties included examining new arrivals, taking control of their possessions and overseeing their appropriation, punishment and living conditions as well as addressing complaints and petitions for indulgences. In 1844, his position was abolished and he retired on a pension of £220 per year. In 1854, Spode returned to England with his wife and two sons. He died in 1858.

PENAL STATION

Penal stations were established to take reoffending convicts for secondary punishment. For over two decades, incorrigible Van Diemonian convicts had been shipped to New South Wales, Queensland or Norfolk Island. In 1822, Lieutenant-Governor Sorell proposed that a penal station be established on Sarah Island in Macquarie Harbour. Convicts were sent there for minor offences such as drunkenness, disobedience, neglect of duty and absence from work, but also for serious crimes such as murder, assault and larceny. Convicts there were subjected to the hardest labour and harshest punishments of the colony. Sarah Island was widely regarded as a hell on earth. In 1825, a second station was built on Maria Island. It closed in 1832. Port Arthur, established in 1833, became Australia's largest penal station. Convicts there worked cutting timber and stone, farming, shoemaking, blacksmithing, tailoring and constructing vessels until the station was closed in 1877.

Sarah Island

James Kelly discovered Sarah Island in 1815 while circumnavigating Van Diemen's Land. A party of 110, including 74 convicts, arrived at the island in early 1822. Land was cleared and an officers' quarters, a military and convicts' barracks, a storehouse and a hospital were built, followed by a tannery, shoemaker's shop, school and further officers' quarters. By 1831, the station was producing £4600 worth of goods annually, but costs were estimated at £8000. The real value of the station, however, was in the convicts who learned skills that enabled them to rejoin society at the end of their sentences and help the colony prosper. Approximately 1150 convicts served time on Sarah Island, including fewer than 30 women. By 1832, the penal station was being wound down, and convicts were transferred to Port Arthur along with surplus stores and equipment. In 1833, it was officially closed and the island was left with nothing but a few stray pigs and goats wandering among the empty buildings.

A Long Hard Voyage

On average it took 27 days to make the 300-kilometre sea voyage from Hobart Town to Sarah Island. At times the ships were delayed by storms and the trip could take longer than three months. Convicts were clapped in leg irons and crammed in on top of cargo. At times they were unable to stand up and remained covered in their own filth. All vessels had to pass through a narrow and dangerous channel known as Hell's Gates. Many had to be guided or winched through to ensure a safe passage.

Solitary for Two

In September 1824, Mary Ann Furze was sent to solitary for seven days. On the sixth day, George Miller was found in her cell but he was acquitted of any charge.

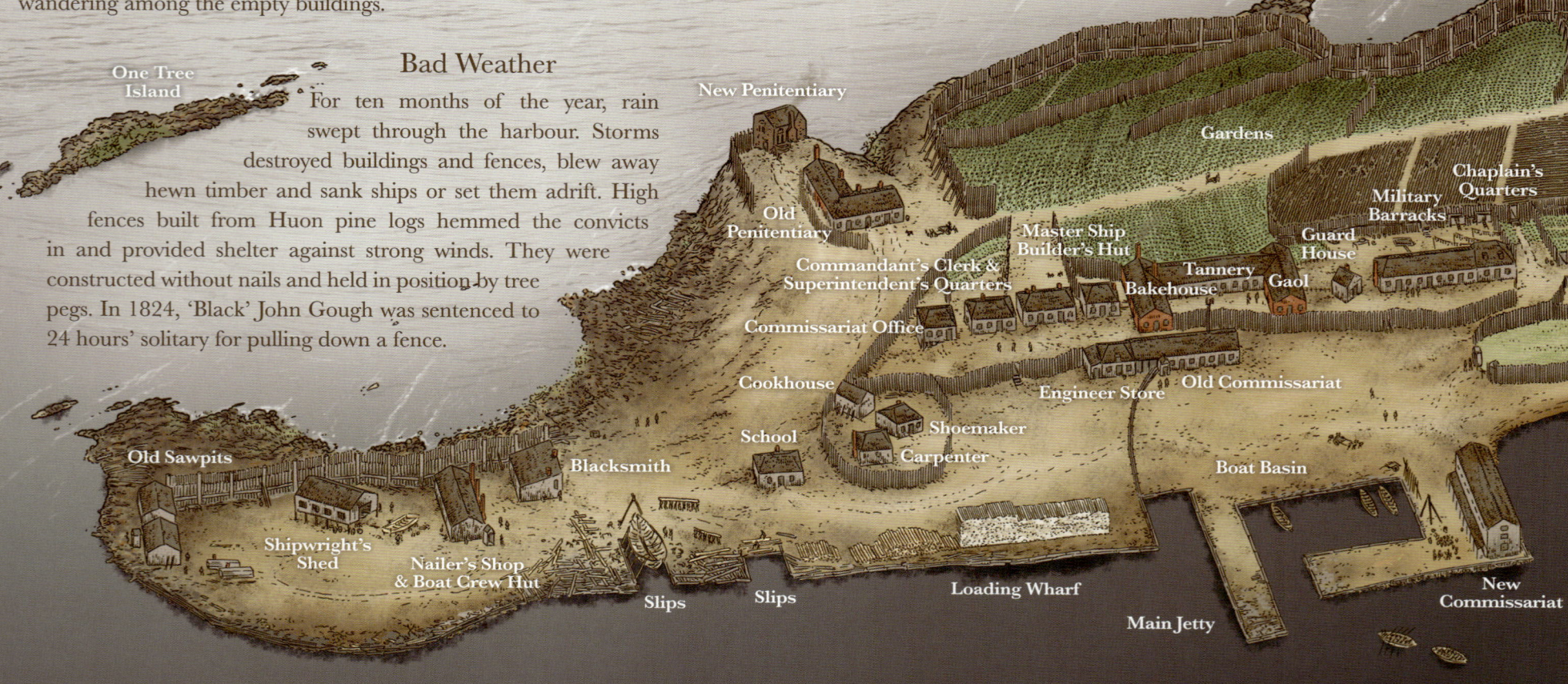

Bad Weather

For ten months of the year, rain swept through the harbour. Storms destroyed buildings and fences, blew away hewn timber and sank ships or set them adrift. High fences built from Huon pine logs hemmed the convicts in and provided shelter against strong winds. They were constructed without nails and held in position by tree pegs. In 1824, 'Black' John Gough was sentenced to 24 hours' solitary for pulling down a fence.

Lashes

In February 1825, Benjamin Bowers was caught crafting a key to the storekeeper's hall door from an impression made in a bar of soap. He received 50 lashes. In 1827, Thomas Morrison copped 50 lashes and eight months in leg irons and was dismissed as watchman for letting convicts make prohibited articles in the blacksmith's shop. In 1828, Thomas Singleton Hawley received 12 lashes for hiding nails in his hat. James Mason lopped off two of his own fingers in 1822 in order to avoid work. He was charged with depriving the government of labour and sentenced to receive 50 lashes.

Daily Routine

The majority of the convicts worked from 7 am to 5 pm between April and October and from 6 am to 6 pm for the rest of the year. Breakfast was from 9 am until 10 am and dinner was from 1 pm until 2 pm. They were given Sunday afternoon off to attend chapel and mend their clothes. Each day the convicts were mustered, inspected and searched for contraband items.

Rations

Food shortages plagued Sarah Island. Each week convicts received 7 pounds of wheatmeal to make bread, salt beef and vegetables when available. A daily ration of 4 ounces of wheat, oat or maize meal was also doled out to make skilly. Convicts carted fresh water by boat to Sarah Island from a creek at Rum Point.

Thomas Day

Thomas Day, a Jamaican born into slavery, was sent to Sarah Island for stealing. He managed to escape with several others, but he was caught and returned to the station. He then served dutifully under Reverend Schofield and Reverend Manton. But after receiving his freedom he was charged with burglary and sent to Port Arthur for another 10 years. Day died in July 1860. It is estimated that several hundred black convicts were transported to Van Diemen's Land. In the records they were termed 'black' and 'of colour'.

Absconders

In 1822, Deputy Surveyor-General George William Evans declared that escape from Sarah Island was next to impossible. Eight weeks later, John Green and Joseph Saunders decamped from a work party. Six more men bolted just six days later. They all disappeared, as did the search party that went after them. In just over a decade, 271 convicts attempted to escape. Those that went overland faced starvation in the bush and some resorted to cannibalism. Runaways on the coastal route risked being found by the harbour pilot or attacked by Aborigines.

Staff at the Station

The first party to arrive on Sarah Island included a military detachment of 17 men and their wives and children. Lieutenant John Cuthbertson was appointed as first commandant in 1821. His duty was to maintain security and ensure convicts undertook hard labour and issue orders. He also served as a judge and could sentence convicts to lashes, solitary confinement or to the chain gang. Convicts were sent to Hobart Town to stand trial for serious offences. A convict clerk dealt with paperwork, and pockets of military posted at the outstations guarded against convict uprisings. The surgeon, with several convict assistants, was responsible for the health of all at the station The pilot's primary duty was to guide vessels through the harbour. A commissariat officer dealt with supplies, a missionary instructed in religious and secular education, and a master shipwright oversaw ship construction. Convicts also served as overseers and watchmen.

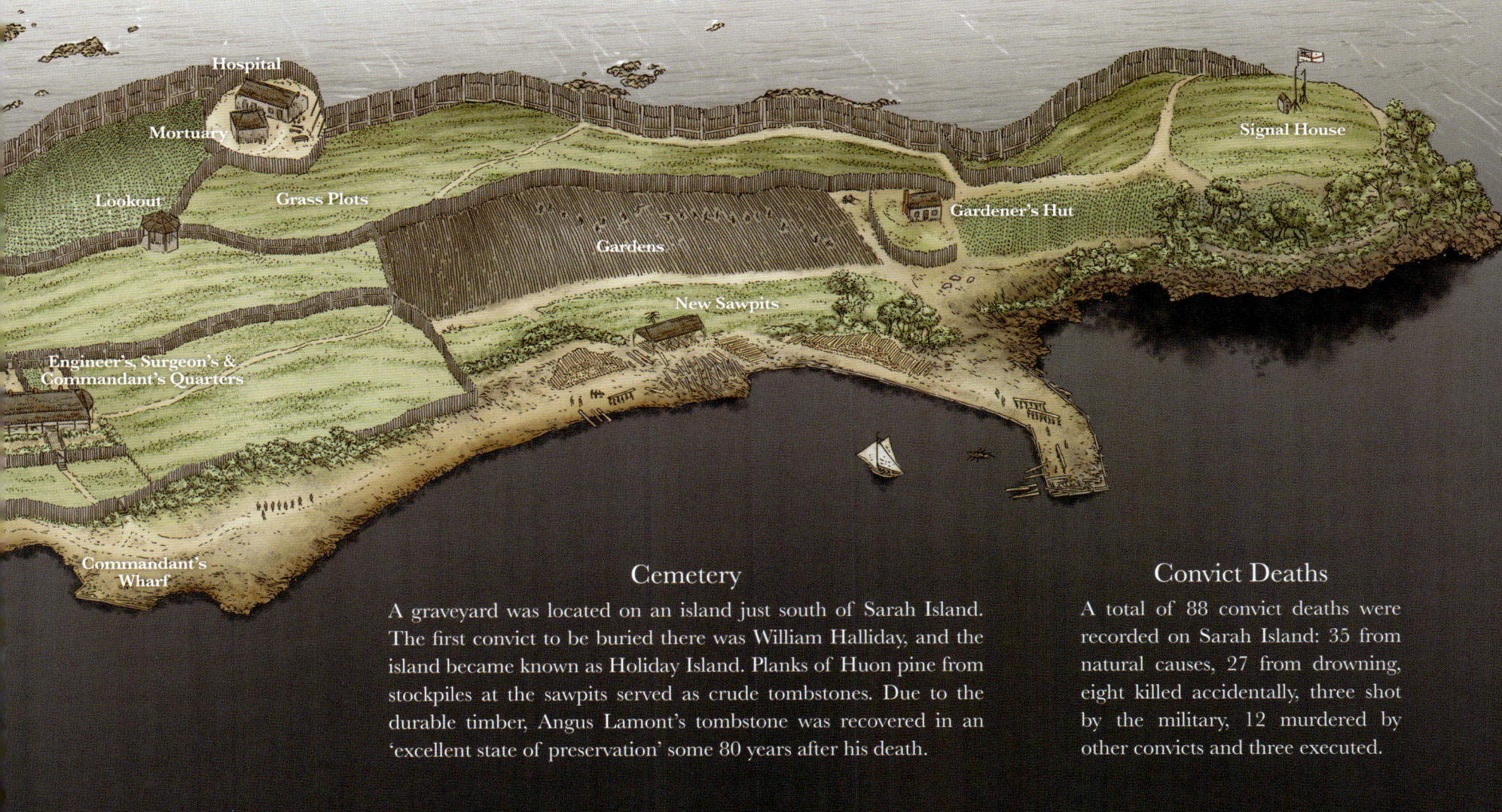

Joseph Geary

Joseph Geary absconded in January 1825 and was speared to death the same day by Aborigines.

In the Stocks

In October 1822, nurse Elizabeth Slater was charged with unbecoming and indecent conduct. She was sent to the stocks for two hours a day for six days.

Cemetery

A graveyard was located on an island just south of Sarah Island. The first convict to be buried there was William Halliday, and the island became known as Holiday Island. Planks of Huon pine from stockpiles at the sawpits served as crude tombstones. Due to the durable timber, Angus Lamont's tombstone was recovered in an 'excellent state of preservation' some 80 years after his death.

Convict Deaths

A total of 88 convict deaths were recorded on Sarah Island: 35 from natural causes, 27 from drowning, eight killed accidentally, three shot by the military, 12 murdered by other convicts and three executed.

William Swallow and the *Cyprus*

In August 1829, the government brig *Cyprus* departed Hobart Town for Sarah Island. On board were 31 convicts, including the infamous runaway William Swallow. En route, 18 of the convicts seized the ship. With a forged set of papers and a newly painted *Cyprus*, renamed the *Friends of Boston*, they set a course to Tahiti. Swallow took command but the journey did not go smoothly. The crew bickered incessantly and some even deserted. After suffering several setbacks, they finally arrived in Japan. There, they were refused permission to land and the ship nearly sank under cannon fire. With the ship leaking, they managed to sail on to China. The *Cyprus* was scuttled to cover their tracks and Swallow washed up in Canton. After eluding the local British authorities in China, he conned his way to a ride back home to England. The *Cyprus* affair was big news in England and Swallow was soon recognised and apprehended. He made history as one of the last men to be tried as a pirate in England. Piracy carried a penalty of death, but Swallow cunningly argued he been forced to take captaincy due to his navigational skills. He avoided execution and was sent back to Van Diemen's Land with no extra punishment. His swashbuckling days ended at Port Arthur where he died in May 1834. Swallow was popular amongst convicts and the convict poet Frances McNamara immortalised him in song. Convicts sang the song of the *Cyprus* for many years.

PENITENTIARY

Penitentiaries were places of punishment and reformation. All three Van Diemonian penal stations had penitentiaries. The oldest was constructed at Sarah Island in 1822. It had six rooms and housed 72 convicts and 12 constables and watchmen. In 1828, a larger penitentiary was built on a headland on the western side of the island. The three-storey stone and brick building perched at the top of a sheer cliff, with a cookhouse and three small constabulary huts nearby. When the Sarah Island penal station was abandoned in 1833, the penitentiary began to deteriorate. In 1846, it was repaired and fitted out with sleeping berths and a chapel, but it was soon abandoned. Today, the ruins are a destination for sightseers.

Shingles
The roof was clad in rot-resistant Huon pine shingles.

Thwarted
In May 1831 several convicts bored a series of holes in one of the penitentiary doors. Their handiwork was discovered and the would-be absconders were rounded up and punished.

Royalty
Carvings of a shield and the royal crown above the initials G.R., the cypher of King George IV, were possibly the handiwork of convicted stonemasons Matthew Tierney and William Pearse.

Murder
In July 1824 Robert Hesp was slain with an axe behind the penitentiary. Thomas Hudson admitted to the murder in order to bring an end to his own unhappy life. He was hanged in January 1825.

Buried Booze
In 1826, Commandant Butler suspected convicts were raiding the commissariat for alcohol. When a pig uprooted a two-gallon keg near the penitentiary, his suspicions were confirmed.

William Buelow Gould
William Gould was born in England in 1801. In 1826, he was convicted of armed robbery and sentenced to seven years' transportation. Gould was made an assistant to the colonial surgeon Doctor James Scott, and he painted botanical specimens. Gould was sent to Sarah Island on two occasions. There, he painted more specimens as well as a view of the island, which included the penitentiary. When the Sarah Island penal station was abandoned, Gould was sent to Port Arthur. He gained his freedom in June 1835, and he continued to paint, mostly on commission, but he also drank heavily and got into trouble. He died in poverty in December 1853.

Charles Henry Theodore Costantini
Charles Costantini was born in 1803 in France. He was a promising medical student in Paris, but he was convicted of forgery and sent to New South Wales. When a snake bit his master's child, Costantini saved the infant's life and he soon sailed to England a free man. However, he was convicted of stealing and sentenced to seven years' transportation. He arrived in Hobart Town in October 1827 and was sent to Sarah Island where he worked as a medical assistant. He also painted several views of the penal station, including depictions of the penitentiary. When caught with art supplies at Port Arthur, however, Costantini was suspected of forgery and sentenced to solitary confinement. He gained his freedom in March 1834, and went on to ply his artistic talents in Hobart Town.

Second Floor

It is likely a ladder provided access to the second floor, which held about 30 men. The daily routine began at daylight. At night, the men were mustered and locked in, at 9 pm in summer and 8 pm in winter.

Thomas Lempriere

Thomas Lempriere was born in January 1796 in Germany. He arrived in Hobart Town in 1822 and married Charlotte Smith. They had 12 children. Lempriere was a storekeeper at various times at the penal stations of Sarah Island, Maria Island and Port Arthur. He wrote a diary, published as the *Penal Settlements of Van Diemen's Land*, with detailed illustrations including one of the new penitentiary. He died in 1852.

Close Quarters

Wet clothes were hung up in any available spot, and most convicts slept on the floor.

First Floor

The first floor held about 30 men. On Monday, Tuesday and Thursday evenings, the first floor served as a school. The chaplain and various others, including Thomas Lempriere and educated convicts, took the lessons. On Wednesday and Friday evenings, sermons were read and the men sang and prayed.

William Schofield

William Schofield was born in June 1793. At age 33 he was accepted by the Wesleyan Methodist Conference as a minister. He was selected to serve in Van Diemen's Land and was stationed at Sarah Island where his duties included a regular service, conversion meetings, evening lectures, singing classes and night school. His efforts had mixed results. In October 1831, John Thompson received 25 lashes for writing improper lines in class and ridiculing the reverend, and Commandant Briggs refused to attend service after finding a sermon disagreeable. Schofield and his wife Martha lived on Sarah Island for four years before they were transferred to New South Wales. He died in June 1878, leaving an estate valued at nearly £50,000.

Warmth

Fires burned day and night in winter.

Ground Floor

In 1833, 55 west-coast Aboriginal people, Toogee, were forcibly detained in the penitentiary before being sent to Flinders Island. Convicts on the floor above poured water through the cracks and urinated on them. Many of the Toogee died there.

George Augustus Robinson

George Augustus Robinson was born in 1791 in England. He was a builder by trade, and he migrated to Hobart Town in January 1824. Relations between colonists and Aborigines were at a crisis point, and Robinson was hired as mediator. Between 1829 and 1834 he travelled Van Diemen's Land, persuading Aboriginal people into captivity. A protectorate, called Wybalenna, was established on Flinders Island. There, Aboriginal people were 'Civilised and Christianised'. The protectorate, however, failed dismally and the mortality rate was high. Robinson left Flinders Island in 1839 to run another protectorate in Victoria, which also failed. Celebrated as 'the protector of Aborigines', Robinson retired in England a wealthy man. He died in October 1866.

51

PRISONERS' BARRACKS

Until the 1820s, male convicts lived in small makeshift barracks or found their own lodgings. In 1822, an official prisoners' barracks was built in Hobart Town. Another was established in Launceston soon after. By the 1840s, the Hobart Town prisoners' barracks was said to resemble a small city. It continued to expand, and by the 20th century the complex housed both male and female prisoners, and it was known as the Campbell Street gaol. It was demolished in 1963.

Arrivals

New arrivals, known was 'new chums', were marched to the barracks at dawn under armed guard. They were lined up and reviewed by the ship's surgeon-superintendent, shipmaster, chief police magistrate, the muster master or comptroller-general of convicts, superintendent of the prisoner's barracks and the lieutenant-governor. Lieutenant-Governor Franklin lectured astride his horse reportedly for two hours to each new group of arrivals.

George Barrel

Between 1828 and 1830 George Barrel was found drunk nine times, once during morning muster for chapel. He received 100 lashes and 49 days on the treadmill.

Bakery

Bread was baked in two large ovens in the bakery and the loaves were distributed in carts. For neglecting to guard his cart, Richard Waters was charged in May 1836 with disobeying orders and he narrowly escaped punishment. Convict baker James Deakin copped 25 lashes for baking 'irregular bread' and a seven-year term for stealing wheat.

Walled In

Housing so many convicts in the colony's capital came at a cost. Robberies increased, particularly during the convicts' free time. After a gang escaped in a stolen boat in January 1827, all inmates were confined to the barracks after dark. The pirates were caught the following year, and in August the barracks' entire population, some 800 people, were marched out to watch them hang. A five-metre high sandstone wall surrounded the barracks to prevent escapes. For scaling the wall in 1822, John Little received 50 lashes. Daniel Gibbs managed to get over with a rope, but he was caught the same day. John Hare took off after boring a hole in his cell wall. When he was caught he received 100 lashes and was sent to Port Arthur for three years.

Staff at the Barracks

The first staff comprised just five men: a superintendent, three constables and one gatekeeper. Twenty years later there were more than a hundred: a superintendent, a chaplain, a dispenser, a blacksmith, five overseers, eight watchmen, 12 bakers and cooks, 20 clerks, 28 wardsmen and 47 wood and water carriers. At this time 872 convicts were housed at the barracks.

Classing the Convicts

Once the barracks were built, new regulations were introduced. Inmates had to wear clothing bearing 'distinctive marks'. Stencilled on their pants and jackets were the letters P.B., standing for prisoners' barracks. They were grouped into three classes; First Class were those ready for assignment, Second Class were those on trial, and Third Class were those undergoing punishment. When Lieutenant-Governor Arthur took up office, he grouped the men into seven classes. First Class were skilled labourers who could live outside the barracks. Second Class were confined to the barracks. Third Class worked on road gangs and Fourth Class on chain gangs. Fifth Class also worked on chain gangs but were kept isolated. Sixth and Seventh Class convicts were sent to penal stations for hard labour. Men in the first three classes could also work for payment.

The Daily Routine

According to convict Linus Miller, the day began with a bell at 4.30 am to wake the men for breakfast. A muster bell rang at 6 am and, following roll call, each man was sent to his gang and marched off to work. Those undergoing punishment remained in solitary or on the treadmill. A chaplain attended convicts each morning and afternoon, and performed a full service twice on Sundays.

William Gunn

William Gunn was born in Ireland in 1800. In 1822, Lieutenant-Governor Sorell convinced him to settle in Van Diemen's Land with an offer of a 162-hectare land grant. Although he held no official title, Gunn led soldiers in pursuit of bushrangers and earned a reputation as a tough and relentless leader. In November 1825, he was shot during a fracas with the Brady gang and his right arm had to be amputated. He was awarded a pension of £70 and a gift of £341 from grateful colonists. In January 1826, he was appointed superintendent of the prisoners' barracks, and it was claimed he knew every convict by name. In 1829 he married Frances Hannah and they had six daughters and three sons. When transportation to Van Diemen's Land ended in 1853, Gunn settled in Launceston and served as police magistrate. His house in Glen Dhu was celebrated for its magnificent lawns, and it was said he possessed the finest rose garden in Australia. Gunn died in June 1868.

Conditions

When James Boyd took over from Superintendent Gunn in 1847, he was appalled to discover convicts smoking and gambling in filthy rat-infested wards. Washing was optional and the privy was in 'the most disgraceful state that can be imagined'. Inmates lacked basic supplies, and some were reduced to eating their food off the ground. Boyd introduced many improvements such as baths, hot water and window shutters.

Linus Miller

Linus Miller was born in New York in 1819. In 1838, he joined the Canadian rebels in an attempt to oust the British from North America. The uprising failed and, after being captured near Niagara Falls, Miller, along with 91 Canadian rebels, was banished to Van Diemen's Land. He arrived in January 1840 and spent four weeks at the barracks where he was forced to beg for clothes. Miller was astonished by the unwholesome conditions and the uncivilised, impious inmates and overseers, including Lieutenant-Governor Franklin whom he described as 'an imbecile old man'. Miller's memoir, *Notes of an Exile to Van Diemen's Land*, was published in 1846.

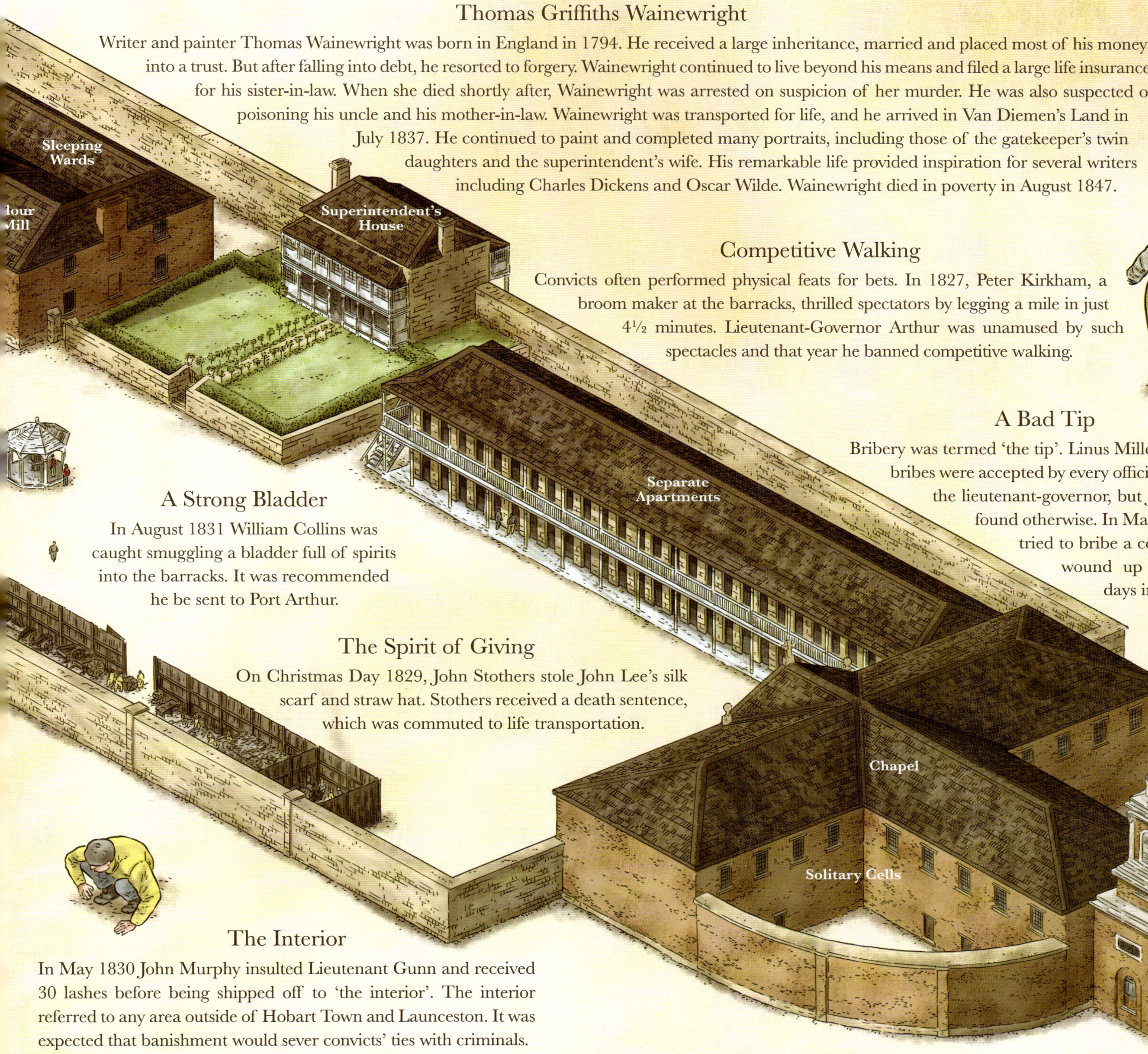

Thomas Griffiths Wainewright

Writer and painter Thomas Wainewright was born in England in 1794. He received a large inheritance, married and placed most of his money into a trust. But after falling into debt, he resorted to forgery. Wainewright continued to live beyond his means and filed a large life insurance for his sister-in-law. When she died shortly after, Wainewright was arrested on suspicion of her murder. He was also suspected of poisoning his uncle and his mother-in-law. Wainewright was transported for life, and he arrived in Van Diemen's Land in July 1837. He continued to paint and completed many portraits, including those of the gatekeeper's twin daughters and the superintendent's wife. His remarkable life provided inspiration for several writers including Charles Dickens and Oscar Wilde. Wainewright died in poverty in August 1847.

Competitive Walking

Convicts often performed physical feats for bets. In 1827, Peter Kirkham, a broom maker at the barracks, thrilled spectators by legging a mile in just 4½ minutes. Lieutenant-Governor Arthur was unamused by such spectacles and that year he banned competitive walking.

A Bad Tip

Bribery was termed 'the tip'. Linus Miller wrote that bribes were accepted by every official, including the lieutenant-governor, but John Hough found otherwise. In March 1853, he tried to bribe a constable and wound up serving ten days in solitary.

A Strong Bladder

In August 1831 William Collins was caught smuggling a bladder full of spirits into the barracks. It was recommended he be sent to Port Arthur.

The Spirit of Giving

On Christmas Day 1829, John Stothers stole John Lee's silk scarf and straw hat. Stothers received a death sentence, which was commuted to life transportation.

The Interior

In May 1830 John Murphy insulted Lieutenant Gunn and received 30 lashes before being shipped off to 'the interior'. The interior referred to any area outside of Hobart Town and Launceston. It was expected that banishment would sever convicts' ties with criminals.

Sleeping Wards
Flour Mill
Superintendent's House
Separate Apartments
Chapel
Solitary Cells

53

PROBATION STATION

In 1840 the probation system replaced the assignment system. Male convicts faced a regime of hard labour, religious instruction and education. Men serving seven- and 14-year terms were grouped into gangs at purpose-built probation stations. Those serving life sentences were sent to Port Arthur. The men worked through progressively lighter stages of hard labour until they were entitled to receive a probation pass. For continual good behaviour they could obtain a ticket-of-leave and then a pardon. In 1844, a similar system was introduced for women, utilising the *Anson* prison hulk. The probation system was unique to Van Diemen's Land. It was designed to reform rather than punish, but due to large numbers, poor planning and a lack of resources, it failed. The probation system ended in 1856.

Superintendent's Quarters

Surgeon's Quarters

Married Soldiers' Huts

Military Barracks

Road to Port Arthur

Life and Limb
In September 1847, Charles Moss was crushed by a falling tree.

Time for Trouble
In January 1848, William Glave was sentenced to two months hard labour for making a sundial.

Salt Water River Probation Station
The first probation station was established in 1841 at Salt Water River on the Tasman Peninsula. Crude huts were built from bark, mud and timber. Officers were posted uphill from the station to maintain security and the social hierarchy. Convicts were grouped into three classes. Those at Salt Water River farmed to generate capital and self-sufficiency. In 1847, approximately 500 men cultivated 93,000 tons of vegetables and 3000 bushels of oats and wheat. The convicts also tended livestock including an estimated 5000 sheep. More than 80 probation stations were built throughout Van Diemen's Land. When convict transportation to Van Diemen's Land ended in 1853, the stations began to be shut down. Some farms were too valuable to waste. Convicts were encouraged to remain as paid probationers to work them. In 1854, Salt Water River was said to resemble 'a very comfortable village'. Eventually the convict workforce became old men, and in 1873 the remaining farms were shut down.

The Daily Routine
Reverend Robert Cooke was the catechist at Salt Water River from 1843 until 1850. He described the daily routine as follows. In summer convicts rose at 4 am, washed and mustered for prayers and breakfast. A doctor tended to the sick while the others marched off to work. Dinner was at noon followed by more prayers and work. After work convicts deemed 'fit' were permitted to attend school, the rest were locked in their barracks. On Sunday they attended service, and books were loaned to those that wanted them. The reverend described the lending of books as 'the only humanising part of the whole system'.

Robbery
In August 1846, Michael Roach and John Dangan absconded from Salt Water River. On the road to the coalmines they robbed Roger Boyle, a teacher and minister. The two convicts were caught and sentenced to death. Dangan was reprieved, but Roach, on account of committing the violent assault, was executed. He was 26 years old.

John Eardley Wilmot
Wilmot was born in February 1783. Due to his expertise in criminal law he was appointed Lieutenant-Governor of Van Diemen's Land in 1843. Wilmot administered the newly established probation system, but he was left without adequate funds. The Colonial Office offered little assistance and disapproved of Wilmot's administration. He was blamed for the inevitable failure of the probation system, and in September 1846 he was dismissed. Wilmot demanded restitution but after falling ill he died in February 1847.

Matthew Forster
Matthew Forster was born in 1796. Following a successful career in the military he moved to Van Diemen's Land with his family in 1831. He served in numerous official capacities including chief police magistrate and chief justice on the executive council. In 1841 he was appointed director of the probation system. Forster was instrumental in establishing the probation system, but he failed to address the system's shortfalls. Faced with the impracticalities of his office, financial woes and poor health, he requested a leave of absence in April 1845. He died in January 1846.

John Edwin Evendon

Evendon was transported for stealing letters containing money. He arrived in Van Diemen's Land in January 1841 to serve a 14-year term. After serving as a schoolmaster he leased the Salt Water River farm in 1861. The lease was revoked soon after and Evendon claimed to have suffered considerable losses. He then worked as a policeman but was sentenced to 18 months imprisonment for misappropriating funds. After gaining his freedom, he remained at Port Arthur with his family and served as a constable, wharfinger, coxswain, semaphore repairer and telegraph operator. When the penal station was wound down he was appointed caretaker and guide on a wage of 5 shillings per day. In 1884, he wrote his memoirs. Although wildly inaccurate, they were used by Port Arthur guides until the 1950s. Evendon died in 1890.

Staff at the Station

Each class of convicts in the probation system contained several hundred men. They were supervised by a superintendent, two or three assistant superintendents, a surgeon, a storekeeper, three overseers, a messenger and members of the military.

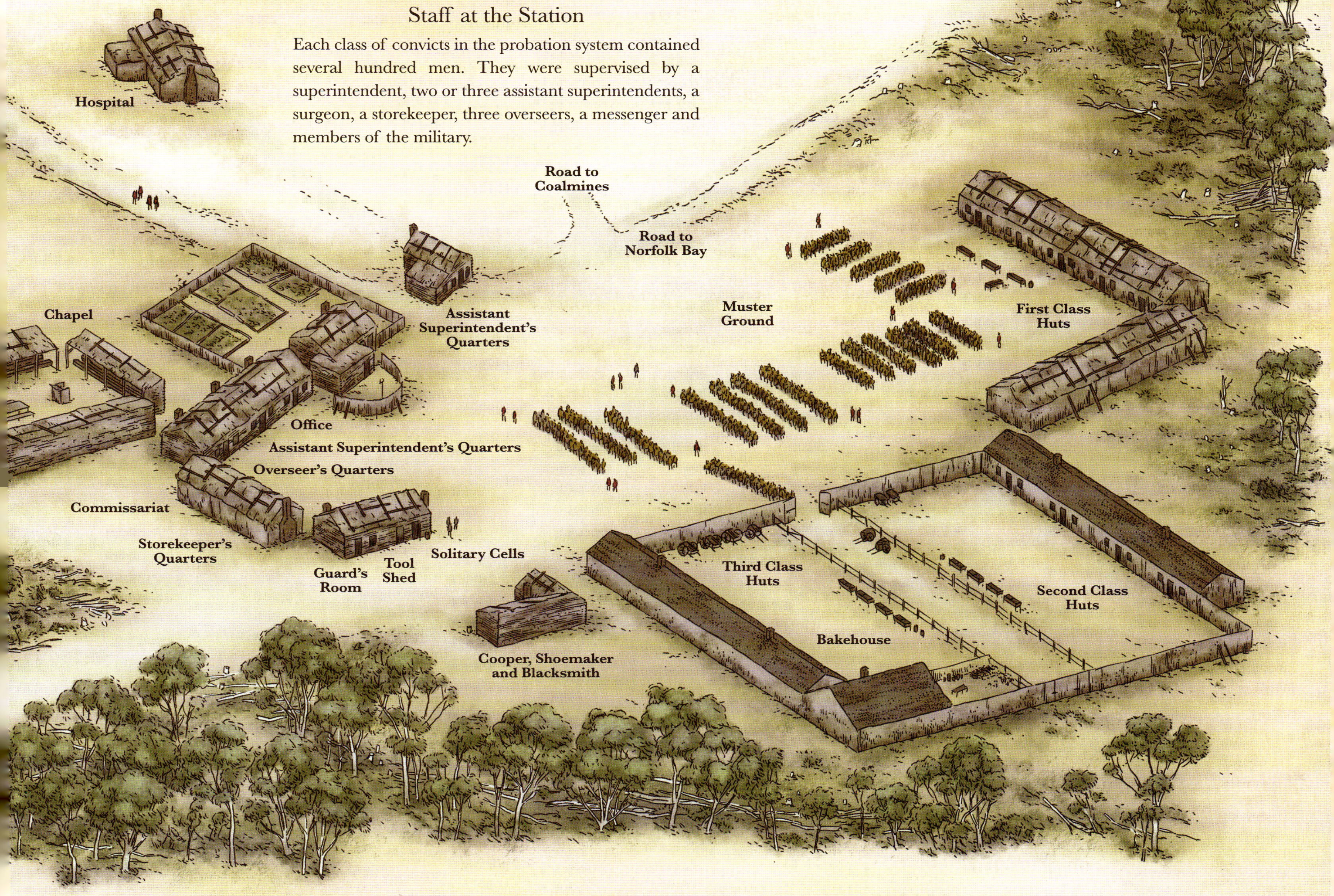

Labels on map: Hospital; Chapel; Assistant Superintendent's Quarters; Road to Coalmines; Road to Norfolk Bay; Muster Ground; First Class Huts; Office; Assistant Superintendent's Quarters; Overseer's Quarters; Commissariat; Storekeeper's Quarters; Guard's Room; Tool Shed; Solitary Cells; Cooper, Shoemaker and Blacksmith; Third Class Huts; Bakehouse; Second Class Huts

PROSTITUTION

Prostitution was commonly termed 'on the town', and brothels were known as 'disorderly houses'. Brothels were illegal but prostitution was not, though prostitutes could be charged with offences such as being absent without leave. In Van Diemen's Land, paid employment was scarce and prostitution was one way women could support themselves. Some masters were even said to have peddled the sexual services of their female servants. By the 1850s, the number of prostitutes per head of population in Hobart Town was said to be higher than anywhere else in the world. It is estimated that at least one in four female convicts engaged in prostitution. Prostitution declined in the 1880s.

Eliza Smith

Eliza Smith was sentenced to seven years transportation for stealing from her brothel keeper in England. She continued to work as a prostitute after she arrived in Van Diemen's Land. Within 12 months, she had been charged with being absent without leave 11 times. In one instance she was found in a disorderly house, and in another she was found in bed with a man. Smith drowned in January 1838.

PUNISHMENT

Punishments were harsh and usually involved inflicting physical pain. But if a punishment was too severe, it could leave a convict unable to work. If it was too lenient, it was thought that it would breed insubordination. There was an effort to standardise punishments. By the 1830s, there were nine categories: reprimand, treadwheel, hard labour by day and solitary confinement by night, solitary confinement on bread and water, hard labour on the roads, flogging, labouring in a chain gang, confinement at a penal station, and execution. Convicts were also punished with privation of indulgences and demotion to a lower class, and they could have their sentences extended. By the 1840s, psychological punishments such as darkness, silence and isolation began to replace corporal punishments.

Iron Collar
Female convicts could be fitted with iron collars with two long prongs that prevented the wearer from sitting or lying down comfortably. Some weighed as much as three kilograms. Iron collars remained in use until the 1820s. Mary Evers was subjected to one for 28 days for abusing the constabulary.

Breaking Stone
Breaking stone was a punishment reserved for the most incorrigible men. At Port Arthur, men were chained while they worked. In May 1841, members of the stone-breaking gang planned to escape by cutting through their irons with a file. The plot was discovered, and Patrick Minnighan suspected James Travis of being an informant and bludgeoned him with a hammer. Travis died in the hospital and Minnighan was executed.

Gag
A gag was a wooden bar put between the teeth and kept in place by a strap around the head. In July 1843, Jane Eskett was gagged at the Cascades Female Factory for riotous behaviour. Some gags were fitted with a breathing hole and forced down the wearer's throat. Reverend Thomas Rogers reported that as convicts struggled to breathe they emitted a 'low indistinct whistle'.

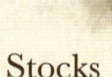

Hair Cropping
Female convicts could have their hair cut or their head shaved. Most women dreaded it, but Ann Wilson defiantly said, 'I don't care if it is cut off fifty times!' The punishment was phased out when the authorities decided that defeminising women was not conducive to their reform. Punishing women was a troubling problem for the authorities.

Stocks
Stocks were an adjustable wooden structure with holes for securing a person's feet. The aim was to publicly shame the victim and make their life miserable. In February 1840, Constable Jones copped 25 lashes for allowing a man in the stocks to puff on his pipe. The *Police Act* of 1837 ruled that a sentence in the stocks could not exceed eight hours. This was reduced to six hours in 1843. Stocks were used until the 1850s.

The Black Box
Convicts on transport ships could be confined to a small portable cell that was like a coffin. Stints in a 'black box', as it was known, ranged from a few hours to a few days. Offenders were forced to stand and at times they were doused with water and the box was suspended from ropes. In 1841, William Thompson was suspended for three hours in a black box. As the ship rolled back and forth, he was tossed about and dunked in the ocean. Sailor John Montagu Smith reported that women were confined to the box on a daily basis, and Smith himself was sent to the box for 12 hours. In the tropics, the heat was stifling and convicts could not be confined for more than four hours at a time.

Flogging

The first flogging in Van Diemen's Land took place in May 1803, when a marine named Edward Westwood received 24 lashes for dozing off at his post. Common sentences for male convicts were between 12 and 100 lashes for crimes such as insolence, drunkenness, neglect of duty and absconding. The maximum that could be awarded by a magistrate was 100 lashes, but an offence could be broken up into separate charges to increase the number. In December 1827, Robert Hansler was sentenced to 100 lashes for absconding, another 100 for stealing the boat in which he escaped and a further 100 for the provisions he took. Female convicts were also flogged. In 1806, Elizabeth Murphy was given 25 lashes for writing an impudent letter. Juveniles received strokes across their buttocks and thighs, which were termed the breech. Regulating a flogging was difficult. Mark Jeffrey claimed to have received such a light flogging that it barely broke his skin. Thomas Berry bled after the second stroke and after the fourth, blood was streaming into his shoes. If the wounds were not treated they could become infected, so salt, lard, lemon and bluestone were sometimes rubbed over the victim's back. Flogging could leave a person scarred for life. Some convicts bore the marks with pride, others with shame. Over time, the punishment was phased out. The flogging of women ceased in 1820, and at Port Arthur flogging ended in 1848. But flogging was not officially outlawed in Australia until 1957.

The Flagellator

Flagellators were responsible for delivering floggings. They were selected from serving convicts of solid build, preferably with a military background. Flagellators differed in attitude and style. Alexander Fraser, known as Big Sandy, made a hole in the ground to keep his heel from slipping. Thomas Jeffries curled the thongs around his victims to tear at the flesh on the chest as well as the back.

A flagellator could lighten the punishment. When Alexander Fraser flogged 13-year-old William Gates he stopped after three strokes, but he was ordered to continue or experience the same fate. In May 1834, John Hearn accepted a bribe to soften his strokes. He was flogged and confined to the barracks for six months.

Flagellators were, as a rule, unpopular. When Henry Ryan was about to be tied to the triangle, he produced a penknife and stabbed Alexander Adams, the flagellator, under his left eye. Adams recovered and Ryan received a life sentence.

The term 'flagellator' was viewed as an insult. In March 1855, Benjamin Marsh was fined £2 for assaulting James Mason after he called him a flagellator. In December 1872, James Hunt referred to Mark Jeffries as a Port Arthur flogger. Jeffries beat Hunt so badly that he died six days later.

The Triangle

A flogging frame, commonly called a triangle, was made from three pieces of scantling joined at the top to form a tripod. Victims were stripped to the waist or denuded completely and securely tied to the frame. Their limbs were splayed to keep the skin on their back taut. Triangles were placed in the muster yard and positioned to ensure that all the convicts had a good view. The triangle was a dreaded object; William Derrincourt carted one to a kiln and incinerated it.

Cat o' Nine Tails

Traditionally a piece of plaited rope was unpicked to leave three strands, which were in turn unravelled to form a nine-tailed whip. Due to the parallel wounds inflicted it was likened to a cat's scratches and known as a 'cat o' nine tails', or simply a 'cat'. The handle of a standard military issue cat was made of wood and covered in blue fabric bound with whipcord. Embedded in the top were nine thongs. Each thong was 30 inches long and had a knot at the end. Cats at penal stations were more severe and known as 'thief's cats'. On Sarah Island, the cat was three times the thickness of the one used in Hobart Town. and the flagellator dragged it through sand and dipped it in salt water after every fifth stroke. Sometimes the knots were strengthened with wire or wax, or lead was woven into the thongs. In 1832, following an inquiry into convict discipline, a 'regulation cat' was decided upon and made standard throughout the colony.

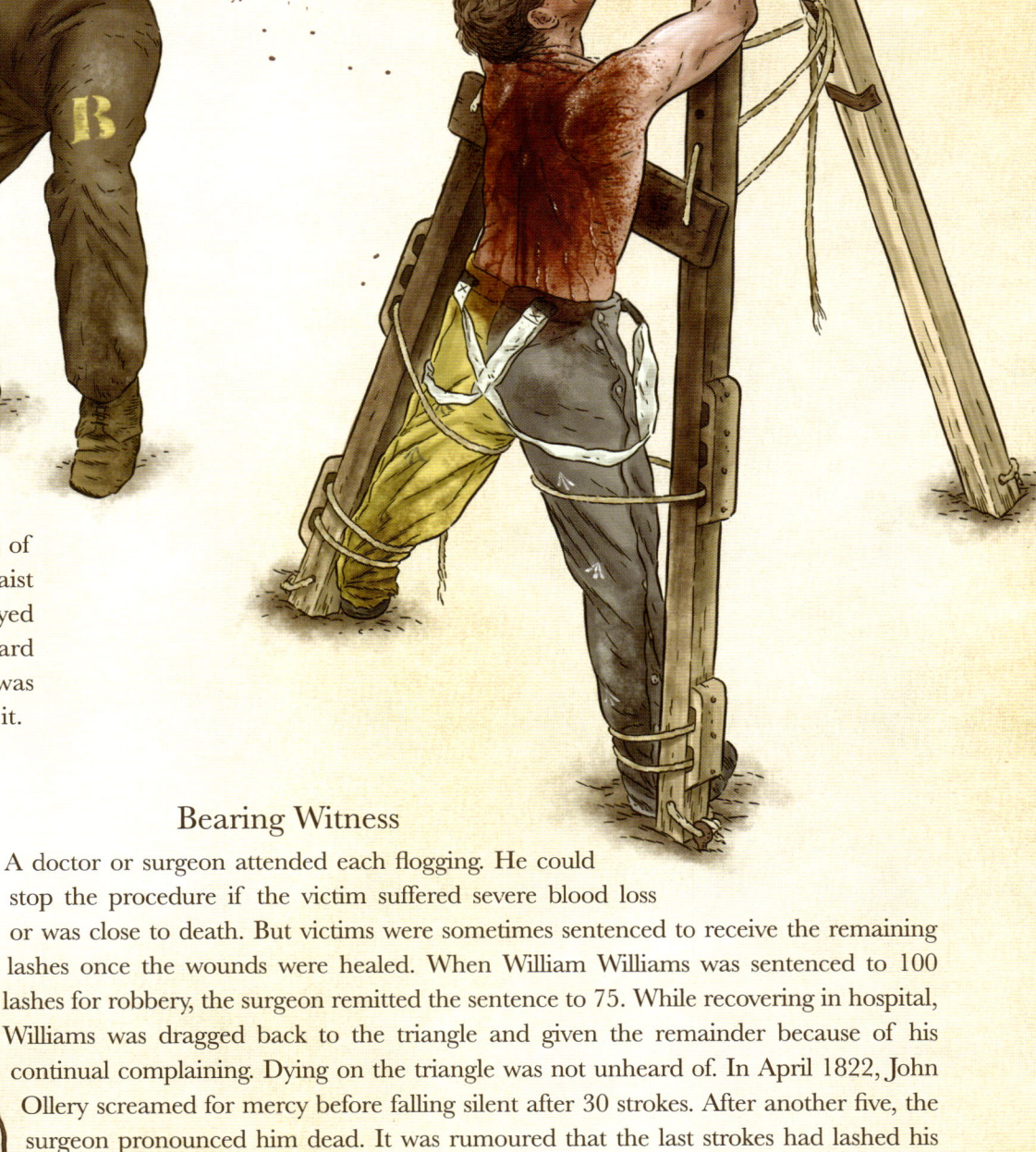

Bearing Witness

A doctor or surgeon attended each flogging. He could stop the procedure if the victim suffered severe blood loss or was close to death. But victims were sometimes sentenced to receive the remaining lashes once the wounds were healed. When William Williams was sentenced to 100 lashes for robbery, the surgeon remitted the sentence to 75. While recovering in hospital, Williams was dragged back to the triangle and given the remainder because of his continual complaining. Dying on the triangle was not unheard of. In April 1822, John Ollery screamed for mercy before falling silent after 30 strokes. After another five, the surgeon pronounced him dead. It was rumoured that the last strokes had lashed his lifeless corpse, but the official report stated that he died in hospital. For the attempted murder of Constable Terry Thomas, Joseph Greenwood was sentenced to 100 lashes and death. He petitioned Lieutenant-Governor Arthur, claiming that it was torture to flog a condemned man, but his pleas were in vain. At the time of his execution his back was still bleeding and, according to John Broxup, crawling with maggots. The public was horrified, and the gruesome ordeal made headlines in Britain.

QUARRY

The first quarry was established at Risdon Brook near Hobart Town in 1803 by Richard Clarke, a colonist and stonemason. As the colony expanded, so too did the need for stone, and quarries were established near most towns.

John Morgan
For rioting on Christmas Day 1834, John Morgan was sent to Port Arthur for three years.

Winning Stone
The process of extracting stone from the earth was known as 'winning'. Convicts cleared the ground with picks and shovels to reveal the rock bed. The surface was probed with a crowbar to find a face from which the rock could be broached or prised loose with wedges and crowbars.

Racketeering
Stone was valuable, and some Van Diemonians bought it illegally to construct their houses. In May 1835, Ross Bridge gangsmen Christopher Bassett, Richard Davis and James Merrett were each given 50 lashes for trading in rough-cut stone. The stonemasons they sold it to were ordered to work for three months in chains. The recipient of the stone, Louisa Abbott, widow of the former deputy judge advocate, escaped prosecution.

Rock Out
Smaller pieces of stone could be carried out of the quarry but larger pieces had to be dragged, carted or hoisted out by teams of convicts.

Broaching
If stone couldn't be levered free, it required broaching. One convict held a jump bar while two others hit it with sledgehammers. After each blow, the bar was rotated slightly and water was poured into the hole to settle the dust and soften the rock. When a line of holes was complete, pointed bars were inserted into each hole and struck with hammers. Eventually the rock cracked and could be levered loose.

Bridgewater Causeway
A quarry established at Black Snake Point for stone for a causeway across the Derwent River became a destination of dread. The work was immense and the treatment of convicts severe. The causeway became known as the 'Bridgewater folly'.

Blasting
If the rock was too hard for broaching it had to be blasted, which was extremely dangerous. Gunpowder was inserted into the rock with a long thin metal pole. When a quarryman ignited the gunpowder, he had to run for his life. Gunpowder was expensive. In November 1821 William Parker, an overseer in a quarry gang, received 50 lashes for stealing and selling gunpowder.

Fully Charged
In October 1830, stonemason Luke Roberts had his sentence extended by seven years for stealing flagstones. Two years later, he split his leg irons and changed out of his government slops in order to sell stone from the quarry. He received 50 lashes. In February 1837, lightning struck his pick and killed him instantly.

Dressing
Stone was dressed, cut into neat blocks, on a wooden bench known as a 'banker'. Stonemasons used chisels, hammers and a ruler called a mason's square. Sandstone was easiest to dress but a good stonemason could work with harder stone, like basalt and granite.

Man Trams

Trams were powered by convict muscle. Although the work was hard, tram running was considered a good job. It broke the monotony of ganged labour, the food and lodgings were better, supervision was minimal and some passengers tipped. When missionary Frederick Mackie rode the rail in 1854, he gave the convicts a small reward. Passengers paid 1 shilling for a one-way trip. The trams made three return journeys each day, each taking about 45 minutes. A party of 10 runners could transport as much cargo as 30 convicts could haul on their backs and they were much faster. Trams could carry half a tonne of coal or timber and large trams could even convey boats across the peninsula. The top speed of a tram on a downhill run was 60 kilometres per hour. Runners perched precariously on the carts on the downhill sections of track.

Rail Woes

In the early 1870s, a railway for horse-powered carts was laid at Port Arthur. In October 1871, John Newby and John O'Brien absconded from their tramroad party. Newby copped three years' imprisonment. John O'Brien received four years' hard labour. By 1877, the railway had been removed and the valuable iron shipped to Hobart Town.

Posting

Joseph Atkinson worked as a carpenter on the Ralph's Bay Neck railway. Commandant Booth kept him hard at work even after his sentence had expired, and Atkinson was forced to lodge a complaint in order to be released.

Dinner Is Served

Ganged convicts were typically divided into mess groups. Each group placed its food in a tagged bag that was dropped into a large communal pot to cook. Basic utensils consisted of a bowl, mug and spoon. A delegate was appointed to divide the meal as evenly as possible in plain view of his messmates. For his troubles he got the leftover fat from the pot, known as slush. In November 1827, Samuel Higgins gave John Onely 5 pounds of bread to have his turn as delegate. When Onely went back on his word he was murdered by his messmates. Any kind of food was very valuable. For giving fat away, Jesse Constable had his sentence extended by two months.

RAILWAY

Commandant Booth proposed a railway be built across the Tasman Peninsula from Norfolk Bay to Long Bay so that the long and perilous sea journey wouldn't be necessary. Lieutenant-Governor Arthur approved the plan, and in June 1836 sawyers and splitters were stationed at Norfolk Bay to begin construction. In July 1837, the seven-kilometre wooden track was completed. It was the first passenger railway in Australia. The line closed in 1858.

Back Breaking

In April 1877, Luke Marshall fractured his spine jumping off a tram on a downhill run. Crippled, he spent the rest of his life in invalid depots.

Nails and Rails

The wooden rails comprised two pieces of quartering nailed together. They were fixed to sleepers with nails forged at Port Arthur.

Charles O'Hara Booth

Charles Booth was born in England in August 1800. In February 1833, he arrived in Van Diemen's Land and was appointed as the commandant of Port Arthur. Booth presided over the Tasman Peninsula and also spent time exploring. His diaries remain a valuable insight into convict life.

RATIONS

The first Van Diemonian convicts were issued just 4 pounds of pork and 7 pounds of biscuit each week. Biscuit, also known as 'hardtack', consisted of flour, water and sometimes salt. It was a durable food particularly suited to long voyages. It could also provide absconders with a meal on the run. In September 1825, Jonathon Smith received 50 lashes and six months in leg irons for smuggling biscuit. The first convicts at the Cascades Female Factory received a pound of bread, a pint of skilly and 2 pints of meat and vegetable soup daily. Skilly, also known as 'gruel', was a paste of flour, water and salt and was generally eaten at breakfast. The first convicts at Port Arthur were issued with a pound of salt beef or 10 ounces of salt pork, 20 ounces of flour for bread and 4 ounces of flour to make skilly. Standard rations were unappetising, but they provided enough sustenance for a convict for a full working day. Convicts were sometimes granted 'luxuries' such as tea and sugar.

Skilly and Water  **Salt Pork, Bread and Water**

ROAD

The first roads were rough tracks through the bush. Convicts felled trees, filled bogs and built the occasional footbridge. The first road between Hobart Town and Launceston followed the route found by Lieutenant-Colonel Paterson in 1807. Governor Macquarie travelled the route on horseback in 1811, naming landmarks along the way. Surveyors retraced the route, marked out distances and erected signs, and a road was built. Using convict labour the road was widened and improved to incorporate bridges, culverts, footpaths and drainage ditches. When Macquarie returned in 1821, he was able to travel the route by coach.

Ganged Convicts

Convicts were sentenced to work in gangs as punishment. Gangs provided a workforce that built much of the infrastructure of the island, including roads. In 1846, it was estimated that 8964 convicts were working in gangs throughout the colony. Gangsmen had the highest mortality rate of any group in the colony.

Carrying Gangs

Convicts were ordered to carry materials such as bricks, shingles, stone and timber. To cart timber, 12 convicts stood either side of a log and heaved it up onto their shoulders. Six of the men then withdrew, leaving the rest to carry on. At Port Arthur, carrying gangs were called 'centipedes'. Some comprised as many as 30 men. Taller convicts took the brunt of the load. Linus Miller, who stood at 6 feet tall, claimed to be nearly crushed with the weight on several occasions.

Portable Huts

Road gangs slept crammed into tiny huts. To save time and money, the huts were fitted with wheels so they could be dragged by gangsmen. The huts were fitted with a small privy so that the men could be locked in from sunset to sunrise. Conditions were so cramped with up to 20 men per hut that they could not all sit or stand at any one time. John Frederick Mortlock likened the huts to animal cages.

Chain Gang

Convicts sentenced to hard labour in leg irons worked in chain gangs. Lieutenant-Governor Arthur described the punishment of hard labour in leg irons as 'as severe as one that could be inflicted on man'.

Road Construction

John McAdam, a Scottish engineer, pioneered road construction. His method, known as 'madamising', involved spreading a crust of stones of a certain size to a depth of 25 centimetres over soil. In 1849 government printer, James Barnard, produced a pamphlet titled *Remarks on the Maintenance of Macadamised Roads*. The chief recommendations were to keep Van Diemonian roads clear of dust, dirt, mud and manure and to make minor repairs as soon as they were required. Maintenance was viewed as relatively light labour that could even be undertaken by children. Thomas Telford, another Scottish engineer, improved surface durability by adding a layer of tightly packed stone known as the Telford layer.

Robert Nottman

Robert Nottman was appointed superintendent of the Roads and Bridges Department. He arrived in Van Diemen's Land in 1822. According to convict Daniel Heustis, Nottman was the most severe taskmaster in the colony. He was rumoured to have once administered 3700 lashes to his gang at Longmeadows before breakfast. In May 1837 he married Harriet Shoobridge, and three years later they reutrned to Scotland.

Biding His Time

In 1829, convict John Allen was sentenced to six months in the Oatlands chain gang for threatening to murder Robert Nottman.

Tools of the Trade

Convicts used shovels, rakes, brooms and hammers. The hammers were used to break the stone, and the size of each piece was checked by passing it through a handheld ring gauge. Horsedrawn rollers were introduced in the 1840s. The stone crusher followed in 1858 and the steamroller in 1860.

Earning His Stripes

For absconding from Robert Nottman's Road Party in May 1832, William Dorton received 50 lashes. He bolted three more times and copped 50 lashes on each occasion.

Van Diemonian Horses

The first horse arrived in Van Diemen's Land in January 1803. It was a mare belonging to Officer John Bowen. By 1820 an estimated 411 horses were in use in the colony. They were extremely valuable; a horse was worth up to £50. By 1827, horseracing was an established entertainment and a course and grandstand had been erected at Ross. In 1851, 'Black' Peter Haley arrived in Van Diemen's Land to serve ten years for horse stealing. A year later his sentence was increased to life for more horse theft.

Thomas Bell

Thomas Bell, born December 1782, joined the 48th Regiment at the age of 17 and by 1813 had been promoted to major. He married Mary Caroline Bourne in January 1806. In August 1817, he arrived in New South Wales with a detachment of the 48th Regiment and travelled to Hobart Town. Bell was appointed acting engineer and inspector of public works. He selected the best mechanics and labourers for government service and oversaw road construction. It is said, however, that he lacked technical expertise, knew little of the colony and delegated much of his work to underlings. He was reputed to be a kind man who did not permit overseers to strike gangsmen. Bell died in June 1866.

William Sorell

William Sorell was born in 1775. In April 1817 he replaced Thomas Davey as lieutenant-governor of Van Diemen's Land. Within 18 months, Sorell had ended the bushranging tyranny of Michael Howe and his accomplices. Sorrel was a popular governor. He established the Convict Department to manage the convict population and was generous in allocating land to colonists. He requested more convicts to work on public works and, as a result, the first convicts were transported directly to Van Diemen's Land from Britain in 1812. In August 1823, however, he was dismissed. Despite his popularity, Sorell was condemned for his private life. He lived with the wife of a fellow officer and had abandoned his own wife and children in England. Sorell died in June 1848.

Mates

John Mortlock noted that dogs made excellent travelling companions. After his hound perished, he traded goods worth 10s for a terrier puppy.

Milestones

Milestones were dotted along Van Diemonian roads. As they were carved in roman numerals, it is doubtful that many people were literate enough to have made much sense of them.

John Mortlock

John Mortlock was born in August 1809. After absconding from school, he travelled to India in the service of the East India Company. In 1840 he returned to England and claimed he had been cheated out of a sizeable inheritance. He broke into his uncle's bedroom, held a pistol to his head and demanded recompense. The gun went off and, although no one was injured, Mortlock was charged with shooting with intent and was sent to Norfolk Island to serve 21 years. In March 1846, he arrived in Van Diemen's Land, and after receiving a probation pass he roamed the colony hawking goods. In 1857, he travelled back to England to seek his inheritance once more, but he was arrested for returning before the expiration of his sentence. Despite a petition for his release signed by 1200 people, he was held in gaol and then transported to Western Australia. Mortlock wrote his memoirs, *Experiences of a Convict*. He was pardoned in 1862 and died a pauper in June 1882.

ROAD STATION

Road gangs were lodged in portable huts, gaols, watch houses and probation stations. In some remote places, where there was lots of work needed, road stations were built. These ranged from semi-permanent huts to large fortified stone-and-brick structures. More than 22 road stations were situated throughout the colony.

An Uphill Battle
Roads that passed over hilly terrain posed considerable problems. Grass Tree Hill is a steep incline, and convicts were set the task of clearing a path for a 10-metre-wide roadway. Cutting a track through bush and steep solid rock beds was extremely hard work. In 1835 an old horse named Captain and four bullocks assisted the convicts. By 1838, two horses and seven bullocks were being used. Large sandstone water troughs for the animals were hewn from solid rock. Two still remain today.

False Message
In May 1837, Henry Kirby boldly knocked on Charlotte Knight's door and said he was a messenger dispatched from Grass Tree Hill to tell her that her husband had been sentenced to the road gang. Knight gave him tea, sugar and bread to give to her beloved, but Kirby made off with the booty. He copped 12 months' hard labour.

Deck of Cards
Edward Desmond was caught with a deck of playing cards and his sentence was extended by two months.

Getting the Boot
In July 1834, Bewley Tuck refused to work until he received a new pair of boots. He copped four months' hard labour in the Grass Tree Hill road gang.

The Grass Tree Hill Road Station
In 1832, Lieutenant-Governor Arthur ordered a road be laid to link Risdon and Richmond. The proposed new road would only shave a few kilometres off the existing route, but it would provide the lieutenant-governor with more convenient access to his estate, Carrington. With so many Van Diemonian roads in need of repair or construction, the scheme was quite controversial. The road became known as the Carrington Cut and reportedly raised the property value of Carrington from £2000 to £16,000. A gang of 50 convicts cleared the land and constructed a road station. In 1834 Lieutenant-Governor Arthur inspected the road station and discovered a leaking, foul smelling barracks. Convict John Leonard claimed to have never suffered such misery. Convicts were half-starved and many had no shoes and barely enough clothes to cover themselves. George Britton had resorted to hunting kangaroo and was punished with 50 lashes. Conditions were so bad that Lieutenant-Governor Arthur revoked his policy of sending convicts to the station directly from their transport ship, feeling that it was too severe a sentence to inflict upon new arrivals. By 1837, the station included a wooden prison barracks enclosed by a log fence, a cell block and a chapel. The buildings perched on terraces that were cut into the steep hill and were accessed by stairs. There was a stone store, a military barracks and quarters for the commandant and superintendent. By 1838, the Grass Tree Hill gang numbered 139, of which 72 worked in leg irons. Progress was slow and the road was not finished until 1841. The station then served as a watch house. It was suggested that the chapel be modified to provide lodgings for ganged convicts on the move, but it was demolished instead. In 1845, a trip to Grass Tree Hill cost 1 shilling and 9 pence if you rode inside the stage coach and 1 shilling and 6 pence if you sat on top. Weary travellers could stop at the 'Help Me Thru the World Inn' at the top of the hill. In time the controversial road became a back road and the station crumbled into ruin.

Road to Ruin
Travellers on isolated roads took their lives into their own hands. In March 1863, two bushrangers held up William Whitton as he walked along Grass Tree Hill road. After stealing £27, they tied Whitton to a tree 50 metres from the road. Two clergymen finally came to his assistance. In June 1855, John 'Rocky' Whelan was charged with robbing William Kearney at Grass Tree Hill. The night before his execution, Whelan admitted to five other robberies in which he had ruthlessly shot his victims through the head.

Grass Tree
Grass Tree Hill derives its name from *Xanthorrhoea Australis*, also known as Southern Grasstree, Blackboy and Kangaroo Tail.

SAWPIT

Timber was placed across a sawpit to be sawn. One convict, known as the 'top dog', stood on top and another, the 'bottom dog', stood beneath, each clasping a handle of a pitsaw. Working with heavy timber and sharp tools was very dangerous, and life as a bottom dog was miserable. Sawdust poured into their eyes, ears and mouth and could lead to lung disease and blindness.

Logging Rafts

At Sarah Island, logs weighing as much as 12 tonnes had to be rolled or dragged to the water's edge where they were chained together to form rafts. The rafts were towed laboriously 23 kilometres back to the station. It was very hard work and convicts stood in the water all year round. Port Arthur was initially formed as a timber cutting station, but by 1846 the Cascades Probation Station had become the main supplier of timber on the peninsula. In 1850 a steam-powered sawmill was established and within six years the surrounding land was stripped bare, and the sawmill was transferred to Port Arthur. By the 1860s, Port Arthur was so denuded that felling gangs had to walk 10 kilometres each day to find trees.

'Logs'

The term logs found its way into convict vernacular. Places of confinement made from timber were called 'logs'. 'Gone for a log' referred to an absconder who had taken to the bush. Arthur Campbell received one week of hard labour for using the term at muster.

Quotas

After meeting weekly quotas, sawyers at Port Arthur were credited for every extra foot of timber they cut. Those who didn't meet the quota were punished. For neglecting his duty in December 1831, John Hartley had to cut an extra 400 feet (130 metres) of timber. His other offences included concealing boards in the sawpit, for which he received 12 lashes, and cutting his partner while sawing, which earned him 18 lashes. Passholders and ticket-of-leave men could earn £20 per week sawing timber. A good sawyer could even earn his freedom. David Dunkley was released for good conduct and unremitting attention to his labour as a sawyer on Sarah Island.

Straight Planks

Logs were mounted onto skids and held in place with wooden chocks or iron staples known as 'timber dogs'. To cut the log straight, a chalk-covered cord was stretched down the length of the log and then released, leaving a white line. The top dog guided the pitsaw along the line as the bottom dog heaved the saw back and forth. It took great skill to cut even planks. John Salmon copped 18 lashes for destroying a Huon pine log while sawing it.

Pitsaw

Timber was cut with a pitsaw, also known as a whipsaw. Pitsaws were 2.5 metres long and the bottom handle was removable so the saw could slip through the cut when the timber needed repositioning.

Escape Craft

In 1825, an escape craft was found buried in the bottom of one of the sawpits at Sarah Island. It was designed to hold up to three men and float at water level to appear as drifting branches whilst being paddled. Boat builder James Reeves gave it a test run and it proved quite seaworthy.

SCHOOL

Alongside religious instruction and trade skills, convicts were taught reading, writing and arithmetic. Particular importance was placed on educating juveniles, but schools also catered for adult convicts. The first school was built in 1822 at the Hobart Town prisoners' barracks. Following the introduction of the Probation System education became mandatory, but the system was far from perfect. Convicts appointed as teachers were not exempt from ganged labour and received no reward for teaching. And, after a hard day's work, many of their students were too tired to learn. Superintendent James Boyd reported that convicts regularly fell asleep in class and some were still unable to read or write after several years of schooling.

Teachers and Equipment

Convicts were taught by chaplains and also by other convicts. Thomas Adams, an ex-soldier and horse thief, taught children at Sarah Island. Schoolrooms were furnished with Bibles, spelling books and instructional cards. Convicts sat at desks and wrote on paper with quills or on pieces of slate with chalk. Equipment was in short supply and commonly dirty, torn and defaced.

Alfred Collins

When 17-year-old Alfred Collins arrived in Van Diemen's Land in 1844, he could neither read nor write. By 1847, he had mastered both. He received 24 hours in solitary for writing a note in which he described Point Puer as a 'little hell'.

63

SHIP

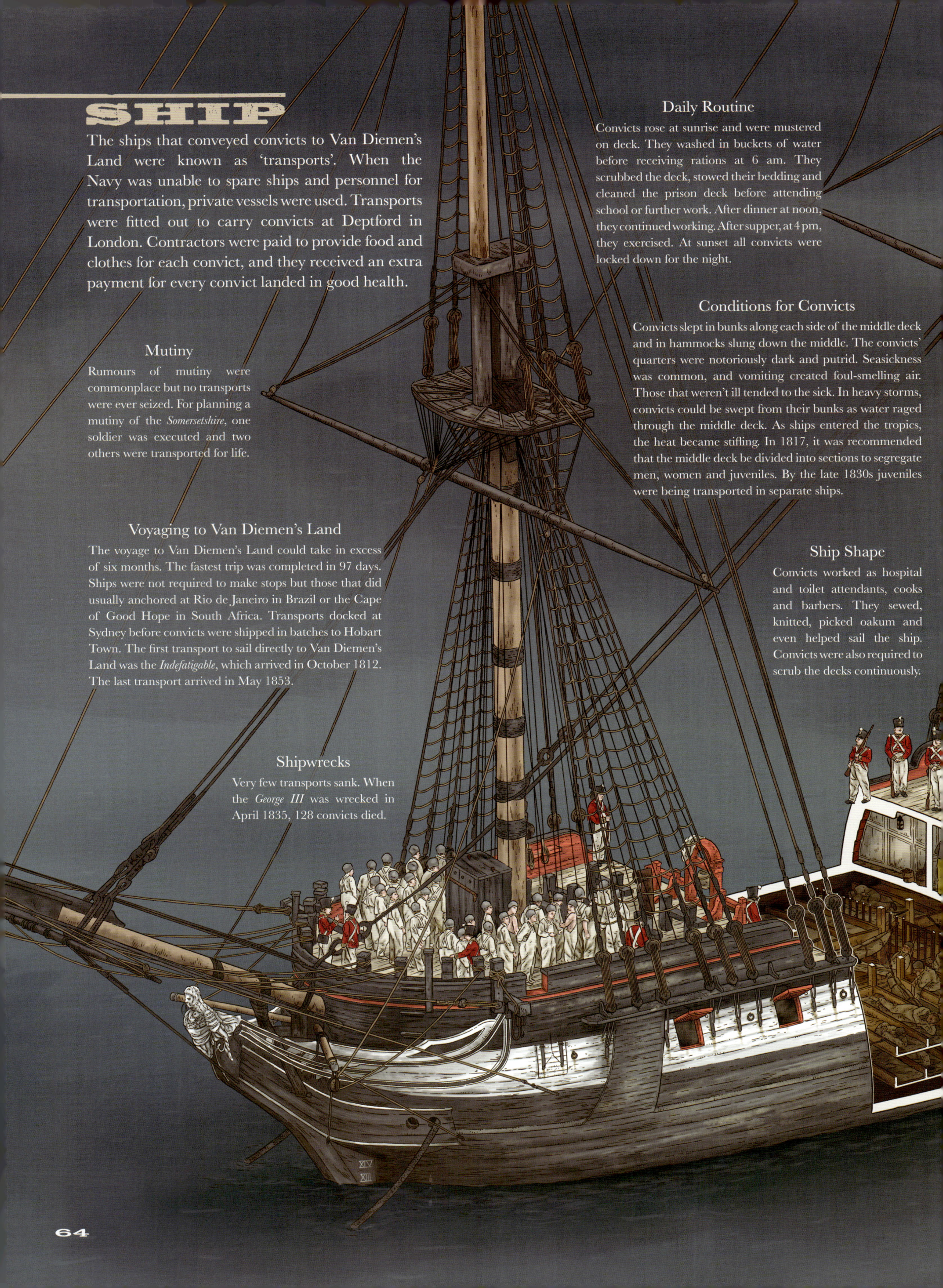

The ships that conveyed convicts to Van Diemen's Land were known as 'transports'. When the Navy was unable to spare ships and personnel for transportation, private vessels were used. Transports were fitted out to carry convicts at Deptford in London. Contractors were paid to provide food and clothes for each convict, and they received an extra payment for every convict landed in good health.

Mutiny

Rumours of mutiny were commonplace but no transports were ever seized. For planning a mutiny of the *Somersetshire*, one soldier was executed and two others were transported for life.

Voyaging to Van Diemen's Land

The voyage to Van Diemen's Land could take in excess of six months. The fastest trip was completed in 97 days. Ships were not required to make stops but those that did usually anchored at Rio de Janeiro in Brazil or the Cape of Good Hope in South Africa. Transports docked at Sydney before convicts were shipped in batches to Hobart Town. The first transport to sail directly to Van Diemen's Land was the *Indefatigable*, which arrived in October 1812. The last transport arrived in May 1853.

Shipwrecks

Very few transports sank. When the *George III* was wrecked in April 1835, 128 convicts died.

Daily Routine

Convicts rose at sunrise and were mustered on deck. They washed in buckets of water before receiving rations at 6 am. They scrubbed the deck, stowed their bedding and cleaned the prison deck before attending school or further work. After dinner at noon, they continued working. After supper, at 4 pm, they exercised. At sunset all convicts were locked down for the night.

Conditions for Convicts

Convicts slept in bunks along each side of the middle deck and in hammocks slung down the middle. The convicts' quarters were notoriously dark and putrid. Seasickness was common, and vomiting created foul-smelling air. Those that weren't ill tended to the sick. In heavy storms, convicts could be swept from their bunks as water raged through the middle deck. As ships entered the tropics, the heat became stifling. In 1817, it was recommended that the middle deck be divided into sections to segregate men, women and juveniles. By the late 1830s juveniles were being transported in separate ships.

Ship Shape

Convicts worked as hospital and toilet attendants, cooks and barbers. They sewed, knitted, picked oakum and even helped sail the ship. Convicts were also required to scrub the decks continuously.

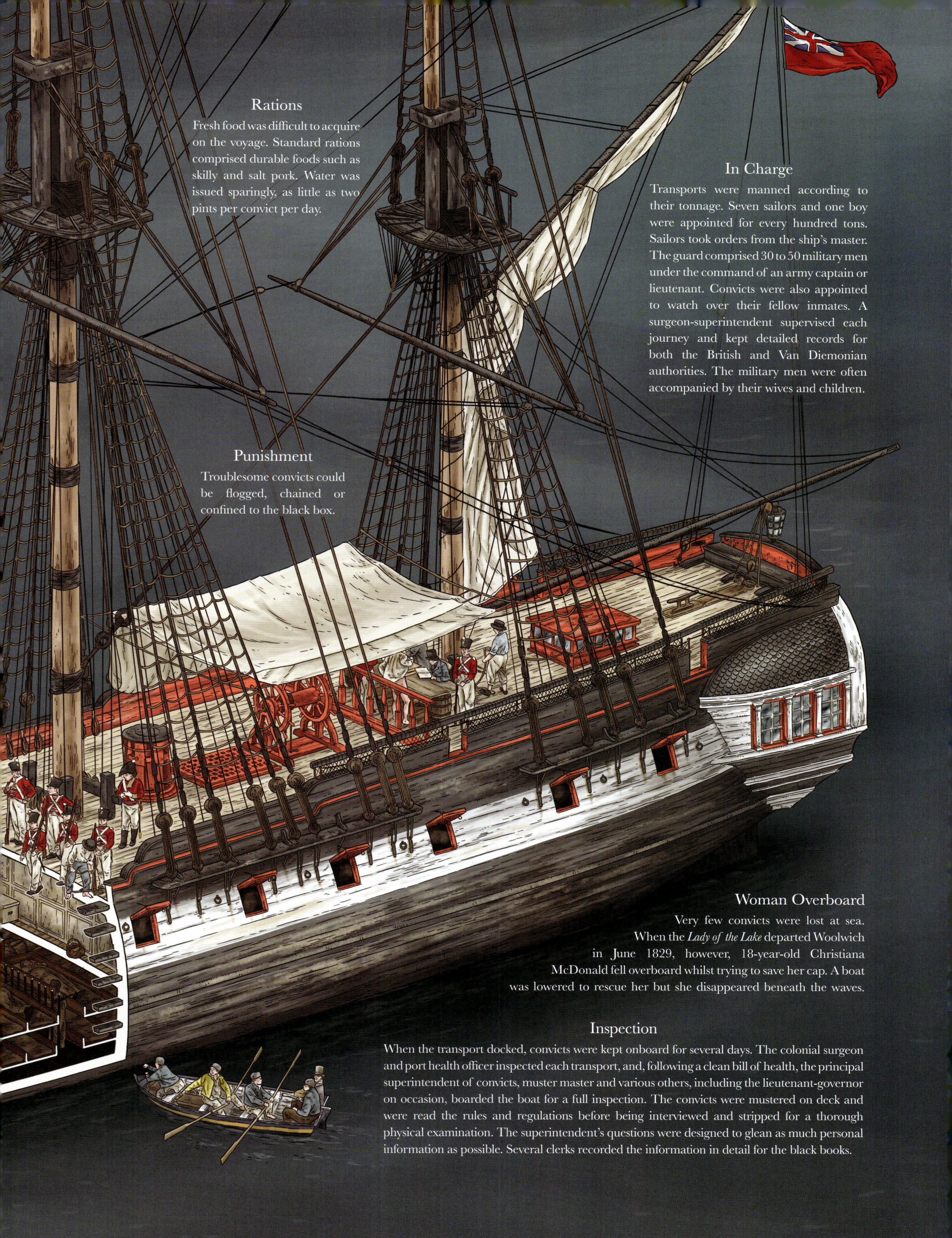

Rations

Fresh food was difficult to acquire on the voyage. Standard rations comprised durable foods such as skilly and salt pork. Water was issued sparingly, as little as two pints per convict per day.

In Charge

Transports were manned according to their tonnage. Seven sailors and one boy were appointed for every hundred tons. Sailors took orders from the ship's master. The guard comprised 30 to 50 military men under the command of an army captain or lieutenant. Convicts were also appointed to watch over their fellow inmates. A surgeon-superintendent supervised each journey and kept detailed records for both the British and Van Diemonian authorities. The military men were often accompanied by their wives and children.

Punishment

Troublesome convicts could be flogged, chained or confined to the black box.

Woman Overboard

Very few convicts were lost at sea. When the *Lady of the Lake* departed Woolwich in June 1829, however, 18-year-old Christiana McDonald fell overboard whilst trying to save her cap. A boat was lowered to rescue her but she disappeared beneath the waves.

Inspection

When the transport docked, convicts were kept onboard for several days. The colonial surgeon and port health officer inspected each transport, and, following a clean bill of health, the principal superintendent of convicts, muster master and various others, including the lieutenant-governor on occasion, boarded the boat for a full inspection. The convicts were mustered on deck and were read the rules and regulations before being interviewed and stripped for a thorough physical examination. The superintendent's questions were designed to glean as much personal information as possible. Several clerks recorded the information in detail for the black books.

SHIPYARD

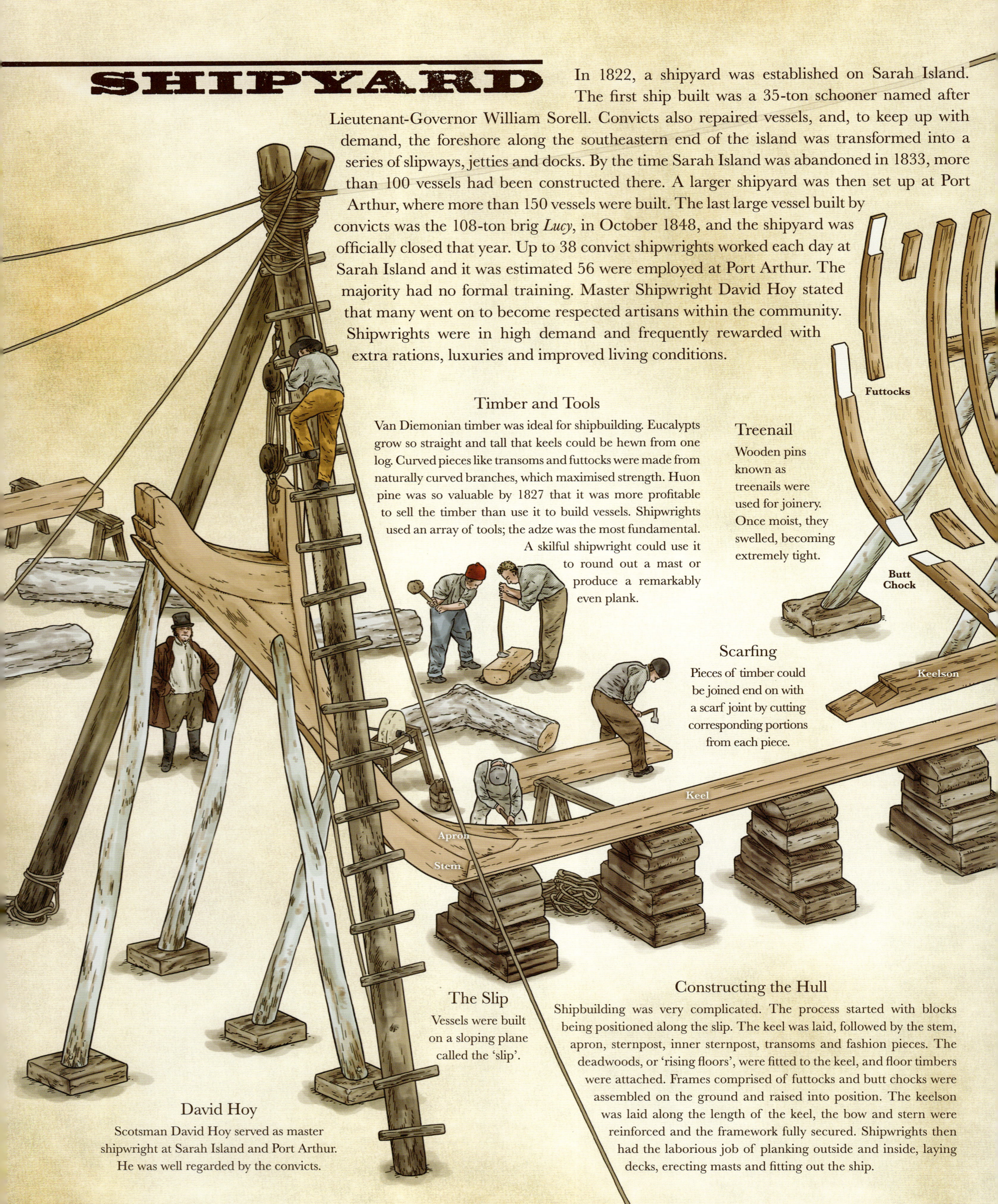

In 1822, a shipyard was established on Sarah Island. The first ship built was a 35-ton schooner named after Lieutenant-Governor William Sorell. Convicts also repaired vessels, and, to keep up with demand, the foreshore along the southeastern end of the island was transformed into a series of slipways, jetties and docks. By the time Sarah Island was abandoned in 1833, more than 100 vessels had been constructed there. A larger shipyard was then set up at Port Arthur, where more than 150 vessels were built. The last large vessel built by convicts was the 108-ton brig *Lucy*, in October 1848, and the shipyard was officially closed that year. Up to 38 convict shipwrights worked each day at Sarah Island and it was estimated 56 were employed at Port Arthur. The majority had no formal training. Master Shipwright David Hoy stated that many went on to become respected artisans within the community. Shipwrights were in high demand and frequently rewarded with extra rations, luxuries and improved living conditions.

Timber and Tools
Van Diemonian timber was ideal for shipbuilding. Eucalypts grow so straight and tall that keels could be hewn from one log. Curved pieces like transoms and futtocks were made from naturally curved branches, which maximised strength. Huon pine was so valuable by 1827 that it was more profitable to sell the timber than use it to build vessels. Shipwrights used an array of tools; the adze was the most fundamental. A skilful shipwright could use it to round out a mast or produce a remarkably even plank.

Treenail
Wooden pins known as treenails were used for joinery. Once moist, they swelled, becoming extremely tight.

Scarfing
Pieces of timber could be joined end on with a scarf joint by cutting corresponding portions from each piece.

The Slip
Vessels were built on a sloping plane called the 'slip'.

David Hoy
Scotsman David Hoy served as master shipwright at Sarah Island and Port Arthur. He was well regarded by the convicts.

Constructing the Hull
Shipbuilding was very complicated. The process started with blocks being positioned along the slip. The keel was laid, followed by the stem, apron, sternpost, inner sternpost, transoms and fashion pieces. The deadwoods, or 'rising floors', were fitted to the keel, and floor timbers were attached. Frames comprised of futtocks and butt chocks were assembled on the ground and raised into position. The keelson was laid along the length of the keel, the bow and stern were reinforced and the framework fully secured. Shipwrights then had the laborious job of planking outside and inside, laying decks, erecting masts and fitting out the ship.

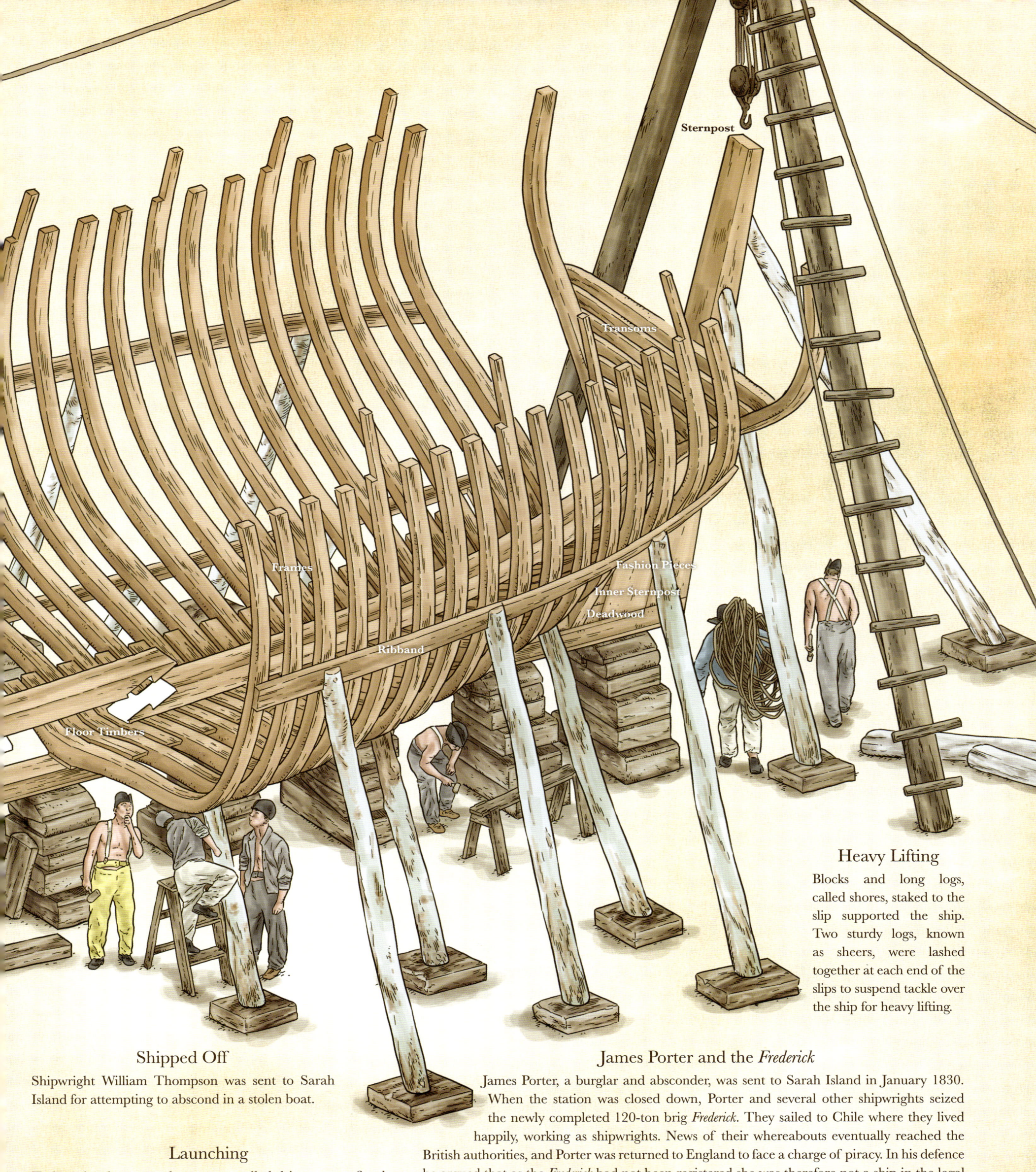

Labels on illustration: Sternpost, Transoms, Fashion Pieces, Inner Sternpost, Deadwood, Frames, Ribband, Floor Timbers

Heavy Lifting

Blocks and long logs, called shores, staked to the slip supported the ship. Two sturdy logs, known as sheers, were lashed together at each end of the slips to suspend tackle over the ship for heavy lifting.

Shipped Off

Shipwright William Thompson was sent to Sarah Island for attempting to abscond in a stolen boat.

Launching

To launch a large vessel, supports, called drivers, were fitted beneath the stem, and a cradle was built at the aft and positioned on rails that ran down the slip. The rails were coated in tallow, oil or soap and a rope was passed from the ship's stern to another vessel moored at sea. When the supports were knocked out, the ship slid down the slip and into the sea.

James Porter and the *Frederick*

James Porter, a burglar and absconder, was sent to Sarah Island in January 1830. When the station was closed down, Porter and several other shipwrights seized the newly completed 120-ton brig *Frederick*. They sailed to Chile where they lived happily, working as shipwrights. News of their whereabouts eventually reached the British authorities, and Porter was returned to England to face a charge of piracy. In his defence he argued that as the *Frederick* had not been registered she was therefore not a ship in the legal sense but merely a bundle of wood. Furthermore, because the seizure had occurred within the confines of a harbour and not on the high seas, it was not piracy, and as there had been no captain in command no mutiny had taken place. Debate over Porter's punishment continued for two years before he was packed off to Norfolk Island. There he penned his memoirs and the tale of the *Frederick* became well known. Porter escaped in May 1847 and was never seen again.

SIGNAL STATION

Signalling with flags enabled messages to be relayed at sea and over long distances on land. Messages were decoded by a signalman equipped with a telescope and codebook. In December 1803, the first flagstaff was erected at Hobart Town to relay information to and from vessels in the Derwent River. When Governor Macquarie of New South Wales arrived in Hobart Town in 1811, he was surprised there was no way to report on shipping within the D'Entrecasteaux Channel. He issued an order to erect the first signal station in Van Diemen's Land on the summit of Mount Nelson. In 1818, another signal station was established at Hobart Town and officially named the Mulgrave Battery.

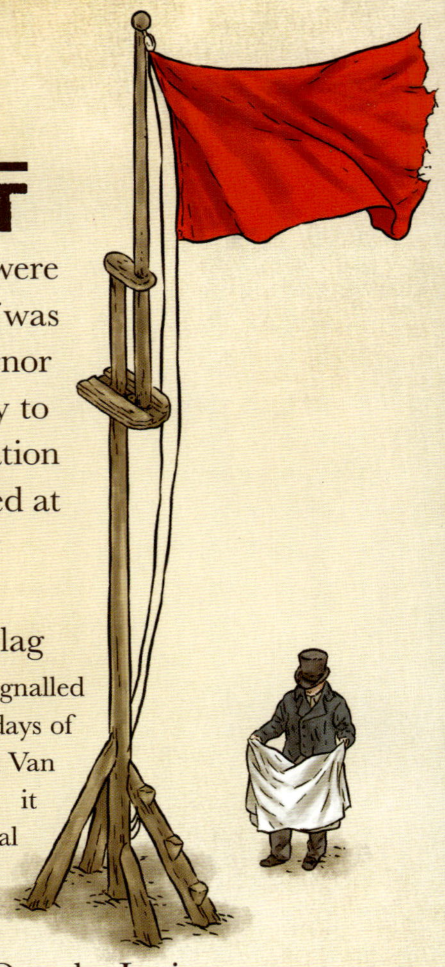

Vessel Signal Flags in 1838

British Man-o-War	London	Liverpool	Scotland	Ireland	Male Convicts
Female Convicts	Sydney	India	Canton	Cape of Good Hope	New South Wales
United States	South Australia	Western Australia	New Zealand	South America	Isle De France
Government Vessel	Colonel	Launceston	Whaler	Twofold Bay	Returning to Port

Raise a Red Flag
A red flag has signalled danger since the days of Ancient Rome. In Van Diemen's Land, it signalled the arrival of male convicts.

Ormsby Irwin
Ormsby Irwin was sentenced to life transportation and arrived in New South Wales in 1809 with his wife Eleanor. In 1814 they got into a drunken brawl with Sergeant Robert Morrow who died of his injuries a week later. The Irwins were charged with manslaughter. Ormsby received two years' hard labour at Newcastle and Eleanor was sent to Parramatta. Following Ormsby's release, he was shipped to Van Diemen's Land where he was appointed as signalman and gunner at the Mulgrave Battery. He received a conditional pardon in 1821.

The Semaphore System

Semaphores consisted of a mast with three revolving arms that could be positioned to represent numbers. The top arms represented units, the middle arm represented tens and the bottom arm represented hundreds. Commandant Booth saw the potential of semaphore for long-distance communication and built a chain of signal stations across the Tasman Peninsula. The system was improved in 1838 when the three arms were replaced with six, allowing numbers up to 999 to be signalled. At that time, nine signal stations enabled communication between Port Arthur and Hobart Town.

Value of Semaphore Arms

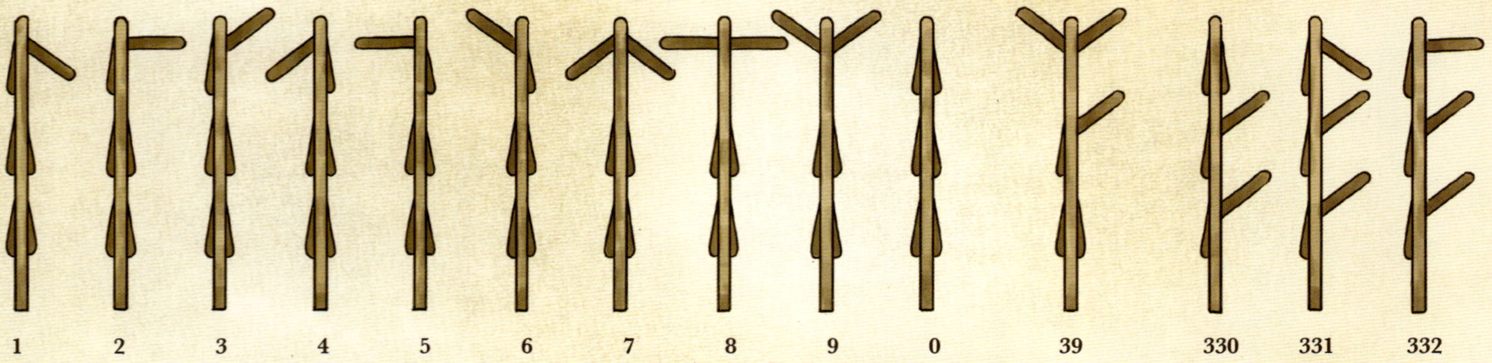

1 2 3 4 5 6 7 8 9 0 39 330 331 332

When Your Number Comes Up
Upon arrival in the colony, each convict was allocated a police number. If they absconded an alarm was signalled at the nearest semaphore and their police number was relayed out. William Derrincourt was number 39. When he absconded, his number was noticed by an overseer who nabbed him the next day. Keeping a watchful eye on the local semaphore was in a colonist's best interests. Number 330 meant 'bushrangers are here', 331 was 'runaways are here' and 332 was 'there is a whale in sight'.

Semaphore No More
A humble semaphore erected at Battery Point was the first in a chain that extended across the colony and all the way to Port Arthur. At the height of operation, 30 semaphores were in use. Following the introduction of the electric telegraph in 1857 and the telephone in 1880, semaphore became obsolete, and most of the stations were completely dismantled. Orders were given to make one final signal that read '343': 'forgotten'. In 1940, the Battery Point signal station was carefully restored and the signal was finally answered 2095: 'remembered'.

Sending Messages

In clear weather a message of up to 20 words could be sent from Hobart Town to Port Arthur and a reply received within 15 minutes. In bad weather an alternative signal station was used or the message was sent by foot to the next station. In high winds, semaphores could not be used at all. When a message was urgent—for example, reporting an absconder—two shots were fired in the direction of the nearest signal station to alert the sentries. Lanterns were hung from the semaphore for night signalling. Commandant Booth invented a code within the code used for secret communication.

Semaphore Tree

In the early 1830s, a giant stringybark was transformed into a semaphore at Port Arthur. The top was lopped off, leaving a 23-metre-high base for the semaphore's arm case. The tree's root system provided good stability in strong winds. To make it more visible, the tree was painted black. A smaller semaphore was built nearby to allow multiple signalling. The semaphore tree was the last in the chain linking Port Arthur to Hobart Town. It was dismantled in the 1870s.

The Life of a Signalman

Experienced signalmen were hard to come by. Literate convicts of good conduct were appointed under the guard of an overseer. Anyone caught sending false messages risked severe punishment. A signalman spent his days in a hut at the foot of the semaphore, on the lookout with his telescope. He had his codebook, signal journal and a gun, and he sent and received messages using the gears to work the arms and hoisting flags.

In the Line of Duty

In April 1840 George Britton, Henry Darkins, Peter Jack and George Hall absconded from the coalmines and arrived at the Halfway Bluff signal station. Constable Henry Miller confronted them, but he lowered his guard when they surrendered, only to be overpowered, bludgeoned with a hammer and handcuffed. The gang took off with Miller's money and some stolen provisions. They were apprehended while building an escape raft at East Bay Neck. Britton received a life sentence and the other three were recommended for a seven-year stretch.

Chequered   **Blue Peter**   **Tricolour**

Semaphore Flags

A chequered flag halfway up the yardarm, or 'half yard', meant that the first number was to be read in the thousands. A Blue Peter flag at yardarm indicated that a signal was about to be sent, but it could also signal that a mistake had been made if flown at half yard. The tricolour flag meant that the number was to be read as a numeral, not as part of the code.

Code Book

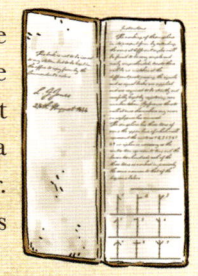

Signalmen were issued a codebook to decode incoming signals and a signal journal to record the messages. The books were treated with utmost care and updated when necessary, with a master copy remaining at Port Arthur. Codes were also published in periodicals to keep the public informed.

Ropes and Chains

Early semaphores were operated with ropes, but they would shrink, stretch or rot. By 1868 ropes had been replaced with chains.

Henry Miller

Henry Miller, a clerk convicted of embezzlement, arrived in Van Diemen's Land in July 1833 to serve 14 years. Despite being described as bad, dangerous and incorrigible, he was appointed constable and signalman. Miller was pardoned in November 1841.

SKILLS

Convicts were divided into two groups: 'unskilled' and 'skilled' labourers. Skilled labourers might include blacksmiths, brickmakers, cabinetmakers, carpenters, clerks, coopers, nailers, nurses, sawyers, seamstresses, shipwrights, shoemakers, stonecutters, tailors and wheelwrights. Unskilled convicts worked as carriers, cleaners, coalminers, domestic maids, errand boys, fencers, gardeners, kitchen hands, lumbermen, oakum pickers, ploughmen, road workers, washermen and washerwomen. Although skilled and unskilled convicts often worked together, unskilled convicts were more likely to be punished and less likely to receive indulgences as authorities believed fear of pain motivated unskilled convicts and that skilled workers were more successfully encouraged through rewards.

69

SOLITARY

Convicts were confined to small individual cells as a form of punishment. Stints in solitary did not usually exceed 30 days for men and 14 days for women. But in December 1817, Isabella Noble, an incessant burglar, was sentenced to three months in solitary. Convicts in solitary subsisted on just bread and water. Despite the depredations, however, some convicts found it a rare chance to rest. At Sarah Island, some men preferred a seven-day stint to one day's hard labour. The psychological effects of solitary confinement were considered greater than those of corporal punishment, and by the 1840s it was the favoured form of punishment. Cells, known as 'working cells' and 'separate apartments', were built to accommodate convicts in solitary while they worked at menial jobs.

In the Dark

Most solitary cells had no window. Those that did had small barred windows. Dark cells, also known as refractory cells and punishment cells, were kept in total darkness and 'dumb cells' were soundproof as well. Convicts could be confined for three days straight before being allowed an hour of exercise. It was an extreme punishment—some convicts preferred to be flogged.

Locked Tight

Cell doors were made from solid timber. Some were fitted with iron cladding on the inside face and edges to make them resistant to arson. Some doors were covered with tacks or nails to ensure the timber could not be chipped away. An observation hole gave a view of the cell and a servery hatch was used to issue rations without having to unlock the door. Doors were locked tight with locks, bolts and heavy padlocks. Despite the precautions, though, some convicts still managed to escape by passing wire around the hasp and feeding it back into the cell. When the coast was clear the hasp was lifted up and bolt drawn back allowing the door to swing open.

Maimed Convicts

Joseph Harrison spent over 200 days in solitary for various offences. In August 1842, he was charged with 'wilfully breaking his wooden leg' and sent to Port Arthur. Maimed convicts were an unwelcome burden. At the insistence of Lieutenant-Governor Wilmot, transportation of maimed male convicts ceased in 1845. Maimed women continued to arrive as it was felt they could still perform domestic duties.

Night Tubs

When they were locked up overnight, or while in solitary, convicts used buckets as toilets. They were known as sanitary buckets, night tubs, urine tubs, necessary tubs and nuisance tubs, and their contents were politely termed 'night soil'. Due to the rank smell, it is likely most convicts tried to hold on until they could use one of the communal lavatories. In the towns, night soil was collected and carted to the nearest cesspit, but it sometimes found its way into the local water supply and was even used as fertiliser. As paper was a precious commodity, it is possible convicts were issued rags or rope for use as toilet paper. It is more likely, however, that they simply did without.

Separate System

The Separate System was designed to isolate convicts. They were placed in individual cells and forbidden to communicate with each other. The aim was to give each prisoner time to think about the error of his ways and improve the course of his life. Separating convicts also prevented them corrupting one another. Chaplains provided religious instruction, and convicts were encouraged to read, write, count and learn a trade. In 1849, a Separate Prison was built at Port Arthur. It consisted of 50 cells, a chapel with 50 individual stalls, 12 exercise yards, two dark cells, a receiving room, a cookhouse and an officers' quarters.

All convicts arriving at Port Arthur had to serve time in the Separate Prison. Those on a life sentence served up to 12 months. When Port Arthur closed in 1877, the Separate Prison was sold. It was restored in 2008 after being destroyed in a fire.

Silence and Isolation

Under the Separate System, convicts were confined to their cell for nearly 24 hours a day. When allowed out they wore a hood. The face covering was only permitted to be drawn back during the daily hour of exercise and at chapel. Inmates were referred to only by their cell number. They wore a grey uniform marked with the letters S.P. and remained five metres apart at all times. Great care was taken to ensure a routine of complete supervision, silence and isolation. Officers in charge communicated with signals and bells and wore slippers in order to move around the prison silently.

Tight Spaces

Separate System cells measured 6 feet by 9 feet. At the Hobart Town Prisoners' Barracks, solitary cells were even smaller. On Sarah Island the cells were smaller again. Female convicts were restricted to a space 7 feet by 2 feet 6 inches at the Cascades Female Factory. At Point Puer, boys were locked in cells 5 feet 6 inches by 3 feet 6 inches. Cells at the penitentiary chapel and the coalmines were notoriously small, but perhaps the most inhumane were located at the Bridgewater Causeway. Each cell measured just 7 feet by 2 feet 6 inches. Convicts were pushed in headfirst and locked behind a barred wooden gate. Stout men were unable to roll over and had to be dragged out by the ankles.

Dennis Doherty

Dennis Doherty was a 'Fenian', an Irish revolutionary bent on establishing an Irish republic. He served time in New South Wales, Norfolk Island and Van Diemen's Land and was one of the first convicts to do time in the Separate Prison. Doherty was regarded as a particularly dangerous inmate. In September 1858, when his cell was unlocked for exercise, he charged out, belted his guard in the face, pummelled him with a stool and nearly choked him to death. He was sentenced to 28 days' solitary and 12 more months at the Separate Prison. Doherty had originally been sentenced to 14 years' transportation when he was just 18 years old, but his stubborn disposition earned him almost 43 years. He was finally released from Port Arthur in February 1876.

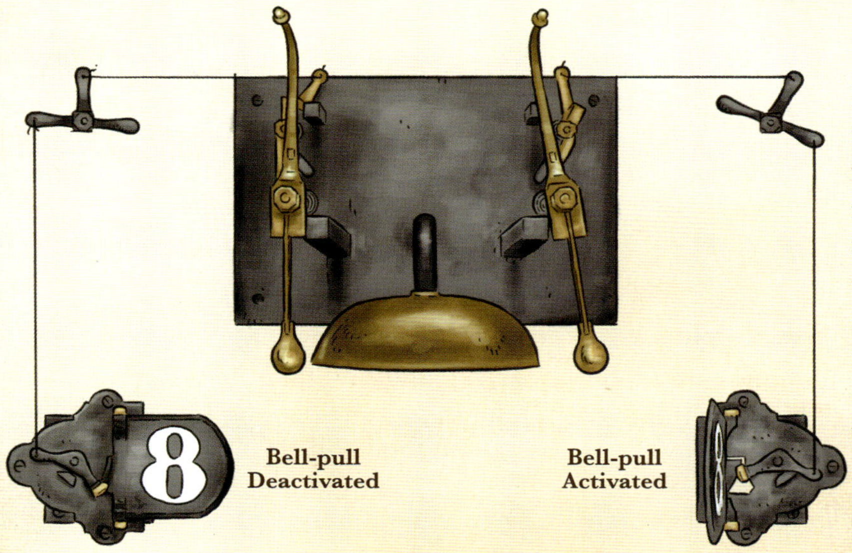

Separate Prison Furnishings

In each cell hung a set of rules that prisoners were expected to adhere to. Cells had to be kept neat and clean. A bell indicated when prisoners were permitted to rise, bed down and put out their lamps. Cells were fitted with a table, stool, night tub, water bucket and a set of shelves for eating utensils, cleaning equipment, a Bible, a prayer book and schoolbooks. Bedding was a canvas hammock, mattress, two blankets and a sleeping rug. Outside each cell was an iron plate with the cell number painted on it. When a handle known as a bell-pull within the cell was turned, the plate flipped out and a long connective copper wire rang the bell to summon the officer on duty.

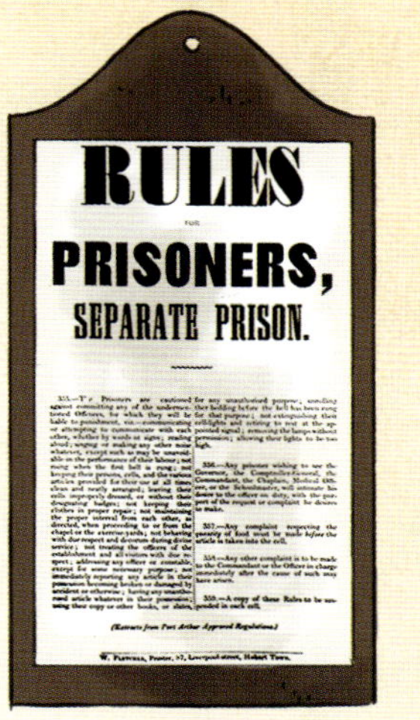

Bell-pull Deactivated

Bell-pull Activated

SUICIDE

Suicide, or 'self-murder', was a sin and a punishable offence. When William Mulhall attempted to hang himself in March 1851, he was charged with misconduct. Suicide was frequently reported as an act of 'temporary insanity' or 'accidental death' to avoid social and religious damnation. Preventing suicide was difficult. In April 1867, William Carter used his hammock straps to hang himself in the Separate Prison. Dennis Collins, a one-legged sailor convicted of high treason for lobbing a stone at the King after his disability pension was revoked, starved himself to death at Port Arthur. Matthew Forster told of convicts entering into pacts whereby one murdered another in front of witnesses, ensuring the death penalty for the murderer and time to repent his crime. At Port Arthur in 1836, a horrified Reverend Butters noted two such instances within the one week. The *Hobart Town Courier* said the large number of suicides was 'too melancholy a proof of the severity of transportation'.

TATTOO

To make a tattoo, an image was pricked into the skin with a sharp instrument, then ink, soot or gunpowder was rubbed into the flesh to leave a permanent mark. Tattooing was popular amongst convicts of all ages. Eleven-year-old John Kennedy bore his initials upon his right arm. Names and initials were the most popular tattoos but convicts also recorded other personal information such as trial dates and sentences. Some images, such as an anchor meaning hope and a heart meaning love, were symbolic. Other tattoos could be religious, patriotic, occupational, humorous or defiant. George Holland had chains tattooed around each wrist. Tattooing could also be a badge of infamy or shame. Army deserters were tattooed with a small 'D' below their left armpit. Convicts tattooed themselves and also each other. John Hill, an ex-sailor, tattooed others for goods such as tobacco. In Van Diemen's Land, where convicts were severed from their family and heritage, and reduced to numbers, tattoos helped them retain their individuality and sense of identity.

Francis Fitzmaurice

Francis Fitzmaurice, a carpenter convicted of stealing clothes, arrived in New South Wales in October 1835 to serve seven years. In June 1843, he was charged with bushranging and transported to Van Diemen's Land for life. The following year, Fitzmaurice and six others absconded from Port Arthur in a canoe made of canvas. A reward of £2 was posted for his capture, along with a complete list of his many tattoos. It was those telltale marks (see below) that were his undoing. In October, he was spotted strolling through Hobart Town. Fitzmaurice was sentenced to Norfolk Island, but during the voyage he and several others broke free of their irons. They sawed their way to the middle deck, but after discovering some beer they got drunk and were quickly caught. After finally gaining his freedom, Fitzmaurice settled in Van Diemen's Land with his wife and children. He died in June 1883.

Chest
The area around the heart was often reserved for symbols of great affection. On the right of Fitzmaurice's chest was Hibernia (the Latin for Ireland) personified. In one hand she holds a harp, another iconic Irish motif, and in the other she clutches the symbols of the union; a rose for England, a thistle for Scotland and a shamrock for Ireland.

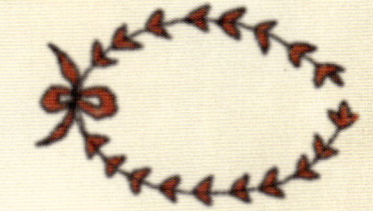

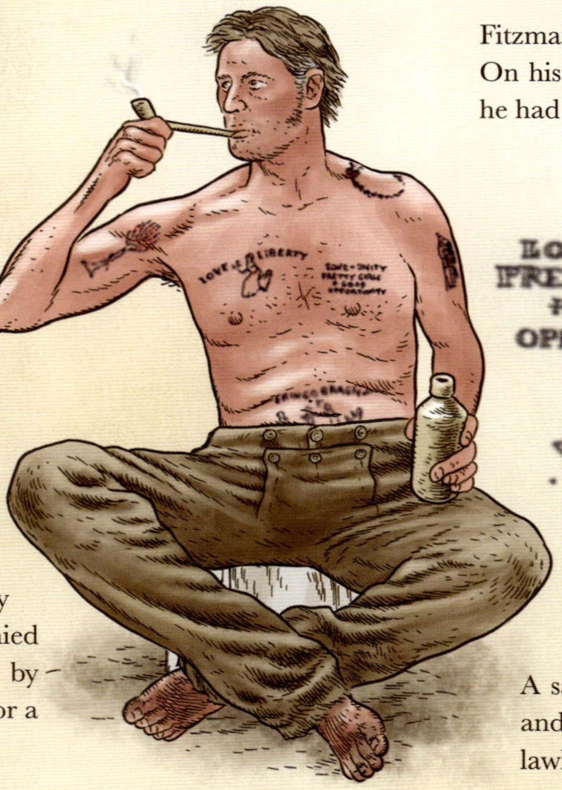

Right Arm
The tree of knowledge encircled by the serpent. Adam and Eve were denied immortality and forced to survive by their own means, a pertinent story for a transported felon.

Belly
Four boxers and the words 'Erin Go Bragh', Gaelic for 'Ireland Forever'. Boxing matches were common tattoos.

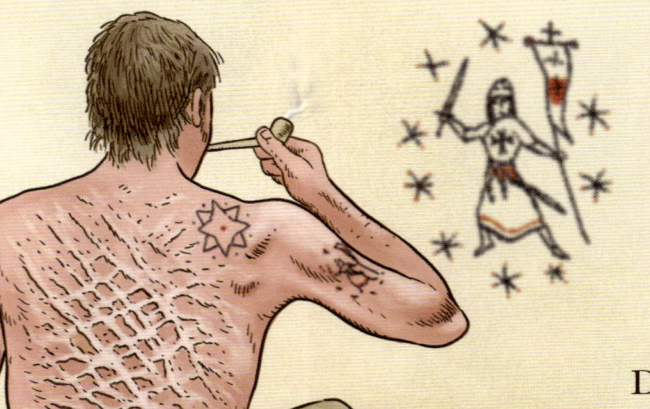

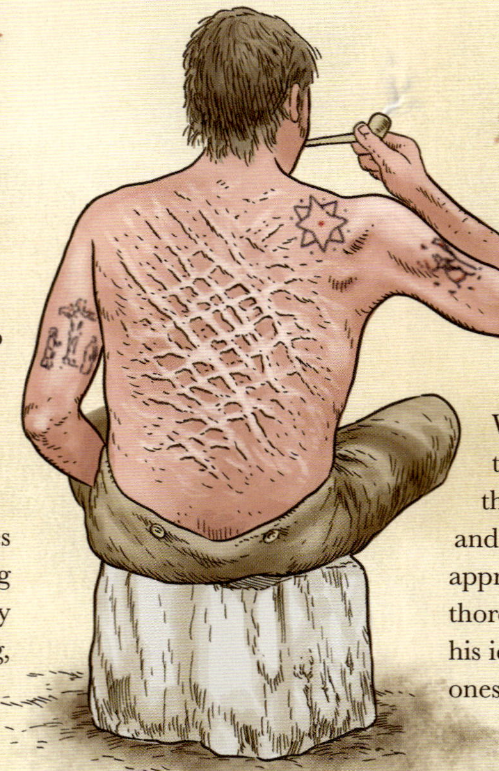

Left Arm
Christ on the cross and two figures praying. Religious tattoos were among the most common images adopted by convicts. They represented suffering, absolution and redemption.

Left Shoulder
Fitzmaurice carried many scars. On his left shoulder was a scar he had encircled in a wreath.

Chest
On his left was 'Love and Unity, Pretty Girls and Good Opportunity.' These optimistic sentiments took on a tragic twist after years behind without such pleasures.

Right Shoulder
A large eight-pointed star. Stars and constellations were points of navigation to ensure a safe voyage.

Left Arm
A sailor clutching a cutlass and a flag bearing the skull and crossbones. A pirate is indicative of rebellion and lawlessness. The skull and crossbones symbolised death.

Right Arm
A Knight of the Templar surrounded by a circle of stars. Images representing secret societies were not uncommon and some convicts bore marks to indicate belonging to an order or fraternity. A knight could also symbolise loyalty, chivalry or courage.

Disappearing Ink
When Fitzmaurice's tattoos were recorded in New South Wales, they included his initials and a mermaid, fish and dish-cloth on the inside of his right arm. On his left arm was a cross, sword, pistol and anchor and on his chest a woman and a ship. By the time he was apprehended in Hobart Town, those images had disappeared. But a thorough examination of his tattoos by several constables confirmed his identity. Although he had replaced many of his tattoos with new ones, his remaining collection had betrayed him.

TICKET-OF-LEAVE

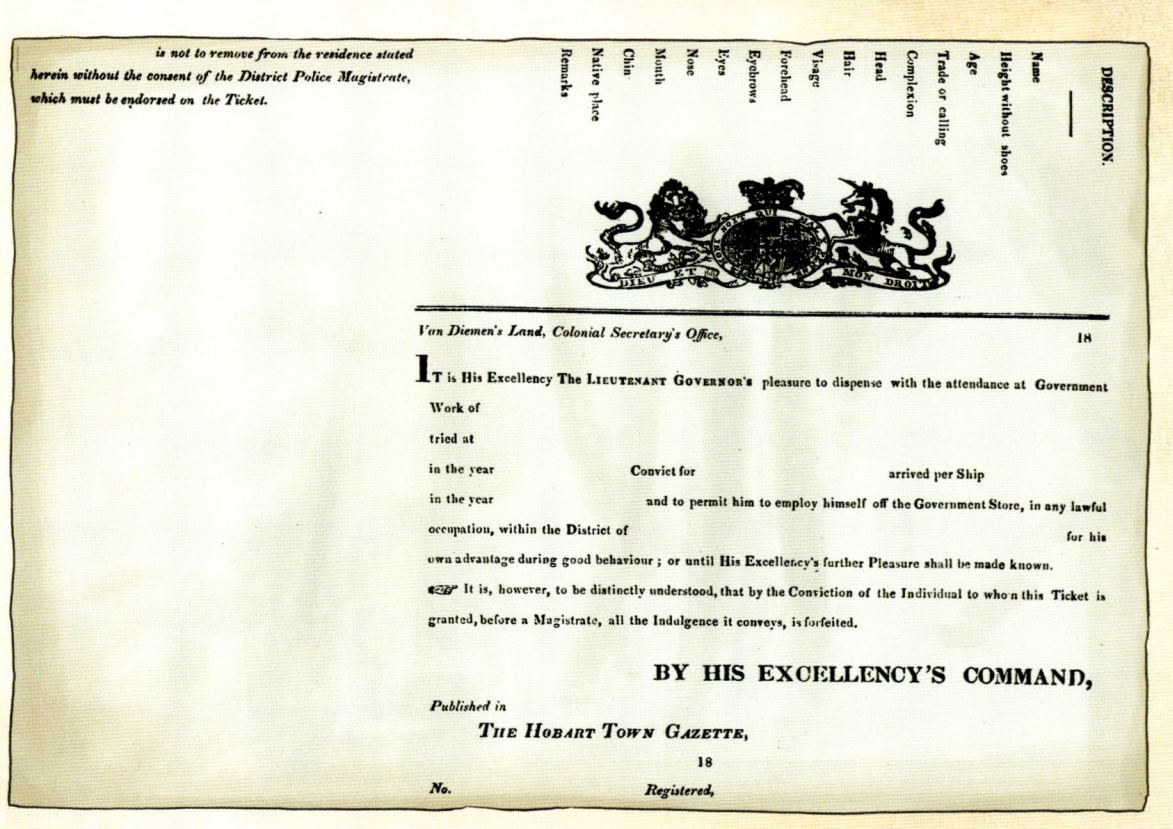

A ticket-of-leave was granted at the lieutenant-governor's discretion. It exempted convicts from labour and assignment. It allowed them to own property and work for a wage. The system was first introduced in New South Wales in 1801. Ticket holders, known as 'paper-men', had to remain within one district, attend a monthly muster and go to Sunday services. Tickets could be revoked for bad behaviour. A convict could apply for a ticket-of-leave after serving a certain time. In later years the required time served was reduced to encourage more convicts to integrate into society. Further allowances were made for those who performed acts of public service, such as apprehending bushrangers. The next step to freedom was a conditional pardon. A pardon was granted by the Crown following a recommendation from the lieutenant-governor; the process could take years. The final step was a free pardon.

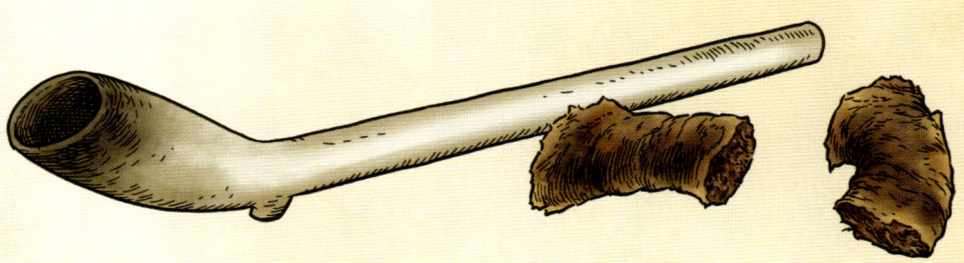

TOBACCO

Although tobacco was issued to convicts as a reward, as a general rule it was forbidden. It became a valued form of currency, particularly because it was concealable and durable. William Derrincourt stated that 1-inch sections of tobacco were worth a bread ration. According to Linus Miller, it was even sold by the puff. Convicts caught with tobacco risked severe punishment. In November 1830, Elizabeth Smith was caught smuggling more than half a kilogram of tobacco hidden in the folds of her petticoat into the Cascades Female Factory and had her sentence extended by three years. In March 1847, William Bennett was executed after he slayed Thomas Shand with an axe for betraying the whereabouts of his stash of tobacco to the authorities. When the tobacco supply at Sarah Island dried up, John Mayo claimed to have lost the will to live and committed a murder in order to bring about his own execution. In 1806, tobacco was worth £1 per pound (half kilogram). By 1846, it was worth 1 penny per pound. Some colonists attempted to grow it commercially, but it required skills that most colonists didn't possess, and the vast majority of tobacco was imported. By the 1860s, tobacco had become standard issue, and convicts at Port Arthur received a daily allowance of 4 drams.

Puffing, Chewing and Snorting

Tobacco pipes were manufactured from fine white clay, which was rolled to size by hand before being moulded, pierced with a thin wire and carefully fired in a kiln. Some pipes were decorated with intricate patterns and the bowls moulded into novel shapes. Pipe making was a skilled profession. Convict Robert Roberts was a clay pipe maker. Pipes were representative of good times and were commonly seen tattooed on the limbs of convicts. Tobacco was chewed in small pieces called 'quids' as well as smoked. In June 1841 Patrick Minnighan was sentenced to death for the murder of James Travis. As the guilty verdict was read out, he disdainfully spat tobacco juice on either side of the Supreme Court desk. Tobacco in powdered form was known as snuff and inhaled through the nose. Snuff was enjoyed by the elite and carried in elaborate snuff boxes. When John Scott attempted to sell a silver snuffbox inscribed 'William Cleland' in August 1849, the jeweller took the box, called for the owner and had Scott arrested.

TRAFFICKING

Trafficking is trade that takes place outside official channels, commonly on the 'black market'. Depots where trafficked goods were received were hot spots. On Sarah Island convicts passed rum, tea and tobacco under the transport ship's hull to the waiting boat crew. Issued items were traded or reworked for the black market. Convicts removed government marks on clothing with soap, which was itself a valuable item. When assigned to wash shirts, William Thompson was given five or six bars for every 100 shirts. He made do with two bars, and sold the remainder. Thompson was also a shoemaker. When convicts were issued new boots, he expertly mended the old ones and resold them as new. Officer James Syme commented that between one third and one quarter of new boots were traded for goods such as tobacco. Preventing trafficking was impossible, especially because those in positions of trust were often the ringleaders.

TREADMILL

A treadmill was a long cylindrical wheel fitted with steps. It was turned as convicts walked the steps. Attached to the wheel axle was a system of gears that turned millstones to grind grain. Treadwheels had no grinding mechanism. They were used solely to punish prisoners.

Productive Punishment

A stint on the treadmill was hard work. A committee investigating the effect on convicts of working on the treadmill reported that when subsisting on a daily ration of gruel, bread and broth, each convict lost approximately 2 pounds, 9 ounces of body weight during a 5½ month period. It was concluded that this was not damaging to their health. During this period the treadmill produced flour at a saving of more than £200 compared to the cost of producing flour in a privately owned mill. The punitive advantages of the treadmill were obvious, but the report could not state conclusively that stints on the treadmill reformed badly behaved convicts. It did, however, conclude that no other system of discipline, such as solitary confinement or flogging, was as beneficial to the public, the government or the convict himself. The report also recognised that the treadmill needed strict management to ensure that it ran smoothly and fairly. It recommended that for every three men on the wheel, there should be two resting; the wheel should not turn for more than 10 hours a day; and the total number of revolutions daily should not exceed 1200.

Leg Irons

Convicts wearing leg irons were expected to keep up even though the chain connecting the two basils prohibited lengthy paces. John Cole was crippled in the left leg and did time on the treadmill in chains. He was flogged for refusing. In January 1847, James Croft was sent to solitary for six days for lobbing his boot into the treadmill in a feeble attempt to jam it.

Van Diemonian Treadmills

The first Van Diemonian treadmill was built in the Hobart Town prisoners' barracks and was operational by 1827. It was divided into two sections: one to punish the general public and military and a larger area for convicts. The wheel measured two metres in diameter and each step was 17 centimetres deep. The axle passed through the southern wall and into the mill room where it was connected to large grindstones. Work often started before sunrise and a large clock regulated the treadmill. After every three revolutions, a bell chimed and the men swapped shifts. Linus Miller recorded that the wheel revolved 14 hours a day and prisoners worked two-hour shifts. Every four minutes, one descended on one end and everyone moved along two steps. It was calculated that 3½ bushels of wheat could be ground every hour, but the *Hobart Town Courier* reported that it was not a particularly viable form of labour, but an effective form of punishment and a good deterrent to would-be lawbreakers. In 1838, a treadmill was constructed in Launceston, and another was built at Port Arthur in 1845. By the late 1850s, treadmills were no longer in use, and they were destroyed or sold.

Resting Stall   **Wheel Booth**

The Dreaded Treadmill

By the 1840s, up to 150 prisoners were crammed into the Hobart Town treadmill room, resulting in daily stints on the wheel of just a few hours each. A sentence on the treadmill was no longer a dreaded punishment but a relief from regular convict work. To remedy this, James Boyd divided the wheel into 25 small booths in the late 1840s, and the room was fitted out with 40 resting stalls so that convicts would be isolated while they worked and rested. Each stall was fitted with a clothes hook, a seat, a mug and a Bible or lesson book. Talking was forbidden, so convicts passed a numbered tablet in a slot in the door to summon an overseer. Another hole in the door ensured convicts could be supervised.

Crime and Punishment

In August 1843, George Meadowcroft, William 'Dido' Driscoll and Charles Baker attacked William Bell in the lavatory adjoining the treadmill room. After pinning Bell down and putting a knife to his throat, they stole several coins that Bell had sewn in his shirt for safe keeping. Driscoll and Meadowcroft were sent to Port Arthur for six years and Baker for five.

Bribery and Generosity

Linus Miller claimed that it was possible to bribe the overseer and be exempted from your shift, or to pay another convict to take your turn. Miller took the shift of a portly prisoner named Thomas Hewitt who struggled to keep pace. His generosity was repaid when Hewitt saved him from a beating. When Jeremiah Pether attempted to bribe the overseer with a forged cheque he was sentenced to seven years at Port Arthur.

James Lovett

In July 1839, James Lovett arrived at the Launceston treadmill, scantly clad, soaked and shivering from the rain. Following a six-hour stint, he complained of being ill but by the time he was transferred to hospital it was too late and he died.

75

UNIFORM

Convicts were issued 'slops', cheap ready-made clothing. A standard uniform for a man comprised a jacket, trousers, striped shirt, boots or shoes and a leather cap. Women were issued a jacket, petticoat, plain dress, apron, stockings, shoes, cap and handkerchief. Clothing was issued twice a year, and convicts were limited to just one set at any time. Uniforms were government property, and a damaged or lost article could result in severe punishment.

Hats and Caps

Headwear included hats of straw, wool and leather. Male convicts were issued a leather cap with peaks that fastened upright. The cap could be worn front-on or side-on, and the peaks could be lowered to provide shelter. When not in use the cap was folded flat. A convicts saluted civil and military officers by raising his hand to his hat or removing it. Hiram Sharp was flogged for not 'doffing his cap'. Hats could also convey defiance. When a convict about to be flogged folded the front peak up and the back peak down, it indicated that he would not flinch. In October 1832, Henry Liddle struck overseer James Burton on the head with an axe. The blow knocked Burton senseless, but the cut was only skin-deep. The surgeon later stated that he was saved by the double band on his leather cap.

Dress Code

In 1814 the parti-coloured uniform was introduced. It consisted of alternating sections of black and white. Parti-colour was highly conspicuous and humiliating, as it likened the wearer to a clown or jester. In 1817, the white was replaced with yellow, long regarded as the colour of disgrace. Usually, recidivists and convicts serving a life sentence wore parti-colour, while those on a short sentence wore a yellow suit. In order to pull pants on over leg irons, a row of buttons ran the length of the outside of each leg. Convicts were expected to keep their clothing buttoned up tightly, but, as a parti-coloured uniform could contain 40 buttons, adhering to the rules wasn't easy. For good behaviour, male convicts could wear a grey uniform. Skilled convicts and those on ticket-of-leave could wear their own clothes. Due to the scarcity of fabric and haphazard issuing practices, convicts frequently dressed in whatever was available and their clothing was anything but uniform.

Footwear

Convicts were issued with shoes in the early years, and later with boots. A basic design with a square toe allowed one boot to fit on either the left or right foot. They were made of leather and stitched by hand. The soles were attached with hobnails. Hobnails also provided grip and some were affixed to form the shape of the broad arrow, which left a tell-tale footprint. Aboriginal trackers could easily track a man by his boot prints. But bushrangers Michael Cody and James Murphy fixed heels to the front of their shoes to try to outwit trackers. Convicts at Port Arthur were issued with two sets of footwear a year and those working in probation stations received up to four per year. Meeting the demand was impossible and many convicts were reduced to covering their feet in rags or going barefoot which, according to Daniel Heustis, left bloody footprints on frozen ground.

Reduced to Rags

Uniforms wore out quickly, leaving many convicts wearing rags. In 1834, John Patching refused to work until he was supplied with more clothing, as he'd been forced to work almost naked. He was punished with one month's imprisonment and four months' hard labour. In 1836, Patching spent three days in solitary for being unable to account for a uniform that had been issued to him a few weeks earlier. Clothing was popular on the black market. In 1838, Patching was charged with stealing several articles of clothing. For his repeated disobedience he copped three years' hard labour in irons.

P A
4 0 3

Numbers and Letters

Uniforms could be marked with a size number of 1 to 4 and an issue number. A register listed the details so that stolen or trafficked items could be traced back to the original recipient. Convicts caught altering or removing their numbers were punished, but some convicts simply turned their uniforms inside out to commit a crime unidentified. Markings were also used to classify convicts. At the Cascades Female Factory the 'crime class' women wore large yellow 'C's on the backs of their jackets and petticoats and right sleeves. Those in 'probation class' bore the yellow 'C' on their left sleeves'. After graduating to 'first class' a female convict could be assigned to a colonist who supplied her with a new set of clothes.

Nicknames

Convicts dressed in yellow were called 'canary birds' while those in parti-colour were 'magpies'. Soldiers wore red jackets and were known as 'lobsters', 'red herrings' and 'bloody backs'. Due to the crisscross pattern of the lacerations inflicted during a flogging, victims were cynically said to have been fitted with a 'checkered vest'.

Flash Is the New Black

Convicts were not allowed to style their hair or wear jewellery. Members of the Flash Mob were said to have worn silk scarves and earrings in an affront to such regulations. Women were not made to wear parti-colour, but troublemakers could be clothed in a punishment dress that is thought to have been entirely black.

Cleanliness

Usually convicts washed daily and bathed once a week under supervision. Convicts were appointed to do the laundry for other convicts, and some were appointed as barbers. Hair was cut once a month and men were shaved twice a week. James Littleton was said to have shaved men very roughly.

The Broad Arrow

Clothing was stamped with the broad arrow and the letters B.O., which stood for the supplier, the 'Board of Ordnance'. After 1855, W.D. (War Department) was stamped on clothing. Marking clothing as government property prevented trafficking and theft.

Making and Mending

Convicts made and mended clothing to supply penal establishments and offset costs. A cloth and weaving factory was established on Maria Island in 1826. Convicts also worked in tanneries to produce leather for making shoes and boots. The goods produced by convicts in Van Diemen's Land were said to be superior to and cheaper than those produced in Britain.

Underwear

Uniforms were unlined and convicts were not supplied with underwear. Underclothes provided a second layer instead. Socks, also known as stockings, were usually made of knitted cloth. In May 1855, Margaret Manning was found wandering the streets of Hobart Town 'dirty and scantily clad' with no shoes or stockings. She was suspected of soliciting and received three months' hard labour.

UNNATURAL CRIME

'Unnatural crime' primarily referred to homosexuality. Convicts were transported for committing sodomy, which was also punishable by death. Hendrick Witnalder was hanged in Hobart Town in February 1863; he was the last man executed for the offence in the British Empire. After the introduction of the Probation System, which grouped men in isolated areas, homosexuality-related charges increased. A report into its prevalence resulted in increased surveillance and plans for beds to be entirely enclosed in wooden slats. Some officials remained in denial of the issue, but the spread of venereal disease was irrefutable. The prevention of unnatural crime was a contributing factor in the closure of coalmines and the introduction of the Separate Treatment System. It was such a taboo that it became one of the leading arguments against transportation. Rape, carnal knowledge and bestiality also fell under the banner of unnatural crime and were punishable by death. In January 1833, Robert Dutchess was hanged for a 'detestable crime' with a mare.

VAN DIEMEN'S LAND

From 1803 until 1853, Van Diemen's Land served as a penal colony to receive British convicts. Under the Assignment System, convicts worked for colonists and lived with their masters or built their own accommodation or rented rooms in the towns. But there were soon gaols, prisoners' barracks, female factories, road stations and penal stations dotted across the island for housing convicts and punishing those who committed further crimes.

Van Diemen's Land was one of the most policed societies in the world. The island was divided into police districts and patrolled by armed members of the field police.

In 1840, convicts were no longer assigned to colonists and were sent to work in probation stations under the Probation System.

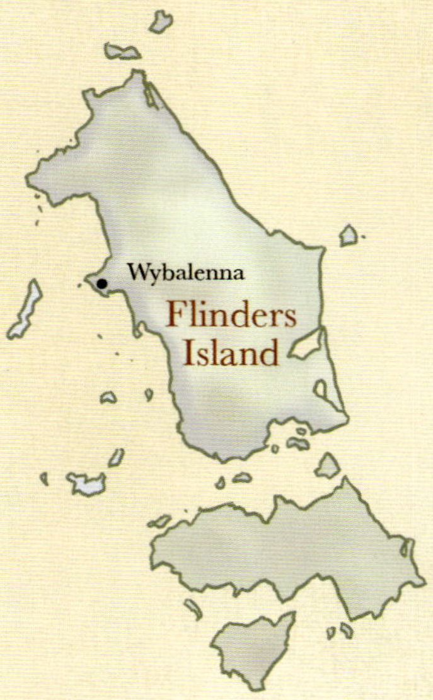

The End of Transportation

By the 1840s, an increasing number of Van Diemonians opposed transportation. The colony was in an economic depression, and running the convict system was costly. Probationary convicts seeking work contributed to high levels of unemployment. It was also felt that grouping men together in remote probation stations had strengthened their criminal ties and led to an increase of 'unnatural crime'. In 1851, the Australasian League for the Abolition of Transportation successfully lobbied for an end to transportation. The last convicts arrived in Van Diemen's Land in 1853. Convicts were then transported to Western Australia until 1868, marking the end of transportation in Australia. In 1856, Van Diemen's Land was officially renamed Tasmania to disassociate the colony from its convict past. Approximately 73,000 convicts were transported to Van Diemen's Land, making up nearly half of the total number of convicts transported to Australia. It has been estimated that between one half and three quarters of today's Tasmanians have at least one convict ancestor.

The Jubilee Medal

In August 1853, a jubilee was held to commemorate the end of transportation. Van Diemonians enjoyed a holiday with fireworks and an enormous cake measuring nearly five metres in diameter. Children were presented with a ticket entitling them to a jubilee medal. In 1855, 9000 medals finally arrived. One side bears the face of Queen Victoria. The other shows an emu and kangaroo beside a coat of arms with St George's cross, the Southern Cross and pastoral, commercial and agricultural emblems. The rising sun heralds a new dawn.

WATCH HOUSE

Watch houses were built to house lawmen and prisoners. They were also known as police stations, guardhouses, receiving houses and lock-ups. Van Diemen's Land was one of the most highly policed societies in the world. More than 40 watch houses were situated throughout the colony, including seven in Hobart Town.

Cliff Fall

The Bothwell watch house sat on a hill by a sheer stone cliff. In December 1854, Chief District Constable Edward Rainsford was found at the base of the cliff. He died three days later.

Writing on the Wall

When William Langley was charged with insolence and neglect of duty and sentenced to seven days' solitary confinement, he carved 'W Langley seven days dec 8th 1841' into his cell wall.

Cash for Booze

In April 1857, Anne Shipley was sent to Bothwell to deposit £9 into the District Savings Bank. Instead she blew most of the cash on booze. She was charged with drunkenness and fined £5.

Gaol Break

In August 1857, Thomas Jones was charged with absconding from the Bothwell watch house and was returned to serve out his sentence.

Red Handed

In July 1862, Constable Hastie watched as Charles Caplin slipped his hand into Bridget McKenna's pocket while she was enjoying a drink in the Ship Tap. Caplin was immediately escorted to the watch house. McKenna offered to overlook the matter, but the constable proved less than compassionate. Caplin was charged with larceny and sentenced to three months' hard labour.

The Bothwell Watch House

In 1849, a military barracks and gaol at Bothwell was converted into a watch house. Three large windows on the eastern face commanded a good view over the township, and an enclosed rear access ensured security. A verandah provided shelter during inclement weather and fireplaces warmed the building. But convicts in the cells had no direct heat. In 1857, the township numbered 1000 and the constabulary numbered nine. In that year the police dealt with more than 360 cases, most of which were the results of drunkenness. By the late 1880s, the building was in disrepair and the roof so full of leaks that prisoners could not be kept in the cells during wet weather. Today, the building is a private residence.

Cut Throat

James Brown, a convict assigned to the Nant distillery in Bothwell, eloped with a married servant. The pair were trailed for 25 kilometres before being caught. Brown was fined £5, but he was unable to pay and was lodged in the watch house to await transfer to the Oatlands gaol. The night before he was due to depart, he was found dead, his throat cut through to the spine with a straight razor. Despite the near decapitation, his death was ruled a suicide: 'self-slaughter whilst in a state of temporary insanity'.

Pilfered Pork

In August 1842 Samuel Hockey pilfered pork from a Bothwell resident and received 12 months' hard labour in chains. His wife, Bridget, was brought up on the same charge with her newborn baby in tow. As her husband had already been charged with the theft, Bridget was acquitted. And the police magistrate of the Bothwell district was condemned in the press for putting a mother and child through such an ordeal.

Christmas Fray
In 1854, Thomas Clarke, John Smith, Henry Jones and James Brown led a mob armed with sticks and staves, to the watch house in order to release a woman imprisoned on Christmas Day. Clarke and Smith received 12 months' imprisonment with hard labour, Jones got six months and Brown got three.

Bushrangers at Bothwell
In 1858, Daniel Stewart, William Ferns, William Thornton and Peter Haley were armed and at large. The gang had connections among colonists and were often helped, but Haley was overpowered by the Phillips family in their hut at Macquarie Plains. A few months later Ferns was captured by Chief District Constable Kidd and transferred to the Bothwell watch house. When another couple betrayed Thornton and Stewart, Thornton was shot and bayoneted in the heart, and he died. The others were sentenced to death. Despite a petition containing 160 signatures calling for their release, they mounted the gallows at Hobart Town in February 1859. They were the last bushrangers to be executed in Van Diemen's Land.

Howell in Despair
Howell Howell arrived in Van Diemen's Land in February 1827 having been transported for life. Despite the hefty sentence he was appointed as a constable on Maria Island. He was dismissed for neglect of duty, but was soon reinstated. At Bothwell, Howell conned a prisoner into absconding so they could share the reward money. He was caught and given three years' hard labour. He made one final foray as a lawman before being dismissed for gross misconduct. It was recommended that he 'never be employed in the police again'.

Fuse
Fredrick Fuse, transported as a 15-year-old for life for stealing silver, spent time as a constable and watch-house keeper at Bothwell.

William Westwood
In August 1845, William Westwood overpowered a Bothwell constable and forced him to assist in robbing a nearby house. The constable escaped and, after meeting up with the Bothwell constabulary and several Aboriginal trackers from New South Wales, he tracked Westwood to Oatlands and arrested him.

Rats and Cats
The term 'rat' was a common insult, sometimes used for a drunk confined to the watch house. Real rats arrived in Van Diemen's Land on ships, and by 1816 they had almost reached plague proportions. One poor child was reportedly gnawed while asleep. Cats were put to work killing rats. They were highly prized for their rat-catching abilities as well as for their companionship. When convicts abandoned the *Frederick* off the coast of South America, they made sure the ship's cat was not left behind. By the 1840s, the cat population was out of control, and feral cats remain a destructive menace today.

WATER
Settlements were chosen for their proximity to freshwater, but remote penal sites often had a limited supply. At Sarah Island, the boat crew fetched water several times a day from the mainland. Wasting it was not tolerated. For destroying freshwater in September 1824, Mary Ann Furze spent seven days in solitary. Convicts were also employed to deliver water by cart. Thomas Carroll worked as a 'waterman' in Hobart Town. In April 1837, he absconded with his master's takings and copped another two years. The government went to great lengths to establish viable waterworks such as aqueducts, dams and wells. In December 1825, two convicts were crushed to death whilst sinking a well at Anglesea barracks. Providing a steady freshwater supply proved to be one of the greatest challenges faced in Van Diemen's Land.

WHALING

Whalers, or whaling ships, were contracted as the first convict transports. Lieutenant John Bowen's party travelled aboard the whaler *Albion* to establish the Van Diemen's Land colony in 1803. During the voyage, Captain Eber Bunker took three whales and commented on how plentiful they were. Van Diemonian whaling was potentially very lucrative, and the British authorities were eager to explore new whaling grounds, but heavy taxes and the possibility of convicts absconding prevented the industry taking hold. Vessels were restricted in their movements and had to be searched for stowaways before being permitted to depart. But the restrictions were lifted in the 1820s, and the first whaling stations were established. Ticket-of-leave convicts were permitted to work for whalers if they signed a bond agreeing to report back within a set time. But they could not man boats or leave the station. Thomas Baynton copped 60 days' hard labour for deserting his post. In 1839, the shore whaling industry peaked with 21 stations catching approximately 1000 whales. The competition for hunting grounds, station locations, supplies and even individual whales was fierce, and the practice of killing calves and pregnant females soon devastated the whale population. In 1847, only nine stations remained with a combined catch of 26 whales. Vessels were refitted to hunt whales at sea and the era of bay whaling ended.

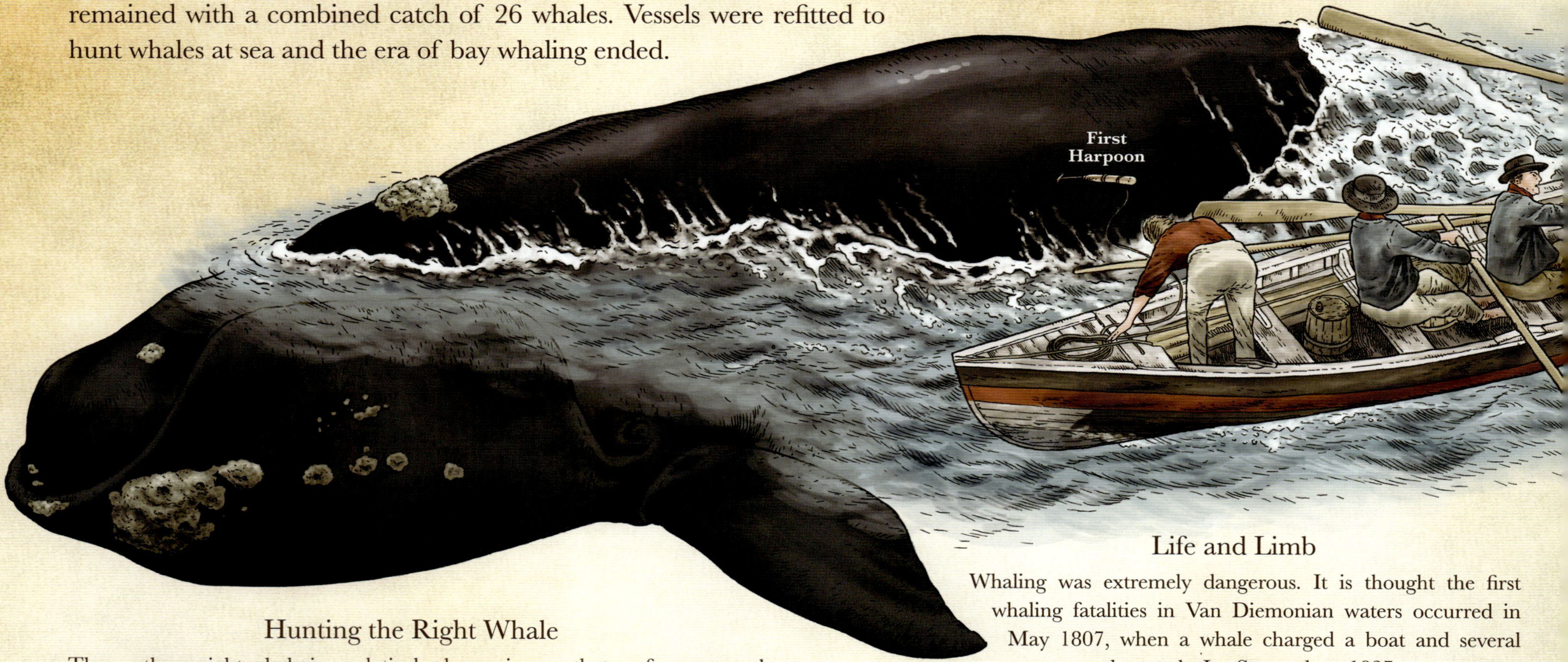

First Harpoon

Hunting the Right Whale

The southern right whale is a relatively slow swimmer that prefers waters close to shorelines. Forty per cent of its body mass is blubber, and its carcass floats. Southern right whales were dubbed the 'right' whale to hunt. Due to the large number of whales close to the coastline, boats could be launched directly from the shore. This was known as 'bay whaling'. Bay whaling boats were double-ended craft to enable propulsion forwards or backwards. They were up to 10 metres in length, made from Huon pine and equipped with sails. Upon drawing near to a whale, the harpooner hurled harpoons into the whale's side. Harpoons were attached to a rope secured in the boat. It could take several hours to tire a whale. A long lance was driven deep into the vital organs to hasten death.

Life and Limb

Whaling was extremely dangerous. It is thought the first whaling fatalities in Van Diemonian waters occurred in May 1807, when a whale charged a boat and several crewmen drowned. In September 1827, a crewman became entangled in rope and was yanked overboard when the whale dived. When the man surfaced, half his leg had been torn off. In August 1839, a whale capsized Captain Henry Wishart's boat. Wishart swam for shore but was attacked by a shark. His remains were collected, pickled in liquor and delivered to his grieving widow. In July 1863, a whale charged the whaler *Maid of Erin*. Three crewmen leapt overboard. One jumped straight into the whale's mouth and was never seen again.

Flensing

Slaughtered whales were towed into shore for flensing, or cutting in. The head was removed and very sharp cutting spades stripped the whale of its blubber. The strips were hauled up the beach with a block and tackle. Whalers had to work quickly as the freshness of the blubber affected the quality of the oil. Flensing could also be done at sea with the whale's carcass lashed to the side of the ship.

Baleen

Inside the mouth of the southern right whale are rows of baleen, which they use to filter food from the ocean. Baleen was commonly called whalebone, and it was used for items requiring strength and flexibility like whips, parasol ribs and corset stays.

Whale Oil

Blubber was cut into small pieces and dropped into a large iron cauldron of boiling oil. A skimmer was used to remove the impurities that floated to the surface. The furnace was fired with wood, but residual blubber was sometimes used to keep it burning steadily, producing a thick, black, putrid smoke. The oil was cooled in vats then siphoned into barrels to be sold. On average a southern right whale produced 6 tuns, and each tun contained 252 gallons. The price of whale oil depended on its colour. Brighter, cleaner-looking oil fetched as much as £45 per tun in 1837. Whale oil was used as fuel for lamps, as candle wax, lubricant, sealant and as an ingredient in the production of soap.

Whales at Port Arthur

Whalers were not permitted near penal establishments. In October 1837, Commandant Booth seized the *Highlander* for whaling off Eaglehawk Neck. The commandant, however, was not averse to whaling himself. When a whale was spotted off Port Arthur in April 1833, he requisitioned the boat crew to give chase. Thomas Earle, a convict on a life sentence, served as harpooner. Despite Earle landing several bloody blows, the whale got away, but the convict crew got to enjoy an hour of 'capital sport'.

Profit Share

Wages were paid as a proportion of the total profit earned from a catch. In 1835, James Kelly paid up to one-twelfth for a headsman and as little as one-sixty-eighth for a labourer.

X

Illiterate Van Diemonians signed their name with the letter 'X'. Not only was it easy to draw but, as it was a sacred symbol, it reflected the signatory's sincerity.

YOKE

A yoke is a wooden frame used to harness draught animals to carts. In Van Diemen's Land, convicts too were yoked to carts. William Gates stated that he was fitted with a leather harness over one shoulder and under the other to pull carts containing up to a ton of broken rock. Martin Cash found it so degrading that he absconded. Convicts were used to do the work of draught animals until the 1860s.

No Yoking Matter

A yoke can be rested across a person's shoulders to carry a bucket. In 1855, William Aldborough copped two years' hard labour for stealing a milkman's yoke.

ZANYISM

In May 1824, William Sylvester was dared to run through the commandant's garden on Sarah Island in just his underwear for some tobacco. He copped 50 lashes and three days' solitary. Outrageous wagers were not unusual. In April 1853, William Wright died after sculling two pints of rum. The zaniest character in Van Diemonian history is, perhaps, Jonathon Burke McHugo, who sailed into Launceston in January 1812. McHugo pretended to be a high-ranking officer and tricked the entire town into letting him take command. When his ruse was discovered, his ship was requisitioned and he was arrested and confined to a lunatic asylum. Like thousands of other convicted British subjects, McHugo's actions contributed greatly to the formation of Van Diemen's Land. After his performance, Governor Macquarie declared Hobart Town the capital and he placed the entire island under the command of a single lieutenant-governor instead of two separate district commanders.

GLOSSARY

abscond escape imprisonment

apoplexy sudden death, such as from a heart attack or stroke

appropriation a convict's placement, or assignment, within the colony

Assignment Board a group of officials who oversaw convicts' appropriation, 1832–40

Assignment System a system of convict management, 1803–40, where convicts were assigned to work for colonists in return for food, clothing and lodgings

bail money or property given as surety that a person released from custody will return

barracks accommodation buildings for male convicts

basils the parts of leg irons that encircle the wearer's ankles

black books registers that list the particulars of each convict

Board of Ordnance the government department responsible for the supply of equipment including munitions, superseded by the War Department in 1856

breeches knee-length trousers

brig a two-masted ship, square-rigged on both masts

catechist a religious instructor

chain gang a group of convicts working in leg irons. Being sentenced to work on a chain gang was one of the most harsh forms of punishment.

colonial secretary a civil servant who acted as an intermediary for the lieutenant-governor

commandant an officer in charge of a penal station

commissariat a government storehouse

comptroller-general the director of the Convict Department, 1843–68

conditional pardon a pardon granted by the Crown on a recommendation from the lieutenant-governor. Recipients of a conditional pardon were free but could not return to Britain.

Convict Department the government department that oversaw all the workings of the convict system, including record keeping, 1818–68

duck trousers trousers made of coarse cloth or canvas known as duck. The term originated from the Dutch word doek, meaning linen canvas.

emancipist a convict who has served his or her sentence or who has received a pardon or conditional pardon

Engineer's Department the government body responsible for engineering works, divided into the Roads and Bridges Department and the Engineer and Architects Department in 1827

flash mob a group of unruly convicts who frequently dressed in a showy style

field police police stationed in outlying areas, largely convicts or ex-convicts, 1826–57

free certificate a document issued to convicts on the completion of their sentence. Recipients could return to Britain.

fox foxes were imported for hunting sport in Van Diemens Land, but never officially introduced

gibbet a wooden frame from which the bodies of executed criminals were suspended in order to deter potential criminals

guinea a gold coin worth 21 shillings

hulk a decommissioned ship converted to a prison

indulgence a privilege granted to convicts, such as a mitigated sentence or tobacco

infanticide the act of killing a baby or infant

interred buried or placed in a coffin or tomb

javelin man a guard appointed to a gaol or court, typically a convict or ex-convict

lieutenant-governor the officer, or chief executive, who governed Van Diemen's Land, subordinate to the governor of New South Wales

kangaroo dog a dog trained to hunt kangaroos

larceny theft

lifer a convict transported for a life sentence

magistrate a civil officer charged with upholding the law. Magistrates governed individual districts and were answerable to the chief police magistrate.

man-o'-war a warship

mess a meal such as breakfast, dinner or supper, also a group of convicts appointed to share a meal

midden a mound of shellfish shells and other foodstuffs discarded over a long period of time by Aboriginal Australians

muster master the director of convict records, also a magistrate, 1827–40s

nailer a person who makes nails

oakum old rope pulled into strands, used for sealing ships' hulls

orlop deck the lowest deck on a ship, situated above the hold

ornithologist a zoologist who specialises in birds

oval the act of reshaping a basil, part of leg irons, so it can be passed over the wearer's feet, also known as ovalling

overseer a person appointed to supervise a gang of convicts, typically a convict or ex-convict

penal station a place of secondary punishment for recidivist convicts

penitentiary a place of imprisonment and reformatory discipline or penance

phrenological examination the study of a person's head or skull in an attempt to find the cause of criminal tendencies

pillory an upright wooden frame for securing a person's head and hands as a form of punishment, used 1803–10s

privy a toilet, typically a small open shed positioned over a pit or bucket

Probation System a system of convict management, where convicts worked at probation stations, used only in Van Diemen's Land, 1840–56

probationary pass a document issued to convicts who had completed a sentence of probation. Recipients could seek paid work.

public works government projects completed using convict labour

recidivist a repeat offender

road station accommodation complexes for road gangs

Royal Engineers the department that oversaw the construction of convict and military establishments, 1835–70s

rustle steal livestock

scantling a thin piece of timber

scuttle sink a ship

semaphore an apparatus for conveying visual signals, used to send messages

skilling a small rudimentary house

skilly thin soup or gruel, typically made from flour and water

stocks a horizontal wooden frame for securing a person's feet as punishment, 1803–50

superintendent of convicts the director of the Convict Department, 1818–43

taproom a hotel or pub, also known as a public house

ticket-of-leave document permitting convicts to live and work for wages under certain conditions, for example, recipients had to reside within a stipulated area

trafficking illegally trading

turnkey person who holds the keys to a penal establishment, such as a gaol

vagrancy wandering homelessness, a punishable offence

Van Diemen's Land Company company formed by English merchants in order to supply British factories with wool. The company still operates today.

voussoirs wedge-shaped pieces of stone that make up an arch in a bridge

War Department the government department responsible for the supply of equipment including munitions

watchman person appointed to keep guard during the night, typically a convict or ex-convict

watch house a building in which prisoners are temporarily held

yardarm pole on which flags were hoisted in the semaphore system

WEIGHTS AND MEASURES

Length and Distance
1 inch – 2.5 centimetres   12 inches per foot
1 foot – 0.3 metres   3 feet per yard
1 yard – 0.9 metres   1760 yards per mile
1 mile – 1.6 kilometres

Area
1 acre – 0.4 hectares

Volume
1 quart – 1.1 litres   4 quarts per gallon
1 gallon – 4.5 litres   8 gallons per bushel
1 bushel – 35 litres

Mass
1 dram – 1.7 grams   16 drams per ounce
1 ounce – 28 grams   16 ounces per pound
1 pound – 450 grams   2250 pounds per ton
1 ton – 1016 kilograms, 1.016 tonnes

Money
1 penny (1d)   12 pence per shilling
1 shilling (1s)   20 shillings per pound
1 pound (£1)
1 guinea – 21 shillings

SELECTED BIBLIOGRAPHY

Alexander, Alison, *Tasmania's Convicts: How Felons Built a Free Society*, Allen & Unwin, Crows Nest, 2010

Boyce, James, *Van Diemen's Land*, Black Inc, Melbourne, 2009

Brand, Ian, *The Convict Probation System, Van Diemen's Land 1839–1854*, Blubber Head Press, Hobart, 1990

Clark, Julia, ed., *The Career of William Thompson, Convict*. Port Arthur Historic Sites, Port Arthur, 2009

Kerr, James, *Design for Convicts...* Library of Australian History in association with the National Trust of Australia and the Australian Society for Historical Archaeology, Sydney, 1984

Laugesen, Amanda, *Convict Words: Language in Early Colonial Australia*, Oxford University Press, South Melbourne, 2002

Maxwell-Stewart, Hamish, *Closing Hell's Gates: The Death of a Convict Station*, Allen Unwin, Australia, 2008

Miller, Linus, *Notes of an Exile to Van Diemen's Land*, McKinstry, Fredonia, 1846

Nicholas, Stephen, *Convict Workers: Reinterpreting Australia's Past*, Cambridge University Press, Cambridge, 1988

Nicholls, Mary, ed., *The Diary of the Reverend Robert Knopwood 1803–1838*, Tasmanian Historical Research Association, Launceston, 1977

Tardiff, Phillip, *Notorious Strumpets and Dangerous Girls*, Angus and Robertson, Sydney, 1990

West, John, *The History of Tasmania*, Angus and Robertson, London, 1981

Archives Office of Tasmania, www.linc.tas.gov.au

Female Convicts Research Centre Inc, www.femaleconvicts.org.au

Founders and Survivors, Australian Life Courses in Historical Context 1803–1920, foundersandsurvivors.org/pubsearch

The Companion to Tasmanian History, www.utas.edu.au/library/companion_to_tasmanian_history/index.htm

Trove, National Library of Australia, trove.nla.gov.au

For a complete bibliography, go to simonbarnard.com.au

INDEX

A
Aboriginal people 2, 8, 9, 18, 34, 41, 51
absconders 3, 16, 20, 21, 49, 50, 54, 72, 80, 83
alcohol 8, 25, 36, 43, 50, 80
amputations 30–31
Anderson, Mary Ann 3
Anson 32–33
Archer, John Lee 6, 12, 36
Arthur, George, Lieutenant-Governor 3, 6, 22, 26, 28, 30, 36, 37, 38, 45, 46, 52, 57, 59, 60, 62
artists 19, 46, 50, 53
Assignment System 2, 3, 78
Australasian League for the Abolition of Transportation 79

B
babies 23, 27, 33
Backhouse, James 30
bakeries 4, 52
bakers 4
Barker, John 5
barracks 15, 44, 52, 54
Barrel, George 52
Batman, John 9
Beattie, John Watt 15
Bedford, William 25
beds 4, 8, 64
Bell, Thomas 61
Bent, Andrew 46
Bigge inquiry 2
Birch, Robert 21
black books 47, 65
black box 56
Black Jack 24
black market 4
blacksmith 5, 42
Blay, Solomon 24, 25
Board of Ordnance 77
Bock, Thomas 46
Booth, Charles O'Hara, Commandant 16, 20, 59, 68, 69, 83
boots 3, 39, 41, 44, 45, 76
Bothwell watch house 29, 80, 81
Bowden, Edmund 33
Bowden, Philippa 33
Bowen, John, Lieutenant 61, 82
Bowles, William 38
boxing 43, 70
Brady Gang 24, 34, 45, 53
Brady, Matthew 3, 8, 9, 20, 35, 45
Bray, William 29
Bread Act 4
brickmakers 40
bricks 40
bridges 6–7
Bridgewater Causeway 71
Britton, George 44
broad arrow 40, 77
Brown, John 28
Brownell, Thomas 31
Bunbury, Henry William St Pierre 18
Burke, Margaret 32
bushrangers 3, 8–9, 16, 17, 28, 34, 35, 37, 41, 45, 53, 81
Butler, Commandant 21

C
Campbell, Mary 37
Campbell Street gaol 52
cannibalism 3, 9
Cascades Female Factory 3, 22–23, 33, 37, 56, 59
Cascades probation station 38
Casey, Cornelius, Doctor 30, 31
Cash, Martin 9, 19, 28, 83
Cashman, Bridget 33
cat o' nine tails 57
cats 81
cells 12, 15, 26, 27, 70, 71, 80
cemeteries 10, 49
chain gangs 56, 60, 61
chains 42, *see also* punishments
chapel 12–13, 22
chaplains 12, 39, 52, 63, 71
children 22, 38, 39, 79
Churton, Ralph 35
Clarke, George 46
classing convicts 22, 32, 38, 52, 69
Clay, George 7
clerks 47, 49
Clifford, Eliza 9
clothes 3, 8, 39, 41, 44, 45, 53, 76
coal 3, 5, 59
coalmines barracks 15
coalmining 14–15
Cockerill, Mary 8
Colbeck, James 6
Collins, Alfred 63
Collins, David, Lieutenant-Governor 11
Colonial Hospital 30–31
commissariat 16–17
communications 68–69
conditional pardon 73
Connelly, Thomas 20
Convict Department 14, 47, 61
Cook, Edward 47
Costantini, Charles Henry Theodore 50
Cox, John 6
Cox, Thomas 3
Cripps, William 4
currency tokens 46
Cyprus 20, 49

D
dancing 43
Davey, Thomas, Lieutenant-Governor 8, 43
Davis, Thomas 31
Davis, William 35
Day, Thomas 49
deaths 14, 15, 23, 24, 31, 33, 49, 51, 57, 64
Derrincourt, William 13, 14, 19, 73
diseases 29, 30, 63, 77
dissidents 16
dog line 18–19, 79
dogs 18–19, 35, 61
Doherty, Dennis 71
Dry, Richard 17

E
Eaglehawk Neck 9
Eaglehawk Neck dog-line 16, 79
education 63
emancipists 19
emus 34
escape craft 20–21, 63
escapes 9, 13, 17, 20–21, 23, 26, 27
Evendon, John Edwin 55
executioner 25
executions 24–25, 28, *see also* punishments
executive council 40

F
farming 54
Fawkner, John Pascoe 20
female convicts 2, 3, 8, 9, 19, 22–23, 24, 27, 32, 33, 37, 43, 48, 55, 56, 57, 65, 69, 77, 80
female factories 3, 9, 22–23, 78, 79
field police 7, 41
First Fleet 11
Fisher, George 31
Fitzmaurice, Francis 72
flagellators 26, 57
flagstaffs 68
Flash Mob 23, 44, 77
Flinders Island 51
floggings 57, 76, *see also* lashes
flour 3, 4, 8, 16, 31, 34, 59, 65, 74
food 3, 4, 8, 16, 26, 36, 39, 48, 52, 59
Forster, Matthew 54
Franklin, John, Lieutenant-Governor 28, 52, 53
Frederick 5, 65, 81
free pardon 73
freshwater 81

G
gags 56
gallows 24–25
gambling 43
ganged convicts 30, 60, 62
gaol keepers 26, 27
gaols 2, 26–27, 78, 79
Geary, Joseph 49
ghosts 26, 28
gibbets 28
Gibbons, John 29
Goodwin, James 20
Gould, William Buelow 50
Government printer 46
graffiti 29
Grass Tree Hill road station 62
gravediggers 10
Greenhill, Robert 3
Greenwood, Joseph 57
Grover, George 26
Gunn, William 53

H
handcuffs 41
hangings 24–25, *see also* punishments
hangmen 24, 25
hard labour, *see* punishments
health 29, 30, 53, 65
Henrys, Catherine 9
Herbert, Daniel 6, 7
hiring depots 33
Hobart Town 8, 10, 16, 22, 26, 31, 32, 41, 45, 46, 55, 58, 68, 78, 83
  commissariat 17
  prisoners' barracks 4, 12, 44, 47, 52, 74, 75
horses 61
hospitals 30–31
Howe Gang 28
Howe, Michael 8, 9, 11, 28, 35, 45, 61
Howell, Howell 81
Hoy, David 66
Hughes, James 14
hulks 32–33
Hunt, George 18
hunting 16, 34
Hurst, James 15
Hutchinson, John, Reverend 23
Hutchinson, Mary 23
huts 35, 60, 78

I
Indefatigable 64
infant mortality rate 23
insane asylum 22, 36–37
invalid stations 36–37, 78, 79
iron collar 56
Irwin, Ormsby 68
Isle of the Dead 10, 11, 20

J
javelin men 24, 26, 41
Jeffrey, Mark 10
Jeffries, Thomas 9
Johnson, John 10
Jones, Francis 21
Jones, John Peyton 18
Jorgenson, Jorgen 7, 35, 43
Jorgenson, Nora 7
jubilee medals 79
juvenile convicts 22, 38–39, 57, 79

K
kangaroos 34, 35
King's Orphan School 39
Knopwood, Robert 11

L
Lacey, Joseph 15
Lake, Thomas 29
Lamb, John 28
Lambe, David 26
lamplighters 18
lashes 4, 5, 18, 20, 24, 26, 27, 31, 40, 43, 48, 51, 52, 57, 58, 61, 62

86

Launceston 26, 30, 74, 78
 commissariat 16–17
 female factory 9
law 40
Laycock, Thomas, Lieutenant 16
leech gatherers 29
leg irons 5, 40, 44, 62, 74
legislative council 40
leisure 39, 43
Lempriere, Thomas 51
Lewis, Richard 37
life expectancy 29
liquor, *see* alcohol
Lord, Maria 19
love tokens 43
Lovett, James 75

M

Macquarie Harbour 20, 48, 78
Macquarie, Lachlan, Governor 6, 17, 60, 68, 83
Madams, William 31
magistrates 11
mail 6
maimed convicts 70
management of convicts 47, *see also* Assignment System, Probation System, Separate System
Manton, John Allen 39
Maria Island 20, 31, 47, 48, 77, 78, 81
marriage 13
Martin, William 8
McConchie, Elizabeth 27
McHugo, Jonathan Burke 83
McKey, John 28
meat 16, 35
medical officer 31
medical treatments 29, 30
Melville, Henry 46
military personnel 31, 44–45, 49, 55, 61, 65
Miller, Henry 69
Miller, Linus 52, 53, 60, 73, 74, 75
miners 14–15
Molesworth Commission 2
money 46
Morgan, John 58
Morgan, Tom 20
Mortlock, John 61
mothers 23, 27, 33
Musquito 8, 9, 24, 34
mutiny 64, 67

N

nailers 5
New Norfolk 30, 36, 37, 78
newspapers 11, 46
nightwatchmen 41
Norfolk Island 9, 17, 27, 37, 61, 67, 72
Nottman, Robert 61

O

O'Brien, William Smith 16
Officer, Robert 37

orphanages 39
overseers 2, 15, 38, 39, 49, 55, 75

P

Paisley, Walter 38
Palmer, Phillip, Reverend 12
pardons 19, 27, 54, 73
parti-coloured uniform 76
Patching, John 76
Paterson, William, Lieutenant-Colonel 16
Pearce, Alexander 3, 24, 35
penal stations 48–49, 78, 79
penitentiaries 50–51
Pickering, Thomas 10
Pickthorne, William 25
piracy 49, 52
Point Puer 21, 38, 63
police 41
Popjoy, John 20
Port Arthur 10, 11, 18, 20, 30, 31, 37, 48, 59, 60, 63, 66, 68, 71, 74, 75, 78, 79, 83
 hospital 30, 31
Port Dalrymple 45
Porter, James 67
priests 11
prison hulks 32
prisoners' barracks 4, 12, 29, 47, 52, 78, 79
probation station 54–55, 78, 79
Probation System 2, 3, 46, 47, 54–55, 77, 78
proclamation board 41
promissory notes 46
prostitution 55
punishments 2, 15, 56–57, 60, 65, 74
 chains 16, 42, 58, 60, 62, 80
 executions 9, 19, 21, 24, 27, 35, 45, 50, 54, 77, 81
 fines 17, 36, 46, 80
 floggings 20, 31, 45, 48, 52, 57, 58, 61, 62, 63, 76
 hard labour 15, 16, 23, 24, 29, 33, 40, 45, 52, 62, 80, 81
 solitary confinement 2, 4, 6, 23, 27, 29, 37, 38, 48, 52, 53, 61, 63, 66
 treadmill 52, 74–75

Q

quarries 58
Quigley, John 37
Quigley's Cage 37

R

railways 59, 79
Randall, Walter 38
rations 15, 19, 26, 36, 39, 48, 59, 65
rats 81
regiments 44, 45
registers of convicts 47, 65
religious instruction 12, 15, 39, 51, 52
rewards 3, 8, 9, 12, 41, 45, 69, 72
Rex, George, Constable 21

Richmond gaol 26–27
riots 23, 36
road gangs 30, 60, 62
road stations 62, 78, 79
roads 60, 62, 78, 79
Roberts, Luke 58
Robinson, George Augustus 34, 51
Ross bridge 6–7
rum 43, 73
Russell, Mary 33

S

Salt Water River probation station 54
Sarah Island 3, 4, 5, 7, 21, 24, 29, 30, 45, 48–49, 50, 63, 64, 66, 67, 70, 73, 78, 81, 83
Savery, Henry 11
sawpits 63
Schofield, William 51
schools 34, 39, 51, 54, 63
Scott, Ellen 23
scurvy 29
sealing 34
semaphore system 68, 69
Separate System 71
Shannon hut 35
shaving 77
sheep 35
ship building 66–67
ships 64–65, 66–67
shipwrights 66
shipyards 66–67
shoemakers 73
signal stations 68–69, 78, 79
signalmen 69
singing 43
skillings 30
skills 2, 69
Skinner, Jane 27
Slater, Elizabeth 23
Smith, Eliza 55
solitary confinement 70–71, *see also* punishments
Solomon, Isaac 41
Sorell, William, Lieutenant-Governor 8, 28, 45, 53, 61, 66
southern right whale 82
Spode, Josiah 47
sports 43
staff 36, 49, 50, 55, 65
stocks 40, 56
stonemasons 10, 58
storekeeper 17, 51
stores 16–17
stowaways 21
suicide 71, 80
Swallow, William 49

T

Tasman Peninsula 59, 79
Tasmania 79
tattoos 72
teachers 51, 63
Tegg 9, 34

Thompson, William 15
thylacines 34
ticket-of-leave 4, 27, 54, 73
timber 63, 66
tobacco 8, 16, 39, 72, 73, 83
toilets 70
tools 4, 5, 61, 66
transportation 2, 64–65, 79
transports 64–65, 82
treadmills 74–75, *see also* punishments
Trinity Chapel 12–13
Turner, William, Captain 6
turnkey 27

U

underwear 77
Underwood, Charles 30
uniforms 39, 41, 44, 76
unnatural crimes 15, 23, 24, 77, 79

V

Van Diemen's Land Company 30
voussoirs 7

W

Wade, Samuel 37
wages 6, 41, 45, 46, 63
Wainewright, Thomas Griffiths 53
Walker, George Washington 30
Walker, Thomas 18
War Department 77
watch houses 78, 79, 80–81
watchmen 49, 52, 65
water supply 81
watermen 81
Waters, Richard 13, 29
weights and measures 17
Westwood, William 19, 81
whaling 82–83
whaling sites 78, 79
Whitehead, James 8, 28
Wilkes, Joseph 5
Wilmot, John Eardley, Lieutenant-Governor 54, 70
Wilson, John Edward 28
windlass 15
women, *see* female convicts
Woodward, George 14
work 2, 14–15, 22, 32, 39, 43, 48, 55, 63, 64, 69, 81
Worrall, Thomas 35

Y

Yerrangoulaga 9

Simon Barnard was born and grew up in Launceston. He spent a lot of time in the bush as a boy, which led to an interest in Tasmanian history. He is an illustrator and collector of colonial artifacts. He now lives in Melbourne with his girlfriend and a little dog.

For answering questions, taking photographs, drawing sketches, measuring distances, forging leg irons, sewing slops, producing caps and gaiters, modelling, allowing me to poke through their homes, offering editorial and artistic advice and providing encouragement and inspiration, I am indebted to the following people: John Laing, Stefan Petrow, Peter MacFie, Ken Lee, Jai Paterson, Michael Smith, Jody Steele, Michael Nash, Richard and Kiah Davey, Chris Leppard, Peter Bell, Peter Dorrell, Michael Sprod, Bob Wright, Alex Scheibner, Will Lincoln, Peter Sinclair, John and Roslyn Hill, Stephen Gapps, Kristin Headlam, Josef Hextal, Jack Callaghan, Cade Butler, Jason Stone, Stuart McKenna, Clinton Rooney, Barry Jessup, Simon Hanselmann, Bernard Caleo, Monty and Tuco. Thank you.

Particular thanks to Amelie Mills, Lyn and Phil Barnard, Jo Bornemissza, Hamish Maxwell-Stewart, Susan Hood, Brian Rieusset, James Boyce, Chris Wallace-Crabbe, Jane Pearson, Michael Heyward, Lorna Hendry, Imogen Stubbs, Chong Weng Ho and Justin Caleo.

The Text Publishing Company
Swann House
22 William Street
Melbourne Victoria 3000
Australia

textpublishing.com.au
simonbarnard.com.au

Copyright text © Simon Barnard 2014
Copyright illustrations © Simon Barnard 2014

The moral right of Simon Barnard to be identified as the author of this work has been asserted.

All rights reserved. Without limiting the rights under copyright above, no part of this publication shall be reproduced, stored in or introduced into a retrieval system, or transmitted in any form or by any means (electronic, mechanical, photocopying, recording or otherwise), without the prior permission of both the copyright owner and the publisher of this book.

First published in Australia by The Text Publishing Company, 2014.
Reprinted 2015 (twice), 2018, 2020

Cover illustration by Simon Barnard, based on an etching known as 'Hobart Town Chain Gang', believed to have been completed in 1831 by convict Charles Bruce, a professional copperplate engraver who arrived in Van Diemen's Land in April 1829 to serve 14 years for housebreaking.

Design by Simon Barnard
Typesetting and additional layout by Lorna Hendry

Printed and bound by Everbest Printing Co

National Library of Australia Cataloguing-in-Publication entry
Author: Barnard, Simon, author, illustrator.
Title: A - Z of convicts in Van Diemen's Land / by Simon Barnard, author and illustrator.
ISBN: 9781922079343 (hardback)
Notes: Includes bibliographical references and index.
Subjects: Penal colonies—Tasmania—History.
           Convicts—Tasmania—History
           Convicts—Tasmania—Social conditions.
           Prisoners—Tasmania—History—19th century.
           Convicts—Discipline.
           Tasmania—History—1803–1877.
Dewey Number: 365.609946

Teaching notes at textpublishing.com.au